HAYDN:
CHRONICLE AND WORKS

HAYDN: CHRONICLE AND WORKS
in five volumes by
H. C. Robbins Landon

★*Haydn: The Early Years 1732–1765*
★ *Haydn at Eszterháza 1766–1790*
Haydn in England 1791–1795
★ *Haydn: The Years of 'The Creation' 1796–1800*
★*Haydn: The Late Years 1801–1809*
(★in preparation)

HAYDN
IN ENGLAND
1791–1795

For
D. Le B. L. and W. G. L.
with much love

Haydn: Chronicle and Works
VOLUME III

HAYDN IN ENGLAND

1791–1795

H. C. ROBBINS LANDON

INDIANA UNIVERSITY PRESS
BLOOMINGTON   LONDON

First American edition 1976 by Indiana University Press

Library of Congress Cataloging in Publication Data

Landon, Howard Chandler Robbins, 1926–
    Haydn: chronicle and works.

    Includes bibliographies and indexes.
    CONTENTS:
    v.3. Haydn in England, 1791–1795.
    1. Haydn, Joseph, 1732–1809.
ML410.H4L26   780′.92′4[B]   76–14630
ISBN 0–253–37003–5   1 2 3 4 5 80 79 78 77 76

Printed in Great Britain

Contents

LIST OF ILLUSTRATIONS 9

PREFACE AND ACKNOWLEDGMENTS 11

AUTHOR'S NOTE 16

ABBREVIATIONS OF BIBLIOGRAPHICAL SOURCES 17

PART I: CHRONICLE 1791–1795 19

    CHAPTER ONE – 1791 21

    CHAPTER TWO – 1792 121

    CHAPTER THREE – 1793 213

    CHAPTER FOUR – 1794 230

    CHAPTER FIVE – 1795 280

PART II: LONDON WORKS 321

    CHAPTER SIX – VOCAL MUSIC 323

L'anima del filosofo (*Orfeo ed Euridice*) 323
Madrigal: 'The Storm' 354
Oratorio fragment: *Mare Clausum* 356
Coro: 'Su, cantiamo' 356
The Ten Commandments and other Canons 357
Occasional works for several voices 361 (Twelve Sentimental Catches and Glees 361; Psalms 364)
Arias with orchestra 370
Arias (duets) with orchestra, of doubtful authenticity 375
Songs 377 (First set of Canzonettas 377; second set of Canzonettas 386; separate English songs 393; Scottish songs 400)
Dr Harington's Compliment – 'What art expresses' 403

    CHAPTER SEVEN – INSTRUMENTAL MUSIC: CHAMBER WORKS 405

Trios 405 (The so-called 'London Trios' for two flutes and violoncello 405; Piano Trios 409)
Works for pianoforte solo 437 (Sonata – Andante con variazioni in F minor 437; Three Sonatas for Therese Jansen 439)
Lost chamber music 452

Notturni for the King of Naples (1790 – adapted for Salomon's concerts of 1791–92) 453

The 'Salomon' Quartets of 1793 (known as Opp. 71 and 74) 455

CHAPTER EIGHT – INSTRUMENTAL MUSIC: ORCHESTRAL WORKS   483

Overture to an English Opera 483

Dance music 483 (Twelve Deutsche Tänze – the Redoutensaal Dances 484)

Marches 487

The 'Salomon' Symphonies and Concertante 490 (catalogue 490; chronology 495; textual problems and their consequence in interpretation 497; position in Haydn's oeuvre and in music history 501)

No. 96 in D ('Miracle') 509; No. 95 in C minor 515; No. 93 in D 518; No. 94 in G ('Surprise') 523; No. 98 in B flat 531; Concertante in B flat 536; No. 97 in C 541; No. 99 in E flat 551; No. 100 in G ('Military') 558; No. 101 in D ('Clock') 567; No. 102 in B flat 582; No. 103 in E flat ('Drum Roll') 594; No. 104 in D ('London'/'Salomon') 609

INDEX   619

LIST OF ILLUSTRATIONS

PLATES

Between pages
16 and 17

I Joseph Haydn, portrait by John
Hoppner, 1791. Royal Collection;
reproduced by gracious permission
of Her Majesty the Queen.

II Joseph Haydn, portrait by Thames
Hardy, 1791. Courtesy, Royal
College of Music, London.

III Johann Peter Salomon, portrait by
Thomas Hardy, 1791. Courtesy,
Royal College of Music, London.

IV Hanover Square, London;
coloured engraving by R. Pollard
and F. Jukes, after E. Dayes, 1788.
Author's collection.

V Ignaz Joseph Pleyel, portrait by
Elisabeth Vigée-Lebrun. Courtesy,
Royal College of Music, London.

320 and 321

1 Joseph Haydn, portrait by George
Dance, 1794. Courtesy, Royal
College of Music, London.

2 Giacomo David(e), anonymous
engraving, c. 1795. Raccolta delle
Stampe A. Bertarelli, Milan.

3 Brigida Banti-Giorgi, anonymous
engraving, c. 1795. Raccolta delle
Stampe A. Bertarelli, Milan.

4 Gertrud Elisabeth Mara-
Schmeling, engraving, c. 1791.
Raccolta delle Stampe A.
Bertarelli, Milan.

5 Johann Nepomuk Hummel,
miniature, c. 1795. Hummel
Archives, Goethe Museum,
Düsseldorf.

6 Figures skating in St James's
Park, pen and ink and
watercolour, $12\frac{1}{4} \times 27\frac{1}{4}$ in. (sight
size), by John Nixon, c. 1790.
Collection of Mr and Mrs Paul
Mellon, Upperville, Va.

7 View of Blackfriars Bridge and St

PLATES

Between pages
320 and 321

Paul's Cathedral, pen and ink and
watercolour, c. 1790; attributed to
Thomas Malton, Junior.
Collection of Mr and Mrs Paul
Mellon, Upperville, Va.

8 George III reviewing the Prince of
Wales's Regiment, by Sir William
Beechey, c. 1794. Sterling and
Francine Clark Art Institute,
Williamstown, Mass.

9 George, Prince of Wales, by Sir
Thomas Lawrence. National
Portrait Gallery, London.

10 Princess Caroline of Brunswick,
engraving by Tookey after
Schroeder. Mansell Collection,
London.

11 Mrs Blair, by George Romney.
Widener Collection, National
Gallery of Art, Washington, D.C.

12 Mrs Elizabeth Billington,
engraving by A. Volpini after V.
Matteini, published 1797. Author's
collection.

13 Muzio Clementi, engraving by
Thomas Hardy, 1794. Raccolta
delle Stampe A. Bertarelli, Milan.

14 Dr Charles Burney, pencil sketch
by George Dance, 1794. National
Portrait Gallery, London.

15 Thomas Saunders Dupuis, proof
copy of an eighteenth-century
engraving. Author's collection.

16 J. L. Dussek, engraving published
in 1793. Österreichische
Nationalbibliothek, Vienna.

17 William Shield, engraving by W.
Daniell after George Dance, 1798.
Author's collection.

18 Joah Bates, engraving by W.
Daniell after George Dance, 1794.
Author's collection.

PLATES	*Between pages*	ILLUSTRATIONS IN THE TEXT	*Page*

19 Samuel Arnold, engraving by Thomas Hardy, 1797. Author's collection. — 320 and 321

Haydn's 'Canon Cancrizanz', 'Thy Voice, O Harmony'. Count Eugen Czernin Archive, Castle Jindřichův Hradec (Neuhaus), Czechoslovakia. — 94

20 William Cramer, engraving by Thomas Hardy, 1794. Author's collection.

Sketches made by Haydn on British paper, including one for the first Redoutensaal Minuet. Burgenländisches Landesmuseum, Eisenstadt, ex coll. Sándor Wolf. — 209

21 Vincent Martin y Soler (Martini), engraving, 1787. Raccolta delle Stampe A. Bertarelli, Milan.

Two pages of the score (Euridice's death scene) from L'anima del filosofo (Orfeo ed Euridice), written out by Haydn's English copyist. Országos Széchényi Könyvtár, ex coll. Esterházy Archives, Budapest. — 346

22 Adalbert Gyrowetz, engraving by F. G. Mansfeld, 1793. Author's collection.

Items from Lord Abingdon's Sentimental Glees and Catches: Glee VII and Catch IX. Author's collection. — 362 / 363

23 Giovan Battista Viotti, engraving by George Chinnery. Author's collection.

Psalm 50, from Tattersall's Improved Psalmody, 1794. British Museum, London. — 368

24 Prince Anton Esterházy, anonymous portrait, c. 1790. Eszterháza Castle, Eisenstadt. Photo Robert Forstner.

Piano Trio No. 36 in E flat, beginning of the slow movement (piano part) of the first edition. British Museum, London. — 429

25 Marie Therese, Princess Esterházy, by Angelika Kauffmann. Hluboká Castle on the Moldau (Frauenberg, formerly Schwarzenberg Castle), Czechoslovakia.

'Notturno 3zo' for the King of Naples (1790), to the autograph of which Haydn later added the introduction (Largo) on British paper. Országos Széchényi Könyvtár, ex coll. Esterházy Archives, Budapest. — 454

26 Title-page of Haydn's Piano Trios, Op. 70, published in 1794. British Museum, London.

Page from the autograph of the String Quartet in G minor (Op. 74, No. 3), 1793. Preussische Staatsbibliothek, Berlin. — 481

27 Haydn's letter to Luigia Polzelli, 14 January 1792. Pierpont Morgan Library, New York (ex coll.) Heineman Foundation.

Page of sketches for the finale of Symphony No. 99. Österreichische Nationalbibliothek, Vienna. — 493

28 The North Terrace, Windsor Castle, looking west; watercolour by Paul Sandby (1730–1809). Collection of Mr and Mrs Paul Mellon, Upperville, Va.

Symphony No. 101, first page of the score from the copy made by Johann Elssler. Országos Széchényi Könyvtár, ex coll. Esterházy Archives, Budapest. — 494

29 Buckingham House (now Palace) seen from St James's Park; watercolour by E. Dayes, 1790. Victoria and Albert Museum, London.

Haydn's autograph note on the title-page of the score of Symphony No. 104, 1795. Preussische Staatbibliothek, Berlin. — 495

'Lord Cathcart's Wee', from a manuscript on paper with watermark date 1807. Author's collection. — 566

Symphony No. 102, page from the autograph of the slow movement, 1794. Preussische Staatsbibliothek, Berlin. — 587

Preface

A CENTURY AGO, the Austrian scholar C. F. Pohl began (in 1875) to publish his three-volume biography of Joseph Haydn, the first large-scale work of its kind about the composer; volume II appeared in 1882, but volume III was unfinished when Pohl died in 1887. The material for this third volume was then entrusted to Eusebius von Mandyczewski, who was (as Pohl had been before him) Custodian of the important Archives of the Gesellschaft der Musikfreunde, Vienna. Mandyczewski also died before being able to complete volume III of Pohl's biography, which was then given to Hugo Botstiber, who completed and published it with Breitkopf & Härtel in 1927.

Pohl's biography, recently reprinted, was for many years the standard work on Haydn. Unlike Spitta's Bach or Jahn's Mozart biographies, however, Pohl's work was never translated, and until the reprint appeared it was very difficult to find a copy in the antiquarian market. Although widely consulted by scholars, Pohl's books were hardly known to the general public, and certainly not in the English-speaking world.

Our knowledge of Haydn's life and works has greatly increased since Pohl's pioneer efforts. Dozens of compositions unknown to Pohl have meanwhile come to light. I need mention only a few, such as the 'Cello Concerto in C (c. 1765?), the Violin Concerto in A (c. 1765?); the *Missa brevis alla cappella* 'Rorate coeli Desuper' (c. 1750?); the German marionette operas *Philemon und Baucis* (1773, revised c. 1776) and *Das abgebrannte Haus* (*DieFeuersbrunst*; c. 1776); and *La fedeltà premiata* (1780), of which opera Pohl knew only fragments. But even more important from the purely biographical standpoint, Pohl knew only a small part of the documents in the Esterházy Archives, which have become generally available to scholars only since about 1958. The autograph letters and other documents from the Esterházy Archives, still in the course of publication, have revolutionized our knowledge of Haydn's daily life at Eszterháza Castle to the point where Pohl's work is now quite outdated. Similarly, the discovery of many musical autographs unknown to Pohl has greatly increased our knowledge of Haydn's early and middle period. Pohl thought, for example, that the so-called *Missa Sanctae Caeciliae* had been composed in the early 1780s, whereas we know now that the work was originally and authentically entitled *Missa Cellensis in honorem Beatissimae Virginis Mariae* – i.e. a Mass composed (like its illustrious companion-piece of 1782, the *Mariazellermesse* – for the great pilgrimage church of Mariazell in Styria – and was, moreover, composed in 1766. Back-datings have also occurred with other major works, such as the *Stabat Mater*, which Pohl dated 1773 but which on the basis of an autograph letter discovered in the 1950s in the Esterházy Archives was actually composed in 1767.

When Pohl was writing his biography, there was no collected edition of Haydn's works. The first attempt, based on Pohl's enormous collection of Haydn sources for the Gesellschaft der Musikfreunde, often entirely written by Pohl himself, was organized by Breitkopf & Härtel in 1907 with Eusebius von Mandyczewski as general editor: but the project collapsed after about ten volumes.[1] A second attempt was begun by the Haydn Society in 1949, and it too collapsed for lack of funds after four volumes had been issued. In the middle 1950s, a third attempt was started by the Joseph Haydn Institut in Cologne, first under the direction of J. P. Larsen and later led by Georg Feder. With some luck, the new collected edition may be completed by (about) the year 2000.

Further, when Pohl was alive, no Haydn Catalogue (in the manner of Köchel's Mozart list) was available, and it was not until 1957 that the Dutch enthusiast, A. van Hoboken, began to publish a thematic catalogue of all Haydn's known works. Volume I (the instrumental works) appeared in 1957, and volume II (the vocal music) was published in 1971. There are difficulties in compiling a definitive scholarly Haydn catalogue in advance of the collected edition. Only a few years after the publication of volume I of Hoboken's Catalogue it was already out of date; but inevitably defective though the catalogue may be, especially volume I, it is much better than not having one at all.

When I was Secretary General of the Haydn Society, there was some discussion with Professor Otto Erich Deutsch concerning a documentary biography of Haydn, such as those which Deutsch had brilliantly compiled for both Schubert and Handel, and was thereafter to complete for Mozart. But as more and more archive material came in from Budapest, Deutsch felt increasingly that in Haydn's case a documentary biography would be of little interest except to the scholar. Moreover, it was soon clear that such a documentary biography would run to at least ten thousand pages, and that many of the documents from the Esterházy Archives – bills for violin strings, horn crooks and oboe reeds – would have to be 'interpreted' for the general reader. A large quantity of such documents, supplied by Prince Esterházy's ex-Archivist, Dr János Harich, have been published in the *Haydn Yearbooks*. Even now (1975), new and mostly unpublished Haydn material is still arriving from the Esterházy Archives.

When it became clear that the official, scholarly collected edition of Haydn's works would probably not be completed before the year 2000, it seemed to me that an interim solution must be found. Towards the end of the 1950s, therefore, I decided to publish an abbreviated *Gesamtausgabe* of Haydn's works, in scholarly but practical form, that is, with performance material for works such as symphonies and operas. This project has occupied me from about 1958 to the present time. The publications include:

    1) a collected edition of all the symphonies;
    2) a collected edition of all the piano sonatas (prepared by Christa Landon);
    3) a collected edition of all the piano trios (all the late trios have been issued at the present time);
    4) a collected edition of all the string quartets (prepared in collaboration with Mr Reginald Barrett-Ayres);
    5) eight of Haydn's operas;
    6) the Masses.

In 1959, I issued the *Collected Correspondence and London Notebooks of Joseph Haydn* (1959), now out of print. This English-language edition was followed in 1965 by an original-language edition edited by Professor Dénes Bartha.

---

[1] Four volumes of symphonies (Nos. 1–40), three volumes comprising all the then known fifty-two piano sonatas, one volume of *Lieder*, and the oratorios *Die sieben Worte*, *Die Schöpfung* and *Die Jahreszeiten*, of which *Die sieben Worte* was issued only in a practical reprint from the original plates.

While preparing the interim edition of Haydn's music, described above, I was steadily collecting material for a full-scale biography. There are, as mentioned earlier, still many unpublished documents in the Esterházy Archives concerning the years up to 1790, and many of these will be appearing in the *Haydn Yearbook*. On the other hand, my researches into the late years of Haydn's life, from the London visits (1791–5) to his death in 1809, while they could not hope to be absolutely complete, were sufficiently ample to enable me to prepare and publish a biography of the later years. Thus I decided to plan the biography in five self-sufficient parts, each of which may be read *per se*; taken together, the five volumes will eventually cover Haydn's entire career. I have found many unpublished letters and documents which shed new light on Haydn's life and works, and equally important on the world in which he lived. The student of eighteenth-century London or Vienna, or of Mozart, Beethoven or Viotti, will, it is hoped, find much that is new (e.g. the hitherto unrecorded first appearance of Beethoven in Vienna in 1795, which happened the very same night that Haydn was presenting to a fascinated London audience the world première of the 'Drum Roll' Symphony). The periods covered by the five volumes planned are listed chronologically as follows:

Haydn: the Early Years (1732–1765);
Haydn at Eszterháza (1766–1790);
Haydn in England (1791–1795);
Haydn: the Years of 'The Creation' (1796–1800);
Haydn: the Late Years (1801–1809).

In the present volume, the first in order of publication, I have incorporated the research from my earlier book on Haydn's symphonies, published in 1955 and long out of print. It was a very specialized work, of little interest to the general reader, but it contained for the first time all the extant programmes and newspaper criticisms of the Salomon and Opera concerts. Pohl's pioneering work, *Haydn in London* (1867), was still useful for its wide background material and for many interesting details, some of which Pohl seems to have picked up orally in England.

In reprinting original documents, I have neither modernized the spelling nor added missing accents: Count von Zinzendorf's Diary in French is particularly careless in the latter respect. Since many of these documents appear here in print for the first time, it was thought that other scholars would find them more useful in their original state. I would like to add here a note on the variations in German spellings. During the period covered by the five volumes, the German language was undergoing a thorough revision, whereby many words previously spelled with a 'C' were now being spelled with a 'K' (thus 'Cölln' became 'Köln', 'Colmar' 'Kolmar' and 'Capell Meister' 'Kapellmeister'). My text attempts to follow this change as best it can: obviously the word in 1760 was 'Capell Meister' (or 'Capellmeister') but in 1800 'Kapellmeister' was the standard spelling. I mention this one example as typical of the problems that confront the conscientious translator.

I have added all Haydn's known correspondence (some of it missing in by 1959 edition of the *Collected Correspondence and London Notebooks*) and all the principal entries of the London notebooks, which have, however, been rearranged in chronological order rather than in the casual order in which Haydn jotted down his remarks.

Those readers who may wish to follow Haydn's life from 1791 till his death in 1809 will realize that the Napoleonic Wars began to play an increasingly important role in the life of every thinking man in Europe. To the twentieth-century mind, it seems nearly incredible that many brilliant intellectuals, including Beethoven, were firmly on the side of Napoleon all through the 1790s. Haydn, however, was not; possibly also because of his strong emotional ties with England. It was no historical accident that it was precisely Haydn who was chosen to compose the Emperor's Hymn.

This book treats of the effects of the war in 1793–5. It was not a war to which England looked forward; indeed, she entered it reluctantly. There is a brilliant article – we would now call it a 'leader' – on this subject in *The Times* for 8 February 1793, which sums up the British – and also, incidentally, Haydn's – attitude at this beginning of what would be the first 'modern' war:

THE APPROACHING WAR

The public mind is now wholly occupied by the great and important question of WAR; and the justification of its NECESSITY is the subject of our present consideration.

We are free to confess, that a war with FRANCE appears to us not only to be founded on the strict rules of retaliation, but also of self-defence against *principles*, which tend to disorganize every existing government, and to destroy all social order. There is not a power in Europe but possesses one common interest to stop the progress of the new political French disease; and the people are equally bound to secure themselves from this pestilential contagion, which for four years past has desolated the finest kingdom in the universe. The approaching war is entered on with reluctance. It is not, as was formerly the case, a war between ambitious Kings, who sacrificed millions of men to ascertain the right of an insignificant town or province; it is not even a war of one nation against another, dictated by commercial interests; but it is a coalition of all regular and well established governments, and of every civilized people, against a system of anarchy, deliberative in its principles, and disastrous in its consequences. . . .

In vain can we attempt to avoid the scourge of war by negociation. But how negociate with a country, without a Government; with an Assembly, without morals; with Ministers who succeed each other with the rapidity of lightning; where one system is immediately overturned, and another substituted in its place, diametrically its reverse: How can Great Britain place any confidence in men, who at the very moment they declare their renunciation of all views of conquest, employ intrigue and violence to unite foreign provinces to their territory; men, who at the time they offer liberty to all mankind, in order to seduce them from their lawful Sovereigns, imperiously dictate laws which the people detest, and arbitrarily harass those who have sufficient fortitude to resist them; men whose lips profess generosity and loyalty, but whose hearts are devoted to riot, confusion, murder and rapine. . . .

And so, although this is a biography of a musician, the thread of history as such could not be overlooked without doing violence to the overall, panoramic view of Haydn in his world; and the reader will, from time to time, find shorter or longer summaries of military and political history, largely taken from contemporary diaries, newspapers, and other such sources, to counterbalance the occasionally very detailed view of Haydn's daily life which must be our principal concern here.

ACKNOWLEDGMENTS
I cannot hope to list here all the persons and institutions to whom, and to which, I am indebted for information, assistance and kindnesses of every sort. I have attempted to thank individuals and libraries in the actual text and footnotes, but would like here to single out a few who have been especially helpful over the many years during which I

have been collecting information for this biography as a whole, and here especially those who have helped with the present volume. Mrs Eva Alberman (London) has given photographs of her valuable Haydn manuscripts – which include Symphony No. 97, no less – as has Mr Albi Rosenthal (London and Oxford), who owns one of the two extant hand-bills of a Haydn concert in England. Mr Fritz Spiegl (Liverpool) has always proved a mine of information. Dr Roger Fiske (London) sent useful notes about Haydn's friend Mrs Hodges. Mr Richard Andrewes (London) was kind enough to examine many British periodicals and to copy their contents or provide photocopies. The late Hans Hammelmann (Vecoli) lent many of his first editions, and Mr Michael Rose (Panzano) was good enough to lend the interesting Haydn manuscripts from the library of Count Papafava. Mr Richard Wadleigh (Rome), my old collaborator at the Haydn Society office in Vienna, sent useful notes on the Orpheus legend. Dr Hubert Unverricht (Mainz) kindly sent me his material, including new information, on J. P. Salomon. Mr Henry Pleasants (London) organized much of the material about Mrs Hunter, and Mr Michael Kassler (Washington, D.C.) sent me his transcript of a diary by Charles Edward Horn which is now in Tokyo. Mr and Mrs F. Gordon Morrill (Florence) were patient enough to read through the whole manuscript and to make countless useful suggestions, and Mr Walter Legge (Saint-Jean-Cap-Ferrat) kindly read over the galley proofs.

I should also like to thank friends and colleagues in museums, galleries and libraries who have helped by providing information and photographs. Of the libraries I should like to single out the British Museum Music Room and Mr O. W. Neighbour, whose efforts on my behalf were numerous and always executed with the greatest efficiency. The Haus-, Hof- und Staatsarchiv in Vienna was host to me for many weeks while I was transcribing the unpublished diaries of Count von Zinzendorf. The Burgenländisches Landesmuseum, Eisenstadt, and its director, Hofrat Dr Ohrenberger, were of great assistance. The Stadtbibliothek in Vienna photographed many unpublished documents for me, including the Archives of the Pensionsgesellschaft and the Bartolozzi correspondence. The Österreichische Nationalbibliothek and its charming director, Dr Franz Grasberger, have proved most helpful, as have the Archives of the Gesellschaft der Musikfreunde in Vienna and the director, Frau Dr Hedwig Mitringer. The following institutions were my hosts on many occasions and also sent me microfilms and information: the Yale University Library, New Haven, Conn.; the Library of Congress, Washington, D.C.; the Preussische Staatsbibliothek, Berlin; the Bibliothèque Nationale, Paris (and my old friend M. François Lesure); the Museo della Scala, Milan; the fürstl. Fürstenbergisches Hofarchiv, Donaueschingen; the fürstl. Thurn-und-Taxis'ches Hofarchiv, Regensburg; the fürstl. Oettingen-Wallerstein'sches Hofarchiv, Harburg; the Benedictine Abbeys of Kremsmünster, Göttweig, Melk, Seitenstetten, Lambach and St Peter (Salzburg); the Augustinian Abbeys of St Florian and Klosterneuburg; the Cistercian Abbeys of Lilienfeld, Zwettl and Heiligenkranz; the Consevatorio Giuseppe Verdi, Milan; the Biblioteca Estense, Modena; and the National Library in Prague.

I should like to reserve a special vote of thanks to the National Library in Budapest and to my many friends and colleagues in the Music Department there who, as well as sending me countless microfilms, were generous enough to photograph material from provincial sources, such as Sopron. The Hungarian authorities were my hosts on five occasions; without their assistance this biography could not have been written.

Finally, I am grateful to all those who have provided photographs for reproduction in the plates (the source of each item will be found in the List of

Author's note

Illustrations on pp. 9, 10). I am especially grateful to Her Majesty the Queen for allowing me to reproduce the famous portrait of Haydn by Hoppner, and to the Royal College of Music, London, for permission to include several of the paintings in its collection, among them the portraits of Haydn and (previously unpublished) Salomon by Hardy. I should also like to thank Mr and Mrs Paul Mellon for providing previously unpublished eighteenth-century views of London in their Collection.

Vienna 1975   H.C.R.L.

AUTHOR'S NOTE

Haydn's music

Vocal music is identified by title and, on the occasion of the first or major reference, by its number in Hoboken's *Haydn Verzeichnis* (vol. II, Vocal Works), Mainz, 1971.

Instrumental music is identified as follows.

Symphonies are referred to by their number in Mandyczewski's list for the publishers Breitkopf & Härtel, which numbering was taken over by Hoboken in his *Haydn Verzeichnis* (vol. I), Mainz, 1955. Symphony No. 95 is thus I:95 in Hoboken's list.

String Quartets are identified by their opus number and, like all instrumental pieces, by the Hoboken number at the first and/or major reference.

Piano Sonatas are listed by their chronological numbering in the *Wiener Urtext Ausgabe*, edited by C. Landon.

Piano Trios are identified by the new chronological numbering in the *Complete Edition of Haydn's Piano Trios*, edited by H. C. Robbins Landon and published by Verlag Doblinger.

Other instrumental works are identified by their customary title (e.g. 'London Trios' and 'Overture to an English Opera') and by their Hoboken number.

References to works by Haydn will be found in abbreviated form, e.g. 'Symphony No. 97/IV, 171–4' – this refers to the symphony's fourth movement, at bars 171–4. The system of pitch notation used is based on middle C being represented by the symbol *c'*.

Instruments (in order of their customary appearance in the orchestral score) are abbreviated thus: Fl. – flute; Ob. – oboe; Cor ang. – cor anglais; Clar. – clarinet; Bsn. (Fag.) – bassoon; Hr. (Cor.) – horn; Trpt. (Trbe.) – trumpet; Trbn. – trombone; Timp. – timpani (kettledrums); V. – violin; Va. – viola; Vc. – violoncello; Cb. (B.) – contrabasso (double bass); Cemb. – cembalo (harpsichord).

Documents

In all documents cited in the text the original orthography – whether in English, German, French or Italian – has been retained. Thus, accents have not been inserted where they were omitted in the original document, notably in passages from the Zinzendorf Diaries. The language of the original document is indicated only in those cases which require clarification. Bibliographical references will be found in an abbreviated form in the text, at the end of quotations and in the footnotes; the full titles of works cited are given on pp. 17–18.

I Joseph Haydn, portrait in oils by John Hoppner, 1791. Royal Collection; reproduced by gracious permission of Her Majesty the Queen. This portrait was commissioned by the Prince of Wales (later George IV), who was a great patron of the arts.

II Joseph Haydn, portrait in oils by Thomas Hardy, 1791.

III Johann Peter Salomon, the famous impresario and violinist, who was responsible for bringing about Haydn's visit to England and for whose concerts at the Hanover Square Rooms Haydn wrote his 'London' symphonies; portrait in oils by Thomas Hardy, 1791.

IV Hanover Square, London, from the north-west; on the east side of the square (on the corner of Hanover Street) were the Concert Rooms in which Salomon's concerts were given. Coloured engraving by R. Pollard and F. Jukes after E. Dayes, 1787.

V Ignaz Joseph Pleyel, the composer who had earlier been a pupil of Haydn's, and who also came to London where he featured prominently in the concert season of 1792; portrait in oils by Elisabeth Vigée-Lebrun.

ABBREVIATIONS OF
BIBLIOGRAPHICAL SOURCES

AMZ	*Allgemeine Musikalische Zeitung*, Leipzig, 1798 *et seq.*
Bartha-Somfai	Dénes Bartha and László Somfai, *Haydn als Opernkapellmeister*, Budapest, 1960.
Carpani	Giuseppe Carpani, *Le Haydine*, Milan, 1812.
CCLN	*Collected Correspondence and London Notebooks of Joseph Haydn*, translated and edited by H. C. Robbins Landon, London, 1959.
Crosse *Account*	*An Account of the Grand Musical Festival, held in September, 1823, in the Cathedral Church of York . . .*, by John Crosse, F.S.A., F.R.S.L., York, 1825.
Da Ponte	*Memoirs of Lorenzo da Ponte*, translated from the Italian by Elizabeth Abbott, edited and annotated by Arthur Livingston; new edition, New York, 1967.
Dies	A. C. Dies, *Biographische Nachrichten von Joseph Haydn*, Vienna, 1810; new edition by Horst Seeger, Berlin, n.d. [1959].
Farington	*The Farington Diary*, edited by James Greig, London and New York, 1923.
Gerber *NTL*	Ludwig Gerber, *Neues historisch-biographisches Lexikon der Tonkünstler*, 4 vols, 1812–14; new edition by Othmar Wessely, Graz, 1966.
Geiringer 1932, 1947, 1959 and 1963	Karl Geiringer, *Joseph Haydn*: Potsdam, 1932; New York, 1947; Mainz, 1959; Garden City, N.Y., 1963.
Griesinger	G. A. Griesinger, *Biographische Notizen über Joseph Haydn*, Leipzig, 1810; new edition by Franz Grasberger, Vienna, 1954.
Grove I, II, III, IV, V	Grove's *Dictionary of Music and Musicians*, first, second, third, fourth and fifth editions.
Hadden	J. Cuthbert Hadden, *Haydn*, London, 1902.
Hase	H. von Hase, *Joseph Haydn und Breitkopf & Härtel*, Leipzig, 1902.
Horányi	Mátyás Horányi, *Das Esterházysche Feenreich*, Budapest, 1959: English edition, *The Magnificence of Eszterháza*, London, 1962
Landon *Essays*	H. C. Robbins Landon, *Essays on the Viennese Classical Style*, London, 1970.
Landon *SYM*	H. C. Robbins Landon, *The Symphonies of Joseph Haydn*, London, 1955.

Landon *Supplement*	H. C. Robbins Landon, *Supplement to 'The Symphonies of Joseph Haydn'*, London, 1961.
Landon *Beethoven*	H. C. Robbins Landon, *Beethoven: a documentary study*, London and New York, 1970.
Larsen *HÜB*	J. P. Larsen, *Die Haydn-Überlieferung*, Copenhagen, 1939.
Lonsdale	Roger Lonsdale, *Dr. Charles Burney, a literary biography*, Oxford, 1965.
MGG	*Musik in Geschichte und Gegenwart* (Allgemeine Enzyklopädie der Musik), edited by Friedrich Blume, Kassel, 1947 *et seq.*
Mörner	C.-G. Stellan Mörner, *Johann Wikmanson und die Brüder Silverstolpe*, Stockholm, 1952.
Olleson	E. Olleson, 'Haydn in the Diaries of Count Karl von Zinzendorf', in *Haydn Yearbook* II (1963–4).
Parke	W. T. Parke, *Musical Memoirs*, 2 vols., London, 1830.
Pohl *H in L*	C. F. Pohl, *Haydn in London*, Vienna, 1867; reprinted, New York, 1970.
Pohl *Denkschrift*	C. F. Pohl, *Denkschrift aus Anlass des 100-Jährigen Bestehens der Tonkünstler-Societät*, Vienna, 1871.
Pohl I, II, III	C. F. Pohl, *Joseph Haydn* (3 vols.): I, Berlin, 1875; II, Berlin, 1882; III (completed by Hugo Botstiber), Leipzig, 1927. All three vols. since reprinted.
Radant *Rosenbaum*	'The Diaries of Joseph Carl Rosenbaum 1770–1829', edited by Else Radant, *Haydn Yearbook* V (1968); also as a separate publication in the original German.
Rosenbaum	'The Diaries of Joseph Carl Rosenbaum 1770–1829'; see Radant above.
Scholes	Percy Scholes, *The Great Dr. Burney* (2 vols.), London, 1948.
Smart	*Leaves from the Journals of Sir George Smart*, by H. Bertram Cox and C. L. E. Cox, London, 1907.
Somfai	László Somfai, *Joseph Haydn. Sein Leben in zeitgenössischen Bildern*, Budapest and Kassel, 1966; also published in English as *Joseph Haydn: his Life in Pictures,* London, 1967.
Spohr	*The Musical Journeys of Louis Spohr*, selected, translated and edited by Henry Pleasants, Norman, 1961.
Thayer I	A. W. Thayer, *Ludwig van Beethovens Leben*, second revised edition (Deiters), vol. I, Berlin, 1901.
Thayer-Forbes	Thayer's *Life of Beethoven*, revised and edited by Elliot Forbes (2 vols.), Princeton, N.J., 1967.
Zinzendorf	MS. Diaries of Count Carl von Zinzendorf, in the Haus-, Hof- und Staatsarchiv, Vienna.

PART I

Chronicle 1791–1795

CHAPTER ONE

1791

It was the afternoon of New Year's Day, 1791, when Haydn first surveyed the long line of chalk cliffs at Dover. He was then aged fifty-eight and was, in the words of Albert Christian Dies, one of the composer's three 'authentic' biographers,

> of something less than medium size. The lower part of his body was too short for the upper, something often to be encountered in small persons of both sexes, but which was very obvious in Haydn's case because he adhered to the old fashioned mode of knee breeches that reached only the hips and not the chest. His facial features were rather regular, and his expression vivacious, fiery, but at the same time moderate, warm and inviting. If Haydn's mood was serious, his features would join his expression to produce an air of dignity; otherwise his look, when conversing, tended usually to be cheerful and amused. I never heard him laugh out loud. Haydn had a moderately strong bone structure; his muscles were not prominent. His hawk line nose (he suffered much from a nasal polyp which had no doubt enlarged this part of his anatomy) and also the other parts of his face were strongly scarred from the pox, and the nose even had pox seams so that each nostril had a different form.

'Haydn considered himself ugly,' continues Dies, 'and told me of a prince and his consort who could not bear his (Haydn's) features, "because", he said, "I was too ugly for them". This presumed ugliness was not, however, in his form but only in his pock-marked skin and the brownish complexion.'[1]

'In his character,' Dies goes on, 'was much cheerfulness, merriness, and a popular, but refined and highly original musical wit. . . .'[2]

Legationsrath Georg August Griesinger, another of Haydn's 'authentic' biographers and in many respects the most reliable of the three, tells us that

> Haydn's stature was small but sturdy and his bone structure solid; his forehead was broad and nicely domed, his skin brown, his eyes vivacious and fiery, the other features strong and sharply defined; and from his whole physiognomy and bearing there radiated prudence and quiet gravity.   [Griesinger, 51]

> An *innocent waggishness*, or what the English call humour, was a principal trait of Haydn's character. He discovered easily and by preference the funny side of a situation, and whoever spent only an hour in his company must have noticed that the native Austrian cheerfulness breathed in him.   [Griesinger, 57]

Both biographers have pointed out the serious and the waggish side to Haydn's complex, and in some respects rather opaque, personality. A Swedish diplomat, the

---

1 Dies, 206f.
2 Dies, 208.

chargé d'affaires Frederik Samuel Silverstolpe, met Haydn at Vienna in 1797 and observed that

> During this conversation [about 'Chaos' in *The Creation*] . . . I discovered in Haydn as it were two physiognomies. The one was penetrating and serious, when he talked about anything exalted [*Erhabene*], and only the expression 'exalted' was enough to show him visibly moved. In the next moment this atmosphere of exaltation was chased away, quick as lightning, from his every-day expression, and he became jovial with a force that showed on his features and which then passed into waggishness. This was his usual physiognomy; the other one had to be induced.[1]

Haydn's cool, shrewd brown eyes were curious about everything he saw in England: the people, the customs, the climate, the music-making, the women (all his biographers stress that he was very fond of women – 'in younger years he is said to have been most susceptible to love');[2] and he kept a series of notebooks, of which three have survived complete and a fourth in extracts, that give us a humorous, sarcastic, naïve, clever and sometimes shocked account of his life in England. It will be observed, as this Chronicle continues, how many different kinds of people became Haydn's friends in England (as much as their different stations would allow): from the Duchess of York to 'Mister March . . . a dentist, coach-maker and dealer in wines . . . a man 84 years old [with] a very young mistress'; from Dr Burney to the Earl of Abingdon (Haydn must have been utterly fascinated to see him put in prison, like any commoner, for a vicious libel); from the violent revolutionary poet and playwright Thomas Holcroft (again Haydn must have watched his treason trial and acquittal with astonishment) to the gentle Mistress Schroeter, the 'amiable widow' whom Haydn might have married had he been single; from the banker Nathaniel Brassey to the naval captain who had the delighted Haydn to lunch on his East India merchantman 'with six cannon' and told the composer how to preserve cream or milk 'for a long time'. Haydn blossomed; nor did the flattery, the adulation of the public, or his constant appearance in the London daily newspapers go to his head. The English loved him, and thought his music the greatest they knew after Handel's.

The England which Haydn so closely observed had, of course, a sharp division between upper and lower classes; but the whole social structure was much different from that of Austria. Haydn, as any thinking man, was intensely aware of the situation in France; and while revolutionary thoughts and even Jacobean mutterings became more and more frequent until the Terror, there was never a serious doubt in men's minds that the monarchy and the system would survive. Part of the reason was the behaviour of the English aristocracy.

> The countryside was dotted with their lovely palaces and noble avenues, the fields and woods of the whole kingdom were open to their horses and hounds, the genius of man, past and present, was brought to decorate their houses and gardens, to fill their libraries with masterpieces of the classical and modern mind in bindings worthy of them, to cover their walls with paintings and tapestries, and adorn their tables with exquisite silver and porcelain. . . . They encouraged freedom of expression and diversity of behaviour, preferring a vigorous existence and the

1 'Haydniana aus Schweden um 1800', by C.-G. Stellan Mörner, in *Haydn-Studien* II, 1 (1969), p. 25.
2 Dies, 209. It has sometimes been said that Haydn had grey eyes; in the oil portraits by Guttenbrunn, Seehas, Hardy and Hoppner – four authentic portraits dating from 1791(?), 1785, 1791 and 1791 respectively – the eyes are clearly brown. In the portrait by Zitterer, *c.* 1795, which Artaria engraved in 1800, Haydn also has brown eyes.

society of their equals to a hot-house tended by serfs. They sent their sons to rough, libertarian schools. . . . At Harrow the Duke of Dorset was always beaten twice; once for the offence and once for being a Duke. . . . Though possessing almost unlimited power, the English aristocracy never attempted to make itself a rigid caste. . . . Save for the eldest male their grandchildren were all commoners with the same prefix as groom and gamekeeper. . . . Because they enjoyed life and seldom stood deliberately in the way of others doing the same, they were popular. They took part in the nation's amusements and mixed freely with their neighbours. They were healthy, gregarious and generous, and had little fear in their make-up. They governed England without a police force, without a Bastille and virtually without a Civil Service, by sheer assurance and personality.[1]

Haydn came to know a great many members of the aristocracy. The king, who was a much more astute and sensitive man than is often realized, asked him to stay in England; and George III's wife offered Haydn a suite in Windsor Castle. Haydn was entertained many times by the Prince of Wales, the Duke of York and especially the handsome Duchess of York. The composer soon became immensely popular; he spent weekends in beautiful houses all over England, and his hosts obviously found him a delightful guest. Haydn's special friend and patron was Lord Abingdon, who took the composer around with him.

But Haydn was not a snob. He said, with simple pride, 'I have been in the company of emperors, kings and many great gentlemen, and I received many a compliment from them: but I do not wish to live on terms of intimacy with such persons and prefer to be with people of my class' (Griesinger, 55). In England, Haydn found a middle class much older, much richer, and with much more influence than in his native Austria. The aristocracy may have been the ones to send Haydn fifty guineas for a ticket to his benefit concert[2] but it was the solid (in those days not stolid) middle class who flocked to Haydn's and Salomon's concerts, cheered their lungs out after the 'Military' Symphony and avidly bought up Haydn's piano trios and English canzonettas. It was from this same large segment of British society that Haydn drew his many English friends, the Mister Marches and Mistress Schroeters and all the other names that adorn Haydn's London notebooks.

If Haydn was drawn to the top and middle level of English society, he was slightly appalled by the bottom. Here, for the first time in his life, he encountered the proletariat, the forerunner of those pitiful creatures that the Industrial Revolution would soon be producing in huge quantities. These men and women, familiar to us from the gruesomely realistic pictures by Hogarth, were tough, dangerous and uncouth. The noise made by this lower class was something new to Haydn: the bunches of street rowdies, yelling songs (which Haydn, fascinated and repulsed, noted in his diary); and the drunken mob, breaking windows and roaring their approval of Lord Howe's great naval victory; the street cries of the violet vendors or lavender girls – all this astonished and perhaps slightly frightened Haydn. The power of the mob was soon to become a new and horrendous force to reckon with in European politics; and this was Haydn's first exposure to it. It was not to his liking.

Haydn's first goal, geographically, was London. Its very size amazed him, but more than that, it was his first experience with a great and worldly metropolis (for Vienna, at that time, was a beautiful but smallish city with walls dating from the time of the last Turkish siege). On the library table in one of the great English country

1 Sir Arthur Bryant, *The Years of Endurance 1793–1802*, London, 1942, pp. 3ff.; reprinted by courtesy of Wm. Collins Sons & Co. Ltd.
2 The Duchess of York in 1795. Griesinger, 33f.

houses to which he was invited, Haydn might have found the following note in *The Sporting Magazine* (January 1794, p. 220):

> Perhaps in no age or country has a metropolis been better characterized than the metropolis of England, in the words of Johnson. 'If you wish to have a just notion of the magnitude of this City, you must not be satisfied with feeling its great streets and squares, but must survey the innumerable little alleys and courts. It is not in the shewy evolutions of buildings, but in the multiplicity of human habitations which are crowded together, that the immensity of London consists. I have often amused myself with thinking how different a place London is to different people. They whose narrow minds are contracted to the consideration of some one particular object, view it only through that medium. A politician thinks of it merely as a seat of government in its different departments; a grazier, as a vast market for cattle; a mercantile man, as a place where a prodigious deal of business is done upon 'Change; a dramatic enthusiast, as the grand scene of theatrical entertainments; a man of pleasure, as an assemblage of taverns, and the great emporium for ladies of easy virtue; but the intellectual man is struck with it, as comprehending the *whole of human life in all its variety*, the contemplation of which is inexhaustible.'

At the beginning of his stay in London, Haydn's life was largely guided by Johann Peter Salomon, the impresario who had gone to Vienna to fetch the composer in December 1790. Since Salomon plays such a decisive role in Haydn's late years – for, as we shall see, that impresario was also responsible for *The Creation* – a few words about his earlier life and character may not be amiss here.

Salomon was born at Bonn in February (christening: 20 February) 1745 at Bonngasse 515, in the same house in which Beethoven was to be born in 1770. By 1758 he had been admitted to the orchestra of the Elector Clement August, and late in 1761 or early in 1762 he made a trip that took him as far as Poland; in 1764 he made a concert tour to Frankfurt-am-Main and Berlin, where he came to the favourable attention of Prince Heinrich of Prussia. Prince Heinrich engaged Salomon as *Concertmeister* but also as a composer of operettas; for if Salomon's name has come down to us primarily as the man who brought Haydn to England, and as an expert violinist and leader, he was also a reputable composer ('ganz passabel', said Haydn of *Windsor Castle*, Salomon's 1795 opera). After Prince Heinrich's band had been dismissed, Salomon possibly visited Paris and then went on to London, where he made his début at Covent Garden Theatre on 23 March 1781. The *Morning Herald* wrote of him, 'He does not play in the most graceful style, it must be confessed, but his tone and execution are such as cannot fail to secure him a number of admirers in the music world.' At first being connected with the Professional Concerts,[1] Salomon later quarrelled with them and

---

1 The Professional Concert – usually referred to in the singular, like the *Concert Spirituel* in Paris – was founded in 1783, and these 'Hanover square great concerts' soon attracted not only the best artists but also brilliant patronage, Haydn's later patron and friend, the Earl of Abingdon, was a prime mover of the 'Professors', as they were often called, and attempted to engage Haydn to come to London and compose for the Professional Concert. The long, involved and slightly sordid story of the Professional Concert's attempt to persuade the composer to visit England, of Haydn's attempt to fob off the Concert with works already known, and of the newspapers' involvement in the scandal, may be read in Cecil B. Oldman's article, 'Haydn's Quarrel with the "Professionals" in 1788' (*Musik und Verlag*, 1968, pp. 459ff.) and in Christopher Roscoe's article, 'Haydn and London in the 1780s' (*Music & Letters*, Vol. 49, No. 3 [July 1968], pp. 201ff.). The animosity of the Professional Concert towards Haydn when the composer arrived in London in 1791 is therefore to a certain extent justified, if we consider that they had attempted, unsuccessfully, to invite the composer to visit England from 1782 to 1788. One interesting sidelight is that Haydn seems to have sent the earliest MS. copies of his Quartets, Opp. 54 and 55 (in reality one opus), to the Professional Concert, which performed them in 1789, as the title page of the authentic Longman & Broderip edition informs us. See the critical edition, prepared by the present writer, for Doblinger. On the history of the Professional Concert, see C. F. Pohl, *H in L*, pp. 15ff.

went his own way, acting as solo violinist, violist, *entrepreneur* and leader. During Gertrud Elisabeth Mara's first season in London in 1784, Salomon led the orchestra and played solos. The *Morning Chronicle*, the next year, writes that

> Salomon's solo, though perhaps not excelling in tone, was in the greatest point, in pathetic impression, excelled by none! Whose violin-playing approaches nearer the human voice? On the whole Salomon is a mannerist, but he has much originality – he is very susceptible – he is a genius.

In 1786, he gave a series of subscription concerts at the Hanover Square Rooms, playing *inter alia* symphonies by Mozart and Haydn. He also became a great specialist in string quartets, in which he was soon not only popular with audiences and the Press, but also impressed Haydn sufficiently to write, as we shall see, the first quartets composed directly for the concert hall rather than the chamber (Opp. 71 and 74, composed in 1793 and performed by Salomon's quartet the next year at the Hanover Square Rooms).

In 1790, Salomon moved to No. 18, Great Pulteney Street, opposite the famous music shop of Broadwood; and it was to this address that Haydn went in 1791, having a room in which to compose at Broadwood's.

We are fortunate in having a detailed description of Salomon's arrival in England from the pen of Charlotte Papendiek (whom we shall be discussing in more detail when she describes Haydn's first concert in London). Mrs Papendiek writes:[1]

> On Friday, February 14 [1783], was the concert for the new Musical Fund, which always took place as early as possible, in order to introduce to the public the foreigners engaged for the season. Salomon was this year the great star. He called upon us, and when Mr. Papendiek returned his visit, he was fortunate enough to find him at home, and cordial friendship seemed at once to rivet them. . . .
>
> Salomon was to play first, and the desk was brought on, as it still continues to be. Then he appeared, introduced [by the composer Carl Friedrich] Abel, [the oboist Johann Christian] Fischer and Mr Papendiek following. [Salomon] was not handsome nor of an imposing figure, but the animation of his countenance, and the great elegance of his manner, soon caught the public eye. Having bowed, he so placed the desk that not the smallest particle of his violin was hidden, and the 'Tutti' of his favourite concerto, by [Rodolphe] Kreutzer, commenced rather mezzo-piano, and increased to a crescendo that drew down volumes of applause. Now came the solo; a repetition of the melody an octave higher, which he played with an effect perfectly sublime. It was in the minor key, and the cadence he introduced was a long shake, with the melody played under – something new, which put Fischer almost into fits. The adagio movement he performed in such a manner that Fischer was heard to say, 'I will play it no more; he has outdone me.' Then the rondo followed in the same key as the first movement, and Salomon introduced one short variation that struck upon the ear in such a manner that it was difficult to keep quiet. Having finished, he returned his instrument to the attendant, but retained the bow, which assisted his graceful bow. Abel, who had been permitted to sit, now rose, and they went off arm in arm. Such a *début* has scarcely ever been experienced. We were jumping from our seats. Schroeder [Johann Samuel Schroeter, whose widow, Rebecca, was soon to become intimate with Haydn] played in the first act, and made a most successful *début* also. His

---

1 *Court and Private Life in the Time of Queen Charlotte: being the Journals of Mrs Papendiek, Assistant Keeper of the Wardrobe and Reader to Her Majesty.* Edited by her Grand-daughter, Mrs Vernon Delves Broughton, London, 2 vols., 1886–7.

graceful and sweet manner of touching the pianoforte found its way to the approbation of the public. . . . [I, 185–7]

[Later in the summer of 1783] Schroeder often breakfasted with us, and if I were pretty well we had a little music in the way of a lesson. Dear Salomon often and often called to plan some entertainment or to practise. See me he always would, which, as Mr. Papendiek was often from home, the world censorious, and all of us warm–hearted, might perhaps as well have been avoided. Yet I am sure that in Salomon's mind only rectitude the most honourable, and sincerity the most pure, had place. Dear friend, we appreciated, we respected, we loved you! Farewell to thy memory. [I, 192]

Salomon was not only a clever and sensitive impresario, he was also generous (giving an extra concert free in 1794 for subscribers), scrupulously honest, and very efficient in business matters. His reputation soon spread back to the Continent from England, and we find complimentary references about him in Forkel's *Musikalischer Almanach für Deutschland auf das Jahr 1782* and the anonymous (perhaps Junker's) *Musikalischer und Künstler Almanach auf das Jahr 1783* as well as in Cramer's well-known *Magazin der Musik* (latter half of 1783). In 1797, a visiting Swede, Gustaf Sehmann, a friend of Silverstolpe's (*vide supra*), wrote an interesting description of Salomon:

[London, 12 September 1797]
. . . His [Salomon's] tone is enchanting and the finest I ever heard; in society without his playing he is less attractive, but does not in any way put one off . . .
[Mörner, 320]

Salomon was an eighteenth-century gentleman; he kept a servant, Johanning, who was later to be of great use to the Spohrs when they lived in London in 1819–20. Johanning acted as servant-cum-interpreter to the Spohrs, and on the last day of their stay, he appeared to take them to dinner 'spick and span in his late master's formal clothes, with white silk stockings and powdered hair'. They dined off Salomon's 'elegant service' and drank a fine *Hochheimer* which Spohr thought must have been from his late master's excellent cellar. Johanning's wife cooked. Spohr also discusses the excellence of the orchestra in London at the Philharmonic Concert, of which Salomon had been a founding member, and especially the string section and the 'precise ensemble playing'. Spohr never heard his symphony so well played (Spohr, 207ff). All this is the great heritage that Salomon left; even now, nearly two hundred years later, only in Britain and America does the leader come in after the orchestra is seated, and receive a round of applause.

Salomon was intensely alert to all new talent. We have been able to discover that he also 'launched' Beethoven's *Septet* during the concert season of 1801;[1] within six weeks it was being called 'the new much admired Septetto' which was performed 'By particular desire' at Salomon's Benefit Concert on 27 May 1801 in a programme which also included Haydn's *March for the Royal Society of Musicians* (composed in 1792 and still in MS. in 1801), the 'Military Symphony' and Mozart as well (*Morning Chronicle*).

This 'original and powerful talent' (Parke, I, 53) improved his position and reputation greatly by getting Haydn to England, but both men made a great deal of

---

1 At Salomon's subscription concert in the King's Theatre on 23 April (*Morning Chronicle*) the new work was announced as follows: 'New Grand Septetto (M.S.) for principal Violin, Viola, Violoncello, Clarinet, Bassoon, Corno and Double Bass, Messrs. Salomon, Pieltain, Dahmen, W. Mahon, Holmes, Leander, Dragonetti, Luigi van Beethoven.' These are all distinguished names familiar to students of Haydn's London sojourns. Haydn, of course, was also on the programme.

money out of the venture. Haydn soon became attached to his clever impresario and remained loyal to him even when the Professional Concert tried to win the composer away. Later, after Haydn left England, he wrote to Salomon as 'Liebster Freund'.

When Salomon died on 26 November 1815, after being thrown from a horse, everyone regretted the loss. Beethoven wrote to his pupil Ries in London (28 February 1816): 'Salomon's death grieves me much, for he was a noble man, and I remember him since I was a child.' This remarkable man and musician lies buried in the cloisters of Westminster Abbey, next to his (and Haydn's) friends Muzio Clementi and William Shield. The tablet says: 'Johann Peter Salomon / Musician / born 1745 died 1815 / he brought Haydn to England in 1791 and 1794.'[1] As will be seen, one of Haydn's first visits was to the publisher John Bland at 45 Holborn, opposite Chancery Lane in the City, where he spent his first night in London while Salomon was preparing quarters at Great Pulteney Street. John Bland had visited Haydn at Eszterháza in 1789 and Haydn had sent him the three 'Flute' Trios (for flute, piano and violin – Nos. 28, 29 and 30, Hob. XV: 16, 15, 17). Haydn published with Bland the Cantata, *Arianna a Naxos*, which was such a success during the season of 1791.[2] The composer also had letters to deliver in London: communications were still difficult and the oncoming Napoleonic Wars would make them more so. One such letter, which is instructive, is from Haydn's friend, the composer and violinist Paul Wranizky (his autograph spelling; contemporary reports usually spelled it Wranitzky):[3]

[page four:] A Monsieur   [across right-hand side: 'Wranizky/
     Monsieur J. Bland   12 dec. 90' from Bland's office]
       a
           Londres

[pages one-two:]
                                         a Vienne 12 December $\overline{790}$
Monsieur!
Je ne vois pas la raison pourquoi vous ne me donnez pas de reponse, sur ma lettre de 7me Aout, étant persuadé, que je Vous faisons des propositions agréables. Je me

---

1 Salomon, after Haydn's second stay, led the orchestra from a fabulous Cremona violin, made in 1578 (the case having been painted by Annibale Carracci) which had been owned by Archangelo Corelli and then by Felice Giardini (who died at Moscow on 17 December 1796). William Sandys and Simon Andrew Forster, *The History of the Violin ...*, London, 1864, pp. 104ff. For the basic biographical material on Salomon, *vide* Grove's *Dictionary*, 1st edition (London 1902, III, 220ff.); Thayer's *Ludwig van Beethovens Leben* (2nd edition, revised by Hermann Deiters, Vol. I, Berlin, 1901, p. 52) where various members of the Salomon family are listed in the *Hofkalender* for 1774 under 'Maître de la Chapelle – Mons. Louis van Beethoven', the grandfather. *Vide* C. F. Pohl, *H in L, passim* and especially pp. 73ff.; Hubert Unverricht, 'Die Kompositionen Johann Peter Salomons: Ein Überblick', in *Hüschen-Festschrift* (Beiträge zur rheinischen Musikgeschichte, Cologne, 1965, pp. 35–42). Salomon's gracious *Romance* in D for violin and string orchestra has been edited by the present writer and published in the series Diletto Musicale of the Verlag Doblinger, Vienna–Munich (No. 471, 1970); it bears an interesting relationship to Beethoven's *Romances*, Opp. 40 and 50, at least one of which, as will be seen, was composed much earlier than its published number indicates. New dates in Salomon's life from Unverricht. There are also interesting details about Salomon to be learned from 'Memoirs of Johann Peter Salomon', in *Harmonicon* VIII (1830), pp. 45ff.
2 'London Printed for the Author & sold by him at No. 18, Great Pulteney Street & at J. Blands Music Warehouse 45 Holborn.' Copy in Esterházy Archives, Budapest (Z 41.088): *Haydn Compositions in the Music Collection of the National Szechenyi Library, Budapest*. Budapest, 1960, item 299 on p. 135. This copy is signed by Haydn (being part-publisher; see also Larsen *HÜB*, 127ff.), as is another one in the King's Music Library, British Museum (R.M.9.d.9).
3 I owe this unpublished letter to the kindness of my old friend Mr Albi Rosenthal, who has always been of great help to me and to whom I am much indebted for many kind favours. The letter, with the rest of my small collection, is now in the Burgenländisches Landesmuseum at Eisenstadt.

donne donc le plaisir de Vous demander encore une fois, si vous ne voules accepter aucune de mes propositions. Mr. d'Haÿden, qui vous remettra cette lettre vous, instruira, si un oeuvre de ma composition soit degne d'etre publié a Londres.

Je vous proposaïs dans ma premiere Lettre trois quintetes toutes nouvelles, ou 6 quatuors concertans, si Vous souhaities de publier l'un ou l'autre oeuvre, puisque je souhaite beaucoup d'être connu à Londres. Les quintetes connais Mr. Haÿden. Demain matin me faira l'honeur Mr. Salomon de venir chez moi pour entendre ces Quatuors, et il Vous ca parlera.

Il y a dix oeuvres deja publié[s], et l'onzième le quel Mr Sieber a Paris va publier sont trois Quintettes compagnons de ces trois, dont je viens de vous faire l'offre.

Si vous souhaites d'entrer en correspondence avec moi, et de faire publier ma musique, vous pouvés être assuré, que Vous trouvés en moi un homme très juste, et très raisonable. Come je supose, que ma Composition aura l'approbation à Londres, j'espere que vous serèz a l'avenir encore genereux avec le prix. Pour cette fois, je me tiens au prix de la premiere lettre. Je vous prie de me donner une prompte reponse pour savoir, prendre ma partie, et j'ai l'honneur d'etre avec l'estime le plus parfait

Votre très humble serviteur
Paul Wranizky
mpria

[page three:]
     addresse
     ————

  Im Dorotheerhof Nro 1142
   im 3ten Stock.
[watermarks: coat-of-arms with a fleur-de-lys at bottom, 'D & C BLAUW']

The next matter which engaged Haydn's total attention was the standard of orchestral (instrumental) playing, and the standard of singing. As far as the instrumental standard was concerned, he could at once see that the average orchestra was about forty strong (*vide infra*), which would grow to sixty by 1795. The difficult technical level of Haydn's 'Salomon' Symphonies – e.g. the octave passage in the violins at Symphony No. 97/IV, 171–4, difficult even now for our greatest orchestras, or the whole Finale of No. 94 – show more clearly than any written testimony how good were the players Haydn had at his disposal. For the Handel Festival in 1791, Haydn could see the excellent standard of British choirs and the enormously effective sound of massed forces; and he would carefully repeat the large size in the Viennese performances of his own late oratorios. There were many famous singers in London, indeed, the greatest the world had to offer, and Haydn wrote new arias or cantatas for many of them: the great castrato, Gaetano Pacchierotti, who so brilliantly launched Haydn's Cantata *Arianna a Naxos* in 1791; Gertrud Elisabeth Mara, for whom Haydn conducted many times; and later Brigida Giorgi Banti, for whom Haydn would compose his greatest cantata, the *Scena di Berenice*; Mrs Elizabeth Billington, to whom Haydn presented, via his friend William Shield, the Terzetto, 'Pietà di me', for two sopranos, tenor, *obbligati* cor anglais, bassoon and horn (which goes up to sounding *b flat*), with orchestra[1]; Giacomo Davide (Davidde; also in England 'David'), one of the

---

1 A work from the Eszterháza years. It is included in the pasticcio *Alessandro* (MS. Gesellschaft der Musikfreunde, Vienna), put together by an Esterházy copyist from Haydn's *La fedeltà premiata* and other works, including 'Pietà di me'. We have been quite unable to find for which occasion Haydn wrote the

greatest tenors of the period, was in England in 1791, and it was for him that Haydn created the title role in his final opera. Local British singers were also trained in the *buona scuola italiana*, for example Miss Sophia Corri, who later married the pianist J.L. Dussek. Miss Corri was born in Edinburgh. Haydn used her services at his benefit concert on 3 May 1792.[1]

Several rooms were regularly used for concerts, as the forthcoming notices will show. Naturally our attention focuses on the Hanover Square Rooms, a building on the east side of the square at the north-east corner of Hanover Street. In 1774, the freehold property was sold by the Earl of Plymouth for £5,000 to Viscount Wenman, who on the same day resold it to a group consisting of Sir John Gallini, Johann Christian Bach and C. F. Abel; Gallini (about whom more later) owned a half, the others each a quarter. They erected a handsome building for assemblies and concerts, with office rooms (one of which was occupied by Salomon), and a big hall (on the second floor) of spacious dimensions. In the *General Evening Post* of 25 February 1794 there is a revealing table of popular London concert rooms, including three the names of which will frequently recur in this Chronicle.

Room	Length	Breadth	Square Feet
King's Theatre			
Concert Room	97	48	4656
Crown & Anchor	81	36	2916
Hanover Square	79	32	2528

The (obviously authentic) measurements given here are at considerable variance with those usually given for Hanover Square, viz. 95 feet by 35; possibly this latter size was that of the Rooms after they were rebuilt in Victorian times. Apart from these large rooms there was also a small room on the north side which was used in those days as a tea-room. The ceiling of the big room was domed and decorated with paintings by Cipriani. Spohr (p. 216) relates that it 'was the custom for the concert-giver to serve his audience refreshments gratis during the intermission between the first and second halves of the programme', and we shall read of a cup of tea being inadvertently poured down Madame Mara's back.

The rooms were opened on 1 February 1775 with one of the Bach-Abel subscription concerts. On 12 November 1776, Sir John Gallini purchased the shares of Bach and Abel, and became the sole proprietor, but Bach's and Abel's concerts continued to be held there until 1782, at which last season (1781) Haydn's Symphony No. 53 in D ('L'impériale') received its first(?) public performance and became, especially the slow movement, the biggest success of Haydn's career up to that time. On New Year's Day, 1782, J. C. Bach died, and Lord Abingdon (also the father-in-law of Sir John Gallini) decided to withdraw his financial support from the Bach-Abel undertaking, which was then discontinued. In 1783, some professors of music formed 'The Professional Concert' (cf. note, p. 24), which played until 1793.[1]

The great hall at the Hanover Square Rooms had excellent acoustics; it was designed to hold 800 persons exclusive of the performers, but at Haydn's extremely

work, which requires *in toto* three French horns (which he almost always had at Eszterháza) but also singers of a quite outstanding flexibility and range. The first performance in modern times was given in 1956 by Charles Mackerras on the B.B.C. Third Programme, with Dennis Brain playing the solo horn and Joan Sutherland in the first soprano part. See Landon, SYM, *addenda*. A critical edition is in preparation with Verlag Doblinger.

1 From the interesting article in Grove's *Dictionary*, 1st edition, London, 1902, Vol. I, p. 661. The author of the article is W.H. Husk.

crowded and successful benefit concert in 1792, '1500 people entered the room'. It was in the Hanover Square Rooms that Haydn would see his greatest triumphs in England: the first concert in 1791, when he instantly established himself; the brilliant success of the 1792 season, particularly of the 'Surprise' Symphony in the sixth concert; and the greatest success of Haydn's career to date, namely the first performance of the 'Military' Symphony in 1794. It is a great pity that this historical monument ceased to be a concert hall after 19 December 1874 (the date of the last concert: how many people, one wonders, would have cause to regret the hall's demise on that day?).

When Salomon drew up the contract with Haydn in Vienna, the impresario was also acting on behalf of Sir John Gallini, the manager of the King's Theatre. Haydn was to compose an opera for Sir John. There is a certain amount of confusion about the actual terms of Salomon's (and Gallini's) contract.[1] Although (as matters turned out) Haydn's new opera could not be given, Gallini had deposited the 5,000 Gulden at Fries & Co. in Vienna and so Haydn received the stipulated honorarium. In the course of the Chronicle, we shall see the curious outcome of the Gallini affair. Suffice it to say here that the king supported a rival opera house, the Pantheon, and declared that two Italian opera houses in London were undesirable. The rivalry between George III and his handsome, dissipated son (later George IV) is well known, and was obviously behind the whole affair.

Salomon had done his advance publicity well. As soon as Haydn had signed the agreement in Vienna, Salomon sent off an open letter to John Baptist Mara, husband of the famous *prima donna* Gertrud. This letter was printed in the *Morning Chronicle* and *St. James's Chronicle or, British Evening-Post* on 1 January 1791, being preceded by a similar announcement with only slightly different word-order in the *Morning Chronicle* of 29 December 1790:

To the MUSICAL WORLD.

London, Dec. 27, 1790.

By a letter just received, on my arrival in Town, from Mr. SALOMON, I am authorised to lay before the Publick an Advertisement, written by Mr. Salomon at Vienna, which he desires may be immediately inserted in the English Newspapers.

JOHN BAPTISTA MARA.

'Mr. SALOMON having taken a Journey to Vienna purposely to engage the celebrated HAYDN, Chapel-Master to his present Highness Prince ESTERHAZY, to come to England, most respectfully acquaints the Nobility and Gentry, that he has actually signed an agreement with Mr. Haydn; in consequence, they are to set out together from Vienna in a few Days, and hope to be in London before the end of December when Mr. Salomon will have the honour of submitting to the Publick a Plan of a Subscription Concert, which he flatters himself will meet with its Approbation and Encouragement.

Vienna, Dec. 8, 1790.'

1 Griesinger (p. 22) says, 'One agreed that Haydn would write an opera for 3,000 Gulden, and in twenty concerts he would receive 100 Gulden for each new composition which he would conduct. Haydn was thus covered to the amount of 5,000 Gulden, and this sum was to be deposited by Gallini in the Fries banking house in Vienna as soon as Haydn landed on English soil. This prudence was not unnecessary, for without it, Haydn would have had to put up with this or that annoyance and his opera, *Orfeo ed Euridice*, would not have been paid for, since it could not be performed in the theatre, which Gallini wanted to open without provisional permission from the authorities.' Pohl (*H in L*, 102ff.) gives different, and perhaps more accurate figures (Salomon would hardly have got up a contract in Gulden): Haydn must compose six new symphonies and conduct them personally; for them he would receive £300; moreover, he would receive another £200 for the copyright and a guaranteed £200 for a benefit concert. Gallini's opera is not mentioned. See also *infra*, p. 77 (footnote).

On 30 December 1790, the *Morning Chronicle* gives a summary description of the musical events to take place in the coming season:

The musical arrangements now making promise a most *harmonious* winter.

Besides two rival *Opera* houses, a Concert is planned under the auspices of *Haydn*, whose name is a tower of strength, and to whom the *amateurs* of instrumental music look up as a *god* of science. Of this concert *Salomon* is to be the leader, and *Madame Mara* the principal singer.

. The professional concert under the able conduct of *Cramer*, is to be reinforced by Mrs. Billington, assisted occasionally by Mr. and Mrs. Harrison.

The Antient concert under the patronage of their Majesties will continue soon after the Queen's Birth-day, with Cramer as their leader and Storace as the principal singer. The *Ladies subscription concert* is to be continued as usual on the Sunday evenings by permission (we hope) of his Grace the Archbishop of Canterbury.

There will be Oratorios twice a week, at the Theatres of Drury-Lane and Covent-garden during Lent.

These with the *Academy of Antient Music* will constitute the principal public musical entertainments of the winter.

On 2 January, the anonymous London correspondent of the *Journal des Luxus und der Moden* sent a report to Weimar:

London, 2 January 1791.
Concerning the present winter amusements in London.

Salomon went on purpose to Vienna and engaged Haydn, who is awaited daily [he arrived that day in fact]. He is to conduct the concert series and a public announcement to that effect has been made. I do not doubt the good success of these concerts. Haydn is quite extraordinarily popular here. His Overtures and Symphonies are constantly performed, and years ago, when Lord Abington [*sic*] was director of the Professional Concerts, they tried to get him [Haydn] over, but he had to refuse at that time, and Graff [Friedrich Hartmann Graff, *Capellmeister* in Augsburg, who received the honorary degree of Doctor of Music, *honoris causa*, at Oxford in 1789] came in his stead. [Jahrgang 1791, VI, 69]

Haydn's arrival was now registered in the *Morning Chronicle* (3 January):

Yesterday arrived at Mr. BLAND's, in Holborn, the celebrated Mr. HAYDN, the composer from Vienna, accompanied by Mr. SALOMON: and we understand the public is indebted to Mr. BLAND as being the chief instrument of Mr. HAYDN's coming to England.

One of Salomon's first gestures was to take Haydn to meet Dr Charles Burney, the great music historian. Burney took to Haydn at once: 'I have had the great Haydn here, & think him as *good* a creature as *great Musician*' (16 February 1791, Burney to A. Young). Burney thereupon had his *History* 'superbly bound' and sent the four volumes accompanied by a poem welcoming Haydn to England. Knowing that Haydn's English was non-existent, Burney had the verses translated into German prose by Christian Ignatius Latrobe, the interesting Moravian composer who also became a friend of Haydn's. Encouraged by Haydn's approval of the poem, Burney expanded it and allowed himself to be 'persuaded by 2 or 3 trusty friends to print it, upon a supposition that it may inform some of our musical folks how great a Man we have at present the good fortune to possess'. In this same letter to Latrobe of 3 March

1791, Burney explains that the verses would be published anonymously:

> I must entreat you to keep my secret or I shall have all the envious brethren on my back, who in the true *spirit du Metric*, imagine all praise bestowed on others, a robery [*sic*] committed on their own little estate (if they have any) in Parnassus. I shall not let even the printer, or *all* my near relations into this secret – therefore Mum's the word.

Dr Burney was many things: a good 'scholastic' composer, a brilliant historian, and a man of much taste, learning and wit. A poet he was not. Burney's old friend, the Rev. Thomas Twining, with whom the historian had corresponded about Haydn for ten years, was very eager to meet the famous composer but he could not withold criticism of the verses, which, he said rather acidly, were 'dry, prosaic, and cataloguish' (Twining to Burney, 4 May 1791). Burney persevered, however, and the expanded poem appeared as a shilling pamphlet of fourteen pages. Its anonymity enabled Dr Burney not only to escape the envy he had prophesied but also to commend the poem to the readers of the *Monthly Review* (June, 1791, vol. vi, pp. 223 ff.), for which Burney wrote criticism.

Haydn carefully guarded the four volumes of Burney's history as well as the presentation copy of the poem (in the expanded version): it is signed on the title page 'From the Author / Dr Burney'. Presumably by the time Burney signed it, the need to preserve the anonymity had ceased to exist.[1]

VERSES

ON THE

ARRIVAL

OF

HAYDN

IN ENGLAND

———

PRICE ONE SHILLING

VERSES / ON THE / ARRIVAL IN ENGLAND / of the / *GREAT MUSICIAN* / HAYDN /

January 1791

Quella Cetra—
Che d'ogni alma a suo talento
D'ogni cor la via s'apri

Metastasio.

[London: Printed for Payne, at the Mews Gate; Walter, Charing Cross: Hookham, Bond Street; and Stockdale, Piccadilly. MDCCXCI.]

On the / ARRIVAL / OF / HAYDN / IN ENGLAND. / —— /
Music! The Calm of life, the cordial bowl,
Which anxious care can banish from the soul,
Affliction sothe, and elevate the mind,
And all its sordid manacles unbind,
Can snatch us from life's incidental pains,

---

1 The information on Burney and Haydn from partly unpublished sources first revealed to the scholarly world in Roger Lonsdale's excellent book, *Dr. Charles Burney, A Literary Biography* (London, 1965, pp. 352ff.). The poem itself is published complete, with minor printers' errors, in Pohl III, 391ff. Our text is from Haydn's copy, now in the Esterházy Archives, Ha. I. 15. It is signed on the title page 'From the Author' (Burney's hand), underneath which Haydn himself wrote 'Dr Burney'.

And 'wrap us in Elysium with its strains!'
To cultivated ears, this fav'rite art
No *new* delights was able to impart;
No Eagle flights its votaries durst essay,
But hopp'd, like little birds, from spray to spray.
No MODULATION did the passions feel,
Whose pow'r could melt the soul or heart congeal;
No MELODY whose novel grace or fire
Could soothe the breast, or noble thoughts inspire;
Nor HARMONY was found, nor COMBINATION,
But what had oft been heard in ev'ry nation.
ITALIA both *Scarlatti's* gave, *Corelli*,
Geminiani, Somis; and *Jomelli*,
Durante, Pergolesi, and *Tartini*,
Vinci, Piccini, Sarti, and *Sacchini*,
Perez, Galuppi, and such gifted men,
as Genius fires, while Science guides the pen.
GERMANIA furnish'd the *Bachs*, and *Gluck*,
With *Keiser, Hasse*, and HANDEL, who forsook
His native soil to charm the British ear,
Gladden each heart, or draw the tender tear;
From Gothic barbarism lift the nation,
and plant a lasting taste of his creation.

These were the gen'ral fav'rites of their days,
The idols of our hearts, and objects of our praise;
But common made by use, and more by thieves,
(And those who pouring water on their leaves,
By a more humble and less dangerous theft,
Extracted all the spirit that was left,)
Were heard with languor, like an oft-told tale,
Nor longer could o'er drowsiness prevail.

Our *Tallis, Bird* and matchless *Purcell*, still
Each sacred dome with sounds seraphic fill;
But grace and elegance, to them unknown,
(Of which elsewhere, no seeds had yet been sown)
With strains impassion'd for the lyric scene,
From foreign fields we are ever forc'd to glean;
And long from these our Instruments were fed,
And Concerts furnish'd with their daily bread;
Till dry and stale became, they ceas'd, at last,
To please and charm us in the ear's repast.

At length great HAYDN's new and varied strains
Of habit and indiff'rence broke the chains;
Rous'd to attention the long torpid sense,
With all that pleasing wonder could dispense.

Artists who long their trade had exercis'd,
No less than feeling ignorance, were surpriz'd
At strains so new, to hand, to eye, and ear,
As made them *Tiros* in their art appear.
Whene'er Parnassus' height he meant to climb,
Whether the grand, pathetic, or sublime,

The simply graceful, or the comic vein,
The theme suggested, or enrich'd the strain,
From melting sorrow to gay jubilation,
Whate'er his pen produc'd was Inspiration!

The tuneful Tribe, for ages yet to come,
In vain for new ideas their harps will thrum;
In vain limp after him with awkward gait;
And try his graceful steps to imitate.
The sportive freaks, so natural to him,
In them with downright affectation seem,
With which himself alone can wield
They wire may draw, or baser metals gild;
As Plagiarists may thrive; but modest men,
In pure despair, will throw away the pen.

Players as seldom have been known to write
As Generals, who plan, in ranks to fight.
SHAKSPEAR, in execution, could at most
But feebly represent his Hamlet's ghost;
But by his wond'rous pen's immortal aid,
All the great Actors of our stage were made:
Our *Bettertons* and *Booths*, our *Wilks* and *Quin*,
And all Thalia's laughter-loving Kin.
GARRICK, with comic sport, and tragic rage,
Taught Shakspeare's self to please a distant age;
With eye and voice, with gesture and with feature,
He best interpreted both him and Nature.
A Proteus in his art, who seem'd design'd
To be the Index of all human kind.

Haydn! Great Sovereign of the tuneful art!
Thy works alone supply an ample chart
Of all the mountains, seas, and fertile plains,
Within the compass of its wide domains. –
Is there an Artist of the present day
Untaught by thee to think, as well as play?
Whose hand thy science has not well supplied?
Whose hand they labours have not fortified? –

Old rules geographic soon were out of date,
When the terrestrial sphere was found oblate:
When wise COPERNICUS the orbs arrang'd,
The system of Astronomy was chang'd:
And new laws of harmony are found,
No treatise, code, or theory of sound,
Whose narrow limits, fixt by pedants vain,
Thy bold creative genius can restrain.
IMAGINATION, which, like garden bird,
Was long forbid the skies, by rules absurd,
Has now broke loose – now takes her airy flight
To explore new world, and regions of delight.

Thy style has gain'd disciples, converts, friends,
As far as Music's thrilling power extends.
Nor has great Newton more to satisfaction

Demonstrated the influence of *Attraction*.
And though to Italy of right belong
The undisputed sovereignty of *Song*;
Yet ev'ry nation of the earth must now
To Germany pre-eminence allow
For *instrumental* powers, unknown before
Thy happy flights had taught her sons to soar.

    Welcome, great Master! to our favour'd Isle,
Already partial to thy name and style;
Long may thy fountain of invention run
In streams as rapid as first begun;
While skill for each fantastic whim provides,
And certain science ev'ry current guides!
    Oh, may thy days, from human suff'rings free,
Be blest with glory and felicity!
With full fruition, to a distant hour,
Of all thy magic and creative pow'r!
Blest in thyself, with rectitude of mind;
And blessing, with thy talents, all mankind![1]

Haydn had brought various letters of recommendation with him, one to the Neapolitan Ambassador, Prince Castelcicala, from no less than King Ferdinand IV, and another from the mighty Austrian Chancellor, Prince Kaunitz, to the Austrian Ambassador, Count Stadion:

[*German*]
Nobly born Count of the Holy Roman Empire!
The princely Esterházy *Kapellmeister* and universally celebrated composer Herr Josef Haiden [*sic*] has been called to London and will remain there for some time. Before his departure he asked me to provide him with a letter of recommendation to Your Grace, which I am especially glad to do since this man, of quite exceptional talents and the most worthy personal character, deserves the best possible recommendation. Your Grace will therefore please extend to him every courtesy and assist him in every possible manner.
    I remain, with every mark of respect,

> Your Grace's
> Obedient Servant
> Kaunitz K[anzler].

      Vienna, the 13th of December 1790
      To Count Stadion[2]

On 8 January 1791, Haydn wrote his first letter from London to his sensitive and intelligent friend, Maria Anna von Genzinger, the wife of Dr Peter von Genzinger, Esterházy's physician. These letters, apart from the intrinsic value of any letter by a great composer, are especially interesting in that they provide us with much information that is not otherwise to be found in the annals of Haydn's English visits. The autographs of all the letters are in the Österreichische Nationalbibliothek, Handschriftensammlung; the translations of these and all the other Haydn letters in

---

1 In Pohl's transcription (III, 394), the last strain, beginning with the word 'Welcome' and ending with 'mankind', is placed in quotation marks (not found in the Budapest copy). Can this strain have been the original 'short' version of the poem?
2 Pohl III, 15, with wrong date (1796 for 1790).

this volume are from CCLN, which we have corrected, when necessary, and brought up to date whenever possible.

[To Maria Anna von Genzinger, Vienna. *German*]

London, 8th January 1791.

Nobly born,
Gracious Lady!

I hope that you will have received my last letter from Calais. I should have written you immediately after my arrival in London, but I wanted to wait a few days so as to be able to write about several things at once. So I can tell you that on the 1st inst., New Year's Day, after attending early mass, I boarded the ship at 7 : 30 a.m. and at 5 in the afternoon I arrived, thank God! safe and sound in Dower [*sic*]. At the beginning, for the first 4 whole hours, we had almost no wind, and the ship went so slowly that in these 4 hours we didn't go further than one single English mile, and there are 24 between Calais and Dower. Our ship's captain, in an evil temper, said that if the wind did not change, we should have to spend the whole night at sea. Fortunately, however, towards 11 :30 o'clock a wind arose and blew so favourably that by 4 o'clock we covered 22 miles. Since the tide, which had just begun to ebb, prevented our large vessel from reaching the pier, 2 smaller ships came out to meet us as we were still fairly far out at sea, and into these we and our luggage were transferred, and thus at last, though exposed to a medium gale, we landed safely. The large vessel stood out to sea five hours longer, till the tide turned and it could finally dock. Some of the passengers were afraid to board the little boats and stayed on board, but I followed the example of the greater number. I remained on deck during the whole passage, so as to gaze my fill at that mighty monster, the ocean. So long as it was calm, I wasn't afraid at all, but towards the end, when the wind grew stronger and stronger, and I saw the monstrous high waves rushing at us, I became a little frightened, and a little indisposed, too. But I overcame it all and arrived safely, without (excuse me) vomiting, on shore. Most of the passengers were ill, and looked like ghosts, but since I went on to London, I didn't feel the effects of the journey right away; but then I needed 2 days to recover. Now, however, I am fresh and well again, and occupied in looking at this endlessly huge city of London, whose various beauties and marvels quite astonished me. I immediately paid the necessary calls, such as to the Neapolitan Ambassador and to our own; both called on me in return 2 days later, and 4 days ago I lunched with the former – N.B. at 6 o'clock in the evening, as is the custom here.

My arrival caused a great sensation throughout the whole city, and I went the round of all the newspapers for 3 successive days. Everyone wants to know me. I had to dine out 6 times up to now, and if I wanted, I could dine out every day; but first I must consider my health, and 2nd my work. Except for the nobility, I admit no callers till 2 o'clock in the afternoon, and at 4 o'clock I dine at home with *Mon.* Salomon. I have nice and comfortable, but expensive, lodgings. My landlord is Italian, and also a cook, and serves me 4 very respectable meals; we each pay 1 fl. 30 kr. a day excluding wine and beer, but everything is terribly expensive here. Yesterday I was invited to a grand amateur concert, but I arrived a bit late, and when I showed my ticket they wouldn't let me in but led me to an antichamber, where I had to wait till the piece which was then being played in the hall was over. Then they opened the door, and I was conducted, on the arm of the *entrepreneur*, up the centre of the hall to the front of the orchestra, amid universal applause, and there I was stared at and greeted by a great number of English compliments. I was assured that such honours had not been conferred on anyone for 50 years. After the concert I was taken to a handsome adjoining room, where a table for 200 persons, with many places set, was prepared for all the amateurs; I was supposed to be seated at the head of the table, but since I had dined out on that day and had eaten more than usual, I declined this honour, with the excuse that I was not feeling very well, but despite this I had to drink the harmonious health, in Burgundy, of all the gentlemen present; they all returned the toast, and then allowed me to be taken home. All this, my gracious lady, was very flattering to me, and yet I wished I could fly for a time to Vienna, to have more quiet in which to work, for the noise that the common people make as they sell their wares in the street is intolerable. At present I am working on symphonies, because the libretto of the opera is not yet decided on, but in order to have more quiet I shall have to rent a room far from the centre of town. I would gladly write you in more detail, but I am afraid of missing the mail-coach. Meanwhile I am, with kindest regards to your husband, *Fräulein* Pepi and all the others, most respectfully.

> Your Grace's
> most sincere and obedient servant,
> Joseph Haydn.

Now I have a request to make of Your Grace. I don't know whether I left the Symphony in E flat, which Your Grace returned to me, in my apartments at home, or whether it has been stolen from me *en route*. I missed it yesterday and need it urgently, and so I beg you to get it from my kind friend, Herr von Kees, and to copy it in your own home on small-sized paper for mailing, and send it here in the mail as soon as possible. Should Herr von Kees hesitate about this, which I don't think likely, Your Grace can always send him this letter. My address is as follows:

> À Mo[ns]:
> Mon: Haydn
> N^{ro} 18 great Pulteney Street.

> [CCLN, 111–13]

Possibly the date of this letter is incorrect. There was a concert on 6 January of the Academy of Antient Music, at Freemasons' Hall, conducted by Dr Samuel Arnold, in which Nancy Storace, Michael O'Kelly and Miss Abrams sang and Salomon was the leader (Pohl: *H in L*, 106ff.); or there was actually a 'grand amateur concert' on the 7th of which nothing seems to be known. We rather incline to the letter being wrongly dated because, on 8 January, Haydn wrote to Prince Esterházy giving all the details of the new opera which, however, he says was not decided upon when he wrote to Madame Genzinger. The symphonies Haydn was working upon were (in that order) Nos. 96 and 95 (for the order, see the comment to the First Concert, *infra*). The one he forgot, and which was to be the subject of much anguished correspondence, was No. 91. *Ritter* Franz Bernhard von Kees (or Keess) was a civil servant and a great music lover, who kept a catalogue of Haydn's symphonies, which is very important for the authenticity, instrumentation and chronology of those works.[1] We shall see that Haydn sent him, from London, the new Symphonies Nos. 96 and 95.

The next letter Haydn wrote was to Prince Anton Esterházy. In it, we learn the title of the new opera and some details of the proposed cast, which may be supplemented by newspapers of the period and Parke's memoirs. The Princess Marie

---

1 Published in facsimile in *Drei Haydn Kataloge* (with foreword and notes by J. P. Larsen, Copenhagen 1941): the original MS. is in the Fürstlich Thurn und Taxis Archives at Regensburg. We believe we have identified Kees's collection of Haydn symphonies, which is partly in Vienna (Gesellschaft der Musikfreunde), partly in Salzburg (Monastery of St Peter) and partly in Regensburg (*supra*): Landon SYM, 36ff.

that Haydn greets is probably Marie Hermenegild, *née* Princess Liechtenstein, whose husband, Nicolaus, was to be Haydn's fourth reigning Esterházy.

[To Prince Anton Esterházy, Vienna. *German*]
Most noble Prince of the Holy Roman Empire!
    I report respectfully that, despite unpleasant weather and a great many bad roads throughout the whole trip, I arrived in London this 2nd of January, happy and in good health. My arrival created a great stir, and forced me to take larger quarters that same evening : I received so many calls that I shall hardly be able to repay them in 6 weeks. Both the ambassadors, *i.e.* Prince Castelcicala of Naples and Herr Baron von Stadion ; and I had the pleasure of lunching with both of them at 6 o'clock in the evening. The new opera libretto which I am to compose is entitled *Orfeo*, in 5 acts, but I shall not receive it for a few days. It is supposed to be entirely different from that of Gluck. The *prima donna* is called Madame Lops from Munich – she is a pupil of the famous Mignotti. *Seconda donna* is Madam Capelletti. *Primo homo* [*sic*] is the celebrated Davide. The opera contains only 3 persons, *viz.* Madam Lops, Davide, and a castrato, who is not supposed to be very special. Incidentally, the opera is supposed to contain many choruses, ballets and a lot of big changes of scenery : the first opera, *Pirro* by Paisiello, will be given in a fortnight. The concerts will begin next month on the 11th of February, and I shall dutifully write Your Highness more about that later. Meanwhile I remain,

Your Serene Highness'
submissive and obedient
Joseph Haydn [m.p.] ria.

London, 8th January 1791.
I take the liberty of respectfully kissing the hands of the loveliest Princess, Your Highness' most charming wife, and also the Princess Marie and Her Highness' husband. My address is, unofficially,

N^ro 18 Great Pulteneÿ Street
Golden Square
London

[CCLN, 113f.]

    The 'official' title of Haydn's new opera was *L'anima del filosofo*. We may now introduce the personnel of Gallini's opera company in the King's Theatre :

Composers: 'Sig. Giuseppe Haydn' and 'Sig. Federici'. Vincenzo Federici (1764–1826) returned to Italy in 1803 and produced a number of successful operas. Lorenzo da Ponte, who was to arrive in London in the autumn of 1792, describes Federici thus :

Federici was a veritable emporium of iniquities. It was enough for a man to have merit, or merely the reputation of having a little, to be hated and persecuted by him.   [Da Ponte, 243]

Federici became conductor of the King's Theatre in 1794, was for a time Banti's lover, and was finally put in prison, from which da Ponte extracted him. The lurid tale can be read in da Ponte's memoirs (pp. 313 and *passim*).

Male Singers: Giacomo Davide ('David' in England and sometimes even in Italy) was the brilliant tenor and founder of a famous family of singers. He was born at Presezzo near Bergamo in 1750 and not only studied singing but also composition under Sala. Parke (I, 140) says he 'possessed a clear and flexible voice, with an extensive falsetto, and an elegant expressive style'. He was to be Haydn's Orfeo, and the composer also wrote a concert aria for him in 1791 (now lost).

Sig. Tajana (Parke I, 140, spells him 'Tajano'), a tenor who sang at the first Salomon Concert in 1791 and frequently thereafter.

Sig. Dorelli, about whom nothing seems to be known. Perhaps he was the not-very-special castrato of Haydn's letter, destined to sing the role of the Genio in Haydn's opera (only one aria!).

Francesco Albertarelli, bass, had been Mozart's Don Giovanni in the Viennese première of 1788 and was thus known to Haydn. Albertarelli sang in several Salomon concerts during 1791. Perhaps Haydn intended the role of Creonte in the new opera for Albertarelli.

Sig. Cappelletti, about whom little is known except that he was to sing at Salomon's first Concert (*vide infra*).

Female Singers: Rosa Lops (Parke I, 140 'Lopps') was to have been Haydn's Euridice; at the rehearsal of Paisiello's *Pirro* on 23 February she was found to be 'a good and finished singer; she has every accomplishment but youth and beauty' (*Morning Chronicle*; H in L, 125).

Madame Pplum [*sic*], about whom nothing is known.

Teresa Poggi Cappelletti (Parke I, 140, 'Capaletto') was also supposed to sing in Salomon's concerts; nothing, otherwise, is known about her.

Signora Maria. Nothing is known of her. Perhaps her name is actually a Christian name and belongs to Signora Sestini who had been in London at least since 1786, when she sang a Haydn song (Pohl, H in L, 96) at a concert.

Signora Maffei is described by Haydn as 'bella, ma poco musica'.

Ballet: Vestris (Gaetano Vestris, who danced 'avec autant de grâce que de noblesse' according to Castil Blaze [Pohl, H in L, 125]), Victor, Casali, Mad. Hilligsberg (about this famous *prima ballerina* we shall read in Haydn's London notebook), Dorival, Mojon (Mozon).

Leader of the Orchestra: Salomon.

Poet: Badini. Carlo Francesco Badini wrote the libretto to Haydn's last opera, and also the text to the charming Italian *Duetti*, 'Guarda qui' and 'Saper vorrei' (1796). Da Ponte describes him as 'surpassing Aretin in satire and destructive gossip, and kept a noose around [the manager of King's Theatre, William] Taylor's neck by virtue of his pen – he had learned English well and was employed as critic on a number of newspapers, whose opinions are accepted as good in London, perhaps to a greater extent than in any other country. The success of Taylor's operas, singers, dancers and composers, depended in great part on Badini's paragraphs.' (Da Ponte, 243).

Most of Badini's newspapers articles were of necessity anonymous, but the following, from the *Oracle* of 30 June 1791, was not; it illustrates Da Ponte's description of his colleague's 'destructive gossip':

> Mr. BADINI having sent a most respectful Letter to Lady MARY DUNCAN entreating her the honour of her Patronage for his Benefit, her Ladyship returned the following curious Note:
>
> *Queen–Ann–Street, West.*
> Lady MARY DUNCAN is not a little surprised at the consummate impudence of BADINI, in daring to have the insolence to send Tickets to her house, without her having sent him orders for it: had she intended going, this *wo'd* have prevented her; nor *dose* [*sic*] she see any *occasion* to employ so bad a Poet as BADINI; he can be

of no service, except to wipe *of* [*sic*] the dust from the Dancers shoes, when they come off the Stage.

THE RETORT COURTEOS
To Lady MARY DUNCAN

My Lady,

When I received your *polite Note*, I happened to be confined with a fever, and as I had just taken a *drastic purge*, your Ladyship's favour was of peculiar service. If your Ladyship should not understand the meaning of that technical word, you may find an explanation in the Pharmacopoeia, that *Doctor Nostrum*, your late Husband, used to keep in his shop.

You express a surprise, my Lady, *at my consummate impudence, in daring to have the insolence of requesting your patronage of my Benefit.* It is true, that the asperity of your Ladyship's furrowed countenance, and the sternness of your presence, might have taught me, that in applying to your Ladyship, I was soliciting the benevolence of *Tisiphone.* I confess myself culpable of a great inadvertence; but as to the double reproach of insolence and effrontery, I am apt to think that it fosters with much more propriety on the Relict of a Scotch Apothecary, who arrogates to herself the pride of a Princess, and the perogative of an Empress.

You are pleased, my Lady, to add, that I am a *bad poet.* I know that your Ladyship constantly wears one of the chief decorations of a learned Judge – I mean *your wig*, my Lady; yet, as your note shews that you cannot spell, I do not think your Ladyship's judgment can have much weight in the Republic of Letters; especially as old women in general are noted for the infirmity of their mental faculties.

The office of *cleaning the Dancers shoes*, which your Ladyship has thought proper to honour me with, being rather too dirty, I beg leave to resign the place into your Ladyship's hands. Your *old wigs*, my Lady, will afford you an opportunity of following that occupation with credit. I thought your Ladyship had only a partiality for the *Cast-Rats*: but I see, that the gentlemen of the Pump are likewise your favourites. It is the Poet alone that excites your Ladyship's aversion. There is no accounting for the whimsies of some Beings. I remember, my Lady, I had once an old B—, that was astonishingly fond of vermin, and had a mortal antipathy against Nightingales and Canary-birds.

I am,

Your Ladyship's

Most obedient humble Servant

BADINI, the Bad Poet.

It is probably idle speculation to guess the names of the anonymous music critics who wrote about Haydn's London concerts in the many newspapers of the period, but given the circumstances we may permit ourselves the luxury of suggesting that Badini himself may have been the anonymous music critic of the *Oracle*, in which the above 'Retort Courteous' appeared, and in which we find so many reports of Haydn's musical activities in 1791–5.

The London newspapers in early January give us a graphic picture of the number and variety of subscription concerts and operas which took place that season. It was, in fact, possible to attend a good concert or go to the opera every night of the week. The *Public Advertiser* of 6 January reports:

> Every thing in the musical kind is now puffed in *alt*! – nothing but superlatives will do the business of fiddles – hence we hear of the *Advent* of Hayden [*sic*], and the *Annunciation of the Blessed Opera* . . .

The paper, on the following day, gives us the complete list:

MUSICAL ARRANGEMENTS FOR EVERY DAY IN THE WEEK, THROUGH THE WINTER SEASON.

Never could this country boast of such a constellation of musical excellence as now illuminates our fashionable hemisphere. No one Metropolis can exhibit such a union of Masters as London now possesses: and therefore as Music will be the chief pleasure of the season, we shall endeavour to give a faithful representation of the Performances.

The Meeting, which through the condescension of the Prince of Wales, was to be held yesterday at Carlton House, may finally arrange the great affair of the rival Operas; but there is no doubt from the auspices, but that it will be settled to give the Opera a national establishment.

In the meantime our Readers may be pleased to see what will be the arrangements of musical pleasures for the week; even if the coalition of the two Operas should not take place.

We shall announce whatever change may be made; at present they stand as follow:

SUNDAY. – The Noblemen's Subscription, is held every Sunday at a different House.

MONDAY. – The Professional Concert – at the Hanover-Square Rooms – with Mrs. Billington.

TUESDAY. – The Opera.

WEDNESDAY. – The ancient music at the rooms in Tottenham Street, under the Patronage of their Majesties.

— – The Anacreontic Society also, occasionally, on Wednesday.

THURSDAY. – The Pantheon. – A Pasticcio of Music and Dancing, in case that the Opera Coalition shall take place; if not, a concert with Madame Mara and Sig. Pacchierotti.

— – Academy of Ancient Music, every other Thursday, at Freemason's Hall.

FRIDAY. – A Concert under the auspices of Haydn at the Rooms, Hanover Square, with Sig. David.

SATURDAY. – The Opera.

This is the arrangement for each week throughout the season; and so full is the town of eminent professors in every department of the science, that there may be a double orchestra found of admirable performers, so as to open two places of musical entertainment every evening.

> If Music be the food of Love, play on,
> Give me excess of it; that surfeiting,
> The appetite may sicken, and so die.' –
> SHAKESPEARE.

On 12 January, Haydn attended a concert of the Anacreontic Society at the 'Crown and Anchor' in the Strand, and his enthusiastic reception there was noticed by *The Times* and the *Gazetteer*:

The meeting of last Wednesday evening was not only the fullest, but the most convivial that has been in this season. The company seemed to be in full glee, and determined to be merry.

Mr. HAYDN, from Vienna, was introduced to the meeting, for the first time, and received by Mr. Hankey, the President, with great civility. On entering the Concert room he was greatly applauded, and the band very opportunely played one of his charming concertos [symphonies]. Perhaps Mr. HAYDN never heard his compositions done so much justice to . . .   [*The Times,* 14 January 1791]

. . . Before the grand finale the celebrated Haydn entered the room, and was welcomed by the Sons of Harmony with every mark of respect and attention. . . .
[*Gazatteer,* 14 January 1791]

Meanwhile the Professional Concert, Salomon's great rivals, had not been idle. Furious at having missed Haydn, whom they had almost persuaded to come to London a few years earlier, they now began to spread rumours of his decline. The stories were sufficiently widely circulated to cause the *Morning Chronicle*, on 13 January, to reply:

THE MORNING MIRROR. "THE GLASS OF FASHION." HAMLET.
So many public Concerts, private Concerts, Operas, Balls, and Music Meetings, as are cut out for the winter, and such a shoal of *eminent* performers as are imported from the Continent, will render a motto from *Shakespeare's* Tempest highly appropriate to this country. –

– The Isle is full of noises,
Sounds and sweet airs, that give delight and hurt not.
Sometimes a thousand twanging instruments
Will hum about our ears.

Upon the arrival of HAYDN, it was discovered that he no longer possessed his former powers. Pity it is that the discovery did not possess the merit of novelty. What less could have been expected from his presence? HORACE mentions some Roman Critics who proceeded upon the same principles of judging,
. . . . Nisi quae terris remota –
. . . . fastidit, et odit.
. . . . absens amabitur idem.
HOR.

Haydn had now had time to examine the pirated editions of his symphonies, most of which he had neither seen nor, perhaps, even heard of: the 'mangled' remains of Symphonies 53, 62 and the Overture Ia: 7, for example. The Forster edition of No. 62 simply leaves out the first movement. In another mangled edition, the second subject of Symphony No. 53's first movement was inserted into the above-mentioned Overture. There are other examples too numerous to elaborate. Haydn must have been horrified. The *Morning Chronicle*, in whose columns Haydn's name was now appearing almost daily, noted, on 14 January:

Since HAYDN's arrival in this country, he has discovered the *remains* of several of his early *Concertos* [i.e. Symphonies] that were first *kidnapped* and afterwards most inhumanely *robbed and mangled* by some of our *Original Composers*. A Jury of *Amateurs* has sat on the *Bodies*, and brought in a verdict – *Wilful murder by persons unknown.*

It was an old tradition, of course. Lady Montagu had seen such things half-a-century before in the literary world, and had written a half-humorous, half-resigned letter about it:

I have seen things I have wrote, so mangled and falsified, I have scarce known them. I have seen poems I never read, published with my name at length; and others, that were truly and singly wrote by me, printed under the names of others.

I have made myself easy under all these mortifications, by the reflection I did not deserve them, having never aimed at the vanity of popular applause. . . .[1]

On 15 January, we read the important announcement of the Haydn–Salomon concerts:

HANOVER SQUARE. MR. SALAMON [*sic*] respectfully acquaints the Nobility and Gentry, that he intends having TWELVE SUBSCRIPTION CONCERTS in the Course of the present Season. The first of which be on Friday the Eleventh of February next, and so continue on the succeeding Fridays. Mr. HAYDN will compose for every Night a New Piece of Music, and direct the execution of it at the Harpsichord.

The Vocal as well as Instrumental Performers will be of the first Rate, and a List of them will appear in a few Days.

Subscriptions, at Five Guineas, for the Twelve Nights, to be held at Messrs. Lockhard's, No. 36, Pall-Mall.

Tickets transferable Ladies to Ladies, and Gentlemen to Gentlemen.

[*Public Advertiser*; *Gazetteer*; etc.]

There was a Court ball at St James on 18 January, the Queen's Birthday. Haydn was present, and from that evening his future in London's aristocratic society was assured. The *St. James Chronicle* reports that the composer, though not yet presented at Court, was, upon entering the room in the company of Sir John Gallini, Mr Wills and Mr Salomon, greeted by the Prince of Wales with a bow, whereupon the eyes of the whole company were directed to the composer and everyone paid his respects. A similar report in the *Daily Advertiser* (20 January 1791) informs us that 'A remarkable Circumstance happened on Thursday Evening'.

In the Ball-Room at St. James's: Haydn, the celebrated Composer, though he has not yet been introduced at our Court, was recognized by all the Royal Family, and paid them his silent Respects. Mr. Haydn came into the Room with Sir John Gallini, Mr. Wills and Mr. Salomon. The Prince of Wales first observed him, and upon bowing to him, the Eyes of all the Company were upon Mr. Haydn, every one paying him Respect.

The next morning Haydn was invited to participate in a concert at Carlton House, and the *Morning Chronicle* of 20 January comments:

THE PRINCE OF WALES CONCERT.

Yesterday his Royal Highness had a Concert at Carlton House, at which were Haydn, Salomon, Jarnowick [Giornovichj], David, and the principal performers, vocal and instrumental. – Such a band for a Chamber Concert it would be difficult for any other metropolis to select. – Detached morsels of the most exquisite modern compositions, Quartetts, Catches and Glees, made up the Miscellany of the Musical Feast.

On 26 January, further details of the Haydn–Salomon concerts were announced in the press:

HANOVER-SQUARE. MR. SALOMON respectfully acquaints the Nobility and Gentry, that his FIRST CONCERT will be on Friday the Eleventh of February next, and continue every succeeding Friday. Mr. HAYDN will preside at the

1 Lady Mary Wortley Montagu (1689–1762) to the Countess of Bute, Brescia, 10 October 1752, in *English Letters of the XVIII Century,* ed. James Aitken, London, 1946, p. 34.

Harpsichord, and will compose for every Night a new Piece of Music. Principal Vocal Performers already engaged are, Signor DAVID, And Signora CAPPELLETTI; the Miss Abrams, And Signora STORACE. Principal Instrumental Performers, First Violin. Mr. SALOMON; Second Violin, Mr. HINDMARSH; Violincello, Mr. BREVAL; Piano Forte, Mr. DUSSECK; Oboe, Mr. HARRINGTON; German Flute, Mr. GRAEFF: Clarinet, Mr. ELEY; Bassoon, Mr. HOLMES; And Pedal Harp, Madame KRUMPHOLTZ.

Besides other distinguished Singers, and Instrumental Performers, who will be occasionally provided in the Course of the Season.

Subscriptions, at Five Guineas, for Twelve Concerts, are received at Messrs. Lockhard's, No. 36, Pall-Mall.

Tickets transferable Ladies to Ladies, and Gentlemen to Gentlemen.

[*Gazetteer*, January 26, 28, February 2 and 5;
Public Advertiser, February 2 and 5; etc.]

The anti-Haydn campaign of the Professional Concert continued, and on 5 February the *Gazetteer* wrote:

MUSIC

The *nine days wonder* about Haydn begins to abate. – He has been *exhibited* at the Anacreontic Society and other music meetings greatly to the amazement of *John Bull*, who expected to hear another *Cramer* or a *Clementi*. – But the truth is, this wonderful *composer* is but a very poor *performer*; and though he may be qualified to *preside* at a harpsichord, we have never heard him celebrated as a leader of a Concert. His pupil *Pleyel*, with perhaps less science, is a more popular composer – from his more frequent introduction of *air* into his *harmonies*, and the general smoothness and elegance of his melodies. How Mr. Haydn and his associate *Salomon* came to overlook the talents of Madame Mara in the formation of their orchestra, can only be accounted for from the proverbial *avarice* of Germany.

Two days later, the Professional Concert opened their subscription series. Haydn was given an ivory disc mounted on a blue ribbon with 'Professional-Concert 1791' on the one side and 'Mr Haydn' on the other, by which he had free access to all their concerts. Haydn was touched and told Griesinger (35) that no such politeness had ever been showed to him in Vienna. Dies (93) relates that at this concert Haydn realized how right he had been to stipulate that his symphonies should open the second part of the programme.

The first act was usually disturbed in various ways by the noise of late-comers. Not a few persons came from well-set tables (where the men, as is the custom of the country, stay in the dining room and drink, after the ladies have left following the conclusion of the meal); they took a comfortable seat in the concert room and were so gripped by the magic of the music that they went fast to sleep.

The programme of the Professional Concert, that night of 7 February, included two Haydn compositions, another courtesy: a quartet and a 'Grand Overture, M. S.' (i.e. a symphony, but from whom did they get it?). The *Morning Chronicle* of the 9th reports on the concert:

THE PROFESSIONAL CONCERT.

The Professors had their first Concert on Monday. This Subscription is honoured by the patronage of the PRINCE OF WALES and Duke of YORK; and which, in our regard for distinguished talents, we trust will compensate to them the loss they have sustained by the death of the Duke of CUMBERLAND. A Concert of such pre-eminent ability, and where the Masters combine their skill, as much for the honour of the Art, as the advantages, deserves the highest protection, as it is worthy of the highest praise.

HAYDN was on Monday evening a witness of the taste and liberality of the Professors, for they selected from his unrivalled works some of his best productions; and he, in return, paid them the honest compliment, that on no occasion had he heard their M.S. Concerto [i.e. Haydn's own symphony] so admirably performed.

Dr Burney was at the concert and Haydn took the opportunity to thank the good doctor for the handsomely bound *History* and the accompanying poem:

Having met the good great man, by accident, at the Professional Concert soon after he had rec^d my present, he took the opportunity of making *fine speeches* innumerable, *viva voce*, & by that means saved himself the trouble of writing a letter, as he told me he intended to do.

[Burney to Latrobe, 3 March; Lonsdale, 353]

Two days later, on 9 February, there was a Concert of Antient Music at Tottenham Street. Haydn must have been fascinated to see that in London, old music, especially Handel, but also Corelli, Jomelli, Graun, Geminiani, and so on, were all cultivated at the various concerts of ancient (or as they usually spelled it, 'Antient') music. There is no doubt that this cultivation of Handel impressed Haydn greatly, even before the monumental Festival concerts later in the season. Dr Burney was there once again:

I afterwards met him at the Concert of Anc^t Music in Tottenham street, whence I carried him home when it was over; & then he repeated & added more *fine things* [about the *History*] on my present, then he c^d have written on ten sheets of Paper.   [ibid.]

On 8 January, the newspapers announced that 'Tickets [for the Haydn–Salomon concerts are] ready for Delivery; the Gentlemen's are Black, and the Ladies' Green' (*Public Advertiser*; also *Gazetteer* on 15 and 17 February). On 10 January, however, the *Public Advertiser* printed a notice in which Salomon postponed his first concert:

HANOVER-SQUARE. Mr. SALOMON'S CONCERT.

SIGNOR DAVID and Signor [a] [?] CAPPELLETTE being prevented from Singing at any Place previous to their Appearance at the Opera, Mr. Salomon, by the Desire of the greatest Part of the Subscribers, has postponed his First Concert, which was advertised for the 11th, to the 25th Inst. that no Opportunity might be lost of hearing those eminent Singers.

Mr. HAYDN will preside at the Harpsichord. . . .

From 19 February, Salomon began announcing the whole of the opening programme:

HANOVER-SQUARE. MR. SALOMON respectfully acquaints the Nobility and Gentry, that his First CONCERT positively takes Place on Friday next, the 25th instant.

PART I
Overture – Rosetti.
Song – Signora Storace.
Concerto (Oboe) – Mr. Harrington.
Song – Signor DAVID.
Concerto (Violin) – Mr. Salomon.

PART II
New Grand Overture – Haydn.
Song – Signora Storace.
Concerto (Pedal Harp) – Madame Krumpholtz.
Song – Signor DAVID.
Full Piece – Kozeluch.
Mr. HAYDN will be at the Harpsichord.
Leader of the Band Mr. SALOMON.
Doors to be opened at Seven, and to begin at Eight o'Clock. Subscriptions, at Five Guineas, for Twelve Concerts, are received and Tickets delivered at Messrs. Lockhard's, No. [36] Pall-Mall . . .

[*Public Advertiser*, February 19, 21, 24; *Gazetteer*, February 19; etc.]

It will be seen that one of the chief differences between this and the final programme that was actually given was the violin concerto at the end of the first half. Originally Salomon himself was to play, but at the last moment he generously and characteristically ceded his place to a French refugee, Madame Gautherot. Salomon later became one of Londons principal supporters of displaced French musicians, and the present Chronicle will show many programmes of which the soloists were refugees from across the Channel. In 1793, we find Salomon leading the orchestra in a benefit for 'Madame la Marquise DUCREST, Emigrée Française' living at No. 34, Great Titchfield Street; the second part of this concert, which was held at the Hanover Square Rooms on 7 June 1793, opened with a 'Grand Overture (M.S.)' by Muzio Clementi (*True Briton*, 1 June 1793). It is one more indication of Salomon's warmly generous personality.

Although the Salomon concerts had not yet begun, Haydn was having a frantically busy life. In demand at one concert after another, composing the new opera and the two new symphonies, the strain began to tell; and, sometime in that spring Haydn took quarters in Lisson Grove, then a quiet suburb with cows grazing in the nearby fields. Apart from the 'guest apperances' at concerts, Haydn also gave lessons 'to various people on the fortepiano, and every lesson was paid for by a guinea' (Griesinger, 35). Said Haydn: 'Da machte ich große Augen' (ibid.; a colloquial translation would be, 'My eyes popped out of my head').

Among these fashionable pupils was Lady Elizabeth Greville, daughter of the Earl of Warwick, one of the few of Haydn's many noble pupils whose names have come down to us in authentic record. In this particular case, the record is Haydn's own: a recently discovered letter to T. Kuffner dated Vienna, 9 July 1799, not in CCLN:

> Now, my dearest friend! you will certainly remember that I had the honour to instruct [*zu instruiren*] your then pupil Lady Elisabeth Greville. I would like to have the permission of her father, the Earl of Warwik [*sic*], to send the Lady a copy [of the printed score of *The Creation*] with her name printed in [the list of subscribers], at no risk to herself, just to show the occasionally doubtful world that I had the fortune to be received kindly also in England. [From the article by H. Unverricht:'Unveröffentliche und wenig bekannte Briefe Joseph Haydns', in *Musikforschung* 1965, Heft 1, p. 40]

Teaching in England was not, however, without its perils. In his lost Fourth London Notebook (1794–5), which we know only in the extracts of his biographers Dies and Griesinger, we read, this time *via* Griesinger, the following note:

> If a singing-, pianoforte-, or dancing-master asks half a guinea per lesson, he demands that an entrance fee of six guineas be paid at the first lesson. This is done

because during the winter many Scots and Irishmen take pride in having their children study with the best teachers, only to find that at the end they cannot pay the fee. The entrance fee is dispensed with if the teacher charges a guinea, but the guinea must then be paid at every lesson. [CCLN, 308]

On 18 February, Haydn played the fortepiano part of his Cantata *Arianna a Naxos*. 'The Ladies' Concert', writes the *Morning Chronicle*, 'was last night held at Mrs Blair's in Portland Place', and that superb street, as usual. '"Outglared the moon with artificial light. . . ."' The success was so great that the work was repeated at a concert of the New Musical Fund, held in the Pantheon on the 24th. At this concert, a band of 300 played a Haydn symphony, and Salomon led a Haydn string quartet. On both occasions, the *Morning Chronicle* commented on the Cantata:

The Musical World is at this moment enraptured with a Composition which Haydn has brought forth, and which has produced effects bordering on all that Poets used to seign of the ancient lyre. Nothing is talked of – nothing sought after but Haydn's Cantata – or, as it is called in the Italian School – his Scena . . . It abounds with such a variety of dramatic modulations – and is so exquisitely captivating in its larmoyant passages, that it touched and dissolved the audience. They speak of it with rapturous recollection, and Haydn's Cantata will accordingly be the musical *desideratum* for the winter. [23 February; Pohl, *H in L*, p. 118.]

. . . The modulation [in the cantata] is so deep and scientific, so varied and agitating – that the company was thrown into extasies. Every fibre was touched by the captivating energies of the passion, and Pacchierotti never, in his most brilliant age, was more successful . . . [26 February; Pohl, *H in L*, p. 119]

Fashionable London was following with interest Gallini's efforts to obtain permission to open the Haymarket Theatre. It looked to Walpole unlikely; on 18 February he wrote to Miss Agnes Bury:

The Rival theater [i.e. Gallini's] is said to be magnificent and lofty, but it is doubtful whether it will be suffered to come to light: in short, the contest will grow politics: 'Dieu et mon droit' supporting the Pantheon, and 'Ich Dien' [the Prince of Wales] countenancing the Haymarket. It is unlucky that the amplest receptacle is to hold the minority! [Pohl, *H in L*, p. 124, note 1]

Naturally, reports of all this activity (or lack of activity, in Gallini's case) spread to the Continent, where fact soon became fiction. We shall see of such a case with the so-called 'Miracle' Symphony. Even in the *Allgemeine Musikalische Zeitung* (hereinafter '*AMZ*') of 1799 (fourth number) there is a story about Haydn in London which the composer himself repudiated to Dies. When Haydn arrived in London, says the report, he was received with great honour by all the musical establishment, 'one certain party excepted' (presumably meaning the Professional Concert). But the rough spirit of the mob manifested itself clearly in one incident. Haydn entered the orchestra of the theatre just before the beginning of a concert. The musicians stood up to welcome him. The connoisseurs in the gallery were astounded at this politeness, but when they heard it was to honour an artist 'and to boot a foreigner, they began to hiss and whistle, crying "Fiddler! Fiddler!" Haydn said: "The musicians in the pit did me much honour but I don't think I heard the hissing, whistling and the words 'Fiddler! Fiddler!''' (Dies, 112f.). Did the incident occur?

On 24 February 1791 there was a concert of the New Musical Fund at the Pantheon, conducted by William Cramer; the hand-bill, from the collection of Sir Joseph Banks and his daughter, has survived (British Museum), and it informs us that Act I opened with a 'Grand Symphony' by Haydn, followed, several numbers later, by an interesting item, viz. the first public performance in England of one of the Quartets from Op. 64, not yet published in London: 'QUARTETTO, Mess. *Salomon, Mountain, Hindmarsch, & Menell* – HAYDN, M. S.' This string quartet, with Salomon as leader, and with the occasional substitution of another member, was to become famous not only for their performances of Op. 64 but, even more, for the 'Salomon' Quartets (Opp. 71 and 74), which they introduced to the British public in the 1794 Salomon concerts.

The Gallini struggle was having highly detrimental effects on the Haydn–Salomon concerts. Salomon had to postpone his opening concert once again, and published an open letter, *inter alia* in the *Public Advertiser* of 25 February 1791 (our source):

HANOVER-SQUARE. Mr. SALOMON'S CONCERTS.

It is with extreme Concern that Mr. SALOMON finds himself obliged to postpone opening his Concerts this Evening.

He thinks it his Duty to state to the Public the unfortunate Situation he stands in.

The Manager of the Opera House having given his Consent, that Signor DAVID should sing at Mr. SALOMON's Concert, even before the Opening of the Theatre, if necessary, Mr. Salomon thought himself justified in publishing the Adver[tise]ment for the opening [of] his Concert this Evening; but the Manager now finding himself compelled, by the Wishes of the highest Characters among the Opera Subscribers, that Signor David's first Appearance in England should be at the Opera House, has thought it necessary to restrain Signor David from singing at his Concert, until he has made his Appearance at the Opera House. Under these Circumstances Mr. Salomon has thought it his Duty rather to postpone his Concert for a few Nights, than to disappoint his Subscribers by the Non-appearance of Signor David.

The Manager has given Mr. Salomon the most positive Assurance, tha[t] the Opera will open at latest on Thursday the 10th of March; and therefore Mr. Salomon's Concerts will open on the following Evening, Friday the 11th of March, and consequently end on the 3rd of June.

Salomon kept the newspapers filled with announcements of the postponed first concert, adding lists of the performers, with changes bringing the public up to date. In the *Public Advertiser* of 4 March there is such a list, with two new entries: 'Violoncello – Mr MENUEL [*sc.* Menel] . . . Clarinet – Mr FLUGER'; the latter entry is interesting, because it shows that there were clarinets in London; yet it seems Salomon did not have two clarinet players in the *tutti* of his orchestra (Mr Fluger obviously being a soloist, used for clarinet concertos) during the 1791 and 1792 seasons. Haydn did not begin to write regular clarinet parts until the 1794 season.

Meanwhile the final programme was announced almost daily in the papers, e.g. on 7, 9, 10 and 11 March in the *Public Advertiser* and on 11 March in the *Gazetteer* as well. Although the King's Theatre in the Haymarket was still closed, Salomon kept his promise and the concert took place.

First Concert: 11 March 1791

HANOVER-SQUARE. MR. SALOMON respectfully acquaints the Nobility and Gentry, that his CONCERTS will open without further delay on Friday next, the 11th of March, and continue every succeeding Friday.

PART I.
Overture – Rosetti.
Song – Sig[nor] Tajana.
Concerto Oboe – Mr. Harrington.
Song – Signora Storace.
Concerto Violin – Madame Gautherot [Composed by Viotti].
Recitativo and Aria – Signor David [Composed by Rusi].

PART II.
New Grand Overture – Haydn.
Recitative and Aria – Signora Storace.
Concertante, Pedal Harp and Pianoforte – Madame
Krumpholtz and Mr. Dusseck,
Composed by Mr. Dusseck.
Rondo – Signor David [Composed by Andreozzi].
Full Piece – Kozeluck [*sic*].
Mr. HAYDN will be at the Harpsichord.
Leader of the Band, Mr. SALOMON.
Tickets transferable, as usual, Ladies to Ladies and
Gentlemen to Gentlemen only.
The Ladies' tickets are Green, the Gentlemen's Black.
The Subscribers are intreated to give particular orders to their Coachmen to set down and take up at the Side Door in the Street, with the Horses' Heads towards the Square.
The Door in the Square is for Chairs only.

People were curious, of course. Some thought that Haydn must have written himself out. Even such a great admirer as the Rev. Thomas Twining had written to Burney on 15 February 1791:

If the resources of any human composer could be inexhaustible, I should suppose Haydn's would; but as, after all, he is but a mortal, I am afraid he must soon get to the bottom of his genius-box.   [Lonsdale 355]

Twining need have had no fear: the genius-box was still bottomless. There are at least three contemporary criticisms of the concerts in London newspapers, one in the *Morning Chronicle* on 12 March:

SALOMON'S CONCERT.

The First Concert under the auspices of HAYDN was last night, and never, perhaps, was there a richer musical treat.

It is not wonderful that to souls capable of being touched by music, HAYDN should be an object of homage, and even of idolatry; for like our own SHAKSPEARE [*sic*], he moves and governs the passions at his will.

His *new Grand Overture* was pronounced by every scientific ear to be a most wonderful composition; but the first movement in particular rises in grandeur of subject, and in the rich variety of *air* and passion, beyond any even of his own productions. The *Overture* has four movements – An Allegro – Andante – Minuet

– and Rondo – They are all beautiful, but the first is pre-eminent in every charm, and the Band performed it with admirable correctness.

Signor DAVID exhibited all the wonders of his voice, and never surely was there heard a tenor of such riches and beauty. His first song was a *Recitativo* and *Aria*, by RUSI; and his second *a Rondo*, by ANDREOZZI.

There was an exquisite *concertante* between M. DUSSECK and Madame KRUMPHOLLZ [*sic*]; Signora STORACE sung two songs in a very fine style.

We were happy to see the Concert so well attended the first Night; for we cannot suppress our very anxious hopes, that the first musical genius of the age may be induced, by our liberal welcome, to take up his residence in England.

The *Diary; or Woodfall's Register*, also on 12 March, writes:

HANOVER SQUARE.

The long delayed Concert, undertaken this year by Mr. SALOMON, took place last night, and was attended by a numerous and very elegant audience. A musical treat, under the immediate direction of the great HAYDN, promised the connoisseurs an exquisite repast, and they were not disappointed . . . A new grand overture by HAYDN, was received with the highest applause, and universally deemed a composition as pleasing as scientific. The audience was so enraptured, that by unanimous desire, the second movement was encored, and the third was vehemently demanded a second time also, but the modesty of the Composer prevailed too strongly to admit a repetition. . . .

The *London Chronicle*, though not generally reviewing concerts, carries the following note in its issue of March 10–12:

HAYDN's CONCERT

The Subscription Concert, under the auspices of the celebrated Haydn, commenced last night at the rooms in Hanover-square. – The attraction of so great a name, with such auxilieries as Salomon and David, cannot fail of success. – The music was extremely well chosen, and it was throughout admirably executed. – The Concertante by Madame Krumpholtz and Mr. Dussek deserves particular mention as a brilliant and elegant performance, and Madame Gautherot displayed much taste and neatness of execution in a very pleasing Violin Concerto, the composition of Viotti. – A new Overture, composed for the occasion by Haydn, shewed that the genius of this great master of harmony is yet in full vigour. Signor David equally astonished and enchanted the audience, and Storace acquitted herself with her usual success.

These are the first of many contemporary criticisms of Haydn's music, and also Haydn the man, in London newspapers. Our Chronicle is largely based upon them. Apart from their obvious importance, historically, we may be permitted to ask ourselves what effect they had in Haydn's time. Actually, such influential newspapers as the *Morning Chronicle* were also read on the Continent, even in Vienna.[1] In those days, 2,000 was regarded as a good circulation. In 1795, the circulation of the *Morning Post*, which we shall be quoting frequently, fell to 350, while that of *The Times* rose to 4,800.[2] But many men read their newspapers in a coffee-house, so that the rather grim figure of 350 does not represent the number of readers.

1 Count Zinzendorf's Diary – a major source of information which we shall discuss in more detail *infra* – has this note for 28 November 1800: 'Selon un article raporté dans le morning-chronicle . . .' Zinzendorf read Gibbon in the original, too.
2 G. M. Trevelyan, *Illustrated English Social History*, Volume III: 'The Eighteenth Century', London 1966 (Pelican Books), p. 218.

Happily, we have another contemporary report, less reliable, perhaps, than the newspapers but interesting all the same: it is the diary of Charlotte Papendiek, whose husband, a flautist, had played in Vienna in 1779 (Haydn may have met him there)[1] and now taught music to the royal family. It is quite clear that the section dealing with the first Haydn-Salomon concert is not entirely accurate, and there is reason to believe that the writer confused the work of 1791 – we shall presently examine which one – with Symphony No. 104. Mrs Papendiek wrote this particular portion of her memoirs in January 1839, shortly before her death. For this reason we have divided the passage in two parts, the second of which is quoted in connection with No. 104 (*infra*, p. 615). Mrs Papendiek writes:

Haydn, long expected, now at last arrived.

Salomon naturally supposing that he would bring with him the symphonies that he intended to open his season with, convened his friends to meet on a fixed morning, and Mr. Papendiek wrote to desire me to go up to hear the performance.

I at once made arrangements to place the three elder children with [a friend]. . . . All my plans were made, when, on the morning of the day on which I was to start, the maid came into my room to tell me that [my daughter] Eliza was far from well. . . . I could not leave the poor little thing that day, so the coach took, instead of my person, a letter to Mr. Papendiek explaining matters.

Letters in return came, regretting the cause of my non-appearance, but telling me that beyond the fact of not meeting my friends there was no cause for disappointment, for there was, after all, no performance on the day specified.

Haydn, immediately on his arrival, told Salomon that he should stay the summer in England, and that as he heard there were to be twelve concerts and two benefits during the season there would be ample time for him to compose his first symphonies after he had had an opportunity of studying the taste of the English. He was determined that his first production should both amuse and please the musical public and rivet him in their favour. . . .

The alarming state of the time kept the King and Royal Family in town, for as the French Revolution gained ground, so revolutionary principles spread here. In almost every town and borough societies were formed, against Government authority, of different ranks and classes of people. In London some of these meetings were called 'The Debating Societies', 'The Corresponding Societies', 'Nights of the People', &c. . . . The city trained bands were put into requisition, and the Artillery Corps, to which my son in later years belonged, then with old Curtis at the head, was also in readiness at a moment's call. . . . All other cities and towns of any note follow the example of London, as is usual. The militia was embodied, attendance was required for practice a given number of days in each month, and they were kept in constant military order so as to be also ready at call if required.

Mr. Papendiek was drawn for the county of Berkshire, and in conformity to the regulations had to find two substitutes, as he could not attend himself. Hatch, the lawyer at Windsor, settled the whole affair for us for 15*l*. [pounds], a small sum for the business, but to us a sad drawback [= sacrifice].

In about a fortnight after the first disappointment Haydn was ready, and I was summoned to hear the first performance. . . . My dress now had to be considered, which had come down to the two muslins and the printed cambrics . . ., the puce

1 Pohl, *Denkschrift*, 59, 90. Papendiek played together with Mozart's friend J. B. Wendling in the intermission of *Judas Maccabaeus* by Handel, given in Baron van Swieten's translation at the Burgtheater on 21 and 23 March 1779. Papendiek is listed as chamber musician to the Margrave of Mecklenburg-Strelitz.

satin being at its last gasp. My blue satin cloak was quite new, and trimmed with a beautiful dark fur. I consulted Mrs. Barlow, who said it was most elegant to wear as a wrap when cold, and on warmer evenings just to hang on more loosely, and she thought that till Easter it would be a dress suitable for any public occasion. A cap to suit I purchased of her for 35*s*., and Kead dressed my hair for 2*s*. 6*d*. as usual, charging the same price if he pinned on.

I sojourned with my husband in his lodgings at Yates's, the perfumer, in Queen's Row, Pimlico, where we could have our breakfast and find a fire on returning there at night. . . . Salomon gave my aunt and family a free admittance to the series of concerts; the same to the Janssen [*sic*] family, the son and daughters being good musician. . . . The youngest Miss [Therese] Jansen, one of Clementi's favourite scholars, afterwards married Bartolozzi, the great engraver, and is the mother of [the famous dancer] Madame Vestris, who certainly inherits the talents of both parents, and as far as acquired knowledge goes, particularly the ornamental branches, does honour to her mother's instruction.

Salomon also offered the same liberal kindness to us, but as I did not live in London [but in Windsor] I did not think it fair to accept tickets for seats that I might not always be able to use, so declined this, but asked that I might be admitted alone or with a friend whenever I could avail myself of the permission on production of my visiting card. I may add here that our friendship continued unclouded till his death in 1815.   [II, 289–94]

The wished-for night at length arrived, and as I was anxious to be near the performers I went early. Mr. Papendiek followed from Queen's House, and I got an excellent seat on a sofa at the right-hand side. The orchestra was arranged on a new plan. The pianoforte was in the centre, at each extreme end the double basses, then on each side two violoncellos, then two tenors or violas and two violins, and in the hollow of the piano a desk on a high platform for Salomon with his ripieno. At the back, verging down to a point at each end, all these instruments were doubled, giving the requisite number for a full orchestra. Still further back, raised high up, were drums, and other side the trumpets, trombones, bassoons, oboes, clarinets, flutes, &c., in numbers according to the requirements of the symphonies and other music to be played on the different evenings.

The concert opened with a symphony of Haydn's that he brought with him, but which was not known in England. It consisted of four movements, pleasing lively, and good. . . .

The second act invarably opened with a new symphony composed for the night. Haydn of course conducted his own music, and generally that of other composers, in fact all through the evening.

The Hanover Square Rooms are calculated to hold 800 persons exclusive of the performers. By the beginning of the second act we concluded that all had arrived who intended to come, and though we knew that Salomon's subscription list was not full, we had hoped for additions during the evening. But no; and I regret to make this observation of my countrymen, that until they know what value they are likely to receive for their money they are slow in coming forward with it. An undertaking of this magnitude, bringing such a superior man from his own country as Haydn to compose for an orchestra filled with the highest professional skill and talent, should have met with every encouragement, first to show respect to the stranger and then to Salomon, who lived among us and had done so much for the musical world, in this case having taken such infinite trouble and incurred so much risk.

Now the anxious moment arrived, and Salomon having called 'attention' with his bow, the company rose to a person and stood through the whole of the first movement.

The effect was imposingly magnificent. The instruments might all be said to have an obbligato part, so perfectly was the whole combination conceived and carried out. One of the movements was to imitate the London cries, and 'Live cod' was to be traced through every instrument that could produce the effect. The cry began the piece and ended it, and Salomon was wound up to a pitch of enthusiasm beyond himself. The public were satisfied, and Haydn was very properly taken up.

His great talent is too well known for me to comment upon it. His twelve grand symphonies were composed expressly for this series of concerts, and he stands unrivalled in this style of composition. . . . Indeed, his amiability, his unbounded talent in many ways, and his humility withal, his liberality, and his every virtue could but bring him friends. [II, 294–7]

Mrs Papendiek has got rather a lot of interesting and first-hand information mixed up. (She also thought Haydn had composed *The Creation* in England.) For one thing, she believed that the year in question was 1792. One possible explanation for that slip is because she may have been using mementos in her possession and chanced on the ticket for Haydn's 1792 benefit concert which she owned, and on which she made notes (*vide infra*, p. 161). She had also forgotten the reason for the delay of the opening concert. And finally, there is the business of 'Live Cod' (which is probably Symphony No. 104), the 'new' symphony at the beginning of the second half, and the performance of an older symphony not yet known in England. The latter did not open the concert, which actually began with a Rosetti symphony, but it is significant that Mrs Papendiek remembered vaguely that an older symphony had figured in the first concert.

Let us examine the least controversial of the points raised in Mrs Papendiek's report, namely the new disposition of the orchestra in Hanover Square. We have confirmation of it, incidentally, in the amusing description of George (later Sir George) Smart in 1794 [*vide infra*, p. 247] in which we hear of Haydn's coming to the timpani player 'at the top of the orchestra'. Haydn's new system seems to have caught on at once, for the London correspondent of the *Berliner Musikzeitung* writes on 6 July 1793 of the oratorio performances when Haydn had already left England:

The arrangement of the orchestra is very good. Right in front is a row of singers; behind them, raised, are the chorus singers; then, directly behind them, the fortepiano, from which everything is conducted, and on the side the violoncelli and double basses, and then the rest of the orchestra in amphitheatre, up to the organ at the top which is used only to strengthen the choruses.

[Pohl III, 11]

It will be seen that this obviously effective plan was the basis for the arrangement of the forces used in the first public performance of *The Creation* in 1799. It was effective not only acoustically but also visually; the only similar arrangement in modern times that this writer remembers is that which the late Dr Fritz Stiedry employed with the New Friends of Music in New York: like Haydn's, the timpani in the middle of the back-stage, raised up; the effect was splendid and acoustically perfect (this was in Carnegie Hall).

The next point is much more complicated. What symphony did Haydn play? The information about this has long been incorrect. The error started with Griesinger (26), who quotes an entry in Haydn's diary as follows: 'In dem ersten Konzert wurden [*sic*] von der neuen Symphonie in D das Adagio repetirt.' Actually what Haydn wrote was very similar: 'in den 1^tn Concert wurde von der neuen Sinfonie in D das Adagio repetirt' (Bartha 512; CCLN 276 is wrong here). Now as it happens, this entry, and the succeeding two entries, refer to the *1792* season and Symphony No. 93. But in its undated version, Pohl (*H in L*) thought it meant the 1791 season. Thus it happened that the first work of the 1791 season was soon described everywhere as No. 93. When this was straightened out, the real symphony was thought to be No. 96, which as we shall see really was composed and performed in 1791. But there is now evidence that Symphonies Nos. 90 and 92 – as we shall see, Haydn forgot to bring No. 91 with him – were also performed at the 1791 season. The evidence is two-fold: (1) *The Times*, on 23 November 1791, carries the following advertisement:

NEW MUSIC
SYMPHONIES IN PARTS
HAYDN's Grand Symphonies, No. 7 and 8, performed at Mr. Salomon's Concert, 1791 each   0/5/0
PIANO FORTE, OR HARPSICHORD
Haydn's Grand Symphonies, performed at Mr. Salomon's Concert 1791, No. 7 and 8, each   0/3/0

It turns out that 'No. 7' = Symphony No. 90, and 'No. 8' = No. 92, which Haydn, as we shall see, played later in the year at Oxford. (2) The actual prints themselves (Landon, SYM 742, source 3) are also marked 'As performed at Mr Salomons concert. Hanover Square'. The arrangement for piano or harpsichord 'with an Accompaniment for a violin' was made by the pianist and composer J. L. Dussek, of whom we shall be speaking in detail below (p. 62).

We know that later in the year Haydn sent two new Salomon Symphonies to his friend Herr von Kees in Vienna (*vide*: Chronicle 14 November 1791, *infra*); and the Kees Catalogue shows us, as its last two entries, Haydn's Symphonies Nos. 96 and 95 (in that order, as Nos. 93 and 94, each marked 'NB Von London/gekom[m]en'). Thus we have the following possible candidates for that famous evening in March 1791: Nos. 90, 92, 95, 96. What evidence do we have:

(1) Haydn's letter to Luigia Polzelli of 14 March 1791, which will be cited *in extenso* later, has the following: 'nel 1mo concerto del Signor Salomone io ho fatto un furore con una nuova Sinfonia, loro hanno fatto replicare l'adagio' (Pohl III, 19 with wrong date: the autograph also has, quite wrongly, the date '4^tro di Marzo', which would place the letter *before* the concert). Haydn, obviously, would not bother to explain to his wily Italian mistress the difference between 'una nuova Sinfonia' *de anno* 1788 (No. 90), 1789 (No. 92) or 1791 (Nos 85, 96). Therefore, the available evidence is negative.

(2) Dies description of Haydn's first rehearsal with Gallini's orchestra – probably identical with Salomon's orchestra (Dies, 84f.):

Haydn's behaviour towards the orchestra that could make or break his opera [*L'anima del filosofo*] was engaging and kindly; he won them over to his side at the first rehearsal. He had laid out a symphony which began with a short Adagio. Three notes of identical pitch opened the music. But since the orchestra played these three notes too forcefully, Haydn stopped the music by waving and 'Sh! Sh!' During the following silence, a German violoncello player quite near to Haydn [see Mrs. Papendiek's description, *supra*] said his mind to his partner in German: 'Hey, he doesn't even like the first three notes, how's he going to like the others?' Haydn was glad to hear German being spoken and took these words as a warning. [Dies explains, in his usual verbose way, how Haydn solved the problem by asking for a violin and demonstrating what he wanted. Can Haydn have wanted three up-bows? We remember the late Sir John Barbirolli having the greatest difficulty with the Vienna Philharmonic Orchestra – never the politest of orchestras – at the Salzburg Festival in 1947 trying to get this effect at the beginning of Symphony No. 92.]

Of the four symphonies that come into question, only No. 92 begins as described by Dies. Thus it would seem that the 'nuova Sinfonia' was No. 92, not yet known in London, and Haydn was none too quick with its presentation, for imported copies of the Le Duc print from Paris were soon to be had in England. Part of this confusion is reflected in the following quotation from Crosse's *Account* (1825):

> . . . We are assured, however, by a friend who knew him [Haydn] previously in Germany, and who has the original MS. scores of some of them [the Salomon Symphonies] in his possession, that the first six, which are not so full as the others, were nearly finished before his arrival here . . . [Crosse, 406n.]

Another typical case how fact became, a decade or two later, mixed with fiction. The report from Crosse is, incidentally, one more reminder that all these seemingly foolish and inaccurate stories often contain a kernel of truth which is only revealed when the whole truth is known to us. It would also seem logical that Haydn, having two 'old' symphonies in his luggage, would naturally present them first, leaving him more time to compose the new ones.

As far as the evidence goes, then, it would seem that No. 92 is the first 'Salomon' Symphony. It is also, we think, significant that Haydn launched it at Oxford: again, this would seem to indicate a highly successful work. It is also noteworthy that Haydn obviously intended to conduct it at Mr Hayward's benefit concert at Oxford on 18 May 1791 – which concert, as we shall see, Haydn could not attend – where it was listed on the programme as Haydn's 'Sinfonia MS in G'.[1]

Haydn's presence was now attracting the notice of the literary world, and we find the famous *European Magazine*, which had printed Haydn's biography in its issue of October 1784, offering the following rather ambivalent poem to Haydn in its issue of March 1791 (p. 230):

IMPORTATION OF HAYDN; OR
THE COMMERCE OF THE ARTS.

The Sages of the Turf have long agreed
To augment the courser's vigour, force and speed,
By frequent mixture of *Arabian blood* –
More pow'rful far than training, rest or food.

    TUSQUIN [Josquin Depres], who choral laws from Flanders brought,
His polyphonic art Italia taught;
Mellifluous tones he first arrang'd, combin'd,
And kindred sounds in harmony entwin'd;
Then bad them mount, and run the sacred race
With curling incense to the throne of Grace.

    LULLI from Italy to France convey'd
The first rude sketches of the Lyric trade;
He furnish'd measures for each dance and song,
With which the nation was enraptur'd long.

---

1 Rosemary S. M. Hughes, 'Haydn at Oxford', *Music & Letters*, XX/3 (July 1939), pp. 242–9.

HANDEL! The mighty Saxon chief sublime,
Britannia's sons subdu'd a second time;
His name is still religion through the land,
Nor had great *Woden* such supreme command.

And now, to ease us of a useless toil,
And fertilize our cold and barren soil,
HAYDN celestial fire and *compost* brings,
And seeds of Genius o'er each fallow flings;
Plants fruits of sweetest savour through the land,
Which (if allow'd to thrive and wide expand)
May well enrich us for an age at least.
Thus in *The Commerce of the Arts* we find
Resources for our wants of ev'ry kind:
If we are furnish'd with the graceful dance,
And draw Apicius' sensual art from France;
If sculpture, architecture, painting come
From Venice, Naples, Toscany, and Rome;
If we are indebted to Italian climes
For all the skill which *vocal sound* sublimes;
If Germany our *instruments* supplies,
And HAYDN from all mortals leads the prize;
Our Bacons, Newtons, Lockes, can Science teach,
Our Poets write, and Theologians preach;
Our Arts and Industry in times of need
Can proud and distant empires clothe and feed –
Parents and friends we find in ev'ry nation,
Where all subsist alike by COMMUTATION.

If Burney's poetical effort was 'dry, prosaic and cataloguish', what are we to say of Haydn as heavenly German dung? Happily, the composer's English will not have been up to this specimen of British wit. Something of the thrill of Haydn's early concerts with his friend Salomon may be caught in the following entry from Dr Burney's memoirs, so ruthlessly destroyed by his daughter Fanny d'Arblay:

> 1791. – This year was auspiciously begun, in the musical world, by the arrival in London of the illustrious Joseph Haydn. 'Tis to Salomon that the lovers of music are indebted for what the lovers of music will call this blessing. Salomon went over himself to Vienna . . . purposely to tempt that celebrated musical genius hither; and on February 25 [*sic*], the first of Haydn's incomparable symphonies which was composed for the concerts of Salomon was performed. Haydn himself presided at the piano-forte; and the sight of that renowned composer so electrified the audience, as to excite an attention and a pleasure superior to any that had ever, to my knowledge, been caused by instrumental music in England. All the slow middle movements were encored; which never before happened, I believe, in any country.   [Scholes II, 110]

The report is useful for one further point regarding the instrument from which Haydn conducted. In most of the 1791 newspapers, it is referred to as a harpsichord; but although the British continued to make powerful and mechanically the best harpsichords the world had ever seen down to the last decade of the century, Burney, a professional musician, says specifically 'piano-forte'; and it may be doubted if Haydn would have chosen the harpsichord when the new English pianos were obviously much more powerful (we shall see that he brought back to Vienna one of the big, new instruments by Longman & Broderip, 'with the additional keys', as the announcements used to read).

A report by Dr Burney brings up another curious point in Haydn's first appearance with a British orchestra. He writes:

> There is a censure levelled at him . . . for making the measure to his new compositions; but as even the old compositions had never been performed under his direction, in this country, till the last winter, it was surely allowable for him to indicate to the orchestra the exact time in which he intended the several movements to be played, without offending the leader or subalterns of the excellent band which he had to conduct.[1]

Strange as it seems to us nowadays, it would appear that it was the leader of the band, i.e. Salomon in this case, who indicated the tempi, and not the composer if he happened to participate. Haydn was used to conducting his own band, sometimes (as in opera) from the keyboard, sometimes (as in the later symphonies) from the violin; and with quiet authority he simply continued to be a conductor at Salomon's concerts, probably giving the 'up-beats' etc. from the keyboard, where he 'presided'. If there was any friction about this procedure at the beginning, as Burney's report seems to indicate, it later died out, for we never hear a similar objection again.

It must have been about this time that Haydn went to call on the Rev. Christian Ignatius Latrobe, the Moravian minister and composer whom Dr Burney had used to translate his poem welcoming Haydn to England. Latrobe describes his meeting with Haydn vividly, in a long letter to Vincent Novello, dated 22 November 1828.[2]

> I was introduced to him [Haydn] by Dr. Burney, who well knew the value I should set upon the personal acquaintance of a man, whose Works I so greatly admired, and of which I may say, that they had been a feast to my soul. I had at that time made scores of about 25 of his Quartettos, from the printed parts, & continued to play them on the pianoforte with tolerable accuracy, as to their internal construction. Whether he perceived, on our first interview, that my admiration of him as the first of composers, in conversation, soon rose to sincere affection for him as a most amiable man, & therefore felt mutual kindness towards me, I will not presume to say, but he was pleased, not long after, to pay me a visit. When he entered the room, he found my wife alone, & as she could not speak German, & he had scarcely picked up a few English words, both were at a loss what to say. He bowed with foreign formality, & the following short Explanation took place.
>
> H. 'Dis, Mr. Latrobe house?' The answer was in the affirmative.
> H. 'Be you his Woman?' (meaning his wife).
> 'I am Mrs. Latrobe', was the reply.
>
> After some pause, he looked round the room, & saw his picture, to which he immediately pointed, & exclaimed, 'Dat is me. I am Haydn!' My wife instantly, knowing what a most welcome guest I was honoured with, sent for me to a house not far off, & treated him with all possible civility. He was meanwhile amused with some fine specimens of Labrador spar [kinds of crystalline minerals, O.E.D.] on the Chimney-piece, which he greatly admired & accepted of a polished slab. Of course I hastened home, & passed half an hour with him in agreeable conversation.

---

1 Rosemary Hughes: 'Dr Burney's Championship of Haydn' in *Musical Quarterly*, XXVII (1941), pp. 95f.
2 British Museum, Department of Manuscripts, Add. 11730, fol. 112. I am grateful to the Museum for sending me a photostat copy of this document, which is reprinted here without alterations.

He gave me his direction & begged me to call on him whenever I pleased, which I considered the more condescending, as he could derive neither honour nor profit by my acquaintance. You may be sure I availed myself of the priveledge, & believe, that we did not grow tired of each other's company. The same friendly intercourse between us was kept up during both his first & second Visits to England. Sometimes I met him at friends' houses, but never enjoyed his Company more than at his own lodging. I now & then found him at work upon the magnificent Symphonies, which he composed for Salomon's Concerts, & tho' I avoided taking up time so well employed, yet he would sometimes detain me, & play for me some passages of a new Composition. On enquiry, hearing from a friend, that I had ventured to compose some Sonatas for the Pianoforte, he desired to hear them. As he observed, that they ought to be printed, I agreed, if he would permit me to dedicate them to him. Of this he has made mention in his own account of his Visits to England [in the biographies of Dies and Griesinger]. These Sonatas [Op. 3, published by John Bland about 1792], with many compositions of better masters, have long ago swam down the stream of oblivion, & made room for a younger fry. Speaking with me of Mozart's death, he added, with that modesty, by which he was distinguished, 'In him the World lost a much greater Master of Harmony than I am.' In general, I never perceived in Haydn any symptoms of that envy & jealousy, which is, alas, so much the besetting sin of musicians.

He appeared to me to be a religious character, & not only attentive to the forms & usages of his own Church, but under the influence of a devotional spirit. This is felt by those, who understand the language of Music, in many parts his Masses & other Compositions for the Church. I once observed to him, that having in the year 1779, when a youth, obtained the parts of his Stabat Mater from a friend, who had found means to procure them at Dresden, I made a score, & became enchanted with its beauty. The study of it, more than of any other Work, helped to form my taste, & make me more zealous in the pursuit of this noble science. He seemed delighted to hear my remarks on a Composition, which he declared to be one of his favourites, & added, that it was no wonder, that it partook of a religious fervor, for it had been composed in the performance of a religious Vow. He then gave me the following account of it. Sometime about the year 1770 [*recte: c.* 1776], (but as to the particular year, I am not sure) he was siezed [*sic*] with a violent disorder, which threatened his life. 'I was', said he, 'not prepared to die, and prayed to God to have mercy upon me & grant me recovery. I also vowed, that if I were restored to health, I would compose a Stabat Mater in honor of the blessed Virgin, as a token of thankfulness. My prayer was heard & I recovered. With a grateful sense of my duty, I cheerfully set about the performance of my Vow, & endeavoured to do it in my best manner. When finished, I sent the score to my dear old friend Hasse, then residing at Venice' (If I am right). 'He returned me an answer which I shall preserve as a treasure to the end of my life. It [the *Stabat Mater*] is full of affection & truly religious feeling, for he was not only my musical, but my spiritual father. The Stabat Mater was performed at Vienna, both in the Imperial Chapel & at other Churches with acceptance, but I dedicated it to the Electress of Saxony [Maria Antonia Walpurgis, widow of Friedrich August II], who was an excellent judge in Music, & Dresden it was done justice to.' – The tears glistened in his eyes, while he gave me this account, of which I have remembered the very words.

More I will not add, than to assure you of my Esteem & thanks for your kind musical presents to me & my children, & wishing, that every possible success may attent your very meretorious endeavors to promote the cause of good music, . . . [etc.]

Three days after the first Salomon concert, Haydn wrote to his mistress, Luigia Polzelli in Vienna. Her sister, Theresa Negri, sang in London (*vide* pp. 64f., 68).

[*Italian, 'Tu' form*]   London, 14th March 1791.
                                                     [autograph, wrongly '4 March 1791']

Most esteemed Polzelli,

I am very sorry for you in your present circumstances, and I hope that your poor husband will die at any moment; you did well to put him in the hospital, to keep him alive. I hope that my Pietro feels better; please tell him to pay better attention to his health and to obey his mother. Dear Polzelli, you will receive one hundred florins [Gulden] from *Mons.* Pierre, the steward-in-waiting to the Prince. As soon as I have given my benefit concert, I shall send you some more. I have written to *Mons.* Pierre that your sister has sent the money, because I don't want him to know that it comes from me. Your sister told me that she will send you something herself. I haven't seen her for some time, because I have a lot to do, with all the concerts and opera, and I am persecuted the whole time by the subscription concerts. Up to now our opera has not yet opened, and since the King won't give the licence, *Signor* Gallini intends to open it as if it were a subscription concert, for if he doesn't, he stands to lose twenty thousand pounds Sterling. I shan't lose anything, because the bankers Fries in Vienna have already received my money. My opera, entitled *L'anima del filosofo*, will be staged at the end of May; I have already completed the Second Act, but there are five acts, of which the last are very short. In order to show the public his theatre, his opera and his ballet, *Signor* Gallini has had the clever idea of arranging, one evening a few days ago, a dress rehearsal in such a manner as if it were the real opening night; he distributed four thousand tickets, and more than five thousand came. The opera, entitled *Pyhro* [*Pirro*], by Paisiello, was very successful. Only our *prima donna* is a silly goose, and I shan't use her in my opera. The ballet was simply magnificent. We now await a yes or a no from the King, and if our theatre is opened, the other theatre, that is, our rivals, will have to close their doors, because the castrato and the *prima donna* are too old, and their opera didn't please anyone. At the first concert of Mr. Salomon I created a furore with a new Symphony, and they had to repeat the Adagio: this had never before occurred in London. Imagine what it means to hear such a thing from an Englishman's lips! Write soon, dear Polzelli, and think of me. I am, and will always be,

                                             Your most sincere friend,
                                             Giuseppe Haydn.

[Address:] Madame Polzelli à Vienna
              im Starnbergischen Freyhaus auf der Wieden N^{ro} 161
[Polzelli added the following note in pencil: 'He will die—an enemy has followed Haydn to London to overthrow him.']

                                                     [CCLN, 115f.]

It is clear from this letter that Haydn no longer intended Euridice in his new opera to be sung by Rosa Lops; possibly he thought of using Teresa Poggi Cappelletti, who contributed to Salomon's concerts. The Paisiello opera *Pirro* had been given its first rehearsal on 23 February, which the Press (and also the Prince of Wales) attended. On 10 March *Pirro* was given as a dress rehearsal in full costume and with lighting. The house was so full that the famous Vestris could not show off his talents to his best ability because even the stage was full of hastily improvised seats; the ballet was *Orpheus & Euridice*, and as we have seen it excited Haydn's admiration. (Pohl, *H in L*, 124f.)

The curious and rather pathetic *postscriptum* by Polzelli shows that false rumours about Haydn's stay in London had been reaching Vienna. We shall see, in a later letter to Frau von Genzinger, Haydn's reaction to some of them. One wonders who among Haydn's enemies – Federici? – can have reported back to Vienna . . . Meanwhile Salomon's second concert took place:

Second Concert: 18 March 1791

HANOVER-SQUARE. Mr. SALOMON'S CONCERT.

THE SUBSCRIBERS are respectfully acquainted, that the Second Performance will be This Day.

PART FIRST

Overture, MAZANT [*i. e.* Mozart?].[1]

Aria, Signor TAJANA.

Concerto (German Flute), Mr. GRAEFF.

Aria, Signora STORACE.

New Quartetto for two Violins, Tenors, and Violincellos, by Messrs. Salomon, Damen, Hindmarsh, and Menel. – Haydn.

PART SECOND

(By particular Desire) the new Symphony of HAYDN will be repeated, as performed on the first Night.

Scena Recitative Aria, Signor DAVID.

Concerto (Bassoon) Mr. KUCHLER.

(Being his first Appearance in England.)

Duetto Sig. David and Sig. Storace – Paisiello.

Full Piece, Pleyel.

Mr. HAYDN will be at the Harpsichord . . .

[*Public Advertiser*, 18 March]

The *Morning Chronicle* of 19 March reports:

SALOMON'S CONCERT.

The second Concert was honoured with the presence of the PRINCE of WALES, who came just in time to join in the triumph of HAYDN. The Concerto [*i. e.* Symphony No. 92], which had so powerful an effect on the Company on the first night, was repeated; and its influence was equally felt. It is a sublime composition – as much from the rich variety of the subject as the grandeur with which it is managed. Every instrument is respected by his Muse, and he gives to each its due proportion of efficacy. He does not elevate one, and make all the rest contributory as a mere accompaniment; but the subject is taken up by turns, with masterly art, and every performer has the means of displaying his talent.

His new Quartetto is exceedingly beautiful, and was well executed.

The celebrated KUCHLER made his first appearance in this country on the *Bassoon*, and performed a very fine Concerto. He is a great accession to the musical band of this kingdom, and, we trust, will be added to the Orchestra of the King's Theatre.

It is impossible to speak of the execution of DAVID in terms of adequate praise. He sung two songs and a duet with STORACE.

Graeff is the flautist and composer J. G. Graeff (Gräf, Gräff, *not* the composer Friedrich Hartmann Graff who received the degree of doctor of music, *hon. causa*,

---

1 The 'Mazant' Overture, if 'Mozart' is the correct interpretation, could be one of the published symphonies, either the 'Paris' (K. 297), the Sieber edition of which will long have circulated to England; of K. 319 in B flat or K. 385 in D ('Haffner'), both published by Artaria of Vienna. K. 385 would make a particularly effective opening.

from Oxford in 1789); in 1797 he published 'Three Quartettos . . . dedicated to Dr Haydn.[1]

If we are correct in our assumption that No. 92 was the first 'new' work of the 1791, it was now repeated at the beginning of the second part. A new Haydn quartet was played in Part One. Op. 64, as we now call them, consists of six string quartets composed in 1790 and 'dédiés a Monsieur Jean Tost', the merchant for whom Haydn wrote a dozen quartets and, it would seem, Mozart his late string quintets. These quartets were not known at all in England, and Haydn not only performed them at Salomon's concerts but also sold them to his friend John Bland, who issued them in June (announcement in the *Morning Herald* on 10 June) as 'perform'd under his [Haydn's] direction at Mr. Salomon's concert, the Festino Rooms Hanover Square'. None of the pieces in Salomon's Third Concert can be accurately identified, though the title 'Grand Symphony' without the additional 'MS' would seem to indicate an earlier symphony. The mysterious Haydn Cantata puzzles us. The authentic manuscript of the Cantata, 'Miseri noi, misera patria' shows (1) that Haydn revised it in England, adding a second flute part, and (2) the M.S. was used by an engraver to 'lay out' his plates. But we have not succeeded in locating any print of the work. Can this have been the 'New Cantata'?

A more likely possibility is the so-called Cantata 'Ah, come il cor', a work which Haydn himself had published with Artaria in Vienna in 1783, but which was actually Celia's great *scena* in Act II of Haydn's *La fedeltà premiata* (1780, performed 1781). That Miss Storace sang the work in question is the more probable because of the fact that the 'Cantata' was reprinted in 1791 by Longman & Broderip, and announced frequently, e.g. in *The Times* on 6 July and in the *Morning Chronicle* on 27 May. Longman & Broderip usually advertised the work as 'Haydn's Cantata' or 'Italian Cantata, with accompaniments' for 5 shillings. They published the score and orchestral parts. Nancy Storace cannot have sung Haydn's popular *Arianna a Naxos,* at least not in its original form; for the work was composed for mezzo-soprano or even contralto, and we should recall that she was Mozart's first Susanna, quite a different kind of voice than that needed for *Arianna*.

Ignaz Pleyel, whose compositions were performed at the Second and Third concerts, was Haydn's 'star' pupil; we shall meet him again when he comes to England (*vide* p. 121). Hoffmeister, the composer of the popular 'La Chasse' played at the Third Concert and of another work at the Eighth Concert, was Franz Anton, better known today as a successful publisher. He founded the firm which would become C. F. Peters, and published works by Haydn, Mozart (the piano quartets) and Beethoven.

Third Concert: 25 March 1791

HANOVER-SQUARE. Mr. SALOMON'S CONCERT.

The Subscribers are respectfully acquainted that the Third Performance will be THIS DAY, the 25th instant.

PART THE FIRST.
Overture – Clementz [*sic*].
Quintetto, for two Violins, two Tenors and a Violoncello,
Messrs. Salomon, Damer [*sic*], Hindmarsh, Bolack [*sic*], and Memet [*sic*]. – Pleyel.
Aria, Signora Storace.
Concerto (Violin) Mr. Salomon.
Aria, Signor David.

1 Linley, London, announced in the *Monthly Magazine and British Register*, Vol. III, January 1797.

PART THE SECOND.
Grand Symphony, Haydn.
Scena, Signor David.
New Concerto Piano Forte, Mr. Dusseck.
New Cantata, Signora Storace. – Haydn.
Full Piece (La Chas[s]e), Hoffmeister.
Full Piece, Pleyel.
Mr. HAYDN will be at the Harpsichord . . .

[*Gazetteer*, 25 March]

The *Gazetteer* reviewed the concert on the following day:

SALOMON'S CONCERT. In the Concert of last night, which was attended by a numerous and fashionable audience, a very charming *Cantata*, the composition of Haydn, was sung by Signora Storace with much elegance of manner. David's *Aria* was greatly admired, as was Dusseck'[s] Piano Forte Concerto. Salomon's violin was highly distinguished in his *Solo*; and a new symphony of Haydn's afforded a new proof of the fertility of this great master's genius in instrumental composition.

The 'New Concerto Piano Forte' by Johann Ladislaw (Ludwig) Dussek brings us to a name that will figure often in these concerts. He was the son of a friend of Haydn's (see p. 138) and was soon to marry the talented singer, Sophia Corri, which marriage would lead to the formation of the publishers Corri & Dussek. Born in Czaslau in Bohemia, Dussek eventually made his way to Holland, Hamburg (where he studied with C. P. E. Bach), Berlin, Russia, Lithuania (with Prince Radziwill, father of Chopin's patron), Paris (where he delighted Queen Marie Antoinette in 1786), Milan (to visit his brother), and back to Paris, in 1788. Shortly thereafter he moved to London and became fashionable immediately, both as a composer and as a performer. His playing must have been remarkable. Eye-witnesses speak of his 'broad and noble style . . ., his method of *singing* on an instrument which possessed no sustained sounds, the neatness, delicacy, and brilliance of his playing' (Fétis, remembering Dussek's performance at the Odéon in 1808); elsewhere we read that 'after the few opening bars of his first solo, the public uttered a general Ah! There was, in fact, something magical about [his playing] . . ., especially in *cantabile* phrases. . . . Dussek was the first who placed his instrument sideways upon the platform'. (J. W. Tomaschek, listening to Dussek at Prague, 1804).

As the composer, he also appears on our Salomon lists with the very first concert (11 March; *supra*), in a Concerto for pedal harp, piano and orchestra; and we have seen that Haydn entrusted to him the arrangements of Symphonies Nos. 90 and 92 for piano (*supra*, p. 54).

Fourth Concert: 1 April 1791

HANOVER-SQUARE. Mr. SALOMON'S CONCERT.

The Subscribers are respectfully acquainted, that the FOURTH Performance will be This Evening:

PART I.
Overture. Girovetz [*sic*].
New Quartetto, M. S. for two Violins, Tenor and Violoncello,
by Messrs. Salomon, Damen, Hindmarch, and Menel. – Kotzeluch [*sic*].
Aria. Signor Tajana.

Concerto Corni Bassetti. Messrs. Divorsack [*sic*], and Springe [*sic*].
Aria. Signor David.

PART II.

New Grand Overture. Mr. S. Hadyn [i.e. MS. Haydn].
Duetto, the Miss Abrams.
Concerto, Pedal Harp. Madame Krumpholtz.
Scena Recitative and Aria, Signor David.
Symphony. Pleyell [*sic*].
Mr. HAYDN will be at the Harpsichord . . .

[*Public Advertiser*, and *Gazetteer*, 1 April]

The *Diary; or, Woodfall's Register* reviews the concert on 2 April as follows:

HANOVER SQUARE.

The Fourth performance of the Concerts under the direction of the celebrated HAYDN and Mr. SALOMON, took place at these rooms last night, and was such as might be expected from the great musical talents employed in the conduct of them.

Of the instrumental pieces, though all excellent, nothing occurred that could bear any comparison with the new overture of HAYDN, which exhibited all the fire and perfection of his genius.

The whole of this charming composition, was received by the most intelligent *amateurs*, with the highest admiration . . .

The most we can say about the New Grand Overture MS. by Haydn is that it was either No. 90, or one of the two new works, Nos. 96 or 95. The Quartet was by the facile and popular Viennese (Bohemian) composer Leopold Koželuch, who maintained a vast correspondence with English publishers for many years and whom Beethoven described in one word – *miserabilis*. We shall hear much more of this curious man in later years. Salomon was clever enough not to stuff the public with Haydn; we often find new works by Haydn's fashionable pupil Ignaz Pleyel (see the Third Concert, *supra*), and there were always the arias by Italian composer to satisfy popular demand. The two basset-horn players, Messrs. Divorsack (Dvořák) and Vincent Springer (*recte*), were touring Europe. Springer, a Bohemian by birth, was a Freemason and together with another basset-horn player, Anton David, he had participated in the first performance of Mozart's *Masonic Funeral Music* (K. 477) in 1785. David, who had been Springer's partner until that period, grew ill and had to reduce his public appearances; his place was taken by Dvořák.[1]

The first piece on the programme was by Adalbert Gyrowetz, a young Bohemian composer who formed his style, as he tells us himself in his well-known autobiography, on Haydn's symphonies. Mozart introduced the attractive young man to Viennese concert audiences, and Gyrowetz then went on to Italy (where he met Goethe in Naples and had long talks with him), wrote music for the King of Naples (lira concertos, such as Haydn had also composed) and then went to Paris. There he found one of his symphonies, in G (Landon SYM, Appendix II, 109, p. 818), already

---

1 See the foreword to our edition, taken from the new collected edition of Mozart's works, of K. 477, separately published by Bärenreiter Verlag in full and miniature score (Tp. 18), 1955. See also a biographical note on David and Springer in Cramer's *Magazin der Musik*, Erster Jahrgang, Zweyte Hälfte 1783 (II, 768ff.), and O. E. Deutsch, *Mozart. Die Dokumente seines Lebens*, Kassel (etc.) 1961, pp. 223ff. Presumably Dvořák was also a freemason.

popular under Haydn's name[1] and published by Sieber; it took poor Gyrowetz some time to convince the French that he, and not Haydn, was the real composer. The frightful events in Paris persuaded Gyrowetz to leave France and seek his fortune in England, where he arrived in October 1789. The Prince of Wales and the Duke of Cumberland took him up, and he soon found publishers, among them Longman & Broderip. Salomon engaged him to compose for the Hanover Square Rooms, and the Theatre contracted an opera, *Semiramis*. The score of this opera was burned with the Pantheon Theatre itself in January 1792, and only the Overture survives. Madame Mara and Pacchierotti were to have sung in it. Gyrowetz tells us in his autobiography how he was helpful to Haydn, introducing him here and there.[2]

Gyrowetz's fatal facility enabled him to rise at meteoric speed. Foreign (Continental) publishers' catalogues of 1790–95 are filled with work after work. His Haydnesque imitations were clever, but shallow and often formless. It took the English some time to realize it – as was also the case with Pleyel. In 1796, Gyrowetz composed a 'New Quartetto Obligato MS.' for Salomon's subscription concert on 24 February, and on 27 February the *Morning Chronicle* wrote that 'The Quartetto was charmingly played, but miserably composed; like almost everything by the same Master (GYROWITZ) it was a collection of passages without meaning, without relation, and consequently without unity.'

On 4 April, the printer Humphrey in London issued a new engraving of Haydn, after a painting by A. M. Ott, 'Painter to the Duke of Orleans', but engraved by the famous Francesco Bartolozzi, with whom Haydn was on friendly terms. Haydn referred to Bartolozzi has having 'corrected' the painting, but the composer obviously thought the sheet a failure. It is a bad likeness (reproduction *inter alia* in Somfai, p. 116, and Geiringer 1947, facing p. 161). Its failure perhaps encouraged other artists to do a better portrait of Haydn; and in fact not only Hoppner's and Hardy's but also Guttenbrunn's are all better than the wretched painting by Ott.

Fifth Concert: 8 April 1791

HANOVER SQUARE. Mr. SALOMON'S CONCERT.
The SUBSCRIBERS are respectfully acquainted, that the Fifth performance will be This EVENING.

PART I.

Overture – Kozeluch.

Aria – Signor Tajana.

Concertant for Clarinet and Bassoon – Messrs. Flieger [*sic*] and Holmes.

Recitative and Aria – Signora Theresa Negri.

(Being her first appearance in this Country.)

New Divertimento, MS. for Two Violins, Two Tenors, One
Oboe, One Flauto, One Violoncello, One Double Bass,
and Two French Horns. – Haydn.

Aria – Signor David.

1 Subsequent to the publication of Landon SYM we have discovered several sources under Gyrowetz's name: from the music collection of the Teutonic Knights at Freudenthal (near Troppau, of Beethovenian fame), where it is No. 1 of five symphonies; this collection is now in the Archives of the Teutonic Knights at Vienna, and its existence was kindly brought to my attention by Fritz Kaiser. A second source under Gyrowetz's name is from Příbram (now Prague National Library XI, A103 'Del Sig. Girovetz'); a third is in the Archbishop of Olmütz's Library in Kroměříž (Kremsier), ČSSR, cat. IV, A101; and a fourth is found in the thematic catalogue of Raigern (Rajhrad, ČSSR) Monastery as No. 143 under symphonies. See also *infra*, p. 503.

2 The most recent large-scale research on Gyrowetz was undertaken by the present author for MGG (see article 'Gyrowetz').

PART II.
By Particular Desire.
The New Overture, M.S. – Haydn.
As performed last Friday, will be repeated.
Recit. and Aria. – Signora Theresa Negri.
Concerto Pedal Harp – Madame Krumpholtz.
Recitative Aria – Signor David.
Full Piece – Rosetti.
Mr. Haydn will be at the Harpsichord . . .

[*The Diary; or, Woodfall's Register*, 8 April]

A short report of the concert appeared the next day in the *Morning Chronicle*:

SALOMON'S CONCERT was last night most numerously attended; and its attraction was more than usually great; for to all the invitations of HAYDN and DAVID, there was the curiosity of a new vocal performer[,] Signora THERESA NEGRI.

Haydn took with him to London some of the *Notturni* for the King of Naples (1790). Originally scored for two *lire organizzate* (a kind of hurdy-gurdy), two clarinets, two horns, two violas and *basso*, Haydn rewrote the *lire* parts for flute and oboe (in one instance two flutes), gave the clarinet parts to violins and added a separate double bass part. At least three *Notturni* in this London version have survived: Hob. 11, 27, 28, and 32; for 11, 27 Haydn wrote a slow introduction, and 11, 32 is scored for two flutes. The autograph of 11, 31, though not rescored, was once owned by the Papendiek family and may have been played in London.

Sixth Concert: 15 April 1791

HANOVER-SQUARE. Mr. SALOMON'S CONCERT.

The Subscribers are respectfully acquainted that the Sixth Performance will be THIS EVENING:

PART the FIRST.
New Overture – Demacchi.
Aria, Signor Tajana.
New Quartetto; M. S. for Two Violins, Tenor, and Violoncello,
by Messrs. Salomon, Damen, Hindmarsh, and Menel – Haydn.
Recitativo e Aria, Miss Corry (being her first appearance in public).
Concerto Violin, Master Bridgetower.

PART the SECOND.
(By particular Desire) the new Overture, M. S. (Haydn)
performed on the first and second nights will be repeated.
Recit. e Aria, Signor David.
Sonata, Piano Forte, Mr. Dusseck, with an
accompaniment, for a Violin, Tenor, and Violoncello, by
Messrs. Salomon, Hindmarsh, and Menel.
Duetto, Miss Corry and Signor David.
Full Piece, Pichl.
Mr. HAYDN will be at the Harpsichord . . .

[*Gazetteer*, 15 April]

The *Gazetteer* on 18 April reviewed the concert as follows:

MUSIC. SALOMON'S CONCERT.

The musical world will rejoice to hear, that the celebrated *Haydn* has determined to fix the seat of his *empire* in this metropolis. The great encouragement of

Salomon's Concert[s], under the *auspices* of Haydn, and his reception every where in private assemblies, has impressed him with a high opinion of the taste and liberality of the English nation.

The performance of Friday was distinguished by the first appearance of *Miss Corri*, who received the rudiments of her musical education under the skilful tuition of her father, which she has cultivated by studying the style of the best singers who have occasionally visited the Italian stage. Her manner seems to have been formed chiefly on that of the celebrated *Marchesi*. Her voice is pleasing and flexible, and it has considerable compass. Her ear is admirably correct; and in her duet with *David* she evinced much skill as a musician. Upon the whole, Miss Corri promises to become a very distinguished ornament of the profession.

The grand Overture of Haydn [Symphony No. 92], which has excited so much admiration, was again repeated; and every time it is heard with new pleasure. Little Bridgetower's violin concerto was a masterly performance; and *Dusseck's* sonata on the piano forte, if it had less *affectation* of expression, would have resembled the affecting simplicity of the much lamented *Schroeter*.

The quartet in the first part was from Op. 64 (see our note after the Second Concert). Miss Sophia Corri was proficient enough for Haydn to use her at his 1792 benefit. The symphony in the second part was No. 92 (if that is the work of the first concert). The most interesting appearance is that of 'Master Bridgetower', who was to go down in history as the man for whom Beethoven wrote the violin Sonata in A (Op. 47) later dedicated to Kreutzer. George Polgreen Bridgetower was, according to Rosenbaum.[1] the mulatto son of the Negro August, a page (Rosenbaum says 'footman') to Prince Nicolaus I Esterházy. The young Bridgetower is reported to have studied with Haydn. In 1789 he played at a Concert Spirituel in Paris, 'not yet ten years old'. Later he and Beethoven quarrelled over a girl and their friendship broke up. On the dedication manuscript of the Sonata, Op. 47, Beethoven wrote: 'Sonata mulattica. Composta per il Mulatto Brischdauer gran pazzo e compositore mulattico' ('Mulatick Sonata. Composed for the mulatto Brischdauer, great lunatick and mulatick composer') with that dreadful punning humour that the composer adopted in his 'unbuttoned' moods.

There is a charming anecdote about Haydn and the Bridgetower family which has just come to light in the unpublished manuscript journal of the composer and singer Charles Edward Horn (1786–1849), a transcript of which was kindly supplied by Mr Michael Kassler of Washington, D.C. The original journal was part of the W. H. Cummings collection and is now in the Nanki Library, Tokyo. Mr Kassler thinks this portion of the journal might have been written about 1845. Here is the portion dealing with Haydn.

> . . . Till we lived in Lambeth Nº 4 Pratt Street my father [Karl Friedrich Horn, the musician, 1762–1830] took of Edward Wetenhall the then celebrated Stock Broker who went to live in Kennington [?] Lane next door the Pilgrem [?] . . . He [Wetenhall] had other peculiarities . . . for instance being very fond of Music and his eldest daughter afterwards Mrs Cairn my fathers best Piano forte Scholar. Hayden when in England when hearing her play dedicated 3 Sonates to her [probably in manuscript] – but Wetenhalls singular Character was such that in his own house – altho appearing a great tyrant – [he] . . . always patronized Musical

1 Joseph Carl Rosenbaum was an employee of Prince Nicolaus II's administration and kept an interesting diary, edited by Else Radant (*Rosenbaum Diaries* – see 16 May 1803 and the concert with Beethoven on 24 May 1803. See also Landon, *Beethoven*, pp. 148ff. and Betty Matthews: 'George Polgreen Bridgetower' in *Music Review,* XXIX/1 (1968), pp. 22ff.

Men . . . It was here in Pratt Street that Hayden was invited by my father with *Dragonetti* the *Prima Contra Bass* at the Opera House to meet *Salomon*. Once the elder *Bridgetower* [George Polgreen's father] – a very dark *creole* or *Indian* – for he was dress'd in robes – and which struck me with such astonishment or fear when I was brought in after dinner that it occasioned Hayden the great and immortal Composer of the Creation to take me upon his knee and this I never forgot altho I did not know Hayden from any other excepting he appeared to me a neat, good natured old gentleman with Ruffels [*sic*] at his Wrists and bosome [*sic*] and a powdered wig with curls on the side seated next my mother and perceiving my alarm at the *oriental looking blackamoor* – he held me closer and this made the impression on me – when I was told the Story some time afterwards, I was informed it was Hayden who held me on his knee. This was the honor that afterwards made so lasting an impression on me . . . .

Bridgetower had arrived with his father in England in 1789, where Mrs Papendiek saw him. She writes:

About this time an adventurer of the name of Bridgetower, a black, came to Windsor, with a view of introducing his son, a most prepossessing lad of ten or twelve years old, and a fine violin player. He was commanded by their Majesties to perform at the Lodge, when he played a concerto of Viotti's and a quartet of Haydn's, whose pupil he called himself. Both father and son pleased greatly. The one for his talent and modest bearing, the other for his fascinating manner, elegance, expertness in all languages, beauty of person, and taste in dress. He seemed to win the good opinion of every one, and was courted by all and entreated to join in society. . . .

[Papendiek II, 134f.]

What is curious is the presence of Father Bridgetower – his name was John Frederick – in England as early as 1789. If he really was the famous 'Mohr August', the personal page to Nicolaus I Esterházy, who died in 1790, how could he have left the Prince's service? Was he dismissed? Did he have leave of absence? We must hope that the present investigation of the Esterházy Archives will perhaps one day reveal some additional facts about the Bridgetowers, whose names are linked with Haydn and Beethoven.

The Schroeter to which the *Gazetteer* review refers is the composer Johann Samuel, with whose widow Haydn was to have a love affair.

On 23 April, Haydn spent a delightful day with his new friend Dr Burney. The following day Dr Burney reports to his old correspondent, the Rev. Thomas Twining:

I [spent] the day yesterday with the dear great & good Haydn, whom I love more & more every time I see as well as hear him. In a small party chiefly of my own family, we prevailed on him to play the 1st Violin to his Instrumental Passione [*The Seven Words of the Saviour on the Cross*], for w^{ch}, though we c^d only perform it in 4 parts, though it consists of 16, yet its effect was admirable as executed by him, in a most chaste & feeling manner. He played the 2^d Violin only to several of his Quartets – while my Nephews played the 1st & Tenor, & a Mr Gun of Cambridge the Violoncello.

[Lonsdale, 354]

A few weeks earlier, the musical prodigy, William Crotch, now organist of Christ Church, Oxford, had written to Burney (8 March; Lonsdale 354, n.6), asking him to arrange a meeting with Haydn; we do not know if the meeting took place, but Crotch was later to play a curious role in the history of Haydn's *Creation* in England, denouncing the work in scathing terms.

This is perhaps the place to supply a few details about the Madame Krumpholz (*recte*) who so frequently figures in the Haydn-Salomon concerts as solo harpist. She was the widow of Johann Baptist Krumpholz, a Bohemian musician who had been a member of Prince Nicolaus Esterházy's band from October 1773 to March 1776, where he is listed as a harpist. He also took composition lessons with Haydn, and later moved to Paris. In the Spring of 1788, his young wife, a far finer harpist than her husband, eloped to London 'with a young man' and settled there; in 1790, Krumpholz drowned himself in the Seine 'at the infidelity and ingratitude of his wife'. It is surprising that we have no compositions by Haydn for either Krumpholz. Johann Baptist had a brother, Wenzel, a violinist, who was one of the first to recognize Beethoven's talents in Vienna.[1]

Seventh Concert: 29 April 1791

HANOVER-SQUARE. Mr. SALOMON'S CONCERT.

The Subscribers are respectfully acquainted, that the SEVENTH Performance will be This Evening.

PART I.
Overture. Girovetz [*sic*].
Aria. Signora Theresa Negri.
Quintetto M. S. for a Violin, an Oboe, two Tenors, and a Violoncello,
by Messrs. Salomon, Harrington, Hindmarch, Polack, and Menel –
Baumgarten.
Aria, Signor David.
Concerto Violoncello. Mr. Menel.

PART II.
New Grand Overture. Mr. S. Hadyn [i.e. MS. Haydn].
Aria. Signora Theresa Negri.
Concerto, Pedal Harp. Madame Krumpholtz.
Recitative and Aria. Signor David.
Symphony, Pleyell [*sic*].
Mr. HAYDN will be at the Harpsichord . . . .

[*Public Advertiser*, 29 April]

The 'New Grand Overture MS' cannot be identified, but by this stage of the 1791 season we are undoubtedly dealing with one of the really new Salomon Symphonies, Nos. 95 or 96; the new work was repeated at the Eighth Concert. In the Seventh, the new Oboe Quintet was by C. F. Baumgarten, a native German settled in England so long that (as Haydn tells us in his notebook), he forgot his mother tongue almost completely. Baumgarten was leader of Covent Garden and also of the Duke of Cumberland's private band.

One of the few programmes of the Gallini concerts which Haydn conducted has recently come to light in German private possession. The long programme gives us a vivid impression of Haydn once again acting as opera *Capellmeister*, though also performing two symphonies and, apparently, the lost Aria he composed for Signor David(e).

1 Pohl, *H in L*, 41ff. Grove's *Dictionary*, first edition (hereinafter 'Grove I'), vol. II, p. 74 (article on the family by C. F. Pohl).

King's THEATRE

THIS EVENING, SATURDAY, April 30,
Will be given a New Collection of
SERIOUS AND COMIC MUSIC,
By Different Composers.
Under the Direction of Mr. HAYDN.
Overture, HAYDN.
SONG. – Signor TAJANA.
Signora SESTINA.
Signor ALBERTARELLI,
Signora CAPPELLETTI.
Song, Signor DAVID – HAYDN.
Duetto, Signor ALBERTARELLI, and CAPPELLETTI
– PAISIELLO.
Overture, – HAYDN.
Song. – Signora SESTINI
Signor TAJANA.
Duetto, – SESTINI and ALBERTARELLI – HAYDN.
Recitative and Song. – Signor DAVID.
Song. – Signor ALBERTARELLI.
Terzetto. – Signor DAVID, CAPPELLETTI, and
TAJANA – TARCHI.
At the end of the First Part,
A DIVERTISSEMENT of DANCING, by

Mons. VESTRIS,	Maddle. HILLIGSBERG,
Mons. VICTOR,	Maddle. MOZON,
Mons. VERMILLY.	Maddle. DORIVAL,

&c. &c.
End of the Second Part will be introduced
A PROVENCALE. By Mons. VESTRIS, And Mademoiselle HILLISBERG,
The other Characters to be performed by ALL THE PRINCIPAL DANCERS.
The Doors to be opened at half after Six o'clock, and the Entertainment to begin
precisely at half past Seven o'clock.
PIT 10s. 6d. GALLERY 5s.
Vivant Rex & Regina!

The amount of music going on during the 1791 season is prodigious. The day that Salomon gave his Eighth Concert (with a new Haydn Quartet from Op. 64), a distinguished rival, Wilhelm (William) Cramer, the leader of the Professional Concert, gave a benefit concert for himself and his family. We give details from a hand-bill in our collection. Part One began with an 'Overture' by Haydn and included Haydn's Cantata, 'Ah, come il core (from *La fedeltà premiata*; score and parts were to be published the same month by Longman & Broderip and would be announced in the *Morning Chronicle* on the 27th), sung by Signor Pacchierotti. Then there was 'Concerto, Violin, Master CHARLES CRAMER, (aged Six Years and an Half)' and the concert ended with 'Symphony, MS. Clementi'. The great Mrs Billington and also Sig. Lazzarini participated as vocal soloists. Counting Pacchierotti, this was formidable competition for Haydn and Salomon.

Although Wilhelm Cramer and his family were – at least *pro tempore* – inseparably connected with the Professional Concert and were thus Salomon's most active rivals, there is no evidence that Haydn bore any resentment against the Cramer family. On the contrary, he thought highly of their respective talents. In 1793, the Professional

Concert went out of business, and when Haydn returned to London in 1794, he and Salomon had the field more or less to themselves. It must have been in 1794 or 1795 that Haydn signed his name in the Album of Mrs Cramer, using as signature the first seven bars of the slow movement from the 'Rider' Quartet (Op. 74, No. 3) in short score. The 'Rider' Quartet was presumably a favourite work of Salomon's 1794 season (Sotheby's sale of 30 June 1964, lot 432).

Eighth Concert: 6 May 1791

HANOVER SQUARE.   Mr. SALOMON'S CONCERT.

The SUBSCRIBERS are respectfully acquainted, that the Eighth performance will be THIS EVENING, May 6.

PART I.
Overture – Rosetti.
Aria, – Miss Corri.
New Quartetto MS. for two Violins, Tenor, and Violoncello.
by Messrs. Salomon, Damen, Hindmarsh, and Menel – Haydn.
Recitative Aria, Signor David.
Piano Forte – Mr. Dusseck.

PART II.
By particular desire.
The New Overture, M. S. – Haydn,
Performed last Friday, will be repeated.
Scena – Miss Corri.
Concerto Violin, Mr. Salomon. – Salomon.
Duetto, Miss Corri, and Sig. David.
Full Piece – Hoffmeister.
Mr. Haydn will be at the Harpsichord . . . . .

[*The Diary; or, Woodfall's Register*, 6 May]

The *Morning Chronicle* reviewed the concert on 9 May:

SALOMON'S CONCERT.

Miss CORRI made her second essay on Friday evening, and again fascinated the audience by the graces and volume of her voice. She sung a Duet with DAVID, and even with all his powers, she maintained her influence on the ear. It is truly pleasant thus to find such an acquisition to our vocal amusement in a country woman, who at the age of sixteen, has the polished manner and execution of the Italian school.

Meanwhile the London critic of the *Journal des Luxus und der Moden* sent the following report to Weimar on 2 May:

London, 2 May 1791.
Salomon's Concert, in which the famous Haydn conducts, and who composes a new Overture for each concert, was opened on 11 March and continues each Friday, and proceeds like the Professional Concert . . . .

[Jahrgang 1791, VI, 351]

The final collapse of Gallini's and Haydn's operatic plans occurs about this time and is related by Haydn's biographer, Dies:

The talk today was about the opera *Orfeo e[d] Euridice* [*L'anima del filosofo*]. I was very pleased to find the opportunity of learning something of this subject. I redoubled my efforts of concentration and became really absorbed. My readers can imagine my surprise when Haydn, instead of furnishing a narrative, wrote the story off in a few words. 'The opera was not performed.' And why not?

Gallini had entered into agreement with several persons to bring about the construction of the new theatre. The contractors had, however, neglected to observe one particular point – whether in ignorance or as because of judgement given by false persons Haydn could not say – namely, to secure permission from King and parliament.

The Theatre now stood, completed, and the orchestra was gathered together to rehearse the opera *Orfeo*. Haydn had distributed the parts, and hardly were forty bars played through, when persons in authority entered and in the name of king and parliament forbade the opera to take place in any fashion whatsoever, not even in the form of a rehearsal. *Orfeo* was, as it were, declared to be contraband, and the worst of it was that the performance of *all* operas in the Theatre was forbidden for the future.

This unexpected blow dismayed not only Gallini but the entire orchestra. Gallini, however, did not leave things in this state but attempted, clever man that he was, to make the occurrence as little damaging as was possible. Through his activity, he was able to get the thing back on its feet to the extent that musical academies [concerts] and ballets could be given in the new Theatre.

[Dies, 96f.]

Haydn had been paid for *L'anima del filosofo*, so that the blow was not quite lethal. On 26 March Gallini had opened with a programme of 'songs and dances', including Vestris and Madame Hilligsberg as members of the *corps de ballet*; we have seen that Haydn thought the ballet to *Orpheus & Euridice* magnificent (the music, apparently, by Federici). Salomon was the leader. A long report of the venture appeared in the *London Chronicle*, of which we quote extracts (26–29 March 1791):

KING'S THEATRE, HAY-MARKET

On Saturday evening this new, noble and elegant structure was opened publicly, but not with the performance of an Italian opera, as has been expected, in conformity to the purpose for which an edifice, grand and capacious beyond all parallel in this country, had been avowedly erected. The entertainment of the evening was a Melange of Music and Dancing, both given in a style of singular superiority and unequalled excellence. The musical parts consisted of two distinct collections, the one serious, the other comic; and both from the works of the first masters, but particularly from those of that fortunate and favourite composer Paesiello. Among the singers were Signor David, Madame Lops, Albertarelli, Madame Capelletti, and Signora Sestini, most of whom were highly applauded, but Signor David, though labouring under a cold, might almost be comparatively considered as the God of Song. Such astonishing flexibility of voice, such command of tones, and such variety of mode of execution, governed by such exquisite taste, were perhaps never before witnessed from a single vocal artist. The novelty of opera performances coming forward on an opera stage in so new a manner, had something not more singular than aukward [*sic*] in effect, but the general sense of the necessity of the case called up a sufficient apology in the mind of every auditor, and when the peculiar skill of the dancers was seen, the company which was elegant, and, in all circumstances considered, greater in number than could reasonably have been expected, joined unanimously in expressions of the most rapturous applause. The historical ballet of *Orpheus and Euridice* is beyond all question one of the first, most interesting and electrical stories ever told through the medium of dancing, and the execution of it was as masterly as ever the eye

71

beheld. The grave, activity, and neatness of the motions of Vestris and Madame Hilligsberg beggar description; nor were Victor, Vermilly, Mozon, and Dorival unmeriting of most commendable notice. The scenes and machinery were grand and beautiful; the sight of the Elysian Fields is alone sufficient to crown a spectator of bounded hopes with felicity.

The house was not quite full. . . . The Prince [of Wales] was in the pit during the last part of the performance, and very warmly united in the general applause to the songs of Signor David. . . .

The question is now fairly at issue between the two rival Theatres. – Persons were sent on Saturday night [26 March] to the different parts of the Theatre, who paid for their admission, to enable them to ground a regular information against the performers on Tuesday next, when Vestris, Hilligsberg, and David, are threatened to be taken into custody under the vagrant act of George II. The event of this contest is looked for with incredible anxiety by the fashionable world.

The succeeding evenings took place twice a week, on Tuesdays and Saturdays. Vocal ensembles by Tarchi, Paisiello, Haydn, Philidor and, of course, the sinister Federici were performed. Haydn wrote a seven-part *Italian Catch* for Gallini which was first performed by the soloists (with Davide) on 'Manager's Night' (Gallini's Benefit), 2 June, and was the smash hit of the Gallini season, being repeated in almost every concert thereafter. Alas, this *Catch*, which Haydn lists in his *Catalogue of Works Composed in England* as 'Maccone for Gallini' (6 sheets, i.e. 24 pages, a large-scale work), is lost. It is difficult to understand how such a thing is possible. But even with Haydn's new Aria for Davide, which was a huge public success, the same thing happened. Vocal works were not so quickly printed as instrumental pieces; and in fact many of Haydn's great vocal pieces survive in only one or two copies (the greatest of them all, the *Scena di Berenice* has survived in the autograph and in an authentic Elssler copy which the present writer happened to find in an English antiquarian catalogue; the work was printed by Mollo in Vienna only in piano score; the full score, unbelievable as it sounds, was not printed until the 1930s).

While Haydn was busy on his opera, a naval officer came to see him one day, 'very polite' says Dies (121f.) 'but not a man of many words'. He quickly explained that

. . . He wanted Haydn to compose two military marches for him. Haydn excused himself, saying that the opera *Orfeo* did not allow him time for anything else, and that he only wrote when he was in good humour, and therefore couldn't tell when the *estro musicale* would visit him, early or late; but if allowed to do so, he would get a clever composer to do the marches and would supervise the work personally.

'The Marches have to be by you. If I had wanted what you suggest, I wouldn't have come to you.' While the officer said that, he played with the guineas in his change purse, several times he lifted a handful and let them roll back into the purse.

'The sound of the gold,' remembered Haydn, 'reminded me that England could be the harvest land for me: so I asked him how much time he would allow for the *estro* to descend on me.'

'Fortnight. And the price?'

'Fifty guineas.'

'My hand on it. I shall come on that day.'

Haydn finished the Marches. The officer came. Haydn sat down at the piano and played the first March in E flat with the greatest expression and emotion. The officer, still as a statue, listened. He doesn't like it, thought Haydn. He finished. The officer said, frigidly 'ancor una volta!'

Haydn had no idea what this all meant, but he played the March a second time and doubled all his efforts thereby. He sneaked a look now and then at the officer, to see if his expression showed whether he liked it. Not a trace! Haydn thought, he doesn't even want to hear the second March. Meanwhile the officer stood up, took out a roll of fifty guineas from his pocket, gave it to the astounded Haydn, took the march, all in dead silence, and wanted to leave.

'Don't you want to *hear* the second March?'

'No!' answered the officer. 'Can't be better than the first. Goodbye. I sail for America tomorrow.'

Of course Haydn thought the English slightly mad. This story, incidentally, also appears in a slightly different form in Carpani's *Le Haydine* (225–7). There, the captain is in the India trade and wanted *one* march for military band, but done in a day, for thirty guineas. Haydn, as soon as the captain left, rushed to the harpsichord and in fifteen minutes, the march was done. Thinking that the captain was not getting his money's worth, Haydn did two more Marches. The captain came, heard the first one, paid the money and wanted to leave. Haydn offered him the others, but the captain would not hear of them: 'Mi piace la prima.' Haydn rolled them up and sent them with a note to the captain's ship: the captain sent them back and Haydn, furious, tore them up.

Ninth Concert: 13 May 1791

HANOVER-SQUARE. The Subscribers are respectfully acquainted, that the NINTH Performance will be This Evening.

PART I.

New Overture, M. S. – Clementi.

Aria, Signora Tajana.

(By particular desire) the new Quartetto, (Haydn,) as performed last Friday, will be repeated.

Cantata, Signora Storace. – Haydn.

Concerto, German Flute, Mr. Greaff [*sic*].

PART II.

Grand Overture. – Haydn.

Recitativo Aria, Signor David.

Concerto, Pedal Harp, Madame Krumpholtz.

Terzetto, Signor[a] Storace, Signor Tajana, and Signor David.

Finale. – Pechl [i.e. Pichl].

Mr. HAYDN will be at the Harpsichord . . .

[*Public Advertiser*; *Gazetteer*, 13 May]

The Ninth Concert, then, opened with a new MS. Symphony by Muzio Clementi, whose name, in garbled form, had earlier graced the programme of the Third Concert on 25 March. The facts of Clementi's life are too well known to require repetition here: we would only remind our readers that in 1782 he had a competition with Mozart who said, rather unkindly, that the Italian had not a *Kreutzer* [farthing] of taste or feeling, and was a mere *mechanicus*.[1] Clementi had moved to England as a young man and there he made a solid career as composer, pianist and teacher. Later he opened up a successful music-publishing house. Haydn and Beethoven did business with him, Clementi bringing out the first editions of Haydn's Quartets Op. 76 and various Beethoven works including the 'Emperor' Concerto (piano Concerto No. 5 in E flat, Op. 73). At the period under consideration, Clementi was composing

---

1 Mozart wrote this almost *verbatim*, and twice, to his father: on 14 January and 16 January 1782. Anderson, *The Letters of Mozart and his Family* II, 792f.

symphonies which, as we shall see, were not entirely successful. In this connection, we would mention a curious story from Dies. Obviously there is some truth in it; it seems clear, however, that the affair happened not at a Professional Concert but quite simply at the Ninth Salomon Concert in 1791. Haydn's memory, in 1805, was no longer reliable.

> [The Professional Concert was losing ground to Salomon's undertaking. The Professionals] wanted to effect a victory over Haydn almost by force. Clementi, probably without knowing the reason, had to compose a symphony, which turned out to be worthy of that great artist. The first part of a concert began with this symphony. The audience greeted it with loud demonstrations of approval. Haydn did not know anything of all this, and had to forego the advantage of being able to enter the competition with new symphony of his own composition: that is what would have been right. But as it was the intention to decrease his fame, they placed an already known Haydn symphony at the beginning of the second part, and thought they would win the day. Their expectations were for naught. The success was unbelievable. Clementi turned white as a sheet and in a few chosen words expressed his displeasure at the (for him) unhappy choice of the Haydn symphony. This occurrence could not long be kept a secret. It passed from mouth to mouth and served not a little to make Haydn's name even more famous.
>
> [Dies, 89]

What will have happened is simply that Clementi will have been offended at the success of a well-known Haydn symphony (notice the wording, 'Grand Overture'). It is easy to imagine an earlier Symphony, such as No. 88, erasing the effects of Clementi's new work. It is not known, incidentally, which MS. Symphony Clementi introduced either here or in the Second Concert of the season 1795 (Opera Concerts. Some of these relatively late-period symphonies were never published and indeed many exist only in fragments. Later Haydn visited Clementi at his country house in Evesham (*infra*, p. 116).

Dr Burney was meanwhile working for Haydn. Originally the latter's benefit concert was to have been held on 7 April, but for unknown reasons it was postponed until 16 May. It was planned to include an Italian oratorio chorus,[1] and Dr Burney wrote to his friend the Rev. Latrobe: 'I am now translating for him, *totidem syllabis*, an Ital. Oratorio Chorus, which is to be performed in English. Success attend him in all his enterprises' (Lonsdale, 353). It may be that Haydn used the translated chorus in one of Gallini's curious concerts.

People were bothering Dr Burney for introductions to Haydn, not least the Rev. Thomas Twining, who on 4 May wrote from Colchester:

> I don't know anything – any musical thing – that would delight me so much as to meet him in a snug quartet party, and hear his manner of playing his own music. If you can bring about such a thing while I am in town, either at Chelsea, or at Mr. Burney's [i.e. Charles Rousseau Burney's], or at Mr. Salomon's, or at I care not where, if it were even in the black hole at Calcutta (if it is a good hole for music) – I

---

1 Probably from *Il ritorno di Tobia* (composed in 1774, revised ten years later): at least two choruses exist in MSS. slightly altered for concert purposes in England: the aria followed by the chorus, 'Ah gran Dio' (MS. score *ex coll.* Landon, Burgenländisches Landesmuseum, Eisenstadt) from the first part and the chorus 'Svanisce in un momento' from the second part (MS. score with the ending changed by Haydn – typically, from soft to loud, as would befit its inclusion in a public concert – in the Royal College of Music [British Museum]). We have not been able to find any copies with English text, however. It is also noteworthy that in the end Haydn did not include any choral piece in his benefit concert. Choruses were altogether hard to come by, as Haydn tells us in a letter to Frau von Genzinger on 24 April 1792 (*vide infra*).

say, if by hook or by crook you could manage such a thing, you should be my Magnus Apollo for the rest of your life. [Scholes, II, 113]

As we shall see, Dr Burney managed to arrange the evening late in May. Haydn's benefit concert was now the musical highpoint of the London season. Announcements for it are found in the *Public Advertiser* on 12 and 16 May and in the *Gazetteer* on the 16th; the latter reads:

HANOVER-SQUARE

MR. HAYDN respectfully acquaints the Nobility and Gentry, that his CONCERT will be THIS EVENING, the 16th instant.

PART I.

New Grand Overture, Haydn.
Aria, Signora Storace.
New Concertanti for Violin, Oboe and Flute Obligati,
Messrs. Salomon, Harrington, and Caravoglia – Haydn.
New Aria, with Oboe, and Bassoon obligati, Signor David – Haydn.
Concerto Violin, Mr. Jiornavichi [*sic*].

PART II.

(By particular desire) the new Grand Overture, – (Haydn) as
performed at Mr. Salomon's first Concert.
Cantata, Signor Pacchierotti – Haydn.
Concertante for Piano Forte and Pedal Harp, Mr. Dusseck, and
Madam Krumpholtz.
Duetto, Signor David, and Signor Pacchierotti.
Finale, HAYDN.
Mr. HAYDN will be at the Harpsichord ...

Fortunately, the hand-bill for this concert (together with a ticket signed by Haydn), from the collection of Sir Joseph Banks and his daughter, could be located in the British Museum. It gives us not only the texts of all the arias, and thus the lost Aria for Davide, but also the final programme. Instead of the new Notturno (for that is what, undoubtedly, the 'New Concertanti' by Haydn must mean), which seems to have been postponed to the Tenth Concert (where it is called 'Concertante'), we revert to the original newspaper announcements' item (not listed above) with the Masonic team of Springer and Dworsack (Dvořák; 'Dworzack' in some newspaper listings).

HANOVER-SQUARE
MR. HAYDN'S NIGHT
MAY the 16th 1791

PART THE FIRST	PART THE SECOND
New Grand Overture – HAYDN	*By particular Desire* the New Grand Overture, *Haydn*, as performed at Mr. Salomon's first Concert
Aria – Signora STORACE	
Concertante for two Corni Bassetti, Messrs SPRINGER and DWORSACK	Cantata – Signor PACCHIEROTTI – Haydn
New Aria, with Oboe and Bassoon obligati, Signor DAVID – *Haydn*.	Concertante for Piano Forte and Pedal Harp, Mr. DUSSECK, and Madame KRUMPHOLTZ
Concerto, Violin – Mr. GIORNOVICHI	Duetto – Sig. DAVID and Sig. PACCHIEROTTI
	Finale – HAYDN

75

[Texts]

RONDO – SIGNORA STORACE *Cimarosa*
    Infelice, ch'io sono! [etc.]

ARIA. Signor DAVID. *Haydn*
    CARA deh torna in pace
    Non ti sdegnar ben mio
    Troppo m'affanna oh Dio
    Le pena del tuo cor,
    Barbaro io vado a morte
    Ah che l'affanno mio
    Mi porta a delinar

CANTATA. Signor PACCHIEROTTI
    Haydn

RECIT.
    Ah come il cor [etc.]

DUETTO
Signor DAVID and Signor PACCHIEROTTI
    Bianchi

RECIT.
    PADRE son teco; [etc.]

DUETTO Gual. Caro Padre a te vicino [etc.]

Printed by H. Reynell, (No. 21,) Piccadilly, near the Hay-Market

Davide's new Aria, perhaps the major lost work of Haydn's London visits, was an immediate success. In the *Morning Chronicle* of 16 May, we read, 'The *song* written by HAYDN for DAVID, and which he sung on Thursday last, is the theme of every Amateur. It can only be equalled by the Cantata [*Arianna a Naxos*] which he brought out at Mrs. BLAIR's.' And *The Times*, on 17 May, carries an announcement of the King's Theatre; in it we read that '. . . Signor David will sing the new Song composed for his benefit by Mr. Haydn, who will be at the harpsichord.'

The violin Concerto played at the end of the first part was by Giovanni Mane Giornovichj (Jarnowick, Jarnowic, Jarnovicki, Jiornavichi), born in Palermo and a pupil of Lolli. He made his début in 1770 at a Concert Spirituel in Paris and was soon a great success there. Always a temperamental and difficult man, he had to leave Paris as a result of some trouble. In 1779, he was engaged by the King of Prussia's orchestra but got into difficulties with Duport and in 1783 left Berlin. About 1786 he was in Vienna and engaged the young Adalbert Gyrowetz to write the tutti passages of his violin concertos. He arrived in London in 1791 and gave his first concert there on 4 May, which Haydn (or Salomon) must have heard and liked. Later Giornovichj and Salomon did not get on well together. Parke (I, 183f.) describes Giornovichj as displaying 'a fine, round and sweet tone; his execution was brilliant, and his style natural and pleasing. His concerto, though difficult, was full of melody, and he played it with great ease.' In March 1796, Giornovichj and the young J. B. Cramer almost had a duel. The *Oracle* of the 23rd reports 'GIORNOVICHI AND *Young* CRAMER have had a serious misunderstanding. A challenge took place; but by the interferrence [*sic*] of friends the difference was happily adjusted.' *The Times* of the 26th amplifies, saying the dispute 'arose merely from the introduction of two persons into the Orchestra of the Opera House. GIORNOVICHI insisted on having them removed. CRAMER, the leader, considering that place as his territory, determined that they should remain. CRAMER's son took up the matter, and the parties were actually preparing to meet in Hyde Park, when they were prevented by the Peace Officers.' We shall see Giornovichj's insolent behaviour at a concert for the Duke of York in 1795 (*infra*, p. 284).

Pachierotti sang the popular Aria from *La fedeltà premiata*, 'Ah, come il core' (which Haydn had issued separately as a cantata). The room was so well filled that in *The Times* of 19 May we read that 'HAYDN's Benefit proved so completely crowded, that during the evening his OWN were the only movements practicable!' A flattering review appeared in the *Diary*, and Haydn himself took advantage of the *Morning*

Chronicle's columns to thank the English for their support of his benefit: it was a nice thing to do and the British will have appreciated Haydn's courtesy. It is said he took in £350 (£200 was guaranteed).[1]

HAYDN'S CONCERT. HANOVER SQUARE.

The great talents of HAYDN received on Monday night a very flattering support at this place, as the room was entirely occupied by a very elegant company, and the apartments contiguous were also well stored with visitors. The instrumental pieces were compositions of HAYDN, and they were performed with great spirit by a very correct orchestra. . . .   [*Diary; or, Woodfall's Register,* 18 May]

Mr. Haydn, extremely flattered with his reception in a Country where he has long been ambitious of visiting, and penetrated with the patronage with which he has been honoured by its animated and generous Inhabitants, should think himself guilty of the greatest ingratitude, if he did not take the earliest opportunity of making his most grateful Acknowledgments to the English Public in general, as well as to his particular Friends, for the zeal which they have manifested at his CONCERT, which has been supported by such distinguished marks of favour and approbation, as will be remembered by him with infinite delight as long as he lives.   [*Morning Chronicle,* 18 May]

With the Gallini season limping towards its bankrupt conclusion, the newspapers nevertheless continue to give us news of the enormous success of Haydn's *Maccone* (as he called it) or *Catch* (as the British newspapers called it), which was repeated time after time. Here is a characteristic announcement in the *Morning Chronicle* (18 May 1791):

KING's THEATRE.
The AUTHOR's NIGHT
TO-MORROW, the 19th instant, will
be introduced to the Public, a new kind of
CONCERT,
With DANCES and DECORATIONS, incidental to
the same. The Entertainment will begin with a New
DIVERTISEMENT,
executed by Maddles. DORIVAL, st. ARMAND, PRO-
VERT, and other Dancers, to introduce the
ANIMATED PICTURES.

First Part of the CONCERT
Signor ALBERTARELLI will sing a new Hunting Song,
Composed by Mr. PHILIDOR. – A Hunt-
ing Symphony [No. 73 in D] by Mr. HAYDN. – Master HUMMEL
will play on the Pianoforte some favourite Airs, with
variations. – A Young Lady, being her first Appearance on any stage, will sing an Italian Song. – Master
CLEMENTS [*sic*] will play a Concerto upon the Violin. –

---

1 Pohl, *H in L*, 129. The entrance price was half a guinea as usual, and Salomon had to pay the bill for the orchestra (and, presumably, the usual refreshments). He tried to shift this sum to Haydn, who, however, quite rightly insisted on the terms of his contact being kept. Pohl's authority for this statement is supposedly the 'Memoir of Johann Peter Salomon' in the *Harmonicon* (VIII, p. 45), wherein we read: 'The terms on which Haydn undertook so long a journey and so responsible a journey were: three hundred pounds for composing six grand symphonies, two hundred pounds for the copyright of them and a benefit, the profits guaranteed at two hundred pounds. The latter produced three hundred and fifty pounds and, as Haydn refused to pay the band, the expense fell on his enterprising countryman.'

Signor DAVID will sing the new Song composed for his
Benefit, by Mr. HAYDN, who will be at the Harpsichord.
As the end of the First Part
A DIVERTISEMENT
By all the principal Dancers, with the charming PAS DE
DEUX, Danced by Mons. VESTRIS and Maddle. HIL-
LESBERG, who will also Dance the favourite
PAS RUSSE.

Second Part of the CONCERT.
A Comic Duetto by Signor ALBERTARELLI and Signora
SESTINI. – A new Overture in the Tragic Style, with
an entire new Cantata, sung by Signor DAVID, both
composed by Signor FEDERICI.
The Concert will finish with Catches and Glees, by the
best English Singers.
At the end of the Second Part, will be exhibited a New
Historical Ballet called
ORPHEUS AND EURIDICE.
The Subscribers are intreated to send their Commands
respecting their Boxes this Day, as from the numerous
applications by non-subscribers [some words omitted?]
– The final arrangement of
the Boxes will then take place.
The Tickets, engraved by Mr. Bartolozzi, will be de-
livered in Lisle-street only, and no where else . . .

As we see, this was a concert featuring 'animated pictures', in the style of
Emma Hamilton's famous 'attitudes'. This was a benefit evening for Carlo Francesco
Badini, and Haydn generously assisted his poet. It was a hunting concert: Signor
Albertarelli sang a hunting song with chorus (by Philidor) and Haydn was represented
by 'a Hunting sinfonie' (obviously *La Chasse*, No. 73), and also by the new Cantata for
Davide, which Haydn himself accompanied. Federici supplied a symphony in the
tragic style and another Cantata for Davide. J. N. Hummel – the child prodigy who
would shortly appear at a Salomon concert – and another child prodigy, the violinist
Clement – also soon to play at a Haydn-Salomon concert – gave concertos. On this
famous evening, there were catches and glees as well,[1] and the evening ended with the
popular ballet, *Orpheus & Euridice*. The handsome ticket was engraved by no less an
artist than Bartolozzi. The series closed on 9 July, without being able to complete the
number of concerts offered to subscribers. (Pohl, *H in L*, 126f.)

Concerning the new *Catch*, we find it in an elaborate announcement placed in the
Morning Chronicle on 1 June 1791:

---

1 Crosse, *Account*, p. 237n. relates, apropos of catches and glees, that 'It will suffice to mention Haydn,
whose visits to England took place when glees were in high estimation. This eminent man became a
member of the *Society of Musical Graduates*, to whom he would often express the great pleasure which he
felt in hearing glees, adding, with a smile, "Ah! if I were to stay long enough in England, I would study
and write glees myself!" and he evinced his respect for the society, by presenting it with a canon on the
first commandment, composed both in three and four parts, which is read forwards and backwards, then
inverted, and sung in the same manner. . . .' We shall hear of the canon in connection with Haydn's
doctorate at Oxford University. Conversely, the popular glee composer, R. J. S. Stevens, assiduously
studied Haydn's new works: the present writer owns Stevens's copy of the Salomon Symphonies in their
first edition as piano trios. Stevens was then at Charterhouse School in London.

KING's THEATRE, HAYMARKET.
THE MANAGER's NIGHT.
TO-MORROW, June 2, 1791, will be
performed,
A CHOICE SELECTION OF SONGS,
ENTIRELY NEW,
with a CATCH (for that Night only),
Composed by the celebrated Mr. HAYDN,
And Sung by the following principal Performers,
Signoras MAFFEI, SESTINI, CAPPELLETTI;
Signors CAPPELLETTI, TAJANA, ALBERTARELLI,
And Signor DAVID.
End of the First Act,
LA MORTE DE HERCULE.
End of the Second Act, a new Dance, composed by Mons.
VESTRIS, sen. called
LA CAPRICIEUSE.
In which Mons. VESTRIS sen. will Dance
THE DEVONSHIRE MINUET.
And the PAS DE TROIS, (from the Follies d'Espagne),
By Mons. VESTRIS, jun., Mademoiselle MOZON, and
Mademoiselle HILLISBERG [*sic*].
And the Two Following Performers will make their first
appearance on that Night,
Mademoiselle AIME and Signor CASALI.
Tickets 10s. 6d. to be had at No. 80, Haymarket.

The *Morning Chronicle* continues to inform us of further performances of this
seven-part (or was it really six- or eight-part?) *Catch:* June 4 ('With an ITALIAN
CATCH,/Composed by the celebrated Mr. HAYDN, / And a new Sextette by Mr.
FEDERICI'), June 6, June 7 ('For that Night only'), June 10 and June 18. At the poet Mr.
Badini's night, the *Catch* was not given (June 17) but it was performed on June 21.

At the Tenth Concert, another of the *Notturni* for the King of Naples (1790) was
first performed in its revised state.

Tenth Concert: 20 May 1791

HANOVER-SQUARE.　　Mr. SALOMON'S CONCERT.

The Subscribers are respectfully acquainted, that the TENTH Performance will
be This Evening.

PART I.
New Overture, M. S. – Hassler [i.e. Haesler].
Aria, Miss Corri.
New Concertino for two Violins, Oboe, Flute, two Tenors,
two French horns, Violoncellos and Double Bass. – Haydn.
Recitativo Aria, Signor David.
Concerto Oboe, Mr. Harrington.
PART II.
Grand Symphony – Haydn.
Sonata, Piano Forte – Mr. Dusseck.
Aria, Miss Corri.
Concerto Violin, Mr. Demachi,
(Being his first appearance in this country.)

Cavatine, Signor David.
Finale, Kozeluch.
Mr. HAYDN will be at the Harpsichord ....

[*Public Advertiser*; *Gazetteer*, 20 May]

The *Diary; or, Woodfall's Register* of 24 May and the *Public Advertiser* of 25 May printed the following notice:

OXFORD.   SUNDAY, May 22.

Hayward's Concert last Wednesday was most numerously attended. Mr. HAYDN, the composer, whose name appeared in the bill, was the attraction of the evening.

No Mr. Haydn, however, appearing, the Music Room was for some time a scene of much confusion and riot; and it was not till after a due apology had been made, that the performances were suffered to go on. It seems, that Haydn had given a solemn promise of attending; and the violation of his word is bitterly and justly complained of in Hayward's *thanksgiving* advertisement.

Three grand musical performances are expected to take place here, in the first week of July ....

Hayward was one of the members of the Oxford band. His announcement, inserted in Jackson's *Oxford Journal* on 21 May, reads as follows:

Mr. Hayward . . . is exceedingly sorry for the Disappointment occasioned by Mr. Haydn's not attending the Musick Room that Evening, contrary to a solemn Promise given, as he had actually said, he would be ready to get into the Carriage with the Singers, and Mr. Buntebart, who was to have come with him at an early Hour; but when the Carriage went to take him up at Lisson Green, near Paddington, he begged Mr. Torezani to acquaint Mr. Hayward, that he was obliged to attend a Rehearsal of an Opera that Morning, but that he would follow afterwards in a Post Chaise, so as to get to Oxford by Seven o'Clock. Why he did not come Mr. Hayward will endeavour to learn, in order to give every satisfaction imaginable to the Company present that Evening at the Room.

[J. H. Mee, *The Oldest Music Room in Europe*, p. 134]

Haydn had to issue an apology, which duly appeared in the local Press at Oxford:

Whereas at the Request of Mr. Jung, an Acquaintance of mine from Vienna, I faithfully promised to play the Harpsichord at Mr. Hayward's Benefit Concert, the 18th, Instant (*which Day I had appointed myself*), but was prevented from coming on Account of a Rehearsal at the Opera House, which lasted from Two till Half-past Four on that Day, I take the Liberty by this Paper to express the greatest Sorrow for not having been able to stand to my Promise. As the University of Oxford, whose great Reputation I heard abroad, is too great an Object for me not to see before I leave England, I shall take the earliest Opportunity of paying it a Visit, and hope at the same Time to make a personal apology to those Ladies and Gentlemen who were kind enough to honour Mr. Hayward with their Company. – Joseph Haydn.

[*Jackson's Oxford Journal*, 28 May; Pohl-Botstiber III, pp. 24f.;
J. H. Mee, *The Oldest Music Room in Europe*, pp. 134f.]

Eleventh Concert: 27 May 1791

HANOVER-SQUARE. Mr. SALOMON'S CONCERTS.

The Subscribers are respectfully acquainted, that the ELEVENTH Performance will be This Evening.

PART I.
Overture. – Rosetti.
Aria, Signora Theresa Negri.
Concerto Violin, Mr. Salomon.
Aria, Signor David.
Concerto Flute and Bassoon, Messrs. Kuieler [*sc.* Kuchler?].
PART II.
New Grand Overture. – Haydn.
Cantata, Signor[a?] Storace. – Haydn.
By particular desire, the New Quttello [Quartetto], M. S.
Haydn, as performed on the 6th Night.
Aria, Signora Theresa Negri.
Concerto Pedal Harp,   Madame Krumpholtz.
Recitative and Aria, Signor David.
Finale. – Rosetti.
Mr. HAYDN wll be at the Harpsichord . . .

[*Public Advertiser*; *Gazetteer*, 27 May]

It is nearly impossible to identify the vocal pieces performed at the Salomon concerts – and not only during this 1791 season but for the remaining seasons in which Haydn actively participated. This is all the more a pity because the vocal texts were always printed on the hand-bill, and if anyone had thought to save these hand-bills, we should know at least all the texts of the lost London arias (such as that for Miss Poole, and so forth) and should, moreover, be able to identify many such items as 'Cantata, Signor [*sic*] Storace. – Haydn', which happens to figure in the Eleventh Concert of the 1791 season. Sometimes the newspaper reviews mention the text or texts of the evening, but often even they are maddeningly silent.

It happens, however, that we have a hint about the work Miss Storace sang at the concert on 27 May. Haydn took back to Austria part of his opera *L'anima del filosofo* (*Orfeo ed Euridice*) in full score, copied on what is known as 'kleines Post-Papier' (small-sized paper for mailing) by the same British copyist who also made the Royal Philharmonic MS. score of Haydn's Symphony No. 98. One number, Euridice's death scene in the second act, was copied separately and also catalogued separately in Haydn's inventory. Both the death scene and the rest of the manuscript passed, after Haydn's death, to the Esterházy Archives and are now in the Budapest National Library.

Euridice's death scene is marked in the following curious way on the Budapest manuscript: 'Cavatina – May 27. in the Opera of Orfeo' (strictly speaking only the 'Aria' should have been marked *Cavatina*: what goes before is a *Recitativo accompagnato*). May 27 may of course refer to 1792, 1794 or 1795; but we doubt it. Haydn tells us that he made the *Orfeo* copy secretly (*vide infra*, p. 324), and the work as such was certainly Sir John Gallini's property. It is too much of a coincidence that 27 May 1791 is the date that Haydn conducted Nancy Storace in an otherwise unspecified 'Cantata' of his composition, and also the date that an English copyist affixed to a score of Euridice's death scene. Finally, the range of this scene is astoundingly similar to that for the role of Susanna in Mozart's *Le nozze di Figaro*. At any rate, we suggest that she may have sung the extract from *Orfeo* that night.

Dr Burney now organized the small musical party at Chelsea College, and Twining was there to enjoy (in Burney's words) 'an excellent Concert for real judges of good Music, unmixed and unannoyed by loquacity; in the Accademia Haydn himself condescended to play the Tenor'. Once again it was *The Seven Words of the*

Saviour on the Cross which Dr Burney thought 'perhaps, the most sublime composition without words to point out its meaning that has ever been composed' (Lonsdale, 355). Haydn was obviously rehearsing for his concert on 30 May, which will soon occupy our attention. Fanny Burney was there, too, and recorded: 'I had the pleasure, one evening at Chelsea, of meeting our ever-valued Mr Twining, and seeing the justly renowned Haydn. There was some sweet music of his performed . . . .'[1]

On 30 May, an extra concert was held, in which Haydn's oratorio *The Seven Words* – listed on the programme as *Passione instrumentale* – was given for the first time in England. The British publishers of the work, William Forster, to whom Haydn sold the work in 1787, will have been especially glad to receive some publicity for it, because *The Seven Words* had been a commercial failure. Forster paid Haydn ten guineas for it, but spent 15s. postage and, it is estimated, a total of £39.5.0. on having the work printed. The first edition consisted of fifty copies(!), which were not sold off until about 1817 or 1818, when another twenty-five were run off, the last of which were, however, disposed of as waste paper. These are sobering facts which show how precarious a business music-publishing was, and that not even Haydn's fame and physical presence in England could sell a 'difficult' work.[2]

News of Haydn's dealings with Forster after the composer's arrival in England are very scarce, for in fact Forster was extremely annoyed with him and took him to court. In the late 1780s, Haydn had sold his latest works not only to Forster but also to Artaria of Vienna, who had promptly sent engraved copies to their London agents, Longman and Broderip. In some cases, Longman's imported Viennese edition had appeared before Forster was ready with his. The second part of the suit with Haydn concerned two spurious piano Trios, actually by his pupil Ignaz Pleyel (*vide infra*, p. 119). In the circumstances Haydn sought, and found, other publishers.

The Seven Words concert was in three parts. It was supposed to have taken place in the King's Theatre but was switched to the Hanover Square Rooms. In the first and third parts a Haydn symphony was given; the second part consisted solely of the oratorio in its original, orchestral version. The vocal soloists for the rest of the evening were Signor Davide and Signora Negri, while the ubiquitous Madame Krumpholz assisted. Salomon was the leader, and Haydn presided at the keyboard (Pohl, *H in L*, 130f.).

The final concert was given early in June:

Twelfth Concert: 3 June 1791

HANOVER SQUARE. Mr. SALOMON'S CONCERT.

The Subscribers are respectfully acquainted, that the TWELFTH and LAST Performance will be To-morrow Evening.

PART I.

Overture. – Girovetz [*sic*].
Aria, Madame de Sisly [*sic*],
(Being her first appearance in public.)
New Concerto Piano Forte, Mr. Dullick [Dusseck].
Aria, Signor David.
Concerto Violin, Mr. Salomon.

---

1 *Diary & Letters of Madame d'Arblay (1778–1840)*, six volumes, edited by Charlotte Barrett with preface and notes by Austin Dobson; Vol. IV, London 1905, p. 459.
2 William Sandys & Simon Andrew Forster, *The History of the Violin* [*etc.*] London, 1864, pp. 310ff.

PART II.
(By particular desire) the New Grand Overture, – Haydn, –
as performed last Friday, will be repeated.
Aria, Madame de Sisley.
Concerto Pedal Harp, Madame Krumpholtz.
Scena, Signor David.
Finale. – Kozeluch.
Mr. HAYDN will be at the Harpsichord . . . .
[*Public Advertiser*, 2 June; *The Oracle, Bells' World*, 3 June]

The last week in May, to be exact from 23 May to 1 June, was given over to a gigantic Handel Festival, 'by command and under the patronage of their Majesties', in Westminster Abbey. There were over one thousand performers, including the cream of all the orchestras and singers; the famous 'large double basses', 'double bass Kettle drums' (tuned an octave lower than normal timpani), double bassoons and massed wind instruments no doubt made a 'sight . . . really very fine, and the performance magnificent; but the chorus and kettle-drums for four hours were so thunderfull, that they gave me a head-ache, to which I am not at all subject.' (Walpole to Sir Horace Mann, speaking of an earlier festival held in 1786.)

The ladies came in full *toilette*, and their head-dress caused much annoyance. The King & Queen, with six royal princesses, came in full Court dress. The orchestra was built up *en amphithéâtre*, in Haydn's system, with Joah Bates sitting at the organ and leading the whole. To his right and left were the two musical prodigies Hummel, of whom we shall speak later, and Bridgetower, both in scarlet uniforms, helping Bates with the registration of the huge organ. The massed rows of trumpets were decorated with banners rich in gold and silver threads.

The first day saw the performance of what is perhaps Handel's greatest oratorio, *Israel in Egypt*, as well as the Coronation Anthem 'Zadok the Priest' and extracts from *Esther, Saul, Judas Maccabaeus* and *Deborah*, and an organ concerto. The second day there were extracts again, an oboe concerto, an organ concerto and anthems. The third day they repeated *Israel in Egypt*, with some pieces from other oratorios; and the fourth day, on 1 June, they did *Messiah*. Haydn had a box near the royal family and was witness to the King, the Queen, and the whole congregation rising to the 'Hallelujah' Chorus. (Pohl, *H in L*, 131ff.)

Haydn was astonished. Of course, he had heard Handel oratorios at van Swieten's concerts in Vienna; but they were nothing compared to the great English tradition; and Haydn often, as we shall see, remembered this Handel Festival. During those days, he must have realized that it was time for him to think of a modern oratorio.

There are many accounts of Haydn's veneration for Handel. One is from his friend William Shield who, in his entertaining and professional book, *An Introduction to Harmony* (London, 1800), tells us the following story:

Travelling from London to Taplow with the Father of Modern Harmony, and having (the preceding evening) observed his countenance expressing rapturous astonishment during the Concert of Ancient music, I embraced the favourable opportunity of enquiring how he estimated the Chorus in Joshua 'The Nations tremble at the dreadful sound.' The reply: 'He had long been acquainted with music, but never knew half its powers before he heard it, and he was perfectly certain that only one inspired Author ever did, or ever would pen so sublime a composition.' . . . . Having been presented with a manuscript score of *Il Ritorno di Tobia* by its Author, I endeavoured to make a suitable return by requesting his acceptance of *Jeptha*: and when I expressed my admiration of the Recitatives in the former, which abound with the finest specimens of the Enharmonic, their Composer proved his liberality and judgment by declaring that 'Deeper and Deeper still' in the latter greatly surpassed them in Pathos and Contrast.

One ought to explain that it was Shield's policy never to mention names in his book; Haydn is 'The Father of Modern Harmony' and Shield loved him, as did many professional musicians in London. Another reference is in Crosse's *Account* (1825), where we read:

At this last Abbey Meeting [in 1791], there was present one auditor, of all men the most capable of appreciating its excellence, the immortal Haydn, then on his first visit to this country; and from it he derived a confirmation of that deep reverence for the mighty genius of Handel, which, to the honour no less of his candid modesty than of his judgment, he was ever prone to avow. The study of Handel fixed his ecclesiastical style, and imparted grandeur and majesty to his ideas, previous to which his early Oratorios do not rank high..... The selections this year were chiefly from *Israel in Egypt*. . . .   [p. 46 n.]

To Giuseppe Carpani, the third of the 'authentic' biographers,

[Haydn] confessed . . . that when he heard the music of Hendl [*sic*] in London, he was struck as if he had been put back to the beginning of his studies and had known nothing up that moment. He meditated on every note and drew from those most learned scores the essence of true musical grandeur.[1]

Salomon's concerts were at an end. The series had been a brilliant success for everyone concerned; it was not hard to persuade Haydn to stay on for another season, and Salomon was soon able to announce a new season 'with the assistance of Mr. Haydn'. The newspapers were lavish in their praises. The *Oracle*, on 8 June, writes:

Mr. SALOMON'S CONCERTS.

Are at length closed for the present season, and due praise must be recorded in the ORACLE.

For Selection, this amusement has had to boast perhaps a taste superior to any of its rivals. – Their execution, though it might be equal, certainly was, either vocally or instrumentally considered, by no means superior.

Mr. SALOMON, as a Leader, is brilliant and neat; but we owe him other obligations – we owe to him the personal knowledge of HAYDN, and of DAVID.

Every lover of harmony will wish a renewal next Season of an entertainment so refined, so highly patronized, and so highly worthy of such patronage.

The *Diary; or, Woodfall's Register* also noted the final concert in its issue of 6 June:

SALOMON'S CONCERT.

This charming entertainment concluded for the season on Friday last at the Hanover Square rooms. . . .

The other exertions of the Concert were worthy of an entertainment in which the great HAYDN took a part, and which was conducted by the taste and genius of Salomon. . . .

The *Morning Chronicle* announces Napier's benefit concert at Hanover Square for 8 June 1791, with the participation of David, Sig. Dussek and Giornovichj, the violinist. The programme included a symphony for double orchestra by J. C. Bach in

---

1 *Le Haydine*, Milan, 1812, 162f.

MS., and there was a 'New Symphony, GIROWETZ' [*sic*] as well as a 'New Symphony, HAYDN'. On 9 June the *Morning Chronicle* printed an enthusiastic review of Napier's concert, especially praising Giornovichj's playing on the violin.

Events in France, meanwhile, continued their sinister course. Haydn will have had the chance to learn something of the Revolution at first hand from a refugee: Madame de Sisley, who sang an aria at the Twelfth Concert. Her husband had perished together with the *Intendant* Bertien, who was a relative, on 14 July 1789. Madame de Sisley soon found herself penniless, and decided to make commercial use of her hobby, singing. She had studied with the best masters, including no less than Nicola Piccinni and Antonio M. G. Sacchini; and her imposing beauty as well as her excellent voice helped her to find a new home in England. Salomon and Haydn were both warm-hearted and generous men, and it is typcal that they launched her at their final concert. (Pohl, *H in L*, 140.)

On 10 June, there was to have been another benefit concert organized by Salomon with Haydn's assistance at the keyboard: this time for the young (born 17 November 1780) Franz Clement. This day saw the publication of *Arianna* (*vide* p. 258n.).

Originally the prodigies Hummell and Clement each intended to give a benefit concert in London, but in the event they decided to merge their efforts. The *Morning Chronicle* (10 June 1791) informs us that of '. . . Master CLEMENT and Master HUMMELL . . . The former, being unexpectedly deprived of the means of giving his CONCERT this EVENING, on account of there being a Performance at the King's Theatre, Haymarket, where all those who were to assist him, are engaged; they have mutually agreed to join their intended CONCERTS in One.' The actual concert, then, did not take place, as was previously stated (Pohl, *H in L*, 141), on 10 June (when Haydn was conducting his *Catch* at the King's Theatre) but on 13 June 1791 (programme in the *Morning Chronicle* of that day) at the Hanover Square Rooms:

PART I.
NEW OVERTURE, MS. – HAYDN.
Quartetto French Horn, Master HUMMELL.
Song, Signora THERESA NEGRI.
Concerto violin, Master CLEMENT, (his Composition).

PART II.
[Haydn's 'Passione Instrumentale', i.e. *The Seven Words* in the instrumental, or rather orchestral version.]

PART III.
Concerto Piano Forte, Master HUMMELL.
Song, Signora STORACE.
Concerto Pedal Harp, Madame KRUMPHOLTZ.
Song, Signor DAVID.
Finale – HAYDN.
Leader of the Band, Mr. SALOMON . . .

Haydn sat at the harpsichord at this benefit concert for his two young friends, one of whom was to enjoy an excellent career – the horn-player, Hummell is not to be confused with J. J. Hummel (*vide infra*), but Clement was later leader of the theatre orchestra in the Theater an der Wien (Schikaneder's theatre in Vienna), in which capacity he came into close contact with Beethoven, who wrote his violin Concerto for Clement in 1806.

Shortly thereafter, Haydn signed his name in Clement's album, quoting a phrase from *The Seven Words*:

Con - su - ma - tum   est

London, d. 22. Junij Ao: 1791   Joseph Haydn
                                                 dein ächter Freund

[The next entry, rather charmingly, reads:]
        Es ist vollbracht! singt Vater Haydn
        Was läßt sich nun noch weiter schreiben?
Aachen, d. 28. September 91.
                Des bewunderungswürdigsten Kleinen aufrichtige Gönnerin
                                Maria Catharina Scholl.
[Autograph: Österreichische Nationalbibliothek, Handschriftensammlung; Pohl III, 23]

Clement was a child prodigy who managed to bridge that fatal gap between childhood and adulthood. His memory was prodigious: Spohr tells a story which is half-true (there is no piano score of *The Creation* printed under Clement's name) but none the less characteristic:

> Clement had a musical memory equalled, possibly, by no other artist. They told me in Vienna that after hearing Haydn's *Creation* several times he had it so perfectly from memory that, with the help of the text, he made a complete piano score. When he brought it old Haydn, the latter's first impulse was to assume that someone had stolen his score or had secretly copied it. After examining it carefully he found it so accurate that he accepted it for publication.
> [pp. 83ff. Vienna, 1812]

Joseph August Röckl, Beethoven's Florestan in the 1806 revival, was stunned by Clement's memory:

> . . . Princess Lichnowsky played the piano from the large orchestral score [of *Leonore*] and Clement, who sat in a corner of the room, accompanied the whole opera from memory on his violin, playing all the solos of the various instruments. Since Clement's uncanny memory was a matter of common knowledge, no one but myself was in the least astonished at this feat.   [Landon, *Beethoven*, 201]

On 15 June, Sophia Corri, the young singer who had made her début at the sixth Haydn–Salomon concert, gave her benefit concert. Salomon was the leader and Haydn was, as usual at the keyboard. By this time, she had fallen in love with the brilliant pianist Johann Ludwig (Ladislaw) Dussek: she was sixteen and he thirty; they were to marry the next year and later founded a music shop and publishing house which Haydn, loyally, patronized. She was not only an accomplished singer but also a good pianist, in which latter capacity she much improved under her husband's instruction. Her concert attracted two interesting reviews, the first from the *Morning Herald* of 16 June:

HANOVER-SQUARE.
The attraction of last night at this place was a Concert for the benefit of Miss Corry, whose family is celebrated for musical talents, and who herself possesses abilities calculated to augment its reputation. The opening piece was a beautiful Overture by Girovetz, a composer of great genius, and proportionate modesty. Miss Corry sung her allotted airs with promising taste and expression. One of

them was a favourite air of Cimarosa, in which Marchesi aquitted himself with singular merit. To follow such a performer, was an arduous undertaking, but Miss Corry succeeded very well.

Storace sung instead of David, who was prevented by illness, and the audience of course made every reasonable allowance. As a performer on the Piano Forte, Miss Corry displayed much ability. A fine manuscript overture of Haydn was highly admired, and it was gratifying to observe with what zeal the audience endeavoured to shew their sense of this composer's exquisite genius, and the modesty with which Haydn received their eager eulogiums.

and the second from the *Oracle* of June:

HANOVER-SQUARE.

Miss Corri, though postponed, has not escaped our attention – At her outset, we praised her skill, and the delicate sweetness of her tone and taste. – We think at present all these considerations improved. – Her benefit, we were happy to see well attended, and the charming execution of the whole, left the loss of DAVID easily compensated by the kind efforts of STORACE.

STABILINI, the Edinburgh Leader, gave a Concerto of his own composition with very superior taste, and a stop exceedingly true indeed. His tone was brilliant, and a considerable applause attended him throughout.

HAYDN'S MS. Overture was highly relished. – The approbation of the audience was received with the utmost modesty by that Gentleman, who himself presided in the Orchestra.

On 18 June 1806, Haydn's biographer Dies paid his twenty-third visit to the composer. Haydn gave him one of the London notebooks.

I opened it up and found a couple of dozen letters in the English language. Haydn smiled and said: 'Letters from an English widow in London, who loved me; but she was, though already sixty years old, still a beautiful and charming woman and I would have married her very easily if I had been free at the time.'

This woman [continued Dies] is the widow, still living, of the famous pianist Schröter [*sic*], whose melodious song Haydn emphatically praised. . . . If he was not invited elsewhere, he usually dined with her.   [Dies, 133f.]

Johann Samuel Schroeter (1750–88) had in 1782 succeeded J. C. Bach as Master of the King's Musick. Rees's *Cyclopaedia* (1819–20) says, 'He married a young lady of considerable fortune, who was his scholar, and was in easy circumstances.' Schroeter published many works for the keyboard and Haydn owned several, which Rebecca probably gave him. It has been doubted if she was really sixty; but in any case she grew to love Haydn and certainly introduced him to a delightful group of people in London. Her first letter reads as follows:

Mrs. Schroeter presents her compliments to Mr. Haydn, and informs him, she is just returned to town, and will be very happy to see him whenever it is convenient for him to give her a lesson. James str. Buckingham Gate. Wednesday, June 29th 1791.

Both Dies and Griesinger relate how even in his old age Haydn loved women. Dies writes:

He freely admitted that he loved pretty women, but he couldn't understand how it happened that in his life he had been loved by many a pretty woman. 'They can't have been led to it by my beauty,' said he. 'You have,' said I, 'something of genius in your face and in your whole bearing, and one likes to see that and knows it's good.' 'One can see [answered Haydn] that I mean weil with everyone.' 'That will have laid you open to attacks.' 'Oh yes [said Haydn], sometimes, but I was clever. . . .'   [Dies, 134]

In July 1791, Haydn received the honorary degree of doctor of music from Oxford University. Happily, we have many documents which tell us, in considerable detail, of the three concerts that took place and of the ceremony itself. The concerts took place in the handsome Sheldonian Theatre, one of Sir Christopher Wren's masterpieces, based on Marcellus's Theatre in Rome and erected in 1664–69; there was room for some 4,000 persons in the building. Griesinger (34) relates:

Dr. Burney suggested to Haydn that he should be given a doctor's degree at Oxford. The ceremony during which the degree was given took place in a cathedral with great ceremony; the doctors enter in procession and put questions to the candidates, if they wish to be admitted and so forth. Haydn answered what his friend Salomon told him to say. The election is put to the assembly from a raised platform; the speaker enlarged upon Haydn's merits, listed his works, and to the question, would Haydn be admitted, there arose a general cry of assent. The doctors dress in a small gown with frills at the collar and they have to wear it for three days. 'I would have dearly liked my Viennese acquaintances to see me in this dress!' The Storace and some other musical friends waved to him from the orchestra. The day after the election Haydn conducted the music. 'I thank you,' he answered [in English], raising the ends of his gown. That caused much jubilation. . . . It happened several times to Haydn that Englishmen went up to him, looked at him from top to toe, and left him saying, 'You are a great man.'

Dies (135f.) relates much the same story but supplies some new details:

Dr. Burney was the moving spirit: he talked Haydn into it and went with him to Oxford. At the ceremony in the University Hall, the assembled company was encouraged to present the doctor's hat to a man who had risen so high in the service of music. The whole company was loud in Haydn's praises. Thereupon Haydn was presented with a white silk gown, the sleeves in red silk, and a little black hat, and thus arrayed, he had to seat himself in a doctor's chair. . . . Haydn was asked to present something of his own composition. He climbed up to the organ loft, turned to the company, took his doctorial robes in both hands, opened them at his breast, closed them again and said as loudly and clear as possible [in English), 'I thank you.' The company well understood this unexpected gesture; they appreciated Haydn's thanks and said, 'You speak very good English.' 'I felt very silly in my gown, and the worst of it was, I had to drag it round the streets for three whole days. But I have much to thank this doctor's degree in England; indeed, I might say everything; as a result of it, I gained the acquaintance of the first men in the land and had entrance to the greatest houses.'

Haydn said this with that openness which is so characteristic of him, so that I simply could not understand how it is possible for such a genius to be so completely unaware of his own strength and to ascribe everything to the doctor's hat and nothing to his art. Self-adulation could not be seen in his words, much less any hidden pride. . . .

The London newspapers carried extensive reports from Oxford:

MUSICALS.

The MUSIC MEETING at OXFORD commenced, for the season, on Wednesday last, in the University Theatre, before a numerous and very elegant audience.

Mrs. Crouch was unfortunately taken dangerously ill on the road, with a sore throat and violent fever. She was left under proper care at Henley, and a physician was despatched to her from Oxford.

The Concert commenced with an Overture and Chorus from Acis and Galatea. 'Total Eclipse' was next sung with great expression by Kelly. One of Pleyel's beautiful quartets followed; in which Cramer, Dance, Blake, and Sperati, distinguished themselves with the best effect. The First Act concluded with an air of Sarti 'Numi possenti Numi', by Storace, who acquitted herself very well.

A New M. S. Overture by Haydn, was to have introduced the Second Act; but as Haydn did not reach Oxford [in] time enough for a rehearsal, one of his former pieces was the substitute, and the Composer himself sat at the Organ. . . .

[*Morning Herald*, 8 July]

The *St. James's Chronicle*, 7–9 July,[1] has a report the opening two paragraphs of which are identical with those of the *Morning Herald* but which continues thus:

The whole was received with strong marks of approbation, which the performances amply deserved. Cramer played and led the band, after travelling all the preceding night. Many of the Professional Band assisted on this occasion.

Dr. Ayrton and Dr. Dupuis wore the Commemoration medals, which his Majesty has graciously permitted them to assume on all occasions.

Haydn was introduced to the audience by Dr. Hayes, and received with a degree of respect and attention worthy [of] his genius.

For the second concert, there was a rehearsal in the morning, so that the 'new' Haydn symphony could be performed: it was Symphony No. 92 in G, which became known as the 'Oxford'. We are thus able to correct an old error: the 'Oxford' Symphony was not substituted for a new one which could not be rehearsed; quite the contrary, another symphony, already known, was substituted for the 'Oxford' in the first concert, on 6 July. We know, incidentally, that it really was the 'Oxford' that was performed as the work of honour through Crosse's *Account* (1825), where on p. 409 he identifies the work *via* the Cianchettini & Sperati score.

Haydn's degree was, of course, entered in the *Catalogue of all graduates* at Oxford as 'Haydn (Joseph), Composer to his Serene Highness the Prince of Eszterhazy, er. D. Mus. July 8. 1791'; while in the *Register of House of Convocation* Haydn's degree is listed as:

Die Veneris octavo die mensis Julli anno Dom. 1791 causa Convocationis erat, ut . . . grata celebraretur publicorum Benefactorum Commemoratio. . . . et ut alia negotia academica peragentur. . . . Proponente. . . . Domino Vice Cancellarie placuit venerabili coetui ut celeberrimus et in re musica peritissimus vir Josephus Haydn ad Gradum Doctoris in Musica honoris causa admitteretur.

[Pohl, *H in L.* 151]

The *Morning Herald* on 9 July carries a full report of events at Oxford:

MUSICALS.

The SECOND PERFORMANCE of the MUSIC MEETING at OXFORD, was more crouded [*sic*] with visitors on Thursday last, than on the preceeding day.

Mrs. CROUCH remains in such a dangerous state at Henley, that all hope of her adding her assistance was relinquished.

---

1 The *Morning Chronicle* and *Diary ; or, Woodfall's Register* bring this and the following reports in almost exactly the same wording.

The Concert began with the Overture to Samson, to which the band did ample justice. Master MUTLOW then sung 'So much beauty' from ESTHER. His voice is good, and his execution tolerable. SPERATI followed with a Solo on the Violincello, in a very good stile, but by no means calculated to eradicate the remembrance of CROSDILL. The next in order was a song by STORACE. '*Quel desir che amor un di*', the composition of her brother, and very creditable to his talents. The first Act ended with a Chorus from ALEXANDER'S FEAST, 'The merry round, etc.' which was well sustained; but the superior energy of the Abbey Chorusses are of too recent date to allow of much impression.

The new Overture of HAYDN, prepared for the occasion, and previously rehearsed in the morning, led on the second Act, and a more wonderful composition never was heard. The applause given to HAYDN, who conducted this admirable effort of his genius, was enthusiastic; but the merit of the work, in the opinion of all the Musicians present, exceeded all praise. DAVID followed, with 'Fell Rage' from Saul, which he sang with great ability, and was unanimously encored.

The musical prodigy, young CLEMENT, then performed a Concerto on the Violin, with such execution, as appeared incredible to those who heard it. – KELLY sung '*Donne chi Vuo Vedere*', an air of Mengozzi, with his usual skill and spirit. – The next was, 'From silent Shades', in Purcell's *Mad Bess*, by STORACE, who was much applauded. – The second Act concluded with 'He gave them Hail-stones'; and at this time *hail-stones* would indeed have been acceptable to the company, as the room was prodigiously hot.

Between the acts, WEBB, BELLAMY, and KELLY, sung a very pleasing Glee.

After STORACE had sung 'Whither my Love', a beautiful Concertante of PLEYEL, began the third act; and CRAMER, DANCE, PATRIA, SPERATI, and BLAKE, rendered the performance fully correspondent with the excellence of the composition.

DAVID followed, with a song of SARTI, well sung, but rather too long. The act concluded with the song, 'Let the bright [Seraphim], etc.' by STORACE, and grand chorus, 'Let their celestial, etc.' from SAMPSON. An attempt was made, to leave out the second part, on account of want of sufficient light; but the young gentlemen of the *Square-Cap* would not suffer the omission.

The band is, of course, conducted by CRAMER, with CONDELL as his *Aid de Camp*; DANCE plays the second Violin, BLAKE is principal Tenor, SPERATI the Violoncello, and PATRIA the Oboe, who all exert themselves very ably. There are besides, BOND, PARKINSON, HACKWOOD, HILL, and others of the Professional Band: so that the combined talents of the Orchestra cannot be exceeded, if equalled, by any other set of performers.

HAYDN expressed himself very handsomely to CRAMER on the manner in which his OVERTURE was performed; and SALOMON, who was present, joined very liberally with the great Composer, in high praise of the spirit, exactness, and promptitude of that very able Leader.

It is expected, that tomorrow (Friday), the University will confer an honorary degree on HAYDN, as a testimony of the high esteem in which his character and talents are held.

To this report we may add the following extract from the *Public Advertiser* of 12 July:

OXFORD, THURSDAY, July 7.

The second GRAND MUSICAL FESTIVAL was this evening highly applauded by a very numerous audience at the Theatre. Haydn's MS. Overture was performed, and met with great approbation. The receipt of this, and the preceding, evening, has cleared the expenses of the preparations; so that whatever money may be received to-morrow evening, will be a well-earned profit to Dr. Hayes.

The next morning the degree was conferred on Haydn in the Sheldonian Theatre (not 'in a cathedral' as Dies says). The *Public Advertiser* of 12 July writes:

FRIDAY, July 8.

The PRIZE PRODUCTIONS were this morning recited at the Theatre, which was immensely crouded [*sic*] on the occasion. After several honorary Degrees had been publickly bestowed, among which that of Doctor of Musick was voluntarily and liberally conferred on Haydn, Mr. Crowe, the Publick Orator, paid the usual compliments, in a Latin speech, to the Founders, &c. of the Institution . . . .

The *Morning Herald* of 11 July tells us not only of the ceremony but also of the concert that evening:

On Friday morning the annual Commemoration took place at OXFORD, when the celebrated HAYDN was admitted to a DOCTOR'S DEGREE in a manner highly flattering to him and creditable to the University, being the free gift and unanimous desire of that learned body.

Between the parts of the Latin and English oration, upon this occasion the band performed pieces adapted to the situation. On the return of the procession from the theatre, and on HAYDN's retiring, the applause which arose, was perhaps equal to any that ever attended a similar occasion.

At five in the evening the concluding Concert took place; and several performers were all well received on their entrance, particularly CRAMER, who was honored with warm tokens of general respect.

The opening piece was the Overture from ESTHER, performed with great spirit. KELLY followed with 'why does the Go[d], etc.' from Samson, with good expression. MATTHEWS and BELLAMY, then sung 'The Lord is a Man of War' tolerably. The next in order was, a beautiful Cantata by HAYDN, who appeared in his gown and conducted it; – this charming air used to be finely sung by MARCHES[I]; therefore STORACE was injudicious in attempting it on this occasion, and indeed, obtained less applause than HAYDN's *Doctorial Robe*. The first act terminated with the Recitative 'Search round the, etc.' and Chorus 'May no rash, etc.' from Handel's Solomon by KELLY. This was repeated.

A new Overture by PLEYEL led on the second act. The composition was much admired and the Band played it with very great correct[n]ess and spirit, though they never saw it till that evening. STORACE then sung. 'The Prince unable to conceal, etc.' from Alexander's Feast, with such *expressive gesture* that the young gentlemen in the *Black Gowns* were highly gratified and unanimously *encored* it. The next was a Concerto on the Violin by CRAMER, executed in his best style, and with such brilliancy that the applause was very great from all quarters. DAVID was followed with 'Comfort ye my People', but not with such success as he gave at the Abbey. This act concluded with the Chorus, 'And the Glory, etc.'.

KELLY before the third act sung an Italian Air, the music of which was not very striking; and he made as much of it as it deserved.

The last act commenced with an Overture of HAYDN, very fine, but well known. HAYDN was not present at this performance. STORACE followed with the Air 'with lowly suite' in which she was very deservedly *encored*. DAVID next sung 'Pensa che in [campo] etc.' an Air of PAESIELLO, but in too flourishing a style of execution with a want of neatness in his divisions. The whole ended with the CORONATION ANTHEM. This was repeated.

When the performers quitted the Orchestra, they were severally greeted with much applause, and CRAMER in particular. It seemed to be the general opinion, that no performance at this place ever went with better success. The company were said to exceed the number of visitors usually present for many years.

Mrs. Crouch who continues at Henley, is pronounced out of danger, and the merit of her recovery is attributed to Dr. HALL of Oxford.

The *Public Advertiser* of 12 July, under the heading 'OXFORD, July 8', describes the final concert:

In the evening, the third, and last GRAND MUSICAL FESTIVAL attracted a crouded [*sic*] and elegant audience to the Theatre.

They were in excellent humour; and when Haydn appeared, and, grateful for the applause he received, seized hold of, and displayed, the gown he wore as a mark of the honour that had in the morning been conferred on him, the silent emphasis with which he thus expressed his feelings, met with an unanimous and loud clapping . . . .

Haydn, methodical as always with money matters, put down the cost of the trip in one of his notebooks (in German, of course, unless otherwise noted):

I had to pay $1\frac{1}{2}$ guineas for having the bells rung at Oxforth [*sic*] in connection with my doctor's degree, and $\frac{1}{2}$ a guinea for the robe. The trip cost 6 guineas.

[CCLN, 274]

He also noted that 'Madam Mara was hissed at Oxford because she did not rise from her seat during the Alleluya [*sic*] Chorus' in *Messiah*.

In July, there was a certain amount of unrest in London and elsewhere. On the 14th, so we are informed by the *European Magazine*:

About one thousand Gentlemen met at the Crown and Anchor Tavern in the Strand, to celebrate the second Anniversary of the French Revolution. . . . The dinner being finished, the following toasts were drunk:
The Rights of Man.
The Nation, the Law, and the King.
The Revolution in France, and may the liberty of that country be immortal.
The Revolution in Poland.
May Revolutions never cease till despotism is extinct. [etc.]

[July 1791, pp. 78f.]

The toasts continued endlessly, including Ireland 'and her Band of Patriots', 'General Washington, and the liberty of North America', etc., etc. 'Many of the principal inhabitants of Liverpool, Manchester, Norwich, Derby, Glasgow, and several other places, also met to commemorate the Anniversary of the French Revolution: but order, harmony, and patriotism ruled the assembled parties.' In London, however, things for a time threatened to get out of hand:

A number of people assembled at the front of Newgate, and with many threats demanded the liberation of Lord George Gordon, that he might participate with his worthy brethren in the celebration of the 14th of July; but, on the appearance of a guard of soldiers, they very quietly dispersed.

About ten o'clock at night a great concourse of pickpockets, &c. assembled near the Crown and Anchor Tavern, and from thence proceeded to break the windows along the Strand, Fleet-street, and various parts of the city; but they were soon dispersed by the Magistrates and Constables, who obliged such persons as had put up lights to extinguish them. [*European Magazine*, July 1791]

At Oxford, people realized that Haydn's doctorate *honoris causa* had been a special thing. A correspondent wrote from Oxford on 15 July to the *European Magazine*:

> Music [at Oxford] has still made farther strides towards perfection. Vulgar annual songs were once considered as almost a part of the institution. Handel's portrait is now to be seen among the sages of the Bodleian repository, and his music is enjoyed, well understood, and even performed by thousands in the University! Can any thing exhibit the improved taste in that divine science so justly, as the degree just given to the modest Haydn by the University – this musical Shakespeare – this musical Drawcausir, who can equal the strains of a Cherub, and enchant in all the gradations between those and a ballad – a genius whose versality comprehends all the powers of harmony, and all the energy, pathos, and passion of melody! who can stun with thunder, or warble with a bird! For the honour at the University be it known, that this honour was conferred without the form of examination, and indeed such transcendant merit deserved the liberal compliment in the way it was conferred.

The *European Magazine* had a wide circulation on the Continent and also in the United States of America. So did another periodical entitled the *Gentleman's Magazine*, which also contained a lengthy description of the festivities at Oxford during July 1791, and Haydn's part in them. Since the report duplicates much material already quoted from the *Public Advertiser*, we shall confine ourselves to quoting only the sections directly concerning Haydn:

> Oxford, July 6 [1791]
>
> ... The second act [of the first concert] should have opened by a new MS overture composed by Haydn, but, not arriving in time for rehearsal, it was deferred till next day, and another piece of the same composer substituted, and received with great applause. ...
>
> ... [July 7] The second Grand Musical Festival. ... Haydn's MS Overture [Symphony No. 92] was performed, and met with great approbation. ... Haydn's new overture, conducted by himself, introduced the second act. It was generally deemed one of the most striking compositions ever heard; and the ingenious author was applauded very warmly. ... July 8 ... The honorary degree of Doctor of Musick was also voluntarily and liberally conferred on Joseph Haydn, Esq.
>
> The Commemoration Speech on this occasion was spoken by the Rev. Dr. Holmes, Poetry Professor. ...
>
> In the evening, the third and last Grand Musical Festival attracted a crowded and elegant audience to the Theatre. They were in excellent humour; ... [etc., a word-for-word reprint of the report from the *Public Advertiser* of 12 July, quoted above.]

Haydn later sent in the canon (see next page), which was also used as the music for the first of the Ten Commandments which Haydn wrote for the Saxon Ambassador in London, Count Brühl. There is an autograph of this canon in the former Castle of Counts Czernin at Neuhaus (Jindřichův Hradec, ČSSR) which we print overleaf in facsimile since it shows the canon's 'realization' (the wrong one is printed in the O. E. Deutsch edition for the new *Gesamtausgabe*).[1]

---

1 *Joseph Haydn Werke*, Reihe XXXI, Kanons für 2 bis 8 Singstimmen, G. Henle Verlag, Munich 1959.

[*Canon cancrizanz a tre*]

Thy voice o Har - mo - ny is di - vine
eniv - id si yn - om - raH o eciov yhT

Thy voice o Har - mo - ny is di - vine
eniv - id si yn - om - raH o eciov yhT

Thy voice o Har - mo - ny is di - vine
eniv - id si yn - om - raH o eciov yhT ★

★To be read backwards   [Pohl, *H in L.* 152]

Haydn was elected a member of the Musical Graduates Society, which has been mentioned above. The Society, which was new, kept records, in which we read:

A new and illustrious member was then added to the list by the University of Oxford, who conferred the Degree of Dr. in music upon the celebrated Haydn, and it was with much concern to Mr. Callcott, who held the sixth meeting at Kensington Gravel Pitts, on the third of August . . . that Dr. Haydn's summer engagements prevented his attendance.   [*Musical Times*, 1 May 1909, p. 298]

Haydn was fascinated with ships, and his relationship to their captains was not only that of supplying marches for the ship's band. In his notebook for the Summer of 1791 we find:

In the month of August [1791] I lunched at noon on an East India merchantman with 6 cannon. I was given a magnificent meal.

In this same month I went with M^r [William] Fraser up the Tems [Thames] from Westminster Bridge to Richmond, where we ate on an island. There were 24 persons in our party, besides a *Feld Music* [wind band].

In England, a large man-of-war is reckoned according to the number of its cannon. Each cannon is estimated at 1,000 lbs.   [CCLN, 275]

Can the captain who keeps intriguingly reappearing in Haydn's notebooks have been the Captain Blount who subscribed to *The Creation*? Haydn noted down a way to keep milk and an exotic recipe from Martinique, the first certainly and the second possibly from one of his 'sea captain' friends:

In order to preserve cream or milk for a long time, one takes a bottle full of milk and puts it in an earthenware pot or copper vessel containing water enough to cover more than half of the bottle, and then places it over a fire and lets it simmer half-an-hour. Then one takes the bottle out and seals it securely, so that no air can escape, and in this way the milk will keep for many months. N.B.: The bottle must be surely corked before it is placed in the water.
This was told me by a sea captain.
Noyan, a drink. Squeezed from nutmeg, rum and sugar. Comes from Martinique in the West Indies, which belongs to France.   [CCLN, 271, 277]

Luigia Polzelli had written to Haydn saying that her husband, Antonio Polzelli, had at last died; he had been an invalid for years. Haydn answered:

[To Luigia Polzelli, Vienna. *Italian, 'Tu' form*]

London, 4th August 1791.
Dear Polzelli!
I hope that you will have received my last letter through Count Fries and also the hundred florins [Gulden] which I transferred to you. I would like to do more, but at present I cannot. As far as your husband is concerned, I tell you that Providence has done well to liberate you from this heavy yoke, and for him, too, it is better to be in another world than to remain useless in this one. The poor man has suffered enough. Dear Polzelli, perhaps, perhaps the time will come, which we

Opposite
Haydn's 'Canon cancrizanz', 'Thy Voice, O Harmony'; the canon is at the bottom in two versions, one marked 'Canone a tre. Auf vierfache arth/Cancrizanz'. Haydn later used the canon for the First Commandment, and there is a note, written in pencil by an unknown hand, 'Die Auflösung [solution] zum Du sollst an Einem Got glauben'; the top of the score is the solution. Note that the canon uses both G and soprano clefs.

both so often dreamt of, when four eyes shall be closed. Two are closed, but the other two – enough of all this, it shall be as God wills. Meanwhile, pay attention to your health. I beg of you, and write me very soon, because for quite some time now I have had days of depression without really knowing why, and your letters cheer me, even when they are sad. Good bye, dear Polzelli, the mail won't wait any longer. I kiss your family and remain always

Your most sincere
Haydn.

Address:] Madame Polzelli Virtuosa di Musica à

Vienne en autriche

abzugeben im Starnbergischen Freyhaus auf der Wieden N^{ro} 161 [This last sentence is crossed out and the postman has written 'nicht auf der Wieden'; Polzelli had already left, but obviously the letter was forwarded and she did receive it.] [CCLN, 107]

Although Haydn had done his best to help the Gallini undertaking in the Pantheon, it was, by the Summer of 1791, obviously doomed to failure. In the *Morning Chronicle* of 17 August we read, 'The Pantheon Opera has been so unprofitable a speculation, that there is little probability of its being resumed. The salaries of the principal Singers and Dancers, it seems, were so great, that there was nothing left for the scene shifters and dressers.'

At the end of one of the London notebooks, Haydn noted 'Mr Bressy [*sic*] N° 71 Lombard Street'; earlier in the same notebook we find a cryptic note:

On 4th August [1791], I went to visit Herr Brassy, the banker who lives in the country, 12 miles from London. Stayed there 5 weeks. I was very well entertained. N.B.: Herr Brassy once cursed, because he had had too easy a time in this world. [CCLN, 271]

As it happened, Haydn expanded on this story to Dies; the house itself where Haydn enjoyed the hospitality of Nathaniel Brassey (*recte*) was called Roxford, about a mile from the village of Hertingfordbury in Hertfordshire; it no longer exists.

Haydn was asked in the most flattering terms by the banker to give lessons in music to his daughter. He gave the lessons and was received with the utmost honour in the house of xxx. Once the entire family of the banker went for several weeks to the country. Haydn was invited there and entertained the company very often with descriptions and anecdotes of his previous life, which was not infrequently at considerable variance with the brilliantly fortunate life the banker had led.

Haydn and xxx were once together, and the latter listened attentively to such an anecdote. Suddenly he jumped up like a madman, yelling the most frightful curses, and swearing that he would kill himself on the spot if he had loaded pistols.

Haydn meanwhile had also got up and yelled for help. 'Just don't shoot me!' He thought he had only one life, and it seemed to him that it was too soon to lose it.

The banker's wife and other people rushed, horrified, to the scene. The banker roared at them, 'Pistols! I'm going to shoot myself.' The people were shaking but tried to calm him down and find out why he had developed those murderous instincts. The banker refused for a long time to give any answer, until finally they asked him with tears in their eyes. Then he repeated the violent oaths and said he wanted to shoot himself because he never knew trouble, misery and poverty; and as he now realized he was not really happy, for all he knew how to do was to stuff himself and drink; he had been surrounded with plenty, and it now disgusted him.

The spectre of Haydn's early poverty returned, even in such idyllic circumstances, to haunt him and his English friends. It cannot be reiterated often enough that Haydn's preoccupation with money had this grim background: he had nearly starved and his entire savings, before he left for London, had been 500 Gulden in cash and a little house in Eisenstadt: not a very good balance for the most famous composer alive.

On 2 September there occurred a lurid event in a London whorehouse: Franz Kotzwara, a musician in Gallini's orchestra, had paid a whore a guinea to hang him as part of a merry orgy; unfortunately Kotzwara died in the process. Haydn cryptically wrote just the name, 'Kozwarra' as the last entry in the First Notebook. But the whole affair, as related by Parke, is interesting much more for Kotzwara's nefarious composing activities. Here, at last, is evidence of a man who was paid to create Haydnesque fakes.

> Kotzwara was a great imitative composer and was engaged by certain music-sellers to compose trios, quartets, &c., in the style of the popular writers on the continent, Haydn, Pleyel, and others; and his productions displayed so accurately the taste and science of his prototypes, that, like the admirable copies of the pictures of the old masters by Renigale, the best judges considered them to be originals. He had been found hanging in a house of ill fame, in a low court leading into Chandos Street, Covent Garden. . . . As it was proved that he was suspended by his own desire, and that neither he nor the parties implicated in the transaction ever contemplated death, [the whores] were acquitted.   [Parke I, 181ff.]

On 17 September, Haydn writes again to Frau Maria Anna:

[To Maria Anna von Genzinger, Vienna. *German*]
Nobly born and gracious Lady!
    I have received no reply as yet to my 2nd letter of 3rd July, which I entrusted to a composer here. Herr Diettenhofer, together with the pianoforte arrangement of a little Andante from one of my new Symphonies, to give to Your Grace; nor have I any answer either about the Symphony in E flat which I asked for; and so I cannot wait any longer to enquire after Your Grace's health, and that of your husband and all your dear family. Could it be that the odious proverb, 'Out of sight, out of mind', is true everywhere? Oh no! either urgent affairs, or the loss of my letter and the Symphony, are responsible. I feel sure that Herr von Keess [*sic*] is quite willing to send the Symphony I asked for, because he said so in his letter to me; but since both of us will have to bear this loss, we shall have to leave it to Providence. I flatter myself that I shall receive a short answer to this. Now, my dear good gracious lady, how is your fortepiano? Is a Haydnish thought brought to mind, now and then, by your fair hand? Does my dear *Fräulein* Pepi sometimes sing poor *Ariadne*? Oh yes! I can hear it even here, especially during the last two months, when I have been living in the country, amid the loveliest scenery, with a banker's family where the atmosphere is like that of the Gennzinger family, and where I live as if I were in a monastery. I am all right, thank the good Lord! except for my usual rheumatism; I work hard, and when in the early mornings I walk in the woods, alone, with my English grammar, I think of my Creator, my family, and all the friends I have left behind – and of these you are the ones I most value. Of course I had hoped to have the pleasure of seeing you sooner, but my circumstances – in short, fate – will have it that I remain in London another 8 or 10 months. Oh, my dear gracious lady! how sweet this bit of freedom really is! I had a kind Prince, but sometimes I was forced to be dependent on base souls. I often sighed for release, and now I have it in some measure. I appreciate the good sides of all this, too, though my mind is burdened with far more work. The realization

that I am no bond-servant makes ample amends for all my toils. But, dear though this liberty is to me, I should like to enter Prince Esterházy's service again when I return, if only for the sake of my family. I doubt whether this will be possible, however, for in his letter my Prince strongly objects to my staying away for so long, and absolutely demands my speedy return; but I can't comply with this, owing to a new contract which I have just made here. And now, unfortunately, I expect my dismissal, whereby I hope that God will give me the strength to make up for this loss, at least partly, by my industry. Meanwhile I console myself by the hope of hearing something soon from Your Grace. You shall receive my promised new Symphony in two months, but in order to inspire me with good ideas, I beg Your Grace to write, and to write a long letter, too, to one who is ever

Your Grace's

most sincere friend and obedient

servant,

Jos : Haydn.

London, 17th September 1791.

My respectful compliments to Herr von Gennzinger and the whole family. Please forgive my taking the liberty of enclosing a letter to Herr von Keess, but I didn't have his address.   [CCLN, 117–9]

Subsequent letters show the little Andante to have been the slow movement of Symphony No. 95 in C minor. Joseph Diettenhofer was a Viennese composer who had lived for some time in England (see also Haydn's letter of 20 December 1791). Haydn was still trying to get Symphony No. 91 in E flat from Frau von Genzinger and/or Herr von Kees. Esterházy's demand for Haydn's return was to compose an *opera seria* in conjunction with the Prince's installation as Governor of the County; the event took place at Eszterháza Castle on 3 August 1791 and was the last great *festa* to take place there. The festivities were celebrated by a handsome engraving (reproduction on p. 157 of Mátyás Horányi's *The Magnificence of Eszterháza,* London 1962) with some gypsy musicians in the right foreground – no doubt to compensate for *Capellmeister* Haydn's absence. In the event, Prince Anton made it up with Haydn, and when they met at the Frankfurt Coronation in 1792, the Prince simply said, 'Haydn, you could have saved me 40,000 Gulden', reputedly the staggering price paid to stage Joseph Weigl's *Venere e Adonis* with an imported Viennese cast.[1]

When it came to banking his newly gained savings, Haydn automatically turned to the Esterházys where, he thought, his money would be as safe as at Fries's banking house in Vienna. In his notebook, Haydn wrote: 'The *obligation* for 1000 fl. deposited with Prince Esterhazi [*sic*] is dated 10 July 1791.' (CCLN, 273).

The Professional Concert now tried to buy Haydn away from Salomon. According to Dies (90) they sent a deputation of six men to Haydn with highly advantageous offers. 'Haydn, however, did not want to break his word to Gallini and Salomon and to hurt them with avaricious greed. Since they had gone to such trouble and great expense on his behalf, the least he could do, he thought, was to let them have the profit as well.' The deputation then appeared a second time, repeating their previous offers and adding that they now had the authority to offer Haydn 150 guineas 'and more' over and above what Salomon had offered. Haydn again refused. Thereupon the Professional Concert launched a publicity campaign against Haydn, some of which we have already seen; Haydn was described as 'written out', weak and

---

1   Dies, 139; Horányi, ibid., 154.

incapable of composing anything new. Therefore they had sent for a vigorous young man who would do it all better – Ignaz Pleyel, once (in the 1770s) Haydn's promising composition pupil and the hope of the new generation. That hope was not realized; but even the great Mozart had spoken flatteringly of Pleyel. In a letter to his father of 24 April 1784, he writes,

> I must tell you that some quartets have just appeared, composed by a certain Pleyel, a pupil of Joseph Haydn. If you do not know them, do try and get hold of them; you will find them worth the trouble. They are very well written and most pleasing to listen to. You will also see at once who was his master. Well, it will be a lucky day for music if later on Pleyel should be able to replace Haydn.[1]

Of course Pleyel's competition was a blow to Haydn and Salomon: not that they had any fear of Haydn's being 'written out', but it was in poor taste to get Haydn's star pupil. As matters turned out, Pleyel behaved very decently and in 1793, the Professional Concert collapsed, leaving the field entirely to Salomon. Besides, although Pleyel was a facile composer and was a good orchestrator, his copies were, inevitably, less enduring that the Haydnesque originals. Pleyel was popular in London, but thinking musicians were annoyed by those Haydnesque traits that Pleyel had magnified out of all proportion; and Dr. Burney found Pleyel's sudden rests, jumping into new keys, etc., used too frequently, while C. F. Pohl sums it up admirably: 'In his later works Pleyel gave himself up to a vast quantity of mechanical writing, vexing Haydn by copying his style and manner without a trace of his spirit, and misleading the public into neglecting the works of both master and scholar. . . .'[2]

Pleyel, having left Eszterháza, went to Italy, where he, like Haydn, Gyrowetz and Sterkel, composed lira music for the King of Naples and Italian opera as well. In 1783 he received the appointment of Chapel Master to the Cathedral at Strasbourg, where Franz Xavier Richter had for years conducted (he did not die until 1789). After returning to France from England in 1792, he was denounced as an enemy of the Republic and had to flee. Cleared of the charges, he opened a music publishing house and piano manufacturing establishment in Paris and printed the first miniature scores of Haydn's symphonies and quartets. The firm still exists in Paris.

By the end of September, if not before, Haydn was back in London: on 26 September 1791, he signed the guest book at Broadwood's piano shop across the street from his and Salomon's lodgings on Great Pulteney Street. During the quiet summer weeks at Roxford, Haydn will have composed Symphony No. 93 and probably some of No. 94 and No. 98, which he now had to complete for the new Salomon season of 1792.

To a certain extent, Haydn was no longer master of his own fame. His reputation began to exist as a thing almost separate from the man. While on the one hand, like all other composers of the period, he had no control of the publication and dissemination of his music once it left his hands; on the other, he was, like all famous men, subjected to intense scrutiny. It could not be thought, of course, that everyone approved of his music; it had been in years past far too controversial for that; but as far as his music was available, it was now being played all over Europe.

---

1 *The Letters of Mozart and his Family*, translated and edited by Emily Anderson. Second edition (Macmillan & Co.), London, 1966, Vol. II, p. 875. Reprinted by courtesy of Curtis Brown Ltd, London, on behalf of the Estate of Emily Anderson.
2 Burney wrote the article on Pleyel for Rees's *Cyclopaedia* (published in 39 vols., 1819–20). Pohl in Grove's *Dictionary*, first edition, London, 1902, Vol. III, 2ff.

Even his operas, those stepchildren of his muse which Haydn loved particularly, were beginning to circulate on the Continent: too late, for they were already 'old' compared to Haydn's own style *de anno* 1791 and, even more, to Mozart's brilliant works. It must have been with a certain sense of nostalgia that Haydn read, in the *Journal des Luxus und der Moden*, whose London correspondent knew the composer personally, the following report:

Brünn [now Brno, ČSSR].
Operas performed in the month of October.
    On the 26th *Ritter Roland* [*Orlando Paladino*] by Haydn, was successful; Mr. Spindler as Roland and Mr. Rothe as his sword-carrier shone with especial brilliance. [Band VI, p. 673]

And a few months later, in January 1793, the Brünn Theatre did *La vera costanza*; the *Journal* (VII, 128) reports 'it pleased less than the beautiful music deserved. But that must be the fault of the performance'.

There was also a certain group of conservatives, both English and German, who regarded Haydn and all 'modern' composers as anathema. Dr. Burney was given a book along these lines to review in the *Monthly Review*; his scathing article came out in the October number (pp. 196–202) and is sufficiently interesting to warrant reproducing it, especially since it seems to be unknown to musical scholars today:

ART. XVIII. *Observations on the present State of Music, in London.* By William Jackson, of Exeter. 8vo. pp. 35. 1s. 6d. Harrison and Co. 1791.

As critical reflections on the fine arts seldom come under our notice, they are a relief to us after the more dry and uninteresting labours of investigation. The remarks of able professors of any art or science come with weight; and from the reputation and productions of the author of this pamphlet, we expected information and ingenuity. Many of his sentiments, however, militate so violently against the general opinion of the lovers and judges of music throughout Europe, and are so decisively delivered, that it seems incumbent on us to examine the principles on which they are founded.

Mr. Jackson boasts a claim to *candour*, for 'not mentioning the name of any living professor'; which will hardly be granted by intelligent musical readers, who can no more help thinking of HAYDN, when *symphonies* are mentioned, than of HANDEL, when *oratorio choruses* are in question. He says, 'if he may judge of the sensations of others by his own,' the public is *not* pleased with what it applauds with rapture. Why does it then applaud? What artist can bribe a whole public? Our House of Lords, which is the highest court of judicature in Great Britain, and from which there is no appeal, is supposed to be out of reach of individual influence; and the enlightened public, in every kingdom, is the supreme judge of such productions of art as are exhibited for its amusement. Cabal and party, in a small circle, may triumph over judgment and good taste: but what, excepting sterling merit, can bias the public at large, for any considerable time?

According to Mr. J. our present musical pleasure is, 'by some awkward and unfortunate circumstances, derived from *polluted sources*'; and, as a wonderful discovery, he tells us, 'that PERFECT MUSIC is the uniting *Melody to Harmony*.' Now this is a *truism* so incontrovertible, that we believe it has never been disputed since the present rules of composition have been invented.

The invariable language of the enthusiastic admirers of Handel, and of every thing ancient in music, has long been, that the moderns *neglect harmony* for air :– but the whole tenor of Mr. Jackson's pamphlet is to prove, that 'melody is best qualified to exist alone, and that modern music has *no air*.' Mercy on us! have we then neither soul nor body? – and have we been so mistaken, as to fancy we have received delight from music, which has neither melody nor harmony to support it? Unluckily for our author, that music which he condemns in so summary a manner, and which, in this country at least, he says, 'is in a fair way of shortly being totally without melody,' is the favourite music of all the most cultivated and polished nations of Europe.

This severe censure is repeated in the next page. 'VOCAL MUSIC had once nothing but harmony to subsist on: by degrees, melody was added; but now it is very near being lost.'

'In the grand opera, *songs* may be considered as *pathetic*, *bravura*, something *between the two*, which has *no name**, and airs called *cavatina*. Generally the last have most melody, and the first sort have least: but it is scarce worth while to ascertain which has most, where all are defective†' This is a brave assertion! – and are all the composers, performers, and bearers, of taste and judgment, to go to Exeter to ask Mr. J. how to please and be pleased? Is there no air, no elegance, no melody, in the productions of a Sarti, a Cimarosa, or a Paesiello? Very few opera airs are now printed, nor indeed were there many performed, in the last year: but that was more owing to particular circumstances, than to the barrenness of the times. Mr. J. perhaps condescends, though, it may be, not with much disposition to be pleased, to go to an opera once in two or three years; and calculates the whole progress of the art by what he happens to hear, or not to hear, during that one night's performance. Surely, prejudice, envy, a provincial taste, or perhaps altogether, prevent candid attention; otherwise, some ingenuity, spirit, grace, and elegance, might have been discovered even in the worst operas, serious or comic, that have been brought on our stage: – but the writer seems wholly to confine his idea of melody to the symmetric measure and monotonous repetition of passages in a Vauxhall ballad, a dancing minuet, or a gavot. A TUNE that can be carried home, and interwoven in an English song, seems the grand *desideratum*.

Now the *tunes* in the English operas of highest favour, which were composed 'when melody still existed,' have been furnished by the Italian opera; and that still continues, as much as ever, to supply our national theatres with melodies which delight both *gods* and men.

Mr. Jackson is equally dissatisfied with the pertinacious adherence to Handel, and with the enthusiasm with which the flights of Haydn into new regions of melody and harmony, are admired. What are we to do? Are we to hear no music in our concerts but elegies, and ballads which the clown "can whistle o'er the furrow'd land," as well as they can be executed by the greatest professor? A liberal and enlightened musician, and hearer of music, receives pleasure from various styles and effects, even when melody is not so vulgarly familiar as to be carried home from once hearing; or even when there is no predominant melody, if a compensation be made by harmony, contrivance, and the interesting combination of the whole.

Our author next anathematizes GLEES, still harping on the want of melody, and treating them, we think with too much severity. As there are merits of various kinds in music, no one species of composition can include them all. Ingenuity of contrivance and modulation acquire the applause of matters: but the public ear is chiefly captivated by pleasing harmony, and graceful melody. To call such

---

* The author surely forgets that there is such a thing frequently in an Italian opera as an *aria graziosa*.
† Why a *cavatina*, which means nothing more than an air without a second part, should have more melody than a pathetic, rapid, or graceful air, we know not. In times when Mr. J. allows melody to have been in its most flourishing state, in *da capo* days, there were no *cavatinas*.

compositions of this class, as afford delight to the lovers and best patrons of the art, STUFF, is not treating either the composers or the admirers of them with the delicacy of a writer whose 'observations are made under *restraint*, and the *fear* of giving offence.'

Mr. Jackson's whole artillery is now pointed against the present *instrumental music.*

'The old CONCERTO (says he) is now lost, and modern full-pieces are either in the form of OVERTURES or SYMPHONIES. The overture of the Italian opera never pretends to much; that of the English opera always endeavours to have an air somewhere, and the endeavour *alone* makes it acceptable.' – Civil again! Richter's eternal repetitions, and Abel's timidity, are praised, for they are no more: – 'but later composers, to be grand and original, have poured in such floods of nonsense, under the sublime idea of *being inspired*, that the present SYMPHONY bears the same relation to good music, as the ravings of a bedlamite do to sober sense.'

Now, might not the ingenious writer as well have said, at once, that the authors of these *floods of nonsense* are HAYDN, VANHALL, PLEYEL, and MOZART, and the admirers of them tasteless idiots, as leave us to guess who he means? If he had gone a little farther, and had assumed the *title*, as well as the style, of SUPREME DICTATOR in the republic of music, what would he have told us that we do not already know? This was one of the times, we suppose, when he '*shrunk from the matter.*'

Modulation, measure, discord, and all such *paltry shifts*, are condemned in the lump; and even poor *Pianissimo*, which, though it moves on tiptoe, with its finger on its lips, and is 'so delicate as almost to escape the ear,' does not escape the lash. Soft and loud, quick and slow, concord and discord, are *all in the wrong*, whenever applied to any thing but ballads and elegies: all other musical productions are *untuneable.*

This complaint of want of *tune* is more usually the croak of ignorance than the voice of knowledge. In the concertos of old masters, of which Mr. J. laments the loss, are there not fugues, and other entire movements, without a single phrase of melody? Yet these had their place, for the sake of variety, and were heard with pleasure. It is the perpetual want of variety which stimulates the composers to try every thing. Old masters did the same, as far as they dared: but so much has been tried, that little now of what is called natural, is left; and art, and sometimes caprice, and whim, are forced to supply the rest. To tread in the steps of our predecessors, in music, would be justly called plagiarism. The public accommodates itself to the music of the times, which chiefly offends those who are old enough to remember that of the last age; which was likewise censured by those of a former period.

We have heard or read somewhere, that Dr. Pepusch, Dr. Greene, and other learned musicians, established the *Academy of Ancient Music* soon after Handel's arrival in England, to check that composer's torrent of innovation, which began to overflow the country. The public, however, for the honour of the nation, not seconding their endeavours, he was suffered to deluge the land; nor have either *drains* or *dums* been since able to diminish, nor to keep in bounds, the streams that flowed from his fountain of invention.

Handel was, at this time, a young man, and little known in any other part of Europe; so that we had the courage and merit of feeling his worth, without adopting it as a foreign fashion: but not to approve and admire Haydn, whose works have been in as great favour at Vienna, Madrid, Lisbon, Paris, and in the several capitals of Italy, as at the court of his patron, Prince Esterhazy, in whose service he had been engaged, as we have been told, for 25 years before he came hither, would have disgraced our musical taste. Indeed, it seems likely that the productions of Haydn will be admired and imitated *all over Europe*, as long as those of Handel have been in England only.

We are not certain that our present musical doctors and graduates are *quite up* to Haydn yet: but the public are so unanimous in applauding, that they cannot help giving at least a silent vote of assent to the justice of the praises so enthusiastically bestowed on him.

Not so Mr. Jackson, who has never been remarkable for failing with the tide of general opinion, on any occasion. He would, perhaps, suppose the whole universe, rather than himself, to be in the wrong, in judging of any of the arts. His favourite style of music has been ELEGIES: but what is an elegy to a tragedy, or to an epic poem? He sees but one angle of the art of music; and to that all his opinions are referred. His elegy is no more than a closet in a palace.

We are nearly in tune with the author, however, where he allows 'QUARTETS and TRIOS to be in a respectable style, as well as concertos for particular instruments.' He condemns, we think justly, the *staggering octaves*, and the perpetual running up and down the keys on the piano forte in *semi-tones*. Once in a year, perhaps, the rapid *ascent* in half-notes may be borne: but *downward*, the effect is as detestable as if the keys were swept with a broom, or as if the performer had taken an emetic; – and yet every *master*, and every *miss*, who is able to atchieve this feat, never omits it at a close, be the piece to which it is applied grave, gay, or graceful.

The abuse of graces in the performance of solo songs, particularly by ignorant singers, is justly censured. Songs, however, have but few notes, and are more open to embellishment than symphonies, where it is usually as much as a performer can do to execute what is set before him. In vocal music, the voice should always have the principal and most interesting melody, to which the accompaniments are subordinate: but the first violin, in a symphony, is a limited monarch; and the power (or principal melody,) is sometimes transferred to the second violin, the hautbois, flute, violoncello, tenor, or bassoon.

Alas! poor Haydn can do nothing right either in the eyes or ears of his present critic. There is a censure levelled at him, p. 25, for marking the measure to his own *new* compositions: but as even the old compositions had never been performed under his direction, in this country, till the last winter, it was surely allowable for him to indicate to the orchestra the exact time in which he originally intended the several movements to be played, without offending the leader or subalterns of the excellent band which he had to guide.

The author's strictures on the injudicious selection of pieces from Handel's works for Westminster Abbey, we recommend to the notice of Mr. Bates, who has certainly studied the works of that composer, and had them performed under his own direction, from his early youth, when a student at Cambridge, to the present time; and this, we should imagine, would qualify him to chuse the pieces best calculated for employing, with effect, 'the largest and best band in the world.'

Though Mr. J. be unwilling that Haydn should march on, yet he says with truth, that 'any thing which helps to fix an art to a *certain point* is destructive to further improvement.' The instance which he gives of the durable effect which an exclusive liking for the music of Lulli had on the public taste in France, is in point.

We have nothing to object to the rest of the pamphlet; on the contrary, we perfectly agree with the author, that the performances in the Abbey should be open to other church composers of the first class, as well as to Handel. There are masses, motets, and psalms, with instrumental accompaniments, by Colonna, Bassani, Steffani, Clari, Lotti, Alessandro Scarlatti, Leo, Duranti, Caldara, Jomelli, Sacchini, Perez, &c. among the Italians; and Fuchs, Sebastian and Emanuel Bach,

Graun, Telemann, Hasse, Haydn, Gas[s]man[n], Rolle, Wolfe, &c. among the Germans; beside our own Purcell, Crofts, Greene, Boyce, and many able harmonists of our country, now living, who might contribute toward varying this magnificent exhibition by new productions, and give an opportunity for the best pieces of Handel to be refreshed by rest, which would increase the eagerness of the public to have them revived, and the pleasure with which they would be heard, after being a little forgotten.

We agree entirely with Mr. J. that so stupendous a band, and so correct a performance, would be of equal advantage to the productions of other great masters of harmony, as well as to those of Handel. It cannot reasonably be supposed, that there is a sufficient number of persons in this kingdom, whose wealth, or zeal for the honour of this great and favourite master, will continue much longer to enable or incline them to attend such an expensive performance year after year, merely to hear the same pieces repeated. Indeed, we have frequently heard of murmurs at the want of variety in the performances of Tottenham-street, particularly since their Majesties have honoured that concert with their presence: for it being well known that our good King hears no music with pleasure, and hardly with patience, but that of Handel, the Directors indulge his Majesty's partiality, so much as to select nine-tenths of the pieces that are performed there from his works; though the concert was originally instituted for the preservation and rivival of the best compositions of old masters *in general*.

The conclusion, therefore, of the pamphlet before us, seems unanswerable, where it is said, that 'the first year of the Abbey-music was a commemoration of Handel, and ought to consist of his works only; but it might at this time, without any impropriety, be open for the works of any other composers.' 'Suppose,' continues our author, 'that, each day, one new instrumental piece, and one for voices, were permitted to be performed? – The experiment might be tried for a year or two. In case of failure the loss would not be great; but, if it succeed, the gain might be immense.' – He then observes, 'the great advantage PAINTING has over MUSIC, in the ease by which its professors may offer their works to the public' attention.'

Our extracts and remarks on this short pamphlet have been extended to an unusual length: as the manifest mixture of spleen and prejudice, with ingenuity and good sense, seemed, in a peculiar manner, to call for discussion and criticism.

D^{r.} B . . . . y.

Concerning Jackson's publication, even the *Morning Chronicle* felt obliged to say, under 'MUSIC' in its issue of 26 July 1791, that 'MR. JACKSON . . . has had the temerity, *indirectly*, to attack the *Shakespeare* of the art, HAYDN, and all the disciples of his school. We must, however, do Mr. JACKSON the justice to mention, that he disclaims the idea of directing the severity of his criticism against any particular artist. *Music*, and not *musicians*, he says, is his object.' There follow extracts of the new book, continued in the issue of 8 August.

Haydn was still needing Symphony No. 91 and wrote again to Frau von Genzinger about it and other matters on 13 October:

[To Maria Anna von Genzinger, Vienna. *German*]

London, 13th October 1791.

Nobly born and gracious Lady!

I take the liberty of making the urgent request that you advance 150 fl. for a short time to my wife, but only on the condition that Your Grace doesn't imagine that since my departure I have become a bad manager. No, my dear gracious lady, God has been kind to me. There are 3 circumstances to blame. First, that since my departure I have repaid my Prince the 450 fl. he advanced me for the journey; secondly, I cannot demand any interest from my bank bonds, because the bonds are in the strong-box which I entrusted to Your Grace's care, and moreover I can't remember their names or numbers and therefore couldn't write a receipt; thirdly, I cannot get at the 5883 fl. which I recently deposited, 1000 in my Prince's hands and the rest at the Count von Fries's, especially since it is English money. Your Grace can see, therefore, that I am still a good manager. This leads me to hope that Your Grace will not refuse my present request, to lend my wife 150 fl. This letter shall be Your Grace's security, and shall be valid in any court. I shall repay the interest with a thousand thanks on my return. Meanwhile I am, most respectfully, with my kindest regards to your husband, *Fräulein* Pepi and all the others,

Your Grace's

most obedient servant,

Jos: Haydn [m.p] ria.

Since I cannot remember the little opening Adagio at the beginning of the Symphony in E flat, I take the liberty of noting the ensuing Allegro:

Shall I be so fortunate as to receive this Symphony by the end of January 1792? Oh yes, I flatter myself that I shall! But how strangely things sometimes come to pass: I think that Your Grace will have received my letter on the very day that I was reading your cruel reproach that Haydn was capable of forgetting his friend and benefactress. Oh! how often I wish that I could be with you at the piano even for a quarter of an hour, and then to have some good German soup for lunch. Well, we can't have everything in this world! May God grant me good health; I've enjoyed it up to now, and I hope that through my good conduct the Almighty will continue to grant it to me. I was very pleased to hear that Your Grace is well. May Providence long watch over you! By the way, I hope to see Your Grace in the course of 6 months: I shall have many things to tell you. [Original language:] Adieu. Good Night – it is time to go to bed. Auf deutsch – gute nacht, es ist zeit zu bette zu gehen, [German:] it's 11:30. One more thing: to ensure the safety of the money, Herr Hamburger, a very good friend of mine, a man of tall stature, who is my wife's landlord, will bring you this letter himself; and you can safely entrust him with the money; but just the same you should get a receipt from him, and from my wife.

Inter alia Herr von Keess writes me that he would like to know my circumstances here in London, because there are various rumours about me in Vienna. From my youth on, I have been exposed to envy, and so I am not surprised that people attempt wholly to crush my modest talents; but the Almighty is my support. My wife writes me, but I don't believe it, that Mozart speaks very ill of me. I forgive him. There is no doubt that many people in London are also envious of me, and I know almost all of them. Most of them are Italians. But they cannot harm me, for my credit with the common people has been firmly established for a long time. Apart from the professors, I am respected and loved by everyone. As for my remuneration, Mozart can enquire of Count Fries for information, with whom I deposited £500, and of my Prince, who has 1000 Gulden, that makes nearly 6000 fl. in all. I thank my Creator daily for this boon, and I flatter myself that I can take home a few thousand more, notwithstanding the fact that I have many expenses, and notwithstanding the costs of the journey. Now I won't bother Your Grace any more. Isn't this handwriting appalling?

How is Pater——? My compliments to him.   [CCLN, 119ff.]

Johann Nepomuk Hamburger was an official ('Registrator') in the Lower Austrian Government and owned a house on the Wasserkunstbastei. 'Apart from the professors' means, probably, the Professional Concert. The 'Pater –' is apparently the Pater Professor of the Schottenstift, which institution owned the Schottenhof, where the Genzingers lived.

On 26 October 1791, Haydn went to a meeting of the Musical Graduates Society, given by Dr Dupuis at Grosvenor Gate, where 'the presence of the new member [Haydn] was highly gratifying to all'.[1]

Early in November Haydn was invited to an official lunch given by the Lord Mayor of London. The description of it in the First London Notebook is a brilliant piece of reportage which shows that like all aspects of England in which noise dominated, Haydn was slightly repelled:

On 5th Nov. [1791] I was guest at a lunch given in honour of the Lord Mayor. The new Lord Mayor and his wife ate at the first table No. 1, then the Lord Chanceler and both the Scherifs, Duc de Lids [Leeds], Minuster Pitt and the other judges of the first rank. At No. 2 I ate with Mʳ Silvester, the greatest lawyer and first Alderman of London. In this room (which is called the geld Hall [Guild Hall]), there were 16 tables besides others in adjoining rooms; in all nearly 1200 persons dined, all with the greatest pomp. The food was very nice and well-cooked; many kinds of wine in abundance. The company sat down at 6 o'clock and arose at 8. The Lord Mayor was escorted according to rank before and also after dinner, and there were many ceremonies, a sword was carried in front of him, and a kind of golden crown, to the sound of trumpets, accompanied by a wind band. After dinner the distinguished company of [table] No. 1 retired to a separate room which had been chosen beforehand, to drink coffee and tea; we other guests, however, were taken to another adjoining room. At 9 o'clock No. 1 rose and went to a small room, at which point the ball began: in this room there is, *a parte*, an elevated place for the high *Nobless* where the Lord Mayor is seated on a throne together with his wife. Then the dancing begins according to rank, but only 1 couple, just as at Court on the King's Birthday, 6th January [*recte* : 4th June]. In this small room there are 4 tiers of raised benches on each side, where the fair sex mostly has the upper hand. Nothing but minuets are danced in this room; I couldn't stand it longer than a quarter of an hour; first, because the heat caused by so many people in such a small room was so great; and secondly, because of the wretched dance band, the entire orchestra consisting only of two violins and a violoncello. The minuets were more Polish than in our or the Italian manner. From there I went to another room, which was more like a subterranean cavern, and where the dance was English; the music was a little better, because there was a drum in the band which drowned the misery of the violins. I went on to the great hall, where we had eaten, and there the band was larger and more bearable. The dance was English, but only on the raised platform where the Lord Mayor and the first 4 numbers had dined; the other tables, however, were all occupied again by men who, as usual, drank enormously the whole night. The most curious thing, though, is that a part of the company went on dancing without hearing a single note of the music, for first at one table, then at another, some were yelling songs and some swilling it down and drinking toasts amid terrific roars of 'Hurrey, H[urrey], H[urrey]' and waving of glasses. The hall and all the other rooms are illuminated with lamps which give out an unpleasant odour. It is remarkable that the Lord Mayor requires no knife at table, for a carver, who stands in front of him in the middle of the table, cuts up everything for him in advance.

1 *Musical Times*, 1 May 1909, p. 298.

Behind the Lord Mayor there is another man who, as is the custom, shouts out all the toasts as loudly as he can; after each shout come fanfares of trumpets and kettledrums. No toast was more applauded than that of Mr Pitt. But otherwise there is no order. This dinner cost £1600; half must be paid by the Lord Mayor, the other half by the two Sherifs. The Lord Mayor is newly elected every year. He wears, over his costume, a large black satin mantle, long and wide, in the shape of a domino cloak, richly ornamented in gold lace bands, especially round the arms. Round his neck he wears a large gold chain like that of our *Toison Order*; his wife has the same, she is Mylady and remains so. A new one is elected every year. The whole ceremony is worth seeing, especially the procession up the Tems [Thames] from Guildhall to Westmynster.

[CCLN, 251–3]

Sometimes Haydn got the strange English customs rather confused. 'On 5th Nov. the boys celebrate the day on which the Guys set the town on fire' is his rather fantastic description (CCLN, 268) of Guy Fawkes' Day. A few days later, on the 9th, Haydn was again a guest of the departing Lord Mayor (CCLN, 269), the 'Farewell dinner' at the Mansion-House: Haydn's host was the Right Hon. John Boydell.

The following note appears in Haydn's notebook:

On 14th Nov. 1791, 2 Symphonies sent to Herr von Keess *per postam*, for which I paid 1 guineas 11½ shillings, and 3 shillings for 2 letters, and 1 guinea for the copying.

[CCLN, 277]

The new Symphonies were Nos. 95 and 96, marked in Kees's thematic catalogue as 'come from London'; hitherto, no trace of these copies could be found in any of the three libraries now containing the remains of Kees's vast library (*vide supra*, p. 37); but in February 1963, the present writer was able to identify some duplicate string parts from a pile of anonymous MS. parts from the cellar of the Gesellschaft der Musikfreunde, in which library the larger part of the Kees Haydn MSS. exists: they are obviously part of the series described in detail in Landon (SYM, 38ff.) and are entitled 'Due Sinfonie Del Sig^r Gius Haydn N° 74 75' (cat. XIII, 6157); no Haydn symphonies later than those two can be found in the series.

Haydn could find no safe way to send the Symphonies to Vienna, as the following letter to Frau Maria Anna shows:

To Maria Anna von Genzinger, Vienna. *German*]

London, 17th November 1791.

Nobly born and gracious lady!

In the greatest haste I beg you to deliver the accompanying parcel, which I have addressed to you, to Herr von Keess, for it contains the two new Symphonies I promised. I was waiting all this time for a good opportunity, but could hear of none, and was therefore obliged to send them by mail. Please tell Herr von Keess that I ask him respectfully to have a rehearsal of both these Symphonies, because they are very delicate, especially the last movement of that in D major, for which I recommend the softest *piano* and a very quick *tempo*. I will write you in more detail in a few days. N.B. I was forced to send both Symphonies to Your Grace, because I don't know Herr von Keess' address. I kiss Your Grace's hands, and with kind regards to your husband and family, I am

Your most obedient servant,
Haydn.

I have just returned from the country today. I have been staying with a Lord for the past fortnight, 100 miles from London.

[Address:]   Madame
        Madame Anne Noble de
          Gennzinger Noble de Kayser.
in schotten Hof, auf   à
der Haupt Stiege   Vienne
    im 2ᵐ Stock   an autriche.   [CCLN, 121]

Concerning the approaching visit of Ignaz Pleyel, the *Morning Herald*, on 22 November 1791, writes that 'PLEYEL, the celebrated composer, certainly visits this country in the course of the approaching musical season. This composer, who is a pupil of the great HAYDN, is becoming even more popular than his master; as his works are characterized less by the intricacies of science than the charm of simplicity and feeling.' This stressing of Pleyel's easy style as compared to Haydn's complexities was a theme which we shall encounter frequently as the 1792 season unfolds.

In the middle of November, Haydn and Salomon made a trip to Cambridge to hear the 'cellist, Dahmen Jr, brother of the violinist, J. A. Dahmen, who had played in the concerts of the 1791 season. Young Dahmen made his first appearance in London on 2 March 1792. The *Cambridge Chronicle* of 19 November reports:

> We understand that the celebrated musical composers. Mr. Haydn and Mr. Salomon, came here last week to hear a private performance on the Violin and Violoncello by Messrs. Dahmen, who are lately arrived from Germany. They expressed the highest [approbation] of the superior skill and abilities of these performers, and immediately engaged them for their concerts in Hanover Square. We are glad to hear that Messrs. Dahmen will have a public concert in Cambridge before they leave this part of the country.
>
> [O. E. Deutsch, *Haydn in Cambridge*, p. 312]

The famous Soprano, Gertrud Elisabeth Mara, gave four farewell performances in Dr Arne's opera, *Artaxerxes*: these took place at the King's Theatre in Haymarket on 17, 19, 21 and 22 November. After that she went to Italy. (At the same time, Mrs Billington and Mr Incledon were singing *Artaxerxes* at Covent Garden.) One aria, with new words by Peter Pindar (John Wolcot), was repeated and the audience wanted Mara to sing it a third time. The *Gazetteer* (21 November) thought that Mara had the slight edge over Billington; in any case Mara made £2,200 for the theatre on these four nights. Haydn was there; we also append his notes about the interior of theatre (written perhaps on another, earlier occasion):

> Before she left for Italy, Mara sang 4 times at the Heymarcket [*sic*] Theatre in the English opera *Artaxerses* by Dʳ Arnd [Arne]. Again she won roars of applause, and she was paid £100 for each appearance.   [CCLN, 277]

Heymarket [*sic*] Theatre
It holds 4,000 persons; the pit, or parterre, alone holds 1,200; 10 persons can sit comfortably in each box. The *Amphy Theater* is entirely round, has four tiers, and to light it there is a beautiful large chandelier with 70 lights: it hangs suspended from the attic, pierces the ceiling, and is situated in the middle of the *Amphy Theater*; it illuminates the whole house, but there are also *a parte* small lustres in the first and 2nd tiers, which are fastened outside the boxes half an ell away.

                                        [CCLN, 274]

Haydn, who had an insatiable curiosity about everything, noted that 'Oranges from Portugal arrive in the middle of November, but they are quite pale and not so good as they are later' (CCLN, 278).

On 23 November, Haydn went to see a marionette opera. There was dancing and music at this 'Fantoccini' entertainment, including a Haydn symphony, Pleyel's *Concertante*, a condensed version of Piccinni's *La buona figliuola* and *Les petits riens* with music by Sacchini and Paisiello. Haydn wrote:

[*English*]
THE THEATRE OF VARIETE'S AMUSANTES, IN SAVILLE-ROW.
[*German*]
On 23rd Nov. [1791] I was invited to go there. It is a marionette theatre. The figures were well directed, the singers were bad, but the orchestra was quite good.
[CCLN, 277]

He will have remembered the famous marionette theatre at Eszterháza, now abandoned and a ghostly memory, if anything, for most people. It must have seemed not only a long time ago – its first big season had been in 1773 – but altogether another world.

That evening, 23 November, the second son of King George III, Frederick, Duke of York, married Princess Friederike Charlotte Ulricke, eldest daughter of the Prussian King Friedrich Wilhelm II. The royal pair had already been married in Berlin, but the British law required that they marry again on English soil. The ceremony took place at seven o'clock in the evening, at Buckingham House (now Palace).

The Duke of York was described by Mirabeau as 'puissant chasseur, puissant buveur, et puissant homme en cordialité pour les femmes mariées, et libre Comme un Seigneur Anglais'.[1] Haydn adored the Duchess at first sight, and she was to become his faithful benefactress and patron. Everybody tried to make the girl feel at home. The handsome Prince of Wales went to greet the couple when they arrived at York House:

> On their arrival at York House they were received by his Royal Highness the Prince of Wales, who came thither about twenty minutes before. The Prince received the Duchess in the Great Hall, with that elegance so peculiar to him; his Highness taking her by the hand, saluted his royal sister, and congratulated her on her arrival in the German language, which the Prince speaks with great perfection.
> ...   [*European Magazine*, November 1791, pp. 323ff.]

The very next day, Haydn was whisked away to Oatlands with the new royal couple:

> On 24th Nov. [1791], I was invited by the Prince of Wales to visit his brother, the Duc du York, at eatland [Oatlands]. I stayed there 2 days and enjoyed many marks of graciousness and honour, not only from the Prince of Wales but also from the Duchess, daughter of the King of Prussia. The little castle, 18 miles from London, lies on a slope and commands the most glorious view. Among its many beauties is a most remarkable grotto which cost £25,000 Sterling, and which was 11 years in the building. It is very large and contains many diversions, *inter alia* actual water which flows in from various sides, a beautiful English garden, various entrances and exits, besides a most charming bath. The Duke bought this country estate for some £47,000 Sterling. On the 3rd day, the Duke had me taken 12 miles towards London with his horse and carriage.
> The Prince of Wales wants my portrait. For 2 days we played music for 4 hours in the evening, that is, from 10 o'clock till 2 o'clock in the morning, then we had supper and went to bed at 3 o'clock.
> [CCLN, 272]

1 Pohl, *H in L*, 163.

The portrait mentioned was to be executed by John Hoppner and is one of the best known likenesses of Haydn; it is in the Royal Collection. The view from Oatlands is also described in rapturous terms by Joseph Farington in 1793:

> The Park of Oatlands rises considerably above the flat country through which the River passes, and is very well wooded. The House is not seen from this part, being situated more than a mile from the Bridge and hidden by trees. . . .
>
> I have seen few situations more beautiful than the line of ground which is called the Terrace, and great taste has been shewn in what now has been done by the hand of Art. A large piece of made water, broad as a fine River, is directed in such a way as to appear to be a part of the Thames although it has no connexion with it. Above the two ends, where it is lost in wood, the real River appears over the trees, and the imagination readily connects them. In the distance St. Anns Hill, Coopers Hill, & Windsor are distinct objects on one side; on the other side Walton double Bridge, Lord Tankervilles, Sunbury, Harrow, & Highgate.
>
> Immediately below the Terrace is an extensive flat country, which is only seen in small proportions, as the Park is well wooded. The water in the Park is about three-quarters of a mile long, and was laid out by the present Duke of Newcastle, who had no assistance in designing it. A lofty and well designed Temple is erected on the Terrace, but is not finished, which is to be lamented as it would make a fine & proper object in this situation, and the view from it most beautiful & extensive. . . .
>
> The House at Oatlands makes not appearance equal to the scenery about it, but being in a great measure hidden among trees, it does not become an object of much notice. Just below the Park the Thames makes a bold sweep, and the point of the angle is called 'Cowey Stakes'; this is the place where Julius Caesar forded the River. It may be half a mile above Walton Bridge. The village of Hawforth is on the opposite side of the Plain.
>
> The Park at Oatlands is about 3 miles round. The long way of it is from Walton to Weybridge, which is about a mile & half. The Duke of York purchased Oatlands from the Duke of Newcastle abt. 5 years ago. He became Lord of the Manor of Weybridge, and some estate is united to it. The Duke of Newcastle had a grotto made which is much admired for the beauty of the workmanship and exactness of the imitation. Before it is a small basin of water. The whole is inclosed by Trees which make the situation secluded. The grotto contains 2 small rooms, and a bathing room, on the ground floor besides passages, and one large room above. All finished in character, with imitations of Icicles, and Shell work.
>
> [Farington I, 9ff.]

The lot of the musician had changed spectacularly in the last generation, even from Haydn's position with Prince Paul Anton Esterházy in 1761; now Haydn was seated next to the Duchess of York. Part of this new treatment was the work of the Prince of Wales. Parke tells us (I, 241) that the later George IV was the first to invite musicians to his dinner table. He was a real connoisseur of music, and especially Haydn's. Sir George Smart tells an amusing story in this connection:

> At one of these concerts I asked Christian Kramer, the master of King George IV's famous band, how it was that the King was so perfectly satisfied with the tempi taken of all Haydn's Sinfonias, His Majesty being so fastidious. 'Why,' said Kramer, 'His Majesty always beats time to every movement. I watch him and beat the same time to the orchestra.'
>
> [Smart, p. 57]

At the end of November there was a scandal with the popular actress, Dora Jordan. The event itself is rather drily told in the *European Magazine*:

THEATRICAL JOURNAL.

On the 26th of November, the Entertainment of Richard Cœur de Lion being intended for performance at the Haymarket, an apology was made for the non-attendance of Mrs. Jordan, who was declared too much indisposed to perform that evening. This excuse being, as it seemed, suspected by some of the audience, a dissatisfaction appeared among them, which was only quieted by the substitution of Mrs. Crouch instead of Mrs. Jordan in the character. In the ensuing week many paragraphs were inserted in the News-papers, charging Mrs. Jordan with want of respect to the public, which occasioned the following letter, addressed to the several Editors, to appear in most of the public prints:

Sir, *Treasury-Office, No. 30, 1791.*
I HAVE submitted in silence to the unprovoked and unmanly abuse which for some time past has been directed against me, because it has related to subjects about which the public could not be interested; but to an attack upon my conduct in my profession, and the charge of want of respect and gratitude to the public, I think it my duty to reply. Nothing can be more cruel and unfounded than the insinuation that I absented myself from the Theatre on Saturday last, from any other cause than real inability from illness to sustain my part in the Entertainment. I have ever been ready and proud to exert myself to the utmost of my strength to fulfil my engagements with the Theatre, and to manifest my respect for the audience; and no person can be more grateful for the indulgence and applause with which I have been constantly honoured. I would not obtrude upon the public an allusion to any thing that does not relate to my profession, in which alone, I may without presumption say, I am accountable to them; but thus called on in the present instance, there can be no impropriety in my answering those who have so ungenerously attacked me, that if they could drive me from that profession, they would take from me the only income I have or mean to possess; the whole earnings of which upon the past, and one half for the future, I have already settled upon my children. Unjustly and cruelly traduced as I have been upon this subject, I trust that this short declaration will not be deemed impertinent; and for the rest, I appeal with confidence to the justice and generosity of the public.
I am, Sir, Your obedient servant,
DOR. JORDAN.

This appeal to the public seemed not to produce entire conviction, as on the 10th of December, when Mrs. Jordan again attempted the character of Roxalana in The Sultan, notwithstanding the very great applause bestowed upon her, some individuals appeared dissatisfied, and disturbance ensued, which was not quieted until Mrs. Jordan had addressed the audience in the following words:
'Ladies and Gentlemen,
'I Should conceive myself utterly unworthy of your favour, if the slightest mark of public disapprobation did not affect me very sensibly.
'Since I have had the honour and the happiness to strive here to please you, it has been my constant endeavour, my unremitting assiduity, to merit your approbation. I beg leave to assure you, upon my honour, that I have never absented myself one minute from the duties of my profession, but from real indisposition. Thus having invariably acted, I *do* consider myself under the public protection.'
This apology was received with bursts of applause, and the disturbance ceased.
[*European Magazine*, Vol. XXI, 1792, pp. 65ff.]

Haydn seems to have been there at the Haymarket Theatre (28 November) when the scandal began; at any rate, here is what he thought about it (London Notebook):

English Fanaticism. Miss Dora Jordan, a mistress of the Duc de Clarens [Clarence] and the leading actress at Drury Lane, wrote to the impresario one evening, an hour before the beginning of a comedy in which she was to play, that she had been taken ill suddenly and therefore couldn't act. When the curtain was raised in order to inform the public thereof, and to say that the management was inclined to give another piece [*Spectacul*], the whole public began to shout that the comedy which had been announced must be given at once, with another actress taking Jordan's rôle and reading with the part in her hand. At the beginning, the management took exception to this plan, but the public became stubborn and its wishes had to be satisfied. Miss Jordan made herself contemptible in the public's eyes because she drove barefacedly in Heÿ [Hyde] Park with the Duc. But she begged for pardon in all the newspapers, and people quite forgave her. [CCLN, 278]

Working in his flat at Great Pulteney Street, Haydn was witness to another dose of 'English fanaticism':

A gang of rowdy fellows sang this song with all their might. They yelled so loudly that you could hear them 1000 paces away from the street, in every nook and cranny. [CCLN, 278]

Haydn was invited to another country house at the end of the month. At one point in his notebook, Haydn notes 'que l'amitié soit aussi solide, silb Pock NB. Lady Blake from Langham (CCLN 254, corrected according to Pohl III, 40; our quotation as it stands, untranslated): 'silb Pock' is, apparently, the German abbreviation for a 'Silber-Pockal', a silver chalice with the French inscription. Haydn left London on the 30th:

On the 30th [November 1791], I spent 3 days in the country, 100 miles from London, at the house of Sir Patric Blak [Patrick Blake, who lived at Langham]; *en route* I passed through the little town of Cambridge. Saw the universities there, which are very conveniently situated, one after another, in a row, but each one separate from the other; each university has back of it a very roomy and beautiful garden, besides beautiful stone bridges, in order to be able to cross the circumjacent stream. – The King's Chapel is famous because of its stuccoed ceiling. It is all made of stone, but so delicate that nothing more beautiful could have been made of wood. It is already 400 years old, and everyone thinks that it is not more than 10 years old, because of the firmness and peculiar whiteness of the stone. The students there bear themselves like those at Oxford, but it is said that they have better teachers. There are in all 800 students. [CCLN, 272]

Was Haydn the second time in Cambridge? Or is the report in the *Cambridge Chronicle* of 19 November, quoted above, a mistake? Possibly Haydn had no time to visit the University when he went to Cambridge with Salomon to recruit the 'cellist.

Haydn was back at his desk on 5 December:

On 5th Dec. [1791] the fog was so thick that you could have spread it on bread. In order to write I had to light the lights at 11 o'clock. [CCLN, 278]

In Vienna, Count Zinzendorf noted that it was foggy, also the next day. In the night, Mozart died. When the news reached London a few weeks later, Haydn was stunned. He never got over it and the tears would spring to his eyes whenever he saw one of the sons. Many years later Wolfgang Mozart *fils* was reported thus by the Novellos:

'Haydn he thinks his father's greatest admirer, and said he never saw him but he wept. . . . Haydn told him that if he (Mozart) went to England first (as Salomon at one time wished) it would be of no use for him (Haydn) to go there as "nothing would do after Mozart's compositions." Haydn often visited them [Constanze and the children] and repeatedly declared that Mozart was the greatest musical genius that ever existed.' Abbé Stadler told Vincent Novello, 'Haydn and Mozart were like brothers. [Haydn said,] "he was a *God* in Music".'[1] Haydn and Dr Burney were one day at Longman & Broderip's shop. Burney later reported the conversation in the 'Mozart' article in Rees's *Cyclopaedia*:

> When Haydn was asked in our hearing by Broderip, in his music-shop whether Mozart had left any MS. compositions behind him that were worth purchasing, as his widow had offered his unedited papers at a high price to the principal publishers of music through-out Europe; Haydn eagerly said: 'Purchase them by all means. He was truly a great musician. I have been often flattered by my friends with having some genius; but he was much my superior.'
>
> Though this declaration had more of modesty than truth in it, yet if Mozart's genius had been granted as many years to expand as that of Haydn, the assertion might perhaps have been realised in many particulars.   [Scholes, 116]

The glee composer, R. J. S. Stevens, walked into the shop just as Haydn was leaving:

> He called on Broderip in the Haymarket, and urged him to purchase *all Mozart's compositions*. Such a genius he never knew.
>
> I *saw Haydn* leave Broderip's shop, after he had made this declaration. Mr. Broderip mentioned Haydn's words to me.   [Scholes, 116]

In far away Eisenstadt, music, on a limited scale, continued at the Esterházy Castle – especially church music, to which end they could get supplementary players from the *Thurnermeister* and the *Regenschori* of the *Stadtpfarrkirche*, Carl Kraus. After Mozart had died they played the *Graduale ad Festum Beatae Mariae* (K. 273) and throughout the MS. parts are remarks like 'Mozartt frantz/Bitt für ihm 1 RosenKrantz' (second violin part) or, on the tenor part, words from the 123rd Psalm (Continental counting), Verse 1: 'Mozart / Requiescat in pace / Ecce quam bonum / quamque jucundum / habitare fratres in unum 792.' They knew what a loss the world had suffered, for they had been trained by one of Mozart's greatest admirers. Haydn was so shaken that all he wrote in his notebook was: 'Mozard starb den 5ᵗⁿ 10ᵇʳⁱ [Decembri]1791.'

Shortly before Mozart died, British newspapers printed reports of the Emperor Leopold II's coronation at Prague; the *Morning Chronicle* for 21 November 1791 carries such a report, mentioning Koželuch's name twice, once as director of a large orchestral concert and once as the composer of a choral cantata written for the occasion; Mozart's name, and *La clemenza di Tito*, are not even mentioned.

By 20 December, the news of Mozart's death had reached London (see letter of that date, *infra*). For the moment, Haydn believed his friend still alive. On the 10th he visited Covent Garden:

> Covent-garden is the National Theatre. I was there on 10th Dec. [1791] and saw an opera called *The Woodman*. It was the very day on which the life story of Madam Bilington, both from the good as well as from the bad sides, was announced; such impertinent enterprises are generally undertaken for [selfish] interests. She sang

---

1 *A Mozart Pilgrimage, Being the Travel Diaries of Vincent & Mary Novello in the year 1829*; transcribed and compiled by Nerina Medici di Marignano, edited by Rosemary Hughes. London, 1955, pp. 92, 170ff.

rather timidly this evening, but very well all the same. The first tenor[1] [space for name left blank] has a good voice and quite a good style, but he uses the falsetto to excess. He sang a trill on high C and ran up to G. The 2nd tenor tries to imitate him, but could not make the change from the falsetto to the natural voice, and apart from that he is most unmusical. He creates a new tempo for himself, now 3/4, then 2/4, makes cuts whenever it occurs to him. But the cahest [cast] is entirely used to him. The leader is Herr Baumgartner, a German who, however, has almost forgotten his mother-tongue. The Theatre is very dark and dirty, and is almost as large as the Vienna Court Theatre. The common people in the galleries of all the theatres are very impertinent; they set the fashion with all their unrestrained impetuosity, and whether something is repeated or not is determined by their yells. The parterre and all the boxes sometimes have to applaud a great deal to have something good repeated. That was just what happened this evening, with the Duet in the 3rd Act, which was very beautiful; and the pro's and contra's went on for nearly a quarter of an hour, till finally the parterre and the boxes won, and they repeated the Duet. Both the performers stood on the stage quite terrified, first retiring, then again coming forward. THE ORCHESTRA IS SLEEPY.

[CCLN, 273f.]

The *Woodman* was composed by Haydn's friend, William Shield. It had proved to be a satisfying success for the composer. The *European Magazine* (March 1791, p. 228) had reviewed it, saying, 'The music of this piece was by Mr Shield, and deserved the applause it received. The performers also were excellent in their several parts.' Shield, according to the article by William H. Husk in the first edition of Grove's *Dictionary* (III, 486f.), 'was perhaps the most original English composer since Purcell. His melodies charm by their simple, natural beauty; at once vigorous, chaste and refined, they appeal directly to the hearts of Englishmen.' He was younger than Haydn by sixteen years. A brilliant string player, he preferred the viola, as did Haydn and Mozart – according to Abbé Stadler, the latter two used to alternate in playing the first or second viola parts in Mozart's Quintets – and left his beautiful instrument, reputedly a Stainer, to George IV. At the time Haydn arrived in England, Shield had been a successful opera composer and for some years engaged by Covent Garden, which post he resigned in 1791 to travel in France and Italy. In 1792 he was back in England at his old post. He met Haydn in 1791 and according to Husk (ibid., 487), Shield 'was wont to say that in four days, during which he accompanied him from London to Taplow and back, he gained more knowledge than he had done by study in any four years of his life.' We have alluded to the Taplow story earlier (*supra*, p. 83). In 1800 he published his well-known *Introduction to Harmony*, followed, a few years afterwards, by an Appendix containing many interesting musical examples, including Haydn and a then unknown piece by Mozart and a quotation from a Beethoven Sonata. Shield was a huge fellow who loved to eat and drink, as his portrait by Dance in the year 1798 shows; he was happily married to Ann Stokes, his 'beloved partner'. He was one of the most sympathetic of all Haydn's many English friends.

---

1 The first tenor was Charles Incledon, and the second tenor was an Irishman named Johnstone (hence there is an Irishman in almost all of Shield's operas). Dr Roger Fiske, who kindly supplied the above information, adds that 'Haydn was not alone in finding Johnstone unmusical, but he had a way with him when it came to singing little Irish songs, and he was popular as a man.' Dr Fiske also discovered that there is in fact no duet in the original version of the third Act. What Haydn heard was 'Together let us range the fields' from Boyce's *Serenata* 'Solomon', which Mrs Billington and Incledon had introduced into *The Woodman* soon after its first performance the previous February. [from CCLN, 274]

The Anacreontic Society, which had been so hospitable to Haydn when he arrived in London, continued, at the beginning of the new season, to pay flattering attention to his music. The first concert of the 1791–2 season took place on 8 December 1791, and the following day we read in the *Morning Chronicle* that

THE ANACREONTIC / Met last Night at the Crown and Anchor. . . . The Orchestra has gained more in selection than it has lost in number. Two Overtures by Haydn, and one by Stamitz were given in the most capital style; as were a Quartetto of Pleyel's and one of Haydn's, by Cramer, Mountain, Blake, and Smith . . . Dr. Arnold [is] the Director.

At these concerts, which began at seven o'clock, 'Supper [was] on the Table at a Quarter before Ten o'Clock'. In the *Morning Chronicle* of 23 December 1791 we read of the second concert in this series: 'Four Overtures from Pleyel, Kozeluck [*sic*], Le Duc, and Mozart were admirably performed by a band considerably fuller than usual, under the direction of Cramer. Two Quartettos, from Pleyel and Haydn, were also given with charming effect by Cramer, Blake, and Smith . . .'.

Haydn was being bothered by Luigia Polzelli for money and she also seems to have accused him of faithlessness. The tone of Haydn's answer, 13 December, shows that he was slowly getting tired of her pettishness: Haydn was now miles and light years away from Eszterháza and was enjoying the company, as we shall see, of many more beautiful, and certainly vastly more intelligent, women.

[To Luigia Polzella, Bologna. *Italian, ' Tu' form*]

London, 13th December 1791

Dear Polzelli!

You gave me quite a shock with you last letter, because I thought my letter had gone astray, and also the money with it. I was so upset that I couldn't sleep for three days, until I received your second letter. I hope that you will never again entertain such cruel suspicions of me, for I esteem and love you as I did on the very first day. I am very sorry for you, and it pains me terribly that I can't do more for you. But be patient, perhaps the day will come when I can show you how much I love you. Write soon, and let me know how your lodgings are, how you are, and if you arrived safely with your two dear sons. Tell Pietro to be obedient and to study hard; if he doesn't, I shan't take him with me. Your sister sends you a thousand kisses; she is still in a most unhappy state: the poor thing now lives in a room, separated from her husband, with whom she is still on bad terms. She will send you a little something. Dear Polzelli, I can't write more today. More another time.

Meanwhile I am your most sincere

Giuseppe Haydn.

[Address:]   Madame
Madame Loise Polzelli,
Virtuosa di Musica
a
Bologna.   [CCLN, 121f.]

As this Chronicle will show, Haydn always had an eye for the ladies: 'it's part of the business', he would tell *Legationsrath* Griesinger (58), calling after the departing friend, 'Many greetings to all the beautiful women!' In England he met many beautiful women, among them a Mrs Hodges. In 1960, Mrs Hodges' great-granddaughter, Miss G. M. Hodges, wrote to the B.B.C. after hearing a programme in which her great-grandmother had been mentioned; she said a portrait of Mrs

Hodges hangs in her ancestral home at Amory Court, Pershore, Worcestershire, that Mrs Hodges does look very beautiful, and that she (Miss Hodges) used to have all her meals looking at this portrait. It was a family tradition that Haydn would come and dine in the house when he visited Clementi at Evesham. In any case, Haydn took back to Vienna one of Mrs Hodges's Songs, 'When from thy sight.' On it, we find this note in Haydn's hand: 'This Song is by Mrs Hodges, the most beautiful woman I ever saw in my life, a great piano player. Text and music by her.' Later, in a trembling hand, 'Requiescat in pace J. Haydn': he kept up with his English friends long after leaving England (Pohl III, 41).

> On 14th Dec. [1791] I dined for the first time at Mr Shaw's. He received me downstairs at the door, and then led me to his wife, who was surrounded by her 2 daughters and other ladies. As I was bowing round the circle, all at once I became aware of the fact that not only the lady of the house but also her daughters and the other women each wore on their headdress *a parte* over the front a most charming curved pearl-coloured band of 3 fingers' breadth, with the name Haydn embroidered therein in gold; and Mr Shaw wore this name on his coat, worked into the very ends of both his collars in the finest steel beads. The coat was made of the finest cloth, and with elegant steel buttons. The Mis^tris is the most beautiful woman I ever saw. N.B.: Her husband wanted a souvenir from me, and I gave him a tobacco-box which I had just bought brand new for a guinea; he gave me his instead. Several days later I visited him, and saw that he had had a silver case put over my box, on the cover of which was very elegantly engraved Apollo's harp and the following words: *Ex dono celeberrimi Josephi Haydn.* N.B. The Mis^tris gave me a stickpin as a souvenir.   [CCLN, 275]

Haydn enlarged a bit on the diary entry to Dies (126f.). We learn that 'Mr S.' was a Member of Parliament, and Haydn was not acquainted with him. The composer received 'a polite invitation' and, curious as he was about everything and everyone in England, he went. 'It was winter, and we were sitting in front of the open fire, at each side of which stood, as is the English custom, a row of chairs, one set for the ladies, one for the gentlemen. The place directly in front of the fire is always empty. Haydn knew the custom and wanted to take a seat on the gentlemen's side, but he was stopped and placed in the middle in front of the fire. Gradually he realized that all the ladies were in white and the men in brown' and told Dies about the bands of 'Haydn'. He 'could not utter a word' for astonishment, gazing first at the ladies, then at the men. Haydn was horribly embarrassed and regained his composure only during the meal, which went on into the small hours. Haydn always kept the stick-pin among his little collection of 'treasures' in Vienna.

At the Tenth Concert of the previous season (20 May 1791), Haydn had conducted a MS. symphony by Haesler, who was to appear, with very mixed reception in the forthcoming season with Salomon's concerts (on 17 March 1792, one newspaper thought he 'evinced extraordinary execution and finished taste'; *The Times*, on 14 May 1792, advised Salomon 'to banish Mr Haesler's concertos: his performance on the harpsichord was the most wretched attempt we ever heard'). Johann Wilhelm Haesler (Hässler) had performed in competition with Mozart in Dresden in April 1789; Mozart thought 'he has done no more than commit to memory the harmony and modulations of old Sebastian Bach and is not capable of executing a fugue properly; and his playing is not thorough'.[1]

1 Anderson, *The Letters of Mozart and his Family*, op. cit., II, 923f.

Now Haesler was in England, and on 16 December the London correspondent of the *Journal des Luxus und der Moden* reported back to Weimar:

London, 16 Dec. 1791.
In the musical world we have here a great organist from Erfurth, Hr. Häseler. It is generally said that he is one of the greatest organists, and not less beautifully he plays the piano-forte; but to perfection and admiration on a good German clavichord [*Claviere*]. Not less beautiful his compositions, which generally please here, too. He has played several times in front of the royal family and especially the King, who otherwise, as is well known, is only for Händel; [the king] specially praised [Haesler's] *Nacht von Zacharia*. He has a wide circle of acquaintances here, and will certainly, with Haydn, very much change and improve the taste of music here.

It is hoped that this massively tactless last sentence did not circulate widely among Dr Burney, William Shield, etc. We shall meet Haesler most interestingly on 30 May 1792, when Haydn conducted a Mozart piano concerto played by Haesler.

On 20 December, Haydn wrote a long report back to Frau von Genzinger:

[To Maria Anna von Genzinger, Vienna. *German*]

London, 20th December 1791.

Nobly born and gracious Lady!

I was very surprised that you did not get my letter at the same time as the 2 Symphonies, for I posted them myself here and gave them every instruction. My mistake was that I didn't enclose the letter in the parcel. That is what generally happens, gracious lady, to those who have too much head work. But I do hope that you will receive the letter somewhat later; if not, I should explain that both Symphonies were destined for Herr von Keess, but with the stipulation that after Herr von Keess had copied them, the scores were to be delivered to Your Grace, so that Your Grace could make a pianoforte arrangement of them, if you felt so disposed. As for the Symphony intended for Your Grace, I shall deliver it by the end of February at the latest. I am sorry to have had to address this large package to Your Grace, but I didn't have Herr von Keess' address; Herr von Keess will of course refund you the postage costs and, I hope, give you 7 ducats *a parte*. Now may I respectfully ask Your Grace to use this money and have the Symphony in E flat, which I ask for so often, and of which I sent you the *incipit* recently, copied on small-sized paper for mailing, and sent to me by mail as soon as possible; for it may be half a year before a courier is dispatched from Vienna, and I need the Symphony very urgently. Further I must bother Your Grace once again; this time it is the last pianoforte Sonata in A flat – that is, with 4♭ signs – with accompaniment of a violin and violoncello, and one other piece, the Fantasia in C [for pianoforte] unaccompanied; please buy these at Herr Artaria's, and have them, too, copied on small-sized paper for mailing and sent here by mail, because these works are not yet engraved in London. Your Grace, however, must be clever enough not to mention a word of this to Herr Artaria, for otherwise he will anticipate the sale here. Your Grace should subtract the costs from the 7 ducats. To come back to the aforesaid 2 Symphonies, I must tell Your Grace that I sent the pianoforte arrangement of Andante of that in C minor through Herr Diettenhofer. It is reported, however, that Herr Diettenhofer either died *en route* or must have met with an accident, and so you can make the pianoforte arrangements yourself, if you are so disposed. The principal part of the letter I entrusted to Herr Diettenhofer described the conferment of the doctor's degree on me at Oxford, and all the honours I received there. I must take this opportunity of informing Your Grace that 3 weeks ago I was invited by the Prince of Wales to visit his brother, the Duke of York, at the latter's country seat. The Prince presented me to the Duchess, the daughter of the King of Prussia, who received me very graciously and said many flattering things. She is the most delightful lady in the world, is very intelligent, plays the pianoforte and sings very nicely. I had to stay there 2 days, because a slight indisposition prevented her attending the concert on the first day. On the 2nd day, however, she remained continually at my side from 10 o'clock in the evening, when the music began, to 2 o'clock in the morning. Nothing but Haydn was played. I conducted the symphonies from the pianoforte, and the sweet little thing sat beside me on my left and hummed all the pieces from memory, for she had heard them so often in Berlin. The Prince of Wales sat on my right side and played with us on his violoncello, quite tolerably. I had to sing, too. The Prince of Wales is having my portrait painted just now, and the picture is to hang in his room. The Prince of Wales is the most handsome man on God's earth; he has an extraordinary love of music and a lot of feeling, but not much money. *Nota bene*, this is between ourselves. I am more pleased by his kindness than by any financial gain. On the third day the Duke of York sent me two stages with his own span, since I couldn't catch the mail-coach.

Now, gracious lady, I would like to take you to task a little, for believing that I prefer the city of London to Vienna, and that I find the sojourn here more agreeable than that in my fatherland. I don't hate London, but I would not be capable of spending the rest of my life there, even if I could amass millions. I shall tell Your Grace the reason when I see you. I look forward tremendously to going home and to embracing all my good friends. I only regret that the great Mozart will not be among them, if it is really true, which I trust it is not, that he has died. Posterity will not see such a talent again in 100 years! I am delighted that Your Grace and your family are well. I have enjoyed excellent health up to now, thank God! but a week ago I got an attack of English rheumatism which was so severe that sometimes I had to cry aloud. I hope soon to get rid of it, however, inasmuch as I have adopted the usual custom here of wrapping myself in flannel from head to foot. I must ask you to excuse the fact that my handwriting is so poor today. In the hope of being consoled by a letter, and with every esteem for yourself and my respectful compliments to your husband, dear *Fräulein* Pepi, and all the others, I am

> Your Grace's
> most obedient servant,
> Joseph Haydn.

Please convey my respects to Herr von Kreybich.

[CCLN, 122–4]

Several points in the letter require explanation. Haydn was trying to sell some already printed music to British publishers before they learned that the works were known. The Fantasia in C (XVII: 4), however, had already been published in 1789 by Longman and Broderip (it was entered at Stationers Hall on 28 November); the piano Trio No. 27 (XV: 14) in A flat was performed by Hummel at a Salomon concert on 20 April 1792, and Haydn sold the work to Longman & Broderip. Diettenhofer did not die: Gerber (*Neues historisch-biographisches Lexikon der Tonkünstler*, 1812, I, 891) reported him still active in London in 1799. The portrait referred to was the one by Hoppner, who had a formidable reputation: his fellow artist Farington thought 'Hoppner is likely to get most reputation by his Portraits of any in that line.'[1] Franz Kreibich (1728–1797), Court Director of Chamber Music under Joseph II, was

---

1 Farington I, 45: 9 April 1794. See also *supra*, p. 110.

formerly a bitter enemy of Haydn (and also Mozart): Haydn was not a man to bear grudges. The references to the Symphonies are Nos. 95 and 96 sent to Herr von Kees, the hoped-for Symphony No. 91 in E flat, and the *Andante* from Symphony No. 95 arranged for pianoforte.

Haydn was certainly understating the point that the Prince of Wales had 'not much money'. William Pitt's memorandum of 22 October 1794 reads:

The total amount of the debts of the Prince of Wales appears to be as follows:

	£
Bonded debt	411,000
Debt to Mr Coutts – [the Bankers]	50,000
To be repaid to the Civil List	30,000
Farther arrears – about	25,000
Arrears of salary	36,000
	552,000

[*The later Correspondence of George III*, ed. A. Aspinall, vol. II, Cambridge, 1963, p. 255]

Haydn's notebook informs us that 'On 23rd Dec. [1791]Pleyel arrived in London. On the 24th I dined with him.' (CCLN, 274.) Just below this entry we learn that 'The Duke of Cumberland had to pay £25,000 in an adultery case': we can imagine the open-mouthed Pleyel as Haydn tried, that Christmas eve, to explain what life was like in London. Certainly they will have talked about Mozart's death.

They will also have had something else to discuss which was not so pleasant for Haydn. In the autumn of 1784, six years before, Haydn had sent three piano trios (XV: 3–5) to his British publisher William Forster, who issued them the next year. The autograph of the G major Trio exists in fragments (No. 3 of Forster's edition; Landon 18) and also in an authentic copy in Kroměříž (Kremsier), and the work is obviously genuine. But the first two trios are just as obviously by Ignaz Pleyel, who published them under his name. De Framéry, in his *Notices sur Joseph Haydn* (Paris 1810), tells the story that Pleyel sent two of his sonatas (i.e. trios) to Haydn, who had just received Forster's request for three sonatas; Haydn took the Pleyel sonatas, added one of his own to them, and sent the batch to London as his own compositions. Meanwhile Pleyel had sold his two works to Longman & Broderip (this edition has not been discovered), as a result of which a legal argument arose between Longman & Broderip and Forster. That such an argument actually took place is known from an archive remark on Haydn's contract with Forster of 1786 (British Museum, Egerton 2380, fol. 12): 'Haydns subjects. D.[ocument] Forster ag^t Longman & [?Broderip; word illegible]. This Paper Writing was shown to Jos. Haydn at the time of his exam. in this Court before me Ja Eyre.' Now Alan Tyson, in a fascinating article on these Trios,[1] has been able to establish that 'Ja Eyre' was Sir James Eyre, since 1793 Chief Justice of the Common Pleas; and that therefore the actual law-suit could not have taken place during Haydn's first London visit but during his second, which date, 1794, is said to be the year in which Haydn and Pleyel came to an agreement over the Trios (again according to Framéry, who had all this information from Pleyel himself). One wonders, therefore, if the subject arose in 1791 or 1792 and what Haydn had to say about it; later he mentioned to Griesinger, for transmission to Breitkopf & Härtel,

1 'Haydn and Two stolen Trios', *Music Review*, 1961, pp. 21ff.

who were preparing the *Oeuvres Complettes* (with the piano Trios), that one of the three Trios was really by his brother Michael – to keep matters in the family, thinks Tyson.

The last day of 1791, Haydn and Pleyel went together to the opera:

> On 31st Dec. [1791] I was with Pleyel in the Pantheon Theatre. They gave *La Pastorella Nobile* by Guglielmi. Mad. Cassentini played the leading rôle and Laza[rini] the *primo huomo*; the thin Calvesi had *l'ultima parte*. The opera did not please. Neither did the ballet, even though the great Hillisberg [Hilligsberg] danced. [CCLN, 266]

Towards the end of his First Notebook Haydn wrote a proverb by Angelus Silesius which obviously attracted him, and which might be called the philosophy of Haydn's old age:

> Wer mit Vernunft betracht' den wechsel aller Sachen,
> Den kan kein glück froh, kein unglück traurig machen.[1]

1 He who wisely observes how all things change cannot be made happy by good fortune or unhappy by bad. CCLN, 267. Identification of Silesius from Niccolò Castiglioni, 'Antologia degli Scritti di Haydn' in *L'Approdo Musicale*, No. 11 (1960), p. 131.

CHAPTER TWO

1792

HAYDN KNEW THAT Mozart's brother-Mason, Johann Michael Puchberg, the banker, had a special relationship to the young composer. Early in January – the letter has survived only in fragments – Haydn wrote to Puchberg in Vienna:

> [*German*]   London, January 1792.
> . . . For some time I was beside myself about his [Mozart's] death, and I could not believe that Providence would so soon claim the life of such an indispensable man. I only regret that before his death he could not convince the English, who walk in darkness in this respect, of his greatness – a subject about which I have been sermonizing to them every single day. . . . You will be good enough, my kind friend, to send me a catalogue of those pieces which are not yet known here, and I shall make every possible effort to promote such works for the widow's benefit; I wrote the poor woman three weeks ago, and told her that when her favourite son reaches the necessary age, I shall give him composition lessons to the very best of my ability, and at no cost, so that he can, to some extent, fill his father's position. . .
>
> [CCLN, 125]

Haydn must have remembered, with a stab of pain, how he and Mozart and Puchberg ('I am inviting only Haydn and yourself') had listened first to piano rehearsals and then to the orchestral rehearsals of *Così fan tutte* in January 1790. Haydn will probably not have known the extent of Mozart's debts to Puchberg (1,000 Gulden, equal to Haydn's annual salary in 1790).[1]

The London newspapers were busy discussing the relative merits of Haydn and Pleyel. On 5 January 1792, the *Public Advertiser* writes:

> Haydn and Pleyel are to be *pitted* against each other this season; and the supporters of each are violent partizans. As both these Composers are men of first-rate talents, it may be hoped that they will not participate in the little feelings of their respective admirers.

What was Pleyel like? The contemporary sources are sparse, unlike those dealing with Haydn at this period in his life. But we have one, written in 1798 from Paris, by Gustaf Sehmann, a friend of Gustav Abraham Silverstolpe (of whom we shall be hearing much more in the course of our study of Haydn). On 22 April 1798, Sehmann writes to Silverstolpe:

> . . . I gave him [Pleyel] the large part of Kraus's [Joseph Martin, the composer] music; that of the Funeral Music for the King delighted him especially; together with his brother he has established a musical printing shop, is a complete Jew as far as prices go, and apart from his talents is rather less interesting. . . .

1 O. E. Deutsch, *Mozart, Die Dokumente seines Lebens*, Kassel, 1961, p. 508. According to Nissen, Puchberg did not ask for his money for several years, and then received it.

On 14 January 1792, Haydn wrote a long letter to Luigia Polzelli, who had now found a position in the Theatre at Piacenza. In his letter Haydn refers to the fire which, on the night of 13–14 January, consumed the Pantheon Theatre and, as we have seen (*supra*, p. 64), the score, except the Overture, of Gyrowetz's new opera *Semiramis* which was to have been performed there. *Semiramis* was well into rehearsal; the decorations had burst into flames while being dried in front of a fire, and the building caught fire and was destroyed. Gyrowetz stood to lose £300. But Lord Bedford generously took things in hand, replacing the musicians' instruments and seeing that Gyrowetz was paid (Pohl, *H in L*, 177f.). Luigia's sister had apparently been in the cast of Guglielmi's *La pastorella nobile*, which Haydn had seen on the last day of the old year. The Signor Negri whom Haydn greets was probably the Eszterháza singer, Domenico Negri, a bass voice who had sung Melibeo in the 1782 revival of Haydn's *La fedeltà premiata* and Rodomonte in the premiere of Haydn's *Orlando Paladino*.[1]

[To Luigia Polzelli, Piacenza. *Italian, 'Tu' form*]

London, 14th January 1792.

My dearest Polzelli! This very moment I received your letter, and hasten to answer it. I am relieved that you are in good health, and that you have found a position in a little theatre; not so much because of the payment but to have the experience. I wish you every possible success, in particular a good rôle and a good teacher, who takes the same pains with you as did your Haydn. You write that you would like to send your dear Pietro to me; do so, for I shall embrace him with all my heart; he is always welcome, and I shall treat him as if he were my own son. I shall take him with me to Vienna. I shall remain in London until the middle of June, not longer, because my Prince and many other circumstances make it imperative that I return home. Nevertheless I shall try, if possible, to go to Italy, in order to see my dear Polzelli, but meanwhile you can send your Pietro to me here in London; he will always be either with me or with your sister, who is now alone and who has been separated quite some time now from her husband, that beast. She is unhappy, as you were, and I am very sorry for her. I see her but rarely, for I have a lot to do, especially now, when the Professional Concert has had my pupil Pleyel brought over, to face me as a rival; but I'm not afraid, because last year I made a great impression on the English and hope therefore to win their approval this year, too. My opera was not given, because *Sig.* Gallini didn't receive the licence from the King, and never will; to tell you the truth, the Italian opera has no success at all now, and by a stroke of bad luck, the Pantheon Theatre burned down just this very day, two hours after midnight. Your sister had been engaged in the last piece; I am sorry for all of them.

I am quite well, but am almost always in an 'English humour', that is, depressed, and perhaps I shall never again regain the good humour that I used to have when I was with you. Oh! my dear Polzelli: you are always in my heart, and I shall never, never forget you. I shall do my very best to see you, if not this year, then certainly the next, along with your son. I hope that you won't forget me, and that you will write me if you get married again, for I would like to know the name of him who is fortunate enough to have you. Actually I ought to be a little annoyed with you, because many people wrote me from Vienna that you had said the worst possible things about me, but God bless you, I forgive you everything, for I know you said it in love. Do preserve your good name, I beg you, and think from time to time about your Haydn, who esteems you and loves you tenderly,

---

1 He was engaged on 8 September 1782, and remained there till the end of 1784. Bartha-Somfai 98, 101, 102, with correction in János Harich, 'Das Repertoire des Opernkapellmeisters Joseph Haydn' in *Haydn Yearbook*, I (1962), 45, 46f.

and will always be faithful to you. Write me, too, if you have seen and spoken with anyone who was formerly in Prince Esterházy's service. Good bye, my dear, that's all for this evening: it's late.

Today I went to see your dear sister, to ask her if she would be able to put up Pietro in her house. He will be received with the greatest pleasure; he can sleep there and have his meals there, too, since I always eat out and am invited out every day; but Pietro can come every day to me for his lessons – I live only a little way from your sister's. I give your sister a bit of money, because I am very sorry for her; she is not exactly poor, but she has to be very economical. I shall clothe your son well, and do everything for him. I don't want you to have any expense on his account; he shall have everything he needs. I shall certainly leave for Vienna in the middle of June, but I shall take the route *via* Holland, Leipzig and Berlin (in order to see the King of Prussia); my Petruccio will always be with me. I hope, however, that up to now he has been an obedient son to his dear mother, but if he hasn't been, I don't want him, and you must write me the truth. I don't want to have an ungrateful boy, for then I would be capable of sending him away at a moment's notice. Your sister embraces you and kisses you thousands and thousands of times. Write me often, dear Polzelli, and remember that I shall be always your faithful
Haydn.

My compliments to *Signor* Negri.

Dear Polzelli, *Signor* Hauder, who is Prince Esterhazy's Master of the Horse, and a rascal, wrote to me that you had sold his harpsichord. I cannot recall that you ever had any other harpsichord than mine. See how they torment me on your account! My wife, that devilish beast, wrote me so many things that I was forced to answer her that I would never go home the rest of my life; and from that moment she was much more sensible. Take good care of this letter.

[Address:]   Madame
   v [ON] LONDON Madame Aloise Polzelli née
        Moreschi.   Virtuosa di Musica
                   à
               Piacenza
     al Theatro
     di Piacenza   en Italiè.

[CCLN, 125–7]

The day that Haydn wrote to *la* Polzelli, the scandalous life of Mrs Billington appeared, and Haydn noted the fact in his notebook:

Today, 14th January 1792, the life of Madam Bilingthon [Billington] was published in print. Her life is exposed in the most shameless detail. The publisher is said to have gotten hold of her own letters, and to have offered to return them to her for 10 guineas; otherwise he intended to print them publicly. But she didn't want to spend the 10 guineas, and demanded her letters through the courts; she was refused, whereupon she appealed, but in vain; for even though her opponent offered her £500, he nevertheless issued this treasure of hers today, and you couldn't get a single copy after 3 o'clock in the afternoon.

It is said that her character is the worst sort, but that she is a great genius, and all the women hate her because she is so beautiful. N.B. She is said, however, to have written the most scandalous letters, containing accounts of her amours, to her mother. She is said to be an illegitimate child, and it's even believed that her own supposed father is involved in this affair.

Such stories are common in London. The husband provides opportunities for his wife so that he can profit from it, whereby he relieves his 'brother-in-law' of £1000 Sterling and more.   [CCLN, 255]

Meanwhile Haydn's new London Symphonies, Nos. 96 and 95, had been played at a big Viennese concert, probably Kees's Christmas Music. We know of the concert's existence through Haydn's letter to Frau von Genzinger of 17 January, and also through a report which mysteriously appeared in the London Press. Zinzendorf in Vienna attended the Kees concerts, but his reactions are no help to us (21 March 1792: 'Au concert de Kees, le P^ce Rosenberg me raproche de n'ete pas venu diner. Je vis le Baron Swieten . . .'). The *Public Advertiser* of 6 February 1792 notes:

HAYDN. At Vienna a Grand Concert has lately been given in honour of this favourite Composer, at which were present the Princes, the principal Nobility, and all the great masters and amateurs; two symphonies composed last winter, for Salomon's Concert were performed, at the end of each an eulogium, written in praise of this extraordinary genius was spoken. The whole was received with a thunder of applause. Mr. Haydn's picture illuminated, was exhibited in the Concert-room, and over the door of entrance were written in the German language,

'Profound Silence'.

The Viennese, at this time, were playing Haydn continually, even if notices of the events hardly got into the Austrian newspapers. On 9 January, for example, *Orlando Paladino* was given in German (*Ritter Roland*) at the Theater auf der Wieden, where Schikaneder was having the success of his career with Mozart's *Die Zauberflöte*.[1] Indeed, many more notices about Haydn were sent from London to the Continent than *vice versa*. On 16 January, the London correspondent of the *Journal des Luxus und der Moden* wrote back to Weimar:

London, 16th Jan. 1792.
Salomon's opposition concert is in the same house, namely Gallini's [at Hanover Square] and will take place on Fridays following [the Professional Concert]. Haydn wrote, too, 12 new pieces for it. Haydn is a man of excellent character, pleasant in society, and has not the least pride of his great musical accomplishments. Haydn was made Doctor of Music by the Faculty at Oxford.
[Vol. VII, 1792, p. 105]

It was already official, then, that Haydn had to keep up with Pleyel's design to offer a new piece of music at each Professional Concert. No wonder that Haydn complains, in his letter to Frau von Genzinger the next day, of his exhaustion:

[To Maria Anna von Genzinger, Vienna. *German*]
London, 17th January 1792.
Nobly born,
Kindest and most gracious Lady!
I ask your forgiveness a thousand times. I own and bemoan that I should not be so remiss in fulfilling my promise, but if Your Grace could only see how I am tormented, here in London, by having to attend all sorts of private concerts, which cause me great loss of time; and by the vast amount of work which has been heaped on my shoulders, you would, my gracious Lady, have the greatest pity on me. I never in my life wrote so much in one year as I have here during this past one, but now I am almost completely exhausted, and it will do me good to be able to rest a little when I return home. At present I am working for Salomon's concerts, and I am making every effort to do my best, because our rivals, the Professional Concert, have had my pupil Pleyel from Strassburg come here to conduct their

1 Pohl III, 62. The translation was by F. X. Giržik (Gierschek).

concerts. So now a bloody harmonious war will commence between master and pupil. The newspapers are all full of it, but it seems to me that there will soon be an armistice, because my reputation is so firmly established here. Pleyel behaved so modestly towards me upon his arrival that he won my affection again. We are very often together, and this does him credit, for he knows how to appreciate his father. We shall share our laurels equally and each go home satisfied.

On the 14th inst., the Professional Concert met with a great misfortune, inasmuch as the new theatre, built only last year – it is called The Pantheon – burned down at 2 o'clock in the morning. The fire was started deliberately. The damage is estimated at more than £100,000 Sterling. So at the moment there is no Italian theatre in London. Now, my angelic[1] and gracious lady, I am going to upbraid you a little, too. How often have I repeated my request that you send me by mail the Symphony in E flat, of which I once sent you the *incipit*, copied on small-sized paper for mailing. I have sighed for it a long time now, and if I don't get it by the end of next month I shall lose 20 guiness. The copy which Herr von Keess has made for me may not arrive in London for 3 [months], or 3 years, because it may be that long before a courier is dispatched. I also asked Herr Von Keess in the enclosed letter to take the responsibility for the whole matter, and if he couldn't, I ventured to transfer the commission once more to Your Grace, because I flattered myself that you would certainly fulfil my urgent request. I further asked Herr von Keess to repay to Your Grace the money expended on his behalf, in order that you have no expenses. Now, kindest and best Frau von Gennzinger, I beg you once more to see to this matter, for you will be rendering me the greatest possible service: I shall explain the reason for all this when we meet, when I shall respectfully kiss your fair hands a thousand times, and repay my debt with gratitude. The celebration you describe in honour of my modest talents touched me very much; but not quite as much as if Your Grace had been completely satisfied by it. Perhaps I can supply this imperfection by another Symphony which I shall be sending Your Grace shortly; I say perhaps, because I, or rather my brain, is indeed exhausted. Providence alone supplies that which my waning powers cannot. I pray to Him daily, for without His assistance I should be a poor creature indeed! And now, my unique and gracious lady, I trust and pray for your indulgence. Oh yes! I can see you quite clearly in front of me, and I can hear you say: 'Well, this time I shall forgive you, you wretched Haydn, but – but!' No, no, henceforth I shall perform my duties far better. I must close now, by saying that as always I hold you in the greatest possible esteem, and shall ever be

> My most gracious Frau von Gennzinger's
> most obedient servant,
> Joseph Haydn.

My respectful compliments to your
husband and all the others.
Please forgive the fact that I always take
the liberty of enclosing the letters to Keess,
but I don't have his address.

[CCLN, 128f.]

On 27 January 1792, the *Oracle* printed the following notice:

HAYDN, though in instrumental composition so *various* and *original*, has yet but slender merit as a Writer for the *Voice*. He once wrote, however, an *Opera* at Vienna, and the late EMPEROR would not hear of its being performed.

1 'Englische', a play on words: 'English' and ''angelic' (= 'englische', as for example in 'der Englische Gruß').

This is a journalistic summary of what happened when Haydn was commissioned by the Court Opera to do *La vera costanza* and which the composer withdrew when he saw that the parts were going to be given to inferior singers (Griesinger, 35). Dies (59f.) says that thereupon Haydn took the problem to his monarch.

'Emperor Joseph saw Haydn's rights in the matter and attempted to intervene, but found unbelievable opposition, so that Haydn declared he would rather not have his opera performed than have to fight against the cabals any longer. Haydn concluded the conversation today with these words: 'I did not give the opera, travelled to my Prince and told him the whole development. The Prince did not criticize my behaviour, but had the opera performed at Eszterháza in 1779.'

The truth of the matter is that the Italian composers in Vienna, and particularly Antonio Salieri, were frightful intriguers: one only need recall Da Ponte's description of his life in Vienna at the time of *Figaro*. Moreover, Joseph II had scant understanding for Austrian music, and Leopold II, now the Emperor, even less. The Austrian public always crept back to the really popular Italian operas, so much easier to understand than Mozart's complicated and sophisticated scores, with their rich woodwind writing. On 7 February 1792, Domenico Cimarosa sat at the harpsichord in Vienna, conducting his new opera, *Il matrimonio segreto*. The opera was an enormous success, much greater than anything Mozart had enjoyed except, possibly, for *Die Zauberflöte*. Certainly Mozart's Italian operas had, particularly in the case of *Figaro*, flaunted political ideas which did not escape astute Austrians: we shall elaborate on this point at another place in our Haydn biography. At any rate, *Il matrimonio segreto* was now the toast of the town, and, what was more important, of the Court. No more 'porcheria tedesca', as the Empress had called *La clemenza di Tito* a few months earlier. Here was good, straightforward Italian opera and none of that over-scored wind writing, either.[1]

The Viennese succumbed completely to Cimarosa. They were to succumb once again, in the years after the Vienna Congress, to Rossini, which caused Beethoven's supporters much anguish. The Viennese were accused of being fickle, of deserting true German music; yet this is understandable, for Beethoven's (and Mozart's and Haydn's) music was dense, often opaque, usually genuinely original. And on the other hand, not only Salieri and Cimarosa, but even more the work of Rossini is the essence of music itself. Beethoven was not being cynical when he said, in 1824, 'Rossini is a talented and a melodious composer; his music suits the frivolous and sensuous spirit of the times, and his productivity is so great that he needs only as many weeks as the Germans need years to write an opera.'[2]

The Italians were to reconquer Europe later with Bellini, Donizetti and lastly with Verdi. All the German textbooks denigrating this music as shallow, facile and vacuous

1 Zinzendorf was at the première (7 February): '. . . Au Spectacle. Il matrimonio secreto nouvel opera de Cimarosa qui etoit lui même au Clavescin et que l'on fait sortir. Joli jeu de la Tomeoni. . . .' On 14 February he again noted 'Belle musique'. 17 March: 'Diné chez l'ambassadeur de Naples avec le grand chamberlain, Pellegrini, le Me Ghiselieri, Casti, Edling, Cimarosa, Sbarra, et Gaspard Mollo [the music publisher], de Duchi di Lusciano, Improvisateur dans un autre genre que Ghiselieri, Poete et musicien, fesant de donner complets et improvisant lentement. . . . Puis il chanta, au clavescin de Cimarosa un morceau de poesi, qu'il a improvisé au partant de minuet et dont il a fait la musique avec une expression superbe.' On 26 May they launched another Cimarosa opera, *Il pittor Parigino*. 'Il est long, la musique de Cimarosa charmante.' Meanwhile Cimarosa was a fêted member of Viennese society, dining out and playing 'au clavescin'. Count Zinzendorf, who never really liked any Mozart opera completely except, interestingly enough, *Così fan tutte*, always had a good word for *Il matrimonio segreto*; he went to a performance on 21 April 1794 and wrote afterwards, 'Cet opera qui m'a toujours plût.'
2 *Thayer's Life of Beethoven*, revised and edited by Elliot Forbes, Princeton, 1967, Vol. II, p. 804.

never really prevented the German, and especially the Austrian audiences from momentarily forgetting the stern music of Sterling German Composers for the delights of music imported from south of the Alps.

The never-ending fight between the German composers and their witty, sarcastic and intriguing Italian colleagues occasioned much comment towards the end of January 1793 in the British Press:

MUSICAL CARICATURE
in
PRIVATE CIRCULATION.

This admirable piece of humour, which is now handing about in the Musical Circles, is a lampoon on the taste which the Germans have introduced, for trick, artifice, surprize, and difficulty, instead of simplicity and nature. The idea is exemplified by a contrast between the German and Italian style of composition. It is entitled, 'Deux Trios en different style, par un Amateur d'Amsterdamme.'

The one has all the perplexity of the modern German; the other all the tenderness of the Italian. It is just possible for a dexterous Musician to play the one, and every body may play the other.

But that which makes the whimsical satire most captivating, is the *Vignette* in the title. A balance and scales are held by the Deity – In the one scale are the simple notes – in the other a vast number of notes covered with flowers. – The three simple notes weigh down the multitude, while, from the sky, Beams of Genius illuminate them, and below a Band of Loves accompany on the violin, the flute, *etc.* in a gay landscape, where doves coo, and lambkins gambol. The other scale is enveloped in gloom, while under it a band of German figures, with immense hats, are bursting their cheeks in blowing the bassoon, the horn, *etc.* – a peacock is singing on a tree – a bear beats time, and there is a full chorus of frogs.

We are not displeased to see this piece of humour; for it must be granted, that the Germans have seen riot in their *instrumentalities*. We wish, however, that the Italians, with all their sacred regard to simplicity, would, now and then, merely for the sake of their characters, indulge in a little novelty. Their melodies would not be worse for being original; and it would very much heighten the charm if their airs occasionally were made unlike one another.

We suspect the author of this piece of genuine satire to be that wicked wit GIARDINI; we have no information, however, on which to ground this conjecture.

[*Morning Chronicle*, 31 January][1]

MUSIC.
'Strange that such discords there should be
Twixt tweedledum and tweedledee.'

The musical rage which has produced such zealous and active contention between rival concerts, is further inflamed by ungenerous animosities, personal and degrading. We lament to see them daily jarring into harsh invectives; so that the science which more than any other is the soother and softener of life, is made to irritate and disturb its feelings. The bitterness of faction is introduced into the scene devoted to harmony, and the soul is agitated by party where it ought to be moved only by the concord of sweet sounds.

1 Dies. (113) tells us of an answer to this satire, made by an organist of the Royal German chapel, who had the following scene engraved in copper: '. . . The best known German composers were placed in a sun, and in its surrounding rays. J. S. Bach stands in the centre; nearest to him, in a circle, are Handel, Graun and Haydn. In each of the farthest rays of the sun, there is to be read the name of a German composer. Under the sun there is an Italian owl, shrinking away from the light of the sun; on the side, however, an Italian capon faces a German cock in antagonistic pose. It is true that Haydn saw this page, and was very satisfied with the place accorded him on it.'

We happily and honourably for our opulence if not for our taste, enjoy for the present season, not only the most sublime and fascinating composers of the world, but the finest performers. There is room enough for them all – for Haydn as well as for Pleyel – for the Professional as well as for Salomon's band; for the Opera in the Little Theatre [the Pantheon had just burned down] as well as the Pasticcio of Chevalier Gallini. But let not our sympathies be wounded by little wretched squabbles. No man whose emotions have been roused by the magic of HAYDN will suffer calumnies to pass on the 'god of their idolatry'; – or if we are to have war, let us have war with wit in it. If it were confined to a sportive display of talents no one would be angry, however keen the conflict. Who for instance could seriously be angry at the exquisite couple of Trios by a Dutch amateur, – Even HAYDN, the Shakespeare of Music, must himself confess that the severity of that satire is as much recommended by its truth as its whim.

[*Morning Chronicle*, 31 January]

It was all very well for the courteous and civilized *Morning Chronicle* to suggest 'war with wit in it', but such a concept would hardly have appealed to the enraged Giardini, who really was the author of the anti-German Trios. Dies (113) tells us: 'There was, you see, a strong counter-party in London, mostly Italians, the *spiritus rector* of which was our old acquaintance Giardini. Giardini sought to make Haydn's music ridiculous, and to this end he printed two Trios . . .', etc., continuing with a description of the 'Deux Trios'.

The following announcement on the last day of January 1792 in the *Morning Chronicle*, where (as noted above) Haydn's name also appeared in another context, is the first public indication that Haydn was working on arranging Scottish Songs. Thereby hangs a tale:

HAYDN.

Nothing, perhaps, can be a stronger instance of the superior genius of this great master than the facility with which he seized the wild, but natural and affecting beauties of the Scots airs now in great forwardness for publication, the taste with which he has entered into their genuine spirit, and the felicity of adaptation, with which he has harmonized, as if the original composers had possessed science enough to add the charm of harmony to their own melodies.

This work will be a striking and lasting proof of how little the merit of HAYDN was confined to inventing, or conquering instrumental difficulties.

[*Morning Chronicle*, 31 January; *Public Advertiser*, 1 February]

Sometime in 1791, Haydn's attention had been drawn to the music publisher, William Napier, who had a numerous family and was in serious financial straits. On 27 May 1791, the *Morning Chronicle* had carried a bankruptcy notice about Napier in which the creditors 'may receive a Dividend of Two Shillings in the Pound, on their respective debts'. Possibly at this point, Haydn stepped in. Dies (158) has one version.

Haydn told me that he had set *50 Scotch songs* to music for the publisher L–. The man was so poor that he could not afford to pay Haydn for them, so Haydn, knowing him to be a worthy fellow, gave him the music as a present. L– published the songs and had such success with them that he found his state suddenly transferred from one of penury to one of comfort.

Griesinger's version (32):

Nepire, an English music-dealer, had twelve children, and was in danger of being arrested for debt. Haydn set for him a full hundred Scottish songs in the modern style, with accompaniments for a bass and a violin, often with the addition of ritornels, etc. These songs sold so well that Nepire was rescued from his pecuniary embarrassments and instead of the 50 guineas which he had paid Haydn for the first instalment, later paid him twice as much for a second.

Messrs. Hopkinson and Oldman, from whose article[1] this information is culled, point out that in the announcement of 3 September 1791 in the *Morning Chronicle* the new volume is mentioned but not Haydn's share in it (though it was said to be 'already in great forwardness'). On 3 November the same journal carries the note:

W. Napier is happy to announce to the subscribers to the Second Volume of the Scots Songs, that the work is now in considerable forwardness; and being anxious to render it worthy of National Patronage, the whole of the Harmony to the Original Melodies will be supplied by Mr Haydn, who has already composed the greatest part of it. Is it permissible, [go on Messrs. Hopkinson and Oldman] to conjecture that Haydn was at first reluctant to have his share in the work made known, but that he afterwards realized that concealment would seriously detract from the value of his gift?

Publication dragged on, however, and it was not until the following 24 May 1792 that the *Morning Chronicle* announced its publication on 1 June. Although there were only 396 subscribers against 484 for the first volume, it would seem that Napier did enjoy something of a success, for traces of a second edition exist. Just before Haydn left England for the last time in 1795, Napier published some more Scottish Songs in Haydn's setting (see 21 July 1795, *infra*).

Although Haydn dined out a great deal, he was interested in prices of everything, including food:

Every canal-lock costs £10,000. [CCLN, 258]
In the month of January 1792, a roasting chicken cost 7 shillings, a turkey 9 shillings, a dozen larks 1 crown. N.B.: a duck, if it is plucked, costs 5 shillings.
[CCLN, 269]

The famous Symphony No. 91 arrived in Brussels, where it got stuck for some obscure reasons known only to the European postal system. Maria Anna von Genzinger had meanwhile organized the copying and shipping to Haydn of his Fantasia in C and the piano Trio in A flat. As far as the *postscriptum* is concerned, Haydn had noted, at the beginning of his First London Notebook, various things for his Viennese landlord, Herr Hamburger, and for other Viennese friends:

[*German.*]

Knitting needle[s], scissors and a little knife for Frau von Keess. For Biswanger, spectacles for someone between 50 and 60 years of age.
For Hamburger, nail-scissors and a larger pair.
A woman's watch chain.
For Frau von Gennzinger, various things.   [CCLN, 251]

[To Maria Anna von Genzinger, Vienna. *German*]

London, 2nd February 1792.
Nobly born,
Most esteemed Frau von Gennzinger!
      Today, 1st [!] February, I received your kind letter together with the Fantasia and the Sonata *a tre*. But I was rather saddened, on opening the parcel, because I

1 'Haydn's Settings of Scottish Songs in the Collections of Napier and Whyte' in: *Edinburgh Bibliographical Society Transactions*, Vol. III, Part 2, Edinburgh 1954, pp. 87ff.

had hoped and believed that the Symphony in E flat for which I have so long and patiently waited would be included. Gracious lady! I beg you urgently to have it copied at once on small-sized paper for mailing and then to send it to me immediately; I shall be only too happy to pay for all the expenses incurred, for God only knows when the Symphonies will arrive here from Brussels. I cannot dispense with this work without great loss. Please forgive me, kindest and most gracious lady, for bothering you so often with this matter; I shall appreciate it very much. I am so burdened with work at present that I simply cannot write to Herr von Keess, and therefore I beg you to apply to him for the said Symphony, and to present my respectful compliments to him. Meanwhile I remain, with kind respects,

> Your Grace's
> most obedient servant,
> [no signature.]

My respects to your husband, the
dear children, and von Kreubich.
Your Grace shall receive a good portion
of the sewing needles.

[Address:]

> Madame
> Madame Anna Noble de
> Gennzinger *née* noble de Kayser
> a
> im Schotten Hof auf
> der Haupt Stiege.
> Vienne
> en autriche.

[CCLN, 129f.]

On the evening of 2 February, there was a benefit concert of the popular composer, Ignazio Raimondi, who was now living in London (he was a year younger than Haydn). The next day, the *Morning Herald* reports on the concert:

HANOVER-SQUARE ROOMS.

Mr. RAIMONDI's Benefit Concert of last night, if not extremely numerous, was at least very scientifically attended, hardly a name of eminence in the world of music being absent. We particularly, and with pleasure, remarked the two great heroes of the ensuing musical campaign, we mean Messrs. HAYDN and PLEYEL, sitting together all the evening, not as contending rivals, but Chiefs associating in the same pursuit.[1]

The celebrated Battle piece of Mr. RAIMONDI, went off with its usual applause, and is an eminent instance of the power of imitation in instrumental music . . . . Madame de' MARIGNY's [Musigny?] Pedal Har[p] was heard for the first time in these Rooms; and if we say that it was heard with interest, even by those who have been accustomed to the exquisite touch of KRUMPHOLTZ, it will be thought sufficient praise.

Salomon announced his series and saw that it was frequently reprinted in a variety of London newspapers:

---

1 There is a copy of this extraordinary piece in the British Museum, g. 161. c. (10.), arranged for piano by Raimondi and with his signature. Can this piece have been the inspiration for the 'Military Symphony'? Haydn, when he heard the Passau arrangement of *The Seven Words* for vocal forces thought he could have written the vocal parts better' Perhaps he thought he could do a battle symphony better, too . . . .

Mr. SALOMON'S CONCERT
HANOVER-SQUARE.

MR. SALOMON most respectfully acquaints the Noblity and Gentry, that his Concert will open on Friday, the 17th instant, and continuing on the succeeding Friday, upon the same grand scale as last year.

Dr. Haydn, who is engaged for the whole Season, will give every night a New Piece of his Composition, and direct the Performance of it at the Piano Forte.

The principal vocal Performers already engaged are, SIGNOR SIMONI, (being his first appearance in England,)

And SIGNOR ALBERT TARELLI [*sic*], MISS CORRI, And MADAME MARA, (who is to return by the middle of March;) Besides other distinguished vocal Performers, who will be introduced in the course of the season.

Principal Instrumental Performers, who will alternately perform Solo Concertos and Concertantes, on their respective Instruments, are, – Violin, Messrs. Salomon and Janievicz – Violoncello, Messrs. Menel, Shram, and Damer [*sic*] – Piano Forte, Messrs. Dussec and Haessler – Oboe, Mr. Harrington – Flute, Messrs. Graeff and Ash[e] – Clarinet, Mr. Hartman – Bassoon, Mr. Holmes – And Pedal Harp, Mesdames Krumpholtz and Delaval.

Subscriptions at Five Guineas for the Twelve Nights are received, and Tickets delivered at Messrs. Lockhart's, Bankers, No. 36, Pall-mall. Tickets transferable, as usual, Ladies to Ladies, and Gentlemen to Gentlemen.

The Ladies' Tickets are red, and Gentlemen's blue.

[*Oracle*, 13, 25, 29 January and 2 February; *Morning Herald*, 2, 4, 9 February; *Morning Chronicle*, 5 January, 2, 4, 10, 13, 15 February; etc.]

The Professional Concert had announced their series, too, and the newspapers continued to discuss the relative merits of Haydn and his erstwhile pupil. On 4 February, the *Oracle* writes:

. . . PLEYEL has, in addition to Fame so worthily won, composed some charming thoughts for the PROFESSIONAL – How they executed, he had no conception, till he heard a *Practice* [*i. e.* rehearsal].

HAYDN '*Princeps Cujus Scientiae*' has also written for SOLOMONS [*sic*], what will never be surpassed, if it be ever equalled . . . .

'On 8th Feb. 1792, the first Ancient Concert took place', says Haydn's notebook, and he left space for the programme, which he never filled in (CCLN, 259). The next day Adalbert Gyrowetz gave his benefit concert, shortly after which he left England, finding that the climate did not agree with him. The programme included an overture, two symphonies and a 'Concertante' for violin, viola and 'cello (Salomon, Hindmarsh, Menel), all by Gyrowetz. Salomon was the leader of the orchestra. Lazzarini and Mrs Billington from the opera sang, and the famous violinist, Felix Yaniewicz, made his first appearance in London. Yaniewicz (Janiewicz), a Pole who had gone to Vienna in the mid-1780s and had made arrangements to study with Haydn, changed his plans when a Polish princess offered to take him to Italy. From there he went to Paris and later to London, which he found much to his liking, settling in England and marrying a Liverpool girl; he died at Edinburgh. Yaniewicz was also a capable composer and a good conductor.

Life was beginning to be very hectic for Haydn, and Rebecca Schroeter was alarmed that he was getting too tired:

Wednesday Feb: 8th 792.

M:D: Inclos'd I have sent you the words of the Song you desired. I wish much to know, HOW YOU DO to day, I am very sorry to lose the pleasure of seeing you this morning, but I hope you will have time to come to morrow. I beg my D: you will take great care of your health, and do not fatigue yourself with to[o] much application to bussiness. My thoughts and best wishes are always with you, and I ever am with the utmost Sincerity M:D your F: et[c].[1]   [CCLN, 279]

The first Professional Concert was announced for 13 February:

PROFESSIONAL CONCERT, HANOVER-SQUARE.

The Committee respectfully acquaint the Subscribers, that the FIRST CONCERT will be on Monday next, February the 13th.

ACT I.
Overture – HAYDN.
Song – Signor LAZZARINI.
Concert Violin – Mr. CRAMER.
Song – Mrs. BILLINGTON.
Grand Symphony, composed for the occasion, Mr. PLEYEL.

ACT II.
Concerto Violoncello – Mr. LINDLEY.
Song – Signora NEGRI.
Concerto French Harp – Madame MUSEGNY [*sic*].
Duetto – Signor LAZZARINI and Mrs. BILLINGTON.
Symphony MOZART.

[etc.]
[*Morning Herald*, 9, 10, 13 February;
Oracle, 7–11, 13 February; etc.]

Haydn was given a complimentary ticket for the whole series, as in the 1791 season. The *Morning Herald* on 14 February noted:

HANOVER-SQUARE.

The PROFESSIONAL CONCERT opened last night with its usual *eclat*, and had such a brilliant train of Subscribers as occupied the Room.

The first Piece was an Overture [i.e. Symphony] of HAYDN, performed with admirable correctness. LAZZARINA [*sic*] sung his favourite air from the Opera of ARMIDA. CRAMER's Violin Concerto exhibited such merit as may enable him to withstand any novelty that may appear against him.

Mrs. BILLINGTON gave the beautiful Air of GYROWITZ [*sic*], which she sung at the benefit of that Composer. The first Act concluded with a very fine Overture composed on purpose for this Concert, by PLEYEL; it abounded with beautiful passages, and was elegant, interesting, and scientific . . . . The PRINCE of WALES came very early in the evening, and seemed highly gratified by the exertions of this admirable band.

On 13 February 1792, there appeared perhaps the most famous and widely copied portrait of Haydn: Thomas Hardy's engraving after his own original portrait in oils. At that time it was owned by John Bland, the music publisher with whom Haydn was on friendly terms; today, the painting hangs in the Royal College of Music. If the engraving misses something of the rather cool, stern-jawed character of the painting and softens the whole in the process of transference, the engraving is technically very

---

1 Abbreviations: 'F.' = Faithful; 'M:D.' = My Dear; 'D.' = Dear.

well done and what the Germans call a 'characteristic' likeness. It was very often copied by Continental engravers. In his notebook, Haydn noted that Hardy, Ott, Guttenbrunn and Hoppner 'painted my portrait' (CCLN, 276), 'Daßie' modelled it in wax. The Guttenbrunn exists in two versions, one owned by Ing. Wolfgang von Karajan in Salzburg (colour reproduction in Landon, *Essays*, 1970) and one owned by Mrs Eva Alberman in London (black-and-white reproduction in Somfai, p. 125): Schiavonetti brought out an engraving (dated London, 1792) based on the Guttenbrunn painting.

Guttenbrunn's name is encountered frequently in the newspapers. On 24 April 1794, the *Morning Herald* carries an advertisement that Guttenbrunn's 'Exhibition of Ancient and Modern Pictures, No. 4 Little Maddx-street four doors down from New Bond-street, is now open every day . . .'. Among the portraits is that of 'the late Queen of France taken from life in the year 1789'. Guttenbrunn, after having worked at Eszterháza in the early 1770s, was sent by Prince Esterházy to Italy; Guttenbrunn's self-portrait, charmingly executed, is in the Uffizi Gallery, Florence (at present in the gallery to the Pitti Palace that runs over the Ponte Vecchio). When Haydn arrived in England, he found Guttenbrunn already established in London.

The wax medallion ('Daßie') is by the well-known Scottish artist, James Tassie (1735–1799); as often, Haydn has in Austrian fashion mixed up 'T' and 'D'. Tassie's portrait of Haydn has not yet been identified, but the artist's work may be seen in many British and American galleries (see Thieme-Becker vol. 32, p. 457; add to the list of galleries the Atheneum, Hartford, Conn.).

Salomon's opening concert took place on 17 February, and we can identify the new Symphony by this entry in Haydn's notebook: 'In the 1st concert, the Adagio of the new Symphony in D was encored' (CCLN, 276, corrected; see Bartha, 512f.), which can only mean No. 93:

First Concert: 17 February 1792

Mr. SALOMON'S CONCERT.
HANOVER SQUARE.

Mr. SALOMON most respectfully acquaints the Nobility and Gentry, that his first Concert will be on Friday next, the 17th instant.

PART I.
Overture, Pleyel.
Song, Mr. Nield.
Concert Oboe, Mr. Harrington.
Song, Signor Calcagni, (being his first appearance in this County.)
Concert Pedal Harp, Madame Delaval.
Song, Miss Corri.

PART II.
New Grand Overture [M. S.], Haydn.
Song, Signor Calcagni.
Concerto Violin, Mr. Janieviez.
Duetto, Miss Corri, and Mr. Nield.
Finale, Gyrowetz.
The doors to be opened at Seven . . . .

[*Oracle*, 15 February; *Morning Chronicle*, 16 February; *Morning Herald*, 15, 16, 17 February; etc.]

Three criticisms from London newspapers show to what a state of excitement the British public had been raised by all this 'harmonious war':

SALOMON's CONCERT

The first Subscription Concert took place last Friday, at Hanover Square.

The established musical judges present all agreed that it went off with surprising effect and rigid exactness. No Band in the world can go better.

A new Overture from the pen of the incomparable *Haydn*, formed one considerable branch of this stupendous musical tree.

Such a combination of excellence was contained in every movement, as inspired all the performers as well as the audience with enthusiastic ardour.

Novelty of idea, agreeable caprice, and whim combined with all *Haydn's* sublime and wonten grandeur, gave additional consequence to the *soul* and feelings of every individual present.

The Critic's eye brightened with additional lustre – then was the moment that the great Painter might have caught – that, which cannot be thrown on the human frame, but on such rare and great occasions.

Calcagni, the *sweet Soprano* just arrived was warmly received, and pronounced to be excellent, particularly in the low notes of his *dulcet* pipe. – His stile is elegant and chaste, joined to a very agreeable figure.

Nield, who is *Harrison's* elegant walk, was remarkably interesting in an air of *Bach's.* – The tones were perfectly flowing and thoroughly in tune.

Miss *Corri* came forward with all the charms and fascination that a most melodious volume of voice, great judgement, and elegant manner and person can give.

Madam *Delaval* struck out with her '*flying fingers*', such effects from the Harp, as confirming all the Poets insist on of the Antients [*sic*] performance on that noble and sublime instrument.

The great Violinist, *Yanievicz*, next demands our highest praise, who wrapt us all in Elysium throughout his whole Concerto; he possesses in a superlative degree a firm real tone, a bow arm capable of giving effect to the wonderful execution that he interlards in his beautiful airs of simplicity and wildness. The *Adagio* gave high pleasure to all the *Cognoscenti*, and the Rondo let all the Ladies on the tip-toe of musical motion – His popularity will be very high no doubt.

The duet between Miss *Corri* and *Nield*, was *duo in uno* – a happy combination of sweetness and skill.

The Orchestra under the direction of SALOMON [*sic*], produced an effect, that may with propriety be said, was A SOUL AND BODY OF HARMONY.

[*The Times*, 20 February]

HANOVER SQUARE

Mr. SALOMON's Concert opened for the season last night to a very elegant audience. The want of room will not permit us to do justice to the excellence of this Concert, which was indeed admirable.

The novelty was, Signor CALCAGNI, first Soprano to the King of Sweden. His voice is full and well toned, and of vast compass. – JANIEICZ [*sic*] played a Concerto on the Violin with such power of execution as astonished the connoisseurs.

The new grand Overture of HAYDN was a composition of very extraordinary merit; and proved that his genius, active as it has been, is as vigorous and fertile as ever. [*Morning Herald*, 18 February]

HANOVER SQUARE

The Concert under the firm of HAYDN and SALOMON commenced for the season last night, before a very brilliance auditory, and was such as might be expected from the union of talents so distinguished. We have not room to expatiate on the merits of this agreeable treat, but it would be highly improper to pass over the excellence of HAYDN's new Concerto [i.e. Symphony], which exhibited all the fire of his bold imagination, and which in the opinion of every musical critic, was a composition at once grand, scientific, charming and original . . . .

Miss CORRI is an improving singer, and only wants a little animation. The other performances merit more praise than we have now an opportunity for allotting. [*Diary ; or, Woodfall's Register*, 18 February]

The following note occurs in Haydn's notebook:

Lord Clermont [Claremont] once gave a large *Soupé*, and when the King's health was drunk, he ordered the wind band to play the well-known song, 'God save the King' in the street during a wild snowstorm. This occurred on 19th Feby 1792, so madly do they drink in England. [CCLN, 276]

The second concert of the Professionals –

PROFESSIONAL CONCERT, HANOVER-SQUARE.

The Committee respectfully acquaint the Subscribers, that the SECOND CONCERT, will be on MONDAY next, the 20th instant.

PART FIRST.
Overture – HAYDN.
Song – Signor LAZZARINI.
New Quartetto, M. S. – PLEYEL.
Song – Mrs. BILLINGTON,
Accompanied by Mr. CRAMER.
New Grand Overture, M. S. – PLEYEL.
PART SECOND.
Concertante for a Clarinet and Bassoon by
Messrs. MAHON and PARKINSON.
Song – Signora NEGRI.
Concerto Violoncello (by particular desire) Mr. LINDLEY.
Terzetto, by Signora LAZZARINI, Signora NEGRI, and
Mrs. BILLINGTON. – – GUGLIEMI.
FULL PIECE.
[etc.]
[*Morning Herald*, 17, 18, 20 February; etc.]

was reviewed in the *Morning Herald* on the 22nd as follows:

Want of room prevented our noticing yesterday the last performance of the PROFESSIONAL CONCERT, on Monday evening, which was indeed highly entitled to a critical praise.

The new compositions were a very fine overture, and a quartetto of PLEYEL, which were warmly applauded. There is certainly much general resemblance in the music of PLEYEL, to the style of HAYDN; but this was to be expected, as the former received his musical education under the latter, and holds his master in laudable reverence.

The Concerto on the Violoncello, by young LIN[D]LEY, was repeated, and so much admired, that the Committee here thought [it] proper to retain him for the season . . . . The room was so well attended, as to shew that 'music has charms to soothe' the rigours of WINTER, with all his present repulsive severity.

At the Second Concert given by Haydn and Salomon, the latest Symphony, No. 93, was repeated, and the new work of the evening was Haydn's *Madrigal* 'The Storm', partly written, no doubt, to silence all the loose talk in the newspapers that Haydn could not write for the voice. The text was by the well-known British author, John Wolcot, who wrote under the pseudonym Peter Pindar.

Second Concert: 24 February 1792

Mr. SALOMON'S CONCERT
HANOVER-SQUARE

Mr. SALOMON most respectfully acquaints the Nobility and Gentry, that the Second Performance will be on FRIDAY next, the 24th instant,

PART I.

Overture, CLEMENTI. – Song, Miss POOL[E].
New Quartetto M. S. for Two Violins,
Tenor and Bass, Messrs. SALOMON, DAMER [*sic*], HINDMARSH,
and MENEL. – Gyrowetz.
Song, Mr. NIELD.
(with an Accompaniment of a Bassoon Obligato, by Mr. HOLMES.)
Concerto, German Flute, Mr. ASH[E].
(Being his first appearance in London.)

PART II.

The new Grand Overture M. S. HAYDN.
(as performed last Friday.)
Song, Miss CORRI.
New Concerto Pedal Harp, Madame KRUMPHOLTZ –
Dusseck.
Song, Signor CALIAGNI [*sic*].
THE STORM.
A new Quartetto, composed by HAYDN, for four voices, and
a Full Band.
Sung, by Miss CORRI, Miss POOL[E], Messrs NIELD, and
BELLAMY.
(The words by an eminent English Author.)
FINALE. [etc.]

[*Morning Herald*, 22, 24 February; *Morning Chronicle*, 22, 24 February;
Oracle, 22, 24 February; *Public Advertiser*, 23 February; etc.]

No less than four daily newspapers now 'covered' the concert, in which (wrote Haydn in his notebook, CCLN 276) 'the first All[egro] and the Adagio of the . . . Symphony were repeated':

SALOMON'S CONCERT.

The second Concert was exceedingly spirited, and by the Overture of the matchless HAYDN, was distinguished above all common competition. It was original, various, and interesting, – and was received with the most marked applause. – And in addition to this, he gave a very wonderful composition from the following words, in which he combined the strongest effects of his art, horror and pity: –

Hark! the wild uproar of the winds, and hark,
Hell's Genius roams the regions of the dark;
    And thund'ring swells the horrors of the main.
From cloud to cloud the moon affrighted flies,
Now darken'd and now flashing through the skies –
Alas! bless'd calm, return, return again.

[*Morning Herald*, 25 February]

HANOVER-SQUARE.

The report of SALOMON's Second Concert last night is briefly an admirable musical treat, and a very numerous and brilliant audience. The instrumental excellence was chiefly a beautiful Quartetto of GYROWETZ; the new grand Overture of HAYDN, and a new Chorus and Quartetto by the same excellent composer.

Mr. Ashe appeared for the first time, and performed a Concerto on the Flute in such a style, as places him on a rank with any of his competitors. Madame KRUMPHOLTZ being ill, a Harp Concerto was played by Madame DELAVAL. Miss CORRI, Mr. NIELD, and Signor CALCAGNI, were the vocal performers, and they all received a flattering portion of applause.

The new Chorus and Quartetto of HAYDN is the first attempt of that great Master on English words, and he has succeeded admirably in representative harmony – his *storm* and *calm* being wonderfully expressed in the composition he has adapted to the following words, which are ascribed to PETER PINDAR . . . [here the text follows]. [*Morning Herald*, 25 February]

MUSICALS.

The second Subscription Concert, under the direction of SALOMON, took place last night at the Hanover Square Rooms, and had a large and splendid auditory.

The prominent excellence in the point of composition, was a charming quartetto of GYROWITZ [*sic*], a new grand overture of HAYDN, which was performed at the last concert, and a new piece entitled THE STORM, composed also by HAYDN. This piece is an exquisite specimen of imitative harmony, adapted to English words; the horrors of a tempest, contrasted with the gradual serenity of a calm, were finely represented, and highly admired . . . .

[*Diary; or, Woodfall's Register*, 25 February]

SALOMON'S CONCERT.

This admirable Concert is a display usually of all the collective Genius in the Country. – Last night its captivations were so numerous, that to particularise them in the present crouded [*sic*] state of the Oracle, is impossible.

HAYDN, of whose wonderful powers rapture alone should be permitted to speak, gave his grand OVERTURE, M. S., himself presiding at the Harpsichord. – We have no hesitation to say, that, for the most powerful effects of the Science, no one of his compositions can compare with it.

His *Storm*, a quartetto accompanied, had a great deal of imitative merit about it – the Performance was perfect; the words were Dr. WALCOTT's [i. e. Wolcot].

Ash[e] is a fine clear flute, of equal execution and taste.

Miss CORRI's *Sposa Amata* had a sweet sensibility and charming style to distinguish the Singer, who was loudly applauded and certainly with sincerest justice.

A very fashionable attendance distinguished the Rooms; and the general effect gave the most entire satisfaction. [*Oracle*, 25 February]

On this same evening, a London music-lover could have also attended (1) Handel's *Redemption* [*sic*] in the Haymarket Theatre and (2) Handel's *L'allegro* at Covent Garden (Pohl III, 46) – good, strong competition which does not, however, seem to have bothered Haydn or Salomon at all.

Andrew Ashe, the flautist who made his début under Haydn, will often appear in this Chronicle: it was he who claimed to have invented the name 'Surprise' for Symphony No. 94 (*vide infra*, 23 March, p. 149).

A few days later, Haydn took the time to write a note to Dussek's father, Johann Joseph, in Czaslau (Bohemia):

My dear Friend!
 I thank you with all my heart that you also remembered me in your last letter to your son. I return the compliment with interest, and consider myself fortunate to be able to assure you that you have, in your son, a most honourable and polished man who is a distinguished musician.
 I love him just as dearly as I do you, and he well deserves it. If you give him a father's blessing, he will continue to be happy, which – because of his great talents – I heartily wish him to be.
 With every respect, I am

Your most sincere friend,
Joseph Haydn.

London, 26th February 1792.

[CCLN, 130f.]

The third Professional Concert was held on the following day; as usual, a symphony by Haydn opened the programme; Pleyel's new MS. symphony which had been performed on the first night was repeated, and a new *Concertante* of his was given its first hearing. The *Oracle* on 28 February notes:

PROFESSIONAL CONCERT.
THIRD PERFORMANCE.

Last night the attractions were as various as fancy could wish for. The novelty of the evening was a *Concertante* by PLEYEL, for six Instruments. The subject extremely easy, airy, and well calculated for the *obligati* of the different Instruments which succeed each other – all varied with profound skill, and producing the most delightful effects. CRAMER led the first Performance with that consummate ability which has placed him in our esteem the first of Leaders.
 The New Grand Symphony of the first night was repeated, and of this and the Concertante it will be sufficiency of praise to say, that HAYDN might own with honour these works of his Pupil. It was the triumph of both – The Master was there, seemingly proud of his Work; the Scholar, himself only second, was very sensibly affected by the applause . . . . The Room was very brilliant indeed, and crouded [*sic*].

The benefit for Mrs Billington took place on 28 February at the Opera: *Orfeo* was given (in English!). It has been said that Haydn painted the English dislike of *opera seria* a little large to dissuade *la* Polzelli from coming over (14 January 1793, '. . . the Italian opera has no success at all now'); the exaggeration for Polzelli's sake may be true, but he was certainly stating a fact. The *European Magazine* (March 1792, p. 218), reviewing the production of 28 February, writes:

It was at first composed by the Chevalier Gluck, but on this its first appearance on the English stage, it received some assistance from the performances of Handel, Sacchini, [J. C.] Bach, Mazzinghi, and others. The music and the performers were entitled to applause, but a serious opera does not seem to agree with the taste of the public. It has, therefore, since been reduced to an afterpiece.

These ominous words may also explain why Haydn did not force the production of his new opera for Gallini, based on that very subject that failed so signally in February 1792. Later in the season, in June 1792, the same magazine reports on another *opera seria*, *Dido*, after Metastasio, with no less a *prima donna* than Madame Mara in the title role. 'It was performed three or four nights only, and then was consigned to oblivion'

– and this despite the efforts of the famous Mara and the 'splendor of the scenery'. .(*vide infra*, 12 June.)

Salomon's Third Concert took place on 2 March:

Third Concert: 2 March 1792

Mr. SALOMON'S CONCERT.
HANOVER-SQUARE

Mr. SALOMON most respectfully acquaints the Nobility and Gentry, that his third Performance will be on FRIDAY, March 2.

PART I.

New Overture, M. S. GYROWETZ.

Song, Signor ALBERTARELLI.

Quartetto for Clarinet, Violin, Tenor and Violoncello,

Messrs. HARTMAN, SALOMAN, HINDMARSH.

and MENEL. – – Michel.

Song, Miss CORRI.

Concerto Violoncello. Mr. DAMER [*sic*] – (Pleyel)

(Being his first appearance in this country.)

PART II.

New Grand Overture M. S. HAYDN.

Song, Signor CALCAGNI.

Concerto Violin, Mr. YANIEWICZ.

Terzetto, Signor CALCAGNI, Signor ALBERTARELLI,

and Miss CORRI – – Tarchi.

FINALE.

[etc.]

[*Morning Herald*, 29 February, 1, 2 March;
Oracle, 29 February, 2 March; etc.]

Haydn's Second Notebook tells us which the new Symphony was: 'In the 3rd concert, the new Symphony in B flat was given, and the first and last Allegros encort [*sic*]': the only B flat Symphony of the period is No. 98. In the Finale of No. 98, there was a solo for 'cembalo' (autograph) which Haydn probably played on one of the big English grand pianos. Samuel Wesley in his *Reminiscences* (1836 *et seq.*) remembered Haydn's playing:[1]

His Performance on the Piano Forte, although not such as to stamp him a first rate artist upon that Instrument, was indisputably neat and distinct. In the Finale of one of his Symphonies is a Passage of attractive Brilliancy, which he has given to the Piano Forte, and which the Writer of this Memoir remembers him to have executed with the utmost Accuracy and Precision.   [B. M. Add. 27593, f. 70]

In later years, this solo would be played by none other than Muzio Clementi: at Salomon's fifth subscription concert in March 1796, No. 98 was given. On 19 March, the *Morning Chronicle* writes that

The last movement of HAYDN's Overture was encored with enthusiasm. The short solo for the forte piano was exquisitely played by CLEMENTI.

1 Our attention was first drawn to Wesley's note in Marion Scott's article 'Haydn: Relics and Reminiscences in England', *Music & Letters*, XIII (1932), p. 126. For a discussion of what instrument was used, see the correspondence columns of the *Haydn Yearbook*, 1965, pp. 182f. It seems ever clearer that a concert grand piano was used in the Haydn-Salomon concerts, and not a harpsichord.

Haydn was being quite artful: first he showed with gentle but convincing persuasion that he could write good vocal music, even in English. A year ago, they were saying in the Press what a 'poor performer' on the pianoforte Haydn was. Now he was once again showing the contrary. Indeed, he cannot have been all that 'poor' in the first place. The great double-bass player, Domenico Dragonetti, speaking to Mary Novello on 29 January 1832 of the relative merits of various composer-pianists, remembered that 'Haydn's playing . . . was good, Hummel, Cramer and the rest he thinks nothing compared with Beethoven's.'[1]

On 2 March 1792, Haydn wrote a letter to Frau von Genzinger. The date may be a mistake, or was added after Haydn had finished the letter; for he says, referring to Symphony No. 93's first performance, that it took place 'last Friday', i.e. on 24 February, when in fact the work had been performed for the second time. But the letter shows Haydn to be an old diplomat with the ladies: how otherwise is one to explain the understatement of all times, when he thanks Frau Maria Anna for the 'prompt and careful delivery' of Symphony No. 91? The news of the stolen piano Sonata was obviously a shock: the work is No. 59 (XVI: 49) in E flat which Haydn had sent to Madame Tost (then Anna de Jerlischek), who had ordered it for Frau von Genzinger. But there were copies circulating that had nothing to do with Haydn's copyist Johann Elssler or the anonymous 'Copyist 63'[2] who did so much work for Haydn before and after the London journeys. For example, one such copy, by an unknown copyist, turned up at a Parisian antiquarian bookseller in 1957 and even bears Haydn's signature: 'Sonata del Jos: Haydn mpria 7^{tia} Martz 791'. Nevertheless the theft must have been particularly galling, since it was published on 31 August 1791 by Haydn's own Viennese house of Artaria & Co. Bearing in mind such fantastic unscrupulousness, it is no wonder that Haydn was a total cynic and Beethoven equally so, having had even more experience of this kind of treatment. Beethoven professed utter contempt at Haydn's attitude, however: 'He [Beethoven] did not have the common education of many of his colleagues and was incapable of selling a second time a MS. for which he had been paid. Papa Haydn had prostituted himself enough in this respect' (Griesinger's letter to Breitkopf & Härtel, 8 December 1802; *Haydn-Studien* I, 1966, p. 92).

[To Maria Anna von Genzinger, Vienna. *German*]

London, 2nd March 1792.

Nobly born and gracious Lady!

Yesterday evening I received your welcome letter and the Symphony I had asked for; I respectfully kiss Your Grace's hands for the prompt and careful delivery. Six days before I had in fact received it through Herr von Keess from Brussels, but the score was much more useful, for I have to change many things for the English public. I only regret that I must bother Your Grace so often with my commissions, the more so since at present I cannot show you how grateful I am. I must confess and admit to Your Grace that this causes me great embarrassment and that there are days in which I am terribly sad; especially because at present I cannot send Your Grace the Symphony which is dedicated to you, for the following reasons: first, because I intend to alter the last movement of it, and to improve it, since it is too weak compared with the first. I was convinced of this myself, and so was the public, when it was played the first time last Friday; notwithstanding which, it made the most profound impression on the audience.

---

[1] A *Mozart Pilgrimage*, op. cit., p. 339.
[2] The term from Bartha-Somfai, p. 423.

The second reason is that I really dread the risk of its falling into other hands. I was not a little shocked to hear the unpleasant news of the Sonata. By God! I would rather have lost 25 ducats than to hear of this theft, and no one except my own copyist can have done it. Nevertheless I hope to God to be able to replace the loss, once again through Madam Tost, for I certainly don't want to incur any reproaches from her. Your Grace must therefore be indulgent towards me until the end of July, when I can have the pleasure of delivering personally not only the Sonata but also the Symphony; *nota bene*, I shall give you the Symphony myself, but the Sonata through Madam Tost. Moreover, I cannot deliver the promised Symphonies to Herr von Kees either, for here too there is a want of faithful copyists. If I had the time I would copy them myself, but there isn't a day, not a single day, in which I am free from work, and I shall thank the dear Lord when I can leave London – the sooner the better. My labours have been augmented by the arrival of my pupil Pleyel, whom the Professional Concert have brought here. He arrived here with a lot of new compositions, but they had been composed long ago; he therefore promised to present a new work every evening. As soon as I saw this, I realized at once that a lot of people were dead set against me, and so I announced publicly that I would likewise produce 12 different new pieces. In order to keep my word, and to support poor Salomon, I must be the victim and work the whole time. But I really do feel it. My eyes suffer the most, and I have many sleepless nights, though with God's help I shall overcome it all. The people of the Professional Concert wanted to put a spoke in my wheel, because I would not go over to them; but the public is just. I enjoyed a great deal of success last year, but still more this year. Pleyel's presumption is sharply criticized, but I love him just the same. I always go to his concerts, and am the first to applaud him. I am delighted that Your Grace and the family are well. Please give my kind respects to all of them. The time is drawing near when I must put my trunks in order. Oh! how happy I shall be to see Your Grace again, to show you how much I missed you and to show the esteem in which, gracious lady, you will ever be held by

Your most obedient servant,
Jos : Haydn.

I hasten to ask Your Grace to present my respectful compliments to Herr von Keess, and to tell him that the press of affairs does not give me time to write, and to explain to him that, for the above reasons, I cannot send him the new Symphonies. I shall have the honour of conducting them at his coming Christmas Concert.

[Address :]   Madame
                Madame Anna Noble de
            Gennzinger, née Noble de Kayser
                          à
                       Vienne
im Schotten Hof.   en autriche.   [CCLN, 131–3]

Haydn also tells us in this letter that he intended to change 'many things' in Symphony No. 91 for the English public. From other Eszterháza works revised for England, such as the Cantata 'Miseri noi, misera patria', we can imagine he might have added a second flute. He probably considered adding trumpets and timpani, missing in the original score.[1]

1 The complete autograph MS. is now in the Pierpont Morgan Library in New York City. Hitherto unavailable, it contains many details not in the other sources. The autograph was first used as the basis for a performance with the New York Philharmonic Orchestra conducted by Pierre Boulez in the spring of 1969. Subsequently an *errata* list has been published, with a description of the source, to be used in conjunction with the Philharmonia (bound score 598; single score 791; full score Haydn–Mozart Presse 176) edition; this *errata* list may be had upon enquiry from Universal Edition.

It may be that Haydn did not have time to make the revisions, and for the following reason. We have seen that Longman & Broderip printed Symphonies Nos. 90 and 92 in 1791 (*supra*, p. 54). Meanwhile, however, Le Duc in Paris had in 1791[1] issued all three works in parts and these parts had been imported to London by Longman & Broderip. At first they sold these Le Duc parts with a Longman slip pasted over the address (a copy in this form of No. 91 in the Henry Watson Library, Manchester; of No. 92 in the Conservatorio Benedetto Marcello in Venice) and then printed their own of Nos. 90 and 92. But they must have procured No. 91, as well, fairly early in 1792 at the very latest; and it was therefore a courtesy on their part to have withheld the sale of it until Haydn could launch the work at Salomon's concert. On the other hand, Haydn must have considered it opportune to perform the work as quickly as possible. The Le Duc prints are very reliable, being engraved from the autographs which Haydn sent to the Comte d'Ogny in 1788 and 1789 (the recently [1956] discovered autograph of No. 92 has Le Duc's name on the second page of music)[2] for transmission to the Loge Olympique. In point of fact, Longman did not even bother to change Le Duc's numbers, which is curious. He was nice enough not to sell No. 9 (=91) until 23 November 1792, when an announcement in *The Times* included No. 9 among the often-advertised Nos. 7 and 8.

On 5 March 1792, the fourth Professional Concert was held:

FIRST ACT.
New Overture – HAYDN.
Song – Signor LAZZARINI.
New Quartetto, M. S. for two Violins, Tenor, and Violoncello,
by Messrs. CRAMER, BORGHI, BLAKE, and SMITH. – PLEYEL.
Song – Mrs. BILLINGTON.
New Overture, M. S. – PLEYEL.
SECOND PART
Concerto French Horn – Mr. PIELTAIN.
Song – Mrs. BILLINGTON.
Concerto Harp – Madame de MUSIGNY.
Song – Signor LAZZARINI.
Finale.
[*Morning Herald*, 3 March; *Oracle*, 3, 5 March; etc.]

PROFESSIONAL CONCERT
Hanover-Square.

There is so much excellence in the general performance of these Concerts, that the brilliant patronage they receive is the necessary operation of eminent talents, employed on admirable materials.

The fine Overture of HAYDN, which opened last night, was, we believe, the first piece he produced after his arrival in this country, at SALOMON's Concert, last year [i.e. Symphony No. 92 in G]. It is a grand composition, and was well supported.

The new pieces of last night, were by PLEYEL; the first a very pleasing Quartetto, to which CRAMER, BORGHI, BLAKE and SMITH did ample justice; the

---

1 Cari Johansson: *French music publishers' catalogues of the second half of the eighteenth century*; with an additional volume of catalogues in facsimile; Stockholm 1955. Facsimile 76, of a Le Duc Catalogue of 1791(?): '[Haydn] Idem second Suite De la Loge Olympique N°. 7, 8, 9 . . . a 4/4.'
2 Facsimile of the first two page of music facing p. 49 in Landon, *Supplement*.

other, a grand Symphony . . . The last piece was a very pretty symphony of GYROWITZ [*sic*], a composer of deserved repute.

Lord ADINGDON [i.e. Abingdon] who was one of the earliest patrons of the charming Concert was last night one of its most applauding auditors. The report of the room, we sincerely hope is ill-founded, which announced the death of poor STORACE.

[*Morning Herald*, 6 March]

MUSIC.

The fourth performance of the Professional Concert at Hanover square, last night, was distinguished for excellent music, and a very brilliant attendance. An overture of HAYDN was the opening piece, and it was a work equally pleasing and scientific....

[*Diary; or, Woodfall's Register*, 6 March]

The programme and the criticisms are given in particular detail because it is probable that they provide one further clue that the Symphony given by Haydn at the first concert of the 1791 season was really No. 92 in G and not No. 96. Obviously, Salomon, who was conducting a rival series, was not going to give the Professional Concert one of his 'exclusive' MS. Haydn symphonies. But No. 92 was no longer exclusive. It had been issued by Longman & Broderip in parts last year (on 23 November 1791, it and No. 90 were announced in *The Times*) and was now in the public domain.[1] That would also explain the designation 'New Overture': it was 'new' but printed, not MS. We also ought to add that the talented British composer Stephen Storace, brother of Nancy (Ann[a] Selina), though afflicted with gout, did not die from that disease until 1796.

On 5 March 1792, the *Morning Herald* announced that 'Miss DALL, who is so deservedly a favourite at the York concerts, is engaged by SALOMON and HAYDN for their concert, as soon as she has completed her Northern engagement'; we hear no more of Miss Dall, however, during the 1792 season.

On 6 March, Haydn was with Mrs Schroeter in the evening. Her letter the next day shows that their relationship had crossed a certain line and become a real love-affair. She sounds like a dear and attractive person from her letters.

March 7th 92.

My D: I was extremely sorry to part with you so suddenly last Night, our conversation was particularly interesting and I had [a] thousand affectionate things to say to you, my heart WAS and is full of TENDERNESS for you, but no language can express HALF the LOVE and AFFECTION I feel for you, you are DEARER to me EVERY DAY of my life. I am very sorry I was so dull and stupid yesterday, indeed my DEAREST it was nothing but my being indisposed with a cold occasion'd my Stupidity. I thank you a thousand times for your concern for me, I am truly sensible of your goodness, and I assure you my D. if any thing had happened to trouble me, I wou'd have open'd my heart, & told you with the most perfect confidence. Oh, how earnes[t]ly [I] wish to see you, I hope you will come to me to morrow. I shall be happy to see you both in the Morning and the Evening. God Bless you my love, my thoughts and best wishes ever accompany you, and I always am with the most sincere and invariable Regard my D:

My Dearest I cannot be happy
till I see you if you know,
do, tell me, when you will come

[CCLN, 279f.]

---

1 Landon SYM (481 *et passim*) requires correction on this important point.

At the Fourth Concert of the Haydn-Salomon season, the new *Concertante* for violin, 'cello, oboe, bassoon and orchestra was first performed, its composition no doubt inspired by the popular Pleyel *concertanti*, one of which had been first performed on 27 February and another (for two violins and orchestra) given on 12 March. Symphony No. 98 was repeated.

Fourth Concert: 9 March 1792

Mr. SALOMON'S CONCERT.

Mr. SALOMON most respectfully acquaints the Nobility and Gentry, that his Fourth Performance will be TO-MORROW, Friday, March 9, 1792.

PART I.

Overture – KOZELUCK [*sic*].

Song, Mr. NIELD.

Concerto, German Flute, Mr. GRAEFF.

Song, Miss CORRI.

New Concerto M. S. for [Violin], Violoncello, Oboe and Bassoon,
Messrs. SALOMON, MENEL, HAR[R]INGTON, and
HOLMES. – HAYDN.

PART II.

(By desire) The New Overture, M. S. HAYDN,
as performed last Friday.

Song, Signor CAIAGNI [*sic*].

New Concerto Pedal Harp, Madame KRUMPHOLTZ
– Dusseck.

Duetto, Miss CORRI and Mr. NIELD.

FINALE.   [etc.]

[*Oracle*, 8 March; *Morning Herald*, 8 March; etc.]

SALOMON'S CONCERT.
FOURTH NIGHT.

Haydn directed for the first time the Performance of a New *Concertante* – the third movement of which seemed expressly calculated to shew the brilliancy of SALOMON'S, and the sweetness of his tone.

The prevailing manner of this Master pervaded every movement – it had all his usual grandeur, contrasted by the levity of airy transition, and the sudden surprises of abrupt rests.

GRAEFF executed a Flute Concerto with very powerful tone and rapidity of finger. It was noticed that he played upon a Flute not of the new construction; it had no greater compass than D below.

Madame KRUMPHOLTZ delighted everybody by the brilliancy of her Harp Concerto. – She is without doubt the first Player we have. – There is an additional charm in manner; that too is her own. – We should wish she might please highly, if we did not know that she certainly would.

Miss CORRI, in a very delicate Air of SARTI,
'Ah non sai qual pena sia',
was universally admired – her style is extremely delicate and pure.

Mr. NIELD acquitted himself very respectably.

Signor CALCAGNI sung from SACCHINI
'non odi il segno'
and a Duo of SARTI with Miss CORRI, very ably. His lower tones are remarkably clear and firm.

The Company were very brilliant.   [*Oracle*, 10 March]

MUSIC.

The last performance at SALOMON's Concert deserves to be mentioned as one of the richest treats which the present season has afforded. A new concertante from HAYDN combined with all the excellencies of music; it was profound, airy, affecting, and original, and the performance was in unison with the merit of the composition. SALOMON particularly exerted himself on this occasion, in doing justice to the music of his friend HAYDN.

GRAEFF played a concerto on the common German Flute, but in a style of uncommon excellence. KRUMPHOLTZ, who has been kept from the Public by illness, made ample atonement for her absence by a delicious concerto on the harp.

NEILD [*sic*], CALCAGNI, and Miss CORRI, were the vocal performers, and they all acquitted themselves very ably.

The room had a very brilliant attendance.

[*Morning Herald*, 12 March]

MUSIC.

Mr. SALOMON gave his fourth Concert on Friday night, in which HAYDN shone with more than his usual lustre.

A new *Concertante*, for a Violin, Violoncello, Oboe, and Bassoon, was performed for the first time with admirable effect. The *solo* parts were finely contrasted with the 'full tide of harmony' of the other instruments, and they were very ably sustained by the respective performers.

The new Overture of the former Friday was repeated; it is one of the grandest compositions we ever heard, and it was most loudly applauded; the first and last movements were encored.

Madame KRUMPHOLTZ played a new Concerto on the harp, which she executed with much elegance. Miss CORRI sung charmingly. She has much the manner of MARCHESI, and with the judicious instruction of her father, she could not have chosen a better model.

It was near twelve o'clock before the concert was finished.

[*Morning Chronicle*, 12 March]

The fifth Professional Concert was held on 12 March, with the following programme:

FIRST PART.
Overture – HAYDN.
Song – Signor LAZZARINI.
Quartetto, M. S. for two Violins, Tenor, and Violoncello,
by Messrs. CRAMER, BORGHI, BLAKE and
Smith. – RAWLINS, Junior.
Song – Mrs. BILLINGTON.
New Concertante M. S. for two Violins, by Messrs.
CRAMER – PLEYEL.

PART SECOND.
Grand Symphony, M. S. – PLEYEL.
Song – Mrs. BILLINGTON.
Concerto Violoncello, Mr. LINDLEY.
Song, Signora NEGRI.
Finale – ROZETTI [*sic*].

[etc.]
[*Oracle* and *Morning Herald*,
12 March; etc.]

PROFESSIONAL CONCERT.

Last Night produced in the first Act two Novelties – A Quartetto by RAWLINS, jun. a very pretty imitation of HAYDN, and of course, promising much.

PLEYEL had written a Concertante for two Violins, to usher into public the young CRAMER, who sustained with great skill the responsive part to his Father, and often when his timidity subsided, evinced his hereditary value. The second movement was highly applauded, and had abundant merit.

LINDLEY is a prodigy of excellence.

Mrs. BILLINGTON executed with wonderful rapidity and sweetness, two charming Compositions –
'Ah non sai mio bene amato',
and in the Second Act, from ANFOSSI,
'Dove povera me'.

LAZZARINI took a Scene from PAESIELLO, and Signora NEGRI one from ANDREOZZI. Of the latter we have to say, that her chaste and feeling style appealed very successfully to *true* taste; there was not much of it, however, in the majority.

[*Oracle*, 13 March]

MUSIC.

The PROFESSIONAL CONCERT held its fifth performance for the present season at the Hanover-Square Room last night, and had a large and splendid train of subscribers. The opening piece was one of the most favourite Overtures of HAYDN, and nothing could be more delicious than the manner in which it was performed.... [*Diary; or, Woodfall's Register*, 13 March]

Haydn's next concert followed on 16 March. The 'Overture M.S. (from last year)' was probably Symphony No. 96 or 95, the others meanwhile having been printed (Nos. 90 and 92, the latter to appear later in the series, at the Ninth Concert on 27 April). The Quartet was probably another from Op. 64. The 'New Recitativo and Aria' sung by Signor Calcagni, a soprano castrato, might have been a scene with Euridice from Haydn's *L'anima del filosofo*: there is evidence on the Budapest copy, made by an 'authentic' English copyist who was also responsible for the Royal Philharmonic score copy of Symphony No. 98, that some of Euridice's music, perhaps the great death scene in Act II, 'Dov'è l'amato bene?' (followed by the Aria, 'Del mio core'), was performed in concert form in London in 1791.[1] If it is not that there are various other possibilities, as there are for the Cantata sung by Miss Corri (*Arianna a Naxos, Miseri noi*, or the unidentified '1 Aria con Orchestra' from the *Catalogue of Works Composed in England*).

Fifth Concert: 16 March 1792

Mr. SALOMON'S CONCERT.
HANOVER-SQUARE.

Mr. SALOMON most respectfully acquaints the Nobility and Gentry, that his Fifth Performance will be THIS EVENING, the 16th instant.

---

1 The Budapest score is from Haydn's library and contains some additions in the composer's hand; it is now Ms. mus. I, 7 of the Esterházy Archives of the National Library. See Chronicle, 27 May 1791, *supra*, p. 81.

PART I.
Overture M. S. (from last year) HAYDN.
Song, Mr. Nield.
Quartetto for two Violins, Tenor, and Violoncello, Messrs SALOMON,
DAMEN, HINDMARSH, and MEMEL [*sic*]. – HAYDN.
Song, Miss POOL[E].
Concerto Violoncello, Mr. SHRAM.
New Recitativo and Aria, Signor CALCAGNI. – HAYDN.

PART II.
New Concerto Piano Forte, Mr. HAESSLER. – HAESSLER.
Cantata, Miss CORRI – HAYDN.
(By desire) the New Concertante, M. S. for Violin, Violoncello, Oboe,
and Bassoon, Messrs. SALOMON, MENEL, HARRINGTON, and HOLMES.
HAYDN. (As performed last Friday.) – – The Storm,
New Chorus and Quartetto, the principal Vocal Parts by
Miss CORRI, Miss POOL[E], Mr NIELD, and Mr. BELLAMY. – HAYDN.
FINALE.

[etc.]
[*Oracle, Morning Chronicle* and
Morning Herald, 14, 16 March]

MUSIC.

There has hardly ever been a more beautiful musical treat than the fifth performance of SALOMON's Concert, at the Hanover-Square Room, last night. No less than six Pieces of HAYDN were performed, exhibiting a richness and variety of genius that far exceed all modern Composers. Of these admirable works, the Concertante and the Storm, were certainly the best.

In the Concertante, SALOMON distinguished himself very eminently. The Storm is a fine effort of musical painting; the vicissitude of the calm, and the tempest are remarkably striking.

A Concerto on the Violoncello was well performed by Mr. SCHRAM.

Mr. HAESSLER, in a Concerto on the Piano Forte, evinced extraordinary execution and finished taste.

Miss CORRI, Miss POOLE, and NIELD, were all deservedly applauded for their Vocal exertions.

[*Morning Herald,* 17 March]

HANOVER SQUARE.

The fifth Performance of the Concerts, under the direction of SALOMON and HAYDN, was held at this place last night, and a more delicious assemblage of harmonic excellencies, we never attended . . . .

HAYDN appeared with usual *eclat,* for six of his own compositions were performed, and they were all character[i]zed by beauty, expression, and originality. Of these pieces, a Concertante, and the fine representation of harmony, entitled, THE STORM, were the most striking; but particularly the latter, which was alternately tremendous and delightful, according to the perdominance [*sic*] of the imitation hurricane, or the approaching calm . . . .

[*Diary; or, Woodfall's Register,* 17 March]

The strain of all this was beginning to tell on a man who, despite robust health and a 'cheerful constitution', was after all within a fortnight of celebrating his sixtieth birthday. His notebook records, laconically, 'On 17th March 1792, I was bled in

London.' Three days later he presided at a concert of the Misses Abrams ('Leader of the band Mr. SALOMON. The Whole to be conducted by Dr. HAYDN'):

A CONCERT
OF VOCAL AND INSTRUMENTAL MUSIC.

ACT I.

Overture – Gyrowetz.

Glee – Stevens.

Song, – Mr. BARTLEMAN.

Quartetto – Messrs. SALOMON, DAME [N], W. ABRAMS, and MENELL [*sic*]
– HAYDN.

Duetto – Miss ABRAMS – Sarti.

Concerto, Piano Forte, Miss E. ABRAMS – Janievicz.

ACT II.

New Overture, M. S. – Haydn.

Quartetto – Messrs. SALOMON, RAIMONDI, MENELL [*sic*], and
GRAEFF – Raimondi.

Aria – Signor CALCAGNI.

Concerto Harp – Mad. DELAVAL.

Terzetto – The Miss ABRAMS – Cimarosa.

Symphonie – Haydn.   [etc.]

[*Oracle*, 15, 17, 19, 20 March]

Underneath this announcement, the *Oracle* printed the following notice:

> The true admirers of HAYDN always forget his Doctorate. First-rate excellence loses all *Prologue* to the NAME.'

Sixth Concert: 23 March 1792

Mr. SALOMON'S CONCERT.
HANOVER SQUARE.

Mr. SALOMON most respectfully acquaints the Nobility and Gentry, that his Sixth Performance will be on FRIDAY next, the 23rd instant.

PART I.

Grand Overture M. S. HAYDN.

Song, Signor ALBERTARELLI.

Quartetto for two Violins, Tenor, and Violoncello,
Messrs. SALOMON, DAMER [*sic*], HINDMARSH, and MEMEL [*sic*]
– CAMBINI.

Scena, Miss CORRI.

New Concerto Violin, Mr. YANIEWICZ.

PART II.

New Grand Overture, M. S. HAYDN.

Aria, Signor CALIAGNI [*sic*].

(By desire) the new Concerto Pedal Harp, Madame
KRUMPHOLTZ – DUSSECK, as performed on the 4th night.

Terzetto, Miss CORRI, Signor CALIAGNI [*sic*], and
Signor ALBERTARELLI.

FINALE.   [etc.]

[*Morning Herald*, 21 March; *Times*,
21, 23 March; *Oracle*, 21, 23 March;
Morning Chronicle, 20, 22, 23 March etc.]

The 'New Grand Overture M.S.' was the soon famous 'Surprise' Symphony –
No. 94 in G, the biggest success of Haydn's career after Symphony No. 53
('L'impériale'); in both symphonies it was particularly the slow movement which was
most popular, that in No. 94 being noted for its surprise kettledrum stroke. Who
named the work 'Surprise'? We find it very soon in English programmes, whereas in
German-speaking countries it was soon entitled 'Mit dem Paukenschlag' (with
the Kettledrum-stroke). Andrew Ashe, the excellent flautist whom we have noticed
before, made the claim to the eye-catching title. In a volume of old programmes
owned by Ashe and with his bookplate, now in the Bodleian Library at Oxford
(17405.d.6[4]), there is a programme of the Opera Concert Room for 9 May 1803
which begins with 'Grand Overture, Surprise'. Ashe has bracketed the 'Surprise' and
added a footnote of his own which reads 'I christened it the *Surprise* when I announced
it for my Benefit Concert at the opera Room, the year it was composed for Salomon's
Concerts at Hanover Square & my valued friend Haydn thank'd me for giving it such
an appropriate Name / A: *Ashe.*' In fact, however, Ashe's benefit concert at the King's
Theatre took place on 8 June 1795 (*vide* Chronicle *infra*), on which occasion Haydn
conducted.

The 'fine printed' quartet is listed below in one review as Haydn, not Cambini;
perhaps there was a last-minute change. There are three reviews in the London
newspapers:

HANOVER SQUARE.

The Subscription Concert under the management of HAYDN and SALOMON,
evidently rises in the esteem of the musical world, for the number of visitors
augments on every performance.

The compositions of last night were chiefly from HAYDN. The opening
Overture was not new, but very fine. A quartetto was also excellent. The third
piece of HAYDN was a new Overture, of very extraordinary merit. It was simple,
profound and sublime. The *andante* movement was particularly admired ....

[*Diary; or, Woodfall's Register*, 24 March]

MUSIC.

The great name of HAYDN, and the general excellence of the Concerts under the
direction of SALOMON, have a suitable operation upon the world of taste and
fashion. The Room was crowded last night, and by a very elegant assemblage.

A new composition from such a man as HAYDN is a great event in the history of
Music. – His novelty of last night was a grand Overture, the subject of which was
remarkably simple, but extended to vast complication, exquisit[e]ly modulated,
and striking in effect. Critical applause was fervid and abundant.

YANIEWICZ, who is a wonderful performer on the Violin, far exceeded all his
former performances, in his Concert of last night.

Madame Krumpholtz gave her last admirable Concerto, and judiciously
omitted the second movement.

Miss Corri is a pleasing singer, but she should try to become more animated;
for her voice and taste, though both good, are considerably affected by a kind of
languid drawl, which too often accompanies her performance.

The concluding piece of GYROWITZ [*sic*] has all the delicacy, taste and science,
for which his works are distinguished.

[*Morning Herald*, 24 March]

SALOMON'S CONCERT
SIXTH NIGHT.

The Selection was uncommonly elegant instrumentally. The first Act commenced with the delightful Overture M. S. HAYDN. – A fine printed Quartetto, also HAYDN [*sic*].

YANIEWICZ, absolutely the most brilliant Performer we have ever heard upon the Violin, played his Concerto in that fascinating style of contrasted strength and beauty, which delights the Amateur.

Miss CORRI, with infinite sweetness and expression, sang a charming Scena; and ALBERTARELLI in his Aria [of] GUGLIEMI, proved what he could do upon the Stage of our Opera.

Act 2d opened with a first performance of the GRAND OVERTURE composed by HAYDN for that evening.

The Second Movement was equal to the happiest of this great Master's conceptions. The surprise might not be unaptly likened to the situation of a beautiful Shepherdess who, lulled to slumber by the murmur of a distant Waterfall, starts alarmed by the unexpected firing of a fowling-piece. The flute obligato was delicious.

Mad. KRUMPHOLTZ played her Harp Concerto like an Angel, omitting the heavy second movement of the *Tom Tom Gongs,* and other funereal Instruments imitated so dolefully of the fourth night.

The *terzetto* [of] GUGLIEMI, from certain classic rests of conception touching the character of ENEAS, we could not taste[,] so perhaps it merited –

Del furor mi sento oppresso,
L'ira mia non so frenar.

[*Oracle*, 24 March]

There is also quite a small literature about this movement in Dies, Griesinger, Neukomm's corrections to Dies, and Gyrowetz's autobiography. It shows how the story lost nothing in the telling.

I asked [Haydn] once in jest if it were true that he wrote the Andante with the kettledrum beat in order to awaken the English public that had gone to sleep at his concert. 'No', he answered me. 'Rather it was my wish to surprise the public with something new, and to make a début in a brilliant manner so as not to be outdone by my pupil Pleyel, who at that time was engaged by an orchestra in London (in the year 1792) which had begun its concert series eight days before mine. The first *Allegro* of my symphony was received with countless bravos, but the enthusiasm reached its highest point in the *Andante with the kettledrum beat. Ancora, Ancora!* sounded from every throat, and even Pleyel complimented me on my idea.'

[Griesinger, p. 32]

Dies refers in his story to the noise made by late-comers to the first part and people going to sleep in the concert after having dined too well; we have quoted that part of the document *supra* (p. 44). Dies also states:

Haydn saw to his annoyance that even in the second part the God of Sleep spread his wings over the company; he saw in this an insult to his muse and resolved to revenge himself, and composed for this purpose a symphony in which he, in the *Andante* – where one would least expect it – arranged to contrast the softest *piano* with *fortissimo*. To make the effect as surprising as possible he accompanied the *fortissimo* with kettledrums. . . . Haydn had told the kettledrummer to take his sticks and use them without any mercy, and the latter fulfiled entirely [Haydn's] expectations. The sudden thunder of the whole orchestra shocked the sleepers, all awoke and looked at each other with disturbed and surprised expressions. . . . [Dies, pp. 91ff. The story goes on, in Dies' usual way, to give details of a woman fainting, etc.]

There is something too incredibly naïve about Dies's story, and among the most interesting rebuttals is one from a German-born piano-teacher and composer, Johann Christian Firnhaber, who later went to St. Petersburg and in 1825 wrote a long letter to the magazine *Der Freimüthige* (XXII, 1825, p. 960) entitled 'Berichtigung, als Beitrag zur Geschichte der Musik'. This letter was intended as an answer to the Dies story, which had been printed as an 'anecdote' in the *Zeitung für die elegante Welt*. Firnhaber writes:

Even non-connoisseurs of music must realize the improbability of such a conduct on the part of the great composer Haydn, and the undersigned permits himself, since he is precisely informed as to the truth of the matter, to offer the following correction . . . Haydn ordered this drum beat to be given six times in rehearsal before he was satisfied with it. I ought to add, incidentally, that he did not conduct the orchestra in the latest mode with a stick in the hand but led, as is the custom with great virtuosi, from a harpsichord or fortepiano. . . . The above-mentioned symphonies I heard in the second season, during the winter of 1793, and when the drum beat occurred in the afore-mentioned Andante, once again the whole auditorium was profoundly shocked [*auf das heftigste erschüttert*], especially the ladies. This time, however, Clementi had taken Haydn's place at the keyboard, and I can add that I never heard anything more perfect than these concerts. Even from this very fact one can see the unlikelihood of the English public's going to sleep during the performance of Haydn symphonies. . . . I can vouch for the above testimony all the more since during my seven-month sojourn in London during the winter of 1792 and 1793, I lived in the same house as Salomon.

[signed:] J. Ch. Firnhaber.

Haydn's pupil of the late 1790s, Sigismund von Neukomm (*Bemerkungen zu den Biographischen Nachrichten von Dies*), has this to say about Dies' version:

This long and rather silly story is really restricted to the fact that H[aydn] had noticed an old man, who occupied the same seat at every concert and who regularly went to sleep at the very beginning. H[aydn] allowed himself the joke of awakening the sleeper by a single drum beat [musical example]– everything else is silly nonsense and not worthy of repetition. [A page earlier Neukomm says:] I should like to remark that all the information I [have] from Haydn, for the most part at our tête à tête conversation over meals, is from an earlier time than that of the visits of my friend Dies; at a time when H[aydn] was strong enough to write that huge work 'Die Jahreszeiten'.

Gyrowetz, in his autobiography (op. cit., p. 75), says:

. . . the [Salomon] concerts often lasted until well past midnight, and so it happened that the ladies not infrequently fell asleep. This suggested to Haydn the idea of composing something which should arose them from their nap, and so for this occasion he wrote the celebrated Andante with the drum beat, as a result of which the ladies were really awakened, and from some was even heard a loud cry. As Haydn was just composing this Andante, Gyrowetz arrived to pay his respects. Haydn was so pleased and delighted with his own idea that he forthwith played the Andante on his square pianoforte, laughing as he did so, and prophesying: 'there the women will jump'. . . .

Haydn's notebook has a curious tale to relate in connection with another concert, which he specifically calls Mr Barthelemon's concert, although his benefit did not take place until 28 May:

On 26th March [1792], at Mr Barthelemon's Concert, an English clergyman was present who fell into the most profound melancholy on hearing the Andante:

etc. [Symphony No. 75 in D, 2nd Movt]

because he had dreamt the previous night that this piece was a premonition of his death. – He left the company at once and took to his bed.
Today, the 25th of April, I heard from Herr Barthelemon that this protestant clergyman had died.   [CCLN, 271f.]

This event made a profound impression in Haydn's mind. To Dies (124f. he said that the concert had taken place at Mr Barthelemon's home – Dies politely kept Barthelemon's anonymity, as he usually did in such cases – which would mean that we are in fact dealing with a kind of 'house concert'. But let us continue with Dies. Haydn said to him: 'Isn't that a strange occurrence?' 'Not more', answered Dies, 'than when a blind chicken finds a kernel of corn.'

On 28 March 1792 we read, in the *Morning Herald*, of a benefit concert at Hanover Square for the singer, Madame De Sisley, 'this evening' with Salomon as the leader; both parts opened with a Haydn Overture and the evening closed with 'Finale, HAYDN' – probably older works since there is no mention of 'M.S.'

On 31 March, Miss Corri gave her benefit concert; the *Diary; or, Woodfall's Register* of 2 April writes:

HANOVER-SQUARE ROOMS.

Miss CORRI's Concert was attended on Saturday evening by a very numerous and genteel audience. . . . A Grand Overture of Haydn's was most powerfully played, and highly relished.
Salomon lead [*sic*] the band with his wonted spirit and ability.

Salomon thought it prudent to postpone his next concert and explained to his public why:

Mr. SALOMON'S CONCERT.

MR. SALOMON being still disappointed in Madame MARA's arrival, has by the advice of many of his Subscribers, who wish to enjoy the additional pleasure of her Performance at all the remaining Concerts, and in hope of meeting the approbation of the Subscribers in general deferred the 7th Concert to April the 13th, the Friday in Easter Week; when Madame MARA, as well as Signor SIMONI, will perform; and that a number of Mr. SALOMON's friends, who, from a variety of circumstances were prevented from subscribing to the whole of the 12 concerts, may not be deprived of the opportunity of hearing such acknowledged merit, he has been particularly requested to accommodate them with Subscriptions for the remaining six Nights; and which, from the deep obligations he feels himself under to those friends, he has the greatest satisfaction in doing . . . .

Haydn will have been delighted at the chance to continue work on his last, great

Symphony for the 1792 season: the bold, aggressive No. 97 in C. He went on seeing the delightful Mrs. Schroeter:

> My D: I am extremely sorry I can not have the pleasure of seeing you to morrow, as I am going to Bleakheath [Blackheath]. if you are not engaged this Evening I shou'd be very happy if you will do me the favor to com[e] to me – and I hope to have the happiness to see you on Saturday to dinner. My thoughts and tenderest affections are always with you and I ever am most truly my D.
>
> Your F: and etc.
>
> April 4th 92.

> My D: with this, you will receive the Soap, I beg you a thousand Pardons for not Sending it sooner, I know you will have the goodness to excuse me. – I hope to hear you are quite well, and have slept well – I shall be happy to see you, my D: as soon as possible. I shall be much obliged to you if you will do me the favor to send me twelve Tikets for your concert,[1] may all SUCCESS attend you MY EVER D: H:[2] that Night, and always, is the sincere and hearty wish of your
>
> Invariable and
>
> James S: truly affectionate
> April 8th 792.
>
> [CCLN, 280]

On 10 April 1792, Haydn wrote to his Prince in Austria, offering his services to the family once again:

> [To Prince Anton Esterházy, (Eisenstadt?). *German*]
> Most Serene Prince of the Holy Roman Empire,
> Gracious Lord and Sire!
>
> Since I must leave England in a short time, I hasten to place my entire faithful services in all matters – as far as I shall be able to fulfil them – at Your SERENE HIGHNESS' disposal. Our concerts will be finished at the end of June, after which I shall begin the journey home without delay, in order to serve my most gracious Prince and Lord again. I am, in humble submission,
>
> Your SERENE HIGHNESS'
> Most humble Joseph Haydn, m.p.,
> *Capellmeister.*
>
> London, 10th April 1792.
>
> [CCLN, 133f.]

We now know, from newly rediscovered London newspapers, that Haydn had made arrangements with Salomon to come back for the 1793 season. We shall see, that the plan had to be changed, as well as an appendix being added thereto, namely to take Beethoven with him. But that the plan was known even to the public, and thus to the newspapers, is shown by the following extract from the *Public Advertiser* on 12 April 1792:

> Haydn finds the *good cheer* of this country in such *concert pitch* with his own *great taste*, that he has declared his intention of concluding the *finale* of his days, with the '*Roast Beef of Old England*'.

---

1 Haydn's benefit concert on 3 May 1792.
2 D: H = Dear Haydn.

Mrs Schroeter wrote to Haydn that day, sensing that he was distracted and overworked:

James St: Thursday April 12th
M:D I am so TRULY ANXIOUS about YOU. I must write, to beg to know HOW YOU DO? I was very sorry I HAD not the pleasure of seeing you this Evening, my thoughts have been CONSTANTLY with you, and indeed MY D:L: no words can express half the tenderness and AFFECTION I FEEL FOR YOU – I thought you seemed out of Spirits this morning, I wish I cou'd always remove every trouble from your mind. be assured my D: I partake with the most perfect Sympathy in ALL YOUR SENSATIONS, and my regard for you is STRONGER EVERY DAY, my best Wishes always attend you and I ever am my D: H: most Sincerely your Faithful
et[c]
[CCLN, 280]

In April 1792, another refugee from the chaos of Paris arrived in London. It was the Tyrolean composer Giacomo Gotifredo Ferrari (1759–1842), who had studied briefly with Paisiello and had settled in Paris in 1786. Ferrari published his memoirs in 1830: *Aneddoti piacevoli e interessanti, Occorsi nella vita di* [etc.; 2 vols., London 1830], and in that same year *The Harmonicon* published lengthy extracts (pp. 368–72, 424–8) in a delightful translation which is reproduced here.

Immediately on my arrival in the city [London], I took a coach to No. 2, Great Pulteney Street, the residence of the composer Pozzi, to whom I had been recommended. Although the streets wore the most melancholy aspect, being clouded with a dense smoke, and the sun bore the appearance rather of the sister planet than of the luminary of the day, yet I drove along in high spirits, at the reflection of the revolutionary horrors from which I had escaped.

Knowing that Haydn was then in London, and that he lived at no great distance from where I lodged, I hastened to pay him a visit. On entering, I addressed him in my Tyrolese *patois*, which not a little amused him. He told me, laughing, that he spoke Italian, and addressed me in that language with sufficient fluency. I paid a sincere and merited compliment to this great man, for whom I felt the deepest veneration. He told me, that till the age of thirty he had been a mere zero in musical knowledge; that he had then the good fortune to study under Porpora, and that to this great master he was indebted for most of what he knew, indefatigable industry having done the rest.

I asked him his opinion of Pleyel, Kozeluch, and Mozart. 'The first two', said he, 'are elegant composers; but as for the other – Ah,' (said he, with a sign of deep emotion) 'Mozart is indeed an eminent writer.' I afterwards requested him to oblige me, by letting me hear some of his latest compositions, and he had the kindness to favour me with his sonata in A flat [the piano Trio No. 27, which Maria Anna von Genzinger had sent him from Vienna, and which had arrived on 2 February 1792; Master Hummel played it at the Eighth Salomon Concert on 20 April 1792], with which I was delighted to excess.

Haydn was a master of great simplicity of character and gentleness of manner, but at the same time there was a considerable degree of humour about him. [There then follows a garbled version of the 'Farewell Symphony' story, in which the last two instruments to leave are described as organ and first violin.]

Soon after Haydn's return to Vienna, he met Prince Lobkowitz, known as the great protector of music, and as a practical connoisseur of no mean talent. He asked Haydn why he had not written an instrumental quintett; the answer was, that he had never dreamt of such a thing till he had heard the celebrated quintetts of Mozart, and that he found them so sublime and perfect, that he could not presume to put himself in competition with such a composer. 'Never mind,' was the prince's reply, 'write me one, and you shall have no cause to complain.' Thus urged, Haydn set himself to work, and some time after laid his manuscript before the prince. Casting his eye over the first page, he found a score of five lines, but of which the fifth was left empty. He thought at first that Haydn had begun the quintett in four parts, intending to add the fifth afterwards, as it was sometimes usual with composers to do. But no: running over the whole manuscript, he always found the same line empty. Then, turning to the composer, he exclaimed, 'Why, my dear Haydn, you have forgot the fifth part!' 'Oh no, your Highness,' was Haydn's reply, 'I have left that for you to fill up; you will do it better than I can.'

The latter story can only have occurred in connection with the Opus 77 Quartets (1799) which were actually dedicated to Prince Lobkowitz; and thus Ferrari can only have heard it second-hand, at best. Nevertheless, it has often occurred that there is a kernel of truth in such anecdotes, wildly improbable though they may at first sound; and we can do no more than print Ferrari's otherwise interesting report and wait for possible further evidence to turn up.

Some days after, [continues Ferrari], I had the pleasure to meet my old friends T. Attwood, J. B. Cramer, Dussek, Sapio &c; and having formed an acquaintance with D. Corri, it was at his house I met the most eminent professors of the metropolis, with many of whom I formed a lasting friendship. Among the number was [J.] P. Salomon, who kindly offered me the freedom of entry to his subscription concerts, in one of which was executed a scena, *Se mi tormenti, amor*, that I had written for Simoni, and which he sung with great success. This piece raised my name here considerably.

In the forthcoming Seventh Concert, on 13 April 1792, Sig. Simoni made his début in London, but no hand-bill of this or the other concerts has survived, so that we cannot say at which of the concerts Ferrari's *scena*, 'Se mi tormenti, amor', was performed. On the other hand, we know that a popular Duet by Ferrari was performed in the Salomon Concert of 3 March 1794, at the Opera Concert of 27 April 1795, and at Cramer's benefit concert on 1 May 1795. The greatest honour for Ferrari, however, was that he figured in the great benefit concert Haydn gave at the Opera House on 4 May 1795, at which the 'London' Symphony was first performed.

The programme for the Seventh Salomon Concert was as follows:

Seventh Concert: 13 April 1792

HANOVER-SQUARE.
Mr. SALOMON'S CONCERT.

MR. SALOMON most respectfully acquaints the Subscribers, that his Seventh Concert will be THIS EVENING, FRIDAY, April 13.

PART I.
New Grand Overture, M. S. HAYDN.
Song, Mrs. [*sic*] CORRI.
Quartetto M. S. for two Violins, Tenor, and Violoncello, Messrs.
SALOMON, DAMER [*sic*], HINDMARSH, and MEMEL [*sic*]. – GYROWETZ.
Song, Signor SIMONI,
(Being his first appearance in England.)
New Concerto Piano Forte. Mr. DUSSECK. – DUSSECK.

PART II.
By desire, the new Grand Overture, M. S. – HAYDN.
As performed on the Fourth Night.
Song, Miss CORRI.
Sonata Pedal Harp, Madam Delaval.
Song, Signor SIMONI.
FINALE – KOZELUCK [*sic*].

[etc.]
[*Morning Herald*, 12, 13 April;
Morning Chronicle, 12, 13 April; etc.]

MUSIC.

The Concerts under the *firm* of SALOMON and HAYDN, were resumed last night at the Hanover Square Rooms, before the usual assemblage of elegant and fashionable visitors. A new Overture of HAYDN had all the taste, richness, and originality, which usually distinguish the compositions of that great master.

The vocal novelty was Signor SIMONI, a very fine tenor. His voice is strong, extensive, and well toned, and he sings with great expression. He was much admired on the Continent, and is in no danger of lessening his reputation in this country.

Mrs. [*sic*] CORRI sung two Italian airs with such taste, that we wonder she has not more musical fame. A Harp Sonata, by Madam DELAVAL, was charmingly performed, and had the support of SALOMON's exquisite accompangment on the Violin. DUSSECK played a Concerto on the Piano Forte, which was wholly recommended by rapid *execution*. The last movement was borrowed from a Russian Air of JARNOVICHI. A Quartetto of GYROWETZ, very pretty in itself, was admirably performed. The band is greatly improved in general spirit and precision. [*Morning Herald*, 14 April]

SALOMON'S CONCERT.

This admirable Concert was further strengthened on Friday evening by the addition of M[r.] SIMONI, a vocal performer who has gained great applause at the *Theatre de Monsieur* in Paris, and who will justly be ranked as one of the finest voices which we have in England. His voice is full, and rich tenor – It is of extensive power and vigorous tone. He sung two songs in a very fine style, and was received with great admiration and applause.

[*Morning Chronicle*, 16 April]

HANOVER SQUARE.

The powerful attraction of the Concert, under the direction of SALOMON and HAYDN, was visible last night, in a large attendance of the fashionable world. . . .

The new overture composed by HAYDN for the evening, was worthy this admirable and original musician. . . .

[*Diary; or, Woodfall's Register*, 14 April]

The first work on the second half was Symphony No. 98. But what of the very first work on the programme? Contrary to all rules, Haydn began an evening with a new work. The explanation seems to be Symphony No. 91 in E flat, which he had received from Vienna. Glancing at it again, he sensibly realized that it could not possibly compete with the 'Grand New Overtures MS.' of the 1792 season: Haydn, in these four years, had developed greatly. So he did what might be expected of a sensible man: he broke his own rule and put the old symphony first, where it still made a good impression. In the next concert, the opening piece was Symphony No. 94 ('Surprise'), the first work on the second half Symphony No. 93. Haydn was now frantically working to complete Symphony No. 97, which explains why there was no new symphony in the Eighth Concert. Mrs Schroeter heard he wrote five hours at a stretch:

> M: D: I was extremely sorry to hear this morning that you was indisposed, I am told you was five hours at your Study's yesterday, indeed MY D: L: I am afraid it will hurt you, why should you who have already produced so many WONDERFUL and CHARMING compositions, still fatigue yourself with such close application. I almost tremble for your health, let me prevail on you my MUCH-LOVED H: not to keep to your Study's so long at ONE TIME, my D: LOVE if you cou'd know how very precious your welfare is to me, I flatter myself you wou'd endeavor to preserve it, for my Sake, as well as YOUR OWN pray inform me how you do and how you have slept, I hope to see you to Morrow at the concert, and on Saturday. I shall be happy to see you here to dinner, in the mean time my D: my sincerest good wishes constantly attend you, and I ever am with the tenderest regard your most
> J: S: April the 19th 92.   [CCLN, 281]

Eighth Concert: 20 April 1792

H A N O V E R - S Q U A R E .
Mr. S A L O M O N ' S   C O N C E R T.

MR. SALOMON most respectfully acquaints the Subscribers, that his Eighth Concert will be TO-MORROW, April the 20th.

PART I.
By particular desire, the New Overture, M. S. HAYDN,
as performed on the Sixth Night.
Song, Miss CORRI.
New Sonata Piano Forte. Master HUMMEL,
with a Violin and Violoncello Obligato, Messrs. SALOMON
and MENEL. – HAYDN.
Song, Signor SIMONI.
Concerto German Flute, Mr. ASH[E].

PART II.
By particular desire, the New Overture, M. S. HAYDN,
As performed on the First and Second Nights.
Concerto Violin, Mr. JANIEWETZ [*sic*].
Song, Signor SIMONI.
FINALE.

[etc.]
[*Morning Herald*, 19, 20 April;
Oracle, 19, 20 April; etc.]

The 'Sonata' played by Master Hummel was the piano Trio in A flat, No. 27 (XVI: 14), which Frau von Genzinger had sent over from Vienna. Johann Nepomuk Hummel, then not yet fourteen years of age, was a child prodigy who had studied with Mozart and became one of the leading pianists and popular composers of his day. Later, in 1804, he became *Kapellmeister* to Prince Nicolaus II Esterházy.

For want of accurate and trustworthy copyists, Haydn was soon reduced to using Rebecca Schroeter as a copyist for a march: it was probably the *March for the Prince of Wales* or its orchestral version for the Royal Society of Musicians (autograph: 1792).

In a letter to Haydn, Mrs Schroeter wrote:

Aprill 24th 792

My D.

I can not leave London without sending you a line to assure you my thoughts[,] my BEST WISHES and tenderest affections will inseperably attend you till we meet again.

The Bearer will also deliver you the March, I am verry sorry, I cou'd not write it sooner, nor better, but I hope my D: you will excuse it, and if it is not passable, I will send you the DEAR original directly: If my H: wou'd employ me oftener to write Music I hope I shou'd improve, and I know I shou'd delight in the occupation. now MY D:L: let me intreat you to take the greatest care of your HEALTH I hope to see you on Friday at the concert and on Saturday to dinner till when and ever I most sincerely am, and shall be your [etc.]

[CCLN, 281]

That same day, Haydn wrote to Maria Anna von Genzinger, suggesting that he might have to go to Frankfurt. This is the first word we have that the composer might be involved in the coronation ceremonies of Franz II as Holy Roman Emperor of the German Nations (Leopold II having died in March 1792). Apparently Prince Anton Esterházy wanted his *Capellmeister* present. The stuttering 'Kreubich' is the composer Kreibich referred to previously.

[To Maria Anna von Genzinger, Vienna. *German*]

London, 24th April 1792.

Nobly born and gracious lady!

Yesterday evening I was delighted to receive your last letter of 5th April, with the enclosed newspaper cutting in which the Viennese are informed of my poor talents. I must admit that this little choral piece, my first attempt at the English language, has earned me considerable credit as a composer of vocal music with the English. It is only a pity that I could not compose more such pieces during my present stay here, but we couldn't have any boy choristers on the days our concerts were held, because they had already been engaged for a year past to sing at other concerts, of which there is a great number. Despite great opposition and the musical enemies who are so much against me – all of whom, together with my pupil Pleyel, tried their very hardest to crush me, especially this Winter – I have gained (thank God!) the upper hand. But I must admit that with all this work I am quite exhausted and wearied, and look forward longingly to the peace which will soon be mine. I kiss Your Grace's hands for your kind solicitude about my person, and just as Your Grace advises, I do not intend to go to Paris at present; but there are other reasons too, which I shall explain to Your Grace when I see you. I am expecting my Prince, to whom I wrote recently, to tell me where I am to go. It may be that he summons me to Frankfurt, but if not, I shall go (*entre nous*) *via* Holland to Berlin, to the King of Prussia, and from there to Leipzig, Dresden, Prague and – at last! – to Vienna, where I shall embrace all my friends. Meanwhile I remain, most respectfully, my kindest

Frau von Gennzinger's
most obedient servant,
Joseph Haydn.

My kind regards to your husband, *Fräulein* Pepi and all the others, no less to Herr von KREUBICH 'I am so gl- gl- glad' that he has the pleasure of enjoying your friendship. N.B. I hope to be able to kiss Your Grace's hands at the end of July. Please forgive my not making an envelope today, but there isn't time.

[Address:]

VON LONDON

Madame
Madame
Madame Anna Noble de
Gennzinger née Noble de Kayser.
à
Vienne

IM SCHOTTEN HOF.   en autriche.   [CCLN, 134f.]

On 26 April there seems to have been a concert at Carlton House in which three Haydn *Notturni* for the King of Naples were performed: Nos. 3, 4 and 7 of the Hoboken list, with the clarinet parts changed to violins, and the lira parts given to flute and oboe, or two flutes. We know, or think we know, of this concert because the MS. parts, with many corrections and additions by Haydn (also signed by him), are still preserved in the (British Museum) King's Library; someone, possibly a player, signed '26 Apr. 1792' (or a slight textual variant thereof) on each work. These *Notturni* would seem to be just the right sort of post-prandial entertainment for the Prince of Wales and his guests.

Haydn was persuaded to allow a letter of his to an instrument-maker to be printed, the next day, 27 April – in the *Morning Herald* – possibly on a business arrangement:

[Open letter to Charles Clagget, London. *English*]

[London, April 1792]

To Mr. *Clagget*, musical Museum, Greek street, Soho. – Sir! I called at your house, during your absence, and examined your improvements on the Pianoforte, and Harpsichords, and I found you had made them perfect instruments. I therefore, in justice to your invention, cannot forbear giving you my full approbation, as by this means you have rendered one of the finest instruments ever invented, perfect, and therefore the fittest to conduct any musical performance, and to accompany the human voice. I wish you to make this known through such channels as may appear to be most advantageous to you. I am etc. Josephus Haydn.

[CCLN, 135]

The 27th was also the day of the Ninth Concert, at which Haydn conducted two symphonies (the second one No. 92) and one of the *Notturni* for the King of Naples in the new London scoring:

Ninth Concert: 27 April 1792

HANOVER-SQUARE.
Mr. SALOMON'S CONCERT.

MR. SALOMON most respectfully acquaints the Subscribers, that his Ninth Concert will be TO-MORROW, April 27th.

PART I.
Grand Overture, M. S. HAYDN.
Divertimenti [*sic*] for Violin, Oboe, Flauto, two Violas, two Corni, Violoncello Obligati [*sic*], – Mess. SALOMON, HARRINGTON, ASHE, HINDMARCH, POLECK, PIOLTAIN [*sic*], LEANDER, MENEL. – HAYDN.
Song, Signor SIMONI.
Concerto Violoncello, Mrs. DAMER [*sc*. Mr. Dahmen].
Song, Madam MARA.

PART II.
By particular desire, the Favourite Overture, – HAYDN,
As performed last Season, on the First and Second Nights.
Song, Signor SIMONI.
Concerto Violin, Mr. JANIEWETZ [*sic*].
Song, Madam MARA.
Finale – HAYDN.

[etc.]
[*Morning Herald*, 26, 27 April;
Oracle, 26, 27 April;
Morning Chronicle, 26 April; etc.]

On 28 April 1792, the *Morning Herald* tells us of a concert 'this present evening' at Hanover Square for the singer Albertarelli, of which Part II opened with a 'Grand Overture, HAYDN'. A few days later there was another benefit concert at Hanover Square, Madame de Musigny's night on 2 May 1792, opening with an 'Overture, HAYDN' (*Morning Herald*, 30 April 1792).

Even as he was completing Symphony No. 97, Haydn still kept an eye on London prices, some of them fantastic:

[*German*] At the beginning of May 1792, Lord Barrymore gave a ball that cost 5,000 guineas. He paid 1,000 guineas for 1,000 peaches. 2000 baskets of gusberes [gooseberries], 5 shillings a basket.   [CCLN, 270]

The time for Haydn's benefit was now fast approaching. The day before, Mrs. Schroeter ordered another six tickets – which meant she was now inviting a party of eighteen, herself included, to the concert – and asked Haydn to dinner on the 5th. Haydn was now scheduled to conduct two nights in succession: at the Tenth Salomon Concert on Friday 4 May, and of course at his own benefit the night before. Rebecca Schroeter wrote on 2 May:

M:D: I am very anxious to know HOW YOU DO, and hope to hear you have been in good health ever since I saw you – as the time for your charming concert advances I feel myself more and more interested for your Success, and heartely WISH every thing may turn out to your Satisfaction. do me the favor to send me six Tickets more. on Saturday my D:L I hope to see you to dinner, in the mean while, my thoughts, my best wishes, and tenderest affections, constantly attend you, and I ever am my D: H: most sincerely and aff. [etc.]

J: S: May the 2^{d} $\overline{792}$.   [CCLN, 281f.]

HANOVER-SQUARE.
For the BENEFIT of Dr. HAYDN.
THIS EVENING, the 3rd of May, 1792,
will be performed a Grand Concert of Vocal and Instrumental Music.

PART I.
Grand Overture, M. S. HAYDN.
Aria, Signor CALCAGNI.
Concertante for Violin, Violoncello, Oboe, Bassoon. Messrs.
SALOMON, MENEL, HARRINGTON, and HOLMES. – HAYDN.
Cantata, Miss CORRI. – HAYDN.
Concerto Violin, Mr. JANEIWETZ [*sic*].

PART II.
Grand Overture, M. S. HAYDN.
Song, Signor SIMONI.
Concerto Pedal Harp, Madam KRUMPHOLTZ.
Song, Madam MARA.
Finale the Earthquake. – HAYDN.

[etc.]
[*Oracle,* 20 April, 1 May;
Morning Chronicle, 30 April;
Morning Herald, 30 April, 2, 3 May; etc.]

Until now, it was not known at which 1792 concert Haydn presented his final Symphony of the season – the brilliantly extrovert No. 97. Curiously enough, new evidence of the 1795 season helps us to establish the point. We shall see that Haydn concluded his Symphonies of the 1795 season with No. 104 which he presented for the first time at his benefit concert on 4 May. We suggest that the same obtained, *mutatis mutandis,* on 3 May 1792, and that Symphony No. 97 in C was the 'Grand Overture, M.S.' at the beginning of Part II. It would have been repeated the next night, at Salomon's Tenth Concert; it was again repeated at the Eleventh Concert (11 May 1792). The Haydn Cantata sung by Miss Corri cannot be identified. The *Concertante* is well known to us, of course, and the Finale 'The Earthquake' is the *Terremoto* ending of the Oratorio, *The Seven Words.*

Mr Albi Rosenthal, to whom musicologists must always be grateful, discovered a ticket for Haydn's 'Night', which he has kindly allowed us to reproduce in facsimile.[1] It is signed '469' on the left and 'Haydn mp.' on the right at the bottom. In a pretty ornamental border, signed 'Macky sculpt.', the whole is printed in blue ink: 'HANOVER SQUARE / *Dr Haydn's Night,* / *On Thursday the 3^d of May 1792* / To begin at 8 o'Clock / *Tickets Half a Guinea each to be had of* / Dr HAYDN, / *N° 18, Great Pulteney Street, Golden Square.*' The ticket was for Mrs. Papendiek, our interesting witness to Haydn's first concert in England, and also his benefit in 1795. On the back she wrote [pencil:] 'Presented to Mrs Papendiek / by Dr Hayden himself / at which Concert ye Dutchess / of York was present for / the first time in England / [ink:] & 1500 people entered the door' – and that in a room which, in Mrs. Papendiek's own words, was 'calculated to hold 800 persons exclusive of the performers'.

That day, 3 May 1792, the *Morning Chronicle* noted that Hardy's portrait of Haydn was being exhibited at the Royal Academy (where there were to be seen paintings of Madame Mara, Madame Gautherot, Madame Krumpholz and Dr Arnold), and that Bland was selling 'a capital print of Mr Haydn' from the painting, and also prints of Salomon and Pleyel.

In the following three, and last, Salomon concerts a *Notturno* for the King of Naples was played in each, the first two not identifiable. The one on 18 May was Hob. II: 32 (known as '*Notturno 8*', but Haydn called it, interestingly, '*Notturno 3^{zo}*', possibly showing that it was the third of another series.) The documents of the period are reprinted here.

---

1 Landon, *Supplement,* facing p. 33. Original size: 12 × 8 cms.

Tenth Concert: 4 May 1792

HANOVER-SQUARE.
Mr. SALOMON'S CONCERT.
The Subscribers are respectfully acquainted, that the Tenth Performance will be
on FRIDAY, May 4, 1792.

PART I.
Overture M. S. HAYDN.
Song, Signor SIMONI.
(By particular desire) the Divertimento, as performed last
Friday, for two Violins, Oboe, Flute, two Tenors, two French Horns,
and Violoncello – Mess. SALOMON, DAMER [*sic*], HARRINGTON, ASHE,
HINDMARCH, POLACK, PIELTAIN, LEANDER, and MENEL. – HAYDN.
Song, Madam MARA.
Concerto German Flute, Mr. GAEFFE [i.e. Graeff].

PART II.
New Overture, M. S. HAYDN.
Song, Signor SIMONI.
Concerto Piano Forte, Mr. DUSSECK.
Song, Madam MARA.
Finale. – HAYDN.   [etc.]
[*Morning Herald*, 2, 4 May; etc.]

[Mrs. Schroeter to Haydn:]

James St Tuesday May ye 8th
My D^t I am extremely sorry I have not the pleasure Seeing you to Day, but hope to
see you to Morrow at one o'clòck and if you can take your DINNER WITH me to
Morrow, I shall be very glad – I hope to see you also on Thursday to dinner, but I
suppose you will be obliged to go to the concert[1] that Evening, and you know the
other concert is on Friday, and you go to the country on Saturday, this my D^t
LOVE makes me more solicitous for you to stay with me TO MORROW, if you are
not engaged, as I wish to have as much of your company AS POSSIBLE. God Bless
you my Dst H, I always am with the tenderest Regard
your sincere and
affectionate [etc.]
[CCLN, 282]

On 10 May 1792, Madame Krumpholz gave her benefit concert in the Hanover
Square Rooms, to which Haydn contributed some new music (as usual, it cannot be
identified):

HANOVER-SQUARE.
For the BENEFIT of Madame KRUMPHOLTZ.
On THURSDAY, May 10, 1792, will be performed,
A GRAND CONCERT of VOCAL and INSTRUMENTAL MUSIC.

PART I.
Overture, M. S. Haydn [*etc.*, with the participation
of Miss Corri, Mr. Dussek playing a piano concerto, Signor
Simoni, Signor Janiewetz].
PART II.
Overture, M. S. Haydn. . . .
Finale Haydn.
[*World*, 7 May 1792]

1 Probably the Academy of Antient Music.

Eleventh Concert: 11 May 1792

HANOVER-SQUARE.
Mr. SALOMON'S CONCERT.

THE Subscribers are respectfully acquainted, that the Eleventh Performance will be on FRIDAY, the 11th of May, 1792.

PART I.
Overture GYROWETZ.
New Divertimento for two Violins, Oboe, Flute, two Tenors, two French Horns, Violoncello, and Double Bass – Messrs. SALOMON, DAMEN, HARRINGTON, ASHE, HINDMARCH, POLACK, PIELTAIN, LEANDER, MENEL, and DRESSLER. – HAYDN.
Song, Signor SIMONI.
Concerto Violoncello, Mr. SHRAM.
Song, Madam MARA.

PART II.
(By particular desire) the New Overture, M. S. HAYDN, as performed last Friday.
Song, Signor SIMONI.
New Concerto Piano Forte, Mr. HAESSLER.
Song, Madam MARA.
Finale – HAYDN.
[etc.]
[*Morning Herald,* 9 May; *Oracle,* 9, 11 May; etc.]

[Fanny Burney, Dr. Burney's daughter, recovering from a kind of nervous exhaustion, writes to Mrs. Francis (later Broome).]

12 May 1792 [also wrongly] 13th [May 1792]
Chelsea College.

. . . Last Night, for the Time, I ventured to a public place. I went to Salomon's Concert, & was quite enchanted by sweet sounds, long strangers to my Ears. It was *My First Appearance in Public* for many Years. – Yet there was no particular applause upon my entrance! – For which reason, finding it so little answer, I do not purpose repeating the same abstinence for quite as long a period in haste.

[From Fanny Burney's Journal for May 1792:]
I went, also, to one of Salomon's Concerts [on 11 May 1792], where I heard most divine Music of Haydn. – & to the benefit Concert of Fischar [*recte*: Fischer, the oboe player], where I heard M[e] Krumpolts [*sic*] play like an angel, & Mrs. Billington sing better than any English singer I ever heard. . . .[1]

SALOMON'S CONCERT.

By far the best of the kind in England, had its ELEVENTH meeting on Friday night. MARA sung in the most enchanting strain, and received general applause. In return, it is her duty to shew every respect to those who contribute to support her, by a decent deportment in the orchestra. Turning her back, and leaning on the harpsichord, has too much the air of negligence and contempt. We are sorry to

---

1 *The Journals and Letters of Fanny Burney* (Madame D'Arblay), edited by Joyce Hemlow & others, Oxford, 1972: Vol. I (1791–2), pp. 144 and 179.

observe, that most of our principal singers need to be often reminded in this respect.

Salomon led the band with his usual spirit and accuracy, but we would advise him to banish Mr. Haesler's concertos: his performance on the harpsichord was the most wretched attempt we ever heard. There might be skill, but harmony was wholly forgotten. [*The Times*, 14 May]

[Mrs. Schroeter to Haydn:]
May 17th
M: D: Permit me to return you a thousand thanks for this Evening's entertainment[1] – where YOUR – SWEET compositions and your EXCELLENT performance combine, it can not fail of being a most CHARMING CONCERT, but independent of THAT, the pleasure of SEEING YOU must ever give me infinite Satisfaction – Pray inform me HOW YOU DO? and if you have SLEPT WELL? I hope to see you to morrow my D: and on Saturday to dinner, till when and always I remain most sincerely my D: L: most Faith[ful] etc. [CCLN, 282]

Twelfth Concert: 18 May 1792

HANOVER-SQUARE.
Mr. SALOMON'S CONCERT.

THE Subscribers are respectfully acquainted, that the Twelfth Performance will be THIS EVENING, the 18th of May.

PART I.
(By desire) the Overture, M. S. HAYDN,
As performed last season, the seventh night.
New Notturno for two Violins, two Flutes, two Tenors, two Horns,
Violoncello, and Double Bass. – Messrs. SALOMON, DAMER [*sic*],
ASH[E], FLORIA [*sic*], HINDMARCH, POLACK, PIELTAIN,
LEANDER, MENEL, and DRESSLER. – HAYDN.
Song, Signor SIMONI.
Concerto Duetto, for Oboe and Bassoon, Messrs.
HARRINGTON and HOLMES.
Song, Madam MARA.

PART II.
(By desire) the Overture, M. S. HAYDN,
As performed the first night this season.
Song, Signor SIMONI.
Concerto Pedal Harp, Madam KRUMPHOLTZ.
Song, Madam MARA.
Finale – HAYDN. [etc.]
[*Morning Herald*, 18 May;
Oracle, 15, 17, 18 May; etc.]

The Symphonies for this last subscription concert were, at the beginning, probably, either No. 95 or 96; and in the second part No. 93. A short criticism appeared the next day in the *Oracle*:

SALOMON'S CONCERT.

FULL as the Oracle is, we will yet give in two lines, the report of Mr. SALOMON's closing Concert. The most varied excellence that was ever combined, as amply

---

1 Haydn seems to have given a musical party at Mrs. Schroeter's or at one of their mutual friend's.
[CCLN, 282]

patronized. HAYDN, SALOMON, MARA, and KRUMPHOLTZ, were applauded last night, as the French say, *à tout rompre*.

And it must have been with a sense of pride mixed with relief that Haydn noted (CCLN, 278), 'On 18th May 1792, the last Salomon Concert was given at Hanover Square.'

Haydn was, of course, at the keyboard to preside over the benefit concert of his friend Salomon on 21 May:

HANOVER-SQUARE.
For the BENEFIT OF MR. SALOMON.
On MONDAY the 21st instant, will be performed a GRAND CONCERT of VOCAL and INSTRUMENTAL MUSIC.

PART I.
Grand Overture, MS. HAYDN.
Song, SIGNOR SIMONI.
Concerto Grand Piano Forte, Mr. DUSSECK.
Song, Madame MARA.
Concerto Violin, Mr. SALOMON.

PART II.
Grand Overture, MS. HAYDN.
Song, Signor SIMONI.
New Concerto Pedal Harp, Madame KRUMPHOLTZ.
Song, Madame MARA.
Finale, the Earthquake – HAYDN.   [etc.]

[*Oracle*, 14, 19 May; *Morning
Herald*, 19, 21 May; *Morning
Chronicle*, 19, 21 May; etc.]

On 22 May, Haydn received a letter from Rebecca Schroeter and wrote one to *la* Polzelli:

[Mrs. Schroeter to Haydn]
M:D: If you will do me the favor to take your dinner with me to Morrow, I shall be very happy to see you, and I PARTICULARLY wish for the pleasure of YOUR company MY Dr LOVE BEFORE our other friends come. – I hope to hear you have SLEPT WELL to Night, and that you are in GOOD HEALTH, my BEST WISHES and tenderest Regards are your constant attendants and I EVER am with the FIRMEST Attachment my Dst H^n

most Sincerely and Affectionately
yours R S:

James S. Tuesday Ev: May 22^d [CCLN, 282f.]

[To Luigia Polzelli, Bologna. *Italian, 'Tu' form*]

London, 22nd May 1792.
Dear Polzelli,
    I received your letter and saw from it that at any rate you are well again. You write that I should get you an engagement at a theatre; I assure you that there is no chance of that in London now, for they don't know whether there will be any Italian opera here next year. The English are not too fond of Italian opera, because they don't understand the language; but I shall do my very best to get something for you when I return to Vienna. I shall send you the money for Pietro very soon, as I promised, and shall let you know the day of my departure from London. The ENGLISH WANT ME TO STAY HERE, BUT THIS IS IMPOSSIBLE AT PRESENT, BECAUSE IT'S

ABSOLUTELY ESSENTIAL FOR ME TO GO HOME, in order to put my affairs in proper order; I left all my things in Estoras [Eszterháza]. My Prince wants me to come to the Coronation at Frankfurt. I shall go there, for I have to take this route home anyway. I shall very soon be sending a trunk with various things for Pietro, and some clothes for you from your sister. Meanwhile farewell; in the hope that God will allow me to see you and embrace you, I am, as always, your faithful

Giuseppe Haydn.

[Address:]   Madame
        Madame Loise Polzelli
        Virtuosa di Musica
           a

Ferma in Posta   BOLOGNA
           EN ITALIE.   [CCLN, 135–6]

We now come to a direct confrontation with Haydn's arch-enemy, the composer and violinist Felice Giardini. Since the Italian seems to have been the leader of an anti-Haydn clique, we might study the sources concerning his character and his qualities as a musician. Parke, who always appears to be an impartial and intelligent observer, writes of Giardini's great abilities, and then adds,

> Giardini was however a man of haughty and capricious disposition, and his vanity being continually flattered by the marked attentions he received from the haut ton, among whom he lived, he was led to imagine that there was no rank in life, however exalted, that would not be proud of his association.   [II, 240]

Giardini had been away, and upon returning to England found he had been supplanted by other composers and other leaders. Parke writes:

> Giardini doubtless expected, on his return to this Country [in 1790], to have shared the public engagements with [the leader of the Professional Concert, Wilhelm] Cramer: but in that he was disappointed, for Cramer had got possession of nearly the whole of them. Giardini, a little chagrined, meeting Cramer, thus sarcastically saluted him: 'How do you do, Mr. Harlequin Everywhere?' To which Cramer, with a smile of triumph, replied, 'Pretty well, I thank you, Mr. Harlequin Nowhere.'   [I, 154]

Haydn tried to be introduced to Giardini. Both Griesinger and Dies relate the story, Griesinger in his pithy way being more accurate, and Dies in his garrulous way being more colourful and prolix:

> A Lord [Abingdon?] took him to the great violin player Giardini. They stood in the anti-chambre, were announced, and heard very clearly that Giardini told his servant, 'I don't want to know that German dog'. The Lord was extremely put out over it, but Haydn only found the episode comical, and soon thereafter he went to hear Giardini play in a concert.   [Griesinger, 35]

During his first eighteen-month stay in London, he [Haydn] attempted, as we have seen, to make the acquaintance of famous musicians. Among them the name of Giardini was known as a violin player who had harvested much fame. Haydn wished to know him personally. His wish was spoken in the presence of a Lord who offered to take him to Giardini. For the Lord it was a pleasant business to be able to introduce two famous men to each other. The Lord and Haydn went there, found a servant in the anti-chambre and asked to be announced. The door remained slightly open; the Lord and Haydn heard quite clearly the decision which Giardini gave his servant in a loud voice, and which in literal translation would be, 'I don't want to know the German dog.'

The Lord was very annoyed about the rudeness of the virtuoso and avoided his company thereafter. Haydn, however, only saw the comical side of the affair, and, even now, it made him laugh whenever the name Giardini was dropped. The latter's curious behaviour did not, however, hinder Haydn from looking for an opportunity to know the man from an artistic side. Soon afterwards, Giardini gave a public concert. Haydn was unrecognized among the audience and admired the skill of the virtuoso, who at an advanced age performed with the fire of youth, and in the Adagio called forth the most gentle tones from his violin and won the audience over to him, so that Haydn gladly forgave his [Giardini's] bad humour and attributed it to his advanced years. [Dies, 107f.]

The concert that Haydn heard took place on Tuesday, 22 May 1792, in Ranelagh Gardens. Giardini's oratorio *Ruth* was given, and between the acts the old veteran played a violin concerto of his own composition. In fact, Giardini, who was born at Turin in 1716, was now seventy-six. He still enjoyed a fine artistic, if otherwise dubious, reputation. William Shield spoke of Giardini in 1798 to the painter Joseph Farington:

He [Shield] spoke of Giardini, who He said, had the finest tone He ever heard, when the strength of it was considered. – In general those who produce fine tones, have not much strength. – Dance observed that Giardini had a narrow mind on the subject of music. – He hated Handel, and the modern 'German compositions'. – When the performance of Handels composition was proposed to be in Westminster Abbey Giardini so far from encouraging affected to sneer at the proposal, and said He would go 2 or 3 miles from the town, as He could then sufficiently hear the effect. [Farington I, 238]

Dr Burney quotes, in Rees's *Cyclopaedia*, from a report on Giardini by a close associate, 'lately come to our hands accidentally':

His disposition is so truly diabolical, that, preferring the evil principle of the Manicheans to the good of the Christians, if it is a matter of indifference to his interest, whether he shall serve or injure an individual, he would always chuse the latter. [Scholes II, 195]

Parke tells us how Giardini's powerful and clear tone made even inferior instruments sound excellent, so that Giardini made a tidy profit selling such inferior instruments to gullible gentlemen (I, 155). But this evening, all Giardini's old friends and patrons turned out to what was obviously going to be a farewell concert (in 1796 he died at Moscow). Parke (I, 154) tells us, 'He did not aim to surprise, but he played with great expression: his tone and taste were exquisite . . . [The] Dukes of Gloucester and Dorset [both old patrons of Giardini] . . . each . . . presented him with a hundred pounds for their ticket.'

After all this, Haydn for once revealed that he could be nasty, particularly when the object was one so thoroughly depressing:

On 21st [*recte*: 22nd] May [1792], Giardini's concert took place in Renalag [Ranelagh Gardens]. He played like a pig. [CCLN, 257]

On 25 May 1792, Haydn seems to have gone to one of the sessions of the famous Warren Hastings trials which had commenced in 1788. Can Haydn have known

Hastings and his attractive German wife, Marian, Baroness Imhoff? Hastings' impeachment trial, which ended in April 1795 with acquittal on all counts, was one of several British law-suits that Haydn followed with increasing interest.

> Hastings' trial which took place last week on 25th May 1792 was the ninety-second meeting in Westminster Hall. Hasting [*sic*] has 3 advocates all to himself. Each of them gets 10 guineas on the day of the meeting. This trial began 4 years ago. It is said that Hasting [*sic*] has a fortune of a million pounds Sterling.
>
> [CCLN, 254]

Salomon had decided to give an extra concert, which for some reason had to be postponed. The documents read as follows:

HANOVER SQUARE.
Mr. SALOMON'S CONCERT.

BY Desire of many of the SUBSCRIBERS, who wish to hear some of those Performances repeated, which have been most admired during the Season, Mr. SALOMON is induced to offer to his Friends, and the Public in general, one more CONCERT on Saturday next, the 26th instant; for which Tickets, at 10s 6d each, may be had at the Rooms. And as many of the Subscribers, from different circumstances, have been deprived of the opportunity of using some of their Tickets in the course of the Season, Mr. Salomon begs leave to assure them, he shall feel himself much gratified, by their doing him the honour of using them on that evening. [*Oracle*, 23, 24 May; *Morning Chronicle*, 23, 24 May; etc.]

HANOVER-SQUARE.

MR. SALOMON most respectfully acquaints the Nobility and Gentry, that having had an Intimation from the Lord Chamberlain of His Majesty's Household, that there would be an impropriety in opening the Rooms To-morrow, his intended CONCERT is unavoidably POSTPONED.

[*Oracle*, 25 May; etc.]

HANOVER-SQUARE.

MR. SALOMON most respectfully acquaints the Nobility and Gentry, that the CONCERT which was intended for Saturday last, will certainly take place on Wednesday the 6th of June, when the most favourite Performances of the season will be repeated. [*Oracle*, 28 May; *Morning Herald*, 29, 31 May; etc.]

On 28 May, Haydn presided over a concert, led by Salomon, for an interesting musician who was a friend of Haydn's. This was François Hippolite Barthélémon, who had lived in England since 1765 and was the son of a French government officer and an Irish lady. Thus the French accents were often omitted from his name in later life, and we follow the local practice. Barthelemon was well known as a composer and a violinist, excelling in the performance of Corelli sonatas. His compositions have not survived, but Haydn thought highly of them. *Jefte in Masfa*, produced during a tour of the Continent in 1776 (it was commissioned by the Grand Duke of Tuscany, later Leopold II), was shown by its composer to Haydn. 'Well, my dear friend,' said Haydn, 'if you'd composed it in Germany, it would have made you immortal' (Pohl, *H in L*, 199). Barthelemon's wife was an accomplished singer, *née* Mary Young, and his daughter, Caecilia Maria, was a pupil of J. S. Schroeter and not only a good organist and pianist but also a composer. (Her Op. 2, Two Sonatas for piano or harpsichord with accompaniments for a German flute, violin and Violoncello was dedicated to another of Haydn's friends and patrons, the 'Dutchess' of York: copy in the British Museum.)

Haydn often went to visit the Barthelemon family in the house at No. 8, Kennington Place, Vauxhall. Haydn and Barthelemon became 'brothers in affection' (Pohl, *H in L*, 199). The daughter preserved various Haydn relics, among other things the Aria 'Son pietosa' (1789) by Haydn, composed for the pasticcio, *La Circe*, in a MS. score by an English copyist.[1] Caecilia Maria wrote on the title page – we omit her eccentric parentheses:

> 'Mio caro Maestro Haydn gave me this Song when I was Caecilia Maria Barthelemon (now Hinchcliffe) often have I sat with him when he play'd his Sweet Canzonetts & he used to shed tears *when he sang* 'The Season comes when *first we met* but you return no more'[2] & I said to him, 'Papa Haydn, Why do you cry?' & he said, 'Oh! *my dear Child.* I do not like to leave my English Friends, they are so kind to me!'

After the word 'Aria' she added '(to be preserved with care)'. She owned a signed copy of both first and second sets of the 'VI Original Canzonettas', and her copies are now in the Stanford Memorial Library in California. The first set is inscribed, 'The Gift of the Author to Cecilia Maria Barthelemon' and over the top of the second page of 'Recollection' (p. 9), 'I heard dear Dr Haydn, sing this, with peculiar expression – with grateful recollection of his English friends.' The 'Second Sett of Dr Haydn's VI Original Canzonettas' is inscribed as follows:

> Cecilia Maria Henslow [apparently a second marriage]. I had the great pleasure to hear the famous Doct. Haydn play & sing his beautiful Canzonetts, (in my youth) in my Dear Father's House at Vauxhall. Oh! what a treat it was! The dear good & respected Haydn was often with us – & express'd much pleasure, when my beloved mother took the upper part (with me) of a Duett of Handels (in his fine Opera of Poro) – She had a fine high soprano voice – & had been (when very young) a scholar of the famous Geminiani.' [Caecilia Maria's daughter added the following:] Given into my hands by my dear Mother. Fanny H. Henslowe.

The concert of 28 May included a Haydn symphony. Barthelemon's pupil Bridgetower played a violin concerto by Viotti; Mrs Barthelemon sang arias by Sacchini and Handel; Salomon, Barthelemon, Hindmarsh and Shram performed a quartet by Barthelemon; and Barthelemon himself played 'by particular Desire' a sonata by Corelli (Pohl, *H in L*, 198f.). We shall see that Haydn once more participated in a Barthelemon concert on 26 May 1794. Examination of the London newspapers after Haydn left England has yielded up an interesting fact. In 1799, Haydn fully intended to compose a violin concerto for Barthelemon: this hitherto unknown fact was revealed in the *Morning Herald* of 16 March 1799. At least we presume Haydn was prevented from sending it from Vienna, for there is no news of the concert taking place. It is just possible, of course, that Haydn did compose the concerto and it is lost – not so incredible if one considers that a Concerto for 2 horns of this late period seem to have completely disappeared, and that, moreover, the famous Trumpet Concerto of

---

1 Burgenländisches Landesmuseum, Eisenstadt, *ex coll.* Landon.
2 Haydn's 'Recollection' from 'Dr. Haydn's VI Original Canzonettas'.

1796 has come down to posterity only in one source, namely the autograph, and that the score was not printed until 1931.

> MR. BARTHELEMON,
> most respectfully begs leave to acquaint his Friends and the Public, that he intends to have a GRAND CONCERT some time in the month of April, Dr. HAYDN having favoured him with a New Concerto for the Violin, of his own composition, from Vienna. – The day, place, and further particulars, will be advertised in due time – Tickets, 10s 6d. each, to be had of Mr. Barthelemon, at his House, No. 8, Kennington-place, Vauxhall; and at the most principal Music Shops.
> [*Morning Herald*, 16 March 1799]

Two days after the Barthelemon concert, J. W. Haesler, of whom we have spoken above (*vide* p. 116) gave his benefit concert at Hanover Square. Haydn presided and Salomon was the leader. Two 'Grand Overtures M. S.' by Haydn were given; Haesler offered a new cantata and performed two piano concerti, one by Mozart and one of his own. 'Haesler', says Pohl (*H in L*, 200f.), 'did not really feel at home in England, although he was much appreciated there. In November 1792, he wrote to his relative at Erfurt, his birth-place, 'the people here [in England] are much too cold, I shall go to Russia";' and in April 1793, the *Berliner Musikzeitung* reports him as 'Harpsichord Player to the Großfürsten of Russia' with a salary of 1000 roubles a year; he died at Moscow in 1822, 'much respected'.

The next day after the Haesler concert Handel's *Messiah* was given as a benefit for the Royal Society of Musicians in St. Margaret's Chapel near the Abbey. The difference between some 300 (*pace* Pohl, Haydn says 200) performers in the much smaller church and 1,000 in the Abbey was felt. In Haydn's notebook we find the following two entries:

> Anno 1791 the last great concert, with 885 persons, was held in Westminster [Abbey]. Anno 1792 it was transferred to St. Margaret's Chapel, with 200 performers. People criticized this.   [CCLN, 271]

> On 30th [*recte*: 31st] May 1792, the grand Widows' Concert, which was given for the last time a year ago in Westminster Abbey with 885 persons, took place in St. Margaret's Church, because of the great expense involved. There were 800 persons at the rehearsal and 2000 at the actual performance. The King gave 100 guineas each time.   [CCLN, 254]

The king and queen were at the performance, and a royal nod suggested that three choruses be repeated, 'For unto us a Child is born', 'Hallelujah' and 'Worthy is the Lamb'. The singers included many of Haydn's friends: Madame Mara, Mrs Harrison (*née* Miss Cantelo), Miss Corri, Miss Poole; Michael O'Kelly, Sale, Bellamy jr., Gore, Knyvett, Webbe, Champness, the young Welsh, and James Bartleman, who began his successful career that Thursday, 31 May 1792. Dr Arnold conducted, Cramer was the leader, and the organist was Dr Dupuis, whose playing Haydn much admired. George Smart saw Haydn one day at the Chapel Royal in St James's. 'He was so pleased with Dr Dupuis's extempore fugues, that meeting the doctor as he came downstairs from the organ loft, after the service, he gave him two kisses in the Ambassadors' Court. This I saw him do', adds Smart rather primly, 'and I was very much surprised at that time at the operation' (Smart, 4).

If Haydn had enjoyed one day's respite from conducting concerts, the day afterwards, 1 June, he was back at the keyboard in Hanover Square Rooms, this time at

Madame Mara's benefit. We have a criticism from the *Morning Herald* and also a couple of lines in Haydn's notebook:

HANOVER-SQUARE.

MADAME MARA's Night will be on Friday the 1st of June, 1792. PART I. Grand Overture M. S. HAYDN. – Quartetto for two Violins, Tenor and Bass, Messrs. SALOMON, DAMER [*sic*], HINDMARSH, and MENEL. – HAYDN. – Aria, Sig. SIMONI. – Concerto Pedal Harp, Mr. MEYER, Jun. – Song, Madame MARA.

PART II. Grand Overture, M. S. HAYDN. – Song, Mad. MARA. (By desire) "From rosy bower" – PURCELL. – Concerto Violin, Mr. SALOMON – SALOMON. – The favourite song in Idalide, Madame MARA, with an accompaniment on the French Harp, by Mr. MEYER, Jun. – Finale – HAYDN . . .

[*Morning Herald*, 29, 31 May;
Oracle, 30 May, 1 June;
Morning Chronicle, 31 May, 1 June: etc.]

MARA'S BENEFIT.

There was a fine show of elegance and scientific visitors at the Hanover-square Rooms last night, to grace the Concert of this accomplished performer. The repast was such as might be expected, considering that it was her night, and that it was under the tasteful arrangement of SALOMON.

MARA sung three airs, one of ARFOSSI [i.e. Anfossi], a fine *bravura*: the second, an irregular, impassioned, and pathetic song by PURCELL; and the third, the delightful *rondeau* from the Opera of IDALIDE. – They were all given in her best syle, and the latter was *encored*.

SALOMON played a Violin Concerto in a manner that may be compared with the most renowned performers. Young MEYER gave a charming Harp Concerto of KRUMPHOLTZ, with admirable skill, though under evident embarrassment from diffidence, and the vexation arising from the breaking of several strings.

The other accidents of the evening, were the fall of an *infirm sopha*, and the consequent *prostration* of some *venerable beaux*, and the *lodgement* of a whole cupfull of hot tea down the neck of MARA, by the sudden movement of some awkward arm.   [*Morning Herald*, 2 June]

On 1st June 1792 Mara gave her benefit concert. They played two of my Symphonies, and I accompanied her, all by myself at the pianoforte, in a very difficult English Aria by Purcell. The audience was very small.   [CCLN, 258f.]

When Haydn woke the next morning, he found a note from Rebecca Schroeter, who liked to write notes the last thing before retiring so that her servant could deliver them early the next day:

My D[r] I beg to know HOW YOU DO? hope to hear you[r] Head-ach is ENTIRELY GONE, and that you have SLEPT WELL. I shall be very happy to see you on Sunday any time convenient to you after one o'clock – I hope to see you my D[r] L on tuesday as usual to Dinner, [crossed out: "and all (?night ? p.m.) with me"] – and I shall be much obliged to you if you will inform me what Day will be agreeable to you to meet M[r] M[tris] and MISS STONE at my house to Dinner, I shou'd be glad if it was either Thursday or Friday, whichever Day YOU PLEASE to fix, I will send to M[r] Stone to let them know. I long to see you my D[t] H, let me have that pleasure as soon as you can, till when and Ever I remain with the FIRMEST attachment My D[r] L:

most faithfully and affectionately
yours [etc.]

Friday June ye 1st 792.

[CCLN, 283]

Haydn's notebook tells us of some events that occurred in London, and to him, on 3 June and 4 June:

On 3rd June, that being the eve of the King's birthday, all the bells in London are rung from 8 o'clock in the evening to 9 o'clock, and so also in honour of the Queen. [CCLN, 259]

On 3rd June 1792, I dined with *Mon*[r] and M[a][d] Mara, M[r] Kely and M[dam] Storace at her brother's Storace. *Sapienti pauca.* [CCLN 254]

Today, 4th June 1792, I was in Vauxhall where the King's birthday is celebrated. Over 30,000 lamps were burning, but because of the severe cold there were very few people present. The grounds and its variety are perhaps unique in the world. There are 155 little dining booths in various places, most charmingly situated, each comfortably seating 6 persons. There are very large alleys of trees, which form a wonderful roof above, and are magnificently illuminated. Tea, coffee and milk with almonds [*Mandlmilch*] all cost nothing. The entrance fee is half a crown per person. The music is fairly good. A stone statue of Handel has been erected. On the 2nd inst. there was a masked ball, and on this evening they took in 3000 guineas. [CCLN, 262]

The Handel statue that Haydn noticed is by Louis François Roubiliac and had been made in 1738: it is now in Novello's publishing house.[1]

On 6 June, Salomon's extra concert was given. The opening work was probably Symphony No. 97, the other Symphony probably one of the well-known ones (No. 94 perhaps?). The 'sehr difficult' Purcell Aria was repeated from Mara's benefit concert. The Gyrowetz Concertante was later published by André of Offenbach-on-the-Main as Op. 34, and is a large-scale work including second flute, oboe and bassoon parts, with horns, trumpets, timpani and strings. Haydn and Salomon performed it again on 12 May 1794. Mrs Schroeter also attended the concert.

HANOVER-SQUARE.

MR. SALOMON'S LAST CONCERT for the Season will be TO-MORROW, Wednesday, the 6th of June.

PART I.
Grand Overture, M. S. HAYDN, as performed on his own night. – Song, Signor SIMONI. – Sonata Pedal Harp, Mr. MEYER. – Song, Madame MARA. – Concerto Violin, Mr. SALOMON. – Song, by desire, 'Rosey Bowers' – PURCELL, Madame MARA.

PART II.
Grand Overture. M. S. HAYDN, as performed at Mr. Salomon's Benefit. – Song, Signor SIMONI. – New Concertante, M. S. for a Violin, Oboe, Flute, Bassoon, and Violoncello Obligati, Messrs. SALOMON, HARRINGTON, ASHE, HOLMES, and MENEL. – GYROWETZ. – Aria, Madame MARA. – By desire, the favourite Air in Idalide, accompanied on the Harp, by Mr. MEYER. – Full piece, HAYDN . . .

[*Morning Herald*, 5, 6 June;
Morning Chronicle, 5 June;
Oracle, 5, 6 June; etc.]

[Mrs Schroeter to Haydn]
My D: I can not close my Eyes to sleep till I have return'd you ten thousand thanks for the inexpressible delight I have received from YOUR EVER ENCHANTING

1 O. E. Deutsch, *Handel, A Documentary Biography*, London, 1955, p. 456.

compositions and your INCOMPARABLY CHARMING PERFORMANCE of them, be assured my D H: that among ALL your numerous admirers NO ONE has listened with more PROFOUND attention, and no one can have such high veneration for your MOST BRILLIANT TALENTS as I HAVE. indeed my D: L: no tongue CAN EXPRESS the gratitude I FEEL for the infinite pleasure your Music has given me, accept then my repeeted thanks for it, and let me also assure you, with heart-felt affection, that I shall ever consider the happiness of your acquaintance as one of the CHIEF Blessings of my life, and it is the SINCER wish of my heart to preserve, to cultivate and to merit it more and more. I hope to hear you are quite well. Shall be happy to see you to dinner and if you CAN come at three o'clock it would give me great pleasure, as I should be particularly glad to see you my D: before the rest of our friends come – god Bless you my D: I ever am with the firmest and most perfect attachment

your et[c].

Wednesday night June 6th $\overline{92.}$ [CCLN, 283f.]

HANOVER SQUARE

To gratify the wishes of his Subscribers, SALOMON last night had an additional Concert for the purpose of repeating the more favourite Pieces of HAYDN, which had been performed through the Season . . . .

  The overtures of HAYDN were warmly applauded, and some of the movements *encored*.

[*Diary; or, Woodfall's Register*, 7 June]

MUSIC.

SALOMON finished his season on Wednesday night, at the Hanover Square Room, with the greatest *eclat*. His own violin concerto, with Young MEYER's fine performance on the harp, and MARA's three grand songs, the last of which, the charming air from IDALIDE, was *encored*, constituted one of the richest harmonic repasts, we ever attended. ASHE's flute was so exquisite in tone, and so correct in performance, that we lamented we did not hear more of it. The instrumental pieces of HAYDN were received with an extacy [*sic*] of admiration; and MARA on quitting the room, had equal honours. A beautiful concertante of GYROWETZ was much and deservedly admired.

[*Morning Herald*, 8 June]

  The first Thursday of June, each year, saw in London the Anniversary Meeting of the Charity Children in St Paul's Cathedral, who marched in a gigantic procession. The sight struck the correspondent of the *St. James's Chronicle* as 'The most sublime, as well as the most generally pleasing sight that can be exhibited' (5–7 June 1794). Haydn's entry in the First London Notebook is undated, but has been generally assigned to 1792 rather than 1791.[1]

  8 days before Pentecost I heard 4,000 charity children in St. Paul's Church sing the song noted below. One performer indicated the tempo. No music ever moved me so deeply in my whole life as this devotional and innocent

---

1 Whitsun in 1792 was on 27 May. The first Thursday in June would have been the 7th. Pohl III, 56f., suggests Haydn meant '8 days after Pentecost' (Whitsunday). The first Thursday in June 1791 is the 2nd, and Pentecost is on the 5th, so that in 1792, the event can have happened '3 days', not 8, before Pentecost. Since the matter cannot be solved with the material at our disposition we leave the event in 1792 where Dies (128), specifically, and Griesinger (24) by implication say it belongs.

N.B.: All the children are newly clad, and enter in procession. The organist first played the melody very nicely and simply, and then they all began to sing at once. [CCLN, 261]

The original chant by John Jones (1728–96) is in the key of D, which suggests that the St Paul's organ was pitched a note higher. Haydn's notation differs slightly from the printed version, which may be seen in Pohl, *H in L*, 214. Another great hymn that was sung on the occasion was 'The Old Hundredth Psalm'. Dies gives us an interesting explanation why Haydn found the Jones chant so particularly moving:

> [Dies cites part of the notebook's entry.] Haydn added verbally: 'I stood there and wept like a child.' . . . He remarked that the voices sounded like angels' voices, and that the fall in the first three bars to low B brought forth a fearsome quality that gripped the heart, as the notes died away in the delicate throats of the children and ended in a hovering breath of a tone; then as it went on, the melody gradually grew in life and strength as it progressed upwards; thus, the melody was full of light and shadow and its effect mighty. [Dies, 130]

Can it be an accident that Part III of *The Creation*, describing the innocence of man, with the three ethereal flute parts, is in the key of E major?

Haydn was exchanging poetry with Mrs Schroeter:

> My Dst Inclosed I send you the verses you was so kind as to lend me, and am very much obliged to you for permitting me to take a copy of them, pray inform me HOW YOU DO, and let me know MY D^t L: when you will DINE with me. I shall be HAPPY to SEE YOU to dinner either to MORROW or TUESDAY whichever is most convenient to you, I am TRULY ANXIOUS and IMPATIENT to SEE you, and I wish to have as much of YOUR COMPANY as possible: indeed MY Dst H: I FEEL for YOU the FONDEST and TENDEREST AFFECTION the HUMAN HEART is capable of, and I ever am with the FIRMEST attachment my D^t Love
>
> most Sincerely, Faithfully
and most affectionately yours [etc.]
>
> Sunday Evening
> June 10 $\overline{792}$. [CCLN, 284]

On the 12th, Haydn went to hear Sarti's *Dido* at the Haymarket Theatre, a performance featuring Madame Mara, which we have noted above (p. 138):

> On 12th June Mara gave her benefit concert in the great Haymarket Theatre; they gave *Dido*, the music by Sarti. N.B.: Only the terzet, a few recitatives and a little aria were by Sarti, the rest was by 6 different other composers. The 1ma *Don[n]a* sang an old aria by Sacchini, *Son Regina etc.*[1] [CCLN, 258]

---

1 While at Eszterháza, Haydn had performed operas by both Giuseppe Sarti (1729–1802) and Antonio Maria Gasparo Sacchini (1734–86).

The next day, he wrote a letter to Luigia Polzelli in Bologna:

[*Italian, 'Tu' form*]
London, 13th June 1792.
My dear Polzelli

I received your letter with the false news about my wife: in fact she is not quite well, but with her usual sicknesses she may, if she pulls through, outlive me by many years. Well, we shall have to leave her fate to Providence. I SHALL LEAVE LONDON AT THE END OF THIS MONTH, and shall write you from Frankfurt. Yesterday I heard that my Prince will go there as Bohemian Ambassador and will arrive on the 25th of this month, together with his musicians. I think, therefore, that I shall have to stay with him for a time. Enough, I shall write you soon, to tell you when your Pietro should leave. Yesterday I purchased a little trunk in which to put the things that we bought together, your sister and I. Pietruccio can then use this same trunk when he leaves Bologna. My dear Polzelli, I hope to see you next year, and to tell you about all the things that have happened to me since I left you; and I hope, as God is my witness. always to be the same to you as I have been. I love you and will always be your faithful

Giuseppe Haydn.

I send your sons many kisses.

My compliments to your dear sister.[1]   [CCLN, 136f.]

On 14 June Haydn went to Windsor and from there to Ascot to see the races:

The castle chapel at Windsor is a very old but splendid building; the high altar cost 50,000 fl. It shows the ascension of Christ in stained glass. This year, 1792, in the side altar to the right, a smaller one, showing Christ appearing to the Shepherds, was completed. This small one is valued more highly than the large one. The view from the terrace is divine.   [CCLN, 276]

On 14th June [1792], I went to Windsor and from there 8 miles to Ascot Heath to see the races. These horse races are run on a large field, especially prepared for them, and on this field is a large circular track 2 English miles long and 6 fathoms wide. It is all very smooth and even, and the whole field has a gentle upwards slope. At the summit the circle stops curving and becomes a straight line about 2000 paces long; along this straight line, stalls of various sizes, or rather an ampitheatre, have been erected, some of which hold 2 to 3 hundred persons. The others are smaller. In the middle there is one for the Prince of Wales and high personages. The places in these stalls cost from 1 to 42 shillings per person. Opposite the Prince of Wales' stall is erected a high platform with a bell over it, on which platform stand several persons who have been specially chosen and sworn, and they give the first signal with the bell for the performers to line up in front of the platform. When they are ready, the bell is rung a second time, and at the first stroke they ride off at once. Whoever is the first to traverse the circle of 2 miles and return to the platform from which they started, receives the prize. In the first Heeth [heat] there were 3 riders, and they had to go round the circle twice without stopping. They did this double course in 5 minutes. No stranger will believe this unless they have seen it themselves. The 2nd time there were seven riders; when they were in the middle of the circle, all 7 were in the same line, but as soon as they came nearer some fell behind, but never more than about [originally '20'] 10 paces; and just when you think that one of them is rather near the goal, and people make large bets on him at

---

1 We know nothing of this second sister, who apparently lived in Bologna [CCLN, 137].

this moment, another rushes past him at very close quarters and with unbelievable force reaches the winning place. The riders are very lightly clad in silk, and each one has a different colour, so that you can recognize him more easily; no boots, a little cap on his head, they are all as lean as a greyhound and lean as their horses. Each one is weighed in, and a certain weight is allowed him, in proportion to the strength of the horse, and if the rider is too light he must put on heavier clothes, or they hang some lead on him. The horses are of the finest possible breed, light, with very thin feet, the hair of their neck tied into braids, the hoofs very delicate. As soon as they hear the sound of the bell, they dash off at once with the greatest force. Every leap of the horses is 22 feet long. These horses are very expensive. The Prince of Wales paid £8000 for one some years ago, and sold it again for £6000; but he won £50,000 with it the first time. Among other things a single large stall is erected, wherein the Englishmen place their bets. The King has his own stall at one side. I saw 5 heats on the first lay, and despite a heavy rain there were 2000 vehicles, all full of people, and 3 times as many common people on foot. Besides this, there are all sorts of other things – puppet-plays, hawkers [*Ciarlatony*], horror plays [*Grusl Possen*] – which go on during the races; many tents with refreshments, all kinds of wine and beer, and many Io-players (in English it is written Eo), a game which is forbidden in London. This horse racing went on 5 days in succession. I was there on the 2nd day; the beginning was at 2 o'clock and it went on till 5, the 3rd day till half-past 6, though there were but 3 Heaths, because it happened twice that 3 riders came in first together, and thus they had to race four times to decide the winner. [CCLN, 255f.]

If Haydn had reached home the next evening, he would have found a letter from Rebecca Schroeter awaiting him:

My Dearest
I hope to hear you are in good HEALTH, and have had an AGREABLE journey, that you have been much AMUSED with the Race, and that EVERY THING has turn'd out to YOUR SATISFACTION pray MY D^{tt} LOVE inform me how YOU do? EVERY circumstance concerning you MY BELOVED H^{dn} is INTERESTING to me. – I shall be VERY HAPPY TO SEE YOU TO DINNER TO MORROW and I EVER am with the sincerest and TENDEREST Regard my Dst H^{dn}

most faithfully & affectionately
yours R: S:

James S. Thursday Even: June ye 14th 792   [CCLN, 284]

Meanwhile, instead of returning directly to London (as Mrs Schroeter's letter seemed to indicate that he would), Haydn went to Slough to see Dr Herschel. William Herschell, as he then spelled his name, was formerly an oboe player in the Hanover Guards, and he came to England just as he was turning twenty-one. He was also a capable composer, and Sotheby's auctioned off a large collection of his music after World War II. His second profession, astronomy, soon began to occupy his life entirely especially after he discovered the planet Uranus. Herschel began his giant telescope in 1785 and completed it on 28 August 1789, the day he discovered the sixth satellite of Uranus; the telescope cost £10,000.

On 15th June I went from Windsor to [blank = Slough] to Doctor Hershel [Herschel], where I saw the great telescope. It is 40 feet long and 5 feet in diameter. The machinery is very big, but so ingenious that a single man can put it in motion with the greatest ease. There are also 2 smaller [telescopes], of which one is 22 feet long and magnifies 6000 times. The King had 2 made for himself, each of which measures 12 feet. He paid him 1000 guineas for them. In his younger days

Dr Hershel was in the Prussian service as an oboe player. During the seven-years' war he deserted with his brother and went to England, where he supported himself as a musician for many years: he became an organist at Bath, but gradually turned more to astronomy. After having provided himself with the necessary instruments, he left Bath, rented a room near Windsor, and studied day and night. His landlady was a widow, fell in love with him, married him, and gave him a dowry of £100,000. Besides this he has a yearly pension for life of £500 from the King, and his wife, at the age of 45, presented him with a son this year, 1792. Ten years ago he had his sister come, and she is of the greatest assistance to him in his observations. Sometimes he sits for 5 or 6 hours under the open sky in the bitterest cold weather. [CCLN, 254f.]

Back in London, Haydn received the usual invitations to dine with Mrs Schroeter:

M:D: I was EXTREMELY SORRY, I had not the pleasure of SEEING YOU TO DAY, indeed my Dr Love it was a very great disappointment to me, as every moment of your company is MORE and MORE PRECIOUS to me now your DEPARTURE is so near – – I hope to hear you are QUITE WELL and I shall be very happy to see you my D^t H^n any time to morrow after one o'clock if you can come but if not, I shall hope for the pleasure of seeing YOU on MONDAY – you will receive this letter to morrow morning[.] I wou'd not send it to Day, for fear you shou'd not be at home, and I WISH to have your answer. God Bless you my D^t Love, once more I repeat, let me SEE YOU as SOON as POSSIBLE[.] I EVER am with the most INVIOLABLE ATTACHMENT my D^t and most BELOVED H.

most faithfully and most affectionately
Yours

Saturday,
R Sch
June y° 16th 792.
[CCLN, 284f.]

It was Haydn's turn to entertain the Society of Musical Graduates, and as his quarters in Great Pulteney Street were obviously too limited, he held the meal at a coffee-house. We do not have a complete list of the company, but they probably included most of the members: Dr Arnold, Dr Aylward, Dr Ayrton, Dr Burney, Dr Cooke, Dr Dupuis, Dr Haydn, Dr Parsons, Mr Bellamy, Mr Callcott, Mr Guise, Mr Hindle, Mr Hudson, and Mr Smith. The *Account*[1] of the Society notes:

1792. Dr. Haydn previous to his leaving England gave the Graduates his dinner on the 20th of June at Parsloes in St. James St. to which at his particular request, Mr. Salomon was admitted, partly as the intimate friend of Dr. Haydn partly as interpreter, Dr. Haydn having not made sufficient progress in the English Tongue. [Scholes, 120]

On 23 June, the Duchess of York gave a garden party which Haydn saw; possibly at that time he wrote down the delicious punch recipe from the Prince of Wales:[2]

[*German*]
The Prince of Wales' punch: 1 bottle champagne, 1 bottle Burgundy, 1 bottle rum, 10 lemons, 2 oranges, 1½ lbs. of sugar.

On 23rd June 1792, the Duchess of York gave a dinner for 180 persons under a large tent in her garden. I saw the same. [CCLN, 270]

1 The *Account* is a manuscript by Dr J. W. Callcott and is in the British Museum, Add. MS. 27693, fols. 6–36.
2 I can personally attest to the excellence of this drink, having served it to a large gathering on St. Stephen's Day 1960 at Buggiano Castello.

The last dated letter – four undated ones exist, none of which we have been able to date from the contents[1] – from Rebecca Schroeter is 26 June (a Tuesday), which means, if the letter is correctly dated, that Haydn was still in London the following Monday, 2 July.

> My D: I hope to hear you are in good HEALTH, and that you SLEPT WELL last Night. I shall be VERY HAPPY to see you on Monday morning – permit me to remind you about M[r] Frasers,[2] and you will be so good as to let me know on Monday how it is settled – God Bless you my D: Love, my thoughts and best wishes are your constant attendants, and I ever am with the tenderest Regard my D: H:
>
> most et[c].
>
> June the 26th $\overline{92}$. [CCLN, 285]

With this letter Rebecca Schroeter disappears as a letter writer from Haydn's life: there are no letters from the 1794–5 period. Were they, perhaps, contained in the Fourth London Notebook, which has come down to us incomplete? Or did the fact that Haydn lived in Bury Street, St James, in 1794–5, very near Mistress Schroeter, remove the necessity of their corresponding? She appears twice more in Haydn's 'official' biography: to her are dedicated three of Haydn's greatest piano Trios, Op. 73 (Nos. 38–40, Hob. XVI, 24–6), in 1795; and she is known to have been a subscriber to *The Creation*. She also helped Haydn with an important contract in 1796 (see *Haydn: the Years of 'The Creation'*), in which she appears as a witness.

On 27 June 1792, Haydn wrote a canon in the commonplace book of a friend then in London, J. C. Falck. The canon contains the same music as that submitted by Haydn for his doctoral degree at Oxford, 'Thy Voice, O Harmony, is Divine' (*vide supra*, p. 94); but here the text is that of the First Commandment' 'Du sollst an einen Gott glauben'. Haydn entitles the work 'Canone cancrizante' with the tempo *Largo*, and it is written in the G-clef; underneath Haydn added 'Glaube Du auch dem Verfasser Jos: Haydn, daß er dein ächter Freund sey. London, den 27ten Juny $\overline{792}$' ('And you, too also believe the composer of it Jos: Haydn, that he is your true friend'). This commonplace book was sold by auction at Sotheby's in London in December 1958, and the Haydn page was printed in facsimile in their catalogue (15–16 December 1958, lot 407).[3]

The important fact of this otherwise pleasant but perhaps inconsequential entry in a commonplace book is that it enables us to date Haydn's set of canons, 'Die heiligen zehn Gebote' (The Ten Commandments, XXVIIa: 1–10) more precisely than was hitherto possible. We know that Haydn wrote it in England, for it is in his *Catalogue of Works Composed in England*; but on the basis of this entry in Falck's volume, we may presume that the canons were completed by June 1792.

In one of the 1791–2 notebooks, there is the following note:

> M[r] Hunter is the greatest and most famous surgeon in London. Leicester Square.
>
> [CCLN, 253]

To Dies, Haydn elaborated:

> In London, Haydn came to know the famous surgeon H[unter], 'a man', said Haydn, 'who almost daily performed surgical operations and always successfully. He had inspected my polyp [in the nose] and offered to free me of this nuisance. I

---

1 CCLN, 285f.
2 Mr Frasers is probably identical with the 'Mr Fraser' mentioned above (see p. 95).
3 I have to thank Mr John Pashby of Sotheby & Co. for sending me the catalogue and for innumerable kindnesses over the years.

had half agreed, but the operation was put off and at last I thought no more of it. Shortly before my departure, Mr. H. asked me to come and see him about some urgent matters. I went there. After the first exchange of greetings, a few brawny fellows entered the room, grabbed me and wanted to force me into a chair. I yelled, kicked and hit until I had freed myself and made clear to Mr. H., who already had his instruments ready for the operation, that I did not want to undergo the operation. He was very astonished at my obstinancy, and it seemed to me that he pitied me for not wanting to undergo the happy experience of enjoying his skill. I excused myself, saying that there was not time because of my forthcoming departure, and took my leave of him.'   [Dies, 125f.]

Just before this passage, Haydn explained that he had undergone several operations to rid himself of this polyp, and even the famous Dr Giovanni Alessandro Brambilla (physician to the Court of Vienna) had been so unfortunate as to remove a bit of the nasal bone without freeing Haydn of the polyp. We shall hear of this polyp as the principal reason given to the British public for Haydn's absence at the beginning of the 1793 season in London.

There were two famous Hunter brothers, William (1718–83) and John (1728–93), both famous doctors, William specializing in the practice of obstetrics and John, as we have seen, in surgery. John was actually the leading surgeon of London and among his many titles, he was (from 1790) Surgeon General and Inspector General of Hospitals; he also published three books, on human teeth, venereal disease and animal oeconomy, any one of which would have sufficed to make anyone else famous. His fame spread widely, and in 1787 he was elected to membership in the American Philosophical Society. In 1771 John had married Anne Home, a talented and sensitive poetess with whom Haydn was on the best of terms and who was to collaborate with the composer during his second London visit to produce the famous two sets of canzonettas. John's portrait was painted by Sir Joshua Reynolds. Haydn will have been much drawn to Dr Hunter, who was honest, un-selfconscious, warm and generous. When Haydn returned to London, Dr Hunter was no more, having dropped dead at a Board Meeting at St George's on 16 October 1793. He was greatly mourned, not least by thankful patients. 'Much concerned,' wrote Farington in his Diary (6f.), 'at an account in the newspaper of the death of John Hunter, to whom I was greatly obliged in the course of last summer for his advice, &c. on account of an incested tumour on my back, which he removed . . . . He mentioned to me once that he had some obstruction or complaint about his heart which he was well assured would cause his death suddenly at some period.'[1]

In Haydn's notebooks of the years 1791–2, there are a whole series of undated entries, including three letters from Mrs Schroeter, which we present here. The notebooks also include, as will be seen a list of all the composers and other musicians with whom Haydn came into contact, which we include as a useful chart of London's musical life, great and small, Mistakes in CCLN have been corrected without comment.[2] Some addresses and unfinished stories – e.g. 'The little story of an errand boy who ate cow dung [*fessa*] [blank: story not filled in]' – and the like have been omitted.

1 About Hunter, see D. Ottley, *The Life of John Hunter*, in *The Works of John Hunter*, ed. J. F. Palmer, 5 vols., London 1835–7.
2 For example the story about the whores in France, Holland and England. I translated 'in England they stay proper all their lives', but I misread 'gut' (proper) for 'Hur' (whore), the German 'g' and Gothic 'H' being very similar.

First London Notebook

[*English*]

Head of June, white Cornelian.							6	guinees
that other white red Cornelian							$3\frac{1}{2}$	guinees
6 Schirts –	–	–	–	–	–	–	8	–
12 deto –	–	–	–	–	–	–	12	–
watch from gold	–	–	–	–	–		30	–
the chen –	–	–	–	–	–	–	1	–

[*German*]

The national debt of England is estimated to be over two hundred millions. Recently it was calculated that if they had to make up a convoy to pay this sum in silver, the waggons, end on end, would reach from London to Yorck, that is, 200 miles, presuming that each waggon could not carry more than £6000.

[CCLN, 253]

N.B.: Mʳ Silvester, *valet de chambre* of the Duchess of York.

[CCLN, 253]

In France the girls are virtuous and the wives are whores; in Holland the girls are whores and the wives are virtuous: in England they stay whores all their lives.

[CCLN, 253]

If anybody steals £2 he is hanged; but if I trust anybody with £2000, and he carries it off to the devil, he is acquitted. Murder and forgery cannot be pardoned; last year a clergyman was hanged for the latter, even though the King himself did all he could for him.

[CCLN, 257]

The City of London consumes 8 times one hundred thousand cartloads of coal each year; each cart holds 13 sacks, each sack holds 2 dry measures [= 3.44 litre]: most of the coal comes from Newcastle. Often 200 loaded ships arrive at once. A cartload costs £2½. [The following sentence was added later, in another ink:] In the year 1795, the coal-measure [*Malten*] or dry-measure £7. Within the last 30 years, 38,000 houses were built.

    If a woman murders her husband, she is burned alive, whereas the husband, on the contrary, is hanged.

    The punishment of a murderer is increased, when sentence is passed on him, by the fact that his body is dissected after his death.

[CCLN, 257]

Once, when an Archbishop of London asked Parliament to silence a learned public preacher of the Moravian religion, the Vice President answered that it could be easily done; just make him a Bishop, and he will remain silent the rest of his life.

[CCLN, 258]

In Oxford Street I saw St. Peter engraved in copper; he was clad as a secular priest [*Weltbriester*] with outstretched arms. The glory of heaven shines on his right side, and on his left you see the devil, whispering in his ear, and with a wind-mill on his head.

[CCLN, 258]

ANECTOD: Just as the director of a grand concert was about to begin the first number, the kettledrummer called loudly to him and said he should wait a moment, since his 2 kettledrums were not yet tuned. The leader could and would not wait any longer, and said he should transpose in the meantime. [CCLN, 259]

When Mr Fox was seeking votes to elect him to Parliament, a citizen said he would give him a rope instead of a vote. Fox answered that he could not rob him of a family heirloom.

Duchess of Devonchire [*sic*], his protector. Anecdote about the foot under her petticoat.

N.B. from *Wurmland*:
     Quoties cum stercore certo,
vinco nel vincor, semper ego maculor.

Ex nihilo nihil fit.

Domine, praxis est multiplex, qui n'intellegit est simplex.

Stella a stella differt claritate, non eadem lux omnibus. Herr! Es ist nicht alles licht was lichtet [Lord! All is not light that lightens.].

Interesse toto mundo
Sin fronte colitur,
Sine satis, sine fundo,
Interque quaeritur.

Mel in ore, verba lactis.
Fel in corde, fraus in factis.
     [Plautus, *Truculentus* 178]

Supernumerarius, das Fünfte Rad am Wagen [the fifth wheel of a waggon].
Mens, ratio, et consilium in senibus est.   [CCLN, 260]

Si nisi non esset, perfectus qualibet esset.

Raro sunt visi, qui caruere nisi.   [CCLN, 261]

In the year 1791, 22 thousand persons died in London.

Lokart [Lockhart], blind organist.

Io vi mando questo foglio
Dalle lagrime rigato,
Sotto scritto dal cordoglio
Dai pensieri siggillato
Testimento del mio amore
[Io] vi mando questo core.   [CCLN, 261]

An apprentice generally works the whole year round from 6 o'clock in the morning to 6 o'clock in the evening, and during this time he has not more than an hour and a half free time at his disposal. He gets a guinea a week, from which he must also feed himself. Many are paid by the piece, but every quarter of an hour of absence is docked.
     Only the blacksmith's apprentices have to work an hour a day longer.
                                                                      [CCLN, 262]

Singers, male and female, in London			*Composers*
Mara	Bacchierotti. Kelly		Baumgarten
Storace	Davide		Clementi
Billington	Albertarelli		Dussek—Dusseck
Cassentini	Dorelli		Girowetz
Lops NB	Lazarini, in the Pantheon		Choris
Negri	Mazzanti	Chelsea College	Burney D^r
Celestini	Morelli		Hülmandel
Choris	Calcagni		Graff
Benda	CROUTSCH		Diettenhoffer
Mrs Barthelemon and her daughter	Harrison		Storace
	Simoni		Arnold
Schinotti			
	Miss Pool		Barthelemon

Mara (see p. 28)

Maffei, bella, ma poco musica [pretty, but not very musical]

Schield*

Capelletti

Miss Barck

Carter*

Devis [Davies], detta Inglesina, la
quale Recitava a Napoli
quando l'aveva 13^{ci} anni[;]
ella è adesso vecchietta ma
ha una buona Scola [called the
English girl, who at the age
of 13 sang at Naples; she is
rather old now, but has a
good technique]

Cramer

Tomich

Frike N^{ro}: 24
BLANFORD STREET
M A N C H E S T E R
SQUARE

M^{tris} Bland

Callcot Scholar

MAD: SECONDA *passabile*

la Trobe—
dedicated his piano
Sonatas to me

Poet Badini

Herrn Hutter
[Moravian Brotherhood]

Mazingi – at the piano-
forte in the Pantheon
Friderici [Frederici]

Burney
Upper   Titchfield
Street

Singers: Mara (see p. 28); Storace (see pp. 37, 61); Billington (see p. 28). Anna Casentini, who married Luigi Borghi, violinist and manager of the Italian opera in London. Lops (see p. 39). Theresa Negri, Luigia Polzelli's sister, appeared in concerts in 1791 (see p. 597). Celestini:?. Choris = the soprano Sophia Corri (later Mrs Dussek; see p. 29). Benda: Felicitas Agnesia *née* Rietz, married Ludwig Friedrich Benda (son of G. A. Benda) and went to London in 1790. Gerber *NTL* II, 768f. Mrs. Barthelemon (see p. 169). Schinotti: ? Maffri, a soprano in Gallini's opera company. Teresa Poggi Cappelletti, soprano in Gallini's opera company, who also sang in the Haydn-Salomon concerts. Cecilia Davies (*c.* 1750–1836), a relative of Benjamin Franklin's, had toured the Continent with her parents and sister Marianne (the celebrated player of the glass harmonica) from 1768 to 1773 (O. E. Deutsch: 'Neues von der Glasharmonika', *Oesterreichische Musikzeitschrift* IX [1954], Heft 12, pp. 380ff.). Seconda is probably Mrs Second from Bath, who sang at least one concert in which Haydn participated (New Musical Fund Concert, 20 April 1795: see Landon SYM 544); she later sang in the first performance of Haydn's *Creation* in London (Pohl *H in L*, 316). Badini (see p. 39). Bacchierotti = Gaetano Pacchierotti (see p. 28). Kelly = Michael O'Kelly, the Irish tenor who (with Nancy Storace) sang in the first production of Mozart's *Figaro* (see pp. 37, 91). Davide (David: see p. 38). Francesco Albertarelli (see p. 39). Dorelli was a male singer in Gallini's company. Lazzarini was a tenor who, apart from singing at the Pantheon, also sang in the Professional Concerts of 1792. Ferdinando Mazzanti. Giovanni Morelli, member of the Italian Opera (see p. 254). Croutsch = Anne Mary Crouch, whose recitative was said to equal that of Mara's. Samuel Harrison, tenor. Simoni was a tenor whom Salomon engaged in 1792; he had previously sung at the *Théâtre de Monsieur* in Paris (Landon SYM 492). Caroline Pool sang at the Haydn-Salomon concerts, and Haydn wrote an aria for her. Miss Barck = the Mistress Park mentioned in one of Haydn's letters (see p. 274). Mistress Bland was born Maria Romani and married George Bland.

Composers: Carl Friedrich Baumgarten (*c.* 1740–1824), see p. 68. Clementi (see p. 73). Dussek (see p. 62). Adalbert Gyrowetz (1763–1850), see p. 63. Choris = Domenico Corri, the father of the Miss Corri mentioned under the singers. Charles Burney (see also pp. 31f.). Nicholaus Joseph Hüllmandel (Strasbourg 1771 – London 1823). Friedrich Hartmann Graff (1727–1795) (see p. 31). Diettenhofer (see p. 98). Stephen Storace (see p. 143). Samuel Arnold (1740–1802), organist at Westminster Abbey; see also p. 177. F. H. Barthelemon (see p. 168). William Shield (1748–1829): see p. 114. Thomas Carter (*c.* 1735–1804). J. B. Cramer (1771–1858), son of Wilhelm, the leader of the Professional Concert. Francesco Tomich, who later arranged many of Haydn's symphonies for piano. Philipp Joseph Frike (or Frick, as it was anglicized; Würzburg 1740 – London 1798). John W. Callcott (1766–1821), one of Haydn's pupils in composition. Rev. Christian I. Latrobe (1758–1836): see p. 57, whose *Three Sonatas for the piano forte* Op. III (J. Bland) were dedicated to Haydn. Joseph Mazzinghi (1765–1839). Burney's name is repeated here probably because of the address in town.

Pianists	Violinists	Violoncellists	Doctors
Clementi	Salomon	Grosdill	Burney
Dushek	Giornovich	Menel	Hess in Oxford
Girowetz	Cramer	Mara	Arnold
Diettenhofer	CLEMENT *petit*	Sperati	
Burney	Barthelemon	Schramb	Dupuis a great organist
Mis Burney	Schield		
Hüllmandel	Hindmarsh, Eng.	*Oboists*	
Graff, also flautist	Scheener, Germ.	Fischer	
Miss Barthelemon	Raimondi, Ital.	Harrington	
Cramer	Serra, from the Marquis DURAZZO	Lolli and his son came from Stockholm.	
Miss Janson	Borghi		
Humel from Vienna	Gionovichi		
Mrs Jansen	Felix Janievicz		
Lenz, still very young	Jarowez		
	Giardini		

Clementi, Dussek, Gyrowetz, Diettenhofer and Burney: see previous note on composers. Miss Burney was his daughter, Esther (Hetty). Hüllmandel: see previous note on composers. J. G. Graeff, not to be confused with F. H. Graff, listed under composers. Miss Barthelemon and J. B. Cramer: see note on composers, Jansen family, see p. 440. J. N. Hummel: see *supra*, p. 78. Heinrich Gerhard von Lenz (*c.* 1764–1839), German pianist who went to Paris in 1784 and to London in 1794, later (1795) to Hamburg. Johann Peter Salomon. Giovanni Mane Giornovichj (Jarnowik; 1745–1804): see p. 76. Wilhelm Cramer: see previous note on composers, also p. 76. Franz Clement (1780–1842): see p. 85. Hindmarsh was a violinist and viola player in Haydn's concerts; his wife was a singer. Scheener: appeared for the first time in London (spelled 'Schenner') in 1781. Ignazio Raimondi (1733–1813), also a composer (see p. 130). 'Serra, from the Marquis Durazzo': Count Johann Jakob Durazzo (1717–94), the well-known theatrical director in Vienna in the 1750s and early 1760s, from 1764 Austrian Ambassador to Venice. Haydn was in contact with him in 1783 and probably before: CCLN 40f. Luigi Borghi was also a composer. Felix Janieviecz (1762–1848) (see p. 131). Jarowez: ? Giardini (see pp. 166–7).

John Crosdill (*recte*; 1751–1825). Menel first appeared as a 'cellist in London in 1789. Sperati first appeared in London in 1787. Johann Mara was the husband of the famous soprano. Schramb: Christopher Shram, who first played in London in 1792.

Doctors: Charles Burney (*passim*). Hess = Dr Philip Hayes (1738–97), Professor of Music at Oxford University. Thomas Saunders Dupuis (1733–96) (see p. 170).

Oboists: J. C. Fischer (1733–1800), also a composer. Harrington played at many of Haydn's concerts. Antonio Lolli (*c.* 1730 [1740?]–1802), well known both as a composer and violinist.

Krumpholz, l'Arpa, Mr Blumb imitated a parrot and accompanied himself admirably on the pianoforte.

Mrs de la Valle, a pupil of Krumpholz:[1] plays rather less well than Madam Krumpholz. Also plays the piano. Her sister-in-law plays the violin very nicely.

M^r. Antis,[2] Bishop and a minor composer.

[CCLN, 262ff.]

Nicolai, *valet de chambre* of the King and a composer.

Hartman, flautist, had to leave England because of poverty, lost his wife by death, and ended up as a ne'er do well.

[CCLN, 266]

Ambassador, Count Stadion.
  Prince de Castelcicala of Naples.
  Marquis del Campo of Spain.

My friend, you think I love you! In truth, you are not mistaken.
In solitude, too, there are divinely beautiful duties, and to perform them in quiet is more than wealth.

---

1 Madame Krumpholz (see p. 68). Madame Delavalle (Delaval) played at the first Haydn-Salomon Concert of the 1792 season.

2 John Antes (*recte*; 1740–1811) was Christian Latrobe's uncle and a third-generation German-American (Moravian), whose mother tongue was German. He collected some interesting Haydn MSS., among them the Six *Scherzandi*. In the tracking down of these Antes manuscripts, I was greatly assisted by my old friend Mr A. Hyatt King, of the British Museum, who in a letter of March 1960 told me of their existence. Subsequently, through the help of Dr Donald W. McCorkle, Director of the Moravian Music Foundation in Winston-Salem, North Carolina, I received a microfilm of all the Antes Haydn copies; to Miss F. M. Blandford, who identified the watermarks of the originals, in the Moravian Theological College, Fairfield, Manchester (England) I am also indebted for many other kindnesses. The Antes copies came into the library of his nephew, Latrobe, and from him were presented to the Moravian Church by his children. See Haydn: *Scherzando* No. 5 (II: 37) in E major, Verlag Doblinger, Vienna-Munich, Diletto Musicale No. 75 (1961), score, p. 7 (ed. H. C. Robbins Landon); also *News Bulletin of the Moravian Foundation*, Vol. III (1959), No. 3, p. 2 (Winston-Salem, N.C.). Antes was not a bishop, but his nephew Latrobe became Secretary '(in England) to the Church and Missions of the United Brethren' and was, of course, what Haydn liked to call a 'Protestant clergyman'. Antes had composed three string trios (two violins and 'cello) shortly before Haydn arrived in England: these trios had been composed in Cairo and were dedicated to the Swedish Ambassador to Turkey and published as 'Giovanni A-T-S, Dillettante Americano'. One has recently been recorded on Columbia Records (USA) 'Odyssey' 23 16 0340. See Donald M. McCorkle, 'John Antes, "American Dilettante" ' (*Musical Quarterly*, Oct. 1956, pp. 486–99).

Begehre nicht ein glück zu gross
Und nicht ein weib zu schön,
Der Himmel möchte dir di[e]s Looß
Im zorne zugestehn.

(Do not desire too great happiness or too beautiful a wife: Heaven might, in anger, grant your wish!)

Wer mit Vernunft betracht' den wechsel aller Sachen,
Den kan kein glück nicht froh, kein unglück traurig machen.

[Angelus Silesius]

(He who wisely observes how all things change cannot be made happy by good fortune or unhappy by bad.)

INTRA IN GAUDIUM.
HABEO, ET NON HABEOR.
RESURGAM.
IN COELO QUIES.

Chi ben commincia, ha la metà dell'opera, ne si commincia ben, se non dal cielo!

[CCLN, 267]

Gott im Herzen, ein gut weibchen im arm,
Jenes macht seelig, dieses gewiß – warm.

[CCLN, 268]

(God in one's heart, a good wife on one's arm,
The one brings salvation, the second is – warm.)

Mit eben einer wärme der ächten freundschaft empfilt sich zu beständigen angedenken [2. Version: 'so viel zum angedenken Ihres'].
Kenne gott, die welt, und dich, liebster Freund, und denk an mich.

With just such a warmth of genuine friendship, I commend myself to your thoughts always [second version: 'I commend myself this much to your thoughts, Your'].) [The text of the canon, which Haydn liked to present to his friends, might be translated: 'Know God, the world, and thyself, dearest friend, and think of me.']

During the last 31 years, 38,000 houses were built in London.   [CCLN, 268]

The Second London Notebook

La risposta del S: Marchesi sopra una lettera del S: Gallini. Nell'anno 1791. 'Ho ricevuto le sua gentilissima lettera, buona Notte.

Marchesi.'

(Sig. Marchesi's answer to a letter from Sig. Gallini, in the year 1791: 'I received your very kind letter. Goodnight, Marchesi.') For Gallini, see p. 59; Luigi Lodovico Marchesi (1754–1829) was a famous castrato.

When a Quaker goes to Court, he pays the door-keeper to take off his hat for him, for a Quaker takes his hat off to no one. In order to pay the King's tax, an official goes to his house during the period when the tax is being collected, and in his presence robs him of as much goods as represent the tax in value. When the disguised thief leaves the door with his goods, the Quaker calls him back and asks him how much money he wants for the stolen things. The official demands just the amount of the tax, and in this way the Quaker pays the tax to the King.

[CCLN, 270]

When 2 persons of opposite sexes receive permission to marry from the secular courts, the clergyman is forced to marry them as soon as they are in the church, even if they have loved without their parent's permission; if he doesn't, the bridegroom and bride have the right, as soon as the clergyman leaves the church, to tear his robes from his body. And then the clergyman is degraded and forever disqualified.

[CCLN, 273]

The City of London keeps 4,000 carts for cleaning the streets, and 2,000 of these work every day.

[CCLN, 275]

The larger traveller's lead pencil costs ½ a guinea.
The smaller one   —   —   5 shillings 6 penz
Pen   6   6 —
[English]

		schilling	penni
Stel Button —	£2 —	2 —	0
a steel girdl — —	1 —	4 —	0
a steel chain —	1 —	11 —	6
2 Secissars 3 Sh: Each	— 6		—
3 — at 6 Sh: Each	— 18		0
1 — at	— —	7 —	6
1 — at —	—	9 —	0
7 Penn Knifes —	1 —	1 —	0

[CCLN, 277]

[Mrs Schroeter's undated letters to Haydn]
My Dearest,
I am quite impatient to know how you do this Morning, and if you slept well last Night – I am much obliged to you for all your kindness yesterday and heartely thank you for it. I earnestly LONG to see you my D^{t}L: and I hope to have that pleasure THIS MORNING. my THOUGHTS and best REGARDS are incessantly with you and I ever am my Dst H:

most faithfully, and most
affectionately yours [etc.]

[CCLN, 285]

M: D: I was extremely sorry I had not the pleasure of YOUR company THIS MORNING as I most ANXIOUSLY wish'd to see you – my THOUGHTS are continually with you, my beloved H: and my AFFECTION for you INCREASES DAILY, no words can express half the TENDER REGARD I feel for you – I hope my D^t L: I shall have the happiness of seeing you to-morrow to diner, in the mean time my best wishes always attend you, and I EVER am with the FIRMEST ATTACHMENT MY D. H. most et[c.].

I am just return'd from from [*sic*] the Concert, where I was very much charmed with your DELIGHTFUL and enchanting COMPOSITIONS, and your spirited and interesting performance of them, accept t[h]en thousand thanks for the great pleasure, I ALWAYS receive from your INCOMPARABLE MUSIC. My D: I intreat you to inform me, how you do, and if you get any SLEEP to Night. I am EXTREMELY ANXIOUS about your health. I hope to hear a good account of it. God Bless you MY H. come to me to morrow I shall be happy to see you both morning and Evening. I always am with the tenderest Regard my D: your

F: and aff.

Friday Night 12 o'clock.   [CCLN, 285f.]

M: D. I am heartily sorry I was so unfortunate not to see you, when you call'd on me this morning, can you my D: be so good as to dine with me TO DAY. I beg you will if possible – you can not imagine how miserable I am that I did not see you – do come to Day I intreat you – I always am M: D: with the tenderest Regard most et[c].

Monday 2 o'clock.   [CCLN, 286]

It is unlikely that we shall ever be able to reconstruct which new and old Haydn symphonies were performed at the first seasons of the Salomon series. We are, as regards new works, better off for the second season, where we are able to identify all the first performances except for No. 97. We do not, however, know the first performance dates for Nos. 95 and 96 in the first season. While No. 92 as the opening work of Haydn's English career seems to be a very likely choice, we do not have any idea when Nos. 90 and 91 were first played, except that the former must have been in 1791 and the latter in 1792.

In contemplating which of the earlier works were performed, we have had certain hints. For Nos. 90 and 92 we have contemporary British editions that tell us the works were played at Salomon's season (1791), and for No. 91 we have the evidence of Haydn's letters to Frau von Genzinger. Here and there we have some other kind of evidence for an earlier work, such as Haydn's own story about Symphony No. 75 and the English clergyman (*supra*, p. 152). Nevertheless it would seem, upon examination of what would appear to be 'new' works launched in England, i.e. works known possibly on the Continent but not in England, that there must be some missing symphonies. It is possibly idle to speculate on what is, after all, largely a matter of statistical interest; and yet there is one particular case in point which transcends the boundaries of statistics because of the fact that there is a large-scale re-orchestration involved.

Of all Haydn's previous symphonies, there remained, of course, a large number of really early works, but it is obvious that they would not do for London in 1791–2. Even a work like Symphony No. 50 might, especially in the slow movement, have sounded a little antiquated for England (No. 50 had, rather curiously, remained unprinted). But there was one single work of the Eszterháza years which was (1) not yet printed;[1] (2) of a big, 'English' scale: we must remember Haydn's remarks about Symphony No. 91, composed only three or four years earlier than 1791–2, that he 'had to change many things for the English public'. There is such a work, and it is No. 54 in G, composed in 1774 and certainly one of the most impressive symphonic works of its time.

We are fortunate in having the autograph manuscript, without which this interesting tale could hardly be told. It is in the Esterházy Archives of the Budapest National Library and was from Haydn's estate (that, too, is an important fact). It is now Mus. Ms. I, 39 and is signed and dated 'Sinfonia. In Nomine Domini. di me Giuseppe Haydn $\overline{774}$.' The autograph shows that there was at first no slow introduction: the MS. begins with the *Presto*. The scoring was originally for two oboes, one bassoon, two horns and strings. After finishing the symphony, Haydn added the second bassoon part in the stave of the first and changed the designation at the beginning of each movement (from 'Fagotto' to '2 Fagotti'). Between 1774 and 1776 Haydn added the introduction and the timpani part. (Göttweig Abbey owns a copy dated 1776 with these hitherto missing items, and there is another source dated 1776 in Laibach – now Ljubljana, Jugoslavia – with timpani and the slow introduction.) In this form, the Symphony was very widely circulated.

At some point, Haydn then added parts for two flutes (originally one but changed immediately; the 3rd and 4th movements right at the start of this revision with '2 Flauti') and two C-trumpets (*Clarini*). There is no other copy anywhere of this version except for a very late (*c.* 1800–1810) set of parts with score, in MS., from the Archduke Rudolph's Collection (now in the Gesellschaft der Musikfreunde), and for the Sieber print. Haydn's autograph of the flute and trumpet parts for the introduction have, of course, not survived except at second hand in the Rudolph and Sieber sources (since the autograph of the introduction altogether is lost). There is no known source of this work in the revised 'big' orchestration prior to about the first decade of the nineteenth century, and Haydn cannot have performed the 'big' orchestration at Eszterháza because he lacked the trumpets except for 1780 (when, however, he still had no second flute). Thus we put forward as a *suggestion* that Haydn did the 'big' orchestration for the first London trip: we say first rather than second, because there are no clarinet parts, though we admit that Symphony No. 102 (composed in 1794) also lacks clarinets; but also because Haydn did not really need any more 'old-new' symphonies during the second trip. He was able to fulfil his contract to Salomon by writing six new quartets (Opp. 71 & 74) and three new symphonies (Nos. 99–101) for the 1794 season, while for the 1795 season (Opera Concerts), there were entirely different conditions prevailing.

Just before Haydn left London, the London correspondent of the Berlin *Musikalisches Wochenblatt* sent a long letter in three instalments (Zweites Heft, Stück XVII–XIX, 1793), and in the following year, on 29 June 1793, the *Berlinische Musikalische Zeitung* began to publish a letter from London:

> Latest Report on Concert- and Theatre-music in London. Extracts from a letter sent from London on 18th May 1793.
>
> The best concert in London is that of which *Salomon* is the entrepreneur, and which is, therefore, known as *Salomon's Concert*. The orchestra consists of 12 to 16 violins, 4 violas, 5 violoncellos and 4 contrabasses, flutes, oboes, bassoons, horns,

---

1 Landon, SYM, 698 (20) notwithstanding. The Sieber print first appeared as 'revue et corrigée' which as we shall see refers to the symphony and not the Sieber edition. See also Hoboken I, 74.

trumpets and kettledrums – about 40 persons in all. The room in which it is held is perhaps longer than that in the Stadt Paris in Berlin, but broader, better decorated, and with a vaulted ceiling. The music sounds, in the hall, beautiful beyond any description. The band is seated *en amphitheatre*. Salomon was always a good interpreter, but now one can say that he is superb. Perhaps, however, the presence of Haydn, who has been here the last two Carneval seasons and personally conducted his symphonies at Salomon's concerts, is in part responsible. In each concert two, often three, Haydn symphonies are played. Madame *Mara* sings two arias; Signor *Bruni*, a castrato from the Italian opera here, the same; *Viotti* or Salomon plays a violin concerto. There is usually, besides this, a concerto for oboe, flute, harp or violoncello – a Concerto Grosso, or a quartet. The whole concert is in two parts, beginning at 8 o'clock in the evening and lasting until 11 or half-past 11. . . . *Harrington*, a Sicilian, and pupil of the late *Lebrun*, is an oboist equally at home in concerti as well as ripieni. He has the nice, round tone of his teacher, but is somewhat weaker in sound. . . . Hindmarsh, an Englishman and pupil of Salomon, plays the viola delightfully. . . .

[Continuation in the issue of 6 July 1793 :]. . . . Mr. *Parke*, an Englishman, plays the oboe not quite so beautifully as *Harrington*, but has a fuller tone. *Lindley*, an Englishman, plays the violoncello as beautifully, as cleanly, and as assuredly as *Hansmann*, but without the latter's fire; he seems, however, to be still very young.

Holmes, an Englishman, plays the bassoon, has the fullest tone I have ever heard, and executes both soli and ripieni very neatly; but he does not on the whole possess the exceptional elegance and class of execution which so delighted me in *Ritter's* playing (in the Königliche Capelle at Berlin). . . .

Haydn's reputation in Germany never reached the heights that it did in England. In fact, the Germans had a very curious attitude towards Haydn's music, an attitude that started when they first began to hear Haydn in the 1760s and has in some respects continued until this very day. On the one hand, they thought Haydn and all Austrian music flighty, frivolous and of a low humour; and on the other, they could not help but be attracted to it for the simple reason that it was irresistible. All this set up a vastly complicated and ambivalent approach to Haydn which is graphically illustrated in a curious little brochure published anonymously (as musical brochures often were in Germany), entitled *Portfeuille für Musikliebhaber, Characteristik von 20 Componisten; und Abhandlung über die Tonkunst*, which is dated, 'Leipziger Ostermesse 1792' (Easter in 1792 coming at the end of the first week of April, this is presumably the date of the brochure's appearance). We cite some extracts from the *Portfeuille*. The writer cannot even wait for the article 'Hayden' before jumping into the fray: he begins at once in the first line of the article on Ditters:

Ditters

Since the time when Hayde [*sic*] changed the tone of Viennese music, or set a new pace, it has actually become more characteristic than ever before, but from the dignity which it enjoyed under Wagenseil, it has too much sunk into triviality [*Tändeley*]. Since Hayde, music has possibly suffered that very change that the theatre has also suffered, but the former certainly to less advantage.

To cause laughter, in whatever way, was the latter's intention, its intention, that is, up to the point when a [Court Councillor Joseph von] Sonnenfels dared to pour out remonstrances and proposals for the throne, or until [Emperor] Joseph [II] felt that he – was Joseph. The comical girl (which part was greatly supported by the author of Harlequin), having been expelled from the theatrical world, has asked permission to be accepted by music; the priest [Haydn], a man who, it would seem, was made for caprice, was softened – reached for the silly thing – and hurled her into his temple; – and since then we laugh over Viennese music.

If, however, the humorous is the genuine, satisfying reaction to music, – if it is not too monotonous to be made national; – if it is not beneath that art, – not too low?

Questions – as you can see.

Had Hayden's [*sic*] caprice, by refining our taste, generally attempted to make music physically more beautiful, more attractive – had he really succeeded in this – then his original mixture would have brought him credit, – to the extent that it would have brought credit to music.

And the cross-fertilization of this style was such that it attracted imitators who, to be capricious (without possessing the actual mixture), had no recourse except to lower their songs down to the level of the street-tune – imitators, then, who directly sought the world's approval by this kind of enticing novelty.

Not seldom Ditters seems to have made Hayden his object for imitation; – and I prefer Ditters, when he is being himself, to Hayde – when he imitates, he is less [than Haydn]. If he [Ditters] has in common with Hayde mostly the same walk, without lift, without panache, he [Ditters] has the advantage that his symphonies are quicker, smoother, more flowing – in short, more like real symphonies than Hayde's; – that he [Ditters] has the advantage, too, in concerti (with the whole concept of which he is in sympathy) of gracing that form with all the strength of pathos and majesty. If Hayde might have more melody: good – Ditters has more harmony. [pp. 28–30]

[There follows a long, tortuously reasoned and pedantically written argument against the rondo form, particular in its dance-like manifestation – pp. 31–5 – ending:] Ditters would appear in a much more favourable light if he himself and his imitators were not so prodigal with this invention [the rondo]. [p. 35]

Joseph Hayden [*sic*]

Capricious is what I called Hayden above. 'Well, what is actually musical caprice?' Yes! That's easily asked! Almost nothing is more difficult than to define a concept which has finally been decided upon (or at least proposed), and to employ it for all the special sides of a special art. [Footnote:]'Why did you call him that?' Because I felt he was so, dear reader; – and because I can trust all of us at last to call a spade a spade. [p. 55]

[There follows a long and humourless treatise on humour, quoting authorities (Rudel and Ben Johnson [*sic*]) to demonstrate that Haydn's humour is not really humour at all.] [pp. 56–63]

No one will contradict that the only dominating attitude or (since we are dealing with music) the only dominating emotion in Hayden is eccentric, bizarre; – and projected without control. Will someone call to witness Hayden's *Adagio*? – good, then it's seriously committed caprice; like the tragic emotions of a Shakespear [!].

Also one thing is certain, that Hayden's humour *in se* does not diminish our respect, for Father Home [*sic*] made a character out of every humorist. [Footnote: Hayden's caprice, I said earlier, had apparently had evil effects on music: right! For if everyone round us wanted to be a humorist, Heaven save us from everlasting laughter or – from fainting.]

Caprice must be the only dominating emotion. But what if you don't find it all the time in every one of Hayden's products, that single, dominating emotion? That is no proof that I have wrongly described a difference in character; but rather that this emotion does not always have the same level at all times, must not always be ascertainable to the same degree; and that humour may have its high and low tides – high and low tides which are fixed or altered by position, by physical and moral influence, and altogether through life's circumstances – but not suppressed; no less than Rabner's emotion as he loses his lands. . . .   [pp. 64f.]

And no ability, no originality, no force suffer more changes, more casual interpretation, than emotion; – because nothing is more dependent upon the sense of feelings. But just name me one single, solitary product of Hayden, in which caprice is not at the bottom of it all! You won't find any.

If there is one single emotion that must never be the reason for apologizing for a symphony, it is *caprice*, which can never be the true basis; and thus Hayden's symphonies, because his emotion is too one-sided, will be less than symphonies.

The richer I find my man in Quatro [*sic*] and related forms. That's the yardstick I measure him by, and promise my respect; if he would only allow Mother Nature (to whom he owes his gifts [*Modification*]) to make her exit.

That Hayden often sins against the rules of counterpoint, I don't hold against him, nor Gretri [Grétry]: for too often subtle theory which is too subtle prevents the composer who adheres too closely to it from larger beauties.

That he actually invented the [melody in] octaves; – is welcome to me; for he can often, without worrying about rightness or wrongness, bring forth big effects; and he has, at least for the ear, the most exact relationship to the simple octave. But since the feeling for the riduculous (according to an experience which is most interesting for the arts) is only pleasant when the soul is empty of every other, especially contrary, emotion, there is no art for which I would less wish humorists than for the art of the note.   [pp. 66f.]

Vanhall

. . . If I compare the very great similarity of Vanhall's violin quartets to those of Hayden, it always appears to me unbelievable that, to be original, two men should be so alike, so closely atuned to another. – And who of the two imitated, who was original?

Vanhall came after Hayden; Hayden therefore cannot have imitated! Moreover, his mixture is much too natural to him, and he is all too true to it. So it was Vanhall imitating, or was he afterwards original? As said, this kind of similarity is never found in nature.

Hayden is that what he is, always: a dash [*Zug*] of Hayden.

Vanhall is that what he is, but not always, – several dashes, then, and with more varied sides to his nature. If he therefore wanted to be original in this *genre* [quartets] like Hayden, he [Vanhal] would have to be so all the time. Even more! – Vanhall's basic emotion in his first violin quartets is often exactly opposite to that of his last symphonies and flute quartets. Apparently, then, Vanhall made Hayden the object to imitate, – and with great luck – did not slavishly imitate him.

[pp. 103–5]

We must bear this kind of scurrilous pamphlet in mind – and there are many others from the earlier period – when we read in the Parke *Memoirs* (II, 27ff.) that Haydn's 'transcendent genius soon enabled him to soar high above all his competitors; and, as envy seldom fails to pursue merit, the German masters became so jealous of his rising fame, that they entered into a kind of combination in order to decry his compositions. Some went so far as even to write pamphlets against his works, complaining of them as wild, flighty . . . and as tending to introduce new musical doctrines. . . . It has often been asserted that the compositions of Haydn are very unequal; that some are replete with elegance and scientific knowledge, whilst others are extravagant to excess.' It is also interesting to see that Haydn's two London journeys had only a delayed effect on the German musical public (by German, we mean German-speaking, of course), nor did his music ever reach the degree of popularity in Germany that it enjoyed in England and to a lesser degree in Austria (though in Austria the scene would soon change rapidly in this respect).

It would be wrong, however, to assert that Haydn was not well known in Germany, for even in 1792 he had a large following among the 'musical masses'. Hamburg, brought up on the stern and brilliantly eccentric music of C. P. E. Bach, eagerly expected Haydn's presence in July 1792. At Westphal's music shop, the new English prints of Haydn's portrait were on exhibition, and the music friends of that cultivated Hanseatic port city hoped, in vain, to catch a glimpse of the celebrated composer.[1]

There are two principal sources for Haydn's visit to Bonn in July 1792. The one is Wegeler's and Ries's book,[2] which has been widely quoted, and the other, even more authentic, has been almost entirely overlooked: we refer to Beethoven's own *Stammbuch*,[3] the only well-known remark in it being the one entered by Count Waldstein about Beethoven receiving Mozart's 'spirit from Hayden's hands'.

According to our first source, Haydn was this time offered a breakfast at Bad Godesberg (next to Bonn) by the Electoral Orchestra, the Elector himself having left Bonn for the Coronation at Frankfurt. What Wegeler does not make clear is whether it was on this visit or (as he seems to indicate) the previous visit at Christmas 1790 (when Haydn and Salomon were en route from Vienna to London) that Beethoven submitted a cantata to Haydn. It was either the powerfully original *Cantata on the Death of Joseph II* (*Cantate auf den Tod Joseph's des Zweiten. In Musik gesetzt von L. van Beethoven*, 1790) or the slightly newer *Cantata on the Elevation of Leopold II to Rank of Emperor* (*Cantate auf die Erhebung Leopolds des Zweiten zur Kaiserwürde, in Musik gesetzt von L. van Beethoven*, 1790). In any case Wegeler reports of this Cantata, whichever it was, that it 'was especially noticed [*beachtet*] by Haydn and its composer encouraged to further study'.

Many later authorities have doubted that this second visit actually took place. We will not quote them simply because their arguments are destroyed by Beethoven's *Stammbuch* and the new evidence that we have of Haydn's being engaged to return at once to London. Their evidence was limited to Wegeler-Ries and the fact that the return trip to Bonn is not mentioned either by Griesinger or Dies.

We must remember that Haydn arrived in Bonn fully expecting, indeed contractually obligated, to return to London in January 1793 to continue writing new works for Salomon (*infra*, p. 230). It must have been decided therefore that Beethoven should go to Vienna in November 1792 and later accompany Haydn to England. That Beethoven actually went to Vienna when he was expected to do so is well known; as for the second part of the plan, the following notice by Beethoven's teacher, Christian Gottlob Neefe, in the *Berliner Musikzeitung* of 26 October 1793 tells us explicitly that Beethoven expected to go to England:

Bonn.

In November of last year [1792] Lud. van Beethoven, the second Court Organist and without doubt one of the first pianists we have, journeyed at the expense of

---

1 *Musicalische Korrespondenz der teutschen Filharmonischen Geselleschaft*, Jahrgang 1792, No. 30.
2 Dr F. G. Wegeler & Ferdinand Ries, *Biographische Notizen über L. von [sic] Beethoven*, Coblenz 1838, p. 10.
3 *Ludwig van Beethovens Stammbuch*, facsimile edition with comments by Dr Hans Gerstingen, Bielefeld and Leipzig 1927. A good transcription in Thayer I, 467–474.

our *Churfürst* to Haydn in Vienna, to perfect under the latter's direction his knowledge of composition. Haydn intended taking him with him on his second trip to London; but nothing has come of this trip so far.

It is quite clear from the documents quoted in this Chronicle that Haydn fully intended to return to England, perhaps for good, and only put his services at the disposal of his Prince Anton Esterházy for the Coronation and afterwards until the composer could settle his affairs. But as we have hinted, there is also evidence from Beethoven's *Stammbuch*. Here is the translation of a poem entered into the book by Christoph von Breuning :[1]

See! Oh friend, Albion calls you.
See! The shady grove, which entices the singer
hasten then without delay
over the surging sea
where a more beauteous grove offers you its shade
and a bard [Salomon] stretches out his hand to you in friendship,
who from our fields
fled to Albion's protection.
There let thy song ring loudly and victorious,
let it ring wildly through the grove, across the waves of the sea
to those fields
whence thou hadst fled with joy.

Bonn, 19bre [Nov.] 1792.

> Think of your friend
> [Christoph] Ed. Breuning.

Now it is quite inconceivable that this trip can have been planned in December 1790 before Haydn had arrived in England; the whole *Stammbuch* shows that it was written after it had been decided (1) that Beethoven should go to study with Haydn; (2) that a trip to England was to be made, with Salomon's blessing and in Haydn's company; and Haydn cannot have thought of taking Beethoven with him until *after* the success of the 1791–2 visit.

There was little time to tarry in the pretty *Residenzstadt* Bonn now, and after talking to Nicolaus Simrock the publisher, Haydn soon left for Frankfurt, where his presence is registered in connection with a curious musical instrument called the 'Harmonica celestina'. The Coronation took place on 14 July, and unlike London, Haydn's presence in Frankfurt was not thought worthy of mention. But we find his name in the *Frankfurter Staats-Ristretto* of 13 July, where a (presumably paid) notice tells us that the newly invented instrument 'has been played and tested by Haydn and thought worthy of his good praises', while in two other Frankfurt newspapers, the *Altes Frankfurter Intelligenzblatt* of 24 July and the *Kaiserliche Reichs-Ober-Postamtszeitung* of 30 July tells us, apropos of the 'Harmonica celestina', 'that it fills a gap which many a great artist was forced to leave empty. Even the great *Herr Capellmeister* Haidn [sic] and the first Imperial *Kapellmeister* [sic: "K" and "C" for "Capellmeister" in the same sentence], who played it and examined it exactly, recognized it for the first in its field.' Salieri was in Frankfurt as part of the royal train,

---

1 Landon, *Beethoven*, p. 57.

together with a large group of musicians from Vienna.[1] On 17 July, Haydn discussed publishing projects with Bernard Schott in the little town of Biebrich on the Rhine, half a day's journey from Frankfurt. Most of these discussions with the German publishers will not have been more than pleasant social chats, for incredible as it sounds, Haydn had very little in the way of new music that he could offer the houses of Simrock or Schott. It was one thing, perhaps, to give Artaria in far-away Vienna a new work which was simultaneously being published in England; but it was another to enter into serious negotiations with publishers so near to England. After all, Gallini owned the rights to *Orfeo* and numerous smaller vocal pieces; Salomon owned the rights to the first six Symphonies for London and probably to the *Madrigal* 'The Storm' and the *Concertante* as well. Apart from these major works, Haydn will not have had many other saleable pieces in his luggage, though it continues to strike one as odd that he did not talk Simrock or André or Schott into some of the *Notturni* for the King of Naples or the insertion arias that he took from old operas for the Eszterháza Theatre and brushed up for England (such as the Cantata 'Miseri noi, misera patria'). But perhaps the German publishers were interested in other *genres* such as chamber music with and without piano, or similar instrumental works which Haydn was not in a position to supply at the moment. In sum, business with the Germans was not yet as interesting as it would later become for Haydn.

According to Pohl, Haydn arrived back in Vienna on 24 July 1792 and took up his old (1790) quarters at Herr Hamburger's house on the Wasserkunstbastei No. 992. The first weeks were spent in unpacking and delivering all the small presents from London, such as knitting needles . . . (Maria Anna von Genzinger seems to have received them all 'for further distribution'.)

[To Maria Anna von Genzinger, Vienna. *German*]
Gracious Lady!
    Since Herr von Keess has invited me for lunch today, I shall have the opportunity to give his wife the knitting-needles I promised her. If, therefore, Your Grace would be good enough to have some sent over, I shall be able to fulfil my promise, for which I kiss Your Grace's hands and remain, respectfully,

Your wholly obedient servant,
Joseph Haydn.

[Vienna] From my home, 4th August 1792.

[Address:]   Madame
      Madame de Gennzinger
             a
         Son Logis.

[CCLN, 137]

---

1 Pohl III, 61. Date for Haydn's Viennese arrival *ibid.*, 62 (no source given) and the address at Hamburger's on p. 64. Wurzbach's *Lexikon* also specifies 24 July 1792. The Schott meeting from Hoboken I, 176. The Simrock meeting from that publisher's announcement in the *AMZ* for October 1810 (*Intelligenz-Blatt*, Anzeige 39); Haydn complained about the many incorrect editions of his symphonies and Simrock promised to issue a corrected edition, which he announced to the world in the *AMZ*, noting that Haydn, 'als [er] bey seiner Zurückkunft aus Engeland zum letztenmal hier [in Bonn] durchreisste [*sic*] . . . mich zu einer korrekten [Ausgabe seiner Symphonien] aufmunterte.' Simrock thus provides us with one more proof of this second visit to Bonn, in July 1792. In August 1795 Haydn travelled back *via* Hamburg, but he will have avoided Bonn, since October 1794 occupied by the French. The first recorded appearance of Haydn in Vienna is a receipt in the Esterházy Archives dated 'Wien den 31st July 1792' signed by Haydn, acknowledging 233 Gulden 20 Kreuzer as his salary from 1 January to the end of July. A. Valkó: 'Haydn Magyarországi Müködése a Levéltári Aktah Tükreben' in *Zenetudomanyi Tanulmányok* VI (1957), 659.

There was no mention of Haydn's return in the Viennese newspapers. As a realist, Haydn will not have expected anything different, for Vienna was still a small, almost rural, city compared to London; but the difference between his position in London and that in Vienna and Eisenstadt will have been forcibly made clear to him almost every day. Although Vienna was, with its population of not more than 270,000 and its famous green belt (the 'Wienerwald'), a third the size of London[1] and lacking the latter's urban accoutrements, nevertheless the 'Imperial and Royal *Hauptstadt*' was the governing centre for a very large and far-flung empire. The shy, new Emperor of this vast realm would soon come to occupy a position of great importance not only as ruler of the Austro-Hungarian Empire but also, with England and Russia, as one of the three principal opponents of Napoleon and his armies. Hardly had Franz II finished the coronation ceremonies at Frankfurt when on 25 July Prussian, Austrian and Hessian armies left Coblenz and began to march on Paris, to free the French capital from the Revolutionary 'Hydra' and to re-establish Louis XVI and Franz's aunt, Marie Antoinette, on the throne of the *fleur-de-lys*.

The first campaign of what would become the Napoleonic Wars ended in defeat for the Allied troops. By the end of September the French had seized the offensive, and General Custine occupied Speyer, Worms on 4 October and Mainz at the end of that month. The French took up winter quarters in Belgium, the Allies in the area Düsseldorf-Cologne. England sent it first expeditionary force to Holland in February 1793.

Franz II was the son of the complex and interesting Emperor Leopold II who would possibly have gone much farther than his brother Joseph II in reforming Austrian politics. But Leopold had died very suddenly in 1792 before being able to do much except settle the political and economic unrest into which Joseph II, with his headstrong *terribilità*, had plunged the monarchy. Joseph had sent for the sixteen-year old Franz to be brought to Vienna, installed him in the Hofburg and started to educate him. He wrote about the youth: 'He is retarded in size and strength and backward in physical skills ... unfit for statemanship ... speaks indistinctly, uses coarse expressions, has a barking voice, and swallows his words. ...'[2] Joseph never really liked Franz, and the young man hardly succeeded in pleasing his difficult uncle. During Joseph's last illness, Leopold (at that time Grand Duke of Tuscany, which province he had brilliantly administered) wrote from Florence to his son to seal all the offices in the Hofburg and pocket the keys. Leopold II had trusted no one.

Franz, writes Mrs McGuigan, was 'a slight youth with a long face, pale blue eyes, protruding lower lip; his public image was cautious, quiet, melancholy; in his portraits he is never seen with the ghost of a smile. In Franz seemed to be reborn the family trait of patient, enduring phlegm, that ability to bear misfortune, humiliation, defeat, to cut his losses again and again and wait out a change of fortune.'

Like almost all the Habsburg family, Franz was very fond of music, though he shared his father's and Uncle Joseph's lack of ability to appreciate the *outré* and the really intellectual. Franz was also extremely conservative and loved fugues. He

---

1 In 1801 the first official census of London was taken; the population in that year was 900,000 (John Summerson, *Georgian London*, London 1962, p. 25). According to the *Nützliches Auskunftsbuch ... Wien 1797*, the population of Vienna was 'wenigstens 270,000'. Allowing for the slight difference in dates, it is safe to say that during the last decade of the eighteenth century London had a population three times the size of Vienna's, which was 'at least' 270,000 in 1797 and growing slowly.

2 Dorothy Gies McGuigan, *The Hapsburgs*, New York 1966, p. 265. Description: p. 274; family and chamber music: p. 279.

preferred Reutter to Beethoven[1] and Michael Haydn to Mozart. But the whole imperial family made music together; Franz played the violin, his wife – Marie Therese, daughter of Ferdinand IV, King of Naples and the Twin Sicilies, and Carolina, and thus his first cousin – sang and was able to sight-read the soprano part of a new Mass by Michael Haydn. It is said that more than one courtier owed his rise in the ministry to his ability to join in the Emperor's house quartet; Metternich later contributed a first-rate 'cello performance. Franz was a born family man, and within the bounds of private life, 'the grave and cautious emperor gave way to the devoted, even lively husband and father. Under the ancient beech trees in the Laxenburg park he was often glimpsed, trundling a wheelbarrow in which rode his epileptic and sadly retarded son, Crown Prince Ferdinand', later known as Emperor 'Ferdinand der Gütige'.

Franz, succeeding quite unexpectedly at the age of twenty-four, lacked confidence in himself, distrusted his own judgements. He was bound, therefore, to lean heavily on his advisers. He gave his former tutor, Count Franz Colloredo, the title of cabinet minister, and he respectfully deferred to the advice of his chief ministers and to that of his brother, the Palatin of Hungary. He kept at arm's length all his father's confidential collaborators. Many of the latters' reports and projects were consigned to the flames.[4] When he appointed Colloredo, the Emperor said, 'I know well that the burden which has been laid on me is too heavy for me, since I am young and have little experience. My only wish is to do good, and I hope that I may be so fortunate as to have my choice fall on righteous men to help me.'[3] Macartney, whose penetrating book on the later stages of the Habsburg Empire provides the best known summing-up of the period politically, writes:

> Francis does not altogether deserve the very harsh judgements which have been passed on him by many later Austrian historians. . . . He was neither a bad man, nor a stupid one. The widespread popularity which he came to enjoy in his later years in Vienna may have been somewhat fictitious: it was largely based on his affability and unpretentiousness . . . and perhaps even more, on his habit of expressing himself in a broad Viennese dialect. . . . Unlike his uncle, he was no militarist. He was shrewd above the average . . . and possessed . . . a sardonic sense of humour . . . but he had in him no trace of his father's genuine constitutional beliefs; he had rather absorbed from his uncle . . . Joseph's unqualified faith in the doctrine of complete Monarchic absolutism . . . [and] his basic conception of the proper relationship between himself and his peoples was completely egocentric.[4]

Haydn, as the Established composer, gradually had a lot to say in the formation of the young Emperor's library (which, fortunately, is almost completely intact). There are, as far as Haydn is concerned, a large quantity of symphonies and other instrumental music, the late oratorios of course, and a valuable collection of arias, some from Haydn's own earlier operas (e.g. *La fedeltà premiata*) and some which he had written for insertion in the operas of other composers given at Eszterháza: the vocal music of the *Kaiserliche Sammlung* is mostly in the Austrian National Library, the instrumental music in the Gesellschaft der Musikfreunde. We also find Haydn's copyist Johann Elssler making copies of Handel oratorios (in the Mozartian

1 'There is something revolutionary in that music!' said Franz about Beethoven (Landon, *Beethoven*, 107).
2 Ernst Wangermann, *From Joseph II to the Jacobin Trials*, London 1969, pp. 109ff.
3 C. A. Macartney, *The Habsburg Empire 1790–1918*, London 1968, pp. 151f.
4 *Ibid.*; reprinted by permission of Weidenfeld & Nicolson Ltd.

orchestration) for the Emperor's Library. The Empress sang a great deal, and this preponderance of vocal music obviously reflects this aspect of life in the Hofburg where, as we shall see, Marie Therese sang Haydn's *Creation* and *Seasons* under the composer's direction.

Franz's position in history was soon complicated by the Napoleonic Wars and by the fear of Jacobin conspiracies at home; in the last lustrum of the century, Austria and particularly Vienna were to change, and not for the better. But we are fortunate in being witness to the last golden era of Viennese culture, when Haydn and Beethoven (often together) dominated the concerts of fashionable Vienna, and when it could be said without exaggeration that the Austrian aristocracy and middle class were the most gifted peoples, musically, in Europe.

On 5 August, Haydn's *Orlando Paladino* was performed in German, as *Ritter Roland*, in the Mannheim Theatre. Since the criticism which has been preserved in the *Annalen des Theaters* reflects the difficulty of staging these Haydn operas a decade after they had been composed, we add it here:

> For some time *Ritter Roland*, an opera with music by the famous Haydn, had been announced to the public and this new production was awaited with impatience. Finally *Roland* was performed for the first time on 5 August. Everything was done to give this piece with all the fantastic splendour that fairytales of this kind require, and our players left nothing undone which might have contributed to the success of the whole. Hr. Demmer was Roland and a success; he sang with fire – and often with expression. If Herr Demmer knew how to use his voice, which is really beautiful; if he attempted to widen his range of taste and to devote somewhat more effort towards declamation and language, he would be more than just a useful member of the company, as far as the opera is concerned.
>
> Mad. Beck had the rôle of Angelika and was generally applauded. In her arias she unites art, taste, fire, fellings – she carried all before her. I would have to single out every aria in her part if I were to describe all the admirable qualities that I found in her singing. Also in the projection of the rôle Mad. Beck showed insight, so rare in singers: her acting was correct and was a success.
>
> I cannot say quite the same for Hr. Epp, who played Medoro. He sang outwardly beautifully, especially the Duet with Mad. Beck, and his aria where he is determined to die; but his acting was cold, and often unconcerned.
>
> Hr. Gern, as King Rodomonte, was successful; but he pleased more at the second performance. This part is not very important; Herr Gern inserted an aria by Reichard in the next performance: thus the rôle gained in interest and Hr. Gern was loudly applauded.
>
> Hr. Leonard played Pasquale, Roland's shield-bearer. He was widely successful because of his comical pose, he sang well. He is our public's darling in rôles of this kind.
>
> Despite everything that the directors had done for the piece at its first performance, and excellent though the music is, nevertheless this opera did not entirely please. The actors were conceded to have done their best. But one found the piece too long; in the original everything is in *recitativo secco*, here all that was changed into dialogue, and it was too often noticed where the grand opera style stopped and operetta began; many parts of the music were incomprehensible to the amateurs [*Nichtkenner*]; and the story itself is dreadfully handled by the poet. Herr Beck therefore received the commission to change this operas and to put a better face on it. He threw out unnecessary and useless scenes, improved the language throughout, and *Ritter Roland* was much more of a success at the second performance (2 September) than it had been at the first. The music was shortened,

too: Mad. Beck omitted an unimportant aria; Hr. Gern inserted a bass aria by Reichard [J. F. Reichardt], and Hr. Leonard the 'Maestro di Cappella' aria by Cimarosa; and then Roland was highly successful. I'm no friend of insertion arias, but here it was not only excusable but really necessary. This music, which on the whole is excellent as far as [accompanied] recitatives, choruses, duets and altogether ensembles are concerned, is one of Haydn's earlier works [1782]; so the style of the arias is rather old-fashioned, and this work appeared just as the taste in music had very much changed. The [inserted] aria of Rodomonte, and Pasquale's 'Maestro di Cappella' aria [by Cimarosa], were the clearest proof of this, and Messrs. Gern and Leonard did well to substitute these arias, which are more to present-day taste, than the original ones.

We have said that Haydn was soon to become the musician of the Austrian Establishment. In this respect, Haydn and Beethoven were to be on different sides of the political fence, Haydn believing to the depths of his soul in the rightness of the cause against Napoleon. It is typical that Haydn should write the *Missa in tempore belli* (1796) and the *Missa in angustiis* (1798) illustrating the war from the Austrian side. He kept a map of the battle of Abukir in his effects. Beethoven consorted with the politically scandal-ridden French Ambassador to Austria, Bernadotte, and planned the 'Eroica' Symphony for Napoleon. Partly this was the difference in generations. But partly, too, Haydn was more experienced, had travelled more and, it might be thought, had a more balanced view of the French situation. Certainly he had witnessed many more first-hand stories about the horrors of Revolutionary Paris than Beethoven, whose politics were much more based on theory and on abstract, Rousseau-like ideas. Haydn's views were shared by many Englishman, including Dr Burney, who in September wrote, 'I can neither think, talk, or write ab^t anything else than the abominations of France.' And like Haydn and many other thinking men of *fin-de-siècle* Europe, he concluded, 'Is this the end of the 18th Cent^y, so enlightened & so philosophical?' Burney thought there was 'no Tyrant so cruel, nor no Sovereign so worthless, as that of the Mob'.[1]

Later in the year (2 December) Burney wrote:

I sh^d think I did the world a signal piece of service, if one night or other, when its inhabitants were all fast asleep, I could, by the wave of a magic wand, wipe away every idea of the [democratic] kind. . . . Let them study mathematics, optics, metaphysics, & all the *ics* & *tics* in the world, except *Politics*. How good-humoured & happy they w^d all come down to breakfast, the next morning.

But from the 'brain-washing' of Dr Burney's harmless type to newspaper censorship and a network of spies was unfortunately a small jump, as we shall see later in the course of this Chronicle.

After the busy and interested London newspapers, Vienna's sleepy official *Wiener Zeitung* must have seemed provincial. Incredible as it sounds, there was at least one Viennese newspaper, *Der heimliche Botschafter* ('The Secret Messenger'), which appeared from 1791–3 in manuscript only, and of which a single copy has survived in the Austrian National Library. In it, Haydn could have read the following notice of 2 October 1792, of which not a single phrase except for the first five (in our translation six) words is true: '*Kapellmeister* Hayden, who has arrived here, is working on the

---

1 Lonsdale, 364. Refutation of democratic ideas: 370.

second part of the favourite opera *Die Zauberflöte* by the late Mozart', while on 15 October, *The Secret Messenger* informed its readers, there would be a new opera by Haydn given at the Court Opera to celebrate the Name-Day of the Empress. Can there have been a plan to produce *L'anima del filosofo*? Or is this another one of the *Messenger*'s tales? No performance took place, in any event.

Pietro Polzelli ('Pietruccio') was now in Vienna studying with Haydn and we have a joint letter by master and teacher to Luigia:

[Pietro Polzelli to Luigia Polzelli (Bologna) with a postscript by Haydn. *Italian: Pietro in 'Lei' form, Haydn in the 'Tu'*]

[Vienna] 22nd October [1792.]

Dearest Mother!

I beg you to forgive me for not being able immediately to answer the letter of 2nd October you sent to me. The reason is that I had kept on hoping to be able to include a little something with it. Dear Mother, I have spoken to *il Sig^r Maestro* Häyde [*sic*] and begged him many times on your account, dearest Mother, but he cannot do more than he has done already. Through *Sig*: Valentino Pertoja[1] of Venice whom you know well from Esterháza, and who is at present here in Vienna on business, *il Sig^r Maestro* Häyden [*sic*] sends you twenty-six florins [Gulden] and 30 xr [Kreutzer] together with this present letter. He says to tell you that he cannot send more at present, because he is incapable of doing so: he has many expenses on my behalf, and also for his own household. Dearest Mother, I must inform you that I shall leave Cristina's[2] house today, since *il Sigre Maes.* Haydn has found a place for me in his own home, so as to have more time to be able to teach me everything. I must further inform you that through the kindness of *Sig^{re} Maestro* Haydn I have found a house where I can earn something: it is at the home of the Countess Weissenwolf,[3] where I teach her own daughter how to play the harpsichord. Thus I hope to be able to help a little, and I shall never fail to do my very best. I am, as always,

Your most obedient son,
Pietro Polcelli [*sic*]

The 22nd of October 1792.

[Haydn's postscript]
Dear Polzelli, Your son has been very well received by my wife, and I hope this situation will continue. Pietro must teach the Countess Weissenwolf's daughter, and he asked me of his own accord to send all the money he earns to his dear mother. I am mortified not to be able to send you any more than these twenty-six florins at present, but I have many expenses. Farewell. I am your most sincere Giuseppe Haydn.

[CCLN, 137f.]

If Viennese newspapers were reticent about Haydn's presence in the Imperial & Royal capital city, people were very much aware of their composer's triumphs in England. Perhaps the most touching honour of all was a pyramid-shaped monument erected in 1793 by Count Harrach, the Lord of Rohrau where Haydn had been born,

---

1 PERTOJA or BERTOJA, violoncellist in the Esterházy band from 1780 to 1788. [CCLN, 138]
2 We do not know who this 'Cristina' was; probably a relative. [CCLN, 138]
3 PRINCE NICOLAUS I had been married to Countess Maria Elisabeth von Weissenwolf (d. 25 February 1790); his second son, Count Nicolaus, had married Countess Maria Anna von Weissenwolf in August 1777, for which occasion Haydn had written *Il mondo della luna*. [CCLN, 138]

sixty-one years earlier. The Abbé Michael Denis, S.J. wrote the text to the large tablet, as Dies (141) tells us:

Dem Andenken
Joseph Haydn's
des unsterblichen Meisters
der Tonkunst,
dem Ohr und Herz
wetteifernd huldigen,
gewidmet
von
Karl Leonhard Graf von Harrach.
Im Jahr 1793.

[The actual tablet has the date 1794.] After Haydn's death a second large tablet was added (but not by the Abbé Denis, for that prolific Viennese poet had died in 1800). On the other sides of the monument, the young (born 1775) poetess Gabriele von Baumberg added the following two verses, the first set to the most popular of all Haydn's symphonic movements (No. 53/II) before the 'Surprise' Andante which, in 1793, was just beginning to be popular on the Continent.

Ihr holden Philomelen,
belebet diesen Hayn,
und lasst durch tausend Kehlen
das Lied verewigt seyn.

The second of these verses was set to the Adagio movement of the string Quartet, Op. 50, No. 1:

Ein Denkmahlstein für Haydn's Ruhm
weiht diesen Platz zum Heiligthum,
und Harmonie klagt wehmuthsvoll,
[daß dieses großen Meisters Hand,
die stets Gefühl mit Kraft verband,]
daß diese Hand einst modern soll.

The bracketed lines are erroneously left out of Dies's quotation (142). Both Dies (141) and Griesinger (36) tell us that Haydn owned a little wooden (Griesinger; Dies says plaster) model of the monument in which two of the sides were still empty. Dies was inspired to fill them in with the following verse:

Dem Nahmen Hayden giebt kein todter Marmor Leben;
Unsterblichkeit muß Er vielmehr dem Marmor geben.

Haydn attempted modestly to decline responsibility for the praise. 'That's too much, I don't deserve so much!' said he. While on the subject of poetry, Griesinger (36) tells us that the Abbé Denis also wrote the following verses, which a lady embroidered on a lampshade which she gave Haydn:

Ihr staunt, daß Orpheus himmlischer Gesang
Einst Thränen aus den Augen roher Menschen zwang.
Bewundert euren Zeitgenossen,
Durch den so oft der Edlen Thränen flossen.

Count Harrach, upon being asked by Dies to explain how the monument came into being, wrote the following letter, which Dies quotes (140f.):

The reason why I had a monument to Haydn placed in my garden was none other than the fact that, having come of age, I wanted to reorganize the flower-, vegetable-, fruit- and pheasant-gardens round my castle – a total of some forty yokes – into, I won't dare say an English park, but at least a proper promenade, in the planning of which economic restrictions had of necessity to play a certain part.

I thought it right and proper, and also honourable for my park, to erect a monument for the so famous J. Haydn in the castle grounds which encompassed his birthplace. Haydn was then in England [so the plan must have been made in 1791 or 1792] and was but little known to me and had no idea of my undertaking; and it was not until two or three years later that he happened to hear that this monument in Rohrau existed and without my knowing it went to see it.

I used a section of my garden which was rather densely covered with leafy trees and a place where the River Laytha [now spelled Leitha], which is rather wide and deep at that point, makes a sudden bend; going backwards, I had a canal deep enough for boats dug and thus created an island which was about a quarter of a yoke in size.

I had this island cleared of underbrush and planted with Lombardian poplar trees, this side of the bank I had planted, however, weeping willows, plane trees, tulip trees and other such foreign species.

On one of the banks is now the monument on three stone steps and consists of a pedestal some ten feet high on which musical trophies have been placed.

Two sides of the monument [this letter was written after Haydn's death] have been used for inscriptions, because they are easily seen. . . .

Haydn offered, in 1804, to see in his will that the monument was cared for, and Count Harrach, not to be outdone, offered to subscribe a trust fund of 500 or 600 Gulden to see that the monument was protected. In any event, it is now in Haydn's birthplace, so beautifully restored by the Lower Austrian Government.

Even in Haydn's lifetime, people went out to Rohrau, and if they were invited to the Harrach Castle – a handsome mediaeval building with old-fashioned towers and a magnificent courtyard – they visited the Haydn monument. Old Count Zinzendorf was invited to Rohrau Castle and remarked, in his Diary for 21 September 1800, 'Une Isle, ou nous passerons en barque pour voir le monument etagé a la memoire de Haydn natif de Rohrau, le monument parmi d'inscription de la composition de l'abbé Denys, en haut sur la corniche des avis avec les paroles. Sur le rivage opposé des beaux Saules de Babylone . . .'. Zinzendorf also noted 'une petite Biblioteque allemande dans la gloriette Hollandoise. M^e est plus riche que Monsieur', concluded the Count. The next morning he noted, slightly annoyed, 'Dejeuné dans ma chambre, du caffé sans Sucre et sans crême.'

Like many great composers, Haydn was fascinated with the mechanical aspects of music-making: we shall be examining this side of his mentality also in connection with the great trumpet Concerto in E flat (Chronicle, 28 March 1800). One of Haydn's hobbies was to furnish the written music for the beautiful clockwork *Flötenuhren* (literally: flute-clocks) which Prince Esterházy's librarian, Pater Primitivius Niemecz, constructed and of which several still exist.[1] Since there is considerable confusion regarding the dating of the clocks both in Hoboken (pp. 827f. of Vol. I) as well as in the late E. F. Schmid's edition,[2] and although part of this information belongs in an earlier volume of this biography, we may state that there is no 1772 clock; the instrument was

1 The 1789 clock (*quondam* 1772) is owned by the Teubner family in Vienna.
2 *Werke für das Laufwerk*, Nagels Musik-Archiv Sonderausgabe Nr. 1, new edition Bärenreiter-Nagel 1954.

made, as two authentic sources inform us, in December 1789. The autograph of XIX: 16, the little *Fuga*, is dated 1789 (the MS. is in the former Czernin Castle in Jindřichův Hradec [Neuhaus], ČSSR) and a copy in the Gesellschaft der Musikfreunde, Vienna, is entitled 'Acht Laufwerck Sonaten Komponiert von Herrn Kapellmeister Joseph Haydn, und in die Walze gesetzt von Primitiv Niemecz Bibliothekar zu Esterhas 1789 in December' (and incidentally the copy of XIX: 32 does *not* belong to this group because it was not composed until 1793!). There are no Haydn autographs or copies which can be dated before the December 1789 clock. There are, from the period under discussion, two signed clocks: one of 1792 and one of 1793. Haydn was not only interested in the little instruments, which sound like little baroque organs, but he also understood their limitations and imperfections: his autographs are always full of instructions for simpler, *ossia* versions of a difficult ornament or a tricky passage.

Many of the pieces are new, but some are arrangements of Haydn's and other composers' popular pieces. For the signed 1793 clock, Haydn gave Niemecz the brand-new Minuet of his half-composed Symphony No. 101, the first movement of which was composed on paper with a British watermark and signed London 1794; and for an unknown clock of 1793, Niemecz received the Finale of Symphony No. 99 in E flat, transposed into F and, of course, shortened (see XIX: 29 and 32). For a contemporary description of Niemecz a few years later, see Chronicle for 20 March 1801, where apparently XIX: 30, a shortened G major version of the 'Lark' Quartet's (Op. 64, No. 5) Finale was played to the listeners' delight and astonishment.

About 10 November 1792,[1] Beethoven arrived in Vienna to study with Haydn. Haydn used to give his pupils his own condensed version of Fux's famous *Gradus ad Parnassum*; one such MS. is extant and belonged to Haydn's pupil, F. C. Magnus. It is dated 22 September 1789 and is in the Esterházy Archives of the National Library in Budapest (Ha. I, 10): 'Elementarbuch der verschiedenen Gattungen des Contrapunkts. Aus dem grösseren Werken des Kappm. Fux, von Joseph Haydn zussamengezogen. Esterhazÿ, d 22^br 7br 1789 F: C: Magnus' (from Haydn's own library). Haydn himself owned a copy of Fux which was very worn and had a multitude of comments in fluent Latin; it was destroyed at Budapest in 1945, but fortunately Pohl made a copy, or rather he entered all Haydn's comments in another copy of Fux which is now in the Gesellschaft der Musikfreunde.[2] Dr Mann describes it succinctly: 'Even a brief examination of this copy reveals a commentary of well-nigh incredible thoroughness and complexity. Haydn more than doubles Fux's own extensive listing of errors and omissions. He elaborates upon point after point, interprets, clarifies, closes every possible gap, and traces every possible inconsistency in Fux's discussion' (ibid., 325). It would almost seem that Haydn intended issuing his own edition of Fux's work, so ample and learned are the annotations.

Beethoven was put to work at simple counterpoint, and in the next year he did about 300 exercises, of which 245 are extant. In 42 exercises there are corrections in Haydn's hand (the MSS. are in the Gesellschaft der Musikfreunde). There is no possible doubt that Haydn was careless in these corrections; indeed, in view of the pedantic thoroughness with which he 'edited' Fux himself, this carelessness appears at

---

1 Thayer I, 321. Gustav Nottebohm, *Beethoven's Unterricht bei J. Haydn, Albrechtsberger und Salieri*, Leipzig–Winterthur, 1873, pp. 21ff.
2 See the useful article by Alfred Mann, 'Haydn as Student and Critic of Fux' in *Studies in Eighteenth-Century Music, A Tribute to Karl Geiringer on his Seventieth Birthday* (edited by the present writer and Roger E. Chapman), London 1970, pp. 323ff. Also 'Beethoven's Contrapuntal Studies with Haydn' by Alfred Mann in *Musical Quarterly*, LVI (1970), pp. 711ff.

times to be completely inexplicable. Occasionally parallel fifths were simply ignored, and some of Haydn's corrections introduce part writing which is worse than the faulty one written by Beethoven. For example, in exercise 34, Haydn marks with a cross the hidden fifths between soprano and alto, but in the correction (marked 'H' and placed at the end) Haydn introduces a hidden octave progression between alto and tenor, and the parallel fifths from bars 4 to 5 in the alto and tenor part are not corrected at all:

No.34

Nottebohm (ibid., 42f.) sums up as follows:

Approximately just as many mistakes remained in those exercises which bear no trace whatever of correction or examination as in those which Haydn corrected visibly. And the number of the uncorrected exercises is much greater than the others, to the extent of about five to one. . . . We have here confirmed the plausible statement of [Ignaz von] Seyfried; Beethoven objected that he was not able to make any progress with Haydn because the latter, far too busy, was not capable of giving the necessary attention to the exercises presented to him.

In 1970, Alfred Mann thoroughly re-examined the manuscripts of Beethoven's studies with Haydn and has come to a different conclusion than Nottebohm. Mann believes that the present source is a fair copy,

a methodical selection made from other manuscripts that may have contained a considerably larger amount of material. . . . It is evident also from a number of details, not listed by Nottebohm, in which Haydn corrects flaws that occurred in transcription and that show a certain carelessness on the part of the student rather than the teacher. . . . While the argument of Haydn's haste in reviewing the manuscript cannot be dismissed – for he bypassed obvious errors in examples that he touched up in other spots – the argument of his inconsistency can be disproved. Haydn's entries show that his attention was directed towards a particular choice of problems, but those he selected, he treated systematically.

Referring to the musical example quoted above, Mann notes that 'Without question . . . the correction is an improvement: the hidden parallels involve no longer an outer part but only inner parts, and the distribution of similar and contrary motion between parts is more evenly balanced than before.' (Mann, 1970, pp. 715ff.)

A point that has been overlooked in all this rather shadowy evidence is the manuscripts of Beethoven's study with Albrechtsberger, the teacher to whom Haydn entrusted his difficult pupil when Haydn had to leave for England. At the beginning, Albrechtsberger adopted a much more methodical approach, but as time went on, Beethoven became as impatient with his new teacher as he had been with Haydn. Nottebohm thought that the lessons with Albrechtsberger were brought to a premature conclusion, even broken off, before the 'course' had been completed. Beethoven was a difficult pupil even with a man as systematic and patient as Albrechtsberger.

Undoubtedly Haydn was not a perfect teacher; but it is perhaps to be doubted, according to the new evidence presented by Mann, that he was a bad a guide to counterpoint as Beethoven always pointedly, perhaps too pointedly, suggested. At another place we shall examine the extremely complicated, ambivalent and even morbid relationship between Haydn and Beethoven; here we would suggest that the lessons began under a shadow and only confirmed that which all the later evidence suggests – that Haydn's and Beethoven's personalities were totally incompatible. The history of their relationship is as cloudy and troubled as the relationship between Haydn and Mozart was sunny and mutually encouraging.

If we may be permitted to break our chronological rule for a moment, we may trace the course of Beethoven's study with Haydn for the year or so which it lasted. Outwardly the two men were on the best of terms. Beethoven was soon in debt; in his little pocket-book (diary) we read: 'On Wednesday the 12th of December [1792] I had 15 ducats.' Elsewhere: 'All the necessary things, for example clothes, linen, it's all gone. In Bonn I was sure I would find 100 ducats waiting for me here [in Vienna], but in vain. I must equip myself completely anew.' Beethoven was dangerously short of money, in fact. In these first months, he wrote down everything. 'Rent 14 Gldn. Piano 6 G. 40 × [*Kreuzer*]. Heat each time 12 × ; meal with wine $16\frac{1}{2}$ Gld.; 3 × for B[eethoven] and H[aydn]. It's not necessary to give the landlady more than 7 Gld., the room is on the ground floor anyway.' He was living, as Carl Holz remembers Beethoven relating,[1] at first in a garret room in the Alserstraße No. 45 at the house of the bookbinder Strauss, 'where', said Holz, 'he lived miserably' ('wo es ihm kümmerlich ging'). In the same house lived Prince Carl Lichnowsky, who was to play such an important role in the young composer's life; but it is doubtful if they met immediately. Beethoven lived at that address until May 1795, perhaps later on the ground floor.

---

1 Notes from this diary and the Holz information from Thayer I, 322ff.

The point is that Haydn was expected to take Beethoven off to London in December, so that the young composer's lodgings and bad financial state were obviously thought to be temporary. Nevertheless Haydn was much impressed by his turbulent pupil, though even at this early state he considered him a Hotspur. Charlotte von Schiller wrote from Bonn on 26 January 1793 (Thayer I, 308, 325n.), 'Haydn has reported to us here that he's going to give him [Beethoven] great operas to compose and soon he [Haydn] will have to give up composing.' The sums Haydn received as a teacher were, after his guinea lessons in London, a bad joke. Beethoven's little notebook has, in December 1792, 'Haidn 8 Groschen' (Beethoven never could spell Haydn's name correctly, which is an interesting point if we consider what a row he made, just before he died, over someone else's mis-spelling of Haydn's name). Later the little booklet contains for 24 October 1793 '22 × für Haidn und mich Chokolade' and on 29 October, 'Kaffee 6 × für Haidn und mich'. The more complicated aspects of Haydn's relationship to Beethoven and *vice versa* will be discussed in another volume. A few documents will, of course, appear in this Chronicle, especially the amusing and curious episode with the composer Schenk (see pp. 217–18).

On 13 November Haydn wrote what would be his last letter to Frau von Genzinger, who would be dead in a little over two months. Even as she was returning the F minor Aria, the fatal disease must have begun

[To Maria Anna von Genzinger, Vienna. *German*]
Gracious Lady!

Apart from wishing you Good Morning, this is to ask you to give the bearer of this letter the final big Aria in F minor from my opera,[1] because I must have it copied for my Princess. I will bring it back to you myself in 2 days at the latest. Today I take the liberty of inviting myself for lunch, when I shall have the opportunity of kissing Your Grace's hands in return. Meanwhile I am, as always,

Y[our]G[race's]

most obedient servant,

Joseph Haydn.

[Vienna]   From my home, 13th November 1792.

[Address:]   Madame

Madame Noble de Gennzinger

a

Son Logis.   [CCLN, 138]

We now arrive at Haydn's first public appearance in Vienna after his return from London. The event was the first masked ball of the Gesellschaft bildender Künstler (Society of Visual Artists, i.e. painters, sculptors), given for the benefit of the Society's widows and orphans. As this Chronicle will often show, Haydn was always the first to give his services to such causes, and the *Ereignis-Protocoll* for this first ball of the Society tells us that Haydn donated twelve Deutsche Tänze and twelve Minuets which he conducted at the Redoutensaal on 25 November 1792. The Society's archives, which are unpublished, were placed at our disposal by the Archiv der Stadt Wien, and contain all sorts of interesting footnotes to Viennese musical life which are herewith presented for the first time.

It is said that the Empress herself asked to have the new Dances arranged for piano. Haydn did the work himself – the autograph manuscript of the piano arrangement for

---

1 Orfeo's aria in the second act of *L'anima del filosofo* [CCLN, 138].

the German Dances is in the Esterházy Archives of the National Library, Budapest (Ms. mus. I. 52) – and sold the rights to Artaria & Co., who issued them with a rapidity quite extraordinary for them: both Minuets and German Dances 'für das Clavier übersetzt' were announced in the *Wiener Zeitung* on 22 December 1792, less than a month after their first performance. The agreement with Artaria reads as follows:

[Receipt to Artaria & Co., Vienna. *German*. Only the signature autograph]

> 15 Kreutzer
> stamp

For the sum of twenty-four ducats I, the undersigned, herewith cede to Messrs. Artaria Comp. here in Vienna all the rights to the Minuets and German Dances which I composed for the benefit of the Artists' Widows Society here, and which were performed at the Redoutensaal Ball on 25th November of this past year. I promise to give the afore-mentioned Minuets and German Dances to no one else, and acknowledge to have received this day the correct sum of twenty-four ducats in cash. Vienna, 7th December 1792.

Attested:

Josephus Haydn.

For 24 ducat pieces
[Artaria's clerk notes: 'Haydn / 108 Gulden / 1792'.]   [CCLN, 139]

The *Ereignis-Protocoll* for the 1792 season – the only one apart from that of 1795 which has been at least partially published[1] – supplies the following information about the money taken in, and the 'Fest' which was afterwards given at Schönbrunn.

The *Protocoll* tells us that Haydn 'als Kunstverwandler' (sympathetic or congenial to the art) offered the Dances without fee to the Society, and adds the interesting bit of information that 'at the request of the Empress' the Dances were arranged for keyboard – as we have seen, by Haydn himself – and presented to the Empress as a token of thanks for her support of the venture. Sebastian Mansfeld, the well-known engraver, fashioned the entrance tickets, and the book-seller Franz Anton Schrämbl printed 2,000 copies of an ode, 'Die Freude winkt: O, kommt zu frohen Tänzen' which was distributed to the guests. The Society sold 2,181 tickets at a profit of 4,521 Gulden, 19 Kreuzer (total income: 5,343 Gulden, 22 Kreuzer). The Emperor was ill but sent 199 ducats. (The poem was also printed in the *Wiener Almanach*, 1794.)

There were two orchestras, one in the Great Hall and one in the Small; the first consisted of forty-three musicians conducted by Johann Patatschny, the second of twenty-seven musicians conducted by Anton Höllmayr, but for this occasion Haydn's Dances, which were performed in the Great Hall, boasted an enlarged orchestra of forty-seven. A week earlier there had been a full rehearsal 'von dem Herrn Kapellmeister Joseph Haiden [*sic*] neu verfertigten Menuetten und Deutschen', which cost the Society 27 Gulden.

In a list 'Bey H: Vice Director haben Billets abgenohmen und bezahlt' (At Herr Vice Director the following tickets were called for and paid), we notice *inter alia*, at the bottom (!) of the list, 'Fürstin Esterhazÿ', who bought six tickets and 'S^re Majestätt die Kaiserin' who bought a dozen tickets at two Gulden each: it is also curious to note that, like the Austrian currency at the period, many people also ordered ball tickets in twelves (or divisions, or multiplications thereof). Under the subscribers, we may also

---

1 Cyriak Bodenstein, *Hundert Jahre Kunstgeschichte Wiens, 1788–1888. Eine Festgabe anläßlich der Säcular-Feier der Pensions Gesellschaft Bildender Künstler Wiens*, Vienna 1888, p. XIII.

note the Archduchesses Maria Anna and Maria Clementina who each bought a dozen tickets but paid '12 Duc:' (twelve ducats) each, and as the fourth entry we again find 'Fürstin Esterhazÿ' but this time with twelve tickets; thus the penultimate entry probably means that at the last minute the Princess needed another six tickets to accommodate her enlarged party of guests.

Princess Kinsky, later of Beethovenian fame, ordered a dozen tickets, and Countess Kinsky two dozen; Count Fries (here spelled 'Frieß'), at whose famous open houses the cream of Viennese musicians played, including Haydn and Beethoven, bought a dozen tickets and paid the curious sum of twenty-seven Gulden. We also note some of Mozart's former patrons listed, in rather incredible spelling, in his 1784 subscription list (Deutsch *Dokumente*, 485–492), and once again appearing in this 1792 list, also in rather optimistic phonetic spelling. 'Comteße Würbm' would appear to be Mozart's 'Würben', a phonetic approximation of Wrbna (a numerous family, of which Count Joseph was *Oberstkämmerer* and Director of the Court Theatre; while Count Eugen Wenzel Joseph was a Privy Councillor and later *Obersthofmarschall*). Baron Waldstätten, an influential member of the Court, whose wife had befriended Mozart when he was trying to marry Constanze, took fourteen tickets.

In a second list, 'Ausgegebene Freÿ-Billets', we find, among the patrons ('Sr Excellenz Herrn Grafen v Ugandi' 12 tickets) and entries such as '8 [tickets] for the two ticket sellers from the theatre', '4. Herrn v Haÿdn', followed by '6. Herrn v Muzarelli', the ballet master. In the coming years, many more musicians and composers would give their services and their names will appear on the list for complimentary tickets.

This Redoutensaal masked ball was the first in a long series of charitable concerts in Vienna, in these last years of the century, to which Haydn would contribute his services *gratis*. Possibly he had been impressed by such concerts in England, and in any event he was following in the footsteps of Handel and the Foundling Hospital charity concerts which constituted the last public appearances of Handel's declining years. Haydn, as we have seen in this Chronicle, was quite rightly very preoccupied with putting aside money for his declining years. The great Mozart had not been dead a year, and his miserable end was the spectre to haunt all musicians forever. Before the new century dawned, the popular Dittersdorf would die in obscurity and poverty in Bohemia. Yet Haydn from 1796 to 1804 would devote much of his concert activity in Vienna to charitable purposes; this relieves the picture, too easily formed, of avarice.

There is some question as to where Haydn composed the new Dances. In his *Catalogue of Works Composed in England* (which we cite from the original English in Dies, 218), we find the following entry: '24 Minuets and german dances'. As we shall see in connection with the great 'Twenty-Four Minuets' for large orchestra (IX: 16), there is some confusion whether Haydn means a total of twenty-four dances or twenty-four minuets *and* an unspecified number of German dances (*infra*, p. 484); but it may be that he actually composed the works in England. The autograph manuscript is lost. There are three sets of sketches: (1) on British paper with a British watermark, in a four-page MS. including an incompleted March in E flat (VIII: 7), there is a sketch for Minuet 1; Burgenländisches Landesmuseum, Eisenstadt; (2) on Italian paper (such as Haydn used in Vienna) there is a sketch for the string Quartet in D (Op. 71, No. 2), the finished autograph of which is dated 1793, and dance sketches, including the Trio of Minuet 1, and Minuet 9 with the Trio; Preussische Staatsbibliothek, Berlin W.; (3) a series of sketches, again on Italian paper, which include Minuets 2 (Trio), 5, 6, 7 (all with Trios) and all the German Dances; Hessische Landesbibliothek, Darmstadt. In the case of (1), it is probable that we are dealing with a red herring: it appears that Haydn must have carried this unfinished March (one of those for the eccentric sea-captain?) back to Vienna with him and begun sketching the first Minuet on it. The presence of all the other sketches on Italian paper would seem clear evidence that the Dances were all composed in Vienna, not in England;[1] the piano arrangements of the German Dances were also written on Italian paper.

The most fascinating area of speculation is what people danced to the *Deutsche Tänze*; and here there is new evidence that suggests, rather sensationally, that the Viennese *waltzed* to this kind of music: a waltz in which the partners still held each other in the old *Ländler* fashion, but which is nevertheless an early version of the dance which would soon conquer Europe.

Here is the evidence for our assertion. We present it in order of importance:

1. The description of the Redoutensaal in Gianluigi de Freddy's *Descrizione della città, sobborghi, e vicinanze di Vienna,* Vienna 1800.[2] There are so many details of interest that we quote the entire document in Italian, but we would single out the passage dealing with the waltz, containing in the *nota*, which reads:

> The dance, which the Germans call in their language *walzen* [to waltz], is the most favoured and the one in most general use throughout the nation. Thus in all the dancing rooms, at all the parties of the nobility, and even in the parties given at Court, it is preferred to all other dances.

There is appended to this footnote a French poem from a Regensburg newspaper of 1798 which demonstrates that 'la Valse' was at that date a well-known phenomenon even in the provincial cities of Germany.

Astute readers will notice that the quiet behaviour of the Viennese crowds are stressed ('. . . malgrada la diversità notabile delle classi le une colle altre alla mescolata regnare il miglior ordine, ed armonia, sicchè rende inutile le cura della guardie di truppa regolata, e dei Commissarj di Polizia . . .'), something that will have occurred to Haydn's cool and observant brown eyes as being in violent contrast to the yelling, obstreperous London mob.

> Il così detto RIDOTTO occupa l'ala del Palazzo Imperiale, che rimane alla sinistra della Biblioteca, e che guarda la Piazza detta Josephplatz.[3] Ivi si danno dall' I. R. Direzione del Teatro pubbliche feste di ballo, ed accademie per solennizzare qualche lieto avvenimento. Era dapprima questo luogo il Teatro pubblico, ove si ammiravano le belle pitture di prospettiva colà eseguite nel 1663 da Lodovico Burnaccini, e poscia da Ferdinando Bibbiena, e vi si rappresentavano in determinati tempi dell' anno Drammi serj Italiani. Venne poscia negli anni 1748 e 1752 sotto il Regno di *Maria Teresa* per opera del *Barone de Lopresti* allora Impresario rifabbricato, e ridotto all'attuale forma per le feste di ballo della Corte, ove non avea ingresso che la Nobilità vestita, giusta una prammatica prescrizione, in bautta di seta nera, o d'altro colore, detta in idioma francese *Dominò*. Sotto il regno di *Giuseppe II.* fu poi renduto comune anche alla altre classi della Cittadinanza, come lo è oggigiorno.
> Due sono le sale destinate al ballo, l'una delle quali avanza l'altra ed in grandezza, ed in bellezza. Sono entrambe tutt'all'intorno illuminate da un'innumerevole quantità de candele di cera, e nel mezzo poi della prima vi hanno

---

1 Contrary to the opinion expressed in Landon, SYM 563.
2 Three vols. in two. Our copy with handwritten corrections and additions; from the library of Ferdinand Raimund with his stamp. Redoutensaal, pp. 276–9.
3 In the original 'Josephstadt'.

A page of sketches by Haydn, made on British paper, which he probably took back to Vienna when he returned there in 1792; in the middle of the page (with 'No. 1' in the left margin) is a sketch for the first of the Redoutensaal Minuets (IX: 11, No. 1).

sette gran lampadarj, e cinque nella seconda. In ciascheduna di queste sta la rispettiva Orchestra provveduta di abilissimi suonatori. Gira attorno della prima sala una galleria fatta costruire de *Giuseppe II.* ove siedono i spettatori, e d'intorno pure a piano-terra delle sale stesse v'hanno a tre ordini di gradini i Sedili, che servono parimenti allo stesso effetto. Al primo piano contiguo alle stesse Sale vi sono quindi alcune camere; le une contengono abiti da maschera da noleggiare, ed i mantelli de' concorrenti in deposito; le altre il caffè, e le ritirate sì per gli uomini, che per le donne. Al secondo poi havvi la Trattoria, e Riposteria, ove si viene servito a prezzi stabiliti nelle Tabelle affisse al muro. Sia nelle une, che nelle altre osservasi un ordine, ed una pulizia molto plausibile.

Questo Ridotto è capace di tre mila e più persone, la cui considerevole folla rende allora poi molesto il divertimento per la difficoltà e di passeggiare, e di trovar luogo. Allor quando non sonovi che 1500 persone riesce molto più divertito, aggradevole, e vago, È questo il solo luogo di Vienna, in cui sia permessa la maschera, e siccome permettesi il mascherarsi in qualunque siasi guisa, purchè sia conforme alle regole prescritte dalla Legge, così vuolsi ancora in vigore di un Sovrano Editto, che ciascheduno debba avere almeno la maschera sul cappello. Queste feste di ballo incominciano ogni anno alla prima domenica dopo il Natale, e durano per tutto il tempo del Carnovale, avvertendo però che nelle due ultime settimane si danno due volte cioè il giovedi, e la domenica. V'hanno poi fra l'anno altre feste di ballo, come nel giorno di S. Teresa, di S. Catterina, e nella Domenica dopo Pasqua di Risurezione e dopo la Pentecoste, il di cui introito va a benefizio delle vedove, e pupilli della società Filarmonica. Altre feste ancora si danno tal volta per festeggiare qualche giulivo avvenimento. Il ballo incomincia dalle nove ore della sera, e dura sino alle cinque della mattina. Il Biglietto d'ingresso si paga due fiorini. È veramente un oggetto di sorpresa, e di soave compiacenza insieme il vedere malgrado un numero sì grande di spettatori, e malgrado la diversità notabile delle classi le une colle altre alla mescolata regnare il miglior ordine, ed armonia, sicchè rende inutile la cura delle guardie di truppa regolata, e dei Commissarj di Polizia, che stanno ivi ad invigliare a riparo di qualunque inconveniente. Spettacolo più bello, a vero dire, non si sa vedere in Vienna di questo, ove l'amore, la gioventù, la bellezza, le grazie spiocano a gara, ove la ricchezza, il buon gusto, e l'indole della moda, sfoggiano in eleganti, e magnifici abbigliamenti, ed ove infine di acquista idea del pacifico carattere di questa brava Nazione. [nota:]Il Ballo, che usasi dai Tedeschi chiamato in lingua alemanna *Walzen*, è il più gradito, ed il più comune in tutta la Nazione. Quindi in tutte le sale di ballo, in tutte le feste della Nobilità, e persino nella feste della Corte si preferisce a tutte le altre questa danza. Un francese ne diede una descrizione accuratissima, la quale uguaglia perfettamente tutta la grazia de' di lei movimenti, e che merita percio d'essere conosciuta.

> L'Orchestre enfin soupire une molle cadence,
> On attendoit la Valse, e la Valse commence.
> Ce ne sont plus ce pas, ce bonds impetueux.
> La scene va changer. En marchant deux à deux,
> Du parquet lentement on mesure l'espace :
> Mais déployant soudain sa souplesse, et sa grace
> Au signal qu'on reçoit, qu'on donne tour-à-tour,
> De vingt cercles pressés on décrit le contour.
> La beauté, que dés-lors le plaisir environne
> Au bras, qui la soutient mollement s'abbandonne ;
> Une tendre langueur se répand sur ses traits,
> Son oeil demi-voilé n'en a que plus d'attraits ;
> Sa bouche de l'amour semble aspirer les flammes.
> Je ne sais à quel point la *Valse* plait aux femmes,
> Je n'ai pas leur secret, mais dans mon jeune temps
> Je pense que par goût j'aurois valsé long-temps.

Mercure de Ratisbone N. 234, de 30. Septembre 1798.

2. *Guide du Voyageur à Vienna ; Vienne chez Artaria et Comp : 1803.* Here we have an 1803 'Baedeker' put out by Haydn's publishers, who were renowned for the beautiful coloured engravings and maps they printed, as well as for their music. Note that the closing hour has been advanced from five o'clock in the morning to six (bread and circuses in the bad Napoleonic times?). But what concerns us is the flat statement that only minuets and waltzes were danced ('Les deux orchestres y exécutent des menuets et des valses ; mais en général on y danse peu' [?]).

La Redoute. Les salles de la redoute sont situées sur la Josephplatz et dans l'intérieur du palais impérial, l'une des deux est très-vaste ; elles servent aux fêtes de la cour ainsi qu'aux bals publics ; ces derniers commencent le premier dimanche de l'année et finissent avec le carnaval. Les salles sont ouvertes à 9 h. du soir et la musique ne se retire qu'à 6 h. du matin. Il étoit autrefois d'obligation d'y entrer masqué ; mais depuis quelques années ceux qui ne veulent point se soumettre à cette gêne se contentent de placer à leur chapeau un très-petit masque, ou plus simplement une carte.

L'entrée à la redoute coute 2 fl. par tête; on y trouve des raffraichissemens de toute espèce et l'on peut y souper dans les salons particuliers qui entourent les grandes salles de danse. Les deux orchestres y exécutent des menuets et des valses; mais en général on y danse peu. Le nombre des personnes qui vont à la redoute augmente à mésure que l'on approche de la fin du carnaval; lorsqu'il n'y en a que 1000, les salles ne sont pas suffisamment remplies; mais quand il s'élève à 3000, la presse y est trop forte et la chaleur étouffante. L. L. M. M. honorent fréquemment la redoute de leur présence.

Le bénéfice de cet établissement appartient à la caisse du théâtre; mais on en prélève une partie en faveur de l'institut des pauvres.   [pp. 206f.]

3. In Sir John Moore's *Journal* (edited in 1904 by Sir Frederick Maurice as 'The Diary of Sir John Moore'), there is a description of a group of British officers travelling through the Tyrol in October 1795, among them Captain Moore. We use the summary which is quoted in Carola Oman's splendid biography, *Sir John Moore*, London 1953.

On a late October day of 1795 the driver of a travelling carriage proceeding through the Tyrol was surprised by peremptory shouts from its occupants. The British officers wanted to stop, to watch the natives dancing the valse. They enjoyed this spectacle twice before the day was out, and the Colonel agreed with the naval Captain that the Tyrolese appeared to great advantage after the Italians, who were really the worst rogues in the world. The women [in the Tyrol] in particular were well dressed, and walked with peculiar smartness; they danced the valse with much grace.   [pp. 127f.]

This report deals with an Austrian province; but it is significant that they were dancing the waltz in the Tyrol as early as October 1795. It is unlikely that the waltz was confined to the Tyrol, of course, and we may consider this unlikely source – a travelling British officer's journal – as one of the earliest dated references to the Austrian waltz known to us. As such it is valuable.

The following reports are four or five years later, but they give us a certain amount of interesting background material.

4. We add here a notice which supplies only local colour. Rosenbaum's Diary of 6 January 1799 (p. 58, with the interesting 'His Majesty's Admonition'):

SUNDAY, 6TH, THE FIRST BALL. . . . In the evening we went [with the Gaßmanns] to Salieri's opera, where I was much annoyed that the opposing party prevented Salieri's being called out after the opera . . .

Balls, especially those at the Redoutensaal, enjoyed great popularity in Vienna and were often organized for charitable purposes, for example in aid of blind performers, etc. Balls were also announced on play-bills, in some instances together with 'His Majesty's Admonition', such as the following: 'Today, Sunday . . . a masked ball will be held in the Imperial and Royal Redoutensaal; the opening is at about 9 o'clock in the evening, and the music will go on until 5 o'clock in the morning. Since it has been noticed for some time that many of the maskers take the liberty, in the press of the crowd, of touching and pinching the ladies, and that the desired delicacy is not always observed in the choice of expressions, such behaviour is, at express Royal command, herewith prohibited.' Theatersmlg. Nat. Bib.

5. The waltz, which took up a lot of room in the crowded redoutes, created a certain amount of confusion. On 16 January 1800 (Rosenbaum, 73) the play-bill contained an announcement regarding the balls: 'For the sake of greater order and convenience, in both of the Imperial and Royal Redoutensäle the so-called waltz will be danced at the sides, and only the quadrille in the centre.'

6. *Crabb Robinson in Germany 1800–1803. Extracts from his Correspondence,* edited by Edith J. Morley, London, 1929. Here we have an interesting description of the partners' stance (still, as pointed out above, using the *Ländler* position).

> [pp. 29f.] ffrankfurt sur Maine 22 Septr 1800 . . . And there is often Musick & Dancing but the dancing is unlike any thing you ever saw – You must have heard of it under the Name of *Walzing* that is Rolling or Turning, tho' this Rolling is not horizontal, but perpendicular. Yet Werter after describing his first Walse with Charlotte says and I say too – 'I felt that if I were married my Wife sho[d] walz (or roll) with no one but myself. Judge – The Male places the palms of his hands gently against the Sides of the ffemale not far from the Arm pits. The female does the same And instantly with as much velocity as possible they turn round and at the same time gradually glide round the room. . . .'

7. British travellers could, of course, reach allied Germany (or indeed Austria) more easily than France, but during the uneasy peace, they rushed over to Paris. George Smart observed at Paris, on 17 July 1802 at a dancing party that 'two charming girls instructed Henry and me how to dance the German waltz, which is all the fashion here' (Smart, 30).

As the old year waned, Haydn was expected in England. The newspapers confidently announced his arrival, together with that of Ignaz Pleyel, who was, however, in danger of his life in France (*supra,* p. 99). The day before Christmas, the *Morning Herald* told its readers that 'SALOMON's Concert, and the Professional Concert, are to be the competitors again – the one with HAYDN, the other with PLEYEL.' The Professional Concert decided to pander to the lowest type of taste and on Christmas Day, the *Morning Post* announced:

PROFESSIONAL CONCERT.
Hanover-Square.
THE Committee respectfully inform the Nobility and Gentry, that the Arrangements for the ensuing Season are nearly completed, and in a few Days will lay before them a list of the Performers.

In the mean Time, they beg leave to say, that in Addition to the usual Performances, Glees, Madrigals, Anacreontics, Pastorals, &c. &c. will be introduced, written and composed by the most favourite Authors, expressly for the Concert, and will be performed by the most approved Singers.

The Subscriptions will remain as usual, Five Guineas each for the Twelve Concerts. . . .

Salomon's series was announced at the same time:

MR. SALOMON'S CONCERT.
Hanover-Square.
Mr. SALOMON respectfully acquaints the Nobility and Gentry, that in addition to the Assistance of Mr. Haydn, Madame Mara, and one of the principal Opera Singers expected from Italy (whose name he will be at liberty to announce in a few days) he will have that of the celebrated Signor VIOTTI.

From the highly flattering Approbation with which his former Concerts have been honoured, Mr. SALOMON is induced to hope, that . . . his Exertions will be thought serving the Patronage and Support of a generous Public.

Subscriptions at Five Guineas each, for the twelve nights. . . .

CHAPTER THREE

1793

On NEW YEAR'S DAY 1793, the *Morning Post* carried a notice of 'WINTER MUSICALS'.

The KING's Concerts have the support of their MAJESTIES. CRAMER leads; the Vocal Performers STORACE, Miss Parke, &c.

The Academy of Ancient Music retains Doctor ARNOLD as conductor, and a better it cannot have; in addition is that incomparable leader, CRAMER. Miss LEAKE, whose vocal skill is rare for her experience, assists as the pupil of the Conductor.

The Professional Concert follows the popular plan this season of introducing Catches, Glees, &c. SALOMON is resolved to make a bold stand against all opposition. He is to have, in addition to MARA and HAYDN, the celebrated VIOTTI, supposed to be the first Violin in the world. He also expects a great addition to his Band, in several of the most approved Performers on the Continent.

ASHLEY takes the lead alone at the Oratorios at Covent Garden during the Lent. He has the strong support of MARA, Mrs. CROUCH, KELLY, NIELD, &c. The Haymarket, of course, can have no Oratorios this Lent.

The Italian Operas are certainly to have a considerable acquisition in the celebrated BRUNI, who has been so great a favourite at all the Courts of Europe, particularly that of Russia.

HARRISON confines the melody of his pipe to his own Concert. It is probable that Mrs. HARRISON will on particular occasions give her assistance.

KELLY sings no where but at the Theatres; as the Italian Operas and Oratorios will occupy so much of his time, that he is obliged to resist all other applications.

Sunday Concerts will be carried on as usual, and thus harmony flourishes in spite of the Parish Associations.

On 11 January 1793, the *Morning Chronicle* announced the first of Salomon's concerts, and here we read for the first time that he was getting slightly uneasy about Haydn's non-appearance.

Mr. SALOMON'S CONCERT, HANOVER-SQUARE.

Mr. SALOMON most respectfully acquaints the Nobility and Gentry, that his First Concert will be on THURSDAY the 7th of February next, to continue on twelve successive Thursdays (Passion Week excepted.)
Composer Mr. HAYDN,
Who, not withstanding a very severe indisposition, will (Mr. Salomon trusts, from the very pressing letters he has written to him to entreat his attendance), fulfil his engagement by assisting at the Harpsichord, as soon as there is a possibility of his undertaking the journey.
Principal Vocal Performers.
Signor BRUNI, first Serious Singer at the Opera.
And Madame MARA. . . .

In later announcements (*Morning Chronicle*, 17, 22, 24 January, etc., *The Times* for 22, 26, 30 January, etc.) it is worth noting that the words 'Piano Forte' are used instead of 'Harpsichord', and that after the word 'journey', the later announcements read: ': – in the meanwhile, his place will be filled by Mr. CLEMENTI'. On 17 January, the *Diary; or, Woodfall's Register* noted that '*Haydn* the great composer is prevented from visiting this country as early as he expected, by a *polypus* in his nose, on account of which he has been obliged to undergo a painful operation, but without the desired success'; and on the following day, the *Morning Herald* has a similar story, probably some kind of Press hand-out from Salomon: 'Poor HAYDN continues in Germany very ill: but composing for England and promising to come over when he can. He is afflicted with the tedious and painful disorder, a *polypus* in the nose, for which he is immediately about to suffer an operation.'

The famous polyp was naturally an excuse. There are, we believe, two reasons why Haydn hesitated, and with him Prince Anton Esterházy (who as we shall see was equally reluctant to let his *Capellmeister* leave a year later). The first was political. The unrest had not really reached Austria to any great extent; but Haydn had experienced the uneasy rumours and Jacobean murmerings in London. A French observer-refugee in 1792 observed in London that 'Aux spectacles on applaudit toujours avec transport *God save the King*; mais on a vu lire plus d'une fois, sans trop de surprise, ou sans trop d'indignation, ces terribles mots tracés en grosses lettres au coin des rues: *no King; no Parliament*.'[1] The British were of course slightly uneasy about the French Revolution, but they tended to think, quite rightly, that King and Parliament would survive. 'The Chief Justice of the King's Bench', runs an 'anecdote' in the *Morning Post* of 11 January 1793, 'was lately lamenting to Lord THURLOW the treasonable disposition of the times, and instanced the expressions which every where appeared on the walls, which, he thought, excited the people to sedition. – "Pshaw", says the Ex-Chancellor, "did your Lordship ever observe that the *obscene* expressions, written upon the walls, excited your *venery?*"'

Most Englishmen were glad to see the new influx of talent from France, with the continual arrival of such great figures as Viotti. 'Nothing less than the demolition of one Monarchy, and the general derangement of all the rest, could have poured into England and settled such a mass of talents as we have now to boast. Music as well as misery has fled for shelter to England...' writes the *Morning Chronicle* on 15 February.

If Haydn had some political reservations about undertaking a new trip to England, the real reason was probably that he had returned exhausted in the Summer and had not really composed enough to leave Austria again in December. Haydn was now sixty and realized that he had to conserve his energies, unlimited though they may have seemed to the English in 1792. He waited for the course of the war to change: it and the Revolution grew steadily worse in 1793. He waited, most important of all, for his travelling trunks to be packed with new music; and that was the case at the end of 1793. Salomon was undoubtedly very annoyed, but the episode seems not to have marred the good *rapport* between the two men.

On 20 January 1793, Maria Anna von Genzinger died, not yet forty-three years of age (not thirty-eight as in Pohl III, 70 et seq.). Haydn had loved her perhaps more than he dared show in his letters. She had occupied a special place in his heart that neither *la* Polzelli nor even Rebecca Schroeter could replace. As Geiringer writes (1947, 119), 'a terrible loneliness... surrounded him like a wall'.

---

1 [M. Meister], *Souvenirs des mes Voyages en Angleterre. Seconde Partie* (Voyage en 1792), Zürich 1795, p. 21.

The day after, on 21 January, they guillotined Louis XVI in Paris. When the news reached Vienna, on the 29th, men were stunned: they had not thought it could happen. The Court was in a state of turmoil, and old Count Zinzendorf reflected the general tenor of the day when he wrote in his diary, 'Quelle affreuse horreur!' If Haydn might still have been toying with the idea of going to England, this new state of affairs will have been a strong argument against travelling.

In February, King George III reviewed the first British·expeditionary force of the new conflict; they passed in front of him on the parade ground at Whitehall. On a white charger, the King, flanked by the Prince of Wales and the Duke of York, benignly surveyed the 2,000 men who were to go to Holland. 'No man living could have guessed [the war's] duration. Before it was to end at Waterloo the youngest survivor of those who sailed that day was to be in his forties' (Bryant, 1). It was not only one of the longest and cruelest wars of European history, but it had many side-effects which no one could have foreseen, such as the change in the Austrian, and especially Viennese, society. It soon began to colour men's lives, and not least, Haydn's. But in February 1793, the long war was still new, and in Vienna society paused to shudder with horror at the execution of the French king; but they went on dancing and going to the opera.

At Prince Schwarzenberg's on the Neuer Markt there was a *souper* for thirteen on 19 February, 'avec les furstenberg, le Jean Lichtenstein, Caroline Furstenberg, nous etions 13. Charmante musique apres le diner de Mozart, die Zauberflöte . . .', wrote Zinzendorf. Others who had not private orchestras could go and see the new production of Paisiello's *La serva padrona* at the Burgtheater. Zinzendorf heard it on 23 February: 'joli musique de Paisiello, qu'ils renderent bien en longueur un peu'. On 12 March, Haydn played at a concert of Prince Lobkowitz (probably Joseph Maria Karl, not the future patron of Haydn's Op. 77 Quartets and Beethoven, Franz Joseph Maximilian); Zinzendorf attended this concert (Olleson, 48).

Haydn had meanwhile started to do something with all the musical treasures he had brought back from England. To Wallerstein, the Court of Prince Oettingen-Wallerstein, an old patron of Haydn's, the composer sent (before March 1793) Elssler copies, with holograph corrections of Symphonies 93, 96, 97 and 98 (with Haydn's 'private' keyboard solo in No. 98 omitted). He now thought, since he would be staying in Vienna at least for the time being, that it was time to present the Viennese with a selection of his newest London compositions. Haydn managed to secure the smaller of the two halls in the Redoutensaal – it is still extant – on 15 March 1793. Newspapers did not report such things but we have two notices, one from Count Zinzendorf (Olleson, 48, plus additions from the MS. Diary), and one from Prince Oettingen-Wallerstein's *Intendant*, who happened to be at that time in Vienna, Major Ignatz von Beecké. Zinzendorf writes:

A 6^h ½ un Concert de Haydn dans la petite Salle des Redoutes. 600 billets, dit–on, a un Ducat. Il etoit charmant, un Adagio surtout. Maffoli et la Tomeoni chanterent. J'étois a coté de M^r de fekete, lorsque M^r d'auersberg vient se mettre a coté de moi et Trautm[annsdorf] me ceda de place. De la chez Mr de la Lippe, ou etoit Lolotte Weißenwolf, fini la soirée seul avec mon amie, qui avoit de la douceur.
   Beau tems.

Haydn was clever enough to engage the popular Irene Tomeoni from the opera as well as the celebrated tenor, Vincenzo Maffolli. No programme for the concert has survived. Beecké writes:

Hier il y avoit le concert au benefice de Hayden dans la petite Sale de la Redoute. On a distribué 400 billets a 1 Ducat. L'assemblée etoit aussi belle et choissie que la Musique. Hayden a fait 3 de ces nouvelles Synfonies, qu'il a envoyé a Votre Altesse. Maffolli et Mad: Tomeoni ont chanté. . . . [Olleson, 49]

This letter identifies the three symphonies as among Nos. 93, 96, 97 and 98 (the four works sent to Wallerstein). If it is thought rather odd that such an important concert should take place without any notice in the newspapers, we would remind our readers that the first public performance of Mozart's *Requiem* (K. 626) had occurred in Vienna a few weeks earlier, on 2 January. Baron van Swieten had put it on for the benefit of Constanze, apparently in the 'Jahn'sche Saal', but the concert's very existence was noticed only in Zinzendorf's Diary and in an obscure Hungarian-language newspaper, *Magyar Hirmondó* (Deutsch: *Mozart, Die Dokumente*, p. 409).

In Beecké's letter, another event in which Haydn participated in March 1793 is mentioned: a performance of Handel's *Das Alexander-Fest* with a new chorus by Haydn. Probably Haydn for this occasion arranged to have his Madrigal 'The Storm' translated into German, and it is more than likely that the translation was undertaken by Gottfried van Swieten, the Imperial and Royal Librarian and the well-known promoter of Bach and Handel as well as the generous patron of Mozart and, at this period, Haydn. Up till 1792, Mozart had been Swieten's composer-in-residence, arranging and re-orchestrating the Handel works that Swieten performed, e.g. *Messiah, Alexander's Feast, Acis and Galatea* and the *Ode to St Cecilia*. Swieten also employed Joseph Starzer, but now that Haydn was back, he seems to have turned to him. We also notice a certain number of Swieten's fair copies in Johann Elssler's hand; Elssler was obviously lent by Haydn to the Baron as a favour. At any rate, even if we cannot date the revision of 'The Storm' into 'Der Sturm', we know that it was performed at the Tonkünstler Christmas Concerts on 22 and 23 December 1793.

Swieten had already at this period the hope that Haydn would compose an oratorio. Johann Baptist von Alxinger wrote and published anonymously a libretto entitled *Die Vergötterung des Herkules*. He offered it to Wieland for publication in the *Neue Deutsche Merkur* on 3 August 1791 and finally published it in the *Österreichische Monatsschrift* (Band III, Prague, September 1793), which contains a preface in which we read: 'Freiherr von Swieten, who himself could shine as a great composer if he had not hidden and pushed aside every service of small size other than his noble efforts for State and Enlightenment, Freiherr von Swieten wanted to lay something in front of the excellent Haydn for him to compose in the spirit and manner of Handel's.' This is the occasion for the present Cantata, whereby the number and even the order of the Arias, Duets and Choruses were prescribed (obviously by Swieten).[1] Haydn did not set the Cantata, but he did rewrite and add a larger wind section, and more woodwind writing, to the Madrigal, for its new German setting.

On 20 March 1793, the young violinist Clement, whom we have met in London, gave a concert (or played a solo perhaps). Zinzendorf writes 'Au Spectacle. Joli Concert du petit Clement du violon. . . .' On the 27th the *Tenebrae* were held, as each year, at court. Zinzendorf thought Mozart's Brother Mason 'Adamberger chanta les lamentations [du Jérémie] mieux que Maffoli', famous though the latter was. On 1 April Zinzendorf went to the opera, Cimarosa's *Amor rende sagace* ('ne réussit pas'), and

---

1 Alxinger was, together with J. Schreyvogel, the editor of the *Monatsschrift*. Wolfgang Amadeus Mozart, *Neue Ausgabe sämtlicher Werke*, Serie X, Supplement, Band 3 (*Alexander-Fest*), Werkgruppe 28 (Holschneider), 1962, p. VIII; also *Kritischer Bericht* (1962, pp. 22ff.) to *Der Messias* (also Holschneider).

a ballet. 'On avoit beaucoup applaudid l'Empereur', noted the old Count with satisfaction. Viennese subjects were quite sure on whose side they were. On 21 April, Zinzendorf notes. '*Tand j'ai sortis* et fit a l'opera *Le gelosie villane*. Rafanelli et Bellantani nouvaux acteurs, le dernier plut beaucoup. La ville *illuminée*.' The next day he went back.

> Le soir a l'opera *le gelosie villane*. Je me rapellois de l'avoir vu a Trieste. Rafanelli joue bien, mais ne chante pas et n'a pas de duets. On a insinué a Bellentani [*sic*: *sc.* Gasparo Bellantani] de ne pas tant appuyer sur la troisième partie que les femmes devient avoir *etroite*, bocca, vitta e potta [botta?].[1] Je me nomme pourtant pas la dernière, et cela n'est pas même de l'opera. La scene du Canapé est jouée avec tant de force, qu'on voit jusqu'aux fesses de la Tomeoni.

The opera itself is not identified: there were half-a-dozen with that title written before 1793, including a famous one of Pasquale Anfossi (1779).

The little theatres outside the city walls also thrived. Schikaneder was still performing *Die Zauberflöte* to packed houses in the Freyhaus-Theater and Wenzel Müller was beginning to launch one after the other of his 200-odd operettas in the Leopoldstadt-Theater. Even Zinzendorf had been persuaded to go to Mozart's opera.

On 4 May Salieri's *Axur* was first performed. Zinzendorf thought 'Les decorations tres belles. L'actrice Seßi a une belle figure, bien mise, mais peu adantages autent.' The Count went again to hear *Axur* on 20 May but his Diary shows that it was the famous Madame Viganò who really fascinated him. Josefa Medina Viganò (*prima ballerina*) and her husband Salvatore (ballet-master) were causing much comment in Vienna at that time. 'Le Ballet de la Vigano, il fit moins d'effet malgré ses gestes, attitudes et habillmens voluptueux.' The city was once again illuminated when the Count left the theatre. Later (14 June) he writes: 'La Vigano avoit cette fois un habée tres longues, cependant elle savoit jetter ses jambes si volupteusement qu'on voyoit beaucoup de ses caleçons blancs, et ses gestes, et le jeu de la physionomie, et comme elle est leste. Il y fermé fort chaud,' concludes the Count.

Meanwhile Haydn was beginning to introduce his brilliant pupil Beethoven to Viennese musical society. In May 1793, the old composer took the young one to Eisenstadt to play for the Esterházy family. We know of the trip only from a passage in the composer Johann Schenk's autobiography. Schenk has mixed up the dates, for (*infra*, line 3) the meeting with Joseph Gelinek, a fashionable pianist, teacher and famous as a composer of variations, is said to happen in July 1792, which is not possible because Beethoven was in Bonn. We have added [1793] but that is also doubtful in view of the chronology of what follows. Probably Gelinek met Beethoven late in 1792 or early in 1793.

> In 1792, His Imperial Highness, Archduke Maximilian, Elector of Cologne, was pleased to send his protegé Louis van Beethoven to Vienna in order that he might study musical composition with Joseph Haydn. Towards the end of July [1793] the Abbé Gelinek informed me that he had made the acquaintance of a young man who displayed a rare virtuosity on the pianoforte, such as he had not heard since Mozart. At the same time he explained that Beethoven had begun to study counterpoint with Haydn more than six months before, but was still at work on the first exercise. He also said that His Excellency Baron van Swieten had warmly recommended the study of counterpoint to him and often inquired how far he had

---

1 Can Zinzendorf have suffered from the Viennese congenital inability to distinguish between 'b' and 'p' (and 'd' and 't' as well)?

progressed in his studies. On Beethoven's writing desk I came across a few phrases of the first exercise in counterpoint. After a cursory examination it was clear to me that in every tonality (short as these were) there were several mistakes. This tended to bear out the truth of Gelinek's above-mentioned remarks. Since I was now convinced that my pupil was ignorant of the primary rules of counterpoint, I gave him the universally known text-book by Joseph Fux, *Gradus ad Parnassum*, so that he might obtain a summary of the subsequent exercises. Joseph Haydn, who had returned to Vienna from London towards the end of the previous year, was engaged in harnessing his Muse to the composition of great new masterpieces. Taken up with these important endeavours, it was clear that Haydn could not easily occupy himself with teaching grammar. Now I was seriously anxious to be of assistance to one so eager to acquire knowledge. Before I began to teach him, however, I pointed out to him that our work together must forever remain a secret. In this regard, I ordered him to copy out once again every passage which I had corrected in my own hand, so that every time that Haydn examined it he would not notice the work of a strange hand. A year later, Beethoven came into conflict with Gelinek, the cause of which I have forgotten. It seems to me, however, that both sides were to blame. As a result of their dispute, Gelinek became angry and revealed my secret. Beethoven and his brothers made no secret of it. . . .

In about mid-May [1793] he informed me that he would shortly go to Eisenstadt with Haydn and would stay there until the beginning of winter. He did not yet know the day of departure. At the beginning of June I went to his house at the usual hour – but my good Louis was nowhere to be seen. He had left me the following little note which I transcribe word for word.

'Dear Schenk,

'I wish that I did not have to depart today for Eisenstadt. I would have liked to talk with you once more. In the meanwhile, you may count on my gratitude for the kindnesses you have shown me. I will make every effort to return them. I hope to see you again soon and to enjoy the pleasure of your company. Farewell and do not entirely forget

your
Beethoven.'
[Landon, *Beethoven*, pp. 60f.]

We may once again break the chronology to add a postscript to the curious story related above. Beethoven's biographer A. F. Schindler relates:

One day in the spring of 1824, Beethoven was walking along the Graben with me, when we met Schenk. Beethoven was beside himself with joy at seeing once more this old friend of whom he had not heard for many years; he seized his hand and dragged him off to the nearby inn called *Zum Jägerhorn* and into the back room which had to be lit up even in the daytime. In order to remain undisturbed he closed the door. Then be began to open up all the secrets of his heart. After complaints about bad luck and description and discussion of misfortunes, events of the years 1793–94 were recalled. Upon which Beethoven broke out into loud laughter, remembering how they both had played a trick on father Haydn, who had never noticed anything. This scene was the occasion of my hearing for the first time about the unusual relationship which had existed between the two men. Beethoven, who at that moment stood at the summit of his art, overwhelmed the modest composer of the *Dorfbarbier* as well as the grand opera *Achmet und Almanzine* and several other *Singspiele*, and who lived by giving lessons, with the most fervent gratitude for the part he had played during his years of study and for his friendly devotion. The leave-taking of the two after that remarkable hour was moving, as if it were for life, and indeed so it was – Beethoven and Schenk never saw one another again after that day.   [Landon, *Beethoven*, 61]

In the peace of Eisenstadt, Haydn was busy composing his new string quartets (the six, which form an entity, have been posthumously divided into two *opera* of three each, Opp. 71 & 74). Beethoven could live very cheaply in a room in one of the many out-buildings of the huge Esterházy Castle, continue to study with Haydn, and play in the evenings occasionally at the Castle, where there was always a willing audience. In fact, the Esterházys were among the first subscribers to Beethoven; they figure in the list of the Op. 1 Trios, Prince Nicolaus to the extent of three copies and 'La Comtesse Jos. [Josephine?]' one. It is odd to think of the two composers together all through the summer at Eisenstadt. Beethoven must have watched Haydn rehearsing and performing his new London Symphonies in Vienna. Now he will have got to know Haydn very well, seeing the 'workshop' and how Haydn fitted into the life of Eisenstadt as princely *Capellmeister* in retirement (for Prince Anton had no orchestra, and supported just enough musicians to perform a small Mass in the Castle Chapel, and some wind-band players for the hunt).

In June, from Eisenstadt, Haydn had to write to the tiresome Polzelli about money (as usual) and other devious manipulations of his ex-mistress:

[*Italian. 'Tu' form*]

Eisenstadt, 20th June 1793.

Dear Polzelli!

I hope that you will have received the two hundred florins [Gulden] which I sent *via* Sig. Buchberg.[1] and perhaps also the other hundred, a total of 300 florins; I wish I were able to send more, but my income is not large enough to permit it. I beg you to be patient with a man who up to now has done more than he really could. Remember what I have given and sent to you; why, it's scarcely a year ago that I gave you six hundred florins! Remember how much your son costs me, and how much he will cost me until such a day as he is able to earn his own daily bread. Remember that I cannot work so hard as I have been able to do in the years past, for I am getting old and my memory is gradually getting less reliable. Remember, finally, that for this and many other reasons I cannot earn any more than I do, and that I don't have any other salary except the pension of my Prince Nicolaus Esterházy (God rest his soul), and that this pension is barely sufficient to keep body and soul together, particularly in these critical times. Your son received the watch from *Sig.* Molton, who however didn't want to give it to him, and made up all sorts of reasons, excuses and lies for not doing so; I had to go to him myself in order to get it. This man is a terrible liar! He told me to my face that he had sent you the 25 florins I had given him four months ago; and he boasted in front of me how much he had done for you, and how he was ready at any time to have you come to Vienna and marry him; you can imagine just what I thought of you! But I am studying this man carefully, to ascertain his true character, and I am getting to know him better and better: tomorrow he is leaving for Poland with his Princess, but he won't slip through *my* fingers with those twenty-five florins! At present I am alone with your son in Eisenstadt, and I shall stay here for a little while to get some fresh air and have a little rest. You will receive a letter from your son along with mine; he is in good health, and kisses your hand for the watch. I shall stay in Vienna until the end of September, and then I intend to take a trip with your son, and perhaps – perhaps – to go to England again for a year; but that depends mainly on whether the battleground changes; if it doesn't, I shall go somewhere else, and

1 J. M. Puchberg: see *supra*, p. 121.

perhaps – perhaps – I shall see you in Naples. My wife is still sick most of the time, and is always in a foul humour, but I don't really care any more – after all, this woe will pass away one day. Apart from this, I am much relieved that you, for your part, are a little more relieved about your dear sister.[1] God bless you and keep you in good health! I shall see to it that you receive what little I can offer you, but now you really must be patient for a while, because I have other onerous debts; I can tell you that I have almost nothing for all my pains, and live more for others than for myself. I hope to have an answer before you leave for Naples. I kiss you, and am your

most sincere
Giuseppe Haydn.

[Address:]   Madame
           Madame Loise Polzelli
             Virtuosa di Musica
     in
Ferma in posta.   Bologna
              en Italie.   [CCLN, 139f.]

Haydn had sold his charming little house in Eisenstadt to realize enough capital when he went to England in 1790; but now that he had returned with a lot of money, he remembered that his wife had found a little house near Vienna, in the territory of the Windmühl near the suburb of Gumpendorf, No. 71 Kleine Steingasse (now Haydngasse, Vienna VI). She wanted Haydn to buy this house so that she could live out her years as a widow in it, as she tactfully put it, and asked Haydn to send her 2000 Gulden for the purpose. Dies, who relates the story (98), quotes Haydn as saying, 'I didn't send her the money she wanted, but waited until I got back to Vienna. When I returned, I saw the little house myself. I liked the still and quiet situation, I bought it, and during my second trip [to London] I had another floor added. My wife', added Haydn rather grimly, 'died about seven or eight years later (1800), and I live in it by myself as a widower.' Haydn must have gone up to Vienna for a couple of days in the middle of August to sign the contract with the former owner, Master Weaver Ignaz Weißgram, Frau Haydn also signed, and they paid 1,370 Gulden: 1,200 'Kaufschilling' Gulden and 170 in 'Leihkauf' (promissory pre-contractual down-payment which was paid out upon signature of contract). The new floor and other changes took until the year 1796.[2] The projected construction had to be approved by the Magistracy, of course:

[To the Vienna City Magistracy. *German*. Copy in an unknown hand in the Vienna City files]
To the worthy Magistracy of the Imperial and Royal capital city of Vienna:
    The undersigned is thinking of slightly enlarging his house, which is situated at No. 71, Kleine Stein-gasse near Gumpendorf, in the territory of the Windmühl property, and therefore comes under the Registry of Landed Property pertaining to your worthy Magistracy. Ground-plan A, attached, shows said enlargement, whereby another storey would be added to the original building. Since your exalted consent is required beforehand, the undersigned begs you to grant it to him; in support of his request, he would point out that:
1mo In this projected construction, good materials would be employed, but altogether it would be planned in accordance with the rules established by the

---

1 Luigia Polzelli had two sisters, one in Bologna and one in London (see *supra*, pp. 59, 175).
2 Pohl III, 72.

Board of Works, and would contribute to improving the general looks of the street. He hopes therefore that his plan will be approved, the more so because 2do By enlarging the building, an increase of tax-money would accrue to the most exalted *orario*.

Vienna, 14th August 1793.
Franz Heiden [*sic*] *Fürstl. Esterhazis.*
Capellmeister and Property Owner in
the Kleine Steingasse No. 71.

[CCLN, 141]

The house had a pretty little garden behind it, and when its reconstruction was completed, it became a handsome and rather spacious dwelling for the Haydns and their servants (Johann Elssler and his family, the Housekeeper, maids and the cook). It is today the Haydn Museum of Vienna and has been beautifully restored by the Museum der Stadt Wien, under whose protection it lies.

In the middle of September 1793, Haydn was invited to a dinner at Schönbrunn Castle, given by the Pensionsgesellschaft bildender Künstler. The protocol records the cost of the banquet, including transportation by carriage from the inner city, to have been 41 Gulden 20 Kreuzer; the guests seem to have enjoyed themselves. In 1792, Haydn had written the Dances for the Great Hall of the Redoutensaal, in 1793 they were by Leopold Kozeluch. The Society's records read:

> Since the *Herren Capellmeister* Joseph Haydn and Leopold Kozeluh [*sic*], the former a year ago, the latter this year, have contributed *gratis* to this Society the Minuets and German Dances for our *Redoute* [ball], the directors have decided to show their gratitude to these two *Herren Componisten* by inviting them to a banquet at Schönbrunn, also with Herr v. Capol, who was of such assistance to us and to whom we are very much indebted, which banquet took place on 17th September 793. These gentlemen, with some of their relatives, and such of the administrators and assessors who happened to be in Vienna at that time, were accompanied to the above-mentioned place, where the noble *Herren Gäste* [guests] expressed their satisfaction, and gave sufficient proof of their further active friendship, to their hosts.

We shall see that Haydn's Dance Music of 1792 was repeated in 1793, but in the Small Rooms of the Redoutensaal.

In October, Count Zinzendorf was again ecstatic about 'La Viganò': on the 19th, '[ils] danserent a ravir leur pas de deux qui me plut extremement', and on the 27th: 'Pas de deux de la Vigano et blanc petit rien bien voluptueux mais l'auditoire moins nombreux.' On the 24th they gave Cimarosa's *L'impresario in angustie*, which had been an utter flop when Haydn had conducted it, together with *Il credulo* by the same composer, during the last season at Eszterháza. It had been one of the very few works ever given at Eszterháza which was only played a single time (June 1790). Zinzendorf thought it 'joli musique' on 24 October and the next day he wrote 'Il est amusant. Bellentani [*sic*],' he thought, was 'bonne caricature.' Later, Haydn was to give to his friend Silverstolpe an Aria which had been inserted by the composer in the Eszterháza performance, 'Il meglio mio carattere'.[1]

---

1 First published in an edition by the present writer from the Silverstolpe copy in Näs Castle (Sweden): Haydn-Mozart-Presse 118 (score) & 119 (parts), 'Aria di Merlina'. About the Eszterháza performance, see Bartha-Somfai, 161, 358ff. and Harich, 'Das Repertoire des Opernkapellmeisters Joseph Haydn in Eszterháza (1780–1790)' in *Haydn Yearbook* I (1962), p. 88.

On 28 October 1793, news of Marie Antoinette's death on the scaffold reached Vienna. Haydn might have felt, like Edmund Burke in his *Reflection on the Revolution in France,* 'I thought ten thousand swords must have leaped from their scabbards to avenge even a look that threatened her with insult. But the age of Chivalry is gone. That of sophisters, economists and calculators has succeeded, and the glory of Europe is extinguished for ever.' 'Dieu, quelle horreur nouvelle!' was Zinzendorf's, and the general, opinion. But despite this grim evidence of Parisian *ferocité* (the Count's description), the war had gone better in the Summer of 1793, at least for the Prussian-Austrian invasion of northern France at the end of July. The Prince of Coburg captured Valenciennes and Mainz fell to the Prussians, but the Prussians and Austrians were soon embroiled in an argument over the division of Poland. Not only England but also the Spanish Netherlands now entered the Allied camp.

Beethoven was still having money troubles, partly because his salary as a member of the Electoral band in Bonn was delayed and would soon disappear altogether as Bonn fell to the French troops and the Elector had to flee to Vienna. Haydn wrote a letter, towards the end of November, which shows his profound insight into Beethoven's genius; the letter was discovered in the Haus-, Hof- und Staatsarchiv of Vienna before the war by the Beethoven scholar, F. Reinöhl (1935) but did not become well known until twenty-five years later.

[Haydn to Maximilian Franz, the Elector of Cologne, Bonn. *German.* Only signature & title autograph]
Serene Electoral Highness!
I humbly take the liberty of sending Your Serene Electoral Highness some musical works, *viz.*, a Quintet, an eight-part Parthie, an oboe Concerto, Variations for the fortepiano, and a Fugue,[1] compositions of my dear pupil Beethoven, with whose care I have been graciously entrusted. I flatter myself that these pieces, which I may recommend as evidence of his assiduity over and above his actual studies, may be graciously accepted by Your Serene Electoral Highness. Connoisseurs and non-connoisseurs must candidly admit, from these present pieces, that Beethoven will in time fill the position of one of Europe's greatest composers, and I shall be proud to be able to speak of myself as his teacher; I only wish that he might remain with me a little while longer.
While we are on the subject of Beethoven, Your Serene Electoral Highness will perhaps permit me to say a few words concerning his financial status. 100 ♯[2] were allotted to him during the past year. Your Serene Electoral Highness is no doubt yourself convinced that this sum was insufficient, and not even enough to live from; undoubtedly Your Highness also had his own reasons for choosing to send him into the great world with such a paltry sum. Under these circumstances, and to prevent him from falling into the hands of usurers, I have in part gone bail for him and in part lent him money myself, with the result that he owes me 500 fl., of which not a Kreutzer[3] was spent unnecessarily; which sum I would ask you to send to him here. And since the interest on borrowed money grows continually, and is very tedious for an artist like Beethoven anyway, I think that if Your Serene Electoral Highness were to send him 1000 fl. for the coming year, Your Highness would earn his eternal gratitude, and at the same time relieve him of all his distress: for the teachers who are absolutely essential for him, and the display which is necessary if he is to gain admission into numerous salons, reduce this sum to such

1 The compositions referred to in this letter have been more or less satisfactorily identified (see Kinsky–Halm, etc.) with the exception of the oboe Concerto in F which is lost.
2 = 100 ducats, or 450 Gulden, not 500 (as in the Elector's answer). [CCLN, 143]
3 = 'Not a farthing'. [CCLN, 143]

an extent that only the bare minimum remains. As for the extravagance which one fears will tempt any young man who goes into the great world, I think I can answer for that to Your Serene Electoral Highness: for a hundred circumstances have confirmed me in my opinion that he is capable of sacrificing everything quite unconstrainedly for his art. In view of so many tempting occasions, this is most remarkable, and gives every security to Your Serene Electoral Highness – in view of the gracious kindness that we expect – that Your Highness will not be wasting any of your grace on usurers as far as Beethoven is concerned. In the hope that Your Serene Electoral Highness will continue his further patronage of my dear pupil by graciously acceding to this my request, I am, with profound respect,

Your serene Electoral Highness'
most humble and obedient
Joseph Haydn
Capell Meister von Fürst Nicolas Esterházy

Vienna, 23rd November 1793.   [*sic*: Nicolaus I died in 1790.]
[The envelope also contained a short letter from Beethoven.]

[CCLN, 142]

[To Haydn from Maximilian Franz, the Elector of Cologne. *German.* Draft in a secretary's hand, corrected in the Elector's hand.][1]

Nomine Serenissimi.

To Prince Esterházy's *Kapellenmeister* [*sic*] in Vienna. d. d. Bonn the 23rd of December 1793 [in a third hand: 'Exped. sequenti.'].

I received the music of the young Beethoven which you sent me, together with your letter. Since, however, with the exception of the Fugue, he composed and performed this music here in Bonn long before he undertook his second journey to Vienna, I cannot see that it indicates any evidence of his progress.

Concerning the money which was hitherto available for his subsistence in Vienna, it is true that this consists only of 500 fl.; but apart from these 500 fl., his salary here of 400 fl. has been paid to him the whole time, so that he will always receive 900 fl. annually. Therefore I do not see at all why his financial circumstances should be as reduced as you have indicated to me.

I am wondering if he would not do better to begin his return journey here, in order that he may once again take up his post in my service; for I very much doubt whether he will have made any important progress in composition and taste during his present sojourn, and I fear that he will only bring back debts from his journey, just as he did from his first trip to Vienna.   [CCLN, 143]

The rudeness and frigidity of Maximilian's answer are surprising in view of the cordiality with which he had greeted Haydn in Bonn at Christmas time in 1790, giving Haydn a *souper* and introducing him to the Bonn orchestra. A recent biography of the Elector[2] suggests that he was aware of Haydn's unsystematic teaching of Beethoven; but this is hardly likely. Moreover, Beethoven, in the enclosed letter referred to at the end of Haydn's letter, had written that he had 'devoted himself this year with all the power of his soul to the furtherance of the art, so as to be able next year to send Your Serene Electoral Highness something which more closely approaches your generosity towards me and your dignity than those sent through Herr Haidn. . . .'

---

1 The original letter, dictated to a secretary, is still more unfriendly: for example, in the last paragraph, the Elector had written: 'for I very much doubt if he can have learnt anything from you. . . .' [CCLN, 143]

2 Max Braubach, *Maria Theresias jüngster Sohn Max Franz*, Vienna-Munich 1961, pp. 252ff.

Unfortunately there is only one explanation for the particular rudeness of the Elector's answer, and it is clearly contained in the words, 'Since, however, with the exception of the Fugue, he [Beethoven] composed and performed this music here in Bonn long before he undertook his second journey to Vienna, I cannot see that it indicates any evidence of his progress.' Haydn had obviously asked Beethoven to give him a parcel of the young man's latest compositions, and what Beethoven had very deviously done was to hand his teacher a fistful of Bonn compositions. Beethoven's duplicity is doubly stupid because the Elector, whatever his faults, was a musical Hapsburg and of course immediately recognized the works; and Beethoven must have known that his patron was musical enough to do so. Of course all this reflected on Haydn, whom the Elector obviously thought was a party to the deceit – also rather stupid on the electoral side, because how could Haydn know which works Beethoven had composed in Eisenstadt and which in Bonn? The episode was, without any doubt, the first to shake Haydn's belief and trust in his pupil; it may even have provided the motive for leaving Beethoven behind on the coming trip to London. It marked the beginning of that mutual distrust which was to take on extremely nasty overtones, especially in Beethoven's attitude, during the coming years, the sorry history of which must wait for detailed examination until a later chapter.

That the Elector did not entertain a bad opinion of Haydn is perhaps seen in a letter criticizing Paul Wranitzky's 'Symphonie caractéristique' to celebrate the Peace of Campo Formio, which Maximilian Franz heard at Ansbach in April 1799. After some caustic remarks on the quality of the music ('also I would have written the piece about the seperate peace in C minor rather than A major'), the Elector concludes: 'Altogether the Symphony would have gone better if an experienced Regens chori – like Haydn – had given the tempo and conducted the whole.'[1]

On 24 November 1793, the Gesellschaft bildender Künstler gave its second annual masked ball in the Redoutensaal. The *Wiener Zeitung* of 23 November (No. 94) announced that the music in the large room would be composed by 'Hofkapellmeister und Hofcompositeur L. Kozeluch', 'in the smaller room the dances will be by the famous and favourite *Kapellmeister* Herr Joseph Haydn and Herr Wolfgang Mozart'. We cannot identify the Mozart works performed, but we can identify those of Haydn: they were the *Deutsche Tänze* (IX: 12) that Haydn had composed for the 1792 season. On the original parts by Elssler that belonged to the Society, entitled 'Tedeschi di Ballo', we find the note 'Aufgeführt 25. Nov. 1792 im Grossen Saal, 1793 und 1820 im Kleinen Saal'. There is no record if Haydn conducted the performance. The patrons, according to the 'Notta. / Über die beÿ H: Vice Rector Pohl ausgegebene Eintritt- / Billets für die am 24ten Nov: 1793 gehaltenen Baal' (Archiv der Stadt Wien), included the Empress (twelve tickets); the Archduchesses Clementine and Amalia (who paid sixteen ducats for their tickets); the Princess Leopoldine – the beautiful daughter of Haydn's patroness, married in 1793 to Prince von Grassalkovic(z) – who bought no less than forty-eight tickets; 'Comteße Würbna' (*vide supra*, p. 207); and members of the Kinsky (Countess 'Kÿnsky' who paid 12 ducats for a dozen tickets), Palffy (a dozen tickets) and Fries (fifteen tickets) families.

The list of 'Freÿ-Billets ausgeben 793' shows a great increase over that of 1792. Haydn only asked for four ('H: v Haÿdn') but Kozeluch asked for a dozen.

In November 1794 Haydn, of course, was in England and did not participate, even *in absentia*, through performances of his various Redoutensaal compositions. Perhaps

---

1 Braubach, op. cit., p. 255

this explains why 'Fürstin Esterhazi' only bought one ticket, according to the 'Notta / Billets zu dem am 23ten Novem. 1794 gehaltenen Redout-Baal / haben beÿ dem Herrn Vice Rector angenohmen und bezahlt'. Under the free tickets we find the two main composers listed as 'H: v Eÿbler Music Compoßitor' with twelve tickets, 'H: v Kozeluch D^{to} [Ditto]' with six, and a mysterious entry which at first seemed inexplicable: 'H: v. Haÿdn D^{to} [i.e. Music Compoßitor] wegen übersetzen two tickets.' 'Wegen übersetzen' means, in contemporary musical language of Vienna, making a piano reduction. In fact the entry is not Haydn but the mysterious Hayda, an organist and composer named Joseph Hayda (see *Haydn Yearbook* I, pp. 211f.) whose *Litany* in C has been erroneously attributed to Haydn. As it happens, Dittersdorf wrote the Minuets and German Dances for the Large Ball Room of the Redoutensaal in 1794, and Joseph Hayda arranged them for piano; his arrangement, once part of the so-called Kaiserliche Sammlung, is now in the Gesellschaft der Musikfreunde and the late Professor Otto Erich Deutsch kindly drew our attention to the MS. (without either of us knowing that one day the Dittersdorf Dances would lead to Hayda and Haydn). In any case, to return to the Redoutensaal Ball of 1794, someone actually collected the tickets, as the distribution list (with numbers) of 'Frey-Billets Anno 1794' for the Society shows: 'Haÿda' with Nos. 174 and 175.

This is perhaps the place to record that one of Haydn's most interesting operas, *La fedeltà premiata*, was in the repertoire in the town theatre at Graz in Styria. It was played in German as 'Die belohnte Treue' during the 1792 and 1793 seasons, very likely from the original performance material of Eszterháza Castle, which Haydn had given to Schikaneder and his company for the 1784 Viennese première of the work, and which had never been returned to the Esterházy Archives. (In fact, it is likely that Haydn did not even own a complete copy of the opera in 1792 and 1793.)

Nearly twenty years earlier, in April 1775, Haydn had conducted the first performance of his oratorio, *Il ritorno di Tobia*, at two benefit concerts for the widows and orphans of the Tonkünstler-Societät in Vienna. The income had been enormous – 1712 Gulden – but the intrigue of Haydn's jealous colleagues had prevented him (rather incredibly even for Viennese colleagues) from becoming a member (see CCLN, 22ff.). Nevertheless he had given the oratorio again in the Easter 'Academies' of 1784, adding two new choruses and revising the work completely. With his usual generosity, he agreed to conduct the Christmas concerts of the year 1793, which were held on 22 and 23 December at the Burgtheater. Here is the programme (with the changes for the second concert given in brackets):

Grand Symphony by Joseph Haydn
Aria (sung by Therese Gassmann)
    [2nd evening Aria sung by Vincenzo Maffolli]
Grand Chorus with German text by Haydn
Grand Symphony by Haydn
Violin Concerto (played by Heinrich Eppinger) [2nd evening: New Terzetto
    for two oboes and cor anglais composed by Went, performed by
    the brothers Johann, Franz and Philipp Teimer.]
Grand Chorus with Italian words by Haydn
Grand Symphony by Haydn
N.B. The Symphonies, and the Chorus with German text, were composed by Herr Haydn in England, who at the request of the Society and out of respectful admiration for the worthy public has consented to direct the orchestra.

[Pohl, *Denkschrift*, 64]

The Italian chorus was probably from *Il ritorno di Tobia*, which oratorio Haydn also plundered for use in his English concerts, as we have seen. The German chorus is, of course, the (van Swieten?) translation, and Haydn's musical revision, of the Madrigal 'The Storm'. Therese Gassmann was to have an important role in Haydn's life when he finally came back to Vienna for good. The daughter of the significant operatic composer Florian Leopold Gassmann, she studied with Salieri and was an excellent high soprano, whose most famous part would be the Queen of the Night. She later married one of Haydn's admirers, Joseph Carl Rosenbaum. Maffolli is the tenor who has often appeared in this part of the Chronicle. The three Symphonies would appear to be those which Haydn had not already introduced to the Viennese public in his March concert at the Redoutensaal. Using the evidence presented in connection with the first concert (where three of Nos. 93, 96, 97 and 98 were given), we may surmise that the Christmas programmes must have included Nos. 94 and 95, and one other, unidentified work. That No. 94 was played is suggested in the Greiner poem quoted below ('ein lauter Pauckenschlag schrecket'). We may therefore assign to these concerts the Viennese première of a Symphony which was soon to be as popular in Vienna as it was in London: 'The Surprise Symphony' (No. 94), or as they called it in Vienna, 'Symphonie mit dem Paukenschlag'.

For a wonder, we have three contemporary criticisms of this concert, which really seems to have created a profound impression on the Viennese. The listeners who also heard Haydn conduct in London can have included the young Adalbert Gyrowetz, who was now back in Vienna and soon to start a successful career as operatic composer for the Vienna Court Theatre.

The *Wiener Zeitung* wrote: 'Haydn himself conducted the orchestra, which consisted of over 180 persons, and the excellent performance moved the public, which appeared in large numbers, to show its complete satisfaction by often repeated and vigorous demonstrations of its undivided approval.' The Society took in the very large sum of 1629 Gulden, 25 Kreutzer [Pohl, *Denkschrift*, 49].

The *Österreichische Monatsschrift* printed the following criticism:

On 22 February [*sic*] was a large musical concert for the benefit of the musicians' widows. They gave the newest symphonies which the great Haydn had performed in London, and gave them as well as they had there, as even Englishmen assured us. The house was extremely full and the success extraordinary. If there is a musician of whom his fatherland can be in every respect proud, it is Haydn. A great, creative, and ever productive genius is in him combined with the most pleasant manner and a modesty which is almost exaggerated; not to speak of a most noble generosity in all that concerns the execution of his art! The late Mozart had no warmer friend, no more ardent admirer. There is only one great artist we know against whom Haydn will allow no fair judgement and that is – himself   [1794, Band I, p. 196]

Later in the journal we find the same poem by Caroline von Greiner (signed with her full name, incidentally) which we will quote *in extenso* in the next review (*ibid*, p. 51). Caroline was the daughter of Haydn's old friend, *Hofrat* Franz von Greiner, and later married the court official Pichler and published famous memoirs. Haydn, it seemed, was predestined to receive appalling dedicatory verses wherever he was. Caroline von Greiner also gave her wretched poem to the *Wiener Theater Almanach für das Jahr 1795*, where on p. 26, we read:

At the concert given by the local Society of Musicians in Advent [*sic* on pp. 22f. the concert is clearly listed as 'Dezember 1793'], those Symphonies were performed under the direction of the immortal Joseph Hayden which the latter composed during his last stay in London. They were received here with just a great a success as in Handel's fatherland. Fräulein Caroline von Gr★, the charming poetess, wrote on that occasion the following poem:

An Herrn Joseph Hayden.
Bey Anhörung seiner sechs neuen, in England verfertigten Symphonien.

Wie rauscht die laute Musik, wie wälzt
im harmonischen Gange
Der Strom der Töne sich reissend dahin!
Kaum folgt das erstaunte Gehör dem kühn
verschlungnen Gesange,
Und fasset seinen erhabenen Sinn!
Der Paucken donnernder Ton, das
Schmettern heller Trompeten
Füllt mit Begeistrung die schwellende Brust.
Wir fühlen uns muthig und kühn vors
Antlitz des Feindes treten,
und hören den lauten Schlachtruf mit Lust.

Doch jetzt verstummt das Geräusch, die
Hirten-Flöten ertönen;
Sie schildern uns sanfter Empfindungen
Glück.
Und rufen mit mächtigem Reitz uns pa-
radiesische Scenen.
Aus einem Land der Unschuld zurück.
Wir hören der Vögel Gesang, in lauen
heiteren Lüften,
Wir hören den fernher murmelnden Bach.
Der Schäfer klaget sein Leid dem Wieder-
hall in den Klüften.
und sympathetisch seufzt dieser ihm nach.
Noch tönt der holde Gesang, der sanf-
tes Entzücken erwecket,
Noch schweben die lieblichen Bilder
uns vor.
Auf einmal schweigt die Musik: ein lauter
Pauckenschlag schrecket
Uns donnernd aus süssen Träumen empor.
Ein Ton, so furchtbar, wie der, der
einst an Israels Spitze
von Iericho's trotzenden Mauern erklang;
Da bebte die thürmende Stadt im tiefer-
schütterten Sitze.
Und Trümmer deckten das Feld entlang.

So spielet. o Hayden, dein Geist allmäch-
tig mit unseren Herzen,
Du rufst mit unwiderstehlicher Kraft
Bald der begeisternden Lust, bald stillen
Freuden bald Schmerzen:
Empörst und bändigst die Leidenschaft.

In diesem regen Gefühl, in dieser heiligen
Stille

> Die nicht ein Odemzug unterbricht.
> Erkenn dein schönstes Lob; der Worte
> reichste Fülle
> Dankt mit so vielem Ausdruck dir nicht.
>
> Und dieser erhabene Geist, der Schöpfer
> von Harmonien
> ist uns Bruder, ein Deutscher wie wir.
> O, fühlten diess Alle wie ich! Du solltest
> uns nimmer entfliehen:
> Kein Albion zöge dich neidig von hier.
>
> Doch willst du uns lassen, vermag kein
> Flehen dich mehr zu erbitten.
>
> Hält nichts dich länger in Deutschland zu-
> rück.
> So geh! wir gönnen ja doch den uns ver-
> wandteren Britten
> Vor allen Völkern der Erde, diess Glück.
>
> Caroline v.G★★

The Viennese, it would seem, feared that Haydn would desert them for ever for Albion. At least that is what Miss Greiner suggests in her rousing final lines.

News of this famous concert was soon brought to England, where it arrived shortly after Haydn himself. In the *London Chronicle* for 15 February 1794 we read:

> *Extract of Letter from Wien, Dec. 28 1793.* On the 22d and 23d, the Society of Musicians gave two grand Concerts for the benefit of its Widows and Orphans. The Orchestra consisting of 180 Persons, under the direction of Heyden [*sic*]. His symphonies composed in England were performed with the greatest success. The first day Henry Eppinger, a young Gentleman Dilettante, played a concert on the violin so admirably, as to exact general and unbounded applause. The second day the three brothers Teimer performed on three different instruments, in a most capital style. They are allowed by all to be farther [*sic*] proofs of the great progress music makes in this country[!].

On 28 December, Swieten's Gesellschaft der Associirten, which he had formed to finance the performances of Handel oratorios, gave a concert, at which possibly *Alexander's Feast* was performed. A textbook of the year 1793 has survived in which Haydn's Madrigal 'The Storm' is printed in German together with Handel's Oratorio. Though it is certain that they were performed together at the March concert, it may, as Edward Olleson thinks, have also been given at the Schwarzenberg Palais on the Neuer Markt on 28 December. If true, it was probably Haydn's last public concert in Vienna before he left for England.[1]

In the year 1793, a German lexicographer issued, in the *Musicalische Korrespondenz der teutschen Filharmonischen Gesellschaft für das Jahr 1792* (published by Boßler in Speyer), a list of the works of Haydn as published by André (Offenbach/Main), Artaria (Vienna), Bland (London), Boßler (Speyer), Breitkopf (Leipzig), Gayl (Frankfurt/Main), Haneisen (Frankfurt/Main), Hummel (Berlin-Amsterdam), Le Duc (Paris), Schott (Mainz), Rellstab (Berlin) and Westphal (Hamburg). The man

---

1 The textbook is preserved in the Gesellschaft der Musikfreunde, 5921 Textbuch 4. See Olleson: 'Georg August Griesinger's Correspondence with Breitkopf & Härtel' in *Haydn Yearbook* III (1965), p. 38. See *supra*, p. 216.

responsible for this colossal undertaking was Ernst Ludwig Gerber, who was later (1812) responsible for the best musical dictionary of the period: the famous *Neues historisch-biographisches Lexikon der Tonkünstler* which appeared in four volumes. Of course, Gerber left out many important printers, such as Huberty (Paris, later Vienna), Chevardière (Paris), Venier (Paris), Guéra (Lyon) and even Torricella in Haydn's own Vienna; but the 'first' Gerber list was the only one of its kind known up to that date. In the foreword, Gerber notes, 'Such a complete catalogue seemed best given to Haydn himself to prepare. But we can have no hope, unfortunately, from that side, because he even told one of my friends, whom I had asked a few years ago to get such a list, the following: "that this was impossible for him. And that moreover many of his works had been burned during the Castle fire at Eszterháza".' As we shall see, Haydn returned to the business of cataloguing his works when it became apparent to him that it would be foolish, even disastrous, for him not to do so.[1]

---

1 Pohl III, 69. Larsen, HUB 54, thinks there has been a confusion between the Eszterháza fire and the two fires at Eisenstadt. It is probable that Haydn was only looking for an excuse not to do such a catalogue.

CHAPTER FOUR

1794

THE TIME HAD COME for Haydn to leave again. We have no details, financial or otherwise, of the new contract with Salomon except that, as we shall see, Haydn had undertaken to deliver six new quartets and some symphonies for the coming 1794 season. This time there were favours to do for English friends: for Dr Burney a good engraved portrait of Metastasio, on whose biography the Doctor was working. Later Burney wrote: 'The admirable composer & worthy man, Haydn, has brought me 2 or 3 of the best prints of Metastasio that have been engraved at Vienna; and I believe I shall have one of them engraved for the 1st vol. of my Memoirs . . .'[1]

Eight days before his departure, Haydn found time to attend a new opera by his god-child Joseph Weigl, Jr, and to write him a letter about it (which was, by the way, immediately published in the *Wiener Theater Almanach für das Jahr 1795*, p. 30). The letter is full of the generosity for which the writer was so much loved:

> [*German*]
> Dearest Godson!
>
> When I took you in my arms after your birth, and had the pleasure of becoming your godfather, I implored Omnipotent Providence to endow you with the highest degree of musical talent. My fervent request has been heard: – It has been a long time since I felt such enthusiasm for any music as for your *La Principessa d'Amalfi* yesterday: it is full of ideas, it has grandeur, it is expressive; in short – a masterpiece. I heartily participated in the well-deserved applause with which it was received. Continue, my dearest godson, to write in this genuine style, so that you may once again convince the foreigners of that which a German can accomplish. Meanwhile, keep a place in your memory for an old fellow like myself. I love you affectionately and am, dearest Weigl,
>
> > Your bosom-friend and servant,
> > Joseph Haydn.
>
> [Vienna] From my home, 11th January 1794.   [CCLN, 143f.]

The recipient was the son of Joseph Weigl, who had been a 'cellist in the Esterházy orchestra, and with whom Haydn had been on the best of terms. The opera was given in the Burgtheater by the successful young composer. Count Zinzendorf thought it also very good when he first heard it on 13 February 1794: 'A l'opera la Principessa d'Amalfi. Jolie musique. Quel che l'uom non puo impedire fa meglio di secundar. O contenti ò non contenti, cont'il fato non si va', a number which specially pleased the old Count.

Haydn had ready with him to take to England the following works: piano Trio No. 31 (XV: 32), the whole of Symphony No. 99 (dated 1793), the Minuets of

---

1 Letter to J. C. Walker of 28 November 1794. Maggs Brothers Catalogue No. 852 (1958), item no. 30.

Symphonies Nos. 101 and 100 (the rest of the two works were finished in England and put down on British paper), the six string Quartets (Opp. 71, 74) and the Sonata (as Haydn calls it on the autograph manuscript) in F minor (XVII: 6) better known under its alternative title 'Andante con variazioni'. An authentic manuscript signed by Haydn gives a third version: 'un piccolo divertimento scritto e composto per la stimatissima Signora de Ployer di me giuseppe Haydn 793'. Barbara von Ployer was the daughter of a Viennese Court Official: *vide infra*, pp. 437–9.

To make Haydn's travelling easier, Swieten loaned the composer a comfortable travelling coach (Griesinger, 37: a direct quotation from Haydn). Prince Anton Esterházy was not in favour of the journey at all, and had to be persuaded. Dies relates the difficulties:

> When Haydn asked permission of Prince Anton [Esterházy] . . . to make a second trip to London, he found considerable difficulties barring the way. The Prince did not require Haydn to perform any duties, but he was well disposed towards him, and was of the opinion that Haydn had acquired enough fame for himself; he should be satisfied with what he had, and at an age of sixty and one years should not expose himself to the dangers of a journey, and to the annoyances arising, in London, out of inflamed jealousies. Haydn of course realized that all these opinions of Prince Anton arose from a noble mind; still, since he knew the extent of his powers, and since a busy life attracted him more than the quiet life in which the Prince had placed him, it was natural that his wishes could not agree with those of the Prince. Besides all this was the circumstance that Haydn had made 12,000 Gulden in cash during his first sojourn in London, and knew that the English public was still very well disposed to his Muse; moreover, he had contracted to write another six symphonies for Salomon, who was no longer in connection with Gallini; finally, he had made very advantageous contracts with various publishing houses: all these and more points were important reasons for him to contradict the wishes of the Prince, who finally sacrificed his will for the benefit of Haydn, and allowed him to make the trip, which began on 19th January 1794.   [Dies, 147f.]

Travelling with Johann Elssler, his faithful servant with the beautiful music script which served Haydn so well, Haydn took the road to Linz and Passau. 'As they reached the Austrian border at Schärding', relates Griesinger (28) 'a customs official asked for his [Haydn's] profession, Haydn said he was a musician [*Tonkünstler*]. What's that? asked the one official. A potter! (*Thon*künstler, Töpfer) said the other one. That's right, said Haydn, and that one who's sitting beside me in the carriage (his servant) is my apprentice' – 'Thon' meaning clay.

Dies tells us of another merry adventure that occurred to Haydn in Wiesbaden.

> In the inn where Haydn was staying, he heard someone next door to his room playing the favourite Andante with the drum beat [Surprise] on the pianoforte. He counted on the player being his friend and politely entered the room from which the music was coming. There he found several Prussian officers, who were all great admirers of his music, and when he finally said who he was, wouldn't take him at his word, that he was Haydn. 'Impossible! Impossible! You Haydn? – A man of such advanced years! – How does that correspond with the fire in your music? – No, we'll never believe it.' They went on in this tone so long, and continued doubting, till Haydn showed them a letter from their King, which he luckily happened to have in his luggage. Now the officers showered him with affection and he had to remain in their company until well after midnight. Haydn was sorry to leave his newly-won friends; he departed and arrived in London as early as 4 February 1794.   [Dies, 149]

Meanwhile Salomon had been busy spreading word of Haydn's arrival and the organization of the 1794 concert season.

MR. SALOMON'S CONCERT, HANOVER-SQUARE.

MR. SALOMON most respectfully acquaints the Nobility and Gentry, that his CONCERTS will open on Monday the 3rd of February next, and continue on every succeeding Monday (Passion and Easter Week excepted).

Dr. HAYDN will supply the Concerts with New Compositions, and direct the Execution of them at the Piano Forte.

Principal Vocal Performers are, MADAME MARA, and Mr. FISCHER, One of the King of Prussia's principal opera Singers, who never appeared in this Country before.

Principal Instrumental Performers, who will play Concertos and Concertantes on their respective Instruments, are – Violins, Signor Viotti and Mr. Salomon – Piano Forte, Mr. Dussek – Oboe, Mr. Harrington – German Flute, Mr. Mr. Ash[e. Pedal Harp, Madame KRUMPHOLTZ.

Besides other distinguished Performers, who will appear occasionally.

Subscriptions at Five Guineas for the Twelve Concerts received, and Tickets delivered, at Messrs Lockarts, Maxtone, Wallis, and Clark, Pall Mall.

The Ladies' Tickets are blue, and transferable to Ladies; and the Gentlemen's are red, and transferable to Gentlemen only.

[*Oracle*, 10, 23, 25 January; *Public Advertiser*, 22 January; *Morning Chronicle*, 10, 16, 21, 25 January, etc.]

It is known that Haydn played almost every instrument in the orchestra, including the kettledrums (which, as we shall see, he demonstrated to George Smart, a member of the Salomon band, in 1794); but as he grew older he became especially fond of the viola, playing, with Mozart, the viola parts of the latter's quintets. Haydn took his viola with him to London in 1794, for we read in the account books of the publisher and violin-maker William Forster for that year: 'Dr Haydn. Putting in order and stringing a tenor' – a statement that, incidentally, shows relations between the two men to have been better than the law-suit between Longman & Broderip and Forster (with Haydn as a witness) might seem to warrant.[1]

CONCERTS, SINGERS, &c.

The Professional is dropt, – in consequence SALOMON's will be entirely unopposed until after Easter, when the promised Concert at the Opera House is to be given.

Thus the HANOVER SQUARE will have had *ten* nights performance completely unrivalled. HAYDN is to be at the Piano Forte, and every nerve is to be exerted to leave an impression deeper than ever of this excellent band.

FISCHER is an admirable Singer – His voice is more *even* than DAVID's; it is a bass running up into a tenor without *falsetto* – it is expected, he will be more to the English taste, than any singer they have ever heard.

HAYDN recommended him many years back to this country, however, other pursuits have kept him till now from the knowledge of our countrymen – Some Italians of fine taste have heard him in private, and they expressed most liberally their astonishment at his science and power.

---

1 *A Mozart Pilgrimage. Being the Travel Diaries of Vincent & Mary Novello in the year 1829*, transcribed and compiled by Nerina Medici di Marignano, edited by Rosemary Hughes, London, 1955, pp. 170ff., and 347. William Sandys & Simon Andrew Forster, *The History of the Violin*, London, 1864, p. 322.

The DOCTOR [Haydn] has been writing with all his original fancy and fertile combination; and the present winter will perhaps give us works, which shall advance even the higher celebrity of HAYDN.

VIOTTI has been selecting some fine thoughts for *Concerto playing*, which for sublimity and simplicity is unequalled – *Duetti*, so much admired between SALOMON and himself, will be of course pursued . . . . [*Oracle*, 25 January]

MR. SALOMON'S CONCERT, HANOVER-SQUARE.

MR. SALOMON most respectfully acquaints the Nobility and Gentry, that Dr. HAYDN's and Mr. FISCHER's arrival in this country having been unexpectedly retarded, he has by the advice of many respectable friends been induced to postpone the opening of his Concerts from Monday next to Monday se'nnight the 10th of February, when the first performance positively will take place . . . .
[*Oracle*, 31 January, 3 February; *Morning Chronicle*, 3 February;
The Times, 3 February; *Sun*, 31 January; etc.]

The celebrated HAYDN's arrival was yesterday announced in the musical circles.

[*Oracle*, 6 February]

First Concert: 10 February 1794

MR. SALOMON'S CONCERT, HANOVER-SQUARE.

MR. SALOMON most respectfully acquaints the Nobility and Gentry, that his FIRST CONCERT will be on MONDAY next, the 10th Instant.

PART I.
Grand Overture, Rosetti.
Aria, Mr. Florio, jun.
(being his first Performance at these Concerts.)
New Concerto, Piano Forte, Mr. Dussek.
Scena, Madame Mara.

PART II.
New Grand Overture, Haydn.
Aria, Madame Mara.
New Concerto, Violin, Signor Viotti.
Scena and Duetto, Madame Mara and Mr. Florio.
Finale.

Dr. HAYDN will direct his Compositions at the Piano Forte.
Leader of the Band Mr. SALOMON.
N. B. Mr. SALOMON is extremely sorry, that Mr. FISCHER is not arrived yet; but he flatters himself that nothing will prevent his performing at the next Concert . . .
[*Oracle*, 8, 10 February; *Morning Chronicle*, 10 February;
Morning Post, 10 February; *World*, 6, 10 February; etc.]

Great as the new string Quartets for Salomon are, Haydn prudently thought he would re-introduce himself to London with a new Symphony: No. 99 in E flat, with clarinets used in a Haydn symphony for the first time. The 'New Concerto' by Dussek is probably identical with the Corri & Dussek print of his '[Second] Grand Concerto in F . . . as Performed at the Professional [and] Salomon's Concerts [and] King's Theatre Haymarket' (with a catalogue dated 1794: British Museum g. 452. (9.)), a fine piece of music which would still prove rewarding to pianists looking for something off the beaten track. Viotti, the great emigré Italian violinist from Paris, from now on appears constantly in this Chronicle. His revolutionary technique, which included making the violin stronger, physically, reinforcing the bass-bar to be able to support the increased pressure of the raised bridge, the neck 'thrown back', as the makers say, and the bow made less curved (again to increase its strength) – all these things contributed to influence not only solo violin playing but orchestral techniques as well. The modern orchestra was born when Viotti came to London and joined forces with Salomon in 1793. Viotti's tone was of the purest and loveliest; he was the last great representative of the classical Italian school, but he had lived in France and carefully studied Haydn's orchestration. In 1793, he had composed the E major Concerto (Giazotto 96), which had been first performed at the Hanover Square Rooms on 7 February; and one week later he had launched the beautiful and richly orchestrated (1 flute, 2 oboes, 2 clarinets, 2 bassoons, 2 horns, 2 trumpets, timpani, strings) Concerto No. 22 in A minor (Giazotto 97), which is still played today with delight. On 7 March the G major Concerto (with small orchestra; Giazotto 98) was performed. He soon became a great friend of William Shield, and we shall see that Haydn got on easily with the great Italian violinist.[1]

No less than four daily newspapers were on hand at the first concert of Salomon's series; the whole of London's non-operatic musical attention was now centered on this series, the Professional Concert having ceased to exist after the abortive 1793 season.

SALOMON'S CONCERT. OPENING NIGHT.

We must of necessity be brief. And after all it may be best, when the *chef d'oeuvre* of the great HAYDN is the subject.

'Come then, expressive SILENCE, muse his praise.'

VIOTTI gave a Concerto, *simple* and *affecting*, like his genius. MARA sang[:] *c'est assez dire.*   [*Oracle*, 11 February]

SALOMON'S CONCERT.

This superb Concert was last night opened for the season, and with such an assemblage of talents as make it a rich treat to the amateur. The incomparable HAYDN, produced an Overture of which it is impossible to speak in common terms. It is one of the grandest efforts of art that we ever witnessed. It abounds with ideas, as new in music as they are grand and impressive; it rouses and affects every emotion of the soul. – It was received with rapturous applause.

VIOTTI produced a new Concerto, in which his own execution was most delicate and touching; nothing could be more exquisite than his tones in the second movement. We have no doubt but both these pieces will be called for again; for they are to be ranked among the finest productions of which music has to boast.

DUSSEK had also a new Concerto on the *piano forte*, in his best manner; and Madame MARA sung divinely.   [*Morning Chronicle*, 11 February]

SALOMON'S CONCERT.

Last night was the first of this years Subscription to this admirable Concert. HAYDN presided at the Piano Forte, and the management of the whole reflects the highest credit on Mr. SALOMON, who has not spared expense to render it deserving of the

---

1 See the excellent full-length study by Remo Giazotto, *Giovan Battista Viotti*, Milan, 1956, with a very useful and accurate thematic catalogue.

patronage it has received. Of Mr. FLORIO we have before spoken in terms of approbation, which his duet the last evening with Madam MARA, fully justified; his voice is strong and impressive, and an excellent Counter-tenor; MARA was never in better voice, and VIOTTI greatly surprised the Amateurs by his Concerto on the Violin. The whole went off with great spirit.

Mr. FISCHER is not arrived; report, however, speaks high in his favour, and he is expected in time for the next performance.

[*Morning Post*, 11 February]

HANOVER-SQUARE.

The Concerts under the management of HAYDN and SALOMON commenced for the season last night, and we were glad to see the taste of the Public manifested in a large and elegant Audience. Indeed, it would be wonderul if a Concert, which can boast the united powers of HAYDN, VIOTTI, SALOMON, and MARA, with an ample and a[d]mirable Band, did not excite a very liberal patronage. The grand instrumental trial of last night was a New Overture by HAYDN, a composition of the most exquisite kind, rich, fanciful, bold, and impressive. VIOTTI displayed all his fine taste and astonishing execution in a Violin Concerto, which, though deeply scientific, was no less pleasing. MARA's excellence is too well known to require eulogium. Her two Airs were from *Anfossi* and *Gugliemi*; she also joined in a Duet with young FLORIO. FLORIO seemed rather indisposed, and perhaps, being a young Performer, was not a little awed by the consciousness of the crowd of Critics that attended. The Concert was worthy of the high name of the Conductor.

[*Sun*, 11 February]

Second Concert: 17 February 1794

MR. SALOMON'S CONCERT.   HANOVER-SQUARE.

The Subscribers are most respectfully acquainted, that the Second Performance will be THIS EVENING, February 17.

PART I.
Grand Overture, Kozeluck [*sic*].
Aria, Mr. Huttenes – Sacchini.
New Quartetto, M. S. for two Violins, Viola and Violoncello
– Messrs. Salomon, Damen, Fiorillo, and Damen, jun. – Haydn.
Scena, Madame Ducrest – Sarti.
(Madama Mara being taken ill with a violent cold and hoarseness.)

PART II.
The Grand New Overture, M. S. Haydn, which was performed last Monday.
Rondo – Mr. Huttenes.
Concerto Violin – Signor Viotti.
Recitative – Aria – Madame Ducrest – Paisiello.
Full Piece.   [etc.]
[*Oracle*, 17 February; *Morning Chronicle*,
17 February; *World*, 17 February; etc.]

It will be noticed that Salomon always had a place for the best of the refugees from France, now arriving in ever-increasing numbers: Madame Ducrest was not only a singer but also a gifted piano player, who appeared frequently in one or the other function. The new Quartet was from the series of six (Opp. 71, 74) but cannot be precisely identified.[1] Symphony No. 99 was repeated; the woodwind *soli* in the slow movement to which the *Morning Chronicle* refers occur at bars 16–26.

SALOMON'S SECOND CONCERT.

Again we found ourselves electrified by that soul of harmony, which pervades this excellent band. The animation and accuracy of the orchestra are highly honourable to the leader, Mr. Salomon, whose attention never wearies, and whose taste and judgement are but rarely equalled. Mr. Huttenes and Madame Ducrest were new performers at this concert. The first was unfortunately heard to great disadvantage, being absolutely hoarse; he is a German, educated in the Italian School, and was lately one of the royal band of Versailles. Of science, taste, and feeling, he gave evident proofs; but whether he have sufficient power of voice for so large an audience, is at present doubted. Those who have heard him, affirm his failure of tone was solely to be atttibuted [*sic*] to the accident of his having caught cold. Madame Ducrest is likewise an unfortunate emigrant, the wife of a man of rank. She gave great satisfaction, especially in the beautiful and popular rondeau, by Paisiello, *Ho perduto il vel sembiante*. Her intonation is uncommonly perfect; and could she delight as much by variety and energy, as she does by her melodious voice, she would be without a rival. Our earnest advice to her is, that she should study passion; which, conveyed in sounds so mellifluous, would produce amazing effects. Viotti played a concerto in a minor key, the composition and performance of which were alike masterly. In style it was neither perfectly ancient or modern, though it partook of the beauties of both. His power on the fourth string is indeed great; but, like power in general, it is liable to abuse. To speak proverbially, 'He harps a little too much on one string.' He played however with uncommon sweetness, feeling, and effect. But the richest part of the banquet, as usual, was due to the wonderful Haydn.

His new quartetto gave pleasure by its variety, gaiety, and the fascination of its melody and harmony through all its movements: and the overture, being performed with increasing accuracy and effect, was received with increasing rapture. The first movement was encored: the effect of the wind instruments in the second movement was enchanting; the hautboy and flute were finely in tune, but the bassoon was in every respect more perfect and delightful than we ever remember to have heard a wind instrument before. In the minuets, the trio was peculiarly charming: but indeed the pleasure the whole gave was continual; and the genius of Haydn, astonishing[,] inexhaustible, and sublime, was the general theme. [*Morning Chronicle*, 19 February]

Another criticism appeared in the *Sun* for 18 February:

HANOVER SQUARE

SALOMON opened his Musical Treasury last night, for the second time this Season, and afforded an elegant Audience a delicious entertainment.

MARA being ill, Madame DUCREST, the wife of an Emigrant French Nobleman, who possessed a high appointment under the late Duke of ORLEANS, made her

---

1 The New Opp. 71–74 Quartets obviously contained some technical difficulties which were so formidable that mention of them is made in the London Press: the *Morning Herald*, on 7 March 1794, notes 'Haydn has been prevailed upon to defer his return to Vienna till summer – he has lately produced a manuscript *Quartetto* of the most complex harmonies, but blended with all the flowing beauties that melody can bestow: – so difficult, however, is this piece in point of execution, as to require all the powers of / Crosdill, with the rapid bow, / Hautboy Parke, or Florio!'

appearance at this place as the vocal substitute. Madame DUCREST deserves public attention, as well for her talents as her misfortunes. She possesses a very charming voice, and sings in a chaste and interesting style. Though capable of much execution, she did not sacrifice feeling and taste.

The other vocal novelty was Mr. HUTTENES, who belonged to the Band of the late KING of FRANCE, before the detestable Revolution which has made such lamentable havock among worth and talents, and produced nothing but barbarism and tyranny. Mr. HUTTENES, under the disadvantage of a very severe cold, displayed great taste and expression. While we applaud his zeal we pity the mortification he must have felt in finding his talents so obscured.

The wonderful new Overture of HAYDN, performed on the first night, was repeated last night, amidst the wondering plaudits of the Audience. The first movement was *encored*.

VIOTTI also repeated his fine Concerto of the former night, which was, if possible, more charming than before.

HAYDN's Overture, which displays exquisite contrivance, was admirably supported by the Band, and had the addition of ASHE's flute.

As SALOMON's Concert is altogether the first ever heard in this Capital, we wonder not at the brilliant patronage it excites.

Haydn must have received two pieces of news about this time, the first something of a shock and the second a pleasant dedication. Prince Anton Esterházy had died, very suddenly, on 22 January. The *Wiener Zeitung* of the 25th had reported:

On the 22nd inst. died here in the 56th year of his age, from the sudden bursting of a pus sack in his rib-cage, Anton Prince of the Holy Rom. Emp. Esterhazy von Galantha, Lord of Forchtenstein, Knight of the Golden Fleece and of the Grand Cross of the St. Stephan Order, Chamberlain to his R. I. Majesty, Lieut.-General-Field Marshall, Captain for the Royal Hungarian Noble Bodyguards, Commander and owner of a Hungarian Infantry Regiment, Erb-Obergespan of the ancient & noble Oedenburger Gespanschaft. The body will be conveyed to the princely Esterházy family vault at Eisenstadt.[1]

Haydn probably knew little of the new reigning Prince, Nicolaus II, and his wife, born Princess Marie Hermenegild Liechtenstein, except the fact that they both knew and appreciated music; he may, however, have already formed that special attachment to the beautiful Princess, who was to play such an important role (discussed in the next volume of our biography) in Haydn's late years.

The second piece of news was the publication, on 5 February at Vienna, of three string Quartets, Op. 1, by Joseph Eybler, a talented composer for whom Mozart and Haydn gladly wrote recommendations (Mozart's on 30 May and Haydn's on 8 June 1790; CCLN, 104). In fact Eybler's early works showed great promise. His teacher Albrechtsberger had written him a handsome letter of recommendation on 24 January 1793:

Attestatum

Since in these enlightened times it is again necessary for a Regens Chori not only to know the church-music style and the necessary Latin as well, but also must be a

1 Prince Anton's death was also reported in the London newspapers (*Sun*, 13 February 1794).

thoroughly trained organ player; and for that reason I declare as an honest man that Herr Joseph Eibler, first, not only knows the two above-mentioned things but also the vocal art and violin playing to a polished degree; secondly, that in composition he is my best pupil; thirdly, that after Mozart he is the greatest genius now that Vienna has; fourthly, I can vouch for his good conduct in the whole world.

Vienna, the 24th of
January 793

Johann Georg
Albrechtsberger I. R.
Court Organist mp.
[seal]
[Austrian National Library, Handschriften-
sammlung 33/108. Autograph]

These were strong words from an Albrechtsberger. But Haydn seems to have thought equally highly of the talented young man. When he announced the new works in the *Wiener Zeitung* Eybler mentioned that the Quartets 'had enjoyed the fortune of so pleasing the famous and also generally popular *Kapellmeister* Haydn that he gave his amiable permission to allow the works to be dedicated to him, and added especially that he would do his very best to see that they are widely distributed.' The works were published by Traeg with an Italian title-page and dedication: a copy of the print is in the Monastery of Schlägl[1] in Upper Austria. Here is one more proof of Haydn's generosity with young musicians, to whom he was always willing to give a helping hand.

In the Third Concert of the Salomon series, we note that Gyrowetz, though back in Vienna, was still supplying Salomon with new music. The 'Grand Overture (M.S.) Haydn' in the second part is an earlier work. The great *basso profondo* Ludwig Fischer, who had a fantastic range from D below the bass clef to *a'*, 'all round, even and in tune' (Reichardt), had been Mozart's first Osmin in *Die Entführung aus dem Serail* – one more of those extraordinary links between Haydn in London and the dead Mozart.[2] The Haydn *Concertante* is the well-known one composed in 1792; this is clear from the description in the *Morning Chronicle*'s review; but what is the flute doing in it (Mr. Ashe, whom we remember from the previous visit)? Did Haydn rewrite the work? Or is this a printer's error, and Mr. Ashe carried over from the Gyrowetz flute Quartet. Wenzel Pichl is the well-known composer whose name often appears in this Chronicle, and who also supplied compositions to Haydn when he was *Kapellmeister* at Eszterháza.[3]

---

1 'Tre Quartetti [&c.] in Casa dell'Autore nella Kumpfgasse Nᵒ 887 o preßa Gius. Traeg nella Singerstraße', the extended foreword dated 'Vienna li 28 febraja 1794'.
2 Fischer – like Haydn and Mozart – was a Freemason, and on 29 April 1794, the *Sun* reports on the annual dinner in 'honour of the Royal Cumberland Free-Mason's School was yesterday held at this place [Free-Mason's Hall] . . . Mr. Fisher, the celebrated German singer, was present, and favoured the Company with an exquisite Song. . .'
3 Fischer material from Grove's *Dictionary*, first edition, I, 528f. Pichl at Eszterháza: Bartha-Somfai 89f., promemoria by Haydn on 23 December 1780, 'Da das letzthin erkaufte Notten Papier theils zur Neuen Opera [*La fedeltà premiata* by Haydn], theils zu denen zwey Neuen Sinfonien [probably Haydn's], und das übrige für die Pichlische Quartetten nun gänzlich verbraucht worden. . . .' Apart from 88 symphonies and 25 operas, Pichl wrote 148 pieces for baryton (a kind of viola du gamba with sympathetic vibrating strings) for Prince Nicolaus I Esterházy. C. F. Pohl's article in Grove I, Vol. II, 751.

Third Concert: 24 February 1794

MR. SALOMON'S CONCERT, HANOVER-SQUARE.

The Subscribers are respectfully acquainted, that the Third Performance will be
THIS EVENING.

PART I.
Overture, Pichl.
New Quartetto (M. S.) for Flute, Violin, Viola, and Violoncello
– Messrs. Ashe, Salomon, Fiorillo and Damen – Gyrowetz.
Aria, Mr. Fischer,
(being his first appearance in this country.)
Concertante for Violin, Oboe, Flute, Bassoon, and Violoncello,
Messrs. Salomon, Harrington, Ashe, Parkinson, and Damen
– Haydn.
Scena, Madame Ducrest,
Madame Mara being still indisposed.

PART II.
Grand Overture (M. S.) Haydn.
Scena, Mr. Fischer.
Sonata, Pedal Harp, Madame Delaval, with an Accompaniment
of a Violin, and Violoncello, Messrs. Salomon and Domen [*sc.* Dahmen].
Finale.   [etc.]
[*Oracle*, 24 February; *Morning Chronicle*, 24 February]

Salomon's Concert on Monday night was crouded [*sic*] to the very extremities of
the room. Madame *Ducrest* sung with great taste, and gave the company no cause
to regret the absence of *Mara*, whose insufferable impertinence, and unbecoming
airs, whenever she appears in an orchestra is such as to disgust even those who most
admire her talents.   [*The Times*, 26 February]

HANOVER SQUARE

SALOMON may say with YOUNG, 'And, Chariot-like, I kindle as I run'; for his
visitors increase every performance, and last night the Room was as full as possible.

The vocal novelty was Mr. FISCHER from *Berlin*, who is the most capital Bass
Singer ever heard in this Country. His voice possesses of tone, and greater
flexibility, than could be conceived possible in a voice of such strength. His first
Song was vehemently *encored*, and he narrowly escaped the fatigue of repeating
the second.

Madame DUCREST again sung instead of MARA, who is still indisposed, and
highly gratified the Audience. She had an *encore* also.

Madame DELAVAL, in spite of two unlucky strings, gave a charming Harp
Concerto, and was beautifully accompanied by SALOMON.

[*Sun*, 25 February]

HANOVER-SQUARE. THIRD NIGHT.

The new Singer made his first appearance in this country, and was received with
unbounded applause.

Mr. Fischer is a deep bass, which with the utmost flexibility ascends into a
counter tenor, and that without the slightest break in the voice.

He combines the two stiles *bravura* and *cantabile* with an ease that astonishes, and executes with the utmost rapidity the most difficult transitions.

The Composer he chose was RIGHINI – the manner of whose composition is difficult, in the *German* way – displaying science rather than feeling.

Madame DUCREST is a very charming singer, and succeeded in the happiest way with an air of *Sarti Cavatina* –

Lunge da te ben mio.

Madame DELAVAL's harp was most cruelly strung. She broke three strings – however, her finger was brilliant, and SALOMON's accompaniment had the sweetest tone in the world. [*Oracle*, 25 February]

SALOMON'S THIRD CONCERT.

The long expected singer, Mr. FISCHER, sung for the first time last night at these rooms. His voice is perhaps in the lower part, the fullest and deepest[-]tone[d] bass we have ever heard, and produces a surprising effect. He is evidently an excellent musician, but his powers may rather be called grand than graceful. He reminded us of Handel's Polyphemus, and is much better capable of inspiring terror, than chearfulness [*sic*] or joy. The effect he produces, however, is highly satisfactory, not only to the man of science, but to the public in general, for the encore of his first air, was universal. He manages the middle part of his voice with most difficulty, but descends from his alto notes to what might almost be called the bottomless deep, with a certainty and fullness of intonation that astonishes.

– A concertante of HAYDN's was performed, the last movement in particular of which gave infinite pleasure, by a mixed expression of tenderness and joy; the first expressed at intervals in recitative, and the latter in the melody, which was delightfully animating. Madame DUCREST gave great satisfaction. We must however repeat our advice to her to study passion. – The room was full even to crouding [*sic*]; and Mr. SALOMON seems at present fully possessed of the patronage his spirited efforts so truly deserve. [*Morning Chronicle*, 25 February]

The 'Terror' had now begun in France, Robespierre executing the leaders of the *sans-culottes* for refusing to submit to its discipline. Dr. Burney told his daughter Fanny, 'There is no talking or thinking of anything else but the tremendous increase of discontent, danger, & unheard of profligacy & horrors.' It seemed to Dr. Burney, and no doubt to Dr. Haydn, that 'Peace, tranquillity, content, benevolence, humility, politeness, and all religious & social Virtues, are not only neglected, but regarded as vices!!' Men were by now thoroughly 'allarmed at the imminent danger of religion, morals, liberty, property, & life' (Lonsdale, 369).

Haydn was now established in comfortable lodgings at No. 1, Bury Street, St. James's, near Carlton House, and also near Mrs. Schroeter's, whose house lay an easy ten minutes' walk through St. James's Palace and The Mall, along St. James's Park, past Buckingham House (now Palace) to No. 6, James Street, Buckingham Gate. He had now completed the second, chronologically, of his new symphonies for Salomon: the ever-popular and brilliant 'Clock', No. 101, again with Salomon's big orchestra including clarinets. The original version, with a beautiful clarinet solo in the first movement, has recently been restored to the score by the present writer.[1]

---

1 Philharmonia bound scores of all the Haydn symphonies, Vol. XII (1968), no. 600, p. XVII.

Fourth Concert: 3rd March 1794

MR. SALOMON'S CONCERT, HANOVER-SQUARE.

The Subscribers are respectfully acquainted, that the Fourth Performance will be THIS EVENING.

PART I.
Overture, Kozeluck.
Aria, Madame Ducrest, Zingarelli,
(Madame Mara continuing still indisposed.)
New Concerto, Oboe, Mr. Harrington.
Aria, Mr. Fischer, Righini.
Concerto, Piano Forte, Mr. Dusseck.

PART II.
New Grand Overture (M. S.) Haydn.
Cavatina, Madame Ducrest, Sarti.
Concerto Violin, Signor Viotti.
Duetto, Madame Ducrest, and Mr. Fischer, Ferrari.
Finale, Chaconna, Fiorillo.   [etc.]
[*Oracle, and Public Advertiser★*, 3 March;
Morning Chronicle, 3 March;etc.]

★ On 1st March 1794, the *Oracle* merged with the *Public Advertiser*: henceforth abbreviated by the former title.

SALOMON'S FOURTH CONCERT.

Mr. Fischer, the new singer, gave us more of the pleasing and less of the grand in his second performance than in his first. He manages a voice of wonderful magnitude, though such voices are usually unmanageable, with great dexterity: this was particularly discoverable in a Duet, which he sang with Madame DUCREST. HARRINGTON played a new Oboe Concerto in a chaste and pleasing stile. DUSSECK played another, the first movement of which was certainly in a very opposite taste; we often heard the master, but we were sometimes reminded of the madman. That he can play with delicacy and expression, so as to delight was evident from his second movement, which was generally applauded, and most by the best judges. – VIOTTI we have never heard with greater pleasure; the sweetness and perfections of his tones were enchanting, as were the feelings they inspired. But as usual the most delicious part of the entertainment was a new grand Overture by HAYDN; the inexhaustible, the wonderful, the sublime HAYDN! The first two movements were encored; and the character that pervaded the whole composition was heartfelt joy. Every new Overture he writes, we fear, till it is heard, he can only repeat himself; and we are every time mistaken. Nothing can be more original than the subject of the first movement; and having found a happy subject, no man knows like HAYDN how to produce incessant variety, without once departing from it. The management of the accompaniments of the andante, though perfectly simple, was masterly; and we never heard a more charming effect than was produced by the trio to the minuet. – It was HAYDN; what can we, what need we say more?

[*Morning Chronicle*, 5 March]

HAYDN, like VIRGIL's fame, *vires acquirit eundo,* has latterly written a symphony, which the connoisseurs admit to be his best work.   [*Oracle*, 10 March]

In the Fifth Concert, we find the name of the distinguished music critic and composer, Johann Friedrich Reichardt. His music is now forgotten but his writings, particularly the travel volumes from Vienna in 1808, contain intelligent, first-hand comments about Haydn, Beethoven and life in Vienna at that time. The 'Clock' Symphony and the new string Quartet were repeated.

Fifth Concert: 10 March 1794

MR. SALOMON'S CONCERT, HANOVER-SQUARE.

The Subscribers are respectfully acquainted, that the Fifth Performance will be on Monday next, the 10th instant.

PART I.

Grand Overture, Reichard[t].
Scena, Mr. Fischer.
(By desire) the New Quartetto, (M. S.) Haydn,
as performed on the Second night. – Two violins, Violo [*sic*],
and Violoncello, Messrs. Salomon, Damea [*sic*], Fiorillo, and Damea [*sic*], jun.
Aria, Madame Mara.
Concerto, German Flute, Mr. Ashe.

PART II.

The New Grand Overture (M. S.) Haydn,
which was performed last Monday.
Aria, Mr. Fischer.
Concerto Violin, Signor Viotti.
Rondo, Madame Mara.
Finale.   [etc.]
[*Oracle*, 8, 10 March; etc.]

SALOMON'S FIFTH CONCERT.

The unremitting exertions of Mr. SALOMON, the spirit and accuracy of the Band, and the supreme excellence of the Performers, added to the support derived from the immortal HAYDN, have produced their intended effect. The Rooms are every night full, and of the best Musical Judges this great City affords. FISCHER sang an Air by SACCHINI, which not only shewed the full power of his voice, but is an excellent specimen of the noble talents of the composer. For our own parts we wish to hear it repeated, and we believe we are not singular in the wish. The masterly performance of VIOTTI exceeded all former sample; his power over the instrument seems unlimited. The grand mistake of Musicians has been a continued effort to excite amazement. VIOTTI, it is true, without making that his object, astonishes the hearer; but he does something infinitely better – he awakens emotion, gives a soul to sound, and leads the passions captive. Madame MARA, who sang immediately after he had ended his concerto, was evidently inspired by what she had just heard. – Delighted as we have often been by the exertion of her wonderful talents, if we except in the *Stabat Mater* of PERGOLOSE [*sic*], we never heard her sing in so chaste, so feeling, and so impressive a style before. HAYDN'S new Quartetto was repeated, and was excellently played, especially by SALOMON. The charming andante of the new overture was encored. Both the compositions are truly worthy of HAYDN.   [*Morning Chronicle*, 12 March]

In the Sixth Concert we have an earlier Haydn symphony, unidentifiable as usual, and the first appearance of Marian(n)e Kirchgässner (Kirchgessner), a blind German artist for whom Mozart in 1791 wrote the exquisite Adagio and Rondo (Quintet) for glass harmonica (K. 617), probably the work she gave at Salomon's concert. We append, after the usual (but this time rather dissatisfied) criticism in the *Morning Chronicle*, a little note we found in *The Times* of 1795 which shows that Miss Kirchgässner stayed on in England and collected royal patronage in the form of Haydn's *Gönnerin*, the Duchess of York. Salomon was persuaded to compose a Quartet for her (glass harmonica and three other parts) which she played, as well as with Mozart's Quintet, at a concert in Königsberg on 14 November 1798.[1]

Sixth Concert: 17 March 1794

MR. SALOMON'S CONCERT. HANOVER-SQUARE.

The Subscribers are respectfully acquainted, that the Sixth Performance will be on MONDAY next, the 17th instant.

PART I.
Overture, PIEHL [*i.e.* Pichl];
Song, Mr. FLORIO;
Concerto Violoncello, Mr. DAMEN, jun.
Aria, Madame MARA;
Terzetto, Madame MARA, Mr. FLORIO, and Mr. FISCHER.

PART II.
Grand Overture (M. S.) Haydn;
Aria, Mr. FISCHER;
Quintetto on the [Glass] Harmonica, Mademoiselle KIRASHGESSNER [*sic*],
(being her first appearance in this Ceuntry [*sic*]).
Cavatina, Madame MARA.
FINALE.   [etc.]
[*Oracle*, 15, 17 March;
Morning Chronicle, 15 March; etc.]

In the announcement of this concert in the *Sun* on 15 March, we find Madame Kirchgessner's name spelled correctly and also the following note:

N. B. Numerous applications having been made for Single Tickets at the Door, by the Friends of Subscribers, without any previous intimation by the Subscribers themselves, Mr. SALOMON feels it incumbent upon him, in order to prevent disappointment to his Friends, to assure them, that no Single Tickets can, on any account whatever, be delivered without an application from a Subscriber, either previous to, or on the Morning preceding the Concert, to avoid the Rooms being too much crowded.

SALOMON'S SIXTH CONCERT.

The only novelty of the evening worth mentioning was the performance of Mademoiselle KIRCH GESSNER [*sic*] on the Harmonica. Her taste is chastened, and the dulcet notes of the instrument would be delightful indeed, were they more powerful and articulate; but that we believe the most perfect execution cannot make them. In a smaller room, and an audience less numerous, the effect must be enchanting. Though the accompaniments were kept very much under, they were still occasionally too loud. Madame MARA, in the second act, gave us pleasure; the air is full of expression and pathos, and she sang it with sweetness, taste, and feeling. Yet we own we could wish she would not too often repeat the same songs, however beautiful; especially as she is a thorough musician, and finds no

1 Hermann Güttler, *Königsbergs Musikkultur im 18. Jahrhundert*, Kassel, 1925, p. 177.

impediment from the labour of learning new airs. The Concert altogether was by no means equal to that of the Monday before.   [*Morning Chronicle,*18 March]

SALOMON'S CONCERT. SIXTH NIGHT.

Mademoiselle KIRASHGESSNER [*sic*] performed upon an instrument little known – the *Harmonica*. It is a conic barrel of glass, which she touches with a truth and feeling so soft, so persuasive, that –
> 'Melancholy marks it for her own.'

Of HAYDN – never to be omitted – an Overture (M. S.) was repeated; and the *second* movement, as usual, encored – For *Grace* and *Science*, what is like it?

[*Oracle*, 19 March]

Under the Patronage of Her Royal Highness The Duchess of YORK.

MISS KIRCHGESSNER's Performance on the Grand Harmonica, No. 57, Poland-street, Soho, every day from 1 till 3, and from 7 till 9 o'clock. Admittance 5s. each person. – Miss Kirchgessner respectfully begs leave to acquaint the Nobility, Gentry, and her friends, that she means to discontinue her performance on the above instrument after the 14th inst. She entertains the most flattering hopes that those Amateurs, who are sensible of the superiority which this instrument so decidedly maintains above all others, it being so happily calculated to convey to the heart the most heavenly sensations, will within this short period manifest the encouragement which they very kindly conceive the abilities of Miss K. deserve, and that patronage of which she has had the honour of receiving already the most agreeable marks.   [*The Times*, 8 May, 1795]

On 20 March 1794, Haydn sat for his portrait to George Dance, who had made a brilliant speciality of profile drawings touched up with red chalk. Acquaintance grew into friendship, and Dance took Haydn to meet many of the artist's friends. Haydn thought Dance's portrait the best of a great many done in England, but it was not engraved until Daniell brought out an accurate print in 1809. The dated drawing is in the Royal College of Music (London), an undated one is in the Haydn Museum (Vienna) and a third version in mirror, is owned by Mr. Edward Croft-Murray, Richmond, England.

On 21 March, Haydn presided at the annual benefit concert of the Misses Abrams, in which it would appear that one of the earlier (or even printed) Haydn symphonies was performed. At the Seventh Concert, another new Haydn Quartet from Opp. 71 or 74 was first performed, and one of the 1791–2 symphonies. Notice, in the *Morning Chronicle*'s report, that Fischer displayed the whole range of his voice (*vide supra*).

HANOVER-SQUARE. MISS ABRAMS' CONCERT.

THIS EVENING, FRIDAY 21, will be performed a Grand Concert of VOCAL AND INSTRUMENTAL MUSIC.

Act I. – Overture, Rosetti. – Glee, Webbe. – Aria, Signor Rovedino. – Sonata Pedal Harp, Madame Grandjean, (being her first appearance in public). – Quartetto, Mr. Nield and the Miss Abrams. – Tarchi. Concerto Piano Forte, Mr. J. B. Cramer – Cramer.

Act II. Grand Overture, Haydn. – Scena, Mr. Nield, Paesiello [*sic*]. – Quartetto, Haydn. – Scena, Madame Ducrest, Piccini. – Finale Chacone, Fiorillo.
Leader of the Band, Mr. Salomon. Dr. Haydn, will precide [*sic*] at the Piano Forte.
[etc.]

[*Morning Chronicle*, 21 March]

Seventh Concert: 24 March 1794

MR. SALOMON'S CONCERT. HANOVER-SQUARE.

The SUBSCRIBERS are respectfully acquainted, that the Seventh Performance will be on MONDAY next, the 24th instant.

PART I.

Overture, Gyrovetz[*sic*]:
Aria, Mrs. HINDMARSH.
CONCERTANTE [Clarinet, Mr. HARTMAN].
Duetto, Mrs. HINDMARSH and Mr. FISCHER;
NEW QUARTETTO, M. S. HAYDN;
for 2 Violins, Viola, and Violoncello, by[1]
Messrs. SALOMON, DAMEN, FIORILLO, and DAMEN, jun.
Scena, Madame MARA.

PART II.

Grand Overture, M. S. HAYDN;
Aria, Mr. FISCHER:
Concerto Violin, Signor VIOTTI;
Cavatina, Madame MARA.
FINALE.   [etc.]

[*Oracle*, 22, 24 March;
Morning Chronicle, 22, 24 March; etc.]

SALOMON'S SEVENTH CONCERT.

The weekly pleasures of the Hanover-Square Rooms were repeated on Monday evening with increasing vigour. FISCHER, by being more accustomed to his audience, gains more confidence, and nightly improves. He is an excellent musician, and his voice is astonishing both in body and compass. He produced a full fair sound on double D, and touched A. in alt. Madame MARA well deserved, and obtained her accustomed applause. Mr. HARTMAN, on the clarinet, was favourably received. Sweetness of tone has been his principle [*sic*] study, and this he has very effectually attained. But musicians who aspire after excellence should never forget that if they want passion, the defect cannot be compensated by any other excellence, however great. VIOTTI again produced the rapturous sensations; he indeed possesses not only sweetness, vigour, and every variety that the bow and the finger seem capable of affording, but he adds the grand ingredient, soul, without which music is either insipidity, trick, or noise. We mention HAYDN last, because among unrivalled excellence itself, he is still supreme: and to SALOMON's praise be it spoken, no man perhaps studies him more ardently, and we may say affectionately. The new Quartet abounded with beauties, and the imagination of SALOMON while playing it, gave continued delight. The Andante Movement of the Overture, was universally encored; and the applause to every movement of it was loud, sincere, and heartfelt.   [*Morning Chronicle,* 26 March]

One day after Salomon's Seventh Concert, the correspondent of the *Journal des Luxus und der Moden* dispatched another report to Weimar, entitled 'On the Present State of Fashion and Music in England', which appeared in July. After praising Salomon for his efforts to foster the best music and artists, and especially for his execution of the quartets of 'our old favourite, Haydn', the article continues:

But what would you now say to his new symphonies composed expressly for these concerts, and directed by himself at the piano? It is truly wonderful what

1 The *Oracle* of 22 March reads, in this line: 'Viola, for 2 Violins Violoncello, Messrs. Salomon. . . .'

sublime and august thoughts this master weaves into his works. Passages often occur which render it impossible to listen to them without becoming excited. We are altogether carried away by admiration, and forced to applaud with hand and mouth. This is especially the case with Frenchmen, of whom we have so many here that all public places are filled with them. You know that they have great sensibility, and cannot restrain their transports, so that in the midst of the finest passages in soft adagios they clap their hands in loud applause and thus mar the effect. In every symphony of Haydn the adagio or andante is sure to be repeated each time, after the most vehement encores. The worthy Haydn, whose personal acquaintance I highly value, conducts himself on these occasions in the most modest manner. He is indeed a good-hearted, candid, honest man, esteemed and beloved by all. [Translation from Hadden, pp. 116f.]

In the Eighth Concert, Haydn conducted the first performance of the third of his new symphonies, No. 100 in G, 'The Military' which, as the criticisms were soon to show, would be the greatest success of his whole career, surpassing even the popularity of 'The Surprise': he had somehow caught the spirit of the day in a miraculous way.

Eighth Concert: 31 March 1794

HANOVER-SQUARE. MR. SALOMON'S CONCERT.

The SUBSCRIBERS are respectfully acquainted, that the Eighth Performance will be on Monday next, the 31st instant.

PART I.
Overture, PLEYEL;
Aria, Mr. FISCHER;
(By desire) The New Quartetto, (M. S.) HAYDN;
which was performed last Monday.
Two Violins, Viola, Violoncello, Messrs. SALOMON, DAMER [*sic*],
FIORILLO, and DAMER [*sic*], jun.
Scena, Madame MARA.
Concerto, Pedal Harp, Madame DELAVEL [*sic*].

PART II.
New Grand Overture, M. S. HAYDN;
Aria, Mr. FISCHER;
Concerto Violin, Signor VIOTTI;
Rondo, Madame MARA.
FINALE. [etc.]
[*Oracle*, 29, 31 March;
Morning Chronicle, 31 March; etc.]

Ninth Concert: 7 April 1794

HANOVER-SQUARE. MR. SALOMON'S CONCERT.

The SUBSCRIBERS are respectfully acquainted, that the Ninth Performance will be on MONDAY next, the 7th April.

PART I.
New Overture (M. S.) REICHARDS [i. e. Reichardt].
Aria, Mr. FISCHER;
Concertante for Clarinet and Bassoon, Messrs.
HARTMAN and PARKINSON.
Scena, Madame MARA.
Sonata on the harmonica, M. KIRCHGESSNER.

PART II.
The New Grand Overture, (M. S.) HAYDN,
which was performed last Monday.
Cavatina, Mr. FISCHER;
Concerto, Violin, Signor VIOTTI.
Rondo, Madame MARA.
FINALE.   [etc.]
[*Oracle*, 5 April;
Morning Chronicle, 5, 7 April; etc.]

SALOMON'S NINTH CONCERT.

Though under the necessity of repeating the same names (for where are their equals?) and the same praises, which never sufficiently express the delicious sensations that these Performers at some moments excite, yet to be silent would be flagrant injustice. What we have on former occasions so ardently spoken, particularly of those first of Performers Mara and Viotti, is again their due, and more if we had it to bestow. Some of the conoisseurs profess to like the playing of Viotti better than his Music. – Judgments differ; we will not pretend to affirm they are mistaken; we can only say, though his Compositions partake of the Old French School, there is yet a richness, unity and grandeur in them, that in our opinion place them far beyond the jigs, quirks and quackery, in which modern music is so apt to indulge. Not that we are the enemies of modern music: it has many essential improvements, but it has no few radical vices. Another new Symphony, by Haydn, was performed for the second time; and the middle movement was again received with absolute shouts of applause. Encore! encore! encore! resounded from every seat: the Ladies themselves could not forbear. It is the advancing to battle; and the march of men, the sounding of the charge, the thundering of the onset, the clash of arms, the groans of the wounded, and what may well be called the hellish roar of war increase to a climax of horrid sublimity! which, if others can conceive, he alone can execute; at least he alone hitherto has effected these wonders.   [*Morning Chronicle*, 9 April]

The review obviously refers to bars 152ff. of the *Allegretto*; the 'climax of horrid sublimity' describes the ominous kettledrum roll (bars 159f.) and the ensuing tutti (bar 161).

While on the subject of kettledrums, there is an amusing anecdote by George Smart on the subject of Haydn and the timpani:

In the year 1794 Haydn came to London for the second time, his first having been in 1790 [*recte* 1791], to conduct his twelve grand symphonies for Salomon's concerts. He conducted some of Salomon's concerts in the Hanover Square Rooms. At that time, and in 1794, the orchestra was at the other end of the room, where the royal gallery now is. This change was made when the 'Antient Concerts' were removed from the Tottenham Street Rooms to those at Hanover Square.

At a rehearsal for one of these concerts the kettle drummer was not in attendance. Haydn asked, 'Can no one in the orchestra play the drums?' I replied immediately, 'I can.' 'Do so,' said he. I, foolishly, thought it was only necessary to beat in strict time, and that I could do so. Haydn came to me at the top of the orchestra, praised my beating in time, but observed upon my bringing the drumstick straight down, instead of giving an oblique stroke, and keeping it too long upon the drum, consequently stopping its vibration. 'The drummers in Germany,' he said, 'have a way of using the drumsticks so as not to stop the vibration' – at the same time showing me how this was done. 'Oh, very well,' I replied, 'we can do so in England, if you prefer it.' It was Haydn, therefore, who first taught me to play the drums, a thing I had never attempted before that day, and have not done often since.

At these concerts I used to play the violin or viola at half a guinea per concert. Garabaldi, a celebrated double-bass player, taught me the violin. Many foreigners were employed by Salomon at these concerts at very low salaries. At the rehearsals most of the professors wore their great coats only, I suppose in order to save their other coats for the performances.   [Smart, 3]

The British public went on cheering Haydn's 'Grand Military Overture (M.S.)' for years. When Salomon performed it on 5 May 1796, the *Morning Chronicle* (9 May) reported, 'We cannot describe the agitation excited through the room by the Grand Military Overture of HAYDN, nor the universal eagerness with which the second movement was encored', while *The Times* (also 9 May) seconded the opinion, saying the work 'was received with the most rapturous applause, and encored by a full and fashionable audience.' Even in 1798, when the Symphony was given at the Opera Concert on 12 March, we find, the next day, the *Morning Chronicle* saying that 'the second movement . . ., in point of grandeur of effect, is truly electrical. It was repeated at the unanimous call of the audience.'

Provincial concerts in England were soon copying the Haydn-Salomon programmes of which one of the specialities was to place a 'new' Haydn symphony at the beginning of the second half. The *Sun*, on 9 April 1794, carries an announcement of a concert given by Mr. Sibly in the Assembly Room at Portsmouth on the 14th, conducted by Joseph Mountain, where Part II began with a 'Grand Sinfonie – HAYDN'.

In April, Master Julien Baux, aged five and a half, gave a concert in the Lyceum, Strand, which included a violin concerto of Giornovichj played by Baux. Later he gave a concert under the protection of the Duke and Duchess of York with symphonies by Haydn, Mozart and the 'Hunting-Symphony' by Stamitz, Baux playing concertos by Giornovichj and Viotti. The exact dates and programmes cannot be discovered (Pohl, *H in L*, 243f.). The *Sun*, on 20 May 1794, contains a short praiseworthy note on Master Baux.

A few days before the Tenth Concert, the famous Brigida Giorgi Banti, a great dramatic soprano, made her sensationally successful London début in the title role of *Semiramide* by Francesco Bianchi (Da Ponte, 259). There were now two equally famous *prime donne* at the London opera, the other being Anna Morichelli. We shall examine their voices and characters later in this Chronicle, when they have to do with Haydn. On 2 May, the devious Vincenzo Federici wrote off a report about both to an unknown correspondent.[1]

A. C.

Londra 2. Maggio 1794

In replica a varie gm^e [gradevolissime] vr^e [vostre] devo dirvi che non ò [ho] mancato di consegnare tutte le acclusemi alla Sig:^ra Morichelli; La medesima unitam^e alla Banti giunsero quì felicemente dopo un pericolosissimo viaggio.

La Banti à [ha] di già debuttato unitamente a Rosselli con grande applauso, sebbene la sudd:^a trovasse molto incommodata dal raffredore. La Morichelli debutterà la settimana ventura, e non dubito che anch'essa farà il più gravi piacere.

---

1 *Katalog der Ausstellung anlässlich der Centenarfeier Domenico Cimarosa's*, Vienna 1901, p. 78. Then in possession of Herr Angelo von Eisner-Eisenhof, the letter is now in the library of La Scala, Milan, from which institution we received a photograph.

Toccante gl'affari nulla posso dirvi per anche di positivo tanto per i Cantanti, che Ballerini. Ò [Ho] onorato le vostre Cambiali, e vi rendo grazie di quanto vi siete compiacciuto di fare per me. Ò [Ho] ricevuto le due Spartiti che mi inviaste col Sig° Robert Herrier, e la Cambiale di £12. – sarà pagata in scadenza.

Devo nuovamente incomodarvi perchè mi facciate il piaccre di spedire a vista Zecchini dodici effettivi a Pesaro diretti al solito Sig:ʳ Abate Teodoro Giommi Segretario d'Udienza, poiche ò [ho] somma necessità che tale somma pervenga al più presto alle di lui mani; Rivaletevene immediatemente sopra di me a giorni dieci vista, Intanto commandatemi dove posso e credetemi constantamente

N°. 15 Fludyer Street   Vr° [Vostro] Affmo⁻ Ser:° ed A. [Amico]
Westminster   V. Federici[1]

The letter is graphic evidence of the clannishness and intricate financial dealings that went on between the Italians in London and the home country. It was a world of its own, closed tightly to outsiders in general and especially to *compositori tedeschi* like Giuseppe Haydn. . . .

On 25 April 1794 the *Sun* carries a review of the Academy of Ancient (rather than 'Antient') Music at Free-Masons' Hall, from which we learn that this year Salomon conducted the series and that, moreover, he had managed to introduce Haydn's music in the programmes – no mean feat, since the Society had hitherto allowed only the music of long dead composers. '. . . The Instrumental Pieces were chiefly from HANDEL and HAYDN. . . . SALOMON has conducted himself most admirably as the Leader. . . .'

Tenth Concert: 28 April 1794

MR. SALOMON'S CONCERT, HANOVER-SQUARE.

MR. SALOMON most respectfully acquaints the Subscribers, that the Tenth Performance will be on MONDAY next, the 28th Inst.

PART I.
Grand Overture, (M. S.) HAYDN.
Aria, Mr. FISCHER;
New Quintetto for 2 Violins, 2 Violas, and a Violoncello,
Messrs. SALOMON, J. DAHMEN, FIORILLO, and WRANIEZKY [*sic*].
Scena, Madame MARA.
Double Concerto for 2 Principal French Horns, Messrs.
W. DAHMEN and ZONCADA;
(Being their first performance in this Country.)

PART II.
Grand Overture (M. S.) HAYDN;
Scena, Mr. FISCHER.
Concerto Piano Forte, Mr. DUSSECK;
Rondo, Madame MARA.
FINALE

[etc.]
[*Oracle*, 26 April; *Morning Chronicle*, 26, 28 April, etc.]

1 [Summary: 'Thanks the recipient for various letters and assures him that he has delivered the enclosures to Mad. Morichelli who, together with Banti, arrived safely after a most dangerous voyage. Banti has had her début together with Rosselli and was a great success, despite a bad cold. Morichelli will have her début next week. Concerning business, he writes concerning various bills of exchange [*cambiali*] which he has paid, also about engaging singers and ballerini. Thanks for the two scores sent through Robert Herrier. Requests the recipient to pay at once twelve *zecchini* to Abbé Teodoro Giommi, Pesaro.']

SALOMON'S TENTH CONCERT.

The novelties of Monday evening were Miss Parke instead of Madame Mara, a quintetto composed by Wraniczky [*sic*], and Messieurs Dahmen and Zoncada, two famous performers on the French horn. The quintet was of the best kind of pleasing common place. Miss Parke improves rapidly; and if her efforts continue, she will become an honour to the divine art she professes; especially as she evidently studies passion, and prefers it to that tinsel, mechanical execution, which repetition soon renders disgusting. Messrs. Dahmen and Zoncada surprised the auditors; and are capable of surprising still more, by producing an echo that deceives the ear, and leads it to suppose the sound comes from a vast distance. This wonderful effect they have reserved for their next performance. Fischer sung in his best and most decided manner. Dusseck played a concerto, the first movement of which abounded in the usual mad flights of the master; the two last were charming, especially the allegro, because of its originality. The overture of Haydn was worthy its sublime and unequalled author: we cannot say more.

[*Morning Chronicle*, 30 April]

The 'pleasing common place' – the Wranizky Quintet – was misprinted on the programme announcement, which led people to think the work was Haydn's. We shall see, in the Eleventh Concert, a Quintet in MS. by Haydn, which has been identified (Pohl, *H in L*, 268) as the spurious work published by André as Joseph Haydn Opus 99 but which is actually by Michael Haydn.

The 'Double Concerto for 2 Principal French Horns' cannot be identified; the word 'Principal' means for a first-horn player (high) rather than second-horn (one even finds eighteenth-century MSS. entitled 'Concerto per il corno secondo'). The two Haydn symphonies were apparently 'old' ones from the 1791–2 seasons.

On 2 May 1794, Haydn gave his benefit concert. There were initial announcements in the newspapers from 19 April ('. . . particulars . . . in due time'). The final announcement reads as follows

HANOVER-SQUARE.

DR. HAYDN most respectfully acquaints the Nobility and Gentry, that his BENEFIT CONCERT will be THIS DAY, the 2d of May Instant.

Part I.
Grand Overture (M. S.) Haydn. Aria, Mr. Fischer. Concerto, Piano Forte, Mr. Dusseck. Scena, Miss Parke.

Part II.
By Desire, the Grand Overture (M. S.) with the Militaire Movement, as performed at Mr. Salomon's Concert, Haydn. Scena, Mr. Fischer. Concerto Violin, Signor Viotti. Aria, Miss Parke.
FINALE, HAYDN.

Tickets, at 10s 6d each, to be had of Dr. Haydn, No. 1, Bury-street, St. James; Messrs. Longman and Broderip, Cheapside and Haymarket; Bland, 45 Holborn; Mr. Williams, Hanover-square rooms. . . .

[*Morning Chronicle*, 2 May; *Oracle*, 1 May; etc.]

HAYDN'S BENEFIT.

Was on Friday last at the Hanover-square Rooms. The Company was numerous and splendid. His grand and most admirable military movement produced its full effect, and every auditor seemed delighted to contribute to do honour to this great man. We cannot help remarking, that the cymbals introduced in the military movement, though they there produce a fine effect, are in themselves discordant, grating, and offensive, and ought not to have been introduced, either in the last movement of that Overture, or in the Finale at the close of the Concert. The reason of the great effect they produce in the military movement is that they mark and tell the story: they inform us that the army is marching to battle, and, calling up all the ideas of the terror of such a scene, give it reality. Discordant sounds are then sublime; for what can be more horribly discordant to the heart than thousands of men meeting to murder each other.

[Morning Chronicle, 5 May]

The first Symphony MS. was probably the popular No. 101, the second one was, of course, No. 100 'with the Militaire Movement'. The reviewer for the *Morning Chronicle* had a jaundiced eye about the extra percussion players, for in 1798 the same writer (or so the style would seem to suggest) complained that in the twelfth and last Opera Concert that 'the *Drummer* and *Cymbol-player* [*sic*], who are principal actors in the piece, instead of *beating*, most cruelly *murdered* the time'. (12 June 1798.) Perhaps these 'extra' players were not always the best.

At the Eleventh Concert, Messrs. Dahmen and Zoncada probably played Anton Zimmermann's *Sinfonia Echo* in E flat. The British Museum owns (Add. 31710) some MS. music (watermarks 1794 to 1805) which is said to have come from the Salomon concerts and is listed as Haydn. The 'Echo' Symphony is contained in the music but the score does not list Haydn's name on the title page (Landon, *SYM*, 814, No. 86; Hoboken I, 256, Es15). Zimmermann was a gifted composer in the service of Cardinal Batthianyi in Pressburg.

Eleventh Concert: 5 May 1794

MR. SALOMON'S CONCERT, HANOVER-SQUARE.

The SUBSCRIBERS are most respectfully acquainted, that the Eleventh Performance will be THIS EVENING, MONDAY, May 5.

PART I

Grand Overture, (M. S.) HAYDN.

Aria, Mr. NIELD.

New Quintetto, M. S. HAYDN.

Scena, Miss PARKE.

Duetto French Horns, Messrs. W. DAHMEN and ZONCADA.

PART II

Grand Overture (M. S.) HAYDN;

Aria, Mr. FISCHER;

Concerto Violin, Signor VIOTTI.

Terzet[t]o, Miss PARKE, MR. NIELD, and Mr. FISCHER.

FINALE.

[etc.]
[Oracle, 5 May, Morning
Chronicle, 5 May; etc.]

SALOMON'S ELEVENTH CONCERT.

Miss PARKE who had before given so much pleasure, sang with no less approbation and effect. The performers on the French-horn answered the expectations that had been formed of them. The echo they produce is a very pleasing deception, and is of the same kind as the art of the ventriloquist, which wholly consists in a calculation of the distance of sounds. Fischer was in full voice, and at each descending note the Audience could not but enquire, What! deeper yet? Viotti played in a grand and impressive style: – he is, indeed, a most finished and masterly performer. The overture of the second act was the favourite one two years ago, and was heard again with infinite delight: the last movement was encored.

[*Morning Chronicle*, 7 May]

The second Haydn symphony seems to have been No. 98 in B flat with the keyboard solo in the Finale which had always been encored in the 1792 season and which was encored on 5 May 1794.

Twelfth Concert: 12 May 1794

MR. SALOMON'S CONCERT, HANOVER-SQUARE.

The SUBSCRIBERS are respectfully acquainted, that the Twelfth and Last SUBSCRIPTION CONCERT for this Season, will be on MONDAY next, May 12.

PART I.

Grand Overture, (M. S.) HAYDN.

Aria, Mr. NIELD.

Concerto, Piano Forte, Mr. BERTIM [*sic*].[1]

Scena, Miss PARKE.

CONCERTANTE FOR VIOLIN, VIOLONCELLO, OBOE, FLUTE,

AND BASSO[o]n, Obligato, GYROVETZ [*sic*].[1]

PART II.

The Grand Overture (M. S.) HAYDN; with the

Militaire Movement.

Aria, Mr. FISCHER;

Duo, (M. S.) for Two Violins, Messrs. VIOTTI and SALOMON.

Rondo, Miss PARKE;

FINALE – HAYDN.

Mr. Salomon is extremely sorry, that Madame Mara's indisposition still continuing, prevents her from fulfilling her engagement to perform at the Concert. . . .   [*Oracle*, 10 May; *Morning Chronicle*, 10, 12 May; etc.]

On 8 May 1794, Wilhelm Cramer's benefit concert at the King's Theatre began with a Haydn 'Overture' (*Morning Herald*, 7 May 1794). While on the subject of such benefits, we might mention Harrison's concert at the 'New Grand Concert Room' in the Opera House on 16 May, with the almost obligatory 'Grand Overture' by Haydn (*Morning Herald*, 14 May).

Salomon's last concert of the season took place on 12 May, and from the criticisms, it is clear that men in London realized more than ever before that these concerts were continually creating musical history; and it must have occurred to more than one astute mind, such as Dr Burney's or Shield's, that these great Haydn symphonies were in fact entering the permanent repertoire with the first night of their respective débûts. Haydn had been persuaded to remain another season, and this fact was apparently announced to the no-doubt delighted audience on 12 May. With Prince Anton Esterházy dead, there was no reason to return and despite his little house in Gumpendorf, Haydn may have been once more seriously contemplating the taking up of residence in a country which was so fond of him and so richly rewarded the products of his fertile pen.

As far as the *Oracle* criticism is concerned, it is not clear to whom the writer refers; probably one of the singers.

1 In the *Sun* for 10 May these names are spelled correctly, viz. BERTINI and GYROWETZ.

SALOMON has had a brilliant season, notwithstanding the *caprice* consequent upon one of his engagements. N. B. This does *not* refer to MARA – she is always ready like BANTI, whatever be her illness.

[Oracle, 13 May]

SALOMON'S CONCERT.

Closed on Monday with no less eclat than it has been continued through the season. A young boy, the son of an Italian named BERTINI, played a concerto of his own composing that evinced a very uncommon maturity of genius. It had indeed been corrected by the famous CLEMENTI, whose scholar young BERTINI is; but both the music and the playing were, for so young a student, far beyond expectation. In addition to a brilliant finger, and good taste, he began his sentences with the accuracy and decision of a master. VIOTTI and SALOMON played a violin duet in a very bold and finished style. Two of the immortal HAYDN's overtures were performed, and were listened to with enthusiasm and rapture. The company were informed that the concerts are to be continued the next season, with some variation but on an equally grand scale; and we cannot take our leave of this concert without declaring it to be our opinion, and the opinion of every impartial musical judge, that the spirit, precision, and genius, that have been displayed at it are worthy of all the favour, fashion, and protection, the public can bestow. To the leader, Mr. SALOMON, the nation is indebted not only for his own excellent performances, but for the bringing forward of excellence at any expense wherever he could procure it, at home or abroad; and above all for having prevailed on the inimitable HAYDN to visit and compose for this country.

[Morning Chronicle, 15 May]

HANOVER-SQUARE.

MR. SALOMON begs leave to present his most sincere acknowledgements to the Nobility and Gentry, for the very great Approbation they have bestowed upon his Concerts; and has the Satisfaction to acquaint them that being honoured with the additional Patronage of the most distinguished Personages, for the next year, they will be continued on a Scale equally grand, but upon a new Plan, which, from the Sanction it has already received, Mr. SALOMON flatters himself will meet with general Encouragement.

Mr. SALOMON'S BENEFIT is fixed for WEDNESDAY the 28th Instant.

[Oracle, 14 May; Morning
Chronicle, 14 May; etc.]

The end of the 1794 season was crowded with events: benefit concerts in which Haydn's name almost invariably appears and at which he occasionally 'presided' at the keyboard. First there was Felice Yaniewicz's benefit:

HANOVER-SQUARE.

MR. YANIEWICZ most respectfully acquaints the Nobility and Gentry, that his BENEFIT CONCERT will be THIS EVENING, WEDNESDAY, the 14th of May Inst.

PART I.

OVERTURE.

Song, Mr. HUTTENES.

New Concerto Violin, Mr. YANIEWICZ.

Song, Miss PARKE.

Concertante for two French Horns, Messrs.

DAHMEN and ZONCADA.

PART II.
Overture, HAYDN.
SONG, MR. HUTTENES.
Concerto Piano Forte, Mr. DUSSECK.
Song, Miss PARKE.
Solo Violin, Mr. YANIEWICZ.
Full Piece.

[etc.]
[*Oracle*, 14 May; *Morning Chronicle*, 12, 14 May; etc.]

On 17 May, there was a brief encounter between Lorenzo Da Ponte and Haydn. It happened that Da Ponte revived his old opera, *Il burbero di buon cuore* (the music by Mozart's former rival, Vicente Martin y Soler [Solar], whose biggest success in Vienna had been *Una cosa rara*), fashioned after Goldoni for the Vienna Opera in 1786. *Il burbero*, adapted and refurbished with some new numbers, was offered to the London public on 17 May 1794. One of the 'new' numbers was the Duet, 'Quel tuo visetto amabile' (between Eurilla and Pasquale) from Haydn's *Orlando Paladino* of 1782; there was also additional material by Vittorio Trento and G. G. Ferrari. Of course, it is possible that Da Ponte got hold of the music from *Orlando Paladino* elsewhere, and it is interesting that Haydn's name never appears once in the *Memoirs*. The Duet was already popular outside the opera. There was a Torricella print of it (copy in the Library of Congress, Washington), and a copy in MS., now in the Conservatoire at Paris, bears the title Teatro S. Moisè, Venice, 1794 (coincidence?). But there is some evidence that Haydn did supply Da Ponte with a copy, because, with Da Ponte's new words ('Quel cor umano e tenero'), it was printed by Haydn's friends, Corri & Dussek, and the composer took back a copy of the print to Austria. We shall see, moreover, that he played the work in his great benefit concert of 1795. The opera itself was not received with particular marks of satisfaction, but the *Oracle* wrote '. . . Of the music, what was in the best possible style was a Duo between Morelli and Morichelli, written by the excellent Haydn.'[1]

It will also have pleased Haydn to have two of the best singers in London interpreting his music. Morelli had participated in Gallini's 'Entertainments' in 1791, singing *inter alia* 'Non più andrai' from *Le nozze di Figaro* in which, said the *Morning Chronicle*, 'though always excellent, [he] was finer than we ever heard him.' Anna Morichelli, thought Da Ponte (252), 'gave a performance that was true, noble, carefully worked, and full of expression and grace', though as a person he loathed her ('Pride, Envy, Money'). She was a great actress, too, and Parke (I, 183) wrote of her that 'both in singing and acting, [she] was admirable, and was greatly applauded.' And so Haydn and Da Ponte are united, for the first and last time, on a three-shilling piece of music published in London in 1794:

'Quel cor umano e tenero / Duetto / Sung by Sg^r Morelli, & Sig^{ra} Morichelli / At the King's Theatre, Haymarket, / In the Opera of / Il Burbero Di Buon Cuore / with an Accompaniment for the Piano Forte / Composed by / Dr Haydn. / The Words by Sig Da Ponte / Ent^d at Stationers Hall Pr. 3^s / Printed for Corri Dussek & Co Music Sellers to her Majesty. No. 67 Dean Street, Soho. . . .'
[From Haydn's own copy, now in the Esterházy Archives of the Budapest National Library, Z 41.611]

1 Alfred Loewenberg: 'Lorenzo Da Ponte in London. A Bibliographical Account of His Literary Activity' in *Music Review* IV/3, August 1943, pp. 177f.

On 19 May, Miss Parke, whom Haydn seemed to like, gave her benefit concert and the composer presided at the pianoforte:

HANOVER-SQUARE.

MISS PARKE respectfully informs the NOBILITY and GENTRY, That HER CONCERT, will be on MONDAY NEXT the 19th instant, at the above ROOMS.

Under the Direction of Mr. CRAMER.

Doctor HAYDN will preside at the PIANO-FORTE.

ACT I.

Overture, HAYDN – Song, Mr. NIELD.

Concerto Violoncello, Mr. LIN[D]LEY – Song, Miss PARKE.

CONCERTANTE (1st Time, M.S.), Violin, Tenor, and Hautboy, by

Messrs. CRAMER, MOUNTAIN, and PARKE – PLEYEL.

Terzetto (1st time), Mr. FISCHER, Mr. NIELD, and Miss PARKE

– PICCINI.

ACT II.

Grand Overture, M.S. PLEYEL. Song, Mr. FISCHER.

Sonata, Piano-Forte, Miss PARKE. Song Miss PARKE.

FINALE.

[etc.]

[*Oracle*, 14 May; *Morning Chronicle*, 15 May, etc.]

Miss Parke's concert was reviewed in the *Morning Herald* on 22 May 1794, and the paper said it 'was honoured by a very distinguished company. It was the most brilliant assemblage of female fashion any public rooms have displayed through the season, an elegant tribute to the highly cultivated talents, so decorously blended with private worth. The compositions of the evening were highly beautiful, and the selection was made with taste and judgement. It opened with one of HAYDN's Overtures; and in the *Instrumental* pieces we must mention PLEYEL with particular praise . . .'.

It will be noticed that the leader was none other than Wilhelm Cramer, the former leader of the Professional Concert. In fact Haydn was not a man to bear grudges, and he must have been interested to play with another distinguished leader, just as he was glad to play with the great Viotti in 1795. Actually Salomon could not have played that night, because he was elsewhere engaged:

WILLIS'S ROOMS, KING-STREET, ST. JAMES'S.

MESSRS. SALE and BELLAMY, Jun. respectfully acquaint the Nobility and Gentry, that their CONCERT will be on MONDAY next, the 19th of May Inst. at the above Rooms.

Leader of the Band, Mr. SALOMON.

Mr. GREATOREX will preside at the Piano Forte.

[A Haydn 'Overture' and 'Full Piece' were played.]

[*Oracle* and *Morning Chronicle*, 14 May]

On 23 May, Viotti gave his benefit, and Salomon was generous enough to let his distinguished rival open each part with a MS. Haydn symphony:

HANOVER-SQUARE. For the BENEFIT of Mr. VIOTTI.

TO-MORROW, May 23, will be a GRAND CONCERT of VOCAL and INSTRUMENTAL MUSIC.

PART I.

Grand Overture (M. S.) – HAYDN.

Aria, Mr. NIELD.

New Concerto Violin, Signor VIOTTI.
Aria, Mr. FISCHER.
Concerto, Piano Forte, Mr. DUSSECK.

PART II.
Grand Overture (M. S.) – HAYDN.
Scena, Madame DU CREST.
New Concerto Violin, Signor VIOTTI.
Terzetto, Madame DUCREST, Mr. NIELD, and Mr. FISCHER.
Finale.

[etc.]
[*Oracle*, 22 May; etc.]

On 23 May 1794, Mr Lee's benefit concert was announced for that evening in the *Morning Herald*, with a programme including two 'Overtures' by Haydn; Haydn would also be included in Mr Lee's benefit concert of 25 May 1795 (*vide infra*).

For his friend Barthelemon, Haydn conducted only his own symphony; (he tended, now, to do that rather than conduct the whole concert). But for Salomon's benefit, Viotti led and Haydn presided the whole time at the pianoforte. Here are four benefit evenings in which Haydn participated:

(I)

HANOVER-SQUARE.
Under the Patronage of his Royal Highness THE PRINCE OF WALES.
MR. BARTHELEMON'S CONCERT will be THIS EVENING, MONDAY the 26th Instant.

ACT I.
Overture, HAYDN.
Song, Mr. BARTLEMAN.
Duetto, for Violin and Tenor, by Master FURTADO,
(being his first appearance in Public) and Mr. BARTHELEMON,
STAMITZ.
Concerto Violoncello, Mr. F. ATTWOOD.
Song, Miss PARKE.
Concerto Violin, Mr. BRIDGETOWER, (Pupil of Mr. BARTHELEMON).
VIOTTI.

ACT II.
Overture, at which Dr. HAYDN will preside at the Piano Forte.
HAYDN.
Concerto, Piano Forte, BERTINI.
Song, Mrs. BARTHELEMON.
New Solo Violin, Mr. BARTHELEMON.
Finale

[etc.]
[*Oracle* and *Morning Chronicle*, 26 May; etc.]

Following the concert, we find this note printed in the *Morning Herald* of 29 May 1794:

Mr. BARTHELEMON begs leave to express his grateful acknowledgements to the Nobility, Gentry, and his friends who did him the honour to attend his Concert at Hanover-square on Monday evening. Also returns his sincerest thanks to Dr. Haydn, Messrs. Salomon, Clemente [*sic*], all the Gentlemen of the Opera Band, and the other Gentleman Professors, Mr. Bartleman and Miss Parke, for their kind exertions on the occasion.

(II)

HANOVER-SQUARE.
For the BENEFIT of Mr. SALOMON.
THIS EVENING, the 28th of May, will be a GRAND CONCERT of VOCAL and INSTRUMENTAL MUSIC.

Part I. Grand Overture, (MS.) Haydn. Aria, Mr. Nield. Solo Violin, Mr. Salomon. Scena, Miss Parke. Grand Concertante.

Part II. Grand Overture, (MS.) Haydn, with the Military Movement. Aria, Mr. Fischer. Concerto Violin, Mr. Salomon. Terzetto, Miss Parke, Mr. Nield, and Mr. Fischer. Finale, Haydn.
Leader of the Band Signor VIOTTI.
Dr. HAYDN will be at the Piano Forte . . .

> [*Oracle*, 28 May; *Times*, 26 May;
> *Morning Chronicle*, 26, 28 May; etc.]

(III)

NEW SUBSCRIPTION ROOM, KING'S THEATRE.
For the Benefit of Mr. GIORNOVICHI.
THIS PRESENT FRIDAY, May the 30th, 1794, will be A GRAND CONCERT.
Leader of the Band Mr. CRAMER.

Act I. Overture, HAYDN. Song, Signor MORELLI. Concerto Violoncello, Mr. SCHRAM. Song, Madame DUCREST. Concertante for Flute, Hautboy, French Horn and Bassoon by Messrs. MONZANI, BEZOZZI, LEANDER, and HOLM[E]s. Devienne. Concerto Violin, Mr. GIORNOVICHI.

Act II.
Concerto Hautboy, Signor BEZOZZI. Song, Signora BANTI. Concerto Piano Forte, Mr. DUSSECK. Song, Signor MORELLI. Concerto Violin, Mr. GIORNOVICHI. Full Piece.   [etc.]

> [*Oracle*, 30 May; *Morning Chronicle*, 28 May; etc.]

(IV)

HANOVER-SQUARE. For the BENEFIT of Mr. FISCHER.
THIS EVENING will be performed a Grand Concert of VOCAL and INSTRUMENTAL MUSIC.

Part I. Grand Overture, (MS.) Haydn. Aria, Mr. Fischer. Quartetto for Flute, Violin, Viola and Violoncello Obligati. Scena, Miss Parke. Concerto Piano Forte, Mr. Dusseck.

Part II. The Favourite Grand Overture, (MS.) Haydn. with the Militaire Movement, (for the last time this season). Scena, Mr. Fischer. Grand Concertante, (MS.) for Violin, Violoncello, Oboe and Bassoon, Obligato, Messrs. Salomon, Dahmen, Jun.[,] Harrington, Macintosch. Haydn. Romance, Mr. Fischer. Duetto, Miss Parke and Mr. Fischer. Finale, Haydn.
Leader of the Band, Mr. Salomon . . .   [*Morning Chronicle*, 2 June]

On 3 June 1794, the *Sun* carried an advertisement by Corri, Dussek & Co.:

DR. HAYDN
Just published,
SIX ORIGINAL CANZONETTAS, with an Accompaniment for the Piano Forte, price 7s. 6d. to be had at the Author's, No. 1, Bury-street, St. James's, and Messrs. Corri, Dussek and Co. Music Sellers to Her Majesty, No. 67, Dean-street, Soho, and Bridge-street, Edinburgh.

Though published anonymously, the words of Haydn's new canzonettas were by Mrs Anne Hunter, widow of the famous surgeon whom he met during the first visit to London. Haydn dedicated the songs to her and signed the original edition; he would certainly be amused to know that such a signed copy of any of his London prints is worth today (1970) £250.[1] The Six Canzonettas in those days cost 7s. 6d. The songs included were:

1) *The Mermaid's Song* ('Now the dancing sunbeams play')
2) *Recollection* ('The season comes when first we met')
3) *A Pastoral Song* ('My mother bids me bind my hair')
4) *Despair* ('The anguish of my bursting heart')
5) *Pleasing Pains* ('Far from this throbbing bosom haste')
6) *Fidelity* ('While hollow burst the rushing winds')

This was the drawing-room music which for the English had a special attraction, and we shall see that apart from the symphonies, Haydn's principal composing activities now turned to piano sonatas, piano trios, songs and other smaller forms. The first set of canzonettas was extremely well received, and remain, with some of the other English songs, his most popular small vocal pieces; Jenny Lind's interpretation of 'My mother bids me bind my hair' was a classic of its time, as are Peter Pears' and Benjamin Britten's today.

In this same announcement of the *Sun* on 3 June 1794, we read, 'here also on Monday next will be published all the favourite Songs and Duets in the Operas, La Venedetta di Nina, Il Burbero di Buon Core....' Haydn's Duet for the latter Opera has been discussed above (*vide* p. 254); this is the announcement for the first publication.

> The Musical Season will conclude with unparalleled eclat by the concert of this day se'nnight, in which all the WHITE BEARS of the musical world are to be united – The BANTI and MORICHELLI are to be heard. FOR THE FIRST TIME TOGETHER. Haydn, Giornovichi, Cramer, all unite their powers in favour of a brother professor, and thus in point both of Vocal and Instrumental excellence, it will defy comparison with any thing that this country ever witness. [*Morning Chronicle*, 9 June]

We shall see that this concert actually took place, on 16 June; but it is doubtful if Haydn personally took part in it. On 10 June, news of a great victory by Richard Lord Howe over the French fleet reached London, 'The Glorious First of June', as it came to be known. Farington tells us (I, 52):

> June 11. – [1794]
> Last night Sir Roger Curtis arrived at the Admiralty from Ld. Howe, announcing a great victory gained over the French fleet of 26 sail of the line, by the British fleet of 25. The Battle was fought on Sunday June 1st. – 6 ships were taken and two sunk, -witht. the loss of one British ship. The papers this morning reported the news.

E. M. Mundy wrote on Wednesday 11 June to Sir Roger Newdigate:

> My Dear Sir, – I cannot resist the Temptation of wishing you all Joy of our great and splendid Victory at Sea. . . . Lord Howe had two actions with the French Fleet; in the last on ye 1st of June he brought them to close Action and took seven Sail of Line of Battle Ships. Six are coming home; one sunk soon after she

---

1 A copy of the signed *Arianna* cantata (Bland 1791; *supra*, p. 27) was offered for sale by Richard Macnutt Ltd, Tunbridge Wells, listed as item no. 75 (with facsimile) in Catalogue No. 102, p. 35 (October 1970).

surrendered [this explains Haydn's figure of seven, *infra*], and one is supposed to have gone down during the Engagement. . . .

We received this News last night at the Opera where Morichelli was singing a favorite song. She was silenced in a Moment, and Rule Britannia called for, which was repeated at least a dozen time, the Audience all standing and huzzaing. . . .[1]

Mundy does not tell us of another occurrence at the opera that same night. We have the story *inter alia* from the *General Evening Post* of 10 June 1794. *La Frascatana* by Paisiello was being performed, and '. . . at the conclusion of d'Eyrille's charming Gallette [an interpolation], Banti having been observed in one of the boxes, was requested to appear on the stage, with which she immediately complied, and gave "God save the King" amidst the plaudits and acclamations of the audience.' Banti's version of 'God save the King' was shortly thereafter published; her ornamentation of the melody provides a unique document of late eighteenth-century vocal performance-practice (copy of the print in the writer's collection).

What Haydn noticed about the news of the 'Glorious First of June' was the violent action of the London mob.

[German][2]
On 11th June [1794] the whole city was illuminated because of the capture of 7 French warships; a great many windows were broken. On the 12th and 13th the whole city was illuminated again. The common people behaved very violently on this occasion. In every street they shot off not only small but also large guns, and this went on the whole night.   [CCLN, 287]

Haydn's description is echoed in the one in Farington's Diary (I, 53):

At 2 o'clock in the morning [June 11] we were knocked up to put out lights. – Many windows were broke. The Illuminations became general. Lord Stanhope's windows were smashed.
June 12. – [1794]
Fuseli came to me . . . and afterwards dined with me – & we walked out to see the illuminations which to-night were general and began early. The streets undisturbed by mobs and no windows broke.
June 13. –
Illuminations were again general this evening – the third night.

The heavy drinking of the English and the violent London mob are two of the aspects of life in England that Haydn really disliked. There are two more entries about Lord Howe:

1794
Milord Chatam [*sic*], President [*sic*] of the War Office and brother[3] of Minister Pitt, was so drunk for 3 days that he couldn't even sign his name, and thus occasioned that Lord Howe couldn't leave London, and together with the whole fleet couldn't sail away.   [CCLN, 298]

---

1 *The Cheverels of Cheverel Manor*, edited by Lady Newdigate-Newdegate. London, 1898, pp. 147f.
2 Unless specified, the Third and Fourth London Notebooks are in German, i.e. all references to CCLN after p. 287.
3 Haydn has confused the two brothers, sons of WILLIAM PITT, SR. (died in 1778): (1) SIR JOHN, 2ND EARL OF CHATHAM, was first Lord of the Admiralty in 1794, though changing to Privy Seal in December of that year; (2) WILLIAM JR. was Prime and War Minister in 1794. Haydn thus gives the name of John but the office of William. Mr. O. W. Neighbour, who kindly supplied this information, adds that 'presumably Howe might have felt the effects of either's drinking.'   [CCLN, 298]

A very good English toast, or drink-your-health: the first 2 words of the 3rd Psalm, 'Lord! How' *etc*: [are they increased that trouble me!], that is, Lord Howe, the great English soldier. [CCLN, 300]

On 16 June the 'White Bears' Concert took place, opening with one of Johann Christian Bach's symphonies (despite the description 'M.S.' it is likely that one of the Op. 18 set was played, No. 1 in E flat and No. 3 in D being particularly well-liked).

At the NEW SUBSCRIPTION ROOMS,
KING'S THEATRE, HAYMARKET.

ON MONDAY next, the 16th of June, WILL BE A GRAND CONCERT, To conclude the Musical Season, by an union of the principal talents, Vocal and Instrumental, in the Metropolis.

ACT I.
Overture for a double Orchestra, M. S. – Bach.
Song, Signor ROVEDINO.
Concertanti for Oboe and Bassoon, Messrs. HARRINGTON and HOLM[E]S.
Song, Signora MORECHELLI [*sic*].
Concertanti for Two Violins Obligati, Mr. GIORNOVICHI and
Mr. TAYLOR, his Pupil.

ACT II.
Grand Overture, – Haydn.
Song, Signor ROVEDINO.
Concerto Violoncello, Mr. LINDLY [*sic*].
Song, Signora BANTI.
OVERTURE.
Leader of the Band, Mr. CRAMER . . .

[*Morning Chronicle*, 10, 13,
14, 16 June; *Oracle*, 14 June; etc.]

On 20 June, Salomon sat for his portrait to George Dance; it turned out very well, the eye pensive and melancholy. Dance's own copy was reproduced for the first time in 1959 (CCLN, facing p. 50). As in Haydn's case, Daniell engraved it, publishing the handsome folio page on 15 August 1810 (reproduced as the frontispiece in Vol. XI of the Philharmonia Edition of Haydn's Complete Symphonies, Vienna 1966).

In the letter from Mundy to Newdigate quoted above, we read, as the last paragraph:

We go on well in Derbyshire with our subscription and have determined to raise a Body of Cavalry consisting of Gentlemen and Yeomen. Sir H. Harpur, Sir Robt Wilmot, Maj^r Banthurst, Cap^m Cheney and I have already offered our services.

Rather incredibly, Haydn was involved in this project. Sir Henry Harpur was in the years 1794–5 Sheriff of Derbyshire and as soon as the regiment was formed, he ordered two marches for wind band from Haydn, who completed them in 1795 (the first survives in dated autograph). Sir Henry published them himself: 'Two Marches composed by J: Haydn M. D. [*sic*] for Sir Henry Harpur, Bart. and presented by him to the Volunteer Cavalry of Derbyshire: Embodied in the Year 1794. London, Printed for Sir Henry Harpur, Bar^t· by Willm· Simpkins, Clements Inn.' The print also included piano arrangements which are so tastefully done that they would appear to have been made by the composer himself.

At this critical juncture in Haydn's life, an important letter arrived from Naples. Dies (155f.) tells us about its arrival in London:

About half a year after Haydn's arrival in London, a letter was sent him in the name of the [then] reigning Prince Nicolaus [II] Esterházy (who was at that time travelling through Italy) from Naples, which contained the news: 'The Prince has named Haydn his *Kapellmeister*, and wishes to restore the whole band again.' Haydn received this news with the greatest pleasure. He had entertained for a long time the warmest sympathy for the Princes Esterházy; they had offered him his daily bread and (what was more important) given him the opportunity of developing his musical talents. Haydn saw, of course, that his income in England was large, and that it by far exceeded that in his fatherland. Moreover, it would have been easy for him to secure any kind of well-paid position there [in England]. Since the death of Prince Anton, he was a completely free man; nothing bound him to the princely house except love and gratitude. It was those things, however, that silenced every opposition and persuaded him to accept the offer of Prince Nicolaus with joy and, as soon as his commitments in London were fulfilled, to return to his native country.

There were probably three important reasons that motivated Haydn's decision to return: (1) The pace at which he lived in England was simply too quick for a man of sixty to be able to keep up for any length of time; he had especially felt this towards the end of the 1792 season. (2) The Terror in France was approaching its ghastly climax, and with the war going badly for the Allies: on 10 July the French occupied Brussels, in August Trier (Trèves) which they successfully defended against Allied counter-attacks, and in October they attacked Holland and drove out the English troops. In view of all this, Haydn thought it was best to be in one's own country and where one's own native language was spoken. (3) Haydn knew that in his old age, he would be taken care of by Prince Esterházy, that he would never starve or lack for bodily comforts; and who, in England would do that for him? Perhaps with some deep-rooted instinct, Haydn sensed that he would live to be (for the times) a very old man and would stop composing. In the event, he did have a comfortable old age, honoured by the Esterházy family (especially the Princess Marie Hermenegild) and by the Emperor too (especially the Empress Marie Therese). His decision was a wise one, even if he had grown very fond of England and his English friends.

Haydn now had a large circle of English friends, who came from all walks of life and enjoyed widely differing professions. For instance:

Mister March is a dentist, *Carossieur* [*recte*: Carrossieur = coachmaker] and dealer in wines all at the same time: a man 84 years old. Keeps a very young mistress. Has a 9-year-old daughter who plays the pianoforte quite respectably. I often ate at his house. N.B.: as a dentist, he makes £2000 every year. Each waggon costs at least £500. As a dealer in wines, I don't imagine his profits will be all that large. He drags himself around on two crutches, or 2 wooden feet.   [CCLN, 291]

We shall meet many other British friends of Haydn as this Chronicle continues.

'At the King's Theatre,' Parke (I, 190) tells us, 'a grand performance was given on the 2d of July, in celebration of the glorious victory obtained by Earl Howe of the fleet of the French republic. The performance consisted of the comic opera, "Le [*sic*] Serva padrona" [by Giovanni Paisiello], with appropriate ballets; after which Madame Banti, who had become extremely popular, sang our national song "Rule Britannia", in which she was vociferously encoured, although her bad English amounted almost to burlesque! This clearly shows that fashion, like love, is blind.'

Haydn was now extremely weather-conscious, a state of mind encouraged by the eccentric English climate:

Anno 1794 there was as beautiful weather in the month of April as there can be in Germany in about the month of July. May, on the contrary, was very cold. Half of June and the whole month of July were very hot, and without any rain; people prayed for rain. In this great heat-wave, a great many people died in the Thames, because they went swimming in it. Some are capable of swimming 2 hours at a time, but when the tide catches them they're lost. Yesterday two fellows were bathing, and suddenly began to fight. They went on shore to box, and one of them received such a strong blow in the stomach that he gave up the ghost forthwith.

[CCLN, 289]

The sight of the day was the ruined French ships which Lord Howe had towed into Portsmouth Harbour. The royal family went down on 26 June to inspect the great French ships, 'all dismasted and in a very shattered condition'.[1] The king inspected the Dockyard, dined with Lord Howe and presented him with a sword and the Order of the Garter. The royal party then boarded the French prizes and saw with their own eyes 'the blood and brains of the killed and wounded [which] had with variegated hue dyed every part of the ships.' On 30 June, after visiting Cowes, the royal party (with Lord and Lady Howe) left Spithead for Southampton.

Haydn decided that he had earned a holiday, and the stories of the sights at Portsmouth had whetted his curiosity. Very early on 9 July, he set off; on the way he stopped at Hampton Court:

On the way to Portsmuth [*sic*] I saw the old Royal Castle at Hampton Court, which is very large and has a garden like that at Estoras [Eszterháza], with three principal allées; there are various splendid statues in bronze, and very fine marble vases; especially beautiful the painting over the main staircase and the ceiling by the artist Verrio.[2] This castle is mostly inhabited by aristocratic widows of the military.

[CCLN, 294]

'The Mail Coach does 110 in 12 hours, that is, one-hundred-ten English miles', wrote Haydn in his Third Notebook (CCLN, 289), which was, says Miss Matthews, 'a hard pace to set over the North and South Downs'; and it was eight in the evening before the travellers arrived at the great Naval base:

On 9th July [1794], I left at 5 o'clock in the morning for Portsmouth, 72 miles from London, and arrived there at 8 o'clock in the evening. Some small earthworks were thrown up 14 miles before Portsmouth; nearby there is a small camp of 800 men; one mile further, in the direction of the city, some 3,500 Frenchmen are quartered in barracks. I inspected the fortifications there, which are in good repair, especially the fortress opposite, in Godsport, which the *gubernium* [= the governors] had had constructed recently. I went aboard the French ship-of-the-line called *le just*; it has 80 cannon; the English, or rather Lord Howe, captured it. The 18 cannon in the harbour-fortress are 36-pounders. The ship is

---

1 Betty Matthews, 'Haydn's visit to Hampshire and the Isle of Wight, described from contemporary sources' in *Haydn Yearbook* III (1965), pp.111-121.
2 On the preceding page Haydn wrote the notes for the above paragraph in pencil, and subsequently erased them (the words 'Court', 'Mahler' [painter], 'Werrio . . . auf der Hauptstiege' [Werrio . . . over the main staircase] are legible). The King's Staircase in Hampton Court was designed by Christopher Wren, and Antonio Verrio painted the walls and ceiling in one huge composition. Sacheverell Sitwell, *British Architects and Craftsmen*, London 1945, p. 59.   [CCLN, 294]

terribly shot to pieces. The great mast, which is 10 feet 5 inches in circumference, was cut off at the very bottom and lay stretched on the ground. A single cannon-ball, which passed through the captain's room, killed 14 sailors.

The Dockyard, or the place where ships are built, is of an enormous size, and has a great many splendid buildings. But I couldn't go there, because I was a foreigner. Hard by is a new and most splendid ship-of-the-line with 110 cannon, called the *Prince of Wales*. The King and his family stayed 3 days in the Dockyard at the *gouverneur's* house. [CCLN, 292]

Ebb-tide and flood-tide every 7 hours. In Spring the tide recedes 14 feet, during the rest of the season only 7 feet.

Every ship-of-the-line, or man-of-war, has 3 masts, likewise a Frigate.
Most of them have 3 decks.
A Brig has 2 masts.
A Cutter has only 1 mast.
Every ship-of-the-line must have at least 64 cannon.
A Cutter has but 14, at the most 16 cannon.
A fire-ship has 2 masts. In the middle of its sails it has 2 large and long cross-beams with round, pointed double irons:

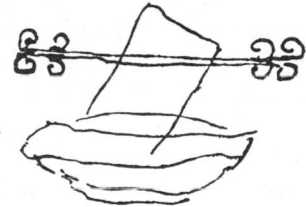

When they come near an enemy ship, this iron grapples the rigging or even the sails, whereupon one sets the ship on fire, so that the other ship which is grappled to it has to burn, too. The crew saves itself in the little lifeboats which they take with them. [CCLN, 289f.]

A Cockswan [*sic*] is a kind of subaltern who, when his Capitain [*sic*] goes to sea, stands at attention next to him. A capitain generally has his special crew, all identically dressed, which he takes with him to his port. At 12 o'clock I was in the neighbourhood of the fleet when the 12 o'clock bells were rung. In July [there follow two or three illegible words] I ate lunch [on a ship?].

[CCLN, 291]

It is said that Juli[u]s Caesar, having had to flee, landed quite by accident on this island, and is supposed to have said: this is the port of the Gods. Godsport. There are 1500 patients in this hospital, among them 300 sailors who were with Lord Howe in the last naval battle. [remark also repeated *infra*] [CCLN, 291]

From Portsmouth, Haydn crossed over to the Isle of Wight, where he was invited to stay at Fernhill as the guest of the Governor, Thomas Orde, 'a cold, cautious, slow and sententious man, tolerably well informed, with a mind neither powerful nor feeble' (Sir Johan Barrington; Matthews, op. cit., p. 114). Fernhill was a pseudo-Gothic edifice but the grounds were beautiful and the view spectacular. In his notebook, Haydn wrote 'Mr Orde *gouveneur* at Fernhall [*sic*] on the Isle of Wight, whose country house commands the most magnificent view over the ocean. L'Isle of Whight', concluded Haydn, with his phonetic spelling, 'is 64 miles in circumference.' (CCLN, 288.) Haydn landed at Ryde (which he spelled, in rapid succession, 'Reid, Reed, port of war opposite Portsmouth, RYDE') and was shown the famous well at Carisbrooke Castle outside Newport. 'The persons who show the castle, generally let down a piece of lighted paper into the well, in order to exhibit it to strangers a singular effect that attends it; a stream of air rushes down into it from the mouth, with such violence as to extinguish the flame long before it reaches the bottom (from the Southampton Guide of 1795; Matthews, 117). Haydn saw the well (CCLN, 300), which he says was 300 feet deep (actually it was probably less) the water was hauled by a large wooden wheel 'driven by a mule'.

'Newport is a nice little town [continues Haydn]; the people look just like the Germans and mostly have black hair.' He also visited a hospital, 'built in the year 1762. At this time there were 1500 patients, among them 300 sailors from the last naval battle.' Haydn embarked from Cowes 'at 4 o'clock in the afternoon for Southampton where I spent the night. It's a little town on a penninsula. From there to Winschester [*sic*], where there is a beautiful Cathedral Church, the altar-piece by [the American artist, Benjamin] WEST [R. A.]. On the way back a good dinner at Feernham', by which Haydn means the pretty old town of Farnham (CCLN, 297, 294), probably at the 'Bush' which was the coaching inn.

In the midst of Haydn's notes about ships and Portsmouth, there is the sentence, 'I met Lauterburg, the famous painter' (CCLN, 292), which implies that the meeting took place sometime during this trip. Philipp Jakob Loutherbourg the younger, a successful stage designer and landscape painter, had lived in England since 1771, was now a member of the Royal Academy and, (said a colleague to Farington [I, 261]), had much improved since Garrick had brought him over from Paris to make stage designs. In 1801 an engraving by J. Landseer after a Loutherbourg drawing of Haydn appeared in a group of musicians ('Tableau'), which is reproduced in Landon, *Essays*, p. 40.

Haydn had lived through three disastrous fires in his life, two at Eisenstadt which had each time destroyed his house, and one at Eszterháza which had destroyed many of his scores. This 'special' interest in holocausts may therefore account for the following entry in the Third Notebook:

> On 23rd July 1794, fire broke out in a master shipwright's dock above London Bridge; the fire spread to a ship with a cargo of nitre, which was docked nearby, and driven by a very strong wind, the fire reached such proportions that it consumed over [at first: '500'] 1200 houses. It lasted from 4 o'clock in the morning to the morning of the next day. The damage is immeasurable, since one single dealer in sugar by the name of Mr Whiting lost £40,000. They are raising a general subscription for the unfortunates. The City Council has had 120 tents erected there as shelters for the poor inhabitants. It is not yet known how many people lost their lives.
>
> By the end of July they have now raised a collection of £10,000 Sterling for the unhappy people.

> [CCLN, 297]

It would seem that in July Haydn was taken to see the Bank of England. The entry in the Third Notebook is dated 15 July but without the year. Previously in CCLN (292), we thought this event must have taken place in 1795, but the evidence is slightly more weighted to 1794: the entry follows the entry of 9 July (trip to Portsmouth),

Loutherbourg and a note about the Dockyard ('. . . I couldn't go there'). The next entry is 28 March 1795 (on Bianchi's *Aci e Galatea*).

On 15th July [1794(?)], I saw the Bank [of England]. There are, first, a *goveneur*, a Deputy or Vice *gouverneur*, 24 *Directores*, and a whole lot of other officials in the department. Mr Dea guided me, and showed me all the treasures. There is a very great fortune in gold ingots, most of which are worth £700 Sterling. There are over one-and-one-half millions in bank notes, some of which are £1000 notes. An enormous amount of Spanish taler. Most of the gold is underground in the vaults. In order to see the main cashier's office, 3 of the directors have to be present, each one of which has his own key. The vaults are exceedingly massive. There are also hidden vaults, which must be very useful in case of a rebellion. To write down all the bills they need 2000 large folio books every year, and on this account there is a very large library which is, however, apart from that very insignificant.

[CCLN, 292f.]

Another undated entry from the lost Fourth Notebook was copied by Dies and records a visit to the dread Tower of London; the Madame Donelli mentioned is perhaps the wife of a singer in Gallini's company, Dorelli (*recte*):

In the company of several friends, Haydn went to see the wild animals in the Tower [of London]. Through carelessness the keeper had left the trap-door to the tiger's cage open. Madame Donelli was fortunate enough to discover this in time, though the keeper rushed to the scene just at the very moment when the tiger had already reached the trap-door. [CCLN, 308]

On 28 July (Haydn writes, wrongly, 29), Haydn went to see *The Mountaineers* and *Auld Robin Gray (a pastorale)*, the music by Samuel Arnold. This entry in the Third Notebook is followed by another anecdote about the premonition of death: we observed one in the earlier London sojourn (*supra*, p. 152):

SPECTAS, ET TU SPECTABERE is the inscription over the curtain in the Little Haymarket Theatre. I was there on 29th July 1794: they gave a National opera, N.B. a piece in Scottish costumes. The men were dressed in flesh-coloured breeches, with white and red ribbons twisted round their stockings, a short, brightly-coloured, striped masons' apron [i.e. kilt], brown coat and waistcoat, over the coat a large, broad ensign's sash in the same style as the apron, and black cap shaped like a shoe and trimmed with ribbons. The women all in white muslin, brightly coloured ribbons in their hair, very broad bands in the same style round their bodies, also for their hats. They perform the same abominable trash as at Sadlers Wells. A fellow yelled an aria so horribly and with such exaggerated grimaces that I began to sweat all over. N.B. He had to repeat the aria. *O che bestie*!

Lord Littledon, a very rich and pious man, had the misfortune to be the father of only one very dissolute son, whom he tried to improve by every possible means. – Eventually he found a most charming wife for his son, but the latter lived with her only 3 months and then sent her back to his father. This behaviour caused the father's death a short while afterwards. But just before he died, the father wrote the son that the latter could sweeten his dying days if he [the son] would divorce his good wife before the father died; the son agreed to do this at once *in forma*, whereupon the old man died peacefully. Scarcely a fortnight went by, however, before the son had a dream, in which his father appeared to him, saying that the son would be a child of death within the very week; and so it happened. The young widow is still alive: but very sad. [CCLN, 294f.]

At the beginning of August, Haydn went on another interesting trip, this time to the fashionable spa, Bath, in company with the flautist Andrew Ashe and the singing teacher and composer Giambattista Cimador, a noble Venetian who became a musician and later formed the publishing firm of Monzani & Cimador. In 1795, his opera, *Ati e Cibele*, was performed at the King's Theatre in London. Haydn stayed at Perrymead – not 'The Pyramids' as in *H in L* –, the house of Venanzio Rauzzini, the famous castrato who had sung Cecilio in Mozart's *Lucio Silla* (Milan, 1772) and for whom Mozart wrote the Motet, 'Exsultate, jubilate' (K. 165) in January 1773.[1] A Roman by birth, Rauzzini had appeared at Vienna in 1767 and had then gone to Munich, where he not only sang but composed operas; in 1774 he made his successful London début; among his pupils were Nancy Storace and Miss Poole. The visit was reported in the *Sun* on 1 August 1794:

> HAYDN is still in this Country, as much respected for his simplicity of his character in private life, as admired for his sublime musical powers. He and ASHE, the ingenious Flautist, are now on a visit to RAUZZINI at Bath.

In his Notebook, Haydn himself has recorded the visit in some detail:

On 2nd August 1794, I left at 5 o'clock in the morning for Bath, with Mr Ashe and Mr Cimador, and arrived there at 8 o'clock in the evening. It's 107 miles from London. The Mail Coach does this distance in 12 hours. I lived at the house of Herr Rauzzini, a *Musicus* who is very famous, and who in his time was one of the greatest singers. He has lived there 19 years, supports himself by the Subscription Concerts which are given in the Winter, and by giving lessons. He is a very nice and hospitable man. His summer house, where I stayed, is situated on a rise in the middle of a most beautiful neighbourhood, from which you can see the whole city. Bath is one of the most beautiful cities in Europe. All the houses are built of stone; this stone comes from quarries in the surrounding mountains; it is very soft, so soft, in fact, that it's no trouble to cut it up into any desired shape; it is very white, and the older it is, once it has been taken from the quarry, the harder it gets. The whole city lies on a slope, and that is why there are very few carriages; instead of them, there are a lot of sedan-chairs, who will take you quite a ways for 6 pence. But too bad that there are so few straight roads; there are a lot of beautiful squares, on which stand the most magnificent houses, but which cannot be reached by any vehicle: they are now building a brand new and broad street.

N.B. Today, on the 3rd, I looked at the city, and found, half-way up the hill, a building shaped like a half-moon, and more magnificent than any I had seen in London. The curve extends for 100 fathoms, and there is a Corinthian column at each fathom. The building has 3 floors. Round about it, the pavement in front of the houses is 10 feet broad for the pedestrians, and the street as wide *a proportione*; it is surrounded by an iron fence, and a terrace slopes down 50 fathoms in successive stages, through a beautiful expanse of green; on both sides there are little paths, by which one can descend very comfortably.

Every Monday and Friday evening all the bells are rung, but apart from this, you don't hear many bells being rung. The city is not thickly populated, and in Summer one sees very few people; for the people taking the baths don't come till the beginning of October, and stay through half of February. But then a great many people come, so that in the year 1791, 25,000 persons were there. All the inhabitants live off this influx, without which the city would be very poor: there

---

1 Deutsch, *Mozart, Die Dokumente*, pp. 128f. On the name of Rauzzini's house at Bath, see Grove I, vol. iv, 191.

are very few merchants and almost no trade, and everything is very dear. The baths are by nature very warm; one bathes in the water, and one also drinks it – generally the latter. And one pays very little: to bathe it costs 3 shillings at all times. I made the acquaintance there of Miss Brown, a charming person of the best *conduit*; a good pianoforte player, her mother a most beautiful woman. The city is now building a most splendid room for guests taking the cure.

The delightful Miss Brown seems to have been the daughter of Abraham Brown (Browne), who had often appeared with Handel (Deutsch, *Handel*, p. 581), while the 'most splendid room' was to be the Pump Room, completed in 1796. At the beginning of this notebook, Haydn jotted down several names and addresses of friends to see in Bath, including the composer Dr Henry Harington (*recte*):

[*English*]
      M^ris^ Bindon   N° 19 great Pulteney
with two Daughters   Str.
                         to Bath

To Honble M^ris^ Brown   N° 3
Burlington Street.   Bath.

Dr Harlinghton   queen Square
      Composer at Bath
[In another hand:]
Mrs Carr – N° 2 Crescent
Miss Gubbins le meme Bath   [CCLN, 287]

Harington wrote Haydn a poem of praise, 'What art expresses', which Haydn, to return the compliment, promptly set to music, first as a song for solo voice, which then turns into a mixed chorus and finally variations for the piano with a *da capo* of the solo vocal section – a typical occasional piece that could have been, and probably was, sung and played at Dr Harington's house. Haydn later sold it to Breitkopf (*infra*, p. 403). The complicated to-and-fro of the poetry inspired Muzio Clementi to say, 'The first doctor [Harington] having bestowed much praise on the second doctor [Haydn], the said second doctor, out of doctorial gratitude, returns the first doctor thanks for all favour received, and praises in his turn the said first doctor most handsomely.'[1]

Haydn's arrival in Bath prompted the *Bath Herald and Register* (9 August) to welcome his arrival as follows:

O had I Jubal's Lyre, says a correspondent, I would sweep the strings, Till Echo Tired with repeating – Haydn treads upon Bathonian ground! And had this place, previous to his arrival, been the seat of discord, it must now be lulled into Peace by the God Harmony – while every Individual who hath Music in his Soul must exclaim with enthusiasm
                  Erit mihi magnus Apollo
                                        [Pohl III, 82]

Dies (127f.), who incidentally tells us, wrongly, that 'Dr Burney led Haydn' to Bath and 'both were Rauzzini's guests for three days', confusing Ashe-Cimador with the Doctor, describes a pleasant gift Haydn composed for his host.

Rauzzini had in his garden a monument to his best friend, who had been snatched from him by death. In the inscription, he lamented the loss of such a true friend,

---

1 Geiringer, *Haydn* 1947, p. 132.

&c., and concluded his lament with the words: 'He was not a man – he was a dog.'

Haydn secretly copied this inscription and composed a four-part canon to the words. Rauzzini was surprised: he liked the canon so much that he had it incised on the monument, to the honour of Haydn's and the dog's.

The 'Canon a quattro' was printed by Pohl (*H in L*, 276):

Orlando Mansfield[1] points out that Haydn has incorporated a famous old chime in his canon (the downward series of thirds) which he must have heard many times, also at Bath where 'every Monday and Friday all the bells are rung' (CCLN, *vide supra*).

Dies also quotes an extract from the lost Fourth Notebook, which tells us that 'On the very day Haydn left Bath, a French emigrant sent him a laurel wreath. This wreath was accompanied by four poems which express nothing other than good will but are

---

1 'Haydn at Bath', *Monthly Musical Record* 58 (1928), pp. 201 ff.

simply too poor to deserve quotation' (CCLN, 308). If the four lost verses are anything like the one printed by a French admirer in the *Bath Herald and Register* after Haydn's departure, one may be thankful for Dies's suppression:

> De l'immortalité Haydn, reçois la couronne,
> Tu ravis tous le coeurs, et le mien te je donne;
> Il devoit cet hommage a tes divins talens,
> Que l'univers entier te rend depuis longtems.
> O toi dont l'amitié a mon coeur nécessaire,
> Me devient Rauzzini, si douce et salutaire!
> Appolon des nos jours, come lui Dieu de Chant
> Reçois ici le prix de ton goût ravissant;
> Tu voix et tes talents, de ce siècle la gloire,
> Sont à jamais gravés au temple de memoire,
> Par leur Admirateur.

On a page of the Third Notebook, a strange hand wrote the following address in pencil:

Mr Hamilton

Rodney Place   Clifton Hill

near Bristol   [CCLN, 290]

Haydn went on to this Mr Hamilton and looked at Bristol:

> On the 6th I went from Bath 11 miles to Pristol [*sic*], to visit Mr Hamilton. The city is very large and half of it, too, is built on a rise. The River [blank: = Avon] flows through the middle of the city, and many hundred merchant ships lie at anchor in the river. There is a great deal of trade, because the open sea can be reached a few hours. The city is also very heavily populated, but otherwise rather dirty; very small streets; a lot of building going on, especially on the hill, which commands the most magnificent views. The churches – there are a great many – are all in the old Gothic style, as they are at Bath, too. In Bath, I saw a vehicle in the form of two sofas for 4 persons; N.B.: 2 persons on each side with their backs diagonally opposite to each other. The drinking and bathing water is especially beneficial for lameness and rheumatism; in Pristol for hectic and consumption. The drinking water at Pristol is very sweet and pleasing. The guests go to Pristol in the Summer, and to Bath in the Winter. The trip there and back cost me 75 Viennese Gulden.   [CCLN, 296f]

He also wrote down an odd Latin inscription 'On a house in Pristol':

CURAS CITHARA TULLIT [*sic*]
MORS JANUA VITAE.

'tiens ta Foy' is the last entry of the Third Notebook; this thought must have been uppermost in Haydn's mind when he went to visit Sir Charles Rich, three miles from Farnham (where Haydn had enjoyed a good dinner a month earlier). Like many of Haydn's English friends, they did not forget him after he had left, and we find Lady Rich subscribing to *The Creation*.

> On 26th Aug. 1794, I went to Waverly [*sic*] Abbey, forty miles from London, to visit Baron Sir Charles Rich, quite a good 'cello player. Here there are the remains of a monastery which has already been standing for 600 years. I must confess that whenever I looked at this beautiful wilderness, my heart was oppressed at the thought that all this once belonged to my religion.   [CCLN, 304]

The horrors of the Terror filled even the stoutest hearts with dread. If the elevation of a whore at the high altar of Notre Dame during the Feast of Reason, presided over by the obscene journalist, Hébert, at Christmas 1793 had appeared not only wicked but insane, the news from the provinces of France in the Summer of 1794 made the blood run cold. At Nantes, five hundred infants were butchered, their mothers first being offered the choice of becoming whores or dying on the spot; at Arras, some 5,000 people were slain; in Paris, gangs of prisoners were dragged through the streets in chains and between two and three thousand were being guillotined every month. Churches and ancient monasteries were laid waste throughout the land.[1]

Now, in September, an assassination plot againt George III was discovered. (A year later, on 29 October 1795, the King was on his way to open Parliament, when a bullet from an air-gun broke one of the windows of his carriage; 'My Lords,' said the courageous old King upon entering the Chamber, 'I have been shot at.')

> In the month of Sept. 1794, there was an attempt to assassinate the King. The principal murderers were very young, one was a clock-maker, the other a chemist. They constructed a kind of blow-pipe from which a little poisoned arrow was to kill the King in the Theatre. The understanding was to start a brawl right under the King's box, during the course of which each of the gang was to raise his stick in the air and threaten to beat the other, whilst the principal rogue was to shoot his arrow at the King. They have discovered another two participants, one of them a bookseller. The clock-maker's name is La Maitre, presumably a Frenchman; the chemist, Higgins. The bookseller is named Joh[n] Smith, the 4th man, Upton. The clock-maker invented the murder weapon.   [CCLN, 298]

The Prince of Wales was having a scandalous affair with Frances, Countess of Jersey, wife of the fourth Earl of Jersey. Farington noted on 8 September:

> The Princess Royal told Lady Beverley before the last entertainment given at Windsor, that the wish of Lady Jersey [to be admitted to the Queen's parties at Windsor] was known at Court, but that it would not be complied with. – When Lady B. went there she was surprised to see Lady Jersey in conversation with the Prince of Wales.   [I, 71]

Haydn put down the latest lines about the affair and made it much dirtier in the German; altogether Haydn must have been a great story teller, and one gets the idea that many of the little lines, beginnings of stories, etc. in the notebooks were there to refresh his memory before going to a convivial dinner party, where Haydn would regale the guests with his English 'anecdotes'.

> [German:]
> The trip into [!] Jersey, or divorce à la mode. [English:] Trip to JERSEY, or – divorce a la mode. [German:] Jersey is the name of the Prince of Wales' new mistress. THAT'S WHAT THEY SAY: *relata reffero* [*sic*].   [CCLN, 299]

On 9 September, Haydn was off again on another trip, this time perhaps to visit Lord Abingdon, whose name appears immediately under the story of Lindley:

> On 9th Sept. 1794, I travelled with a bridal pair. The man was named Lindley, organist, 25 years old; his wife 18, with very good features – but both of them stone-blind. The old proverb, 'Love is blind', does not apply here. He was poor, but she brought him a dowry of £20,000 Sterling. Now he doesn't play the organ any more.

1 Bryant, *The Years of Endurance*, p. 116. Assassination attempt on George III, Oct. 1795: p. 141.

Lord Avington [Abingdon] had an organ built in the church on his estate. When the Archbishop of the diocese heard about it, he wrote a letter reproving him for having done this without his knowledge, inasmuch as one cannot do such a thing without previously informing the authorities. He got an answer: The Lord gave it, and the Lord can take it away again. This is most ambiguous, but very good. [CCLN, 300f.]

> Salomon und David waren grosse Sünder,
> Hatten schöne weiber, machten viele kinder.
> Da Sie nicht mehr konnten und kamen in das alter,
> macht der Eine Lieder, und der andere Psalter. [1]

N.B. Lord Avington set it to music, but miserably: I did it a bit better.
[CCLN, 299]

It was perhaps on this occasion that Haydn began to write an English Oratorio, Nedham's translation of Selden's *Mare Clausum* (Joannis Seldeni *Jurisconsulti Opera omnia, Tam edita quam inedita. In tribus Volumnibus*. Londini MDCCXXVI, p. 1179, Vol. II: *Mare Clausum, seu de Dominio Maris*.) Haydn actually finished two whole numbers in full score, a powerful bass Aria, 'Nor can I think my suit is vain' and a Chorus, 'Thy great Endeavours' with large orchestra. Lord Abingdon later gave the MS. to his friend and fellow-flautist T. Monzani, who presented it to the British Museum, which institution added this note:

'Nor can I think my suit is vain'; a song and chorus, in full score, composed by, and in the autograph by Joseph Haydn, in the year 1794, at the desire of the Earl of Abingdon, and by him given to T. Monzani, the celebrated flute player, who in 1821 presented it to the British Museum. Mr. Monzani states that it was intended to form part of an oratorio, but that Haydn never did more towards its completion .... [Add. 9284; Pohl, *H in L*, 310]

The reason why Haydn did not finish is probably two-fold: (1) in February 1795 Lord Abingdon disappeared from circulation in a rather spectacular manner, the circumstances of which will interest us; (2) Haydn, though he might be 'predestined for bad poetry' (Griesinger), may have taken umbrage at this really fourth-rate text ('For England has great wealth posses'd by sea's access, and thereby blest with plenties not a few, which next the virtue of thy watchful eyes will her secure from foreign miseries . . .'). Haydn was undoubtedly fond of England and the English. He loved her ships and lusty sea-captains who gave him splendid lunches, and he was on her side politically; but to set this kind of verse to music as an oratorio may have seemed a dubious undertaking to him. The newspapers were, interestingly enough, aware that he was working on it that Summer. 'Music', wrote a newspaper not identified by Pohl (*H in L*, 309) 'but for Haydn, would be *dumb* among us. He is writing for the best of all possible concerts. Nor has he given up his idea of Oratorio. He will there

> All but equal him [Handel]
> Whom thunder has made greater.

---

1 'Salomon and David were great sinners / had beautiful wives and made many children. / When they couldn't do it any more and grew old, / the one wrote songs and the other wrote psalms.' The play on names (Salomon = Haydn's impresario; David = the famous tenor, DAVIDE, who was always referred to as David in England) is obvious. The poem is written down with many corrections and improvements, which suggests that Haydn was probably the author (or translator?).

It was probably at this time that he helped the amateurish Lord Abingdon with some catches and glees, the Earl composing the vocal parts and Haydn the accompaniments. Later this too was given to Monzani, who published it with the following title page: 'Twelve Sentimental Catches and Glees, For Three Voices Melodized by the Right Honble. The Earl of Abingdon, The Accompaniments for the Harp or Piano Forte by the celebrated D^r. Haydn, Being a Gift of his Lordship to M^r. Monzani. for his Benefit. Entered at Stationers Hall. Price 10^s. 6^d. Sold by M^r. Monzani N°. 16, Dean Street, Piccadilly [etc.].'

The British newspapers were still following Haydn's career not only from the musical but also the social standpoint. On 23 September 1794 the *Sun* informs us that 'HAYDN is still in this Country, and is now tolerably well acquainted with our language. We are not surprised that he should wish to remain secure in this happy Island, where his genius is received with due honour.'

One of the most interesting of Haydn's English friends was Thomas Holcroft who had been, successively, stable-boy, shoemaker, tutor, actor, playwright poet and amateur politician. He was definitely one of Fox's followers, and his connection with some of the corresponding societies, such as the Constitutional Society, were in sympathy with the principles of the French Revolution and ultimately brought them under the suspicion of the Government. The *Morning Chronicle* printed his interesting poem to Haydn on 12 September 1794, the only verse in connection with our composer which it is possible to read without cringing; the poem was reprinted in the *European Magazine* in its issue of September 1794 (p. 214) and also in the *Gentleman's Magazine* of January 1796 (pp. 65f.).

TO HAYDN

WHO is the mighty master, that can trace
Th'eternal lineaments of Nature's face?
'Mid endless dissonance, what mortal ear
Could e'er her peal of perfect concord hear?
Answer, Oh, HAYDN! strike the magic chord!
And as thou strik'st, reply, and proof afford.

Whene'er thy Genius, flashing native fire,
Bids the soul tremble with the trembling lyre,
The hunter's clatt'ring hoof, the peasant-shout,
The warrior on-set, or the battle's rout,
Din, clamour, uproar, murder's midnight knell,
Hyaena shrieks, the warhoop scream and yell –
All sounds, however mingled, strange, uncouth,
Resolve to fitness, system, sense and truth!
To others noise and jangle; but to thee
'Tis one grand solemn swell of endless harmony.

When dark and unknown terrors intervene,
And men aghast survey the horrid scene,
Then, when rejoicing fiends flit, gleam and scowl,
And bid the huge tormented tempest howl;
When fire-fraught thunders roll, and whirlwinds rise,
And earthquakes bellow to the frantic skies,
'Till the distracted ear, in racking gloom,
Suspects the wreck of worlds, and gen'ral doom;
Then HAYDN stands, collecting Nature's tears,
And consonance sublime amid confusion hears.

T. HOLCROFT

It must have been about this time that Haydn sent to his Revolutionary-minded friend the following letter in his inimitable English, dealing with two songs: Holcroft translated Haydn's *Lied* 'Eine sehr gewöhnliche Geschichte' into English and perhaps this is one of the '2 Songs', while the canon might be the Oxford 'Thy voice' or perhaps one of the new 'Ten Commandments' for Count Brühl.

[To Thomas Holcroft, London. *English*]

[London, 1794 or 1795]

Dear Sir!

I tack me the liberty to Send you the Canon, and the 2 Songs and if is possible, I self will come to you to day, o[r] to morrow. I was oblieged to tack a Medicine to Day, perhaps I see you this Evening.

I am

Sir with the greatest Respect

Your
Oblig Ser^v
Haydn

[Address:] M^r. Holcroft

[CCLN, 144–5]

In November, Thomas Holcroft was indicted for High Treason, along with a large group of similar hotheads. Farington says, quoting some local gossip,

Holcroft had a son who he is said to have treated with great severity. The lad ran away & went on board a ship, & being traced by his father who went to the ship, blew his brains out on his father approaching him. Holcroft is avowedly a man of the most loose principles with regard to religion. [I, 75]

British justice soon showed, however, that England was the home of liberty, for almost all these free-thinkers were acquitted, Holcroft on 1 December. He always preserved his loyalty to Haydn, even when confronted with Mozart. In his entertaining memoirs,[1] we read, on 10 July 1798:

Left my Card for C. –Mr. B. called. Has adopted the cant which from Germany has spread to England, of affirming Mozart to be a greater man than Haydn. In Germany, his theatrical pieces have given Mozart his great popularity: he was undoubtedly a man of uncommon genius but not a Haydn. His life indeed was too short.

Holcroft was also a friend of Salomon's, as the entry for 20 October 1798 shows:

When I returned home, found Salomon, who accompanied Fanny with his usual feeling and enthusiasm. Spoke in raptures of Haydn, which well accorded with my own sentiments. Staid till one o'clock, and occasioned me to eat too much supper.

On 4 November:

Music at Mr. Mackenzie's. Haydn's symphony quintetto [Salomon's arrangement of the London Symphonies, perhaps] and Mozart: both men of uncommon genius, but the latter impatient after novelty and superior excellence, often forgets the flow of passion in laboriously hunting after new thoughts which, when thus introduced, have the same effect in music, as the *concetti* of the Italians have in poetry; and for these Mozart is frequently extolled as superior to Haydn.

1 *Memoirs of the late Thomas Holcroft*, edited and completed by Hazlitt, London, 1816, II, 269; III, 54, 61.

In March 1799, Holcroft left England to settle in France, but he was lonely there, and in 1802 Farington, visiting Paris, tells us that

> ... Opie informed me that Holcroft, the author, who went abroad with strong prejudices founded upon political notions is become quite national to England. In painting, – in acting, – &c. &c. He will admit of no comparison on the part of France; in short after having taken leave of his Country He is preparing to return to it. [II, 10]

Holcroft was quite well known on the Continent. The following report was made, slightly incredulously, by Crabb Robinson, the late eighteenth century diarist, whose diary later became much quoted.

> ffrank-furt sur Main Sunday 22^d Mar: 1801 ... Mad: de la Roche – have I ment^d her to you? I forget – She is spoken of in the Life of Wieland ... At her house I have seen another of the German Literati ffrau V. Kalb – The fair friend of Schiller and John Paul Richter – She knows a little English And made Enquiries after the Author of a Book which interested her she said more than any one in the Eng: Language – Anne St. Ives [by Thomas Holcroft, 1792].
> [op. cit., (*vide supra*, p. 212), pp. 6off.]

Crabb Robinson himself was furious over Holcroft's translation of *Hermann und Dorothea*:

> Jena 1st and 2^d June 1803 ... it was with real indignation that I read the Monthly Review of Holcroft's translation of Herman & Dorothea by Göthe – I felt a sort of shame for the Reviewer, for Holcroft & myself – For myself because I confess that whoever reads that Article & knows nothing besides of Göthe, is justified in despising Göthe .... That Holcroft who has shewn himself to possess so much original Talent, sho^d be capable of making such verses And giving us instead of the *living Grace* of the original, a *putrid carcase* is quite a riddle to me ....
> [op. cit., pp. 124ff.]

From being a violently controversial man, Holcroft has almost noiselessly disappeared from history, literary or otherwise; but he was certainly a colourful addition to the strikingly varied group of friends Haydn had gathered round him in two short trips to England.

On 13 October, Haydn attended a performance of *Hamlet* at Covent Garden. In the fifth act a funeral ode, which Haydn's friend William Shield had set to Shakespeare's words, was sung, and after *Hamlet* was over, the pantomime *Harlequin and Faustus* was given. The *Oracle* of 14 October reviewed the performance and noted that 'the amiable Haydn, as a genius second to no one, sat in a side box' (Pohl, *H in L*, 277).

Another English family with whom Haydn was on friendly terms was that of the oboist John Parke, who played in the Prince of Wales's band. His younger brother William was oboist at Covent Garden and later wrote his celebrated *Musical Memoirs,* which have been so often quoted in this Chronicle. Mistress Parke was the daughter of John and often sang at the Haydn–Salomon concerts; Haydn had presided at her benefit concert earlier in the year; she was twenty-one years old at this point. The two prints mentioned in Haydn's letter are listed under No. 46 of the catalogue of Haydn's legacy. The letter is undated by Haydn, but at the bottom of the sheet is the note '22 Oct. 1794' followed by another note (in a different hand) 'The celebrated Musician, D^r. Haydn'.

[To (John?) Parke, London. *English*]

[London, 22nd October 1794]

I am much obliged to you for the two so charming Prints, I tack me the liberty to Send for the Mistris Park a little Sonat, and to come to Her next Friday or Saturday between 1 and 2 o'clock. I am

Your most obedient S^t
Haydn

[Address:]   Mr Park
       Piccadilly N^r 32.   [CCLN, 144]

William Gardiner, the music-lover and factory owner from Leicester who in 1804 was to send Haydn six pairs of cotton stockings with various Haydn melodies woven into them, relates in his amusing memoirs, *Music and Friends*, how the composer entered the London music shop of a certain Howell. We presume the encounter took place during the second London visit, when Haydn's English had progressed sufficiently to carry on such a conversation.

> One morning a neat little gentleman came into his [Howell's] shop and asked to look at some pianoforte music, and laid before him some sonatas by Haydn which had just been published. The stranger turned them over and said, 'No, I don't like these.' Howell replied: 'Do you see they are by Haydn, Sir?' 'Well, Sir, I do, but I wish for something better.' 'Better,' cried Howell indignantly, 'I am not anxious to serve a gentleman of your taste,' and was turning away when the customer made it known that he was Haydn himself. Howell, in astonishment, embraced him and the composer was so flattered by the interview that a long and intimate friendship followed. [Geiringer 1947, pp. 128f.][1]

Lord Abingdon had a friend, Sir Walter Aston, Bart., Eighth Lord of Forfar, County Forfar, in the Scottish Peerage; he was married to Anne, *née* Hutchinson, and they lived at Preston in the township of Hitchin in Hertfordshire. It appears that on or for a visit to Preston, Haydn took as a 'hostess' present a couple of delightful and sophisticated *Divertimenti* for two flutes and violoncello. Some years later, in 1799, our ubiquitous friend T. Monzani issued them as follows: 'Two Original Trios for two German Flutes, and Violoncello, Composed while in England by D^r. Haydn . . . . This Trio [IV: 1 in C] was Composed for Sir Willoughby [*sic*] Aston B^t. who generously gave it to Mr. Monzani for Publication . . . . This Trio [IV: 2 in G] was composed for

---

1 This story also appears in Carpani's *Le Haydine*, without mentioning the name of the music shop. Otherwise, however, Carpani's anecdotes about Haydn in London bear examination only with considerable scepticism. In one of them, a 'rich milord' asked to have lessons from Haydn at a guinea each. The milord brought along a Haydn work which he proceeded to demolish as not adhering to the rules of strict counterpoint, etc. Haydn defended his work up to a point but finally gave up, saying that he perceived that the milord wished to instruct him (Haydn), 'Excuse me! I'm not in a position to pay you a guinea a lesson.' The most interesting story in Carpani concerns the concerts of Antient Music. Haydn praised the institution but 'confessed to me [Carpani] that many of these compositions that had thrilled him when he had heard them for the first time in his youth, afforded him considerably less pleasure upon rehearsing them so many years later, no matter how beautiful and praiseworthy they may once have seemed to him.' Carpani is responsible for the very doubtful story of the Reynolds portrait of Mrs Billington as St Cecilia. 'The painter has made a great mistake; he has pictured you listening to the angels. He should have pictured the angels listening to you.' There is also the totally spurious story of Reynolds painting Haydn for the Prince of Wales. (Can Haydn have confused Reynolds with Hoppner: It seems most unlikely.) We cannot bring ourselves to accept these pretty anecdotes as truthful, but we concede, as does their editor, that behind all the gossip there may have been an element of fact. See the interesting article by Vernon Gotwals, 'Haydn in London again' (*Music Review* XXII/3 [August 1961], pp. 189ff.), from which these extracts have been quoted. The interested reader may in that article examine all these stories *in toto*.

the Earl of Abingdon who generously gave it to Mr. Monzani for Publication.' We shall examine these 'London Trios', as they are now called, *infra* p. 405). Walter Aston started life as a watchmaker. The *Gentleman's Magazine* said of him, 'His Lordship, who had been in trade in the early part of his life was an inoffensive man of a rather convivial turn.' We cannot explain how Monzani came to call Aston by the wrong Christian name of Willoughby: *The Peerage of the British Empire* by Edmund Lodge (London, 1834, p. 31), and also *The Complete Peerage* are quite clear that his name was Walter. (See also Geiringer 1947, p. 128.)

In his London Notebook, Haydn remembered the visit as follows:

On 14th Nov. 1794 I went with Lord Avingdon [Abingdon] to Preston, 26 miles from London, to visit the Baron of Aston; he and his wife love music.

[CCLN, 304]

A week earlier the *Sun* had printed a short notice about the coming season:

SALOMON, it is said, means to carry on his Concert this winter, and as the Professional Concert is *no more*, it is probable that he will have a very flourishing season. The name of HAYDN is a powerful charm in his favour; but with the aid of musical novelties from so great a composer, he may bid defiance to competition. [*Sun*, 7 November 1794.]

On 25 November, the *Sun* carried an important announcement: the publication of 'Trois Sonates pour le Piano-Forte avec Accompagnement de Violon & Violoncello. Composées & Dédiées a son Altesse Madame la Princesse Douarière Esterházy *née* Hohenfeld' by Longman & Broderip. They are the piano Trios Nos. 32–34 (XVI: 18–20) in A, G minor and B flat, the first of a long and distinguished series which, together with the last three piano Sonatas for Therese Jansen (Nos. 60–62), constitute Haydn's pianistic legacy. Can these have been the 'sonatas by Haydn which had just been published', and which Haydn was shown in the music shop of Mr Howell?

It was a polite gesture on Haydn's part to have dedicated the new Trios to Prince Anton's widow, *née* Countess Marie Therese von Hohenfeld [*recte*]; she later married Karl Philipp, Prince von Schwarzenberg.

Sometime in 1794, but probably after the concert season was finished, Haydn wrote at least one (in E flat No. 62, XVI: 52) and possibly more of the set of three piano Sonatas for Therese Jansen, later married to Gaetano Bartolozzi. We shall examine both the interesting Miss Jansen as well as the music for her, *infra* (see pp. 309 and 439).

On 15 December Haydn was invited to Joah Bates's house. Bates had conducted the great Handel festival in 1784. A graduate of King's College, Cambridge, he was a warm admirer of Handel's and in 1794 the conductor of the Antient Music in London. In 1780 he had married Miss Sarah Harrop, the singer, who was born in Lancashire of humble parents and who was an inspiration to the factory girls of northern England. In the lost Fourth Notebook, Haydn wrote:

On 15th Dec. 1794, I visited Mr. Baze, who conducts the Ancient-Concert from the organ and plays quite well; his wife has a very pleasant, flexible voice, her pitch is very true and her pronunciation clear; she has Bachierotti's [Pachierotti] way of singing, but her shake is a little too rapid. [CCLN, 304]

The Farington Diary has an interesting confirmation of this. On 29 November, Farington notes 'Mrs. Bates (late Miss Harrop) to sit to him [George Dance]' and on 16 December we read:

Wm. Dance introduced Haydn, the Composer of Music last night to Mr & Mrs Bates at their home in John Rd., Bedford Row. – Mrs Bates sung some of Haydn's songs, in so admirable a manner as drew from him the warmest eulogiums. – He had never heard them sung so well. – Mrs. Bates [1741–1811] is about 40 years of age, – Dance thinks her a very sensible woman. [I, 76]

On 18 December 1794 the *General Evening Post* carried an announcement the quotation of which will prove to be self-explanatory: 'This Day were published by PRESTON . . . THREE SONATAS . . . dedicated, by permission, to Dr. Haydn, By T. Haigh.' One of the many works dedicated to Haydn by friends and pupils, these Sonatas will be discussed briefly in connection with Haydn's last piano Sonatas (*vide infra*, 450).

It was now known that the great *prima donna* Banti would participate in the new concerts which were being planned by Salomon and members of the Opera as the old year drew to a close. Haydn was, of course, curious to hear *la* Banti and on 18 December he wrote to his colleague Viotti as follows:

[To Giovan Battista Viotti, London. *Italian*, 'Lei'.]
My most excellent Friend!
    You will excuse me, wanting for every reason to hear our dear Banti tomorrow, but since we poor *Maestri* cannot spend half-a-guinea so frequently, that I ask you to have the goodness (if it is possible) to procure a ticket for me from Dr. Deller, who the last winter did me the favour of letting me attend the theatre *gratis*: I am sorry not to have had the honour of seeing you the last time at your place; I hope to see you another time. I am with every respect
Your
Oblig. Ser.
Haydn.

Bury Street, 19th Dec. 794.
[Address:] M^r: Viotti.   [not in CCLN; *Haydn Yearbook* IV, 202]

Since Haydn would write his greatest single vocal piece for Banti, it behoves us to hear contemporary opinions on her voice. Da Ponte has a lot to say about her, prejudiced of course (as Da Ponte was about everything) but always interesting and often brilliant:

The opera season [of 1794] was almost half over when two famous rivals came to London: the Banti woman, at that time one of the most celebrated singers in Europe in serious parts, and la Morichelli, equally celebrated in comedy. They were neither of them any longer young, and never had they been enumerable among the great beauties: but the one was much sought after and exorbitantly paid for the splendours of a glorious voice, the single gift she had receive from Nature . . . . They had therefore both become idols of the public but the terrors of composers, poets, singers, and impresarios . . . . Which of them was the more dangerous and the more to be feared, is a question not easy to decide. Equal in their vices, their passions, their iniquities, their wickedness of heart, they were women of totally different, even contrary, dispositions . . . . Banti . . . was an ignorant, stupid, insolent woman. Accustomed from early girlhood to singing in cafés and about the streets, she brought to the Opéra, whither her voice only had elevated her, all the habits, manners and customs of a brazen-faced Corsican. Free of speech, freer of action, addicted to carousals, dissolute amusements and to the bottle, she showed herself in the face of everybody for what she was, knowing no measure, no restraints; and when anyone of her passions was stirred by difficulties or opposition, she became an asp, a fury, a demon of Hell, capable of upsetting an empire, let alone a theatre.   [*Memoirs*, 251–3]

Banti at that time had as a lover the oboe-player Giuseppe Ferlendis for whom Mozart composed his oboe concerto in C (K.314) in 1777, and who was to play with Haydn in 1795 (about whom the composer wrote in his Third Notebook, 'Ferlendis, oboe player, is mediocre' [CCLN, 301]). Parke says of her:

> Giardini being asked his opinion of Banti, previous to her arrival in England, said, 'She is the first singer in Italy, and drinks a bottle of wine every day.' [Earlier Parke noted] the voice of Banti evinced sweetness, power, and flexibility. Her execution was rapid and neat, and she was equally excellent in the bravura and cantabile style of singing; she was besides a graceful actress ....   [I, 183]

We have seen that Banti made her début at London in April 1794. At that time, the newspapers were full of notices about her, and the *General Evening Post* on 26 April 1794 writes as follows:

KING's THEATRE

> The Musical World were gratified on Saturday evening by the first appearance on the BANTI, and it is but justice to say, that her performance was worthy of her fame. Her first *bravura* song literally electrified the audience; in the succeeding efforts she shewed that her powers in the *Cantabile* are equally transcendent. To these, she adds a degree of intelligence and attention to the business of the scene, which interested every careful Auditor in her success ...

The *Sun*, on 28 April 1794, says of Banti's first appearance that she

> laboured under so severe and so evident a cold, that her promtitude to come forward . . . deserves high commendation. Not withstanding this oppression of her talents, she fully displayed the powers of a very great Singer. Her voice is peculiarly sweet, and seems to be of great compass. Her taste is admirable . . . she is also a good Actress . . . There is something interesting and elegant in her person, though she is by no means to be considered as a beauty . . .

Domenico Dragonetti, the great double-bass player, who was away on the Continent and was to return early in 1795 with two fellow Venetians, the composer Bianchi and the engraver Bartolozzi,[1] later expressed his opinion on Banti to Mary Novello in 1832: 'Banti he thinks the most wonderful of singers, and related his astonishment at her wonderful memory, as she could not read a note of music, or a word of print, yet hearing an air once played over, and that but indifferently, she sang it most divinely.' Not everyone was so enthusiastic. Haydn's friend George Dance heard her on 3 July and the next day Farington reports: 'George Dance came in the evening. He heard the Banti at the Opera last night and does not think her equal to Mara. She has a very fine voice and a good ear, but has no knowledge of musick. He thinks her action, which has been much extolled, very mediocre' (Farington I, 59f.).

From Crosse's *Account* (229n.) we learn that Madame Banti had £1,400 and a benefit in 1794, an enormous salary.

On 22 December 1794, the *Sun* announced that 'This Day was published' a work to which Haydn contributed: the Rev. William D. Tattersall's *Improved Psalmody, Vol. I [all published] The Psalms of David from a Poetical Version by James Merrick . . . with new music collected from the most eminent Composers*, printed by T. Skillern, London, 1794.

---

1 Oliver Strunk, 'Notes on a Haydn Autograph', *Musical Quarterly* XX, 2 (April 1934), pp. 195f. Dragonetti from *A Mozart Pilgrimage*, p. 339.

Haydn was given a silver plate, on which the following note was engraved, which Haydn copied in his Third Notebook:

In the year 1794
Dr Haydn, Dr Arnold, Mr John Stafford Smith, and Mr Atterbury declared their readiness to cooperate with Dr Cooke, Dr Hayes, Dr Dupuis, Dr Parsons, Mr Calcott, the Rev^r Osborne Wight, Mr Webber, Mr Shield, and Mr Stevens in their Exertions towards perfecting a work for the Improvement of Parochial Psalmody.
    as a Small Token of esteem for
    his abilities and of gratitude
    for his Services this Piece of
    Plate is presented to Doctor Haydn
[in another hand:] by W. D. Tattersall.   [CCLN, 290]

We have met almost all the composers listed here. The exceptions are Dr Benjamin Cooke, composer and organist of Westminster Abbey who had died in 1793; Dr (later Sir) William Parsons, pupil of Sacchini, was Master of the King's Musick; John Stafford Smith was an organist and composer; as was Samuel Webbe.

Salomon had come to a momentous decision: he was going to relinquish his concerts and merge forces with the Opera. In a very long open letter to the Press, he gives his reasons for so doing, the principal one being the difficulty of finding singers willing to cross the English Channel. The great Salomon concerts were at an end, then – but not, in fact, for very long, for in 1796 Salomon found that he could start them up again. Haydn was not particularly worried, since the new organization had obviously come to him at once and secured his services; and moreover he admired and liked Viotti. He had composed in preparation for the new organization one of his very greatest symphonies, No. 102 in B flat, which is signed London, 1794; and he could look forward to the new year with his usual cheerful confidence.

CHAPTER FIVE

1795

Hanover-square, January 12, 1795.

MR. SÀLOMON respectfully presents his acknowledgments to the Nobility and Gentry who have hitherto done him the honour to support his Concert; he feels the most lively sentiments of gratitude for the protection which they gave him in the arduous undertaking; and it is with real regret that he is under the necessity, from circumstances which he has it not in his power to control, to decline the further continuance of the establishment.

In the present situation of affairs on the Continent, Mr. Salomon finds it impossible to procure from abroad any Vocal Performers of the first talents, but by the influence of terms which an undertaking like his could by no means authorize him to offer; and it would be a presumption, of which he is incapable, to solicit the patronage of the Nobility and Gentry to an inferior entertainment.

It was an essential object in his original undertaking to promote the character of the profession by the union of its most splendid talents; and, he flatters himself, that he speaks the sense of the best Connoisseurs when he presumes to say, that in his essays he succeeded to an extent that gave unprecedented distinction to the Concert. At the present moment, therefore, when from circumstances incompatible with a single and circumscribed undertaking he is obliged to relinquish his favourite idea, he is happy to find a cordial disposition to take up and further the plan of a National School of Music becoming the taste and grandeur of this kingdom, in a quarter which necessarily possesses the means for that purpose.

As a professional man he wishes well to the new establishment of a grand and regular Concert at the Opera; to which, from the exclusive union of all the talents of the Theatre, a foundation would be given that no other undertaking could equal; and which is further to be supported by many eminent masters, whom in a very liberal and handsome manner he is invited to join, that they may unite their efforts for its perfection. – Mr. Salomon hopes that his labours have not been altogether useless, if they have tended to give rise to an institution which promises so much in favour of his art; and the Nobility and Gentry, his subscribers, will not lament to see the powers of the most splendid of his associates combined with talents worthy their union.

Mr. Salomon owes too many obligations to Dr. Haydn, to suffer this opportunity to pass without offering him his public acknowledgments for the advantages he derived from his unparalleled genius, and which he is happy to say, is not to be left unexerted in the service of the Public. To Mr. Viotti, and to all the other Professors, who honoured him with their assistance, he returns also grateful thanks, and rejoices to find, that all, equally animated by the love of the Profession, cheerfully enter into the Arrangement that has been formed.

[*Morning Chornicle*, 14, 15, 16, 17 January; *Oracle*, 16 January; etc.]

It was definitely the letter of a civilized and cultivated eighteenth-century gentleman.

Haydn had been a brilliant operatic *Capellmeister* for many years at Eszterháza, but he had a very jaundiced attitude towards Italian composers – whose works he had ruthlessly 'adapted' and 'improved' for Esterházy – and he was distinctly weary of coping with hysterical opera singers. Da Ponte has some horrendous tales to tell of William Taylor, the director of the London Opera, and Haydn's comments are equally pungent:

> The *Entrepeneur* of the Haymarket Theatre, of which the Duke of Pedfort [Bedford] is the principal figure, pays that miserable cur Taylor £21,000 Sterling every year for the expenses of the opera house; which sum is never sufficient, so that a group of various Lords, bankers, merchants &c. (but in all more than 200 of them) helps out. Moreover the house brings in not less than [at first: 'two hundred'] £500. The present contract was established in 1791 and lasts for 17 years. Each backer gets 15 percent annually, but he loses the capital entirely after the 17 years are up.   [CCLN, 297f.]

Another of Haydn's tales is about Dr Arnold. Haydn had the correct essence of the story but the wrong theatre. Dr Roger Fiske kindly informed me of the sequence of events. Samuel Arnold wrote *The Banditti* for Covent Garden in 1781. The opera failed; Covent Garden then staged it the next year as *The Castle of Andalusia*, and it stayed in the repertoire for a good half century with no benefit to its composer.

> Dr. Arnold composed an opera for the Drury Lane Theatre; since the backers were afraid that it would not be successful, Dr. Arnold agreed to give it three times at his own expense. He spent over seven-hundred pounds on it; the backers, however, payed a lot of people each time to hiss the opera. Finally Arnold let the backers have the opera and the costumes for two-hundred pounds, and they thereupon performed it, with some alterations – better costumes and scenery – and earned twenty-thousand pounds with it in the course of one year; the publisher alone earned some five-thousand pounds, and the poor composer lost five-hundred. O, what swindlers!   [CCLN, 306f.]

But if Haydn was going to have to do business with the London Opera, he had to swallow his prejudices; and Haydn, being a shrewd man, did just that. The first thing was to write down a list of the composers and principal singers, and we find such a list on CCLN, 301: 'Banti, Rovedino, Morichelli, Morelli, Brida, Braghetti, Bianchi, Martini, Ferlendis, Dragonetti, Harrington, Taylor, impresario, Neri, poor castrato.' He added to new operas which were in the repertoire: Gluck's *Alceste* and Bianchi's *Semiramide*, in which Banti had made her début. Most of the names are already familiar to us. Francesco Bianchi, the composer, whose opera *Aci e Galatea* Haydn thought over-orchestrated (*infra*, p. 298), was nevertheless good enough so that, according to Crosse's *Account* (69n.), 'Haydn used to keep a leaf of his works turned down for reference to soothe his mind when disturbed.' Bianchi committed suicide in 1810. Martini = Vincente Martin y Soler. The third composer mentioned is Dr Harington, whom we have seen in Bath. Of the singers, Carlo Rovedino was a bass and a friend of Da Ponte's; Brida (Haydn: 'a good youngster') a tenor; about Braghetti we know only that he was a member of the King's Theatre. The other names are instrumentalists: Ferlendis the oboe player and *amante* of *la* Banti, Dragonetti the double-bass player whom Beethoven admired. When George Smart was in Vienna in 1825, he wrote, 'The double-bass here [at St Michael's Church] had four strings and Mittag said some had five, but with three Dragonetti does more than I have yet heard.' (Smart, 112).

The New Year saw numerous announcements of the so-called Opera Concert:

OPERA CONCERT, KING'S THEATRE.

THE Nobility and Gentry are respectfully informed, that there will be, in the Great Room of this Theatre,

NINE CONCERTS BY SUBSCRIPTION.

To be held every MONDAY Fortnight, commencing on MONDAY, the 2d of February next.

In this Concert it will be the Study of the Proprietor to combine the most eminent talents, Vocal and Instrumental, now in England.

Composers.
Dr. HAYDN. Mr. MARTINI.
Mr. BIANCHI, and Mr. CLEMENTI.
From whom there will be at least Two New Pieces of Music
for each Concert.

Vocal Performers.
Madame BANTI, Madame MORICHELLI,
Signor NERI, Signor MORELLI,
Signor BRIDA, Signor BONFANTI,
And Signor ROVEDINO.
who are all engaged not to perform out of the Theatre.

Solo Performers.
Mr. SALOMON, Mr. DUSSECK,
Signor DRAGONETTI, Mr. SCHRAM,
Mr. LIN[D]LEY, Mr. ASHE,
Mr. HOLMES, Mr. HARRINGTON,
And Mr. VIOTTI.

The Chorusses under the Direction of Dr. ARNOLD, Organist of his Majesty's Chapel, who will himself preside at the Organ.

At the Harpsichord, Dr. HAYDN and Mr. FEDERICI.

Leader of the Band, Mr. CRAMER.

The whole to be under the Direction of Mr. VIOTTI, who will also occasionally furnish new Pieces of Music . . . .

[*Morning Chronicle*, 2, 7, 16, 17, 19, 20, 21, 22, 23, 24, 25, 26, 28, 29, 30, 31 January; 2 February; *Oracle*, 16, 17, 21 January; *The Times*, 29 January; etc.]

Plans were being made for the Prince of Wales's marriage to the unfortunate Caroline, Princess of Brunswick (Braunschweig), and Haydn's advice was sought about the music.

On 21st Jan. 1795, I dined with Dr. Parsons. There arose an argument which of the Doctors, Parsons, Dupuis, or Arnold, should conduct the orchestra for the Handel Antiphon at the Prince of Wales' marriage. Dr. Parsons is Master of the King's Band, the other two are Court Organists. In England, however, the organist is the head in all the churches, and the singers are subordinate to him. Each of the three wanted to be the principal conductor. When I was forced to express my opinion, I said: The youngest organist should play the organ; the other should conduct the singers who are subordinate to him; and Dr. Parsons should conduct the Instrumental Performers; and since the singers always have the preference over the instrumental players, one of them should place his chorus on the right, the other on the left. They didn't want that, however, and so I shook the dust off my feet and went home.   [CCLN, 305]

In the event the various Doctors followed Haydn's advice. The marriage, as we shall see, took place in April, and the music included Handel's 'Sing unto God' (Wedding Anthem, which had been composed for George III's father, then [1736] Prince of Wales). Dr Parsons directed the King's Band (leader: William Cramer) and was principal conductor; Arnold and Dupuis conducted the huge choir, and Dupuis also played the organ (Pohl, *H in L*, 299).

People seemed to be pleased with the new Opera Concert. The *Morning Chronicle* wrote, on 24 January:

> The whole world cannot produce such a combination of Musical talents as the Opera Concert presents to the Amateurs; and, as SALOMON candidly owns in his Advertisement, it is the foundation of a Musical School in England, worthy the taste and opulence of the Nation. The Great Room will conveniently accommodate 800 Subscribers; and to this number is limited.

Being the subject of such constant adulation, Haydn received all sorts of gifts of music, such as Dr Burney's 'XII Canzonetti a due voce in canone'. Fellow composers also dedicated works to him, and on 25 January 1795, Alexander Campbell, a Scottish organist, gave Haydn 'Twelve Songs' and signed the title page (Somfai, 120). Haydn kept almost all these relics and we shall meet many of them again in the catalogue of his music library.

Haydn now came more and more to the attention of the Royal family. In the Fourth Notebook, is his description:

> On 1st February 1795, I was invited by the Prince of Wales to attend a musical soirée at the Duke of York's, which the King, the Queen, her whole family, the Duke of Orange &c. attended. Nothing else except my own compositions was played; I sat at the pianoforte; finally I had to sing, too. The King, who hitherto could or would only hear Handel's music, was attentive; he chatted with me, and introduced me to the Queen, who said many complimentary things to me. I sang my German song, 'Ich bin der verliebteste'. On 3rd Feb., I was invited to the Prince of Wales'; on 15th, 17th and 19th Apr. 1795, I was there again, and on the 21st at the Queen's in Buckingham House. [CCLN, 532]

There are many descriptions of this event, which must have been one of the highpoints of Haydn's whole life. There is even a report from the official *St James's Chronicle* (3 February):

> ... Last night the Prince of Wales gave a grand Concert and Supper, at Carlton-House [*sic*] to their Majesties, the House of Orange, the Princess Royal, the Duke and Duchess of York, Dukes of Clarence and Gloucester, all the junior Princesses, and Princess Sophia of Gloucester, and a select party of the Noblesse of both sexes.
>
> Previous to the Concert, the King went over to Carlton-House for the first time.
>
> The Concert was led by Salomon. The Musick consisted chiefly of Haydn's Symphonies, and a Concerto, played by Viotti ....

By far the most interesting description is in Parke's *Memoirs*, where the date is wrongly given as 2 March:

> ... His Royal Highness the Duke of York gave a grand concert of instrumental music, March 2nd, at York House, Piccadilly [*sic*], (where the Albany Chambers now stand,) at which their Majesties and the Princesses were present. Salomon led the band, amongst whom Cervetto, the elder Parke, Shield, myself, Dance, Blake, and Haydn, who presided at the piano-forte. Jarnovicki was to have played a

concerto on the violin, by desire of Her Majesty, who had never heard him perform; but on coming into the room just before the music commenced, and perceiving Salomon there, (to whom he bore a violent hatred,) Jarnovicki vented his spleen by leaving the house immediately. This insolent foreigner, who suffered professional jealousy to supersede the respect due to the queen of a great nation, deserved punishment for his presumption. When we had tuned our instruments, and were waiting for the signal to begin, His Royal Highness the Duke of Gloucester (brother to the King) entered the room, and fixing his eye on a respectable double-bass player, belonging to the Italian Opera, named *Jouvre*, who had been several years in England, suddenly exclaimed, 'There's a Frenchman!' and hurried out of the room. It ought not to appear extraordinary that persons of such exalted rank should have been mistrustful in times when the blind fury of the French Revolution had been so cruelly levelled at royalty, and when several instances had occurred of the British government finding it necessary to send Frenchmen out of the kingdom, one of whom, on taking leave of his friend, (an Italian musician,) said, 'Fare ye well; I shall be back again in a fortnight with my friend *Buonaparte.*' Their Majesties, however, and the Princess, sat in the room during the whole of the concert.

At the end of the first part of the concert Haydn had the distinguished honour of being formally introduced to His Majesty George III., by His Royal Highness the Prince of Wales. My station at the time was so near to the King, that I could not avoid hearing the whole of their conversation. Amongst other observations, His Majesty said (in English) 'Doctor Haydn, you have written a great deal.' To which Haydn modestly replied, 'Yes, Sire, a great deal more than is good.' To which the King neatly rejoined, 'Oh no, the world contradicts that.'

After his introduction, Haydn, by desire of the Queen, sat down to the piano-forte, and, surrounded by Her Majesty and her royal and accomplished daughters, sung, and accompanied himself admirably in several of his *Canzonets*. The gracious reception Haydn experienced from the King was not only gratifying to *his* feelings, but flattering to the science he professed; and while it displayed the condescension and liberality of a great and good monarch, it could not fail proving a powerful stimulus to rising *genius*.

The following weeks I attended a grand instrumental concert given by the Prince of Wales at Carlton House to their Majesties and the whole of the royal family. Haydn presided at the piano-forte, and Salomon led the band, which consisted of the same performers as at the Duke of York's. The magnificence of the scene on this occasion was truly fascinating. The exalted rank of those present, the splendour of the dresses, and the elegance and beauty of the ladies, all combined to strike the beholder with admiration and delight. I had permission that night to enter the room while the whole of the royal family (seventeen in number) were at supper. The King and Queen sat at the head of the table, and the branches of the royal family nearest to them, according to their seniority, while the Prince of Wales occupied a seat opposite to his royal parents, doing the honours of his table with all that elegance for which he has ever been so highly distinguished. I frequently attended the concerts of the Prince of Wales, in one of which I played a concerted piece for the oboe composed by Haydn [*Notturno* for the King of Naples, *vide* 1791–2 *passim*], and was honoured with the distinguishing appro-bation of His Royal Highness, who, whilst playing the violoncello, called two foreign noblemen to him to listen, and repeatedly exclaimed 'Bravi – the finest tone in the world!' I had the satisfaction several times of meeting Haydn at Carlton House, at music parties, where, after the concert was ended, an elegant supper invited us to partake of its gratifications. The attention we experienced at Carlton House proceeded from Mr. Bect, then maitre d'hotel, successor to Mr. Weltjee, who had retired to his house and grounds at Chiswick Mall.   [I, 196ff.]

Haydn elaborated the evening of 1 February orally to Griesinger, also including events from other evenings:

Haydn had very much wanted to have something of his played at the annual large music concerts which the King put on, in which nothing but Handel's compositions was put on the stands. They raised his hopes, but soon an order was given that at these concerts nothing younger than music composed thirty years before could be performed. During his second stay in England, however, Haydn got his way. One of his symphonies was played and excellently so by the King's Band. Now the King wanted Haydn to play a Handel Psalm on the organ; Haydn, who had diligently studied Handel's works, fulfilled this wish to general satisfaction.

He had to play for the Queen several times, and she gave him the manuscript of a German oratorio by Handel, the Erlöser am Kreuz [the MS. Haydn owned now in the Nationalbibliothek, Vienna], the only one he had written in that language [the so-called *Brockes Passion*]. One evening, after Haydn had played on the pianoforte for a long time to the Queen, the King, who always spoke German [*sic*], said that he knew Haydn was once a good singer, and he would like to hear him sing a few German songs. Haydn pointed to the joint of his little finger and said: 'Your Majesty, my voice is only this big now.' The King laughed, and then Haydn sang his Song, 'Ich bin der verliebteste.'

The King and Queen wanted to keep him in England. 'I will give you rooms in Windsor for the summer,' said the Queen, and then she added slyly, squinting at the King, 'and then sometimes we'll make music tête à tête. 'Oh! I'm not jealous of Haydn,' said the King, 'he's a good honest German man'. 'To keep that reputation,' answered Haydn, 'is my greatest pride.' Upon repeatedly being pressed to stay in England, Haydn gave as excuses that he was bound to the house of his Prince through gratitude, and that he couldn't forever be separated from his fatherland or from his wife [!]. The King offered to have her sent over. 'She won't even cross the Danube, let alone the ocean,' said Haydn. He remained steadfast, and thought this was the reason why the King never gave him anything. Of the Royal family, only the Duchess of York came to his benefit concert, but she sent him fifty guineas. He was, on several occasions, received by her in a very friendly way, for she knew how much her father, the King of Prussia, thought of Haydn. At the Prince of Wales's he conducted twenty-six concerts, and the orchestra often had to wait for several hours until the Prince rose from table.   [Griesinger, 33f.]

The mysterious German Song, 'Ich bin der verliebteste' is nothing other than a translation of 'Transport of Pleasure' (later: 'Content') from the Second Set of Canzonettas, on which Haydn must have been working at this time (also on words by Mrs Hunter). We ought perhaps to add here a word of the size and constitution of the orchestra that played at Carlton House. Parke (II, 320) tells us that the Prince of Wales's music parties 'were never calculated to shock the ears of the ladies with the shrill notes of the trumpet, or the infantile cannon of the kettle-drums. They were entirely instrumental, and might without impropriety be termed chamber music.' This explains the reason for the appearance of those Haydn *Notturni* for the King of Naples at Carlton House (*supra*, p. 159); no doubt Haydn also had his newest Quartets performed there.

We have seen that Haydn, alone of living composers, had entered the programmes of the Antient Music in 1794. Now, a year later, we find him still represented. The *Sun* of 30 January 1795, reviewing a concert of Antient Music the day before, tells us that 'A beautiful new *canzonet* by HAYDN, sung by Miss POOLE, was very much admired . . .'. The work in question was obviously one of the Six Canzonettas published in 1794.

The 1795 season was now about to begin. The first new work that Haydn offered to the subscribers of the Opera Concert was the majestic and brilliant Symphony No. 102 in E flat, which he had composed in 1794. The slow movement was, probably later, used in the piano Trio No. 40 in F sharp minor (Hob. XV: 26) which Haydn published as one of three with Longman & Broderip and which was dedicated to Rebecca Schroeter. Was this mysterious movement with its gigantic reserve of strength a favourite of hers?

During the Finale, a chandelier crashed to the floor. Dies heard the story from Haydn, but this was confused with Symphony No. 96, which is known in England as 'The Miracle' (it is still so unknown in German-speaking countries that it has no nickname except when the English title is translated). Neukomm, however, in his *Bemerkungen zu den biogr. Nachrichten von Dies* is sceptical of the whole thing. 'I never heard anything of this anecdote,' he says, 'either from Haydn, or later, in England.'

First Concert: 2 February 1795

The Orchestra will consist of more than Sixty Instrumental Performers, besides the Solo Players . . . .

CONDITIONS of the SUBSCRIPTION.

Four Guineas for Nine Performances. Tickets to be transferable. – Ladies' to Ladies, and Gentlemen's to Gentlemen. – A single ticket will be delivered for the nine nights, and the Subscribers to write on the back of it the name of the Lady or Gentleman to whom they transfer the same.

Subscriptions are received at the Banking House of Messrs. Ranson, Morland, and Hammersley, in Pall-Mall, and at Messrs. Longman and Broderip's, in the Haymarket and Cheapside; who will give receipts, which will be exchanged for the proper ticket, at the Office of the Theatre, adjoining Union-Court every Day. The Ladies' Tickets are green, the Gentlemen's red.

N.B. As the Tickets are transferable, the number of Subscribers is necessarily limited to the accommodation of the room.

The First Performance will be on MONDAY, the 2d of February, 1795.

PART FIRST.
A Grand Overture, MS. – Haydn.
Duetto, Signor Rovedino, and Signor Morelli – Cimarosa.
Concerto Bassoon, by Mr. Holmes – Devienne.
Song, Madame Morichelli – Gazaniga.
Concerto, Piano Forte, by Mr. Dusseck – Dusseck.
Quartetto, Madame Morichelli, Mr. Kelly, Signor Rovedino,
and Signor Morelli, MS. – Martini.

PART SECOND.
A new Grand Overture, composed on the Occasion, by – Haydn.
Song, Signor Neri, in Castor e Polluie [*sc*. Castore e Polluce] – Bianchi.
Concertone, Mr. Dragonetti – Dragonetti.
Song, Madame Banti in Scipione Affricano – Bianchi.
New Concerto, by Mr. Viotti – Viotti.
Terzetto, Signor Neri, Mr. Kelly, and Madame Banti, MS. – Piccini.
FULL PIECE.

The Doors to be opened at Seven . . . .

The Nobility and Gentry are most respectfully informed, that the KING's DOOR, adjoining Union court, will be open for the general resort of the Company, and in order to prevent confusion, the Subscribers are earnestly requested to give positive Directions to their Servants to set down and take up with their Horses' Heads towards Pall-mall; and at the desire of many of the Subscribers, the Door in Market-lane will also be opened for the accommodation of the Company.

In reply to numberless applications which have been made at the office, the Public are entreated to observe, that it is an unalterable rule in this Concert, (conditioned on the part of the Subscribers) that no Tickets shall be granted for the night, and no Subscriptions divided; neither will Tickets be issued at any period of the Season under the full Subscription.

The office will continue open all this day and evening, for the delivery of the Subscribers' Tickets.

[*The Times*, 2 February, etc.; *Oracle*, 26, 28, 29, 30 January, 2 February; etc.]

When Haydn appeared in the orchestra and seated himself at the Pianoforte, to conduct a symphony personally, the curious audience in the parterre left their seats and pressed forward towards the orchestra, with a view to seeing Haydn better at close range. The seats in the middle of the parterre were therefore empty, and no sooner were they empty but a great chandelier plunged down, smashed, and threw the numerous company into great confusion. As soon as the first moment of shock was over, and those who had pressed forward realized the danger which they had so luckily escaped, and could find words to express the same, many persons showed their state of mind by shouting loudly: 'miracle! miracle!' Haydn himself was much moved, and thanked merciful Providence who had allowed it to happen that he [Haydn] could, to a certain extent, be the reason, or the machine, by which at least thirty persons' lives were saved. Only a few of the audience received minor bruises.'

This occurrence I have heard in various versions, almost always with the additional fact that the symphony has in London been given the complimentary name. 'The Miracle'. It may be that this is true, but when I asked Haydn about it, he said: 'I know nothing of that.'   [Dies, 95f.]

OPERA CONCERT.

The first concert of this new establishment took place last night. It is impossible to speak of this concert in higher terms than M[r]. SALOMON, whose judgment will not be disputed, delivered in regard to it, when he candidly owned, that comprehending all the great talents, vocal and instrumental now in England, all competition must sink before it. It is certainly such an assemblage as no Country in the World can now exhibit, and we have no doubt but the success will answer the liberality of the undertaking.

It cannot be expected that so numerous an Orchestra could play with the same spirit and accuracy on the first night, and indeed the first time of their performance in this Hall, for we understand they did not rehearse here, as they will hereafter; yet this remark applies only to the first act, for the new Overture, composed by the inimitable HAYDN, was performed in a masterly stile, as it most richly deserved to be. His genius, as we have frequently before had occasion to remark, is inexhaustible. In harmony, modulation, melody, passion and effect, he is wholy [*sic*] unrivaled [*sic*]. The last movement was encored: and notwithstanding an interruption by the accidental fall of one of the chandeliers, it was performed with no less effect.

The new Concerto of VIOTTI, both in composition, execution, and taste, was a capital performance: each movement gave great pleasure, but especially the *adagio*, which, for sweetness of harmony, we have scarcely ever heard surpassed.

Madame BANTI was truly captivating, notwithstanding a severe cold, the effects of which nothing but her genius could have conquered. We never heard a Singer, whose intonation is so perfect. Of her execution, taste, and feeling we have often spoken with rapture, but never in adequate terms.

[*Morning Chronicle*, 3 February]

As might be expected, the Opera Concert introduced a great deal of vocal music into its programmes, more than in Salomon's concerts; but there was still plenty of instrumental concertos. Of the composers on the first programme, Domenico Cimarosa hardly needs an introduction. François Devienne, himself a flautist and bassoonist, wrote many works with solo woodwind parts which were popular in their day; he also introduced improvements of a technical nature to wind instruments and was a predecessor of the great Theobald Böhm ('Böhm Flute'). Giuseppe Gazzaniga was a successful Italian operatic composer whose works Haydn had conducted (and 'improved') at Eszterháza, while Martini is Martin y Soler. Both he and Bianchi were 'house composers' of the London opera. Domenico Dragonetti had returned from his travels to the Continent and was giving concertos on that unwieldy instrument of which he was such a master.

Haydn was now writing for an orchestra of sixty, almost the size of a modern orchestra if we imagine that the woodwind and brass family are more numerous in today's orchestras. Probably the woodwind were doubled frequently in Haydn's symphonies. Some of the original parts of the 1795 Symphonies have survived, in a set of the Salomon Symphonies Haydn sold to Prince Fürstenberg at Donaueschingen. These MSS. were discovered by the present writer in 1957.[1] The flute part of Symphony No. 103 was marked by Haydn to show the players when only one should be playing ('Solo') and when all of them should play ('Tutti'). Presumably Haydn will have used four flutes, four oboes, four clarinets, four bassoons and perhaps even four horns and four trumpets – as he was to do in *The Creation* performances in Vienna – which makes twenty-four wind instruments, with the kettledrums, twenty-five. This means that there will have had about thirty-five strings (perhaps in the composition of ten first violins, nine seconds, six violas, five 'cellos, five double basses?).

The day after the first Opera concert (2 February 1795) there was a concert at Carlton House. In the *Morning Herald* of 4 February we read, under the headline 'FETE AT CARLTON-HOUSE', that 'Last night, the PRINCE of WALES gave a Grand Concert and Supper . . . . previous to the Concert, the KING went over Carlton-House for the first time. – The Concert was led by SALOMON. The music consisted chiefly of HAYDN's symphonies, and a Concerto, played by Viotti . . .'. Two days later, on 6 February, the same newspaper reports a curious incident to which Parke, in his memoirs, also refers obliquely (*supra*, p. 283), but names Giornovichj, not Yaniewicz:

At the first Concert given at *Carlton-House* to the ORANGE Family, a *fiddling fracas* gave a *bar* of *discordance*: SALOMON, in attempting to mount the leader's stool, was jostled from it, by the indignant JANIEVICZ. The PRINCE observing this inharmonic contest, walked up, and learning the cause, immediately told the latter, that SALOMON was, as usual, to direct the band, and that a concerto was all that was required of him, Mr. JANIEWICZ: this, however, the latter very *modestly* declined performing; and therefore, packing up his fiddle, *scraped* off, to the astonishment of all present.

---

1 Landon, *Supplement*, 33 ff. Their textual importance is discussed in detail in the Philharmonia Complete Haydn Symphonies, Vol. XI & XII (Philharmonia 599 and 600).

Parallel to these concerts was another series, given every Friday evening at the King's Theatre Concert Room: here, the programmes were, in keeping with the Lenten period, primarily devoted to church music. Dr Arnold conducted from the organ, and Federici sat at the pianoforte; Cramer was leader of the band, which numbered some 200 persons. Madame Banti, Miss Leake, Signor Brida, Signor Rovedino and Mr Harrison were the principal singers. Several Haydn symphonies were given, and were placed, as usual, at the beginning of the second part of each programme. Contrary to the crowded Opera Concert, this series played to nearly empty houses. (*Oracle*, 2 March; Pohl, *H in L*, 289f.)

If Haydn must have watched the respective trials of Warren Hastings and his friend Thomas Holcroft with much interest, on 7 February there was an even more sensational case at the Court of King's Bench: Lord Abingdon on trial for libel. The very idea of trying a Lord must have seemed fantastic to Haydn, used to the practically unassailable position of the aristocracy in Austria. It is as if, *mutatis mutandis*, they had put Baron van Swieten on trial. . . . We have an interesting report of how British justice was 'seen to be done' from a report in the *Sporting Magazine* for February 1795:

EARL OF ABINGDON
As the EARL OF ABINGDON once held a first-rate situation in the Sporting World, and may still be considered not wholly unconnected with it, we shall lay the following particulars before our readers, in which it gives us some concern to find that his Lordship has unluckily run on the *wrong side of the* Post . . . .

In the Court of King's Bench, on Saturday, February the 7th, Mr. Erskine prayed judgment upon the Earl of Abingdon, who had been convicted last term, of writing and publishing a false and scandalous libel upon the character of Mr. Thomas Sermon, an eminent attorney, of Gray's Inn.

The Earl of Abingdon came into court, attended by Mr. Estwicke, a member of parliament, who had made an affidavit in justification of his lordship. The affidavit was read, and contained a sort of repetition of the calumny for which his Lordship had been prosecuted.

Lord Kenyon said that this was a most scandalous affidavit, and ought not to have been read. The learned Judge admonished Lord Abingdon to conduct himself in Court with propriety, and to dismiss from his mind that malevolence which had placed him before the Court for judgment.

Lord Abingdon then rose to address the Court as counsel in his own cause. He said that in consequence of the verdict found against him by the Jury, he must beg the affidavit he had made to shew cause why the information ought not to have been filed against him, to be then read. This affidavit was accordingly read, after which his Lordship said he had only a few words to offer to the Court. He complained that there was not a Counsel to be found who would plead his cause. Not even money would induce them to defend him. This was the reason he had been his own Counsel, Like Diogenes he had gone about with a lanthorn in search of an honest man, but could not find such a character. Lawyers, he said, whether honest or dishonest, would always keep together. If he had wanted an advocate for a parliamentary reform, he should have found a willing and zealous one in Mr. Erskine; but being a friend to the constitution of the country he was deprived of his assistance. His Lordship made several strong observations against the conduct of Mr. Sermon, and added, that though he venerated the law, he would never fail to manifest his indignation against those lawyers who were the scourges and pest of society.

Mr. Erskine, as counsel for the prosecution, addressed the Court in a most able and energetic speech. He said, that in praying the judgment of the Court upon the defendant, he should not be led astray from the case by the personal and unjust observations that had fallen from the noble Lord. The libel, of which he stood convicted, was of the most scandalous and malignant nature. He had thought fit to introduce the calumny; first, in his speech in the House of Lords, as a Peer of Parliament, and afterwards sent it in manuscript to several newspapers. He had made the House of Peers the medium through which he had endeavoured to overpower and ruin the reputation of a private citizen; but, thank God, the law was no respecter of persons, and would not permit the proudest Peer to calumniate the humblest individual with impunity. The tranquillity and happiness of human life depended upon the protection of the reputation of honest men. With respect to the insinuations thrown out by a noble Peer against him (Mr. Erskine) he could only say that they were false. He cared not for his insinuations. He was descended from as good a family as the noble Lord; but why talk of rank? the quality of the offender called down upon him an aggravation of punishment. The noble Lord had thought fit to complain that he could find no barrister to defend him; not to defend him in the manner he had proposed they should defend him, or as he had defended himself. It was to their honour that they refused to do so, for his defence was a new calumny. The noble Lord had brought a Member of Parliament into Court with him, who had made an affidavit that was a libel, for which he was liable to have an information filed against him. Mr. Erskine added a variety of other strong observations upon the case, and said the defendant's conduct and deportment, both at the trial, and on that day, gave him very little claim to the clemency of the Court.

Mr. Garrow made an able speech on the same side. He lamented that the noble Lord, in his journey with his candle and lanthorn, in search of an honest man, had not thought of a peer who wanted at least, a little discretion and propriety of conduct.

Lord Kenyon said, he was at a loss to tell whether the affidavit that had been produced and read in Court was more pregnant with wickedness or folly. It was certainly a very ill-advised affidavit. His Lordship ordered Lord Abingdon to be committed to the King's Bench Prison, and brought up again the last day of the present Term.

His Lordship was brought into the Court of King's Bench to receive judgment for a libel on Mr. Sermon, on Thursday. Previously to sentence being passed, he requested leave to say a few words. He Apologized for his intemperate language to Mr. Erskine and the Bar on the day when he was last brought up. Mr. Erskine expressed his willingness to accept the apology, which he trusted would have a proper effect on the Court.

His Lordship was sentenced to three months imprisonment in the King's Bench, and a fine of 100*l.* [pounds] and to find security for his future good behaviour. [pp. 261–3]

In such a way, the Earl of Abingdon made his exit from Haydn's life, escorted to prison by police officers. Haydn later (1795) dedicated his Second Set of Canzonettas to Lady Charlotte Bertie, Abingdon's wife.

The second concert took place a few days after Lord Abingdon's disgrace:

Second Concert: 16 February 1795

OPERA CONCERT, KING'S THEATRE.

THE Subscribers are most respectfully informed that the Second Performance will be on MONDAY next, the 16th Instant . . .

PART I.
Overture, MS. – Federici; Song, Signor Brida – Andreozzi; Duetto Concertante, Mr. Viotti and Mr. Salomon – Viotti; New Song, Madame Morichelli (composed here for the occasion) – Martini; New Symphony for the occasion – Clementi.

PART II.
Grand Overture, MS. – Haydn; Duetto Notturno, Madame Banti and Signor Rovedino – Bianchi; Concertone Double Bass, Dragonetti – Dragonetti; New Song, Madame Banti (composed here for the occasion) – Bianchi.

FINALE. [etc.]

[*Oracle*, 6, 14, 16 February; *Morning Chronicle*, 7, 8, 9, 10, 11, 12, 13, 14, 15, 16 February; etc.]

OPERA CONCERT. SECOND NIGHT.

We can only notice a few of the numerous excellencies that were produced here last night, by the splendid talents that are united in this Concert. Signor BRIDA sung like a master; but we wonder that with so good a voice, he should prefer the bravura to the cantabile. The Duo, by VIOTTI and SALOMON, we may safely affirm, could not have been better performed by any other two men existing – perhaps not so well. Masterly as VIOTTI truly is, SALOMON was no less sweet, various and impressive. MARTINI's new song was given with taste and gaiety by MORICHELLI, and was encored. The new Symphony by CLEMENT[I], did honour to his science and his genius. To write what is worthy to precede the wonders of Haydn is no easy task, yet this he successfully executed. The introduction was an Adagio of a grand and appropriate style; the succeeding Allegro had numerous beauties of melody and modulation; the slow movement was a canon, in four; and which in this species of composition is very rare, was no less sweet than scientific; and the last movement, continuing the same subject in rapid time, exhibited great learning, and perhaps too much contrivance. The musician, like the poet, cannot be too fearful of being seduced by the playfulness of fancy from the passion and subject of his story. We hope CLEMENT[I] will preserve in this majestic style of composition, for which few indeed are equally capable. What shall we say of HAYDN, and the sublime, the magic Overture, with which he began the second act? The rapture it gave cannot be communicated by words: to be known it must be heard. DRAGONETTI amazed all the musical cognoscenti by his Concertante on the Double Bass. At first it was Callibran [*sic*] singing a Cantabile; and afterwards, in the language of Bottom, a 'Lion that roared like any Nightingale!' For execution, it was almost past [b]elief; and for tone, infinitely more pleasant than was ever before thought possible. BANTI sang a beautiful Cantata, and a Bravura, both by BIANCHI, and, as usual, was adored; especially in the Cantata.

[*Morning Chronicle*, 17 February]

OPERA CONCERT, KING'S THEATRE

The Second Grand Concert, resulting from the union of the talents that formed the PROFESSIONAL and SALOMON's Concert, took place at this Theatre last night. Large as the Concert Room is, it was nearly filled by a very elegant audience. The entertainment was in the highest style of musical excellence.

BANTI sung in her best manner. Her first air was a new composition of BIANCHI, who sat at the harpsichord. The air was finely conceived. The recitative was particularly impressive, and the air admirably blended tenderness and spirit. – MORICHELLI, in a pretty air of MARTINI, had the luck to get an *encore*.

Nothing could be more correct and annimated [*sic*] that the Duet between VIOTTI and SALOMON.

The only other instrumental novelty was a symphony by CLEMENTI, the middle movement of which was a charming expression of tenderness. One of the exquisite overtures of HAYDN, introduced at SALOMON's Concert last year, was performed on this occasion, and received with the warmest applause. The second movement was *encored*.

Altogether this Concert is perhaps the best that has ever graced the annals of harmony. [*Sun*, 17 February]

KING'S THEATRE.
New Room.

On Monday night the Concert at this place was attended by the most fashionable company. A new Cantata, set on purpose by Signor Bianchi, for Signora Banti, was introduced in the second part of the Concert, and the audience were at a loss which to admire most, the execution, or the composition. The other singers acquitted themselves with sufficient credit; but the rules of discretion oblige us to make proper allowances for the humble predicament in which they all find themselves, when in competition with the Queen of the Quavers, the matchless Banti. – Signora Morichelli received some applause in a new song, set by Signor Martini, the harmony of which afforded an exquisite delight to the Connoisseurs. We cannot, however, omit observing, that the modulations were not sufficiently disguised, for we had an opportunity of tracing them to the celebrated Polacca, sung by Signora Banti, in the [pasticcio of] Serva Padrona. This circumstance was certaintly not very favourable to the singer, and did more honour to the judgment of the composer than to his invention; yet while Signor Martini borrowed from such a composer as Bianchi, we shall ever be ready to excuse his plagiarism. [*Star*, 17 February]

In analyzing this programme, we wonder if the Dragonetti *Concertone* was not cancelled at the last minute in the First Concert, because it seems odd that he would play what is presumably the same piece at two successive concerts. Unfortunately only one single hand-bill of the 1795 concerts has survived (but it is the most important: Haydn's benefit) so we cannot tell any last-minute changes, made between the first newspaper announcements (which were obviously not changed) and the actual concert. The Haydn Symphony was, as we gather from the *Sun*, either No. 99 or – more likely – No. 101 ('The Clock'), the slow movement of which was usually repeated (whereas of No. 99 it was usually the first movement that was encored).

It is not generally known that Haydn also participated in the oratorio concerts held at the King's Theatre, but such was the case. In the *Sun* of 21 February we read:

ORATORIOS

King's Theatre.

This Theatre was opened last night with the Oratorio of *Debora and Sisara*, composed by the celebrated GUGLIELMI . . . BANTI sung 'Angels ever bright and fair', in a style of exquisite sweetness, and without that excess of decoration with which the Italians are in the habit of profaning the grand simplicity of HANDEL. She was properly *encored*.

The grand manuscript overture of HAYDN at which himself [*sic*] presided, went off with spirit and precision, and was warmly applauded.

We cannot, of course, identify the Haydn Symphony. At the Third Concert, Symphony No. 100, the great success of the 1794 season, was played for the first time in the 1795 season, and it was noticed that the large size of the band was giving difficulty. Of the new composers, Gluck and Reichardt need no introduction and

Lindley's concerto is not further identified. Johann Friedrich Eck was the son of a musician in the famous Mannheim Orchestra and grew to become one of Germany's great violinists. Reichardt said of him that he never heard a better one with the single exception of Salomon. Eck published several violin concertos, and is also known for his involvement with the extremely dubious Mozart violin Concerto, K.268.[1] In 1801, he married a wealthy and titled woman and retired to France. Eck also had a brother, Franz, who became Spohr's teacher.

Third Concert: 23 February 1795

OPERA CONCERT, KING'S THEATRE.

THE Subscribers are respectfully informed that the Third Performance will be THIS PRESENT MONDAY, the 23d Instant.

The Fourth Performance on MONDAY, the 2d of March; the Fifth, on MONDAY, the 16th of March; and the Sixth (on account of the Easter Holidays), will be deferred, by desire of the Subscribers, to MONDAY, the 13th of April.

FOR THIS EVENING.

PART I.
Overture, M. S. Reichar[d]t. Duetto, Madame Morichelli, and Signor Brida: Paesiello [*sic*]. Concerto Violoncello, Lindley. Song, Madame Morichelli: Cimarosa. The favourite Overture, Iphigenia: Gink [i.e. Gluck].

PART II.
Great Militaire Overture, M. S. Haydn. Rondo, Madame Banti, in Achile in Sciro: Paesiello [*sic*]. Concerto Violin, Mrs. Guilberg [*recte*, Gillberg] (being her first performance in this country): Eck. Cantata, Madame Banti: Bianchi.

FINALE. [etc.]

[*Oracle*, 23 February; *Morning Chronicle*,
19, 20, 21, 22, 23 February; etc.]

OPERA CONCERT

King's Theatre

We are happy to see this fine combination of musical talents properly supported. The room last night was attended by a large and elegant company, and the Entertainment was adequate to the assemblage attached.

Of the instrumental pieces HAYDN's *Military Overture* was the most conspicuous. This excellent specimen of imitative harmony was originally performed at SALOMON's admirable concert. It was highly applauded last night, and the second movement *encored*.

Madame GUILBERG, who made her first appearance in this country as a Violin Performer, is really a musical wonder. Her tone, taste and feeling deserve great commendation. There was a remarkable neatness and precision in her execution, and she gave the *Double Stop* with considerable skill. She is by a birth [*sic*] a Swede. Her person and manner are very interesting.

BANTI not only deserves great praise for the excellent singing, but for the liberal kindness with which she encouraged the fair stranger. [*Sun*, 24 February]

OPERA CONCERT.   THIRD NIGHT.

In a room so spacious, with a band so select, and singers and solo performers, whom we doubt if all Europe can excel, no wonder that the highest pleasure is received; and that a select, elegant, and well judging audience should be

---

1 For the latest literature on this subject, see *The Mozart Companion* (edited by Donald Mitchell and H. C. Robbins Landon), London, 1956, p. 218.

assembled. The company last night was brilliant beyond example. Of the music and the musicians, with very few exceptions, we cannot well speak too highly. In the first Act, Madame MORICHELLI sang an excellent song, composed by Cimarosa; and the famous Overture, by Gluck, to *Iphigene en Tauride* (a noble composition) was played with great spirit and effect.[1] The Grand Symphony of Haydn, with the Military Movement, which never fails to astonish and enrapture, and which, as usual, was encored, began the second act. We know not by what accident, but, though the sublimity of the composition overcame every little defect, we have heard it performed more accurately. Another time, no doubt, the band will be more determined, and more precise in their time. A Lady of the name of GUILBERG, a native, as we are informed[,] of Germany, played a Concerto on the Violin. Her youth and beauty, added to a delicate, though rather feeble tone, a brilliant shake, and great neatness of execution, interested her hearers, who expressed their approbation with repeated plaudits. The Adagio in particular (composed by Viotti, much to his honour) she played in a chaste and charming style. Madame BANTI sang first a most delicious Rondeau, by Paisiello; and afterward repeated the Cantata she sang at the last concert. It is a noble composition by Bianchi, and as a proof of its excellence pleased even more the second time than the first. Madame BANTI did it justice: it was extasy to listen to her sweet, powerful, and impressive notes.   [*Morning Chronicle*, 24 February]

The day of the Fourth Concert, 2 March 1795, was an important one in the history of music. One event was in London, where Haydn conducted the first performance of his great 'Drum Roll' Symphony (No. 103 in E flat), which 'excited the deepest attention'. The other event is a new discovery, and it happened in Vienna: Ludwig van Beethoven made his début at the Lobkowitz Palace. It was not at the young Prince Franz Joseph Maximilian's, Beethoven's patron and Haydn's too, who was a lad of twenty; but at the concert given by the 'old Prince'. Our source for this event is the Diary by Count Zinzendorf, who at this stage always refers to Prince Franz Joseph Maximilian and his wife (*née* Princess Caroline von Schwarzenberg) as 'les jeunes Lobkowitz' (even when in their teens, they were giving concerts; on 19 February 1793, Zinzendorf noted, 'au petit concert *chez les jeunes* Lobkowitz'). Zinzendorf was in some respects slightly cynical about music, and we have seen that he did not like Mozart much at the beginning; nor do we find him liking Beethoven much better, except this first time, when the young man's impact seems to have been enormous.

'De la au Concert du P^ce Lobkowitz, ou un nomé Bethofen de Bonn fit tous sentir' is the entry in question. If one may hazard a guess what Beethoven played, it might have been the 'Alla ingarese, quasi un capriccio', the original title on the autograph of what would much later be renamed by Schindler 'Wuth über den verlorenen Groschen' (Op. 129). Recent examination of the autograph, in a private collection in Rhode Island,[2] has shown that the watermarks and paper used permit a dating as early as 1795.

It would have seemed incredible to anyone, perhaps even to Beethoven himself, that he would soon tower over music as no other man had ever done before; that he would topple even Haydn's image forever. It would have seemed equally impossible that the great Haydn Symphony (actually being performed for the first time in London, probably at that very moment) would be, a hundred years later, described as

---

1 It seems certain that *Iphigénie en Aulide* (not *Tauride*) was played.
2 Erich Hertzmann, 'The Newly Discovered Autograph of Beethoven's *Rondo à Capriccio*. Op. 129' in *Musical Quarterly*, Vol. 32 (1946), pp. 171ff.

a 'pygmy' (*Encyclopaedia Britannica*) compared to Beethoven. Yet who knows what stirrings of ambition, what hidden drum-beats of pride, what hopes will have filled the head of that young firebrand, as he walked home to the Alserstrasse that night through the cold, moonlit streets of Vienna, looking up at the snowy Kahlenberg and Leopoldsberg rising against the horizon?[1]

Fourth Concert: 2 March 1795

OPERA CONCERT, KING'S THEATRE.

THE SUBSCRIBERS are most respectfully informed, that the Fourth Performance will be THIS present MONDAY, the 2d of March. (The Fifth Performance the 16th of March; and the Sixth, on account of the Easter Holidays, will be deferred, by desire of the Subscribers, to Monday, the 13th of April.)

FOR THIS EVENING.

Part I. Overture, M. S. Reschard [i. e. Reichardt]. Song, Signor Morelli: Mozzart [*sic*]. New Concerto, flute, Mr. Ashe: Ashe. Song, Madame Morichelli: Haydn. Overture, Demonshoont [i. e. Démophoon]: Vogel.

Part II. New Overture, composed here for the occasion: Haydn. Song, Signor Brida: Bianchi. Concertante, two violins, Mr. Viotti and his Scholar, Mr. Libon: Viotti. Song, Madame Morichelli: Gazzaniga. New Terzetto, composed here for the occasion, Madame Morichelli, Signor Brida, and Signor Morelli: Martini. Finale, under the direction of Mr. Viotti.   [etc.]

[*The Times*, 2 March; *Morning Chronicle*,
28 February, 2 March; etc.]

OPERA CONCERT.   FOURTH NIGHT.

This Concert is very deservedly in high fashion, and must necessarily increase the fame it has acquired. – BANTI is unfortunately ill, and her admirers, or rather adorers, were deprived last night of that exquisite delight which her uncommon talents afford: but MORICHELLI was no unworthy substitute. She is now better acquainted with her auditors; the timidity, which at first repressed her powers, is worn off, and she displays much science, taste, and feeling. The symphony, by VOGEL, is a grand movement, is but little known in this country, was well executed, and highly approved. Another new Overture, by the fertile and enchanting HAYDN, was performed; which as usual, had continual strokes of genius, both in air and harmony. The Introduction excited the deepest attention, the Allegro charmed, the Andante was encored[,] the Minuets, especially the Trio, were playful and sweet, and the last movement was equal, if not superior to the preceding. VIOTTI and his scholar, Mr. LIBON played a Concertante for two Violins, which gave great satisfaction. The talents of Viotti are well known; and the youth, his scholar, discovers an ear uncommonly chaste and delicate. His body of tone is not yet sufficient; but it will become more powerful when he gains greater confidence; it scarcely can be more sweet. The Concertante, as a composition, has great merit, and does honour to its author, Viotti. The new Terzetto by MARTINI was charmingly sung by BRIDA, MORELLI, and Madame MORICHELLI, is composed in the best Italian style, and adds to the well established reputation of its author.

[*Morning Chronicle*, 3 March]

OPERA CONCERT.

This admirable Concert afforded last night another proof of the improving taste of the Town by the very large Audience which attended it. BANTI was prevented by

1 Zinzendorf, last entry for 2 March: 'Il a neigé la nuit sur les montagnes. Vent de NO qui seche et emenat du froid et un beau clair de lune.'

imposition from appearing, a circumstance that was of course a considerable draw-back on the general entertainment, but however, the excellence of the whole furnished a very rich repast.

ASHE made his first appearance at this place and performed a Concerto on the Flute with all the skill which has raised his reputation so deservedly high. His second movement was STORACE's pretty Air of *Lullaby*, to which the variations by ASHE are beautiful.

A Concertante for two violins by VIOTTI and his pupil, Mr. LIBON, was one of the most charming treats of the evening. It is praise enough for Mr. LIBON to say, that he made a very respectable figure, even on so near a comparison with his master.

HAYDN's new Overture was much applauded. It is a fine mixture of grandeur and fancy.

MORELLI and BRIDA were severally excellent, and MORICHELLI never sung better. Her first Air was a beautiful movement from one of HAYDN's well-known Overtures. The room had abundance of rank and fashion.

The second movement of HAYDN's new Overture was encored; and CRAMER's skill each time received a distinct plaudit. [*Sun*, 3 March]

Johann Christian Vogel was a gifted operatic composer born in the same year as Mozart but who died even younger, in 1788, at Paris. The Overture to *Démophoon* was apparently a great success, for it was repeated at the next concert, where Haydn's Symphony No. 102 was also repeated.

Fifth Concert: 16 March 1795

OPERA CONCERT, KING'S THEATRE.

THE SUBSCRIBERS are most respectfully informed, that the FIFTH PERFORMANCE will be THIS EVENING, the 16th instant.

The SIXTH (on account of the Easter Holidays), will be deferred, by desire of the Subscribers, to MONDAY, the 13th of April.

[The detailed programme for 16th March is not given.]

[*Oracle*, 16 March; *Morning Chronicle*, 16 March; etc.]

OPERA CONCERT. FIFTH PERFORMANCE.

Our Readers surely will not blame us that we are to be frequently obliged to repeat praise; when it is so eminently merited, silence would be injustice. Among other delightful pieces, for the selection of which the subscribers are indebted to the director, VIOTTI, we again were charmed, or rather shaken, by the grand opening symphony to Demaphoon [*sic*]; MORELLI had a comic song in his usual bold and characteristic stile, and was encored. Mr. SCHRAM performed a concerto on the violoncello: his tone good, his hand firm, his knowledge of the finger board great, and his musical science undoubted. His contrasts of forte and piano we thought too uniform; whatever is regularly foreseen is mechanical: and light and shade should oftener melt and mingle than discover hard and determined outlines. MORICHELLI sang both her duet, with MORELLI, and her song, excellently; the duet was encored. In the first act, BANTI was either ill, or out of spirits; we believe the former: but in the second, more perfect, more impassioned, more divine singing, perhaps was never heard. The delicacy of her execution and sweetness of her tones, the accuracy of her taste, and the enchanting discrimination of her feeling, were incomparable. SALOMON's violin concerto was performed in so masterly a manner, with so much expression, variety, and genius, that it were a misfortune not to have heard him. In his cadenza particularly, few men are his equal. CLEMENTI furnished a new Overture; and afforded ample proof that, well as his fame was established, he rises in his compositions.

The ALLEGRO was truly *joyous*, the Andante was an animated conversation, in which the cheerful, the serious, and occasional touches of the grand, were charmingly intermingled, yet the subject preserved. – The Minuets were alive, and the last movement equal if not superior to the rest.

The first of the new overtures by HAYDN, was repeated; and with an accuracy and effect that were highly honourable to the band: and especially to the leader, Mr. CRAMER. He is indeed most commendably attentive, and the accuracy and effect of the band nightly improves. Of the Overture, what can be said more than that the best judges seem to doubt whether HAYDN himself ever surpassed it. The last movement was encored; and the Adagio still more deservedly ought to have been. *[Morning Chronicle,* 17 March]

Perhaps the main reason why there are no more detailed newspaper announcements of the Opera Concerts, once the season was in full progress, was because the series was sold out. In a significant announcement printed by the *Morning Herald* on 10 March 1795, we read 'OPERA CONCERT./WANTED, Tickets, particularly Ladies Tickets, for the next Concert, and for the residue of the season. Apply to Mr. Hookham, No. 15, Old Bond-street.'

Haydn noted Madame Mara's concert on 24 March twice (Third Notebook):

On 24th March 1795, Mara gave her Benefice Music [benefit concert] in Hanover Square. Yaniewish [*sic*] conducted; Clementi sat at the pianoforte. She had to bear the expense. [CCLN, 302]

On 24th March 1795, Mara, having returned from Bath, gave her Benefic-Music [benefit concert] in Hannovers Room [Hanover Square Rooms]. There were not more than 60 persons in the audience. It is said that she never sang better than at that time. Janiowick conducted. – Mr Clementi sat at the pianoforte, and conducted his new grand Symphony, without success. After the concert was over, Madam Mara gave a *Soupé* in the adjoining room. After 12 o'clock Mr Mara, very confident, walked in the door, came forward, and asked for a glass of wine. Since Madam Mara saw quite clearly that her husband was raging, and feared the consequences, she turned to her lawyer, who was at the table, and he said to Mr Mara: You know our laws; you will have the goodness to leave this room at once, otherwise you will have to pay £200 tomorrow. The poor man left the company. Madam Mara, his wife, went the other day to Bath with her *Cicisbeo*, but I rather think her obstinacy makes her despicable to the whole nation. N.B.: M. Florio.[1] [CCLN, 288]

The programme on that occasion was as follows:

PART I.
Grand Symphony (M. S.), Mozart.
Aria, Mr. Braham.
Quartet, Haydn.
Aria, Madame Mara – Andreozzi.
Concerto flute, Mr. Ashe – Ashe.
Aria, Madame Mara – Nasolini.

---

1 G. FLORIO was a flautist who first appeared in London in 1782. The son of Pietro Grassi Florio, former member of the Dresden band who left Dresden in 1756 to go to Paris and then London, Florio jun. was Madame Mara's *cicisbeo*. She took him to Germany in 1803 and performed several of his compositions. See J. J. Engl, *Haydns . . . Tagebuch . . . 1794 and 1795,* Leipzig 1909, p. 42 and Pohl, *H in L,* p. 372.

PART II.
New Grand Overture, M. S. – Clementi.
Aria, Mr. Braham.
Concerto Violin, Mr. Yaniewicz – Yaniewicz.
Aria, Madame Mara.
Full piece – Haydn.

[Pohl, *H in L*, pp. 236f.]

The newest production at the London Opera was Bianchi's *Aci e Galatea*, which was first given on 21 March. Da Ponte tells us of the scandals under which it was born:

[Bianchi] suggested to Banti, instead [of Da Ponte's *Merope*], another opera which he had written in Italy; and the woman had the shamelessness to tell the manager [Taylor] that it was a new creation and to insist that it be called and believed such, even by people who had seen it in Venice, many, many [*sic*: première at Venice in 1792] years before. Then, suddenly, it was announced with great pomp in all the newspapers and on all the bulletins that 'Madame Banti would give a second proof of her rare talents in "Acis and Galatea", an opera written especially for her in London by the celebrated composer, Francesco Bianchi.'
   Unfortunately for me, I happened to own the libretto of 'Acis and Galatea' which had been printed in Venice; and I was imprudent enough to say as much to Federici. He told the singer, she the composer, the composer the manager, trying to make him believe that it was all an imposture which I had cooked up. Taylor came to my office, his face redder than a rooster's comb, and demanded to see the libretto; but as he had no red-hot poker in hand to 'poke' me, I begged him to have a chair, and handed him a bottle of port instead. Then when he seemed a little calmed, I picked up the libretto in question and laid it on the fire, promising him not only to hold my tongue, but to make speedy reparation for my ill deed. Taylor was not always blind. . . .
   It was my task, meantime, to print the libretto. I sent the opera to the printer announcing it as new and with the same paragraph which had been published in the newspapers. But all those precautions were of little avail. Dress rehearsal came on: partisans and flatterers all cried: 'Beautiful! – Sublime! Divine!' But when the opera went on stage, though the room was packed with hands paid to applaud, and though Banti, before the performance, ate a hundred roasted chestnuts and emptied a full bottle, not a single piece of music pleased, and, despite all efforts made, it was not performed more than twice thereafter. [*Memoirs*, 255f.]

This is what Haydn had to say of the performance, and of the rowdy mob – this time in the galleries and not on the streets – of which he was so deeply distrustful:

On 28th March 1795, I saw the opera *Aci & Galathea* by Bianchi. The music is very rich in parts for the wind instruments, and I rather think one would hear the principal melody better if it were not so richly scored. The Opera is too long, especially since Banti has to keep everything going all by herself; for Brida is a good youngster with a beautiful voice but very little musical feeling; and Rovedino, and the good old Braghetti, and the wretched *Seconda Donna* – they all deserved, and received, not the least applause. The orchestra is larger this year, but just as mechanical and badly placed as it was before, and indiscreet in its accompaniments; in short, it was the 3rd time that this Opera was performed, and everyone was dissatisfied. It happened that, when the 2nd Ballet began, the whole public suddenly became dissatisfied and yelled 'off – off – off', because they wanted to see the new Ballet which Madam Hillisberg [*sic*] had given at her *Benefice* 2 days earlier. – Everyone was embarrassed – there was an interval lasting half an hour – until at last a dancer came forward and said, very submissively: 'Ladies and Gentlemen: since the performer Mr. Taylor cannot be found, the whole Ballet Company promises to perform the desired ballet next week, for which, however, the Impresario must pay Madam Hillisberg £300.' That satisfied them, and they then yelled, 'go on – go on'; and thus the old Ballet was then performed. [CCLN, 293]

The 'old Ballet' was *Paul et Virginie*. The *Sun* in its issue of 30 March 1795 describes this very scene as in Haydn's notebook and concludes, 'The delay in the Performance occasioned the Company to remain in the great Room till a very late hour.'

The review of the new opera by Bianchi, *Aci e Galatea*, in the *Morning Herald* was rather more favourable than the note in Haydn's diary: '. . . In Italy he is generally considered as the first disciple of JOMELLI, and we had an opportunity to distinguish, through out his performance, JOMELLI's peculiar refinements. The overture was in the grand style of HAYDN, but softened in the exquisite manner of SACCHINI; the second movement in particular was truly enchanting.' (The bad chorus and wretched scenery were severely criticized. 23 March 1795.)

The following documents are self-explanatory; they are printed here in the order given because the newspaper announcement obviously preceded Haydn's refusal.

FREE-MASON'S SCHOOL.
Under the Patronage of His Royal Highness the PRINCE of WALES.
      In Aid of the FUND for completing and furnishing the SCHOOL-HOUSE in St. George's Fields, for the Reception and Maintenance of One Hundred poor Female Orphans and Children of distressed Free-Masons.
      A GRAND CONCERT of VOCAL and INSTRUMENTAL MUSIC will be performed at FREE-MASONS' HALL, on MONDAY the 30th of March, 1795.
under the Direction of Dr. ARNOLD and Dr. DUPOIS [*sic*].
Principal Vocal Performers,
Miss Parke, Miss Leake, and Mrs. Harrison. Mr. Nield, Master Welch, Mr. Sale, Mr. Gore, Mr. Page, Mr. Leate, Mr. Guise, Mr. Vincent. Leader of the Band, Mr. Cramer.
Principal Instrumental Performers.
Messrs. F. Cramer, Parke, Lindley, Mountain, Smart, and Sons; Sowerbys, Leanders [*sc.* Leander], Hyde, Lyon, Boyce, &c., &c.
Double Drums, Mr. Ashbridge.
      A Grand Overture, Dr. HAYDN, under his Direction.
      In Part the First – A Concerto on the Violoncello, By Mr. Lindley. In Part the Second – A Concerto on the German Flute, By Mr. Ashe . . . [etc.]
                                        [*Oracle*, 25, 28, 30 March;
                                        Morning Chronicle, 30 March; etc.]

On 30th March 1795 I was invited by Dr Arnold and his associates to a grand concert in Free Maisons [*sic*] Hall: one of my big symphonies was to have been given under my direction, but since they wouldn't have any rehearsal, I refused to cooperate and did not appear. [CCLN, 289]

Haydn's notebooks inform us that the Prince of Wales was married on 8 April 1795. Two days later, on the 10th (a Friday), Haydn 'presided' and Salomon led at a concert for the Prince of Wales. This concert is confirmed by the *St. James's Chronicle*. Haydn says he was also at Salomon's new opera, *Windsor Castle* on the 10th. No doubt he attended, because his *Overture to an English Opera* (which according to the *Entwurf-Katalog* he composed in 1794) was performed. However, it seems doubtful that all this happened on the 10th, seeing that (1) the opera had been on for several days and (2) if we are to believe an announcement in *The Times* which indicates that a 'Grand Overture by Dr. Haydn, and performed under his immediate direction' was given on the 10th at Willis's Rooms for the benefit of Mr. Danby, 'Who has been confined more than 7 months by a severe illness. . . .' Leader of the band was Cramer, and Dr. Arnold presided at a 'Grand Piano Forte' (*The Times*, 8 and 10 April). Here are the relevant documents:

> On 8th Apr. 1795, the marriage took place between the Prince of Wales and the Princess of Brunswick. On the 10th, I was invited to a musical soirée at the Prince of Wales' in Carlton House. And old Symphony was played, which I accompanied on the pianoforte; then a Quartet; and afterwards I had to sing some German and English songs. The Princess sang with me, too; she played a Concerto on the pianoforte quite nicely. [CCLN, 305]

> . . . On Friday night there was a Musical Party at Carlton-House, for the entertainment of the Princess of Wales. Her Royal Highness is particularly fond of Musick, and performs herself. Haydn and Solomon, with some of the Princesses Household, were present. The Princess with engaging affability played a Concerto on the Piano Forte. . . . [*St. James's Chronicle,* 11–14 April (also *verbatim* in the *Sun*, 13 April)]

> On 8th April 1795, the Prince of Wales married the Princess of Brunswick. On the 10th I was at the Covent Garden Theatre – to see the big Spectacul [*sic*] – WINDSOR CASTLE, THE MUSIC BY SALOMON QUITE PASSABLE. The decorations – costumes – scenery, and the enormous amount of people on the stage are exaggerated. All the Gods of Heaven and Hell, and everything that lives on the earth are in the piece. [CCLN, 299]

COVENT-GARDEN THEATRE.

WINDSOR CASTLE – *grand masque.*

The introductory matter to the masque is by Mr. Pearce. He is not successful in the tragic diction, clogging his lines with unmeaning epithets. The LYRIC province he fills with better powers. The BLACK PRINCE and the MAID of KENT, the illustrious EDWARD and his COURTIERS, occupy the scene, but not long enough to take hold upon the mind.

They are speedily forgotten in the NUPTIALS of PELEUS and THETIS, which NOVERRE, SALOMON, and the MANAGER, have adorned with prodigality. The grouping is uncommonly excellent and picturesque; and the DANCERS executed their steps with amazing grace and neatness. BYRNE seemed to have stolen
'Atalanta's better Part'.

The MUSIC is very beautiful; and the first movement of the OVERTURE bespoke the style and fancy of HAYDN in notes, which no other genius ever could so combine.

For detail, we have unluckily no room; the bill of the day, however, may be fully trusted.

THESPIS.
[*Oracle*, 7 April]

. . . Piece in two Acts, called *Windsor Castle* . . . The Music, principally by SALOMON, is grand and impressive. The overture has all the fire and genius to be expected from HAYDN. . . . [*Evening Mail*, 6–8 April]

... the Overture was composed by the celebrated HAYDN. ... [discusses the Ballet by Noverre]   [*Sun*, 7 April]

[In an announcement for *Windsor Castle*, we read] 'The Overture composed expressly for the occasion by/Dr. HAYDN'.   [*Sun*, 8 April]

THEATRE ROYAL, COVENT GARDEN.
THIS Evening will be presented
LIFE'S VAGARIES
To which will be added, a new Drama, called,
WINDSOR CASTLE.
The overture composed expressly for the occasion by Dr. Haydn, as is the rest
OF THE MUSIC BY MR. SALOMON. ...
[*The Times*, 21 April]

Covent Garden, April 16./WINDSOR CASTLE./
A new piece in two acts, entitled *Windsor Castle*, in honour of the Royal Nuptials, was produced this evening. The marriage of Edward the Black Prince with his cousin the Countess of Kent, is the subject applied to the present happy occasion.
The fable is told in one act. ...
The second act includes the masque of Peleus and Thetis, supposed to be given in honour of the celebration of these nuptials.
The scene of the celestials in full assemblage, witnessing the marriage, with the various groups on the stage, forms a spectacle of uncommon grandeur. ...
The overture to the drama selected from Pleyel.
The overture to the masque composed expressly for the occasion by Dr. Haydn; as is the rest of the music by Mr. Salomon; except the glee, and Song, 'May the Prince and his Bride', which are composed by Mr. Spofforth. ...
The dialogue is interspersed with several other songs, duets, and choruses; also a concerto on the harp by Mr. Jones, bard to his royal highness the Prince of Wales. ...
[The words of two songs were reproduced later in the issue. Some dialogue is also reproduced in the May issue, p. 105.]
[The *Sporting Magazine*, April 1795, pp. 33f.]

The musick [to *Windsor Castle*] is principally by Mr. Solomon [*sic*], the Overture by Dr. Haydn, and a beautiful Glee by Mr. Spofforth. ...
[*European Magazine*, April 1795, p. 272.]

It is from the review in the *Sporting Magazine* that we learn exactly where the new Haydn Overture was placed. However, when Salomon published the opera, the Haydn Overture was omitted; on the other hand, Haydn himself seems to have attached it to his opera *L'anima del filosofo*. In the opera's autograph (Preussische Staatsbibliothek, Berlin), the Overture is present, partly by English copyist and partly by Haydn himself; the Overture is also present in the only complete copy of the opera known, the Conservatoire de Musique in Paris. The fact of this Overture to Salomon's Masque turning up in Haydn's *L'anima del filosofo* is not quite so mysterious as it first seems: probably it was added to make the opera complete and thus to fulfil the letter of the contract with Sir John Gallini. More curious is that the main theme of the fast section (given out by the solo oboe) contains clear reminiscences of Orfeo's big Aria in

F minor from Act II of Haydn's opera, 'In un' mar' d'acerbe pene', to wit the passage in the relative major:

Overture to an English Opera (Ia: 3)

L'anima del filosofo, Atto 2do, Aria

In 1796, Salomon replaced the Haydn Overture with one of his own. The opening work of his first concert at Hanover Square Rooms, 18 February 1796, began with 'New Overture to Windsor Castle' by Salomon (*Morning Chronicle*, 15, 16, 17, 18 February), and the *Morning Chronicle* on 23 February thought 'the Overture, composed by SALOMON for the after-piece called *Windsor Castle*, being played with every advantage, produced its full effect, and is highly creditable to its author.' In the announcement of the sixth subscription concert, for 31 March (*Oracle, The Times, Morning Chronicle*), in which a 'Grand Overture (M.S.) Haydn' opened the second part, we read: 'N.B. This Overture adapted for the Piano Forte, with an accompaniment of a Violin and Violoncello, ad libitum, is to be had at the Rooms, price four shillings, as is also the Opera of Windsor Castle, composed by J. P. Salomon, price 8s.' It was in the first part of this concert, incidentally, that Clementi conducted a revised version (see also *infra*, p. 305) of his Symphony which had been first played at the Opera Concert on 16 February 1795. The *Morning Chronicle* registered increased approval:

> A grand Symphony by CLEMENTI, written for the Opera Concert last Season, was performed with alterations this evening; and produced a very sensible and captivating effect. The second movement was loudly encored; and not only the Musicians and Connoisseurs, but the whole room, were equally warm in their expression of pleasure and approbation.   [2 April 1796]

Windsor Castle Overture was again the beginning of the Eighth Concert on 14 April 1796, and on the 16th, the *Morning Chronicle* actually lumped Haydn and Salomon together, saying 'the Orchestra played the Overtures of SALOMON and HAYDN with their usual sweetness, grandeur, and effect' – the highest praise a composer could expect from a London critic of that year.

To return to our 1795 season, the Sixth Concert took place on 13 April; no exact programme has survived, but from the review it would seem that an earlier Haydn symphony, such as Nos. 99 or 101, was given.

Sixth Concert: 13 April 1795

OPERA CONCERT – KING'S THEATRE.

The Subscribers are most respectfully informed that the Sixth Performance will be THIS EVENING.   [*Morning Chronicle*, 13 April]

OPERA CONCERT. SIXTH NIGHT.

The selection for last Monday evening, was made with that happy discrimination which the director, Viotti, has shewn through the whole course of these Concerts.

The Concertante for wind instruments was performed with much taste and accuracy. HOLMES is unrivalled on the bassoon; and we never heard the horn so well in tune, throughout, as it was on this occasion played by LEANDER.

Neither of these Performers, however, are yet sufficiently determined in finishing their sentences; and musical performers, like actors on the stage, are frequently unintelligible, at the close of their periods. – If they knew how great a defect this is, they would certainly exert themselves and reform. A Quartetto, sung by MORICHELLI, BRIDA, ROVEDIN[O], and MORELLI, produced a very great effect on the auditors; and is a signal proof of the powers of the composer, CHERUBINI, who discovered in it taste, melody, harmony, passion, and unity. MARTINI wrote a new song for Madame MORICHELLI, which was remarkable rather for its energy, than for that playful gaiety which is the general character of his compositions. Madame GUILBERG played a violin concerto: and, after anticipating the general favour, by her youth and beauty, secured it by the delicacy of her performance. We must however acknowledge, we should prefer the masculine and matured powers of VIOTTI, or SALOMON. Madame BANTI was encored in a delightful Air; and, by the variety which she displayed in repetition, gave increasing pleasure. We must not forget the Overture of HAYDN. This wonderful man never fails; and the various powers of his inventive and impassioned mind have seldom been conceived with more accuracy by the Band, or listened to with greater rapture by the hearers, than they were on this evening.   [*Morning Chronicle*, 15 April]

At that Sixth Concert, we are introduced to a man of whom both Haydn and Beethoven thought highly, Luigi Cherubini, whom we will meet in Vienna ten years from now. The work, as usual, cannot be identified.

Haydn's name was not missing from the big charity concert on 20 April, or the benefit concert of Madame Gillberg, or at that of his friends, the Misses Abrams.

NEW MUSICAL FUND.

Under the PATRONAGE of their Royal Highnesses the PRINCE of WALES and DUKE of YORK.

At the KING'S THEATRE, in the HAYMARKET.

ON MONDAY the 20th of April, 1795, will be performed A GRAND MISCELLANEOUS CONCERT of Vocal and INSTRUMENTAL MUSIC.

For the BENEFIT of the NEW MUSICAL FUND, established for the relief of DECAYED MUSICIANS, their WIDOWS and ORPHANS, residing in England.

Leader of the Band Mr. CRAMER.

Conductors, Dr. HAYES and Dr. MILLER.

Dr. HAYDN will preside at the Forte Piano.

Mr. GREATOREX at the Organ, erected for the occasion by Mr. ELLIOTT, with the Long Movement.

N. B. The Band will consist of Four Hundred Performers for which an Orchestra will be erected on the Stage.

Act First.
Grand Chorus in the Dettingen Te Deum – Handel.
Song, Mr. Bartleman.
Concerto, Grand Forte Piano, Mr. Smart, jun. – Cramer.
Song Mrs. Second, from Bath.
Concerto Violoncello, Mr. Lindley.

Song, Madam Banti, accompanied by Mr. Cramer on the Violin.
Concerto, German Flute, Mr. Ashe.
Air and Grand Chorus, 'Glory to God' – Handel, Mr. Harrison.

Act Second.
Grand Symphony, M. S. – Haydn – and performed under his immediate direction.
Song, Madam Storace.
Pleyel's celebrated Concertante (by desire), Messrs. Cramer, F. Cramer, Smith, Ling, jun., H. Smart, etc.
Song, Mr. Harrison.
Concerto Violin, Madam Gillberg, being her third public performance in England.
Song, Mrs. Harrison.
Grand Chorus, 'How Excellent' – Handel.

[etc.]
[*Oracle*, 14, 16, 18, 20 April;
Morning Chronicle, 14, 16, 18, 20 April;
Sun, 14 April; etc.]

New Rooms, OPERA HOUSE.
For the BENEFIT of MADAME GILLBERG.
On THURSDAY NEXT, the 23d of April,
Will be performed
A GRAND CONCERT of VOCAL and
INSTRUMENTAL MUSIC.

PART I.
Overture, REICHARDT.
Song, Signor ROVEDINO.

Quartetto for a Clarinet, Violin, Tenor and Violoncello obligati, Mess. HARTMAN,
CRAMER, PIELTAIN, and SCHRAM.
Song, Signor BRIDA.
Concerto Violin, Madame GILLBERG. – Eck.

PART II.
Grand Overture, HAYDN.
Concerto Piano Forte, Mr. BERTINI. – Bertini.
Song, Madame BANTI.
Concerto Violin, Madame GILLBERG. – Viotti.
Finale.
Dr. HAYDN will be at the Piano Forte.
Leader of the Band, Mr. CRAMER.
Doors to be opened at Seven, and the Concert to begin at
Eight o'Clock.
[Tickets were to be had at Mad. Gillberg's, 10 Duke-street, Portland Place, etc.]
[*Morning Herald*, 20 April 1795]

NEW ROOM, OPERA HOUSE.

MISS ABRAMS most respectfully begs leave to acquaint the Nobility and Gentry,
that Her CONCERT is fixed for FRIDAY NEXT, the 24th Inst . . .
ACT I.
Overture – Pleyel.
Glee.
Quartetto – Messrs. Cramer, F. Cramer, W. Abrams, and Lindl[e]y – Pleyel.

Scena – Signora Storace, Bianchi.
Concerto Flute – Mr. Ash[e].
Song, Mr. Harrison.
Sestetto – Mrs. Harrison, Mr. Harrison, Mr. Bartleman, and the
Miss Abrams – Zingarelli.
ACT II.
Grand Overture – Haydn.
Glee.
Song – Mr. Harrison.
Concerto Violoncello – Mr. Lindley.
Mad Bess – Signora Storace – Purcell.
Finale.
Leader of the Band, Mr. CRAMER.
Dr. HAYDN will preside at the Piano Forte.

[etc.]
[*Oracle*, 21, 23, 24 April; etc.]

At the Seventh Concert, we find united the names of Clementi, Gluck, Haydn, Mozart, Cimarosa, Viotti and Guglielmi; Haydn with the repetition of the 'Drum Roll' Symphony No. 103, which had been first given on 2 March, and Clementi with a revised version of his Symphony which had first given on 16 February (and would be repeated, as we have seen, at Salomon's 1796 subscription concerts). On 1 May, we find Haydn at Cramer's benefit concert. Two days previously, on 29 April, Beethoven had played his B flat piano Concerto (later Op. 19) in the intermission of a Tonkünstler Societät oratorio by Cartellini in the Burgtheater, Vienna – his first real 'public' appearance after the semi-private affair of 2 March (*supra*, p. 294).

Seventh Concert: 27 April 1795

OPERA CONCERTS, KING'S THEATRE.

The Subscribers are most respectfully acquainted that the SEVENTH PERFORMANCE will be this evening; Monday, the 27th Instant.

N. B. The remaining two Concerts will be (by desire of the Subscribers) the 11th and 18th of May . . . .   [*Morning Chronicle*, 27 April]

OPERA CONCERT. SEVENTH NIGHT.

In the mention that we have made of the Subscription Concerts, circumstances have confined us to a barren recapitulation of the pieces performed, and the general sensation produced. From the enquiry into the merits and demerits of the pieces and performers, to which we are strongly inclined, we are deterred by the pressure of other circumstances, more immediately within the province of a daily paper. The following is the list of the last performance. The famous Overture to Iphigenia, by GLUCK; a Duetto, by FERRARI, sung with great character by ROVEDINO and MORELLI; a new flute Concerto, by ASHE, well written and well performed, especially the middle movement; two songs by BANTI, and composed by CIMAROSA and GUGLIELMI; (to the astonishing powers which the singer displayed we can do no justice: we can only express admiration and surprise)[;] an air of the ballad kind, by MOZART, sung by MORICHELLI; a new Violin Concerto by VIOTTI, who played with a degree of power and energy, unexpected even from him (in his hands this little instrument is itself an Orchestra), and two Overtures, one by CLEMENTI, performed before, but re-written and essentially improved (the best musical judges allow it to be a masterly performance, full of passion and rich in thought, but in some places somewhat too abrupt in its modulations), and another Overture, by the great master of the art, HAYDN, which had been performed once before, and was repeated with additional effect and pleasure.

The Room, though the largest in London, was crowded. No wonder, the musical powers of all Europe are at present there collected.

[*Morning Chronicle*, 29 April]

NEW ROOM, KING'S THEATRE, HAYMARKET.

For the BENEFIT of Mr. CRAMER.
ON FRIDAY NEXT, the 1st of May, will be performed.
A CONCERT
ACT I.
Overture – Gluck.
Song – Mr. Harrison.
Duetto for Violincello [*sic*] and Violin, by Messrs.
Lindley and Cramer – Stamitz.
Song, Mr. Harrison.
Concerto Violin, Master Charles Cramer.
Song, with a Violin, by Mrs. Cramer and Signora Banti.
Concerto Piano Forte, Mr. J. B. Cramer.

ACT II.
Grand Overture, MS. Dr. HAYDN who will preside at the Piano Forte.
Duetto, Signor Rovedino and Signor Morelli – Ferari.
Concerto Violin, Mr. Cramer – Martini.
Song, 'Angels ever bright, etc.' Signor Banti – Handel.
Concerto Violoncello – Mr. Lindley.
Finale.   [etc.]

[*Oracle*, 27, 29 April, 1 May;
Morning Chronicle, 28 April, 1 May; etc.]

It will have been noted that Gluck's *Iphigénie en Aulide* Overture was having a sudden rise in popularity, establishing it as one of the best-loved eighteenth-century overtures; in 1796, London would see the opera *Iphigénie en Tauride*.

The big event of the season was Haydn's benefit concert on 4 May, perhaps the greatest concert of Haydn's life. By a strange coincidence, we are informed of what exactly took place, through three documents, two of them discovered after the publication of Landon SYM (1955): (1) Haydn's Fourth Notebook; (2) the criticism in the *Morning Chronicle*, discovered by Richard Andrewes when he was undertaking research for this present book; (3) the hand-bill, owned by Mr Albi Rosenthal. At this spectacular concert, two new pieces by Haydn were played for the first time, Symphony No. 104, 'The 12th which I have composed in England', wrote Haydn on the autograph, perhaps with a certain sense of destiny; and the beautiful *Scena di Berenice* for *la* Banti, one of the great cantatas of the century and the model for Beethoven's *Scena* 'Ah, perfido!' composed a year later in Prague. Some of the greatest singers in the world participated, not only *la* Banti but also *la* Morichelli, her great rival, and Morelli. The Duet is the music that we have noted above in connection with *Il burbero di buon cuore* and the 1794 season, but it is interesting to observe that Haydn here restores the *original text* of the Duet from *Orlando Paladino*, 'Quel tuo visetto amabile' rather than the adapted Da Ponte words: obviously the original words fitted the music better.

Ferlendis was the only less than first-rate artist (we have seen that Haydn describes him as 'mediocre'), but apparently he was sold with *la* Banti in what, in the present language of advertising, is called a 'package deal'. We shall shortly see that he played on the cor anglais at a concert with Banti.

That night in London, men thought that music had reached its apogee, at least in the instrumental sphere. Dr Burney (8 May to Susan Phillips) considered the new symphonies 'such as were never heard before, of any *mortal's* production; of what Apollo & the Muses compose or perform we can only judge by such productions as these' (Lonsdale, 355). The hand-bill (facsimile in Landon, *Supplement*, facing p. 48) also affords us an insight into the opinions of a typically cultivated listener of the time, for there are handwritten comments on the programme.

[Benefit Concert, 1795]

NEW ROOM, OPERA HOUSE.

DR. HAYDN most respectfully begs leave to acquaint the Nobility and Gentry, that his CONCERT is fixed for MONDAY next, the 4th of May. Part I. Overture, M. S. – Haydn. Song, Signor Rovedino. Concerto, Hautboy, Mr. Ferlendis (from Venice, being his first performance in this country), Ferlendis; Duetto, Madame Morishelli [*sic*] and Signor Morelli – Haydn. New Overture – Haydn.
Part II. Military Sinfonie – Haydn. Song, Madame Morichelli. Concerto Violin, Mr. Viotti – Viotti. New Scena, Madame Banti – Haydn.
Finale. [etc.]

[*Oracle*, 28 April, 2, 4 May; *Morning Chronicle*, 28 April; etc.]

The hand-bill

NEW ROOM, KING'S THEATRE
Dr. HAYDN's Night.
MONDAY, MAY 4, 1795
PART I

	[*MS. comments*]
Overture, MS. – *Haydn*	Very good
Song, Sig. ROVEDINO – *Ferrari*	nothing
Concerto Hautbois, Sig. FERLANDIS, from Venice, (being his First Performance in this Country) – *Ferlandis*	*astonishing fine command of the instrument, but degenerated into mere foolish trick*
Duetto, Madame MORICHELLI and Sig. MORELLI – *Haydn*	
New Overture – *Ditto*	very noisy

PART II

Military Symphony – *Haydn*	grand but very noisy
Song, Madame MORICHELLI – *Paisiello*	
Concerto Violin, Mr. VIOTTI – *Viotti*	Most delicate caution [?] but very little music in the composition

New Scene, Madame BANTI – *Haydn*
FINALE

[*Texts*]
Song. Sig. ROVEDINO – *Ferrari* [There follows the whole text, beginning] 'Or dell' avverse sorte [,] amata Berenice . . .'

DUETTO, M. MORICHELLI and Sig. MORELLI. – *Haydn* [Text,] 'Quel tuo visetto Amabile . . .' [Lists names of characters in *Orlando Paladino* who sing this duet, viz. Eurina & Pasquale]

Morelli's short part diverting in the buffo stile.

SONG, Madame MORICHELLI – *Paiesello* [Text beginning,] 'Crudele, or colei piangi . . .'

Nothing more than a decent second opera singer

NEW SCENE, Madame BANTI – *Haydn*.

Berenice che fai? [etc.]

Recitative very finely composed.

[Later, aria:] Non partir bell'idol mio [etc.]

Something of a pleasing air

Me infelice che fingo?

Recitative I think [True.]

[etc.]

Ends with an air in the minor key. Banti has a clear, sweet, equable voice, her low & high notes equally good. Her recitative admirably expressive. Her voice rather wants fulness of tone; her shake is weak and imperfect –

☛ The Subscribers to the Opera Concert are respectfully informed, that two remaining Subscription Concerts will be on the 11th and 18th of next Month, (the 25th being Whit-Monday [)].

At the request of a very great number of the Subscribers, there will be Two additional Concerts upon *Wednesday*, the 27th of May, and *Wednesday*, the 3d of June, (the Concert of Antient Music being over on the 20th of May) for which nights two separate Tickets will be delivered for *One Guinea*; and the Subscribers to this Concert will have a preference for themselves and their friends until the 18th of May, after which the Subscription will be open for the Public. At these Concerts, Mr. FERLENDIS, from Venice, will play (for the first time in this country) upon the English Horn.

The Criticism

HAYDN. – It is with pleasure we inform the public, that genius is not so totally neglected as some people are too apt to confirm. The Benefit of Haydn, was at the Great Concert Room of the King's Theatre, on Monday night; and attended, not only by the best judges and dearest lovers of Music, but by a distinguished and crowded Assembly. More than half the pieces performed were of Haydn's composition, and afforded indubitable marks of the extent and variety of his powers. Nothing was ever more truly comic, or more in the Italian Buffo stile, than his Duet, sung by Morelli and Morichelli. The Scena, by Madam Banti, was no less Italian, and still more masterly; because the stile of composition is of a grander kind. He rewarded the good intentions of his friends by writing a new Overture for the occasion, which for fullness, richness, and majesty, in all its parts, is thought by some of the best judges to surpass all his other compositions. A Gentleman, eminent for his musical knowledge, taste, and sound criticism, declared this to be his opinion, That, for fifty years to come Musical Composers would be little better than imitators of Haydn; and would do little more than pour water on his leaves. We hope the prophecy may prove false; but probability seems to confirm the prediction.   [*Morning Chronicle*, 6 May]

[Haydn's Notebook]

On 4th May 1795, I gave my benefit concert in the Haymarket Theatre. The room was full of a select company. a) First part of the Military Symphony; Aria (Rovedino); Concerto (Ferlandy) for the first time; Duet (Morichelli and Morelli) by me; a new Symphony in D, the twelfth and last of the English; b) Second part of the Military Symphony; Aria (Morichelli); Concerto (Viotti); *Scena nuova* by me, Mad. Banti [*English*:] (She song very scanty). [*German*:] The whole company was thoroughly pleased and so was I. I made four thousand Gulden on this evening. Such a thing is only possible in England. [CCLN, 306]

There is an undated entry about this time in the Third Notebook which provides an interesting link to the Romantic world of the nocturne: it is in Haydn's colourful English, and reads 'Field a young boy, which plays the pianoforte Extremely well' (CCLN, 301); at this point Field was a pupil of Muzio Clementi's.

On 8 May Dragonetti, the great double-bass player, gave his benefit concert.

CONCERT ROOM, KING'S THEATRE.

Mr. DRAGONETTI'S CONCERT

MR DRAGONETTI begs leave most respectfully to acquaint the Public, the Nobility, and Gentry, that is Concert Night will be on Friday next, the 8th instant, at the New Room, Opera House.

Part I Overture, Iphigenia – Gluck; Song, Mr. Morelli – Pozzi; Concertante, Harrington, Monzani, Holmes and Leanders – Devienne; Song, Madame Banti – Cimarosa Cappricio, Double Bass, Mr. Dragonetti – Dragonetti.

Part II Overture, M. S. – Haydn; Duetto, Signor Rovedino and Morelli – Ferrari; Concerto Violin, Mr. Viotti; Cantata, Madame Banti – Bianchi; Concertone, Double Bass, Dragonetti – Dragonetti; Finale.

Tickets, 10s. 6d. to be had of Mr. Dragonetti. No. 29, Suffolk-street, Charing-cross [etc.) [*Morning Chronicle*, 6 May]

We lack detailed programmes for the next two, and last, subscription concerts:

Eighth Concert: 11 May 1795

The Subscribers are most respectfully acquainted, that the Eighth Performance will be This Evening, Monday, the 11th instant. N. B. The last Subscription Concert will be on Monday next, the 18th instant (The 25th being Whit-Monday.) . . . . [*Morning Chronicle*, 11 May]

On 15 May, at 'Mr HARRISON'S NIGHT, NEW ROOMS, KING'S THEATRE . . .' Banti sang and a 'symphony, Haydn' ended the concert. [*Oracle*, 14 May]

On 16 May, Haydn was a witness at the marriage between Therese Jansen and Gaetano Bartolozzi at St. James's Church, Piccadilly. The other witnesses were Charlotte Jansen, Gaetano's father Francis (Francesco) Bartolozzi, the famous engraver, and Maria Adelaide de la Heras.[1] Before taking leave of Miss Jansen, we might add here the story of how Haydn's lost violin Sonata 'Jacob's Dream' (which he still had in his Viennese library when Elssler catalogued the contents) came to be written. We have the story from Dies:

In London he [Haydn] was closely acquainted with a German musical dilletante who had acquired a skill on the violin that bordered on virtuosity, but had the bad habit of forever playing the highest notes close to the bridge. Haydn decided to

1 Strunk, op. cit., 196.

make an experiment, in which he would try to see if it were not possible to cure the dilletante of his habit and give him a feeling for a solid way of playing.

The dilletante often visited a Demoiselle J.X, who played the pianoforte with great dexterity, which he generally accompanied. Haydn in all secrecy wrote a Sonata for the pianoforte with the accompaniment of a violin, entitling the Sonata 'Jacob's Dream', sealed it, without signing his name, and saw it reached Demoiselle J.X by a safe hand; and she did not wait to try what seemed to be an easy sonata, together with the dilletante. What Haydn had prophesied came to pass. The dilletante got stuck in the highest notes, where there was much passage work; and as soon as Demoiselle J.X was able to follow the idea of the unknown composer, who saw Jacob in his dream, and how the dilletante on this ladder soon made heavy going of it, was uncertain, tripped, stumbled and fell, she thought the situation so amusing that she could not resist laughing; while the dilletante cursed the unknown composer and boldly entertained the opinion that he couldn't write for the violin.

It was not for five or six months that it became known that Haydn was the composer of the Sonata, and then he received a present for it from Demoiselle J. [Dies, 154f.]

The last subscription concert was held on 18 May, followed by two extra concerts, the first of which took place on 21 May and was reviewed in the *Morning Chronicle* four days later.

Ninth Concert: 18 May 1795

The Subscribers are most respectfully acquainted, that the last Subscription Performance will be This Evening. . . . [*Morning Chronicle*, 18 May]

OPERA CONCERT.

The nine Subscription Nights at the Opera Great Room closed on Monday. Notwithstanding the Fete at Windsor, the Company was numerous and chosen. The Band performed with its accustomed spirit and power, and the performance gave no inferior degree of satisfaction. VIOTTI, in particular, was never heard to greater advantage. [*Morning Chronicle*, 21 May]

NEW ROOM, KING'S THEATRE, May 13, 1795.

THE Nobility, Public, and Gentry, are respectfully acquainted, that at the request of a very great many of the Subscribers, there will be Two additional CONCERTS, the First on THURSDAY, the 21st instant, and the second on MONDAY, the 1st of June, on which night will be performed,

FIRST NIGHT
Part I. Overture, double Orchestra, MS. – Bach. New Song, Signor Brida – Martini. Concerto Bassoon, Mr. Holmes – Holmes. New Rondeau, Mad. Banti – Bianchi. Concerto, Mr. Dragonetti – Dragonetti.

Part II. Overture, MS. – Haydn, New Duetto, Mad. Morichelli and Signor Morelli – Martini. Concerto Violin, Mr. Viotti – Viotti. Song, Mad. Banti, accompanied on the English Horn by Mr. Ferlendis – Zingarelli. FINALE.

SECOND NIGHT
Part I. Overture, double Orchestra, MS. – Bach. Song, Signor Rovedino – Paessiello [*sic*]. Concertone, Dragonetti – Dragonetti. New Scena, Madame Banti – Haydn. Concertante.

Part II. Overture, MS – Haydn. Quartetto, Mad. Morichelli, Signors Brida, Rovedino, and Morelli – Cherubini. Concerto on the English Horn (for the first time in this country), by Mr. Ferlendis – Ferlendis. New Song, Mad. Banti – Bianchi. FINALE. [etc.]

[*Oracle*, 14, 16, 18–21 May; *Morning Chronicle*, 14–16, 18, 21 May; etc.]

OPERA CONCERT.

Of the two additional Subscription Concerts, the first was distinguished by the introduction of an instrument called (we know not why) the English Horn; the power, tone, and utility of which we are persuaded are highly excellent. It is a tenor instrument, new (as far as our enquiries could extend) to the musical world, or at least only partially known; but with a sweet, full and articulate tone. Signor Ferlendis performed, both on this and the Hautboy, with great feeling and effect. Salomon played a Violin Concerto [a change of programme] with a delicacy, feeling, and variety, that were truly delightful. Haydn was indisposed, and could not conduct his grand sinfonia; the middle movement of which was most deservedly encored. [*Morning Chronicle*, 25 May]

Having confirmed that the cor anglais was unknown in England, one wonders about the exceptionally low English horns required in the death scene of Act II in Haydn's *L'anima del filosofo*, composed in 1791. In Euridice's Cavatina 'Del mio core' there are two English horns, which descend in solo passages to E flat and once even to D in the bass clef; and moreover there is evidence that this very number was performed at one of the Salomon concerts in 1792. We have here music for a special English horn, perhaps with the kind of extension that Mozart's friend Stadler added to the clarinet and basset horn.

Pursuing the problem of the cor anglais in London, we note that the *True Briton*, in its issue of 16 June concerning *Semiramide* at the Opera, adds 'with an additional new Song, composed here for the occasion by BIANCHI, to be sung by Madame BANTI, accompanied by the English Horn, Violoncello, French Horns [later issues: 'Horn'] and Bassoon Obligati, by Messrs. FERLENDIS, LINDLEY, LEANDERS, and HOLMES.'

This extraordinary combination of *obbligati* wind instruments reminds us of Haydn's Terzetto, 'Pietà di me', for two sopranos and tenor, with *obbligati* cor anglais, bassoon and horn (XXVb:5). Although the English source of this work, now in the British Museum, suggests that Haydn gave it to Mrs. Billington, the peculiar disposition of the wind instruments, and especially the presence of the cor anglais, would seem to suggest Banti and her lover Ferlendis – see also p. 278. Pleasant though it would be to assume such a connection, however, we must bear in mind that the Terzetto exists in an Eszterháza pastiche largely copied by Johann Schellinger before 1790 and including several pieces from Haydn's *La fedeltà premiata*. 'Pietà di me' remains something of a mystery, stylistically and chronologically, and being of a pre-1790 vintage can only concern us marginally here.

On 25 May 1795 the *Morning Herald* announces for 'this Evening' a benefit concert at King's Theatre, New Rooms, for Mr Lee, with Wilhelm Cramer as leader and Greatorex at the piano. Act I began with 'Overture, Haydn' and Master Field played a piano concerto.

On 26 May, Da Ponte and Soler ('Martini') collaborated on a new opera for London, *L'isola del piacere*. Da Ponte tells us that

the first act . . . was a marvellous success, both for the composer and for me. This was not the case with the second act. Martini was not very hard to please in the matter of women. He took a fancy to a servant girl, young, but neither pretty nor interesting, while, at the same time, he was courting and feigning passion for the *primma donna buffa* [Morichelli], who might in truth have been his mother, not to say, his grandmother. [Soler put out that he was covering up for Da Ponte, who was really the girl's lover.] . . . Martini, nevertheless [after Da Ponte treated the matter as a joke], left my house and went to live with Morichelli. . . . [Morichelli then] insisted that . . . the second act of my opera should have a mad scene [because she had been such a success in Paisiello's *Nina pazza per amore* in Paris]. . . . The whole spectacle failed, accordingly. . . .   [*Memoirs*, 257f.]

Haydn, too, was not impressed:

L'Isola del piacere BY MARTINI
The Overture from *L'Arbore di Diana*, a lot of old stuff from *Cosa rara*; and he had a very unsuccessful benefit concert.   [CCLN, 301]

The day after the première, Haydn's principal publishers in London, Longman & Broderip, went bankrupt. The *Sun* carried this announcement on 27 May:

BANKRUPTS
James Longman and Francis Fane Broderip, of Cheapside, London, and of the Haymarket and Tottenham-Court-Road, Middlesex, musical instrument makers, to surrender May 30, June 6, July 7, at one, at Guildhall. Attorneys, Messrs. Herne and Peace, Paternoster-row, London.

Haydn's other main London publishers, Corri & Dussek, in which Da Ponte was also involved, did no better; Da Ponte maintains he lost 'just a thousand with those two wretches' (*Memoirs*, 327) and continues: 'Dussek, *insaluto hospite*, went to Paris. Corri went to Newgate.'

Perhaps Haydn was relieved to read, on 2 June 1795 in the *Sun,* that at Longman & Broderip's, 'business is carried on as usual'.

On 29 May, Haydn presided at his friend Miss Corri's concert, now Mrs. Dussek:

NEW ROOMS, KING'S THEATRE.

MADAME DUSSEK begs leave to inform the Nobility, Gentry, and her Friends in General, that HER CONCERT is fixed for THIS EVENING the 29th inst.
Leader of the Band, Mr. GIORNOVICHI.

Part I. Overture, Dr. Haydn under his own direction. Concerto Oboe – Mr. Harrington. Song, Andr[e]ozzi – Mr. Nield. Piano Forte Concerto – Mr. Dussek. By Dussek. Song, Mrs. N. Corri, from the Edinburgh Concert (being her First Appearance).

Part II. Grand Overture, Haydn. Song, Madame Dussek – Dussek. New Concerto Violin, Mr. Giornovichi – Giornovichi. The Grand March in Alceste, arranged as a Glee[!] – By Dussek. New Concerto Pedal Harp, Madame Dussek – Dussek. Finale . . .   [*Oracle*, 29 May; *Morning Chronicle*, 29 May]

Meanwhile some changes were introduced into the final concert at the Opera. The symphony by J. C. Bach (perhaps it was a misprint, since it appeared at the first concert, too) and Haydn's *Scena di Berenice* were dropped:

OPERA CONCERT, KING'S THEATRE.

May 26, 1795.

THE LAST PERFORMANCE THIS SEASON
WILL be on MONDAY NEXT, the First of June.
PART I.
Overture – Vogel. Song, Signor Rovedino – Paessiello [*sic*]. Concertone. Dragonetti – Dragonetti. New Rondo, Madame Banti – Bianchi. Concerto Violin, Mr. Salomon – Salomon.

PART II.

Grand Military Overture, M. S. – Haydn. Song, Madame Morichelli – Cimarosa. Concerto on the English Horn, or Voce Umana (for the First Time in this country), Mr. Ferlendis – Ferlendis. The Favourite Rondo (by most particular desire), Madame Banti – Cimarosa. Finale. [etc.]

[*Oracle*, 29, 30 May and 1 June;
Morning Chronicle, 27, 29, 30 May
and 1 June]

The day before, 30 May, Haydn noted it 'was such a bright day that you could read anything at 9 o'clock in the evening' (CCLN, 287). On 3 June, Haydn gave a helping hand to the oboist Hindmarsh:

Mr. HINDMARSH's NIGHT.

Hanover-Square Rooms.

THIS EVENING, June 3, will be a GRAND CONCERT, under the Direction of Dr. HAYDN. Act I. Overture, Stamitz. – Glee, four voices. – Quartetto Obligato, for Flute, Violin, Tenor and Violoncello, Mess. Ashe, Hindmarsh, R. Ashey, and C. Ashley, Pleyel – Song, Mr. Nield (accompanied on the Bassoon by Mr. Holmes). – Concerto, Alto Viola, Mr. Hindmarsh. – Song, Mrs. Hindmarsh, Cimaroso [*sic*]. Act II. Grand Overture, M. S. Haydn. – Glee, four voices, – Concerto Oboe, Mr. Harrington – Song, Mrs. Hindmarsh, Bianchi. – Finale.

[*The Times*, 3 June]

On 5 June, Haydn was a guest of the Burneys and this time he also gave Fanny a memento: obviously she had asked for it. It is an arrangement for two trebles and two basses of sixteen bars from a string quartet in E flat (unidentified), signed by Fanny Burney 'June 5th, 1795. Recd. from Dr. Haydn, 1795' (Scholes II, 114f.). Three days later Haydn made his last recorded appearance at a London concert hall.

NEW ROOMS, KING's THEATRE.

Mr. ASHE's CONCERT.

ON MONDAY, June 8, 1795, will be a Grand CONCERT of VOCAL and INSTRUMENTAL MUSIC; at which Madame MARA has kindly consented to perform.

Leader of the Band Mr. CRAMER.

Pianoforte, Mr. CLEMENTI; and Dr. HAYDN will preside during the Performance of his Grand MS. Sinfonia.

Act I. Grand Overture, MS. Clementi; Song, Mr. Nield. Concertante Flute, Oboe and Bassoons, Messrs. Ashe, Harrington and Holmes, Devisme. Scena, Madam Mara; Giodaniello. Concerto, Mr. Ashe, in which will be introduced an Air to evince the possibility of producing regulated double Sounds on the German Flute. Ashe.

Act. II. Grand Sinfonia, MS. Haydn. Scena. Madam Mara; Gugliemi. Concertante (by particular desire) for two Flutes, both Instruments to be performed by Mr. Ashe; Ashe. New Concerto Violin, Mr. Viotti; Viotti. Aria, Madam Mara, Andreozzi. Full Piece. [etc.]

[*The Times*, 19, 21, 23, 26, 29 May,
2, 4, 6 and 8 June]

Haydn, remembering her benefit concert on 24 March, wrote:

Madam Mara gave a 2nd concert under the auspices of the flautist Ashe. The house was quite full; I sat at the pianoforte. [CCLN, 303]

On 13 June the *Morning Chronicle* announced the publication of three new piano Trios (Nos. 35–37, XVI: 21–3), in C, E flat (with a particularly striking middle movement which also exists in an authentic copy as a solo piano piece) and D minor, dedicated to the reigning Princess Marie Esterházy, *née* Princess Liechtenstein, and published by Preston & Son at the wholesale warehouse, 97 Strand.

One of the last musical programmes of the season containing works by Haydn was the rather fantastic evening announced *inter alia* in the *True Briton* on 18 June 1795. We read:

UNDER THE PATRONAGE OF
HIS ROYAL HIGHNESS THE PRINCE OF WALES
Order of the Evening Meeting for
READING AND MUSIC,
To be held at the NEW LYCEUM, HANOVER-SQUARE,
THIS PRESENT EVENING, JUNE 18,
in Honour of Their Royal Highness the PRINCE
and PRINCESS of WALES.
At Seven o'Clock – A LECTURE on ASTRONOMY,
illustrated by a large Transparent Diagram.
Eight o'Clock – ITALIAN, FRENCH, and ENGLISH READING.
Half past Eight – MUSIC, Vocal and Instrumental
Leader of the Band, Mr. RAIMONDI.
Mr. CLEMENTI will preside at the Piano Forte.
Overture – Dr. HAYDN.
Song, Miss DUFOUR.
Concerto, Piano Forte. Miss MᶜARTHUR, CRAMER
Song, Signor TRISOBIO.
REFRESHMENTS
ITALIAN, FRENCH, and ENGLISH READINGS:
Sinfonia – HAYDN.
Concerto, Violin, Master PINTO SAUNDERS –
GIORNOVICHI.
Duet, Miss DUFOUR and Signor TRISOBIO.
FINALE.
    Admission Tickets, to Non-Subscribers, 5s. for Ladies and 7s. 6d. for Gentlemen, to be had of [etc.]

For the next two months Haydn lived quietly in London. He does not make note of any extensive travels in England, and there are very few dated observations in his Third or Fourth Notebooks. There is probably a very simple explanation for this reticence, namely that Haydn was busily composing. He had entered into profitable negotiations with several London publishers, as we have seen. After he had left London, a number of his new works appeared in the autumn. On 9 October 1795, the *Morning Chronicle* announced Longman & Broderip's publication of the newest piano Trios (Nos. 38–40, XV: 24–6), Op. 73, dedicated to Mrs. Schroeter and containing the soon very famous 'Rondo, in the Gypsies' stile'. A few days later, on 14 October, the *Sun* announced 'Dr. Haydn's Second Set of English and Italian Canzonettas' dedicated to Lady Charlotte Bertie, the wife of Lord Abingdon, and 'Three Quartettos' Op. 72 dedicated to Count Anton d'Apponyi. Haydn must have been working on the Trios and Songs in 1794 and 1795: a sketch of the slow movement to the 'Gypsy Rondo Trio is on British paper with the watermark, 'Portal & Bridges/1794' and 'G[eorgius] R[ex]'.

And we have seen that Haydn used to sing a German version of 'Transport of Pleasure' (later: 'Content') while he was in England.

The new songs, most of which became favourites in the English drawing rooms and remained so for many years, are:

1. *Sailor's Song* ('High on the giddy bending mast')
2. *The Wanderer* ('To wander alone')
3. *Sympathy, after Metastasio* ('In thee I bear so dear a part')
4. 'She never told her love' (from Shakespeare's *Twelfth Night*)
5. *Piercing Eyes* ('Why asks my fair one')
6. *Transport of Pleasure* ('What though no high descent')

The sixth *canzonetta* originally appeared with the title, and the first words, as above, and there are strong musical grounds for thinking that it was this original version that Haydn set to music. For some reason not immediately apparent – can Lady Charlotte have thought the original text slightly immodest? – new words and a new title were soon applied to the song and the plates altered. The new title is:

6. *Content* ('Ah me, how scanty is my store!')

The poems were written or selected by Mrs. Hunter, who once again chose to remain anonymous. Mrs. Hunter wrote Haydn a farewell poem and the composer set it to music; 'O tuneful voice' is Haydn's nostalgic and lovely farewell to the country that liked him so much. Perhaps the greatest of Haydn's English canzonettas is, like 'O tuneful voice', a separate piece. It is entitled 'The spirit's song' and Haydn thought it was by Shakespeare. 'O tuneful voice' was given to Breitkopf & Härtel and published in 1806, while 'The spirit's song' came out in a German version in *c.*1801 and an English-German version in 1803, the latter published by the Verlag des Kunst- und Industrie-Comptoir in Vienna. It is very curious that there are no contemporary English editions.

The string Quartets, like the songs, were published by Haydn's friends, Corri & Dussek. The Quartets are the ones composed in 1793 for the Solomon concerts of 1794 and known nowadays as Opp. 71 & 74. J. L. Dussek made an arrangement as 'Sonata[s] for the piano forte, with accompaniments for a violin & bass, ad libitum' dedicated to the Princess of Wales, and which seems to have come out before the quartet edition: Haydn took back (or was sent) at least two sets of parts, and they appear in the catalogue of his music library.

Sometime in May or June, Dr. Burney was invited to dinner at Lord Macartney's, and perhaps Haydn was there, too; for in the Third Notebook we find the following entry:

Lord Macartney was sent as Ambassador to China.

Pekin [*sic*] is the capital – Gehol the Emperor's residence, 150 miles from Pekin. The wall of Pekin is 2,000 miles long. The city is not paved. The longest street is 6 miles long and 130 feet broad. The wall is 26 feet high and some 15 feet broad, at the base 20 feet. Every 150 paces along this wall there is a tower 15 feet high and 45 feet long; there are 45,000 of them in all. The present Emperor is 83 years old. Everyone prostrates himself at his feet.

The King of England wanted to open commercial intercourse with China, but he received a negative answer. The Emperor sent George some verses which he himself had written in his [the King's] honour.   [CCLN, 299f.]

Or perhaps Haydn got the information from Dr. Burney.[1] But both Lord Macartney and his wife later subscribed to *The Creation*.

The Third Notebook contains a number of the usual Latin aphorisms that Haydn liked, but also a good deal of English poetry, possibly potential song texts. One is called 'The Ladies' Looking Glass':

> Trust not too much to that Enchanting Face[,]
> Beaty's [*sic*] a charm, but soon that charm will pass.
>
> [CCLN, 303]

Haydn actually set it to music as a tiny song (the autograph also contains a miniature contra-dance, or as Haydn would call it, 'Contry Dance') – the kind of thing you might bring with you as a hostess present to a Mistress Shaw or Mistress Schroeter.

Still fascinated by London, we find an undated entry about the Cattle Market which was then held at Smithfield:

> Bartholomew Fair is generally held at the cattle-market, in the City; it goes on for 3 days. There are Berchtesgaden wares [toys] to be had there, and all sorts of plays are given, little comedies, juggling, tight-rope-walking, hawkers [*Carlatonerey*], dentists; and all sorts of riff-raff are there. [CCLN, 300]

Haydn was now getting his packing cases ready. In the partially lost Fourth Notebook he made a catalogue, in English, of all the works he had composed in England. It is a formidable list, on any count, but in the number of pages, Haydn seems to have pursued a system which was only known to himself. We reproduce the list and the explanations as in CCLN 309ff.

[Catalogue of all the works Haydn wrote in and for England between 2nd January 1791 and 1795] [*English*]

Orfeo, opera seria.[1]	110 sheets
6 Symphonies.[2]	124 —
Concertant Symphonie.[3]	30 —
The Storm. Chor.[4]	20 —
3 Symphonies.[5]	72 —
Aria for Davide.[6]	12 —
Maccone for Gallini.[7]	6 —
6 Quartettes.[8]	48 —
3 Sonates for Broderip.[9]	18 —
3 Sonates for Preston.[10]	18 —
3 Sonates for Miss Janson.[11]	10 —
1 Sonate in F minore.[12]	3 —
1 Sonate in g.[13]	5 —
The Dream.[14]	3 —
Dr. Harringtons Compliment.[15]	2 —
6 English songs.[16]	8 —
100 Scotch songs.[17]	50 —
50 Scotch songs (for Nepire).[18]	25 —

1 Burney to his daughter Fanny: 'Three huge assemblies at Spencer House; two dinners at the Duke of Leeds'; two clubs; a *déjeuner* at Mrs. Crewe's villa at Hampstead; a dinner at Lord Macartney's; two ditto at Mr. Crewe's; two philosophical conversations at Sir Joseph Banks's; Haydn's benefit; Salomon's ditto, etc., etc. What profligacy! But what *argufies* all this festivity. – 'tis all vanity and exhalement of spirit. I am tired to death of it all, while your domestic and maternal joys are as fresh as the roses in your garden.' [Scholes II, 115]

2 Flüte divert.[19]	10	—
3 Symphonies.[20]	72	—
4 Song for Thattersal.[21]	6	—
2 Marches.[22]	2	—
1 Aria for Miss Poole.[23]	5	—
1 God save the King.[24]	2	—
1 Aria con Orchestra.[25]	3	—
Invocation of Neptun.[26]	3	—
10 Commandments (Canons).[27]	6	—
March – Prince of Wales.[28]	2	—
2 Divertimenti a più voci.[29]	12	—
24 Minuets and german dances.[30]	12	—
12 Ballads for Lord Avingdon.[31]	12	—
Different songs.[32]	29	—
Canons.[33]	2	—
1 Song with the whole orchest.[34]	2	—
Of Lord Avingdon.[35]	2	—
4 Contrydances [sic][36]	2	—
6 Songs.[37]	2	—
Overtura Coventgarden [sic][38]	6	—
Aria per la Banti.[39]	11	—
4 Scotch songs.[40]	2	—
2 Songs.[41]	1	—
2 Contrydances.[42]	1	—
3 Sonates for Broderip.[43]	[see note]	

Summa 768 sheets.

The catalogue is reproduced in Dies in the original English, but without the number of sheets, and with various cryptographic abbreviations ('for P—'). Griesinger prints the list in German, but with the number of sheets ('Blätter') and with the names written out. Differences between the two sources are noted below. For purposes of comparison, Carpani's biography (in the English translation of the Stendhal piracy) occasionally proved useful (Carpani's Italian biography, *Le Haydine* . . . Milan 1812 = Stendhal, *Vie de Haydn* [published under pseudonym, L. A. C. Bombet], Paris 1814; English translation, *The Life of Haydn*, London 1817, pp. 328f.). The number of sheets which Haydn lists is often inaccurate. Sometimes Haydn seems to mean four pages for a sheet: the *Scena di Berenice* (= Aria per la Banti, 39) has in fact 11 double sheets, or 44 pages. At other times, however, this four to one relationship does not apply. The *Sinfonia Concertante* (2) is listed as having 30 sheets. The autograph has 40 sheets (80 pages).

1 *Orfeo*, or as its actual title reads, *L'anima del filosofo*, was composed in the first six months of 1791.

2 Symphonies Nos. 93–98 (1791–1792).

3 *Sinfonia Concertante* in B flat (1792).

4 The autograph is entitled *Madrigal* (1792).

5 Presumably Symphonies Nos. 99–101 (1793–1794).

6 The aria is lost.

7 The *Maccone* is either lost or unidentified.

8 The so-called Op. 71 & 74 (a silly method of identification, inasmuch as all six were written at one time and as an entity), Vienna 1793.

9 Haydn wrote three sets of pianoforte Trios (they were published as 'Sonatas') for Longman and Broderip: Nos. 32–4 (published in 1794), Nos. 38–40 (published in 1795) and Nos. 43–5 (published in 1797).

10 Pianoforte Trios Nos. 35–7 (published in 1795). In Dies 'P—'.

11 In Griesinger 'zwey Sonaten' (two Sonatas). Probably pianoforte Sonatas Nos. 60–62, but possibly the pianoforte Trios Nos. 43–45, which are dedicated to her. Stendhal also lists '3', not 2 works.

12 The so-called *Andante con variazioni*, the autograph of which is entitled *Sonata* (1793). For pianoforte solo.

13 The pianoforte Trio No. 31 in G, Hoboken XV: 32, published by Preston in 1794. For years

this work has been considered a violin Sonata, but the authentic Preston edition shows clearly that Haydn wrote it as a Trio.

14 This piece, called 'Jacob's Dream', was for violin and pianoforte; it seems to be lost.

15 Haydn wrote this piece in Bath for Dr. Henry Harington. See also *supra*, p. 267.

16 Probably the first set of *VI Original Canzonettas* (see *supra*, pp. 257–8), published in June 1794.

17 The Scotch songs for Napier, the first set of which included 100 settings. They appeared in the autumn of 1791.

18 The bracketed part appears only in Griesinger '(für Nepire)'. The 50 songs constituted a second volume (see 17). Cecil Hopkinson and C. B. Oldman, 'Haydn's Settings of Scottish Songs in the Collections of Napier and Whyte' (*Edinburgh Bibliographical Society Transactions*, Vol. III, Part 2, pp. 85ff).

19 Two *Divertimenti* for 2 flutes and 'cello: Haydn wrote three such works in 1794: Hoboken IV: 1–4 (of which No. 4, containing one movement, obviously belongs to another work).

20 Presumably Symphonies Nos. 102–104 (1794–1795).

21 In Dies '4 Song for S–', in Stendhal '4 Songs for F.', in Griesinger 'Vier Gesänge für Thallersal'. We presume Griesinger misread Haydn's handwriting, and have therefore simply altered the 'll' to 'tt'. See pp. 364ff., for a description of the psalms which Haydn arranged.

22 The Marches for Sir Henry Harpur. See Karl Haas, 'Haydn's English Military Marches' (*The Score*, No. 2, Jan. 1950, pp. 50ff.).

23 In Dies '. . . for Mss. P—'. The Aria is lost.

24 Haydn's setting is lost.

25 The Aria cannot be identified, and is presumably lost.

26 Aria and chorus from an unfinished Oratorio, *Mare clausum*, which Haydn started to write for Lord Abingdon in 1794. Autograph in the B.M. See *supra*, p. 271.

27 These Canons were written for the Saxon minister in London, Count Brühl. The autograph in the Gesellschaft der Musikfreunde is in my opinion a copy Haydn made for himself.

28 This March, Haydn's best, survives in two versions, one for wind band (the Prince of Wales' version) and one for orchestra (the version Haydn made for the Royal Society of Musicians), 1792.

29 Haydn here appears to count two arrangements of Notturni which he wrote for the King of Naples in 1790; in fact Haydn rewrote some four such Divertimenti, and played them in the Salomon concerts of 1791 and 1792.

30 These 24 Minuets and *Deutsche Tänze* are probably identical with the Redoutensaal dances of 1792: see also pp. 205–6. They may be the '24 Menuetti' (IX:16); see *infra*, p. 486.

31 Dies '. . . for Lord A—'. The pieces have been mentioned above (see p. 272).

32 The 'Different songs' cannot be identified.

33 It is almost impossible to say which canons Haydn refers to: possibly the canon he wrote for his Doctor's degree at Oxford ('Thy voice, O Harmony, is divine'), and the German Canon which he entered in one of the London Notebooks (see p. 185).

34 The 'Song' cannot be identified.

35 Dies '. . . Lord A' Probably songs, or one of the Divertimenti for 2 flutes and 'cello (see also note 19 and p. 275).

36 The 'Contrydances' are apparently lost.

37 Probably the second set of *VI Original Canzonettas*, published in the Autumn of 1795.

38 The Overture to Salomon's *Windsor Castle* (first edition, edited by the writer of these notes, published by the Universal Edition, Vienna). Haydn's *Entwurf-Katalog* lists the work as 'Musik zu einer Englischen opera, 1994' (i.e. 1794), but *Windsor Castle* was first performed in the Spring of 1795. See also pp. 300–2.

39 The *Scena di Berenice*, 1795.

40 The '4 Scotch songs' cannot be identified.

41 The '2 Songs' are possibly 'O Tuneful Voice' and 'The Spirit's Song', English Songs which are not part of the twelve Canzonettas.

42 The two Dances are lost.

43 This entry is missing in Griesinger, but it appears in Dies and also in Stendhal ('3 Sonatas for Broderich'): see note 9.

A great stillness had now settled round the famous Haydn in London. People were away at their country houses. The newspapers were full of the war, and Haydn's name was hardly mentioned except in publishers' advertisements. One of the very last times we hear of him is in the *Morning Herald* for 20 June 1795: 'DR. HAYDN expects his recal [*sic*] daily to Vienna: – the EMPEROR, it is hoped, requires the presence of this celebrated *harmonist*, to prepare a new *Te Deum* on a general peace!'

On 13 August, Haydn and Salomon made a written agreement about the copyright to the first six London Symphonies (which was followed by one for the second six but not, rather strangely, until February 1796):

[Agreement with Johann Peter Salomon, London. *German*. Only the signature autograph]

The undersigned herewith testifies that, according to the agreement signed this day between myself and Herr Johan [*sic*] Peter Salomon, the afore-mentioned Herr Salomon shall have the exclusive rights pertaining to the following specified Overtures which I composed for his concerts; and that I hereby renounce any further claims whatever on him, now or at any other time. The afore-mentioned Overtures have the following *incipits*:

Executed at London this 13th of August 1795.

Joseph Haydn [m.p] ria.

[Agreement with Johann Peter Salomon, London. *German*]

Vienna, 27th February 1796.

I, the undersigned, testify and declare that Herr Salomon shall be in perpetuity the sole owner and proprietor of my last six Symphonies, of which 3 are of the year 1794, and the last 3 of the year 1795,[1] and promise on my honour to make no other but personal use of them.

Josephus Haydn [m.p] ria.

[CCLN, 146]

On 15 August 1795, Haydn left England, never to return.[2] Haydn had come away with a small fortune. Griesinger tells us that the composer

made through his three-year sojourn in England some 24,000 Gulden, of which about 9,000 were used for the trips, for his stay, and for other costs. . . . Haydn often repeated that he first became famous in Germany through England . . . [p. 35]. [He] considered the days spent in England the happiest of his life. He was everywhere appreciated there, it opened a new world to him, and he could, through his rich earnings, at last escape the restricted circumstances in which he had grown grey: for in the year 1790 he had owned barely 2,000 Gulden capital.' [p. 23]

1 Haydn refers to the dates when the works were first performed, not necessarily when they were composed (No. 99 was written in 1793.) The last six London Symphonies are Nos. 99–104. [CCLN, 146]
2 Dies, 159. I suggest that Dies has this exact date from an entry in the partially lost Fourth Notebook, something in typical laconic fashion such as 'Am 15ten Augustii reiste ich von London ab.'

In his travelling cases, there was also a little manuscript libretto of an oratorio called 'The Creation' which Salomon had pressed into Haydn's hands before he left. With pounds of music, a parrot, a piece of coconut shell embellished with silver trimmings (a gift from Clementi), and with his faithful servant and copyist Elssler, Haydn passed through the English countryside in August. Perhaps he felt, like Henry Swinburne[1] returning, that 'the country [was] in high beauty', and perhaps the sexagenarian Austrian was also struck with the 'limpidity of the streams, neatness of the gardens, beauty of the women, and elegance of almost every vehicle'.

On 8 September 1795, the Austrians heard he was returning:

> According to letters from Hamburg, the princely Esterházy *Kapellmeister* Herr Joseph Haydn, that universally esteemed and indeed very great composer whose excellent compositions are everywhere received with the greatest approbation, arrived there from London on the 20th of last month [August], continuing his journey to Vienna the next day.
>
> [*Pressburger Zeitung* No. 72, 8 September 1795]

Neukomm (*Bemerkungen* to Dies's biography, p. 29) tells us Haydn spent the night in Passau, the pretty border town in Germany, where on that evening were given *The Seven Words* in a new arrangement made by the local Chapel Master of Passau Cathedral, Joseph Friebert, who added a choral part to Haydn's instrumental music (and also some recitatives). Neukomm then goes on: "H. was satisfied with the perf. but added quite simply (in his usual modest way), 'the vocal parts, I think, I could have written better.'" He was very soon to do so.

Haydn probably passed through Linz, where he could have heard a performance of *Orlando Paladino* at the local theatre.[2] This theatre was having financial difficulties; perhaps *Orlando* was too difficult for the reduced local forces; at any rate, the critic of the *Rheinische Musen* thought so:

> Pieces Performed [at the Linz Theatre] from 1 May to the End of August 1795.
> ... 13. Orlando Paladino, Op[era] in 3 A[cts]. Music by Haydn. Herr Hater as Roland was really something horrible to hear; and moreover we must register that the orchestra had to help the singers along, for in our opinion the music certainly wasn't written for this cast.   [Zweiter Jahrgang, Erster Band, Mannheim 1795]

Orlando Paladino was the only Haydn opera to achieve a rather wide circulation in this period. We have seen above that it was performed at Vienna, Brünn and Mannheim and reviewed in Continental journals. Just as a matter of record, it was performed also at Prague by the Wenzel Mihul Company in 1791, at Dresden (Hoftheater) and Pillnitz (Schlosstheater) in 1792, at Frankfurt-am-Main and Graz in 1793 and 1794. Many further performances followed from 1796 to 1805, some of which were criticized in local journals; these criticisms will be examined in later volumes of our biography.[3]

Early in September, Haydn reached the Imperial and Royal capital to take up his duties with Prince Nicolaus II Esterházy.

---

1 *Letters Written at the End of the Eighteenth Century* (part of a series: 'Secret Memoirs of the Courts of Europe'), reprint of the 1840 edition (Charles White), Philadelphia, n.d., Vol. II, 60. The entry is dated Canterbury, 12 June 1781.
2 Fritz Fuhrich: *Theatergeschichte·Oberösterreichs im 18. Jahrhundert*. Vienna 1968, p. 229 records the première at Linz on 2 December 1794, and notes that there were five performances. Probably the work was already withdrawn when Haydn would have reached Linz in late August. Linz also did one of the last recorded performances of Haydn's *La fedeltà premiata* (première on 24 April 1799).
3 Ludwig Wendschuh, *Uber Jos. Haydn's Opern*, Rostock, 1896, pp. 101f.

1 Joseph Haydn, pencil sketch with traces of red crayon, by George Dance. This version – one of two – is inscribed 'March 20th 1794 Geo. Dance'; the other, from Dance's own collection, is now in the Historisches Museum der Stadt Wien. Haydn considered this portrait to be the best likeness of himself during his stay in England.

2, 3 Two outstanding singers, for both of whom Haydn wrote arias, and who made regular appearances at the Salomon and Opera Concerts in London: Giacomo David(e) and Brigida Banti-Giorgi. Both after engravings by an anonymous Italian artist, c. 1795.

4 Gertrud Elisabeth Mara-Schmeling, the famous soprano; engraving marked 'Castelli delin.' and 'dal Piano sculp.', *c.* 1791. Below the portrait is inscribed the legend 'Mad.ª Elisabetta Schmeling Mara, / che canto in Venezia l'Anno 1790 / Nel Nob:ᵐᵒ Teatro di S. Samuele.'; above it is a Latin inscription, 'Semper honos, nomenque tuum, Laudeqsue manebunt. Virg.'

Below
5 Johann Nepomuk Hummel, miniature (diameter 2⅝ in.), *c.* 1795; signed (on the arm of the chair) 'Nanette Rosenzweig'.

Both Mara and Hummel appeared at the Salomon concerts: Mara was one of the great sopranos of her day and Hummel, a child prodigy and pianist, later succeeded Haydn as Kapellmeister to Prince Nicolaus II Esterházy.

SCENES IN LONDON AT THE TIME OF HAYDN'S VISIT TO ENGLAND

6 Figures skating in St James's Park, in front of Horse Guards Parade, pen and ink and watercolour, by John Nixon, c. 1790.

7 Blackfriars Bridge and St Paul's Cathedral, pen and ink and watercolour, attributed to Thomas Malton (the Younger), c. 1790.

8 King George III reviewing the Prince of Wales's Regiment, oil painting by Sir William Beechey, c. 1794; also shown on horseback are (left) the Prince of Wales and (right) his brother, the Duke of York.

9 The Prince of Wales (later George IV), portrait in oils by Sir Thomas Lawrence.

Haydn was received by the Prince of Wales and by other members of the royal family on many occasions (see pp. 109–10); the prince commissioned the portrait of Haydn by Hoppner (colour pl. I), executed in 1791.

10 Princess Caroline of Brunswick, who married the Prince of Wales in 1795; engraving by James Tookey after Schroeder.

11 Mrs Blair, a great patroness of music in London, at one of whose concerts in 1791 Haydn's cantata *Arianna a Naxos* was performed; portrait in oils by George Romney.

12 Mrs Elizabeth Billington, the famous soprano to whom Haydn probably presented his extremely difficult *Terzetto*, 'Pietà di me' (autograph now in the British Museum); engraving by Angelo Volpini, after a drawing by Veronica Matteini, published in Florence by Lasinio, 25 March 1797.

13 Muzio Clementi, the well-known Italian composer who had settled in England as a young man and whose reputation was overshadowed by that of the newly arrived Haydn; portrait painted and engraved by Thomas Hardy, and published by John Bland (the music publisher at whose house Haydn spent his first night in London) on 31 October 1764.

14 Dr Charles Burney, the noted composer and music historian, to whom Haydn was introduced shortly after his arrival in London, and who was the moving spirit behind the award of an honorary doctorate to Haydn by Oxford University; pencil sketch by George Dance, 1794.

Above, left
18 Joah Bates, the well-known organist and conductor, whose wife Sarah (*née* Harrop) impressed Haydn with her singing ability; engraving by William Daniell, after a pencil drawing by George Dance, 20 December 1794.

Above, right
19 Samuel Arnold, the famous Handelian conductor who invited Haydn to participate in a 'grand concert' in March 1795 (an invitation which Haydn refused because of lack of rehearsal time); portrait painted and engraved by Thomas Hardy, published by F. Linley in 1797.

20 William Cramer, leader of the Professional Concert, who led the band which Haydn conducted in the Sheldonian Theatre, Oxford, in July 1791; portrait painted and engraved by Thomas Hardy, published by John Bland in 1794.

24 Prince Anton Esterházy, whose
reign from 1790 to 1794 covered
the greater part of Haydn's stay
in England; anonymous portrait
in oils, *c.* 1790 (detail).

25 Marie Therese, Princess
Esterházy, *née* Countess Hohenfeld,
who was married first to Prince
Anton Esterházy and later to Prince
Karl Philipp Schwarzenberg;
portrait in oils by Angelika
Kauffmann (detail).

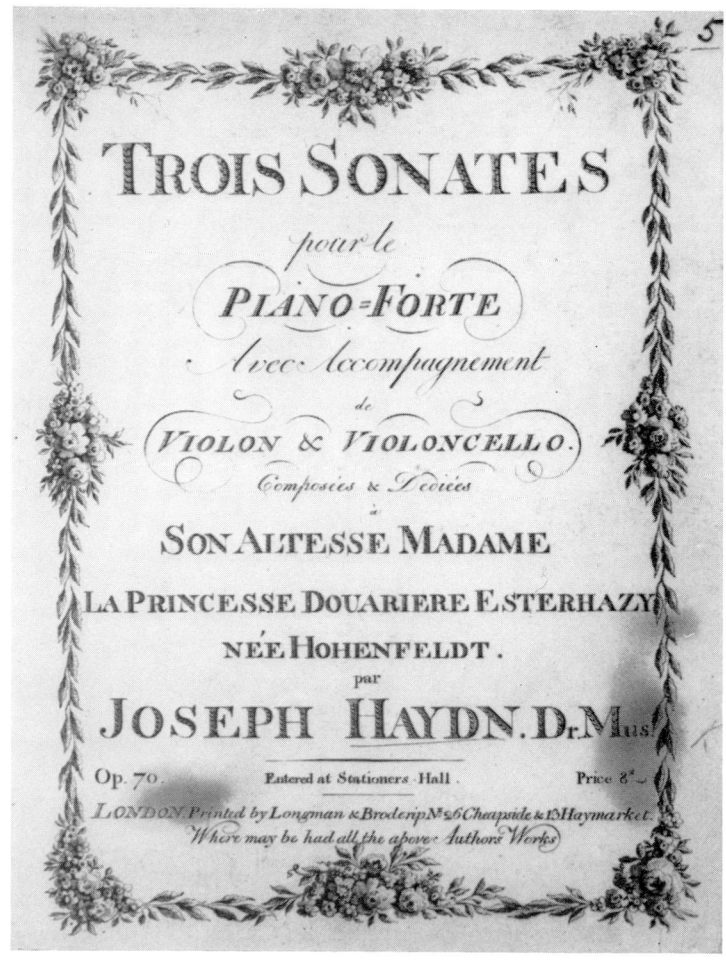

TROIS SONATES

pour le

PIANO=FORTE

Avec Accompagnement

de

VIOLON & VIOLONCELLO.

Composées & Dédiées à

SON ALTESSE MADAME

LA PRINCESSE DOUARIERE ESTERHAZY

NÉE HOHENFELDT.

par

JOSEPH HAYDN. Dr.Mus.

Op. 70.   Entered at Stationers Hall.   Price 8ᵃ

LONDON Printed by Longman & Broderip Nᵒ 26 Cheapside & 13 Haymarket.
Where may be had all the above Authors Works

26 Title-page of Haydn's three
Piano Trios, Op. 70, dedicated
to Marie Therese, Princess
Esterházy, who had been
widowed by the time these 'Trois
Sonates' were published by
Longman & Broderip in
November 1794.

Londra ai ____ di gennajo 17__

Carissima Polpli mia! in questo momento che ho ricevuto la tua lettera...

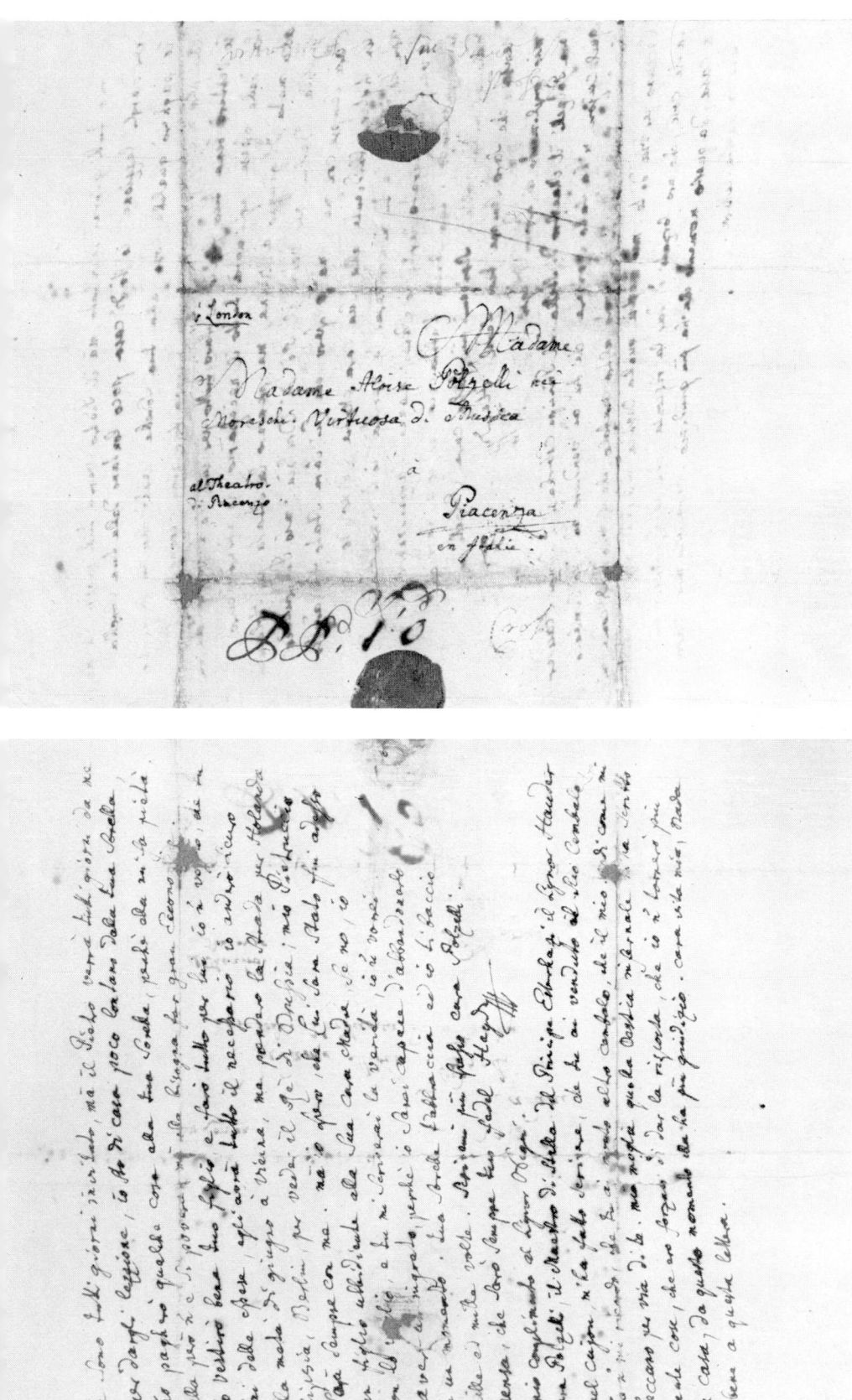

27 Letter written by Haydn on 14 January 1792 to Luigia Polzelli in Piacenza (for translation see p. 122).

28 The North Terrace, Windsor Castle, looking west, watercolour by Paul Sandby (1730–1809);
when Haydn visited the castle in June 1792 he admired the view from the terrace.
29 Buckingham House (now Palace) seen from St James's Park, watercolour by E. Dayes, 1790;
in 1794-5 Haydn lived within a short distance of the royal residence (see p. 240).

PART II

London Works 1791–1795

As we have seen in the Chronicle, Haydn's *Catalogue of Works Composed in England* also includes, naturally, pieces written in 1792 and 1793 for the next London season, for instance the Quartets for Salomon of 1793 which were dedicated to Apponyi. Strictly speaking, the Redoutensaal Dances of November 1792 cannot be described as works 'composed in or for London'; but Haydn did not make this fine distinction, and we have followed him in making a single group of all the works composed between January 1791 and September 1795. And it is certain that this whole period, even the Viennese interlude of 1792–3 (which was not supposed to happen anyway), is dominated by the impressions of England and its musical life.

CHAPTER SIX

Vocal Music

WE HAVE SEEN THAT the number of sheets ('Blätter') of Haydn's catalogue is inaccurate. But taking it as a basis – and we are forced to do so because of the many lost works – it will be very surprisingly found that the amount of vocal music is proportionately large: 321 'Blätter' are vocal music, the remaining 447 instrumental. Considering that for posterity, the English part of Haydn's life means the twelve Salomon Symphonies, and perhaps the quartets and trios, the sheer amount of vocal music Haydn composed in England is impressive. Much of it is obviously occasional and some of it is lost. But Haydn began his catalogue with the opera, and we follow him.

L'anima del filosofo (Orfeo ed Euridice)
(XXVIII: No. 13)

Opera seria in four (five?) acts by C. F. Badini, composed January–May(?) 1791.
First performance of complete opera: Maggio Musicale, Florence (principal parts: Tygge Tyggeson, Maria Callas, Boris Christoff, cond. by Erich Kleiber), 1951.
First recording of complete opera: Haydn Society HSLP 2029 (principal parts: Herbert Handt, Judith Hellwig, Alfred Poell, cond. by Hans Swarowsky), 1950.
Cast: Orfeo (tenor), Euridice (soprano), Creonte (baritone; later tenor), Genio (coloratura soprano), Pluto (minor part: bass), Baccante (minor part: soprano), Primo corista (minor part: bass), secondo corista (minor part: bass), terzo corista (minor part: bass), quarto corista (minor part: tenor), quinto corista (minor part: soprano). Chorus (in various combinations, using S–A–T–B).
Orchestra: 2 fl., 2 ob., 2 cor ang., 2 clar., 2 bsn., 2 hr., 2 trpt., 2 trbn., timp., solo harp, str., harps. (continuo) and possibly organ for figured bass in final number.

THE SOURCES

The incomplete autograph is in the Prussian State Library in Berlin. It is not in any particular order. An authentic manuscript, partly on small 'post paper', by an English copyist which Haydn also used to make the score of Symphony No. 98 in the Royal Philharmonic Society's Library (on deposit at the British Museum), with some corrections and additions by Haydn, is in the Esterházy Archives at Budapest (from Haydn's library). It, too, is not in chronological order and is not complete; but it contains some things missing in the autograph (e.g. the little recitative which precedes Creonte's big C major Aria at the end of Act II) and also some helpful hints as to where the pieces belong. For example, the beginning of Act II (the 'Amorini' chorus which Haydn adapted from *Orlando Paladino*) is unmarked by the English copyist, but at the top of the page, Haydn himself added 'Coro' and to the right, 'Atto 2do'. In 1805,[1] Haydn persuaded Breitkopf & Härtel to issue eleven of the best numbers 'which he had

---

1 Hase 49, using information from Griesinger's letters to Breitkopf, a part of which has not survived.

secretly arranged to be copied; the copyist did not have time to do the Overture'. This little quotation (Haydn to Griesinger to Hase) shows that Haydn probably made the little copy on 'post paper' which is now in Budapest in this secretive manner. It is questionable if Haydn ever had the whole opera in his hands when he left England in 1792. Some of the eleven scenes, which Breitkopf issued in piano score in 1806 and in score a year later, are not contained either in the autograph or in the Budapest copy (from which, possibly, they were removed to send to Breitkopf?). Haydn did a certain amount of selling of *Orfeo* arias in scores copied by Johann Elssler: Mrs Peploe acquired one in 1797 from Haydn, along with some other London and post-London works, and we have seen that Frau von Genzinger had the F minor Aria of Orfeo from Act II (*supra*, p. 205). There are a few such separate scores extant, e.g. from the Aloys Fuchs Collection in Göttweig Abbey, Lower Austria. But there was no complete copy. On the basis of the three incomplete scores, the writer and Richard Wadleigh, also of the Haydn Society, reconstructed the chronology of the opera, using the hints from the Budapest copy and such indications in the text itself as were of help (obviously Orfeo's Aria, 'Perduta un'altra volta', had to come in Act IV, where he loses her the second time). This version was the basis of the Vienna recording and Florence performance. Then Professor J. P. Larsen brought our attention to a MS. copy of the opera in four volumes owned by the Paris Conservatoire de Musique. We subsequently examined this copy and found (a) that it is in chronological order and must have been made from Gallini's autograph by some French copyist in the early nineteenth century (local French paper with the almost illegible watermark 'RENEROL' or 'PENEROL'); (b) that it is the most complete of all the sources and probably contains the entire opera. One secco, that after Euridice's death, is contained only in this source. The chronological order of Landon-Wadleigh was confirmed in Acts I, II (except for the missing secco) and IV exactly; in Act III there are some differences.

As it appears in this source, *L'anima del filosofo* makes a complete opera and appears to be a self-contained entity. Haydn wrote to Luigia Polzelli in March 1791 that the new opera would have five acts, the last three short; did Badini and Haydn condense the last three into two? What can the fifth act have possibly included? Until fresh evidence comes to light – and it is unlikely that it will – we are safe in asserting that Haydn's last opera has come down to us complete and in four sources the combination of which provides us with a textually reliable score.

The Paris source, which we herewith present, is entitled 'L'anima del Filosofo / o sia / Orfeo e Euridice / Di Giuseppe Haydn / Atto 1°' (= Vol. I), D.5514.

Atto I°
Sinfonia = Overture to Salomon's *Windsor Castle* (*supra*, p. 299). As we noted, Haydn said there was not time to copy the Overture, which he seems later to have added to the Gallini MS. But it seems rather odd that having delivered the opera in 1791, he should go to the trouble to add an Overture to it three or four years later knowing it would not be played. Or is it possible that Haydn, to fulfil the contract, actually composed the Overture in 1791 and used it in 1794 for the 'English Opera'? Yet the work is dated '1994' (*sc.* 1794) in the *Entwurf-Katalog*. It is also interesting that Haydn seems not to have had a copy of the work when he returned to Vienna, but inexplicable that Salomon never printed it. Perhaps it was after all the property of Gallini himself.

2 fl., 2 ob. 2 bsn., 2 hr., 2 trpt., timp., str. C minor ⟶ C major. *Largo*: Presto (with slow introduction).

Recitativo acc. Euridice, 'Sventurata, che fò?' 2 ob., 2 bsn., 2 hr., str. (E flat ⟶ dominant of C), leading into

Coro ed Euridice, 'Ferma il piede, O Principessa!', as above but with male chorus (ten., bass, 2 pts.), C minor.

Recitativo acc. Euridice, 'Che chiedete da me?'. Str. F major.

Aria. Euridice, 'Filomena abbandonata'. 1 fl., 2 ob., 2 bsn., 2 hr., str. F major.

Recitativo secco, Un corista; un' altro; un' altro (3°); Orfeo; Euridice; 'Cieli! Soccorso!'

Recitativo acc. Orfeo, 'Rendete a questo seno'. harp, str. B flat leading to Aria Orfeo, 'Cara speme!'. 2 fl., 2 ob., 2 bsn., 2 hr., str. B flat.

Recitativo secco. Un corista; Euridice; Orfeo; 'O prodigio'.

Coro (ten., bass), 'O poter dell'armonia'. 2 ob., 2 bsn., 2 hr., str. C major.

Recitativo secco, Creonte; Corista; un'altro corista; 'Ah, chi sa dirmi'.

Aria Creonte, 'Il pensier sta negli oggetti'. 1 fl., str. E major.

Recitativo secco, Orfeo; Euridice; Creonte; 'Grazie agli Dei'.

Duetto Euridice – Orfeo, 'Come il foco'. 1 fl., 2 ob., 2 bsn., 2 hr., str. G major.

Atto II°

Coro (Amorini: sop., alt.) 'Finche circola il vigore', 2 ob., 2 bsn., 2 hr., str. A major.

Recitativo secco, Orfeo, 'Adorata consorte'.

Coro (as above) with Euridice & Orfeo, 'Finche circola' &c., same orch. leading to recit. acc. (Euridice, 'Numi, che ascolto?'). A major ⟶ G major.

Recitativo secco, Un corista; Euridice, 'Ecco Signor!'

Recitativo acc. Euridice, 'Dov'è l'amato bene?' 2 ob., 2 bsn., str. B flat ⟶ E flat.

Cavatina Euridice, 'Del mio core'. 2 cor. ang., 2 hr., str. E flat.

Recitativo secco, Corista, 'Con Euridice estinte'.

Recitativo acc. Orfeo, 'Dov'è quell'alma audace'. 2 ob., 2 bsn., 2 hr., str. D major ⟶ C major ⟶ C minor.

Aria Orfeo, 'In un mar d'accerbe pene'. 2 ob., 2 clar., 2 bsn., 2 hr., str. F minor.

Recitativo secco, corista (4°), Creonte; 'Euridice, Signor!'

Aria Creonte, 'Mai non sia inulto'. 2 ob., 2 bsn., 2 cor., 2 trpt. on the stage, timp., str. C major.

Atto III°

The order of the 4th–7th numbers are different from the Wadleigh-Landon version; after the *da capo* of the opening chorus, we had the order: secco 'Che sarà mai d'Orfeo', Aria Creonte, secco 'Venerata Sibilla', Aria Genio; while, as will be seen, the MS. requires that the order of the two arias, with their previous *secchi*, be transposed.

Coro (SATB), 'Ah, sposo infelice'. 2 ob., 2 clar., 2 bsn., 2 hr., str. E flat.

Recitativo secco, Orfeo; Creonte; 'Al cielo te ne voli'.

Coro 'Ah sposo infelice' da capo (Shortened), E flat.

Recitativo secco, Orfeo; Genio; 'Venerata Sibilla'.

Aria Genio, 'Al tuo seno fortunato'. 2 ob., 2 bsn., 2 hr., 2 trpt., timp., str. C major.

Recitativo secco, Creonte; corista; 'Che sarà mai d'Orfeo'.

Aria Creonte, 'Chi spira e non spera'. 1 fl., 2 ob., 2 bsn., 2 hr., str. A major.

Recitativo secco, Orfeo, 'Costanza a me'.

Coro (SATB), 'La giustizia in cor regina'. 2 ob., 2 bsn., 2 hr., 2 trpt., timp. D major.

Recitativo secco, Orfeo, Genio, 'Dove mi guidi?'

Coro da capo.

Atto IV°

Coro (SATB), 'Infelice ombre'. 1 fl., 2 ob., 2 bsn., str. F minor.

 Recitativo secco, Orfeo, Genio, 'Che ascolto, oh Numi?'

 Coro di furie (TB), 'Urli orrendi'. 2 fl., 2 ob., 2 bsn., 2 hr., 2 trbn., str. D minor.

 Recitativo secco, Orfeo, 'O Signor'.

 Coro (TB), 'Trionfi oggi pietà'. 2 fl., 2 ob., 2 bsn., 2 hr., 2 trpt., timp., str. D major.

 Recitativo secco, Pluto; Orfeo; Genio; 'O della Reggia mia'.

 Balletto. 1 fl., 2 ob., 2 bsn., 2 hr, str. D major.

 Recitativo secco, Orfeo; Genio; 'Quai dolci e care note'.

 Coro (SATB), 'Son finiti le tue pene'. Orch. = Balletto.

 Recitativo secco, Genio; Euridice; Orfeo; 'Sovvengati la legge'.

 Recitativo acc. Orfeo, 'Perduto un altra volta'. 1 fl., 2 ob., 2 bsn., 2 hr., str. B flat

⟶

 Aria Orfeo, 'Mi sento languire'; same orch. E♭.

 Recitativo secco, Orfeo, 'Barbaro infido amore'.

 Coro di Baccanti (SA), 'Vieni, vieni, amato Orfeo'. 1 fl., 2 ob., 2 bsn., 2 hr., str. A major.

 Recitativo secco, Orfeo; Baccante; 'Perfide, non turbate'.

 Finale: Orfeo, Coro di Baccanti (SA), 'Bevi, bevi in questa tazza'. 2 fl., 2 ob., 2 bsn., 2 hr., 2 trpt., 2 trbn., timp., str. (organ?). A major ⟶ F major ⟶ D minor.

THE STORY AND ITS HISTORICAL BACKGROUND[1]

The main source for Badini's libretto was Ovid's *Metamorphosis* (Books IX and X), especially the ending, i.e. from the second death of Euridice, to the tearing apart of Orfeo's body by the Thracian Maenads and its floating away to sea. This also appears in Milton's *Lycidas* (where it was also probably borrowed from Ovid). The ending as an orgiastic-tragic theme is more according to the various early legendary sources than the standard happy ending found in most of the known operatic versions (Monteverdi, Peri, Gluck, etc.).

The legend of the man who descends to the nether world to recover his woman (wife or sister) is common to the mythology of many parts of the world.

Badini's story presupposes a certain amount of knowledge about what happened before the curtain goes up. Orfeo, the famed singer of antiquity, son of the River God, Oeagrius, is not married to Euridice, a Princess and the daughter of King Creonte. (Creonte's kingdom is not identified in Badini's libretto, but in other versions of this legend he generally appears as King of Thebes.) Before the opera opens, Creonte had promised Euridice's hand to Arideo, who never appears in the opera at all. Euridice was not in agreement with her father's plans, for she fled from Arideo's coarse attentions. It is at this point that the first act of the opera opens.

The Genio seems to have been an invention of Badini, though the figure is evidently derived from the sibyls, or any one of the numerous soothsaying oracles prevalent in Greek mythology. It is uncertain where Badini found the sources for Creonte, but in any event he is probably the Theban king, not the one of the Oedipus-Antigone legend. Our Creonte is indirectly connected with the Orpheus legend via

---

1 This section is taken from two sources: (1) Joseph Haydn: *Orfeo ed Euridice* (*L'anima del filosofo*), Analytical Notes, Haydn Society, Boston 1951, pp. 49ff.; which portion of those notes was compiled by Richard Wadleigh; and (2) information sent to the author by Richard Wadleigh in November 1970. The author would like to thank his friend and collaborator of many years for the research which is herewith presented.

Heracles, who was the husband of Creonte's daughter, Megara, and Heracles is connected with Orpheus inasmuch as Eristeus (Euristeo) was the man who forced the twelve labours on Heracles. Arideo (= Aristeus = Eristeus) was the son of Apollo and Cyrene. He was a demi-god of various forms of husbandry, especially bee-keeping. In Virgil's 4th *Georgic*, there is a reference to the fact that the other Dryads, to avenge Euridice's death, killed off all his bees; but that he later appeased the nymphs and obtained new bees from the carcasses of bulls. He is definitely connected with the Orpheus legend and in most versions is responsible for Euridice's death, as in our opera. Generally Euridice is found as a Dryad (tree nymph) in the sources.

Act I.
Scenes 1/2. Euridice, fleeing alone and disconsolate from the advances of Arideo, is discovered bewailing her plight at the edge of a dark forest. She is about to enter the forest but the chorus warns her that the inhabitants of the forest are more ferocious and dangerous than wild beasts. In the aria 'Filomena abbondanata' Euridice says that she does not care; even if she were to be sacrificed in savage rites by the forest people, this fate would be no worse than that from which she has just escaped. She again attempts to enter the forest, from which the inhabitants emerge to seize her. The chorus calls for help, summoning Orfeo, who appears, and taking his lyre, sings an impassioned aria 'Rendete a questo seno', entreating the forest people to give him back his beloved. His singing is so beautiful that even the hungry tigers are appeased. Euridice is rescued, to the amazement and joy of the chorus. The two lovers make their way to Creonte's palace, while the chorus sings in praise of harmony.

Scene 3. Creonte's throne room. Creonte asks his followers if anyone knows what has happened to his beloved daughter, who has fled from the palace. The chorus leader (*corista*) tells him of the events in the preceding scene, adding that Orfeo has saved the life of Euridice, and that she loves him. Creonte agrees to their union, although he would have liked to keep his promise to Arideo. In the aria 'Il pensier stà negli oggetti', he philosophises on the inability of man to be master of his own fate. The two lovers then appear, and ask for a father's consent to their marriage. The King gives them his blessing and departs, leaving the two to sing a long love duet, which closes the act.

Act II.
Orfeo and Euridice are married and are found surrounded by a chorus of 'Amorini divini', happily singing. They are suddenly disturbed by a commotion off-stage. Orfeo leaves Euridice to investigate the origin of the disturbance, but while he is gone, an emissary of Arideo, who is lurking in the vicinity, attempts to carry off Euridice to his frustrated master. As she attempts to flee, Euridice steps upon a poisonous snake which bites her foot. The poison quickly spreads throughout her body, and with her dying breath, Euridice sings the beautiful Aria 'Del mio core'. Orfeo, returning, finds her lifeless body, and in desperation sings the long *scena* concluding with the Aria 'Dov'è quel alma audace'.

Creonte then appears with his court, and when he is informed of events, he sings the war aria with on-stage trumpet fanfares, 'Mai non sia inulto'.

Act III.
Scene 1. At Euridice's grave, Orfeo, Creonte and the chorus mourn the death of Euridice. Virgins strew flowers on her tomb. Orfeo bewails his fate, saying that now that Euridice's eyes are closed forever, his world is dark.

Scene 2. Orfeo in desperation consults a Sybil. In answer to his entreaties, a spirit (Genio) appears who, while advising Orfeo to take his fate philosophically, reveals to him, in the course of a *bravura* aria, 'Al tuo seno fortunato', that he may attempt to enter the underworld and bring back Euridice to the upper world.

Scene 3. Creonte, expressing sympathy for Orfeo, sings another philosophical aria, 'Chi spira e non spera' to his followers.

Scene 4. The Genio accompanies Orfeo into the cleft leading to the underworld, while the chorus 'La giustizia' tells Orfeo that the Gods are kind to him.

Act IV.

The scene – and it should be remarked here that in the various scores there are no indications of scenic divisions, which we have added on the basis of the words, and as the music would seem to require – represents both banks of the river Lethe, which divided the world of the living from the world of the dead (the Elysian fields). As the act begins, a lugubrious chorus tells of the souls of the damned who must wait a hundred years before entering the Elysian fields. Orfeo, led by the Genio, appears at the far bank of the river and is about to cross it in Charon's boat when the Furies appear and try to prevent his landing. Orfeo's pleading softens their hearts, and Pluto himself appears and allows Orfeo to pass. A ballet and chorus of souls appear, among which is Euridice. The Genio reminds Orfeo of the condition imposed upon him; namely, he must not look at Euridice until they have reached the upper world. Orfeo, stretching his arms behind him feels for Euridice's features; but Euridice, apparently not knowing the condition, places herself in front of Orfeo so that he cannot avoid seeing her. The Genio, sensing the impending disaster, leaves Orfeo to his fate. Euridice is once more lost to Orfeo, who sings a long aria, 'Perduto un altra volta'. Then a group of Bacchae (followers of Bacchus, who indulged in orgiastic rites, slaying all who opposed them) appear, and make advances to Orfeo, inviting him to join in their celebrations. Orfeo replies to them with rough words, and announces to them that he forever renounces the pleasures of the female sex. (In the *Metamorphosis*, Books IX and X, Ovid clearly states that after the second death of Euridice, Orfeo abandoned himself to homosexual practices, and thereby incurred the wrath of the Bacchae who tore him to pieces; Badini seems to have followed this rather closely.) Angered by Orfeo's refusal, the Bacchae give Orfeo a cup filled with poison, which he drinks. Orfeo dies in agony, while the Bacchae go into a furious frenzy of delight. But as they prepare to tear his body in pieces, a storm arises on the river Lethe – we must remember that Orfeo's father is the River God – and drowns the frenzied women, and Orfeo's body is borne upon the waters, to find rest on the isle of Lesbos.

THE LIBRETTO

Badini's libretto is a conventional eighteenth-century *opera seria*, with all the attitudes, exclamations ('Che vedo? O Numi!') and underlying philosophy that we know from many such similar books. It is in part felicitously, even occasionally poetically, expressed: 'Delle vaghe pupille l'amorose faville, ah dove sono?', sings Orfeo in Act II after finding's Euridice's corpse; or the opening chorus of Act IV, 'Infelice ombre dolenti cento lustri varcar dobbiamo, meste e pallide e languenti senza mai trovar pietà.' In part, too, Badini has a real sense of dramatic rhythm: in Act IV, when Orfeo is poisoned by the Bacchae (Baccanti), he says a few broken words: 'Oimè! Che già nel seno mi serpe un rio veleno. Sento mancar la vita! Il ciel s'oscura . . . finirà con la morte ogni sciagura . . .' (. . . original). There is no grand aria *à la* Donizetti; he is dead in two minutes, and the Baccanti, peering over his body, sorrowfully sing, 'Dead is the Thracian bard.' On the other hand, Badini has done nothing to heighten the drama of Euridice's death in the same act, and Haydn has not improved the situation. The chorus sings, 'Son finite le tue pene, ma se miri la tua sposa, perderai l'amato bene,' Euridice is led on, and in a brief secco Euridice and Orfeo have a short conversation; he looks at her, and the Genio says, 'Oimè, che veggo, o Numi? Giunto è il momento reo, Tu sei perduto, io t'abbandono, Orfeo.' Still, it is inexplicable that Haydn did not save the situation dramatically: as we shall see, he made it worse.

The key figure of the principal title *L'anima del filosofo* is Creonte, who in Act I sings 'Il pensier stà negli oggetti, da lor nasce ogni desio, son tiranni i nostri affetti e vantiamo libertà. Così augel talor si crede di spiegar all'aure il volo e'il meschino, avvinto al piede, serba un laccio, e non lo sà' (roughly: 'The thought is in the objects, from them every desire springs; our emotions are tyrants and yet we boast of liberty. So does the falcon's flight at dawn oft think to reach the heavens when, poor wretch, his foot is chained, and he knows it not'). Or when discussing Orfeo in Act II, after the initial chorus has been repeated, Creonte says to his follower, 'Il è stupo, che giunge il disperato affetto di valor fedele a così grave eccesse; chi perde il caro ben, perde se stesso.' ('He who is forced to submit to such a desperate affliction of faithful valour, to such grave excesses, is rendered senseless; he who loses the loved one, loses himself!' might be a free translation.) This is Metastasio bathed in the still cooler waters of the Age of Reason; but it makes for an oratorio rather than an operatic libretto.

The choice made by Haydn and Badini from among the available singers reveals careful thought. Of course, the title role was in excellent hands, for the way Haydn composed Davide's music shows what a versatile and remarkable singer he must have been. It is not quite clear who was to sing the Genio: possibly the castrato, 'who is not supposed to be very special' (Haydn to Prince Esterházy, 8 January 1791), Sig. Dorelli (*supra*, p. 39). The original Euridice, Madame Lop(p)s, seems to have displeased Haydn when he got to know her voice, for on 14 March 1791 he was writing to *la* Polzelli, 'Only our *prima donna* is a silly goose, and I shan't use her in my opera'; perhaps he was thinking of using Teresa Poggi Cappelletti, who sang in Salomon's concerts of the season (which Madame Lops did not). Originally, as we have seen in the Chronicle, Haydn thought that 'The opera contains only 3 persons', Lops, Davide and the castrato. Thus the part of Creonte seems to have been an afterthought, which may explain why there is the curious fluctuation between tenor and bass clef in his music (*vide infra*).

What Haydn found immediately interesting was the widespread use of the chorus, which he had not been able to have at Eszterháza in Italian operas (though local forces could be, and were, recruited for choruses in the German marionette operas). In Badini's libretto, the chorus occupies several functions simultaneously: first, it acts in the Greek fashion as a permanent commentator on events, and as such it must have been planned to have it present on the stage for most of the opera. Second, it sometimes takes actual part in the drama, as when in the Fourth Act it is the Chorus of the Furies and later the Baccanti which poison Orfeo and are later drowned. As such, the chorus plays a much greater role in Badini's opera than in any of the earlier works on the subject such as Francesco Bertoni's *Orfeo ed Euridice* (which Haydn had conducted at Eszterháza in 1788 and 1789) or Gluck's opera (not, as we have seen, a success in London in 1791), or in the aberrations of the Gluck work such as the one by Antonio Tozzi (changes in the libretto by Marco Coltellini, who had worked for Gluck and supplied the libretto for *L'infedeltà delusa* in 1773) for Munich in January

1775. In fact there is reason to think that the concept of English oratorio materially influenced, if not the presence of, at least the large role assigned to, the chorus in *L'anima del filosofo*. In a sense, the chorus is the real *protagonista principale* of the piece, and there can be no doubt but that Haydn poured into the choruses all his skill and affection.

THE KEY STRUCTURE

The opera is in progressive tonality, not like Haydn's earlier works (e.g. *L'infedeltà delusa* [1773] or *L'incontro improvviso* [1775], which begin and end in C major and D major, respectively) or Mozart's mature works which, from *Idomeneo* on, are all centred round one key. In this respect, Haydn's last opera looks forward to *The Creation*, also in progressive tonality, but for a different reason, as we shall see. *L'anima del filosofo*, if we except the problematical Overture, begins in E flat and ends in D minor.

The key sequences of the fixed numbers are:
Act I – E flat major; C minor; F major; B flat major; C major; E major; G major.
Act II – A major; (G major); E flat major; D major; C major; C minor; F minor; C major.
Act III – E flat major; C major; A major; D major.
Act IV – F minor; D minor; D major; B flat major; E flat major; A major; (F major); D minor.

One strong tendency reveals itself in this interesting and rather subtle scheme: Euridice makes her appearance in E flat, dies in E flat, is generally mourned (Act III choruses) in E flat and specifically by Orfeo in Act IV. Thus there is, as a result of this concentration on Euridice and E flat, a distinctly Neapolitan–sixth outline in the whole opera in general (E flat to D minor) and specifically in Act III, the crucial one as far as her eventual rehabilitation is concerned; the two lovers in the event ruin their opportunity, but in Act III we do not yet know this (Act III: E flat to D major).

ORCHESTRATION

The orchestration of *L'anima del filosofo* is much larger than that of the contemporary symphonies. For one thing, Haydn had clarinets. But they must have been imperfect instruments, because he uses them throughout with a very good sense of their colour but with a great deal of caution; the clarinet parts of Symphonies Nos. 101 and 104 are equally cautious, while those of Nos. 99 and 103 are a little more adventurous, perhaps because his players were better on B flat than on A instruments. In *L'anima del filosofo* the clarinets are also used sparingly, in fact only in Orfeo's F minor Aria in Act II ('In un mar d'accerbe pene'), where they appear for the first time; then in the mourning choruses of Act III. We have seen that Haydn wrote parts for two cors anglais; these instruments are used soloistically in Euridice's death aria, where as we have seen they go down to D in the bass clef. But we are told that London had no knowledge of the instrument before Ferlendis arrived in town with *la* Banti from Venice and demonstrated the cor anglais in 1795. Obviously this difficult question cannot be solved with the evidence at our disposal; but we know Haydn was always a great orchestral experimenter and innovator, and he may have persuaded the oboe players to get his favourite cors anglais specially constructed. Haydn had always had a particular affinity for this tenor oboe and had used it to great effect in many of his vocal works (and in Symphony No. 22 and other instrumental pieces) in the 1760s and 1770s, in particular in several operas. It is, of course, possible that in 1795 the London critics had never before *heard* a cor anglais, but the oboe players in that international city must have known of the instrument's existence, since its use was fairly widespread on the Continent. That Haydn had a special instrument in mind is clear from the extended range downwards.

Haydn's trombones are used, with chilling effect, only in the Furies' Chorus and in the final dénouement: there are two, one in the alto clef and one in the tenor, corresponding to two instruments of different size (he does not use the bass trombone here). The solo harp part, which appears just once in Orfeo's first Aria, was presumably intended for the famous Mrs Krumpholz; if Haydn might have forgotten her playing from Eszterháza, he could have renewed acquaintance with it almost from the moment he arrived in London, and particularly at the First Salomon Concert. Like most eighteenth-century harp solo parts, it does not sound characteristic to us; neither do Mozart's in the Concerto for flute and harp, K. 299, or indeed the many Dussek works expressly written for Mrs Krumpholz. The typical rolling arpeggios and the sonorous bass notes (as at the beginning of another *Orfeo*, by Stravinsky) were obviously not yet known to *settecento* harpists or their composers. Haydn only wrote once more for the harp, in the incidental music to *Alfred*; and in the composer's autograph, the part is, curiously, left blank.

For the rest, the orchestration is on the same brilliant level as the first Salomon Symphonies. It is particularly effective in the choral pieces, and in the end of the work; there we find the typical pattern of repeated semiquavers in the upper strings and relentless bass line in quavers. We also note its heavy brass section (how the trumpets cut through the texture like knives!), and its doom-ridden ending with the ghostly flutes – all this is fully the equal of anything of the period. The ugly sound of the orchestra, with its high, piercing trombones, in the Furies' Chorus is also characteristic, and reveals quite a different side of Haydn's personality than do the more well-known symphonies.

THE CHORAL WRITING

The libretto often dictates that only women, or only men, sing in a certain number, or part of a number. Haydn had the usual choral structure of S-A-T-B, but when it was divided, he kept the writing two-part: this was obviously to make it easier to learn for the singers who, unlike those in the oratorio concerts, had to sing from memory. There are some magnificent four-part choruses, especially the gravely sad and beautifully laid-out entrance chorus of Act IV, 'Infelice ombre'; and the men's choruses (e.g. the beginning of the opera, 'Ferma il piede', and the Furies' Chorus in D minor) are very effective. There is a certain amount of balance problems with the purely female chorus at the end of the opera; in the D minor Allegro, the chorus enters on the notes d''[1] (sop.) and d' (alto), against the whole orchestra, with timpani, $f\!f$; it is very difficult to hear the singers come in, unless the chorus was very much bigger than one might imagine. Haydn had never written anything like it before, and there was no chance to try it out in rehearsal; perhaps he would have adjusted something if he could have heard it.

Even in the two-part choral writing, Haydn manages to get much variety through imitation and by polyphonic writing. The beginning of the choral entry in the Furies' Chorus is characteristic:

[1] The system of pitch notation here used is based on middle C being represented by the symbol c'. See note on p. 16.

as is the following passage from the first Baccante chorus, just before the Finale:

The great choral entry in the opening number of Act IV may serve as an example of all that is 'in the best possible taste' (as they said about Haydn's Duet in *Il burbero* in 1794) in this opera – see example opposite.

One of the most effective choral numbers is the opening; Euridice begins with a quiet *recitativo accompagnato* in E flat, all alone on the stage (the chorus, if on the stage, is in the background and, as it were, invisible). She is at the edge of a thick wood, and suddenly a men's chorus appears, the music switches to C minor, and they warn her not to enter the wood, full of people more ferocious than wild beasts – nameless horrors, who even then are rushing down from the mountains to attack her ('Mostri vi

sembran legname, alme selvagge. Vedi costor, che scendono dal monte. Fuggi, fuggi
...'). It is a genuinely frightening piece of music, rushing forwards like Euridice to her
doom. We shall not defend you,' warn the chorus. 'Leave me in peace' ('Per pietà, deh
lasciatemi'), cries Euridice, and to the warning, 'Fuggi, fuggi, fuggi', dying away in
the distance, the music itself slips away to nothing. It is as if Haydn, with some hidden
intuition, had glimpsed a ghastly world of fear and doom into which he never had to
enter, but of whose existence his subconscious was grimly aware.

On a quite different level, we find the mourning chorus (and its shortened *da capo*)
at the beginning of Act III. It is interesting to point out parenthetically that Haydn
seems to have thought of clarinets, at least in *L'anima del filosofo*, as instruments of
sorrow; for he uses them, as we have seen, only in the preceding Aria of Orfeo
mourning Euridice's death; the clarinet there sings sorrowfully to the words of the
eternal harpist, 'Questi son lugubri avanzi, spoglie infauste, ch'io rimiro.' Here the
clarinet is a prominent orchestral member accompanying first the women's chorus,

then the men, then the women, then the men, soon joined by the women to conclude as a four-part chorus. 'Ah sposo infelice, perduto hai per sempre la cara Euridice, il core del tuo cor,' they sing, in E flat major, key of majesty but also key of *tristezza* (Mozart's great Symphony K. 543; Haydn's Symphony No. 99; but also the middle part of Mozart's *Maurerische Trauermusik*, K. 477). Altogether, the choral sections of the opera reflect almost every kind of emotion, particularly of the stronger sort.

THE WRITING FOR THE SOLO VOICES

With the exception of Madame Lops, for whom in the end Haydn probably did not write the part of Euridice (*vide supra*), most of the cast were Italians. Haydn had been dealing with Italian singers for many years at Eszterháza, and experience had made him a great diplomat with them. Dies (pp. 85–7) tells us,

> Haydn saw with much pleasure that even the Italian singers, though their ears and throats from earliest childhood were used to the operatic style of their country, which was always melodious but tended to avoid complications and dissonances; even they took pains not to mistake his (very often) sudden modulations and changes of pitch, and sang his music with grace. Naturally the Italian singers often let him know that they had undertaken such difficulties only as a special favour to him; even the most famous made no exception, and when Haydn went from the usual harmonies to less usual ones, when he described an emotional situation not just by loud noise but by a surprising and emotional modulation, they remarked that such passages were very difficult to sing. [Dies then goes on to say how the singers in Italy tyrannized their composers and conductors, and that the connoisseurs soon came to judge such music 'tailor written' for the singers as being very attractive to the senses but deprived of any inner life.] Haydn did not contradict all these remarks which I introduced into the conversation, but he added that one must take the particular time into consideration. 'Because later', he added, several Italians raised themselves above the usual routine of their country; they were at home in all the spheres of harmony and with facility, for instance Cherubini [who was just at that time, 9 December 1805, in Vienna].

Haydn was obviously thinking not so much of his singers at Eszterháza, who while good and occasionally famous (e.g. Constanza Valdesturla or Guglielmo Jermoli) were not international stars like Davide or Banti: Haydn was also clever enough to write that which lay well for their voices, and you can tell more what Davide's voice was like from examining the present opera, and what Banti's capacities were from *Scena di Berenice*, than from almost any contemporary description, however gifted.

Orfeo's music

Orfeo's (Davide's) first Aria shows many sides of his voice. First we have his expressive recitative, with harp and accompanying strings. Then we have the harp's music given to the strings and the tempo changes from adagio in cut time to 'largo assai' in cut time (slower, perhaps?); Orfeo enters on a long held *f''*, culminating in a pause (*fermata*), which shows the comfortable top of his voice and also his sustaining power (see example opposite at top of page). We then have a series of crotchets obviously designed to show his shining and powerful middle notes in a slow marching pace (to triplet accompaniment) – see opposite, centre.

We soon notice that Haydn cultivates Davide's middle range; he has the very occasional high note, but *a flat'* seems to have been his comfortable top; at the end of

the Duet in Act I he reaches *b′* (all these are sounding pitches, they are of course written an octave higher). But if Davide's speciality was not ringing high notes, he had an unbelievable low register, which Haydn fully exploits in Orfeo's last Aria in Act IV; here we have low A's, low B flats, and reached by jumps:

Returning to the first Aria, we find Haydn in the allegro section, now displaying his leading man's flexibility. It is awesome to behold:

At the end of the Aria, Haydn even takes his *primo uomo* up to *b flat'*:

Nothing in the rest of the opera contains any music for Davide as florid as this except for the Duet at the end of Act I, where we find difficult passages which require very good intonation and great agility from both singers, e.g.:

Orfeo's greatest Aria is without question the big Scena in Act II after Euridice's death, a typical *bravura* piece from an *opera seria* but with many brilliant touches. From D major, when Orfeo returns to the stage and does not immediately see the dead Euridice, we proceed to G and then to C major. Then he sees her, the music swerving to A flat, D flat, back to A flat, with a cadence in E flat. There then begins the customary slow aria-like section which is destined to be interrupted: in this case it is in C major, with solo oboe, and is more of an accompanied recitative. After a cadence to C minor, the Aria itself, in F minor, an old favourite key of Haydn's, begins. And here we find really original ideas: up to now, the music could have been from any good *opera seria*; now we are immersed in Haydn's special language, the old *Sturm und Drang* key of the great Quartet Op. 20, No. 5, composed nearly thirty years before; of the *Sinfonia La Passione* No. 49 (1768); of the bass aria in Act I of *L'infedeltà delusa* (1773). As for the following enharmonic modulations, we can imagine Davide after the rehearsal telling Haydn that he had sung all those b double-flats, c flats, etc. just to please the composer:

Vocal music

Without any doubt, the most moving of Orfeo's laments comes in a *secco* recitative between the two mourning choruses; here was the great opportunity for Davide to show all his skill and powers of projection in the lowliest musical form of the *opera seria*:

Orfeo's last Aria, in Act IV after Euridice's death, might have saved Badini's weak death scene, where as we have pointed out, Euridice dies in a secco. But what are we to make of this calm, almost placid *recitativo accompagnato*, to the words, 'lost another time'?

And despite its marking 'allegro agitato', the Aria proper is musically speaking out of place. Considering the force of what went before (the Furies' Chorus and the opening Chorus of Act IV), and the end of the opera, this dramatic lapse is as inexplicable as it is unfortunate. The words, too, are at painful variance with the lilting tune:

339

The Aria itself, taken out of context, is an admirable piece of music and even develops not only harmonic ingenuity but real strength in the middle part. But here it holds up the action, and does not grip us in the way that such an intrusion into the main plot must, if it is to be tolerable.

Euridice's music

Euridice opens the opera with a slow *recitativo accompagnato*, which sets the action but does not particularly tell us much about her voice. The chorus, with her taking part, has music which suggests that she must have had a ringing dramatic soprano voice. The ensuing recitative tells us not much more, and the first big Aria is distinctly cool and rather conventional. If up to now it might be thought that Madame Lops was a big, dramatic soprano, this Aria displays her agility. Like Davide, she seems to have had a powerful low range, and Haydn, after a long coloratura section, gives us a chance to hear Madame Lops' chest notes:

Rather interestingly, Haydn starts the slow section in the tonic, of course, modulates to the dominant, and then *stays* in the dominant for the whole beginning of the Aria. It is a curious but effective device. We are also shown that Madame Lops possessed a high c, which means that as far as pure range is concerned, she equalled Banti (for whom Haydn wrote from *b flat* to *c′′′*). And yet, there is something distinctly unenthusiastic about this first Euridice Aria; probably by now Haydn had come to have grave reservations about that 'silly goose', as he was soon to describe her to Polzelli. One particular passage, however, deserves to be singled out. It comes at the end of a cadential passage in F major, but as will be seen, the key changes at once to the minor:

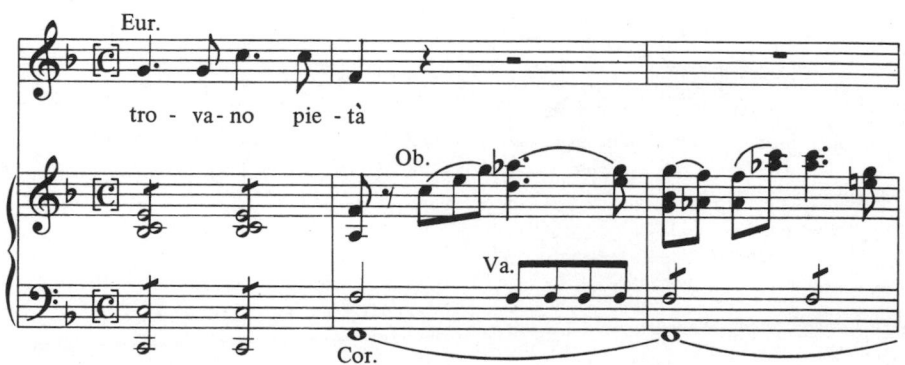

This is the first of a series of warnings in Haydn's music as to what will be the end of Euridice (rather like the slightly sinister introduction of the Passion Chorale into Bach's *Christmas Oratorio*). There are three such warnings and all are built upon the same pattern: sudden plunge into the minor a pedal point, a *piano* context, all before Euridice's death, and only in her or in Orfeo's music; Creonte has his premonitions, too, but not of this particular kind. The second time this warning occurs is in Orfeo's first Aria, and the third time in the concluding Duet of Act I; it will also be observed that the horns, in each case, contribute to the pedal point; in the first two cases, the text is as sombre as the music; in the third the lovers are all wrapped up in themselves and only the audience hears this third and last warning.

Euridice's great moment comes in the second act, after she has been bitten by the snake; she then sings a short accompanied recitative and aria. It is the highpoint of her part and the climax of the opera. Like so much of Haydn's finest music, it is exquisitely simple. Dramatically it is very much to the point: short, poignant and expressive. The opening recitative has a sextuplet accompaniment, dry as the rustle of autumn leaves with a 'dying fall', while the upper line, with its appoggiature, graphically tells us of the poison spreading through her body:

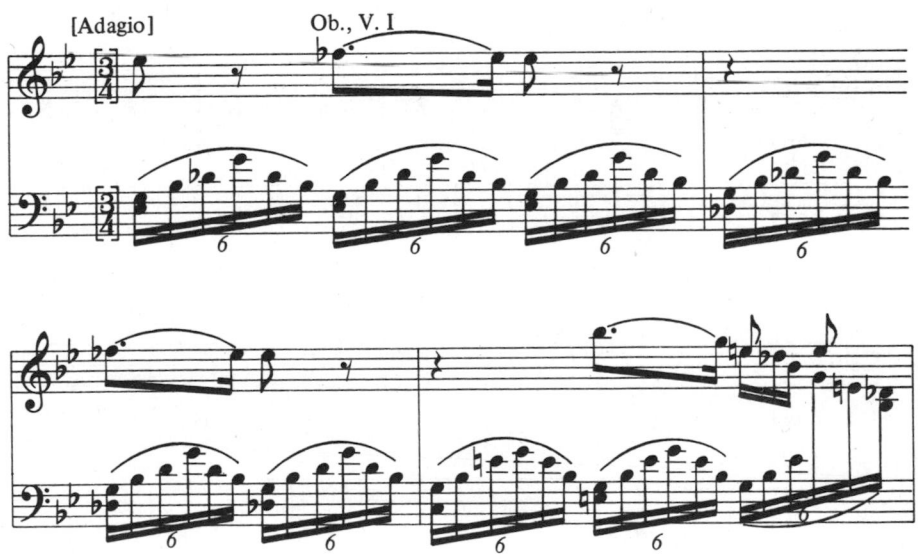

while the recitative's end shows us the breath coming out of her dying lips in little gasps:

The Aria is so short that Haydn calls it *Cavatina*, as he would do in a great tenor aria 'Dem Druck erlieget die Natur' in *The Seasons* ten years later. Euridice's Largo in cut time is a great masterpiece of understatement. The melody seems to be the summing-up, the quintessence of every Italian opera melody:

in its simplicity, elegance and *cantilena*; while the nine bars of the contrasting middle section seem to contain all the sorrows of the world in them:

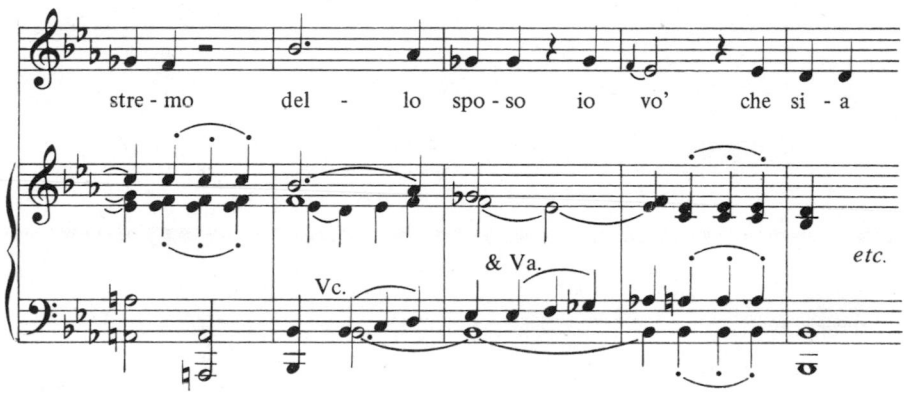

The very end contains the extraordinary English horn solo down to D in the bass clef, symbolizing the last breath of life coming in feeble sighs from the dying *Principessa* (below). To all intents, this scene is Euridice's farewell to the opera; she appears, it is true, in the brief *secco* in Act IV, but as we have seen, that scene is a distinct anticlimax.

345

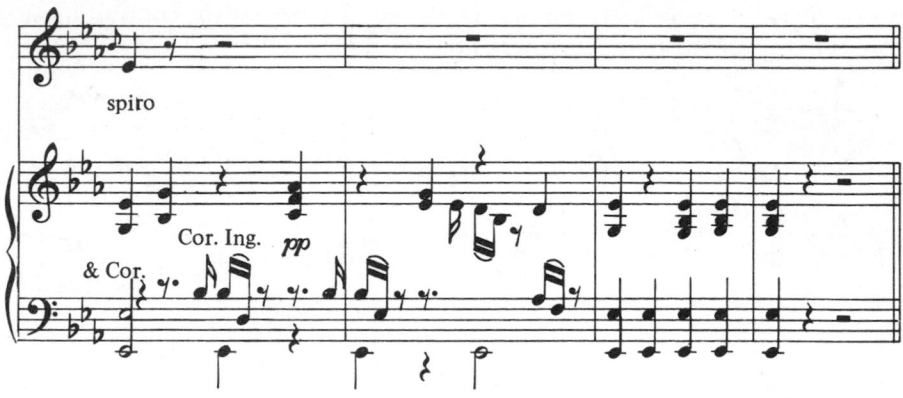

spiro
Cor. Ing.
pp
& Cor.

Two pages from the score of *L'anima del filosofo* (*Orfeo ed Euridice*) – Euridice's death scene from Act II – written out by Haydn's English copyist; from the composer's library. The textual correction in Italian is in Haydn's own hand.

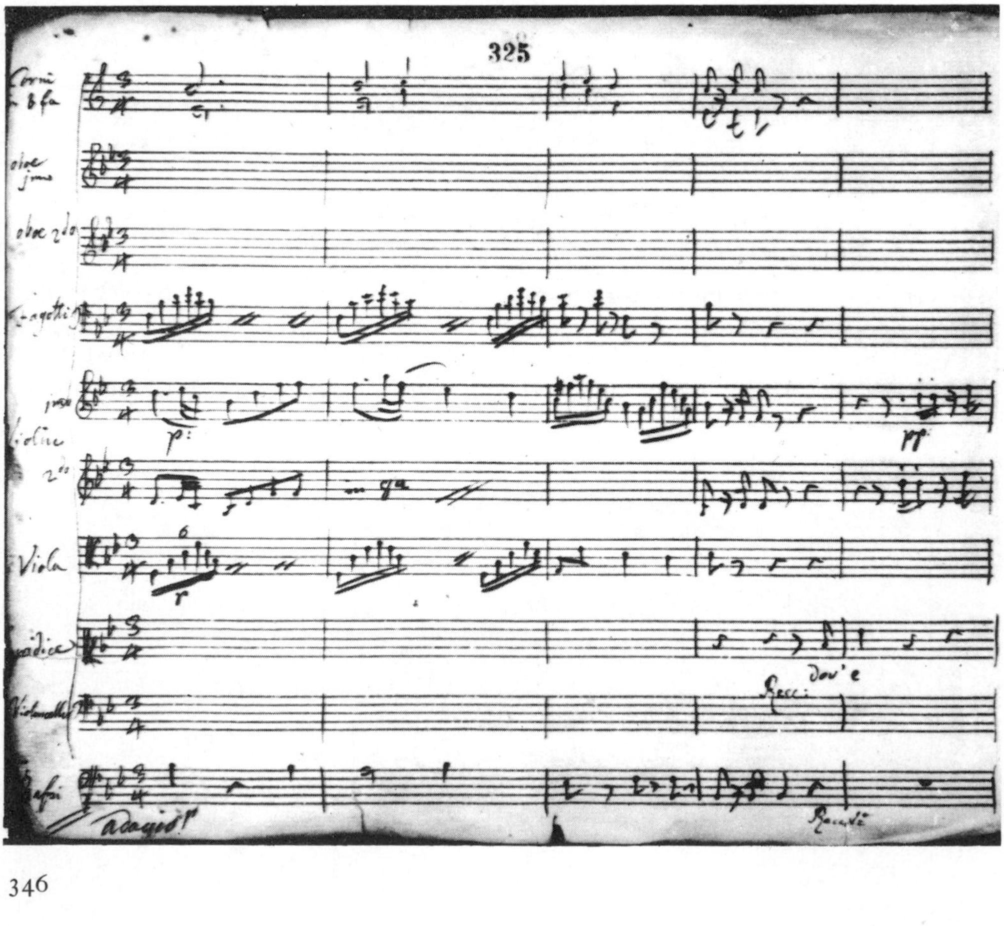
325
Viola
dov'e

Creonte's music

Creonte, as was suggested above, may have been an afterthought. It is curious that something seems to have happened between Acts I & II, where the part is for a baritone, and Act III, where the Aria in A is written in the tenor clef; but actually the *tessitura* of the earlier arias is rather high, and in the concluding C major Aria of Act II Creonte is expected to sing a thoroughly exposed *f'* twice. It may be that the use of the tenor clef in the Act III Aria is a mere technical convenience, to avoid the use of the ledger lines, of which the notation in the bass clef would involve a great many: the range now extends to *f sharp'* and down only to *c sharp* in the bass clef. Perhaps the singer was a high, light baritone.

His greatest Aria is unquestionably the one in Act I, 'Il pensier sta negli oggetti', in the rather unusual key of E major (which Haydn very much liked, much more so than Mozart,[1] for instance). It is the 'filosofo' part of the title with humanistic and Freemason overtones. It is philosophically and musically like much of *Die Zauberflöte* – which of course postdates Haydn's opera by half a year. The text inspires Haydn to a fine bit of imitation; the falcon not knowing it is chained, of which idea the flute's line is vividly descriptive (see overleaf).

---

1 An interesting parallel is the E major Aria, with many Masonic undertones, 'In diesen heil'gen Hallen' from *Zauberflöte*.

Creonte's second Aria is the 'revenge' piece at the end of Act II, one of Haydn's typical C major 'war' arias of which the best example is in *La vera costanza* and others are in *Armida*; previously Haydn had used his trumpet-substitutes, the C alto horns; here we have both trumpets and horns, the latter of course in C basso (since C alto horns were practically unknown outside the Austro-Hungarian monarchy). The trumpets do not appear until the middle of the Aria, when they are, as the text indicates, on stage. It is an effective moment and Haydn does not disappoint us:

Creonte's third and final Aria, 'Chi spira e non spera', is more conventional than either of the others.

Genio's music

The Genio has only one Aria, the great C major *bravura* piece, 'Al tuo seno fortunato', with a massive orchestral accompaniment including trumpets and drums. After the Queen of the Night's 'Der Hölle Rache', this Genio Aria is one of the great coloratura *tours-de-force* of the late eighteenth century. It has phenomenally difficult coloratura passages, but also long and beautiful melodic lines. As a separate piece, it should prove enormously effective; the top range is *e'''*, a note below the famous *f'''* of Mozart's Aria in *Die Zauberflöte*. Here is a specimen of what the Genio is expected to sing:

The minor parts

Of the minor parts, those of the first *corista* and Pluto, both for bass-baritone, are the most interesting; but neither has an aria and both roles as well as the other *corista* parts were obviously sung by members of the chorus.

Haydn's *L'anima del filosofo* is basically a magnificent failure – despite unforgettable moments and points of real dramatic interest, particularly in the Fourth Act. Part of its lack of success is undoubtedly because Haydn has no opportunity to revise it; part is the libretto's static, oratorio-like quality; part consists of the dramatic miscalculations, e.g. the *corista* explaining to Creonte, towards the end of Act II, everything we have just seen ourselves on the stage; or inexplicably the second death of Euridice, when Badini and Haydn completely miss the opportunity for another dramatic highpoint. *L'anima del filosofo* lacks the pithy concentration of Haydn's earlier *L'infedeltà delusa* (a perfect example of operatic timing from beginning to end), and it also wants the timeless and ageless quality of Act II in *La fedeltà premiata* where, particularly the tenor *scena* and Celia's great 'Ah, come il core' seem to hang suspended in time and space. There is almost none of that operatic tension in *L'anima del filosofo*. Opera seria was paradoxically a still popular but dramatically doomed and old-fashioned vehicle. It was what princes and emperors expected for marriages and coronations, and even the great Mozart had to compose music to an old Metastasian drama – somewhat modernized by Mazzolà – *La clemenza di Tito* in this very same year (1791) for the Prague coronation ceremonies of the Emperor Leopold II.

But neither was the world a place for *opere serie* any longer, nor was Haydn much interested in the form as such. His strength had been Italian opera in the *buffa* style with elements from *opera seria*; his greatest gifts lay in the portrayal of comic parts, especially in the 'underdog' – something which always opened the flood-gates of his immense reservoir of inspiration. What moved Haydn, and thus moves us, is the beggar-woman (in reality Hanswurst) in *Das abgebrannte Haus*; or Colombina's E major Aria in Act II of the same opera, which she sings after the house has burned down and she is left utterly destitute. Badini's stylized and slow-moving libretto offered no such opportunities, and there are only parts of Euridice's role, and more of Orfeo's, that seemed to have seized his imagination. Despite the length of time which its composition demanded in 1791, the opera's non-performance hardly affected Haydn's English career. Nor could it be said that *L'anima del filosofo* is in any way a central work in Haydn's mature style. Although it would be wrong to judge Haydn's artistic life in the 1770s and 1780s without his operas, which are often his most important works of that period, the late Haydn could, and in fact until 1951 did, exist almost entirely without his final stage piece.

The 'almost' in the above sentence refers to the extracts published in 1806 by Breitkopf & Härtel. The opera was announced in the October issue of the *AMZ*, following an interesting note on the final, unfinished Quartet (known as Opus 103).

> Orpheus und Euridice, heroische Oper, in Musik gesetzt von Joseph Haydn, (Ital. und deutscher Text. Klavierausz. Preis 2 Thlr. 12 Gr.). A work that Haydn composed in his finest and most brilliant period, when he was living in London and writing his world-famous, great symphonies there; and which was, because of special circumstances, not mounted on the stage and also not quite completed; but those pieces which were finished, and herewith presented for the first time, are so full of intellect and expression, partly large-scale and brilliant, partly graceful and

tender scenes, arias and choruses, such as have hardly ever graced a large theatre. Leipzig in Oct. 1806.   Breitkopf & Härtel's music publishing house.

In due course the full score was also printed (announcement in the *Intelligenz-Blatt* of the *AMZ* for 29 July 1807, price 4 Thaler). On 3 December 1806, the *AMZ* carried the following anonymous criticism of *Orfeo*:

The public has already been informed about the history of this very valuable work. The great master wrote it, in fact, during his sojourn in London, at the same time that he was writing the series of his greatest and most perfect symphonies, through which he has especially gained the admiration of the whole educated world,[1] and where, it would seem, he found himself for the first time, as a man and as an artist; – and where at last those who had an immediate effect on his career received him in the liberal fashion which he would long have deserved. The opera was to have been staged during Haydn's stay in London; but certain circumstances prevented the directors from doing so. Haydn did not proceed (as far as can be judged from the fragments here presented) with the rather good libretto in the usual fashion, i.e. a hack libretto hastily knocked together and where one begins at the beginning and sews the whole length piece for piece. On the contrary, after receiving the whole libretto, he set to work on single pieces of importance, his choice depending on how he felt disposed and attracted on the one or the other day. And so it is that we have these pieces, which do not by far constitute the complete opera and thus are of no use for the theatre (unless perhaps one inserts, now and again, single movements in other operas), but are the more valuable for private delight. The more valuable I say: for these are almost entirely large-scale, fully developed pieces: and of a kind that contain very little stage atmosphere [*Scenisches*] and are almost without any 'action' whatever. They are also, with the exception of one single aria, for the two principal voices, the soprano and the tenor, and for the chorus; the pieces employ the two principal voices thoroughly, it is true, but in such a wise as befit the noble, tragic circumstances and also the composer's dignity. Thus they have far more claim to profound emotion and a sympathetic [*seelenvollen*] performance than an exaggerated range for the voice, vastly complicated passages, and so on: things which composers and singers without wit and heart like to call bravura and greatness. Some of the pieces here presented belong quite certainly to the most beautiful things for voice Haydn has ever written. We present, by way of conclusion, the contents of the whole:

No. 1. An aria for Euridice in the style of the modern Italians, so long as they still compose really heroic operas; well and rather brilliantly composed. ['Filomena abbandonata' from Act I.]

No. 2. A chorus of the Furies, very characteristic, written in a spirited and expressive fashion. The vocal part is only for two parts, both low voices. It creates a strange, imposing effect: and if we consider it as a separate piece, as it is here, one would very much have wished that it had pleased the composer to continue the ideas and develop them further – but on the stage of the theatre that would not have been possible. [Chorus of the Furies from Act IV.]

No. 3. A short, pleasant, gentle Aria for high bass voice, in form like a small rondo, simple, easy, very smooth and completely matched to the text, which is very good here. [Creonte's Aria from Act I, 'Il pensier sta negli oggetti'.]

---

1 [Footnote in the original article] The reviewer takes the liberty of pointing out that these symphonies are the declared favourites – in Petersburg as in Naples, in Moscow as in Madrid, in Paris and London as in Lisbon and Stockholm, in the whole of Germany as in – Philadelphia. Who can claim such a fame as Haydn's? Is it not something wonderful to speak in a language that the whole educated world understands?

No. 4. A Scene for Euridice, only three pages long, very simple and without any obvious tricks at all, but really more valuable than many an act of a much applauded opera. The whole cavatina has a vocal range almost all within an octave and moves just in crotchets; but sung, with a beautiful voice, just the way the composer intended, and was able to express in his few notes, it cannot fail to strike deep into the heart of any sensitive person. [Euridice's death scene in Act II, 'Dov'è l'amato bene?' ending with the Aria (Cavatina), 'Del mio core'.]

No. 5. is a grand Scene for Euridice again, with the chorus which interrupts and accompanies her and is again only for two low vocal parts. The Scene is simple, grand and effective, more in the German than the Italian manner. [Scena 'Sventurata, che fò!' and Chorus with Euridice in Act I, 'Ferma il piede, O Principessa'.]

No. 6. consists of a large-scale Scene, also passionate, for Orpheus, not without strength and originality but, it would seem, not the equal of the great Scene. [Orfeo's Recitative and Aria in Act IV, 'Perduta un' altra volta' with the Aria, 'Mi sento languire'.]

No. 7., again for Orpheus, and in the original it was accompanied by an obbligato harp part. This is once again one of those pieces for head and heart which only a great master can produce and which, if performed properly, cannot be heard without sympathy and emotion. It is actually composed in the more noble Italian manner but is somewhat richer in the accompaniment than that manner demands. [Orfeo's Recitative and Aria in Act I, 'Rendete a questo seno' with the Aria, 'Cara speme!'.]

No. 8. consists of a very large-scale and richly worked out Duet for Orpheus and Euridice, the character of which may be most easily explained to the reader if we say that it approaches to the well-known Mozart Duet 'Meinetwegen mußt du sterben' from *Die Entführung* – only it does not quite have the inner warmth of the latter, and the roles are more similar to each other. [Duet at the end of Act I, 'Come il foco'.]

No. 9. is again a long, highly developed and affective Scene for Orpheus which is rather like No. 6. [Orfeo's Recitative and Aria in Act II, 'Dov'è quell' alma audace' with the Aria, 'In un mar d'accerbe pene'.]

No. 10. A soft Chorus of Souls on the Lethe (only for soprano and alto voices) with single solos for Orpheus; then the Chorus introduces a musical pantomime, to which is added a concluding violent Chorus. [Finale from Act IV, 'Bevi, bevi in questa tazza'.] The last piece is

No. 11. A very ingenious but quite simple, noble and moving Chorus of Souls in Orcus (F minor), in four parts throughout and worked out with very simple accompaniment. This Chorus is again a small masterpiece, and as far as I personally am concerned, I would say it is the crown of the whole set, though it only takes up two pages. It is just what the persons, the situation and the text require, and I cannot do better in words to describe it than to quote a few lines

> Infelice ombre dolenti!
> cento lustri varcar dobbiamo,
> meste, pallide e languenti,
> senza mai trovar pietà.

> Weh uns armen, bleichen Schatten!
> treiben fünfmal hundert Jahre
> auf den Wellen, und ermatten
> ohne Rettung, unbeklagt!

[Opening Chorus of Act IV]

One can see in the words at that same time that the German translator has worked with intelligence and taste; but one rather imagines (which upon closer examination of the work turns out to be the case several times) that his words are not everywhere comfortably fitted to the music.

The piano score is very well done – it is sufficiently complete but is also playable and flowing. The work is well printed.

In the ensuing numbers of the *AMZ*, we read of successful performances of some of these single numbers. In the *AMZ* of 6 January 1808, the Leipzig correspondent tells us of a performance of the Scena and Chorus with Euridice from the First Act, 'Sventurata, che fò!' – the beginning of the opera, in fact – which 'made a lively, strong effect; the connoisseur will, particularly in the recitative and in the connection between the chorus and the solo voice, recognize the ingenious and experienced master.' The big Recitative and Aria of Orfeo in Act I, 'Rendete a questo seno' was performed at Leipzig on 30 January 1809 (*AMZ* of 8 February) which the Leipzig correspondent of the *AMZ* found 'excellent' (*vortrefflich*). In 1808, the entire Breitkopf selection had been given at Königsberg on the stage.[1]

But as the critic of the *AMZ* had rightly observed, the fragmentary publication of the opera was of no use to opera houses; and contrary to his hope that the pieces would become popular in private concerts (or as concert arias), even these extracts – which, after all, contained the essential numbers of the opera – became forgotten. Although it is curious to think that Euridice's death scene remained so popular in England that there was even an ancient gramophone record of it still extant half a century ago.[2]

Madrigal: 'The Storm'
(XXIVa: No. 8)

The great German musicologist Ernst Ludwig Gerber, who corresponded with Haydn, made an interesting observation in his 'Haydn' article for the *Neues historisch-biographisches Lexikon der Tonkünstler*[3] in connection with the origins of the libretto to *The Creation*, 'Since Handel's death', says Gerber,

> there had been resting a vocal libretto [*Sing-Gedicht*] in England put together from Milton's *Paradise Lost* and called *The Creation*, because it was thought that only the singer of *Messiah* could have been expected to provide this text with an harmonic garb worthy of it. Meanwhile Haydn appeared in London, and recalled, with his great and powerful works, the giant strength of Handel. One's hopes were once again raised, and they hoped to see this poem worthily set to music also by Haydn; they looked for it, and gave it to Haydn to compose. . . .

Now it seems unlikely that Haydn's purely instrumental music, even the great London Symphonies, would have brought to mind the 'giant strength' of Handel. It must have been Haydn's vocal music, and more specifically his choral pieces, that awoke the hope for a worthy successor to the Saxon composer. As we have shown in the preceding Chronicle, however, Salomon and Haydn found it difficult to get boys for the chorus, and the English public of 1791–5 probably knew Haydn's choral writing from two choruses out of *Il ritorno di Tobia* (*supra*, p. 74), from the occasional works such as the lost Catch for Gallini, and principally from this Madrigal, 'The Storm', which was such a success at its première in the 1792 season. In the Chronicle,

1 Ludwig Wendschuh: *Über Haydns Opern*, Rostock, 1895, p. 113.
2 Sung by J. Sonnenberg (alto) on Polydor 66083. F. F. Clough and C. J. Cuming: *The World's Encyclopaedia of Recorded Music*, London 1952, p. 270.
3 1812–14. New edition in facsimile (edited by Othmar Wessely), Graz 1966, Vol. II, p. 543.

we have seen how frequently Haydn is praised for his terrifying effects, the man 'who can stun with thunder' or who can, as Thomas Holcroft wrote, 'bid the huge tormented tempest howl'; these are hardly emotions which would be aroused by the Salomon Symphonies. On the other hand, they do fit this grandiose short choral piece, with its bold harmonies, its tremolo strings (particularly effective in the return to the 'storm' section after the first 'blessed calm' interlude) and its majestic sweep. Like the brilliant chorus 'Svanisce in un momento', the Madrigal is divided into several sections, a stormy part and a strongly contrasting slow part. In form, both works show the same overall pattern: storm – calm – storm – calm. In the Madrigal, Haydn sets the words 'Bless'd calm, return, return again' to a hymn-like, slowly moving music almost like a church anthem and heightens the contrast by having the four soloists sing the words; whereas the tempest section, 'Hark! The wild uproar of the winds, and hark; Hell's Genius roams the regions of the dark' (etc.) was for the chorus.

As we have suggested in the Chronicle (*supra*, p. 226), 'The Storm' was rather heavily revised, new instruments added, and the woodwind writing enlarged, when Haydn mounted the work in 1793 in Vienna. Unfortunately, there is no critical edition; but happily, Haydn himself furnished the final revised version to Breitkopf & Härtel which Griesinger personally took to Leipzig in the Spring of 1802[1] and which the Leipzig firm published in October 1802 (*Intelligenz-Blatt* to the *AMZ* of 6 October 1802), but only with German and Italian words. Haydn's original manuscript of 1792 is in the Esterházy Archives and it was the basis for the supposedly critical edition published jointly by Editio Musica, Budapest and the Doblinger Verlag in Vienna-Munich.[2] Unfortunately this new edition used only the autograph and not the many other authentic sources still available, and in the autograph are missing the brass and timpani parts for which there was no room on the twelve-stave paper Haydn used; these brass and timpani parts, probably written on separate sheets, as was Haydn's custom, are now separated from the manuscript, but the other authentic sources show clearly that they were part of the original London version (while conversely the clarinets and trombones, which Salomon did not have in his 1792 band, were added in Vienna). Rather unbelievably, the new Musica-Doblinger score just includes, as the orchestral part, the flutes, oboes, bassoons and the string parts found in the autograph. Performers wishing to perform the original English text will therefore use the choral (and vocal soloist) material of the new edition as far as it goes, and add the late orchestration if they wish to from the Breitkopf score. Since there is no doubt that the revision is a distinct improvement in the sound and in the overall layout of the orchestration too, there is no particular merit in the *Urfassung* except as an historical curiosity. The revised version is also published by Doblinger (edited by Franz Burkhart).

If we seem to owe the existence of the English *Creation* libretto to the success of the Madrigal in London in 1792 et seq., it had a similar effect on a man who was also responsible for the oratorio's existence: Gottfried van Swieten, who appears to have made the German translation. The success of the Madrigal in Vienna in 1793 will have not only pleased the Baron (who despite being a stiff aristocrat and possessing a rather frigid manner was surprisingly modest and self-effacing when it came to his translations) but suggested to him that Haydn might have the makings of a great

---

1 Edward Olleson, 'Georg August Griesinger's Correspondence with Breitkopf & Härtel' in *Haydn Yearbook* III (1965), p. 37.
2 Edited by Ferenc Szekeres. Full score, 1969. See our review of this edition in *Haydn Yearbook* VIII (1971).

oratorio composer. Thus it would seem that this Madrigal occupies a very central position in Haydn's music composed in or for London – indeed, it is probably no exaggeration to say that we owe to its success the last three oratorios of Haydn, i.e. the revised choral version of *The Seven Words*, *The Creation* and *The Seasons*. Quite a feat for a choral piece lasting less than a quarter of an hour!

Oratorio fragment : Mare Clausum
(XXIVa : No. 9)

Lord Abingdon's idea (see Chronicle, p. 271) also served its purpose in that it set Haydn's mind on an oratorio book, though not one interesting enough to stimulate the full unfolding of his talents. The first of the two extant pieces is an F major Aria, 'Nor can I think my suit is vain', for bass solo and full orchestra with trumpets and timpani, which enter when Haydn modulates to the dominant (C) with fine effect. Like all Haydn's music for the bass voice, it 'sings itself', as Crosse maintained (*Account*, 198). The second number is a big chorus in D major, 'Thy great endeavours to increase the Marine power', with the same large orchestra and with the upper vocal part surprisingly written in the G (not the soprano) clef: this seems to have been already common practice in English choral writing and Haydn, always quick to adopt any technical innovation to make the player's or singer's task easier, immediately changed the old tradition. The choral writing is natural and as always well laid out, while the style of the piece is the kind of brilliant and festive movement which would later become typical for Haydn's D major joyous choruses in the *Nelson Mass* or the two late oratorios. The work was not published until the 1970s.[1] The two single movements would make excellent concert pieces for someone looking for late Haydn which is to all intents and purposes completely unknown to the general public. The relatively easy choral parts recommend the second number to amateur choral groups.

Coro : 'Su, cantiamo'

The opening number of Act II of *L'anima del filosofo*, the Amorini Chorus 'Finche circola il vigore', has an interesting history which we have saved until now because that music is the same as the present little Chorus. Actually the music is one of the few things among the London works which Haydn borrowed from one of his earlier (pre-London) works, in this case from the Finale of his Eszterháza opera, *Orlando Paladino* (1782). One is puzzled by this extremely isolated case of Haydn's self-borrowing until one studies the libretto of the earlier opera. It is always listed as by the Eszterháza house poet Nunziato Porta, but Porta – as was almost always the case in Haydn's opera librettos – actually borrowed an earlier book, printed anonymously in Vienna in 1777 (copy in the present writer's library), but in fact by none other than Carlo Francesco Badini; the music of this 1777 setting was by the well-known Italian composer Pietro Guglielmi. If possibly Haydn was not aware of Badini's part in the Eszterháza *Orlando Paladino*, it may have arisen in conversation with Badini in 1791 when he and Haydn were working on *L'anima del filosofo*; for it seems too much of a coincidence that Haydn used this Finale from the earlier opera twice in London.

In the *L'anima del filosofo* setting, the music is scored for two oboes, two bassoons, two horns in A, strings and 'Amorini 1mo' with 'Amorini 2do' (both, interestingly, in the G-clef: see our remarks about the chorus in *Mare Clausum*, *supra*). The new 'Su,

---

1 The new edition was prepared by the present writer in 1959 but was postponed many times in favour of other tasks more urgent and perhaps more important (e.g. Symphonies 1–49) to the Doblinger Verlag : Diletto Musicale 90.

cantiamo' setting is enlarged to include flute, two oboes, two horns in A, two trumpets in A (*sic*: more of this shortly), timpani, strings (no separate viola part; under the Basso is Haydn's note 'Viola col Basso') and three vocal parts, soprano, tenor, bass, with indications for soli and tutti. The autograph manuscript – the only source known to exist – is in the Royal College of Music in London (MS. 706, fol. 115–119) and is entitled by Haydn 'Coro'. A later hand noted 'Terzettino Haydn. Original Score'. The manuscript contains the usual twelve staves and the watermarks are British: fleur-de-lys, horizontal chain lines and 'J LARKING': paper which we know elsewhere from works composed by Haydn in 1791, e.g. Symphony No. 95, Symphony No. 96, and also *L'anima del filosofo*. If we try to find the work in the catalogue of the pieces Haydn composed in London, we shall at first seek in vain; but it is probably one of the 'Maccone for Gallini 6 [sheets]' or possibly one of the 'Different songs 29 [sheets]'. It would be the kind of work Haydn supplied for the Gallini concerts in 1791, almost none of which can be identified. The text (see Hoboken II, 433), with its reference to 'viva il Presidente', may refer to a meeting of some society, musical or otherwise.

The most striking feature of the present little Chorus is the use of A trumpets. We shall see that Haydn started to write 'English trumpets' in G for the 'Surprise' Symphony (No. 94) but changed to C trumpets after the first movement. With G trumpets the players are constantly in a very high register, way above many of the wind instruments, and the first trumpet, if he plays written *f''* and *g''* is at sounding *c'''* and *d'''*; the textural problems that this high *tessitura* impose on the overall orchestration are almost superhuman. And here we find Haydn writing for an A trumpet. High A? If so, the problems of *tessitura* are really formidable: even the common written note *e''* becomes *c sharp'''*. But it is possible that these trumpets are not high instruments at all; if Haydn was, in 1792, to write for B flat trumpets, why could the players not easily attach a half-note crook to the B flat instruments and lower them to A trumpets? It seems to be the only sensible explanation. If it is true, we have the first known use in music of low A trumpets, the typical kind of instrumental innovation for which Haydn was always being reproached. We must once again remember the words of Parke (II, 27) who wrote, in 1830: 'That Haydn displayed some novelties in the *notation* of his writings, must be acknowledged; but that he invented that mode for the convenience of the orchestral players is equally well known.' Bold as this innovation for the trumpet was, however, Haydn was to give us an even bolder one in the year 1796, in his famous Concerto in E♭ for trumpet and orchestra which will be examined elsewhere.

Like the chorus from *Mare Clausum*, this 'Su, cantiamo' contains no very difficult writing for the voices and is thus highly to be recommended to amateur choral societies as yet another unknown, and delightful, piece of late Haydn; the solo parts can be given to the leaders of the soprano, tenor and bass sections of the chorus. Like so many of Haydn's larger vocal compositions written in or for London, 'Su, cantiamo' was not published at the time and its first appearance in print had to wait till the 1970s.[1]

'The Ten Commandments' (XXVIIa: Nos. 1–10) and other Canons

Haydn was the last of the great contrapuntists and nowhere does he reveal his consummate mastery more clearly, less pretentiously and with less apparent effort than in his canons, most of which would seem to have been composed in his later years. We

---

1 First edition, prepared by H. C. Robbins Landon, for Doblinger Verlag.

are indebted to the *AMZ*, which in its review of the Breitkopf & Härtel edition of Haydn's *Forty-two Canons* as well as the *Ten Commandments* (12 December 1810, pp. 1006ff.), and to which we will be returning shortly, for revealing the origins of the *Ten Commandments*. They were written, said *AMZ*, 'during his last stay in London, for the then Saxon Minister, Herr Graf Brühl'; and this information obviously comes from Griesinger, to whom Haydn gave the autograph manuscript in 1808. The Saxon Minister in London was Count Hans Moritz von Brühl, who died the same year as Haydn, 1809.

In Haydn's *Catalogue of Works Composed in England* the works are listed as '10 Commandments (Canons) 6 [sheets]' but although Haydn lists them in English, which language he was obviously speaking and writing quite fluently by August 1795 (when presumably the catalogue was compiled), he wrote them in German. The autograph manuscript, from Griesinger's collection, which is now in the Gesellschaft der Musikfreunde, would appear to be Haydn's *Handexemplar*, for (1) he must have given an autograph (or a verified copy?) to Count Brühl in London and (2) the present autograph is written on Italian paper – not British – and would thus seem to have been put down in Austria in 1793. On the other hand, we have seen (*supra*, p. 178) that the First Commandment was composed at least by the end of June, 1792. Perhaps Haydn sketched them in 1792 and wrote the final draft in Austria. Underneath Canon No. 1 in the autograph is the following note: [Griesinger's hand:] 'Zum Andenken für Herrn v Griesinger'/[Haydn's shaky hand:] 'Von Jos: Haydn mpria 1808'.

Haydn obviously felt a certain compunction in allowing the work to be published, for having offered the work to Breitkopf & Härtel via Griesinger in December 1803, the composer then changed his mind and stipulated that it could only be published after his death. Whether this compunction was the result of some agreement with Count Brühl or for other reasons is not clear in the Griesinger correspondence.[1] Griesinger noted, in a letter of 14 December to Leipzig, '. . . he also promised me his last Mass [*Harmoniemesse*, 1802], and the 10 Commandments in a 4-part canon, an earlier work, that no one has; the text is from the old Catechism, but it would be easy to fit under the music better chosen expressions. . . .' And on 4 January 1804, we learn that 'The 10 Commandments are also arranged for the piano by him', which statement Griesinger changed on 22 August 1804 as follows: '. . . he cannot make up his mind about letting the Canons go; an accompaniment for piano, which he showed me, belongs to them'. This mysterious accompaniment or the piano arrangement, whichever it was, cannot be satisfactorily explained; all the canons that Haydn wrote were for *a cappella* voices.

In 1809, Clementi in London brought out an edition of the *Ten Commandments* in English, for which purpose Clementi himself seems to have made the translation: his supposed autograph of the works was given to the present writer by Albi Rosenthal many years ago and is now in the Burgenländisches Landesmuseum, Eisenstadt. Since it can be easily demonstrated that Clementi's source for the music was slightly different from Haydn's autograph, it is probable that the English version of the music derives from Count Brühl's source. In reviewing the Breitkopf & Härtel edition, *Die heiligen zehn Gebote als Canons*, the *AMZ* reviewer wrote *inter alia*:

> The character of these pieces is, as the text requires, almost throughout a solemn one [*feyerlich*], and the composition is simple and easy. . . . The Canons are, by the way, *all* without accompaniment, and in two-, three-, up to eight-parts [this refers

1 Olleson, op. cit., pp. 44ff.

to other Canons, also reviewed]. . . . The great artist, who more, perhaps, than anyone else of the modern age, understood not only with simple means but also *in a restricted genre* [original in italics: *'in enger Bahn'*] to express himself completely and easily, has made only very moderate demands in the *vocal parts*: any feminine, and any masculine, voice, who is not just a high tenor or a low bass voice, can perform these Canons. . . .

All Haydn's Canons have been admirably presented by the late Otto Erich Deutsch in the new Haydn *Werke* of the Henle Verlag (Reihe XXXI, 1959, with the 'kritischer Bericht' separately), the *Ten Commandments* also including the Clementi translation. There are also several practical editions available, both in the original German and in various English translations (a good one, by Jean Lunn, for Edition Peters 6999, New York City, 1966).

THE TEN COMMANDMENTS

First Commandment. In three parts, a Canon *cancrizans*, which as we have seen was identical with the Canon Haydn sent to Oxford University. The facsimile (*supra*, p. 94) shows not only Haydn's solution of the Canon but also the 'secret' notation, using both C and G clefs. C major, *alla breve*. This canon can be sung forwards or backwards, either right side up or upside down: it is of an outward simplicity that belies the dazzling technical knowledge which went into its composition.

Second Commandment. In four parts, G major, 3/4. Haydn's sunny attitude towards religion is also reflected in these Canons; here the 3/4 metre and the *fz* marks combine to lighten and enliven the music.

Third Commandment. In four parts, B flat major, 3/4. Presumably Count Brühl, the British representative of Catholic Saxony, was a Roman Catholic like Haydn. The repeated b-flats in the second and third bars, and the line of bars 4/5 in the example below have a strong feeling of Gregorian chant, the musical language of the Sabbath. Later, the flowing quavers serve to brighten the texture, as indeed many a Haydn Mass has brightened a Sunday service.

Fourth Commandment. In four parts, E flat major, 3/4. One of the longest and most beautiful Canons, the subject of which must have been particularly close to Haydn's heart, for we know how he revered and loved his parents. The first notes of the theme seem to recall a montage of old Haydn melodies in E flat: the main theme of the 'Philosoph' (Symphony No. 22/I), that same Symphony's Minuet, and a host of other E flat works by other composers from Bach to Mozart. In some unfathomable way, Haydn has created a musical movement which sounds 'parental', as if we knew the melody from our childhood; but of course this is an illusion, for the tune is quite different from its possible ancestors.

Fifth Commandment. In four parts, G minor, *alla breve*. In an austere key, and with an old sequence from Baroque times (up until the entrance of the second voice), this short movement recalls the atmosphere of *The Seven Words*.

Sixth Commandment. In five parts, C major, 6/8. There can be little doubt that there is a sly sense of humour to Haydn's views on adultery; first the lilting six-eight metre, then the nagging little a-flat dissonance in the fourth voice's entry, and the e-flat entrance of the third voice in the coda – all this is in Haydn's best mock-heroic style; as an honest man, the lover of *la* Polzelli could not do otherwise. . . .

Seventh Commandment. In five parts, A minor, *alla breve.* Concerning this Canon there exists an old tradition according to which Haydn humorously 'stole' a melody by another composer as the basis for 'Du sollst nicht stehlen' (Pohl III, 328), but while this was the sort of joke that Haydn might well have played, no one has yet discovered the real composer of the melody. The possible stealing apart, this intricate and subtle Canon develops some highly original harmonies as it progresses, approaching at times almost to poly-tonality.

Eighth Commandment. In four parts, E major, 3/4. As always with the key of E major, Haydn has reserved his most majestic thoughts for this 'false witness' Canon: the g natural in the sixth bar of the third voice is a brilliant stroke for illuminating 'false' (*falsch*).

Ninth Commandment. In four parts, C major, *alla breve.* Coveting one's neighbour's wife was, like adultery, rather amusing to Haydn, who had indulged in this sin more than once in his life; his handling of this text is witty and highly original. It is the only Canon of the series to have a tempo mark, Largo, no doubt to ensure that the humour comes through. The score is full of modern-sounding expression marks, 'hairpins' (the crescendo–cum–decrescendo), terraced dynamics, staccato dots over crotchets, and a long crescendo at the beginning – all this adds up to a brilliant and rather cynical Canon which, no doubt, Count Brühl and his circle will have well appreciated.

Tenth Commandment. In four parts, F minor, *alla breve.* In Haydn's favourite 'austere' key of F minor, this gravely beautiful Canon ends the cycle in the same serious mood in which it began. There is a coda, with a pedal point on the tonic followed by one on the tonic, which gives an air of finality to the whole; and the old-fashioned ending, in F major, is somehow very moving.

On the whole, the *Ten Commandments* are one of the most successful of the many occasional pieces that Haydn composed in the London period.

OTHER CANONS

It is difficult to ascertain which other canons are included in Haydn's English Catalogue under 'Canons 2 [sheets]'; but apart from the Oxford University 'Thy voice, O Harmony, is divine' (XXVIIb: No. 46), they probably included two others: (1) the 'Turk was a faithful dog and not a man' (XXVIIb: No. 45) which has been printed *supra* (p. 268); and (2) the little Canon, 'Kenne Gott, die Welt und dich, liebster Freund' (XXVIIb: No. 13) which was entered into one of the London Notebooks (*supra*, p. 185); the latter was printed in the *AMZ* after the review of the Canons referred to earlier, but with the slightly different, and also authentic, text 'Denke mein, und liebe mich, o dann bin ich stets um dich'. 'And by way of conclusion', writes the *AMZ*, 'instead of anything further, we give Haydn's last request and word of farewell, as it reads here, and as it certainly, most certainly, will be as faithfully observed by every friend of Art as he himself observed it in his own works!' Perhaps Thomas Holcroft, who received a canon from Haydn (*supra*, p. 273), and who was fluent in German, was one of the several recipients of the 'Kenne Gott' alias 'Denke mein' Canon.

Occasional Works for Several Voices

Most of these works, as far as they can be identified from Haydn's *Catalogue of Works Composed in England*, seem to be lost, e.g. the Catch which was so popular in the Gallini season of 1791 (part, or the whole, of the 'Maccone for Gallini' with its six sheets?), and probably the 'God save the King'. The following have survived:

TWELVE SENTIMENTAL CATCHES AND GLEES

Twelve Sentimental Catches and Glees, For Three Voices Melodized by the Right Honble The Earl of Abingdon, The Accompaniments for the Harp of Piano Forte, by The Celebrated D^r. Haydn. Being a Gift of his Lordship to M^r. Monzani, for his Benefit. Entered at Stationer's Hall. Price 10^s. 6^d. Sold by M^r. Monzani, N°. 16, Down Street, Piccadilly. M^r. Balls, N°. 1, Duke Street, Grosvenor Square, & at T. Skillern's, N°. 17, S^t. Martins Lane [copy in the writer's library].

There is no watermark date on this copy, and the only newspaper announcement of the works we could locate was in *The Times* of 24 October 1800 where Monzani & Cimador advertise the works as 'Twelve Catches and Glees, harmonized with a Piano-Forte Accompaniment by Dr Haydn price 5s', which suggests that the issue with the title page as listed above was perhaps slightly later: a similar confusion exists with regard to the Monzani edition of the London Trios for two flutes and violoncello (see Hoboken I, 464 and *infra*, p. 405) which was announced a year earlier, in 1799. In Haydn's *Catalogue of Works Composed in England* the works are called '12 Ballads for Lord Avingdon [*sic*] 12 [sheets]'.

We have seen that Haydn had a rather jaundiced view of Lord Abingdon's abilities as a composer (*supra*, p. 271), and one could not describe these products as works of genius; yet in all fairness Abingdon's *Sentimental Catches and Glees* (XXXIc: No. 16) are rather pleasant little pieces that show its composer was a good amateur musician. Haydn's accompaniments, which at the beginning of No. 1 are marked 'Harp or Piano-Forte', are mostly restricted to very simple three- or four-part lines which can be read at sight by any amateur with a minimum of training, and which have little ritornellos at the end of most pieces. The vocal parts are for three voices, all in the treble clef.

A 'Catch' originally meant a round for three or more voices, without accompaniment, written like a puzzle canon in one line; that is, not in score. The word derived from the fact that the singer had to take up or 'catch' his part at the right time. The Catch started its life in Elizabethan England and became in the course of time a very complex affair which required skill and rehearsal from the performer; later the words were constructed so that by crossing the various parts and with mispronunciations, all sorts of comical effects could be introduced; this practice led to some very indecent Catches during the period of Charles II, which, it seems, were also accompanied with gestures and mimics.

The Earl's Catches are all conveniently printed in score and are to be performed as follows: the first voice starts alone and reads through line no. 1, returning to sing line no. 2 (the explanation for the '2' at the end of no. 1's part), at which point the second voice enters; after the third voice has entered and the Catch has been sung complete, the pianist or harp-player finishes with the ritornello. The majority of the works in the print is in fact Catches, and the texts are the usual sentimental poetry of which we have seen several examples in Haydn's Notebooks; one of the texts is in Italian but all the others are English. As an example, we reproduce No. IX, a Catch in A major.

Nº IX. CATCH.

Moderato

2

Tell CORINNA, fince we parted,
I have never known delight;
And fhall foon be broken hearted,
If I longer want her fight.

3

Tell her, how her lover mourning,
Thinks each lazy day a year;
Curfing ev'ry morn returning,
Since CORINNA is not here.

The 'Glee' is a more recent addition to the English tradition, and its name derives from the Anglo-Saxon word for music, *gligg*. It might be described as a degenerated madrigal; usually for three men's voices, the Glee contains many typical elements of the mid eighteenth-century instrumental music: the stress on the vertical (harmonic) rather than the horizontal (contrapuntal), a great many full and half cadences, short phrases (as the words change) and not enough rhythmic unity. It naturally interested composers to find a way to make more unified and organized Glees, and a whole

Two items from Lord Abingdon's *Sentimental Glees and Catches*: (left) Catch IX; (above) Glee VII.

school soon grew up consisting of men who composed practically nothing else. Foremost among them was Samuel Webbe (1740–1816), but there were also men like R. J. S. Stevens (*supra*, p. 78), whose Glee 'Ye spotted Snakes' erases all the inherent mistakes which we have enumerated above by casting the whole Glee in sonata form; and Mozart's pupil Thomas Attwood. There were Catch and Glee clubs throughout England, the most famous being the Glee Club in London which was formed in 1783 and during the period of Haydn's sojourns in that town used to meet at the Crown and Anchor or the Freemasons' Tavern. In 1793, another Glee Club in London was formed, of which Haydn's friend Shield was a member, and W. T. Parke another; in his *Memoirs* (II, 175), Parke tells us 'it was held on Sunday evenings at the Garrick's Head Coffee House in Bow Street, Covent Garden, once a fortnight, when we amused ourselves by singing the works of the old and modern masters, after which we sat down to supper'. It is very likely that Shield will have taken Haydn along to such a Glee Club meeting, and perhaps they will have tried out some of his Lordship's productions while that gentleman was languishing in prison.

As a typical example of the Earl's and Haydn's Glees, we reproduce here No. VII, A Glee in G major with a *minore* middle section, which shows that these modest pieces will have served well to whet the appetite of Haydn and the other guests who might have sung them before being served a hearty dinner by his Lordship. Abingdon may have been an amateur but he was one with all the good taste which was so much a part of *fin-de-siècle* Georgian London.

PSALMS

We have seen that in December 1794, there appeared Volume One of the Rev. William Dechair Tattersall's *Improved Psalmody* and that Haydn contributed to it. along with a number of British colleagues. It is a pleasant thought to consider Haydn, a staunch Catholic, putting his services at the disposal of the Church of England in an atmosphere of religious freedom and tolerance typical of the British at that time. Haydn's contribution consisted of six Psalms (XXIII: Nachtrag), all (like the whole of the *Psalmody*) for three voices and using Merrick's metrical poetry. In the Preface, Tattersall mentions

> Dr. HAYDN (who may be looked upon as naturalized in this country, from having taken his degree at one of our Universities, and who may be justly esteemed the most celebrated composer of the present day); Dr. ARNOLD, Mr. JOHN STAFFORD SMITH, and Mr. ATTERBURY, having allowed me the honour of reckoning them in the number of my respectable coadjutors, they will, I trust, excuse my mentioning thus publicly the offer they have now made me of their services, and permit me to assure them, that I am happy to obtain their consent to add their names to my list. . . .

The principal contributors were, as this 'address' makes clear, Dr Hayes, Dr Dupuis, Dr Parsons, Mr Callcott, the Rev. Osborne Wight, Mr Webbe, Mr Shield, and Mr Stevens. In the preliminary 'Advertisement', Rev. Tattersall explains the purpose of the publication:

> The design of the Editor in this undertaking, is not only to silence the many ludicrous reflections, that are perpetually cast upon our psalmody, but to fulfil the wishes of many able writers, who, though they have published treatises in defence of the Church of *England*, have at the same time recommended an amendment in this part of the service. If the psalms had never undergone any material alteration, it might perhaps have been thought dangerous to bring forward any thing, that should have the appearance of innovation. But alterations, both partial and

general, have already been allowed without ill consequence; and as most of the Rules of our Church have seen and declared the necessity of some further amendment, and have been desirous to encourage such a plan, the period, perhaps, may not be far distant, when it shall be deemed worthy of consideration, in what manner it ought to be effected. In proof of his position, that the adoption of Mr. MERRICK's version is desirable, it will suffice for the Editor to produce the sentiments of those right reverent Prelates, who have expressed their admiration of the original work, and of others, who have since honoured him with their observations on his alteration of that valuable performance. . . .

Concerning the type of melodies for these settings, the Rev. Tattersall notes:

. . . We are all perfectly agreed that plainness and simplicity are the grand criterion, that ought to guide us. . . .

Haydn contributed six to this collection of twenty-five psalms:

(1) *Psalm 26*, Verses 5–8. 'The Psalmist declares his Love for GOD's House and determines to bless GOD'. First line: 'How oft, instinct with warmth divine'. F major 3/2 – F minor – F major. 'Slow'.

This is the second longest of the settings that Haydn contributed. The first thing that strikes us is the familiarity of the melodies, both the principal one in F

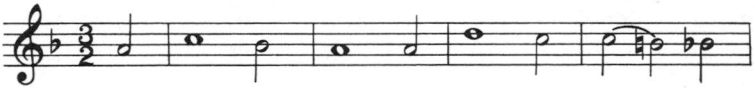

as well as the theme in F minor

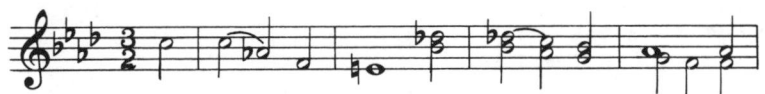

They sound almost like a dozen eighteenth-century melodies, and since this feature occurs in almost all six settings, it is clear that Haydn is trying to create 'prototype' themes suitable for congregation singing. It is the same principle that we noted in his setting of the Fourth Commandment – a deliberate attempt to sound 'parental'. When Haydn reaches the relative major of F minor, the A flat melody also sounds familiar:

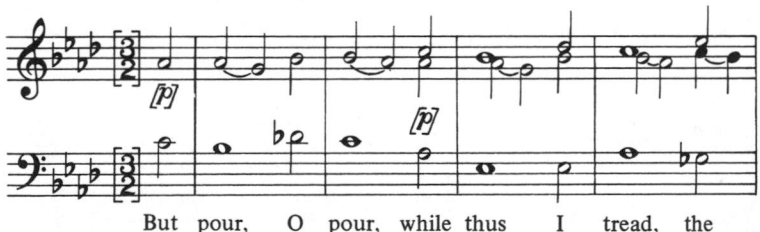

But pour, O pour, while thus I tread, the

[*cf.* Haydn: *Missa Cellensis in honorem B.V.M.* of 1766, 'Et vitam venturi' fugue.]

But though Haydn seems to be quoting from some previous work, such as the 1766 Mass, we shall actually discover that these psalms sometimes contain tunes which were later incorporated into the last masses and oratorios. Here we seem to have the kind of pattern used in dozens of fugues and in particular sections with pedal points. The form of this Psalm is A–B–A and there are 77 bars. It is in general the kind of writing to which Haydn will again have recourse when composing the part-songs of the late 1790s.

(2) *Psalm 31*, Verses 21–24. 'The Prayer of the Psalmist being accepted, he exhorts the good to rely on GOD's help alone.' First line: 'Blest be the name of Jacob's God'. E flat, 3/2, no tempo.

This is a typically Anglican hymn which sounds as if we had known it since childhood, twenty bars of sturdy E flat major in the three-two time that Haydn uses in four out of the six psalms (the other two are in barred C [₵]). It is constructed in four-bar phrases, like many such hymns, and is easy to remember. It opens as follows:

(3) *Psalm 41*, Verses 12–16. 'A Prayer for the divine Favour, and an Exhortation to Praise'. First line: 'Maker of all! be thou my guard.' D major, barred C, no tempo.

This Psalm is the most elaborate of Haydn's settings, running to four pages of score and 93 bars. Haydn's first and third settings are *durchkomponiert*, that is, all the verses are composed, while the others are in the usual manner of hymns in which the subsequent verses are sung to identical music. Psalm 41 is also the closest in musical content to the part-songs of Haydn's post-London years. The opening bars serve as a kind of introduction and are brought back, with the beginning and end altered, to conclude the work:

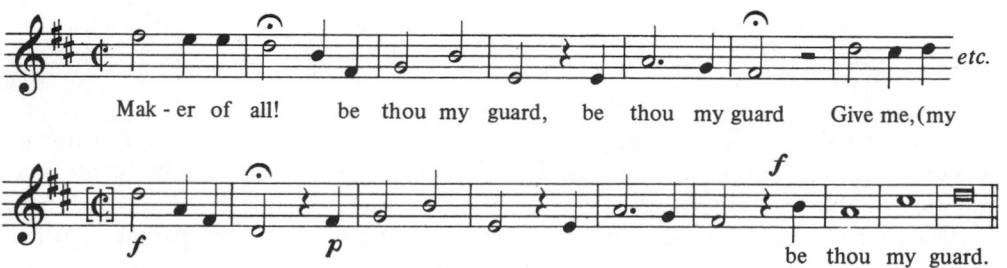

Haydn then proceeds in free imitation:

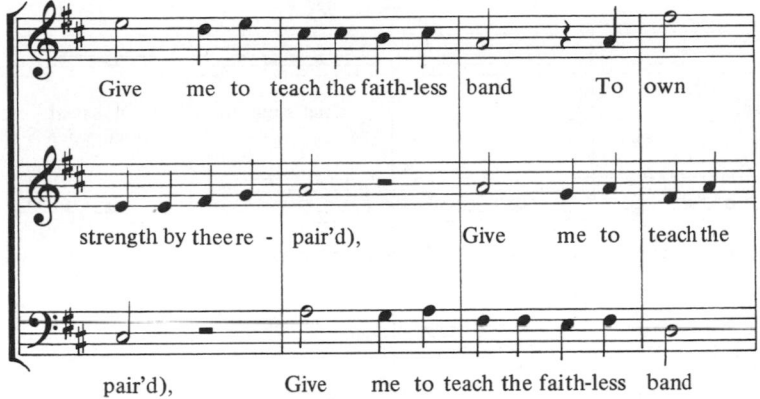

There is a passage just before the end which excites the composer's imagination; the words 'One song of oft repeated praise', of which not only is the entry in free ('repeated') imitation but the whole is also 'repeated', *piano* and with the parts interchanged. It is the kind of word-painting, a legacy of the Baroque, at which Haydn was always highly adept.

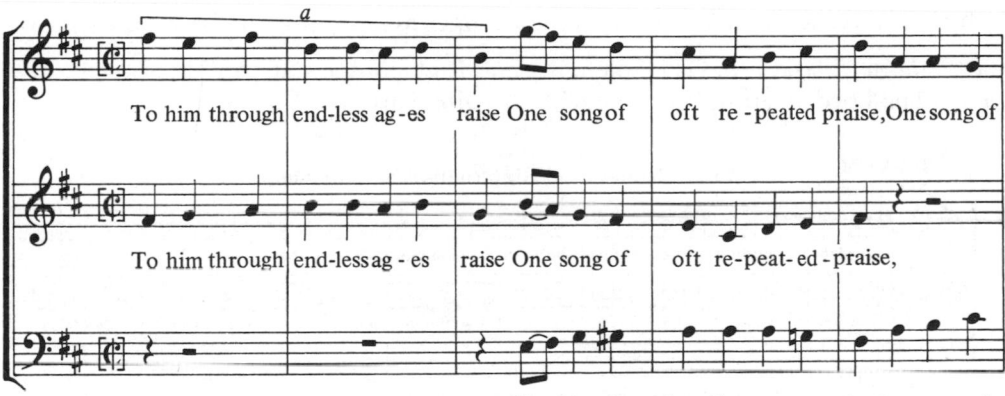

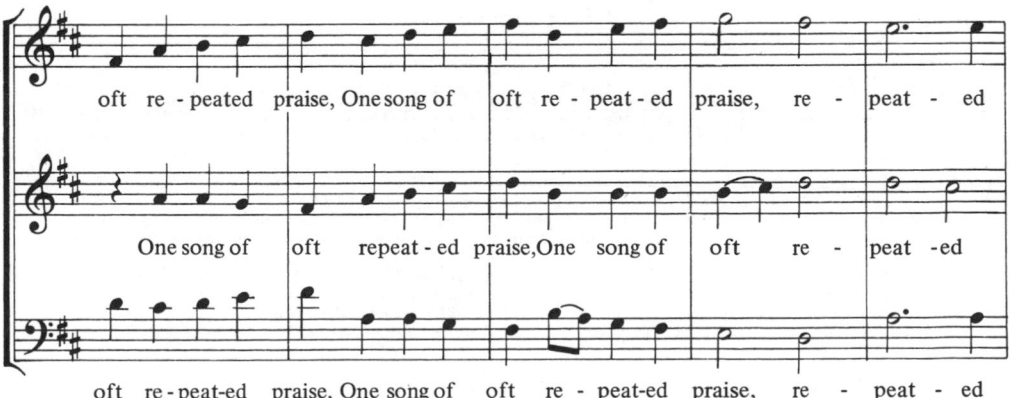

Haydn's method of holding the musical fabric together by interrelated motivic fragments is just the same as in his instrumental music: observe how bracket 'a' from the beginning is woven into the passage quoted above. This is the most ingenious and complicated of Haydn's settings and undoubtedly one to suggest (at least to his unconscious mind) that such a form could be adapted to German-language part-songs, both sacred and secular. It cannot be accidental that upon his return to Austria, we find Haydn writing a whole series of 'mehrstimmige Gesänge' the musical language of which is startlingly similar to that of these longer psalms, and especially Psalm 41.

(4) *Psalm 50*, Verses 1–6. 'The Solemnity and Righteousness of GOD's Judgment'. First line: 'The Lord, th'almighty monarch'. C major, barred C, no tempo.

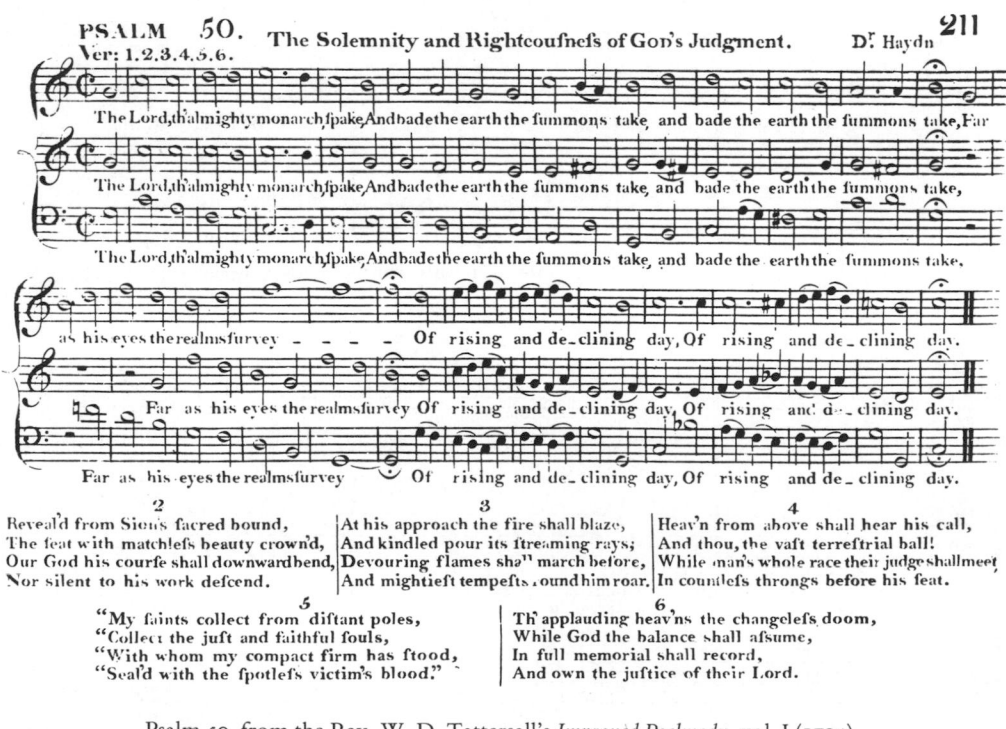

Psalm 50, from the Rev. W. D. Tattersall's *Improved Psalmody*, vol. I (1794).

The relationship between this martial Psalm and 'The Heavens are telling' from *The Creation* is strong (and not merely in the intervallic similarity of their respective openings). Psalm 50 is put together with the swift and sure efficiency of the professional: the march-like opening is effectively balanced by the imitation to fit the words 'Far as his eyes the realms survey' (wherein note the *cancrizans* relationship between first and third voice) and the word-painting with which Haydn composes 'Of rising and declining day', where the general pattern shifts to crotchets. In its open simplicity, Psalm 50 shows the hand of the master; we quote it complete as an illustration of the whole series.

(5) *Psalm 61*, Verses 6–8. 'The King praises GOD for the Safety of himself and his Descendants.' First line: 'Long life shall Israel's king behold'. E flat major, 3/2, no tempo.

Another sturdy E flat hymn, of immaculate construction. We note how carefully the melodic line is carried from point to point, the stresses being well calculated. The central note *e flat''* is stressed at the beginning of four-bar periods nos. 1, 2 and 3 and at the *end* of period 4. The *ductus* leads *e flat''* ⟶ *f'*; *e flat''* ⟶ *b flat'* for the first two periods. For the third Haydn increases the melodic tension by rising to *g''* before proceeding to *f'*, and the final time, the initial *e flat* is changed to *g'* so that *e flat* is not reached until the end (preceded by another stress-point, *f''*, to prepare the cadential *e flat*). The construction of the melody shows the same attention to detail that we will find in the greatest quartets and symphonies, and yet these psalms are but occasional pieces. The melody reads as follows:

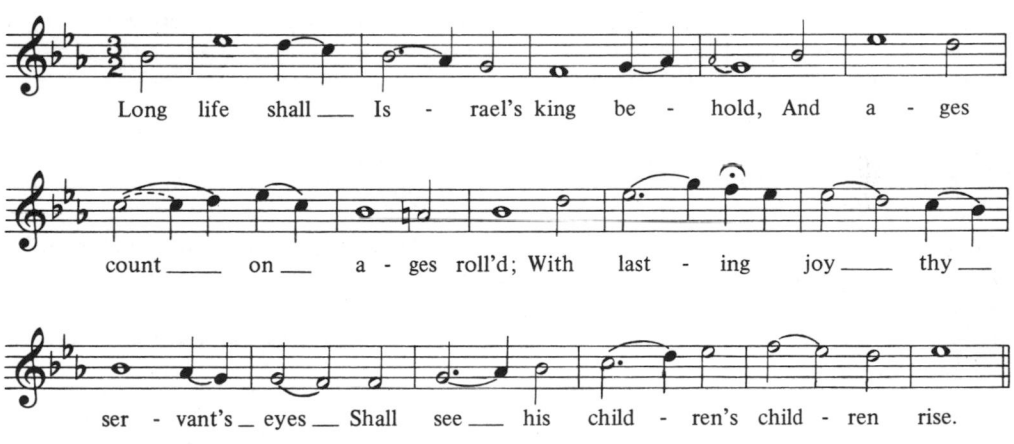

(6) *Psalm 69*, Verses 13–17. 'An earnest Address for speedy relief and Succour'. First line: 'O let me in th'accepted hour'. A major, 3/2, no tempo.

Another melody which sounds very familiar. Its familiarity is on several levels, first because it is almost identical with the Canzonetta 'Pleasing Pains' from the second set. If the first part reminds us of Philemon's Canzonetta 'Ein Tag der allen Freude bringt', the second part ('In pray'r to thee my spirit pour') is almost a quotation from the 'calm' section of Haydn's Madrigal, 'The Storm'. While of course it is doubtful if anyone in London had heard *Philemon und Baucis* at Eszterháza, the majority of the concert-going public had 'The Storm' fresh in their ears, for it had been successfully performed in 1792, two years before publication of these psalms. Obviously the 'quotation' was unconscious, but it shows Haydn's attempt to create a popular vocal style to go hand in hand with the popular instrumental style of which he was an acknowledged master. In the event, the Reverend William Dechair Tattersall's *Improved Psalmody* was not much of a success at the popular level, for Volume Two never appeared and there is no record of Volume One going into a second edition. This is doubly surprising in that Volume One was dedicated 'with Permission to the King'. Thus it was that Haydn's attractive English Psalms never achieved wide currency and it was the later choral works that made his popular vocal style internationally accepted. The melody of Psalm 69 reads as follows:

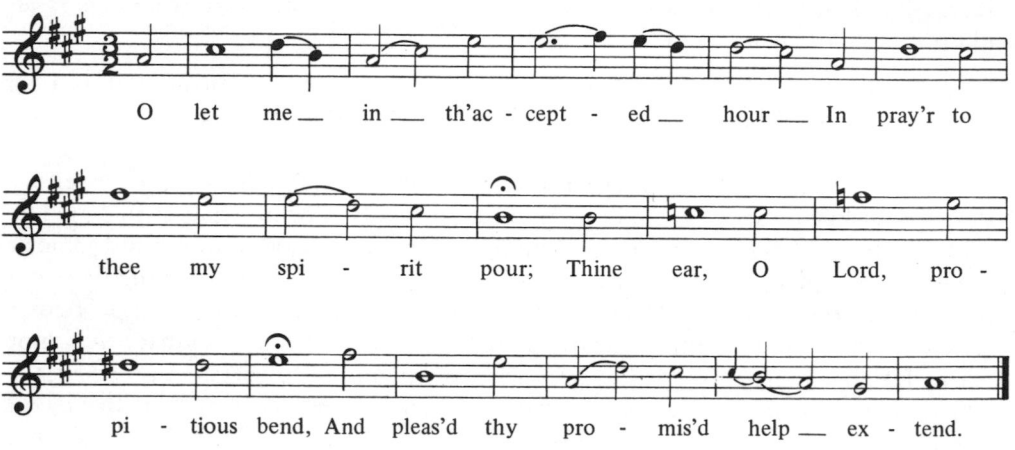

There is no modern edition of *Improved Psalmody*; the above examples are taken direct from the first edition, of which a fine copy is owned by the British Museum. A modern edition of the Haydn settings is in preparation (1972) by the writer of these notes (Broude Brothers, New York).

Arias with Orchestra

(1) Aria ('Cara deh torna in pace') for Davide (tenor) and orchestra with oboe and bassoon *obbligati*, first performed at Haydn's Benefit Concert on 16 May 1791. Lost. That it was on a very large scale, even bigger than the famous *Scena di Berenice* is shown by its entry in Haydn's own Catalogue, where it is given as having 12 sheets (*Scena di Berenice*: 11 sheets), i.e. nearly fifty pages. Considering Davide's beautiful music in *L'anima del filosofo*, it is a great pity that this major vocal work has not survived. Hoboken *deest*.

(2) Aria (text unknown) for Miss Poole (soprano) with orchestra. Probably composed in 1792, when Miss Poole was engaged by Salomon for the season. Listed in Haydn's Catalogue as having five sheets. Presumably lost. Hoboken *deest*.

(3) '1 Aria con Orchestra. 2 [sheets]' from Haydn's Catalogue. This Aria cannot be identified and is presumably lost, because it is too small to fit as a description for No. 7. Hoboken *deest*.

(4) '1 Song with the whole orchest. 2 [sheets].' This Aria, too, cannot be identified and is presumably lost; and it is also too small to be No. 7. Hoboken *deest*.

(5) Recitative and Aria for Signor Calcagni (soprano castrato) with orchestra (Hoboken *deest*), first performed at the Fifth Salomon Concert of the 1792 season on 16 March. The adjective 'new' attached to the work on the announcements for the concert suggest that it may have been specially composed for the occasion; it may, of

course, be identical with Nos. 3, 4, 6 or 7. If, however, the programme bill of the concert should come to light, we would immediately be able to identify it because the hand bills always listed the words of each vocal piece given.

(6) 'Cantata a Voce Sola con V° [Violino] Composed for the Duke of Bedford' (Hoboken *deest*). This interesting and hitherto unknown information comes from a manuscript catalogue of the Joseph Warren Collection in London dated 1849 and now owned by Cecil Hopkinson, Esq., London, who kindly allowed me to consult it. On p. 181 there are two Haydn MSS. listed, the above entry about the Cantata for the Duke of Bedford and then 'Cantata a Voce Sola Teseo mio ben [Aria from the Cantata *Arianna a Naxos*] believed to be in the aut. of Haydn'. The Fifth Duke of Bedford, Francis, was very left-wing and an associate of Fox's. Farington (I, 37f.) notes 'it was surprising a man in the Duke of Bedford's situation should join the Democratic party in times like the present [27 January 1794]. [Lord Inchiquin] said he believed it was owing to a pique subsisting between him and the Prince of Wales'. Later Farington quotes Samuel Whitbread as saying that 'the Duke of Bedford is rather a shy than a proud man, – is easy with his acquaintance, but cannot be familiar & general with strangers' (I, 265). The Duke was one of the most outspoken critics of Pitt's policies and rose in the House of Lords during the Summer of 1794 to ask for a resolution in the Lords that George III should be petitioned either to end the war or 'be graciously pleased to state what the object of it was' (Bryant, op. cit., p. 116); some idea of his financial situation may be gathered from his contribution to the Finance Bill (which passed the Commons on 5 January 1798) of £100,000. Another of Haydn's interesting acquaintances in England, and yet another one from the opposition side; can Holcroft have introduced Haydn to the democratically minded Duke of Bedford? It is unfortunate that this Cantata has completely disappeared, as has the autograph of *Arianna*.

(7) Revision for London of the Cantata 'Miseri noi, misera patria' (XXIVa; No. 7). A detailed list of the small-scale changes may be seen in our edition of the work for Doblinger (Diletto Musicale 17 [1960]; miniature score Stp. 161 [1969]): they concern mostly an enlarged first flute part. Actually, Haydn's original score included two flutes but they have separate parts only in three bars (96–98) of the score. This cavalier treatment of the flutes (or rather separate flute parts) often occurs in Haydn's music, but perhaps not in as extreme a form as this. For London, Haydn added a first (!) flute part for the opening pages of the Cantata, the whole wind section for the cadence of the first part (bars 36 and 37, just before the Largo) and one bar (18) of the bassoon part. Otherwise, Haydn's additions consist of supplementary dynamic marks, e.g. the characteristic *pp* at the end of the 'Largo assai's' opening ritornello (bar 76), and an occasional slur or staccato.

(8) *Scena di Berenice* (XXIVa; No. 10). Title of the autograph: 'Scena/composta/per la Signora Banti/di me giuseppe Haydn mpria', the date at the top of the first page of music: 1795. First performed at Haydn's Benefit Concert on 4 May 1795. Text from Pietro Metastasio's *Antigono*, first set to music by Hasse for the Carneval season at Dresden in 1744: Act III, Scene VII. The work was not printed in London during Haydn's stay there, but when he returned to Vienna he occasionally sold or gave a manuscript copy to a travelling singer, for example the British singer Mrs Peploe (of whom Burney thought so highly), who signed her textually interesting copy of the score in December 1797. It was, rather curiously, first printed by Tranquillo Mollo, a former partner in Artaria & Co., early in 1806 but with piano accompaniment only

(plate no. 1439, announced in the *Wiener Zeitung* on 8 February 1806);[1] we do not know where Mollo received his engraver's copy, possibly from Haydn.

In Metastasio's drama, this scene shortly precedes the grand dénouement and the end of the opera: Berenice, abandoned by her lover Demetrio, contemplates her lonely fate. Pursued by confused and tormented ideas, the opening recitative describes in Metastasio's most elaborate language Berenice's nearly hysterical state. In the first Aria, which is (as is customary in the *scena* form) broken off,

> Non partir, bell'idolo mio;
> Per quell'onda all'altra sponda,
> Voglio anch'io passar con te.
> Voglio anch'io . . .

she implores her absent lover not to part for the shores of Lethe without her. After another section of recitative, the big Aria begins,

> Perché, se tanti siete
> Che delirar mi fate,
> Perchè non m'uccidete,
> Affanni del mio cor?
>
> Crescete, oh Dio, crescete,
> Fin che mi porga aíta
> Con togliermi di vita
> L'eccesso del dolor.

Death only can remove such an excess of grief, such burdenings of the heart. It is a strong text in the best *opera seria* tradition, and one which Haydn calculated would give him a fitting structure for music worthy of the great Banti. He was not mistaken.

A measure of what happened to Haydn in England may be gathered from a comparison of this *Scena di Berenice* with the Cantatas, 'Miseri noi' (*supra*, No. 7), or even with *L'anima del filosofo*, composed only four years earlier. There is, in the 1795 *Scena* a boldness of concept, a self-confidence, a sense of dramatic design which place the work on the level of the other two greatest *scene* of the period, Mozart's *Scena e Rondo* 'Ch'io mi scordi di te' (K. 505) for Nancy Storace, the 'most mature love-letter ever written in music' (Paul Hamburger) and Beethoven's 'Ah, perfido!' of 1796, which takes Haydn's work as its direct model (not only in overall design, but also in the progressive tonality which – like Haydn's – modulates upwards a minor third: Haydn's from D major to F minor, Beethoven's from C major to E flat). It must have been a perfect show-piece for *la* Banti, too: one wonders if she appreciated its harmonic and structural subtlety; she certainly will have immediately grasped the dramatic force and the consummate skill of the vocal writing.

As we have mentioned above, there are two principal and authentic manuscript sources for this work:

(1) Haydn's autograph manuscript (now in the Vienna Stadtbibliothek, shelf-mark M H 4074/C), which was previously owned by Haydn's pupil Sigismund Neukomm and later by Ignaz Moscheles. It would seem that Banti received a copy (probably by Elssler, who was with Haydn in England during the second visit) and Haydn retained the original, for there are some rather curious and in part important changes which Haydn made after 1797, when he was back in Vienna, on the MS.

---

1 Alexander Weinmann, *Verlagsverzeichnis Tranquillo Mollo* (Beiträge zur Geschichte des Alt-Wiener Musikverlages, Reihe 2, Folge 9), Vienna 1964, p. 54.
2 *The Mozart Companion*, ed. by H. C. Robbins Landon & Donald Mitchell, London 1956, p. 356.

(2) The second source is a score by Elssler, obviously copied from the autograph manuscript, which Mrs Peploe acquired along with several other vocal pieces by Haydn in December 1797: the copy, *ex coll.* Landon, is now in the Burgenländisches Landesmuseum at Eisenstadt. What is interesting and textually valuable about this copy is the fact that the later changes of the autograph were *not* incorporated into the MS. by Elssler, and thus the changes must be dated post 1797. The changes were probably made for the soprano Anna Milder, Beethoven's first Fidelio (Leonore), who participated in a concert at the Augarten on 22 September 1803. In a criticism in the *Zeitung für die elegante Welt*, the description of the Haydn aria that Milder sang enables us to identify it as the *Scena di Berenice* (*Haydn Yearbook* V, 115): ' . . . An aria by Metastasio, set to music by Haydn, was excellently sung by Mlle. Milder, whose voice is extremely lovely; the aria is distinguished by its boldly, imperious spirit and high pathos.' There is no other *scena* by Haydn which can fit this description, for it is out of the question that Haydn would have used part of this only Metastasio opera *L'isola disabitata* (1779), 'old fashioned' as it would have been considered, for a showpiece destined for Milder in 1803. This Augarten Concert was possibly the occasion when Haydn made the remark, often quoted in the Beethoven literature,[1] to Milder, 'My dear child! You have a voice like a house.'

The first change, chronologically and in importance, occurs at the very beginning of the Scena: Haydn crossed out the first three bars. It is at first glance hard to see why he thought this necessary, particularly in view of the fact that the excised music is part of a subtle and complex attempt to provide a motivic unity to the whole opening part of the work; indeed we find the very opening notes repeated at different intervals in bars 7/8 and 9/10. We have a suggestion for the cut which, we hope, will not be considered too frivolous: at the Augarten Concerts, audiences were (as they are today at summer concerts) probably noisy, and Haydn may have thought his *piano* opening would be lost in the chatter.

It is very interesting to observe the way in which Haydn ties the long and loose recitative together to make it a stylistic and musical entity; and as we might expect from him, the basic method is by putting small motives to work for the larger whole. We have seen that the beginning, in its uncut version, continues to dominate the first dozen bars. At bar 4 (the opening, if the cut is made), the orchestra plays the rhythmically taut figure ♩. 𝅘𝅥𝅯𝅘𝅥𝅮𝅘𝅥𝅮𝅘𝅥𝅮 | ♩ [etc.]; at bar 12, the orchestra introduces two derivatives of the figure, *viz.* ♩. 𝅘𝅥𝅯𝅘𝅥𝅯 followed by 𝅘𝅥𝅯𝅘𝅥𝅯 and then 𝅘𝅥𝅯𝅘𝅥𝅮𝅘𝅥𝅮𝅘𝅥𝅮 | ♩ ♩ . After we have modulated to E flat (about which more anon), the last of these derivatives continues to bind the music together: see bars 47–8, 49–50, and also 51–2, 61–2, 62–3 and 66–7, where Haydn reverts to the original rhythm of bar 4, omitting the opening dotted crotchet.

The tonal structure of the Scena is also intricate and beautifully accomplished. On a large scale, the scheme is as follows:
Recitative (*Allegro*) D major 4/4 time, modulating through the dominant and submediant to C sharp minor ⟶ B flat major (new key signature), modulating to E flat major, A flat major and C minor to ⟶ C major (*Adagio*; new key signature) barred C; this section being like a little aria, with oboe and bassoon obbligato, but the vocal part shows that we are still in the overall recitative section; modulation to G

1 *Inter alia* in *Thayer's Life of Beethoven* (ed. Forbes), Princeton 1967, I, 383.

major and then to ——→ Aria (*Largo*) E major in barred C (new key signature), modulating to B major and, in a brilliant enharmonic change (which will be discussed below) to the dominant of——→ E flat major: Recitative (new key signature), breaking off the course of the slow Aria and modulating to the dominant of——→ F minor: Aria (*Allegro*: new key signature), barred C.

During his second London visit, Haydn was becoming ever more attracted to the relations of keys by thirds, and not only the overall tonal structure of the *Scena di Berenice* is that of a minor third but as can be seen, the cycle of modulations within the work has a strong 'third-related' feeling (e.g. D to B flat, C to E, and so forth).

We would point out two particularly striking modulations, both enharmonic: the first is the modulation from the first section's end to the new key of B flat, which is accomplished as follows:

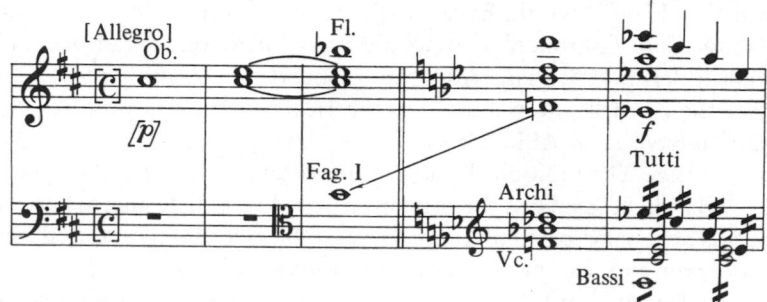

The sensitive orchestration – notice the magical entrance of the strings – assists this bold stroke. The second enharmonic modulation was so daring that Haydn thought it necessary to instruct the copyist and players that the oboe and first violin actually had 'NB: the Same Tone', an admonishment that we will encounter in a similar passage in the slow movement of Symphony No. 102. Here Haydn breaks off the slow Aria in E, and the dramatic effect is of course heightened by the *crescendo* (see opposite).

The slow Aria in E has all the noble simplicity and classic purity of melodic line which we have observed in the death scene of Euridice. The orchestration is breathtakingly beautiful: the viola's doubling of the vocal part when the latter enters at bar 96 is a stroke of genius, for the middle range of the soprano's voice is coloured darkly by the viola two octaves below and in its lowest register; similarly, the horns' entrance is beautifully timed. The orchestration of the whole Scena, in fact, reflects the spirit of the second London visit as much as the late Salomon Symphonies. Up to the quick F minor Aria, Haydn restricts himself to flutes, oboes, bassoons, horns and strings. Originally he intended to have C trumpets and kettle-drums (C and low F) for the Aria, but he only got as far as writing the indications; on the other hand, he introduced clarinet parts which he uses cautiously – we shall have more to say on this subject in connection with the second set of London Symphonies, *infra* – but with his usual sense of colour (see the suave line at bars 193ff.). The Aria is full of those beautiful touches that seem to illuminate everything that Haydn composed in those golden years 1794 and 1795. The second section in the relative major, in which the clarinet solo mentioned above occurs, is as smoothly flowing and glowingly orchestrated as the opening is jagged and rather severely scored. Haydn introduces Banti's soaring high C just once (bar 231), but this virtuoso flight is carefully related, thematically, to the beginning of the section in the relative major (cf. bars 230–1 with 183–4): everything is part of a well-ordered **system**, even the *prima donna*'s high C. The last pages of this great Aria return the gaunt atmosphere of the beginning, to underline which we find Banti displaying the bottom range of her voice (bars 302ff.), the strings accompanying in 'broken' chords, and the woodwind (without the clarinets) entering to provide a cold, silvery wash over the whole.

The *Scena di Berenice* is a great tribute to the Italian art of singing and one of Haydn's finest vocal pieces. A new edition (Landon) is published by Doblinger.

Arias (Duets) with Orchestra, of Doubtful Authenticity

The trade in spurious vocal works by Haydn was nothing like that of his instrumental works, except for masses and smaller church music, of which there exists a vast quantity (over 100 spurious masses). There are, however, not very many forged or doubtful Haydn arias, and most that do exist are very difficult to date. The *Recitativo e Rondo* (XXIVa: B1) 'Se ti perdo' for soprano and orchestra with solo viola and cor anglais, of which a MS. by the copyist of the Kees Catalogue exists in the Fürstenberg Archives in Donaueschingen Castle (Mus. ms. 667), seems to be a rather late (*c.* 1790) work. But Haydn's name was added locally: the Viennese MS. was delivered to Donaueschingen as anonymous, which is very curious. Interesting, indeed beautiful, though the piece is, we cannot bring ourselves to believe that it is by Haydn. For one thing, the principal influence would seem not to be Haydn but Mozart, and the Mozart of *La clemenza di Tito* at that, though of course the use of a solo cor anglais is very atypical of Mozart.

An attractive, bright little Aria (XXIVb: Es2) in a Viennese copy entitled 'Favorite Arias [*sic*] Del Sig[re] Gius. Haydn 794 [= 1794]' in piano score with the text

'Come lasciar potrei' (Donaueschingen Mus. ms. 668) is a straight copyist's forgery. It is an Aria from the popular opera by Giovanni Paisiello, *Il rè Teodoro in Venezia*, produced at Vienna on 23 August 1784. Mozart attended the first performance (Deutsch *Dokumente* 201). Artaria issued the Aria under Paisiello's name as No. 1 of 'Racolta delle migliori Arie, Duetti, e Terzetti . . . Trasmessi per il Clavicembalo o Forte Piano.'

The most curious work of all is a new discovery. It comes from the interesting Biblioteca Papafava, an old family of the Padovan aristocracy whose collection contains many works by the Viennese school (including some authentic editions of early Beethoven).[1] Among the sizeable Haydn collection is a manuscript score of the late eighteenth century, on Venetian paper (watermarks: 'REAL', letters COZ, the firm of Olibro, Comici & Zucchetta: see Landon SYM, 612, watermark 38) of a work entitled 'D'Emirena la voce/Scena con strumenti ed/Aria/del Sig: Giuseppe Haydn'. We give the *incipits* here:

[*Recitativo*] *Andantino*. Sop. solo, 2 oboes, 2 horns (later in Italian horn notation for E flat, viz. written as they sound, in bass clef), 2 violins, 2 violas, [Violoncello-Basso].

[*Aria*] *Largo moderato*.

at the end of which a second soprano (Emirena) joins, leading to a

---

1 Our thanks must go to Mr Michael Rose, who brought this collection to our attention, and also to Count Papafava for lending me this manuscript and some other works to study.

[*Duetto*] *Allegro.*

There is, of course, not a shred of outside evidence which could assist us in dating this work or in establishing its authenticity. All three works here discussed do not figure in any known records of Haydn's operatic activity at Eszterháza, so there exists the slender possibility that if any of them are genuine, they were composed in or for London. If the existence of a long Scena for soprano, which ends up as a Duet, seems rather improbable, we must not forget the famous Terzetto, 'Pietà di me' (two sopranos and tenor); Haydn seems to have found a market in London for even such *outré* objects as that (and what did they do with the solo cor anglais part in the Terzetto if no one in England knew of the instrument's existence before Ferlendis arrived? *Vide supra*, p. 311). The internal evidence of this interesting piece from the Papafava Library is once again not such as to warrant its authenticity: there are some features that are very Haydnish and others that are perhaps less convincing.

Mr Richard Macnutt has discovered an important new source for this work, which he found in the British Museum (Add. 29967) and a description of which he kindly sent me. In this new source, the work is attributed, no doubt correctly, to Giuseppe Sarti: 'D'Ademira la voce. Scena e Rondo. In Venezia l'autunno 1787 nel teatro di S. Benedetto. Del Sig. Giuseppe Sarti.' Apart from the different heroine (Ademira for Emirena), the music and text are identical. *Ademira* by Angelo Tarchi, a young contemporary of Haydn's, was first given at La Scala in Milan on 27 December 1783. In the autumn of 1787 it was revived at the Teatro S. Benedetto, Venice, with 'additional music' *inter alia* by Sarti.

Songs

Haydn's English Songs may be conveniently separated into several groups, as follows: (1) The First Set of Canzonettas (1794). (2) The Second Set of Canzonettas (1795). (3) Separate English Songs (probably all 1794–5). (4) The Scottish Songs for William Napier (1791 & 1795).

1. THE FIRST SET OF CANZONETTAS (1794)
(XXVIa NOS. 25–30)

It seems clear that Haydn's intention was to compose technically easy songs which could be sung at sight by any educated music-lover and played on the piano *a prima vista* by the average lady of musical inclination. This appeal to the amateur had also marked Haydn's German *Lieder* of the 1780s, which were technically even simpler, since the right hand of the accompaniment was generally the vocal line, too, and the ritornelli were severely restricted in scope (something of an exception were 'Dir nah ich mich, nah mich dem Throne' with its ten-bar introduction and the slow five-and-a-half bar introduction to 'Das Leben ist ein Traum', both from *XII. Lieder . . . II. Theil* published by Artaria in 1784). Haydn's earlier *Lieder* had not been entirely successful, for the texts were generally second-rate – in accordance with the prevailing bad literary taste in Vienna at the time – and some of the criticisms in German literary and musical journals had been distinctly unfavourable. The English texts by Mrs Hunter, although in the pastoral-cum-sentimental English tradition, are far better than Haydn's previous German texts. Musically, too, the English Canzonettas are worlds away from the *kleinbürgerliche* literary trash which Haydn, who like Leonardo used to call himself 'un uomo senza lettere', indiscriminately set to music.

In the first of the series, 'The Mermaids' Song', we are surprised to see a twenty-one bar ritornello (with a bad printing mistake in the first chord, right hand, of bar 17, where the top note is *a'* instead of *c''*), with Haydn's favourite triplet rhythm. The text is:

> Now the dancing sunbeams play
> On the green and glassy sea;
> Come, and I will lead the way,
> Where the pearly treasures be.
>
> Come with me and we will go
> Where the Rocks of coral grow,
> Follow, follow, follow me.
>
> 2^d Verse
> Come, behold what treasures lie
> Far below the rolling waves,
> Riches hid from human Eye
> Dimly shine in Ocean's caves.
>
> Ebbing tides bear no delay[1],
> Stormy winds are far away.
> [Come with me etc.]

The vocal part is very often separate from the accompaniment's right hand, and while the piano part is simple, it is also ingenious. To the words 'Come with me and we will go where the Rocks of coral grow', Haydn sets up a 'following' pattern with rather sophisticated dissonances:

If the opening Canzonetta is rather bland, the second one, 'Recollection', used to bring tears to Haydn's, and presumably to his listeners', eyes when he sang it (*supra*, p. 169).

> The Season comes when first we met,
> But you return no more.
> Why cannot I the days forget,
> Which time can ne'er restore.
>
> O! days too fair, too bright to last,
> Are you indeed for ever past?

1 In Anne Hunter's *Poems*, London 1802, p. 104 these lines are reversed.

(2ᵈ Verse)
The fleeting shadows of delight
In memory I trace;
In fancy stop their rapid flight,
And all the past replace.

But Ah! I wake to endless woes,
And tears the fading Visions close!

Haydn's setting is dignified and has a curiously remote quality which lends a slightly impersonal quality to the words. Is it accident that the music, following the words, 'Why cannot I the days forget, which time can ne'er restore'; seems to recall the Minuet of Symphony No. 97, the triumphal closing work of the 1792 season?

['Recollection']

[Symphony No. 97]

'A Pastoral Song', the Third Canzonetta, is one of Haydn's few songs which has become immortal, partly because it was sung by all sorts of famous people in the nineteenth century such as Jenny Lind, partly because it is a great miniature work. Like all these songs, 'My Mother bids me bind my hair' is in strophic form, the second verse being fully 'written out' in the first edition. Pohl (*H in L*, 312), quoting an article in the

Quarterly Musical Magazine and Review,[1] suggests that the words were originally written to a Pleyel Andante from one of his sonatas and that Haydn changed the order of the verses round and began with the second. We beg leave to doubt this theory: knowing of Haydn's friendship for the Hunter family, and considering that Mrs Hunter wrote the words of both Canzonettas especially for Haydn, as well as the dedication of this authentic first edition to her, we find it very unlikely that Haydn would have permitted himself – *un'uomo senza lettere* – the luxury of transposing Mrs Hunter's stanzas.

> My Mother bids me bind my hair
> With bands of rosey hue,
> Tye up my Sleeves with ribbands rare
> And lace my Boddice blue.
>
> For why, she cries, sit still and weep
> While others dance and play.
> Alas! I scarce can go or creep
> While Lubin is away.
>
> (2^d Verse)
> 'Tis sad to think the days are gone,
> When those we love were near;
> I sit upon this mossy stone
> And sigh! when none can hear.
>
> And while I spin my Flaxen thread
> And Sing my simple lay,
> The Village seems asleep or dead,
> Now Lubin is away.

Part of the Song's attractiveness lies in the chaste beauty of the middle parts, which almost seem to suggest string quartet writing:

The copy in the British Museum (K. 8. g. 6. 1–2) has some additional ornaments added locally by hand, e.g. at the words 'Lubin is away' (six bars before the end of each section), the original has

---

1 III (1821), p. 155. See also *Notes and Queries*, 1858, 2nd. Series No. 120, p. 313.

while B.M.'s additions read:

Probably this represents the kind of improvisational ornaments which were the rule in those days.

Canzonetta IV is entitled 'Despair', and the words read as follows:

> The anguish of my bursting heart,
> Till now my tongue hath ne'er betray'd.
> Despair at length reveals the smart
> No time can cure, no hope can aid.
>
> (2ᵈ Verse)
> My Sorrows verging to the Grave,
> No more shall pain thy gentle breast.
> Think! Death gives freedom to the Slave,
> Nor mourn for me when I'm at rest.
>
> (3ᵈ Verse)
> Yet if at eve, you chance to stray
> Where silent sleeps the peacefull dead,[1]
> Give to your kind compassion way,
> Nor check the tears by pity shed.
>
> (4ᵗʰ Verse)
> When e'er the precious dew drop falls
> I ne'er can know, I ne'er can see;
> And if sad thought my fate recalls
> A Sigh may rise, unheard by me.

If 'My mother bids me bind my hair' is unquestionably the most popular of these six songs, 'Despair' is much the greater work of art; to some critics, indeed, it ranks among Haydn's greatest songs, and one biographer calls it 'the best song Haydn ever wrote'.[2] 'The bold independent piano prelude clearly indicated the line that Schubert was to resume twenty years later.' The Song also foreshadows Haydn's old age: the *crescendo* to c flat presages the beginning of the 'Crucifixus' in the *Nelson Mass* ('Credo', bars 28f.), while the extraordinary stabbing ninth chord, which Haydn brings in three times (notice the typical *fz* stress), looks forward to a touching passage in Haydn's last, unfinished Quartet ('Op. 103'). 'No time can cure, no hope can aid' an old man's failing powers, the Quartet's 'Andante grazioso' seems to tell us. See examples overleaf. The use of E major for a solemn text is also typical: it was one of Haydn's favourite keys, as we have seen in *L'anima del filosofo*, for expressing special emotions (*supra*, p. 334).

---

1 Anne Hunter's *Poems*, London 1802, p. 105: 'Where peaceful sleep the silent dead', and two lines later 'tear' for 'tears'. Verse 4 begins: 'Where 'er the precious drop may fall', 'And if sad thoughts my fate recall.'

2 H. E. Jacob: *Joseph Haydn, His Art, Times, and Glory*, New York 1950, p. 225. Bitterly criticized by Haydn scholars for its amateurishness, its historical–novelish approach (Haydn, listening to his Symphony No. 92 at Oxford: '. . . at the close of the exposition . . . the maestro closed his eyes. Then he opened them again, savouring the second movement . . .' 'When he finished playing the last chords of the funeral cantata, Beethoven swung round in his seat . . .'), the Jacob biography is not completely without merit or sensitivity; but it must be used very carefully.

[Canzonetta IV: 'Despair']

On the very early British Museum copy, the title for Canzonetta V is left blank; but from later copies of the print and other sources, we know it to be 'Pleasing Pains', another pastoral poem which Haydn, characteristically, sets in six-eight time. As in

[Quartet, Op. 103/I]

Canzonetta I, the music soon breaks into triplets, a device to which Haydn often has recourse in filling out a passage or a transition.

> Far from this throbing [*sic*] bosom haste
> Ye doubts, ye fears, that lay it waste.
> Dear anxious days of pleasing pain,
> Fly, never to return again.
> (2[d] Verse)
> But ah! return, ye smiling hours,
> By careless fancy crown'd with flowr's;
> Come, fairy joys, and wishes gay,
> And dance in sportive rounds away.
> (3[d] Verse)
> So shall the moments gayly glide
> O'er various[1] life's tumultuous tide;
> Nor sad regrets disturb their course,
> To calm oblivion's peaceful source.

In this Canzonetta, Haydn writes a different accompaniment to the second strophe; and the third verse, while basically a musical return, in the piano part, to the first, has still other variants. The melody seems to be of the kind we think we know from somewhere else; and indeed it looks partly backwards to the slow section of the Madrigal 'The Storm' and partly forwards to the fast section of the Kyrie in the *Schöpfungsmesse*. On the whole, Haydn's placid music suits the placid text; only once, for the words 'Dear anxious days of pleasing pain', do we get a short excursion into the minor key. 'The Mermaids' Song' and 'Pleasing Pains' are the weaker works in the set.

1 In Anne Hunter's *Poems*, London 1802, p. 94 'varying'.

383

The concluding Canzonetta, 'Fidelity', is the most original and forward-looking (in the broader sense) of the whole series. The text reads:

> While hollow burst the rushing winds
> And heavy beats the show'r,
> This anxious aching bosom find[s]
> No comfort in its pow'r.
>
> For ah! my love it[1] little knows
> What thy hard fate may be;
> What bitter storms of fortune blow,
> What tempests trouble thee.
>
> A wayward fate hath spun the thread
> On which our days depend,
> And darkling in the checker'd shade
> She draws it to an end.
>
> But whatsoe'er may be our doom
> The lot is cast for me;
> For in the world or in the Tomb,
> My Heart is fix'd on thee.

Haydn opens in the old *Sturm und Drang* key of F minor, the right hand crossing down into the bass clef, *fortissimo*, and he seems to drop into his old 1772 style for the music to fit 'This anxious aching bosom finds no comfort.'

We soon see that this Song is not strictly speaking in the strophic form at all, but is a combination of *durchkomponiert* and strophic. We modulate to the relative major, where the music begins more and more to take on the character of a real song. If the beginning was slightly operatic, what follows in A flat is a German *Lied*:

The music modulates back to the dominant of F and suddenly we plunge into F major, and a variant of the theme in A flat quoted above; it is altogether remarkable how Haydn knits the Song together by similarity in the vocal part: it is all built round a very few melodies or fragments of the one melody, if you will. The piano accompaniment has also become more independent and less like a frustrated orchestra.

---

1 First edition: 'is', which makes no sense. 'It' in *Poems*, p. 109. Above 'bursts the rushing wind'. Below 'bitter' storm . . . blows'.

Haydn returns briefly to F minor, without, however, changing the key signature (which is now firmly that of F major); but soon we are back with the beautiful F major melody and its hauntingly lovely piano aftermath, the c sharp of which is so original. The final ritornello is full of the suspensions that show that Haydn's heart was completely atuned to the mood of this poem. It is certainly his greatest achievement in the song form to date and a real link to the enchanted world of Franz Schubert.

2. THE SECOND SET OF CANZONETTAS (1795)
(XXVIa: NOS. 31–36)

The first thing that strikes one about the Second Set of Haydn's English songs is the fuller accompaniment of the piano: fuller not only in the broader sense but also in the spacing of chords. Passages such as this one, with the Clementi-like layout – see arrows – of the third in the lower octave), hardly occur in the First Set.

The fuller accompaniment is also a reflection of Haydn's increased preoccupation with the piano. Indeed, piano sonatas and trios dominate the last two years of Haydn's stay in England, and it is natural that some of this interest in the keyboard should appear in the Canzonettas' accompaniments. Although the strophic form still continues to be the predominant form of the Songs, it will be observed that the repeats are almost always varied, sometimes greatly; and one of the songs ('She never told her love') is *durchkomponiert* in the most modern fashion. If anything, the Second Set is on still a higher level than the first, possibly because Haydn's English was now fluent and he was more capable of appreciating the subtleties of the poetry.

Canzonetta I has always been a popular song; it was part of Elisabeth Schumann's repertoire, for example, at a period when even Haydn's English Songs were as good as forgotten. 'The Sailor's Song' is one more proof of Haydn's fascination for the sea and the men who sailed on it, whether captain or tar.

> High on the giddy, bending Mast
> The seaman ferles [*sic*] the rending sail;
> And fearless of the rushing blast
> He careless whistles to the Gale.
>
> Rattling ropes and rolling Seas,
> Hurly, Burly; Hurly, Burly;
> War nor Death can him displease.
>
> The Hostile Foe his Vessel seeks,
> High bounding o'er the Raging Main;
> The Roaring Cannon loudly speaks,
> 'Tis BRITAIN's Glory we maintain.

Haydn, as we have seen, was all on the British side anyway, and so he hardly found it difficult to enter into the swashbuckling, patriotic atmosphere of the poem. Musically, we notice the 'military' use of horn fifths even in the opening ritornello (opposite, top). In this Song, Haydn is also much freer with the words, and we find him 'manipulating' the text as he ws accustomed to do in his Italian operas. After a rousing passage with martial, dotted accompaniment to summon up British glory on the seas (which is, strictly speaking, the end of the poem), Haydn returns to the music of the *a* strophe the text as he was accustomed to do in his Italian operas. After a rousing passage with poetry. Thus the form is not at all a simple, repeated strophe. We have: twelve bars of ritornello; then strophe *a* (comprising verses 1 & 2) which remains in the tonic;

strophe *a'*, which modulates to the dominant and ends in the martial cadence (''Tis Britain's Glory we maintain'); we then return to the middle of strophe *a*, picking up the music with the lead-in scale one bar before the text 'Rattling ropes' etc., and continuing to the end.

Canzonetta II ('The Wanderer') has the following text:

> To wander alone, when the moon faintly beaming,
> With glimmering lustre darts thro' the dark[1] shade,
> Where Owls seek for covert, and night birds complaining,
> Adds sound to the horror that darkens the glade.
>
> 'Tis not for the happy: come, Daughter of sorrow,
> 'Tis here thy sad thoughts are embalm'd in thy tears,
> Where lost in the past, disregarding tomorrow,
> Theres nothing for hopes and nothing for fears

Haydn sets the poem in G minor, a rare key for him, and he catches at once the spirit of the lonely wanderer ('alone' = bare, two-part writing):

There is also strangely menacing music to the section 'Where Owls seek for covert, and night birds complaining':

1 *Poems*, 1802, p. 101: 'dim'. Later, 'nor regarding tomorrow' and 'for hopes, there's nothing for fears'.

This is a strophic song, but the second part introduces a harmony to the previous two parts of the ritornello, and also when the piano accompanies the voice (''Tis not for the happy' etc.). It is obvious that a strophic setting brings with it the danger of the additional poetry not fitting the music, but Haydn has been very careful, and the new words, 'Where lost in the past' etc., also fit the menacing music quoted above. 'The Wanderer' is a good example of Haydn's ability to set a mood by the simplest of means.

Canzonetta III, 'Sympathy', has the following note in the first edition: 'Translated from the Italian of Metastasio'. The words are as follows:

> In thee I bear so dear a part,
> By love so firm am thine;
> That each affection of thy heart,
> By sympathy is mine.
>
> When thou art griev'd, I grieve no less,
> My joys by thine are known.
> And ev'ry good thou wouldst possess,
> Becomes in wish my own.

This Song, too, is in no simple strophic form, but in a much more sophisticated derivative. The key is in Haydn's favourite key of E major, and in the ritornello the downward scales remind us oddly of Creonte's A major Aria in Act III of *L'anima del filosofo*:

[*L'anima del filosofo*]

After the end of the first verse and an ending on the dominant, Haydn begins the next verse by a most surprising modulation into E minor ('When thou art griev'd') – see opposite. He then works round to the ritornello and the passage with the scales (not used in the accompaniment of the first verse), now used to accompany 'And ev'ry good thou wouldst possess'. The Song ends with the material previously used to end verse one, but transposed into the tonic.

Haydn's musical contemporaries appreciated the delicately balanced form and the subtle use of motifs to bind the whole together. 'Sympathy' was reprinted in the first year of the *Allgemeine Musikalische Zeitung* (1799) as *Beilage 12*.

['Sympathy']

thou art griev'd I grieve no less

Canzonetta IV ('She Never Told Her Love') is the most brilliantly original of the six, no doubt because of the inspiration, and responsibility, of a Shakespeare text: the first edition carefully notes 'By Shakespear'. Haydn creates a little *scena* to describe Viola's words in *Twelfth Night* (Act II, Scene 4):

> ... She never told her love,
> But let concealment, like a worm in the bud,
> Feed on her damask cheek . . . .
> [line omitted]
> She sat like Patience on a monument,
> Smiling at grief . . . .

The whole little masterpiece – in the first edition, the engraver required exactly two folio pages – is written in the then very novel *durchkomponierte* fashion, that is, the words and meaning dictate the course of the music. Actually, the form is very carefully worked out, as we might expect. By having a very long ritornello, Haydn is able to lay before the listener the basic material he will use in the song. The work is in the unusual (for Haydn) key of A flat and is marked 'Largo assai e con espressione'. The dynamic markings are much more elaborate than usual, with swell signs, *diminuendo* signs, and so forth: often visible evidence of Haydn's being emotionally involved with a piece of music (*vide infra*, Symphony No. 102/II, or piano Trio No. 36/II). Examining the ritornello, we see that Haydn has linked the beginning of the vocal entrance to the three chords of bars 2–4 and 12–14, which after their use as the accompaniment to the word 'Love, She [never told her love]' never appear until the very last bar of the piece.

The passage of the ritornello at bars 8–9 (with the lead-in notes of bar 7) turn out to be the music for 'She sat like Patience'. The entrance of the vocal part quite unexpectedly and on a six-four chord is highly original, and so is the false cadence to introduce the word 'grief'. The English used to call Haydn 'The Shakespeare of Music': the composer tried his very best, in this Canzonetta, to live up to the compliment.

Some of the Songs we have been considering look forward to Haydn's later vocal style, and Canzonetta V ('Piercing Eyes') could be from *The Creation* or, even more, *The Seasons*: the kind of simple, folk-like melody which the composer was soon to make immortal.

> Why asks my fair one if I love?
> Those eyes so piercing bright,
> Can ev'ry doubt of that remove,
> And need no other light.
>
> Those eyes full well do know my heart,
> And all its workings see,
> E'er since they play'd the conq'ror's part,
> And I no more was free.

In fact *The Seasons* has two direct quotations from this Song, and *The Creation* a strong hint. The beginning of the piece turns up in Simon's Air with the solo horn from *The Seasons* (No. 10); the following phrase is very like the end of the ritornello in 'with verdure clad' ('Nun beut die Flur') from *The Creation*, while the end of the Song's ritornello appears in part note for note in 'Komm, holder Lenz' from *The Seasons*.

In form the 'Piercing Eyes' resembles 'Sympathy' in its emancipation from the strophic form, and Haydn's skill in weaving a whole out of the various motives (mostly presented in the ritornello) is no less skilful than before.

The final Canzonetta. 'Transport of Pleasure' (Hoboken *deest*) was first published with that title and the following words:

> What though no high descent I claim,
> No line of Kings or race divine;
> Not all the mighty Sons of fame
> Can vaunt of joys surpassing mine.
>
> Possess'd of blooming Julia's charms,
> My heart alive to love's alarms,
> Transported with pleasure, I'm blest beyond measure,
> Such raptures I find in her arms.
>
> (2d Verse)
> What though no robe of Tyrian dye,
> No gold of Ophir I can boast,
> Nor fields, nor flocks, yet rich am I
> In wealth the gods might envy most.
>
> For mine are blooming Julia's charms,
> While Love my throbbing heart alarms,
> Transported with pleasure, I'm blest beyond measure,
> And } die with delight in her arms.
>   I }

In the last line, Haydn twice uses the 'I' version and twice the 'And' version; in the last page, we see him 'manipulating' the text very freely, e.g. 'and die with delight in her arms, and die in her arms, I die transported with pleasure, I'm blest beyond measure', etc. In this last Canzonetta, Haydn returns to the more usual strophic form. The fact that 'Transport of Pleasure' is the sixth of the series does not necessarily mean that it was composed last; in the Chronicle (*supra*, p. 285) we have seen that Haydn used to sing a German variant of this Song in A flat entitled 'Ich bin der Verliebteste (XXVIa:

36 bis). Whether he wrote the German version (published at Vienna in 1794) before or after the 'Transport of Pleasure' cannot at present be established, but one thing is certain, namely that the 'Content' variant (XXVIa: 36) was added to a later edition of Corri & Dussek. The original English words fit the music too well, as the very first words show (where Haydn incorporates both 'high' and 'descent' in the music):

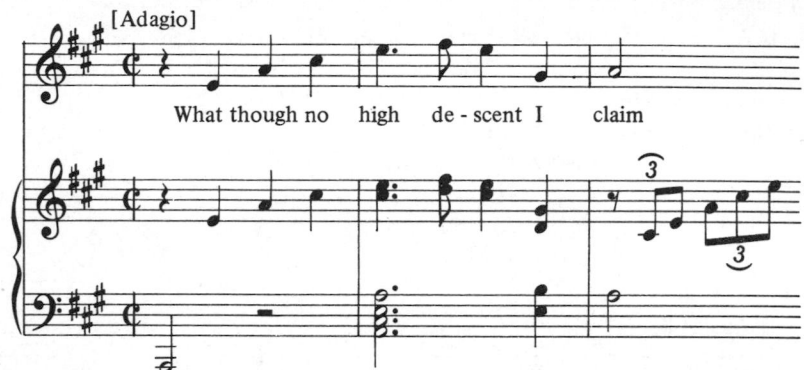

Whereas the new text of 'Content' does not fit nearly so well. Similarly the unison fanfare Haydn writes to the words 'alive to love's alarms' do not fit the words '[this heart] has e'er ambition known'. When the passage returns a second time, the original words will be seen to fit brilliantly '[Love] my throbbing heart alarms'.

We suggested in the Chronicle that Lady Bertie may have found the text to this song offensive, and there is no doubt that Haydn has if anything accentuated the erotic content, especially towards the end, where Haydn, having achieved a rather breathless series of triplets ('transported with pleasure, I'm blest beyond measure'), drops to *pianissimo* and in the third–last bar, slows the tempo to 'più adagio' in what Lady Bertie might have considered a post-coital slackening. The substitution must have happened rather rapidly, for copies of the first edition with the 'Transport of Pleasure' text are much rarer than those with the 'Content', the words of which are:

> Ah me, how scanty is my store!
> Yet for myself I'd ne'er repine,
> Tho' of the flocks that whiten o'er
> Yon plain, one lamb were only mine.
>
> 'Tis for my lovely maid alone
> This heart has e'er ambition known;
> This heart, secure in its treasure is
>   bless'd beyond measure,
> Nor envies the monarch his throne.
>
> (2[d] Verse)
> When in her sight from morn to eve,
> The hours, they pass unheeded by;
> No dark distrust our bosoms grieve,
> And care and doubt far distinant sly.
> 'Tis for my lovely maid alone [etc.]

It is actually probable that Haydn supervised the setting of this second version, because the words are metrically speaking well fitted to the music. When Artaria published their edition of 'Sechs Lieder beym Clavier zu Singen mit deutschem und englischem

Texte. Die Musik ist vom Herrn Joseph Haydn. 4ter Theil. In Wien bey Artaria und Comp.' (the Second Set of Canzonettas), the 'Content' version is used and also translated into German. The original English version is, however, preferable, for the obvious reason that the text and the music are better allied.

During Haydn's absence, Artaria of Vienna had published a German translation of the first six Canzonettas (announced in the *Wiener Zeitung* in August 1794). When Haydn returned from England in 1795, the war with France had interrupted communications between England and the Continent. At least the resulting chaos seems to explain the fact that it was not until 1798 that the Second Set of English Canzonettas was printed on the Continent. The First Set had meanwhile become popular. Following Artaria's first German edition, André reprinted the German version in 1794, and in 1799 they made a second edition which included the original English text as well. In April 1798, André published the Second Set with the original English text and a German translation by Daniel Jäger. In July of the same year, Artaria brought out the same works with the English words and the Jäger translation. Hoboken (II, 261) states that the Artaria edition is the first with the German words; but André indubitably preceded his Viennese colleagues by three months. The *Allgemeine Musikalische Zeitung* of March 1799 printed a review of the Artaria edition:

> *Sechs Lieder beym Klavier zu singen, mit deutschem und englishem Texte. Die Musik ist vom Herrn Joseph Haydn.* Vierter Theil.

In Wien bey Artaria und Comp. In Querfolio, 5½ Bogen stark.
It is a blessing for the lover of true Art when, among the piles of Songs to be sung at the piano, he sometimes receives something to read and hear which distinguishes itself from the usual run-of-the-mill. Such works are without any doubt these six Songs by *Jos. Haydn* who, despite his increasing age, has been able to keep pace with the progress of Art and Taste, and who has up to now preserved his enviable reputation in the sphere of the greatest and most successful composers.

The title might suggest Songs of the lowest order: but they differ from the usual sort by a rather more noble poetry and composition; and they have an unfussy [*unverkünstelten*], expressive line that flows from a sensitive heart. The piano accompaniment is not very difficult but is well defined.

The first is a sea song ('Sailors Song') and has two strophes with the music written out; the second strophe, though it is on the whole the same melody as the first, introduces here and there appropriate changes, in the melody as well as the accompaniment. This kind of approach may be seen in the other Songs of this kind. The second Song with the title 'The Wanderer' is solemn and slow; it creates a deep impression because of its original and moving composition. The third is called 'Sympathy' after Metastasio and is sensitively set. The fourth, from Shakespear, begins 'She never told her Love', and has much pathos; the vocal part enters, after an important introduction, unexpectedly and beautifully. The fifth, 'Piercing Eyes', is a very naive Allegretto; and finally the Sixth, 'Content', is distinguished by its beautiful and moving vocal line. These Songs, which have the German text over the English, will be certain to please all lovers of sensitivity.

3. SEPARATE ENGLISH SONGS (1794–5?)

Probably quite a number of Haydn's 'occasional' English songs have disappeared. In the London Catalogue, we find '6 English songs 8 [sheets]', '6 Songs 6 [sheets]', which we assume meant the two collections of Canzonettas. We might identify '2 Songs' as being two of the three listed here, but this is unlikely because Haydn listed both songs as going on one sheet; and except for 'Trust not too much', each of the other two are longer than one sheet. But what happened to 'Different songs 29 [[sheets]'? Unless Haydn meant orchestral arias, it would seem that posterity has lost a large number of English songs, and probably from the second visit, when Haydn's English was sufficiently improved to enable him to come to grips with setting that language to music.

One such 'occasional' Song is the little 'Trust not too much' (XXXIc: No. 17) of which the autograph, together with a Country Dance, is in the Vienna Nationalbibliothek. For some odd reason, the Song was omitted from Max Friedländer's volume of the Breitkopf & Härtel *Gesamtausgabe* (Serie XX, Band 1, 1932) and was not actually printed until the Henle Verlag issued the volume of songs in the new Collected Edition (*Werke*, Serie XXIX, Band 1, 1960, edited by Paul Mies). Undoubtedly, Haydn wrote many such songs, perhaps as 'hostess gifts', which are now irretrievably lost. The melody, which is surprisingly like a folk–tune, and a British folk–tune at that, also turns up as the beginning of the Divertimento ('London Trio') No. 2 (IV: 2), with which composition we shall be dealing below.

One of the very finest of Haydn's songs is 'The Spirit's Song' (XXVIa: No. 4) which Haydn thought was by Shakespeare. It is particularly curious that this profound and original work was not printed in England when Haydn was there, and even more curious that the first edition had to wait till the early years of the nineteenth century. As late as the autumn of 1800, Haydn was giving away MS. copies in Elssler's hand – one went to Lady Hamilton when she visited Eisenstadt. It is signed in her hand 'given to Lady Hamilton by the most/excellent Haydn at eisenstadt at the/princip Esterhasy sept 9th 1800' (from a photostat kindly supplied by William Reeves, London). Perhaps, like the piano Sonatas for Therese Jansen, Haydn was somehow bound not to print the work; there is hardly any other explanation for witholding such an easily saleable masterpiece.

The first edition – if it is that – is shrouded in mystery. It is a German translation with the words 'Horch! Horch! liebe auf mein Wort' and appeared in the Viennese house of Tranquillo Mollo & Company about the year 1801. This was the period when Artaria's great publishing firm was splitting up. It appears, according to Alexander Weinmann (*Vollständiges Verlagsverzeichnis Artaria & Comp.*, Vienna 1952, item 967), that Haydn's Song was originally scheduled for publication by Artaria, but after the firm split up, Tranquillo Mollo & Co. received the work as part of the settlement. Mollo, again according to Weinmann (*Verlagsverzeichnis Tranquillo Mollo*, Vienna 1964, p. 39), published the work as No. 167. In the Hoboken Catalogue, however, it is decisively stated (II, 267) that there is no plate number on the edition, which reads: 'Aria/mit Begleitung des Klaviers/von/Joseph Haydn/167/—24 X^r./Wien bey T. Mollo u. Comp.' Since however the publication number is included in the title page, we may trust Weinmann's dating of 1801. Plate number 166, a *Chanson Bacchique* by Pierre-Jean Garat, was announced in the *Wiener Zeitung* on 25 March 1801, while plate number 169, the second Livraison of Beethoven's Quartets Op. 18, was announced in the same newspaper on 28 October 1801.

We have been at some pains to establish the presumed first edition, because two years later, in 1803, the Kunst- und Industrie-Comptoir in Vienna issued what appears to be an authentic edition with German and English text (announced in the *Wiener Zeitung* on 5 November 1803). The title reads: 'Des Geistes Gesang./(THE SPIRIT's SONG)/Gedicht von Shakespeare./mit Deutschem und Englischem Texte,/in Musik gesetzt von JOSEPH HAYDN/[Pl. No.] 303./30 Xʳ./Im Verlage des Kunst- und Industrie-Comptoirs/zu Wien, am Kohlmarkt N° 269 (copy in Budapest National Library K 2119). It is interesting that the Song should have been so popular in Vienna as to warrant a new edition, and a new translation (for the new edition begins 'Horch, Horch was dein Treuer spricht'), two years after the Tranquillo Mollo edition.

There is an even more curious mystery to the bilingual edition, namely the attribution to Shakespeare. Who made the attribution? Did Haydn really think he was setting Shakespeare? And above all, how (as we shall see) can the *AMZ* have called the poem 'well known', when apart from Haydn's MS. copies of the Song, the verse was first published by the real author, Mrs Anne Hunter, in her *Collected Poems of 1802* (pp. 107f.)? Obviously Mrs Hunter gave the poem to Haydn to set to music. She cannot have suggested it was by Shakespeare. Possibly after Haydn left England, he mixed it up in his mind with a real Shakespeare Song from *Twelfth Night* that Mrs Hunter had given him, and that he had set to music in the Second Set of English Canzonettas ('She never told her love'). The authentic Elssler MS. for Lady Hamilton mentions no poetic author.

Mrs Hunter's poem is one of her best, however, and inspired Haydn to do his best. The text reads:

> Hark! what I tell to Thee:
> No sorrow o'er the tomb!
> My spirit wanders free,
> And waits till Thine shall come.
>
> All pensive and alone,
> I see Thee sit and weep,
> Thy hand upon the stone,
> Where my cold ashes sleep.
>
> I watch Thy speaking eyes,
> And mark each falling tear;
> I catch Thy passing sighs,
> E're they are lost in air.
> Hark! what I tell to Thee, &c., &c.

In its issue of 30 May 1804 (pp. 595f.), the *Allgemeine Musikalische Zeitung* devotes a short review to the bilingual Viennese edition of the Kunst- und Industrie-Comptoir.

> Not much more than a *Bogen* [4 sheets] of music, a few lines of text (the well-known and excellent verse: Hark, what i tell to thee): and yet one can promise oneself much pleasure from it if one has a feeling for simplicity and nobility. Even in a trifle, the master reveals himself. To remark on details is superfluous, otherwise we would particularly note the passage where [bars 83 *et seq.*] the accompaniment has the ritornello [bars 34 *et seq.*] once more but now with the voice added. The German translation and the outward look of the print are both very good.

Once more, Haydn chooses one of his old favourites: the key of F minor. The sombre ritornello sets the mood, but does not prepare us for the surprising entry of the voice on the submediant. The words 'My spirit wanders free' are set in unison accompaniments which move 'freely' from F to G flat, G natural, A flat, A and B flat, so that the modulation into B flat minor sounds unexpected. The next ritornello has a rhythmically taut sequence, the one the *AMZ* referred to:

The music modulates into the relative major (A flat) for the next part of the text ('All pensive', etc.), and Haydn uses all the rest of the poem at this point. He then modulates slowly back to the tonic and we have a recapitulation, using the first four lines of the poem. When Haydn gets to the musical example quoted above, the voice continues instead of pausing, as it did the first time:

Haydn closes 'The Spirit's Song' with yet another variant of our music, this time with the principal line in the bass part:

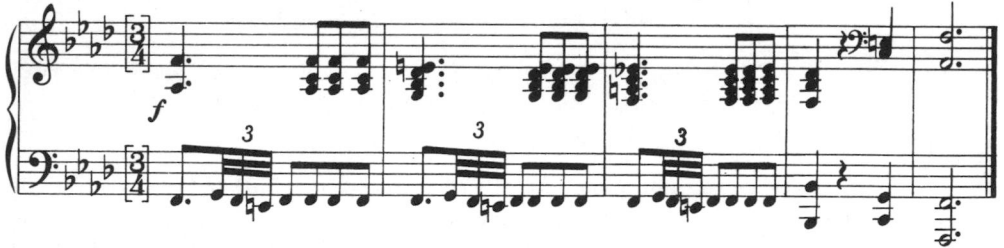

Haydn, perhaps believing that he was setting Shakespeare, once again, as in 'She never told her love', gave us the very best he had to offer.

Undoubtedly the last of Haydn's English Songs is the single work 'O Tuneful voice' (XXVIa: No. 42). We first hear of it not from English sources, but from a letter of Griesinger to Breitkopf & Härtel (Pohl III, 233) which seems to have been written early in 1803 or possibly at the end of 1802. Clementi had visited Vienna in 1802, with his young pupil Field, and had asked Haydn for some of his unpublished works. Haydn found some, but loyally offered them first to Breitkopf & Härtel, with whom he was in close business relations. Griesinger mentions piano Sonata No. 61 (51) In D; then '2. an Aria (Adagio) on an English poem, in which Mistress Hunter . . . said good-bye to Haydn' and 'What Art expresses'. Breitkopf & Härtel took all three, and issued

O tuneful voice' in 1806. The *AMZ* reviewed the print in its issue of 5 March 1806 (pp. 367f.):

> *O süsser Ton etc. (O tuneful voice) Gesang mit Begleitung des Pianoforte, in Musik*
> *gesetzt von J. Haydn.* Leipzig, bey Breitkopf und Härtel. (Pr. 6 Gr.)
>
> A trifle, in which one may constantly recognize the master! Haydn wrote this Song during his sojourn in England for a lady of quality, and it appears herewith in print for the first time. The text is actually more or less like the well known Scottish ballads, but (as the text readily allows) Haydn treats it almost like a tragic scene – simple and yet rich, noble, gentle, with many a new aspect in the writing of the elaborate accompaniment and the very flowing line of the soprano. The German translation is masterly – following, on the whole, the sense of the original, very near in the message and tone, unforced, flowing, and without having to change a tiny note. The little work, which quite certainly will be received joyously by everyone who loves a simple and noble song, is also correctly and beautifully printed.

As will be gathered, Breitkopf & Härtel have earned our thanks by printing Mrs Hunter's original text, which otherwise would not have survived except in the revised version of *Poems* (1802). The fact that the Song was not printed before 1806 is partly due to the private nature of the poem and partly, perhaps, because Haydn thought a certain amount of time should elapse before he published his farewell message to Mrs Hunter.

The extraordinary powerful impact of the Song makes us wonder about Haydn's true feelings towards Mrs Hunter and vice versa: nothing in the other English songs for which she wrote or selected the text – with the exception of 'The Spirit's Song' – quite prepares us for the intimate, profoundly emotional language in which 'O Tuneful voice' is couched. Critics have been rather puzzled why Haydn should have set to music a farewell poem in his honour; but surely the explanation is, first, to return a pretty compliment and secondly, to say in music what you cannot in words (as one Viennese newspaper wrote when Mozart's *Figaro* was allowed while the Beaumarchais play was still banned). Haydn also treated the whole as his farewell to England, the land which had adopted him and had brought out the best he had to offer; in a wider sense the Song seems, as Marion Scott once observed, to be a hymn in praise of music itself.[1]

As in 'She never told her love' and 'The Spirit's Song', Haydn has the voice enter in a highly unconventional way, with a diminished seventh leading to a six-four chord, certainly the most startling and dramatic of any vocal entrance in Haydn's songs. He leads up to this entrance with a ritornello in which the surging triplet rhythm is established at the very beginning and continued throughout the entire accompaniment (see overleaf, top).

As the writer of *AMZ*'s criticism notes, the vocal line is particularly beautiful and smoothly flowing – in strong contrast to the triplet unrest of the accompaniment. When Haydn reaches the dominant, he introduces an unexpected modulation to the words 'still vibrate on my heart'. Notice the characteristic bass part in the accompaniment at the word 'heart' (see overleaf bottom), which returns many times and slightly reminds us of the violoncello line in Symphony No. 102/II, also in triplets.

---

1 'Some English Affinities and Associations of Haydn's Songs' in *Music & Letters* (January 1944).

['O tuneful voice']

At the end of this section in the dominant, a ritornello leads to D flat and a beautiful modulation which once again brings to mind Symphony No. 102/II (bars 38/9), a movement very close in spirit and technical execution to this Song:

From a firm close in C minor, Haydn modulates back to the recapitulation, but brings in the vocal part much earlier, in fact only one bar after the reprise begins in the accompaniment. There is in fact no end to the novelty of this piece, both in detail as well as its grand tonal scope. The rich chromatic writing of the following passage in the recapitulation reminds us of another extraordinary slow movement, wherein triplet rhythms and tonal boldness dominate: piano Trio No. 36/II (see bars 9–10):

In short, a great masterpiece in miniature, and a tribute to Anne Hunter, whose verse could unlock such a vein of poetic feeling in the old Haydn; a tribute to England, too, the land that 'brought out the best' in the composer (Karl Geiringer, 1947, dedication) and opened the floodgates of his inspiration. Mrs Hunter's text reads:

> O Tuneful voice, I still deplore
> Thy accents, which I hear no more,[1]
> Still vibrate on my heart!
> In Echo's cave I long to dwell,
> And still to hear that sad farewell,
> When we were forced to part!
>
> Bright eyes! O that the task were mine,
> To guard the liquid fires, that shine,
> And round your orbits play,
> To watch them with a vestal's care!
> To feed with smiles a light so fair,
> That it may ne'er decay.

4. THE SCOTTISH SONGS

There has been an enormous amount of literature on a part of Haydn's output which, even by his most fervent admirers, cannot be said to be really significant. What began, for Napier, as a favour became, as matters turned out, a very lucrative undertaking, namely to provide accompaniments for piano, violin and violoncello, and later 'symphonies' or ritornellos, for Scottish folk-songs which, of course, existed only in an unaccompanied state. As we have seen in the Chronicle, Haydn first provided songs for the bankrupt Scottish musician and music publisher William Napier. Haydn's work for these first arrangements was considerably less than that later required for George Thomson, for the Napier songs have no 'symphonies' at the beginning or concluding ritornellos. Moreover, the keyboard part is not written out at all but is laid out as follows: each song is contained on two pages; on page one the music is in three lines, the top line for the violin, the second and third lines (connected by a brace) for the vocal part (second line) and figured bass (third line). One verse of the text is included, while the remaining verses are placed on the otherwise blank folio page opposite. Haydn's violin parts are professional and done with his usual good taste, and the added figured bass is simple and tasteful; but the late eighteenth-century idea of treating a Scottish folk-song fills twentieth century folk-song experts with horror. The more ribald texts were Bowdlerized, and the whole made suitable for the drawing-room.

The first volume of the Napier edition, with music by Haydn's friends and colleagues Samuel Arnold, William Shield, Charles Thomas Carter and F. H. Barthelemon, came out on 1 February 1790. It contained an interesting note about the performance of the songs:

> The accompaniment of a Scottish song ought to be performed with delicacy . . . .
> The full chords of a thorough bass should be used sparingly and with judgement, not to overpower, but to support and raise the voice at proper pauses. Where, with a fine voice, is joined some skill in instrumental music, the air, by way of symphony, or introduction to the song, should always be first played over; and at

---

1 *Poems*, 1802, p. 103: 'Those accents which, tho' heard no more'. The last two lines of verse one read: 'And still would hear the sad farewell, Wherever were doom'd to part.'

the close of every stanza, the last part of the air may be repeated, as a relief to the voice. In this symphonic part, the performer may show his taste and fancy on the instrument, by varying it *ad libitum*.

In other words, Napier's edition expected the performers to supply the ritornellos and concluding instrumental pieces. The presence of a violoncello is nowhere mentioned, but presumably it was often used at informal performances in private homes. Thus Haydn's share, like that of his predecessors, was really limited to choosing the basic harmonies and providing a violin accompaniment of the kind fashionable in piano trios of the period. It is to be doubted that Haydn's English, or rather Scottish, was in 1791 sufficiently fluent to understand many of the texts – even Napier thought it prudent to include a Glossary of the more *recherché* words – and presumably Haydn got someone to help him out with the more obscure phrases (Napier himself? Burney? Salomon?). If the texts were Bowdlerized in some cases, Haydn's (and his colleagues') settings try to force the music into the London drawing-room, too, and they even succeeded in removing much of the Highland charm and idiosyncrasies by clothing the songs in 'modern' garments. On the whole it was a hopeless task, and posterity has shown little interest in Haydn's, or even Beethoven's, settings of the British national folk-songs; but if the public has not taken kindly to them they have proved, as we suggested, a musicologist's delight. Long before any semblance of order had been brought into Haydn's divertimenti for orchestra, string trios, piano trios, operas, insertion arias, etc. British musicologists had provided us with admirable *catalogues raisonnés* of all the printed editions (Napier, Whyte, Thomson) of the Scottish, Welsh and Irish Songs; and Karl Geiringer made a thorough study, an extract of which was published in 1949.[1]

The title page of Napier's Volume Two reads: 'A / Selection / of / Original Scots Songs / in / Three Parts. / The Harmony by / Haydn / Dedicated by Permission / to / Her Royal Highness the Duchess of York / Vol. II. Pr. L 1 : S 6 : D o. / London / Printed for Willm. Napier, Music Seller to their Majesties, / N°. 49 Great Queen Street, Lincoln's Inn Fields. / Neele sc. Strand.' [1792]. 396 subscribers are listed for this set of 100 Scottish Songs. Vol. III [1795] was dedicated to the Queen and has, otherwise, an almost identical title page. There is no subscribers' list to Vol. III.

The Preface to Volume II contains some interesting information which is worth quoting:

> The favourable manner in which the First Volume of Scots Songs was received by the Public, has induced the Editor to continue the Work on the same plan.
>
> In the selection of the Airs, he has endeavoured to trace the Original Melodies, as far as they can be ascertained; and in this he has carefully studied the simplicity of their character, by rejecting the AFFECTED Graces and Variations, which had taste or caprice had introduced into many of the most popular Songs.
>
> The difficulty of harmonizing those wild but expressive Melodies, so as to preserve their Effect, has been acknowledged by the most skilful musicians. In the present Volume, the Editor considers himself as peculiarly fortunate in having engaged the superior talents of the celebrated HAYDN, by whom the whole of the

---

1 Cecil Hopkinson & C. B. Oldman: 'Thomson's Collections of National Song, with special reference to the contributions of Haydn and Beethoven'; in *Edinburgh Bibliographical Society Transactions* Vol. II, Pt. 1 (Session 1938–9), Edinburgh 1940; the same authors': 'Haydn's Settings of Scottish Songs in the Collections of Napier and Whyte', same *impressum*, Vol. III, Pt. 2 (Sessions 1949–50, 1950–51), Edinburgh 1954; Karl Geiringer: 'Haydn and the Folksong of the British Isles', *Musical Quarterly* XXXV (2 April 1949), pp. 179ff.

Harmonies to the following Songs is composed; and he trusts they will be found worthy of the exalted patronage, and cultivated taste, to which they are respectfully presented.

Of the genius and character of the Scots Music, so much has been said in the Dissertation prefized to the First Volume, that little remains for the Editor to add.

He has only to request that those, who are not skilled in the THEORY, as well as in the PRACTICE of Music, will not *hastily* decide on the merit of the following performance. Whatever objections may be imagined, on the first trial, he is confident they will vanish, in proportion as the performer becomes more ready and correct in the execution.

The original Words, to many of the Songs, being unfit for a work of this nature, others have occasionally been substituted; and in this the Editor has been favoured with the assistance of several gentlemen, distinguished in the literary world, particularly by Dr. WOLCOT, the elegance of whose compositions, in Song writing, has been equalled only by the humour of the productions that have given celebrity to the name of PETER PINDAR.

The Editor would be wanting, in a due sense, of the merits of those eminent artists, HAMILTON and BARTOLOZZI, were he not gratefully to acknowledge their liberality in the design and elegant execution of the characteristic Frontispiece to this Volume.

[From a copy in the author's possession.]

Behind the words of the fifth paragraph, concerning the performance of these Scottish Songs, we may sense a certain uneasiness. Although, as we have suggested, Haydn's settings followed the same general lines as those of his predecessors, his musical thinking was apparently more complex than theirs, and Napier was slightly worried whether the accompaniments for Volume II might prove too difficult for amateurs. This raises a whole problem, at the root of which lies, we believe, the fundamental lack of success not only of Haydn's arrangements but of the whole undertaking, whether the musical 'editing' was entrusted to a Haydn or Beethoven, or to composers of the second order (most of them, however, skilful professionals such as Ignaz Pleyel or William Shield). Since the publication of Scottish folk-songs in the 1790s (and later) coincided with a new interest in 'National Melodies', we may perhaps go beyond Napier's publications to examine the whole nature of the idea, which must have seemed so propitious to the publishers of that age.

We shall see that George Thomson was also much worried that Haydn's accompaniments would prove too difficult for the average amateur, and to Beethoven he lamented on the dearth of good musicians in Scotland. It would seem that all the publishers of these National songs were in some doubt as to the kind of public who would purchase and perform the volumes: they hoped for a wide amateur sale, and in that they were mostly mistaken. They published (at least Whyte and Thomson did) separate violin and violoncello parts, which were very often not purchased, so that we have many incomplete sets, without the string parts, in the libraries of the world today. All these publication ventures were no doubt well intended, but they all fell short of their intended goal: to circulate these National songs throughout the kingdom and to make them genuinely popular. Not even Haydn, or later Beethoven, were able to do that, because the basic premise was mistaken. The accompaniments, and later the symphonies and ritornellos, were at frequent, and often violent, odds with the contents, musical and poetic, of the songs. Part of the reason for this discrepancy was because Thomson, and presumably Whyte, sent their composers only the melodies, without the words: an arrangement which would seem insane to any modern folk-song arranger, schooled in the methods of Bartók and Kodály. Also, the publishers were continually forcing their composers to make everything simpler, to rewrite even slightly difficult ritornellos, etc. 'Allow me to mention,' writes Thomson to Haydn (20 December 1802, CCLN 223), 'that if you find any of the Airs fit for an accomp^t similar to that in your 1st Canzonet in C, published by Corri & Dussek [i.e. "The Mermaids' Song"], I am particularly fond of that kind of easy motion in accomp^t . . .': as if this were the ideal kind of accompaniment for a rough Scottish song! No doubt professional musical standards in Scotland were not what they were in London, but it was really of no interest to Beethoven to hear (September 1813: Hadden, *Thomson*, 330), *in re* the Razumovsky Quartets, 'Alas! my friend, we have not. in Scotland a dozen persons (professionals included) who could take a part in these quatuors, and not one who could play *correctly* the *violino primo* of any of the three!' All these factors mitigated against Haydn's efforts for the Scottish National songs; and it is curious that the second batch of arrangements which he delivered to Napier – fifty instead of one hundred – and which Napier issued in 1795 as his Volume III, did not have the success either of Volume II (Haydn's) or Volume I (various masters). Volume III is the rarest of all Napier's series, even although the settings were all by Haydn and the volume was dedicated to Queen Charlotte.

Volume I is described by Napier as 'adapted for the Harpsichord, with an accompaniment for a violin'; both Volumes II & III describe the accompaniments as 'in three parts' (*vide supra*, the third part was obviously the violoncello). A complete thematic catalogue, and a description of the prints and their variants, may be found in Hopkinson-Oldman 1954, and to that excellent work we refer interested readers. None of the autographs of Haydn's Scottish Songs for Napier has survived. Volume II of Napier's series was published by the Henle Verlag in the new *Collected Edition of Haydn's Works* (Reihe XXXII, Band 1, 1961, edited by Karl Geiringer)[1] and Haydn's first 100 Scottish Songs are thus readily available to the student.

5. DR HARINGTON'S COMPLIMENT ('WHAT ART EXPRESSES')
(XXVIb: 3)

It is a happy accident that this *pièce d'occasion* has survived; Haydn took back a copy to Austria and, as we have seen in the Chronicle (*supra*, p. 267) sold the work to Breitkopf & Härtel, who issued it in 1806. The piece is so curiously constructed that it can only have been intended for 'home consumption'; it is difficult to imagine how it could be performed publicly today. It begins as if it were a song, in slow tempo ('Poco Adagio'), with a hymn-like melody preceded by a short ritornello. After announcing the theme with a soprano solo, the piano has another ritornello which sounds like the first of a set of variations on the tune. Then the chorus enters (written in four parts, the top lines in G-clefs, as was usual in England, and the tenor in the tenor clef). The choral statement is no longer than that of the soprano solo. There is a double bar at the end of this section, and turning the page we find a piano solo entitled 'Variazione', the music mostly moving in sextuplet rhythm. After a dozen bars, the music moves into A minor and a slower metrical division: here we seem to be in the adagio movement of a late piano sonata:

---

1 An interesting review of the volume by Eugene Hartzell in *Haydn Yearbook* II (1963–4), pp. 98ff.

[Poco Adagio]

And to conclude this extraordinary, almost 'improvised' piece, the solo soprano again enters with the main theme, but the piano part continues its variations, and again in predominantly triplet rhythm. Breitkopf &Härtel published the English text and also a German translation. The original words read:

> What Art expressed and what Science praises
> Haydn the Theme of both to Heaven raises.

Although 'Dr Harington's Compliment' was quite obviously written for an evening's entertainment, it is touching to see the loving care with which Haydn composes this occasional piece. Breitkopf's first edition reads:

'*Der Tausenden so oft Freude gegeben* | (What art expresses etc.) | *für Gesang und Pianoforte* | *An Doctor HARRINGTON, zu Erwiderung* | *der von ihm an J. Haydn gerichteten Verse und Musik* | *von* | J. HAYDN. | [line] | *Bey Breitkopf & Härtel in Leipzig* | *Pr. 8 Gr.*'

CHAPTER SEVEN

Instrumental Music – Chamber Works

Trios

THE SO-CALLED 'LONDON' TRIOS FOR 2 FLUTES AND VIOLONCELLO (IV: 1-4).
(1794)

Trio No. 1 in C (IV: 1). I *Allegro moderato*. II *Andante*. III *Finale: Vivace*.
Trio No. 2 in G (IV: 2). I *Andante*. II *Allegro*. Later the *Finale* to Trio No. 3 was added when this Second Trio was presented to the Earl of Abingdon.
Trio No. 3 in G (IV: 3). I *Spiritoso*. II *Andante*. III *Allegro* (the last movement also used as *Finale* to Trio No. 2.
Trio No. 4 in G (IV:4). A single movement – *Allegro*.

We have seen in the Chronicle (*supra*, p. 275) that in November 1794 Haydn and Lord Abingdon went to visit one of the Earl's friends, Baron Aston (Sir Walter, Eighth Lord), who had a house near London. It was probably for this occasion that Haydn wrote his 'London' Trios, as they have come to be known in modern times, for the curious combination of two flutes and violoncello. At any rate he gave one of the Trios to Abingdon and one to Aston, because when Abingdon's friend T. Monzani published an edition of two of these Trios in January 1799 – it was announced in *The Oracle and Public Advertiser* on 2 January – he made a note as to the provenance of each one. For the First Trio he noted: 'This Trio was Composed for Sir Willoughby Aston B^t. who generously / gave it to Mr Monzani for Publication', and for the Second, 'This Trio was composed for the Earl of Abingdon who generously gave / it to Mr Monzani for Publication.'

Let us examine briefly the sources. For Trio 1 we have Haydn's autograph in the Berlin Staatsbibliothek, signed 'di me Giuseppe Haydn mp. London 7̄9̄4'. It is together with Trio 2 (only the Andante-Allegro movement); there is no 'Fine Laus Deo' at the end of Trio 1, but there is that final 'signature' at the end of Trio 2. The autograph bundle consists of 9 sheets (*Bogen*). In Haydn's *Catalogue of Works Composed in England*, we find the entry '2 Flüte divert. 10 [sheets]', which obviously refers to the above autograph (9 sheets) plus one sheet for, perhaps, the Finale of Trio 3 that Haydn tacked on to Trio 2. Trio 3, the autograph of which was formerly in the Berlin Staatsbibliothek but was lost at the end of World War II, and Trio 4, a single movement which survives in a copy by Johann Elssler on British paper signed by Haydn 'Trio per due Flauti e Violoncello. Nro. 2' (changed to 'Nro. 3'), do not figure in the *Catalogue of Works Composed in England*. The autograph of Trio 3 was not dated, but it was on British paper with the watermark 'J WHATMAN 1794', as Larsen notes. The Elssler copy of Trio 4 is in the Berlin Staatsbibliothek.

Trio 1's autograph contains two versions of the slow movement, one 39 bars and one 45. Hitherto, Haydn scholars have automatically considered the long version to be

Haydn's final one, and it was adopted by the editors of the new editions, except for K.-H. Köhler, who published both. But the evidence is not entirely clear. Here are the two beginnings (A and B):

[Version A]

[Version B]

In the autograph, the 'B' version has 39 bars, the 'A' version 45. But if we examine the Monzani 1799 edition, which may be presumed to represent the authentic British version of the Trio, it will surprise us to see that although Monzani has the dotted pattern of the 'B' version, and also the 'B' version of flute I in bar 3, he has a 45-bar movement. This comes about as follows: up to bar $20\frac{1}{2}$ Monzani's text is basically the 'B' version; from the upbeat to 21, however, Monzani has the 'A' version to the end (the last eleven bars of both are identical), except that when the theme returns at (Monzani's reckoning:) bars 28–9, it is dotted as at the beginning of version 'B', and not as in the autograph. All this is very mysterious, and it makes one wonder that Haydn should have taken the immense trouble to write *three* different slow movements to this tiny Divertimento. But as Pierre Boulez has said apropos of genre pieces such as the London Trios, '. . . I cannot help feeling that a great composer reveals himself also – and in a very engaging manner – in works which are like family portraits, snapshots, in relation to large study portraits.'[1]

1 Translated by Felix Aprahamian on a CBS record: 72785 (1970). Our thanks to our old friend O. W. Neighbour, Esq., of the British Museum for help in sorting out the textual problems of the Monzani print.

In the autograph's 'A' version, Haydn intended to repeat the first section and gave a double version to the 'cello (left) which was suppressed in the 'B' version (right).

Obviously the bottom line is to lead back to the beginning in G major, the top line to continue. To print both of them as if the 'cello were to play both simultaneously, as does the new (1959) Köhler edition, is inadvisable.

In the autograph bundle, the little G major Trio 2 has just the one movement, going from andante to allegro. In the Monzani edition, as we have seen, the Finale of Trio 3 was added. The great Austrian scholar, Eusebius von Mandyczweski, when preparing these Trios for the Breitkopf & Härtel *Gesamtausgabe* – his MS. score is in the Gesellschaft der Musikfreunde library – proposed another idea. He combined Trio 4, obviously a single movement and from its layout an opening one at that, with Trio 2 into one work and renumbered the others. In his proposed version for the (now defunct) Breitkopf G.A., we should have had: Trio = IV: 1; Trio 2 = IV: 3; Trio 3 = IV: 4 plus IV: 2. This very ingenious scheme takes in all the extant movements, but we cannot know if it was what Haydn intended.

To continue going through the works and following the sources, Trio 3 (IV: 3) is a complete autograph manuscript and was not printed until the Lenzewski edition early in this century, while Trio 4 (IV: 4) is obviously a fragment. Considering the sources as we know them now, Mandyczewski's solution is a clever compromise. One might consider offering two new versions of Trio 2, the Monzani one (*supra*) and that of Mandyczewski. At any rate, it is astonishing to see with what care Haydn worked on these little Divertimenti, and how many problems, textual and otherwise, these four pieces have managed to create.[1]

Haydn obviously knew of the flute's immense popularity in France and England: next to the harpsichord (piano) and singing, it was the most popular musical instrument of the amateur; and indeed, before 1750 it is probable that the flute was even more popular than the harpsichord among cultivated amateurs. It also represents, in many ways, the pastoral scene, the Rousseauian 'Back to Nature', the Petit Trianon, and the hazy world of a Watteau garden party. Haydn had always preserved a special affection for the flute and had used it lovingly in chamber and orchestral works all his life. With these 'London' Trios, he says farewell to the flute as a part of chamber music.

The Trios are delightful. Haydn manages the organization of the two flutes with airy mastery; nor is the second flute neglected, for these are not the string trios of the

---

1 CCLN 309. Hoboken I: 463–5. Larsen HÜB 264f. A. Kopfermann: 'Zur Veröffentlichung des Haydnschen Flötentrios' in *Die Musik*, Jg. 8, No. 16 (May 1909) with the score of IV: 2. Pohl III, 317 (where the works are treated in Botstiber's usually cavalier fashion). Geiringer 1947, p. 278 (discussing the two slow movements of Trio 1). C. S. Smith: 'Haydn's Chamber Music and the Flute' in *Musical Quarterly* XIX (1933). *Time Magazine* (5 April 1971, p. 37), where the London Trios are, however, erroneously listed as 'all-string works'. New editions: Trios 1, 3, 4 ed. Gustav Lenzewski, Vieweg-Verlag, Berlin (n.d.); 1–4 in parts, ed. Leo Balet, Nagels Musikarchiv 1931. 1–3 in score and parts, ed. K.-H. Köhler, Edition Peters, Leipzig 1959. Dr Köhler omitted Trio 4 which, he maintains, exists only in a 'fragmentary copy' (Hoboken I, 465: 'an extremely careful and rigidly precise [copy]') and is of dubious authenticity ('Wegen Echtheitszweifeln') – although it was written by Elsser in England on British paper and signed by Haydn. We must sadly point out that Haydn scholarship is bedevilled by incomprehensible attitudes such as that one. See C. S. Smith, 'Haydn's Chamber Music and the flute – Part II', *Musical Quarterly* XIX 4 (October 1933), pp. 449–51.

1750s, where the second violin is a real stepchild. The two flute parts cross each other, they gambol about in playful and sometimes quite difficult semiquaver patterns. It all sounds extremely easy, but the Trios are the works of music's most experienced craftsman. Haydn even finds time to introduce imitations, some of them of a rather serious bent, such as at the beginning of the development section in Trio 1.

Trio 2 is based on the little Song, 'Trust not too much' which we noticed (*supra*, p. 394) in the previous section dealing with vocal music. The interesting and unconventional side of the melody, which has a very English flavour to it, is its breakdown into five plus five plus four bars (in the Song with another four bars' concluding ritornello). Haydn wrote sophisticated variations on this pastoral-like tune, stressing the asymmetrical, five-bar side to the theme. Thus the final, Allegro variation is constructed: 5 + 5 to the double bar, then 2 + 2 for a middle section and concluded by 5 + 5 bars.

The opening of Trio 3, Spiritoso, has gay, march-like rhythms; but in some respects it is the most elaborate, contrapuntally, of the 'London' Trios. The opening bars are so constructed that they work ideally in imitation: so that when Haydn writes

it can be made to serve him as follows, when he reaches the dominant:

The development section, as in that to Trio 1, is surprisingly serious: surprising because these are supposed to be pastoral divertimenti. It was the same side of Haydn revealed in the early wind band Divertimenti of 1760 when he introduced in the Trio of a Minuet the 'Incipit Lamentatio' Gregorian plain-chant. When the recapitulation begins, the whole theme is treated canonically with itself, as in the example quoted above from the exposition. It is this fastidious attention to detail, even in 'minor' works of the period, that make the whole London – and of course post-London – period of Haydn's life so valuable. Incidentally, we find the same canonic treatment and in fact a theme similar to that of Trio 3/Spiritoso, in the March for Prince of Wales, with which we shall be dealing *infra* (p. 488).

The fate of the 'London' Trios mirrors *en miniature* that of most of Haydn's music. When Monzani brought out his 'Two Original Trios for Two German Flutes and Violoncello. Composed while in England by D^r. Haydn' he also published an arrangement for the piano 'with a German Flute Accompt. ad Libitum'. The two works were obviously popular enough to warrant Clementi & Co. issuing a new edition, and similarly on the Continent, Artaria published them, probably from the Monzani edition, in 1805. The Trios soon fell into oblivion, however, so that when

Kopfermann brought out Trio 2 in the magazine *Die Musik* in 1909, it was a real discovery. The Balet edition reintroduced the 'London' Trios into the chamber music repertoire and went through several editions; even gramophone recordings were made before and after the war. In the standard literature, the works were usually dismissed as inconsequential (Pohl-Botstiber, Geiringer), but they continued to have a flourishing life of their own; so much so that Edition Peters could contemplate a rival edition in 1959. We read recently (1971) that San Francisco street musicians have Haydn's 'London' Trios in their repertoire and that these works 'get the biggest audiences and make the most money': a purpose for which Haydn certainly did not intend them but which illustrates how music of this charm, vitality and technical mastery will survive despite the works' temporary eclipse in the nineteenth century.

SONATAS (TRIOS) FOR PIANOFORTE WITH THE ACCOMPANIMENT OF A VIOLIN AND VIOLONCELLO

These sonatas are here arranged in chronological order and with the numbering of the new critical edition, Doblinger Verlag, 1970 *et seq.* prepared by the present writer.

Trio No. 31 in G (XV: 32) 1792–3? Published in 1794 by Preston and Bland in London. I *Andante*. II *Allegro*.

Trios Nos. 32–34 (XV: 18–20) 1793–4? Published in 1794 by Longman & Broderip (entered at Stationers Hall on 15 November 1794; announced in *The Sun* on 25 November 1794). Dedicated to Princess Dowager Marie Therese Esterházy, *née* Countess Hohenfeld.

Trio No. 32 in A. I *Allegro moderato*. II *Andante*. III *Allegro*.
Trio No. 33 in G minor. I *Andante – Presto*. II *Adagio ma non troppo*. III *Presto*.
Trio No. 34 in B flat. I *Allegro*. II *Andante cantabile*. III *Finale : Allegro*.

Trios Nos. 35–37 (XV: 21–23) 1794–5? Published in 1795 by Preston (entered at Stationers Hall on 23 May 1795; announced in the *Morning Chronicle* on 13 June 1795). Dedicated to Princess Marie Esterházy, *née* Princess Liechtenstein.

Trio No. 35 in C. I *Adagio pastorale – Vivace assai*. II *Molto Andante*. III *Finale : Presto*.
Trio No. 36 in E flat. I *Allegro moderato*. II *Poco Adagio*. III *Finale : Allegro*.
Trio No. 37 in D minor. I *Molto Andante*. II *Adagio ma non troppo*. III *Finale : Vivace*.

Trios Nos. 38–40 (XV: 24–26) 1794–5? Published in 1795 by Longman & Broderip (announced in the *Morning Chronicle* on 9 October 1795; entered at Stationers Hall on 31 October 1795; announced in the *Public Advertiser* on 18 December 1795 as 'New Music just published'; sketch for the slow movement of Trio No. 39, owned by Messrs. J. A. Stargardt of Marburg/Lahn, is on British paper with the watermarks 'Portal & Bridges / 1794' and coat-of-arms / 'G R'; but the sketch is on a sheet listing all the incipits of Haydn's 'Salomon' Symphonies – see Landon SYM, 436 – which suggests that the work was written sometime between May and August 1795, May being the date when Symphony No. 104 was first performed and August 15 being the date when Haydn left England for good.) Dedicated to Rebecca Schroeter.

Trio No. 38 in D. I *Allegro*. II *Andante*. III *Allegro ma dolce*.
Trio No. 39 in G. I *Andante*. II *Poco Adagio*. III *Finale : Presto* ('Rondo, in the Gypsies' stile').
Trio No. 40 in F sharp minor. I *Allegro*. II *Adagio* [using the slow movement of Symphony No. 102 in B flat, 1794]. III *Finale : Tempo di Minuetto*.

We can now establish which of the late trios were composed in or for England between about 1792 and 15 August 1795. They are those we have listed above. In Haydn's *Catalogue of Works Composed in England*, the last entry, according to Dies, was '3 Sonates for Broderip'. Griesinger removed this entry, probably thinking that it was a repetition of an earlier entry, '3 Sonates for Broderip'. Griesinger probably took the trouble of adding up Haydn's number of sheets. Haydn has the sum of 768, but the figures listed add up to 771 without the '3 Sonates for Broderip' at the end. Possibly Haydn added this last entry without the number of sheets; these Trios (Nos. 38–40) were probably the last thing he wrote and delivered to his publishers before he left England. The remaining five trios, Nos. 41–5 of the new edition, consisting of two single works and a set of three (also for Longman & Broderip), do not figure in Haydn's *Catalogue of Works Composed in England* and there is much supporting evidence that they were composed in Austria between 1795 and 1797. Thus they are not works which fall within the scope of this volume, though there is evidence that four of the five works were destined for English publishers.

Trio No. 31 was known to us until 1957 as a violin Sonata; with the publication of Hoboken's Catalogue, Volume One, in 1957, we learned that the work was conceived and published in London by Preston as a piano Trio; the date of publication was suggested by the dated watermarks: 1794. Subsequently Alan Tyson was able to show that there also existed another British print of the Trio, also with the watermark date 1794: J. Bland, a publisher with whom Haydn was on friendly terms. Tyson suggests it is 'possible . . . that both editions are in a sense authentic. That is to say, an understanding may have been reached between Preston and Bland whereby the former was to be allowed to publish an edition for general sale, while the latter was to include it in his periodical series [*Le tout ensemble*]', of which it figures as No. 38. (No. 39, by the way, was Haydn's Trio No. 27, which Master Hummel had introduced to London in the Haydn–Salomon concert of 20 April 1792 and which Longman & Broderip issued the same year. Obviously the Bland was, in this case, a reprint.) It is probable that Preston, not Bland, was the original publisher. There are a few textual points, at any rate, that suggest that Bland copied from Preston's plates and not vice versa.

By all counts, Trio 31 is the earliest of the London series; but exactly when it was written cannot be established. In the letter to Frau von Genzinger dated 2 March 1792, Haydn talks of the stolen Sonata for Madame Tost and also of replacing it (Chronicle, *supra*, p. 140). It has been suggested that Trio 31 is the replacement. It is also the only candidate for the entry in Haydn's Catalogue '1 Sonate in g 5 [sheets]' (CCLN 309). We also presume that Haydn delivered a copy of the work to his Viennese publishers Artaria before he left for the second London journey: Artaria brought out the work as 'Sonate pour le clavecin ou Piano-Forte avec accompagnement d'un violon . . . Oeuvre 70', announcing it in the *Wiener Zeitung* on 14 June 1794. By omitting the almost superfluous 'cello part, they started the legend of this work as a violin Sonata.

In its easy-going, *divertimento*-like opening, Trio 31 reminds us of another two movement keyboard work for London: the Sonata for piano No. 61. The opening Andante movements of both seem to recall an earlier Viennese *Gemütlichkeit* which perhaps seems slightly *déplacée* in the glories of the second London sojourn. The second movement is also emotionally uncomplicated but rhythmical and formally terse, much more in the 1794 style than the opening Andante. The violin part is hardly of a brilliance such as we know from the 'Kreutzer' Sonata, but it is absolutely independent. Of course all Haydn's piano trios except perhaps the final three for Therese Bartolozzi (*née* Jansen) were written with anonymous amateurs in mind. And this explains why the piano writing is generally on a higher technical level than the string writing: piano amateurs were becoming a race of their own, with brilliant techniques and a special flair for expressive effects. Many of these amateurs were women and their only claim to the amateur state was that they did not play the piano for money: artistically they were on a superbly professional level. Therese Jansen was one such lady pianist; later such feminine talents as Madame Marie Bigot and Baroness Dorothea von Ertmann were to elicit words of praise not only from Haydn but also from Beethoven. In London of the mid 1790s, Haydn must have found the amateur string players of a rather limited technique, whereby the violinists were obviously better than the 'cellists. The title pages of the first editions of Haydn's trios describe their inner layout quite precisely: 'with accompaniments for a violin and violoncello'. The 'cello parts are basically a late eighteenth-century descendant of the *basso continuo* in the Baroque trio sonata, as Haydn's own early keyboard trios show very strikingly. Haydn's late trios, then, are really piano sonatas with string accompaniment, and until this basic fact of their construction is understood and appreciated, we shall have difficulty in placing them correctly not only in the history of the piano trio but also in Haydn's own *oeuvre*. It is useless to expect the innovations *in sound* that we have come to expect from Haydn's orchestral and choral music, and also from his string quartets. The amateur recipients were a deliberate limitation on the string parts, and thus on the works as piano *trios*.[1] Once, however, we have rid ourselves of this initial prejudice, it will be seen by any sensitive student of the period that Haydn's late piano trios are magnificent works of art that in many respects go further than the late symphonies: in the exploration of third-related keys, something that Haydn could on the one hand pursue in large operatic finales for Eszterháza such as in Acts I and II of *La fedeltà premiata*, and on the other in intimate chamber music such as these piano trios.

We believe, moreover, that Haydn's late piano trios have not even been examined in the light of other contemporary evidence except for Mozart and Beethoven where, particularly in the latter, the 'cello parts are much more independent than those of Haydn. Again, Beethoven was writing for one time and place (in the case of his Opus I Trios: Vienna, 1795), whereas all except possibly one of Haydn's late piano trios were destined for England between 1794 and 1797. It would in fact seem that there was a great difference in the two markets; and while Haydn may have been one of music's greatest innovators, he obviously thought that works commissioned by British publishers for amateurs, or at least amateur string players and semi-professional pianists, were not the place to run against the prevailing tradition. Indeed, many of the tremendous innovations within the structure of these trios may stem from the obvious limitations of writing the string parts for the amateurs, i.e. with great technical simplicity.

If we examine the other trio productions of British publishers in the mid 1790s, the extraordinary similarity to Haydn's trio writing becomes at once similar. The

---

1 Trio 31: Alan Tyson: 'New Light on a Haydn Trio (XV: 32)' in *Haydn Yearbook* (1962), pp. 203–5. Hoboken I, 717f. Marie Bigot: Pohl III, 239. Dorothea von Ertmann: A. F. Schindler: *Beethoven as I know him* (ed. D. W. MacArdle), London 1966, pp. 209–11 and, more recently, G. R. Marek: *Beethoven: Biography of a Genius*, New York 1969. On the music of Haydn's piano trios, there are three serious studies: (a) D. F. Tovey's article on Haydn in *Cobbett's Cyclopedic Survey of Chamber Music*, London 1929; (b) Cecil Gray: Analytical Notes to *A Limited Edition of Haydn Trios*, The Parlophone Company, Ltd., London, 1940; (c) Charles Rosen: *The Classical Style*, London and New York 1971, pp. 351–365. See also A. Craig Bell: 'An introduction to Haydn's Piano Trios' in *Music Review* 1955.

daughter of Haydn's friend, the violinist Barthelemon, both of whom have figured in the preceding Chronicle, published chamber music which has a distinct relationship to the kind of amateur writing we have been discussing. Caecilia Maria Barthélémon published herself 'Two Sonatas for the Piano-Forte or Harpsichord, With Accompaniments, For the Violin, German Flute & Violoncello, Dedicated by Permission to Her Royal Highness The Dutchess [*sic*] of York . . . Opera seconda' [etc.] the *impressum* reads 'To be had at all the Music Shops' and the first edition, of which the British Museum owns a copy, is signed 'C M Barthelemon'. In these works, the extremely simple technical level of the 'accompaniments' may be noted, as opposed to a relatively advanced piano part. The same type of writing obtains in Gyrowetz's Three piano Trios Op. 9, dedicated to Miss Townsend and published by Longman & Broderip *c.* 1793 (they are entitled 'Three Sonatas for the Piano Forte or Harpsichord, with Accompaniments for Violin and Violoncello'). But perhaps an even more interesting parallel is J. P. Salomon's first editions of the London Symphonies for piano trio, issued jointly by Salomon himself and Corri & Dussek, of which Haydn owned a set.[1] These very successful arrangements were designed for the average concert-going lover of music who could be expected to find a violinist and 'cellist amongst his friends. The piano part is the leading member of the group, almost to the extent that the works could have been, and perhaps were, played, or at any rate practised, without the string parts. Easy though the violin part is, the 'cello part is ridiculously simple. It was the commercially expedient way to lay out a piano trio in those days. The same thing can also be observed in J. L. Dussek's arrangements for piano and violin of Symphonies 90 and 92 (November 1791: see Chronicle, *supra*, p. 54): the piano part has the lion's share of the music and the violin is secondary.

Having now, as it were, established and, we hope, explained the technical limitations of these late piano trios, we may now proceed to a more positive analysis of their great features; which we propose to do, series for series, the G major work having been the only single work of the 1794–5 period.

During his first visit to London, Haydn quite obviously had no time to compose trios. In 1791, he composed his huge *opera seria*, *L'anima del filosofo*, 'presided' at all the Salomon concerts, for which he furnished two new symphonies and various other works, and also 'presided' at all the ill-fated Gallini concerts. For the 1792 season, he had to compose four big-scale symphonies, the Concertante (also a large work), the Madrigal 'The Storm', and several vocal works. We have seen that Haydn was exhausted by the winter season of 1792 and eager to return home to Vienna. Understandably, there was no room for piano trios in the 1791–2 season. But there were obviously agreements with London publishers for trios to be delivered in what both Haydn and they (as well as Salomon) thought would be the 1793 season. We have seen how that proposed visit became delayed for a year, and we recall Dies's explanation (Chronicle *supra*, p. 231) and especially the interesting detail, that Haydn 'had made very advantageous contracts with various publishing houses [in London]' which he naturally wished to fulfil. In view of the sudden and prodigious flow of piano trios from Haydn's pen during the years 1794 and 1795, we can be confident that we owe the existence of Haydn's late trios primarily to the astute business acumen of the two London publishing houses of Preston, and Longman & Broderip.

1 Haydn's copies are now in the National Library at Budapest, from the Esterházy estate. *Haydn's Compositions in the Music Collection of the National Széchényi Library Budapest*, 1959, pp. 148f. Salomon's arrangements were entered at Stationers Hall as follows: Nos. 1–4 (97, 94, 98) on 25 June 1796; Nos. 5–6 (95, 96) on 1 July 1796; Nos. 7–1 (99–104 but not in that order) on 30 September 1797. I am indebted to Dr Alan Tyson for the dates from Stationers Hall.

We also owe the piano writing to Haydn's contact with the new British grand pianos, which were a spectacular advance on the Viennese pianos that he had known hitherto. Since it is only of recent date that we are beginning to study in depth the eighteenth century piano and its ramifications on the piano music of the period, a few words about the British pianos of the mid 1790s may not be amiss, particularly since Haydn, as it happens, was the man destined to begin a long and for both countries profitable exchange of pianos and pianistic concepts between England and Austria, in the course of which J. B. Cramer, Muzio Clementi, Johann Nepomuk Hummel, Beethoven and others were to play decisive roles.

Mozart had developed an entirely new method of piano writing, especially in his concertos which, as these great works gradually spread through Europe, were to create a profound impression and decisive influence. Mozart's instrument had been a Walter (Walther) with a pedal attachment. Walter also serviced the keyboard instruments at Eszterháza, as we know from dated receipts in the Esterházy Archives at Budapest. Haydn had written in July 1790 (CCLN 107), 'It is quite true that my friend Herr Walther is very celebrated, and that every year I receive the greatest civility from that gentleman, but between ourselves, and speaking frankly, sometimes there is not more than one instrument in ten which you could really describe as good, and apart from that they are very expensive.' Haydn preferred the lighter touch and 'very agreeable' mechanism of the pianos by Schanz. If, as has been assumed, the Walter piano found in Liszt's birthplace came from the Esterházy Castle at Eisenstadt, there is some reason to agree with Haydn,[1] because that instrument, now in the Haydn Museum after having been painstakingly restored by Professor Josef Mertin, is definitely deficient in sustaining power in the treble register. The Walter pianos of c. 1785 and c. 1795 in the Vienna Kunsthistorisches Museum are indeed spectacular instruments; Mozart's own Walter piano, now in the Mozart Museum in Salzburg, has been too heavily restored to judge its original tone. But it was a characteristic of the pre-1800 Viennese pianos to have a lovely, darkly metallic sound in the low register; to have a singing, warm tone in the middle; but to be thin sounding and weak in construction in the upper register. The standard range was five octaves, from f' to f''', though occasionally an instrument with an extra two keys, up to g''', was made in Vienna; but composers did not write for it and the extra 'g' (as it was called) was of sufficient rarity to warrant the fact being mentioned when someone sold such an instrument through the *Wiener Zeitung*: 'zwey große Forte piano, wovon eines bis ins G geht' (28 February 1798). Basically the Viennese fortepiani of the 1780s and 1790s were beautiful but fragile instruments, and fragile also in their construction.

Haydn had been introduced to a whole new race of British (native or adopted) pianists in 1791–2: J. L. Dussek, J. B. Cramer, Muzio Clementi, and amateurs with a spectacular technique such as Therese Jansen. Obviously we have to rely on contemporary criticisms to judge what their piano playing was like; but perhaps it will suffice if we remember Beethoven's high opinion of Cramer, as quoted in the Wegeler-Ries *Notizen*: 'Among the pianists, he praised one as being an excellent player: John Cramer. All the others meant little to him.'[2] We have in Carl Czerny an

---

1 As we write this paragraph, the famous 'Hummel Inventar' of 1806 has just been rediscovered in the Hummel Archives, and Frau Maria Hummel, who has been of the greatest help and kindness in this as in many other matters, has given us permission to publish it. The Hummel Catalogue of 1806 also contains a list of the pianos at Eisenstadt, from which it will be seen that all the 'old fashioned' eighteenth-century pianos had been thrown out: there is not even one Walter instrument listed.

2 F. G. Wegeler & F. Ries: *Biographische Notizen über L. von [sic] Beethoven*, Coblenz 1838, p. 99. Czerny taken from H. C. Robbins Landon: *Beethoven, a documentary Study*, London 1970, p. 62.

interesting description of many of these pianists:

> Clementi's manner is distinguished by the regular position of the hands, a firm touch and tone, clear fluent execution and a correct declamation, and also in part by great velocity and dexterity of the fingers.
>
> Cramer's and Dussek's manner: beautiful *cantabile*, avoidance of all coarse effects, a surprising smoothness in the runs and passages as a substitute for fluency, which is less necessary in their works; also a beautiful legato linked to the use of the pedal.
>
> Mozart's school: clear and markedly brilliant playing based more on staccato than legato; a witty and lively execution. The pedal is rarely used and never necessary. . . . Mozart's manner, which was so excellently perfected by Hummel, was more suited to the German *fortepiani* which combine a delicate and shallow touch with a great clarity, and thus are best adapted for general use and use by children. . . .

In the development of the piano between 1780 and 1820, Vienna and London played a major role. An exchange of each other's new devices and effects was brought about by the travelling virtuosi. Cramer and Clementi came to Vienna, Haydn and Hummel came to London; a Broadwood piano was given to Beethoven in 1817 (it arrived in 1818). Paris, too, was to enter this friendly competition; the Erard instruments of 1803 owned by Beethoven and Prince Lichnowsky were of considerable influence, and Beethoven radically changed his Third Piano Concerto (autograph: 1800) after the French instrument's arrival. But at the moment Paris, and indeed most of France, was in the throes of The Terror and its aftermath, so that French musical instruments were out of the European scene for the next few years.

The English grand pianos (*piano forme clavecin* was the French term, to distinguish it from the more usual spinet-form of piano so popular in France and England) differed in several important respects from the Viennese instruments. In the first place, the overall construction of the British instruments was more robust and mechanically superior (the beautiful brass hinges were a tribute to a sea-faring nation whose ships boasted the finest brass fittings in the world), the 'corpus' was usually placed on a secure wooden trellis with sturdy cross-beams, as opposed to the graceful but fragile Louis XVI legs of the Walter instruments. The English action was far heavier than that of the average Austrian or German piano; solider and less likely to go out of tune, but lacking the pearly evenness of the best Stein or Walter keyboards. Even Streicher, the piano manufactor and Beethoven's friend, complained of the heavy action of his Broadwood – 'the tone was beautiful but the action too heavy.'[1]

The principal difference in the pedals (knee pedals for the Viennese) was the damper. On Viennese instruments, these dampers (*Pianozug*) were often split into two, one for the lower and one for the higher register; the dampers when applied had an intriguing but very muffled sound which, however, could be gradually raised to create a kind of crescendo. When on 'full,' the overtones practically disappeared and the whole sound appeared to be lined in cotton wool. The English instruments, on the other hand, had a unique device called the *sopra una corda*, by which the piano hammers could be shifted so that they hit only one string. By operating the pedal gradually, the

---

1 Thayer-Forbes II, 695. In 1792 Rellstab in Berlin sold 'English fortepianos of a much larger *corpus* than usual, and of a tonal beauty such as has not yet been seen in Berlin; they go to *a'''*.' In the *Journal des Luxus und der Moden* of 1794, the London correspondent writes on 25 March 1794, 'Broadwood makes the finest large fortepianos in harpsichord shape [i.e. grand pianos]; the usual price for such an instrument is from 70 to 80 guineas.' Horst Walter: 'Haydns Klaviere', *Haydn-Studien* II (1970), Heft 4, p. 269, n. 92.

hammers could be shifted so that they hit one string, then two strings (and then three, as far as the instruments had three, which in 1795 they generally did for the upper notes); fascinating effects could be made by using half or all the *sopra una corda* (so that, as it were, the hammers hit about one-and-a-half strings) in conjunction with the sustaining pedal – which was standard equipment on both Viennese and English pianos. The *sopra una corda* is markedly different from the Viennese damper in that the former cuts down the number of strings used but does not smother the tone, while the latter smothers the tone but the number of strings remains constant. It is interesting to see, from the astute F. S. Silverstolpe (whose correspondence illuminates so much of Haydn's activity in Vienna at the turn of the century), how the *sopra una corda* arrived at Vienna:

> The only commission of my Count that I have been able to execute is about the piano: but I flatter myself that I have done it well. – I found one at the same instrument maker from whom I got the other one, that is, Walther. It is from the same wood and has the same outward look as the previous one but has great advantages as far as tone and strength are concerned. Usually each key has only two strings. But here there is a new and excellent invention: if one raises the left knee and activates a pedal, the key hits three strings all at once, by which one gets a forte that is superior to that of the earlier pianos, for now the tone [of the forte] is more like the piano tone and thus more natural. The invention was made long ago in England but was not imitated here till now. . . .[1] (5 June 1802).

As if the music of the late piano trios and sonatas did not bear eloquent enough witness to Haydn's interest in the new kind of English piano, we have still more evidence. Haydn brought back with him from England a handsome Longman & Broderip piano, which was sold after his death for 700 Gulden. Vincent Novello, visiting Abbé Stadler in 1829, saw the instrument:

> The Abbé then walked across the room and opened a Grand Piano Forte which he informed me was the instrument that belonged to Haydn. It was one of Longman & Broderip's, the compass from FF in the bass with the added keys up to C in alt [*c''''*]. Haydn had brought it with him from England and had retained it till death, when it came into the possession of l'Abbé Stadler. The latter told me he had often heard Haydn play upon it when he used to call to see him. I need not add that I sat down and played with peculiar pleasure.

When Haydn returned to Vienna in 1795, bringing with him the handsome new 'Grand Piano Forte' by Longman & Broderip, he already had a piano in his possession, one by [Wenzel?] Schanz, a Viennese manufacturer whose instruments Haydn, as we know, preferred to those of Walter. Haydn sold his Schanz for 200 ducats – an enormous sum – to someone in the year 1809. Apart from the British piano, Haydn soon (1801) received another large piano from the Parisian firm of Erard; Beethoven was to receive one, too, in 1803, and so was Prince Lichnowsky. We mention these Viennese and French pianos in Haydn's possession to show the composer's familiarity with European keyboard instruments. The Schanz has completely disappeared, and the Erard was last seen a hundred years ago in an attic in Rohrau, used by Haydn's descendants as a flour bin. The Longman & Broderip piano (or an identical one) survives in private possession in Vienna.[2]

1 Mörner 390. Abbé Stadler and Vincent Novello: *A Mozart Pilgrimage*, p. 157 & note on p. 347. Note that Walter seems to have constructed a kind of 'reverse' *sopra una corda*.
2 Walter, 'Haydns Klaviere' op. cit., pp. 280–3.

The *sopra una corda* device, known in England as the 'shifting pedal', produced a fascinating effect because of the vibrations of the unused strings, which resounded sympathetically and with an ethereal *timbre*. It was not until Beethoven's Fourth Concerto (1807) that we find that composer specifically requiring the *sopra una corda*, but there were obviously many times when Beethoven's earlier music, and Haydn's late piano music, benefited from this great innovation. Beethoven will no doubt have first heard the effect when trying out Haydn's new Longman & Broderip piano in 1795. Unfortunately, the modern grand piano cannot reproduce this effect, nor does it even approximate to the overtone-rich, delicate, metallic sound, of the late eighteenth-century fortepiano, compared with which the Steinway and Bechstein are crude, clumsy pieces of Victorian pomposity.

Mozart's piano playing was celebrated in its day, but we have seen that Czerny thought Mozart's playing 'based more on staccato than legato'. Beethoven also thought Mozart's playing lacked legato. 'Beethoven said [once] to Czerny that he had heard Mozart play; [Mozart] had a delicate but choppy touch, with no legato, which Beethoven at first found very strange, since he was accustomed to treat the pianoforte like an organ.' Another time, Czerny tells us: 'Beethoven, who had heard Mozart play, later said that his touch was neat and clean, but rather empty, flat, and antiquated.'[1] Haydn, as we know, considered Mozart the greatest musical genius of all time. Griesinger (56) tells us Haydn's very words: 'Mozart's loss is irreparable; I will never forget his piano playing so long as I live – that went to the heart.' Obviously Haydn was talking of Mozart's musical mind, not so much his technique. Then, taste had greatly changed after Mozart's death, and especially was this true of London, where as we have seen a whole group of pianists had grown up almost entirely with only the vaguest knowledge of Mozart's music or his piano playing. It is probably true that the English school owed its existence to Clementi. Mozart had spoken harshly of Clementi in 1782 – 'He has great facility with his right hand. His star passages are thirds. Apart from that he has not a penny's worth of taste or feeling; he is a mere *mechanicus*.'[2] But more than a decade had passed, and no doubt Clementi's technique, too, had changed. Moreover, the centre of the British piano world had passed to a younger generation, many of them Clementi's personal pupils, all of them influenced by his technique and his compositions. There is some other evidence that even the great Mozart's technique had been surpassed. One of the distinguished contributors to Grove's *Dictionary* was A. J. Hipkins, who managed to find someone who had actually heard Mozart play. Hipkins tells us:[3] Mozart 'was yet not a piano-forte-player in the sense that Clementi was. . . . The late Herr Saust, who heard Mozart play, told the writer that Mozart had no remarkable execution on the instrument, and that, for instance, he would not have compared, as a virtuoso, with Dussek.'

The decade 1781–1791, when Mozart was in Vienna, was the period when Haydn was most influenced by Mozart's playing and his way of writing for the piano. One only need compare Haydn's Concerto for fortepiano or harpsichord in D, Opus 21 (XVIII: 11), published in 1784 but probably composed about 1781, with the

1 The first Czerny quotation from an interview with Otto Jahn in Vienna on 15 September 1852; the second from L. Nohl: *Beethoven. Nach den Schilderungen seiner Zeitgenossen*, Stuttgart 1877, p. 9. The translations from *The Mozart Companion*, ed. H. C. Robbins Landon & Donald Mitchell, London 1956, 33 n. 3.
2 Letter of 16 January 1782. Anderson vol. ii, 793. We have always compared Mozart's original German in the new definitive Deutsch-Bauer edition and have occasionally changed a small phrase of the Anderson translation.
3 Grove I, vol. ii, 717.

'Genzinger' Sonata in E flat No. 59 (XVI: 49) composed in 1790, to see how profoundly Haydn assimilated Mozart's piano technique. Confronted with an entirely new technique in London, much more brilliant (with those typically Clementian thirds and octaves in the right hand, the use of fast-moving triplets and sextuplets, the more sophisticated adaptation of the old 'Alberti' or broken bass chords, etc.), Haydn adopted the skeleton of the language and made it his own. The confrontation with Clementi the pianist and composer came not only through the public concerts at which they sometimes, particularly in the Opera Concert of 1795, participated together, but even more directly through Miss Therese Jansen, Clementi's pupil. In June 1794 Clementi dedicated to her 'Three Sonatas for the Piano Forte', Op. 33, which Longman & Broderip published; the third of these also exists as a piano Concerto, and it was known in Vienna, too, where the only copy (as a Concerto) is preserved; it was signed by Beethoven's secret teacher of 1793, 'Johann Schenck / 1 Javier [*sic*] 1796'. Even the most cursory glance at these three Sonatas for Miss Jansen will show (1) the difference between them and the Mozartian technique; and (2) how much Haydn benefited from these late Clementi keyboard works.[1]

If we examine Haydn's Op. 70, dedicated to the Dowager Princess Esterházy, we may find many pages which bear eloquent witness to the new type of piano writing. For example, the beginning of 'Sonata III' (Trio No. 34), an Allegro of great majesty and brilliance. Here we notice Haydn exploiting (bar one, r.h.) the very top notes of most late eighteenth-century pianos: Haydn's own Longman & Broderip went up further to c'''', but these 'extended keys', as they were referred to in contemporary English language, were so rare on the Continent as to be practically non-existent, and Haydn, thinking of a market outside England, sensibly limited his upper range of writing to the usual f'''. The extraordinary effect of the opening is not only the exploitation of the very top register but the simultaneous use of the low register as well, the one being marked *legato* and the other *staccato*. Notice Haydn's wide skips in the r.h. of bar 4, again using the top register (f'''); and how well he has calculated the length of time that the low B flat can sound in the bottom note of the l.h. in bars 5–10; by repeating it at the beginning of each bar. Haydn keeps up the wide and at the same time dense range of sound. The student will also see that the violin part, while not virtuoso, is absolutely essential, adding independent patterns of its own (e.g. the downward scale in bars 5 and 7); while the 'cello part provides a constant touch of colour and strength to what would have been a wiry, delicate and metallic bass sound in the piano. What is so typically second-London-period about this proud page of music is not only the change in layout of the piano – its exploitation of the whole keyboard and the easy virtuosity of the writing – but the enormous self-confidence of such a passage as bars 5ff. Haydn may have had his doubts about where the trio, as a form, was going prior to his London visits; now he knew precisely what he wanted, and what the London public wanted, and was able to please both.

Being a private form, as opposed to his 'public' symphonies and even the 'public' string quarters of the 1794 season (Opp. 71, 74), Haydn was freed from certain

---

1 Riccardo Allorto: *Le Sonate per pianoforte di Muzio Clementi: Studio critico e catalogo tematico*, Florence 1959, esp. pp. 120f. Haydn owned a set of Clementi piano trios, apparently op. 27 or 29, which is listed in the Elssler *Verzeichniss musicalischer Werke* . . . as No. 121 'Clementi. Three Sonatas for the Pianoforte or / harpsichord with an accompaniment for a Violin / and Violoncello, London. groß fol: gebunden.' The description fits either op. 27 or 29, both published 1791, 1793 respectively, op. 27 by Longman & Broderip, op. 29 by J. Dale. Allorto, pp. 114–118. Alan Tyson: *Muzio Clementi Thematic catalogue*, Tutzing 1967.

impedimenta that automatically went with music composed for a large public audience. This is, of course, an obvious point but it needs to be made. Quoting an extension of the opening subject of Trio 36 (XV: 22), Charles Rosen, one of the few recent critics of Haydn's trios with something new and profound to say about them, writes:[1]

> . . . This feeling of spacious, relaxed, almost improvised expansion is almost never found in the symphonies, and rarely in the quartets. This is why the tempo mark for the majority of opening sonata movements in the trios is Allegro moderato, occurring almost twice as often as Allegro. Not only is the organization looser than that of the quartets, but also the effects are broader, with a brilliance and a massiveness that the sonatas for piano solo never reach and only approach in the early C minor [Sonata No. 33, XVI: 20 of 1771] and the two very late ones in E flat major [Sonatas Nos. 59 & 62, XVI: 49 and 52, 1790 and 1794 respectively].

When Haydn arrived in London in January 1791, he was not only confronted by the physical presence of the new British grand piano, the characteristics of which we have been at some pains to describe and analyze, but he must have had many discussions with other 'eminent professors' such as Dussek and Clementi. Piano teachers, too, were at pains to stress the new characteristics of the piano, as opposed to the spinet-form of the instrument, or the harpsichord. Pianists were also aware that a good player could produce a fine *legato* from the piano, something which occupied Beethoven's thoughts, too. The *European Magazine* of 1796 carried a series of reports by a piano teacher signed 'J.B.'; although published in 1796, the series was written earlier. It is entitled 'Desultory Remarks on the Study and Practice of Music, addressed to a young lady while under the tuition of an eminent master, written in the years 1790–1 and 2'. 'J. B.' seems to have resided at Bath. In a letter to the *European Magazine* signed 'Bath, 5 Dec. 1796' the writer mentions that 'Haydn, Clementi, Giornovicchi and many other of the eminent Professors of Music' admired the young lady's 'skill, taste, and expression.' She was a pupil of J. L. Dussek's. We have not been able to identify either 'J. B.' (Joah Bates?) or the young lady. 'J. B.' writes:

> Much must depend on the Inherent Powers of an Instrument. That richness, that dignity of Sound, which a GRAND PIANO FORTE will yield, under the hands of a spirited and judicious Performer, cannot be produced from the feeble SPINET, or the quilly tinkling HARPSICHORD; but as you have at command the best Modern Instrument, improved to a state of excellence, it has all the properties of Tone. . . .
> The mellow, impressive, Organ-like Tone is superior in significance and effect to that quilly and vapid Sound produced by the generality of Piano-Forte Players; those even who are *vastly* admired for what is called Execution, in an age wherein Rapidity of Finger is held to be the Criterion of capital performance. . . .[2]

It will be noted that Haydn, in these late piano works, cultivates assiduously a smooth *legato* technique, which can be seen in many places, for instance in the principal subject of Op. 70, No. 1.

Earlier in the Chronicle (*supra*, p. 159), we have seen Haydn attesting to the excellence of Charles Clagget's pianos in London. We have a final testimony of this kind that Haydn made privately to another London piano manufacturer, William Stodart (one of whose instruments, owned by Mr Edward Croft-Murray in Richmond, was used for a programme in the series prepared by the present writer for the British Broadcasting Corporation in 1958 entitled 'The Unknown Haydn').

1 Op. cit., p. 357; reprinted by permission of Faber and Faber Ltd and the Viking Press, Inc.
2 *European Magazine*, 1796, pp. 180f.

Haydn called [in the year 1795] at his [Stodart's] shop in Lad Lane to see it [an 'upright grand pianoforte in the form of a bookcase'] and expressed himself delighted with the new possibilities it foreshadowed in case-making and with the quality of the tone.[1]

Thus it is clear that Haydn's newly awakened interest in the piano, and in music for that instrument, was the result of his English trips and the many and varied contacts with pianos and pianists that occurred from 1791 to 1795. We may now proceed to the actual music of Op. 70, the first-fruits of this new contact with the keyboard.

The first of the Op. 70 series is in A major, and like the great majority of these late trios, has three movements (sometimes the second leads into the third, a typical feature of the trios that you never find in a Haydn symphony, for the simple reason that audiences then applauded between movements at public concerts). It starts out with three *forte* chords, much in the manner of the 'Salomon' Quartets of 1793. Unlike such chords at a public concert – and we must remember that the 1793 Quartets were designed for and played at London public concerts in 1794 – these at the beginning of the Trio were not so much stately curtain raisers as foils to set off the cantabile main theme, which begins very unassumingly and on the up-beat. The across-bar phrasing

is therefore 'set up', as it were, by the three on-the-beat opening chords which are, of course, not repeated when the music returns for the *da capo* after the first double bar. We shall note a similar, non-repeated opening chord at the beginning of Trio 38.

The innocuous beginning is part of Haydn's grand scheme. As bland as is the opening, the development section is extremely involved. Take the following modulation, which begins after a half-close in the dominant of F sharp. What follows would appear to be an enharmonic plunge into the dominant of E flat but in reality it is a Neapolitan preparation for the six-four chord of D minor. The fabric of this musical material is, as one might suspect in late Haydn, all derived from earlier material. The principal theme was

whereas the triplet figure had its origins in what used to be called, in nineteenth-century textbooks, the 'bridge passage'. Following the half-cadence in the dominant of F sharp, we find the bass (left hand of the piano) utilizing the first three notes of the main theme, while the violin *simultaneously plays the cancrizans in augmentation*; even the triplet figure in the piano's right hand is merely a spacing-out of the figure. Students of the history of mean versus tempered tuning will have noticed that while the piano and violin are noted in E flat, the 'cello is still in sharps, another proof, if one were needed, that not only is all late eighteenth-century music with piano written in equal temperament, but also music without piano. Haydn generally took the easier

---

1 Rosamond E. M. Harding: *The Piano-Forte. Its History traced to the Great Exhibition of 1851*, Cambridge 1933, pp. 6off.

notation *for the players*, as did occasionally Mozart (when rewriting the oboe parts in the Finale of the G minor Symphony K. 550, he notated them incorrectly in flat keys rather than in the original sharp-key notation which was correct but extremely difficult for the players to read).[1]

1 W. A. Mozart: *Neue Ausgabe sämtliche Werke*, Serie IV, Werkgruppe 11, Sinfonien Band 9 (Landon), Kassel 1957, pp. XI and 177 plus *kritischer Bericht*.

The A minor *Andante* is in three-part form (A–B–A'), the third part elaborately varied with almost extravagant ornamentation in the piano r.h., again straining the upper register of the instrument constantly. The middle 'B' section is in A major with one of those pre-Schubertian lyrical melodies that Haydn was then beginning to use quite frequently. The strength and, one might say, comforting beauty are partly based on the fact that most of the harmonies are in root position:

At the end of the 'A″' section there is a pause, as if for more extravagant piano figurations; in fact we go straight into the Finale, a procedure we shall frequently encounter. The Finale itself is a kind of Gypsy Rondo in three-four time. It will be seen that of the London piano Trios after No. 31 in G, almost all are in three-four (one is in six-eight and two in two-four), and the same applies to the Trios of 1795–7. Connoisseurs will notice that Haydn has now begun to use the accent (>), partly to replace the *fz* but partly to establish a less violent marking than *fz*. The Hungarian (Eastern European) elements of this Finale are, first, the strong syncopations in the main theme, and secondly, the little acciaccature[1] that are used cadentially:

In terms of its formal construction the movement is original, too: it is neither a sonata nor a rondo nor a sonata-rondo nor an A–B–A. Basically the movement is two-part. The first 28 bars ('A') are a-b-a, going from I-V-I as if it were a rondo. The next section ('B') uses the syncopations from the main theme and indeed most of its basic rhythms, but is a kind of new section all the same; it modulates from the tonic to the dominant but ends in a V[7] chord with a pause. We then have the beginning again, but at the end of what might be called the recapitulation we plunge again into the 'B' section, which is however extended like another development. The whole is linked together by the Hungarian syncopations and by the brilliant bravura work of the piano. We note the repeated octaves in the l.h. which will now become a regular feature of these late trios, and indeed of Haydn's late piano style. This Finale is a genuinely new and original substitute for the usual three-four 'Tempo di Minuetto' with which many of the contemporary trios closed, Haydn's included (e.g. Trio 30 with flute instead of violin, 1790). We suggest that Trio 32's successful Finale paved the way for the famous Gypsy Rondo, just as earlier in his career Haydn often tries out an experiment and, finding it successful, repeats it even more brilliantly.

The second Trio (No. 33) of the set is in G minor. In each of the three sets of trios of the 1794–5 period, there is one work in the minor key, a much higher percentage than in the 'public' symphonies (only one Paris Symphony and one London Symphony) and only one each of the Quartets of 1790 ('Op. 64'), 1793 ('Op. 71, Op. 74') and 1796–7

---

1 We use the term as in Callcott's *Musical Grammar*, London 1806, p. 225. 'The Acciaccatura or Half Beat, is also used with great effect in [the Terzett from Mozart's *Zauberflöte*, 'Seyd uns zum zweytenmal'; example follows: No. 16, bar 1, Viol. I]'.

('Op. 76'). Haydn's use of the minor keys in his late works has been a source of puzzlement, even exasperation, to many scholars and critics, including Tovey. Having been brought up on the enormous minor-keyed movements of Beethoven, and the anguished works of Mozart, especially in this very G minor, nineteenth-century critics found that Haydn had somehow begged the issue by ending his late-period minor-keyed works in the major. Having rediscovered the *Sturm und Drang* period of Haydn and his contemporaries, which flourished in Austria from about 1766 to 1773, and which contained passionate music in the minor keys, modern critics on the whole decided that the later Haydn somehow lacked the single-minded dedication of this earlier period. And it is perfectly true that Haydn never quite regained the dour sound of the Sinfonia 'La Passione' (No. 49) or the furious concentration of the outer movements in the C minor Symphony No. 52. Even the rhapsodic, texturally dense C minor piano Sonata of 1771 stands dramatically isolated among its fellows, just as the contrapuntally intricate string Quartets of Op. 20 in the minor key (Nos. 3 & 5) represent to a certain extent an emotional cul-de-sac – at least judging from Haydn's later career.

In fact it seems clear that Haydn's attitude towards the minor key changed sharply: it was deliberately no longer one of emotional commitment in the sense of the 1772 symphonies and quartets. That is not to say that Haydn's later music was not emotionally committed, but rather that his sense of values had undergone a complete metamorphosis. If in the process his music lost some of the intensity, single-mindedness and even naked power of the period 1766 to 1773, it gained in sophistication of technique, in integration of style and above all in balance. Many of Haydn's *Sturm und Drang* works are flawed masterpieces: they penetrate deeply into the essence of music but occasionally at the expense of formal symmetry. The great *Missa Cellensis in honorem B. V. M.* of 1766 rises to heights of nobility and grandeur, but it is too long as a whole and there are some disproportionately lengthy single movements; the same applies to the *Stabat Mater* of 1767. In taming his nervous energy, Haydn lost something of his erratic brilliance; but he must have recognized that it was easy to fall into the trap of a Franz Beck, one of the most brilliant and original musical minds of the 1760s, whose youthful promise, never tamed and never subjected to the rigours of a Haydnesque self-discipline, died away in a half-century of provincial sloth.

In this vast shift of values, Haydn's attitude towards the minor key had so shifted as to make the G minor of Haydn's Op. 20, No. 3 (1772) emotionally light years away from the G minor of this Trio of 1794. Even the Symphony 'La Poule' (No. 83, 1785) begins like a great *Sturm und Drang* work, only to subside to Hanswurst comedy with the second subject and its clucking oboe accompaniment; the movement ends in G major, and Haydn never returns to G minor at all. Here in the Trio, there is no such stylistic shock. We begin with an Andante movement in double variation form which is much more a piano solo than the other music of this set: cf. the beginning of Trio 34, quoted above. The mood is wary and the music rather angular; but the breadth of the melody, although Baroque in spirit and almost as dotted as a French overture, is remarkable in that it extends from d' to the top of the average piano's range, f'''. It is interesting to observe how carefully Haydn has laid out the basic melodic line so that the first melodic highpoint comes at bar 5 with the $e\,flat'''$, while the second, purposely stronger, changes $e\,flat$ to $e\,natural'''$ and then reaches the top f''' only to plunge down the scale to $b\,flat$ below middle C. The closing passage in the relative major, linked to the preceding material by that dotted figure in bar 14, is to be of great importance: Haydn takes the music and reshapes it as the subject of the second variation section.

Formally this movement resembles closely the double variation form of the famous Sonata in F minor ('Andante con variazioni' of 1793) composed the year before: group I tonic minor: group II tonic major, with the alternation continuing. In the Sonata we have a famous coda to end the work; in the Trio, a different procedure is adopted. Group II of the Trio, in the tonic major, is marked *cantabile* and is further contrasted with the first group in that there are no dotted figures whatever. The second variation of the group II music turns into a Presto and is a lively and spirited extension of the previous material, now in six-eight time (bars 1–16).[1]

The second movement is in the submediant, as it was in Symphony No. 83 (1785): one more flirtation with third-related keys. This 'Adagio ma non troppo' is in Haydn's favourite three-four time, with an intricate and highly ornamented melody in the piano's r.h., the strings accompanying like the orchestra of a piano concerto. The whole movement, serenely beautiful, is what one might call an un-slow adagio, not a tautology in Haydn: the pulse of the movement is seen to be quavers rather than crotchets right at the beginning, and as early as bar 3 we have semiquaver sextuplets which become the basic pulse of the music for most of the movement. By using this sextuplet rhythm, Haydn is able to set up a Baroque sequence, after the close on the dominant, which is an extenuation of the material, as it were, across all the barlines: aurally it is hardly possible to distinguish the bar-lines at all. This tiny sequence, incidentally, a total of six bars, is all there is by way of a 'middle section' to the movement: thus it resembles the overture form without a development as in Mozart's *Le nozze di Figaro*. There the economy was dictated by theatrical necessity (long overtures to comic operas are usually self-defeating), here by the fact that the exposition and recapitulation have long written-out repeats, e.g. the closing music which consists of a bar, repeated (a-a) with a third cadential bar added (a-a-b), the whole three bars then played again with the piano in the upper octave. To avoid prolixity, Haydn simply reduces the whole middle part to half-a-dozen bars (23–30).

The bluff presto Finale in six-eight returns to the time signature of the first movement's conclusion. The Finale is in sonata form, the second subject being clearly derived from the first, and is in the tonic minor; but for the recapitulation, the composer turns to G major, in which key the piece ends. The piano's r.h. has the opening statement of the theme, and also its appearance in the relative major, in octaves; but they lie very well in the hand, as do the broken octaves in the transition (bars 19f.). All the brilliant-sounding figurations in the piano are actually much easier than they sound: subtle flattery for the amateurs (the opposite of a work like Mozart's Concerto K. 503, which sounds much easier than it is).

We have spoken of the first movement of Trio 34, the most virtuoso of the set. The second movement begins with a piano solo marked, in the first edition, 'The left hand alone': it is a 20-bar passage in the austere two-part counterpoint that Haydn always appreciates. As the variations unfold, we see that the theme is capable of much ornamentation. The first variation has the violin doubling the top part of the piano l.h. at the octave, while the piano r.h. adds a new series of figurations. In the third variation, the piano is still playing 'left hand alone', but the figuration has become more rapid (semiquavers), while the violin has a brand new melody above it. In the final variation, the tempo has now increased by having the piano r.h. play in

---

1 For an excellent analysis of how Haydn develops this material, see Rosen, op. cit., pp. 83–7, where the original material of group II is placed over the six-eight Presto extension.

demisemiquavers. The whole movement is a typical example of Haydn's subtle art of the variation. It is in G major, the submediant.

The Finale is one of the three–four *deutscher Tanz*-like movements with which Haydn prefers to conclude his late piano trios. It is more robust than a comparable 'Tempo di Minuetto' but not so robust as some of the late examples of the form. The middle section is a solo for the violin in the (for strings) rather awkward key of B flat minor; the music sounds twenty years before its time, like a piece of Austrian *Biedermeier*, and here we realize how different this kind of movement is from a minuet. A kind of rustic waltz, it will have sounded decidedly exotic in England (bars 33–46). The work ends with a short passage like a *perpetuum mobile* in slow motion: six bars repeated, growing 'sempre più forte' and ending abruptly with two *ff* chords – the kind of effect that Haydn obviously did not think workable with a full orchestra.

In May 1795, Preston registered at Stationers Hall the three new Haydn piano Trios (35–37) dedicated to the new reigning Princess Marie Hermenegild Esterházy, wife of Nicolaus II. It was for the Princess that Haydn would compose his last six masses (1796–1802); we know that she was fond of Haydn and made his old age comfortable in many small ways. The dedication of these Trios suggests a mutual sympathy that antedates her becoming the reigning Princess Esterházy.

The first of these Trios is No. 35 in C, a bold, forthright work in the usual three movements. It begins with a slow introduction which Haydn marks 'Adagio pastorale' (in six-eight time). It is one of the shortest of his introductions – we are not counting the chord or chords that introduce many of the Salomon Quartets of 1793 – but it efficiently sets the stage for a large-scale work. Like Symphony No. 98, the thematic material is largely that of the ensuing 'Vivace assai'; but like Symphony No. 97, not all the relationship between the introduction and the movement proper is immediately apparent. When we arrive at the dominant, the main theme appears again: almost always a warning that there is more thematical material coming and/or that there will be large-scale extension or development in the rest of the time allotted before the double bar. The repetition of the principal theme in the dominant is a way of postponing other thematic material, of increasing the motivic tension. Here, we suddenly find ourselves in the middle of a country scene with peasants stamping out a dance to the tune of the bagpipes:

Now, and only now, do we really understand the description 'pastorale' for the beginning. During the remaining material before the double bar we notice a further connection with the introduction. It is a superb example of the subtle way in which Haydn is now able to bind a seemingly loosely constructed movement together.

Stylistically we notice the many repeated series of broken octaves in the bass line of the piano:

It is also worthwhile recalling the amount of personal taste which the performers were expected to inject into the music. Although there is a good 'skeleton' of phrasing marks – quite enough for the intelligent performer even if reading *a prima vista* – there are practically no dynamic marks at all. They appear only in the development section and consist of three *fz* (for all three instruments) and one *p cresc. f* in the piano part: the lead-back to the recapitulation. Otherwise there are no dynamic marks at all in the whole movement. There are also none whatever in the second movement until five bars before the end (*piano* in all instruments), and hardly any in the Finale except for some *fz* and a short section in the piano part at the beginning of the second part which is marked at first *piano* and then *forte*. This extreme austerity with regard to the dynamic markings of the late trios is rather odd. Public works like symphonies, especially when *not* played by Haydn's own orchestra at Eszterháza, had to be marked efficiently as far as dynamic range; and so did the string quartets which would be played by a 'new' quartet in London; but apparently Haydn thought his British amateurs possessed enough taste to be able to shape the dynamic content of his new trios with only the minimum of hints.

The slow movement, marked 'Molto Andante' and in barred C time, is an entirely new kind of form: written straight through with no double bar and no repeat signs, it is a kind of variation on a single theme. The melody itself consists of a very regular four plus four bars (progressing I-I; V-V♯) the quiet strength of which derives largely from the frequent use of chords in their root positions. It is another example of Haydn's great violin tunes which are found with ever increasing frequency in these late trios. Bars 8–16 are an ornamented version of the theme for piano solo, 17–24 the theme again varied in the tonic minor (with modulations to E flat and C minor), 25–34 the theme still differently varied in G major again. At this point one would expect a strong contrast: a section in the minor with new thematic material, or something similar. But Haydn is pursuing another monothematic movement, and so we have the theme in the violin, in E minor, modulating to C major (bars 40ff.) and a piano solo, again modulating back (bars 52ff.) to the main theme as it was at the very beginning. Since bars 52–67 are identical with bars 1–16, and the succeeding bars 68–86 identical with 17–34, we have what sounds like a typical A–B–A form, except that the whole movement is securely based on one single melody. The last seven bars (lengthened rather cleverly into sounding like eight by having the final bar divided into two minims, each with a hold) are a tiny codetta. The movement is an effective contrast between the two robust outer movements.

The Finale (Presto) might be from a larger instrumental work, almost a symphony. It reminds one faintly of Symphony No. 97's Finale, though of course the Trio is in a much smaller formal scale. It is in what one might call Haydn's sonata-finale form: it is sonata in the sense that we have a rough approximation of exposition (with a very rudimentary closing subject in the dominant just before the double bar, as in Symphony No. 104/I; this tune also appears just before the end of the movement), development (which modulates to the subdominant and then slowly round to V^7) and recapitulation. It is a finale in that the subject is a rondo-like theme in two-four time and also in the fact that the first eight bars have a repeat sign, as if the form were rondo rather than sonata.

The second Trio (36) is unquestionably the greatest that Haydn has composed hitherto. It is also on a very large scale: the first movement, in Haydn's characteristic trio speed of 'Allegro moderato', consists of 234 bars (as against 160 bars of Trio 35's 'Vivace assai'). It has a leisurely, almost improvisatory style that soon becomes typical of these late trios. Part of the solidity comes from Haydn's use of sextuplets in two-four time: indeed sextuplet subdivisions assume an increasingly dominant role in time signatures of two-four and four-four. Bars 1–15 have as their quickest denomination straight semiquavers, but bars 16–45 have semiquaver sextuplets in one or the other part throughout, and so do bars 107–132 and 138–149 of the development section. These sextuplets have the paradoxical effect of urgent forward motion (as they do in Beethoven's triplets) and at the same time of massive repose: forward motion when they are written, for example, thus:

and repose when they are an accompanimental figure, as in the example opposite. The second passage, from the development section, is based on the broad and important subsidiary theme; and it, in turn, is the logical outcome of the main subject: (1) between bars 1 and 2 is an upward jump of a fourth, just as there is in the second subject; (2) the 'accompanying' violin figure in broken arpeggios is the nucleus for the

piano's accompaniment to the second subject, at first

and later turned round as in our example. Moreover, the leading figure

is based on two figures already seen in the exposition, the dotted figure (shortened) in the transition (bars 19–23), and the three quavers at bars 36 and 38 – also the transition. The whole is a gigantic series of connected small motifs, but Haydn has managed to make the end result sound spacious, broad, improvisatory. The important role of the violin will be seen even in the few musical examples here quoted; also Haydn's new device of crossing the hands, something he had attempted in 1790 with piano Sonata 59, much to the discomfort of the recipient, Maria Anna von Genzinger, who was unable to play the passage in question (CCLN, 108).

As the reader will have gathered, mediant and submediant key relationships, within the movements and between, have come to play an important part of Haydn's tonal scheme in these late trios. Thus it is perhaps no longer a surprise to find the second movement of this extraordinary Trio in G major, the mediant. What is, however, surprising is the violent emotion that wells up throughout this intensely personal,

rhapsodic 'Adagio ma non troppo', so personal that it sometimes borders on the eccentric. With one sweep Haydn has achieved a new kind of piano style: broad in sound yet terse in organization, with a free and brilliant piano part for which nothing in the whole of Haydn's previous *oeuvre* has remotely prepared us. Again, a triplet undercurrent pervades the whole Adagio, and this gives a curiously unsettled, uneasy rhythmic background that verges often on the ominous and only resolves itself in the final bar of music.

The Adagio seems to have started life as a piano piece. At least this would seem to be the explanation for a manuscript in the Esterházy Archives (Ms. mus. I. 151, from the Haydn Legacy) signed by Haydn and with one important holograph addition (*fz* at bar 57) and at least one very significant cancellation. The MS. was copied by Johann Elssler on English paper with an English watermark, presumably in 1794. We suggest that the Elssler MS. represents an earlier version[1] for the following reasons: the published version is far more elaborately marked, as far as dynamics are concerned, and it is very unlikely that Haydn would have written the elaborate version first and then dropped all these essential dynamic marks afterwards. Moreover, one change, when the right hand crosses the left and proceeds down to the bottom of the piano's range, would seem to have been made for the player's benefit: the printed version is distinctly easier, for the skip between *F sharp'* and *d'''* with no break in between is really very tricky. Conversely, it would be highly unlikely to have rewritten the printed text and made it more difficult for the Elssler MS. The passage in question also illustrates the intensely rhapsodic style of the movement (bars 17–19).

We would also draw attention to the extraordinary scale passage in the piano's r.h. which rushes up in crescendo. Formally the movement is closely allied to the Adagio of Symphony No. 102, which Haydn turned into part of the piano Trio in F sharp minor (No. 40). Both trio movements are in *adagio* sonata form, and both are marked by the constant motion of triplets in the accompaniment. But although the G major Adagio from Trio 36 is outwardly in two parts, there is a strong tripartite feeling about the movement: after modulation to the dominant and a *legato* secondary subject, Haydn moves (bar 35) straight back to the tonic and begins the second part with the first subject in the tonic. Within four bars we are, however, well 'off-tonic' and clearly in a development section: there are a whole series of syncopated dynamic patterns and a long and ingenious lead-back to the tonic and the opening thematic material, so that we have the feeling of a recapitulation. The resolution of the final bar is brilliant and satisfying; the piano's l.h. and the strings sit on a G major chord marked with a pause, and after half-a-bar's rest, the piano has a G major arpeggio with the penultimate note *f sharp'*. The *f sharp* is at first extremely shocking, but when it moves to *g'*, nothing could have established the tonic (after such a harmonically unsettling movement) so securely and with such economy of means.

In keeping with the large-scale construction of the Trio, Haydn has a big Finale: 186 bars based on a kind of *deutscher Tanz*, with complicated off-beat rhythmic patterns and an almost eccentrically brilliant modulation at the beginning of the development section. After the usual cadence in the dominant, Haydn begins at once to modulate in a series of virtuoso arpeggios for the piano's r.h.: B flat ⟶ C minor ⟶ F minor ⟶ D flat major (which only appears in six-four spacing) ⟶ [*change of key signature from three flats to three sharps*] C sharp minor (in six-four spacing) ⟶ A major; and in A major we remain for several bars, establishing what is probably the first pivot in *tritonus* in the Viennese classical style: E flat to A major to E flat. In the middle of the development, still in three sharps, the theme is introduced in E major. This flirtation with the flattened supertonic is something we shall encounter in another work and under different circumstances: Sonata 62 (*infra*, p. 451). Tonally, the centre

---

1 It is published complete as an appendix to the Doblinger critical edition (Diletto Musicale 486, 1970, pp. 36–40).

The beginning of the slow movement (piano part) of the Piano Trio No. 36 in E flat, one of three Trios dedicated by Haydn to Princess Marie Josepha Hermenegild Esterházy, *née* Princess Liechtenstein, and published as Op. 71 in May or June 1795.

of this Finale expands the possibilities of the tonic-dominant relationship way beyond anything hitherto known except in huge operatic finales such as Haydn's *La fedeltà premiata* (1780) and in Mozart's operas from 1782–1791. The feeling of improvisation is further enhanced by a little cadenza for the piano just before the closing material, which provides a grounding to the particularly Romantic and rather nostalgic harmonies of the bars immediately preceding (160–70).

With the D minor Trio 37, Haydn's use of the 'minor' key reaches a point of no return. D minor is used only as the key of the first section of the double variation form in the opening movement; the movement ends in the major, the key of the alternating section. The second movement is in B flat: here a word might be inserted about the ambiguity of such keys in late Haydn. Since these movements in the minor key often end in the major, the use of what would be (in the minor) the relative major is actually no longer that but a third-related key, i.e. the flattened submediant. Of course, the sound of the tonic minor is still 'with us', and this creates a rather subtle ambivalence. In Trio 37, the Finale is in D major. There is only one point in this disintegration of the minor key in which Haydn can go even further, and that is the use of the tonic minor *only* for the slow introduction, as in Symphonies Nos. 98, 101 and 104. There is no doubt that Haydn's ruthless attitude towards his old *Sturm und Drang* minor keys – D minor has, in Haydn, no less a noble past than in Mozart: the *Sinfonia Lamentatione*, the lost *Missa Sunt bona mixta malis* of *c.* 1768 and the string Quartet Op. 9 No. 4 of *c.* 1768 are among the better known examples of the older master – is deliberate. Indeed, the previous Trio in E flat (36) goes much farther in the emotional scale than does this vivacious and brilliant D major piece.

Students of Haydn will have noticed the subtle difference, now, between *fz* (*forzato*) and the accent, of which the latter plays an ever more important role in the musical syntax. The violin and piano r.h. both have the following at the beginning of the first announcement of the section in major:

fz > *fz* > *fz* > | etc.

Altogether, Haydn's trio style is now extremely personal, and brought with it a need for change in the syntax. Occasionally, one feels Haydn's inspiration stronger than can be contained in the traditional notation, especially in the works to follow the present set.

Some of this fascinating and wilful eccentricity may be seen in the beginning of the slow movement. The ornaments have become so intricate that they almost obscure the basic tempo entirely: it is not until the violin takes over at the end of bar 8 and the piano settles down to legato semiquavers in the r.h. that we begin the sense 3/4 as the basic time signature. The curious *fz* in the piano, especially on the third beat of bar 6, should be noted; but even more the totally unexpected jump to the top of most people's piano, *f‴*, in the middle of bar 5. The skittishly irregular grouping of '11' in piano r.h., bar 7, is also typical.

In a sense, it is clear why the concept of the minor key and its doom-ridden, or at least anguished, emotional content would be out of place here, as it would in any such *Midsummer Night's Dream* atmosphere. Haydn's rhythmic displacement is also coupled with a new and enriched sense of chromatic passings notes, as in the final part of the slow movement. After another extravagant cadence for the piano (49), we have one of these bar-displacing, rhapsodic passages with extremely personal chromatic lines

(50–52) ending with yet another six-four cadence and trill. The final bars, in the tonic minor, have a quietly impersonal sadness about them (49–56).

The Finale is a racy and texturally lean movement (the theme is in Haydn's severe two-part writing, the violin as usual doubling the left hand), characterized by the off-beat accented return to the theme. It is a *bravura* piece for the piano which lies very well in the hand and sounds, as so often in the late trios, more difficult than it actually is (semiquavers at bars 38–50, also later, in recapitulation: notice how the violin's line, in contrary motion, serves to increase the tension). Another chromatic lead-back shows Haydn's sense of dynamic timing. The context is *forte*. Haydn presumes that the piano's l.h. will have died away automatically to *piano* by bar 92, so that, once the string's sound has ceased, Haydn has only to mark *piano* for the piano's r.h. and a kind of *subito p* will ensue: it all looks effortless. The *fz* is one of the off-beat accentuations which will lead us to the main subject (bars 83–93).

As suggested above, there is some evidence that the brilliant group of Three Trios Op. 73 dedicated to Rebecca Schroeter was one of the last things Haydn completed in the Summer of 1795 before he left England for ever. As a set, Op. 73 is the finest achievement of Haydn's trio style hitherto, and like all Haydn's truly popular music, it covers a large range of the composer's emotional gamut. In fact the three works are remarkably different. The D major (No. 38) is a bold, enormously forceful Trio, full of the new pianistic technique Haydn had now mastered and made his own; the G major Trio (39) turned out to be Haydn's most popular piano piece, because of the 'Gypsy Rondo' Finale; while the F sharp minor Trio (40) is arguably Haydn's greatest tragic work in the instrumental *oeuvre* of the second London period – worthy to rank with the *Scena di Berenice* or Symphony No. 102, the slow movement of which it shares in common.

One of the devices, almost rhetorical in effect, by which Haydn gains dramatic unity in the first movement of Trio 38 is the use of the fermata or pause. There are no less than ten fermate and one whole bar of rest *in lieu* of a fermata during the development section in this Allegro as opposed, for example, to one (just before the recapitulation) in Trio 40/I and none in Trio 36/I: two other movements similar in form. The opening theme is so quiet that Haydn thought it prudent to begin with a single *forte* chord, as in the string Quartet in E flat, Op. 71 No. 3; in both cases there is a pause after the chord, to lengthen the effect of the chord itself and to heighten the suspense before the actual movement begins. It is interesting to observe how Haydn binds the whole movement together from the material of the first subject: there is really no second subject in the strict sense, and the closing material (bars 57ff.), which also appears in the recapitulation, is the first thematic material not obviously drawn from the first subject. It will be noted that bars 13ff. derive most closely from the beginning. The violin part comes from the accented *staccati* of bars 4–5 (10–11), while the 'cello (with piano l.h.) and piano r.h.'s lines follow the *Urlinien* of the first subject (piano r.h. and violin *f sharp'–d''*; 'cello and piano l.h. *d–f sharp*). The way Haydn uses rhythm to accelerate the movement forward is also characteristic: from a crotchet pace at the beginning, we slide into quavers (bars 13ff.) with an occasional semiquaver until the semiquavers dominate for two whole bars (24–5). After a dead stop we begin again: crotchets to quavers but then to triplet quavers, which dominate for the next ten bars, again leading to a complete stop. But if, as we say, the closing material of the exposition does not seem to come directly from the first subject, it does appear to derive from its extension. When Haydn introduces the first subject in the dominant, he adds a little triplet figure (bars 47ff.).

In turn the figure at 57ff. and its repetition depend on this triplet figure which may be said to develop out of the bass line of part of the theme: bars 3ff., viz. *b–a–g–f sharp–e–(c sharp)–d*. Thus

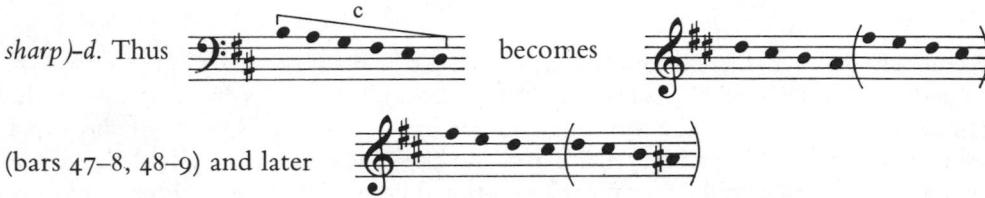

becomes

(bars 47–8, 48–9) and later

This example provides a typical study of Haydn's now effortless ability to unite a movement by means of small motifs from one single theme. The highpoint of the development turns out to be C major, which Haydn reaches in a long series of modulations dominated by triplets or sextuplets (quavers): A minor ⟶ F major ⟶ G minor ⟶ dominant of A ⟶ 4/2 position of dominant of C. Having reached such a remote key, he then has to move slowly towards the recapitulation, which he does via a long passage in B minor. He is so far 'off-tonic' that a brief sally into D major (98) hardly strikes one as the tonic at all (which it is not, in the context). In the recapitulation Haydn once again indulges in some spectacular hand-crossing (163ff.).

After this particularly brilliant and scintillating first movement, we have a very sober Andante on the tonic minor with the dotted Baroque rhythm to which Haydn again and again turns as a strong contrast to the modernity of an opening Allegro. Surprisingly, the modulation is to the dominant minor, and from there (in the second part) to the dominant minor of the dominant (i.e. supertonic: E minor). After a very varied recapitulation (theme in the 'cello and piano's l.h.), we appear to prepare for yet another variation, instead of which the fermata on the dominant seventh leads straight into the Finale. Haydn manages to establish another point of unity in this concluding *deutscher Tanz* ('Allegro, ma dolce'): the whole middle section of this A-B-A form is once again, like the slow movement, in D minor. The contrast is heightened by another factor, too: the A section is all *p* and mostly in two-part writing, with only the end and half-a-dozen bars in the middle in three parts (in the piano); while the B section, which is based on the same thematic material, is all *forte* and with usually more than two parts. The piano part is much more jagged here, and exploits the top range of the instrument as well as the bottom. The mechanics are simple, but the effect is of great richness, variety and virtuosity.

Trio 39 became an enormous favourite, first in England and immediately afterwards on the Continent. Whereas all Haydn's greatest successes had been, interestingly enough, with slow movements – from Symphonies Nos. 53 ('L'impériale'), 63 ('La

Roxelane') and most recently with No. 94 ('Surprise') and 100 ('Military') – he now scored equally effectively with a Finale. In some of his London works, it will be noted that a whole work may be built round a single climax of some sort: this is particularly the case with his chamber music, and it may be said that the whole beginning and end of the Quartet in E flat Opus 71, No. 3 is geared to the fantastic passage in the slow movement for all the instruments in the highest register (*pp* and *stacc.*). To a certain extent this is even true of Symphonies 94 and 100, the slow movements of which were deliberately designed for, and were eminently successful in, bringing down the house.

Like Haydn's old *sonata da chiesa* works of the 1760s, this famous 'Gypsy Rondo' Trio opens with a slow movement. If we consider the character of the Finale, it may be that Haydn really did write all the rest of the Trio to precede it. The opening Andante is a particularly lovely, open set of variations, or rather double variations in the customary major-minor fashion: except that the minor sections are built upon exactly the same theme, in G minor, as the beginning in G major. The second of the variations is in E minor and is a brilliant violin solo. All these are features we shall encounter *mutatis mutandis* in the Finale.

The slow movement, i.e. even slower than the opening, is a 'Poco Adagio' in the submediant major (E), a key to which the second variation of the preceding movement looks forward. As we see, Haydn is now constructing these late trios in far more cyclical a way than had ever been the case before. The form of this subtle and melodically rich 'Poco Adagio' is also interesting. The middle section moves to the subdominant, A major, where we have another of Haydn's ravishing violin tunes, marked *cantabile*. The piano's accompaniment is rich, the r.h. in triplets (quavers), the l.h. in stately octaves (neatly avoiding those notes which did not exist on the piano of that day, i.e. lower than F''). Haydn, as it were, begins the Trio slowly, slows it up for the second movement, and then slows up the second movement for the violin solo, preserving throughout a quiet accompaniment of triplet quavers as accompaniment. All this retardation accentuates the effect of the Finale. As always, the 'cello is sparingly used but its voice is felt throughout and sometimes, as in the penultimate bar, it sounds through everything in an independent line.

Haydn calls the Finale, in the authentic Longman & Broderip print, 'Finale. Rondo, in the Gypsies' stile'. There is a huge literature on the origins of the various melodies Haydn puts into this celebration of Eastern European folk-music.[1] We may sum it up in the words of the late Hungarian scholar, Ervin Major, who notes that the melodies used by Haydn are 'of particular significance for the history of Hungarian music: the dance melodies woven into [the Trio] belong to our earliest hitherto known recruiting [*verbunkos*] dances: among our more notable records, only the Hungarian dances of József Bengráf (1790) and four Hungarian dances in the 'Hadi és más Nevezetes Történetek' are of an earlier date'. Haydn actually makes no distinction between Hungarian and Gypsy music: that is to say, between the 'Rondo all'Ongarese' from the piano Concerto in D (XVIII: 11 of *c.* 1780) and the 'Rondo, in the Gypsies' stile' of 1795. The melodies are primarily those used for the recruiting of

---

1 Ludwig Koch: *Joseph Haydn, 1732–1932; Bibliographie als Festgabe der Budapester Stadtbibliothek*, Budapest 1932. Ervin Major: 'Ungarische Tanzmelodien in Haydns Bearbeitung' in: *Zeitschrift für Musikwissenschaft* Jg. XI, Leipzig 1929; ditto: *Magyar táncdallamok Haydn feldolgozásában*, Zenei Szemle, 1928; ditto: 'Magyar elemek a 18–19. századi európai zenében' in: *Magyar muzsika*, 1936; ditto: 'Népdal és verbunkos' in: *Zenetudományi Tanulmányok* I. kötet Akad. Kiadó, Budapest 1953. Quotation from Major 1928. See also: E. F. Schmid: *Joseph Haydn*, Kassel 1934, p. 288. Bence Szabolcsi: 'Haydn und die ungarische Musik', *Bericht über die internationale Konferenz zum Andenken Joseph Haydns*, Budapest 1959 [1961], pp. 159ff.

soldiers by Austrian officials, who employed Gypsy bands to entice the peasants from the fields to the *Wirthshaus*. There, they made their mark on a slip of paper, the significance of which they hardly will have realized, dazzled as they were by the gorgeous white uniforms, seduced by the strains of the most interesting 'folk music' in Europe and plied with the local *Tokay* wine. That Haydn knew many such tunes and loved them is self-evident in his music from the 1760s to the end of the century: also we must not forget that significant engraving of Eszterháza Castle in August 1791 (from a drawing by Carl Schütz), wherein we may clearly see a Gypsy band playing in the right-hand lower corner.[1]

A parallel source for some of the Gypsy melodies in the Haydn Trio turns out to be included in 'Originelle Ungarische Nationaltänze für das Clavier', a series issued by the Vienna 'Chemische Druckerey' in four volumes beginning about 1805. Volume One includes the following tunes (as No. 6) known to us from the 'Gypsy Rondo': bars 67ff., 128ff.; in other words the 'minore' sections. The 'Chemische Druckerey' version is in D minor and is otherwise slightly different, but the melodies are clearly the same. Probably Haydn was remembering another (Eszterháza?) version, and he certainly relied on his memory rather than on any written text. This extract from the Vienna print – copies are in the British Museum (incomplete), Budapest National Széchényi Library and the Österreichische Nationalbibliothek – is conveniently available in a modern reprint and we may therefore abstain from musical examples: *Magyar Táncok Haydn Korából/Ungarische Tänze aus Haydns Zeit*, ed. Bence Szabolcsi and Ferenc Bónis, Budapest 1959, p. 16.

By now we have come to expect each set of late Haydn trios to include a work in the minor key; but nothing quite prepares us for the gaunt power of Trio 40 in F sharp minor. We have observed that Haydn's philosophical attitude towards the minor key changed fundamentally from the great *Sturm und Drang* works of the late 1760s and early 1770s. If many of the works in minor of the 1780s and early 1790s seemed to betray the high principles of Haydn s first manhood, we must be reminded once again that by the 1780s Haydn was actively pursuing different aesthetic principles than those which had guided him earlier, principles in which the wildly personal, eccentric and single-minded energy of *anno* 1772 no longer had the same validity for its creator. But Haydn changed again, and changed profoundly, in the London years, and the present F sharp minor Trio is a startling proof of that change. The nervous brilliance of twenty years earlier has turned into controlled energy; the anguish and real loneliness of the 'Farewell' or 'Trauer' Symphonies have been transmuted into a quiet sadness; the intellectual precocity of the double fugue *à la* Opus 20 Quartets has mellowed into an effortless technique which hardly ever reveals the craftsman's seams; and forty's flashing genius has become a sexagenarian's wisdom and humanity.

It is true that we should guard against biographical interpretations of Haydn's music; yet we cannot restrain from noting that this series was dedicated to Haydn's intimate friend, Rebecca Schroeter, and that the opus represents, quite literally, Haydn's farewell not only to her but to the gracious and civilized country she so charmingly represented. In a work which is so serious, and without any trace of Haydn's usual humour, we need not look far beyond the chaste dedication to realize that in this great Trio we have, *in nuce*, Haydn's touching, unsentimental but profoundly sad tribute to England and his English friends.

1 Detail shown in László Somfai: *Joseph Haydn: his Life in Pictures*, London, 1967, p. 61.

The Allegro begins quietly, but there is that characteristic rhythmic build-up that is so much part of the texture of these late trios: from what is primarily a pulse of quavers, a small semiquaver fragment gradually achieves great importance:

In the bridge passage, the semiquaver passage becomes:

The second subject is also *piano* and in the expected relative major; before it arrived, the rhythms shifted from primarily quavers to semiquavers (as in the bridge passage), then to semiquaver triplets. After the second subject, the triplets continue in the accompaniment. The development proceeds from the dominant of B minor to B minor, C minor and then D sharp minor, which Haydn changes enharmonically into E flat minor (also changing the key signature to three flats), even suggesting the fingering for the violinist (a very rare occurrence at this period). This whole part of the movement is based on the bridge passage (see overleaf), via C sharp minor and a whole bar's hold on a diminished chord, the recapitulation (which strictly speaking is in E double-sharp minor) begins quietly. It is altogether a serious movement, to which the many subsidiary sections in off-tonic minor keys attest.

The 'Adagio cantabile' is the same music as in the Symphony No. 102's slow movement, where, as will be seen, it is in F major rather than F sharp major and is heavily and brilliantly orchestrated (with muted trumpets, covered timpani and an

[Trio No. 40/I: Allegro]

obbligato 'cello part). Unless this movement was originally composed for piano solo (piano trio?) all by itself, as was the case with Trio 36's slow movement (and also piano Sonata 60's slow movement, which we shall be discussing shortly), there now seems little doubt that it was, in the Symphony, a favourite of Mistress Schroeter's and thus the Trio version a reworking of the Symphony and not, as was often previously asserted, vice versa. It is interesting to observe the things that Haydn considered unfit for piano trio: many of the very detailed accents (>) are replaced by the less subtle *fz*. This is curious; one would have thought that the orchestral players would have needed a sharper dynamic marking. In the opening five bars of the Trio's version we can observe that all the piano's *fz* marks are accents in the orchestral score, and that at bar 3, the piano's *e natural* was marked in the violins of the score with an accent, not the next *d sharp* (which in the Longman & Broderip print is missing but is there in the recapitulation, at bar 31): similarly the Beethovenian *crescendo* going through all of bar 5 to end in *piano* at bar 6, is in the score a 'hairpin' (< >). But the sum total is that this remarkable and very tense music[1] sounds in its way just as beautiful for the intimate chamber as for the concert hall. Because of the intense quality of the music, however, Haydn prefers in the Trio version to present the first half of the music only once: in the Symphony, it comes twice, the second time with the muted trumpets and covered timpani, but also with the horns, and altogether more massively orchestrated. Obviously Haydn considered the orchestration of primary importance, so that without it, he thought the repetition better omitted.

After the subdued and leashed power of the extraordinary 'Adagio cantabile', Haydn adds a serious, rather subdued 'Tempo di Minuetto'. There are no dynamic

---

1 Rosen, op. cit., p. 361, notes: 'Without Haydn's varied orchestral sonority, the melody seems more personal and unrolls like an improvisation. The skeleton is very simple, with the melody defining an ornamental and expressive arabesque and a descent down the notes of the scale from D♯ back to the tonic note. Yet it not only sounds eccentric but appears to accelerate. The acceleration is real: the first beat of the second measure plays the arabesque twice as fast. The irregularity is part of the acceleration: the high note of each measure is successively closer to the first beat, and the arabesque occurs twice in the third measure, where the movement is slowed by making the last appearance almost as a written-out *ritenuto*. Even with a melody of such personal emotion, there are all the signs of a controlled energy.'

marks whatever throughout the whole Finale except for a crescendo sign leading to *forte* shortly before the end. Cecil Gray notes[1] that

> the treatment and development of the first phrase of the theme, with its characteristic 'turn', is almost symphonic in style and extent. Its perpetual recurrence dominates all sections of the movement from beginning to end, binding them all into an indissoluble whole. Its recurrence, moreover, tends to increase in frequency as the movement progresses, until in the coda the rest of the theme almost disappears from view.

Rosen, speaking of this Finale, considers that with it 'the genre is transformed by a melancholy so intense it is indistinguishable from the tragic'. It is a movement of great power and of an almost 'private' emotion, far removed from the public image that he had left behind at the Opera Concerts – the *fortissimo* crash of the 'Military Movement' and the great good spirits of Symphony No. 104's Finale. Here, in this lyric and rather reserved Trio in F sharp minor is quite another side of Haydn's personality *de anno* 1795. It is the same rapid metamorphosis that so fascinated the Swedish diplomat F. S. Silverstolpe in 1797; we have quoted the passage (*supra*, p. 22), but we would repeat the beginning apropos of the F sharp minor Trio. 'During the conversation,' writes Silverstolpe, 'I discovered in Haydn as it were two physiognomies. The one was penetrating and serious, when he talked about anything exalted, and only the expression "exalted" was enough to show him visibly moved. In the next moment this atmosphere of exaltation was chased away, quick as lightning, from his every-day expression, and he became jovial. . . .' Any student of Haydn will have observed this at times violent disparity in his music: we need only think of the introductions to Symphonies Nos. 101 and 104 and the following allegros. But nowhere do we find this 'Erhabene' side of Haydn's genius more poignantly, more intimately and more compellingly put forward than in this private, yet published, Trio in F sharp minor for Mistress Rebecca Schroeter.

Works for Pianoforte Solo

Of Haydn's smaller works for pianoforte solo, we have mentioned the first version of the slow movement of Trio 36. A similar case is the earlier slow movement of Sonata 60, which will be discussed *infra*. Apart from these two adagio movements which later formed part of larger works, the principal smaller piano piece of the London period is one of Haydn's most popular Variations, that in F minor (XVII: 6). Although it consists of one single movement (rather long, 228 bars, lasting, with all the repetitions performed, about a quarter of an hour), Haydn entitled it 'Sonata' on his autograph manuscript, and also listed it in his *Catalogue of Works Composed in England* as '1 Sonate in F minore 3 [double sheets]', which incidentally agrees with the number of sheets in the autograph (6 sheets or 12 pages, the title page blank except for the word 'Sonata': the MS. is in the New York Public Library, and came from the Artaria collection in Vienna).

The MS. is dated 'di me giuseppe Haydn mpria 793' and is written on oblong Italian music paper, but like other works composed at Vienna between the two London visits, Haydn reckoned it among his London works. It seems that it was composed for one of Mozart's most talented piano pupils, Barbara ('Babette') von Ployer, daughter of the Salzburg *Hofagent* in Vienna, Gottfried Ignaz von Ployer. Zinzendorf had written in his diary under the date 23 March 1784 '. . . puis au Concert

---

1 *A Limited Edition of Haydn Trios*, London [1940], p. 15. Rosen, 362.

de l'agent Ployer, ou j'entendu sa fille toucher de Clavecin a merveille'. Mozart had, a month earlier, composed his piano Concerto in E flat K.449 for her, and on 13 June 1784 Mozart organized a concert for the famous composer Giovanni Paisiello, who was passing through Vienna; the concert took place at the Ployers' summer house in Döbling, a suburb of Vienna, and Barbara played the new Mozart piano Concerto in G, K.453, and the Sonata for two pianos, K.448, together with Mozart.[1] Barbara's Commonplace book (*Stammbuch*) included an otherwise unknown Mozart *Trauermarsch* for piano, K.453a, entitled 'Marche funebre del sig^r: Maestro Contrapunto'. The book was in the Mozarteum until it was stolen in the confusion of the final days of World War II (1945); it included a version of the *Canon cancrizans* 'Du sollst an einen Gott glauben' (First Commendment), dedicated 'Von Ihrem Verehrer und/ Bewunderer/Joseph Haydn mpria'. The entry, which is fortunately preserved in a facsimile published by Roland Tenschert,[2] seems to have been made about 1793, perhaps together with the dedication of the Variations. The dedicatory MS., signed by Haydn, is in the Music Collection of the Austrian National Library. It is entitled: 'Un piccolo divertimento, Scritto e composto per la Stimatissima Signora de Ployer da me giuseppe Haydn $\overline{793}$'. It is perhaps significant that Haydn did not have the work published in England in 1794 or 1795. It would seem that it was one of those works written specifically for someone who held all the rights for a certain number of years; Beethoven was to compose many such works in this fashion, probably following his teacher's example. We shall see that Haydn's Sonata 60, composed for Therese Jansen in London, did not circulate on the Continent, for this and similar reasons. Haydn, however, did take a copy to England of the new 'Divertimento' (or Sonata, or Variations, whichever title is preferred), and no doubt he allowed his friends, such as Therese Jansen or Rebecca Schroeter, to make copies and perform the work in private. In February 1875, there was a London auction at which was sold: 'Sonate F minor for the pfte consisting of 11 pages [autograph: 12 pages, of which one without music] oblong folio signed by Haydn. This Sonata was written by Haydn's Secretary [Johann Elssler] for Mrs Montlieu and signed by Haydn when in Ldn.' We have unfortunately been unable to find this authentic copy, and also unable to identify Mrs Montlieu.

The work was in fact not printed until January 1799, long after Haydn's return from England. Artaria & Co., brought it out as 'Variations pour le clavecin [*sic*] ou piano-forte composées et dediées a Madame la Baronne Josephe de Braun par Joseph Haydn oeuvre [ink:] 83'. Baroness Braun was the wife of the banker and industrialist Peter Freiherr von Braun, later (1794–1806) director of the Court Theatres (Burgtheater, Kärntnerthortheater) at Vienna, under whose advocacy Beethoven's *Fidelio* was performed. His wife was a fine amateur pianist, and in the same year, 1799, that Haydn dedicated to her the Variations, Beethoven dedicated to her the piano Sonatas in E and G, Opus 14; two years later, he dedicated to the Baroness the Sonata for horn and piano, Opus 17.

One used to think that this beautiful piece, which is now known to most people as the 'Andante con variazioni' in F minor, was inspired by the death of Maria Anna von

1 Deutsch, *Mozart, Die Dokumente*, pp. 198, 200, 259. Larsen HÜB, 42. Hoboken I, 791ff. The *Urtext* Peters edition does not use the New York autograph but is based on the Ployer copy (edited by Kurt Soldan), whereas the new *Urtext* edition for the Henle Verlag (Sonja Gerlach) uses the autograph and all the other known authentic sources, as does the new edition (1975) by Franz Eibner (Wiener Urtext Ausgabe).

2 *Frauen um Haydn*, Vienna 1947, facsimile facing p. 128. Also Tenschert, 'Unbekanntes Autograph eines Canons von Jos. Haydn' in: *Die Musik* XXI/4 (Jan. 1929) pp. 253–7, also with facsimile. T. Frimmel: *Beethoven-Handbuch*, Leipzig 1926, I, 58f. (**Braun family**).

Genzinger (26 January 1793). Possibly this is one reason for the totally unexpected and violent emotion of the coda; but there may be a more plausible explanation for what Larsen calls 'the most beautiful and mature example of the typically Haydnesque double variation form', namely in the person of the original dedicatee: Barbara von Ployer. She was Mozart's talented pupil – the second, K.453, of the two piano concertos he composed for her shows that she must have been an exceptionally sensitive artist – and in a sense this, Haydn's first major piano piece after he had returned from England, is a real tribute to Mozart and his piano playing that 'went to the heart'. The double variations are in Haydn's typical minor-major relationship. He worked over the autograph considerably, polishing and adding. Originally there was a different ending in F major after the second variation (reproduced in Hoboken I, 791), which was cancelled when Haydn later noted 'Von hier Da Capo aber ohne Repetition'. The coda was at first only fifty-seven bars long. It contains the most eccentric, brilliant and moving piano writing of Haydn's career to date: it is of course totally conceived for the fortepiano and Artaria's addition 'pour le clavecin' is as fatuous as similar additions to Beethoven's piano music of the period. The ending is great tragedy: simple, short, unaffected and (in a technical sense as well) unadorned, the right hand quietly fading away in last reference to the octave jump that dominated so much of the music before. These Variations mark the beginning of the great, final period of Haydn's interest for the piano, which produced the late trios and sonatas.

The *Allgemeine Musikalische Zeitung*, in its issue of May 1799, carried a 'short notice' (*kurze Anzeige*) of the Artaria edition; the *AMZ* forgot to mention the publisher:

> *Variations pour le Clavecin ou Pianoforte, comp. et déd. à Mad. la Baronne Josephe de Braun, par Joseph Haydn.* Oeuv. 83. (Preis 1 Fl.)
> A sorrowful [*schwermüthiges*] Andante in F minor, varied as only a Master can, which sounds almost like a free improvisation. Even the first section is not easy, and one can thus expect that the further development will bring with it difficulties. Occasionally, and in particular as far as the suggestions for a new approach to the piano's sound are concerned [*in Rücksicht der Vorzeichnungen für neues Klang-geschlecht*], the difficulty is such that even better players will not bring it off at once. But once again, a rewarding contribution to the literature.

Following Artaria's first edition of January 1799, the 'Andante con variazioni' was reprinted by André in Offenbach as Op. 94 (announced locally on 20 September 1799) and in the *Musical Magazine* by Spehr. Simrock of Bonn transposed it into E minor, for some odd reason, and issued it in September 1799. Viguerie of Paris printed the work as Op. 94 (locally announced in November 1799), and Pleyel as Op. 91; the Parisian editions are entitled 'Caprice ou Variations pour le Forté-Piano'. Clementi and his associates brought it out in London in 1802 (locally announced in April of that year), the delay probably a result of the Napoleonic Wars and the confusion they created. From this large selection of reprints, we may guess that Haydn's Variations met with critical and amateur approval throughout Europe. It was one of the first Viennese works to combine the pianoforte schools and techniques of England and Austria, and it combined them with rare perfection.

THREE PIANO SONATAS FOR THERESE JANSEN

These sonatas were composed in London in 1794 (and 1795?). Latest critical editions, using all known MS. and authentic printed editions, by C. Landon (*Wiener Urtext*

Ausgabe of *Haydn: Sämtliche Klaviersonaten*, Vol. III, Vienna 1964, pp. 79–124, including the original version of Sonata 60/II); and by G. Feder, Henle Verlag, 1973.

Sonata No. 60 in C (XVI: 50), composed in 1794 or 1795 for Therese Jansen. First published by Caulfield in London *c.* 1800 with a dedication to Mrs Bartolozzi (*née* Jansen). I *Allegro*. II *Adagio*. III *Allegro molto*.

Sonata No. 61 in D (XVI: 51), composed in 1794 or 1795 for Therese Jansen. First published by Breitkopf & Härtel in 1805 from a MS. supplied by Haydn. I *Andante*. II *Finale: Presto*.

Sonata No. 62 in E flat (XVI: 52), composed in 1794 (autograph) and with title 'Sonata composta per la Celebra Signora [*sic*] Teresa de Janson [*sic*] – In Nomine Domini – di me giuseppe Haydn mpria Londra 794.' First published by Artaria & Co., Vienna, in December 1798 with a dedication to Mademoiselle Madelaine von Kurzböck; it is not known where Artaria received their engraver's MS., for it differs from the text of the autograph. Published from the autograph MS., with a dedication to Mrs Bartolozzi, by Longman, Clementi & Co. in November 1799 (announced on 29 October 1799 in *The Times*: 'In a few days will be published a new Sonata for the Piano Forte by Dr Haydn'). I *Allegro*. II *Adagio*. III *Finale: Presto*.

In Haydn's *Catalogue of Works Composed in England*, the piano Sonatas are listed, but Dies and Griesinger present conflicting evidence: the former has '3 Sonates for Ms. Janson [*sic*]', while the latter has 'Zwey Sonaten für Miss Janson 10 [sheets]'. But we actually have three, not two, Sonatas; the autograph and first English edition of No. 62 specifically mention Miss Jansen (Mrs Bartolozzi), as does the authentic English edition of No. 60; while Griesinger wrote to Breitkopf & Härtel in 1803 (Pohl III, 233), offering various works that Haydn had not yet published, including as the first item 'An Andante and Finale for piano, which Haydn composed for a lady in England, who kept the original and instead gave Haydn a copy she had written'; this was published by Breitkopf as the Sonata [No. 61] Op. 93. The list of sheets can only mean, in this case, double sheets (four pages to a sheet); because the autograph MS. of No. 62 alone contains ten sheets.

Therese Jansen, whose name has figured briefly in the preceding Chronicle (*supra*, p. 309) and in connection with the piano trios (*supra*, p. 413), was *inter alia* the subject of a brilliant article entitled 'Notes on a Haydn Autograph' which Professor W. Oliver Strunk published in the *Musical Quarterly* in April, 1934 (Vol. XX, No. 2, pp. 192–205). The article, which we shall be quoting frequently in connection with the late piano Sonatas, was inspired by the rediscovery of No. 62's autograph. In it, we learn interesting biographical details about Miss Jansen, of which a summary is here presented.

Miss Jansen's name occurs in the list of musicians Haydn met in London (CCLN 265) – she is listed among the 'Pianists' – and of course in Haydn's *Catalogue* just quoted; but until the appearance of Strunk's article, she seems to have escaped the serious attention of Haydn scholars. Since she was the recipient not only of the composer's final piano solo music but also of his final works for piano trio, Miss Jansen was obviously worth a detailed investigation.

Therese was the daughter of a famous dancing master from Aachen (Aix-la-Chapelle), where she was born about 1770. A highly successful pupil of Clementi, Therese soon made a successful career teaching. Her brother Louis, although trained as a dancing master, was also a composer, and began publishing his own music in 1793 with three piano Sonatas, Op. 1. An anonymous pamphlet entitled *Memoirs of the Life,*

Public and Private Adventures of Madame Vestris (the daughter of Mrs Bartolozzi, *née* Jansen), published in London in 1839, tells us that as a teacher, Miss Jansen 'was eminently successful; so much so, indeed, that she and her brother . . . realized rather more than two thousand pounds per annum. They resided at No. 14, Great Marlborough-street. . . .' By 1793, Therese was celebrated enough to receive from J. L. Dussek the dedication of his Opus 13, three Sonatas for piano and violin; later he would dedicate to her, in 1800, a Grand Sonata for pianoforte Opus 43. We have seen that in June 1794, her former teacher Clementi dedicated three piano Sonatas to her (*supra*, p. 417).

In 1795, as we have seen in the Chronicle, Therese married Gaetano, the son of the famous engraver Francesco Bartolozzi, who had produced a stipple engraving of Haydn soon after the composer arrived in England (*supra*, p. 64). Gaetano became a picture dealer and, as the *Memoirs* inform us:

> general trader in everything that might present itself in his various journeys to and from Italy. Indeed he was so very successful that in a few years he accumulated an independent fortune and purchased an estate near Venice, with a country residence about fifty miles distant from that celebrated city. . . . Signor Bartolozzi was a very fine violin and tenor [viola] player and could boast of having introduced into this country [England] the very first double-bass player in the world – Signor Dragonetti. . . .

After two miscarriages, the couple produced a daughter, in May 1797, who was destined to become the famous dancer Madame Vestris. Shortly afterwards, Bartolozzi wound up his affairs, selling his stock of prints, drawings, copper plates etc. at Christie's in June 1797. A few months before departing, Mrs Bartolozzi had given to Longman & Broderip the latest Haydn piano Trios which the composer had dedicated to her. The *Memoirs* then inform us that Bartolozzi and his wife went first to France, where he left his wife and infant daughter in the 'care of a friend of the Jansen family, the Marquis del Campo, Ambassador to the Court of England from the King of Naples [*recte*, of Spain]. In due time, Mrs Bartolozzi joined her husband in Vienna', where Bartolozzi had gone 'to prepare for the reception of his wife'. We cannot date Bartolozzi's arrival in Vienna exactly, but Haydn soon entered his name in the list of the subscribers for *The Creation* as 'Mr Bartolozzi Junr N° 30 Poland Street London'. Presumably Therese arrived in Vienna sometime in 1798, possibly early in 1799.

Great must have been her surprise to find Messrs. Artaria & Co. doing a profitable trade with 'her' great E flat Sonata. Whether Haydn supplied the engraver's copy or not cannot now be determined, but it seems very likely: where would Artaria otherwise have got hold of a copy? Probably Haydn was not expecting Mrs Bartolozzi's visit in Vienna, and moreover he had no doubt calculated that with the chaos of the Napoleonic Wars, she would not have heard that Artaria had issued the work. Mrs Bartolozzi will likewise have been puzzled to see Artaria marketing just the slow movement of 'her' Sonata in C major, which in fact the Viennese publisher had issued in June 1794 as a separate 'Adagio per Clavicembalo o Piano-Forte' – obviously an earlier and, from the standpoint of dynamic marks, more 'primitive' version of the Sonata's second movement which Haydn left with Artaria before leaving the second time for England. It is clear that Haydn had certain qualms about these 'Jansen' Sonatas, for he did not publish any of them before December 1798 – a good four years after the work (No. 62) had been composed; and on the thematic list of piano music that Breitkopf sent Haydn for approval, the composer wrote over the *incipit* of No. 60, 'not to be printed'; while it was not until 1803 that Haydn dared to offer the D major Sonata No. 61 to Breitkopf, probably realizing that Mrs Bartolozzi had not printed it.

And what did Mrs Bartolozzi do, seeing in Vienna the whole of one, and part of another, of her Haydn Sonatas already printed? It appears that she acted swiftly. Perhaps she was carrying with her the autograph of Haydn's Sonata No. 62; or perhaps she could instruct relatives in London where to lay hands on it. At any rate, she arranged for the autograph to be delivered to Longman & Broderip, now Longman & Clementi, who engraved the Sonata directly from the autograph – the MS. still shows the red crayon marks and other notes that Longman's engraver made when laying out the plates – and announced its publication in *The Times* on 29 October 1799. The title page of the authentic edition read in part 'A New Grand Sonata for the Piano Forte Composed Expressly for M^{rs}. Bartolozzi by Joseph Haydn, M.D. Op. 78. . . .'

Why did not Mrs Bartolozzi engrave the other two works? There are several possible explanations. One is that she did not have the music with her and could not tell her relatives in London where to find it in her possessions left behind. Another is that she extracted a promise from Haydn not to publish No. 60 (did Haydn even own a copy of it?), of which she obviously owned the world copyright. Haydn respected this wish. As for No. 61, it is the least brilliant and altogether the least interesting of the three, and possibly Mrs Bartolozzi did not consider it worth publishing, or worth imposing a non-publication ban on it for Haydn. It is, in any case, curious that she never did publish it. As for No. 60, technically the most advanced of the three, she had it published as soon as she returned to London. From Vienna, the Bartolozzis proceeded to Venice, where Napoleon's troops soon (as the *Memoirs* inform us) 'deprived Bartolozzi of his estates and forced him to return to England'. In *The Times* of 8 January 1800 we read that 'Mr. Bartolozzi, jun., respectfully informs the Ladies and Gentlemen who have formerly honored him with their patronage and recommendation, that being now returned from Italy, he means to resume giving Lessons in Drawing.' Towards the end of the year, Therese gave the C major Sonata to the engravers. The authentic first edition reads: 'A Grand Sonata for the Piano Forte Composed Expressly for and Dedicated to M^{rs}. Bartolozzi by Haydn . . . Op. 79 . . . London. Printed for, and to be had of the Proprietor 82 Wells Street and of the Publishers J. and H. Caulfield 36 Piccadilly. Where may be had just published Peace, a Grand Characteristic Sonata for the Piano Forte by L. Jansen. . . .' The edition was signed by her 'T. Bartolozzi.'

Before leaving our brief excursion into the rather complicated world of Miss Jansen and Haydn's last three piano Sonatas, we would mention still one final reason why the composer, or anyone else, hesitated to publish the C major Sonata on the Continent: and that was the greatly extended range of the keyboard at the top. Haydn writes, in the Finale, up to *a'''*; but until about 1805, most Continental pianos still had the old five-octave range with *f'''* as the top upper range (very rarely extending to *g'''*, as we have seen). No one, in fact, could play either the actual notes or the *sopra una corda* effects in the first movement which we shall be discussing shortly. The 'additional keys' (as they were called) do not figure in Beethoven's Sonatas until the 'Waldstein' of 1805.

Strunk thought that the chronological order must be: E flat (No. 62), D major (No. 61), C major (No. 60). He probably thought so because of the *sopra una corda* effects, the 'additional keys' and the extremely advanced dynamic markings in the C major Sonata. But pedantically speaking, we *know* that the slow movement of No. 60 was composed before Haydn left Vienna in January 1794, since Artaria printed it in

June 1794. Therefore No. 60 was presumably started first, while Haydn was in Vienna in 1793. The character of the D major would suggest its being considered by the composer as a sort of 'buffer' between the large-scale works in C major and E flat major. But if it seems likely that Haydn may have finished No. 60 last, there is no doubt that the majestic E flat work is in many respects the summing-up of all Haydn's solo keyboard music: a Janus-like work which is in the one hand a final golden harvest but on the other looks far forward to the world of Schubert (with the flattened supertonic slow movement, an almost unbelievably bold stroke). Morphologically, it is difficult to choose an exact chronological order for the two major works of this trilogy.

Sonatas 60–62

The dry, witty opening of Sonata 60 shows, in its relaxed expansiveness, that this will be a large-scale Allegro. It is interesting to observe how Haydn broadens and 'opens' the theme, which begins in two parts and adds a third only towards the end. The repetition is made brilliant by the arpeggio chords that so suited the instrument, while the upper line is already varied. One thing leads to another, one thing grows out of another: the main theme continues when Haydn reaches the dominant, but constantly enriched and developed. From the main subject:

comes the transition, where the octave skip in the bass of bars 1ff. is retained in a slightly different rhythm, while the progression of thirds in the r.h. is directly related to the progressions in thirds at bars 5 (with upbeat) to 7:

443

The same combination of thirds and octaves, accelerated, then appears later in the dominant:

It can be seen that the closing material of the exposition is closely related (1) to the opening theme but also (2) to the passage at bars 35ff. quoted above. The ninth skip in the main theme – E to F, D to E – is transformed into the ninth progression from *e″* to *f sharp″* in the closing material, and the progression *g″–d‴* of bars 35 and 36 becomes the same progression at bars 51–2 *g′–d″*. It will also be noted that the accompaniment figure of bars 10ff. in the l.h. is used in bars 47ff. Even the progression in the l.h. of bar 9 is used later (e.g. in bar 16, l.h.). Despite this rigorous intellectual display, the music retains a sparkling freshness which seems to belie its tense motivic development. The development section modulates to A flat major, where Haydn introduces a famous and much discussed passage:

A similar and particularly beautiful 'open Pedal' passage occurs also in the recapitulation, also based upon the main subject:

Not knowing the constitution of Haydn's English piano, many commentators have been misled by the indication 'open Pedal' to imagine Haydn wanted the sustaining pedal held down during these two passages. Even allowing for the relatively short duration of sound generated by a late eighteenth-century piano, such a use of the sustaining pedal would be wrong, blurring the music in a quite absurd way. Of course, what Haydn wanted is the *sopra una corda* effect. In bars 73–4, the *sopra una corda* pedal is, obviously, lifted at once after the third note of bar 73 ; but in the next section (bars 120–123), Haydn presumably wants the pedal gradually lifted at the beginning of bar 124, in such a way that the semiquavers sound normally 'pianissimo'. The fact that this *sopra una corda* effect was not available on Continental pianos may have been (as we have pointed out above) one of the reasons why no one published the Sonata in Austria or Germany. Those who know Haydn's previous sonatas will realize the enormous increase of dynamic marks in this movement, particularly of the *crescendo-diminuendo* kind (as in the example of bars 33ff. quoted above), quite different from the 'terraced' dynamic levels of the composer's earlier music for the keyboard. Sonata 60, especially the first movement, goes further in this respect even than Sonata 62 (where in the opening Allegro there are whole long sections with very few dynamic marks, e.g. bars 44–78, the development section, which contain but three *pianos*, three *fortes*, two *fz* marks, and one *decrescendo* to *piano*). Such a series of violent dynamic marks as in the development of Sonata 60 (notice the refined use of *piano* in the r.h. and the explosive off-beat *fz* in the l.h.) is brilliant proof of the far-reaching effect these new British pianos and their composers had on Haydn's late pianistic style (bars 76–81).

The first critical edition of Haydn's piano Sonatas was brought out by Karl Päsler and published in 1918 in three volumes by Breitkopf & Härtel as Series XIV of the *Gesamtausgabe*. Alas, Päsler's brilliant and pioneer efforts hardly had any practical repercussions: his impeccable texts were never republished in a popular edition, and even his new chronology was scarcely recognized for many years. A semi-scholarly edition of the Sonatas by C. F. Peters partially used Päsler's research, but to all intents and purposes, his volumes remained accessible only to scholars, and were hardly known among performers. (Even a great musician like Vladimir Horowitz, when recording Sonata 62 in a scintillating performance for H.M.V. about 1932, never even glanced at the Päsler edition and probably never realized its existence.) We mention all this because students may now acquire the Päsler text in the reprint by Lea pocket scores; in many respects his edition is completely superseded – he did not know the autograph of Sonata 62, for instance – but there is one particularly useful point in examining the slow movement of Sonata 60 which Päsler's edition makes specially clear.

We noted that Artaria brought out, in June 1794, the first version of this Adagio for pianoforte alone: in this form it was also reprinted in the *Oeuvres Complettes* which, conversely, did not include the complete version of the Sonata. In the new critical edition by C. Landon, the early version is printed as an Appendix, which enables pianists to play it; whereas Päsler, whose edition was primarily for scholarly purposes, managed to include both the principal text (i.e. revised version) and, by smaller print, the earlier version at the same time.[1]

It is revealing to compare the two texts. Apart from different note values (quaver instead of crotchet, etc.) and an occasional change of rhythm (as in the grace-note figure of bars 7 and 40), the main change is once again in the dynamic marks. Here we have a parallel in the Adagio from Trio 36, which was also composed before the rest of the Trio (and as a solo piano piece). In both the Trio's *Urfassung* and in this Adagio of Artaria's version, there are hardly any dynamic marks at all. To be precise, we find in the Artaria text two *fz* marks (C. Landon has added another at bar 39) and two *pianos*; a similar paucity of dynamic indications obtained in the original piano version of the Adagio in Trio 36. Did Haydn expect his Viennese players to know how to 'grade' such a slow movement dynamically? Or do we have another display of dynamic marks for the more subtle and complicated English pianos? It is difficult to say. There is one other curious detail to point out. In bars 6 and 7, Haydn doubled the bass line at the lower octave in the Artaria; in the English edition, this is removed. The parallel passage is slightly different, in that Haydn doubles the low A in the English edition but not the ensuing B flat. Were the basses of British pianos so much more powerful than their Viennese counterparts that Haydn felt obliged to remove some of the sound from the overall texture? We include the first eight bars of the Päsler text so that readers may see this passage and also the kind of differences between the two texts: the differing notation of the appoggiature in bar 7 is very curious at first glance, but in fact what Haydn has done is to adjust the passage according to the recapitulation, where Artaria's rhythm is different from that of the exposition (see opposite). At any rate this fantasia-type of slow movement, which sounds like an improvisation but is actually in 'slow-movement sonata form', i.e. with a very short 'development' section (10 bars, in the event) is admirably suited to set off the dry brilliance of the opening Allegro and the scherzo-like humour of the Finale.

Formally this very original third movement ('Allegro molto') is related to the Minuet of Symphony No. 97 (1792) in that all the repeats are written out. We have seen that Haydn experimented widely with three-four Finales in the late piano Trios, but in those works the tempo was generally slower, more like a German Dance. Here we have a kind of scherzo such as the composer was to adopt in the late string Quartets of Op. 76 and 77. The feeling of a finale is enhanced by the grotesque false cadence at bar 10 – as if the music were to go into E – something which would hardly take place so soon after the beginning of a real scherzo. Haydn had, as is well known, experimented with calling the minuet movements of the string Quartets Op. 33 (1781) 'Scherzi'; but they remain minuets in feeling and in tempo. The Minuet of Symphony No. 94 (1791)

1 Haydn: *The Fifty-Two Sonatas in 4 Volumes*, Vol. IV, New York 1959, pp. 97–100.

[Sonata No. 60]

is marked 'Allegro molto', but this Finale to Sonata 60 may lay claim to being Haydn's first real (though hybrid) scherzo. Formally the movement is worked out as follows: A (24 bars, modulation to dominant) – A (exactly repeated, but written out) – B (modulation back to tonic via dominant of D minor, dominant of G minor, dominant of C, 24 bars) + A¹ (45 bars) – B + A¹ (exactly repeated, but written out). In the B section, the false cadence at the beginning is expanded to further buffoonery and is followed by the passage where Haydn uses the 'additional keys' up to *a'''*. The movement stops suddenly in the middle of a *piano*: the first edition is very clear about that (bars 155–84).

The smaller-scale Sonata 61 is, like Sonata 58 (XVI 48, *c.* 1788–9) and Trio 31, in two movements; both works remain in the tonic throughout. Flanked by the great Sonatas in C major and E flat, the D major has always been the stepchild of the trilogy. Perhaps, however, Haydn intended this contrast deliberately. The little Sonata 61 is as much of a foil *in toto* between Sonatas 60 and 62 as is, for instance, the slow movement of Sonata 60 between its powerful outer movements.

The form of the opening Andante is new again. This time Haydn expands the 'slow movement sonata form' (with a short or almost non-existent 'development') as follows: instead of what is basically an A–A¹ form, we now have a tripartite A–A¹–A², each beginning in the tonic: A consisting of 43 bars with the last two bars simply modulating back to the tonic and A¹ (36 bars, the last two again transitional), while A² contains 32 bars. Notice the diminution of the sections: 43 : 36 : 32. The form was undoubtedly dictated by the lyrical content, which looks forward almost to the world of the German or Austrian *Biedermeier*. The melody in octaves exploits the sonorous treble register of the British piano, which was obviously more resonant and more solid in tone than its Continental sisters (bars 10–22).

The second movement is another kind of scherzo (Finale: Presto) in three-four time but with whole series of off-beat (mostly third-crotchet) accents which again show, if any further proof were needed, how effortlessly Haydn's late pianistic style merges with Beethoven's piano music of the outgoing eighteenth century. One notes again how Haydn carefully juxtaposes his old *fz* with the new accent sign (bars 23b–47). Formally, we note that in this scherzo bars 1–23 are repeated (with a sign), while the B–A¹ section is repeated too but the whole written out. If Sonata 60's Finale was wiry and grotesque, No. 61's is deceptively quiet, even faster moving (not only in the actual tempo but because of all the syncopations, which propel the music forward in a far more nervous way). It is a brilliant *tour-de-force* and did not go unnoticed in London; for although Mrs Bartolozzi did not, as we have seen, print the work, she must have played it often to her friends. One of Haydn's English pupils, Thomas Haigh (*c.* 1769–1808), who studied with the master in 1791–2,[1] published a set of 'Three Sonatas for the Piano-Forte, Composed & humbly dedicated to Dʳ. Haydn... Op. VIII' (Preston & Son, 97 Strand), which were brought out during the second visit – Haydn owned a copy (Elssler's *Verzeichniss musicalischer Werke...* British Museum Add. 32070, fol. 10ʳ item 15) – and in which two of the three works are in two movements and remain in the tonic key throughout (Sonata I, A major and Sonata II, D). The order of tempi is different, though, because Haigh in the first Sonata starts with an 'Allegro vivace' and concludes with a *Larghetto (Espressivo, con Variazione*

1 Grove I, i, 644 (William H. Husk); *Musik in Geschichte und Gegenwart* V, 1329–1331 (Charles Cudworth; with list of works).

[*sic*]), while for the second he begins with an 'Allegro moderato' and concludes with 'A celebrated Irish Air arrang'd as a Rondo' (Presto). Nevertheless, the two-movement form is striking and would seem to derive from our Sonata or the Trio 31 (or possibly Sonata 58, which Bland had issued in 1791). Haydn's use of octaves in Sonata 61, which we have noted, was also appropriated by Haigh, and we find in Sonata III ('Allegro moderato', a three-movement work) the octaves not only in the bridge passage but also, very like Sonata 61's passage, in the subsidiary theme:

When the little Haydn Sonata appeared in Leipzig, the *Allgemeine Musikalische Zeitung* No. 44 of 31 July 1805 included a 'Kurze Anzeige' of the new work:

Sonate pour le Pianoforte composée par Joseph Haydn. Oeuvre 93.
    Leipsic, chez Breitkopf et Haertel. (Pr. 8 Gr.)
This Sonata really appears before the public for the first time; but it is probably from a much earlier period of this master, and perhaps was an occasional piece for someone who was not yet a trained pianist but still wanted to play something by Haydn. It consists of two movements only: a simple, *cantabile* Andante, as are found in many early Haydn piano works, and a Finale, which displays the pretty bloom of a happy muse but also the profound science as revealed to us, richly and luxuriantly, in the best *later* works of this kind – on a small scale but unmistakable even to the eye which is only slightly trained. If the little piece is thus primarily to be recommended to less trained players, it has nevertheless *some* attractive features for the more serious friends of the art.

When Professor Strunk announced to the scholarly world in 1934 the rediscovery of Sonata 62's autograph, he believed it to have been totally unknown to previous Haydn scholarship. Actually, the autograph had been mentioned, and a short description given, in John Crosse's much-quoted *Account* of 1823 (published two years later), wherein we read that the work had been '. . . written for Madame Bartolozzi, the original MS. of which is now lying before us' (p. 406). The hope that we might, one day, find the other two autographs (Nos. 60, 61), and those of the last fifteen piano Trios, of which all except one (No. 41) and a tiny fragment of another (No. 42) have totally disappeared, seems nowadays rather remote. We mention this because, although Haydn's English publishers were the most accurate of his career, there are

449

probably at least some details from Haydn's MSS. – not least the precise years of composition – which never reached the printed page. But the first English edition of Sonata 62, which we have seen used the actual autograph MS. as engraver's copy, is a model of accuracy and legibility: far more useful than the Artaria edition, which may have been corrected hastily by the composer (it contains some 'supplementary' dynamics missing in the autograph) but is on the whole just not in the running, textually speaking. In defence of Artaria, it ought to be said that Haydn may have taken back to Austria only a partially accurate copy – we should recall that he owned only Mrs Bartolozzi's MS. copy of No. 61 – and restored some of the missing points by memory. This would explain, on the one hand, the missing *decrescendo* sign to *p* in bar 16 of Artaria's edition of the opening Allegro (perhaps it was missing in Haydn's copy, too), and also the discrepancy in the rolled chords of the opening theme and its repetitions: here the autograph has only rolled chords in the l.h. of the first crotchet of bar one, whereas Artaria has them in both hands and much more frequently: who added the roll signs?

During the last ten years of Haydn's life at Eszterháza, he wrote only about half-a-dozen piano sonatas (we do not count the reworking of an early Sonata, No. 57 [XVI: 47]). One of the finest of these is the delicate and carefully worked-out Sonata for Maria Anna von Genzinger (No. 59 [XVI; 49] completed in 1790), also in E flat major. If we compare the beginnings of the two Sonatas, we may see at one glance the enormous difference. No. 59 opens as if it were made for the delicate *Hammerklavier* of Walter or Schanz: there is also a slow sense of time about the music. There are rarely more than two or three parts, and there is a sense of cultivated, intellectual *Hausmusik* about the whole. The beginning of No. 62 is another world: the massive brilliance of the opening springs out from the page, and even if Miss Jansen did not play the work in public (that is, in the Salomon or Opera Concerts), this is a 'public' Sonata on the grand scale. How profoundly Haydn's technique has changed may be seen from the easy way in which the 'Clementi thirds' of the r.h. (bars 4–5) have been smoothly integrated into Haydn's style. There is even a slightly flashy brilliance to the run at bars 9–11 which stresses the virtuoso quality of the music and also its 'public' character. This is music for a great pianist, not the delicate but (dare we say it?) perhaps slightly amateurish fingers of Madame von Genzinger. Of the increased dynamic range we have spoken often before, but it is apparent in every line of the later work, with its *decrescendo* sign (bar 5), the off-beat accent (bar 6), and also in the exploitation of the whole range of the instrument.

Sonata 62 is so well known that we shall limit ourselves to a brief note of some interesting details. In the development, the modulation is so startling as to surprise even the connoisseur of Haydn used, as he must be, to the composer's limitless interest in remote keys. After the usual close in B flat (the dominant), we move in a swift modulation to C major (again the sub-mediant relationship to the tonic!), then to F major, to G minor (mediant to the tonic, still in third-related distance), then back to C minor, to A flat and to a close on the dominant of G. At this point Haydn simply moves without preparation into E major, the Neapolitan major (or flattened super-tonic). This key is so outrageously off-tonic that unless one knows the overall scheme of the Sonata, the excursion, though brilliantly prepared and brilliantly resolved (in a bold modulation back to E flat and the recapitulation), seems merely eccentric *à la* C. P. E. Bach. What Haydn is doing, of course, is in a most subtle and cunning way to prepare us for the even greater shock of the whole slow movement being in the

Neapolitan major, E. Just before the final bars, Haydn introduces another seemingly weird modulation:

This piece of apparent eccentricity also has to do with the coming E major (in which the notes would be C natural, or B sharp, followed by B natural, A, G sharp, A). The whole movement is marked not only by pianistic brilliance but also by extreme economy of form and an ever-present sense of tautness: much more so than in the expansive Sonata 60's opening Allegro.

The intensely rhapsodic Adagio goes further in being improvisational, fantasia-like and intense than any slow pianoforte movement before the *post*-London piano Trios, especially those – obviously no coincidence – for Mrs Bartolozzi (Trios 43–45, published in London in 1797). These other works for Therese Bartolozzi fall outside the scope of this volume, but we would stress that they are definitely the descendants of this extraordinarily personal, profound and totally unconventional Adagio: we shall encounter an even more violent expression of this *fantasia*-type slow movement in Trio 44, while in Trio 45, another great E flat work, we shall note that the slow movement is in B major (by this time Haydn is, however, exploring enharmonic relationships, so that B major is none other than the submediant of D sharp major = E flat major). Haydn, to return to Sonata 62, tames his Neapolitan major relationship by a simple but yet devastatingly effective means: The middle section of the movement is in E minor and modulates to the relative major, G: which in turn is the mediant of E flat and a key to which Haydn has pointedly referred in the development section of the first movement. The rhythmic freedom of this movement is so extraordinary that the music seems to burst the bar-lines. It will be noted that this rhythmic elasticity is much aided by the dynamic marks (as in bar 46's *crescendo*), while his use of the small notes (auxiliary notes) is almost waywardly 'free'. All this intimate yet public display is a far cry even from the great slow movements of the Salomon Symphonies: the Sonata contains thoughts that are simply not feasible for or suitable in orchestral music (bars 45–53).

The Finale is a highly compact and technically demanding Presto which rounds off in a particularly satisfying way Haydn's last and probably greatest solo keyboard Sonata. In the development section the music, which is now moving in a relentless series of semiquavers (the semiquavers continue from bar 128 to the pause at 170 without ceasing for a single beat), Haydn takes up a Scarlattian device that he had briefly introduced in the exposition and now continues in a thrilling series of sequences (bars 148–73).

It is not too much to assert that Mozart's C minor Sonata (K.457, with or without the Fantasia K.475, 1784 and 1785 resp.), Haydn's final E flat Sonata of 1794 and Beethoven's 'Pathétique' Sonata Op. 13 of 1799 were the most influential piano sonatas of the eighteenth-century's final quarter. All three had a profound effect on the early Romantic composers and established, in three radically different ways, different but equally great approaches to the problem of the piano and its capabilities.

The *Allgemeine Musikalische Zeitung* (I, No. 33, 15 May 1799) carried a review of the Artaria edition which had been published in December 1798. In the new periodical, which was already very widely read, such a review will have helped greatly in disseminating the new Sonata, and in fact the work was quickly reprinted by André of Offenbach (1799), Simrock of Bonn (1800), Hummel of Berlin (1803–4?), in the Boßler *Musikalisches Magazin* (*c.* 1800?) and by Viguerie of Paris (1799) – thus becoming one of Haydn's most widely circulated piano works.

> *Grande Sonate pour le Clav. ou Pianof. comp. et dédié a Madem. de Kurzbeck,* par Joseph Haydn. Oeuv. 82. (1 Fl. 30 Xr.)
>
> Grand Sonata, rich and difficult as well, both in content and in its manner. It is true that the reviewer must copy the exclamation that perhaps others have said a hundred times before – *Haydn* is inexhaustible and will never grow old. What a highly personal way we find here, once again! No copying his own style. Whoever is capable of playing this Sonata (a really fine piece truly written for the connoisseur) – his early works in the form hardly compare at all for difficulty – whoever can play it perfectly and with precision, without missing a single bit, he can truthfully say about himself: I can play. It creates a very good impression of the lady mentioned on the title page that the venerable *Haydn*, who won't have the time or inclination to pay empty compliments, should dedicate such a Sonata especially to her.

Although Magdalene von Kurzböck (Kurzbeck) properly belongs in the final chapter of Haydn's life, a few words about her may not be amiss here. She was the daughter of the Viennese publisher and writer Joseph Kurzböck, whom Empress Maria Theresa raised to the nobility. She was a pupil of Clementi's and probably had a technique similar to that of Therese Jansen. Haydn was very fond of her and dedicated to her not only this Sonata but also the E flat minor piano Trio (No. 41, 1795).

LOST CHAMBER MUSIC

As far as Haydn's *Catalogue of Works Composed in England* informs us, the principal lost piece of chamber music is the work described in the foregoing Chronicle (p. 310) as for piano and violin. In his *Catalogue* Haydn lists it as 'The Dream 3 [double sheets or 12 pages]'. As we have remarked several times in the course of this study, it is extremely odd that this no doubt interesting work was never printed. The autograph, which Miss Jansen seems to have owned, has never been located. Even more strange is the fact that Haydn himself took back to Vienna a copy of the 'Dream' and kept it as late as about 1805, for it figures in the list of music from the composer's library that Johann Elssler drew up. Here, it is listed (British Museum Add. 32070, fol. 23ʳ) under 'J. Haydn's Verzeichniss geschriebener musicalien' under 'Jos. Haydn' as item 40. '*Jacobs Dream.* Ein *Allegro* fürs *Piano forte*' (ital. = Latin, the rest in Gothic script). This description is at odds with that in Dies (piano and violin); is the MS. that Elssler saw a different version? Although most of the Haydn MSS. (but by no means all) eventually became the property of the Esterházy Archives, 'Jacob's Dream' did not. Unlike the lost London Arias, which seem to have perished with the singers for whom they were written, there is the remote possibility that we may find 'Jacob's Dream' in a contemporary copy.

In Haydn's *Catalogue* there are listed '2 Divertimenti a più voci 12 [double sheets]'. Actually the composer performed and revised at least four and possibly five of the extant eight Notturni in the Salomon Concerts of 1791 and 1792. The principal revision consisted in adding a new double-bass part: the original version had only one bass line (sometimes marked 'Basso' but apparently for a violoncello only: the autograph of Notturno IV is signed by Haydn 'Notturno in C/a/2 lire / 2 Clarinetti/ a viole / 2 corni / e / Violoncello / di me giuseppe Haydn mpria / 790 / per la Sua Maestà il Re di Napoli'). The two lira parts were given either to flute and oboe, or in one case to two flutes (Notturno III); while the two clarinet parts were usually played by two violins, though as we shall see that the authentic parts from the King's Library (now British Museum) of three such works specify in one of them (Notturno IV) clarinets *or* violins. Haydn seems to have forgotten at least two such revisions in his *Catalogue*, and his number of double sheets cannot be explained satisfactorily. Notturno III of the 2nd set (*vide infra* for Professor Ohmiya's new chronological order) exists in autograph and contains 24 single sheets (or 48 pages), which would account for the 12 double sheets of Haydn's two Divertimenti. The autograph of Notturno IV contains 18 single sheets (36 pages), while the authentic copy of Notturno III of the 1st set, obviously copied from the now lost autograph, contains 20 single sheets (40 pages). Apart from adding the double bass parts, Haydn also inserted a slow introduction to Notturno III of the 2nd set.

Professor Makoto Ohmiya, who is at present (1972) preparing the Notturni for the Joseph Haydn Institut's *Werke*, has worked out a new chronological list of the Notturni which we present here.[1] Although the detailed examination of these delightful and sophisticated works must belong to an earlier volume of our biography, we feel it convenient for readers who might examine the works in their revised state, and in conjunction with their performances in London, to know the new order at this stage.

FIRST SET OF NOTTURNI (1788–1790)
Notturno I (II: 25): no record of a London revision.
Notturno II (II: 26): no record of a London version.
Notturno III (II: 32): MS. score by an Esterházy copyist, Bibliotheca Musashino Academiae Musicae, Tokyo (AM 109). Revised by Haydn for London, with a new double bass part. Christopher Papendiek owned a contemporary sets of parts. This is the only known Notturno in which the two lira parts were given to two flutes for the London performances.
Notturno IV (II: 31). Autograph, formerly owned by Christopher Papendiek, now the property of Dr Grumbacher in Basel. There are, curiously, no indications of the revision for London. But in the King's Library there are authentic parts signed by Haydn and dated (locally) 26 Apr. 1792 for clarinets or violins, with a new separate double bass part, and the lira parts given to flute and oboe.
Notturno V (II: 29): no record of a London version.
Notturno VI (II: 30): no record of a London version.

---

1 'New Order for the "Lyra-Notturni" of Joseph Haydn' in *Tone & Meditation* (Festschrift for Prof. Nomura), Tokyo 1969, pp. 67ff.

SECOND SET OF NOTTURNI (1790?)

Notturno I (Hoboken *deest*): presumed to be lost.

Notturno II (II: 28): MS. parts in the King's Library signed by Haydn and dated (locally) 26 Apr. 1792; with parts for two violins, a new double bass part, and the lira parts for flute and oboe.

Notturno III (II: 27): Autograph in the Esterházy Archives. The *Largo* introduction added later on English paper with English watermarks while at the beginning of what was the original *Allegro*, Haydn has changed the lira parts to flute and oboe; the clarinet parts are here given *a priori* to violins (as they seem to have been for Notturno II, of which parts in the Esterházy Archives are for 2 violins, not clarinets and there is a new double bass part added throughout (except, of course, to the new introduction, which included them from the first). King's Library owns parts signed by Haydn and dated (locally) 26 Apr. 1792 (the London version).

There are five programmes of the Salomon Concerts during 1791 and 1792 which include what are obviously Notturni for the King of Naples. They are: (1) 'New Divertimento' of 8 April 1791; with double bass. (2) 'New Concertino' of 20 May 1791; with double bass. (3) 'Divertimenti' [*sic*] without double bass of 27 April 1792. (4) 'New Divertimento' with double bass of 11 May 1792. (5) 'New Notturno' with double bass and two flutes mentioned on 18 May 1792, i.e. Notturno III of the first set. Possibly the 'New Concertino' was one of the Concertos for two lire, two horns, two

'Notturno 3^{zo}' for the King of Naples (1790), to the autograph of which Haydn later added the introduction (Largo) on British paper.

violins, two violas and 'Basso' of 1786; in which case Haydn also added a double bass part. If this actually was a Concerto and not a Notturno, we then have four occasions on which we know Haydn gave Notturni: these performances match the number of revised works, i.e. four. Haydn also played some of them at the Prince of Wales's, from whose possession they passed, when he became George IV, into the King's Library. The fourth work, of which the Prince of Wales owned (it seems) no parts, remained in Christopher Papendiek's possession (Notturno III of the 2nd set), who may have found the work useful for Queen Charlotte's private concerts. We note that Papendiek also owned the autograph of Notturno IV and that it does not contain a new double bass part. Can this have been the work performed on 27 April 1792, where there was no double bass part, and later revised again to include the new double bass line?

Once more we note that Haydn did not publish any of these Notturni. Did he feel obliged to the King of Naples not to do so? Most of these exquisite pieces of enlarged chamber music were first published in the 1930s, one in 1946 (Notturno VI) and one in 1959 (Notturno I of the 1st set).

The 'Salomon' Quartets of 1793,
dedicated to Count Anton Apponyi and known as Opp. 71 and 74.

SIX STRING QUARTETS FOR TWO VIOLINS, VIOLA AND VIOLONCELLO (III: 69–74)

Composed in Austria in 1793 (autograph of each 'Quartetto') dated 1793. Latest critical edition: part of the Complete String Quartets published by Doblinger Verlag, Vienna: Opp. 71 & 74 edited by the present writer (1972). Published by Corri, Dussek as Op. 72 and Op. 74 (announced in *The Sun* on 14 Oct. 1795 [Op. 72] and in the *Monthly Magazine* for February 1796 [Op. 74]). J. L. Dussek arranged the works for piano trio, but only one, the first (minus the Minuet), seems to have been printed by Corri & Dussek. That edition is marked 'as performed at M^r. Salomon's Concert', and Haydn owned a copy, or rather two copies. Within a week of Corri & Dussek's first announcement, Artaria in Vienna brought out the first three works as Op. 73 (announced on 21 Oct. 1795 in the *Wiener Zeitung*; the second set, Op. 74, was announced in the *Wiener Zeitung* on 30 April 1796; Haydn owned a copy of the second Artaria set, which suggests that he was involved in its publication).

Quartetto in B flat ('Op. 71, No. 1'). I. *Allegro*. II. *Adagio*. III. *Menuet & Trio: Allegretto*. IV. *Finale. Vivace*.

Quartetto in D major ('Op. 71, No. 2'). I. *Adagio–Allegro*. II. *Adagio*. III. *Menuet & Trio: Allegro*. IV. Finale. *Allegretto–Allegro*.

Quartetto in E flat ('Op. 71, No. 3'). I. *Vivace*. II. *Andante con moto*. III. *Menuet & Trio*. IV. *Finale. Vivace*.

Quartetto in C ('Op. 74, No. 1'). I. *Allegro*. II. *Andantino*. III. *Menuet & Trio: Allegro*. IV. *Finale. Vivace*.

Quartetto in F ('Op. 74, No. 2'). I. *Allegro spiritoso*. II. *Andante grazioso*. III. *Menuet & Trio*. IV. *Finale. Presto*.

Quartetto in G minor ('Op. 74, No. 3'). I. *Allegro*. II. *Largo assai*. III. *Menuet & Trio: Allegretto*. IV. *Finale. Allegro con brio*. The Corri & Dussek edition have as a tempo for the first movement 'Allegro non troppo' which would appear to be an afterthought added later by Haydn. This Quartet is known as 'The Rider'.

We have seen in the Chronicle for 1791 that Haydn performed his then new string Quartets known as Opus 64 at the Salomon Concerts; they were a success and we have also seen that they were immediately printed by John Bland in June 1791. It will have been noted that Salomon not infrequently played MS. quartets in his concerts: it was a new idea for Haydn, used as he was to the quartet being essentially a private form for connoisseurs, to be performed in intimate surroundings. In Mozart's 'Akademie' concerts in Vienna, or in those by the Tonkünstler-Societät – among the few groups of the 1790s for which complete programmes have survived – it was not the custom to introduce string quartets or, as Salomon had done when introducing 'Master Hummel' in 1792, piano trios. The Viennese passion for the quartet form was gratified in the semi-private concerts of the nobility, or in private homes such as Mozart's (where Haydn heard for the first time the great quartets dedicated to him by his younger contemporary). We do not know whether it was Salomon who suggested the idea to Haydn of writing a new series of quartets for what Salomon imagined would be the 1793 season, or whether Haydn himself decided to do so.

By now, there was a steady shift in the fashion of dedicating such new works. Previously, the publisher often made the dedication, but as the eighteenth century waned, the composer gradually came to reserve this privilege for himself. It was a tactful way to thank a patron for favours, and apart from that it could serve as a mark of friendship and esteem for someone. Haydn's dedications fulfilled both these divergent tasks, as Beethoven's were to do in the near future. Some of Haydn's dedications during the London period are to patrons present and past, such as members of the Esterházy family, especially the princesses; but also there are tokens of affection for Mistress Schroeter, a mark of esteem for Miss Jansen, and in the case of the present Quartets, a remembrance for Haydn's Masonic sponsor, Count Apponyi.

Anton Georg, Count Apponyi (1751–1817) is described on the title page of the authentic Corri & Dussek first edition of our Quartets as 'Chambellan actuel de Sa Majesté Imperiale Royl. Apostol. et supreme Comte du Comitat de Tolna au Royaume d'Hongarie'. After having become a Freemason on Christmas Eve of 1784 – Mozart was present at the ceremony in the Viennese lodge *Zur wahren Eintracht* – Apponyi sponsored Haydn's entrance into the Brotherhood in 1785. Apponyi was also a member of van Swieten's Viennese 'Gesellschaft der Associirten' for the promotion of 'old' music (Bach, Handel, etc.). It is reported by Dr Franz Wegeler and Ferdinand Ries in their *Biographische Notizen über L. von [sic] Beethoven* that in 1795, at a soirée at Prince Lichnowsky's in Vienna, 'Count Apponyi asked Beethoven to compose a quartet for him for a given compensation, Beethoven not yet having written a piece in this genre' – a commission which, as we shall subsequently see, Beethoven did not accept for a variety of reasons, though at the repeated instigation of Wegeler, there appeared for Apponyi the Op. 3 Trio and the Op. 4 Quintet. Apponyi's commission must have been an indirect result of the Haydn Quartets.[1]

Haydn brought the autographs with him to England, or so one presumes. It may be that he had Elssler make parts and took those instead. As was his custom, Haydn corrected the parts, probably after the first rehearsals and performances, and it was from these parts, not from the autograph, that Corri & Dussek engraved their first edition. There are numerous details which show the kind of editorial additions Haydn is known to have made in the extant authentic parts for the Salomon Symphonies.

---

1 O. E. Deutsch: *Mozart und die Wiener Logen*, Vienna 1932, p. 29. Wegeler-Ries, *Notizen* . . . Coblenz 1838, p. 29 (translation from Thayer-Forbes, op. cit., I, 262). Theodor Frimmel: *Beethoven-Handbuch*, Leipzig 1926, II, 33. CCLN, 48f. O. E. Deutsch: *Mozart, Die Dokumente*, op. cit., p. 290. For a letter from Count Razumovsky about these works, sent to Russia about the middle of 1795, see the next volume of this biography.

Some of these additions are significant, such as the tempo qualification he made in the first movement of the 'Rider' Quartet in G minor: the autograph has only 'Allegro', the authentic first edition 'Allegro non troppo'. As we hinted above, the Artaria edition, which Haydn owned, seems to be partly authentic; just possibly Haydn furnished the engraver's copy. When the *Wiener Zeitung* announced the Quartets, we read: 'Three entirely new [*ganz neue*] Quartets op. 73 composed by J. Haydn . . . 3 f. [Gulden]. For some time music lovers have expressed the general wish to receive new Quartets by this great master. This edition is distinguished by particular accuracy, clarity and legibility.' Our slight reservation about the authenticity of the Artaria edition is because of a letter that our old acquaintance Gaetano Bartolozzi wrote to Artaria on 6 October 1795. In it, Bartolozzi writes that he is sending to Artaria's Hamburg agents the three latest Haydn Quartets in the Corri & Dussek edition together with the arrangement of the first one for piano trio by Dussek. Bartolozzi further notes that these Quartets were printed half-a-year earlier. In this case, the announcement of the new Quartets in *The Sun* on 14 October is rather curious. Perhaps, after all, Artaria received not a *manuscript* from Haydn but the first pulls, or even proofs, of Corri & Dussek's edition. It is worth recalling that the London edition appeared in two parts, and if the first set was really ready before Haydn left London, he could easily have given it, or a copy of it, to Artaria as soon as he returned. Note, too, that Artaria's second set did not appear until the end of March, while Corri & Dussek's second set appeared in February. Textually, the Artaria set is closer to the Corri & Dussek edition than to the autograph; but that would be the case anyway, if Haydn included his post-autograph corrections made in London. Bartolozzi's letter reads:

Vienna Sig^r Artaria, e Co:
Dietro alla commissione ricevuta con la grata vostra de di 5 p° scad^e, spedisco in quest' oggi p^r ordine vostro alli Sig^{ri} Brentano Bovara, & Urbieto [*recte*: the firm of Brentano, Bovara & Urbietta, Artaria's Hamburg agents] una cassetta contenente li 3 nuovi Quartetti di Haydn, e la già contrass^{te} stampe. . . . Credei pure di farci cosa grata, unindovi uno delli tre nuove Quartetti Haydn, trasportato per il Cembalo da Dussek, con l'accompagnam^{to} di Violino, e Basso. Siate sicure che al momento che usciranno gl'altri tre vi li rimetterò con tutte sollicitudine. Mi meraviglio però che li suddetti Quartetti non sono ancora pervenuti costì, mentre quì sono stati stampati che sono più di cinque mesi. Se aveste qualche nuove opere postume per il Cembalo del divino Mozart, mi farete somme grazie di mandarmele con la prima occasione che vi si presente. Fratanto pronto sempre ad agni vostro pregiato comando, con vera stima u.b.l.m.

Gaetano Bartolozzi

[with a bill for music and various prints, etc.]

[Stadtbibliothek, Vienna, I. N. 67955/3.]

The new Corri & Dussek Quartets finally appeared, and there follow extracts from three final letters by Bartolozzi to Artaria on the subject:

Vienna Sig^{ri} Artaria, e Comp:

Londra $\overline{pmo}$ Marzo 1796
Con la grata $\overline{vra}$ de dì 27 Gen:° p p° mi trovo favorito della prima di Cambio per £8.10.0 St^e. . . . La settimana scorsa furono publicati li tre altri nuovi Quartetti di Haydn; ed essendomi presentate la bella occasione d'un mio amico Mr de Harring [*sic*], che per costì parte quest'oggi; ve ne rimetto una copia, che dal sud^{to} vi sarà consegnata, e per la quale vi compiacerete di accreditarmi de scellini 8 . . .

[Stadtbibliothek, I. N. 67955/4.]

Vienna, Messrs Artaria e Co:

Londra 26 Aprile 1796

Senza care vostre vi confermo l'ultima mia $\overline{pmo}$ Marzo p p°, sperando che a quest'ora avrete recevuti li tre nuovi Quartetti di Haydn, trasmessivi costì col mezzo dell'amico mio Sig Haring [*sic*], del che ne attendo li vostri riscontri . . .

[Stadtbibliothek, I. N. 67955/5.]

Vienna, Sig^{re} Artaria e Co:

Londra 19 Agosto 1796

. . . . Mi rincresce di sentire il modo con il quale il Sig^r Haring esequi la Commissione dei Quartetti Haydn, dopo di avergli tanto raccomandato di rimetterveli in persona. Scusate la mia cattiva scelta del Messaggiere. Se mai ne ritrovaste uno migliore costì vi pregherei di mandarmi un esemplare dei 6 Quartetti di Mozart dedicati a Haydn.

Conservatemi la pregiata vostra amicizia, e corrispondenze, e con la più vera stima u.b.l.m.

Gaetano Bartolozzi.

[Stadtbibliothek, I. N. 67955/6.]

We see that Bartolozzi sent to Vienna the second set of the Corri & Dussek edition of Haydn's Quartets (= Op. 74 in our reckoning). The works were given on 1 March to a courier named Häring (the banker and violinist who figures in Haydn's correspondence? CCLN, 95n.) who seems not to have delivered them himself, and also to have done so in a less than courteous manner. What is interesting in all this affair is to determine how textually independent Artaria's edition is. We recall that Artaria issued the first set in October 1795 (*Wiener Zeitung*: 21 October), just as Bartolozzi was sending off the first Corri & Dussek set. Bartolozzi sent the second set in March, and Artaria issued their second set on 30 April 1796 (*Wiener Zeitung*). It seems therefore unlikely that Bartolozzi's copies can have served Artaria as engraver's texts. Here is a curious mystery which we cannot explain satisfactorily.

Although as we noted the Artaria editions are closer to the British print, textually, than they are to Haydn's autographs, still there are differences: the change in tempo of the 'Rider Quartet' that we found in Corri & Dussek is not found in the Artaria print. Until more evidence comes to light, it would seem that Artaria engraved from a corrected set of MS. parts probably furnished by the composer.

The character of these Quartets is primarily determined by a fact which curiously seems to have escaped all the Haydn biographers: these 'Salomon' Quartets are the first works of their genre by any of the three Viennese masters – Haydn, Mozart, Beethoven – to have been composed deliberately for the public concert hall. As such they are entirely different from the leisurely, more 'detailed' and much more intimate works which Haydn had previously written for the Austrian connoisseurs. In the works *de anno* 1793 Haydn paints with a broad brush. To see graphically the difference between a typically 'Viennese' Quartet of 1790 (though it may have been, and probably was, composed in Eszterháza) and the world of the music for J. P. Salomon, one only need compare the first movement of Op. 64, No. 1 in C, with any of the first movements of Opp. 71 or 74. The immensely sophisticated, slow-paced, almost epicurean unfolding of the 1790 work is contrasted with the high-powered, nervous brilliance of the 1793 pieces. The *Gemütlichkeit* of the 1790 style has disappeared entirely. Everything about the 'Salomon' Quartets is more intense; the slow movements are 'slower' (think of the 'Largo assai' of the 'Rider' Quartet in G minor), the quick movements are more restless and seem to belong to the glittering concert world of a huge international metropolis. Geiringer has on several occasions pointed out the almost orchestral technique of these London Quartets. Actually, the reason why they are 'orchestral-sounding' is partly their broad layout, their 'public' character. Another technical aspect reflects the great leader for whom the Quartets were composed; for Count Apponyi was the dedicee, to be sure, but the prime mover of the actual music was Haydn's leader. From documentary evidence at our disposal, in a letter of 1795, it is evident that Haydn may have received the initial commission for these Quartets in 1793 from Count Apponyi, who reserved all the Viennese rights for a certain period; but technically his eye was on Salomon and the Hanover Square Rooms rather than on Apponyi and his chamber.

Salomon was undoubtedly a greater violinist than Luigi Tomasini: and certainly the German was a more international musician and aware of all the latest technical devices just then being imported to London by Viotti, a refugee from chaotic Paris. Salomon's virtuoso technique and his skill as the leader of the quartet, to which contemporary critics often gratefully refer, will have been great sources of inspiration for Haydn. The Quartets are, in a very real sense, 'Salomon's Quartets': they bear the unmistakable imprint of his strong personality. To a certain extent, therefore, these great and powerful Quartets are an excursion, a detour, from the normal path of Haydn's development as a quartet composer. Quartets were, from the time Haydn invented the form as we know it, designed for the minority. Here, in 1793, are works not only for the majority but also expressly written for a famous violin virtuoso. The first violin often dominates the texture: not in the manner of Haydn's earliest quartets, and not, let us hasten to add, to the exclusion of the other instruments. It is almost as if we felt the very spirit of Salomon as we listen to these bold and intensely masculine works. The first violin's leadership is not in the number of notes, the difficulty of the passage work, or the height of the position (though we shall have an astounding example of the latter in the slow movement of Op. 71, No. 3): it is a kind of 'moral' domination, a state of affairs difficult to assess, but which the sensitive listener will immediately perceive upon studying these Quartets.[1]

It is perhaps superfluous to add that the division, by most eighteenth-century publishers, into two *opera* is not authentic and, on the contrary, wrong. Haydn wrote the six Quartets as a single *opus* and we retain the customary opus-number (which derives from Pleyel's numbering) only for purposes of ready identification to those who know and cherish this music. The order of the Quartets within two *opera* represents that of Haydn's autograph MSS. and the authentic first edition of Corri & Dussek.

One of the features that distinguish the 1793 Quartets is the introduction with which Haydn in five out of six cases begins the opening movements. (The sixth case is the 'Rider' Quartet which, having a very strong G minor 'introductory' beginning, does not need one: there is, as we shall see, a direct parallel to Haydn's only Salomon

---

1 There is not much useful literature on Haydn's London Quartets, considering their importance in the composer's *oeuvre*. A short list of the essential references follows. Geiringer 1932, pp. 57f.; 1947, pp. 278f. Cecil Gray: *The Haydn String Quartet Society*, London 1932 *et seq.* (eight volumes). Robert Sondheimer: *Haydn: A historical and psychological study based on his quartets*, London 1951 (tendentious and of little use to the Haydn scholar). László Somfai: 'A Klasszikus Quartellhangzás Kialakulása Haydn Vonósnégy-eseiben' in *Zenetudományi Tanulmányok* (VIII. Kötetéból), Budapest 1960, pp. 381ff.; 'A bold enharmonic modulatory model in Joseph Haydn's string quartets' in *Studies in Eighteenth-Century Music: A Tribute to Karl Geiringer on his Seventieth Birthday*, London 1970, pp. 370ff. Rosemary Hughes: *Haydn's String Quartets*, London 1966 (also the article in the Penguin Book on *Chamber Music*). A comprehensive study may be expected in R. Barrett-Ayres's new book on Haydn's quartets, now in preparation at Barrie & Jenkins, London, as we write [1972]. D. F. Tovey has a useful survey in *Cobbett's Cyclopedic Survey of Chamber Music*, London 1929. The theses are listed in the Bibliography (*Haydn: the Late Years 1801–1809*).

Symphony in a minor key, No. 95.) Seeing that *none* of Haydn's earlier quartets begins with any kind of an introduction, these 1793 works stand out conspicuously in this respect. In the later quartets (Op. 76 and 77, Op. 103 being unfinished), the only one to begin with a rhetorical flourish is Op. 76 No. 1, clearly a link in this and other respects between the London works and the rest of the great series of Op. 76 (1796–7). The introductions in Opp. 71 & 73 are of three kinds: (1) a flourish consisting of one or more chords (Op. 71/1, 71/3, 74/1); (2) a real though very short Adagio beginning as in Op. 71/2; (3) or the eight-bar unison opening of Op. 74/2, which is a brilliantly new idea to be examined below: suffice it to say here that Op. 74/2's first eight bars fulfil a dual function, that of being an introduction although in the principal tempo and as well providing a violently condensed thematic pattern for the rest of the movement.

These introductions obviously have a close relationship to the main distinguishing feature of the six works, i.e. their having been written for public concerts. Symphonies, especially Haydn's but also those of his contemporaries such as Mozart, Gyrowetz or Pleyel, often began with an introduction – one of Mozart's (K.504) assuming enormous proportions. Chamber music, at this period, was less inclined to slow introductions (Mozart's 'Dissonant' Quartet K.465 is the exception rather than the rule), possibly because the audience for whom it was written was presumed to be more attentive, more intellectual and less in need of being reminded, as in theatre symphonies, that the piece was about to begin and that conversation should, hopefully, cease. Apart from these external considerations, most of Haydn's slow introductions also serve to set off a first subject that begins softly. This is the case with Haydn's late Symphones Nos. 93–96, 98–101, 103–104 and also with the Quartets Op. 71/1, 71/3, 74/1 – thus illustrating that the public symphonies and in this case the public quartets are designed from the same cloth. The introductions for the quartets are generally too short to permit thematic allusions to what follows, but as we have hinted, that to Op. 74/2 is a major exception.

There are a few other important points general to most of the 1793 Quartets. One is again perhaps linked with their being public Quartets, and that is the deliberately 'popular' character of the melodies: by that we do not suggest that Haydn had recourse to folk tunes as he did with many of the late symphonies, but there is a clear tendency in these Quartets to easily recalled and comfortably shaped melodies. This is particularly true of the minuet movements. Here we notice the emergence of what might be called a 'concert minuet', which is bolder, also quicker (two of the tempi in the 1793 Quartets are actually marked Allegro),[1] gradually approaching the presto three-in-a bar which we find in Op. 76/1. The third-related keys which we have noted so frequently in the piano works, and which we will observe in the Salomon Symphonies (Nos. 99, 104), appear in the 1793 Quartets: not only in the slow movement of Op. 74/3 (principal key: G minor [G major], 'Largo assai' in E major) but also in the Trios of Op. 74, Nos. 1 and 2 (No. 1 in C, Trio in A; No. 2 in F, Trio in D flat major).

There is also a strong tendency to concentrate the major emotional centre of a given Quartet in the slow movement. Here, the scholars have curiously divergent opinions. Cecil Gray (op. cit. III [1933], 16) informs us, apropos of Op. 74 No. 3's 'Largo assai': 'The slow movement in Haydn's symphonies is frequently the most important, but seldom in the quartets. That of Op. 33, No. 6, is an exception and, as it happens, so is this one – the longest as well as the most beautiful of the four

1 Op. 71/2; here Hoboken has 'Allegretto' (I, 421), but autograph and Corri & Dussek both have 'Allegro'; Op. 74/1 also 'Allegro'.

movements, beautiful though they all are.' On the other hand, we read in Pohl III (312, in this case obviously pure Botstiber):

> Contrary to his symphonies, in the Haydn quartets the focal point is transferred to the slow movement. Many of the slow quartet movements are the central point, the crown of the whole work; they show Haydn the melodist, who knows how to sing from the depths of a full heart, at his finest. These adagio movements sometimes flow along like a broad and majestic river, full of greatness and full of comfort. Examples of such beautiful adagio movements are in the first and second 'Apponyi' Quartets [Op. 71, Nos. 1 and 2], also the sixth (Rider Quartet) . . .

Even when our attention to the slow movement is not directed by an intrinsic melodic or emotional concentration, it may be achieved by other means, as in Op. 71/3, where a fantastic passage for all the instruments in their highest register, *pianissimo* and *staccato*, stands out in such bold relief as to be the highpoint, in some respects, of the whole work.

The relative positions of Gray and Botstiber are only apparently tautological. What is clear from a study of Haydn's late-period music is that the centre of emotional gravity begins to shift altogether to the slow movement, whether in symphony or quartet. After 1795 Haydn wrote no more symphonies, and in the Quartets Op. 76 – in particular the last three – the slow movements contain the quintessential emotions of their respective works. But even the slow movements of the London symphonies and quartets show distinct trends in this general direction; they were also the immediate reason for many of Haydn's greatest popular triumphs – witness the 'Surprise', 'Military' and 'Clock' Symphonies. The first movements of both quartet and symphony are mostly clearly designed for the connoisseur; even in deliberately popular and successful works, we find highly esoteric enharmonic passages (generally to render more easily playable a modulation which, if expressed in real notation, would lead, as in Trio 40/I, to a recapitulation in E double-sharp minor or in Op. 71/3/I to a recapitulation in F double-flat major, rather than the 'heard' keys, respectively, of F sharp minor and E flat).

Finally, we would add that although these 1793 Quartets represent the apex hitherto of Haydn's classical, humanistic, popular chamber music, there are definite tendencies, in the harmonic breadth of his language as well as in specific formal effects (such as the 'ostinato' technique of the slow movement in Op. 71/2, which looks forward to Schubert) that strikingly presage the world of the German Romantics. From his beginnings as the inheritor and cultivator of a great Baroque tradition, Haydn's style has, rather incredibly, moved to pre-classical (in the early 1760s), to a Romantic crisis general to Austrian music of the late 1760s and early 1770s, to a polished classicism of the 1780s, and has now reached a synthesis of classical and early Romantic elements which would soon become the basis of Beethoven, Schubert, Weber and the whole world of European music which emerged after the Congress of Vienna. The great 1793 Quartets are clearly the dividing point, in the chamber music of the Austrian classical composers, between what is known as 'high classical' and the early Romantic movement with which, as we shall see, Haydn would be closely allied when he returned to Vienna to become the doyen of European music in 1795.

The Allegro of Op. 71/1 begins with five *fortissimo* chords, a preface to the suave theme which is given out *mezza voce* (a favourite dynamic designation in late Haydn string quartets). This movement is a supreme example of the composer's monothematicism: there is no second subject, not even an attempt at one. The whole music grows inexorably out of the principal subject which, being the only one, is very long and divided into several sections. As always when the *piano* (in this case *mezza voce*) opening of such a subject is very short – and here it is 5 bars and the first part of a sixth – the ensuing passage in the tonic is not only loud but very long: we shall see the same procedure in Symphony No. 94/I. Here in the Quartet, the music remains in the tonic, with only an occasional modulation, for 31 bars. Everything in the movement is on a big scale: the music reaches a V of V cadence in bar 38, and from bar 39 to the double bar at 69 everything is in the dominant (again except for minor excursions). In these brief examples the reader may follow the logic and intellectual tautness of Haydn's thought. The main subject begins as follows:

The main 'motif' of this subject, in the first violin, appears so often and so conspicuously that we have not thought it necessary to mark it as such. On the other hand, the first bar of the second violin, and bar 4 of the first violin, apparently accompanimental (in the first case) and cadential (in the second), are of great importance in what follows. The 'b' figure will also appear as a separate fragment. In the *tutti* that follows there appears another seemingly inconsequential little figure

which will also appear later. A curiously ominous passage in *piano* appears after this *tutti* which uses fragment 'b'.

The first part of the main theme is repeated but it is now *forte* and to it is added a tail which was not there before, making it a ten ($9\frac{1}{4}$)-bar theme. There follows still another *tutti*, based on the 'a' figure:

When the dominant arrives we are simply given a variant of the main theme, with a new gliding accompaniment:

In the extension of this pseudo-second-subject, we have another fragment

which appears in imitation in the second violin and viola immediately thereafter. This 'c' figure is, at the beginning of the development section, combined with the first two bars of the main subject:

Even the closing tutti of the exposition is clearly based on previous material, fragments 'a' and 'd':

We have gone to some pains to show, though incompletely, how very closely-knit is the fabric of this typical opening Allegro.

The tenderly restrained Adagio, in the simplest of three-part forms (the original 'A' section with repeat signs ||: 1–8 :||: 9–20 :||) is only 57 bars long but is so closely conceived as to the part-writing and the harmony that its intensity makes it seem much longer. The hairpin dynamic signs under the first two bars are typical of the increased attention that Haydn now gives to his dynamic marks to aid in the expression. Again, we must remember that Haydn's quartets had up to now been written for his own private circle of friends and patrons; if the outer world was able to eavesdrop, by means of the printed editions, on this music, it was with no guarantee as to a proper execution of such details; for Haydn's scores were often skeletal and left a great deal to the player (as obtained even in the late piano trios). But the 1793 Quartets were for strange players, and contain, as do the Salomon Symphonies, a great many more aids to the players than ever before. In the construction of the main subject (itself also in tripartite form, a–b–a′), we note the third-related shift from the end of the first 'a' section to the beginning of the 'b': C major to A flat. The recapitulation is varied by the addition of many appoggiature to the theme and its counter-theme. Connoisseurs in London will have noticed the striking similarity, *mutatis tonaliis*, between this lead-back

and a similar passage in the slow movement of Symphony No. 88 in G, a popular work in London since it had been issued by Longman & Broderip in 1789 after its successful British début a few months before in the Professional Concert:

The sturdy Menuet is marked by the relentless pace of its bass line in crotchets. It was Cecil Gray who first (op. cit. III [1934], 21) drew attention to the subtle way in which Haydn links together the whole Quartet by means of a single fragment. We deliberately refrained from quoting the passage in question from the first movement, which first appears in the *tutti* after the *piano* part of the principal subject. There the first violin has:

Here the Menuet begins as follows:

In the *da capo* of the Menuet, the top line gets the fragment in question

thus accentuating its importance. The 'cello then gets it, ending the Minuet proper. In the spirited and dashingly elegant Finale, Haydn introduces the figure in violin I at bars 37–9:

It is probable that such thematic affinities are unconscious on the part of the composer; nevertheless, as Cecil Gray asserts, 'One such occurrence might perhaps be dismissed as a mere chance resemblance, but two would be stretching the arm of coincidence too far for credibility.'

The arch *pianissimo* ending, preceded by several references to a mock sentimental diminished chord over a tonic pedal point (upper lines G flat, E flat, A), is particularly effective.

The D major Quartet Op. 71/2 is the most brilliant of the series in its outer movements and also the one where Salomon's virtuosity is perhaps most exploited. There are whole bars of semiquavers in the first violin part of the opening Allegro which verge on being a violin concerto (bars 24ff.), and the octave passages at bars 99ff. are difficult to keep in tune. In this work, the slow introduction serves the opposite function from that which it usually fulfils: whereas in most of the other works, the chords are devised to set off a *piano* first subject, here the first subject is a brilliant *forte* which stamps its way in octave leaps from 'cello up to violin I. The octave leaps, indeed, keep appearing in one guise or another throughout the movement. In one such passage, we have a fascinating example of Haydn's making what sounds like a purely *bravura* passage – an interstitial episode – an integral part of the whole. The octaves of the opening bars of the Allegro

are altered and used as the subsidiary parts in Salomon's virtuoso solo (we quote from bars 30ff.):

It is altogether unbelievable to which uses Haydn manages to put these octaves. Here they are, once again inverted, during the recapitulation.

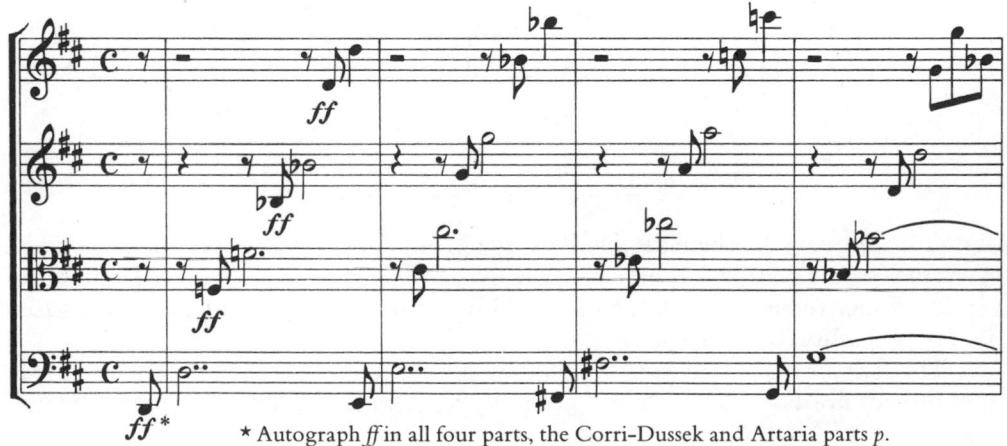

* Autograph *ff* in all four parts, the Corri-Dussek and Artaria parts *p*.

Here Haydn manages to return to an old Baroque device of combining an aural effect with a double visual one: double visual because the beguiling pattern of the printed page is repeated by the four players on the stage; aural for the obvious reasons. Since one can only assimilate a limited amount of such high powered music, Haydn keeps the movement astonishingly short: the development section covers only bars 53–70. But both exposition and the second half are to be repeated.

The 'Adagio cantabile' begins very slowly, that is to say at the slowest basic pulse of the tempo: the first violin has the theme in crotchets (tempo: 3/4) over held dotted minims. This is partly, of course, to establish a wide contrast after the unabated intensity of the first movement. The basic tempo soon dissolves into smaller divisions, but a majestic calm seems to pervade the whole movement, which is, incidentally, *durchkomponiert* without any double bars whatever. Here, one feels, is the essence of the Viennese classical slow movement in all its developed purity (a tautology which students of Haydn will understand, like his remarks 'innocentamente' or 'semplice' over a theme):

The form of this particularly lovely *Adagio* is a kind of A–B–A but all the thematic material derives from the opening, so that the end result sounds more like an ostinato or a set of variations. Haydn's technique of varying the main theme by arabesques, by appoggiature, and by changing rhythms is highly sophisticated, as is the harmonic pattern. After the modulation to the dominant, we move into the six-chord of the dominant (E) minor, then in a *crescendo* to C major (the flattened mediant), a six-chord in F and via an augmented sixth (bass A sharp) to the six-four of the dominant and a cadence on E. All this, apart from the highly Romantic sound of the harmonic turn, would not be all that remarkable if it were not for what happens at the end of the

467

invisible double bar-line (bar 35). From E major, we slide by one passing-note in the 'cello (D natural) suddenly into C major, which was stressed in the passage mentioned above. Haydn now remains in C major for half-a-dozen bars. We again realize the amount of third-related key structures also within these movements; and not only third-related but also *bimodally* third-related. That is, the diatonic triad might be altered chromatically to include a key not originally part of the home key. In our case, A major is the home key, but we have seen that Haydn once lightly and once seriously moves into C. He does it, of course, from E major; but the point is that the C sharp common to both A and E major is bimodally altered to C natural. This concept is part of Haydn's expanded concept of third-related keys, which (according to his new precepts) could be altered either enharmonically, whereby in E flat major we might modulate to B major, which is a third related key of D sharp major, or else, and even more radically, in the bimodal system we have just observed.[1]

The Menuet, marked 'allegro' and almost like a scherzo in feeling – though still three-in-a-bar, not one-in-a-bar – is a lively example of the new 'concert minuet', in which the Trio seems almost to be the same movement, i.e. not a separate piece, as was earlier the case. The Finale starts out like a witty Haydn rondo, but in a curiously slowish tempo: allegretto. The form is A (subdivided a–b–a) – B (*minore*) – A but then the tempo suddenly jumps forward to allegro and we return to the virtuoso violin writing of the first movement. The *staccato* runs in the first violin are later joined by all the other instruments, *ff*, and the end, a brilliant flourish, is another sparkling tribute to Johann Peter Salomon's art.

The first movement of Op. 71/3 in E flat (which starts dramatically with a single chord, followed by a fermata) has been the subject of an interesting analysis by László Somfai, the brilliant Hungarian scholar who has made a special study of Haydn's string quartets. We are dealing here – and we have roughly touched upon the matter in the first movement of Trio 40 – with Haydn's enharmonic modulations in the development section which land him in the enharmonic equivalent (mostly in flats, in Trio 40 in sharps) of the tonic for the recapitulation. Using what Somfai calls 'enharmonic deceptions', the composer 'remains within the keys playable on strings and finally the recapitulation is sounded in the key of the exposition.'

This is primarily a monothematic movement:

(the first subject) is also the basis of all the principal thematic material in the dominant:

1 See Louise E. Cuyler: 'Tonal Exploitation in the Later Quartets of Haydn' in: *Studies in Eighteenth-Century Music* (Geiringer Tribute op. cit.), pp. 136ff.

The development starts in E flat minor and, in Somfai's plan (op. cit. 1970, pp. 373f.) is

Haydn is descending into the enharmonic flat range and here moves in a distance of minus four fifths from E flat minor to B minor (expressed thus but strictly speaking C flat major). Somfai adds: 'The transition to the enharmonic spelling proceeds stepwise and this ensures a comparatively clean intonation. This is Haydn's innovation: there are no enharmonic progressions from G flat to F sharp or from E flat to D sharp. The different instruments perform the intervals, familiar and relatively easy to perform, of an augmented second (E flat–F sharp in the viola, bars 121–3; in V. I bars 123–5) while the third (note D) of the B minor chords is entrusted to the open string (V. II bar 125, Va. bar 126). He even takes care that the third and fifth of the B major chords presented in the mixed spelling (B–E flat–E sharp) should not sound simultaneously with the root of the triad, i.e. with the basic note B (*cf.* bar 123) so as to avoid a "false" major triad.'

(The last bar of the musical example begins a passage in B minor which contains a famous case of the viola providing a 'false bass'. Sir Donald Tovey, in his brilliant Haydn article in Cobbett's *Cyclopedic Survey of Chamber Music* [London, 1929, Vol. I, 518], calls this 'an astonishing miscalculation' and continues: 'Where Haydn miscalculates in these mature works, the error really lies in the viola part. In [Op. 71, No. 3] the one possible and perfectly satisfactory correction consists in substituting a rest for the first quaver in [bars 129 *et seq.*].' We wonder if this passage is not a miscalculation but a bold experiment; it seems very unlikely that music's greatest craftsman could miscalculate in 1793, at least in the structure of a string quartet.)

It will be noted that the descent into flat keys is usually a characteristic of works in *flat* keys. Such enharmonic deceptions occur in these late Quartets primarily in the development sections, as in the E flat Quartet Op. 76/6's slow ('Fantasia') movement, in the first movement of the last completed Quartet in F Op. 77/2, and in the B flat 'Andante grazioso' of the D minor Quartet Op. 103. Where such enharmonic descents occur in works in sharp keys, it will be found that very often the actual modulation takes place within a 'flat' context; thus in the G major Quartet Op. 76/1, there is such a modulation in the Finale, but the Finale starts in G *minor* and the modulation begins in the key of the relative major, B flat. It is characteristic that the ascent into enharmonic sharp regions usually occurs in works in sharp keys, as in the first movement of Trio 40 in F sharp minor.

Here, then, in Op. 71/3's first movement we have a recapitulation which is actually in F double-flat major, in the course of which third-related keys play once again a decisive role (E flat minor to C flat minor [B minor]). Naturally all this darkens the texture of the music greatly; and we shall see, by the time the recapitulation is finished, that this darkening in the development presages an even darker, indeed eerie, passage at the beginning of the coda. Haydn wants the second part of the movement repeated, and we would point out how brilliantly he composes the last bars before the repeat sign so that they effortlessly modulate back to the E flat minor of the beginning of the development – or to this part of the coda, also significantly in E flat minor, which appears like a breath of icy air. It is characteristic of Haydn that he is able to dispel this atmosphere within a few bars, notably by the trills, first upwards in violin II, then downwards in both violins (291–315).

It has been observed that the adagio movements of many of Haydn's late quartets form the central point of the work in question. Here the composer even manages to create such a focal point with what seems at the outset, to be one of his smoothly flowing andante variations (it is marked 'Andante con moto', and the 'con moto' might, in the autograph, be a slightly later addition). In the theme, the autograph has the interesting word 'licenza' at bar 3 of the second violin. When Haydn uses the word 'licenza' (or more frequently 'con licenza') it is usually to remark on the fact that he has deliberately broken some grammatical rule. We will find a striking example of *con licenza* in the 'Qui tollis' of the *Missa in tempore belli* (1796). Fortunately we have Haydn's own words on the subject. When Dies (61) interviewed the composer on 23 May 1805, the biographer asked him if he had formed any rules with the help of which he could ensure the public's approval. Haydn answered: 'In the heat of composition I never thought about that; I wrote what seemed good to me and corrected it afterwards according to the rules of harmony. I never used other tricks [*Kunstgriffe*]. Now and then I took the liberty of offending, not the ear, but the usual rules of the textbooks, and signed these passages with the words *con licenza*. They cried aloud, 'A mistake!' and wanted to prove it with Fux. I asked my enemies if they could prove it by ear, that it was a mistake. They had to answer 'no' 'My own ear', Haydn continued, 'hears no mistake in those passages; quite on the contrary, I find it sounds beautiful. That is why I asked for permission to be able to sin against the rules.' He made a similar remark about his ear, of which he rightly thought highly – consider the finely planned enharmonic modulations which we have been analyzing – to Griesinger (60). 'The ear, by which I mean an educated one, of course, has to decide [such matters], and I consider myself as worthy [*befügt*] as another to create rules in this respect.'

Here, the *licenza* at the beginning of our slow movement is to document the octaves between first and second violins (F–E–F) but even more the tritonal interval between the E natural of the violins and the B flat of the 'cello (1–16). We have here an $a–b–a^1$ form, in which the unconventional harmonic direction may be noted. The music modulates to F (the dominant) but continues at once to the mediant, D, which is ambiguously expressed in that there is no third, and thus one is uncertain if mediant minor or major is meant. In the second part, we begin in the dominant of C, and the C, supertonic, is also ambiguous, first appearing to be C minor but then moving to C major and back to the tonic. This harmonic ambiguity is a feature of much late Haydn, and we shall encounter another striking example in the introduction of Symphony No. 97, and of course the greatest and most extended series of such ambiguities in the 'Chaos' introduction to *The Creation*.

After the opening section, we have $8 + 16$ bars in the tonic minor, each part repeated, and then an unrepeated *da capo* of the opening section. Thus, although the *minore* part is clearly based on the opening thematic material, we have a combination of variation form with A–B–A. As the movement progresses, we see that Haydn has put forward a new adaptation of variation, to wit a double A–B–A movement. Section IV is a variation of A ($a^1–b^1–a^2$) with repeat signs; there then follows a variation of B, also in B flat minor (but with different modulations: originally the music ended at the first double bar in F minor, but now we modulate to D flat). This new B^1 section is also split up into $a^1–b^1–a^2$ (or rather $c^1–d^1–c^2$), but the c^2 is broken off and we enter into the A section, again varied.

A(a–b–a^1) B flat   →   B(c–d–c^1) B flat minor   →   A *da capo*   →

||: 8 :||||: 8 :|| ||: 8 :||||: 16 :|| no repeats

A^1 (a^1–b^1–a^2) B flat →   B^1 (c^1–d^1–[c^2]) B flat minor

||: 8 :||||: 8 :|| ||: 8 :|| 8 breaking off and moving without c^2

into   →   A^2 B flat   →   Coda (based on a) in B flat
       $8 + 12$ 28 bars.

The surprise is what Haydn does with the A^2: the theme strikes off into the three upper strings' highest register, *staccato assai e piano*. It is an enchanted fairy-tale world and constitutes one of the most original strokes ever to have come from Haydn's fertile pen. This is the centre of the whole Quartet, to which Haydn has led up and from which (in a sense) he now leads down in the last two movements. Haydn often follows a rather quick slow movement with a much slower minuet than usual. The most famous case is in the 'Military' Symphony where the 'Military Movement' (Allegretto in barred C) is followed by the slowest Menuet, marked 'moderato', of the Salomon Symphonies. In Op. 71/3, the Menuet has no marking but is obviously the same kind of slow dance movement as that of the 'Military'. The lively Finale (Vivace) introduces a *fugato* in double counterpoint, with the first violin having the countersubject in running semiquavers and the second the theme. Altogether this is a very contrapuntal movement, despite its homophonic beginning. The Coda even introduces a *stretto* passage with the main theme over a dominant pedal point. This is a characteristic movement in sonata-rondo form which keeps returning to the tonic for each new main section; in this, and in its contrapuntal excursions, Op. 71/3's Finale is a precursor to the famous Finale of Symphony No. 101, to be composed at the beginning of the coming year (1794).

If Op. 71/3 has never been one of the more popular works from this sextet, the ensuing Quartet in C, Op. 74/1, has always been much admired and, after the 'Rider' Quartet (Op. 74/3), the most performed of the series, at least in the twentieth century. One of the reasons for Op. 74/1's success is perhaps the powerful underlying motivic unity not only of the first movement – this was to be expected – but of the whole work. The unity operates on several levels, and as it is rather complicated to explain, even with musical examples, we will occasionally move from one movement to another to illustrate a particular facet of its operation. The work opens with a held, off-tonic (in fact dominant seventh) chord, a bold innovation. It serves, of course, to establish the tonic in a simple and effective way, and this is necessary because the main theme is almost Mozartianly chromatic. The chromaticism is grounded by a 'cello pedal point in quavers which is, however, also altered chromatically when the theme is repeated. The progression from *b'* to *e'''* in half steps will be a central point of the work's unity, and also the theme's *Urlinie* from *c''* to *g''*.

The continuation of the theme is a free imitation between three of the parts. Notice that in the first violin part of the opening (quoted above) we find the juxtaposition F natural to F sharp; we also find it in the continuation:

This is a derivative of the changing chromatic line at the beginning (C–C sharp, E flat–E). The main theme appears in the dominant, followed by a series of semiquavers in the violins, of which the second violin part will prove essential:

The main theme appears yet again in the dominant, this time to introduce what might be termed the second subject, which is relatively unimportant, appearing only in the recapitulation (as in Symphony No. 104's opening movement) and not otherwise – at least not yet. The countersubject in the first violin part at bars 43–4 is also important for the role it will play in the development section:

At this juncture we shall interrupt the analysis of the first movement and proceed to the Menuet and Finale (Vivace), since they both utilize material from the exposition of the first 'Allegro moderato'. First the Menuet's theme:

Again we have the progression from C to C sharp. In the Finale, after the announcement of the main theme, we have the following passage, marked by the same progression at a different interval: (F to F sharp), which however drops to the literal quotation of C–C sharp):

Particular attention should also be paid to the lower lines (bracketed). When we reach the dominant, a variant of the above quotation appears, still haunted by the chromatic progression:

The second subject of the Finale is not yet freed from the chromatic progression, which by now could be termed almost an obsession with its inventor:

If this point of 'chromatic progression' unity may seem on the face of it obvious, Haydn also has more devious methods. As an interesting case in point – the Quartet has many, of which we mention just a few – we may take the beginning of the Finale. Apart from the virtuoso manner in which Haydn handles the repetition (*staccato assai*) of the main subject, we may note that it is clearly a derivative of the closing material in the first movement's exposition (bars 45ff.). If we mentally transpose that passage into C, we will note the striking similarity of the bracketed part of the theme to the *tr* figure (bar 46) in violin I of the earlier quotation (including the upbeat). As if to stress the connection with the first movement, Haydn then gives us the theme again but *staccato* (bars 1–23). The link to the first movement is further cemented by the following passage in the Finale's exposition, just after we have firmly established the dominant key:

The connection with bars 35ff. of the first movement is clearly felt although the two figures – both have been bracketed – have slightly different endings. Their similarity is suggested, too, by the fact that both are announced by the second violin, while the first in each case has a countersubject.

476

To return to the first movement, the development is, except for a brief reference to the material originally announced in bars 35ff., dominated by the first subject and also by its countersubject. The first violin figure at bar 43 assumes ever greater proportions:

The first five notes of the countersubject are now inverted:

Thus we see the tremendous motivic concentration not only in this *Allegro moderato* but also throughout the Quartet.

477

The 'Andantino grazioso', says Cecil Gray[1], 'is one of these movements in which the genius of Haydn comes near to that of Mozart . . . The airy grace and charm, the serenity and poise, the whole allure, of the first symmetrical eight bars are decidedly Mozartian, but only Haydn would have followed them up and completed them with an irregular five-bar phrase.'

It will be noted how deftly Haydn used the viola & 'cello line of bars 9–10, first as an accompaniment, then in the first violin (bars 12–13), which seems to continue the bass line. This bass lines also appears when the music reaches the dominant at bars 28 and 29. The bracketed part at bars 14–15 and 18–19 (c′) seems to foreshadow bars 29–31 of the Finale which has been quoted above.

The second subject, if one cares to call it that, is beautifully and subtly related to the beginning (bars 1–22). Haydn takes the intervallic essence of bars 3–4 and 6–7 –

in the first violin  and

– and proceeds to turn them into the dialogue between first violin and 'cello (bars 38ff.). This particularly exquisite section appears three times in all, and as the movement unfolds, it is ever clearer that even the viola of bars 38ff. is an expansion of the viola at bars 14ff. In its almost feminine sensitivity, this gracious *Andante* (a literal translation of the tempo) is in fine contrast to the vitality and virility of the quick outer movements. Once again, in the Quartet as a whole, Haydn has successfully combined great melodic, motivic and intervallic tension with tender lyricism, and warmth of expression.

Haydn has thought up a new kind of introduction to the first movement of Op. 74/2: here the 'Allegro spiritoso' starts with what appears to be the main theme. It is only after the half close and fermata that we realize that the first eight bars are an introductory flourish. This, in *forte* unison, provides material for the real main subject (1–18). This is another monothematic movement, which is to say the lion's share of the action is given to the first subject, but a wealth of subsidiary material is introduced so that the new entries of the principal thematic substance may stand out more boldly. It is also a very symphonic-sounding movements, partly because of the chordal nature of the theme. In all six works of this set, one notices the increased role given to trills, not in the usual cadential function but as a device often used to increase the sound and volume of a note; frequently three of four instruments have a trill simultaneously, and this happens nearly half-a-dozen times in this exposition alone; while the four semibreves of the first violin with a trill on each, just before the end of the exposition, stand out as an effective and almost Falstaffian touch. The boisterous humour of this 'Allegro spiritoso' is also increased by the 'false' lead-backs and lead-ons at the end of the exposition's double bar: unison cadence on the note C, then (lead-back) two minims in *piano* for all instruments, D flat–E natural, leading back to F, or (lead-on), two minims in *piano* C sharp–E which leads, quite unexpectedly to the medium major of C, that is, A major (again a third-related key, and this time a pivot key, because A is third-related not only to C but also to the home key, F). There now follows a dense contrapuntal passage using the main theme and also a countersubject (the figure with the grace note in violin I at bars 111f.). Students of Haydn will notice a similarity, not

1 Op. cit. VII [1938], 21.

only in the triadic 'head' of the theme but also in the contrapuntal extension, with the development of Symphony No. 98 in B flat (1792), first movement (bars 110–30).

This enormous development section, with its large-scale contrapuntal exploitation of the main subject, is the central part of the movement. It is also, like its counterpart – Symphony No. 98 – particularly serious, moving from one long passage in the minor to the next: A minor, see the above example; then a succession of keys, mostly tinged with minor, leading to C minor, then to E flat and to a long pedal point on the dominant of D minor, ending in a unison passage on the note *a* which is identical with the rhythm of bars 7 and 8 – a clever device to remind us that the eight-bar introduction is essential even in such a small detail. With one more jocose modulation in unison (*piano* semibreve unison notes *d–e*) we are back in the tonic and the recapitulation. We would quote one more passage, a use of the main theme over a 'cello pedal point in broken quaver octaves (bars 206–16) so powerful and so driving that one is again reminded of the fact, emphasized above in the Chronicle, that Beethoven was probably at Eisenstadt in the Summer of 1793 when this very work was being composed; and in any case he will have heard it countless times in the Autumn of 1795 and early in 1796, when this set of quartets will have been the rage of intellectual Vienna.

In the suave and elegant theme and variations that follow (marked 'Andante grazioso') Haydn seeks, and successfully, to lower the level of boisterous humour and (in the development) thematic tension which characterized the opening *Allegro spiritoso*. The theme is indicated 'mezza voce', the dynamic mark used for this and the slow movement of the following 'Rider' Quartet, Op. 74/3, but frequently employed elsewhere in the series, as well. As a novel element in this 'Andante grazioso' we have a whole variation led by the solo *second* violin, while in the next (and last) variation we have a delicate semiquaver accompaniment for solo viola, later given also to the 'cello. In the *Menuet* we return to the high comedy of the opening movement, but we note the dark-hued Trio in the flattened submediant, with a long lead-back to the *da capo* such as we shall encounter in Symphonies Nos. 99 and 104. The Finale (Presto), a brilliant rondo with strong development sections – not a sonata rondo in the classical scheme of the Salomon Symphonies but a far cry from Haydn's rondos of the late 1770s and early 1780s. The theme is one of those sensationally popular tunes which caused Breitkopf & Härtel to issue it (and the slow movement), together with a batch of late symphonic movements, in an arrangement for piano: 'XII petites pièces pour le Clavecin ou Piano-Forte' (Leipzig 1799?).

As if to balance the monothematicism of the first two movements (the first because the composer willed it so, the second because of the form), Haydn now builds a Finale in which not only the first subject returns, rondo-like (1–16), but we also have a strange and Balkan-like second subject in C minor, presented twice, which appears no less than three times, the second time in D minor and the third time in F minor. It is the strongest possible contrast to the flippant first subject and as such is extremely effective. Towards the close of the movement the first violin breaks into triplet arpeggios and passage-work, another tribute to Salomon (whose presence is perhaps less felt in this Quartet than in many of the others).

The famous and epoch-making Quartets of Op. 20 (1772) contained two particularly sombre works in minor keys. But apart from this one exception – and Op. 20 is an exception at almost every level – Haydn from Op. 9 (1769?) onwards reserves precisely one work in the minor for each series of six. This is the case in Opp. 9, 33, 50, 54–55 (one *opus* as in the case of 71–74), 64 and 76. One can see that after about 1772

Haydn had very precise ideas as to how many works in the minor should be introduced in every *opus*. In the late piano trios composed as sets of three we have seen, on the other hand, that he placed one work in the minor key for each set of three.

In recent years, Haydn's later symphonies and strings quartets in the minor key have come in for some harsh criticism, particularly Op. 74/3 in Bea Friedland's *Haydn's 'Sturm und Drang' Period: a Problem in Esthetics* (Dissertation, Queens College, New York 1968). This is because on the one hand, these critics have misjudged Haydn's intent as regards the minor key in the classical scheme (as opposed to his views in the *Sturm und Drang* period, the culmination of pre-classical aesthetic concepts), while on the other they have, particularly as regards Op. 74/3, overlooked the obvious fact that the central message of the work is not in its outer movements – as was the case with Symphony No. 95 in C minor (1791) – but in its slow movement ('Largo assai'). We may have misjudged Haydn's intention: his contemporary audiences did not. We have no less than five contemporary editions of the slow movement (variously entitled 'Andante', 'Adagio' and 'Largo') arranged for piano: in Vienna, two editions came out within a fortnight of each other, Traeg's announced in the *Wiener Zeitung* on 31 May 1797 and Hoffmeister's in the same journal on 14 June (can Haydn have made the arrangement himself?). And in the year of Haydn's death, this movement was used as the last part of a Cantata for voices and orchestra entitled 'Der Versöhnungstod' (arranged by J. A. Schulze) and published by Breitkopf & Härtel.

There is no slow introduction to the opening Allegro because the theme itself is so powerful and its presence so immediate as to require nothing to prepare it (bars 1–23). The later addition of 'non troppo' to the original tempo Allegro comes from the first violin of the authentic Corri & Dussek edition, and we do not doubt that it is authentic. The fact that it was added only to the first violin does not mean much: the first violin determined the tempo and was in a real sense the 'leader'. Moreover, composers were generally more attentive to the proofs of the first violin than to the others: Mozart's proof-reading of the great Quartets dedicated to Haydn was almost entirely confined to the first violin part.[1]

We say that there is no introduction: but the first eight bars might be construed as such in the same way as the beginning of the preceding F major Quartet. (1) They never reappear directly again, not even in the recapitulation; but (2) they are used in a fragmentary state together with the triplet figure of bars 21ff. at the beginning of the development.

The triplet figure is perhaps a clue as to why Haydn thought it prudent to add 'non troppo' to the Allegro: one can always tell an over-hasty performance by the pace of these triplets, which turn out, incidentally, to have a major function throughout the movement. The second subject, played first by violin I on the d-string and then by violin II, is an almost unsettling contrast to the sombre first subject (by which we mean the *piano* section, not the opening with the grace notes). It is the same abrupt contrast (bars 55–64) as we have noted in Symphony No. 83 and will note with No. 95. The recapitulation is reached by a particularly felicitous lead-back, starting (still in the development) with the triplets which have dominated the music to an extraordinary extent: from bars 21–106, there have been triplets in every bar except for 15 bars, so that their sudden withdrawal from the scene creates a marked retardation of the basic pulse. Their absence throws into sharp relief the gradual emergence of the principal

1 The first edition was published by Artaria in 1785 with the famous preface dated 1 September. See Alfred Einstein's critical edition for Novello & Co., London, 1945 as part of 'The 10 Celebrated String Quartets by Mozart, First Authentic Edition in Score'.

subject, first to lead into, and then dominate, the beginning of the recapitulation (bars 104–37). The second subject is in G major, in which key the movement ends. This also makes more plausible the key of E major for the slow movement, it being the submediant major of G major. That is why, too, the following Minuet is in G major and not G minor. Could there be more conclusive proof that the Quartet was actually planned round its extraordinary 'Largo assai'?

If one were to select the single greatest movement of this sextet, the present 'Largo assai' would be the obvious choice. It is so striking, formally, harmonically, and in richness of conception, that it dwarfs the rest of the work – and we believe that this was Haydn's intention. Such a violently intense piece of music could only, accordingly to Haydn's aesthetic principles, be set off by movements less intense, less demanding. Formally, the movement is in A–B–A¹ form, the B section being in the tonic minor (E) and illuminated by a poetic transition back to the recapitulation. The beginning of the Largo has two harmonic highlights, the first one the incredible chord, *ff*, of the recapitulation has a finely elaborated first violin part, but nothing prepares us for the dominant of C major at bar eight – enough to make a lesser composer immortal in one *fortissimo* stroke; while the other, equally prominent by being marked *pianissimo*, is the drop from C sharp minor to what appears to be the Neapolitan sixth of F sharp but actually presages a modulation to the dominant (seventh) of E, a progression in which that sinuous, *Tristan*-like viola part adds a darkly rich gush of colour. (Cf. bar 12.) The recapitulation has a richly elaborated first violin part, but nothing prepares us for the gigantic inspiration of the *tremolo* re-interpretation of bars 12–13:

A page from the autograph of the String Quartet in G minor, Op. 74, No. 3 (1793) – the slow movement (Largo assai).

We gradually begin to work our way back to G minor and (curious thing to observe in a key so doom-ridden by Mozartian interpretation!) normality via the Trio of the Minuet: again notice Haydn's grand scheme, to take us from E major (six 'fifths' in the circle-of-fifths relationship away from G minor) to G major (Minuet) with a middle part (rather longer than the Minuet proper) in G minor, finally arriving back at the tonic minor for the Finale.

Critics have always asserted that this Quartet was called the 'Rider' because of the bouncing appoggiature of the opening bars of the *first* movement; but we beg leave to observe that the 'riding' rhythm is all in the opening bars (1–14) of the Finale ('Allegro con brio') – not that the matter is of any importance to the music either way.

This is a well balanced movement, with a distinct second subject of which much is made in the development, even to combining it and juxtaposing it with the first. The gruff, even violent atmosphere (cf. the *ff* outburst at bars 83 ff.), in which the first violin manages to play almost a concerto-like role, gradually gives way to G major when the second subject arrives in the recapitulation. Within a few bars the whole mood of the G minor opening – not to speak of the rhapsodic and poetical atmosphere of the slow movement – has disappeared, leaving a serenely joyous conclusion: it is rather like the description, so penetrating, of Haydn by the Swedish visitor to which we have twice before alluded – the two physiognomies of Haydn, one severe and stern, the other jovial and light-hearted. The direct confrontation of both elements has always made twentieth-century (or indeed most nineteenth-century critics after Beethoven's death) critics slightly uncomfortable; but it remains a significant trait of Haydn's many-sided and, over the years, profoundly changing character.

It is hard, after so many years, to imagine the effect of these new string quartets on young musicians in London at that time, but as it happens we have a touching tribute in the form of an unpublished letter from Haydn's admirer, the Italian composer Giovanni Battista Cimador (born 1761), to his friend Alessandro da Ponte (apparently no relation to Lorenzo), dated 10 October 1794. Filled with delight by these new works, Cimador, who apparently had access to Haydn's autograph scores (we recall that the young Cimador was in Bath with Haydn in August 1794), enclosed a copy of the Largo from – what would be – Op. 74, No. 3, in score, adding: 'Eccovi, caro amico, un pezzo che deve entusiasmare tutti gl'adoratori di quel divino uomo che l'ha fatto. . . .'[1]

---

1 Letter formerly in the Heyer Collection, Cologne; sold by Leo Liepmannsohn and included in his Catalogue of 5–10 May 1927 (item no. 414), where the spelling 'entusiastare' is used, wrongly. This same spelling also occurs in another reference to this letter, in the undated Lager-Katalog 23 of K. H. Henrici, Berlin, item no. 241. The letter, if recovered, would be of great interest. In it (according to the summary in the Henrici catalogue) Cimador speaks of his personal relationship to Haydn and adds a special word about the Mozart Quartets, Op. X, dedicated to Haydn (K. 387, etc.): '. . . che dedicò a Haydn . . . sono capi d'opera . . .: ma, quantunque io adoro Haydn, trovo che non gli stanno al di sotto'. The letter, consisting of three full pages, also discusses the London Opera, Banti, the forthcoming arrival of Bartolozzi, Dragonetti and Bianchi, and the political situation ('. . . in questa terribile situazione dell' Europa').

CHAPTER EIGHT

Instrumental Music – Orchestral Works

Overture to an English Opera
(1794: Ia: 3)
[Orchestration and *tempi*: see *L'anima del filosofo – sinfonia*]

The probable origin of Haydn's *Overture to an English Opera* and its (unlikely) connection to his opera *L'anima del filosofo* (1791) has been discussed in the Chronicle (*supra*, p. 299) and also in connection with the opera. Haydn's entry in the *Entwurf-Katalog* for the work, 'Overture to an English Opera 1994 [= 1794]', is probably correct and refers to Salomon's *Windsor Castle*, which was performed in April 1795. As we have noted, it is curious that Salomon (or Gallini, who may have owned the work if it was in fact composed earlier than 1794) never printed the Overture which, one would have thought, could have been a great success as a concert piece. It was not printed until 1952 (edited for the Haydn-Mozart Presse by the present writer) an extraordinary fate for a late-period orchestral work by Haydn.

The work opens with a majestic slow introduction in C minor (Largo) which uses the whole orchestra, with dotted rhythms like a French 'Ouverture', while the charming Presto section begins with a theme for solo oboe which actually appears in *L'anima del filosofo* and has been quoted above in the Chronicle (*supra*, p. 302). In this nearly monothematic Presto – the second subject is treated in very perfunctory fashion – there is a spirited development section and a rousing little codetta with held notes in the brass instruments, just before the end, which sound surprisingly like a nineteenth-century theatre overture. The Overture is a minor work but like everything Haydn touched during his London sojourns it is beautifully constructed and at its modest level very effective.

Dance Music

Haydn's *Catalogue of Works Composed in England* lists the following dance music: '24 Minuets and german dances 12 [double sheets] . . . 4 Contrydances [*sic*] 2 [double sheets] . . . 2 Contrydances 2 [double sheets]'. Except for one which is certainly authentic and one that is possibly authentic, these six 'Contrydances' have, alas, disappeared. The genuine one was submerged at the end of a little autograph manuscript owned by the Austrian National Library, the first part of which contains the short Song, 'Trust not too much' (which has been mentioned above, p. 394). The second part is what would appear to be a 'Contrydance'. We have no other genuine Haydn country dances with which to compare this single specimen, but we do have an old MS. in the Gesellschaft der Musikfreunde containing 'Contredanze per il Clavi Cembalo Del Sigre. Giuseppe Haydn' (IX: 29) which the late O. E. Deutsch published in 1930 – there is no guarantee that they are authentic – and which are certainly of the period. Formally these dances are very similar to Haydn's, including the repeated notes at the end of each section, so that we may presume that our little piece really is a piano sketch for one of the lost six Country Dances:

The other is 'The Princess of Wales's Favorite Dance by D[r]. Haydn' offered by Alan Tyson, with facsimile, as 'a somewhat mutilated, and probably truncated, form of a *genuine* country dance by Haydn' in the *Haydn Yearbook* I (1962), 198f., 202.

The major works of dance music of the London period are the Twenty-Four Minuets and German Dances that Haydn lists in his *Catalogue of Works*. There are two candidates for this group of works among the late orchestral dances by Haydn that have come down to us. One would be the magnificent set of Twenty-Four Minuets (IX: 16) for large orchestra (including clarinets and Turkish instruments) which exists in one single set of MS. parts in the Berlin State Library, who acquired it from Artaria together with a large amount of Haydn autographs and copies in the nineteenth century. These great Minuets were not published until 1972.[1] The second candidate for the group is the Twelve *Deutsche Tänze* and Twelve Minuets composed for the Redoutensaal in Vienna in November 1792, and there are several reasons why these latter must be considered the works in question: (1) We know they were performed in November 1792 in Vienna because Artaria published them almost immediately thereafter. (2) if Haydn had composed not only these Redoutensaal Dances but also the Twenty-Four Minuets during the period 1791–5, he surely would have indicated both in his English Catalogue. Thus we presume that the Twenty-Four Minuets must have been composed *after* September 1795, when Haydn arrived back in Vienna. They cannot very well have been composed before, since they include 2 flutes, 2 clarinets and 2 trumpets, instruments which Haydn did not have all at once in Eszterháza, and stylistically they are very much works of the late 1780s or, more likely, 1790s. We have therefore treated these Minuets in another place.

TWELVE DEUTSCHE TÄNZE (IX: 12) and TWELVE MINUETS (IX: 11)
For 2 flutes, 2 oboes, 2 clarinets, 2 bassoons, 2 horns, 2 trumpets, timpani and strings without viola (1792); and Twelve Minuets (IX: 11) for *flauto piccolo* (in No. 7's Trio), 2 flutes, 2 oboes, 2 clarinets, 2 bassoons, 2 horns, 2 trumpets, timpani and strings without viola (1792). Modern edition of the *Deutsche Tänze*: edited by O. E. Deutsch, Kistner & Siegel, Leipzig 1931. Modern edition of the Minuets: edited by E. F. Schmid,

1 Verlag Doblinger, Vienna-Munich, edited by H. C. Robbins Landon. The first modern performance of some took place in the Haydn Festival at Eisenstadt held in September 1971.

Kistner & Siegel, Leipzig 1940 under the title 'Katharinentänze' (for St. Catherine's Day, when the works were first played in 1792: see Pohl III, 65).

These are practically the only orchestral dances by Haydn to have entered the modern repertoire (albeit rather tardily, as we have seen), and the only ones to be recorded complete in our day (Haydn Society, 1950). By any count, they are among the greatest pieces of their kind to come out of the Viennese classical school, which is saying something if one knows the magnificent dance music that Mozart, Schubert and Beethoven have left us. It happens that we have a series of sketches for all the *Deutsche Tänze* and some of the Minuets – the sketches have been listed above (p. 207) – which show the care with which Haydn approached even this light music during this late period. In fact the whole Viennese classical school seems to have had a special affection for dance music, and there is no doubt that the Viennese delight in dancing was their prime inspiration. These beautiful miniature creations by Haydn, Mozart, Schubert and Beethoven led directly to the lyric waltzes of Lanner and the burst of inspiration that followed with the Strauss family. It is a grand tradition to which the Redoutensaal Dances contributed twenty-four particularly felicitous compositions. Mozart took the trouble to list his dance music in his own thematic catalogue, but Haydn did not – neither the *Entwurf-Katalog* nor the Elssler Catalogue of 1805 contains any of the dance suites. We are fortunate that a great selection, though by no means all, of Haydn's mature orchestral dance music has survived; though their survival was largely a matter of chance and most of the works have come down to us in one source only. Apart from the authentic piano arrangements, the *Deutsche Tänze* (IX: 12) exist only in the former Redoutensaal collection of the Pensionsgesellschaft, now housed in the Austrian National Library. These MS. parts, lacking violin II but with corrections by Haydn, are entitled 'Tedeschi di Ballo' and are the original ones used in 1792. The Minuets (IX: 11) exist in two authentic sources: (1) the original performance material from the Redoutensaal collection of the Pensionsgesellschaft (Austrian National Library), entitled 'Dodeci Menuetti di Ballo 1792', with corrections by Haydn and (2) an authentic set of MS. parts from the Artaria Archives, now in the Berlin State Library (without the *flautino* part).

The Minuets are based on the key of D major, that is No. 1 and No. 12 are in that key, and so is the beginning of the second part, No. 7. The first five Minuets move in third-related keys, as follows: No. 1 in D; No. 2 in B flat; No. 3 in G; No. 4 in E; No. 5 in C. Having moved down in thirds, Haydn now breaks the scheme: No. 6 in F; No. 7 in D (beginning of second part), No. 8 in E flat, No. 9 in C; No. 10 in G; No. 11 in E flat, No. 12 in D.

This interest in third-related dance suites is not new in Haydn: the Artaria 'Six Allemandes' of 1787 (IX: 9) has the following scheme: No. 1 in B flat, No. 2 in G, No. 3 in E flat, No. 4 in C, No. 5 in A, No. 6 in D – again a downward succession of thirds broken off so as to end in D major (No. 5 to No. 6 making the dominant to tonic relationship). If the attractive *Deutsche Tänze* (IX: 10) published by Hoffmeister in Vienna and Amon in Heilbronn about 1793 are authentic, they too illustrate an interest in linking the dances together, but this time not by third-related keys but through the circle of fifths, to wit: No. 1 in D, No. 2 in G, No. 3 in C, No. 4 in F, No. 5 in B flat, No. 6 in E flat; while the second part again breaks the scheme: No. 7 in G, No. 8 in A and Nos. 10–12 in D.

The key-scheme of the *Deutsche Tänze* of 1792 is more conventional: No. 1 in G, No. 2 in B flat, No. 3 in G, No. 4 in C, No. 5 in A, No. 6 in D, No. 7 in G, No. 8 in D, No. 9 in B flat, No. 10 in C, No. 11 in F, No. 12 in D. Although in progressive tonality

(G to D), it is clear that these Dances were designed to fit with the Minuets (in the home key of D). We have no idea which of the two groups of works was played first, or if they were split up into groups of six each and interspersed.

The Minuets vary in the number of bars: 16, 20, 22 and 24 bars, while the Trios contain 16, 20 or 22 bars. In the great Twenty-Four Minuets (IX: 16) the number of bars of the Minuets ranges from 16 to 32 but also includes 18, 20, 22, 24, 28 and 30 bars, and the Trios vary from 16 to 20, 24 and 28 bars. We mention this to show that the conventional eight and sixteen-bar divisions, no longer hold true. The layout of the *Deutsche Tänze*, on the other hand, is much more constricted. They are usually in sixteen bars; in one case (No. 8) we have twenty and the Coda of No. 12 is also twenty. There is only one Trio (to No. 4) and it contains twenty bars, too.

Two outstanding features of these Redoutensaal Dances are immediately apparent: the one is the endless amount of beautiful, lyrical, witty, brilliant and rhythmically enticing tunes that Haydn is able to produce. The sketches show that for every accepted tune, he wrote at least one that was either rejected or put aside. There are no less than twenty-four delightful melodies that Haydn never seems to have used at all (not twenty-six as in Hoboken I, 561–3; two, Nos. 11 and 23, were actually used, and for IX: 11, No. 9). The other principal feature of these works is the inventive, sparkling orchestration. Those who are fortunate enough to own the Haydn Society recording, which was made with the entire first-desk members of the Vienna Philharmonic Orchestra conducted by Hans Gillesberger (1950), will remember the exquisite playing of the late Leopold Wlach, first clarinet, in the Trio of Minuet No. 2:

The accompaniment, in the waltz rhythm (*l–u–u*), is a look far into the future, of Emperor Franz Joseph's early years and the first flowering of the Viennese *Walzer*.

The German Dances are orchestrated in a more transparent way. The Minuets are in a slower tempo and more massively scored: not with more instruments, for the orchestra of both sets is identical except for the *flautino* (not used in the German Dances); but the Minuets are more like symphonic minuets, as are the Twenty-Four Minuets (IX: 16). The German Dances are *sui generis*, with all kinds of fascinating details, such as No. 8, where the music ends with the violins dashing down the scale and simply stopping at the end – this is the sort of thing not found in the Minuets:

Apart from the Twenty-Four Minuets, which we have tentatively placed in the immediate post-London years, *c.* 1795–7, these Redoutensaal Dances are the last of Haydn's many efforts in the genre. There is possibly no more spectacular way to judge Haydn's growth as a musician and artist than to compare the earliest known set of his dance music, Twelve Minuets (known as the 'Seitenstetten Minuets' [IX: 1] from the fact that the autograph was found in that Benedictine Monastery of Lower Austria), composed in the 1750s, with the Redoutensaal Dances of 1792. From these bright works of the outgoing Baroque to the splendours of the late Dances is to see, in miniature, the ripening of the whole Viennese classical school. As Mozart said about another Haydn *Gelegenheitsstück*, 'Auch in der unbedeutendsten Posse lässt sich ein Meister nicht verkennen'.[1]

The Redoutensaal Dances were also acquired by Prince von Fürstenberg at Donaueschingen Castle, and hereby hangs a tale. For much to our astonishment we find that instead of the German Dances IX : 12 another set has been substituted, namely IX : 13. The Minuets IX : 11 (which really were for the Redoutensaal) are marked on the title page: '12 Neue Menuetti/für d Clavir übersetz/Componirt/von H; Herrn Capellmeister/Joseph Haydn/aufgeführt in den k : k : Redoutensaal in Wienn 792'. The MS. is, as the title informs us, a piano arrangement, and would at first glance seem to be a copy of the Artaria print, which appeared in December 1792; since the piano arrangement of IX : 13 (the German Dances of 1792 for the Redoutensaal) exists in Haydn's autograph, we may with confidence assume that the piano version of IX : 11 (Minuets) which Artaria published is Haydn's own. So far, the Donaueschingen MS. would seem to be a routine Viennese copy of an Artaria print; but if we examine it more carefully, we find that most of the MS. was copied by none other than Johann Schellinger, the former princely copyist at Eszterháza; it is also dated at the end '$\overline{793}$' (a second copyist wrote from No. 5 Trio to Minuet No. 7, inclusive). Now as for the German Dances which should have been IX : 12 and are in fact IX : 13 : they are entitled '12/deutsche Tänze/aus d k : k : Redouten Saale/auf d clavir/gesetzt/J. Haydn 792', and Schellinger wrote the title page and the first page of music, another copyist the rest. Was Haydn using Schellinger as a copyist? It would seen the natural answer. Perhaps Artaria was using him, or – a faint third possibility – Schellinger was operating on his own. The interesting thing, however, is that textually Schellinger seems – at least in the case of IX : 11 – to be working from the autograph (there are accuracies therein that do not appear in Artaria) and *not* from Artaria. But most of all, IX : 13, for which there is. no other source except a duplicated MS. in Donaueschingen, seems to be an authentic copy and therefore the work is authentic (which we did not, really, know hitherto). Since Donaueschingen acquired all the Salomon Symphonies from Haydn, there is no reason to think that these interesting piano arrangements, in the case of IX : 13 unique copies, are anything but authentic. Professor Franz Eibner, who drew our attention to the MSS., is preparing a critical edition.

Marches

It seems scarcely believable that Haydn found time to compose marches while he was in England; but he did, and they are partly listed in his *Catalogue of Works* as follows: '2 Marches 2 [double sheets] . . . March – Prince of Wales 2 [double sheets]'.[2] Three

---

1 *Wiener Schriftsteller- und Künstler-Lexikon*, Vienna 1793, p. 59.
2 Karl Haas, 'Haydn's English Military Marches' in: *The Score*, No. 2, January 1950, pp. 50ff. Critical edition: *Joseph Haydn: Samtliche Werke für Blasinstrumente: Märsche* (edited by the present writer), Verlag Doblinger, Vienna-Munich 1960 in Diletto Musicale 34. The *March for the Royal Society of Musicians*, also edited by the present writer, is published in the same series as Diletto Musicale 98. The piano arr. of the 'Derbyshire Marches', by Haydn, are published in *Haydn* (Great Composers Series) by H. C. Robbins Landon, Faber, 1971.

complete Marches for wind band, one incomplete March for wind band, and one of the complete Marches arranged for full orchestra, have survived. They are as follows:

(1) MARCH FOR THE PRINCE OF WALES IN E FLAT (VIII: 3) for 2 clarinets, 2 bassoons, 2 horns, trumpet, serpent [and percussion instruments] with Trio. London, 1792(?).

(2) MARCH FOR THE ROYAL SOCIETY OF MUSICIANS IN E FLAT (VIII: 3 bis) for 2 flutes, 2 clarinets, 2 bassoons, 2 horns, 2 trumpets, strings [and percussion instruments] with Trio. London, 1792.

(3) MARCH IN E FLAT (VIII: 7) for 2 clarinets, 2 bassoons, 2 horns, trumpet and serpent. London, 1792(?).

(4) MARCH NO. 1 FOR THE DERBYSHIRE CAVALRY REGIMENT IN E FLAT (VIII: 1) for 2 clarinets, 2 bassoons, 2 horns, trumpet, serpent and 'Militair Instrumente' (percussion: the stave is, however, not filled in). London, 1795.

(5) MARCH NO. 2 FOR THE DERBYSHIRE CAVALRY REGIMENT IN C (VIII: 2) for 2 clarinets, 2 bassoons, 2 horns, trumpet, serpent [and percussion instruments]. London, 1794(?).

The *March for the Prince of Wales* has become popular in our time, since Karl Haas printed the score for the first time in *The Score* in 1950 and conducted a superb recording of it for Parlophone (long deleted). Although the autograph has disappeared, there are several authentic sources including a score, partly autograph, for the orchestral version (*infra*). The incomplete original performance material is in the King's Library (British Museum); there is a sketch, rather complete, to the Trio in the Berlin State Library; and recently the French antiquarian dealer M. Marc Loliée turned up what is probably the rest of the Berlin sketch, again rather complete, of which he was kind enough to supply us with a photograph (by this time our edition had, unfortunately, already appeared). Perhaps it might be better to term the sketch a first draft of the autograph, for it is so complete that it could be used for an edition. The Loliée MS. is of the March proper.

It is, actually, a very unmilitary March, with a lovely passage for the clarinets (clarinet II in its low, *chalumeau* register, with 'Alberti'-bass figures that so well suit the instrument). In the second part, there is a marvellous solo for the trumpet (bars 24–6) which, though just an octave skip prefaced by the dotted figure that dominates the whole March, cuts through the orchestral texture in a way that Johann Strauss's trumpets often do. At the end there is even a little canon based on the main subject. In the Trio, the beautiful clarinet writing again claims our attention, as indeed the subtle layout of the wind instruments throughout.

Having to supply a short work for the Royal Society of Musicians, Haydn reorchestrated the March. He had a copyist 'lay out' the score by first writing out the wind-band version. Haydn then added the 'Flauti' and strings, changed the trumpet parts from 'Clarino' to 'Clarini' and wrote at the beginning of the serpent part, 'bleibt aus' (to be left out). The March's autograph, still owned by the Society, is entitled, not in Haydn's hand, 'Grand March composed expressly for and presented to the Royal Society of Musicians, London, by Joseph Haydn, Mus. Doc. Oxon. 1792. (Original Score)' and is signed and dated by Haydn on page two, 'N.[omine] D.[omini] London di me giuseppe Haydn 792'. In the orchestral version, the second bassoon takes over the serpent part for the Trio.

The incomplete March in E flat (VIII: 7) exists in Haydn's autograph, Burgenländisches Landesmuseum, Eisenstadt (*ex. coll.* Sándor Wolf), where it occupies one page of a sheet containing sketches to the Redoutensaal Dances and other dance movements. The MS. is written on British paper with a British watermark. The March breaks off after eight bars, of which the eighth, crossed out, has only the parts for the two clarinets filled in; the rest of the work was reconstructed for the Doblinger edition by the present writer. This spirited March would almost seem to be the first draft, or *Urversion*, of the *March for the Prince of Wales*: the same dotted upbeat, the same kind of *cantabile* passage for the clarinet, the same unmilitary, lyric atmosphere. It is not known if Haydn ever finished the March: no other source exists except that in Eisenstadt.

The circumstances surrounding the commission to compose marches for Sir Henry Harpur and the Derbyshire Cavalry Regiment have been discussed in the Chronicle. The Volunteer Cavalry was 'embodied' in 1794, but Haydn's marches were composed a year later: at least one of the autographs is so dated. The autograph of No. 1, entitled 'March' and signed and dated 1795, is in the Esterházy Collection of the National Library, Budapest and comes from Haydn's legacy. The autograph of No. 2, also entitled 'March', is in the Burgenländisches Landesmuseum, Eisenstadt (*ex. coll.* Sándor Wolf). Both are written on British paper and the two MSS. make up four pages each, or a total of eight pages, exactly the 2 double sheets listed in Haydn's English Catalogue. (The autograph of *the March for the Royal Society* also consists of eight pages, which equals the 2 double sheets listed for the *March for the Prince of Wales*, the autograph of which presumably numbered eight pages too; Haydn obviously considered the two versions as one work.)

The first March is the more massive of the two – there is only one bar of *piano* in the whole work – with an effective tonic pedal point at bars 18–20, where the bassoons, horns, trumpet and serpent hammer out the dotted rhythm in alternating groups. The second March is more lyrical and much more transparently scored, with a charming *piano* section for clarinets, bassoons and horns alone. Both Marches have no trios, both contain one new feature: the trumpet often has its own triplet rhythm ♪♪♪ against the dotted figure ♪.♪ in other instruments. This never occurs in the other marches and seems to have been a speciality of the trumpet player in Sir Henry's wind band.

If any further proof were needed of Haydn's minute attention to detail and his concern for the aural success even of such little marches, we need only study the textual problems of these two Derbyshire pieces. In the presumably authentic private edition that Sir Henry printed, and which also includes the authentic piano arrangements by Haydn (No. 2's autograph is in the Berlin State Library):

> Two Marches composed by J: Haydn. M.D. for Sir Henry Harpur, Bart. and presented by him, to the Volunteer Cavalry of Derbyshire; Embodied in the Year, 1794. London, Printed for Sir Henry Harpur, Bar^t. by Willm. Simpkins, Clements Inn.

there are astounding differences between Haydn's autograph and the first edition. The interested reader can see the principal ones listed by footnotes in our edition of No. 2; for the changes between autograph and print of No. 1 are so widespread that they could not be thus shown. It would seem that the printed edition contains Haydn's final thoughts, which means in effect that he painstakingly revised the works after having completed the autograph manuscripts. Nothing could more tellingly reveal this 'scholarly' side of Haydn, who always set great store in making the final revisions to a work after the first performances(s). We shall see that he revised the whole end of his penultimate Symphony (No. 103, 1795) and that even the great choral works of the 1790s were subjected to the same keen self-scrutiny. In that, too, may be seen the *Hand des Meisters* . . .

The Salomon Symphonies and 'Concertante'
Catalogue, arranged in the presumed chronological order.

SINFONIA No. 96 in D ('The Miracle'), London 1791. I *Adagio – Allegro*. II *Andante*. III *Menuetto & Trio (Allegretto)*. IV *Finale: Vivace (assai)*. 2 flutes, 2 oboes, 2 bassoons, 2 horns, 2 trumpets, timpani, strings. Principal sources: (1) Autograph, dated London 1791, Royal Philharmonic Society (British Museum); (2) MS. parts by Johann Elssler, Princely Oettingen-Wallerstein Archives, Schloss Harburg (Bavaria) with corrections and additions in Haydn's hand, copied before March, 1793; (3) MS. parts by Johann Elssler, Princely Fürstenberg Archives, Schloss Donaueschingen; (4) MS. parts by Johann Elssler, Esterházy Archives, National Library, Budapest, with corrections and additions in Haydn's hand; (5) printed parts by Robert Birchall, London based on Salomon's orchestral material; (6) printed parts by André, Offenbach (February 1795); (7) printed parts by Artaria, Vienna (April 1795). The supposedly autograph piano reduction of the first, third and last movements (Landon SYM, 755 source 2) is not autograph; it is now owned by Dr. Fritz Moldenhauer of Spokane, Washington. There are also arrangements for piano trio of all twelve London Symphonies made by J. P. Salomon and published by him, as well as his arrangements of all twelve for flute, 2 violins, viola, 'cello and piano, of which the autographs are owned by Mr. Alfred Newman in Hollywood, California, and which Salomon published more or less simultaneously in his own edition in London and also at Simrock's in Bonn. Both arrangements are sometimes useful in establishing the texts.

SINFONIA No. 95 in C minor, London 1791. I *Allegro moderato*. II *Andante*. III *Menuet & Trio*. IV *Finale: Vivace*. 2 flutes, 2 oboes, 2 bassoons, 2 horns, 2 trumpets, timpani, strings (with solo violin and solo 'cello). Principal sources: (1) Autograph, dated London 1791, Royal Philharmonic Society (British Museum); (2) MS. parts by Johann Elssler, Esterházy Archives, National Library, Budapest (wanting the first bassoon part); (3) MS. parts by Johann Elssler, Princely Fürstenberg Archives, Schloss Donaueschingen; (4) printed parts by Robert Birchall, London, based on Salomon's orchestral material; (5) printed parts by André, Offenbach (February 1795); (6) printed parts by Artaria, Vienna (April 1795).

SINFONIA No. 93 in D, London 1791. I *Adagio – Allegro assai*. II *Largo cantabile*. III *Menuetto & Trio*. IV *Finale: Presto, ma non troppo*. 2 flutes, 2 oboes, 2 bassoons, 2 horns, 2 trumpets, timpani, strings. Principal sources: (1) Autograph, last seen by the Haydn scholar C. F. Pohl at the Court Book Shop of Eduard Leibrock in Braunschweig in *c.* 1870: The MS. was formerly owned by Artaria & Co., who certified its authenticity on 14 June 1834. It was entitled 'In Nomine Domini. . . . Londini $\overline{791}$'. (2) MS. copy of the autograph by an Esterházy copyist, Esterházy Archives, National Library, Budapest (from Haydn's legacy); (3) MS. parts by Johann Elssler, Princely Oettingen-Wallerstein Archives, Schloss Harburg (Bavaria) with corrections and additions in Haydn's hand, copied before March, 1793; (4) MS. parts by Johann Elssler, Princely Fürstenberg Archives, Schloss Donaueschingen; (5) printed parts by Robert Birchall, London, based on Salomon's orchestral material; (6) printed parts by André, Offenbach (June 1796); (7) printed parts by Artaria, Vienna (July 1796).

SINFONIA No. 94 in G ('The Surprise'; 'Mit dem Paukenschlag'), London 1791. I *Adagio cantabile – Vivace assai*. II *Andante*. III *Menuetto & Trio: Allegro molto*. IV *Finale: Allegro di molto*. 2 flutes, 2 oboes, 2 bassoons, 2 horns, 2 trumpets, timpani, strings. Principal sources: (1) Autograph, dated London 1791, Berlin State Library; last page of first and all the second movt., Library of Congress; (2) MS. copy of the autograph by an Esterházy copyist, Esterházy Archives, National Library, Budapest (from Haydn's legacy); (3) MS. parts by Johann Elssler, Princely Fürstenberg Archives, Donaueschingen; (4) printed parts by Robert Birchall, London, based on Salomon's orchestral material; (5) printed parts by Artaria, Vienna (June 1795); (6) printed parts by André, Offenbach (August 1795).

SINFONIA No. 98 in B flat, London 1792(?). I *Adagio – Allegro*. II *Adagio*. III *Menuet & Trio: Allegro*. IV *Finale: Presto*. 2 flutes, 2 oboes, 2 bassoons, 2 horns, 2 trumpets, timpani, strings (with solo violin) and solo harpsichord (only end of Finale). Principal sources: (1) Autograph, the signature and date torn off, Berlin State Library, from the library of Ludwig van Beethoven; 4 pages of the Finale, containing bars 75–128, are missing; the MS. was removed for safe-keeping during World War II and has disappeared; (2) MS. score by a British copyist whom Haydn used during the first London visit (he also copied the Esterházy Archives score of *L'anima del filosofo*); apparently a copy of the autograph; Royal Philharmonic Society (British Museum); (3) MS. parts by Johann Elssler, Princely Oettingen-Wallerstein Archives, Schloss Harburg (Bavaria) with corrections and additions in Haydn's hand, copied before March, 1793; (4) MS. parts by Johann Elssler, Princely Fürstenberg Archives, Schloss Donaueschingen; (5) printed parts by André, Offenbach (February 1796); (6) printed parts by Artaria, Vienna (July 1796); (7) printed parts by Robert Birchall, London, based on Salomon's orchestral material.

CONCERTANTE in B flat (known as the *Sinfonia Concertante* Op. 84), I: 103. London 1792, I *Allegro*. II *Andante*. III *Finale: Allegro con spirito*. Solo instruments: oboe, bassoon, violin and violoncello. Orchestra: 1 flute, oboe [II] *ripieno*, 2 bassoons, 2 horns, 2 trumpets, timpani, strings. Principal sources: (1) Autograph, dated London 1792, Berlin State Library; (2) MS. parts by Johann Elssler, Esterházy Archives, National Library, Budapest; consisting of two sets of complete parts from Haydn's legacy (where there are two separate sources listed, both, as here, entitled 'Concertino') but with three oboe I and three bassoon parts; the one set with a few corrections and additions in Haydn's hand; (3) printed parts by André, Offenbach (May 1796); (4) printed parts by Artaria, Vienna (July 1796).

SINFONIA No. 97 in C, London 1792. I *Adagio – Vivace*. II *Adagio, ma non troppo*. III *Menuetto & Trio: Allegretto*. IV *Finale: Spiritoso* (later altered to *Presto assai*). 2 flutes, 2 oboes, 2 bassoons, 2 horns, 2 trumpets, timpani, strings (solo violin in III/Trio). Principal sources: (1) Autograph, dated London 1792, Mrs Eva Alberman ('heirs of Stefan Zweig'), London, from the auction by Gerd Rosen, Berlin, April 1951; (2) MS. parts by Johann Elssler, Esterházy Archives, National Library, Budapest; the MS. contains corrections in Haydn's hand, *inter alia* the change in IV's tempo; (3) MS. parts by Johann Elssler, Princely Oettingen-Wallerstein Archives, Schloss Harburg, with additions and corrections in Haydn's hand; copied before March, 1793; (4) MS. parts by Johann Elssler, Princely Fürstenberg Archives, Donaueschingen; (5) printed parts by André, Offenbach (April 1796); (b) printed parts by Artaria, Vienna (July 1796); (7) printed parts by Robert Birchall, London, based on Salomon's orchestral material.

Sinfonia No. 99 in E flat, 1793. I *Adagio – Vivace assai*. II *Adagio*. III *Menuetto & Trio: Allegretto*. IV *Finale: Vivace*. 2 flutes, 2 oboes, 2 clarinets, 2 bassoons, 2 horns, 2 trumpets, timpani, strings. Principal sources: (1) Autograph, Berlin State Library (now unavailable: see No. 98 [1]); the first page of music is signed 1793 and the whole is on Italian (not British) paper; the outside title page signed 1794, the year of the first performance; (1a) sketches to the Finale, Austrian National Library Vienna; (1b) Haydn's autograph arrangement of the Finale for musical clock, Berlin State Library; (2) MS. copy of the autograph by Johann Elssler, the title page containing Haydn's autograph note '16 bo. [Bögen]', Esterházy Archives, National Library, Budapest, from Haydn's legacy; (3) MS. parts by Johann Elssler, partly on British paper and partly on Italian, Princely Fürstenberg Archives, Donaueschingen, being – in the case of the woodwind, brass and timpani parts – Haydn's authentic British orchestral material, to which was later added a set of string parts in Vienna: (4) MS. parts by Johann Elssler with a note in another hand 'ricevuta da lui medesimo / in segno d'amicizia', Esterházy Archives, National Library, Budapest; (5) printed parts by Simrock, Bonn (February 1801); (6) printed parts by André, Offenbach (1801); (7) printed parts by Robert Birchall, London, based on Salomon's orchestral material.

Sinfonia No. 100 in G ('Military'), London 1794 (the Minuet on Italian paper and probably composed in Vienna or Eisenstadt, 1793). I *Adagio – Allegro*. II *Allegretto*. III *Menuet & Trio: Moderato*. IV *Finale: Presto*. 2 flutes, 2 oboes, 2 clarinets, 2 bassoons, 2 horns, 2 trumpets, timpani, Turkish instruments (triangle, cymbals, bass drum, possibly also tambourine), strings (2 violas in II). Principal sources: (1) Autograph (minus II), Esterházy Archives, National Library, Budapest, from Haydn's legacy; (1a) Autograph of the second movement arranged for flute, 2 oboes, 2 bassoons, serpent, 2 horns and 2 trumpets with 'tamburo', entitled 'March', Captain Rudolph Nydahl, Stockholm; (2) MS. parts by Johann Elssler, Esterházy Archives, National Library, Budapest; (3) printed parts by Robert Birchall, London, based on Salomon's orchestral material; (4) printed parts by Gombart, Augsburg (February 1799); (5) printed parts by André, Offenbach (March 1799), with many of the printer's errors of the Gombart edition corrected; (6) printed parts by Artaria, Vienna (Spring 1799?); (7) printed parts by Sieber, Paris (April 1799).

Sinfonia No. 101 ('The Clock': in 1798 Traeg issued II as 'Rondo . . . Die Uhr', which shows that the subtitle was known that early) in D, London 1794, but the autograph written on two types of paper – British and Italian – so that we may assume that part of the Symphony was composed in 1793 in Austria. I *Adagio – Presto, ma non troppo* (later: *Presto*). II *Amiante*. III *Menuet & Trio: Allegretto*. IV *Finale: Vivace*. 2 flutes, 2 oboes, 2 clarinets (not listed in the *instrumentarium* of the autograph but one solo passage still visible in I: 324ff with indication in 323 'Clar', and the clarinet parts, with a correction by Haydn in Donaueschingen, *vide infra*), 2 bassoons, 2 horns, 2 trumpets, timpani, strings. Principal sources: (1) Autograph, dated London 1794, Berlin State Library (now unavailable: see No. 98 [1]); (1a) sketches to the Minuet, Austrian National Library; (1b) Haydn's autograph arrangement of the Minuet for musical clock, Berlin State Library; (2) MS. copy of the autograph by Johann Elssler, the title page containing Haydn's autograph note '20½ Bögen', Esterházy Archives, National Library, Budapest, from Haydn's legacy; includes the clarinet parts, also in the *instrumentarium*; (3) MS. parts by Johann Elssler, Esterházy Archives, National Library, Budapest, from Haydn's legacy; the string parts on British paper and used for the first performance, and subsequent performances as well; the players' names noted:

A page of sketches for Symphony No. 99 (1793), in which Haydn introduced clarinets for the first time; these sketches, for the finale, are numbered by Haydn. Note, on line six, Haydn's abbreviations for the clarinets ('clar:', 'clarin') and, on line nine, the timpani entrance ('Timp:'). The sketches are reproduced in their entirety in *Joseph Haydn: Critical Edition of the Complete Symphonies*, vol. XII, Vienna, 1968, pp. 402 ff.

V. I 'Mr. Salomon', V. II 'P. Dahmen', Va. 'Fiorilo & Slezak'; no clarinet parts and the passage in I: 324ff. rewritten to avoid their solo passage; with duplicate string parts; (4) MS. parts by Johann Elssler and another copyist, Princely Fürstenberg Archives, Donaueschingen; with the clarinet parts corrected by Haydn, and with other holograph corrections and additions; (5) printed parts by Robert Birchall, London, based on Salomon's orchestral material; (6) printed parts by André, Offenbach, [Autumn?] 1799, based on a MS. copy still in the André Archives (M 12478); (7) printed parts by Gombart, Augsburg (Spring 1799); (8) printed parts by Artaria, Vienna (Autumn 1799?).

Sinfonia No. 102 in B flat, London 1794. I *Largo – Vivace*. II *Adagio*. III *Menuet & Trio: Allegro*. IV *Finale: Presto*. 2 flutes, 2 oboes, 2 bassoons, 2 horns, 2 trumpets, timpani, violoncello solo (in II), strings. Principal sources: (1) Autograph, Berlin State Library, dated London 1794 on the first page of music and 1795, the date of the first performance, on the title page; (2) MS. parts by Johann Elssler with corrections and additions in Haydn's hand, Princely Fürstenberg Archives, Schloss Donaueschingen; the wind and timpani parts on British paper and used in the London concerts, the strings on Italian paper and added subsequently; (3) printed parts by Simrock, Bonn (February 1801); (4) printed parts by André, Offenbach (1801); (5) printed parts by Robert Birchall, London, based on Salomon's orchestral material.

The first page of the score of Haydn's Symphony No. 101, from Johann Elssler's copy; the autograph had no room for the clarinet parts which were added by the composer on spare sheets of paper, since lost. These parts are, however, included in the authentic MS. score from Haydn's own library.

SINFONIA No. 103 in E flat ('Drum Roll'), London 1795. I *Adagio – Allegro con spirito*. II *Andante* (later: *Andante, più tosto Allegretto*). III *Menuet & Trio*. IV *Finale: Allegro con spirito*. 2 flutes, 2 oboes, 2 clarinets, 2 bassoons, 2 horns, 2 trumpets, timpani, strings (with solo violin in II). Principal sources: (1) Autograph, dated London 1795, given to Luigi Cherubini by Haydn in February 1806 and signed again: 'Padre del celebre Cherubini / ai 24:ᵗʳᵒ Febr: 806', now British Museum, London; (2) MS. parts by Johann Elssler with corrections and additions in Haydn's hand, Princely Fürstenberg Archives, Schloss Donaueschingen; the wind and timpani parts on British paper and used in the London concerts, the strings on Italian paper and added subsequently; (3) MS. parts by Johann Elssler and others, lacking the Minuet, Esterházy Archives, National Library, Budapest; (4) printed parts by André, Offenbach, [Autumn?] 1799, based on a MS. copy still in the André Archives (M 12476); (5) printed parts by Gombart, Augsburg (Spring 1799); (6) printed parts by Artaria, Vienna (Autumn 1799?); (7) printed parts by Robert Birchall, London, based on Salomon's orchestral material.

SINFONIA No. 104 in D ('London' / 'Salomon'), London 1795. I *Adagio – Allegro*. II *Andante*. III *Menuet & Trio: Allegro*. IV *Finale: Spiritoso*. 2 flutes, 2 oboes, 2 clarinets, 2 bassoons, 2 horns, 2 trumpets, timpani, strings. Principal sources: (1) Autograph, on cover Haydn's title '795/ The 12th which I have composed in England', signed again inside, London 1795, Berlin State Library; (2) sketch to the last movement, sold on

Detail from the title page of Symphony No. 104 with Haydn's autograph note 'Sinfonia in D. The 12th which I have composed in England.' (1795).

11/12 June 1974 at the auction house of J. A. Stargardt, Marburg/Lahn, catalogue No. 393 (*vide infra*, p. 615). (3) MS. parts by Johann Elssler with corrections and additions in Haydn's hand, Princely Fürstenberg Archives, Schloss Donaueschingen; the wind and timpani parts on British paper and used in the London concerts, the strings on Italian paper and added subsequently; (4) printed parts by Simrock, Bonn (February 1801); (5) printed parts by André, Offenbach (1801); (6) printed parts by Robert Birchall, London, based on Salomon's orchestral material.

CHRONOLOGY

There is an autograph sheet written by Haydn, listing the *incipits* of all twelve London Symphonies. It was sold at the 'XXXVII. Autographen-Versteigerungs-Catalog Leo Liepmannsohn' as No. 91 (Berlin, 4 and 5 Nov. 1907), then formed part of the Westley Manning Collection in London, was sold at Sotheby's on 12 October 1954 (item 207), and is now owned by Messrs. J. A. Stargardt of Marburg/Lahn. The sheet is British paper with a dated watermark 1794 and includes as well Haydn's sketch for the slow movement of the 'Gypsy Rondo' Trio No. 39; here the Symphonies are listed as follows:

795	in E mol [103]	in D [104]	in b fa [102]
794	[101]	in E mol [99]	in g [100]
792	[94]	[98]	[93]
[originally '791']			
791	[95]	[96]	[97]

Obviously this catalogue was drawn up in the late Spring or early Summer of 1795, after the final Opera Concert. It only purports to show the years in which the various Symphonies were first performed, not the date of composition (e.g. No. 99 was composed in 1793, No. 93 in 1791, etc.); it is also not in chronological order within these years, because we know that No. 94 was certainly not the first work of the 1792 season; and it misplaces No. 97 in the 1791 season, whereas the dated autograph informs us that it was a 1792 work. Thus, the catalogue is not much use to us. Overleaf, in tabular form, is the chronological list with explanations.

495

Work	Date on Autograph	First performance	Other Data
96	London 1791	1791 season (or 11 March 1791? See Chronicle)	Entered in Herr v. Kees's Cat. as having come from London.
95	London 1791	1791 season	Ditto.

N.B. We cannot determine the internal chronology of these 1791 Symphonies. In the Kees Catalogue they are listed as 96–95 (in Kees Cat. Nos. 93 and 94 resp., 'NB Von London gekom[m]en').

Work	Date on Autograph	First performance	Other Data
93	London 1791	17 Feb. 1792	Haydn's Diary and its nearly exact quotation by Griesinger. Haydn wrote: 'In the first concert, only the Adagio of the new Symphony in D was repeated.').
94	London 1791	23 March 1792	Local Press describes slow movt. Haydn withheld this work till after No. 98 and the *Concertante* had been performed.
98	London 1792(?)	2 March 1792	Haydn's Diary, giving key.
Concertante	London 1792	9 March 1792	Programme in London newspapers.
97	London 1792	3 or 4 May 1792	One assumes that Haydn saved the new work for his own benefit on 3 May and repeated it on 4 May (see Chronicle).
99	[Austria] 1793	10 Feb. 1794	Criticism in *Morning Chronicle* 19 Feb. refers to the solo woodwind passage in II.
100	London 1794	31 March 1794	Criticism in *Morning Chronicle* 9 April.
101	London 1794	3 March 1794	See Chronicle.

N.B. The internal chronology of Nos. 100 and 101 cannot be established: both autographs contain sections composed in Austria, and while No. 101 was played first, the fact that No. 100 contains as II a reworking of an older (1786) Concerto for 2 lire would suggest that strictly speaking at least part of the new Symphony was composed before No. 101, though the latter was probably completed before No. 100.

Work	*Date on Autograph*	*First performance*	*Other Data*
102	London 1794	2 Feb. 1795	See Chronicle.
103	London 1795	2 March 1795	*Morning Chronicle* specifically mentions Introduction in its review of 3 March.
104	London 1795	4 May 1795	See *Morning Chronicle*'s review of 6 May.

The information on the watermarks of those Symphonies of which the autographs, formerly in the Berlin State Library, are now in Eastern Europe and unavailable, was provided by two sources: (1) the notes which Professor J. P. Larsen made before World War II and which he kindly placed at our disposal; (2) the notes which the late Professor Helmut Schultz made before World War II, kindly made available to us by Messrs. Breitkopf & Härtel, Leipzig. Photographs of two Symphonies, Nos. 99 and 101, were fortunately made for the Hoboken Photogramm-Archiv of the National Library, Vienna before the MSS. disappeared, while of the third missing work, No. 98, Messrs. Breitkopf & Härtel, Leipzig, made available to us an exact copy, with copious notes on the watermarks, changes, first drafts, etc. in the MS., made by Professor Schultz before World War II.

The literature on the London Symphonies is so vast that even a complete listing would require many dozen pages. We have therefore been obliged to limit ourselves here to works which have concentrated on the London Symphonies *in general*, we have then provided each Symphony, as it is discussed, with a small and rigorously selective list of specialized articles.[1]

TEXTUAL PROBLEMS, AND THEIR CONSEQUENCE IN INTERPRETATION

The first inkling that all was not right with Haydn's Salomon Symphonies could be realized from the publication in the 1930's of some of these works by Edition Eulenburg, then Leipzig. No less than two new editions appeared of No. 103, the final one edited, as was most of the series, by the late Dr. Ernst Praetorius in February 1938;

1 Apart from Pohl H in L, CCLN and Landon SYM, see Helmut Therstappen: *Joseph Haydns symphonisches Vermächtnis* (Kieler Beiträge zur Musikwissenschaft), Wolfenbüttel 1941. On the dating of the Artaria prints, the latest work on the subject, and the most reliable, is A. Weinmann's *Vollständiges Verlagsverzeichnis von Artaria & Comp.*, Vienna 1952. On dating the Simrock prints, and their textual significance, see Hubert Unverricht: 'Die Simrock-Drucke von Haydns Londoner Sinfonien' in: Beiträge zur Rheinischen Musikgeschichte, Heft 52, Cologne 1962. On the dating of the André prints, which the writer ascertained in the actual André Archives at Offenbach, see: Wolfgang Matthäus: 'Das Werk Joseph Haydns im Spiegel der Geschichte des Verlages Jean André' in: *Haydn Yearbook* III (1965), pp. 54–110. The latest critical edition of all twelve Salomon Symphonies and the *Concertante* is published in full score and parts by the Haydn-Mozart-Presse of the Universal Edition (1961 *et seq.*); the same editions, with notes, in Vol. X, XI and XII of the Philharmonia Edition of the Complete Symphonies. Nos. 99–104 are also published in the Henle *Joseph Haydn Werke* (Reihe I, Bd. 17, 18, 1963, 1964); the Haydn-Mozart-Philharmonia series edited by the present writer, the Henle publications by Hubert Unverricht. The Philharmonia series is also available separately (not only in bound volumes). Of the vast amount of general literature, we would single out the chapter entitled 'The Popular Style' in Rosen's book (*op. cit.*, pp. 329–50). Concerning the eastern European melodic origins of Haydn's late Symphonies, there has been little on the subject published since W. H. Hadow's *A Croatian Composer*, London 1897 (using the research published by F. Kuhač, Zagreb, 1880); and it is now unlikely that we shall discover anything more on the subject, since the tradition has practically died out in the eastern European villages where researchers once found such unlimited source material among the peasants.

here for the first time in modern history, the clarinet parts of the Trio were restored. In Praetorius's edition of No. 96, which did not use the autograph or any authentic MS. sources, it became nevertheless clear that there were two completely different sets of trumpet and timpani parts. Astonishingly, these interesting Eulenburg editions, though widely distributed among music students and conductors, had no effect whatever either on the scholarly world – there is no mention of the problem in Larsen's pioneer book, *Die Haydn-Überlieferung* (1939) – or in the practical sense. Conductors went on playing these famous late works in the same old Breitkopf & Härtel or Peters editions. This is the more surprising since Breitkopf & Härtel had engaged the late Dr. Helmut Schultz to carry on the symphonic series of the *Gesamtausgabe* (which had reached No. 49 by 1933) and also to prepare good 'working editions' of some of the later works. Schultz published *inter alia* new editions of Nos. 95 and 96 – not, alas, using the British Museum autographs – but having had access to the Esterházy parts. And to any conductor using these new scores, it must have appeared that there were grave textual differences between them and the old accepted versions. In particular, it must have seemed curious that in Schultz's edition the trumpets and timpani of No. 96 were (with a few exceptions) those 'new' parts first mentioned and printed as *ossia* reading in the Eulenburg score. One would have thought that with two new scores of No. 96, conductors would have been puzzled and curious to pursue the matter. But the matter was greeted with total indifference. At this very period, His Master's Voice (The Gramophone Company) recorded Haydn's Symphony No. 96 for the first time with Bruno Walter and the Vienna Philharmonic Orchestra – but in the old version that everybody knew. The war then put an abrupt stop to textual investigations of Haydn's symphonies, as pursued in splendid isolation by Doctors Praetorius and Schultz.

Having first studied these problems as best as the conditions allowed, which meant via such revised Eulenburg and Breitkopf scores – and they soon became exceedingly rare – as existed, the present writer later made an investigation of the whole textual problem of Haydn's first Salomon Symphonies, the results of which he published in 1954.[1] Including a detailed list of corrections to the Eulenburg scores, he came to the conclusion that 'the scores and parts of certain of the first six "Salomon" Symphonies and *Sinfonia Concertante* in everyday use are flagrant falsifications of Haydn's own texts.' In this article, attention was drawn *inter alia* to the newly discovered Elssler parts, with Haydn's corrections, of Symphonies 93, 96, 97 and 98 in Harburg Castle, till then unknown to the musical world.

In 1954, however, there were many discoveries still to be made. The Esterházy materials were only partially available, and photographs of all of them did not arrive from Budapest until some years later. In 1958 and 1959, we were able to announce in the *Music Review*[2] our discovery of a whole series of authentic parts of the Salomon Symphonies, corrected by Haydn and partly on British paper with the watermark date '1794', at Donaueschingen Castle. Still later, we persuaded the British Museum's Music Room to purchase a series of printed editions by Robert Birchall which proved to be based on Salomon's long-disappeared orchestral material. All this new information, and other important material by German colleagues on the significance and chronology of the earliest printed editions of the Salomon Symphonies, could be

---

1 'The original versions of Haydn's first "Salomon" Symphonies' in: *Music Review*, Volume XV, No. 1 (1954), pp. 1–32.
2 Vol. XIX No. 4 (1958, pp. 311–19) and XX No. 1 (1959, pp. 56–70).

incorporated in the first critical edition, which was published between 1961 and 1967 by the Haydn-Mozart Presse of the Universal Edition.

The history of how these great works came to be falsified in the offices of Messrs. Simrock, Breitkopf & Härtel, Bote & Bock, Le Duc, etc. cannot concern us here; the changes are all spurious, done without Haydn's knowledge or approval, and most of the worst cases (Nos. 96 and 98) appeared after his death. (Haydn knew Le Duc's score of No. 98 and found the series unfortunate, but having omitted the trumpets and timpani of No. 98 entirely it did not sin in that respect except by omission.) The restoration of the authentic texts brought with it certain questions of interpretation which are perhaps worth recalling.

Since Nos. 96 and 98 were, to all intents and purposes, reorchestrated by these publishing hacks in the nineteenth century, we might do well to examine some of the problems briefly. By the time these corrupt texts had entered the public domain in the second quarter of the nineteenth century, replacing the older and partly authentic editions such as Birchall, André, Artaria, Simrock's older parts (they were later revised and 'brought up to date', i.e. in line with the new spurious texts), Gombart, Imbault, Sieber, etc., symphonies were no longer played without a conductor. In the eighteenth century, the leader, that is, the *Konzertmeister* of the first violin section, had held the performance together; although Haydn conducted his Salomon Symphonies from the keyboard, this old *quasi-continuo* tradition was already obsolete and in most performances of the works in large centres like Paris, Berlin, St. Petersburg or Vienna, a piano was no longer used for Haydn's or Mozart's later symphonies. Thus there arose the need for full scores. Since everyone knew that the late eighteenth-century and early nineteenth-century orchestral parts were full of printing errors and also did not even agree with each other – an orchestra could not have played a correct performance of Symphony No. 96 using the Birchall and Artaria parts simultaneously – not only was a score needed but also parts which agreed with the score. As Breitkopf & Härtel, for example, gradually came to print revised scores and parts of the late Haydn symphonies, taste had changed enormously and these works were no longer the main staple of orchestral repertoire that they had been from about 1795 (as far as they were printed) to 1815. People had forgotten what Symphony No. 96, or 98, had sounded like when Haydn had conducted it in London or Vienna. The recasting of these two particular symphonies concerned not only their trumpet and drum parts but also (in the case of No. 96) the bassoon parts. There were changes in the harmony, even in the very melodies themselves. In the Minuets of Nos. 94 and 96 a note was changed in the melody, and for the whole orchestra; in No. 96 the last note of bar 7 in the Minuet should be G but it was corrupted to F sharp, necessitating changing almost all the subsidiary parts as well; while in No. 96, the last note of bar 3 (and bar 31) read G sharp (fl., ob. I, v. I) and E sharp (ob. II, v. II) instead of the G and C natural that Haydn wrote.

Some of these changes had arisen because of the faulty printing of the older editions: when Artaria had, in No. 96/II, bar 72, a B natural in the bassoon and a B flat in the second violin, a later editor realized that one of the two readings was wrong and he mistakenly opted for the B flat version, thereby creating a chord that Haydn never wrote. But the widespread rewriting of the trumpet and timpani, as well as the bassoon parts of Nos. 95 and 96, the flute parts of No. 96, and so on – all this was the result of quite another concept.

Mozart's late symphonies did not start circulating throughout Europe until the last five years of the eighteenth century, and they reached most of the great capitals together with Haydn's late symphonies, to be followed very quickly by Beethoven's first two symphonies (which were well known all over the Continent by 1805) and then by the Eroica. As Beethoven's symphonic *oeuvre* gradually dominated the musical world, the editors of the German publishing houses deliberately attempted to bring Haydn's orchestration of Nos. 96 and 98 into line with the more conventional sound of his illustrious friend Mozart and erstwhile pupil Beethoven. The high trumpets of Haydn were radically different from Mozart's much lower trumpet writing, and different again from Beethoven's, who wrote loudly for the trumpet but not in such a high *tessitura* as Haydn. Similarly the timpani parts that Haydn wrote were altered to sound tamer and less prominent. It was a process to make Haydn sound more like Mozart (in particular) and also more like the orchestration fashionable in 1815. Nos. 96 and 98 are not the only cases: an even more sensational recasting of the trumpets and timpani took place in Symphony No. 48, where some editor grafted on to Haydn's lean orchestral fabric a set of trumpet and drum parts in the late Mozartian manner. Naturally Haydn's orchestral personality was strong enough to survive these intrusions, but in the process that personality was, obviously, altered. It was the same kind of repainting that Giotto's frescoes in Santa Croce in Florence suffered at the hands of *ottocento* restorers: it was well meant, no doubt, but it did Giotto no good and created a totally false overall impression. It did similar harm to Haydn. Indeed, it is hard for most conductors nowadays to return to the robust orchestration, with piercingly high trumpets, and to the much sharper dynamic marks (many of the *ff* and *fz* were removed by the editors) of Haydn's own scores. The fact that Haydn's own orchestration is so much better than those of the hacks seems to make little difference. One would have thought that the original orchestration of No. 96's slow movement would have seemed, even at first glance and to a person only faintly musical, vastly more effective: here the editors *removed* the trumpet and timpani parts entirely (adding them, to make up for it, to the introduction of the first movement, where Haydn had left them silent). Yet it was not until 1960 that a recording of the original version was undertaken, and that as part of a subscription series that never reached the broad public at all (Max Goberman conducting the Vienna State Opera Orchestra for the Library of Recorded Masterpieces, New York). This warped view of Haydn's late style was drastically confirmed by another famous work, the *Nelson Mass* (1798), which existed only in a bowdlerized version first issued by Breitkopf & Härtel in 1803 and mindlessly reprinted ever since until 1963 (first *Urfassung* version published by Schott & Co. together with Edition Eulenburg): here, too, the high trumpets were cruelly mutilated and the whole score reorchestrated in a manner calculated to remove the acid bite and lean sound of the original.

It was thus obvious that many famous conductors grew up with a view of Haydn as warped as the scores they persisted in using. The late Sir Thomas Beecham, who steadfastly refused to acknowledge that all was not right with Haydn's Salomon Symphonies, was one of those many misguided conductors whose aural view of Haydn – that is to say, the one they transmitted, often with lavish affection and great sophistication, to the general public – was at radical variance with what the original scores contained. His refusal to conduct from these original scores was by no means obstinacy; to have done so would have been totally to destroy the image of Haydn with which he was brought up, in the old 'accepted' versions of Breitkopf, Peters (etc., *ad nauseam*).

The effects of these *Urtext* scores have not yet been fully felt. The first movements of Haydn's symphonies are often taken at far too quick a pace nowadays; and the same objection was raised again and again by the London correspondent of the *Harmonicon* in the 1820s and early 1830s. But the bad texts were and are partly responsible for this faulty speeding. If we observe what Haydn wrote at the beginning of the 'Vivace assai' in No. 94/I, a too quick tempo is out of the question:

The 'hairpin' marks of the first violin will be unplayable if the movement is taken at the tempo used by Arturo Toscanini at the end of his life (and preserved on a R.C.A. Victor recording); and in fact the 'hairpin' was not on Toscanini's score and was thus ignored. The usual editions vary between nothing and the significant

– a phrase which would of course allow the adoption of a much quicker tempo; there are other variations in the old editions, but they all conspire to falsify this deliberately time-restricting 'hairpin'. It is this kind of nineteenth-century tradition which has coloured most musicians', and the public's, idea of Haydn's style. The ramifications of these false texts have indeed gone far beyond their wrong notes, wrong dynamic marks, wrong phrasing and wrong orchestration – though the sum total of those is awesome enough; they have contributed to create a picture of Haydn with the crooked made straight and the rough places plain.

THEIR POSITION IN HAYDN'S OEUVRE AND IN MUSIC HISTORY

We have seen in the course of this book that the London period of Haydn's career was distinguished by a large number of masterpieces in all genres, ranging from opera to cantata (*scena*), from choral works to song, from piano trio to solo keyboard works, from flute trio to string quartet and from *sinfonia concertante* to symphony. Yet despite the high level of the other works, it is, when the final balance is made, the London Symphonies which have remained the favourites of the public and which seem to most people to contain the essence of Haydn's personality. In fact, it was almost exclusively these symphonies, of all Haydn's vast output, that remained alive in many countries. In German-speaking lands, the late oratorios were always deeply loved, and in Catholic Austria and Bavaria, the masses were played on Sunday after Sunday and often proved to be the only contact that the poorer classes of those parts of German-speaking Europe had with Haydn's music. In Anglo-Saxon countries, however, the public has always been deeply suspicious of Haydn's (and Mozart's) church music: we can trace the early disapproval even in the pages of the *Harmonicon* (published between 1823 and 1833), whose reviewers regarded Haydn, otherwise, with the greatest veneration. This same disapproval extended to *The Creation* and *The Seasons* as well, to the extent (as we shall see in a later volume of this biography) that the Oratorio *The Seasons* was never given in England at all in its entirety until many years after Haydn's death.

The situation was not the same during Haydn's lifetime, or at least not to the same degree. Although Haydn's religious music (until the arrival of *The Creation*) was almost totally unknown in England in the eighteenth century, much of Haydn's secular vocal music was known and appreciated there. Especially the two sets of English Canzonettas were widely sung for many years. In the Austro-Hungarian Empire, Haydn's masses were enormously popular and created whole schools of local composers who imitated, often with great success, their illustrious models. It was the *Nelson Mass* rather than the London Symphonies that exerted the most profound influence on Bruckner's formative years, and the Upper Austrian composer's Mass in D minor would not have existed in its present form without the *Nelson Mass*. The chamber music of Haydn, too, was also widely played in the years before and after 1800. It is true that the string quartet, and even more the late piano trio, were never designed for the broad public but for connoisseurs; yet there were, obviously, many more such connoisseurs in 1800 than there were in 1900 or in 1970. Not only Haydn's string quartets were widely reprinted all over Europe in the late eighteenth and early nineteenth centuries, but also those of his followers such as Gyrowetz and Pleyel, whose chamber music enjoyed a vast public on an international scale. Even the Haydn piano trios were reprinted and, obviously, sold all over Europe.

Haydn introduced his London Symphonies to Vienna as soon as he returned, the first time in 1792, the last and final time in 1795. But somehow, except for the 'Beliebte Symphonie mit dem Paukenschlag' and one or two others, the London Symphonies never really caught the public's imagination in Vienna to the extent they had done so in England and were to do so elsewhere, particularly in France and Germany. Conversely, *The Creation* and (to a slightly lesser extent) *The Seasons* were profoundly appreciated and highly successful in Vienna, becoming the basis of a whole new choral tradition there and in the province of the Empire. Vienna was in some respects very wedded to the voice in general and to German-speaking vocal productions in particular. The only successes at a really popular level which Mozart ever enjoyed in his lifetime in Vienna were *Entführung* and *Zauberflöte*; by 'popular level' we mean in particular the lower classes of the musical population. The aristocracy may have (once) flocked to *Le nozze di Figaro* (though it afterwards much preferred *Una cosa rara* and *Il matrimonio segreto*) and to Mozart's subscription concerts in the Mehlgrube (though later Mozart could not raise more than one name, van Swieten's); but it was the German operas, and especially *Die Zauberflöte* in its off-*Hoftheater* production, that appealed to a whole new group of the Viennese populace who had probably remained in almost total ignorance of Mozart's other, and especially instrumental, productions. This situation was also reflected in Haydn's late, German-speaking choral music. It dominated a geographical segment of Europe where Bach was still unknown and Handel hardly played except through the efforts of a van Swieten. When *The Creation* had to match its force with that of the Bach Passions and B minor Mass, as well as Beethoven's *Missa Solemnis* it was inevitable that some of *The Creation*'s initially explosive popularity must abate. But while the progress of Haydn's late oratorios might in some countries be compared to a rocket which explodes into light only soon to disappear, the London Symphonies were tougher; and if their initial launching was often, as in Vienna, perhaps less dramatic than had been the case in England, they managed to survive better than almost any other group of Haydn's works.

It is true that the London Symphonies took a long time to penetrate the Italian peninsula. This was partly because all northern music was regarded in Italy with great scepticism, and partly because the Italians were now technically so far behind the rest of Europe that they could hardly play Haydn's late symphonies at all. They were soon to find *The Creation* full of technical difficulties and they could, shortly after Haydn's death, hardly manage *Don Giovanni* at all when it was attempted at the Scala. Haydn's symphonies arrived in Italy first through the Austrian governers of such cities as Milan and Florence (later Modena and Venice, too). We know that Rossini studied assiduously Haydn's symphonies, and one of the surprising contents of Verdi's library at Sant'Agata near Busseto is his well-thumbed collection of Haydn's symphonies in MS. parts. But all this happened after Haydn's death, so that it is almost true to say that *The Creation* was cultivated in Italy before the symphonies (which, Dies assures us, were as good as unknown at Rome in 1794 and not at all appreciated when heard). On the other hand, Spain had always had a long tradition of Haydn's music and had boasted a series of direct connections between members of the great Spanish noble houses and the composer himself, so that his symphonies were known and appreciated there long before they entered – if they ever entered more than very superficially – the culture of the Italian peninsula.[1]

Part of the effect of Haydn's symphonies lay in their vast number; that is to say, the effect was cumulative. Some composers strike with a single work, even a single symphony (César Franck); but in Haydn's time, a composer's reputation usually depended on a large number of compositions, especially if they were instrumental works. It is now well known that Haydn's symphonic production, once thought to be uniquely vast, is matched by that of his contemporaries such as Dittersdorf, Vanhal and Ordoñez; and even Mozart's symphonic *oeuvre*, considering that he died at thirty-five, is very extensive. But Dittersdorf and Vanhal had, by 1795, become old-fashioned composers, whose works were almost all forgotten (Dittersdorf's operas were an exception: they were still given in German-speaking countries), while Ordoñez and his contemporaries (Leopold Hofmann, Wagenseil, Gassmann, etc.) were in 1795 hardly names except to church musicians in the Austrian provinces and lexicographers such as Gerber or Burney. Haydn's symphonies, on the other hand, had not only survived but except for the very early works were played constantly all over Europe. Thus the arrival of these London productions, preceded by some ninety genuine (and an equal number of spurious) symphonies, seemed to musicians to represent the crowning efforts of Haydn's symphonic muse. We mention the spurious symphonies because, especially in France where publishers had for years foisted on the public large numbers of such unauthentic pieces, the public and even the trained musician obviously found great difficulty in deciding which of these many works were by Haydn and which by his pupils and followers. In 1788 Sieber had printed (as Haydn) a symphony by Adalbert Gyrowetz (I: G3) which Gyrowetz, when he arrived in Paris a year later, claimed as his own, though the Parisian musicians were at first highly sceptical.[2] Great is our astonishment, however, to find a London pupil of Haydn's, the composer Thomas Haigh (about whom we have spoken *supra*), arranging this Symphony about 1795 or 1796 ('A Grand Symphony of Dr. Haydn's') for pianoforte and having it published about 1797 (on paper, however, with a watermark date 1795) by Culliford, Rolfe & Barrow in England, immediately to be reprinted in the Summer of 1797 by André of Offenbach ('Grande Sinfonie pour

---

1 For a recent survey of Haydn in Spain, see Georg Feder: 'Manuscript sources of Haydn's works and their distribution' in: *Haydn Yearbook* IV (1968), pp. 133f.
2 Adalbert Gyrowetz: [*Selbst-*] *Biographie. Lebensläufe deutscher Musiker. Vide supra*, p. 64. Haigh print: Matthäus op. cit., 73f. Culliford, Rolfe & Barrow print in the Bodleian Library, Oxford, dated 1797.

Piano Forté à deux mains arrangée par Haigh: Etrennes pour le Dames Livre 38'). If not even a talented pupil of Haydn's could tell the difference between Gyrowetz and Haydn, imagine the confusion among French and German musicians, who knew Haydn's music only at second hand, through local prints and MS. copies of uncertain parentage.

In this respect, therefore, the London Symphonies not only represented the *non plus ultra* of Haydn's symphonic style, but they were also indubitably genuine works. Publishers, perhaps only accidentally but perhaps knowingly (they having been among the principal sinners in marketing spurious Haydn), often described the London Symphonies as (to take a typical English early edition) 'Celebrated Overture Composed for and Performed at M^r. Salomon's Concert' or (to take a typical André early edition) 'Grand Sinfonie pour plusieurs instrumens, composée par Joseph Haydn, Docteur en Musique, Oeuvre 98me. Liv. I. (Cette Sinfonie a été éxécutée pour la première fois au Grand Concert, dit de Salomon, à Londres sous la direction de l'auteur) . . .' [= Symphony 104].

Some of Haydn's earlier symphonies had reached the intellectual, orchestral and virtuoso level of the London compositions, e.g. Nos. 82, 86, 88 and 92 of the works for Comte d'Ogny and the Parisian concerts; but on the whole, the scintillating brilliance of the Salomon Symphonies had, with the exceptions noted (and perhaps one or two others), remained unapproached in the composer's previous efforts. A part of the increased brilliance is no doubt the result of the stimulation by audience and orchestra in London, but as an intellectual *tour-de-force* the 'Oxford' Symphony (1789) remained unsurpassed. In the minds, at least, of English audiences, the 'Oxford' was automatically placed among the ranks of the Salomon Symphonies, since it was probably the first work Haydn introduced in the 1791 season of Salomon's concerts and since, in any case, it had been the work played to celebrate Haydn's receiving the doctoral degree at Oxford in July 1791. Once again, it is the very number of London Symphonies, twelve masterpieces, that secured for all time Haydn's reputation as a symphonic composer. If we add the 'Oxford', which British audiences certainly did, to the number, we have thirteen works which immediately entered the repertoire and never really left it, except occasionally, since then.

In his earlier years, Haydn was naturally susceptible to various outside stylistic influences, and we know that he heard and studied a great deal of contemporary music in his formative years. It is indeed possible to trace a number of influences on Haydn's instrumental style up till the middle 1760s; later, he became profoundly affected by Italian comic opera, and his operatic works, including all the holograph additions to those works by other composers performed at Eszterháza Castle, naturally reflect this influence. Italian *opera buffa* soon cast its long shadow not only on Haydn's operas but on his instrumental works as well. The opening of Symphony No. 61 (1776) is unthinkable without the *opera buffa* style, and it is perhaps significant that the work's date coincides exactly with a profound change at Eszterháza, whereby from 1776 to 1790 Prince Nicolaus maintained a regular operatic season in Hungary. For a time, Haydn's whole thinking, and most of his best thoughts, went into opera productions of one kind or another. But from 1784, when he composed his last opera for Eszterháza, to 1791, the whole operatic routine for Prince Nicolaus began to sour the composer's life, making him bitterly intolerant of the operas by his Italian contemporaries on the one hand, and on the other increasing his longing to leave the not-so-splendid isolation of Hungary and to concentrate on writing music nearer his heart. Thus the break in 1790, occasioned by Prince Nicolaus's death, was a real release from his position which had, by accident and circumstances, become that of an operatic *Capellmeister*.

A great deal has been written about the influence of Haydn on Mozart and vice versa. If there had been any principal influence on Haydn from 1781 to 1790 (for before that he can hardly have known any significant works by Mozart), it must have been that of Mozart's music, which we know Haydn loved and admired more, perhaps, than that by any other composer. Yet if we examine Haydn's music, even his operas, from 1781 to 1790, impartially and knowing – this is an essential point – all his major works of the period, it would be a bold man who would assert that this was the period in the composer's life when his music was most profoundly influenced by that of his younger contemporary. If anything, Haydn's reaction to Mozart's music was partly negative: that is, the older composer ceased writing operas after 1784, except for *L'anima del filosofo*, a commissioned work, and an *opera seria* at that; he never wrote a string quintet; and he stopped writing piano concertos after about 1782 (the D major Concerto was published in 1784 but is probably somewhat earlier). We shall see Beethoven adopting a similarly negative, 'withdrawing' attitude in the case of his erstwhile teacher – and to a certain extent vice versa. Haydn's style was, by 1781, firmly established and the works he composed in the ensuing decade all show a steady, unwavering line which comes almost exclusively from his own already huge *oeuvre*. In fact it is astonishing what Haydn did not take from Mozart. We know that the elder man heard *Le nozze di Figaro* (letter to Maria Anna von Genzinger of 9 February 1790) and intended to stage it at Eszterháza in 1790, getting as far as the initial performances; we know that he heard *Don Giovanni* because of his famous defence of the work quoted in the *Allgemeine Musikalische Zeitung*, that he was at the rehearsals of *Così fan tutte* in December 1789 and January 1790[1], and that he participated in performances of all the major string quintets.[2] The MS. parts of the last three Mozart Symphonies, as well as the great C major *Missa* K.337 and the 'Coronation' Mass K.317 in the Esterházy Archives (not to speak of much other church music, including a skilful arrangement of *Thamos* choruses as Motets) also show a certain knowledge of Mozart's music apart from the operas and quintets; and of course we know that he heard the string Quartets Mozart dedicated to him. We mention all this because it is difficult to assess exactly how much of Mozart's music was known to Haydn before he left for England. We cannot prove that he ever heard a Mozart piano concerto, though it is very likely, and we do know that Haydn much appreciated Mozart's piano playing. Apart from the piano concerto, we can see that Haydn knew a limited, but characteristic, selection of Mozart's music; and we have been deliberately over-cautious, for Mozart must have shown the older man much that was unpublished and had only been played once or twice. That the two exchanged such unpublished, or one might say 'unavailable' music, is known from the evidence of Mozart's autograph copy of a passage from Haydn's *Armida* (1784); the autograph of the Mozart copy is in the University Library, Bonn.

Yet there is, in Haydn's music of the 1780s, little tangible evidence of all this exposure, direct and indirect, to Mozart's style. Altogether, the two composers' influence on each other has been greatly overanalyzed: every five-bar phrase in Mozart must be attributed to Haydn and every chromatic passing-note in Haydn laid

---

1 Mozart's letters to Puchberg, Nos. 1113 and 1115 in the Deutsch-Bauer edition; Anderson II, 934f.
2 Abbé Stadler to the Novellos, *A Mozart Pilgrimage*, op. cit., pp. 170ff.

to Mozart. The influence of Haydn on Mozart is mostly formal. As Mozart often said, he learned how to write quartets from Haydn, and the famous letter of dedication in the Opus X 'Haydn' Quartets sums up Mozart's debt. From that point on, however, Mozart's enlarged harmonic spectrum; his peculiarly individual method of orchestration (whether his martial C major density or his opaque writing in, for example, E flat or G minor); his philosophical attitude, if we may call it that, about operatic characterization; and the alarming undertones of much of his music – all these are things that hardly figure in Haydn's style at all, and certainly not in the 1780s. Haydn not only remains aloof from all these Mozartian trends, but he continues along the paths which he, perhaps the eighteenth century's greatest innovator, had himself so carefully laid out. By the time Haydn was sixty, in London (March 1792), Mozart was dead and his international influence yet to come. Haydn, on the other hand, was distilling the essence of his own wiry style. We notice an increasing trend towards third-related keys, enharmonic key-relationships, daring tonal exploitation of the development section and an ever more complex motivic relationships within a movement – in short, towards a purer intellectual approach. If anything, Haydn draws further away from the sensuous Mozartian sound. We should not be led astray by the outward brilliance of Haydn's late orchestration, for it conceals an increasingly austere approach to music. Haydn stopped writing symphonies in 1795 because he thought he had said all he could in the form: there is something forbiddingly final about 'The twelfth I have composed in England' on the title page of No. 104. Yet he went on with string quartets, where his ideas could be presented with, as it were, the bare minimum in instrumental clothing. There is a cerebral purity, a dry quality, about some movements of the Opus 76 Quartets which would be ill-suited in a symphony. On the other hand, Haydn had new and large-scale ideas which, he considered, would be better fitted to oratorio and mass than to the symphony. It never seems to have occurred to him to expand the symphonic form beyond its then conventional length of about half-an-hour; he preferred to gather his laurels with more than one hundred symphonies and to proceed to different forms involving human voices. All this has very little indeed to do with Mozart. If anything, Mozartian influence is more to be felt – this is the strongest word one would wish to use – in the post-1795 works than before. Even then, it is nearly minimal.

Haydn's London Symphonies created a fourth 'wave' of imitations. In his earlier works, we can trace three distinct schools of *seguaci*. The first grew up round Haydn's pithy and highly experimental works of the 1760s; he found admirers and imitators among the many composers living in the Austro-Hungarian Empire. *Kleinmeister* in the provincial monasteries and princely houses wrote symphonies *à la* Haydn which were, often as not, copied by Austrian scribes and sold abroad as Haydn and printed as such in Paris; but also the better-known composers, such as Dittersdorf, Ordoñez and Leopold Hofmann were not uninfluenced by Haydn; and his brother Michael certainly started symphonic life in Grosswardein (now Oradea Mare in Roumania) in 1760 copying the church-sonata productions of his brother's (such as Symphonies 5 or 11). Then, during the Romantic Crisis of the late 1760s, Haydn's new symphonies in the minor keys attracted wide attention: one of their most talented imitators was J. B. Vanhal, who occasionally succeeded in creating works almost the equal of the originals; the other was the young Mozart, who in the Symphony K. 183 produced an interesting copy of a Haydn *Sturm und Drang* symphony. When Haydn had perfected his first 'popular' style in the early 1780s, he found that certain movements, particularly slow movements such as the Andante from Symphony No. 53 and 'La

Roxelane' from No. 63 of the same name, became international best-sellers. This deliberately *volkstümlich* style, with its bright and easily remembered melodies, but also its skilful motivic development and sparse but effective orchestration, created the most lasting of all the schools hitherto mentioned. Haydn's pupil Ignaz Pleyel became one of the most successful purveyors of this popular style, and so did Adalbert Gyrowetz, who (as he himself tells us in his autobiography) took Haydn for a model and almost succeeded in reaching the popularity of the original. Hoffmeister was another Viennese composer who took over many attributes of this 1780-style from Haydn; and even Mozart, particularly in his first Viennese works of the early 1780s, often modelled a Finale directly on Haydn's high-spirited music: the Finale of the piano Concerto in D (K.451) is almost a Haydn copy, and the tune of the newly composed Finale (K.382) to the early (K.175) piano Concerto is also cast in the popular vein of Haydn's rondos. Other examples, and Mozart's transformation of them, must belong in another place.

The fourth series of Haydn's symphonic imitators must not be regarded as a mere continuation of the third. Naturally Gyrowetz, to choose one example, was influenced by the London Symphonies, and he witnessed the first two seasons there in London as one of the contributors to Salomon's concerts; but Gyrowetz began life by studying the Haydn symphonies of the late 1770s and early 1780s; and his works of the 1790s, though modified by what he heard in London in 1791 and 1792, were basically continuations of a style formed on Haydn's of a decade earlier. The same is true of Pleyel. In the last years of the eighteenth century, there arose a school of young composers who modelled their symphonies on the latest products of Haydn's style, and specifically on the London Symphonies. In Germany, where Haydn's latest symphonic works were much admired by public and *cognoscenti* alike, a whole series of pseudo-Salomon-Symphonies came into being. Most of these works have long since been forgotten, but at least one suddenly acquired a new – and unexpected – lease of life.

When Haydn sent, at the end of 1792 or early in 1793, four of his London Symphonies to the Court of Prince Krafft Ernst von Oettingen-Wallerstein, one of the 'cellists in the Wallerstein band was a talented young composer named Friedrich Witt, who had been born in 1771 and engaged at Wallerstein on 21 January 1790. He studied composition with Rosetti, the Wallerstein *Capellmeister*. Witt fashioned his first symphonic efforts directly on Haydn's London Symphonies, and one of these early Witt works is a Symphony in C of which the principal model was Symphony No. 97 by Haydn, though there are also traces of Symphony No. 93 – both works that had been sent by their composer to Wallerstein Castle. Witt wrote other symphonies, all of which show strong leanings towards the London series, and eight such works were published by André beginning in 1804. As early as 1794 Witt was performing his own symphonies at Potsdam, so we may assume that he began writing them in 1793 at the latest. The Symphony in C major was acquired along with another work in D major by Göttweig Monastery in 1825. It was also acquired by a musical society in Jena, and thereby hangs the tale.

This society at Jena, the Akademisches Konzert, apparently purchased several Witt symphonies, but in the course of the years, the title page of the C major became separated from the parts and someone in the nineteenth century thought it was composed by Beethoven. On the (then anonymous) parts, someone added 'Par Louis van Beethoven' to the second violin part and 'Symphonie von Bethoven [*sic*]' on the 'cello. In 1909, the late Professor Fritz Stein 'discovered' the work, which he entitled

'Jena Symphonie' and published under Beethoven's name. It was not until 1957 that Witt's authorship could be definitely established.[1] Because of the attribution to Beethoven, a miniature score of the Witt Symphony is available and may be studied as an interesting and by no means untalented copy of the Salomon Symphony style. Apart from this Witt copy, there are many others by English, French and Austrian *Kleinmeister* which, like the Witt Symphony in C, reproduce not only the thematic material but even the modulations and the orchestration. These are reproductions. It is more profitable to turn to the *Großmeister* and their assimilations. Of these the greatest are, as might be expected, Beethoven's first two Symphonies, first performed in 1800 and 1803, respectively. For Beethoven, though for many years he considered Mozart the greatest composer, did not adopt his style except in works deliberately modelled on Mozartian originals, e.g. the piano Quintet Op. 16 and the first three piano Concertos. Otherwise Beethoven's orchestral style is taken almost entirely from Haydn: this should be apparent to anyone who studies Haydn's and Beethoven's symphonies and then compares Schubert's Symphony No. 5 with its Mozartian models. (There were also many Mozartian followers among the *Kleinmeister*, such as Anton Eberl or the anonymous Frenchman who wrote the interesting Symphony attributed to Mozart as K. 311a.) Beethoven must have felt that Mozart's style, except perhaps in his piano writing, was inimitable and represented to a certain extent a cul-de-sac; imitating Mozart, one could only write pure (or as it might be adulterated) Mozart, whereas with Haydn – as he himself had shown – the symphonic style was capable of endless development, variation and metamorphosis. One of the curiosities of Haydn's fifty years of composing is the way in which his style constantly changes, adapting itself like a chameleon but with a resilient self-sufficiency. When the definitive study of the second half of the eighteenth century's musical life has been made, it will be realized how little Haydn owes to any outside influence after the 1770s and how much almost every composer living from 1770 to 1810 owes to Haydn. His style was nourishing and capable of endless transformation.

In the first decade or two of the nineteenth century, Haydn's late symphonies were overplayed. They were almost, but not quite, played to death. The study of Haydn's gradual decline in popularity must occupy the final chapter of any serious and objective biography but cannot concern us here except marginally. The decrease in his popularity may be traced in part to other causes – to a fundamental change in taste and to the gradual misunderstanding of his musical language. Adagios that seemed immensely sad and full of wisdom to men in 1795 sounded attractive but slightly superficial, *nichtssagend*, to the Romantic generation of 1825. One of the reasons for this trend away from Haydn was the direct result of overplaying his London Symphonies. They may have been the most influential symphonic music written in the late eighteenth century, but by overexposure to them, the public's ear became slowly blunted to their beauties. In the music journals of Europe published after the Vienna Congress of 1815, one notices an increasing irritation with these Haydn symphonies. No one disputed their importance, but after a time their constant repetition seemed due more to the slothfulness and inertia of orchestral leaders and managers than to the prevailing taste of the audience. Yet the public was still fascinated by a great unknown Haydn composition. In 1838, Felix Mendelssohn gave a series of

---

1 See our article, 'The "Jena" Symphony' in: *Music Review* 1957, reprinted in our *Essays on the Viennese Classical Style*, London 1970, The relevant literature may be found in that article. The miniature score of the 'Jena' Symphony is published by Breitkopf & Härtel.

so-called 'historic' concerts at the Leipzig Gewandhaus, and on 22 February he included several works by Haydn (not, one notes, London Symphonies . . .): the 'Farewell' Symphony, parts of *The Creation* and piano Trio No. 43 in C, which Haydn had composed shortly after his final return to Austria. Felix writes to his sister Rebecka on 24 February 1838 *inter alia*: '. . . [The Finale of Symphony No. 45] is a curiously melancholy little piece. Beforehand we played the Haydn C major Trio, and people were quite bowled over [*des Todes verwunderten*] that something so beautiful could exist, and yet it was printed long ago by Breitkopf & Härtel [in the *Oeuvres Complettes*] . . .'[1]

We are in a better position as regards Haydn's Salomon Symphonies. The 'Surprise', 'Clock', 'Drum Roll' and 'London' may be still overplayed, but not so the other works. A whole new generation of relatively unprejudiced listeners is there to rediscover anew their radiant freshness, and in the versions written by the composer rather than some well-meaning hack at a German publishing office. It is time to wipe the slate: to reconsider their intrinsic importance, to recapture their optimism and message of faith. For they are one of the great legacies of eighteenth-century Enlightenment.

Symphony No. 96 in D ('The Miracle') (1791)

Mrs Papendiek (II, 290) informs us of an interesting detail concerning Haydn's arrival in London. 'Haydn . . . told Salomon that he should stay the summer in England, and that as he heard there were to be twelve concerts and two benefits during the season there would be ample time for him to compose his first symphonies after he had the opportunity of studying the taste of the English. He was determined that his first production would both amuse and please the musical public and rivet him in their favour.' We know that Haydn considered that Symphony No. 91 needed to be altered to bring it into line with the 'English taste', but apart from adding trumpets and drums it is difficult to imagine what needed to be changed in the older (1788) work. And if we now proceed to what is probably Haydn's first English Symphony, it is equally difficult to see what makes this delicately orchestrated work different, let us say, from the 'Oxford' with which he apparently introduced himself to the public at the Hanover Square Rooms. Perhaps in Mrs Papendiek's quotation Haydn was simply making excuses in order to gain more time.

All the London Symphonies except for No. 95 open with a slow introduction, but this is not really a 'new' device for England, since it was used in the previous Paris works with considerable frequency (Nos. 84, 85, 86, 88, 90, 91 and 92). In No. 96 we may note that Haydn withholds the trumpets and drums until the first *tutti* of the Allegro, so that eighteenth-century listeners were not sure, until bar 25, whether the Symphony was one with trumpets and timpani or not. In bar 3 we note Haydn's very personal use of the turn (with three auxiliary notes), a Berenson 'fingerprint'. The turn has two distinguishing features: (1) it is accompanied by a phrase progressing a third upwards and (2) it occurs in slow tempo. This is not the only use that Haydn has for a turn, but it is one of his characteristic ones, and we shall encounter another particularly poignant example of it in bars 66–74 of the 'Incarnatus' of the *Missa in tempore belli* (1796). We show overleaf some typical examples which occur in the London Symphonies.

1 Susanne Grossmann-Vendrey: *Felix Mendelssohn Bartholdy und die Musik der Vergangenheit*, Regensburg 1969, p. 161.

Mrs Papendiek, in her report on the first concert, specifically mentions Haydn's obbligato use of the instruments. One does not know to which symphony she refers, but in No. 96 the wind instruments are used with great freedom and the whole score is marked by an orchestral transparency which is apprent even in the introduction. Here we modulate into D minor and the oboe, and only the oboe, has a long *crescendo* leading to a *forte*; and again the oboe has a kind of cadenza leading to a pause and the Allegro.

It will be observed that Haydn now takes great care to bind the slow introduction to the rest of the movement. In most cases this is done thematically, and we shall see a particularly subtle example in No. 103. Here in No. 96 Haydn has employed an equally interesting method, for the prominence of the solo oboe part in the opening Adagio looks forward to its brilliant solo in the Trio. We may also note that the solo oboe's reversed pedal point (the *crescendo* referred to above) is matched by a real pedal point in the horns shortly afterwards (bars 12–15). The same procedure may be observed in the Menuetto (horns' pedal point, bars 5–8, oboe's reverse pedal point, bars 14–16), where the instruments' order is reversed but, interestingly, the note values or length of pedal point are almost exactly the same, and in 3/4 time, too.

The Allegro begins with its own accompaniment. Apropos of this curious procedure, we have a note by no less a man than Giovanni Simone Mayr, the once celebrated operatic composer whose treatise on Haydn, though most interesting, is hardly known at all.[1] As it turns out, Mayr's treatise is in part taken *verbatim* from Rochlitz's famous review of *The Creation* in the *Allgemeine Musikalische Zeitung* IV (1802), pp. 385ff., which is reproduced *in toto* in the next volume of our biography, giving readers a chance to compare Mayr's elegant adaptation (translation) of the thoughtful original. Mayr writes, 'Non hanno questi *Allegri* tavolta neppure un *tema*, e sembrano di cominciare in mezzo; e nulladimeno trovasi in essi ad onta di tutta la leggerezza una fluidità, un ordine, che annunziano sempre la mano maestra.' The Allegro of No. 96 certainly begins 'in mezzo', and it is hard to believe what importance the 'leading note'-figure of the first violin will have: (here repeated notes *a'*). Whole sections of the first movement are cemented together by this little motif. In the first *tutti*, which separates the double announcement of the main subject, the rhythm appears in the timpani (bars 27f.), but in the second *tutti* it becomes more prominent and is repeated in each bar by the 'cellos and basses. Gradually it begins to pervade everything, even transition to the dominant (bars 50, 53–56) and the second subject itself:  . The 'fragmented'

first subject is further dissected. Its first phrase (i.e. bar 4 of the subject) terminates in three repeated notes *e''* ( ) ; we find the identical notes attached to the second subject (see the musical example). Finally, in the accompaniment to the first subject, there is the following rhythmic figure (bar 21:), which Haydn soon turns into . The movement is an almost classic example of motivic economy based on a theme-less first subject, where however the rhythm is of all-pervading importance. The development section has a long *tutti* in C major, where the bassoons and bass line have still another combination of motivic fragments, viz. with to make , which combined rhythm now assumes a vital role. The development seems to end with the large *tutti* beginning, as we say, in C major; it ends on a long sequence in the V of B minor and two whole bars of rests. (These rests have been the subject of much discussion, and Erich Leinsdorf recently announced publicly that he thought it necessary to remove one of the bars of rest!) There then follows an extremely comical *fausse reprise* in the subdominant. After the real recapitulation, there is a magnificent *tutti* which is far

1 *La Creazione del Mondo . . . da eseguirsi nel nuovo Teatro della Società nell'occasione della fondazione del Pio Instituto Musicale. Con una prefazione e notizie storiche della vita e delle opera del Compositore Estese Da G. S. M. Bergamo, Dalla Tipografia Sonzogni 1809*, p. 11. A copy in the writer's possession; another in the Library of the Biblioteca di S. Cecilia, Rome.

more intricate than the first one of the movement (which it purports to repeat): here we find a spectacular exchange of the ♩♫ ♪♪♩ between horns and trumpets (which, we must recall, were situated way up at the apex of Haydn's pyramidal orchestra; the effect was not only aural but also visual), while the opening fragment of the main theme is played simultaneously. This splendid effect was one of those mutilated eyond recognition in the nineteenth-century adaptation. There is one final point, which occurs at the very end: a violent plunge, *fortissimo*, into D minor (the *ff* marking was a tradition of Haydn's London performances; it is contained only in the autograph and the Birchall print), with the whole orchestra participating. Even here, Haydn's preoccupation with fragments of the themes follows us, the timpani and bass line hammering out the ♩♫ ♪♪♩ rhythm. Haydn directs not only the exposition to be repeated but also the second part, probably because the movement seems so short (though it is not: over 200 bars). This sense of brevity is brought about by the extreme concentration on short motivic fragments. It is curious to think that this Symphony and No. 95 must have arrived at Vienna just as Mozart lay dying.[1] But the music of this exhilarating and bright D major Symphony is worlds away from the *Spätstil* of the *Zauberflöte* and the *Requiem*. Nothing could be more dissimilar.

Giovanni Simone Mayr (*via* Rochlitz) says of Haydn's slow movements:

> Gli *Adagj* [*sic*] e gli *Andanti* hanno le forme più varie. Per lo più sono vasti, e mostrano una fisonomia di stile grande. Richiedono però un'esecuzione brillante e vivace, non essendo della spezie sentimentale ed affettuosa, anzi respirando piùttosto uno spirito nazionale di gajezza e di umoristico, il quale non può restare lungo tempo d'un carattere serio e languente (op. cit., p. 11).

Here we have the prototype of the late symphonic slow movement, 'non essendo della spezie sentimentale ed affettuoso' but orchestrated enchantingly and with the same luminously 'open' feeling that we noted about the first movement. Again we observe the obbligato use of the wind instruments, which accompany the repetition of the main subject (bars 5ff.). Like the first Allegro, this Andante starts off as if it would have dropped the trumpets and timpani (which the later arranger actually did!); one is delightfully surprised to find them joining in the first *tutti*. After what is basically an a–b–a announcement of the first section, each entry of the main theme being decked out with new garlands from the wind section, we break off the main theme and enter a long passage in the minor. Based on a fragment of the main theme, this minor excursion is treated like a *fugato* and gathers great momentum as it proceeds. The introduction of a minor 'middle' section (sometimes not exactly in the middle) is a feature that will occur in the slow movements of Nos. 93, 94, 95, 97, 98, 100, 101, and 104 and thus may be considered typical of the London Symphonies. The repetition of the opening section is not fully written out in the autograph, and Haydn, as he often does, uses the words 'etc: come Sopra' to indicate to the copyist to repeat the exact notes of the opening (this 'come Sopra' occurs at bar 51). Up to the end of this repetition the movement has proceeded as normally as Haydn's fertile invention ever allows anything to proceed 'normally'. We have had an A–B–A form of which, as we have seen, the A was subdivided into a–b–a. But what now occurs is unexpected and elevates the movement to being one of the most original and inspired of the Salomon series. A short variation on the final a section leads to an elaborate cadence and a six-four chord, just as if we were in a concerto rather than a symphony. At this point, one

---

1 Haydn sent them by mail on 17 November; they would have arrived in Vienna on 1 or 2 December. Haydn's trip to London in 1794 took from 19 January to 4 February 1794.

might call the rest of the movement a gigantic coda, or if one will, cadenza (bars 69 [with upbeat] – 89). The concerto-like atmosphere is astoundingly made more real by the introduction of two solo violin parts, just like the *concerto grosso* of a century earlier. In addition, the whole woodwind section is used like the *concertino* which thus consists, if one wishes to spell out matters, of two solo violins, solo flute, two solo oboes and bassoons; while the *ripieno* consists of strings and two horns. The cadenza even ends with a gigantic series of trills, entering one after the other in oboe I, flute I and bassoon I. The end of this movement also includes a highly Romantic modulation from G major to E flat through the augmented sixth pivot, a passage which, as we mentioned earlier, was stupidly 'edited' in the nineteenth century so that the augmented chord was changed to a I⁶ chord by flattening the note *b* in violin II and bassoon II:

This extraordinary *cadenza-cum-coda* is a brilliantly original stroke of genius. We believe that here we may also have the first concrete example of Haydn's attempting to cultivate the 'English taste'. In his own previous *oeuvre*, especially in the works of the 1760s, we find several examples of this *concerto-grosso*-technique – and not only in the famous trilogy of 1761, *Le Matin, Le Midi* and *Le Soir*, but also in the organization of such a movement as the Adagio in Symphony No. 36 in E flat (*c.* 1761–5?), where there are two solo parts (*concertino*), violin and violoncello, accompanied by a *ripieno* of strings. But such escapades had long since disappeared from Haydn's symphonies. Having arrived in London, Haydn will have taken note that here was a flourishing tradition of 'Antient Concerts', where the *concerti grossi* of Corelli, Geminiani and, especially, Handel still held the affections of the conservative-minded and tradition-conscious British public. Is this *concerto grosso* episode in Symphony No. 96 not

Haydn's charmingly expressed tribute to this great tradition, still kept alive in many London concerts? One is tempted to think so.

Haydn may have thought that he was writing 'English' symphonies, and perhaps in the last part of the slow movement he had done so. In this irresistible and captivating Menuetto, however, he wrote a movement of which the roots, the rhythm and the expression are all purely Austrian. It was the great tradition of the Redoutensaal, which must have been as good as unknown in England except through such minuets of Haydn and his pupils as were known there. It is a symphonic minuet in the grand style, but with that indefinable Austrian 'thing', the secret of which has persistently eluded non-Austrian composers for some two centuries. And if this so basically kinetic music is purely Austrian, what are we to say to the pure *Ländler* – what Haydn would have called 'Contrydance' – of the Trio, for solo oboe and accompanied in strict 'waltz rhythm' by the strings? It was a graceful and lovely tribute to the country of Haydn's birth:

Simone Mayr's (Rochlitz's) comments on Haydn's minuets in general seem to fit peculiarly well to our Symphony (which, incidentally, Mayr undoubtedly knew).

> I *Minuetti* poi sono talmente fregiati di tesori d'arte pratica e di genio, che in un solo *Minuetto* di HAYDN, trovasi una ricca miniera di dottrina e di genialità da poterne ornare un'opera grande formando essi una spezie particolare e stando sul firmamento musicale come piccioli corpi scintillanti di una luce vivissima.

The same intelligence and cultivation of language also informs Mayr's (Rochlitz's) comments about the last movements. 'Gli ultimi *Allegri*,' he writes:

> poi o *Rondò*, in cui HAYDN mette in opera tutti li mezzi e tutte le forme, che gli presentano la misura, l'armonia, ed il *Ritmo* (nel maneggio di cui niun altro lo agguaglia), consistono generalmente in piccoli periodi, li quali giungono per mezzo d'una elaborazione diligente ed artifiziosa al sommo grado del comico in cui egli è del pari inarrivabile. In mezzo e nel fine sono questi pezzi pieni di vita, di spirito e di condimento, e spirano una libertà, forza ed arditezza, che incantono e sorprendono anche l'orecchio più versate. Vi si trova soltanto ogni apparenza di serietà per renderci la leggerezza del delizioso giuoco de' suoni più inaspettata, e per ingannarci da tutti i lati, finchè stanchi d'indovinare ciò che viene, o che potessimo immaginarci, ci sottomettiamo a discrezione del compositore; e quell'

umoristico (*vis comica*), quella gajezza sì pura, sì maliziosetta, piena di spirito, e di certa onestà, unita alla fantasia più traboccante ed alla forza di dottrina più profonda ci trasporta in un mare di belle modulazioni, alle di cui dolci, inesprimibili impressioni, non può resistere nè l'intelletto, nè il sentimento.

Mayr sums up by saying that these 'quadri romanzechi' have a character which might be summed up in two words: '*artificiosa popolarità* = ossia *popolare* (intelligente, insinuante, trasfusibile) *pienezza di arte*' (op. cit., pp. 11f.).

Haydn thought to ask Maria Anna von Genzinger to press upon Herr von Kees the fact that he 'have a rehearsal [!] of both these Symphonies [Nos. 96 and 95], because they are very delicate, particularly the last movement [of that] in D, for which I recommend the softest *piano* and a very quick tempo . . .' (letter of 17 November 1791). Haydn originally marked the Finale 'Vivace' but later added 'assai' to the tempo to ensure 'a very quick tempo'. Basically this whirlwind movement is one of the composer's characteristic rondo movements, but the various subsections are ''developed' as in sonata form. The main group, or first A, is subdivided with repeat marks, i.e. ‖: 8 bars :‖‖: 20 + 20 bars :‖ and we shall see this same kind of division in
　　　　　　a　　　b　　a
the opening material of No. 97's Finale. The B section is a long section in the minor, the same kind of diversion that we have already seen in the slow movement and will see in subsequent final movements such as that to No. 101 ('The Clock'). The whole movement, in No. 96, is strictly monothematic and there is not even a hint of a second subject. C section introduces, once the a section of the theme has been announced, a kind of development where the theme is used contrapuntally with itself. There then occurs a kind of recapitulation of the main a–b–a section but without repeats, which leads to a pause and a new kind of cadenza, this time for the whole wind band. It is a presage of the long and intricate wind band soli which we shall encounter in an extended and famous passage in the first movement of No. 97 in C, and once again in the slow movement of No. 99 in E flat – a section that so inspired the players that the critic of the *Morning Chronicle* was moved to comment upon it. Like the opening movement, the Finale of No. 96 is marked by what appears to be a great overall brevity, but it is, as far as the actual count goes (239 bars), a long movement and Haydn has once again used extreme economy of thematic material to produce a sensation of concision.

It was a highly auspicious beginning of a new career in a strange country.

Symphony No. 95 in C minor (1791)

There are several ways in which to judge the popularity of the individual Salomon Symphonies, at least in London. One is the reaction in the daily newspapers, and we have seen in the Chronicle that some of the works were far more popular than the others, especially the 'Surprise' and 'Military'. Symphony No. 104, and indeed the other works first played in the 1795 season, did not have time to become really popular by the time Haydn left England – No. 104 can only have been played a few times towards the end of the 1795 season. Another measure of the various works' popularity may be gleaned from a rather unexpected source: namely, Salomon's first editions for piano trio. These were first printed as a joint endeavour between Salomon and the publishers Corri & Dussek, and Salomon's address was his office at the Hanover Square Rooms. Naturally, some of the works far outsold the others, particularly the 'Surprise' and 'Military', the first two works to receive nicknames in England. Salomon later changed his address to 34 Clipstone Street. Thus it happened that when people had sets of all twelve works bound up, they often had individual works with different publishing addresses; the plates also started to wear thin, and one can see graphically how they wore out for the most popular works. In examining the bound volumes, one usually notices that No. 95 still remained in its first edition (which was, moreover, signed by Salomon). So did No. 96, which suggests that it cannot have been the popular work so often repeated after its first performance in March 1791; for the 'Oxford' Symphony was not one of those arranged by Salomon for piano trio but had been issued, for popular 'drawing-room' consumption, in an arrangement by Dussek for piano and violin in November 1791. No. 96's slow sales as shown by the evidence of the bound volumes is another hint, albeit negative, that the 'Oxford' may have been the work which Haydn played in the opening concert of the 1791 season (see p. 143).

At any rate, No. 95 was one of the slowest sellers of the twelve in Salomon's piano trio edition, and this fact tells us that it cannot have been a very popular piece, at least compared to most of the other symphonies. It has never become a favourite, either, and many attempts to resuscitate it have been connected with the fact that being in C minor, it later basked in the reflected glory of Beethoven's Fifth Symphony, with which work, however, it could ill stand comparison on any level. Even compared to the violent emotion in the outer movements of Haydn's own earlier Symphony No. 52, not to speak of the great Mozart piano Concerto K. 491, No. 95 does not measure up. The very fact that it was the only work in a minor key among thirteen London productions (i.e. counting the Concertante) tells us a great deal about its initial lack of success. No doubt London audiences would have found the violence of a Mozart K. 550 way out of the ordinary not to mention the D minor piano Concerto K. 466; but No. 95, which begins as if it were to be a huge and dramatic piece in C minor and then (except for the Minuet) turns out to be much tamer than expected, was also not the way to English hearts; it was, in short, an experiment that Haydn took great care never to repeat. Perhaps its lack of success is because it was something of an unsuccessful compromise.

The first movement is a slow *alla breve* ('Allegro moderato'), the warning is because of the triplets and also such figures as  which would sound hurried if the barred C is taken too quickly. There is no slow introduction, also the only time this ever happens in a London symphony (though it occurs again in the Concertante which, being a concerto, is another kind of work entirely). The beginning is so impressive that no curtain-raising adagio was needed:

Those of the London audience who knew their earlier Haydn, and in particular the previous C minor Symphony No. 78, will have realized that these first five notes were designed for large-scale contrapuntal elaboration; and they were not disappointed. The motivic development of the first subject is the most striking thing about this movement. Even when modulating to the relative major, the first theme is used with itself contrapuntally, and of course it is still more expanded in the development. There is, in No. 95, a highly polished second subject, which introduces the triplets and then succumbs to them entirely: we are reminded of the same device in the 'Rider' Quartet's first movement. In the development these two widely contrasting themes are placed side by side, but the result seems to be primarily to increase the rather jerky and unsettled feeling engendered by the bars of rest in the main theme and now part and parcel of the whole fabric. The retransition to the recapitulation provides a nice touch in that the first five notes of the main subject, having been used so frequently in the course of the movement, are now omitted. The music then modulates to C major and stays in that key till the end of the movement. The telescoping that we noticed with the main theme in the recapitulation is continued; the big bridge passage is dropped, and the first subject's *piano* part slides elegantly into the second subject and the tonic major at the same time. The second time round, Haydn provides a magical wash of colour by having a solo violin play one of the countersubjects (bars 139ff.). There is a short coda in a splendid outburst of C major, to which the whole brass section and timpani contribute a slash of brilliance to a martial outburst in which only they are marked *ff* (bar 148), the others (except the triplets of the first violin) having *fz* (a strong accent). And yet there is something unsatisfactory about this movement as an aesthetic whole. Perhaps we are conditioned to expect greater things from a 'Grand Symphony in C minor', and possibly we overreact to the tame qualities of the second subject and the rather windmill-tilting triplets which occupy so much of the movement (63 bars out of 165). One ends by being slightly confused as to the music's basic message.

There is no such confusion about the even tamer E flat 'Andante cantabile' variations – Haydn called it 'a little Andante from one of my new Symphonies' (CCLN 117) – which constitute the slow movement. The trumpets and drums are dropped, and the atmosphere is much more like an andante of ten years earlier. It is charming and beautifully constructed but nothing to compare either with the Adagio of the 'Oxford' or the Andante of its chronological fellow No. 96. One interesting feature is the use of the solo violoncello in the second variation, lying wonderfully in the upper register (as do all Haydn's solo 'cello parts in that range) and once again – like the oboe in No. 96 – a presage of the famous solo in the Trio to come.

The gaunt and powerful Menuet lays claim to being the finest of all four movements. It has a real sense of unity which the Symphony as a whole may be thought to lack, and it seems to exploit the ferocious side of C minor in a way which makes us long for what Haydn could have done with such a Symphony if he had felt himself able to. In this striking and original movement, the orchestration of the Minuet proper, which features an independent 'cello part in relentless octaves and a high viola part, is as trenchant as the basic thought.

The Trio is a technically demanding 'cello solo, fulfilling the promise of the *Andante*'s second variation; it is famous among 'cellists and they play it with delight. Perhaps it is not unkind to say that as a whole the Trio is more interesting to the player than to the audience. As a concept, this kind of solo is, like the *concerto grosso* in No. 96, a throw-back to a much earlier technique: to such concerto movements as Haydn's Symphonies No. 13/II (for solo 'cello) or No. 24/II (for solo flute). Such a solo is perhaps something of an anomaly in a work of this kind, which is *in toto* more massively symphonic than No. 96; perhaps that is why the oboe solo in No. 96's Trio succeeds, having been preceded and to be followed by pieces of music filled with obbligato woodwind writing.

The Finale of No. 95 is a Vivace in barred C, and like the Trio, we are now firmly in C major and remain in that key, except for the usual modulations, till the end of the work. Formally, this is Haydn's last orchestral attempt at a 'fugued' movement in the manner of Mozart's 'Jupiter'. The fugal sections take the place of the normal bridge passage to the dominant, and instead of a second subject and development the fugue continues until the recapitulation and also figures, though briefly, in the recapitulation. The material for all this contrapuntal virtuosity is the first five notes of the main subject, and Haydn makes an exhilarating and highly effective movement out of it. By this time we have forgotten that this is a C minor Symphony, of course, but the vivacious conclusion is perhaps better suited to Haydn's English mood than the kind of minor-major rondo that concluded the earlier C minor Symphony No. 78. Can this C major burst of triumph have been one of Beethoven's models for the conclusion of the Fifth Symphony?

Naturally, we hear the Finale of No. 95 with different ears than did Haydn's audience in 1791, and we do not mean, in our case, only the knowledge of Beethoven's Op. 67; we know, as the London public did not, that the inspiration for No. 95's Finale is the conclusion of Mozart's 'Jupiter' Symphony. With its majestic tones ringing in our ears, it is difficult to hear Haydn's Finale with unprejudiced ears.

If Symphony No. 95 is generally considered the least successful of the London Symphonies, the fault is no doubt partly Haydn's, for having produced a half-tame, half-grand C minor composition, but also ours, for being unable to hear it without the 'heavy footsteps' of K. 491, K. 551 behind and Beethoven's Op. 67 in front – grossly unfair in the case of Beethoven, of course, but hardly to be changed any more.[1]

Symphony No. 93 in D (1791)

Haydn had now had half a year to observe conditions in London, and this new Symphony, with which he opened the 1792 season, may be considered the first result of his experience in the previous 1791 concerts. The introduction (Adagio) opens with a flamboyant *fortissimo* unison for the whole orchestra which is so devastatingly effective that one wonders that there is no precedent for it in any of Haydn's (or Mozart's) previous symphonies. The effect comes from holding the minims, by means

of a fermata, to much more than their usual values: ♩ ♪ │ ♩ ╏ │. The effect on

Salomon's audience must have been electrifying. As if to match this theatrical beginning, Haydn then gives us a striking modulation, whereby the note A functions as the pivot from

1 This is the first London Symphony in our chronological arrangement that was analyzed by Sir Donald Francis Tovey in his famous series of programme notes which were gathered together in essay form by the Oxford University Press. Tovey's understanding of Haydn was, for his time, almost unique and was probably considered exaggerated and eccentric. His analyses remain the finest collection of their kind on Haydn. *Essays in Musical Analysis*, 6 vols., London (O.U.P.) 1935 et seq.

V of I to a six-chord in E flat: the sense of mystery and withheld power is increased because the E flat section contains no chords in the root position.

The 'Allegro assai' opens with one of Haydn's melodies that was born popular; for many people in obscure American villages, this tune became their introduction to Haydn by way of its arrangement as a Protestant hymn – a rather unlikely fate for such a cheerful tune:

The accents Haydn noted are extremely subtle: during all the dynamic marks of the first violin in the example just quoted, the second violin (and presumably the unmarked 'cello & bass) are *pp*. This 'Allegro assai' is one of Haydn's most regular, in that there is a real second subject which also appears in its proper place in the recapitulation:

What is most irregular is the development section. After three bars of modulation, Haydn is in E minor and introduces what appears to be a new subject; this five-note phrase then proceeds to dominate matters during the entire development section except for a brief reference to the second subject just before the final retransition to the recapitulation. It can be demonstrated with some conviction that this 'new subject' – the kind of thing Mozart did in his Symphony in B flat, K. 319, with the 'Credo' theme, which is new to its development section – is in fact pasted together from two fragments, one from the first and one from the second subject. But it might with some justification be said that the average listener could hardly make this kind of analysis aurally, though there is a curious and very strong feeling that this five-note figure is well known to us. It is, however, one of the few times that Haydn's developmental figures are not immediately recognizable not on paper but to the ears of the average educated listener. We quote the beginning of the development where this five-note figure is first introduced:

Throughout this movement one has the constant feeling of self-confidence, and this in turn generates a sense of power that is displayed in an almost un-Haydnish way in the massive cadence during the coda, where the whole orchestra crashes down in chords on the first beat: ♩ 𝄾 𝄾 | ♩ 𝄾 𝄾 | ♩ 𝄾 𝄾 | ♩ 𝄾 𝄾 | (bars 252ff.). There is indeed a considerable difference between this worldly and powerful movement and the music of the 1791 season. At the opening night, as Haydn's diary informs us, the slow movement was repeated; at the second concert, the Madrigal 'The Storm' was repeated, and also the first *and* second movements of No. 93. Haydn had certainly succeeded in guessing the English taste. . . .

The 'Largo cantabile' in barred C opens with another stroke of great originality; having heard it, one wonders why no one ever thought of it before. The music is announced by a solo string quartet, and it is not until bar 9 that the strings, 'Tutti ma piano', and a solo bassoon repeat the theme in 'normal' orchestral colours. The rests between the notes of the theme itself ♩ ♪ ♪ ♩ ♪ ♪ | ♩ ♬ ♪ as well as the trill are all destined for dotted treatment in the grand Baroque manner. The movement is a new kind of variation form but *durchkomponiert* and without any double bars or repeat signs: new, because Haydn has here combined variation with rondo form, creating a fascinating hybrid that would be called 'variation rondo form' if he had composed more examples of it and made it more popular. The theme is always repeated in the tonic; in between the theme's announcement, we wander into other keys and introduce material that is new but often related to the theme. The first such 'excursion' is in G minor and in the Handelian manner, with dotted figures and chain trills, such as would awaken delightful *déjà-entendu* feelings in British hearts. Excursion Two slides into quaver triplets and introduces us to a delightful solo timpani passage (bar 30), again a presage of more to come. It will have been noted that Haydn very often gives us a hint of some instrument's coming prominence (thus the oboe solo in No. 96/I's introduction foretelling the great oboe solo in the Trio, and the solo 'cello in No. 95/II preparing the way for the Trio); here he gives us the first taste of what will become a famous timpani solo towards the end of the movement. This Excursion Two continues with a ravishingly beautiful oboe solo, which grows magically out of held *d″* minims to curve gracefully over the accompanying orchestra. The effect is highly operatic, almost like the beginning of the slow section in some great *scena*. When the theme comes back it is carefully transformed to continue producing these triplets as an accompaniment in the second violin. In fact the theme is immediately transformed into a huge orchestra crescendo, one of the most powerful of the first Salomon Symphonies, and we modulate in slow waves from G minor to B flat and to the dominant of G in a spellbinding decrescendo (marked 'sempre più piano'); arriving at the penultimate announcement of the theme. This whole section is bound together by the ubiquitous triplets, which lend a sense of unity to this brilliantly constructed Adagio. The feeling of unbroken line is further enhanced by a last and poignantly beautiful oboe solo (still in triplets: bars 67ff.), reminding us of that instrument's previous solo. The final announcement of the theme is marked *forte* but breaks off to introduce a kind of cadenza in which the timpani have an effective solo (bars 73 ff.). Following this passage of suspended motion, the bassoons let out a most obscene and ridiculous *ff* note, *C′* (two octaves below middle C), which is one of the few times that Haydn ever indulged in Rabelaisian humour. It is an extremely comic effect. The whole movement indeed has a joviality and high spirits that complements very effectively the swashbuckling outer parts of the Symphony.

Haydn is now beginning to speed up his minuet sections. Those of 1791 were still in the slower 'Viennese' tempo (as indeed befitted such a delightfully Austrian dance movement as No. 96/III), but now we find 'Allegro' more prominent than the older 'Allegretto'. No. 93/III is *Allegro* and so is No. 98/III, while No. 94/III is *Allegro molto*; only No. 97 is marked with the slower tempo. Together with this increase of tempo goes a certain incisiveness and the same very symphonic approach that already distinguished No. 92/III ('Oxford'). In No. 93/III we observe an interesting attempt to link the *Menuetto* to the first movement, and by means of the latter's important second subject. The accompaniment is identical even to the staccato dots

and the melodies have the same *Urlinie* in both cases:

In the second part we note another prominent timpani solo, this time a long *pp* roll. The layout of the score is highly original here, the two oboes and two violins echoing each other and a double pedal point being executed by the flute in repeated quavers (in itself an almost Mahlerian effect) at *d‴* and the timpani three octaves below (bars 31–38).

In the Trio we find ourselves in the middle of a sumptuous pageant, with the wind band and timpani thundering out a series of fanfares on the note *d*. Each time the strings answer in some unexpected key, the first time in B minor, the second time in G. It is a curiously aggressive and almost exhibitionistically masculine movement which obviously had a profound effect on Beethoven.

Haydn seems to have had this Symphony in mind for Frau von Genzinger: he had promised her a new symphony early in 1790 (CCLN 99) but although he had written Nos. 95 and 96 in between, it was No. 93 that he thought, as we see, to dedicate to her.

> I cannot send Your Grace the Symphony which is dedicated to you, for the following reasons: first, because I intend to alter the last movement of it, and to improve it, since it is too weak compared with the first. I was convinced of this myself, and so was the public, when it was played the first time last Friday; notwithstanding which, it made the most profound impression on the audience. The second reason is that I really dread the risk of its falling into other hands . . .

(letter of 2 March 1792, probably misdated, because 'last Friday' would be 24 February, at which No. 93 was repeated; but it is clear that No. 93 is meant; CCLN 131).

We have no means of knowing if Haydn ever found the time to revise the movement, or if what we now have is still the first, 'uncorrected' version. As it stands, however, it is difficult to see any weakness and certainly not any feebleness, so perhaps the original version was really discarded. It is in sonata form and marked 'Presto, ma non troppo', but its Finale character is assured by the light metre (2/4) and by the way in which the movement is laid out, the first section being in Haydn's customary scheme of ‖: a :‖‖: b + a :‖ and ending on the tonic. There is a long
    16 bars 26 bars 8 bars
transition to the dominant, and then a repetition of the first subject in that key – all as might be expected; what follows would appear to be the closing material in the dominant, a broadly spaced *tutti*. At the end of the *tutti* we are surprised to find a fully-fledged second subject and one, moreover, clearly related to the subsidiary theme of the first movement and also the passage in the Minuet quoted above (see overleaf).

521

The lead-back to the recapitulation has always been the delight of connoisseurs: from a *tutti* ending in the dominant of the mediant (bass: *c sharp*), a solo cello repeats the octave skip (*piano*) twice, whereupon Haydn simply jumps *fortissimo* into unison D and the recapitulation. Like many details of this Symphony, this sliding into the tonic from a pivotal leading note (in this case: V of III = leading note of I) is something which Beethoven would put to excellent use. The coda introduces still another timpani solo, once again a *pp* roll (269) on a tonic pedal point and again unsupported. At the end of this coda, the oboes, bassoons, horns and trumpets blare out the theme (supported by timpani) in a last rousing fanfare to echo the sound of the Trio (the second horns and trumpets had to fake the written *d'*, sounding *e'*, which were not on valveless brass instruments . . .) and conclude one of Haydn's most extrovert, hearty and eminently successful attempts at *le goût anglais*.

Symphony No. 94 in G ('The Surprise'/'Mit dem Paukenschlag') (1791)

This is, and for at least a century and a half has been, Haydn's most celebrated piece of music, rivalling the popular affection for *The Creation* in German-speaking countries and surpassing it in the Anglo-Saxon world. It is certainly the most over-played Haydn symphony and one of the most hackneyed pieces in the whole repertoire of classical music. It has only been saved from an even 'worse' popularity by not having been arranged as a jazz tune, in the manner of Mozart 'Symphony No. 40' or (in earlier years) the Sonata K. 545. Because of its being so overplayed, Haydn biographers have not treated it kindly, possibly because of a simple case of overexposure.[1] The public, as is well known, finds it easier to love and remember a piece of music with a history, a nickname, one connected with an anecdote. It is scarcely an accident that Edition Eulenburg, when it began to issue the lesser-known Haydn symphonies in miniature score, printed 'The Oxford' before Nos. 90 and 91, 'L'ours' before No. 80, 'Der Schulmeister' before Nos. 52 or 54 (both far greater works), 'Maria Theresa' before No. 47 – and so forth; the list is long and slightly depressing. On the other hand, it must be recalled that Symphony No. 94 had no name at all when it was first performed

1 The vast individual literature about No. 94 – programme notes, etc. – is mostly worthless. In recent years, there has been a notable tendency to take the work as a whole and even its famous second movement much more seriously. See *inter alia* D. C. Johns: 'In Defence of Haydn: The "Surprise" Symphony revisited' in *Music Review* Vol. XXIV No. 4 (Nov. 1963), pp. 305ff., also Guy A. Marco: 'A Musical Task in the "Surprise" Symphony in *Journal of the American Musicological Society* XI' (1958), pp. 41ff.

in 1792; and the 'Surprise' in the second movement was hardly the sole reason for the work's immediate popularity in London. If we examine the whole Symphony with critical impartiality, it is clear that it has special qualities in all its movements – not only the Andante – that places it somewhat in a class by itself, at least in the first series of the Salomon Symphonies. It is, obviously, the second movement which propelled it into the small group of really popular Haydn compositions; and it will be seen that the Andante is a particularly beautiful, elegant and in part stirring piece of music which every bit deserves the fame it enjoys.

The first thing that sets it apart from its companions of the 1791–2 season is, of course, the key – G major. This pastoral key, a great favourite in eighteenth century music of all genres, had already been the vessel for some of Haydn's finest symphonic ideas: Symphony No. 54 (1774), possibly a work revised for London, was outstanding for its time, and Symphonies Nos. 88 (1787?) and 92 ('Oxford', 1789) are the two works that might be considered the greatest immediate precursors of the 'Surprise'. With the limitation of the trumpets in G – a subject to which we will return in a moment – Haydn scored these earlier G major Symphonies with trumpets in C. This gave a curious orchestral colour to the brass parts of these pieces and taxed Haydn's imagination to overcome the technical drawbacks. Mozart tackled the problem in a symphony only once: in the magnificent theatrical Overture in three connected movements (K. 318), where he used four horns and two trumpets. (The timpani part in the autograph of K. 318 was added later to the autograph and is in the very curious pitch of high G and [normal] D.) K. 318 achieved hardly any circulation in Mozart's lifetime, however, and thus the full orchestra in G major was, as far as most European musicians were concerned, a Haydn invention – which historically speaking it was, since Symphony 54 (1774) precedes Mozart's K. 318 by five years.

Haydn originally started to write the autograph of Symphony No. 94 with trumpets in G, the so-called 'English' trumpets referred to in Altenburg's famous treatise of 1795;[1] in Italy they were called 'trombe piccole'. Since their diatonic scale did not begin until sounding *g″*, their limitations were really very extreme in an age where the *clarino* register had almost entirely disappeared except in remote provincial pockets. Their 'useful' notes, *de anno* 1791–2, were:

which meant that their upper notes were in an extremely high range of the orchestra and that the trumpets would tend to cut through the texture even in *forte* passages. The sounding *c‴* being impure (it could be 'lipped up' to *c sharp‴* more easily), its use at this fearfully high range was dubious. Haydn wrote the whole opening movement of No. 94 with G trumpets, and he was very careful to use them mainly up to written *e″* (= *b″*); only once does he employ the tricky sounding *c‴* (I: 214); but he must have decided that they would be too difficult to play and perhaps also too shrill; for having completed the opening movement he changed to C trumpets and wrote, at the first entrance of the original (G) trumpet parts in the autograph (I: 21), 'a parte' over the stave, crossing out the discarded parts. The C trumpet parts for I are on a separate sheet at the end of the MS. By the time he reached the third and fourth movements, Haydn put C trumpets in the score: the slow movement would have had parts in C as a matter

---

1 *Versuch einer Anleitung zur heroisch-musikalischen Trompeter- und Pauker-Kunst...*', Halle, 1795, p. 11.

of course. The original G trumpet parts are printed as an Appendix to the Haydn-Mozart-Presse (Philharmonia) score.

It is difficult to assess to what extent a composer's attempt to unify such a multi-movement Symphony as the present one is conscious and to what extent unconscious. Obviously the idea of linking the introduction of No. 98 to the main body of the movement by means of straight thematic association is conscious. The fact that the 'Vivace assai', the Minuet and the Finale of No. 94 all begin on upbeats and all have a centre of gravity round the note B may be design or it may be entirely unconscious, it is also curious that all the examples shift the centre from B to G within (at the most) $1\frac{1}{2}$ bars:

The first of 'second subject group' (more of this later) in the first movement is also centred round the note B, moving to G, and so is the second of this group:

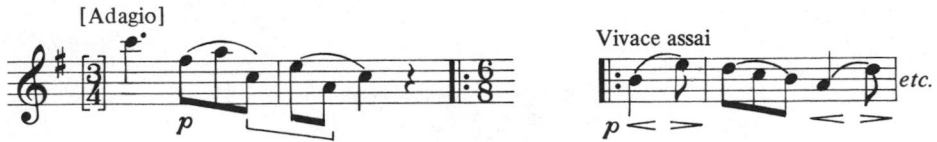

Similarly, there is a mysterious feeling of great unity between the introduction and the 'Vivace assai'. Haydn makes up for the differences in metre (introduction 3/4 and 'Vivace assai' 6/8) by subdividing the 6/8 in such a way that it starts out sounding like

$$\frac{3}{4}\;\text{♩}\;\;\text{♩}\;|\;\text{♩}\;\text{♩}\;\text{♩}\;|\;\text{♩}\;\;\text{♩}\;|\;\text{♩}\;\text{♩}\;\text{♩}.$$ This illusion is aided by the end of the in-

troduction, which deliberately blurs the final bar lines so that the upbeat at the beginning of the 'Vivace assai' sounds more like a downbeat:

The importance of this final phrase of the introduction is made clear when the main theme is led in for the second time:

The intervals *c'''–a''–f sharp''–c''–e''–a'–c''* return in the above quotation and particularly the bracketed section (*c''–e''–a'*) of the Adagio is stressed in the lead–back. It is hard not to believe that all this intervallic and motivic interconnection is part of an overall scheme to unify this Symphony; but whether conscious or unconscious, there is a definite feeling of strong underlying unity between all the movements of this work, so that even the second movement becomes linked to the rest of the piece.

There is one final point which should be made in connection with the underlying unity of the Viennese classical style, and that is the fact, first examined and then put into practice by Richard Strauss when he was conducting at the Munich Opera, that all the large-scale works of Haydn, Mozart and Beethoven are conceived in one basic tempo which is then subdivided as the movements succeed one another. According to this theory, all the great operatic Finales of Mozart's Viennese masterpieces (i.e. from *Entführung* to *Zauberflöte*) are in one basic pulse which is divided according to the tempo indication. This one *Urtempo* also applies to whole symphonies (of which a specially obvious example would be Mozart's 'Linz' Symphony in C, K. 425). The theory has much to recommend it. It is obvious that the Finales of Haydn's *La fedeltà premiata*, Acts I & II, are constructed in this manner, and since they are the earliest large-scale multi-movement operatic finales of the Viennese classical school, having been composed in 1780, it is probably correct to assume that the same principle would also apply to symphonies. The 'Surprise' is a work which lends itself particularly well to this treatment.[1]

Symphony No. 94 begins with a pastoral introduction, the only one of the first set of London Symphonies to open *piano*; years of subsequent symphonic writing have possibly blunted our ears to the originality and freshness of the beginning, for wind band *soli* marked 'cantabile'. The gradual drift away from the tonic begins at the end of bar 8, so that at the beginning of bar 10 we are in F minor, the beginning of bar 11 in B flat (I^6), the beginning of bar 11 in C (I^6) and the beginning of bar 12 in the dominant. This darkly coloured modulation is started in the bass line under a series of repeated quavers in octaves (violins I, II)

---

1 We have detailed knowledge of this theory of the basic underlying tempo in the Viennese classical school from Professor Hans Swarowsky, a former associate of Richard Strauss. Professor Swarowsky explained the principle to us on many occasions.

and it will not have failed to escape the notice of the astute musician that this springboard to the 'off-tonic' later occurs in the 'Vivace assai' when the main subject, itself off-tonic, is approached, for instance:

The first subject is one of Haydn's very shortest, and in its harmonic pattern it is similar to that of No. 86 (also off-tonic, also only a few bars in length); and if we have studied that previous work for Paris, we will expect a large *tutti* to establish the tonic and a repetition of the main theme. That seems to be what happens in No. 94: 14 bars of a rousing orchestral flourish and then after another four bars' transition the main theme over again, with a countersubject in the oboe. But there is one significant difference: in No. 86, the *tutti* turned into a bridge passage and modulated to the dominant; in No. 94, we are still in the tonic when the theme is reintroduced. The whole procedure is then repeated: bridge passage to the dominant and then the main theme in a brilliantly ambivalent tonal position of appearing to be in F major for a moment before moving deftly into the dominant of the dominant:

The shortness and tonal instability of the first theme leads Haydn to balance it with a very long section in the dominant and a second subject group which consists of two distinct theme. No. 94, then, is almost unique in Haydn's symphonic *oeuvre* by having three main subjects. They have been quoted above.

In the development Haydn introduces another great innovation: the G drum is tuned to A at the end of the exposition (the player is given plenty of time to retune, and plenty of time afterwards to get his instrument back to the tonic). Haydn can, by this operation, have drums in the tonic and dominant key for his long episode in D minor during the development section (bars 123ff.). This tremendous 'leap forward' into later orchestral practice is clearly marked in Haydn's autograph but was later changed (not in Haydn's hand: is it Salomon's?) to fit the un-retuned drums of G and D. Elssler's parts at Donaueschingen have the grim dissonance G at bars 131–2 and D at 133–4, while modern (i.e. nineteenth-century) editions usually have D throughout 131–4. The score by an Esterházy copyist which is a copy Haydn had made when he returned from England in the Summer of 1792 has the original A version unchanged, which shows that the change was made later. No doubt this innovation will have created utter chaos in most orchestras, whereas Haydn could explain what he wanted verbally to the London players (bars 131–6).

The last and perhaps wittiest of the ambiguous preparations for the main theme is that of the actual recapitulation, which is reached in the following passage (the tail end of a full cadence in B minor for the whole orchestra):

Once more there is an extraordinary allusion to the introduction. It is the beginning of that veiled and brooding modulation in the *Adagio*:

which in the recapitulation of the 'Vivace assai' is turned into the following (notice the *ff* marking for the woodwind and brass, to make the reference to the repeated *g*'s clearer):

Originally there was no 'Surprise' in the Andante and the first 32 bars of the present score were, in the original MS., twice eight bars with repeat signs. The original version is printed as an Appendix to the Haydn-Mozart Presse (and Philharmonia 794) score. There are three highly indicative markings that should help conductors in understanding the movement's character. The one is the description of the main theme in the autograph as 'Semplice'. This sort of nursery tune is very difficult to write so that it sounds effective, 'child-like' and innocent; Haydn had composed a similar kind of movement many years before, the second movement of the 'Schoolmaster' Symphony No. 55, where we also find the indication 'Adagio, ma semplicemente' (which meant in that case totally without vibrato, the subsequent indication for which is 'dolce'). The movement is also Andante and not Allegretto; almost everyone nowadays takes it too quickly, which automatically destroys many of Haydn's delicate effects. The third point is more subtle: it is the use of *tenuto* on the crotchets. How necessary this *tenuto* is (writing the unadorned crotchet was obviously insufficient) may be seen in the many performances where despite this warning the notes are not held to the very end. This *tenuto* also serves another function. By holding the note to its full length, the melodic stress does not simply end there, as it otherwise would, but carries on to the next phrase. Thus each one of the crotchets serves the dualistic purpose of forming the end of one phrase and leading in the beginning of the next.

The first variation is in two groups of eight bars, both repeated. It is the beginning of a gradual build-up of melodic, rhythmic and orchestral tension-cum-relaxation which shows Haydn the supreme master-craftsman. Here the theme is presented in the middle strings and the first violin, once joined by the flute, have a counter-subject.[1] The second variation is in the tonic minor and only the first eight bars are marked with a repeat sign. From there to end of the movement everything is *auskomponiert*. The entrance of the brass and timpani at bar 65 mark the climax of a steady increase in tension during the minor section. From steady quavers we move unobtrusively to semiquavers in the accompaniment (53-4) and, at the beginning of the *minore*'s second

part to 𝅘𝅥𝅮𝅘𝅥𝅮 𝅘𝅥𝅯𝅘𝅥𝅯𝅘𝅥𝅯 𝅘𝅥𝅮𝅘𝅥𝅮 𝅘𝅥𝅯 . Variation three (bars 75ff.) returns to *piano* but the

increased rhythmic division in semiquavers is continued during the oboe solo, while the second part returns to the original slower quaver pulse but shifts the attention to a ravishingly beautiful solo passage for first flute and first oboe. Variation four (bars 107ff.) is a march with the trumpets and horns thundering out the theme *fortissimo* and the basic pulse still more increased by having the violins move in sextuplet semiquavers. The off-beat triple stops by the second violins, violas and 'cellos adds one further element of excitement to this stirring section. Its repetition (bars 115ff.) is a startling contrast – just strings and bassoons *col basso*, and the score is marked 'pianissimo e dolce'. The march resumes, moving majestically towards a massive *fermata* on a deceptive cadence. The ending is as if a sudden veil had been drawn across this scene of pageantry, blurring the outlines and merging the colours: it is a magical effect, giving the music some of the ephemerality, the lingering sadness that we find in Watteau's *fêtes* (see example overleaf, top).

The only other time Haydn had ever used such a quick tempo for a minuet was in Symphony No. 28 (1765): No. 94's Menuet ('Allegro molto') seems to be a Breugelian dance, but although the oboes, horns, second violins and violas have the | 𝄽 𝅘𝅥 𝅘𝅥 | rhythm to contrast with the strong first beat of trumpets, timpani and basses, the effect is much more like a lusty, perhaps rather crude, peasants' dance than

---

1 We would point out a printing error in bar 38. Here the full score is correct but the miniature scores (bound and separate) have for flute and violin I as penultimate note *c'''* and *c''* instead of *d'''* and *d''*

the waltz with the rhythm of which it has obvious affinities. The Trio, a wispy, rather droll piece for bassoon and strings, is carefully bound to the Menuet by the association of a quaver scale (going in inverted direction in the Trio) and by intervallic association.

The Finale is one of the most sophisticated examples of a sonata rondo that Haydn (or anyone else) ever composed. If one examines the phrasing of the main theme, it is immediately apparent that by shifting the accents to the 4th and 2nd quavers the music divests itself of what would otherwise be a conventional four-squareness.[1] Formally this movement is one of two basic kinds of sonata rondo which Haydn favoured during the London period. The one is monothematic (No. 97/IV is a very characteristic example) and ours is duo-thematic, with a broadly contrasting second subject. After the announcement of the second subject, instead of a double bar and then a development section, No. 94/IV dispenses entirely with the double bar and then modulates back to the tonic and a restatement of the main theme. Schematically this may be expressed as follows:

	Exposition			*Development*

A	B 2nd subj.		close	
a – b – a				a

$(I – V – I) \rightarrow (I \rightarrow V) \longrightarrow (V) \longrightarrow (V) \longrightarrow (I) \rightarrow$
bars: 1–38 38–74 75–87 87–99 (100–103) 103*ff.*

The rondo character is suggested by the return to the main theme and the tonic key, but there follows a lively and extremely virtuoso development as in strict sonata form. There is even a *fausse reprise* of an unexpected kind. After this afore-mentioned development section, Haydn returns once again to the main theme (bar 145), but its progress is immediately broken off by a new development in G minor which dashes its way through another kaleidoscopic series of modulations and arrives back at the main theme by a series of *perpetuum mobile* figures (bars 178ff.). After the second theme there is a gigantic timpani solo (bar 233) which roars out of a tonic pedal point – this solo was later Bowdlerized, but Haydn's original text is not only in the autograph but also in

---

1 For a fascinating rhythmic analysis of this theme, see Grosvenor Cooper and Leonard B. Meyer: *The Rhythmic Structure of Music*, Chicago & London, 1960, pp. 65ff. This book is altogether essential reading for any serious student of music analysis.

the Esterházy Archives copy and in the authentic MS. parts at Donaueschingen Castle by Johann Elssler. People were, no doubt, disturbed by the dissonance at bar 235 (timpani's G against A flat in the bass line); for those, we suggest changing the G at bar 235 to D. It may be that Haydn later changed his mind and removed the effect, for the Birchall print (and indeed the other early printed parts) have, for bars 233–5,

It seems to us, however, that the original version is far more piquant (bars 222–7).

This is a phenomenal movement, combining as it does an orchestral technique of a superb calibre, a freedom of form (uniting the qualities of sonata and rondo) and a treatment of the thematic material that satisfies the intellectual and fascinates the audience. It is the great summing up of a distinguished line of such Haydn Finales in G major, a key that always seems to bring out that fascinating and typically Viennese ability to combine rigorous intellectual discipline with great outward beauty. It would be a bold man who would dare give the palm to the triumvirate of G major Finales from the years 1787–1791: No. 88, No. 92 ('Oxford') or No. 94 – the latter in a Symphony which has justly become a symbol for all Haydn's music.

Symphony No. 98 in B flat (1792?)

This is the first symphony, and as far as we can tell the first work altogether, in which Haydn uses trumpets and kettledrums in the key of B flat. Mozart never used them in a B flat symphony. Perhaps the use of brass in this key was an English speciality, though the tradition existed in Salzburg. Haydn's brother Johann Michael used them in a Symphony in B flat dated 29 January 1788 (Perger 28) and also in church music twenty years before (preserved in autograph). The tradition was hardly known in Vienna for instrumental works, however, and it was not till Haydn returned there and introduced his various B flat London works with trumpets and drums (No. 98, Concertante, No. 102) that the practice became general. It is a curious detail but worth mentioning. Mozart actually used trumpets in B flat (for example in the Aria 'Come un scoglio' from *Così fan tutte*), and possibly the fact that he wrote no symphonies in that key after K. 319 may explain their absence in his symphonies. Moreover, B flat orchestral works in Austria were usually either 'chamber symphonies' or (for example) piano concertos with B flat alto horns but no trumpets or timpani. Although Haydn's many previous B flat symphonies lack any indication of alto or basso for the horns, there is no reason to think that his orchestral palette for B flat was any different than Mozart's. The only indication of alto for horns that exists before 1791 is for C horns, and that frequently because there were almost never trumpets at Eszterháza (1780 was an exception) and the C alto horns took over the function of the trumpets. In England, however, there seems to have been no tradition for alto horn playing, certainly not in C and probably not in B flat either. Haydn's friend William Shield, discussing the pitch and transposition of all the horns in 1800[1] writes: 'Corni in B♭. . . . The length of a B flat Horn renders the tone very dead, in consequence of which Compositions in this key are often accompanied with E flat Horns', and goes on to add an example with the top line the 'written notes' and the bottom line 'real tones', from which it is abundantly clear that B flat horns were played basso. The subdued brilliance of trumpets and horns

1 *Introduction to Harmony*, London, Printed for the Author, p. 95.

in that key gives the orchestral sound a kind of solemn elegance, quite different from the clear, shining colour they have in D major or the martial excitement they generate in C major, at least in Haydn's treatment of that key. From this point in Haydn's career, B flat major with the full orchestra plays a major role, not only in symphonies but particularly in the late Masses (*Missa Sancti Bernardi de Offida* of 1796 and the Masses of 1799, 1801 and 1802) and the two late Oratorios, *The Creation* and *The Seasons*.

No doubt the brass and timpani in B flat lend to this work a heaviness and weight which accord well with the serious atmosphere of the Symphony as a whole. The orchestral colour seems to have disturbed nineteenth-century musicians because this is the second London work in which the entire trumpet and timpani parts were rewritten; Haydn's original parts were first published in modern times by the present writer (*Music Review* 1954). Bad though these rewritten parts are throughout the arranger outdid himself in two places: he is scandalously inept in the heavily brass and timpani-accented Minuet, the texture of which he ruined, and criminally negligent in the last part of the Finale; there, at bars 344ff., the trumpets double the horns at the beginning when the music is *forte*, giving a shining gloss to the top of the orchestral sound and later they are fastidiously lowered a little in pitch when the whole passage is repeated in a momentous *piano* to *crescendo*; all this studied treatment of the brass parts was ruthlessly destroyed by the editorial hack. It is hard to believe that anyone could have been so unmusical. See p. 534 *infra*.

In keeping with the spirit of the work, the Adagio introduction begins in B flat minor and announces the Allegro's main subject at once, or at least the first four notes of it. This literal pre-announcement of the principal theme occurred in 1788, with Symphony No. 90 in C, and both are part of Haydn's efforts to bind the introduction more closely to the movement proper. We shall see in the final Symphony of 1792 (No. 97) an even more compelling, though concealed, effort which, in turn, will lead to the most complicated relationship between introduction and allegro that Haydn attempted, No. 103.

It will be noted that the introduction has the notes unbound (or with *staccati*) and marked with *fz* under the minims, whereas in the Allegro the melody is elegantly phrased in *legato* slurs. Both facets of the theme appear side by side when the music reaches the dominant and the main subjects is introduced again: ♩ ♩ |♩. ♩ |♩ ♩ ♩ ♩. The enormous size of the exposition is apparent not only in *fz fz fz p*

the number of bars (16 to 131 as compared to 61 bars in No. 95 and 65 in No. 96, the latter counted from the end of the introduction, of course), but also in the length of time Haydn stays in the dominant. By bar 55 he is in the middle of the modulation to the dominant but since he has already arrived at V of V we may say with confidence that from this point to the double bar at 131, the music is firmly in F major. In such a passage as that of bars 75ff. (later repeated in a slightly changed form), the intervals of a sixth, third and fifth are all plainly derived from the main subject, which contains (in order) two third progressions, one fourth, one sixth, one fourth, one fifth, one fourth and one fifth:

The second subject is put off until bar 106; it is a long oboe line in semibreves accompanied by rather restless quavers in the upper strings and broken off by an upwards scale in the first violin which derives from the end of the first subject (beginning of the bridge passage: bars 32f.). The long oboe arc is resumed after the interruption and leads to the double bar. In the recapitulation this second statement is given unexpectedly and with a lovely effect to the flute. The serious intention of this Symphony is immediately made even more clear in the development section, which is an elaborate and contrapuntally involved working-out of the first subject and other material from the exposition's long section in the dominant. There was a constant feeling of restlessness throughout the exposition; this restlessness now turns rather ominously to anxiety in a way quite unprecedented in Haydn's recent career. Verbal description being at best a cloudy substitute for the actual music, one must simply refer to bars 145ff. from the development where this feeling of *Angst* is suddenly behind all those *forzati*.

Tovey, in his brilliant essay on this Symphony, thought that great slow movement (Adagio), the main theme of which is inspired by 'God save the King', was Haydn's lament on the death of Mozart; and un-Mozartian though the other five London Symphonies of 1791–2 undoubtedly are – not to speak of the Concertante – there are aspects of this beautiful Adagio in No. 98 which might be construed as a tribute to the composer of the 'Jupiter' Symphony and especially its Andante. The same troubled and restless undertones that we have observed in the opening Allegro of No. 98 also inform this Adagio, and the music rises to a crisis almost amounting to panic in the development section, repeating the pattern of the first movement and also

using the same technical device, viz. the first notes

of the principal subject. The recapitulation enters to the accompaniment of a solo 'cello, whose lonely sound adds a sense of autumnal beauty to the music. When the theme enters the last time, the first oboe has the theme and the first violin has a staggering E flat, creating a sudden ambiguity and poignancy.

This flash of inspiration was, like many things in this Symphony, destroyed by the hacks in the nineteenth century. In one score we have examined (Cranz), the original plate had what Haydn wrote in the first violin part, and one can see that it was subsequently changed to *f'*, which is what *die Herren* Gyrowetz or Pleyel or Wranizky would have written. We shall never know if Haydn really composed this profoundly personal movement in private memory of his dead young friend; but if he did, it is the greatest epitaph that Mozart, who lay in a nameless Viennese grave, would ever receive.

The Menuet is heavily symphonic, with a dark swirl of colour in the *soli* for wind band and timpani at bars 4–6 and a series of *forzati* towards the end that culminate in an explosive *ff* at bar 50. The Trio omits horns, trumpets and drums so that the folk-tune of a melody will stand out in all its innocence.

This is the largest, most complex and ambitious symphonic Finale of Haydn's career up to now and is only matched in quite another sphere and with another purpose by the Finale of Mozart's 'Jupiter'. Haydn's Presto has 386 bars, and the first 147 are to be repeated, a total length of some eleven minutes. The entire Symphony is thus nearly thirty-five minutes in length even at our tempi which are certainly quicker than those Haydn and Salomon would have chosen. After the double bar, preceded by a fermata which must apply, one assumes, only to the *second* time round, the music drops into A flat major and the totally unexpected pleasure of a series of solo violin passages for Mr. Salomon. These 'Salomon soli' are not just confined to the section after the double bar; after a big *tutti* the solo violin enters again and in a very extended solo section, he carries the music back to the recapitulation and announces the main theme himself. If the London audience was already on its tiptoes, Haydn has still more sensational effects in store for us. In keeping with the enormous size of the Finale as a whole, the coda is equally huge. It begins with the upbeat to bar 328 and the tempo is retarded to 'più moderato'. The main theme sounds, at first, like a lunatic slow-motion copy of itself, but after the seventh bar, the music lunges ahead by the notational trick of having been written in semiquavers. This 'più moderato' has, in effect, had the opposite effect of speeding up the music in a most exciting way. In the middle of this bustle of semiquavers, Haydn introduces an orchestral effect which is intoxicating: the brass and timpani seem to interrupt and then to take over the pattern of exchange between the bass line and the top woodwind. The whole thing is then repeated with different emphasis and *piano*, leading (as Salomon's quintet arrangement suggests) to a huge *crescendo* – the autograph and the authentic MS. parts are rather fragmented here as to what happens after the *piano* (bars 343–56).

It must have been thought, that historic night of 2 March 1792, that Haydn had now reached the end of his limitless invention, and the end of the Symphony. But, no doubt to the utter incredulity of the London public, Dr. Haydn now proceeded to display his talents on the fortepiano (still marked, of course, 'Cembalo Solo' in the autograph). One needs only a modicum of imagination to conjure up the cheers of delight and the stamping that greeted this dexterous display on the part of the world's greatest living composer (see extract opposite, top).

The extract follows the text of two principal sources: (1) the autograph manuscript; (2) the authentic copy, by Haydn's London copyist of 1791 and 1792, in the Royal Philharmonic Society. It will be noted even in the extract – the interested reader may easily consult the complete text in the full or miniature score (Haydn-Mozart Presse or Philharmonia or Eulenburg) – that Haydn wrote down the pianoforte part for an instrument the top range of which was the usual Continental *f'''*.

But that is not, apparently, what 'Dr. Haydn used to play'. For the British sources show us a text in which the piano's top note is g'''. We printed in facsimile a contemporary British source for this passage in Volume XI (p. XXVI) of the *Complete Symphonies*, but since this interesting text was not included in our edition of the actual music, we add it here, complete, for those who may wish to perform Haydn's text for the instrument 'with additional keys'.

'N.B. Upon an Instrument with additional keys, and when there is a Violin to accompany it the Violin may Play the Treble part, and the Piano-Forte the following eleven bars, which Dr. Haydn used to play.'

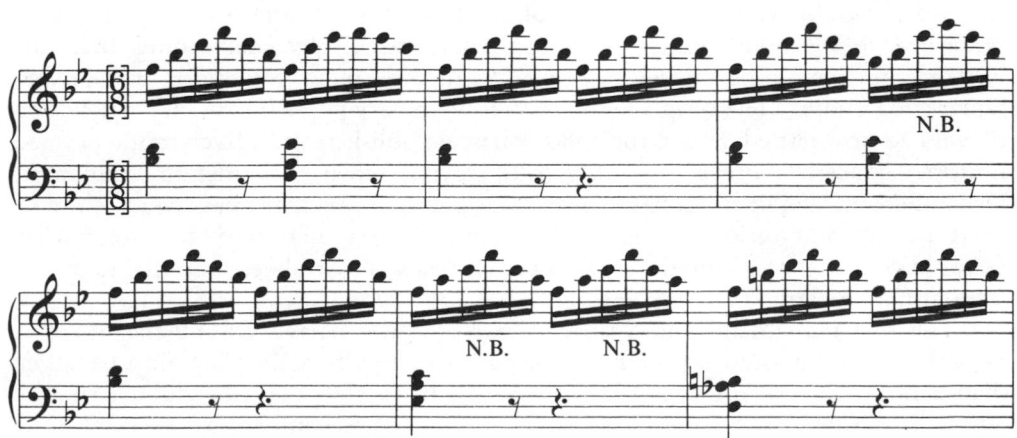

Concertante in B Flat (1792)

The autograph is entitled 'Concertante' but in subsequent years it became known as 'Sinfonia Concertante'. The presumably authentic André print, announced in May 1796, was entitled 'Sinfonie concertante', and the Artaria edition, which followed André's in July, was issued as 'Grand Simphonie Concertante'. Both these editions were preceded by that of Imbault (also put forth as 'Sinfonie Concertante') in Paris, which was announced in the Frankfurt newspaper *Staats-Ristretto* in April 1796. Shortly before Haydn's death, the *Chemische Druckerei* published the work, anonymously arranged as a 'Grand Sestetto' for two violins, two violas and two violoncellos or violoncello and double bass.

The autograph shows that the work was composed or at least put down on paper in considerable haste and under a certain amount of stress. The orchestration is so unusual for Haydn, as is the form – he never wrote another multiple concerto unless one includes the very early work for violin and harpsichord (XVIII: 6, composed in the 1750s?) – that one is tempted to ascribe its presence to outside factors. They are not hard to find. Haydn's erstwhile pupil, Ignaz Pleyel, had arrived with a trunk full of music to be given at the Professional Concert; and among this batch was a Concertante for six solo instruments and orchestra which Pleyel conducted at the Hanover Square Rooms on 27 February (*vide* Chronicle). It was a *symphonie concertante* for violin, viola, violoncello, flute, oboe, bassoon and orchestra which Pleyel published in his own edition ten years later, specifically mentioning that this 'Quatrième Simphonie concertante' was 'composée pour le Concert d'Hanover-Square de Londres'. The *symphonie concertante* was a very popular form in Paris, where Pleyel had now settled, and in the 1780s Parisian publishers did a lively trade in these multiple concertos. Pleyel probably told Haydn, when they met in London in December, that the Professional Concert was going to perform a new concertante of his (Pleyel's) composition. No doubt Salomon urged Haydn to show the world what *he* could do in the form, and the result is the Concertante for oboe, bassoon, violin and 'cello usually referred to as 'Op. 84'.

The first movement is in a slow Allegro (C, not barred C) and the mood is expansive, as one would expect in a multiple concerto where the scale must be larger than a normal work for one solo instrument. Naturally, the solo violin part was especially written for Salomon, who (as the Press notices inform us) excelled in it.

Haydn was never much attracted to the concerto form after his youth, when he wrote many harpsichord and organ concertos and *concertini* for himself and his pupils, and works to please the Esterházy virtuosi (such as the violin concertos for Luigi Tomasini). In 1783, he had written his last concerto – as far as we know – before the London trip: the famous 'Cello Concerto in D. After that we know only the present Concertante, the great Trumpet Concerto of 1796, and the *incipit* of a lost Double Concerto for two horns in E flat. (The promised but apparently unwritten violin Concerto for Barthélémon has been noted above, see p. 169.) It is rather surprising that he was not persuaded to write a concerto for Salomon, but although Haydn gladly cultivated almost every known form of musical activity while in London (except, for obvious reasons Catholic church music), he did not touch the solo concerto. With the present Concertante, Haydn could compose another symphonic work interwoven with four solo parts. He attacked the problem with gusto and wrote one of the eighteenth century's most interesting multiple concertos.

The principal theme contains once more those Haydnish turns-on-the-note in a phrase progressing a third upwards:

Haydn approaches the form with his usual unconventionality, for hardly have we reached the first *tutti* and a half cadence on V than soloists begin to come in. Their first entrance is a kind of *trompe l'oreille*. All the solo instruments enter but as part of the orchestral tutti (that is to say: *all* the violins, *all* the 'celli and the orchestral oboe I and bassoon), and immediately afterwards the *real* soli slide in unobtrusively (bars 26–33). All this takes place during the first orchestral ritornello. The solo quartet once again breaks into the *tutti* at bars 41–2. Apart from the delightful break with the conventional concerto opening, this procedure gives all the solo instruments, and especially the wind instruments, time to warm up: Haydn will do the same with the solo trumpet in the 1796 Concerto.

The *tutti* finally ends in a tonic cadence, and the real solo section begins. The treatment of the four soloists is what we would expect from a master craftsman: the theme itself, so suited to the *legato* quality of the string instruments, is given to solo violin and solo 'cello, while an adaptation of the original first *tutti*

is given to the wind instruments, accompanied by the orchestral horns (see overleaf). The long exposition ends at bar 126 and the music slips from dominant to the flattened submediant of the dominant, D flat which is, of course, the same key as the flattened mediant of the tonic (B flat). From there we move slowly to E flat minor – everything about this broad movement moves almost in slow motion as far as harmonic and formal divisions are concerned, though the appearance of a fast tempo is maintained by the interjection of semiquavers; then to F minor and a long passage in the dominant of C minor. At this point the soloists modulate to the dominant of G minor, and Haydn intended a long excursion of 36 bars which were to swing round gradually to

the exposition. This was cut in the autograph before it got beyond the first draft and replaced by a miniature *tutti* of three bars and a further transitional bar for the solo violin, at which point we are back in the recapitulation.[1] One has noted the almost total domination of the development section by minor keys, something that also happens in the other B flat work of the 1792 season.

Haydn provides his own cadenza: the four performers could hardly have been expected to improvise one. It is a model of what such a cadenza ought to be: just the right length (35 bars), using segments of previous material but with a nice harmonic surprise at bar 247.

The formal construction of the quiet Andante is also dazzlingly original. The four solo instruments are accompanied only by the strings and, of the rest of the orchestra, the flute, an oboe and the two horns. Except for four bars in the middle (33–6) there are no ritornelli in the movement whatever! This innovation is probably unique in late

1 This 'sketch is reproduced as Appendix II of the critical score (Haydn-Mozart Presse 193 or Philharmonia 805 or in Vol. X of the bound volumes). Haydn had already made a cut of four bars – these were, contrary to the later cut, already fully orchestrated before they were removed – in the ritornello in the dominant, at bar 118. This first cut is a spirited modulation to the supertonic of the dominant and back again to the dominant, and it is difficult to see why Haydn made it; this cut is printed in Appendix I of the score. The second cut, on the other hand, is an improvement.

eighteenth-century concerto writing; it is almost like hearing a piece of enlarged chamber music such as the Notturni for the King of Naples. The orchestral accompaniment is so discreet that when the ritornello finally makes its brief appearance on the scene, it sounds almost like an intrusion on this quietly pastoral dialogue between the four instruments. At the beginning Haydn writes a *b flat'* for the solo bassoon but, in case he could not manage this high note, provided him with an *ossia* an octave lower (bar 3).

The Finale ('Allegro con spirito') opens with one of Haydn's 'Kehraus'-sounding rondo themes, but before it has a chance to develop into a proper melody, it interrupts itself to introduce Mr Salomon in the perhaps unexpected role of an impassioned Italian operatic *diva*. Haydn marks the solo violin 'Recitativo, adagio' (see example overleaf, top).

This is a procedure that we find in Haydn's earliest works for Prince Paul Anton Esterházy in 1761: the *Divertimento à Nove Stromenti* (II: 17) in C for clarinets, horns and strings and the Symphony 'Le Midi' No. 7, both of which have elaborate mock-recitatives: in the Divertimento – which is published in a new edition by Doblinger – the 'Recitativo' comes as the third movement, in the Symphony as the second. In the notation of the solo violin part – for in these early works the dramatic soprano part was assigned to that instrument – we notice that Haydn partly writes out the appoggiature

539

[Concertante: Finale]

and partly indicates them, especially in the Symphony, by the kind of grace notes that he also used in vocal music (drops of a third):

which meant, of course, to *omit* the first F sharp and sing

By 1792, however, Haydn was taking no chances and wrote out all the vocal appoggiature, which incidentally provide striking proof that these drops of a third were inevitably and always changed to an appoggiatura – we mention this because there has been a great deal of amateurish and ill-founded talk in the British press of recent years that singers did not make these changes. People did *not* sing phrases like

in the late eighteenth century. We have recently located another instance of a mock-recitative in a set of Three Concertos printed in Italy *c.* 1780–1790, of which unfortunately the title page and the solo part is missing. As it happens, this otherwise disastrous state of affairs does not affect the point we are making, which is the presence of such mock-recitatives in Concerto I's Larghetto:[1]

1 The *incipit* of the first movement is:

The other two concertos are in F and B flat. The Allegro spiritoso parts are in oblong format and are by an Italian engraver and printed on paper from the mill of Galvani Fratelli in Pordenone. Our copy is signed twice 'Ad uso della S^{ra}: Co: Anna Roverella' [*Signora Contessa*, etc.].

Recitativo col flauto

V. I

Here is proof that the appoggiature were also sung in Italy, in case it might be thought – the enemies of appoggiature will go to any lengths to disprove the existence of the practice – that this tradition extended only to Austria and the British Isles.

This amusing instrumental *recitativo* – who cannot think that this was the inspiration for the great double bass recitative in Beethoven's Ninth Symphony? – turns into that which the movement promised to be: a light-hearted, deftly orchestrated, and (for the soloists) brilliant piece of virtuoso writing. There is a spectacular piece of fireworks for Salomon which, being the kind of writing suited only for strings, the 'cello then gets a few bars later (violin: 125ff., 'cello: 155ff.). Haydn seems to have cut out the beginning of these particularly difficult passages, for all the printed editions remove bars 135–8 and 165–8. Yet it would seem that these cuts were only made because the London players experienced difficulty with the places in question, for the authentic Elssler parts in the Esterházy Archives show neither of the cuts. The autograph is also without any trace of them.

Unlike the London Symphonies, the Concertante dropped out of sight in the nineteenth century, after having enjoyed a considerable initial success: apart from the earliest editions (in parts) by André, Artaria and Imbault of 1796, the work was reprinted by Sieber in Paris and, in 1799, by Forster in London, in which latter edition it was entitled 'the celebrated concertante Sinfonia, performed at Mr. Salomon's Concert'. An arrangement by L. W. Lachnith for pianoforte, flute, violin and 'cello was published by Imbault in Paris in 1796; Lachnith arranged all the first London Symphonies for this combination, anticipating Salomon's arrangements for piano trio by three months. In the twentieth century the Concertante was published in score and parts by Breitkopf & Härtel, heavily arranged by Hans Sitt, the German composer, and since then it has taken on a new lease of life. It was first recorded in the 1930s by *Oiseau Lyre* with Charles Münch conducting the Société des Concerts du Conservatoire de Paris. After World War II, the Concertante, like all Haydn's concertos, suddenly became extremely popular, especially in France.

Symphony No. 97 in C (1792)

This is Haydn's last symphony in C major, the end of a long series that the composer began about 1760, when still in the service of Count Morzin, with Nos. 32, 33 and possibly slightly later No. 20. As distinguished from the customary kind of C major symphony with oboes and horns (Nos. 2, 9 or 25) this other type in the same key includes trumpets and kettledrums. It is some time, indeed, before Haydn uses those instruments in any other key except C major, so that C becomes for Haydn what D major was for Bach – a 'festival' key. When Haydn became director of the Esterházy establishment, he found no trumpets in the orchestra, and it was some time before he composed any more 'festival' symphonies. Gradually he evolved a clever substitute for trumpets, namely horns in high C (C alto), which together with timpani produced a brilliant orchestral effect. Occasionally Haydn was able to recruit trumpets as well, and the combination of C alto horns and trumpets (at the same pitch) proved to be an intoxicating sound in Symphony No. 56 (1774). In the years from about 1768 to 1788, we have a long series of C major 'festival' symphonies, including Nos. 38, 41, 48 ('Maria Theresa'), 50, 56, 60 ('Il Distratto'), 63 ('La Roxelane'), 69 ('Laudon'), 82 ('L'ours') and 90. Beginning with an orchestra of oboes, horns and/or trumpets, kettledrums and strings (with bassoons *col basso*), this group was gradually widened to include a flute as in No. 41 (where it only plays in the slow movement) and an obbligato bassoon as in No. 56 (also only the slow movement, though it otherwise was expected to double the bass line). By No. 69, the orchestra includes two bassoons with an independent part throughout, and by No. 82 there is an obbligato flute part in all movements. Symphony No. 90 is the last such 'festival' symphony to require C alto horns (though as we have seen, in London they probably played them in C basso when Haydn conducted the work there in 1791). No. 97 uses the usual Salomon orchestra (pairs of woodwind without clarinets, C basso horns, trumpets and timpani with the customary strings) and carries this peculiarly Haydnesque type of symphony to a final burst of glory.

The Adagio introduction carries a step further Haydn's experiments with uniting the introduction to the rest of the movement. At this stage the introductions are still relatively short, so that a complicated thematic relationship with the ensuing Vivace, or with the rest of the Symphony, cannot be expected; and yet Haydn manages to unite the Adagio with what follows in a more indirect way than the procedure of more-or-less direct quotation observed in No. 98. Here the basic melodic line, stripped of its ornaments, appears in the closing material of the exposition (bars 97ff.) and, much more directly, in the coda (bars 240ff.). The tonally rather ambiguous accompaniment of the passage when it first appears in the introduction – ambiguous because of the E flat in violin II – is reproduced in the dominant but (for obvious reasons) more explicitly in the coda, where the thought is also extended:

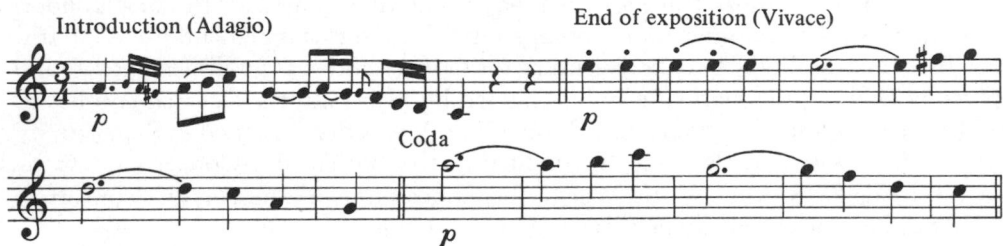

The accompaniment that leads into the first violins' note *a′* is a repeated middle C in the second violin, and this figure is then transferred to the melody at the end of the exposition. It is also worth noting that there is a definite three-part feeling to the introduction, mostly brought about because the music modulates from I to V and back again, and because the two complete bars quoted (they are bars 2, 3 and the first note of 4) at the beginning also finish off the Adagio and go straight into the Vivace.

The Vivace seems to reflect, in its exuberant and aggressive hammering-out of the tonic triad, the triumph of Haydn's first visit to London. It is immensely self-assured music and orchestrated in a flamboyant way, with prominent kettledrums. The first subject – which recalls the opening of No. 56 in the same key – starts to develop itself almost immediately, even as the music moves to the dominant. Out of

from the very beginning there comes

(bars 40ff.)

and out of

develops this section of the bridge passage:

Before he reaches the dominant we have a most extraordinary skeleton outline of a Neapolitan sixth in G without the crucial note C. It must have sounded very *outré* in 1792:

The first three notes of each bar are reinforced by the woodwind, thus stressing the progression of a minor second (C sharp to D, D to E flat). There is a comical second subject, almost a waltz tune, with the bassoons quacking out the ♩ ♩ ♩ rhythm. The almost jarring discrepancy between the heroic first subject and the Hanswurst comedy of the second is a pattern which will repeat itself with uncanny emotional accuracy in the Menuetto and Trio later in the Symphony. The only ambiguous moment, apart from the 'Neapolitan' chord quoted above, is the coda, which repeats the fleeting harmonic ambiguity of the introduction. The development goes to the opposite extreme, for it introduces one of the most subtle, evasive and complex ideas of Haydn's symphonic career. Using the first subject, Haydn moves without a break from the dominant (G) to the pivotal E flat (the flattened third of the tonic as well as the flattened sixth of the dominant), which turns out to be the Neapolitan sixth of D. Having reintroduced the Neapolitan relationship so curiously stressed in the exposition, Haydn proceeds to introduce its latent ambiguity into the following famous passage for the solo woodwind (solo flute and the two oboes), often quoted in textbooks on orchestration for its remarkable sense of woodwind colour and its accompaniment of the strings using, as we realize, a fragment of the first subject. The Neapolitan aspect is now combined with the first subject, i.e. a jump of the fourth (*a′* to *d″*) which we know so well from earlier, plus the upward minor second (flute, bars

543

124/5) from the 'Neapolitan' modulation quoted earlier. This relationship of the flattened II to I is now spun out. What makes the whole so remarkable is the strings' accompaniment, which gradually breaks down the sense of passing bar lines completely. Haydn does this by bringing in the dotted figure on the first beat (bars 129f.), upsetting its previous upbeat function. The on-the-beat announcement follows the last 'entry' (in the bass line) by five beats of rests, sufficiently long to start the confusion. The long *legato* lines of the upper woodwind are thus free to float, almost 'beat-less'. The series of entries up the strings at bars 130ff. is further calculated to break down the three-four rhythm. It is done in such an efficient way that unless one is following with a score, the 'entry' of the 'cello-bass at 134–5 hardly sounds like an upbeat any longer.

The coda is as long as the development is, relatively speaking, short. Exposition ran from bar 14 to bar 107, development to 167, recapitulation to about 244 (about because the coda now merges with the recapitulation), the coda from about 245 to and including 293, thus being only a dozen bars shorter than the development. It is a beautifully proportioned movement and certainly the boldest-sounding of the first six London Symphonies; it is also a work which had, perhaps, more influence than any other of its fellows. Its orchestral layout was obviously the model for Beethoven's First Symphony and a host of minor works written at the turn of the century.

To counteract the square, firmly on-the-beat quality of the first subject, we have seen that Haydn introduced a very complicated system of rhythmic displacements during the development to break down the bar lines. Nevertheless the outstanding feature of the first movement as a whole was its violently forceful first subject, definitely on the beat. The rest of the Symphony is, significantly, made up of movements the principal subjects of which are *all* introduced by an upbeat: this obtains in the 'Adagio, ma non troppo', in both Menuetto and Trio, and in the Finale. That Haydn should go to such extremes to offset the impression of metric squareness and solidity in the first movement shows what a powerful effect he expected it to have. The opposite was the case in the 'Surprise', where the terrific strength of the second movement (all very much on the beat and in march-like two four tempo) suggested to its composer to form all the other principal subjects of the first, third and fourth movements with strong upbeats.

The rhythmic displacement that Haydn now imposes on the slow movement of No. 97 is so strong that the second and fourth beats often seem to tower over the first and third. This is of course a deliberate design. Bars in which the woodwind and horns appear only as ¢ 𝄽 ♩ ♩ 𝄽 , and in which the strings are phrased ♩ │♩ ♩ ♩ ♩ , are designed to foster this displacement of the strong beats. Another feature of this movement which is immediately repeated in the Minuet is that everything is written out and there are – except in the F minor part – no repeat signs. This procedure is so rare in Haydn's symphonies that there can be no question that the middle movements were especially so designed and were conceived in some respects as an entity. In fact there is some evidence that Haydn may have put off composing the first movement until the last three had been completed: the autograph of the first movement ends with 'Laus Deo', a note of quiet thanks that Haydn otherwise reserved for the conclusions of his scores. In any case, the whole of Symphony No. 97 is a strong unity.

The Adagio is formally a set of free variations. Variation II introduces triplet arabesques in the first violins, Var. II is in F minor and it is here that the trumpets and timpani first enter in this movement. Var. III introduces one of Haydn's boldest orchestral devices: the violins move into a semiquaver pattern and the autograph directs them to play 'al ponticello', high on the bridge. This gives a nasty, aggressive, metallic sound which must have staggered the London public in May 1792: it also requires a brilliant orchestral technique and Haydn did not import this spectacular device when he took the Symphony back to the Continent. There are no 'ponticello' remarks on any of the authentic sources except for those destined for England (i.e. also including Salomon's arrangement for quintet and the ever-reliable Birchall print). This particular passage is marked *forte*, and when Haydn repeats it *piano*, he varies the sound by requesting 'vicino al ponticello' (near the bridge). This huge *ponticello* section extends in Haydn's autograph – which, incidentally, was unknown to Haydn scholars until its rather mysterious reappearance at the Berlin auction house of Gerd Rosen in 1951 – from bar 85 (with upbeat) to and including bar 127. The coda is one of the most beautiful parts of Haydn's late orchestral scores: the 'naturale' of the violins in bar 128, cancelling the 'ponticello' instructions, comes with an incredible sense of relief after the Beckmesser chattering. It is typical that this whole 'ponticello' section was not printed in any modern score until that of the Haydn-Mozart Presse (1965). Over repeated semiquavers in the upper strings and 'portato' repeated quavers in the 'cellos and basses, Haydn has the first flute and first oboe spin out a fragment of a previous thought, while the bassoons fill in the tenor harmony. It is suddenly a great wave of emotion, quite unexpected in this otherwise extroverted Symphony, which rises to a *fortissimo* climax at bar 145 and then dies away. The two chords that Haydn rather surprisingly uses to cut off this wave of almost uncontrolled emotion (though nothing in Haydn, as we know, is really uncontrolled) reminds us that in those days London audiences were accustomed to applaud after individual movements. Later, at the end of Symphony No. 101's slow movement, Haydn originally ended with a loud chord which, as we shall see, he later suppressed.

The Menuetto, as we noted, is *durchkomponiert* and so is the Trio. This allows Haydn to vary each repetition which was otherwise purely mechanical. We return to the rousing C major 'bloody red' of the first movement, except that there is a constant attempt to soften the aggressive sound by constructing the melody with long legato phrases. The theme is first presented in this way, which seems to make the Minuet curiously symphonic and dignified. It is definitely not a quick movement (as was No. 94's 'Allegro molto' Minuet). Thus the two middle movements gradually slow down, and then bring up, the quick tempo of the outer movements in a graceful curve. The main theme, originally so *legato*, is then presented *piano* and *staccato*, then very *staccato* with slashing *fz* accents. There is a startling timpani entrance, *solo* and *forte*, which crashes into the middle of a *piano* passage (twice: at bars 36 and 62). The Trio is again a violent contrast, returning to the doggerel of the first movement's second subject. Here it is an almost aggressively Austrian dance complete with yodel-like accents, the melodic construction of which shows, as always with Haydn when he is being 'semplice' or 'innocente', extreme sophistication and an uncanny sense of poise.[1]

The melody is as follows:

---

[1] This movement has been much quoted by Haydn scholars, *inter alia* in Schmid 1934, p. 300 ('There one hears the stamping and the shouting of the peasant inn . . .'). For a subtle analysis of the Trio's rhythmic structure, see Cooper-Meyer, op. cit., pp. 83–7. Rosen, pp. 342f.

It is first given to solo oboe, solo bassoon and the strings; the accompaniment later includes two horns which, like the bassoons in the first movement's second subject, play the ♩ ♩ ♩ accompaniment. But at the end, Haydn introduces a fantastic orchestration with 'Salomon Solo ma piano' (a humorous warning to the vigorous German leader) and the trumpets and timpani entering quietly. Rosen, who quotes this section, says of it. 'The oom-pah-pah of a German dance band is rendered with the utmost refinement, amazingly by kettledrums and trumpets *pianissimo*, and the rustic *glissando* (a sort of glottal stop on the first beats) is given a finicky elegance by the grace

notes in the horns as well as by the doubling of the melody an octave higher with the solo violin. These details are not intended to blend, but to be set in relief: they are individually exquisite.'

The end of the Trio has elicited much comment; we quote it below with some of the preceding material to set it in perspective (bars 104ff.).

Haydn originally marked the Finale 'Spiritoso' and later, probably after he had left London in 1792, changed the tempo to 'Presto assai'. This is a sonata–rondo, such as we have seen in Nos. 94 and 96, but (like No. 96) without any second subject. In earlier

Menuetto da capo

works, such as Symphonies Nos. 85 or 88, Haydn generally preferred to have a full tripartite statement in the exposition, as follows:

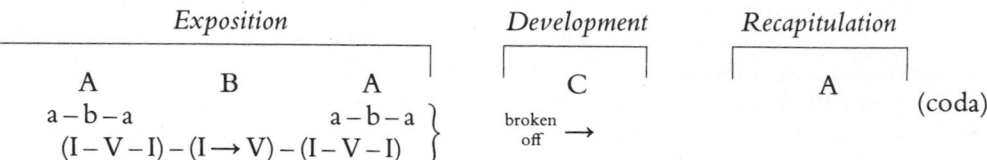

The formal scheme of No. 97's Finale is somewhat different in that the repetition of the a–b–a is shortened by having the development interrupt the 'A' section in the manner of the old *fausse reprise* joke (where in the development section the main subject was introduced in the tonic but then broken off and further worked out). It is part of Haydn's constant sense of surprise. Among the many unexpected things in this racy and high spirited Finale is the incredible sound of the two horns in the 'b' section, hammering out the accompaniment – a series of repeated quavers on the note G – in *forte*, against the melodic instruments' *piano*. The loud accompaniment is then transferred to the trumpets and kettledrums. When Haydn reaches the repetition of 'A', the 'b' is cancelled and the development begins ('C') in C minor:

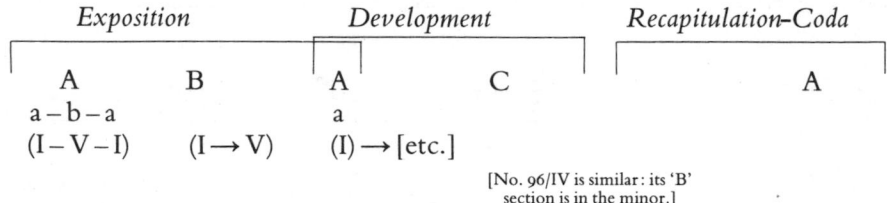

[No. 96/IV is similar: its 'B' section is in the minor.]

Just before the end of this ebullient movement Haydn introduces a double fermata, the second time with the whole orchestra (including a timpani roll) rising in a crescendo and sinking again back to *piano*: ⁀p | ⁀p. . This was an effect that would be much copied, in this and other contexts, by the coming Romantic school. A small textual point: the timpani roll is marked ⁀𝄐. Of course Haydn does not expect the drummer to play 𝅘𝅥𝅯𝅘𝅥𝅯𝅘𝅥𝅯 𝅘𝅥𝅯𝅘𝅥𝅯𝅘𝅥𝅯 but a roll (which Haydn sometimes writes ∿ as at the beginning of Symphony No. 93). We mention this point because the abbreviation of two semiquaver 'crosses' through the stem was obvious in 1792 but is apparently no longer obvious to players outside Vienna. Altogether this Finale is in many respects – formal, orchestral and in spirit – a prototype for fast-moving rondos with an extended development section and a truncated exposition. As far as anything in Haydn is 'typical', No. 97/IV is a typical late-period sonata-rondo. Its influence is also felt in Haydn's own instrumental works of the coming years: the Finales of the C major Quartet Op. 74 No. 1 (1793), the Trio for pianoforte, violin and 'cello No. 35 (1794–5?) and even the London Trio in C for 2 flutes and 'cello (1794) all owe part of their formal construction, their melodic patterns and above all their *esprit* to Symphony No. 97's brilliant conclusion.

And with this gay and forceful Symphony, Haydn completed the first six Salomon Symphonies, setting a new standard of symphonic excellence which would only be surpassed by his own second series for London. Many commentators have justly pointed out that as a work of art, the 'Oxford' Symphony No. 92 (1789) reaches a pinnacle of formal sophistication and pure physical beauty that place it on the same level as the first six London Symphonies. The excellence of the 'Oxford' is not to be disputed, and if one wanted to describe the principal new feature of the works composed in England, it would probably be a certain panache, a sparkling brilliance which is partly orchestral. If there were any criticism to be made of the 'Oxford', it would be that the trumpets and timpani, which were possibly added later – how much later is a difficult question, for they are already in the Wallerstein manuscripts that Haydn sent off from Eszterháza in 1789 – seem in the quick movements to be rather superimposed on the rest of the orchestral layout. That astute nineteenth-century French critic, E.-M.-E. Deldevez,[1] comparing them to the superbly integrated trumpet and timpani parts of Symphony No. 102, thought those of the 'Oxford' spurious; they are not, but they are not always felicitous. An analysis of the problem will be put forward in an earlier volume of this biography, however, this situation never occurs even in the first series of London Symphonies. In this one respect, therefore, these works for Salomon's concerts of the 1791 and 1792 season represent an even finer *Auslese* of their composer's abilities as a symphonist than all but a very few of their chronological precursors. Apart from the 'Oxford', we would say that only Nos. 82, 86 and 88 can compare with the finest of the first London set (such as No. 98). Hardly anyone except their creator would have imagined that he would now surpass even their excellence in a second series destined for the same friendly capital.

Haydn wrote his last six Symphonies between 1793 and the Spring of 1795. He was now indisputably the doyen of European composers; there was no one to touch him. Haydn was too wise and too sensitive not to realize the responsibilities that such a position of crowded isolation (if we may use the apparent tautology) brought with it, and he rose to the occasion in a way that hardly even his most fervent admirers could have dreamed. The heady success of the 1792 London season seemed to have released in him as yet untouched well springs of inspiration and fertility. High as was the standard of his first Salomon Symphonies that of the second is even higher – and this enlargement occurs in every sense. The slow movements now reach depth of profundity that the earlier symphonies only occasionally suggest (e.g. the great Capriccio in No. 86). The orchestration is also fuller, not only generally but specifically in that clarinets now enter Haydn's symphonic scores for the first time. He had not had these instruments at Eszterháza except for a brief period in the 1770s, and for some curious reason he never used them in symphonies of the time (though they appear in the recently resuscitated German *Singspiel*, *Das abgebrannte Haus* [*Die Feuersbrunst*]). He had written some early *divertimenti* with clarinets, e.g. the *Divertimento à Nove* (II: 17) in C, but the instruments he had at his disposal – they were C clarinets – seem to have been technically unsatisfactory; he hardly used them in instrumental music until the Notturni for the King of Naples composed in 1790, where incidentally he again uses only C clarinets. The history of Mozart's peculiarly effective use of clarinets was bound up with the Stadler brothers, who developed the *chalumeau* or lower register of the instrument and also made mechanical improvement in it and the basset horn. Otherwise, apart from Vienna, the clarinets even in the 1790s

---

1 *Curiosités Musicales*, Paris 1873, p. 20.

were rather primitive instruments and Haydn used them with a certain amount of circumspection in the Symphonies of 1794 and 1795. We will examine the technical aspects of Haydn's clarinet writing in connection with Symphony No. 99 in E flat, *infra*.

Released from the provincial cage of Eszterháza – where everybody had soon known (via the publishing world) what he was doing, but he himself remained a prisoner – Haydn soon developed an almost seismographical, or perhaps one should say mesmeric, ability to sense what the public wanted. If he soon managed to create an instantaneous and international hit in the form of the 'Surprise' Symphony in 1792, he surpassed himself with the 'Military' two years later; and what is so extraordinary about the huge public success of the latter's slow movement is that it comes from an *earlier work* (part of a Concerto for two lire written for the King of Naples in 1786). Haydn was now so sure of himself that he could pick and choose among his 'unpublished' works, seeking out a piece which had not reached a public except that present at Eszterháza, or at the private concerts of King Ferdinand and his friend Norbert Hadrava from the Austrian legation in Naples. Haydn knew, obviously, that this movement, reorchestrated for the London public and provided with a new coda, would be another smash hit. His withholding both No. 94 and No. 100 until their respective seasons had been well in progress shows how carefully he gauged the public pulse, just as he had always stipulated that his new symphonies should be played *after* the interval. All this is partly instinct and partly showmanship, but Haydn's ability to seek out such a hit from among his earlier works is an astonishing tribute to his knowledge of the London, and indeed the European, public temper. It is also a tribute to the composer's perspicacity that he was writing such music in 1786, destined (at least as far as Haydn or anyone else then knew) for an eccentric King and his cronies in a faraway capital and in a sense a stillborn child. It took London to release this movement from an unmerited obscurity and Haydn's judgement to know that it had within it the seeds of a gigantic public success.

There were some works among the last six 'Londons' that were never supposed to be great popular successes: these were the 'private pieces' for connoisseurs which reveal in a special and intimate way the innermost thoughts of their composer. Perhaps Mozart's G minor Symphony, K. 550, was such a private work; at any rate it did not become popular until the composer was dead, and was not really considered the essence of the 'demonic' Mozart until the Romantic period. Haydn's Symphony No. 102 is also such a piece. Haydn could afford to write a symphony for himself, as it were, after the great success of the 1794 season. No. 102 has never become a popular work in the sense of the 'Surprise' and 'Military'; no doubt Haydn would have been very surprised if it had. It rights the balance of the last six Salomon Symphonies, revealing in its fantastic intellectual power (the first movement) and in its brooding ambivalence (the second movement) a part of the composer that could not have shown itself to this extent in the crashing Turkish music of No. 100 or the virtuoso brilliance of No. 101 ('The Clock').

The greatest orchestral and formal experimentor of the eighteenth century could not, even at this stage of his life, rest on his laurels. In one work we must have muted trumpets and covered drums, something that had been used in theatrical music (*inter alia* by Mozart in *Idomeneo*, which was still unpublished) but never in a classical symphony (No. 102); in another we must organize the most complex interrelationship between a slow introduction and the main movement since Mozart's K. 543 (No. 103), and in that same Symphony, there is a beginning which is without question the most original (and ominous) beginning of a Symphony, certainly of its period, possibly of all time – the strange drum roll that has given the work its name. The use of the Turkish music in No. 100 is again something used in operatic music, especially Viennese operas with a 'Turkish' twist such as Haydn's *L'Incontro improvviso* (1775) and Mozart's *Entführung* (1782), but never in a classical symphony. If we are to have monothematic Finales, it is now on a grand scale and of an intensity (No. 103/IV) unreached until the first movement of Beethoven's Fifth Symphony. And for the last time in a symphony, Haydn can enjoy melodic excursions into the folk-lore of eastern Europe, creating wild confusion among ethnographical researchers (are they Croatian, Hungarian, Gypsy, these Balkan tunes?) but delight among London's *fin-de-siècle* audience (No. 103/II). Haydn's own melodies have become almost indistinguishable from folk-tunes: is the melody of No. 104/IV a London street cry, a Croatian folk-tune or Haydn's own creation? We shall probably never know, given the time interval (1795–1972) and the almost complete disappearance of such tunes among eastern European peasants. And in one sense, the matter is of historical interest only, considering the melodic structure of Haydn's London Symphonies as a whole. These exotic excursions, if we may quote Bence Szabolcsi in another (Mozartian) context, are a part of the great heritage that Haydn enjoyed as a member of the Austro–Hungarian Empire; but they are reserved for special occasions, like the Turkish music of No. 100.

In sum, these last six Salomon Symphonies are on the one hand a magnificent summing-up, the great harvest of nearly half-a-century, while on the other they open endless new vistas for other and later composers to explore – not least among them Beethoven, who inherited this glorious symphonic tradition and was destined to carry it to new and remote spheres.

Symphony No. 99 in E Flat (1793)

Haydn thought he would return to London in 1793. We do not know when in that year he composed this Symphony, but he must have discussed with Salomon the enlargement of the orchestra to include clarinets, for although the London newspapers of the previous seasons had listed clarinet players (Mr. Eley and/or Mr. Fluger or Flieger in 1791 and Mr. [Carl] Hartman a year later, the latter praised for his sweetness of tone in the *Morning Chronicle* during the 1794 season), they seem to have been soloists rather than regular members of the band. From 1794, clarinets were a regular feature of the Salomon orchestra, and also in the Opera Concert of 1795.

We have mentioned that Mozart's clarinet writing was profoundly influenced by the excellence of the Stadlers, especially Anton, who made mechanical improvements on both clarinet and basset horn, significantly to enlarge their tonal compass in the lower register. It is now known that the lost authentic version of Mozart's Clarinet Concerto in A was for an instrument with a range extending lower than the instrument now in general use; originally it was composed, but not completed, for a basset horn in G. Stadler specialized on the *chalumeau* register, as we have noted, and it is questionable whether this lower range had been exploited by any other player to that extent. Certainly Mozart's clarinet writing did not create a 'school' for some time, and one wonders if apart from the Stadlers there were other clarinet players capable even of playing some of Mozart's more difficult parts, such as the solo basset horn parts in *La clemenza di Tito*. It is curious that neither Haydn nor Beethoven really followed the Mozartian trend, though Haydn's parts are often closer to Mozart's – especially those composed in the late 1790s in Vienna. In the Trio of Minuet No. 9 from the

Twenty-Four Menuetti for Orchestra composed about 1795–7, we find Haydn writing the very characteristic clarinet II part:

a passage which exploits all the liquid beauty of the instrument when used as an accompaniment and in the low register. It is, moreover, problematic how many of Mozart's clarinet works Haydn can have heard by 1793: hardly the Concerto, and hardly any of the chamber music. The Esterházy band owned MS. copies of Mozart's last three symphonies, but they can scarcely have been acquired in 1788–90 because there were no clarinets and no trumpets in the band and they could not have played K. 543 at all, and K. 551 only by leaving out the trumpet parts. (This raises the question how Haydn performed *Le nozze di Figaro* in 1790 at Eszterháza when his band had no clarinets . . .) Haydn might have seen the scores at Mozart's house. If the G minor Symphony was revised by the composer for the Tonkünstler concerts in April 1791 to include clarinets, Haydn can only have seen the revised score at the widow's when he returned in 1792. There is no evidence that there were any performances of the G minor Symphony in Vienna in the years 1792–3, when Haydn was there. Haydn's use of the clarinets in No. 99 is nonetheless so idiomatic that one is astounded that he had never used the instruments in orchestral music before. It is interesting to note that the clarinets in this Symphony are much more freely used than in the other works of the 1794 season; for in No. 100 they figure only in the slow movement and in No. 101 they are used with extreme reticence. It was not until Haydn wrote another E flat Symphony, the 'Drum Roll', that he allowed the clarinets so much freedom. Probably they were unexceptional players in London and their instruments rather crude, not nearly reaching the advanced level that we find even in the orchestral scores of Mozart's operas for the Viennese court theatres.

That Haydn appreciated the sustaining quality of the clarinet in its bottom register is shown by the opening of Symphony No. 99, where the second clarinet holds down low *E flat* (a sixth below middle C) as a pedal point under the rest of the orchestra, the bassoons rising above it as the *piano* enters (bars 1–4).

During the 1791–2 seasons, Haydn had composed no symphonies in *E flat*, and he had never composed an *E flat* symphony with a large orchestra, that is with two flutes (rather than one) and with trumpets and kettledrums as well as clarinets, Compared even to the late-period Symphonies Nos. 84 (1786) and 91 (1788), No. 99 sounds immensely richer. E flat was always a favourite key of the Viennese classical style. In it, wind instruments take on a peculiarly satisfactory sonority, and even the trumpets, despite their high *tessitura*, blend excellently with the rest of the wind choir. Haydn here writes for the timpani in real sounding notation, and with a signature containing two flats; in the late-period B flat works with timpani, he uses a signature with one flat – a great innovation, this, because the timpani were usually written in transposing notation (C–G), as in Mozart's Symphony in E flat K. 543. In the two final E flat Symphonies of the second London series, Nos. 99 and 103, Haydn left to posterity the first symphonic works of the Viennese classical masters using that key with the full orchestra of the time. In this respect, too, they created a profound impression on Continental symphonic thought, as did Mozart's K. 543 when it finally began to circulate in the late 1790s.

The slow introductions of the second Salomon set are miniature masterpieces. If they cannot be said to grow in size, they seem to grow in scope; they remain introductions but they manage to create for themselves an atmosphere all their own. In No. 104 there is even a complete, though miniature, ternary form. Here in No. 99, there are two distinct elements which, despite the Adagio's seemingly self-contained little form, look forward to the rest of the movement and to the rest of the Symphony. One is the curious thematic relationship with the main subject of the slow movement:

Here Haydn seems to be experimenting along the lines of what would later be known as the twelve-note technique, treating 'rows' of notes as if they could be interchanged at will. To facilitate the reader's ability to see this interrelationship, we have transposed the *Urlinie* of the introduction into G major (placed in parentheses) next to that of the Adagio. The subtle relationship between the two melodic elements is further enhanced by the dotted rhythm which appears in both instances. Apart from this link to the slow movement's melody, we may note the modulation, via an enharmonic change from C flat to B natural and the incredible key of E minor, to the third-related key of C (in this case minor). The introduction seems to be leading permanently to C minor rather than E flat, and the dominant of C is stressed for four bars ending in a unison half-cadence wherein the note G is placed in a prominent light. This double stress of the principal third-related keys in E flat – C and G – looks forward to (1) the key of the slow movement in G major and (2) the key of the Trio in C major, which in turn is again brought to our vivid attention in a striking modulation to C major in the middle of the slow movement (bars 40 et seq. which we shall analyze later for other reasons). Haydn extricates himself suavely from his trend to C in the introduction by a long-held woodwind and horn chord on the dominant seventh of E flat, a reminder of the sonorous qualities of the solo wind choir in E flat on the one hand and, once again, a presage of the incredible wind band solo in the slow movement. In this introduction, however, all these hints about the future are done with great subtlety and are as nebulous (and as real) as the beginning of *Rheingold*: but in retrospect, it is 'all there'.

We noted, in the final Symphony of the 1792 season (No. 97), the fact that the second, third and final movements used subjects with upbeats to counteract the strong on-the-beat character of the first movement's main subject. The same delicate balance may now be observed in the organization of the first and second subjects of all those Symphonies in the second London set that begin with a movement in four-four or barred C; those beginning in six-eight time (Nos. 101 and 103) raise different problems which will be discussed later. Nos. 99, 100 and 104 all begin with squarely on-the-beat main subjects and all three have second subjects beginning on the fourth (or up-)beat. To accentuate the second subject's arrival in Nos. 99 and 100, Haydn begins with the accompaniment, as the Viennese waltz was to do countless times and with equally telling effect. In No. 99 the first subject begins:

and continues with a *tutti* in which Haydn's new and broad orchestral layout may be observed, even to a divided 'cello and bass part and a bassoon part independent of it. The horns and trumpets also have separate parts and altogether the score gives the impression of great attention to orchestral detail throughout. Haydn begins to break the four-four squareness of the theme even in the bridge passage. How he does it is typical. The first impetus is given by the timpani, which have at bar 33 ♩ ♫.♩♩ ♩ ♩, the *fz* obviously (since no one else has it) to draw attention to itself. Immediately this new dotted rhythm is taken up by the other instruments at the interval of every two bars, while a new pattern emerges, viz. ♩ ♩ ♫♫♫, which alternates with the dotted rhythm quoted above. Consequently there is all during the long transition to the second subject a variety of rhythm which begins even at this early stage to act as a foil to the first subject, which keeps appearing either in fragments or in motivic derivatives. Such a melodic derivative even ushers in the second subject, where we note Haydn's new accent (>), taking the place of *fz*, now reserved for stronger effects (bars 69–75). Now the one thing to bind together these two wholly (or seemingly wholly) disparate subjects is the accompaniment. When the first subject made its initial appearance, the second violin played:

– clearly the father of the violas's accompaniment to the second subject. Thus, during the development section, Haydn is able, by keeping this quaver accompaniment running in the orchestra, to move from the second subject to the ♩ ♩ ♪♫♫ figure noted above in the bridge passage and a derivative of the first subject. The delicate balance between the first and second subject is maintained in the middle of the movement by the fact that once the development gets under way – after four bars based on the first subject's opening two bars – the first subject is never quoted directly until the recapitulation, and then without its *piano* beginning. In the coda, which is yet once more based on the irresistible second subject, the horns are used with great ingenuity. Horn II is used in the bottom register to accompany the second subject, using the stopped note sounding A flat (which means that this Continental technique, produced by inserting the right hand into the bell of the instrument to lower – in this case – the natural note B flat, had reached England by the 1790s). In the next *tutti* the first horn soars up to sounding *e flat''* (bars 177–89), a sure way to increase orchestral tension (and it creates a quite different 'inner' tension from that produced if the same effect is given to the trumpet, as every student of Wagner's scores knows very well. Notice the sudden *ff* with which the first horn's high note coincides; like most *ff* markings in Haydn, they apply for a *limited* space of time, in this case about four bars (and a crotchet of a fifth). Still one more horn trick appears just before the end: the 'walking' octaves that Haydn had already made famous in the Finale of the 'Oxford' Symphony. Here (bars 191ff.) they are given to second horn, as was the tradition, but also doubled by bassoon I; and this pattern is used to accompany the final reference to the first subject, which had been almost submerged after its brief reappearance in the recapitulation.

The Adagio, in the mediant (G major), is certainly one of the greatest slow movements Haydn ever composed. It is filled with an extraordinary wealth of detail and is also one of the most beautiful sounding adagios in all his late symphonies. The most striking thing in the first section, apart from the sheer beauty of the opening theme, is the big wind band solo that arises out of the establishment of the dominant key. It was carefully prepared beforehand, since the second part of the main subject was given to the solo woodwind. The wind band, in this case, consists of a solo flute, two oboes and two bassoons (later only one); the clarinets in C are used mostly to double the melody of the violins or for sustaining notes, but never alone. Clarinets in C were (and are, insofar as they are used at all, as in the occasional French provincial band) military instruments and their tone is rather strident; Haydn is thus careful to keep them in the background in a movement which, unlike No. 100's Allegretto, is not at all of a military but rather a songfully lyric character. We have noted in the Chronicle that the press singled out this woodwind passage for special comment, and it must have made a profound impression not only on the London public but also all over the Continent (where many provincial orchestras will have experienced the same difficulty in playing it that we know was also the case when Mozart's operas began to circulate in the smaller towns of German-speaking Europe). The movement is in sonata form, and quite regularly constructed with another lyrical subject which is introduced after the famous wind band solo. There is then a double bar and the first section is to be repeated; it is an essential repeat, too, if the large second part, without repeats, is to appear in its correct proportion. There are 34 bars of the first part and 64 of the second, or very nearly double the length.

Haydn has scored the movement up to now for flutes, oboes, clarinets, bassoons, horns and strings. The trumpets and timpani are silent. But now Haydn introduces a gigantic orchestral surprise (which, typically, coincides with a harmonic turn that he wished to stress: the introduction of C major, which was mentioned above, in connection with the beginning of the Symphony). The second part starts for strings only, continuing a thought from the second subject's conclusion. A large orchestral *crescendo* coincides with a slow, measure-for-measure modulation into C major, and when Haydn reaches a point where it is harmonically feasible, to wit bar 40, he marks the whole orchestra *ff* and the timpani enter, also *ff*, with stupendous effect. (The general *ff* does not extend, in a stroke of Mahlerian subtlety, to the horns and trumpets, which are 'filling' and are not supposed to drown out the other wind instruments; the timpani's *ff* is a theatrical effect, of course.) The entrance of the trumpets and timpani is obviously a grandiose gesture, and it is also primarily one of colour. The timpani are tuned in C and G, and the trumpets are in C, which means that without any question their entrance, and tuning, were designed for this particular moment, though Haydn very cleverly uses both instruments later in the movement despite their unnatural tuning: unnatural, actually, only for the timpani since the trumpets would not have been in G (see our comments about the 'Surprise' Symphony's first version, *supra*). It is a measure of Haydn's incredible skill that we hardly notice at the end of the movement that the drums are in the tonic and *sub*dominant. He also manages to create a very sinister effect later in the movement by having the horns and trumpets batter out a jarring accompaniment in seconds. The texture of Haydn's fabric has become very closely woven by this time: the frightened 'jumping' bass line comes from the bass line at the very close of the exposition (bar 33). It was, after all (see bars 81–4), a Symphony in Time of War . . .

Haydn's symphonic minuets become steadily more sophisticated in 1793–5. After experimenting with speeding up the dance form in the Symphonies of the 1792 season (Nos. 93, 94, 98), Haydn now returns to the slower Allegretto tempo for the works of the 1794 season, even going as far as Moderato in No. 100 (where the tempo has other considerations, however, which will be examined *infra*). Slowing up the tempo in this fashion allows Haydn to be massively symphonic on the one hand – quite the opposite of the light, fleeting one-in-a-bar scherzos of Beethoven's Symphonies Nos. 1 and 2 – while on the other he can easily slip into the kind of *Ländler* that we find towards the end of the first part of No. 99's Menuet. Here we find the basses pushing out a *forzato* at the beginning of every bar, just as in today's Tyrolean dance band, while part of the wind band indulges in the ♩ ♩ rhythm that the *Ländler* was to bequeath to the waltz. To break this tap-room beat, Haydn uses *inter alia* the trumpets and timpani; the timpani hit the first crotchet and then move into a kind of semiquaver roll for four bars, while the trumpets have a pattern extending over two bars. The whole section is a study in Haydn's method of adapting Austrian dance rhythms for (as it were) the international concert public, something in which Johann Strauss was also to become a great expert.

This passage does not return again: it is an effect that Haydn considered should be used only once. The second part of the minuet form has now become a kind of development-cum-recapitulation in sonata form style, but of course on a very limited scale: here, fragments of the minuet's main theme are used to modulate through G flat major (never reached in its root position) and G minor to the 'recapitulation'. The restatement is no simple *da capo* any longer but continues the development, just as in Haydn's own larger movements in sonata form. The wind section is used differently, and this time the horns have their own accompaniment, the first horn rising to sounding *g″*. The music comes to a halt in a series of accents which serve to twist the music at this point from off-beat three-four into two-four time:

♩ | ♩ ♩ ♩ | ♩ ♩ ♩ ♩ ♩ | ♩ ♩ ♩ ♩ ♩ | $\widehat{♩}$ etc. The Trio is introduced
fz   *fz*   *fz* *fz*   *fz* *fz* *fz*

by a little oboe flourish on the note G, a pivot from E flat to C major in which latter key the Trio is written. It is a melancholy little dance, for oboe solo (later with bassoon solo) and strings, *legato* and singing (the oboe is marked *cantabile*). There is a long lead-back to the Menuet (with some pretty clarinet writing) in which Haydn gradually shifts both the phrasing and the accents from the Trio's rhythm –

♩ | ♩ ♩ ♩ | ♩ ♩ | ♩ ♩ ♩ | ♩ – to that of the Menuet. First we have

♩ | ♩ ♩ ♩ | ♩ ♩ , then ♩ ♩ ♩ ♩ | ♩ ♩ which all at once becomes ♩ | ♩ ♩ ♩ | ♩

and we are back in the Minuet. It is a new device to unite more closely minuet and trio, and one that we are more likely to find in Haydn's chamber music, in which off-tonic trios need to be brought back to the main key by such a transition (e.g. Quartets Op. 77, Nos. 1 and 2, 1799).

We have a complete set of sketches for the Finale to Symphony No. 99 (pp. 492–3).[1] They provide one of the few glimpses into Haydn's workshop and were probably saved from the wastepaper basket by Johann Elssler. It is significant that these sketches are to movements (1) written in Vienna in 1793 in preparation for the next London journey and (2) used by their composer in musical clocks of 1793. The clock also includes an arrangement of the string Quartet Op. 71, No. 2 in D, Finale, the autograph of which is in the Gesellschaft der Musikfreunde. The autographs of the clock arrangements of Nos. 99 and 101 are in the Berlin State Library and may be seen in E. F. Schmid's edition, Haydn *Werke für das Laufwerk* (first issued in Hannover in 1931, 2nd revised edition Kassel 1954) as No. 29 (= No. 101/III) and No. 32 (= No. 99/IV). On the clock, the works are transposed from D to F (No. 101) and from E flat to F (No. 99). The Quartet is also transposed from D to C. The other works for the clock of 1793 come from other, earlier compositions or are newly composed (such as XIX: 26).

The sketches are mostly jotted down on one stave, sometimes on two, rarely (where contrapuntal extension requires it) on four staves. Here and there we find indications for instruments, e.g. the delightful clarinet run in thirds at bars 168–170 and, interestingly, even the timpani at bar 245. Here the sketch has just the timpani for bars 245–7 and the first violin part, all without dynamic marks. In the finished score, Haydn marks the timpani *ff* to show that its entry is thematic, as indeed it had been earlier, at bars 120ff. The sketches are what we would expect from Haydn at the summit of his career: coolly efficient, precise and clear, with surprisingly few discarded first thoughts or serious alterations. The whole movement was obviously in his mind, and orchestrated, too; while the sketches, which he numbered in sections – since they extend over several pages – simply served as a handy shorthand 'skeleton' map of the entire proceedings; for they go through the movement, right up to the end (which, characteristically, was at first several bars shorter).

As a piece of music, this Vivace is as typical of Haydn's late-period finales as anything in the last dozen symphonies. Cast in the usual sonata-rondo form (i.e. returning to the tonic before the development starts), it has two subjects, both full of mirth and wit. The second is based upon the first in a vague way, much as Haydn's slow introductions offer us the cloudy contours of themes and patterns to come. The subsidiary theme includes solo passages for all the woodwind and also the horns. In the recapitulation even the second horn has a solo, which reminds us once again that all the greater masters of the Viennese classical school, even Beethoven, were fond of writing solo sections for the stepchildren of the orchestra: thus, Mozart for the second trumpet in one of the trios of the 'Haffner' Serenade K. 250 or Beethoven for the posthorn in the delightful 1795 Dances for the Redoutensaal (or indeed the fourth horn in the Ninth Symphony's slow movement). In the development we are treated to a closely

---

1 First published by the present writer together with the sketches for the Minuet to Symphony No. 101. The six pages are reproduced from the original manuscript in the Music Collection of the Austrian National Library, Codex 18987, on pp. 402–7 of the Complete Haydn Symphonies Vol. XII (Philharmonia 600, 1968). Leopold Nowak published a facsimile of the sketches to No. 99's Finale, and his reconstruction of what might be called an imaginary 'fair copy' thereof, in *Haydn-Studien* II (1970).

worked contrapuntal display of the first theme, the beginning even *in stretto* at the interval of one bar and the end combining the theme *recte* and in inversion:

In the middle of the recapitulation there is a series of fermate and the main subject is treated to a mock-serious excursion, a pseudo-sentimental journey which actually slows down to adagio (bar 187). The same thing had happened in Symphony No. 97's Finale, where the effect was perhaps more on mock-heroic lines; but here, like everything else in the movement including the vigorous contrapuntal treatment in the development, the result is a grand parody. As all these effects whirl past us, we are scarcely aware of the terrific concentration and expert craftsmanship that enabled this Vivace to sound as light as it does. As in all such quick Haydn finales, the movement is put together with great structural economy, so that there is not one bar too many.

Symphony No. 100 in G ('Military') (1794)

We may suspect that such a work as the 'Surprise' Symphony was written, as it were, round the famous slow movement; with No. 100 we know this to have been the case. And not only that: Haydn composed, or in the case of the slow movement rewrote, the middle movements before he started the outer parts of the Symphony. He began with the Allegretto, which from bars 1–148 and 151–2 (up to the trumpet solo) come from Concerto No. 3 (VIIh: 3) in G for the King of Naples, second movement, marked 'Romance: Allegretto'. It is scored for the two lire parts, accompanied by two violins, two violas, and bass line. The Concerto was first published in 1932 by Edition Adler in Berlin, edited by Karl Geiringer, and again in 1959, directly from the authentic score in the Esterházy Archives, by the present writer (Diletto Musicale 43, Doblinger). The latter edition is in print and may be consulted for a detailed comparison with the 'Military' slow movement. We shall examine some of the changes Haydn made *infra*. The autograph of the second movement has not survived with that to the rest of the Symphony (Esterházy Archives), possibly because there was none in the strict sense. It may be that Haydn had Elssler copy the score of the Concerto's *Romance* on large-sized paper and made the necessary changes on the copy. In any case, the original manuscript, whatever it was, of the famous 'Military Movement' has disappeared; having been the most celebrated piece of music Haydn wrote during the second London sojourn, he may have left it in England as a keepsake.

The first of the other movements that Haydn composed was the Menuet. At least the autograph is written on Italian paper such as Haydn used in Vienna in 1793, while the first and last movements are on British paper. Having almost a quick piece – the tempo is Allegretto – with all sorts of extra effects (Turkish music, clarinets, trumpet solo, and so on) as his 'slow movement', Haydn took care to write a slow Menuet (Moderato) so that in a certain sense the two middle movements could act together as a block round which he could fashion the first and last sections. A very quick minuet such as that in the 'Surprise' ('Allegro molto') or even one of the Allegro minuets in the other works of 1791–5 would have meant that there was hardly any 'slow' music at all; thus, the deliberate slow tempo and the accent on the quavers rather than the crotchets such as was the case with No. 99. In No. 100 we have, then, a case of Haydn's deliberately focussing attention on the 'Military Movement' not only by the more obvious means which we shall discuss shortly but also in the organization of the other movements. By now, he was a supreme master of the popular style; in No. 100 he created his greatest triumph, at least as far as the European public of the day was concerned. Although it was later to be rivalled by the 'Surprise', until 1805 or thereabouts the 'Military' was the most popular symphony ever composed. Before 1803 it was published in parts by (in alphabetical order) André (two editions, the first in 1799) in Offenbach/Main, Artaria of Vienna, Gombart of Augsburg, Hummel of Berlin and Amsterdam, Imbault of Paris, Monzani & Cimador in London (using André's plates), Pleyel in Paris, Sieber in Paris and in numerous arrangements all over Europe. It was the example *par excellence* of a composition being totally integrated in the society that first heard it; perhaps it was the last time in musical history when the public completely understood and appreciated great music at its first performance. From Beethoven to Stockhausen and from Schubert to Berio, the fatal gap has always since existed.

Haydn's introduction (Adagio) is once again attached to the rest of the Symphony by various thematic associations. The first is the delicate relation between the introduction's opening 'theme' and the Allegro's first subject. It will be seen that the introduction's melody rises from *d″* to *g″* and back to *d″*, and that we then have the interval

a′ b′ twice. All this is a hazy, half-remembered vision of the crisp main theme in the Allegro:

The next point of connection is the large and ominous *crescendo* that begins in G minor at bar 14 and continues to the *ff* in bar 16, bringing in the whole orchestra with a timpani roll. The strings then lapse into *piano* and another *crescendo* begins at bar 18. This double *crescendo*, either directly in the minor key or in a modulation leading to a minor key, is distinctly freighted with a heavy sense of foreboding. The same pattern, much extended, appears at the beginning of the development section: a double *crescendo* (bars 137–8, 150–1) in and leading to the minor in both cases, with the same underlying feeling of foreboding. Finally, there is a sharply (in some cases double) dotted, French Overture rhythm that grows more insistent as the Introduction unfolds; it reappears throughout the Trio.

The first subject of the Allegro, which we have quoted above when it reappears in the strings, is first given only to solo flute and two oboes; it is a fascinating sound, looking forward to the 'toy' music of Rimsky-Korsakov and the ballet music of Tchaikovsky. The scoring, or rather the layout, of the first *tutti* shows how much Salomon's great orchestra has influenced Haydn the composer: solid middle parts in slow motion (horns, trumpets, viola); the second violins in a 'broken' pattern of quavers which then unobtrusively slide into a slower motion, doubling the first oboe and strengthen its interesting countersubject; the 'cello pounding out the bass line in 'walking' octaves and the bass itself providing an impetus to each first beat by dropping an octave. It is symphonic scoring which sounds brilliant and uses the whole orchestra to every instrument's individual advantage (bars 39–48).

The second subject has been likened to the 'Radetzky March' by Johann Strauss the Elder, composed in the aftermath of the Viennese revolution of March 1848.[1] Even writers who did not sense the relationship noted, as did H. E. Jacob in his book on the Strauss family, that the '[Radetzky March] has something familiar about it.' Our idea of military music is, as we pointed out in connection with Haydn's marches *supra*, quite different from that of the late eighteenth century as well as the period up to 1848 known to Austrian history as the *Vormärz* ('pre-March'). But if Strauss sounded military in his day perhaps Haydn's theme

sounded military to the public of 1794 et seq. At any rate, it certainly sounded like a popular tune, and it was introduced, like the second subject of No. 99/I, with a tap-room accompaniment over a pizzicato bass. Of course Strauss was deliberately quoting Haydn: the time (barred C) and the key, D major (because in the Haydn we are now in the dominant) is the same, and besides, No. 100 was still a very popular Symphony in *Vormärz* Vienna. But perhaps both Haydn and Strauss were not writing military music at all. In those days of revolution in 1848, Haydn's music sounded to many like a lost paradise. Franz Gernerth wrote: 'Just after the three days in March I played several Haydn symphonies on the piano with a friend, and I cannot describe what a sorrowful [*wehmütigen*] feeling these magnificent masterpieces made on me. Their message sounded to me like a paradise of freedom in this time of oppression . . .' Can Johann Strauss, Father, have been quoting Haydn in this sense rather than linking a 'Military Symphony' with a military man (i.e. Radetzky)?

That Haydn intended something curiously ambivalent with his 'Radetzky' subject is made abundantly clear in the development section: ambivalent in two senses. First, because the innocent-sounding theme immediately begins to take on the ominous character of the *crescendo* in the introduction, and secondly because all the modulations

---

1 Pohl III, 305. H. E. Jacob: *Johann Strauss: A Century of Light Music*, revised ed., London 1949, p. 137. On the development of the 'Military' Symphony, see Oscar Wappenschmitt: 'Die Durchführung im 1. Satz von Haydns "Militär-Symphonie": Eine Studie' in *Die Musik* 8. Jahr, Heft 16 (1909), pp. 243–250. Gernerth: *Allgemeine Wiener Musik-Zeitung*, 8, 1848, No. 48. See Clemens Höslinger: 'Der überwundene Standpunkt: Joseph Haydn in der Wiener Musikkritik des 19. Jahrhunderts', *Beiträge zur Musikgeschichte des 18. Jahrhunderts*. Eisenstadt 1970, p. 134.

and *crescendi* lead to quite different tonal goals than the music first allows us to believe. Notice another link to the introduction, namely that a timpani roll accompanies the climax of each of the two modulations, just as the drums underlined the first of all these threatening *crescendi*. The tonal ambivalence takes place as follows. The exposition ends in D and after two full bars of silence (and three beats of another bar as well), the second theme begins in B flat but soon starts to establish C minor. Here the first *crescendo* begins. At its climax, with a kettledrum roll, the music shifts suddenly away from C minor into D minor, but all through this series of modulations there are almost no chords in a root position so that each key that Haydn establishes seems uncertain and even menaced by the next modulation. The momentum starts again, *piano*, in D minor (though still not in root position), and the same *crescendo* is repeated a note higher, with the same climax, timpani roll and sudden change towards E minor, the arrival of which is procrastinated by seventeen bars. It is not until Haydn settles into E minor that we begin to sense its relative major, and our tonic, round the corner. The recapitulation is chopped short to such an extent that we are suspicious: the exposition ran for 100 bars, of which the last 17 bars were 'closing material', or the final *tutti*, while the recapitulation runs – first and second subject, with all the truncated bridge passages – to 37 bars. What Haydn is doing is to prepare for the biggest and most flamboyant coda of his symphonic *oeuvre* hitherto. This spectacular conclusion starts out its promising course by jumping without preparation into E flat, the flattened submediant. This, too, was foretold at the beginning of the development, where Haydn moved from D to its flattened submediant and gave us a large grand pause to help us remember the effect. In this fifty bars we are treated to a display of orchestral fireworks unprecedented in Haydn's career. We are even given the intoxicating sound of the violins racing away in quavers with only the sound of horns, trumpets and kettledrums hammering out tonic and dominant chords behind them (bars 256–8 with lead-in and lead-out). It is one of the first times that a symphony orchestra was used as a pure, virtuoso instrument and as such it presages many such pages in the nineteenth century; but through it all we are constantly aware of previous thematic fragments and derivatives. It is virtuosity on a magnificent scale, but never empty virtuosity.

Once Haydn saved the trumpets and drums until the slow movement of a symphony (it was No. 88, 1787); their entrance must have electrified musicians all over Europe. In No. 99 we have seen a similar instance of withholding these instruments until the middle of the second movement. In No. 100, Haydn does an equally unprecedented orchestral trick, or rather a double trick. In the first place he introduces two clarinets in C, which play only in the Allegretto. In the second, he has arranged a battery of 'Turkish' instruments such as were used by Austrian composers in exotic operas with Turkish subjects (*vide supra*, p. 551); this percussion group enters the fray together with the trumpets and kettledrums when the music turns from C major to C minor at bar 57. There are two sets of percussion parts: (1) those contained in the authentic set of MS. parts by Johann Elssler in the Esterházy Archives, a source which is textually very close to the Birchall print; the reader is referred to the notes in Vol. XII of the *Philharmonia Complete Haydn Symphonies* for further details. Since these percussion parts are indubitably genuine, we have included them, and only them, in the new critical edition. On the Elssler title page, a 'Tambourine' is mentioned but there is no part for it in the MS. Perhaps it improvised a part reading over the shoulder of one of the percussion players. Elssler has actual parts for triangle, cymbals and bass drum. (2) The textually different parts contained in the earliest André and other German, French and Austrian prints. The interested reader may consult both percussion parts, Elssler's and the Germans', in the new edition of *Joseph Haydn Werke* (Henle Verlag, 'Londoner Sinfonien, 3. Folge'). Since no concrete evidence as to the authenticity of *any* of these German prints has been brought forward, we believe that only the parts as found in the Elssler MS. have a claim to complete genuineness. Since the percussion parts were often left out of MS. and printed copies of the work, we wonder if those of the German prints are not 'improvised' by someone who remembered where they all entered but could not remember the actual 'notes' (if such can describe percussion parts). Unfortunately our only autograph of this second movement, as a March for wind band and 'tamburo', does not help us in solving this particular problem. For a clever piece of arranging, however, music lovers should not miss this March, which was first published in the afore-mentioned Henle edition.

Haydn completely reorchestrated the 'Romance' of the Concerto, dropping the title as he did so. In 1786, when the Concerto was composed, Haydn was much interested in the *Romance*, using an old French song, 'La gentille et jeune Lisette' as the basis for the *Romance* in the Symphony No. 85 ('La Reine') composed about 1785 or 1786 for Le Concert de la Loge Olympique in Paris. Both movements are themes and variations on the melody, and that of the Concerto for the King of Naples also sounds like a French folk-song. In 1785, Mozart and Haydn were particularly intimate, and it is not surprising to find the younger composer using a *Romance* as the slow movement of the piano Concerto in D minor K. 466, first performed the night that Haydn was initiated into the Freemasons. The simple, folk-song construction of the typical Romance's theme is also found in Beethoven's two beautiful Romances for violin and orchestra (1798: this earlier date will be explained in the subsequent volume).

Not only did Haydn reorchestrate the *Romance*, he also had to compose new inner parts as he did so. Perhaps the most striking alteration concerns the endings of the individual sections in the Concerto. Haydn originally had three crotchet rests of silence in such places (bars 8, 16, 36, 56, etc.) which are in the 'Military' version deftly filled – so deftly, in fact, that the earlier version sounds empty once we have assimilated the later one into our unconscious minds. Who can imagine

after having heard the later version?

There is no doubt that the 'Military' text is vastly smoother and more poised 'at the joints'; even where the original had something to connect two sections, such as the minim at bar 44, Haydn later added a rhythmic lead in the horns ♩ ♩ ♩ | 𝅝.

The use of C major is also connected with 'Turkish' or 'Janissary' instruments: it was the key of Mozart's *Entführung* where there are also C clarinets. For Haydn, this almost chamber-musical use of the wind instruments (before the 'Turkish' instruments enter) also reminded him of another set of works for King of Naples, namely the Notturni, which in their original orchestration had many of the elements found in the second movement of No. 100: 2 lire, 2 clarinets in C and divided violas (the lira parts would be divided up, in a reorchestration, between flute and oboe). Once the original sound of these solo wind instruments has begun to penetrate, and this occurs after their extensive solo sections in bars 8–16 and 36–56 of the first 'A' section, we realize that the 'toy' music of the opening Allegro, for solo flute and oboes unaccompanied, was nothing but another one of Haydn's announcements of things-to-come. It might be noted how utterly different is the effect of the solo wind band here – martial, witty, light-footed and even rather exotic-sounding – compared with the Romantic, *legato* wind band solo in the slow movement of No. 99. The Allegretto thus continues the 'toy' music of the opening Allegro, leading us even further into some 'Sleeping Beauty' world of unreality and marmalade skies (bars 116–22). This great emphasis on the wind section of the orchestra was what undoubtedly suggested to Haydn to make an arrangement of this popular movement for military band and 'tamburo'.

The Concerto movement ended at bar 152 but two bars have been added (146 and 147) in the symphonic version. The solo trumpet call, which is given to the second trumpet (though the sources are not absolutely clear on this point and it is just possible that Haydn meant 'a due'), has a curiously sinister sound by being so low. The fanfare seems to have been well known. Whether it was Austrian or British cannot be established any more, but it was clearly an 'Allied' fanfare. Arnold Schering, the well-known German scholar, maintained that the fanfare was still known to the Prussian (= German) cavalry in 1939 as 'Paradepost'.[1] The drum roll is known to us from the *crescendi* in the first movement and becomes a symbol of unrest, uneasiness, fear. We shall encounter it again as it is presented here: solo. The unexpected use of A flat major to follow this drum roll on the note C also increases the feeling of anxiety: this is the real climax of the trumpet fanfare and drum roll – a 'false resolution' like the art of war. Audiences of 1794 shivered at this 'climax of horrid sublimity'. Even the actual ending is preceded by ambivalent harmonies – A flat keeps entering the resolution into C major (bar 179 in the bassoon, bar 181 in second oboe and bassoon): the parallel was obvious to everyone in the audience at Hanover Square Rooms that March night in 1794 when 'shouts of applause' greeted the conclusion of this *Allegretto*.

The construction of the Menuet is unusual, first because of its slow tempo (Moderato), the reasons for which have been discussed above, and secondly because the first section is not repeated and ends in the tonic. Actually this 'A' section consists in itself of an eight-bar theme which is first given out *forte* and then *piano*, with different inner parts, different articulation (bar 3 quavers *staccati* and bar 11 slurred) and different orchestration. This places the stress on the (repeated) second section, and a very symphonic treatment of the material. It is more like a sonata-form development than almost any of the other minuets of the 1791–2 season, though we can see the trend in many of the previous works. It was, however, not carried this far. The quaver passage which we noted was phrased differently when repeated in the 'A' section is now used as a counterpoint in the bottom and inner voices. If the Menuet is serious, the Trio sounds once more an alarming note in the second part. The stress on the dotted rhythm that so much sounds like a French overture was perhaps a reference to the enemy across the Channel; no one can have missed the martial undercurrent to the ♪♫♩♫♩♩ rhythm or the reference to G minor.

---

1 'Bemerkungen zu Joseph Haydns Programmsymphonien' in: *Peters Jahrbuch* XLVI [1939], p. 18, footnote 4.

If we judge the middle movements of No. 100 as an entity, and the sources seem to allow that, the Finale must occupy a position of special importance. Not only does it restore the fast tempo of the opening barred–C Allegro – for, as we have seen, the two middle movements are moderately quick but never slow – but it is the longest final quick movement in any Haydn symphony to date except for No. 98, which is even longer: we say 'quick movement', because earlier works with slow sections such as Nos. 45 or 67 do not fall into this particular category. No. 100's Presto is also on a huge formal scale. Bars 1–49 are in the usual ‖ : A : ‖‖ : B A : ‖ scheme, and the bridge-

8 bars   33 bars   8 bars
I   →V   →I

passage begins thereafter in the tonic. It is a sonata rondo, then, on an unprecedented scale, with a very extended middle section (if one wishes to lump everything that Haydn does into this category) lasting from bar 50 to bar 218 (the recapitulation, with upbeat from 217). There is a final and particularly 'shocking' timpani solo in the middle of this section (bars 122–3), after a big cadence in D major. Like the first movement of No. 45, the second subject is introduced in this huge middle section and is characterized by a series of acciaccature ♪♪. The timpani solo ushers in the development, where we find an exceptionally wide range of keys, even for late Haydn: D major → F major → A flat → D flat (enharmonically changed to C sharp minor) → E major (F flat) → E minor (F flat minor) and back to the dominant of G. The strong third-related tendency will be noted, also the fact that the recapitulation is actually in A double-flat major which Haydn avoids by shifting from flats to sharps in the middle. At bar 265 Haydn brings in the Turkish instruments again; they are not marked in the autograph, where there was no room for them on the already crowded twelve-stave paper Haydn had at his disposal. The *Morning Chronicle*'s correspondent did not approve of the cymbals (by which he meant all the extra percussion, no doubt) in this last movement (5 May 1794: *supra*, p. 250). Haydn obviously thought it made an effective conclusion to this extroverted but brilliantly planned Symphony. (The Finale's percussion parts are, fortunately, preserved in the Elssler parts now in Budapest, as well as being found in slightly altered form in the early German, Austrian and French prints.)

The principal theme of the Finale soon proved to be as popular as the 'Military Movement'. It is apparently a case in which a Haydn melody became a folk-tune. In a letter by Mr. Fritz Spiegl of 16 February 1957, we learned that the tune of the Finale appeared in at least three mechanical organs of the early nineteenth-century as 'Lord Cathcart' (or 'Catheart') together with other English country dances. Mr Spiegl was kind enough to copy the theme from one of the musical clocks, reproduced opposite. In March 1957, we sent this information, thanks to the kind efforts of Mr. A. Hyatt King of the British Museum's Music Room, to the English Folk Dance and Song Society, who wrote the following note:

> ... I have found 'Lord Cathcart' as a country dance in two collections, and also the tune in one of our nineteenth-century MS. tune books. Details as follows:
> LORD CATHCART –
>   *as* LORD CATHCART'S WELCOME in *Treasures of Terpsichore* . . . being a Collection of all the most popular Country Dances . . . together with all the new Dances for 1809. By T. Wilson, London, 1809.
>   *as* LORD CATHCART'S WELCOME TO SCOTLAND in *Wheatstone's Selection* of Elegant and Fashionable Country Dances, Reels, Waltzs [*sic*], *etc.* for the Ensuing

[Musical clock theme]

Season, with an Accompt. for the Piano Forte or Harp by Augs. Voigt, *etc.* Sold by C. Mitchell, at his Musical Circulating Library and Instrument Ware rooms, 51, Southampton Row, Russel [*sic*] Sqre. [*n.d.*, but between 1808–1814).

as LORD CATHCART in a manuscript book of country dance tunes, *etc.* which is not earlier than the first decade or so of the nineteenth century.

Lord Cathcart is presumably Sir William Shaw, tenth Baron Cathcart and first Viscount and Earl Cathcart (1755–1843) who after a distinguished military career was created Viscount Cathcart in 1807 and appointed C. in C. Scotland presumably in the same year . . .

At present it seems that 'Lord Cathcart' is derived from Haydn's melody rather than vice versa

concludes the Secretary of the Society Miss Sara Jackson.

The present writer found in 1958 another contemporary MS. of the 'Cathcart' version in a pile of old songs which Mr. Hermann Baron kindly presented to us. Here the Song is entitled 'Lord Cathcart's Wee' and is in B flat major. The paper on which the MS. was written is British and bears a dated watermark 1807. It is reproduced overleaf.

If we assume that Haydn's Finale was the source of this arrangement (and for the moment we must resist the temptation to think that he wove into his famous Symphony an English folk-song), we note that the arranger, whoever he was, had to create a 'middle section', since Haydn's symphonic extension (bars 9 et seq.) would not do for the purpose of a folk-song adaptation. What is interesting in the musical clock's version is, apart from the ornaments that well suited the little instrument and abound in Haydn's own pieces for *Flötenuhr*, the 'inégal' notation (= sound) of bar 7, the way the

clock would interpret ♪♪ ♪ ♪♪ ♪

Before leaving mechanical adaptations of this Symphony, we should note that the Allegretto was one of the pieces on Johann Nepomuk Mälzel's mechanical instrument, the 'Panharmonicon', constructed a few years after Haydn's death. (Some sources

'Lord Cathcart's Wee', from a contemporary manuscript (on paper with watermark date 1807). See p. 565.

suggest that Mälzel had the whole 'Military' Symphony on a cylinder but this seems very improbable.)[1]

No. 100 was one of the first Haydn symphonies to be reviewed in the then new *Allgemeine Musikalische Zeitung* (April 1799, pp. 422=4):

RECENSION

Grande Simphonie à plusieurs Instruments, composée par J. Haydn.

Oeuvre 9. Augsbourg chez Gombart et Comp. (Prix 3 Fl.)

The fashion in which J. *Haydn* composed symphonies is as well known and well appreciated as almost anything in the musical world. It would be therefore quite unnecessary to say anything further about this Symphony, composed in London by the great master, except that it is one of the finest he has written. It is somewhat less learned, and easier to take in, than some of the other newest works by him, but it is just as rich in new ideas as they. The effect of surprise cannot perhaps be pushed further than it is here, when in the second movement we are utterly surprised by the full Janissary music in the minore – up to that point one had no idea that these Turkish instruments were part of the Symphony's scoring. But here, too, we see not only the inventive but also the prudent artist. The Andante [*recte*: Allegretto] is in fact conceived as a whole: for despite all the pleasantness and lightness with which the composer in the first part attempts to distract attention from the coming coup, it is laid out and worked out like a march. That at least should be a hint to imitators, who no doubt are at this very moment planning to shower us with symphonies with Turkish music. . . . [There then follows a list of appalling printer's errors, 'not even mentioning many a smaller error'.]

1 Thayer: *Beethoven* (Forbes), I, 559ff. The 'Military Movement' was a favourite of other clockmakers as well.

Symphony No. 101 in D ('The Clock') (1794)

This is the third of the four D major Salomon Symphonies. There are many obvious advantages to the key, not least its sonority for the strings where the empty strings are useful in chords, but also its fine effect for the brass and timpani. A large part of Professor Jan LaRue's thematic catalogue of all eighteenth century symphonies is in D major, and two of Mozart's last six symphonies (K. 385, 504) are in that key. It was very much a 'public' key in the eighteenth century, though not so much in Austria (where big Church Masses, festive symphonies and 'Applausus' cantatas tended to be in C major) as in Germany and Italy.

Symphony No. 98 had opened with a slow introduction in the tonic minor, and Haydn now repeats the idea in No. 101 and later in No. 104. The mysterious, portentous D minor opening is unique in Haydn's symphonies hitherto: it is orchestrated in 'grey' tones, too – no clarinets, no brass and timpani. Thematic illusions to the Presto are as clouded as the mists that seem to surround the introduction. The slowly rising scale at the beginning

might seem to be the ghostly predecessor of the Presto's first theme

and, perhaps, of a curious little phrase that rounds off the second subject in both exposition and recapitulation:

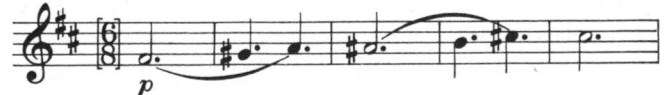

Similarly, the second violin part in this passage from the introduction (which is also the only lower voice and is thus particularly exposed)

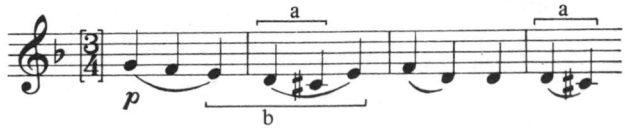

would seem to be responsible for the second subject, the feminine cadence of which, in turn, is related also to the first:

To feel this hidden relationship between the second violin's phrase in the introduction and the second subject, it is only necessary to imagine the D minor phrase in D major and in six-eight. Apart from these deliberately nebulous references, this magnificent introduction serves as perhaps no other (except possibly No. 99) to raise one's expectancy, to prepare one for the beginning of the Presto (which by the way Haydn at first marked 'Presto, ma non troppo', later cancelling the 'ma non troppo' – thus showing that he wanted a really fast pace). This Adagio is a typical instance of the Richard Strauss precept that all basic *tempi* in the Viennese classical masters larger works are the same, i.e. in this case it is obvious that ♩. of the Adagio = ♩. of the Presto, an easy relationship that, however, might be placed in doubt if one were to worry too much about the 'ma non troppo'. It is also one more instance of Haydn regarding six-eight and three-four as mutually compatible (as we have seen in No. 94/I and will see again, with startling clarity, in No. 103/I).

Six-eight is a most unusual tempo for an opening movement. Haydn had tried the effect in Symphony No. 67 in F, a work of great originality and daring which also has a Finale with a large slow insert. Six-eight was, in the 1760s, rather a Finale tempo (as in Haydn's Symphony No. 16) and became in the 1780s an equally successful conclusion on a larger scale, such as Mozart's 'hunting' rondos (in the horn concertos or the piano Concerto in E flat K. 482) which were, in turn, based on Haydn's 'La Chasse' Finale of Symphony No. 73 (published at Vienna in July 1782). Mozart, perhaps as a compliment to the older man, wrote the first movement of the B flat 'Hunt' Quartet (K. 458), one of the six dedicated to Haydn, in six-eight. In No. 101's opening Presto we have a six-eight movement on the largest possible scale (over 300 bars, the exposition to be repeated). Haydn has of course realized the 'light' metric nature of six-eight – which is why it is an ideal finale metre – and the thematic material of the movement is so light as to be almost inconsequential until we realize Haydn's broad scheme. The nature of the opening subject required the broad introduction with which Haydn provided it; only after this expanse of D minor could the anacrustic opening theme make any impression. Because of the movement's thematic frailty, he begins extending the main subject motivically, developing it, all during the very long bridge passage to the dominant. This is nothing unusual in late Haydn symphonies, but the extent and depth of this development so early in the movement shows us that Haydn is compensating for his metre by heavily symphonic treatment. The second subject is no contrast at all to the first: he makes things as difficult as possible for himself. Yet because the second subject seems to grow out of the foregoing material, there is a sense of unity throughout. We have seen that thematic connections between the introduction and the second subject, but the relationship between the two subjects of the Presto is also strongly latent:

and becomes even clearer when Haydn modulates back to the beginning of the exposition (there are two endings, of which this is the first):

The characteristic interval of a ninth in the main theme (*d*) appears as part of the closing material (*tutti*) following the second subject:

and is immediately augmented a bar later. Another such procedure is when Haydn takes the end of the first subject and alters it in various ways, for example:

The elaboration of all these motivic fragments is so fascinating and proceeds at such a dizzy pace that one soon forgets how slender is all the actual material from which this massive symphonic edifice is constructed. There are also interesting dynamic effects which serve to propel the music forward, such as two different uses of *ff*. On the one hand, Haydn uses the marking towards the end of the exposition only in the horns, trumpets and kettledrums as a means of bringing them into the foreground and thus infusing the already rich and agile score with a sudden blaze of colour (bars 101–108). Another use of *ff* is to lash out a bold modulation, such as occurs at bar 190 in the middle of the development section; again, we must remember that *ff* in Haydn's scores are of short duration (as can be seen by the fact that he is able to use *fz* for the wind parts in the same bar: *fz* in the strings would, however, have meant ♪♪♪ ♪♪♪ to most players, whereas *ff* meant a louder [loudest] level throughout all six notes). The *ff* leads, as it were, to the entrance of the clarinets, horns, trumpets and timpani, which have been silent for half-a-dozen bars and add one further wave of sound to the *ff* (*fz*) climax. The passage is remarkable for the attention to orchestral detail which characterizes this robust, vigorous, yet delicately balanced Presto. (The use of the triad [bracket *e*] discussed above will be seen in context here.)

The second movement, Andante, has given the Symphony its name, 'The Clock'. Considering that it is one of Haydn's most played works, surprisingly few people have gone to the trouble of investigating either the Symphony as a whole or even the form of the Andante. In 1798, the Viennese publisher Johann Traeg issued the movement in a piano arrangement entitled 'Rondo . . . Die Uhr'. Rondo is in fact the nearest description of this new and fascinating hybrid form that Haydn has created for this Andante. On paper it looks almost like a typical Haydn finale, for example that of Symphony No. 96: the same A–B–A opening section followed by a big 'minore' ('C') and a return to the 'A' section. But whereas in a typical finale the return to the 'A' section is fairly regular, here the presentation of 'A' following the 'minore' is radically different. It is actually so different that Geiringer (1947, 290) describes the movement as a 'mixture of variation and rondo'. This is particularly true of what happens after the 'minore': the 'A' section is given with a completely different orchestration (theme in the first violins, the accompaniment so laid out that it straddles the first violin by having the 'tick-tock' split up at the interval of two octaves instead of thirds). The beginning was a stroke of genius, with its clock-like accompaniment, but the variation with the straddled violin theme is even more brilliantly original. Writing about this kind of language in general, Rosen (96f.) notes that:

> The buffoonery of Haydn, Beethoven, and Mozart is only an exaggeration of an essential quality of the classical style. This style was, in its origins, basically a comic one. I do not mean that sentiments of the deepest and most tragic emotion could not be expressed by it, but the pacing of classical rhythm is the pacing of comic opera, its phrasing is the phrasing of dance music, and it large structures are these phrases dramatized. . . . If the taste for the comic in music grew in the second half of the eighteenth century, this was at least in part because the development of style had at last made a genuinely autonomous wit possible. The incongruous seen as exactly right, the out-of-place suddenly turning out to be just where it ought to be – this is an essential part of wit. . . . Clarity of articulation is essential to this kind of comedy. The contrast between the melodic and accompanying parts in classical style . . . allows us the delicious moment in Haydn's 'Clock' Symphony when the accompaniment is transposed into the upper register [and] where the double meaning is made even more evident by giving the figure to the solo flute and bassoon.[1]

Tracing the formal scheme of the movement thus far we have:

$$\|: A \qquad :\|\|: \quad B \qquad\qquad A \qquad :\| \; C \text{ ('minore')}$$
$$\text{(I) (10 bars)} \qquad (\to V \to I) \text{ (13 bars) (I) (11 bars)} \qquad (Ib \to \flat VI - V)$$

A^1–B^1–A^1. There then follows a bar of silence; the main theme then begins in E flat, modulates to the tonic and a new statement of the 'A' section begins which, unlike the fragmentary statement in E flat, turns out to be a complete A^2–B^2–A^2 with a concluding coda; this final time, the principal tripartite statement is for full orchestra (strings ff) the first time (A^2) and again for full orchestra the last time, but slightly differently orchestrated (higher trumpets) and a new, penetrating timpani part, *inter alia*). Thus the graph is only very approximate and can give but an inadequate idea of Haydn's apparently limitless ingenuity, wit and craftsmanship. The 'C' section is also a not very accurate description of an extremely powerful 'minore' which is closely based on rhythmic figures already known to us: the dotted 'Baroque' pattern of bar 4, the 'clock' accompaniment and the demisemiquavers of bar 3.

Among the many original ideas – formal, orchestral and otherwise – in this Andante, we would draw attention to one small but characteristic detail. The main

---

1 Reprinted by permission of Faber and Faber Ltd and The Viking Press, Inc.

theme begins with its accompaniment. This is a device we have seen in No. 96/I, but here it is more closely allied to the popular second subjects of Nos. 99 and 100, the dance tune beginning with its accompaniment. No. 101's melody is not a dance tune but it is very definitely a folk-tune-like march, a slow dance in two-four time. It is enlightening to see what Haydn does with this one bar of introductory accompaniment. The first time it reappears Haydn leads into it with the first violin, providing a smooth joint which is at the same time comic because it seems as if bar 24 is the beginning of the melody, whereas of course it is still the bar of accompaniment; but this is not really made clear until the first violins and flute take up the actual theme at bar 25. When the music goes into E flat, the accompaniment becomes for a moment so fragmentary that we are as unsure of the music's progress as we are unsure where Haydn is going tonally:

The final time, just before the last big *tutti*, the accompaniment is given to the lower strings but also to the horns in a high register; this time the joke is that the horns go on sounding this accompaniment right through the whole texture of the *tutti*, which they are easily able to do because of the high *tessitura* in which the part is written, the marking *ff* and the doubling by other wind instruments (bars 133–6). Haydn's coda is a delightfully sentimental farewell to the 'clock' (bars 144ff.). Like many of the epilogues in J. S. Bach's chorale preludes, the sentimentality is achieved by a tonic pedal point and some such chordal progression as

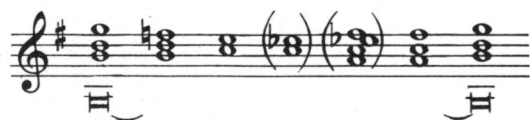

Haydn ended many late slow movements on such a pattern, e.g. Nos. 94 and 97 of the first Salomon series. Here, the music quietly stops its ticking with three soft *piano* chords. But this was a graceful afterthought. Instead of the last two bars, Haydn originally planned a different ending (see overleaf) which is found, cancelled, on the autograph. We know that London audiences, less inhibited than today's woeful grandchildren of Victorian custom, applauded between movements, also after adagios. The kind of loud chord that Haydn originally planned was of the sort that we find at the end of No. 97's or No. 99's Adagio; now, having won the applause of his career with No. 100's Allegretto, Haydn could afford to indulge his sense of what was fitting (as opposed, let us say, to what Mr. Salomon might have preferred . . .) and the

[Symphony No. 101: Andante, ending]   [Original ending in autograph]

---

slow movements of Nos. 101, 102 and 104 all end quietly. No more concessions were necessary.

The Menuet of Symphony No. 101 is the longest of all twelve Salomon Symphonies. We are no friend of long rows of statistics, but in this particular case a list of the bar lengths of all twelve works shows two facts at once: the prodigious length of No. 101's third movement and also Haydn's incredible variety. As far as the length is concerned, No. 97 has no repeats either in the Minuet or in the Trio, and thus only Nos. 99 and 102 – both highly developed symphonic minuets – come anywhere near the scope of No. 101 (see table opposite).

The richness and variety of 'The Clock' Minuet are everywhere apparent – not least in the orchestration. The divided violas at bars 4–8 (later repeated in the recapitulation) are rare in this context, and even more unexpected is the timpani solo at the beginning of the second section (bars 29–38).

Symphony		Minuet	Trio	
93		46	52	
94		62	27	
95		56	28	
96		52	32	
97	(no repeats)	68	48	
98		60	41	
99		68	50	
100		56	24	(first part minuet: no repeat)
101		80	80	(first part trio: no repeat)
102		66	40	
103		48	32	
104		52	52	

Haydn takes great pains to establish a balance between the strong up-beat of the theme and the normal beat of three four. This is partly accomplished by *fz*, as in bars 29–38, and also at the very beginning of the Minuet: ♩ | ♩ ♩ ♩ | ♩ ♫♫ | and partly by displacing the whole stress: ♩ ♩ | ♩ ♩ | ♩ ♫♫ (etc.) or by *fz*⏤ *fz*⏤ introducing even series of quavers (bars 65–72). In the latter passage, the rhythmic organization of the score is particularly deft: the violins carry on in quavers; the clarinets have crotchets; the oboes have ♩ | ♩ 𝄾 ♩ | ♩ 𝄾 ; the bassoons and bass line ♩ ♩ | ♩ ♩ , the violas and horns ♩ ♩ | ♩ ♩ and the trumpets and timpani (except for one establishing crotchet of the timpani on the first beat of bar 66) have the rhythm of the oboes. The general effect of this passage is one of intense kinetic subtlety and yet vibrant rhythmic activity. One notes how all these diverse and in part contradictory strands are resolved in the cadential formula at bar 71, to which the timpani give a conclusive underlying stability (see example overleaf).

The beginning of the Trio based on the bracketed portion of the this example, has been the cause of much controversy among scholars and musicians. Here is what Haydn wrote:

[Symphony No. 101 : Minuet]

The next time this passage is repeated (and the repeat is written out) the strings change to (V. I, II. Va.) *g″*, *c sharp′* and *e′* at bars 102–3, which would be 86–7 in the first statement; at 104 the inner strings have a slight difference because of the previous part-writing.

Now there is no question about Haydn's intentions. The autograph is not only clear but the repeated bars are numbered over the first violin part. The dissonant version is also in the Elssler copy of the score (Esterházy Archives) and in the original set of London string parts (on British paper and with the musicians' names on the title pages – see our short catalogue, *supra*) which form part of the authentic MS. parts in the Esterházy Archives. This was also the version that Haydn sent to Donaueschingen Castle. Later, however, someone changed the Donaueschingen MS. When the change entered the sources and if it was with Haydn's approval, we cannot say; at any rate, we find it in Salomon's trio arrangement, in his quintet arrangement, and in the Birchall print. The whole thing is, of course, a huge joke. The music begins yet again with the accompaniment, but it seems as if the soloist – in this case the flute – has forgotten to come in; and when he does, there is the dissonance in the strings who seem to be blissfully unaware of what is going on above them. The next time, they 'get it right'. Possibly this was a joke which did not come off. But since it was obviously what Salomon and his orchestra played at the first performance, there seems no reason to accept the change, which was certainly made later and is, until better evidence is uncovered, of doubtful authenticity. At the end, this village band makes another mistake: the horns come in with a pedal point too early (bar 154), sitting placidly on octave 'd' although there is a dominant seventh harmony a bar later. We shall see later that Germany's leading musical journal took great offence at this and other passages in the Symphony. It was the kind of Austrian humour which did not go down well in the old *Reich*. Beethoven was to remember all this tomfoolery when writing the peasants' dance in the 'Pastoral' Symphony wherein the oboe comes in on the wrong beat. Schindler tells us:[1]

> . . . Beethoven asked me if I had noticed how village musicians would often fall asleep while playing, sometimes let the instrument sink and not play for a while, then wake up with a start, make a few hearty blasts or blowings at random, yet usually in the right key, and then go back to sleep again . . . There were dances in which the 3/4 measure suddenly gave way to a 2/4 bar. In the 1820s I still used to hear such dances in villages within a few hours' distance of the capital, such as Laab, Kaltenleutgeben, Gaden, and others.

In the Trio of the 'Clock', Haydn has given us a delightful view of such a village band in the 1790s – complete with sleepy strings, delayed entrances, wrong entries and hurdy-gurdy effects.

The Finale lays excellent claim to being the greatest symphonic last movement of Haydn's career. It is pre-eminent even in a series of twelve scintillatingly brilliant finales. Formally it is the descendant of No. 94's effervescent Finale except that No. 101 hardly has any second subject; everything is based on the main theme. In the dominant the place of the second subject is taken by a pure derivative of the first:

The music starts developing immediately. In the following tutti (still in dominant) we notice that under the glittering series of quavers in the first violins, the basses of the orchestra are pounding out the first three notes of the main subject:

1 *Beethoven as I knew him* (ed. Donald W. McArdle), London (Faber and Faber Ltd) and Chapel Hill (University of North Carolina Press), 1966, p. 146.

We return to a slightly varied restatement and then comes perhaps the most impressive of all Haydn's many 'minore' sections in a finale. This one is ferocious beyond all expectations, its enormous energy assisted by furious quavers throughout, sometimes in the middle parts, sometimes on the top. It starts out like a real 'C' section but by the time we are in the relative major the first theme emerges from the boiling mass of quavers:

And attentive listeners will have heard that the flutes, oboes, bassoons, horns, trumpets and timpani have a direct quotation, though only rhythmic, of the main theme when the minor section begins: ♩ ♩ | ♩ ▬, which for a time only the kettledrums sustain – another of many instances when Haydn assigns important functions to this instrument, the effective qualities of which took on an entirely new dimension in Haydn's late symphonies. After this display of D minor we would expect a restatement; but no, Haydn has in store for us a *fugato* based on the main theme, which rushes away *pianissimo* in a long section full of *Midsummer Night's Dream* fantasy: an inspiration which was to have a profound effect on Mendelssohn.

The *fugato* spreads into a large-sized orchestral *tutti*, with the countersubject in the clarinets and lower strings with bassoon. After a last farewell to the main theme (with the usual 'farewell' tonic pedal point and I_4^6–I_5^{b7} harmonies),[1] there is a rousing conclusion and, incidentally, Haydn's last use of an old and much-loved symphonic device: to end the movement with three repeated chords preceded by a rest (and a cadential formula), usually

(the bracketed portion is a deviation found in No. 101). This was the formula that ended (in reverse numerical progression) Nos. 95, 92, 89, 88, 87 (without the preceding cadential formula), 85, 84 (in two-four time), 83 (in twelve-eight time, also no cadential formula) and 80. There are finales of greater monothematic tension (such as No. 103's), of greater wit (such as No. 102's), of greater contrapuntal dexterity (such as No. 95's): but none in which all these elements are combined with such fantastic virtuosity, such real panache, as in the 'Clock's' Vivace.

In the September 1799 issue of the *Allgemeine Musikalische Zeitung*, Gombart's edition of Haydn's Symphonies Nos. 101 and 103 was reviewed. The three Symphonies that made up Gombart's Op. 91 also included the 'Military' (No. 100) which had been reviewed earlier in *AMZ* and is quoted above by us). After quoting the title page and giving a short résumé of the movements in each work, the review continues as follows:

> The reviewer does not know very well the first of these Symphonies [No. 100], which was reviewed in this journal (No. 17) earlier, but he has not only heard the last two several times but also has the scores in front of him. He must admit that he found, in these Symphonies, as in all the works by this intelligent and ingenious

1 The 'farewell' aspect of the harmonies is not only because it is the last entrance of the theme and has these typically Haydnesque progressions but it also recalls a real farewell scene in a Haydn opera, namely the last act of *Le pescatrici* (1769). There, we find the same pedal point as Eurilda and Lindoro prepare to set sail. See the piano score (Universal Edition), pp. 319f.

composer that have appeared for the last twenty and more years, an inexhaustible genius to understand and admire. But as an *objective* reviewer he must also make the frank confession that he found in these Symphonies not only superficial but really important points of carelessness, which, he must candidly admit, made him really rather shy and embarrassed in view of his opinion of the great man, who is esteemed and loved almost throughout the length and breadth of Europe. Of course he is well aware how positively and with every good reason the first men and judges of music regard *Haydn*; among these men he would only mention a *Mozart*. Without investigating or being able to judge to what extent these opinions were and are perhaps more fanciful than truthful . . ., he is nevertheless glad to believe that if one melted down himself and a few dozen other reviewers, there would not by any means emerge a *Haydn* – to quote *Mozart* [who had said the much quoted remark to someone who was criticizing Haydn, 'if the two of us were melted down together, there would not by any means emerge a *Haydn*'].
Despite this, he not only believes but is firmly convinced that many a work by *Haydn* would not only not lose but on the contrary would certain profit if these mistakes, so easy to avoid or correct, had been avoided or corrected. He knows, moreover, that perhaps several of these mistakes must be laid to *copyists, engravers* and *pirate engravers* – not to *Haydn*; but he intends to lay before the public only some passages from these Symphonies to be examined and judged, and he has his reasons for believing that *Haydn* wrote them just as they appear, except that unnecessary instruments have been here omitted.

In the six-eight Presto of the 2nd Symphony [No. 101, bars 111–4]:

[We quote from *AMZ*, in which the faulty Gombart print is followed, for example in rewriting all Haydn's *fz* as *sf*.] In the 4th bar of this example it seems that *Haydn* has chosen the unprepared doubling of the dissonant fourth in viola and bassoons and the following unmelodic progression of the viola to the seventh in order – to avoid hidden fifths. Moreover:

[No. 101, bars 166–8]. Compare this example with the previous one. In the earlier example a hidden fifth is avoided with fear, but here there are three consecutive fifths one after the other [marked in the horn; the fifths are with the bass. In both cases, apart from small differences in the spelling of dynamic marks, *AMZ* is really quoting correctly. Interestingly, the Birchall print corrects this horn fifth by changing bar 167, the 2nd of the example, to written *d″*]. Moreover:

[No. 101, bars 237–9.] Would it not be much better if the 2nd violin went with the first in *unisono*? For if the trumpeters and horn-players, who apart from the oboists also have the timpani as assistants, play even half-heartedly, the listener will not hear much of the *f″* in the flutes and first oboe. [This passage, too, is as Haydn wrote it; this passage has never proved to be a problem in any performance heard by the present writer.]

In the following very attractive Andante in two-four, in which *Haydn* was previously so fortunate and is here, too, as much as ever before, we find in the *minore* section some harmonies which actually did not please the reviewer but which may be very beautiful and excellent according to a *certain new* system; to please the admirers of this system, the reviewer includes them here. They are the following [No. 101/II, bars 46; 50–54]:

[Again, these passages are substantially correct. The dissonance in the trumpets in the first example was changed by Birchall to written *g′*; in the second example, the trumpets in Birchall were changed at 51 to read  , thus avoiding the dissonance. In fact, Haydn also liked these harsh clashes between brass and strings and there is every reason to believe that the autograph meant what it said, especially as there are no such changes in the authentic MSS. Consider the following dissonance in the horns from Symphony No. 47, Finale, bars 162f., where the horns have sounding *a′* against B flat a semitone away:

Haydn could perfectly well have written *g'*, sounding *d'*, and have thus avoided the dissonance entirely.]

To this belongs this passage, too, with which the *minore* of the 'Finale vivace' begins [No. 101/IV, bars 138–141]:

[Here *AMZ* does not mark his objection with a little cross as he did previously, but he obviously meant the fifths between first oboe and bass, i.e. *a'' + d*, *b flat'' + e*, and he probably disapproved of the bassoon's doubling the *b flat* at bars 140f. as well.]

Several times the horns in this passage at the end of the Minuet's Trio are probably printed wrongly [No. 101/III, bars 149ff.]:

[We have discussed Haydn's 'village band' horns at this point in the score. Birchall changes the horns in bars 154–6 to read as follows:

– can Salomon have read the *AMZ* review before passing the proofs of the Birchall engraving? It almost seems so in view of the changes which only Birchall has.]

The rest of the *AMZ* review will be appended to Symphony No. 103. We have no idea what Haydn thought of this *AMZ* review, which he certainly will have read, since we know he subscribed to the journal; he was not a man to write letters of protest to a German musical journal.[1]

Symphony No. 102 in B flat (1794)

No. 102, the first of the three Symphonies for the Opera Concert of 1795, was composed the previous year. In many respects this great work opens a whole new avenue of symphonic thought which hardly anyone except Beethoven – certainly not Schubert – chose to explore. The principal element, not new in Haydn's previous *oeuvre* but hardly exploited to this extent hitherto, is the enormous sense of concentration thematic, motivic, orchestral, formal, with which No. 102 is infused. This is not to say that No. 102 is necessarily shorter than its fellows (though in fact it is slightly shorter than its numerical partners, Nos. 101 and 103) but that Haydn is working so tightly with his material that the overall impression is one of brevity. No. 102 is also Haydn's loudest and most aggressive Symphony, at least in the outer movements. In the opening Vivace there are stretches of *forte* that continue for bars at a time, and all at a very high level of tension. Except for the repetition of the main subject in *piano* (upbeat to 31–37), the exposition runs *forte* from bar 23 (with upbeat) for the next fifty bars, until the second subject enters; and there is a similar stretch from the middle of the development, bar 192, *ff*, which except for a tiny interruption just before the recapitulation (mainly to bring in a huge timpani *crescendo*) continues to the second subject at bar 263. As if to balance this *forte* display of tension, the slow movement introduces tension of another kind, with the dynamic level muted (also literally, in the trumpets) but with, if anything, an increase in the feeling that the music gives us of vast, unleashed power held tightly in check. It is a movement with many levels of emotion, and one of the most complex slow movements Haydn ever wrote. But although Haydn repeats the first section of the Adagio, the movement as a whole shares the intellectual compression of the outer movements. Here, too, is concentration on the highest level. Altogether this Symphony might be considered the most intellectual and certainly the most powerful of the London series. Sir Donald Tovey thought it, No. 104 and the Quartet in F, Op. 77, No. 2, Haydn's greatest instrumental works. Some critics, indeed, consider No. 102 Haydn's greatest Symphony.

Haydn made few significant changes in the texts of his Salomon Symphonies when he returned to Austria in the Autumn of 1795, but it just happens that there are a number of such alterations in this work. A word must be said in preface to Haydn's changes which he liked to make in the original performance material. Much of this material for the late works has survived, e.g. for *The Creation* and the last six Masses, also for parts of the London Symphonies (e.g. the wind parts of Nos. 102–4 in Donaueschingen Castle, which are written by Johann Elssler on British paper with the watermark 1794). Many of these alterations – the additional phrasing, *staccato* mark and, especially, an accent *fz* – are found only on the parts and not on the autograph. In the case of the changes in No. 102, Haydn took the considerable trouble to enter them on the autograph manuscript. The first of these changes is in the orchestration of the introduction, one of Haydn's greatest and most profound. Many critics have been

1 An oblique reference to this review by Haydn is discussed in the next volume of this biography.

struck by the similarity in feeling between this Largo, with its unison opening (marked with a fermata and a 'hairpin' dynamic mark < >), and the beginning of *The Creation*, also a Largo (the Description of Chaos). There is the same feeling of great space, of cosmic loneliness (perhaps, really, Haydn's view of eternity through Herschel's giant telescope). Originally Haydn scored these two ⌢̇ for the gaunt, monkish sound of horns, trumpets, timpani and strings (bars 1 and 6). This is the sound which greeted the audience at the Opera Concert when the Symphony was first performed but also the only way British audiences heard the work for many years. As it happens, the Donaueschingen performance material of this work contains not only the wind and timpani parts on 1794 British paper but also the strings, so that we have as it were an authentic record of No. 102 as performed by Haydn in London in 1795. We also have the Birchall print which follows the London tradition. When Haydn returned to Austria, he added the wind parts for this opening (and bar 6), carefully scratching out the rests in the autograph and inserting the appropriate notes. Since he never took the trouble to tell Salomon of this change, the Birchall print gives us the unchanged London version. Although there is much to recommend the original London version of these bars, we have deferred to Haydn's later wish and printed the score as he changed it (in the new critical edition for the Haydn–Mozart Presse and Philharmonia).

The introduction continues with the following five notes which appear later in the middle strings and then in the basses. During the Vivace Haydn seems to touch on the outline of the five notes in the very theme itself but later quotes it exactly, much accelerated of course, at the end of the exposition (bars 72ff.) and later in the recapitulation: there it is in the tonic. Each time this little phrase is repeated several times so that the reference is made clearer:

The organization of the thematic material in the Vivace shows a power and concentration equalled only by the first movement of Symphony No. 88 (1787). Haydn achieves the unity and diversity of his subjects by contrapuntal means, as he had done in No. 88/I. The first subject[1]

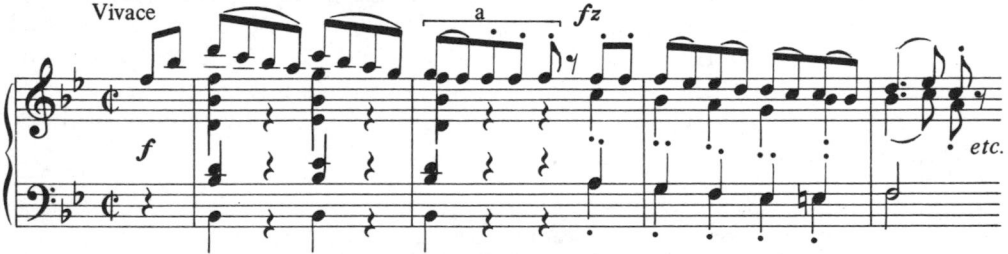

has a powerful upbeat, which Haydn accents in the second part of the opening phrase with a *fz*. The interplay between the accented upbeat and the natural stress of the first beat is exploited by Haydn throughout the exposition; in bars 39ff. we find

♫♩ ♫♩ , and at bars 49ff. ♫| ♫♩ ♫♩ corresponding to the first and second
fz *fz*   *fz*   *fz*

1 For a penetrating analysis of the rhythmic organization of this first subject, see Jan LaRue: *Guidelines for Style Analysis*, New York 1970, p. 111.

part of the theme. In the bridge passage to the dominant, the motif marked 'a in the first subject is worked into an inner part with itself and its inversion, and this corresponds to what is going on above and below this motivic transformation, namely a six-note phrase which is presented simultaneously with its inversion in the bass line:

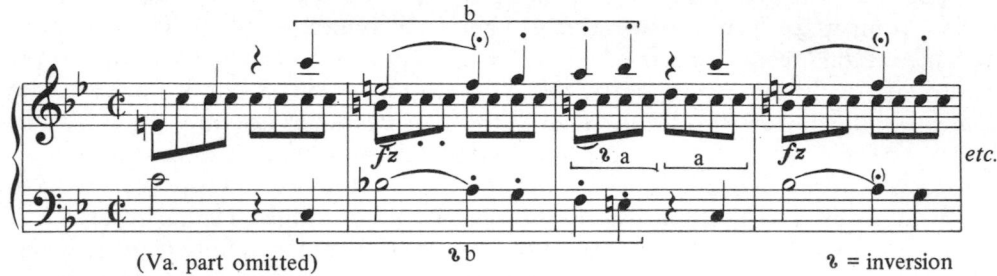

(Va. part omitted)   ℔ b   ℔ = inversion

We have noted that dance-tune quality of the second subjects in the first movements of Symphonies Nos. 99 and 101. Here in No. 102 we have a different kind of second subject. If those in Nos. 99 and 101 were marked by strong up-beats as opposed to the square on-the-beat quality of their first-subject partners, here in No. 102 the same principle in reverse is observed, viz. strong-on-the-beat accents for the second subject:

But whereas the second subjects of Nos. 99 and 101 were designed to release some of the tension generated by the previous part of the exposition, here in No. 102 the opposite obtains. Full of tension though the first subject and its extension was, the second increases the tension. Partly this is the huge contrast between *fortissimo* and *piano*, partly it is the automatic on-the-beat accents and partly the use of rests. In the closing material of the exposition, Haydn has already established a developmental technique with motives from the previous thematic material. The second violin part of the bridge passage which used motif 'a' and its inversion is now placed in the 'cellos and basses, over which is motif 'b' in inversion and immediately afterwards 'b' inverted plus 'a', viz.:

The development is a new milestone in the history of sonata form. Many of Haydn's earlier developments had reached high levels of tension, but nothing quite to compare with this. For one thing, the *forte* character of the main subject necessitates its being presented at the recapitulation in the role of a conqueror. Thus by its very nature it required a different approach than the witty, *piano* themes such as figured in other sonata movements with striking development sections such as Nos. 88, 92 or 100. In

No. 102, the two widely contrasting themes are interwoven in a deadly serious combat, which reaches a climax in the D minor canon. Even the main subject is stripped for battle:

If all this material was first examined intellectually in the exposition it is now treated dramatically in the development. The second subject is given wide scope here, as wide as the tonal field on which all this drama is enacted (C minor → E flat → dominant of F minor → A flat → B flat minor → C minor → D minor → G minor → C minor → C major → C minor → modulation back to the recapitulation). As the tension mounts, we may observe the means by which Haydn produces his battle. Rhythmic acceleration is one such device; the second subject is speeded up to prepare the way for the moment of greatest motivic tension, a closely worked canon which begins in D minor:

etc.

The momentum stops by means of a grand pause at bar 184, and the first subject now comes in C major, *piano*, which is broken off by the orchestra in a *fortissimo tutti*. This *tutti* carries the music slowly towards B flat major and the recapitulation, a phenomenal tribute to Haydn's ability to start the tension increasing all over again after such a climax as the canon. But Haydn's sense of broad structure is of an unfailing genius in this movement and indeed throughout the Symphony, and just when the music seems not to be able to stand any more pressure from within, Haydn abates the dynamic level, introduces a long drum roll (four bars) with a crescendo and propels the music over the top and into the recapitulation. In order not to break the dramatic tension, Haydn simply skips the *piano* repetition of the main subject – which in any case we have just experienced in C major in the development – so that the music can continue to roll forward in one unbroken *forte* wave to the gates of the second subject. Here (bars 238–52) are the off-beat *forzati*, too, that will colour the whole of Beethoven's writing, and the virtuoso treatment of brass and timpani (bars 243ff.) which will create *scuola* for the next fifty years. At the end of the exposition, the timpani had suddenly roared out, *fortissimo*, at the end of a long roll (bar 104); now, at the end of recapitulation, they mark out the upbeat to the first subject:

It is a device that Haydn will repeat at the end of the Symphony, binding the whole together: a detail, perhaps, but the fingerprint of genius. The ending of the first movement illustrates the compact force with which this whole movement is informed, various motivic fragments being woven into the music up to the very last.

We have seen that Haydn also used the Adagio as the middle movement of the F sharp minor piano Trio No. 40. There is something special about the symphonic movement in Haydn's entire *oeuvre*, and this extends even to the autograph manuscript, which has its own otherwise blank title page with only the word 'Adagio' in Haydn's hand; at the head of the actual music is 'In Nomine Domini' with which he was accustomed to begin his manuscripts. We now come to a very important later (Austrian) addition to Haydn's score, namely the use of mutes for the trumpets and timpani. These signs ('Con Sordini' for the trumpets and 'Con Sordino' for the 'Tympani' which Haydn usually wrote in the singular, 'Tympano') are missing from the Donaueschingen parts on British paper and also from the Birchall print, and unless Haydn gave then instructions to the effect orally, they are later additions. Mozart, when requiring mutes for *Idomeneo* in Munich, found difficulty in obtaining them and had to write to Salzburg to get them; the chorus 'O voto tremendo' includes parts for muted trumpets and muffled drums (for that is what the term 'con sordini' means for the timpani; in some cases, the word 'coperti' was used). Haydn incidentally can hardly have heard *Idomeneo*, which apart from the Munich première (and the following performances) was only given privately at the Palais Auersperg in Vienna during Mozart's lifetime. Like Mozart, Haydn may have found it difficult to organize the necessary trumpet mutes in London. The mutes, in any case, alter the character of the instruments completely, giving them a rather sinister, snarling tone which is very startling. As he often does with exotic instrumental effects, the muted trumpets and covered drums do not enter immediately: they are held back until the repetition of the first section, at one point (bar 56) the trumpets hold a single note (middle C) after the rest of the orchestra has stopped playing, a strange jet of dark colour. The use of muted trumpets and covered timpani in a symphony is one of Haydn's most daring orchestral innovations. It seems to have been an Austrian speciality.

The movement is a free variation form of a kind as unique in Haydn's symphonies as the orchestration (of which more later). The formal freedom is such that although on paper the Adagio looks perfectly normal, in practice it sounds like a rhapsody or, as the composer often called such movements, 'Capriccio'. Part of this rhapsodic atmosphere comes from the eccentric theme, with its constant rhythmic displacements, part comes from the equally eccentric orchestration; part from the harmonic range, which surpasses anything that Haydn had written in a symphony; and part comes from the exaggerated dynamic marks – orgies of *crescendi, decrescendi, forzati,* little accents, and so forth. The score sometimes looks like a work written fifty years later. The formal scheme is as follows:

A¹   A²   A³   A⁴

I → V   I → V   ♭III (flattened mediant major) → I + coda.

Haydn scores the first 'A' section (16 bars) for flute, oboes, bassoons and strings. In the middle of bar two, our ears are assailed by a new sound, a solo violoncello which soon begins to establish for itself a brooding series of triplets which give still another shade of dark to a colour already opaque and misty. One notes, too, that the wind instruments are used in a very full and free fashion, so that the shades of the orchestra all run together to form a vague and blurred painting. The sense of dark-hued yearning that this extraordinary Adagio calls forth reminds one – if there is such a thing as a visual transfer of music to painting – again and again of the humanity, subtlety and tenderness of Watteau.

A page from the autograph of Symphony No. 102 in B flat (1794) – the slow movement (Adagio). Note that Haydn entitles the bass line 'Bassi continui'; the trumpets ('Clarini') and timpani are marked 'con sordino'.

Originally Haydn started to write horn parts (bars 6–8) but then cancelled them. They, the muted trumpets and the covered timpani enter at bar 17. This cancellation of the horns is one of the many changes that we may observe on the autograph manuscript. Haydn was becoming more and more fastidious. At first he planned a gorgeous wash of colour to lead in the wind section at bar 17, viz.:

Later he substituted the most drastic of all contrasts: silence. But he may have wanted to save the effect for bar 26 (where there had been silence the first time, at bar 10): the sound of the oboes, bassoon, muted trumpets and drums is very unsettling. There was also more use of the muted trumpets: at bars 36–8, the first trumpet had an intriguing part

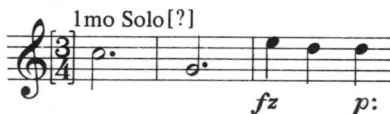

which coincided with a staggering enharmonic modulation – so unusual in 1794 (or rather 1795 when the players first saw it) that Haydn took the trouble to write, across the flute at bars 37–8, 'The Same Tone' ('Tune'? but probably he meant 'der selbe Ton', the same note). Again, it seems that Haydn's fastidious sense of orchestration decided the muted trumpets would make a better effect if they entered at bar 39, when the orchestral motion is at a standstill except for the swaying triplets of first and second violins. In the bar of retransition to the recapitulation, the dissonance was so odd-sounding to the band at Donaueschingen that they altered the 'cello part to read as follows:

Towards the end of the recapitulation, a deceptive cadence leads, at bar 54, to a *fortissimo* section in D flat major – a curiously disquieting effect underlined by the timpani rumbling below in sextuplet semiquavers which sound as inexorable and alarming as the Parisian tumbrils. It is after this D flat section that the trumpet enters on its middle C, snarling after the rest of the orchestra is silent (bar 56). The music gradually dies away, *sempre più piano*, to the ending, *pianissimo*. An emotionally ambivalent movement, this *Adagio* is of a visionary greatness. Generations of future musicians and music-lovers would find in it nourishment, comfort and inspiration.

Haydn made two significant changes in the fast Menuet (Allegro). At 46–9, he originally had the following:

The final version was made before the first parts were copied, or at any rate before Donaueschingen was made on its 1794 British paper. On the other hand, Haydn made another change in the orchestration of bars 31ff. after he had arrived back in Austria; the 'London' version is preserved in Donaueschingen and in the Birchall print. They have the following wind parts at 31–4:

The final version of 31–4 as well as 46–9 (or rather 46–8 since 49 was not changed) is as follows:

This quotation also illustrates a point in the recapitulation of the main theme. When Haydn first presented it, the orchestra reinforced the first beat of bars 1 and 2 with chords. The second time there is a delightful contrary motion in the flutes and bassoons and a new part for the horns, whose fetching quavers in bar 45 add a new and saucy lilt to this marvellous peasant dance: one can almost sense the tramping Breugelian wooden feet on the 'one' beat. It is also typical that Haydn should accent not only the first beat to relieve the anabrach tendency but also the anabrach itself the second time the theme is presented (*fz* at bar 42). There is a triple series of *ff* markings towards the end of the Menuet, stressing its heavily symphonic character. It is altogether fascinating to observe how Haydn manages to retain the dance character as well as making his minuets thoroughly symphonic.

The Trio looks forward far into the nineteenth century: its doubling of the oboe and bassoon at the octave with the first violin in between is Brahmsian. The role of the flute, which only plays a cadential drop of the third, reminds one of the *ars combinatoria* permutations. It is a curious effect and also slightly unsettling, like the permutations in the Trio of Mozart's 'Jupiter' Symphony.[1] What is this *commedia dell'arte* clown doing

1 See Leonard G. Ratner's interesting article, '*Ars combinatoria*: chance and choice in eighteenth-century music' in: *Studies in Eighteenth-Century Music: A Tribute to Karl Geiringer on his Seventieth Birthday*, London 1970, p. 359.

at this stately, beautiful dance? The clown, at any rate, is no more comic than Watteau's *Gilles*. In this quietly persuasive Trio, we feel that Haydn, like Watteau himself, is 'tendre et peut-être un peu berger'. . . .

The similarities between Beethoven's Fourth Symphony in B flat and the present work are many and on a deep level. Their two Finales are also much alike, even to the slowing-up of the main theme just before the end. They are also part of the great *opera buffa* tradition, which had such a profound and decisive effect on Haydn's symphonic style in the middle 1770s. No. 102's Finale is high comedy, and its success is perhaps the more surprising if one considers that the movement caps one of Haydn's most learned and serious symphonies.

Formally it is a sonata-rondo, that is with the 'development' starting in the tonic, and it is almost completely monothematic. There is a kind of second subject which is accompanied by repeated quavers in the manner of a 'parlando' Italian aria (bars 78ff., 234ff.). It is even funnier the second time, when Haydn has the trumpets holding a fifth through the texture, only to break into *fz* as they hold the notes: ♩ ♩ ♩ ♩ / *fz fz fz fz*. It is pure *buffo*. Since the effect of much Italian comic opera rests on the unexpected, this aspect of such a Finale is most important. Even the way the main subject gets to the dominant, via D minor, is entirely unexpected and amusing. The chattering woodwind in the 'b' section of the a–b–a opening is also *opera buffa*. Later the theme even stutters, first at bars 109f., where the middle strings first have ♪ | ♩ 𝄾 before the second violin starts out in earnest with its pattern of semiquavers ♪ | ♫♫ ♫♫. Then the music hiccups before the main theme comes in the second time:

The 'chattering' woodwind part is now reinforced by timpani (bars 140ff.), which adds a Falstaffian swagger to the whole. In the 'development' section, the music touches A major for a moment. It seems that it was this passage that inspired the Viennese correspondent of the *Allgemeine Musikalische Zeitung* to write the following note, dated Vienna, 1 May 1799:

> . . . Haydn once again directed two brand new [*ganz neue*] Symphonies at Count F's [Fries] that are very interesting. They are among his finest but are so atypical that one is dumbfounded by the composer's extraordinary powers of invention. The following is especially to be relished. The rondo theme of the one begins in B flat, modulates very easily into A major within a few bars and closes again right afterwards just as easily in B flat. [Jahrgang I, col. 544]

Pohl III (148) thought the correspondent meant 'As dur' and not 'A dur', i.e. A flat, and that the Symphony must have been No. 98, where the solo violin enters at the beginning of the development in A flat. Edward Olleson[1] thinks No. 102's Finale must be meant. What is interesting is that the Symphony was so unknown in Vienna in 1799.

---

1 'Haydn in the Diaries of Count Karl von Zinzendorf', *Haydn Yearbook* II (1963–4), pp. 56f., where Zinzendorf hears a concert at Count Fries on 5 April 1799. 'Le Concert dans un beau salon tres sonore. Toute la ville y etoit . . . <u>Symphonie</u> de <u>Haydn</u> . . .'

In this 'development' (which we place in quotation marks because it is really more of a pseudo development), there is a mock *fugato* on a derivative of the main subject, and then the two violins chase each other into the recapitulation, which Haydn deliciously varies by marking the first violins' entrance with a whiplash *fz*. The stuttering reaches a climax just before the end. The music slows down (the *ritardando* is written out in the score) and leaves the first violins to play a slow-motion phrase of the main subject. It is the next thing to Shakespearian humour, and even the sentimental *piano* repetition of the *ff* and *fz* passage has a poise and grace to it that is like the end of an Elizabethan comedy bars (272–97).

As the music hiccups (♪♪) and stutters its way to the end, even the kettle-

ff

drums tap out the first three notes of the main theme ♫ | ♩, just as they had done at

the end of the first movement. It is the most sensational of all Haydn's 'joke' finales, and we have completely forgotten how the Symphony began, the solemn profundity has turned to midsummer madness, just like the oft-quoted Swedish description of Haydn himself, with his lightning-swift facial changes. Symphony No. 102 is a miniature autobiographical sketch of its composer; it contains in its four movements the quintessential Joseph Haydn.

Symphony No. 103 in E Flat ('Drum Roll'/'Mit dem Paukenwirbel') (1795)

As Haydn was composing Symphony No. 102, he may have come to the momentous decision to stop writing symphonies after the 1795 season was finished. It is significant that he firmly resisted all offers to write a symphony after 1795, even the charming invitation from the Concert des Amateurs in Paris of 1802 (see CCLN 211). But whenever he did come to that decision, it was probably before he wrote the final-sounding 'The twelfth I have composed in England' on the title page of No. 104's autograph. It is perhaps not too far-fetched to consider the last three Symphonies in this light of finality: in each, Haydn intended to display another facet of his seemingly endless inventiveness. In No. 102 we have a Symphony which starts out as a serious, learned work and ends up with a display of Haydn's symphonic *opera buffa* technique. The slow movement was a daring experiment in new orchestral timbres. In No. 103 we have a number of novel experiments, too: the construction of a slow introduction connected to the main body of the movement in a fashion more complex and at a deeper level than any eighteenth-century symphony except Mozart's K. 543 in the same key; the composition of a monothematic finale of a tighter construction and a more relentless unity than any movement before the first of Beethoven's Fifth Symphony; and the conscious use of popular tunes throughout. The dance-like quality of the first subject is carried a step further in the popular cast of the second, with its oom-pah-pah accompaniment. In the Menuet there is even the imitation of a yodel. The themes of the second movement are profoundly eastern European, and whether they are in fact Croatian, Hungarian or Gypsy is in a sense immaterial to the Symphony. The theme of the Finale has also been traced as a folk song from Croatia. The point is Haydn's integration of them into the language of the international classical style, just as robust Hungarian dishes found favour with the fastidious Viennese aristocracy; they were a piquant change from the everyday fare. And there is one last detail in this Symphony that sets it off from its numerical fellows: the extended violin solo, probably written for the distinguished leader of the Opera Concert

Orchestra, Giovan Battista Viotti, with whom Haydn was on friendly terms. It is written, however, to delight the leader of any band, since it displays his tone, his musicianship and his good taste rather than any sort of empty virtuosity.

The introduction starts with a timpani roll. It is one of the most original beginnings of all symphonic music and we can well believe the correspondent of the *Morning Chronicle* that it 'excited the deepest attention'. Haydn marks the drum roll 'Solo' and 'Intrada' but assigns no dynamic mark to it. Nor does the London performance material at Donaueschingen (the timpani part is on British paper, written by Johann Elssler in London in 1795). Obviously there has to be a dynamic mark, but its complete absence here and at the repeat near the end of the movement suggests that Haydn may have left the dynamic 'interpretation' up to the performer. But what did the Viotti Orchestra play? The arrangement for piano trio by Salomon has < >, and this 'hairpin' has become the traditional way of performance. On the other hand, Salomon's quintet arrangement which also exists in his autograph, has *ff*, presumably followed by a long *decrescendo*. When this reading was first adopted in modern times by the late Hermann Scherchen in 1950, it proved enormously effective. Charles Rosen (op. cit., p. 348) disapproves of our having incorporated this *ff* reading into the main text of the new edition, giving the 'hairpin' as an alternate reading. He prefers the 'hairpin' version and adds, 'if the new edition is surely unwise to accept the *fortissimo* attack suggested by the piano quintet arrangement of 1797, it is certain that the timpanist should make this a very long and effective roll.' Probably no further source material will come to light to clarify the matter, and conductors may at present choose between Salomon's two oddly contrasting versions.

Without knowing the score, and listening to a performance with closed eyes, no one could possibly tell the metre of the opening:

It is as mysterious as the 'Be fruitful' passage from *The Creation*, but also full of foreboding; the oblique reference to the 'Dies Irae' plainchant may not have struck Anglican audiences, but it was clear to the Catholic world, and of course Haydn's earlier symphonies have the occasional reference to Gregorian chants (*incipit Lamentatio*, and so forth). The wind band chord clarifies the tonal world of the introduction at bar 6, but not the metre, which remains formless until the two violins start to play at bar 14; and even then it takes some time to establish a clear triple time.

The integration of this extraordinary Adagio into the main 'Allegro con spirito' proceeds at several different levels. Just before the second subject is introduced, we find a passage which reads as follows:

It takes us a while to realize that this theme is a speeded-up version of the opening notes of the introduction. Haydn places it squarely in context by having it follow in the recapitulation immediately after the whole introduction is brought in; and then we recognize it immediately, not least because it is now in the tonic:

In the middle of the development there is a half-cadence on the dominant of C (bars 107–111); it is sufficiently insistent to make us remember the end of the introduction, also a half-cadence on the dominant of C. Haydn then proceeds to bring in another speeded-up variant of the opening bars:

After the second subject in the recapitulation, the music changes mood in a series of tremolos which become increasingly sinister and menacing, dying away in a questioning diminished chord; whereupon the introduction itself enters. It is as dramatic as the last act of *Don Giovanni*, and another astonishing innovation, as new as the grim timpani roll that announced the 'intrada' once again.

The opening subject of the 'Allegro con spirito' has that curious division of accents which served Haydn often when trying to relate a three-four introduction to a six-eight allegro. We have seen an earlier example in Symphony No. 94/I. The upbeat character of this tune

is so pronounced that as in the beginning of the introduction, it is some time before we understand the music's pulse – here, in fact, it is in six-eight and not three-eight

. The up-beat feeling is further enhanced by the phrasing. (How necessary the introduction was in Haydn's scheme can be seen if one starts the Symphony with the 'Allegro con spirito'!) The metre resolves itself with the *tutti*, and Haydn's *Ländler*-like second subject, this time no stepchild in the scheme, is very much on the beat (we quote the recapitulation, in the tonic):

The integration of these two subjects, with their strongly contrasting rhythmic stresses, into a symphonic plan which is also calculated to include the introduction, presupposes as complex a structure as Haydn ever set out to erect. When dealing with an intellectual problem as variegated and deep-rooted as this, Haydn's music on the surface tends to sound extremely compact, even terse. It is astonishing that he could write a first movement so complicated, so many-sided and with so many structural problems to solve, and yet remain within the customary length. If anything, No. 103 is shorter than its companions. No. 94/I, which is not much quicker in tempo, contains 17 bars' introduction and 240 bars of 'Vivace assai', while No. 103/I requires a longer introduction (39 bars) but only 189 bars of 'Allegro con spirito'. It is not quite fair to compare Nos. 102 and 104 with No. 103, because both the even-numbered works have allegros in barred C, which in this case is slightly quicker than six-eight (No. 102 = 22 plus 289, No. 104 = 16 plus 278); but even allowing for this difference, No. 103's allegro is more compact.

Haydn originally marked the double variation slow movement Andante but later added 'più tosto Allegretto'; he made this change long after having left England, because all the London sources have only Andante, and so do the Continental MSS. and prints. This double variation, in alternating minor and major, drops the clarinets entirely. Haydn's players in London were patently not the best, and we shall see that even in the transmission of the sources there are problems with the clarinets which suggest strongly that these players were the weakest link of the 1794–5 British orchestras.

We now come to the problem of the melodic origin(s) of the two principal themes in this movement. Obviously we are forced to rely on the evidence of nineteenth-century researchers, since (as we have pointed out earlier) the peasants who used to sing such tunes no longer do so; villages in Hungary, where Kodály and Bartók found old people who could still remember the ancient folk-songs transmitted orally from generation to generation, now have other problems and different songs. The industrial revolution and two great wars have almost wiped out the living tradition of eastern European folk-song, despite the frantic efforts by the authorities to stem the tide. We learned some of the difficulties of tradition versus the demands of modern life on a long tour in the Roumanian provinces in the Autumn of 1960: one could see the old and noble traditions crumbling before one's eyes, defeated by the wireless, the tractor and the collective farm. We may mourn this passing of perhaps Europe's greatest, and certainly its most original, folk-song tradition, but our mourning is of necessity historical. With such totally altered social and economic conditions, how could one hope to keep alive (except artificially) a folk-song tradition hundreds of years old which was grounded in now forgotten wars, long forgotten invasions and (almost) forgotton feudal life?

Unfortunately, nineteenth-century researchers did not have the scientific accuracy or the impartial sympathy of a Bartók or Kodály. National prejudices and anti-Austrian (= anti-Imperialist) feelings coloured many of their findings. The Croatians tried to make Haydn a Croatian, the Hungarians a Hungarian. It was stupid and unhistorical but these researchers were caught up in a process over which, to some extent, they had no control. But it is to be doubted if the entire evidence of a Kuhač is to be dismissed out of hand. There is no doubt that the south Slavonic peasants did sing melodies extremely similar to those of No. 103's slow and final movements; just as there is no doubt that the whole *ductus* of the first subject is profoundly, completely 'eastern European'. The raised F provides a melodic line which is part of the Balkans' life-blood (E flat to F sharp to G and back again). Thus we can do nothing else but present the evidence as assembled by Kuhač in his monumental 'South Slavonic Popular Songs' and translated by Sir W. H. Hadow's little book.[1]

Kuhač established that the first subject of No. 103/I is Croatian (Kuhač III, 92; Hadow 46), and that the two melodies of No. 103/II are based on two folk-songs of the Oedenburg district, 'Na Travniku' and 'Jur Postaje' (Kuhač III, 100ff., Hadow 46). Oedenburg (Sopron) was the nearest large town of the Eszterháza district, and there are in the whole region Croatian, Hungarian and German villages. The two melodies are very similar and may derive from some common melodic root, now unknown.

[Haydn]
Andante più tosto Allegretto

Na Travniku

---

1 F. Kuhač: *Josip Haydn i Hrvatske Narodne Popievke*, Zagreb 1880; W. H. Hadow: *A Croatian Composer, Notes towards the study of Joseph Haydn*, London 1897 (reprinted in W. H. H.'s *Collected Essays*, London 1928).

An interesting point of orchestration is that Haydn relies heavily in both melodies on the bottom *contra*-C of the 'cellos and double basses, which once again proves that either he had five-string double basses with low C as the bottom string, or they tuned the three-string basses differently:

This old-fashioned orchestration is perhaps connected with the use of the old folk-songs. As the movement progresses, the orchestration, curiously, gets more and more modern, almost as if Haydn were escorting the old tunes through music history. *Maggiore II* (bars 85ff.) is the elegant violin solo, while *Minore III* brings in the trumpets and kettledrums for the first time in this movement. By now Haydn also always connects their entrance with some kind of surprise; it was a simple but always devastatingly effective device. *Maggiore III* is enchantingly orchestrated, with the 'toy music' that we remember from the 'Military' Symphony (see example overleaf). From this point to the end, the music remains in C major. There occurs in this section perhaps the largest deceptive cadence in Haydn's career. After a big *tutti*, there appears to come one of his beautiful, sentimental endings – over the tonic pedal point we remember so well from similar passages (such as in No. 97/II). At the very last minute the music modulates into E flat and the whole mood is broken. It is another of Haydn's jokes, and it is well prepared, the arrival in E flat being preceded by a *crescendo* which grows across two bars and arrives *fortissimo*. The final statement of the *maggiore* section has not only the murmering bass line

but an enormous timpani roll, also with a *fz* at the beginning of each bar. The whole movement strikes one as a (highly successful) attempt to write another 'Military' march-like movement which would bring the house down; for this reason the

[Symphony No. 103: Andante-Maggiore III]

sentimental journey was broken off and we end with rousing fanfares. We note once again the delicate balance between the very learned and the very popular. The first movement was a complicated formal structure filled with popular tunes, but still a serious movement on an unprecedentedly complex scale. The second movement is directly 'popular' but uses exotic eastern European melodies; it is so exotic that one expects to have the clarinets in C and the Turkish instruments of No. 100 – but that would have been a lesser composer's trick. Haydn was content to show to himself – because no one in London can have known the original melodies and only a few experts will have caught the 'Slavonic' twist of the raised fourth or the pentatonic construction of the second subject – how exotic eastern European tunes could serve to make an unabashedly popular set of double variations. In short, Haydn had done it again. The sheer abundance and fertility of his last three Symphonies will have astounded both connoisseur (like Dr. Burney) and the general public alike. No one had ever written such a series of symphonic works which were instant successes with press, public and *Kenner*.

By the time we reach the Menuet (the clarinets rejoining the band), it is clear that in some respects we are dealing with a folk-song symphony. If it is true that Haydn attempted to display his art in three final supreme efforts, it may be that this concentration on genuine popular melodies in No. 103 is quite deliberate. For here we have a genuine Austrian yodel:

Haydn presses the point home when, just before the first double bar, the 'yodel-rhythm' of bar two appears isolated in second clarinet, bassoons and horns, followed by its repetition in the upper woodwind. The joke

is made even more explicit when the yodel is turned gracefully into 'art music' and used as an elegant modulation to C flat major. (For the violins the composer adds the extra warning, 'legato'.)

The Trio was a unique opportunity for the clarinets to display their tone. Though Haydn is very cautious to double them with violins, the effect is very characteristic nonetheless. But something went wrong somewhere. The early German editions simply drop the clarinets in the Menuet entirely, and we shall see that in those editions the clarinets are very defective elsewhere in the Symphony. Were the London clarinets players unable to cope with these parts in the Trio? Haydn, interestingly enough, did not change the autograph, and we also have part of the London performance material (including, as it happens, the clarinets) copied out by Elssler in 1795 and later sent with newer string parts to Donaueschingen Castle. In the Elssler MS., the clarinet parts are as found in the autograph, which suggests that at the first performance they played what was written. Perhaps Salomon dropped the parts in the Menuet and Trio later (if indeed he was responsible for the André first edition of 1799), or perhaps the other German editions were made from unauthentic and unauthorized copies.

The Finale is one of the longest (386 bars) of all twelve Salomon Symphonies, precisely the length of Symphony No. 98's Finale, too. But whereas No. 98 ended with a delightfully diffuse Presto, No. 103's 'Allegro con spirito' is possibly the most concentrated movement of its kind Haydn ever wrote. It is based, according to Kuhač (III, 82; Hadow 46), on an old Croatian song entitled 'Divojčica potok gazi':

Haydn had the clever idea of starting the movement with a rousing horn call, almost like a hunting symphony. It turns out that this horn call is the accompaniment of the first part of the main theme:

The entire movement is based on the first subject (which continues, of course, into an a–b–a form). The transitions, most of the *tuttis*, the second subject – it is all derived from this tune or segments of it. It is a sonata rondo with very extended development. It is also one of the few times that Haydn made a major change in a finished composition. After the autograph was completed – perhaps even after the first performance – Haydn cut out the passage just before the final *tutti* (shown opposite and overleaf).

It is hard to see why he thought this witty passage in C flat, prepared by two whole bars of rests, would hold up the course of the movement; C flat was also a major excursion in the Menuet (quoted *supra*). But no one was more rigorously self-critical than Haydn, and out the whole section went (see p. 605).

The Finale is without doubt one of the great *tours-de-force*, formally speaking, of Haydn's career: the creation of a long movement on a single theme in which our

interest never flags; on the contrary, it is a Finale of unusual tension and strength. It is difficult to select details from a movement in which all the parts are so magnificently fashioned, but perhaps one seemingly insignificant one will show how carefully the fabric is constructed. Part of Haydn's great success, and later Beethoven's, in movements that generate this kind of tension is the rhythmic acceleration that accompanies a passage in which the tension is built up. Beethoven's Eighth Symphony has recently (by Cooper and Meyer) been selected for a brilliant analysis along these lines. We will confine ourselves to one quotation: the ending of the Symphony in the timpani part (which by the way is quite different from the 'cello and bass line). Here

603

[Symphony No. 103 : Finale]

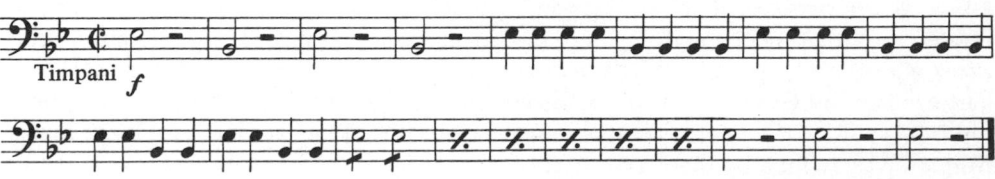

one can see in a few bars how meticulously Haydn handles even this lowly member of the orchestra to increase the tension as the Symphony draws to an end:

[Symphony No. 103 : Finale – see p. 602]

it is the kind of detail that Beethoven certainly did not miss. It is also the sort of highly sophisticated craftsmanship that almost always distinguishes the work of a great musician, great painter or great sculptor. *Deo Matematica . . .*

We may now continue our quotation from the *AMZ* review of Gombart's edition (Op. 91) of Haydn's Symphonies 100, 101 and 103, which we broke off at No. 101 (pp. 576–82).

As far as the third Symphony is concerned, some instruments must be missing throughout, probably the clarinets, as can be seen in several passages in the Finale and *inter alia* in the following extract from the first movement:

[Here, at bars 139–41, the clarinet parts really are completely missing. They are, as we see, not placed in any other instruments.] Moreover, this Symphony is much more carefully and diligently worked out than the second [No. 101]. Only in the last 'Allegro con spirito' there are again some careless passages, for example:

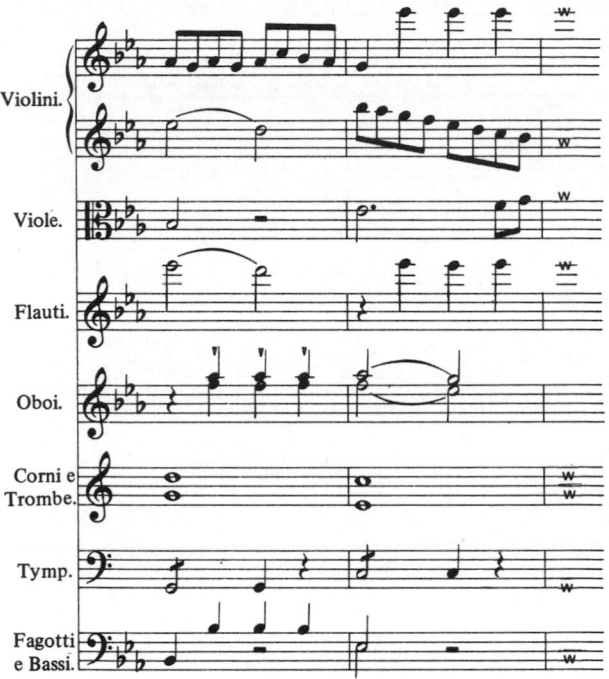

[This passage, bars 300ff. is substantially as Haydn wrote it, apart from the timpani being rewritten in old-fashioned transposing notation and the clarinets left out. *AMZ* objects to the way in which the violins are unresolved, i.e. the progression in bars 2–3 of the example from *d'''* to *b flat''*, also probably to the clash between oboes and trumpets at bar 3 and the doubled third between oboes and horns-trumpets at bar 5, and in the latter the part writing.]

[In the following two passages, bars 342ff. and 368ff., *AMZ* objects (1) to the dissonance between the bass line and the first violins, E flat against E natural; and (2) to the unresolved dissonance in the first violin, *d'*; both passages are marked with a cross; both are, again, substantially what Haydn wrote.]

608

All these mistakes and imperfections can of course be noticed during a good performance only by the attentive listener; they get lost, as it were, in the *melée*. Except that in *Haydn* there should not really be anything that ought to be lost in the *melée*; in a man of whom it is rightly expected and demanded – that *everything* is good. The reviewer regrets extremely that neither space nor time allows him in a similar fashion to point out the beauties and perfections in the Symphonies, which even among *Haydn*'s are two of the finest, and in which once again he found many a seemingly unimportant detail interesting and significant. Finally, we list here only *some* of the worst sins of the copyist or also the engraver. [There follow three columns of *errata*.]

We would register the astonishing fact that Gombart seems to have delivered No. 103 without *any* clarinet parts at all, for the *AMZ* notes, '*Clarinetti* missing altogether.' We do not wish to dwell any longer on the clarinet problem of No. 103, since we have Haydn's autograph and the authentic Elssler MS. at Donaueschingen Castle; but the history of these instruments in our Symphony will make an interesting footnote one day. Otherwise, we would note that *AMZ*'s objections to Haydn's grammatical oversights are the beginning of a long tradition in which German critics were to object to many details of this sort in late Haydn, especially in *The Creation* and *The Seasons*. When Haydn stopped composing they were to turn their objections to Beethoven. The kind of dissonance in which the violins have E natural against the basses' E flat was obviously intended since it happens twice in succession; a few years later no one would have noticed the passing dissonance, and certainly *AMZ* would not have thought it worth all that space. Some aspects of late Haydn were beginning to move faster than the critics, especially the Germans, understood. At this point the public was still easily attached to these new works. But in a few years not only the German critics but also a part of the public could no longer keep pace with Beethoven. These *AMZ* objections are perhaps the first hint of clouds on the horizon.

Symphony No. 104 in D ('London'/'Salomon') (1795)

It was not on the whole a typically eighteenth-century practice to attempt a motivic or melodic interrelationship between the various movements of a sonata, a quartet, a trio or a symphony. The very attempt at diversity would seem to preclude such a procedure. But as the eighteenth century drew to a close, we can observe a conscious attempt to make instrumental works more cyclic, though it may be doubted if many of Haydn's and Mozart's efforts were as cyclic as modern analysis tends to suggest. In Mozart's last four symphonies, however, there seems little doubt that he attempted to create a deeper element of unity within each work, achieved as one might expect by melodic, motivic and intervallic means. We have seen in the foregoing analysis of the Salomon Symphonies that Haydn was also at pains to unify his music in such a manner. The last London Symphony is without question the most spectacular example of such a procedure in a Haydn symphony. Here the interrelationship is fixed by three principal intervals, the fifth, the fourth and the second. These are established with the greatest possible emphasis in the fanfare that begins the Symphony. A small textual point: after the *ff* opening, which sets up the fifth above and the fourth beneath, the first violins put out the interval of the second. Since this happens in a piano text, Haydn later made a significant dynamic change in this passage after he left England (it is not contained in the Birchall print): he changed [C] ♫♩ |- ♫♩ |- ♫♩ |
p

to read *fz p* on each entry, thus drawing our attention to the figure. In order to show the extraordinary connection between all four movements we append the following graph in which all the themes have been presented in the tonic (rather than their first appearance, if they are second subjects, in the dominant).[1]

It is quite obvious that these intervallic relations cannot be fortuitous. We have quoted only those of the principal subjects, but the student will soon see that there are many

1 Friedrich Heller 'Haydns "Londoner Symphonie", D-Dur', Eine Analyse' in *Beiträge zur Musikgeschichte des 18. Jahrhunderts* I, 2, Eisenstadt 1971, pp. 182ff. Papendiek II, 297. Kuhač III, 98–100. Hadow 43, Schmid 290. 310f., Rosemary Hughes, *Haydn* (1950), p. 190.

more throughout the work. The whole has what the Germans call a 'quintig' or 'fifthy' character, which is often made more apparent by the accompaniments. It is a remarkably early attempt to produce an entire Symphony round three intervals.

Perhaps the introduction is the greatest of all Haydn's symphonies. It has an inevitable, inexorable quality about it which is only really apparent after the first movement, and indeed the whole Symphony, has been heard. Naturally it establishes the intervals; it also 'sets up' the opening theme, which appears in a much more important context following the stern D minor beginning. Never was a Haydn Adagio more vital to the construction of the whole. The lead into the Allegro is made more important by adding the Neapolitan sixth after the unexpected drop, not to the fourth A but to the fifth G (bars 12–16).

The main theme is in the great 'singing *allegro*' tradition of the Viennese classical school, in turn a synthesis of northern intellectual principles with southern (Italian) vocal melodies. We have quoted bar 19 (above) from the autograph; Haydn later uses

four tall *staccati*, as he gets into the movement and uses ♩ ♩ ♩ ♩ | ♩ ♩ | more and

more as an isolated motivic phrase; the three, however, give a subtle 'leading rhythm' to the next bar, and is the rhythmic basis for the transitional figure

Since Haydn intends to do so much with the opening theme, or at least a part of it, the second subject is postponed to the very end of the exposition; instead, almost the whole of the first subject appears in the dominant (bars 65ff.). This 'epilogue'-like quality of the second subject, here and elsewhere in Haydn's works, has always slightly puzzled critics, coming as it does so late in the formal scheme, almost as if it were an afterthought. It is very much an integral part of the subtle increase and decrease of stress, however, and is carefully designed to 'ground the tension' (Rosen) of the opening subject. It does this by being very much off the beat (also the accompaniment) and by being much more of a popular cast; it is postponed because the development will immediately start the first subject's tension again and will continue it, almost without break, till the recapitulation. It is just long enough to divide the exposition's earlier tension with the even greater tension of the development.

The development has always been much admired, for its overall 'sweep' and also for the concentration of its motivic basis (the six notes, bars 19–20, of the first subject) – though of course other elements of both subjects are used, too. The little theme at the end of the second subject – in our quotation of it above, we have given the recapitulation's version of it at bars 270f. – is combined with an accompaniment which, although it is only four repeated crotchets to each bar, contrives to sound like a derivative of bar 19. This illusion is fostered by the bassoon which plays (bars 120ff.)

♩ ♩ ♩ ♩ | ♩ ♩ |. Even repeated thirds in the second violin (139ff.) can be seen to come directly from accompanying parts of the exposition (bassoons, bars 50ff.). As far as the 'sweep' is concerned, Haydn achieves this by slow-moving modulations: B minor, E minor, C sharp minor → E minor, B minor, dominant of D. Almost the whole section is, as we see, in minor keys, an obvious foil to the predominantly major construction of the exposition and recapitulation. The symmetry of the development is an echo of the introduction, where the music went from D minor to F major and back to D minor – a self-contained harmonic element. In the development the centre of gravity shifts to the submediant, and that is the principal key until just before the recapitulation. In both introduction and development, the music goes away from the harmonic centre and returns to it ⌐⌐. It is harmonically the same inexorable pattern established by the whole tone of the introduction. The top of the modulatory arc in the development is when Haydn returns to B minor from E minor, and at the crucial juncture the timpani enter for the first time since the end of the exposition. (There is also a *ff* here for all instruments in Birchall's print, but no sign of the *ff* in the autograph or Donaueschingen; it is a sensitive and sensible dynamic addition, but did Haydn make it? Or is it the kind of thing he 'conducted' and was later transmitted to us by Salomon? The *ff* is also in the Salomon trio arrangement.)

The sense of development is continued in the recapitulation. It is not only that even the main theme is wonderfully varied by giving the second group of eight bars to solo flute and oboes, but the whole previous scheme is profoundly changed. The transitional figure quoted at bars 50ff. is now altered back to its original state as found in the main subject

And following this tutti, there is still more straight development of the main subject to take the place of its unaltered repetition as we encountered it in the dominant during the exposition (bars 244–52). Following the appearance of the second subject, the first is yet again brought in to take the place of the little codetta in the exposition. The last bars concentrate on the fifth interval, the horns sounding out the skeleton of the whole in semibreves

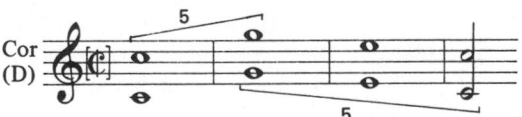

This was immediately preceded by the following:

The last three chords of the movement are in D without any third, another skeletal presentation of the fifth:

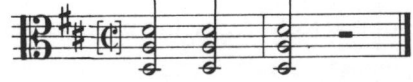

It is by now a point that hardly anyone with a basic musical education – which probably ninety per cent of Haydn's audience on 4 May 1795 enjoyed – could have missed.

The simplicity of the Allegro's formal pattern, and its effectiveness, are obvious. The following Andante, one of Haydn's best loved and most admired, is equally simple: a–b–a¹ A (tonic major) B (tonic minor) A¹. Haydn was aiming for the grandeur that comes with absolute formal simplicity. The main subject is orchestrated only for bassoons and strings; it has become so much a part of our musical heritage that we have forgotten what a perfect example of Viennese grace, warmth and craftsmanship it is. The contours are just irregular enough to be new and interesting; the *fz*, which happen twice in the first eight bars, break the symmetry but add two new points of stress where, without them, one would tend to accent, if only slightly, the next quaver, i.e. the beginning of bars 3 and 7. The little codetta (bars 33ff. quoted above) over a tonic pedal point is in itself a tender farewell, which Haydn will enlarge to heart-breaking dimensions at the end of the movement. 'B' is a 'minore' section, excitingly and mysteriously introduced by the main subject in minor: the *tutti* then breaks in with D minor and is, in a word, overwhelming. Never, perhaps, – not even in the magnificent 'Clock' *minore* – has a contrast of this kind in Haydn been prepared with more finesse and executed with more effect. Later, there is a bar of silence when Haydn reaches what ought to have been the cadence of his modulation to B flat; and this 'gran pausa', too, is immensely effective. In the recapitulation of the 'A' section there occurs one of the composer's grand flights of imagination. (Haydn rewrote bars 106ff.: originally the digression was to be even more longer and involved. The cancelled version, as much as can be read, may be seen in the appendix to the Haydn-Mozart Presse or Philharmonia score.) It is this kind of 'leap forward' into time that cause the distinguished German writer and musician E. T. A. Hoffmann to equate Haydn with 'romantic music'. It is, in fact, the great link between *Wiener Klassik* and *deutsche Romantik*; it made the change from Haydn to Weber less abrupt than we perhaps realize.

Rosemary Hughes writes so perceptively about bars 102–25 that it would be a pity to use any words but hers. After the apparently normal recapitulation, 'the opening melody . . . suddenly floats clear of the earth in an effortless modulation into a remote and luminous region somewhere between A flat and D flat, hovers there for a while, then clouds over enharmonically into C sharp minor, and quietly spirals down again through F sharp (major and minor) into the calm and steady daylight of the home key.' At the end the little cadential passage mentioned above (bars 33ff.) is expanded into a coda of sudden poignance. Perhaps it was very hard, after all, to say farewell to one of music's greatest forms.

The Menuet establishes the gay tone that will predominate for almost all the remaining music of the Symphony. The *fz* accents of the main theme are almost as pointed as in Gypsy music:

But withal it is highly symphonic. There is an innovation that rounds out all the timpani effects of the Salomon Symphonies: a long *crescendo* that begins *pp* and propels us with great excitement back into the *reprise*. At the end of the first phrase there had been a long trill in the melody instruments, but also, incredibly, in the first horn (playing, however, sounding *e'* since it could not negotiate *c sharp*):

This trill now assumes the character of a huge joke. It stops the music dead and then continues, twice as large as life, to round off the final cadence. We are in the grotesque world of comic opera, and a combination of Hanswurst and Harlequin at that:

The Trio, lightly scored (flute, oboes, bassoons, strings), is like a half-remembered country dance, 'tendre et peut-être un peu berger', with a lilting upbeat which for some odd reason manages to sound nostalgic and far-away. It is in the flatted submediant (B flat) but has as a coda a beautiful modulation back to D major and the *da capo*.

The Croatians claim the melody of the Finale, with its drone bass and the characteristic repeated notes of bars 10 (and 18). Kuhač says it is 'commonly sung' by the Croatian colony in Eisenstadt and also in Kopház near Eszterháza. In point of fact there really are Croatian villages, even today, in the district between Oedenburg (Sopron) and Eszterháza; E. F. Schmid names Homok (Amhagen) and Hidegség as well as Kopház (Kohlnof). In the last century since Kuhač produced his monumental research, this tradition has all but died out in these Croatian villages; and it is unlikely that the traveller today would hear Haydn's melody in the local inn.

Similarly, Eisenstadt was until very recently surrounded by villages with a predominantly Croatian population. Schmid names Trauersdorf, Oslip, Stinkenbrunn, Zillingtal, Wulkaprodersdorf, Siegendorf, Zagersdorf and Klingenbach. Haydn really could have heard such a melody there and imported it to London.

But there is an English tradition, for which we can locate no evidence, that the tune is a London street cry, variously identified as 'Hot Cross Buns' or 'Red Hot Buns'. We know that Mrs. Papendiek mixed up several of the Haydn-Salomon concerts in her memoirs. She says that at the opening concert of the 1791 season, Haydn conducted a new symphony. 'One of the movements was to imitate the London cries, and "Live cod" was to be traced through every instrument that could produce the effect. The cry began the piece and ended it, and Salomon was wound up to a pitch of enthusiasm beyond himself. The applause was great.' At the first concert of 1791, the two candidates for the 'new' Symphony were No. 92 (which cannot have incorporated 'Live cod', having been composed in Hungary in 1789) or 96, which is not known to have any such cry. Can Mrs. Papendiek mean the Finale of No. 104? 'Through every instrument that could produce the effect' may be an oblique reference to the fact that the horns finally get the melody at bars 221ff. And the movement really ends with the 'cry', if it is one: bars 309ff. We put all this vague and contradictory evidence before the public without being able to offer a word of encouragement. Even if we think that the tune sounds Balkan, with its repeated notes, it may after all have originated with the fishwives in London.

As this volume goes to press, a sketch to the Finale has turned up (*vide supra*, pp. 494–5). Through the kindness of Messrs. Stargardt in Marburg/Lahn, we are able to describe the sketch in detail. On one side of the page, which is a twelve-stave piece of English music paper, there are six and one-half pages of a sketch written in four staves in D minor, which may belong to an incompleted work. On the other side of the page we find the following sketch to the Finale. We see two interesting facts from this sketch: (1) that the principal theme was, in this first draft, much more asymmetrical and much more like a genuine folk-tune from the Balkans:

N. B.

and (2) that Haydn immediately conceived this theme as the basis for contrapuntal extension. In the event, the countersubject is different from the one here sketched:

The accompaniments to the theme – still in its original state of asymmetry – were at first in triplets and sextuplets, much in the manner of a string quartet or piano trio. Haydn soon decided that the theme would have to be reset into a more 'classical' mould and that the countersubject(s) would have to run in even crotchets and quavers. But the sketch does lend credence to the folk-tune origin of the theme.

Whatever its origins, it is a down-to-earth melody with a real drone bass such as Haydn had used with great effect in the Trio of Symphony No. 88. As the broadest possible contrast there is a long lyrical theme as the second subject, the phrasing of which is widely different from the small-segmented opening tune:

There is also a closing subject, here quoted when it makes its appearance in the recapitulation (bars 108ff.). This is, then, a sonata movement on a very substantial scale, with a development section which starts auspiciously by combining effortlessly the first and third subjects in double counterpoint:

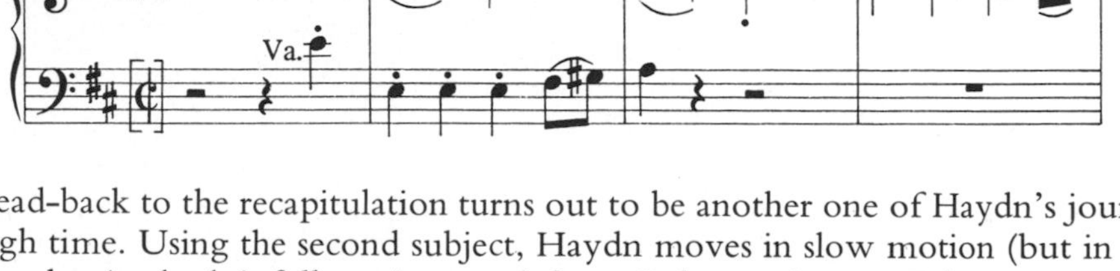

The lead–back to the recapitulation turns out to be another one of Haydn's journeys through time. Using the second subject, Haydn moves in slow motion (but in strict tempo: the *ritardando* is fully written out) from C sharp minor to F sharp minor. The latter key is never touched in root position so that Haydn can by a deceptive cadence slide into the recapitulation:

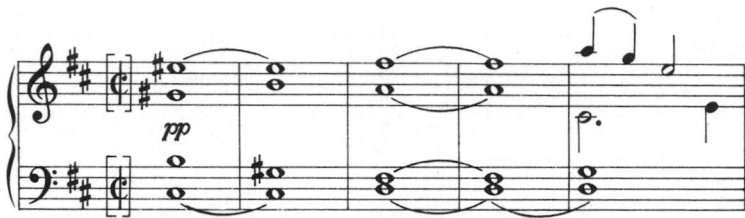

Haydn seems to linger sentimentally over this movement. Any excuse will do to prolong it: a little episode for the first flute and oboes – the last 'toy' music; a diversion in minor (bars 287ff.). But the time is up, and in a last *tutti*, broadly spaced, with the timpani thundering out the tonic pedal point in quavers, Haydn brings to a close this music, of which it might be said, like Florence Cathedral, that it was evidence of a heart expanded to much greatness. The last bars, *Deo Matematica*, are the fourth, the second and the fifth.

The autograph closes: *Fine Laus Deo*.

Haydn's impact on British musical life had been enormous; it was not for many years that a foreign musician, or indeed any musician, would equal it. Conversely, the London works – especially the Symphonies – formed the most lasting part of Haydn's *oeuvre. The Creation* became a controversial work in England, but never the 'Surprise', 'Clock', 'Military' or 'Drum Roll' Symphonies. One might have thought that Haydn would have been well content to rest on his laurels, and it is astonishing to see the final burst of creative activity that was to round off Haydn's last years in Austria, the investigation of which will be the principal feature of the subsequent volumes of this biography.

Index

Principal references are shown in bold type; references to artists, engravers etc. in captions to the plates are indicated parenthetically, e.g. (*pl. 5*). In documents cited in the text, variant forms (and misspellings) of proper and place names are frequently found; such variations and alternatives are shown in parenthesis, e.g. 'Erfurt(h)', 'Abingdon (Adington; Avingdon)' etc., as appropriate. For abbreviations of musical instruments, see p. 16.

Aachen 440
Abel, Carl Friedrich 25, 29, 102
Abingdon (Adingdon; Avingdon, etc.), Earl of (Lord) 22f., 24n., 29, 31, 143, 166, **270-2**, 275f., **289f.**, 317f., 356, **361-4**, 405
Abingdon, Countess of (Lady Charlotte Bertie) 290, 314, 392
Abrams, Miss (?) 37
Abrams, Miss E. (pianist) 148
Abrams, Miss W. (viola player) 148, 304
Abrams, Misses 44, 63, 148, 244, 303, 304f.
Abukir (Aboukir) 198
Adam, J. (*pl. 21*)
Adamberger, Valentin (tenor) 216
Aime, Miss (dancer) 79
Aitken, James 43n.
Akademisches Konzert (Jena) 507
Alberman, Eva 133, 491
Albertarelli, Francesco **39**, 69, 71, 78, 131, 139, 148, 150, 160, 162f.
Alberti, Domenico 417, 488
Albrechtsberger, Georg 204, 237f.
Allgemeine Musikalische Zeitung (Leipzig) 47, 194n., 351-4, 358, 360, 388, 393, 395, 397, 439, 449, 452, 505, 511, 560n., 566, 576-82, 593, 605-9
Allorto, Riccardo 417n.
Altenburg 524
Altes Frankfurter Intelligenzblatt 193
Alxinger, Johann Baptist 216; *Die Vergötterung des Herkules* 216
Amalia, Archduchess 224
American Philosophical Society 179
Amon (publisher, Heidelberg) 485
Amsterdam 228, 559
Anacreontic Society 41f., 44, 115
Ancient (Antient) Music, Academy of; Concerts of 31, 37, 41, 45, 83, 102, 131, 162n., 213, 247, 249, 275n., 276, 285f., 308, 513
Anderson, Betty 73n., 99n., 116n., 416n., 505n.,
André, J. J. 172, 194, 228, 250, 393, 439, 452, 490-5, 507, 536, 559, 561, 601
Andreozzi, Gaetano 49f., 146, 291, 297, 312f.; Aria 291, 297, 312f.; Rondo 49f.; Scena 146
Andrewes, Richard 306
Anfossi (Arfossi), Pasquale 146, 171, 217, (233), 235; Aria (unid.) 171, (233), 235; 'Dove, povera me' 146; *Le gelosie villane* 217
Ansbach 224
Antes (Antis; A-I-S; Dilettante Americano), John 184; Three Trios (str.) 184n.

Apponyi, Count Anton 314, 322, 455, 456
Aprahamian, Felix 406n.
Archiv der Stadt Wien 205, 224
Aretino, Pietro 39
Arne, Thomas 108; *Artaxerxes* 108; 'Rule Britannia' 259, 261
Arnold, Samuel 37, 115, 161, 170, 177, 182f., 213, 265, 279, 281ff., 289, 299, 364, 400, *pl. 19*; Auld Robin Gray 265; *The Banditti* 281; *The Castle of Andalusia* 281
Arras 270
Artaria & Co. 22n., 60n., 117, 140, 194, 206, 210, 228, 371, 377f., 392f., 394, 408, 410, 437-43, 446f., 466n., 480n.
Ascot 175f.
Ashbridge, Mr (musician) 299
Ashe, Andrew 131, 136f., 149, 157, 159, 162-4, 172f., 232, 238f., 242, 266f., 282, 295f., 297, 299, 304f., 313; Concerto (fl. and orch.) 295f., 305, 313
Ashley (singer) 213
Ashley, Mr (musician) 299
Aspinall, A. 119
Aston, Sir Walter (Willoughby), Lord of Forfar 275f., 405
Atheneum (Hartford, Conn.) 133
Atterbury, Mr 279, 364
Attwood, F. ('cellist) 256
Attwood, Thomas 155, 364
Auersperg (Auersberg), M. 215
Auersperg, Palais (Vienna) 586
Augsburg 31, 492-4, 559, 566
August (page at Eszterháza) 66
Austria 22f., 81, 124, 126, 153, 189, 192, 195-8, 206, 211f., 214f., 222, 231, 254, 289, 320, 358, 368, 407, 410, 413, 422, 434, 439, 445, 448, 492, 501-3, 506, 508f., 514, 520, 541, 545, 550, 556, 561, 563f., 567, 575, 582f., 586, 591, 598, 601, 618
Austrian National Library (Österreichische Nationalbibliothek) 35, 86, 196, 198, 211, 238, 285, 394, 483, 492f., 557
Austro-Hungarian Empire 195, 348, 502, 506, 551
Aylward, Dr 177
Ayrton, Dr 89, 177

Bach (family) 33
Bach, Carl Philipp Emanuel 62, 103, 192, 450
Bach, Johann Christian 29, (54), 55, 81f., 87, 138, 260, 310, 312; Aria (unid.) 54f.; Symphony for double orchestra 81f., 87, 260, 310, 312; Symphonies (Op. 18, Nos. 1 and 3) 260

Bach, Johann Sebastian 11, 103, 116, 127n., 216, 341, 359, 456, 502, 541, 571; *Christmas Oratorio* (*Weihnachts-Oratorium*) 341; Mass in B minor 502; Passions 502
Bach-Abel subscription concerts 29
Bacon, Roger 56
Badini, Carlo Francesco **39f.**, 79, 182f., 323f., 326, 328f., 339, 351, 356
Balet, Leo 407n., 409
Balkan tunes 479, 551, 598, 615
Bank of England 264f.
Banks, Sir Joseph 48, 75, 316n.
Banthurst, Major 260
Banti, Brigida Giorgi 28, 38, 248, 253, 257-61, 277, **278**, 281f., 286, 288f., 291-6, 298, 303-13, 317, 330, 334, 340, 371f., 374f., 482, *pl. 3*
Barbirolli, Sir John 55
Bärenreiter-Verlag 63, 201
Barlow, Mrs (dressmaker) 52
Baron, Hermann 565
Barrett, Charlotte 82n.
Barrett-Ayres, Reginald 12, 459n.
Barrie & Jenkins (publishers) 459n.
Barrington, Sir Johan 263
Barrymore, Lord 160
Bartha, Dénes 12, 53, 133, 221n., 238n.
Barthelemon (family) 168f.
Barthelemon, Caecilia Maria (also Hinchcliffe and Henslow) 168f., 182f., 412; Sonatas (Op. 2) 169, 412
Barthelemon (Barthélémon; Barthelomon; etc.), François Hippolite 152, **168-70**, 182f., 256, 400, 412, 537; *Jefte in Masfa* 168; Quartet (str.) 169
Barthelemon, Mrs (*née* Mary Young) 168, 182, 256
Bartholomew Fair 316
Bartleman, James 148, 170, 256, 303, 305
Bartók, Béla 403, 598
Bartolozzi, Francesco 64, 78, 278, 309, 402, 441
Bartolozzi, Gaetano 52, 276, 309, 441f., 457, 482
Basel (Basle) 453
Bassani, Giovanni Battista 103
Bates (Baze), Joah 83, 103, **276f.**, 418, *pl. 18*
Bates, Mrs (*née* Sarah Harrop) 276f.
Bath 177, 183, 266-9, 281, 297, 303, 318n., 418, 482; *Bath Herald and Register* 267, 269
Batthianyi, Cardinal 251
Baumberg, Gabriele von 200
Baumgarten (Baumgartner), Carl Friedrich **68**, 114, 182f.; Quintet (ob., v., 2 va., vc.) 68
Baux, Julien 248
Bavaria 490, 501
Beaumarchais, P,-A.-C. 397
Bechstein (piano makers) 416
Beck, Franz 422
Beck, Herr 197
Beck, Madame 197f.
Beckmesser (from *Die Meistersinger*) 545
Bect, Mr (maître d'hotel, Carlton House) 284
Bedford, Francis, Duke of 122, 281, **371**
Beecham, Sir Thomas 500
Beechey, Sir William (*pl. 8*)
Beecké, Ignatz von 215
Beethoven, Ludwig van 13, 24, 26f., 61, 63, 64n., 66-8, 73, 85f., 114, 126, 140, 153, 192f., 196, 198, 202-5, 207, 215, 217-9, 222-4, 242, 281, 294f., 303, 305f., 372, 376, 381n., 402f., 410f., 413-8, 422, 426, 436, 438f., 442, 448, 456, 458, 461, 479, 482, 485, 491, 500, 505, 507f., 516, 518, 521f., 526, 541, 544, 551, 556f., 559, 562, 570, 582, 586, 593f., 603, 609.
WORKS:
'Alla ingarese, quasi un cappriccio' ('Wuth über den verlorenen Groschen'; Op. 129) 294;
Aria, 'Ah, perfido!' 306, 372;
Cantate auf den Tod Joseph II, and *Cantate auf die Erhebung Leopolds II. zur Kaiserwürde* 192;

Concerto (oboe and orch.) 222;
Concertos (pf. and orch.): — No. 1 (Op. 15) 508; — No. 2 (Op. 19) 305; — No. 3 (Op. 37) 508; — No. 4 (Op. 58) 416; — No. 5 (Op. 73; 'Emperor') 73;
Concerto (v. and orch.; Op. 61) 85;
Deutsche Tänze (1795) 557;
Fidelio 86 373, 438;
Fugue 222;
Leonore, see *Fidelio* above;
Missa Solemnis 502;
Parthie (wind band) 222;
Quartets: — (Op. 18) 394; — (Op. 95; 'Razumovsky') 403;
Quintets: — (string; Op. 4) 456; — (unid.) 222; — (wind instr. and pf.; Op. 16) 508;
Septet (Op. 20) 26;
Sonata (horn and pf.; Op. 17) 438;
Sonatas (pf.): — (Op. 13; 'Pathétique') 451; — (Op. 14) 438; — (Op. 53; 'Waldstein') 442;
Sonata (pf. and v., Op. 47; 'Kreutzer') 66, 410;
Symphonies — (No. 1) 508, 544, 556; — (No. 2) 508, 556; — (No. 3; 'Eroica') 198, 500; — (No. 4) 593; — (No. 5) 516, 518, 551; — (No. 6; 'Pastoral') 575; — (No. 8) 603; — (No. 9; 'Choral') 541, 557; ('Jena', see Witt, Friedrich);
Trios: — (pf., v., vc.; Op. 1) 219, 411; — (string; Op. 3) 456;
Variations (pf.; unid.) 222
Belgium 195
Bellamy (Bellami), Mr (singer) 90f., 136, 147, 177
Bellamy Jr (singer) 170, 255
Bellantani (Bellentani), Gasparo 217, 221
Bellini, Vincenzo 126
Bell's World 83
Benda, Felicitas Agnesia (*née* Rietz) 78
Benda, G. A. 78
Bengraf, Joszef 433
Berchtesgaden 316
Berenson, Bernard 509
Bergamo 38, 511
Berlin 24, 27n., 62, 76, 109, 118, 123, 158, 188, 207, 228, 239, 301, 323, 405, 414n., 452, 488, 491-5, 499, 545, 557-9; Staatsbibliothek (Preussische Staatsbibliothek; Deutsche Staatsbibliothek) 207, 301, 323, 405, 484, 488, 491-4, 557
Berlinische Musikalische Zeitung ('Berliner Musikzeitung') 53, 170, 188, 192
Berlinisches Musikaliches Wochenblatt 188
Berio, Luciano 559
Bernadotte, General J.D. J. 198
Bertie, Lady Charlotte see Abingdon, Countess of
Bertien (Intendant) 85
Bertini, (Bertim) Jr 252f., 256, 304; concerto (pf.) 252, 256, 304
Bertoni, Francesco 329
Beverly, Lady 270
Bezozzi, Mr (oboist) 257
Bianchi, Francesco 248, 278, 281f., 286, 288, 291-4, 298f., 305, 482; *Aci e Galatea* 265, 281, 298f.; Aria (unidentified) 291f., 295, 311, 313; Aria (sop., with obbl. cor ang., bsn., hn., vc.) 311; Cantata (unid.) 293f., 309; 'Caro Padre, a te vicino' (duet) 75f.; *Castore e Polluce* 286; *Duetto Notturno* 291; Rondo (unid.) 310, 312; Scena (unid.) 305; *Scipione Affricano* 286; *Semiramide* 248, 281, 311
Bibiena, Ferdinando Galli 208
Biblioteca di Santa Cecilia (Rome) 511
Bibliotheca Musashino Academiae (Tokyo) 453
Biebrich/Rhine 411
Bigot, Marie 411n.
Billington (Bilingthon), Elizabeth 28, 31, 41, 69, 108, 113, **123,** 131f., 135, 138, 142, 145f., 163, 182, 275n., 311, *pl. 12*

Bindon, Miss 267
Birchall, Robert 490-5, 512, 531, 545, 561, 582, 583, 586, 591, 609, 612
Biswanger, Herr 129
Blair, Mrs 47, 76, *pl. 11*
Blake (musician) 89, 115, 142, 145, 283
Blake, Lady 112
Blake (Blak), Sir Patrick 112
Bland, George 183
Bland, John (publisher) 27, 31, 58, 61, 132, 161, 183, 228, 250, 258n., 409f., 449, 456, (*pls. 13, 16, 19, 20*)
Bland, Mrs (Maria Romani) 182f.
Blandford, F. M. 184n.
Blaze, Castil 39
Blount, Captain 95
Blumb, Mr 184
Bodenstein, Cyriac 206n.
Bodleian Library (Oxford) 149, 503n.
Bohemia 62f., 68, 138, 207
Böhm, Theobald 288
Bolack (Poleck), Mr (musician) 61, 159
Bologna 115, 165, 175, 199, 220
Bond, Mr (musician) 90
Bonfanti, Signor (singer) 282
Bónis, Ferenc 434
Bonn 24, 191-3, 194n., 205, 217, 222-4, 294, 439, 452, 490, 492f., 495, 505
Borghi, Luigi 142, 145, 182-4
Boßler (publisher) 228, 452
Bote & Bock 499
Botstiber, Hugo 80, 407n., 409, 461
Boulez, Pierre 141n., 406
Boyce, Mr (musician) 299
Boyce, William 104, 114n.; Serenata, 'Solomon' 114n.
Boydell, John 107
Braghetti, Prospero (singer) 281, 298
Braham, Mr (singer) 297f.
Brahms, Johannes 592
Brain, Dennis 29
Brambilla, Giovanni Alessandro 179
Brassey (Bressy), Nathaniel 22, 96
Braubach, Max 223n.
Braun, Josepha, Baroness 438
Braun, Peter von 438
Breitkopf & Härtel 11f., 16, 119, 140, 228, 267, 315, 323, 351, 354f., 358, 394, 396f., 403f., 407, 440f., 445, 449, 479f., 497-500, 508n., 509, 541
Brentano, Bovara & Urbietta 457
Brescia 43n.
Breugel, Pieter (the Elder) 529, 592
Breuning, Christoph von 193
Breval, M. ('cellist) 44
Brida, Signor (tenor) 281f., 289, 291, 293, 295f., 298, 303f., 310
Bridgetower, George Polgreen **65-7**, 83, 169, 256
Bridgetower, John Frederic 66
Bristol (Pristol) 269
British Broadcasting Corporation (BBC) 29n., 115, 418
British Evening Post see *St. James's Chronicle*
British Museum 27, 48, 57, 75, 119, 130, 159, 177n., 184n., 233, 251, 271, 318n., 323, 370, 377, 380, 382, 406n., 412, 434, 448, 452, 488, 490f., 494, 564
Britten, Benjamin 258
Broadwood (piano makers) 25, 99, 414
Broderip, Francis Fane 113, 312, 316f., 317n., 318n., 410
Broude Brothers (New York) 370
Broughton, Vernon Delves 25n.
Brown(e), Abraham 267
Brown, Miss 267
Brown, Hon. Mrs 267
Bruckner, Anton 502
Brühl, Hans Moritz, Count 93, 275, 318n., 358-60
Bruni, Signor (singer) 189, 213

Brünn (Brno) 100, 320
Brussels 129f., 140, 261
Bryant, Sir Arthur 23n., 215, 270n., 371
Buckingham House (Palace) 109f., 240, 283, *pl. 29*
Budapest 27n., 35n., 81, 146, 188, 202, 206, 254, 323f., 355, 395, 412n., 413, 433n., 459n., 489, 490-2, 494, 564
Buntebard, Mr 80
Burgenländisches Landesmuseum 27n., 74n., 169n., 207, 358, 373, 488
Burgtheater (Vienna) 51n., 215, 225, 230, 305, 438
Burke, Edmund 22
Burkhart, Franz 355
Burnaccini, Lodovico 208
Burney, Dr Charles 22, 31ff., 32n., 45, 49, 56f., 67, 74f., 81f., 88, 99, 100-4, 113, 117, 163, 167, 177, 182-4, 198, 230, 240, 252, 262, 283, 307, 313, 315f., 371, 401, 503, 600, *pl. 14*; XII Canzonetti 283
Burney, Charles Rousseau 74
Burney, Esther (Hetty) 183
Burney, Fanny (later Mrs D'Arblay) 56, 82, 163, 240, 313, 316n.
Bury, Agnes 47
Bute, Countess of 43n.
Byrd (Bird), William 33

Caesar, Julius 110, 263
Cairn, Mrs 66
Cairo 184n.
Calais 36
Calcagni (Caliagni, Caiagni), Signor (singer) 133f., 136, 139, 144-8, 160, 182, 370f.
Caldara, Antonio 103
Callas, Maria 323
Callcott (Calcott, Callcot), John W. 95, 177, 182f., 279, 364, 421n.
Calvesi, Signor (singer) 120
Cambini, G. M. G. 149
Cambridge 67, 103, 108, 112, 119, 236, 419n.
Cambridge Chronicle 108, 112
Campbell, Alexander 283; Twelve Songs 283
Campo, Marquis del 184, 441
Campo Formio, Peace of 224
Canterbury 320n.
Capol, Herr von 221
Cappelletti (Capelletti; Capeletto), Teresa Poggi 38f., 44, 45, 59, 69, 71, 79, 182, 329
Cappelletti, Signor (singer) 39, 45, 69, 79
Caravoglia, Mr (flautist) 75
Carisbrooke Castle (Newport, I.o.W.) 264
Carlton House 41, 43, 159, 240, 283ff., 288, 300
Carnegie Hall (New York) 53
Carolina, Queen (of Naples) 196
Caroline, Princess (of Brunswick, later Princess of Wales) 282, 300f., 314f., 484, *pl. 10*
Carpani, Giuseppe 73, 84, 275n., 317n.
Carr, Mrs 267
Carracci, Annibale 27n.
Carter, Charles Thomas 182f., 400
Cartellini, C. A. 305; Oratorio, *Gioas Re di Giuda* (305)
Casali, Signor (dancer) 39, 79
Casentini (Cassentini), Anna (*née* Borghi), 120, 182
Castelcicala, Prince 35, 38, 184
Castelli (artist) (*pl. 4*)
Casti, Giovanni Battista (poet) 126n.
Castiglioni, Niccolò 120n.
Cathcart (Catheart), William (Lord) 564f.
Caulfield, J. & H. 440, 442
Celestini (singer) 182
Cervetto, Mr (musician) 283
Champness, Mr (singer) 170
Chapman, Roger E. 202n.
Charles II (of England) 361

Charity Children 173f.
Charlotte, Queen (of England) 23, 25n., 31, 41, 43, 83, 104, 170, 172, 213, 270, 283-5, 403, 405
Charlotte Augusta (Princess Royal) 270, 283
Charterhouse School 78n.
Chatham, Earl of 259
Chelsea College 81, 163, 182
Chemische Druckerey (Vienna) 434, 536
Cheney, Captain 260
Cherubini, Luigi 303, 334, 494; Quartetto (vocal) 303
Chevardière, de la (Paris publisher) 229
Chianchettini & Sperati (publisher) 89
China 315f.
Chinnery, George (*pl. 23*)
Chopin, Frédéric 62
Christ Church (Oxford) 67
Christie's (auction-house) 441
Christoff, Boris 323
Cimador, Giambattista **266f.**, 361, **482**; *Ati e Cibele* 266
Cimarosa, Domenico 87, 101, 126, 148, 198, 216, 221, 286, 305, 309;
    WORKS:
    Amor rende sagace 216;
    Aria (unid.) 87, 293, 305, 309, 313;
    Il Credulo 221;
    Duetto (unid.) 286;
    L'impresario in angustie 221;
    'Infelice, ch'io sono' (Rondo) 75f.;
    Il matrimonio segreto 126n., 502;
    Il maestro di cappella 198;
    Il pittor Parigino 126n.;
    Rondo (unid.) 313;
    Terzetto (unid.) 141
Cipriani, Giovanni Battista 29
Clagget, Charles 159, 418
Claremont (Clermont, Lord 135
Clarence (Clarens), Duke of 112, 127
Clari, Giovanni 103
Clemens August, Elector of Cologne 24
Clement, Franz 78, **85f.**, 90, 183, 216; Concerto (v. and orch.; unid.) 85
Clementi (Clemetz), Muzio 27, 44, 46, 52, 61, 69, **73f.**, 116, 136, 139, 151, 182f., 214, 253, 256, 267, 282, 291, 297f., 302, 305, 309, 313, 320, 358f., 386, 396, 408, 413f., 416-8, 439, 441f., 450, 452, pl. 13; Concerto in C (pf. and orch.) 417; Sonatas (pf., Op. 33) 417, 441; Symphony (Overture; unid.) 12, 61, 69, **73f.**, 136, **291f., 297f., 302, 305**, 313; Trios (pf., v., vc.; Op. 27, Op. 29) 417n.
Clough, F. F., and Cuming, C. J. 354n.
Cobbett's Cyclopedic Survey of Chamber Music 411n., 459n., 470
Coblenz (Koblenz) 195, 413n., 456n.
Coburg, Prince of 222
Colloredo, Franz, Count 196
Colmar 13
Cologne (Köln) 13, 195
Colonna, Giovanni Paolo 103
Coltellini, Marco 329
Columbia Records (C.B.S.) 184n
Concert des Amateurs 594
Concert Spirituel (Paris) 24n., 66, 76
Condell, Mr (musician) 90
Conservatoire (Paris) 254, 301, 324
Conservatorio 'B. Marcello' (Venice) 142
Cooke, Dr Benjamin 177, 279
Cooper, Grosvenor, and Mayer, Leonard B. 530n., 545, 603
Copenhagen 37n.
Corelli, Archangelo 27n., 33, 45, 169, 513
Corri (Choris), Domenico 66, 155, 182f.
Corri, Mrs N. (singer from Edinburgh) 312
Corri (Corry, Choris), Sophia (marr. Dussek) 29, 62,

65f., 70, 79, 86f., 131, 133f., 139, 144f., 147-50, 152, 155-7, 160-2, 170, 182f., 312
Corri & Dussek (Corri, Dussek & Co.) 62, 233, 254, 257, 312, 315, 392, 403, 412, 455-9, 460n., 466n., 480, 515
Covent Garden 24, 31, 68, 108, 113f., 137, 213, 274, 281, 300, 317, 364
Coutts (bankers) 119
Cowes 262, 264
Crabb Robinson, see Robinson
Craig Bell, H. 411n.
Cramer, Carl Friedrich (ed. of *Cramers Magazin der Musik*) 26, 63n.
Cramer, Charles, Jr (violinist) 69, 76, 145f., 304, 306
Cramer, François (Franz; violinist) 299, 304
Cramer, J. B. 76, 140, 155, **182f.**, 244, 303, 305f., 314, 413f., Concerto (pf. and orch.; unid.) 244, 303, 306, 314
Cramer, Mrs (violinist) 70, 306
Cramer, William (Wilhelm; leader) 31, 44, 48, 69, 76, 89-91, 115, 132, 135, 138, 142, 145f., 166, 170, 183, 213, 252, 255f., 258, 282f., 289, 296f., 299, 303-6, 311, *pl. 20*
Cranz (publisher) 534
Crewe, Mr and Mrs 316n.
Croatia(n) 551, 594, 598, 602, 614
Croft-Murray, Edward 244, 418
Crofts (composer) 104
Crosdill (Grosdill), John 90, 183f., 236n.
Crosse, John (*Account . . .*) 55, 78n., 84, 89, 278, 281, 356, 449
Crotch, William (organist) 67
Crouch (Croutch), Anne Mary 89, 92, 111, 183, 213
Crowe, Mr 91
Crown & Anchor (tavern, London) 29, 41, 92, 115, 364
Cudworth, Charles 448n.
Culliford, Rolfe & Barrow (publisher) 503
Cumberland, Duke of 44, 64, 68, 119
Cummings Collection 66
Curtis, Sir Roger 258
Custine, General 195
Cuyler, Louise E. 468n.
Czernin, Counts 93
Czernin Castle 202
Czerny, Carl 413, 416

Dahmen, W. (horn player) 249-51, 253
Daily Advertiser 43
Dal Piano (engraver) (*pl. 4*)
Dale, J. 417n.
Dall, Miss 143
Damen (Dahmen; Damer; Domen; Damea; etc.), J. A. (violinist) 60-2, 70, 108, 136, 147f., 155, 162f., 164, 171, 235, 242, 245f., 249, 493
Damen (Damea) Jr ('cellist) 26n., 108, 131, 139, 159, 235, 239, 242f., 245f., 257
Damen, Messrs 108
Danby, Mr 300
Dance, George 114, 167, **244**, 260, 276, 278, (*pls 1, 14, 17*)
Dance, Mr (violinist) 89, 127
Dance, William 276
Daniell, William (engraver) 244, 260, (*pls 17, 18*)
Da Ponte, Alessandro 482
Da Ponte, Lorenzo 38f., 126, 248, 254, 298, 306, 311f.; *Merope* 297
Darmstadt 207
David, Anton (basset-horn player) 63
Davide (David, Davidde), Giacomo 28f., **38f.**, 41, 43-6, 48-50, 60-6, 68-73, 75f., 78-85, 87, 90, 182f., 232, 271n., 316f., 329, 334-8, 340, 370, *pl. 2*
Davies (Devis), Cecilia 182f.
Davies, Marianne 183

Dayes, F. (*pls IV, 29*)
Dea, Mr 265
Deiters, Hermann 27n.
Deleval (de la Valle, Delavel), Madame 131, 133f., 137, 148, 156, 184, 239f., 246
Deldevez, E.-M.-E. 549
Deller, Dr 277
Demachi (Demacchi), Giuseppe (violinist and comp.) 65, 79; Symphony (unid.) 65
Demmer, Herr (singer) 197
Denis (Denys), Abbé Michael (S. J.) 200f.
Depres, Josquin (Tusquin) 55
Derby 92
Derbyshire 260; Derbyshire Cavalry Regiment 260, 488f.
Deutsch, O. E. 12, 63n., 93, 108, 121n., 172n., 183, 207, 216, 225, 266n., 359, 376, 416n., 438n., 456n., 483, 505n.
Devienne (Devisne, Devisme), François 257, 286, 309, 313; Concertante (fl., ob., bsn., hn.) 257, 309; Concertante (fl., ob., bsn.) 313; Concerto (bsn. and orch.) 286
Devonshire, Duchess of 181
Diary; or Woodfall's Register, The 50, 63, 65, 70, 76f., 80, 84, 89n., 135, 137, 143, 146f., 149, 152, 156, 173, 214
Dies, Albert Christian 21, 44, 46-8, 54, 58, 71f., 74, 87f., 96, 98, 116, 126, 127n., 128, 150-2, 166, 173n., 174, 178f., 192, 200, 207, 220, 231, 261, 265, 267f., 286f., 309f., 317f., 319n., 320, 334, 410, 412, 440, 452, 470, 503
Diettenhofer (Diettenhoffer), Joseph **97f.**, 117, 182f.
Ditters von Dittersdorf, Carl 189f., 207, 225, 503, 506
Doblinger, Verlag 16, 24n., 27n., 29n., 184n., 355, 356n., 357n., 371, 375, 409, 428n., 455, 484n., 487n., 489, 539, 558
Dobson, Austin 82n.
Donaueschingen 288, 375, 487, 490-5, 527, 531, 574, 582, 586, 588, 591, 595, 601, 609, 612
Donelli (Dorelli?), Madame 265
Donizetti, Gaetano 126, 328
Dorelli, Signor (castrato) 39, 182f., 265, 329
Dorival, Mlle (dancer) 39, 69, 72, 77
Dorset, Duke of 23, 167
Dover (Dower) 21, 36
Dragonetti, Domenico 26n., 67, 140, 278, 282, 286, 288, 291f., 309f., 312, 441; Capriccio (cb.; and orch.?) 309; Concerto (cb. and orch.) 310; Concertone (cb. and orch.) 286, 291f., 309f., 312
Dresden 58, 116, 158, 297n., 320, 371
Dressler, Mr (double-bass player) 163f.
Drury Lane Theatre 31, 112, 281
Duncan, Lady Mary 39f.
Ducrest, Marquise 46, 235f., 241, 244, 256f.
Dufour, Miss (singer) 314
Duport, Jean Pierre 76
Dupuis, Thomas Saunders 89, 106, **170,** 177, 183, 279, 282, 299, 364, *pl. 15*
Durante (Duranti), Francesco 33, 103
Durazzo, Count Johann Jakob 183
Dussek (Dusseck), Johann Ladislaus 29, 44, 49f., 54, **62,** 65, 70, 75, 82, 84, 86, 131, 136, 138, 144, 148, 155f., 162, 165, 182f., 232f., 241, 249f., 254, 256f., 282, 286, 312, 315, 331, 412-4, 416, 418, 441, 455-8, 515, *pl. 16*; WORKS:
Concertante (pedal harp and pf.) 49f., 75;
Concerto (pf. and orch. unid.) 62, 82, 155f., 241, 249f., 254, 256f., 286, 312;
Concerto (harp and orch.) 312;
Grand Sonata (pf.; Op. 43) 441;
Second Grand Concerto in F(pf.) 233f.;
Sonata (pf.; unid.) 79;
Three Sonatas (pf. and v.; Op. 13) 441;
Quartet (Sonata; pf., v., va., vc.) 65

Düsseldorf 195
Dvořák (Divorsack; basset-horn player) 63, 75

Eck, J. F. 293, 304; Concerto (v. and orch.) 293, 304
Eberl, Anton 508
Eck, Franz 293
Edinburgh 29, 129, 131, 257, 312, 401
Editio Musica 355
Edition Adler 558
Edition Eulenburg 497-500, 523, 534
Edling 126n.
Eibner, Franz 438n., 487
Einstein, Alfred 480n.
Eisenstadt 27n., 74n., 97, 113, 153, 169n., 195, 207, 210, 217-21, 224, 229n., 237, 264, 358, 373, 394, 413, 479, 484, 488f., 560n., 610n., 614
Eisner-Eisenhof, Angelo von 248n.
Eley, Mr (clarinet player) 44, 55
Elliott (organ builder) 303
Elssler (Elßler), Johann 72, 140, 196, 215f., 221, 224, 231, 309, 320, 324, 372f., 394, 405, 407n., 417n., 428, 438, 448, 452, 456, 485, 490-5, 527, 531, 541, 557f., 561f., 564, 574, 582, 595, 601, 609
Engl, J. E. 297n.
English Folk Dance & Song Society 564
Epp, Herr (singer) 197
Eppinger, Heinrich (violinist) 225, 228
Erard (piano maker) 414f.
Erfurt(h) 117, 170
Erskine, Mr (barrister) 289f.
Ertmann, Dorothea, Baroness von 411
Esterházy (family) 98, 217, 219, 237, 261, 285, 456; band (orch., virtuosi) 68, 199n., 230, 537, 552; copyist 453, 490, 527; establishment 541; Princes 35, 98, 261, 285, 394; for individuals, Archives, Castle, see below
Esterházy, Countess Josephine 219
Esterházy, Count Nicolaus 199
Esterházy, Prince Anton 30, 37, 89, 98, 105, 122f., 153, 158, 166, 175, 193, 214, 219, 221, 223, 231, 237, 252, 261, 276, 329, *pl. 24*
Esterházy, Prince Nicolaus I 66-8, 97, 102, 126, 133, 199n., 201, 219, 223, 238n., 281, 504
Esterházy, Prince Nicolaus II 38, 66n., 157, 219, 237, 261, 320, 424
Esterházy, Prince Paul Anton 110, 539
Esterházy, Princess Leopoldine (later Grassalkowic[z]) 224
Esterházy, Princess Marie Hermenegild (*née* Princess Liechtenstein) 38, 237, 261, 314, 409, 424
Esterházy, Princess Marie Therese (*née* Countess Hohenfeld) 38, 205-7, 225, **276,** 409, 417, *pl. 25, (pl. 26)*
Esterházy Archives 11, 27n., 32n., 67, 81, 146, 188, 194n., 202, 206, 225, 254, 323, 355, 412n., 413, 428, 452, 454, 489-94, 505, 531, 541, 558, 561, 574
Esterházy Castle (Eisenstadt) 113, 219, 413; see also Eszterháza
Eszterháza (Estoras; Esterhas; Esterhaz; etc.) Castle 11, 27, 28n., 98, 109, 115, 122, 126, 133, 141, 166, 187, 194, 196, 199, 202, 221, 225, 229, 238, 262, 264, 281, 288, 311, 329, 334, 356, 369, 377, 411, 413, 425, 434, 450, 458, 484, 487, 504f., 531, 549f., 598, 614
Estwicke, Mr (M.P.) 289
European Magazine 55, 93, 109-11, 114, 138, 272, 301, 418
Evening Mail 300
Evesham 74, 116
Exeter 100
Eybler, Joseph 225, 237f.; Quartets (string; Op. 1) 237f.
Eyre, Sir James 119

Fairfield (Manchester) 184
Falck, J. C. 178
Falstaff 478, 594
Farington, Joseph 110, 118, 167, 179, 258, 264, 270, 274, 276f., 278, 371
Farnham (Feernham) 264, 269
Feder, Georg 12, 440, 503n.
Federici (Friderici), Vincenzo **38**, 60, 71, 182, 248f., 282, 289, 291, 298; Cantata (unid.) 78; *Orpheus & Euridice* (ballet) 59, 71, 78; Overture (Symphony; unid.) 291; Overture in the Tragic Style 79; Sextet (unid.) 79
Fekete, M. de 215
Ferdinand, Crown Prince (later Emperor) of Austria 196
Ferdinand II (IV) of Naples 35, 65, 79, 99, 159, 161, 194, 196, 284f., 318n., (441), 453-5, 539, 549f., 562, 563
Ferlendis (Ferlendy), Giuseppe 278, 281, 307-11, 313, 330, 377; Concerto (cor ang. and orch.) 311f.; Concerto (oboe and orch.) 307
Fernhill (house, I.o.W.) 263
Ferrari (Ferari), Giacomo Gotifredo **154f.**, 241, 254, 306; Aria 'Or dell' avverse sorte' 307; Duet (unid.) 155, 201, 306, 309; Scena, 'Se mi tormenti, amor' 155
Fétis, F. J. 62
Field, John 309, 311, 396
Fiorillo (Fiorilo; viola player) 235, 239, 241f., 245, 493; Chaconna 241, 244
Firnhaber, Johann Christian 151
Fischer (Fischar), Johann Christian 25, 163, 183f.
Fischer, Ludwig 232, 235, 238-47, 249-52, 255-7
Fiske, Roger 114n., 281, 323
Florence (Italy) 133, 195, 323f., 417n., 500, 503, 618
Florio (Floria), G. (flautist) 164, 236n., **297**
Florio, Jr (singer) 233, 235, 243
Florio, Pietro Grassi 297n.
Flötenuhren (musical clocks) 201f.
Fluger (Flieger, Flugar; clarinet player) 48, 64, 551
Forbes, Elliot 126n., 373n., 566
Forfar, Lord of, see Aston, Sir Walter
Forkel, J. N. 26
Forster, William 42, 82, 119f., 541
Foundling Hospital 207
Fox, Charles 181, 272, 371
Framéry, de 119
France 22, 55, 64, 92, 95, 99, 103, 114, 180, 198, 214f., 222, 234-6, 240, 260, 270, 272, 274, 293, 393, 407, 414, 441, 502-4, 541
Francis, Mrs (later Broome) 163
Franck, César 503; Symphony in D minor 503
Frankfurt-am-Main 24, 98, 156, 166, 175, 192-4, 212, 228, 274, 320, 536
Frankfurter Staats-Ristretto 193, 536
Franklin, Benjamin 183
Franz (Francis) II, Emperor 14, 158, 195-7, 206, 211, 217, 261, 318
Franz Joseph (Francis Joseph) I, Emperor 486
Fraser (Frasers?), William 95, 178
'Fräulein Pepi', see Genzinger, Josephine
Freddy, Gianluigi de 208
Freemasons 63, 238, 347; — Hall (London) 37, 41, 238n., 249, 299; — lodge 'Zur wahren Eintracht' (Vienna) 456
Freemason's Tavern (London) 364
Freimüthige, Der 151
Freudenthal 64n.
Freyhaus Theater (Vienna), see Theater auf der Wieden
Friebert(h), Joseph 320
Friederike Charlotte Ulricke, Princess of Prussia (Duchess of York) 22f., 109f., 118, 161, 169, 177, 243f., 248, 283, 285, 401, 412
Friedland, Bea 480
Friedländer, Max 394
Friedrich August II (Elector of Saxony) 58

Friedrich Wilhelm II (King of Prussia) 76, 109, 118, 123, 158, 231, 285
Fries (Frieß), Moritz, Count 105, 207, 224, 593
Fries & Co. (bankers) 30, 59, 98
Frike (Frick), Philipp Joseph 182f.
Frimmel, Theodor von 189n., 456n.
Fuchs, Aloys 324
Fuhrich, Fritz 320n.
Fürstenberg, Prince 215, 288, 487
Fürstenberg, Princess Caroline 215
Fürstenberg Archives 275, 490ff.
Furtado, Master 256
Fuseli, Henry 259
Fux (Fuchs), Johann Joseph 103, 202, 218, 470

Gaden 575
Gallini, Sir John 29, 38, 43, 47f., 54, 59, 68, 70, 72, 74, 77f., 81, 96-8, 122, 124, 128, 138, 182, 186, 194, 231, 254, 265, 301, 316, 324, 354, 357, 361, 412, 483
Galuppi, Baldassaro 33
Galvani Fratelli 540
Garabaldi, Mr (double-bass player) 248
Gardiner, William 275
Garat, Pierre-Jean 394; *Chanson Bacchique* 394
Garrick, David 34, 264, 364
Garrow, Mr (lawyer) 290
Gassmann (family: Therese, sister, mother) 211
Gassmann (Gasman; Gaßmann), Florian Leopold 104, 226, 503
Gassmann, Therese 211, 225f.
Gautherot, Madame (violinist) 46, 49f., 161
Gayl (publisher) 228
Gazetteer, The 42-6, 48, 62f., 65, 67, 73, 75, 80f., 108
Gazzaniga (Gazaniga), Giuseppe 286, 288, 295; Aria (unid.) 286, 295
Geiringer, Karl 64, 202n., 214, 267, 275, 400, 403, 407, 409, 459n., 468n., 558, 570, 592
Gelinek, Joseph (Abbé) 217f.
Geminiani, Francesco 33, 45, 169, 513
General Evening Post 29, 259, 277f.
Gentleman's Magazine 93, 272, 276
Genzinger, Maria Anna von (Gennzinger, Marianna; Marianne; *née* de Kayser) 35-7, 60, 74n., 97f., 104-8, 117f., 124f., 129f., 140f., 154, 157-9, 187, 194, 205, 214, 324, 410, 417, 426, 438f., 450, 505, 515, 521
Genzinger, Josephine von ('Fräulein Pepi') 37, 97, 105, 118, 158
Genzinger, Peter von (physician) 35, 98, 125, 130
George II (of England) 72; as Prince of Wales 283
George III (of England) 23, 30f., 41, 51, 59, 71, 83, 89, 92, 104, 106, 109, 117, 122, 170, 172, 186, 213-5, 262, 270, 283-5, 288, 315, 371, *pl. 8*
George IV (of England; see also Wales, Prince of) 30, 110, 114, 455
Gerber, Ernst Ludwig 118, 182, **228f.**, 354, 503
Gerlach, Sonja 438n.
Germany 56, 108, 189, 191ff., 214, 247, 262, 264, 273, 294, 319f., 352, 445, 502ff., 507, 561f., 567, 575, 582, 601, 609, 611
Gern, Herr (singer) 197f.
Gernerth, Franz 560
Gerstingen, Hans 192n.
Gesellschaft der Associirten (Vienna) 228, 456
Gesellschaft (Pensionsgesellschaft) bildender Künstler (Society of Visual Artists, Vienna) 205, 221, 224, 485
Gesellschaft der Musikfreunde (Society of Friends of Music, Vienna) 11, 28n., 37n., 107, 188, 196, 202, 225, 228n., 318n., 358, 407, 483, 557
Gewandhaus (Leipzig) 509
Ghisaliere, M. 126n.
Giardini, Felice 27n., 127f., **166f.**, 183f., 278; *Ruth* 167; Concerto (v. and orch.; unid.) 167

Giazotto, Remo 234n.
Gibbon, Edward 50n.
Gillberg (Guillberg), Madame (violinist) 293f., 304
Gillesberger, Hans 486
Giodaniello (prob. = Giordaniello = Giuseppe
    Giordani) 313; Scena (unid.) 313
Giommi, Abbate Teodoro 249
Giornovichj (Giornovichi; Jarnovik; Jiornavichj; etc.),
    Giovanni Mane 43, 75f., 84., 156., 183., 248, 257-60,
    283f., 288, 312, 314, 418; Concerto (v. and orch.;
    unid.) 76, 248, 257, 312, 314
Giotto 500
Giržik (Gierschek), F. X. 124n.
Glasgow 92
Glee Club (London) 364
Gloucester, Duke of 167, 283
Gluck, Christoph Willibald 33, 38, 138, 281, 292f., 306,
    309, 326; *Alceste* 281; *Iphigénie en Aulide* (Overture)
    293f., 306, 309; *Iphigénie en Tauride* 293f., 306; *Orfeo*
    138, 326
Goberman, Max 500
Godesberg, Bad 192
'God save the King' 135, 214, 259, 317, 318n., 361, 533
Goethe (Göthe), Johann Wolfgang von 63, 274;
    Hermann und Dorothea 274; *Werther* 212
Goldoni, Carlo 254
Gombart (publisher, Augsburg) 492ff., 559, 566, 576,
    605, 609
Gordon, Lord George 92
Gore, Mr (musician) 170, 299
Gosport (Godsport) 262f.
Göttweig Abbey 188, 324, 507
Gotwals, Vernon 275n.
Graeff (Greaff; Gräf; Gräffe; etc.), J. G. (flautist) 44,
    60f., 73, 131, 144f., 148, 162, 183; Concerto (fl. and
    orch.; unid.) 60f., 73
Graff, Friedrich Hartmann 31, **60f.**, 182f.; Three
    Quartets (1797) 61
Gramophone Company, The (H.M.V.) 445, 498
Grandjean, Madame (harpist) 244
Grassalkovicz, Prince von 224
Graun, Carl Heinrich 45, 104, 127n.
Gray, Cecil 411n., 437, 459n., 460f., 465, 478
Graz 225, 320, 354n.
Greatorex, Mr (pianist) 255, 303, 311
Green, Maurice 104
Gregorian chant 359, 408, 595
Greiner, Caroline von (marr. Pichler) 226-8
Greiner, Franz von 226
Grétry, André-Ernst-Modeste 191
Greville, Lady Elizabeth 46
Griesinger, Georg August 21, 23, 30n., 44, 46, 53, 58,
    87f., 115, 119, 126, 128, 140, 150, 166, 173n., 192, 200,
    228n., 231, 271, 285, 317n., 318n., 319, 324, 355n.,
    358, 396, 410, 416, 440, 471, 496
Grossmann-Vendrey, Susanne 59n.
Grosswardein (Oradea Mare) 506
Grove's Dictionary 27n., 29n., 68n., 99n., 114, 238n.,
    266n., 416n., 448n.
Grumbacher, Dr 453
Gubbins, Miss 267
Guéra (publisher, Lyon) 229
Guglielmi, Pietro 122, 135, (148), 150, (233), 235, 292,
    305, 313, 356; Aria (unid.) 148, 150, 233, 235, 305;
    Debora & Sisara (Oratorio) 292; *La pastorella nobile*
    122; *La vera costanza* 356; Scena (unid.) 313;
    Terzetto (unid.) 135, (148), 150
Guillberg, Madame (violinist), see Gillberg
Guise, Mr (musician) 177, 299
Gumpendorf (suburb of Vienna) 220f., 252
Gun, Mr ('cellist) 67
Gustav III (King of Sweden) 121, 134
Guttenbrunn, Ludwig 22n., 64, 133

Guttler, Hermann 243n.
Gypsy music 421, 431, 433f., 495, 551, 594, 613
Gyrowetz (Girovetz; Gerovetz; etc.), Adalbert **62-4**, 68,
    76, 82, 85f., 99, 122, 131f., 136f., 139, 143, 148, 150f.,
    155f., 163, 172f., 182f., 226, 238f., 245, 252, 460, 502-
    4, 507, 534
WORKS:
    Aria (sung by Miss Billington) 131f.;
    Concertante (v., va., vc) 131;
    Concertante, Op. 34 (fl., ob., bsn., v., vc. and orch.)
    172f., 252;
    Quartet (unid.) 64, 136f., 155f., 239;
    Semiramis 64, 122;
    Symphony in G (formerly attr. to Haydn) 63f., 503f.;
    Symphony (Overture; unid.) 62, 68, 82, 85f., 131,
    133, 139, 143, 148, 163, 245;
    Three Trios, Op. 9 (pf., v., vc.) 412

Haas, Karl 318n., 487n., 488
Habsburg Empire 85
Hackwood, Mr (musician) 90
Hadden, J. C. 246, 403
Hadow, W. H. 497n., 598, 602, 610n.
Hadrowa, Norbert 550
Haesler (Hassler; Haessler; etc.), Johann Wilhelm 79,
    116f., 131, 147, 163f.; Cantata (unid.) 170;
    Concerto (pf. and orch.; unid.) 116, 163f., 170; *Die
    Nacht von Zaccharia* 117; Symphony (Overture;
    unid.) 79
Haigh, Thomas 277, 448f., 503; Three Sonatas (pf.) 277,
    448f.
Hall, Dr 92
Halle 524n.
Hamburg 62, 183, 192, 194n., 228, 320, 457
Hamburger, Johann Nepomuk 105f., 129, 194
Hamburger, Paul 372
Hamilton, Gavin 402
Hamilton, Lady 78, 394f.
Hamilton, Mr 269
Hamlet, see under Shakespeare
Hampton Court 262
Handel (Händel), G. F. 12, 22, 28, 33, 45, 51n., 56, **83f.**,
    91f., 100-4, 117, 127n., 137f., 167, 169f., 172, 196, 207,
    216, 227, 228, 240, 249, 267, 271, 276, 282f., 285, 292,
    303f., 306, 354, 356, 502, 513, 520; Festival 28, 83, 276
WORKS:
    Acis and Galatea 89, 216, (240); Chorus (unid.) and
    Overture 89;
    Alexander's Feast 89, 91, 216, 228; 'The merry round'
    89; 'The prince unable to conceal' 91;
    L'allegro 137;
    Anthem, Wedding: 'Sing unto God' 283;
    Aria (unid.) 169;
    Brockes-Passion 285;
    Concertos: — (oboe and orch.; unid.) 83; — (organ
    and orch.; unid.) 83;
    Coronation Anthem: 'Zadok the Priest' 83, 91;
    Deborah 83;
    Esther 83, 90f.; Overture 91; 'So much beauty' 90;
    Israel in Egypt 83f., 91; 'He gave them hail-stones' 83;
    'The Lord is a Man of War' 91;
    Jeptha 84; 'Deeper and deeper still' 84;
    Joshua 83; 'The Nations tremble' 83;
    Judas Maccabeus 51n., 83;
    Messiah 83, 91; 'And the Glory' 91; 'Comfort ye, my
    people' 91; 'For unto us' 170; 'Glory to God' 304;
    'Hallelujah' 83, 91f., 170; 'Worthy is the Lamb' 170;
    Ode to St. Cecilia 216;
    Por(r)o 169;
    Redemption (*Messiah*) 137;
    Samson 89-91; 'Let the bright Seraphim' 90; chorus,
    'Let their celestial' 90; Overture 90; 'Total eclipse' 89;

'Why does the God' 91;
Saul 83, 90, (304); 'Fell rage' 90; 'How excellent' 304;
Solomon 91; 'Search round' 91; 'May no rash
intruder' 91;
Te Deum, 'Dettingen' 303;
Theodora 91, 292, 306; 'Angels ever bright' 292, 306;
'With lowly suite' 91
Handt, Herbert 323
Haneisen (publisher) 228
Hankey, Mr (president) 41
Hanover Square (London) 43ff., 54, 60ff., 79f., 82-7,
124, 130ff., 142ff., 168, 170-3, 213, 232ff., 239ff.,
249ff., 255-7, 280, 297, 313, pl. IV
Hanover Square Room(s) 25, (29f.), 41, (52), 64, 82, 84,
130, 137, 147, 152, 156, 162, 170f., 173, 234, 239ff.,
297, 302, 313, 459, 509, 515, 536, 563; see also
Hanover Square and New Lyceum
Hanover Street 29
Hansmann, Herr ('cellist) 189
Hanswurst (Hanswurst Comedies; Harlequin) 189, 274,
351, 422, 543, 614
Harburg Castle 490ff.
Harding, R. E. M. 419n.
Hardy, Thomas 22n., 64, 132, 161, (pls. III, 13, 19, 20)
Harich, Janos 121, 122, 221
Häring, (Haring; Harring), Herr (violinist) 457f.
Harington (Harlington; Harrington), Dr Henry 267,
281, 316, 317n., 403f.
Harmonica celestina 193
Harmonicon 27n., 77n., 154, 501
Harpur, Sir Henry 260, 318n., 489
Harrach, Karl Leonhard, Count 199-201
Harrington, Mr (oboist) 44f., 49, 68, 75, 79, 131, 133,
144, 147, 159f., 162-4, 172, 183f., 189, 232, 239, 241,
252, 257, 260, 309, 313
Harrison, Mrs (née Cantelo) 31, 170, 213, 299, 304f.
Harrison, Samuel (tenor) 31, 134, 182f., 289, 304f., 306
Harrow 23
Hartford (Conn.) 133
Hartman, Carl (clarinet player) 131, 245, 304, 551
Hartman (flautist; = Carl Hartman?) 184
Hartzell, Eugene 403
Hase, Hermann von 324
Hasse, J. A. 33, 58, 104, 371; Antigono 371
Hastings, Warren 167f., 289
Hatch, Mr (lawyer) 51
Hater, Herr (singer) 320
Hauder, Signor (employee of Prince Esterházy) 123
Haus-, Hof- und Staats-Archiv 222
Hayda, Joseph 225; Litany in C 225
Haydine, Le (G. Carpani) 73, 84
Haydn, Franz Joseph: portraits pls. I, II, 1; see also
separate index of compositions, pp. 637-40
Haydn, Johann Michael 120, 196, 250, 251, 506, 531;
Quintet Op. 99 (2v., 2va., vc.), wrongly attr. to
Joseph Haydn 250f.; Symphony (Perger 28) 531
Haydn Institut (Cologne) 12, 543
Haydn-Mozart Presse 141n., 212n., 525, 529, 534, 538,
545, 583, 613
Haydn Museum (Eisenstadt) 413; see also
Burgenländisches Landesmuseum
Haydn Museum (Vienna) 221, 244
Haydn Society 12, 323f., 326n., 485f.
Hayes (Hess), Dr, Philip 89, 91, 183f., 279, 303, 364
Haymarket Theatre, see King's Theatre
Hayward, Mr 55, 80
Hazlitt 273n.
Hébert (journalist) 270
Heilbronn 485
Heimliche Botschafter, Der 198
Heinrich, Prince (of Prussia) 24
Heller, Friedrich 610
Hellwig, Judith 323

Hemlow, Joyce 163n.
Henle, G. (publisher) 35n., 359, 394, 403, 438, 440,
497n., 562
Henrici, K. H. 482
Henslow(e), Fanny 169
Heras, Maria Adelaide de la 309
Hermann und Dorothea (Goethe), see under Goethe
Herne & Peace, Messrs (lawyers) 312
Herrier, Robert 249
Herschel (Herschell; Hershel), William 176f., 583
Hessische Landesbibliothek 207
Hertzmann, Erich 294n.
Heyer Collection 482
Hidegség 614
Higgins (chemist) 270
Hilligsberg (Hillisberg; etc.), Madame (dancer) 39, 69,
71f., 120, 298f.
Hill, Mr (musician) 90
Hindle, Mr (musician) 177
Hindmarsh (Hindmarsch), Mr (violinist) 44, 48, 60-2,
65, 68, 70, 131, 136, 139, 147f., 155, 159, 162-4, 169,
171, 183, 189, 313
Hindmarsh, Mrs 79, 245, 313
Hipkins, A. J. 416
Hoboken, A. van 12, 16, 188n., 194n., 201, 251, 371,
391, 394, 407n., 411, 438, 454, 460, 486, 497
Hodges, Miss G. M. 115f.
Hodges, Mrs 115; Song, 'When from thy sight' 116
Hoffmann, E. T. A. 613
Hoffmeister, Franz Anton 61f., 70, 480, 485, 507; 'La
Chasse' (Symphony) 61f.; Symphony (unid.) 70
Hofkalender (Bonn) 27n.
Hofmann, Leopold 503, 506
Hogarth, William 23
Hohenfeld, Countess, see Esterházy, Princess Marie
Therese
Holcroft, Thomas 22, 272-4, 289, 355, 360, 371
Holland 62, 123, 158, 180, 195, 215, 260
Höllmayr, Anton 206
Holmes, Rev. Dr (poet) 93
Holmes (Holms), Mr (bassoon player) 26n., 44, 64, 131,
136, 144, 147, 160, 164, 172, 189, 257, 260, 282, 286,
303, 309-11, 313; Concerto (bsn. and orch.) 310
Holschneider, Andreas 216n.
Holz, Carl 204
Home, Anne, see Hunter
Homok 614
Hopkinson, Cecil 129, 318n., 371, 401n., 403
Hoppner, John 22n., 64, 110, 118, 133, 275n., (pl. I).
Horace 42
Horanyi, Matyas 98
Horn, Charles Edward 66
Horn, Karl Friedrich 66f.
Horowitz, Vladimir 445
Höslinger, Clemens 560n.
House of Orange 283
Howe, Richard, Lord 23, 258f., 262
Howe, Lady 262
Howell (music shop) 275f.
Huberty (publisher) 229
Hudson, Mr (musician) 177
Hughes, Rosemary 55n., 57n., 113n., 459, 610n., 613
Hüllmandel, Nicholaus Joseph 182f.
Hummel, J. J. 228, 452, 559
Hummel, Johann Nepomuk 78, 83, 85, 118, 140, 154,
157, 183, 410, 413, 456
Hummel, Maria 413n.
Hummell, (Master) L. C. (horn player and pianist) 85
Humphrey (printer) 64
Hungary, Hungarian 421, 468, 504, 551, 594, 597f., 615
Hunter, Anne (née Home) 179, 258, 285, 315, 378ff.,
395-7, 400
Hunter, Dr John 178f., 258

Hunter, William 179
Hüschen-Festschrift 27n.
Husk, W. H. 29n., 114, 448
Hutchinson, Anne 275
Huttenes, Mr (singer) 235-7, 253f.
Hyde, Mr (trumpeter) 299
Hyde Park (London) 112

Imbault (publisher) 499, 541, 559
Imhoff, Marian (Baroness; marr. Hastings) 168
Inchiquin, Lord 371
Incledon, Charles 108, 114n.
Ireland 92
Italy 38, 63, 99, 102f., 108, 114, 122, 131, 133, 207f., 212, 261, 334, 442, 502f., 524, 540, 567, 611

Jackson, Sara 565
Jackson, William 100-4
Jackson's Oxford Journal 80
Jacob, H. E. 381n., 560
Jäger, Daniel 393
Jahn, Otto 11, 416n.
Jahn'sche Saal (Vienna) 216
Jansen (Janssen; family) 52, 440
Jansen, Charlotte 309
Jansen, Louis 440; Sonata, Op. 1 (pf.) 440
Jansen (Janson), Therese (marr. Bartolozzi) 52, **183**, 276, 309, 316f., 394, 411, 413, 417, 438, **439ff.**, 456
Jarnowick, see Yaniewicz
Jarowez (violinist) 183f.
Jena 507f.
Jermoli, Guglielmo 334
Jersey, Earl of 270
Jersey, Frances, Countess of 270
Jindřichův Hradec (Neuhaus) 93, 202
Johanning (Salomon's valet) 26
Johanning, Frau 26
Johansson, Cari 142n.
Johns, D. C. 225n.
Johnson, Samuel 24
Johnstone, Mr (tenor) 114n.
Jomelli, Niccolò 33, 45, 103, 299
Jones, John 174; Chant for St Paul's Cathedral 174
Jones, Mr (composer) 301
Jonson, Ben 190
Jordan, Dora 110-2
Joseph (Giuseppe) II, Emperor 118, 125f., 189, 195, 208
Josephsplatz (Vienna) 208 (wrongly as 'Josephstadt'), 210 ('Josephplatz')
Journal des Luxus und der Moden 31, 70, 100, 117, 124, 245, 414
Jouvre, M. (musician) 284
Jugoslavia 188
Jukes, F. (engraver) (*pl. IV*)
Jung, Mr 80
Junker, C. F. 26

Kaiser, Fritz 64n.
Kaiserliche Reichs-Ober-Postamtszeitung 193
Kaiserliche Sammlungen 196, 225
Kalb, Frau von 274
Kaltenleutgeben 575
Karajan, Wolfgang von 133
Kärntnerthortheater (Vienna) 438
Kassler, Michael 66
Kauffmann, Angelika (*pl. 25*)
Kaunitz, Wenzel Anton, Prince 35
Kead (hairdresser) 52
Kees (Keess; Keeß), Bernhard Ritter von 37, 54.,98, 105, 107, 117, 124f., 130, 141, 194, 375, 496, 515

Kees, Frau von 129
Keiser, Bernard 33
Kelly (O'Kelly; Kely), Michael 37, 90f., 170, 172, 182f., 213, 286
Kensington Gravel Pits 95
Kenyon, Lord 189f.
King, A. Hyatt 184n., 564
King's Band (King's Musick) 87, 279, 283
King's Chapel (His Majesty's Chapel) 282
King's College (Cambridge) 276; Chapel 112
King's Library (Music Library) 27n., 159, 453f., 488
King's Theatre (Haymarket) 26n., 29, 38, 47, 60, 69, 71f., 76-9, 82, 85, 108, 111, 137, 149, 174, 213, 233, 252, 254, 257, 260f., 265f., 278, 281f., 286
Kinsky (Kynsky), Countess 207, 224
Kinsky, Princess 207
Kinsky-Halm, A. 222n.
Kirchgessner (Kirchgässner; Kirashgessner), Marianne 243f.
Kistner & Siegel (mus. pub.) 484
Kleiber, Erich 323
Kleine Steingasse (now 'Haydngasse', Vienna) 220f.
Klingenbach 614
Knyvett, Mr (singer) 170
Koch, Ludwig 187n.
Kodály, Zoltan 403, 598
Köhler, K.-H. 406f.
Königliche Kapelle (Berlin) 189
Königsberg 243, 354
Kopfermann, A. 407n., 409
Kopház (Kohlnof) 614
Kotzwara (Kozwarra), Franz 97
Koželuch (Kozeluck, etc.), Leopold 46, 49, 62f., 64, 80, 83, 113, 115, 144, 154, 156, 221, 224, 235, 241; Quartet (str.) 62; Redoutensaal Dances 221, 224; Symphony (Overture; unid.) 64, 115, 144, 235, 241
Kramer, Christian 110
Kraus, Carl 113
Kraus, Joseph Martin 121; Funeral Music for Gustav III of Sweden 121
Kreibich (Kreybich; Kreubich), Franz 118f., 130, 158
Kreutzer, Rodolphe 25, 66, 410; Concerto (v. and orch.; unid.) 25
Kreutzinger, Joseph (*pl. 21*)
Kroměříž (Kremsier) 64n., 119
Krumpholz, Johann Baptist 68, 171; Concerto (harp and orch.; unid.) 171
Krumpholz (Krumpholtz), Madame (harpist) 44, 46, 49f., 63, 65, (68), 73, 75, 81, 83, 85, 131, 136f., 144f., 148-50, 161-5, 184, 232, 331
Krumpholz, Wenzel 68
Kuchler (Kuiler), Mr (bassoon player) 60, 81
Kuffner, T. 46
Kuhač, F. 497n., 598, 602, 610n., 614
Kuhnel, Mr (bassoon player) 60, 81
Kunst- und Industrie-Comptoir (Vienna) 315, 395
Kurzböck, Joseph 452
Kurzböck, Madelaine (Magdalene) 440, 452

Laab 575
Lachnith, L. W. 541
Ländler 208, 212, 514, 556, 597
Laibach (Ljubljana) 188
La Maitre 270
Landon, Christa 12, 16, 439ff.
Landseer, J. 264
Langham 112
Lanner, Joseph 485
Larsen, Jens Peter 37n., 229n., 324, 407n., 497f.
LaRue, Jan 567, 583n.
Latrobe, Christian Ignatius 31, 45, 57f., 74, 182f.; Sonatas, Op. 3 (1792?) 58

Latrobe, Mrs 57
Laxenburg Castle 176
Laytha (now Leitha), River 201
Lazzarini (Lazarini), Signor (singer) 69, 120, 131f., 135, 142, 145f., 182f.
Lazzarini, Signora (singer) 135
Lea (pocket scores) 446
Leake, Miss (singer) 213, 289, 299
Leander (Leanders), Mr (horn player) 26n., 159, 162-4, 257, 299, 303, 309, 311
Leate, Mr (singer) 299
Lebrun, Ludwig August (oboist) 189
Le Duc, Simon (publisher and composer) 55, 115, 142, 228, 499; Symphony (unid.) 115
Lee, Mr (musician) 256, 311
Leeds, Duke of 106, 316n.
Leibrock, Eduard 490
Leinsdorf, Erich 511
Leipzig 123, 158, 189, 228, 352, 354, 358, 397, 404, 407n., 433n., 438, 449, 456n., 479, 484, 497ff., 509
Lenz, Heinrich Gerhard von 183
Lenzewski, Gustav 103
Leo, Leonardo 103
Leonard, Herr (singer) 197.
Leonardo da Vinci 378
Leopold II, Emperor 113, 126, 158, 168, 195, 351
Leopoldstadt-Theater (Vienna) 217
Libon, Mr (violinist) 295n.
Library of Congress (Washington, D.C.) 254, 491
Library of Recorded Masterpieces 500
Lichnowsky, Prince Carl (Charles), 204, 414f., 456
Lichnowsky, Princess (*née* Countess Thun) 86
Liechtenstein (Lichtenstein), Prince Jean 215
Liepmannssohn, Leo 482, 495
Lind, Jenny 258, 379
Lindley (Linley; Lindly), Mr ('cellist) 132, 135, 145, 189, 255, 260, 282, 293, 299, 303-5, 311
Lindley (blind organist) 270
Linley, F. (London publisher) 61n., (*pl. 19*)
Ling, Jr (musician) 304
Linz 231, 320
Lippe, M. de la 215
Lisbon 102, 352n.
Lisson Grove 46
Liszt, Franz 413
Lithuania 62
Littledon, Lord 265
'Live Cod' (London street-cry) 53, 615
Liverpool 92
Lobkowitz, Caroline (Princess; *née* Schwarzenberg) 294
Lobkowitz, Franz Joseph Maximilian, Prince 215, 294
Lobkowitz, Joseph Maria Karl, Prince 154f., 215, 294
Locke, John 56
Lockhart (Lokart; blind organist) 181
Lodge, Edmund 276
Loewenberg, Alfred 254n.
Loge Olympique, Concert de la (Paris) 142, 562
Loliée, Marc 488
Lolli, Antonio 76, 183f.
London, see under names of buildings, institutions etc.; City of 106f.
London Chronicle 50, 71f., 228
Lonsdale, Roger 32, 45, 49, 67, 74, 82, 198n., 240, 307
Longman, James 141
Longman & Broderip 24n., 57, 61, 64, 69, 82, 113, 118f., 142, 232, 250, 276, 286, 312, 314, 316f., 317n., 318n., **415f.**, 417, 433, 436, 441f., 464
Longman, Clementi & Co. 440, 442
Lopresti, Baron de 208
Lops (Lopps), Rosa (soprano) **38f.**, 59, 71, 182, 329, 334, 340
Lotti, Antonio 103
Louis XVI (King of France) 195, 215, 237

Loutherbourg (Lauterbourg), Philipp Jakob 264
Lower Austrian Government 201
Lusciano, Duchi di 126n.
Lulli, Jean-Baptiste 55, 103
Lunn, Jean 359
Lyceum, Strand 248
Lyon 229
Lyon, Mr (musician) 299

MacArdle, D. W. 196n.
Macartney, C. A. 196n.
Macartney, Lord (and Lady) 315f.
Macintosch, Mr (bassoon player) 257
Mackenzie, Mr 273
Mackerras, Charles 29n.
Macnutt, Richard 258, 377
Madrid 102, 352n.
Mälzel, John Nepomuk 565f.
Maffei, Signora (singer) 39, 79, 182
Maffolli (Maffoli), Vincenzo (singer) 215f., 225
Magazin der Musik 26, 63
Maggs Brothers 230n.
Magnus, F. C. 202
Magyar Hirmondó 216
Mahler, Gustav 521, 555
Mahon, W. (clarinet player) 26n., 135
Mainz 195, 222, 228
Major, Erwin 433n.
Malton, Thomas (the Younger) (*pl. 7*)
Manchester 92, 142, 184n.
Mandyczewski, Eusebius von 11, 16, 407
Mann, Alfred 202-4
Mann, Horace 83
Mannheim 197, 293, 320
Manning, Westley 495
Mansfeld, F. G. (*pl. 22*)
Mansfeld, Sebastian 206
Mansfield, Orlando 268
Mara, Johann Baptist 30
Marburg/Lahn 495, 615
March, Mr (dentist) 22f., 261
Marcellus, Theatre of (Rome) 88
Marchesi, Luigi Lodovico (castrato) 66, 87, 91, 145, **186**
Marco, Guy A. 225n.
Marek, George 411n.
Maria, Signora (Sestini?) 39
Maria Anna Walpurgis (Electress of Saxony) 58
Maria Ludovika (Empress; wife of Leopold II) 126
Maria Theresa (Empress) 208, 452
Marie Antoinette (Queen of France) 62, 133, 195, 222
Marie Therese (Empress; wife of Franz I) 196, 199, 205f., 224, 261
Martin(i) y Soler, Vincente, see Soler
Martinique 95
Matteini, Veronica (*pl. 12*)
Matthäus, Wolfgang 497n., 503
Matthews, Betty 66, 262n., 263f.
Matthews, Mr (singer) 91
Maurice, Sir Frederick 211
Maximilian Franz (Elector of Cologne) 192, 217, 222-4
Mayr, Giovanni Simone 511f., 514f.
Mazant (= Mozart?) 60
Mazzanti, Ferdinando 182f.
Mazzinghi (Mazingi), Joseph 138, 182f.
Mazzolà, Caterino 351
McArthur, Miss (pianist) 314
McCorkle, Donald W. 184n.
McGuigan, Dorothy G. 195
Mecklenburg-Strelitz, Margrave of 51n.
Medici di Marignano, Nerina 113n., 232n.
Mee, J. M. 80

Meister, M. 214n.
Mendelssohn-Bartholdy, Felix (430), 508f., 576; *A Midsummer Night's Dream* - incidental music (Shakespeare) 430, 576
Mendelssohn-Bartholdy, Rebecca 509
Menel (Menal; Menall; Memel; etc.), Mr ('cellist) 48, 60-2, 65, 68, 131, 136, 139, 144, 147f., 155, 157, 159f., 162-4, 171f., 183f.
Mengozzi, Bernardo 90; Aria, 'Donne, chi vuo vedere' 90
Mercure de Ratisbone 210
Merrick, James 278, 364f.
Mertin, Josef 413
Metastasio, Pietro 32, 138, 230, 329, 351, 371-3, 389, 393
Metternich, Clemens, Prince 196
Meyer, Leonhard B. 228n.
Meyer, Mr (harpist) 172f.
Michel (probably Joseph Willibald Michl) 139; Clarinet Quartet (unid.) 139
Mies, Paul 394
Mingotti, Regina 38
Mihul, Wenzel 320
Milan 62, 84n., 234n., 248n., 266, 503
Milder, Anna 373
Miller, Dr Edward 303
Milton, John 326, 354
Mirabeau, H.-G. R. (Comte de) 109
Mitchell, C. 565
Mitchell, Donald 293n., 372n., 416n.
Mittag, Herr 281
Modena 503
Moldenhauer, Fritz 490
Mollo, Gaspard 126n.
Mollo, Tranquillo 72, 371, 394
Molton, Signor 219
Montagu, Lady Mary Wortley 42f.
Monteverdi, Claudio 326
Monthly Magazine and British Register 61n., 455
Monthly Review 32, 100ff., 274
Montlieu, Mrs 438
Monzani, Teobaldo (flautist) 257, 271f., 275f., 309, 361, 405-8
Monzani & Cimador 266, 361, 408, 559
Moore, Sir John 211
Moravian (Herrnhutter) 31, 57, 180, 182f.; — Brotherhood, Church, Music Foundation, Theological College 184n.
Morelli, Giovanni 182f., 254, 257, 281f., 286, 295f., 303, 305-10
Morichelli, Anna 248, 249n., 254, 259, 277, 281f., 286, 291-6, 303, 305-13
Morley, Edith J. 212
Mörner, C. G. Stellan 22n., 26, 415n.
Morning Chronicle 25, 26n., 30f., 39, 42-4, 47, 49f., 60, 65, 69f., 76-9, 84f., 89n., 96, 127-9, 131, 133, 136, 139, 147f., 156, 160f., 165, 168, 172, 213f., 232-5, 238-58, 272, 280, 282, 288, 291, 293-7, 299, 302-14, 409, 496, 515, 551, 564, 595
Morning Herald 24, 61, 86, 89, 91, 108, 130-7, 139, 142-9, 152, 156f., 159-65, 168-73, 214, 236n., 252, 255f., 258n., 288, 304, 311, 318
Morning Post 50, 213, 233, 235
Morzin, Count 541
Moscheles, Ignaz 372
Moscow 27n., 167, 170, 352n.
Mountain, Joseph (violinist and conductor) 48, 115, 248, 255, 299
Mozart, Constanze 113, 207, 216
Mozart sons (fils) 113
Mozart, Wolfgang, Jr 112f.
Mozart (Mozard; Mazant[?]; etc.), Wolfgang Amadeus 11, 13, 25f., 39, 51n., 58, 60f., 63, 73, 99f., 102, 105,
112-6, 118f., 121, 124, 126, 132, 154, 157, 170, 192, 196, 199, 204, 207, 215-7, 224, 226, 232, 237f., 242f., 248, 254, 266, 273, 278, 293, 295-7, 305, 311, 330f., 334, 347, 349, 351, 353, 359, 364, 372, 376, 397, 411, 413f., 416f., 419, 420n., 421n., 423, 430, 437-9, 451, 456-8, 460, 472, 478, 480, 482, 485, 487, 499-503, 505-8, 512, 516-9, 523-6, 531, 533f., 549-52, 555, 557, 562, 567f., 570, 577, 586, 592, 594, 609
WORKS:
Aria (unid.) 295, 305;
Concerto (clar. and orch.; K.622) 551;
Concerto (fl., harp and orch.; K.299) 331;
Concertos (hn. and orch., various) 568;
Concerto (oboe and orch.; K.314) 278;
Concertos (pf. and orch.): — (K.175) 507; — (K.449) 438; — (K.451) 507; — (K.453) 438; — (K.466) 516, 562; — (K.482) 568; — (K.491) 516, 518; — (K.503) 423;
Concerto (v. and orch.; K.268; doubtful) 293;
Fantasia (pf.; K.475) 451;
Graduale ad Festum Beatae Mariae (K.273) 113;
Masses: — in C ('Coronation'; K.317) 505; — in C (K.337) 505;
Maurerische Trauermusik (*Masonic Funeral Music*; K.477) 63, 334;
Motet, 'Exsultate, jubilate' (K.165) 266;
Operas: *La clemenza di Tito* 113, 126, 351, 375, 551; *Così fan tutte* 121, 126n., 505, 531; *Don Giovanni* 39, 503, 505, 596; *Die Entführung aus dem Serail* (*Il Seraglio*) 238, 353, 502, 526, 551, 562; *Idomeneo* 330, 550, 586; *Lucio Silla* 266; *Le nozze di Figaro* 81, 126, 254, 397, 423, 502, 505, 552; *Die Zauberflöte* (*The Magic Flute*) 124, 126, 199, 215, 217, 347, 349, 421, 502, 512, 526;
Quartets (string): — (K.387 etc.) dedicated to Haydn 456, 480, 505f.; — (K.458 in B flat; 'Hunt') 568; — K.465; 'Dissonant') 460;
Quintet for glass harmonica (K.617) 242f.;
Quintets for strings 114, 505;
Redoutensaal Dances 224;
Requiem (K.626) 216, 512;
Rondo (pf. and orch.; K.382) 507;
Scena, 'Ch'io mi scordi di te' (K.505) 372;
Serenade in D (K.250; 'Haffner') 557;
Sonatas (pf.): — (K.457) 451; — (K.545) 523;
Sonata (2 pf.) in D (K.448) 438;
Symphonies: — (K.183) 506; — (K.297; 'Paris') 60n.; — (K.311a; spurious) 508; — (K.318) 524; — (K.319) 60n., 519, 531; — (K.385; 'Haffner') 60n., 567; — (K.425; 'Linz') 526; — (K.504; 'Prague') 460, 567; — (K.543) 334, 505, 550, 552, 594; — (K.550) 420, 505, 516, 523, 550, 552; — (K.551; 'Jupiter') 505, 517f., 534, 552, 592; — (unid.; Overture) 60, 115, 132, 248, 297;
Thamos, König von Aegypten (music to drama by Gebler; K.345) 505;
Trauermarsch (K.453a) 438
Mozarteum (Salzburg) 438
Mozon (Mojon), Mlle (dancer) 39, 69, 72, 79
Müller, Wenzel 217
Münch, Charles 541
Mundy, E. M. 258-60
Munich 38, 266, 329, 355, 526, 586
Musical Fund 25; see also New Musical Fund
Musical Graduates Society (Society of Musical Graduates) 78n., 95, 106, 177
Musicalische Korrespondenz der teutschen Filharmonischen Gesellschaft für das Jahr 1792 192n., 228
Musical Magzine 439
Musical Times 95
Music & Letters 24n., 139n.
Music Review 66n., 119, 254n., 275n., 498n., 508n., 523n., 532

Musigny (Marigny; Musegny; etc.), Madame (harpist) 130, 132, 142, 160
Musikalischer Almanach für Deutschland auf das Jahr 1782 26
Musikalischer und Künstler Almanach auf das Jahr 1783 26
Musik und Verlag 24n.
Mutlow, Master (singer) 90
Muzarelli, Signor (dancer) 207

Nagel (music publisher) 201n., 407n.
Nanki Library (Tokyo) 66
Nantes 270
Napier (Nepire), William 84f., **128f.**, 317, 318n., 377, 400ff.
Naples 56, 63, 126n., 182, 184, 220, 261, 352n., 549
Napoleon 13f., 27, 195, 197f., 442
Näs Castle 221
Nasolini, Sebastiano 297; Aria (unid.) 297
National Library (Prague) 64n.
National School of Music (England) 280, 283
National Széchényi Library (Budapest) 15, 27n., 81, 146n., 188, 202, 206, 254, 346, 395, 412n., 434, 454, 489–94
Neapolitan sixth 330, 419, 450, 481, 543, 611
Nedham (Needham), Marchamont 271
Neefe, Christian Gottlieb 192
Negri, Domenico 122f.
Negri, Theresa (singer; Luigia Polzelli's sister) **59**, 64f., 68, 82, 85, 115, 122f., 132, 135, 145, 182
Neighbour, O. W. 259n., 406n.
Neri, Signor (castrato) 281, 286
Neuhaus, see Jindřichův Hradec
Neukomm, Sigismund von 150f., 286, 320, 372
Neue Deutsche Merkur 216
Neuer Markt (Vienna) 215, 228
Newcastle 180
Newcastle, Duke of 110
Newdigate, Sir Roger 258, 260
Newdigate-Newdegate, Lady 259n.
New Friends of Music (New York) 53
New Lyceum (Hanover Square, London) 314
Newman, Alfred 490
New Musical Fund 47f., 183, 303f.
Newport (I. o. W.) 264
Newton, Sir Isaac 56
New York 53, 141n., 359, 370, 381n., 411n., 438n., 446n., 480, 500, 583n.
New York Philharmonic Orchestra 141n.
New York Public Libraray 437
Nicolai (valet) 184
Nield (Neild), Mr (tenor) 133f., 136f., 144f., 213, 244, 251f., 255, 257, 299, 312f.
Niemecz, Pater Primitivus 201f.
Nissen, Georg Nikolaus von 121n.
Nixon, John (*pl. 6*)
Nohl, Ludwig 416n.
Nomura, Professor 453n.
North America 92
Norwich 92
Notre Dame (Cathedral, Paris) 270
Nottebohm, Gustav 202n., 203
Novello, Mary 140, 278
Novello, Vincent 57, 113, 172, 415
Novello & Co. 480n.
Novellos (Mary and Vincent) 113n., 505n.
Noverre, Jean Georges 301
Nowak, Leopold 557n.
Nützliches Auskunftsbuch . . . Wien 1797 195n.
Nydal, Rudolph 492

Oatlands 109f.

Odéon (Paris) 62
Ocdcnburg (Sopron) 598, 614
Oedipus–Antigone legend 326
Oettingen-Wallerstein, Krafft-Ernst, Prince von 215f., 507
Oettingen-Wallerstein Archives 409ff.
Offenbach-am-Main 172, 228, 439, 452, 490ff., 559
Ogny, Comte d' 142, 504
Ohmiya, Makoto 453
Oiseau-Lyre (gramophone co.) 541
'Old Hundreth Psalm' 174
Oldman, Cecil B. 24n., 129, 318n., 401, 403
Olleson, Edward 216, 228n., 355n., 358n., 593
Olmütz 64n.
Oman, Carola 211
Opera band (London; King's Theatre, Haymarket) 76, 256, 280, 594f.
Opera concert (room; King's Theatre, Haymarket) 29, 149, 155, 188, 248, 251f., 278f., 280, 417, 437, 450, 495, 551, 582
Opera house (London; King's Theatre, Haymarket) 31, 38f., 41, 47, 67, 76-9, 80, 155, 213, 232, 259, 281
Opie, John 274
Oracle 39, 76, 83f., 87, 125, 130-3, 136-9, 142, 144-8, 150, 157, 160f., 163-5, 171f., 232-5, 239-47, 249-57, 260, 274, 280, 282, 287, 289, 291, 293, 295f., 299f., 302, 304-7, 309, 311-3, 405
Orange, Duke of 283, 288
Orde, Thomas 263f.
Ordoñez, Carlos d' 503, 506
Orleans, Duke of 64, 236
Orpheus & Euridice (ballet) pasticcio by various composers, see under Federici (the principal composer)
Oslip 614
Österreichische Monatsschrift 216, 226
Österreichische Nationalbibliothek, see Austrian National Library
Ott, A. M. 64, 133
Ottley, D. 179
Ovid 326ff.
Oxford (Oxforth) 31, 55, 61, 67, 78n., 80, 88-95, 112, 117, 124, 149, 163, 178, 183f., 273, 318n., 359, 381n., 503n., 504; Oxford band 80
Oxford Journal 80
Oxford University Press 518n.

Pacchierotti (Bacchierotti), Gaetano 28, 41, 47, 64, 69, 75f., 182f., 276
Padua 376
Page, Mr (singer) 299
Paisiello, Giovanni 38f., 59, 69, 71f., 91, 101, 109, 146, 154, 215, 235f., 244, 259, 261, 294, 307f., 310, 312, 376, 438
WORKS:
Achile in Sciro, Rondo from 293f.;
Arias: — Crudele, or colei piangi' 308f.; — 'Pensa che in campo' 91; — (unid.) 310, 312;
Duet (unid.) 60, 69, 293;
La Frascatana 259;
Nina, pazza per amore 312;
Les petits riens (music by P. and Sacchini) 109;
Pirro 38, 39, 59;
Il re Teodoro 376
Recitative and Rondo (Aria) 'Ho perduto il vel sembrante' 236;
Scena (unid.) 146, 244;
La serva padrona 215, 261
Palermo 76
Palffy family 224
Palmer, J. F. 179n.
Panharmonicum 565

Pantheon (London) 30, 41, 47, 64, 96, 120, 122, 125, 128, 182,
Papafava, Conte 376f.
Papendiek (family) 65
Papendiek, Charlotte 25f., 51-4, 67, 161, 509f., 610n., 614f.
Papendiek, Christoph(er) 25f., 51f., 453, 455
Papendiek, Eliza 51
Paris 24, 28, 55, 62-4, 66, 68, 76, 99, 102, 119, 131, 142, 154, 156, 158, 183, 195, 198, 222, 229, 234, 254, 264, 270, 274, 297n., 301, 312, 317n., 352n., 414, 439, 452, 492, 499, 503f., 506, 509, 527, 536, 541, 549n., 559, 562, 588, 594
Park (Barck), Miss see Parke
Parke, John 274, 283
Parke, Miss (singer) 182f., 213, 250-7, 274, 299
Parke, William 26, 37, 39, 76, 97, 110, 166f., 189, 191, 236, 255, 261, 274, 278, 283, 285, 288, 299, 357, 364
Parkinson, Mr (musician) 90, 135, 239, 246
Parlophone (gramophone co.) 411n., 488
Parsloes Restaurant 177
Parsons, William 177, 279, 283, 364
Pashby, John 178n.
Päsler, Karl 445f.
Passau 130n., 231, 320
Patatschny, Johann 206
Patria, Mr (oboist) 90
Pearce, Mr (actor) 300
Pears, Peter 258
Peking (Pekin) 315
Pellegrini, Signor 126n.
Pensionsgesellschaft bildender Künstler (Vienna), see Gesellschaft bildender Künstler
Peploe, Mrs (singer) 324, 371, 373
Pepusch, Dr Johann Christoph 102
Perez, Davide 33, 103
Perger, Lothar 531
Pergolesi (Pergolese), Giovanni Battista 33, 242; *Stabat Mater* 242
Peri, Jacopo 326
Perrymead (house; Bath) 266
Pertoja (Bertoja), Valentino 199
Pesaro 249
Peters, C. F. 61, 359, 407n., 409, 438n., 445, 498, 500, 563
Philadelphia 320, 352n.
Philharmonia miniature scores (Universal Edition) 141n., 240n., 260, 288n., 497n., 525, 529, 534, 538n., 557n., 561, 583, 613
Philharmonic Concert (London) 26
Philidor, François André 72, 77f.; 'Hunting Song' 77f.
Phillips, Susan 307
Piacenza 122
Piccinni (Piccini), Nicolà 33, 85, 109, 244, 255, 286; *La buona figliuola* 109; Scena (unid.) 244; Terzetto (unid.) 255, 286
Pichl (Pechl, Piehl), Wenzel 65, 73, 239, 243; Symphony (Overture) 65, 73, 239, 243
Pichler, A. E. 226
Pieltain (Pioltan), Mr (horn player) 26n., 142, 159, 162-4, 304
Pierpont Morgan Library (New York) 141n.
Pillnitz 320
Pindar, Peter, see Wolcot, John
Pitt, William, Sen. 259n.
Pitti Palace (Florence) 133
Plautus 181
Pleyel, Ignaz 44, 60-4, 68, 82, 89-91, 97, **99**, 102, 108f., 115, 119-22, 124f., 128, 130-3, 135, 138f., 141f., 144-6, 150, 154, 158, 161, 212, 246, 255, 301, 304, 313, 380, 402, 439, 459, 502, 507, 534, 536, 559, *pl. V*
WORKS:
Concertante (fl., ob., bsn., v., va., vc.; *Quatrième*

Symphonie concertante) 138, 144, 536;
Concertante (unid.) 90, 109;
Concertante (2 v. and orch.) 138, 144-6, 304;
Concertante (ob., v., va.) 255;
Concerto (vc. and orch.; unid.) 139;
Quartet (2 v., va., vc.; unid.) 89, 99, 115, 135, 142, 304;
Quartetto obligato (fl., v., va., vc.; unid.) 313;
Quintet (2 v., 2 va., vc.; unid.) 61;
Sonata (unid.) 380;
Symphony (Overture) (unid.) 60, 62f., 68, 91, 115, 132f., 135, 138, 142, 246, 255, 301, 304;
Trios (pf., v., vc.) formerly attr. to Haydn 82, 119
Ployer, Barbara (Babette) von 131, 437
Ployer, G. I. von (Hofagent) 437
Plymouth, Earl of 29
Poell, Alfred 323
Pohl, C. F. 11-13, 24n., 27n., 30n., 32n., 35n., 37, 39, 47, 51n., 53f., 59, 68n., 77n., 78, 80, 82f., 85, 89, 94, 99, 109n., 112, 116, 122, 124n., 137, 168-70, 173n., 174, 182, 194, 202, 214, 225f., 229n., 238n., 248, 250, 268, 271, 274, 283, 289, 298, 360, 379, 396, 407n., 409, 440, 461, 485, 490, 497n., 560, 593
Pohl (Vice-Rector) 224f.
Polack (Bolack, Poleck, etc.), Mr (viola player) 61, 68, 159, 162, 164
Poland 24, 92, 219, 222
Pollard, R. (engraver) (*pl. IV*)
Polydor (gramophone co.) 354
Polzelli, Antonio 59, 95
Polzelli, Luigia (*née* Moreschi) 54, 59, 95f., 115, 122f., 138, 165f., 175, 182, 199, 214, 219f., 324, 329, 340, 360, (*pl. 27*)
Polzelli, Pietro (Pierino) 59, 115, 122, 165f., 175, 199, 219
Ponte Vecchio (Florence) 133
Poole, Caroline 81, 136, 147, 170, 182f., 266, 285, 317f., 370
Pordenone 540n.
Porpora, Nicolà 154
Porta, Nunziato 356
Portfeuille für Musikliebhaber 189
Portsmouth 248, 262-4
Potsdam 507
Pozzi (composer) 154, 309
Pplum (Blumb?), Madame (singer) 39
Praetorius, Ernst 497f.
Prague 62, 113, 158, 216, 306, 320, 351
Presezzo 32
Pressburg (Bratislava) 251
Pressburger Zeitung 320
Preston 275f.
Preston & Son (music publisher) 277, 314, 317n., 409f., 412, 424, 448
Pribram 64n.
Princeton 373n.
Professional Concert (London) 24, 27, 29, 31, 41, 44f., 47, 69f., 74, 98, 106, 122, 124f., 131f., 135, 138, 141-3, 146, 166, 183, 213, 232f., 276, 291, 464, 536
Professional Concert-band (orch.) 89f., 128
Professors (= Professional Concert) 24n., 44, 248, 256, 280
Provert, Mlle (dancer) 77
Prussian Army (Cavalry) 222, 563
Public Advertiser 40, 43-6, 48, 60, 63, 68, 73, 75, 80f., 83, 90-3, 121, 124, 128, 136, 153, 232, 241, 405
Puchberg (Buchberg), Johann Michael 121, 219n., 505n.
Purcell, Henry 33, 90, 104, 114, 171-3, 305; *Mad Bess* 90, 305; 'From rosy bower' 171; 'From silent shades' 90

Queen's House 52

Rabelais, François 520
Rabener (Rabner), G. W. 191
Radant, Else 66n.
Radziwill, Prince 62
Rafanelli, Signor (singer) 217
Raigern (Rajhrad), Monastery of 64n.
Raimondi, Ignazio 130, 148, 183, 314;
  'Battle Symphony' 130;
  Quartet (2 v., va., vc.; unid.) 148
Raimund, Ferdinand 208n.
Ranelagh (Renalag) Gardens 167
Ranson, Morland & Hammersley (bankers) 286
Ratner, Leonard G. 592n.
Rauzzini, Venanzio 266-9
Rawlins (Rawlings), Thomas, Jr 145; Quartet (2 v., va.,
  vc.; unid.) 145
Razumovsky, Andreas (Count, later Prince) 403, 456n.
R.C.A. Victor (gramophone co.) 501
Redoutensaal (Redoute; Ridotto; Vienna) 208-11, 215f.,
  221, 224-6, 318, 484-7, 514, 557
Rees's *Cyclopaedia* 87, 99n., 113, 167
Reeves, William 394
Regensburg (Ratisbon) 37n., 208, 509n.
Reich (German) 575
Reichardt (Reichard), Johann Friedrich 198, 238, 241,
  246, 293, 295, 304; Symphony (Overture; unid.) 242,
  246, 293, 295, 304
Reinöhl, F. 222
Rellstab, J. K. F. 228, 414n.
Renigale (painter) 97
Reutter, Georg, Jr 196
Reynell, H. (printer) 76
Reynolds, Sir Joshua 179, 275n.
Rheinische Musen 320
Rich, Sir Charles and Lady 269
'Richard, Coeur de Lion' (play) 111
Richmond 95, 244
Richter, Franz Xaver 99, 102
Richter, John Paul 274
Ries, Ferdinand 27, 192n., 413n., 456
Righini, Vincenzo 241; Aria (unid.) 241
Rimsky-Korsakov, Nicolay A. 560
Ritter, Herr (bassoon player) 189
Robespierre, M. F. I. de 240
Robinson, Crabb 212, 274
Roch, Madame de la 274
Rochlitz, Johann Friedrich 511f., 514
Röckl, Joseph August 86
Rohrau 199, 201
Rolle, Johann Heinrich 104
Rome 56, 88, 503, 511n.
Romney, George (*pl. 11*)
Roscoe, Christopher 24n.
Rose, Michael 376
Rosen, Charles 411, 418, 423n., 436n., 497n., 545n., 546,
  571, 595, 611
Rosen, Gerd 491, 545
Rosenbaum, Joseph Carl 66, 211, 226
Rosenberg, Prince 124
Rosenthal, Albi 27n., 161, 306, 358
Rosenzweig, Nanette (*pl. 5*)
Rosetti (Rozzetti; Rösler), Francesco Antonio 45, 49, 53,
  65, 70, 81, 145, 233, 244, 507; Overture (Symphony;
  unid.) 45, 49, 53, 65, 70, 81, 145, 233, 244
Rosselli (singer) 248
Rossini, Gioacchino 126, 503
Rothe, Herr (singer) 100
Roubiliac, Louis François 172
Roumania 506, 598
Rousseau, Jean-Jacques 198, 407
Rovedino, Carlo (singer) 244, 260, 281, 286, 289, 291,
  298, 303-7, 309f., 312
Roverella, Anna (Contessa) 540n.

Roxford 96, 99
Royal Academy 161, 264
Royal College of Music 74n., 132, 244, 357
Royal Cumberland Free Mason's School 238n., 299
Royal Philharmonic Society 146, 323, 490, 534
Royal Society of Musicians 157, 170, 318, 488
Rudel 190
Rudolph, Archduke, Collection (Vienna) 188
Rusi 49f.; Recitative and Aria (unid.) 49f.
Russia 62, 170, 195, 213, 456n.
Ryde (Reid; Reed; I. o. W.) 264

Sacchini, Antonio Maria Gasparo 33, 85, 103, 109, 138,
  144, 169, 174, 235, 242, 279, 299; Arias: — 'Non odi
  il segno' 144; — 'Son regina' 174; — (unid.) 169, 235,
  242; *Les petits riens* (with Paisiello) 109
Sadlers Wells 265
St. Armand, Mlle (dancer) 77
St. Ives, Anne 274
St. James's (London) 43, 170, 255
St. James Chronicle, or British Evening Post 30, 43, 89, 173,
  283, 299f.
St James's Park 240
St Margaret's Chapel 170
St Michael's (church, Vienna) 281
St Paul's Cathedral (London) 173f.
St Petersburg 151, 352, 499
Sala, Nicolà 38
Sale, Mr (singer) 170, 255, 299
Salieri, Antonio 126, 193, 211, 217, 226; *Axur* 217
Salomon, Johann Peter 13, 23, 24-8, 30f., 36, 39, 45-52,
  54-60, 61-71, 74-6, 77n., 78f., 84-6, 88, 98f., 108,
  112f., 116, 118, 124, 128, 130f., 133-7, 139, 141-57,
  159-65, 168, 170-3, 177, 182f., 184n., 188f., 192f.,
  213f., 230, 232-53, 255f., 260, 271n., 273, 276f., 279f.,
  283f., 287f., 291-3, 296, 299-303, 305, 311f., 315,
  316n., 318f., 323f., 331, 334f., 370, 374, 401, 409f.,
  412, 419, 424, 450, 453-6, 458f., 464, 466, 468, 471,
  479, 483, 490-5, 497-500, 504, 507-9, 515f., 518, 527,
  534, 536f., 539, 541, 545f., 548-51, 553, 560, 571f.,
  575, 582f., 595, 601f., 609, 612-5, *pl. III.*
  WORKS:
  Concerto (v. and orch.; unid.) 171, 173, 312;
  Quartet (for glass harmonica; lost) 243;
  Romance in D (v. and orch.) 27n.;
  Windsor Castle: — Overture by Haydn 24, 299-302,
  324, 483; — New Overture by S. 302
Salzburg 37n., 55, 133, 413, 437, 531, 586
Sandby, Paul (*pl. 29*)
Sandys, William, and Simon Andrew Forster 27n., 82n.,
  232n.
San Francisco 409
Sansculottes 240
Sapio, Mr (musician) 155
Sarti, Giuseppe 33, 89f., 101, 144, 148, 174, 235, (239),
  240, 376f.
  WORKS:
  Arias: — 'Ah non sai qual pena' 144; — 'Numi,
  possenti Numi' 89; — (unid.) 90;
  Cavatina, 'Lunge da te ben mio' (239), 240;
  Dido (138), 174;
  Duet (unid.) 148;
  Scena, 'D'Ademira la voce' 376f.;
  Scena (unid.) 148
Saunders, Master Pinto (violinist) 314
Saust, Herr 416
Saville Row (Theatre of Varietiés Amusantes) 109
Saxony 318n., 354, 358f.
Sbarra, M. 126n.
Scala, La (Milan) 248n., 503
Scarlatti, Alessandro 33, 103
Scarlatti, Domenico 33, 451

Schanz, Wenzel 413, 415, 450
Schärding 231
Scheener (Schenner; violinist) 183
Schellinger, Johann 311, 487
Schenk, Johann 205, 217-9, 417; *Achmet und Almanzine*
    218; *Der Dorfbarbier* 218
Scherchen, Hermann 595
Schering, Arnold 563
Schiavonetti, Luigi 133
Schikaneder, Emanuel 85, 124, 217, 225
Schiller, Charlotte von 205
Schiller, Friedrich von 274
Schindler, A. F. 218, 294, 411n., 575
Schinotti (singer) 182
Schlägl (Monastery) 238
Schmid, E. F. 201, 433n., 484, 545n., 557, 610n., 614
Scholes, Percy 56, 75, 113, 167, 177, 313, 316n.
Scholl, Maria Catherina 86
Schönbrunn (Castle) 206, 221
Schott, Bernhard (Schott & Co.) 194, 228, 500
Schottenstift 106
Schrämbl, Franz Anton 206
Schreyvogel, J. 216n.
Schroeder (artist) (*pl. 10*)
Schroeter (Schroeder), Johann Samuel 25f., 66, 87, 168
Schroeter, Rebecca 22f., 25, 87, 131f., 143, 153f., 157f.,
    160, 162, 164f., 171-4, 176-9, 186f., 214, 240, 286, 314,
    409, 431, 434, 436f., 438, 456
Schubert, Franz 12, 381, 385, 421, 443, 461, 485, 508,
    559, 582; Symphony No. 5 – 508
Schulze, J. A. 480
Schultz, Helmut 497ff.
Schumann, Elisabeth 386
Schütz, Carl 434
Schwarzenberg, Joseph, Prince zu 215
Schwarzenberg, Karl Philipp, Prince zu 276
Schwarzenberg Palais (Vienna) 228
Scotland 402f., 565
Scott, Marion 139n., 397
Seconda (Second), Mrs (singer) 182f., 303
Seehas, Christian Ludwig 22n.
Sehmann, Gustaf 26, 121
Seitenstetten (Monastery) 486
Selden, John 271
Sermon, Thomas 289f.
Serra (violinist) 183
Sessi (Seßi), Marianna 217
Sestini (Sestina), Signora (singer) 39, 69, 71, 79
Seyfried, Ignaz von 303
Shakespeare, William 34, 41, 49, 93, 104, 128, 190, 274,
    315, 389f., 393-5; *Hamlet* 41, 274; *A Midsummer
    Night's Dream* 291 (see also under Mendelssohn); *The
    Tempest* 42, 291; *Twelfth Night* 389, 395
Shaw, Mr 116
Shaw, Mrs 116, 316
Shaw, Sir William, see Cathcart
Sheldonian Theatre (Oxford) 88ff.
Shield (Schield), William 27f., 83f., (113), 114, 117, 167,
    182f., 234, 252, 274, 279, 283, 364, 400, 531, *pl. 17*;
    The Woodman 113
Shram (Schramb; Schram), Christopher ('cellist) 131,
    147, 163, 169, 183f., 257, 282, 296, 304
Sibly, Mr (musician, Portsmouth) 248
Sieber, Jean Georges 28, 60n., 64, 188, 499, 503, 541, 559
Siegendorf 614
Silesius, Angelus 120, 185
Silverstolpe, Frederik Samuel 22, 26, 221n., 415, 437,
    (482)
Silverstolpe, Gustav Abraham 121
Silvester (lawyer) 106
Silvester (valet to Duchess of York) 180
Simoni, Joseph 131, 152, 155-7, 159-65, 171f., 182f.
Simpkins, William 260, 489

Simrock, Nicolaus 194, 439, 452, 490, 492-5, 497n.
Sisley (Sisly), Madame de (singer) 82f., 85, 152
Sitt, Hans 541
Sitwell, Sir Sacheverell 262n.
Skillern, T. 278
Slezak, Mr (viola player) 493
Slough 176
Smart, George (later Sir) 53, 110, 170, 212, 232, 247,
    299
Smart, H., Jr 299, 304
Smith, C. S. 407n.
Smith, John (bookseller) 270
Smith, John Stafford (musician) 279, 364
Smith, Mr ('cellist) 115, 142, 145, 177, 304
Smithfield (London) 316
Société des Concerts du Conservatoire (Paris) 541
Society of Musical Graduates, see Musical Graduates
Society of Visual Artists (Vienna), see Gesellschaft
    bildender Künstler
Soldan, Kurt 438n.
Soler (Solar), Vincente Martin y 254, 282, 286, 288,
    291f., 295, 303, 306, 310, 311f.
    WORKS:
    L'arbore di Diana 312;
    Aria (unid.) 291f., 303, 310;
    Il burbero di buon cuore 254, 258;
    Concerto (v. and orch.; unid.) 306;
    Duetto (for soprano and bass; unid.) 310;
    L'isola del piacere 311f.;
    Quartetto (soprano, tenor and 2 basses; unid.) 286;
    Terzetto (soprano, tenor, bass; unid.) 295
    Una cosa rara 254, 312, 502
Somfai, László 64, 133, 221n., 238n., 434n., 459n., 468f.
Somis, G. B. 33
Sondheimer, Robert 549n.
Sonnenberg, J. J. 354n.
Sonnenfels, Joseph von 189
Sophia, Princess (of Gloucester) 283
Sopron, see Oedenburg
Sotheby & Co. 70, 176, 178, 495
Southampton 262, 264
South Slavonic popular songs 598
Sowerbys, Mr (musician) 299
Spain 184, 441, 503
Spanish Netherlands 222
Sperati, Mr ('cellist) 89, 183
Spehr (printer) 439
Speyer 195, 228
Spiegl, Fritz 564
Spindler, Herr (singer) 100
Spithead 262
Spitta, Philipp 11
Spofforth, Reginald 301; Glee 301; Song, 'May the
    Prince and his Bride' 301
Spohr, Ludwig 26, 29, 86, 293
Sporting Magazine 24, 289, 301
Springer (Springe), Vincent (basset-horn player) 63,
    75
Staatsbibliothek, Berlin (Preußische), see under Berlin
Stabilini, Signor (violinist) 87; Concerto (v. & orch.;
    unid.) 87
Stadion, Count 35, 38, 184
Stadler, Abbé Maximilian 113f., 415, 505n.
Stadler, Anton 311, 551
Stadler brothers (clarinet players: Anton and Johann)
    549, 551
Stadt Paris (Berlin) 189
Stainer (instrument makers) 114
Stamitz (?) 115
Stamitz, Carl 248, 256, 306, 313; Duet (v. and va.) 256;
    Duet (v. and vc.) 306; 'Hunting Symphony' 248;
    Symphony (Overture; unid.) 313
Stanford Memorial Library 169

Stanhope, Lord 259
Star 292
Stargardt, J. A. 409, 495, 615
Starzer, Joseph 216
Steffani, Agostino 103
Stein, Fritz 507
Stein, K. A. (piano maker) 414
Steinway & Sons 416
Stendhal (M. H. Beyle) 317n., 318
Sterkel, J. F. X. 99
Stevens, R. J. S. 78n., 113, 148, 279, 364; Glee, 'Ye spotted snakes' 364; Glee (unid.) 148
Stiedry, Fritz 53
Stinkenbrunn 614
Stockhausen, Karlheinz 559
Stockholm 142n., 183, 352n., 492
Stodart, William (piano maker) 418
Stokes, Ann (marr. Shield) 114
Stone, Miss, Mr, Mrs 171
Storace, Anna Selina ('Nancy') 31, 37, 44-6, 49f., 60-2, 73, 75f., 81, 85, 87-91, 143, 213, 266, 304f., 372
Storace, Stephen 90, 143, 172, 182f., 296; Aria, 'Quel desir che amore un di' 90; Lullaby (Aria) 296
Strasbourg (Strassburg) 99, 124, 183
Strauss (bookbinder) 204
Strauss (family) 485
Strauss, Johann, the Elder 488, 556; 'Radetzky March' 560
Strauss, Johann, Jr 560
Strauss, Richard 526, 568
Stravinsky, Igor 331; *Orfeo* 331
Streicher, J. A. (piano maker) 414
Strunk, Oliver 278n., 309n., 440ff.
Stuttgart 416n.
Styria 111, 225
Sultan, The (play) 111
Summerson, Sir John 185n.
Sun (newspaper) 233, 235f., 239, 243, 248f., 252n., 257f., 272, 276, 285, 292f., 296, 299, 301, 304, 312, 314, 409, 455, 457
Sutherland, Joan 29n.
Swarowsky, Hans 323, 526n.
Sweden 221n., 293, 594
Swieten, Gottfried van (Freiherr; Baron) 51n., 83, 124, 216, 226, 228, 231, 289, 355, 456, 502
Swinburne, Henry 320
Szabolcsi, Bence 434, 551
Szekeres, Ferenc 355n.

Tajana (Tajano), Signor (singer) 39, 49, 60, 62, 64f., 69, 73, 79
Tajana, Signora (singer) 73
Tallis, Thomas 33
Tarchi, Angelo 69, 72, 139, 244, 377; *Ademira* 376f.; Quartetto (unid.) 244; Terzetto (unid.) 69, 139
Tartini, Giuseppe 33
Tassie (Daßie; Deßie – spellings used by Haydn; *vide* CCLN 276; Bartha 513), James 133
Tattersall (Thallersal; Thattersal), Rev. William D. 278, 317, 318n., 364f., 370
Taylor, Mr (violinist) 260
Taylor, William 39, 281, 298f.
Teatro S. Benedetto (Venice) 377
Teatro S. Moisè (Venice) 254
Teimer, Franz 225, 228
Teimer, Johann 225, 228
Teimer, Philipp 225, 228
Telemann, Georg Philipp 104
Tenschert, Roland 438n.
Teubner family 201n.
Teutonic Knights, Order of 64n.; Archives 64n.
Thayer, A. W. 27n., 126n., 202n., 205, 373n., 414n., 456n., 566n.

Theater an der Wien (Vienna) 85
Theater auf der Wieden (Freyhaus Theater; Vienna) 124
Théatre de Monsieur (Paris) 156, 183
Theatre of Varietés Amusantes, see Saville Row
Theatrical Journal 111
Therstappen, Helmut 497n.
Thomson, George 400-3
Thurlow, Lord 214
Thurn und Taxis, Princely Archives (fürstl. Archiv) 37n.
Times, The 14, 42, 50, 54, 61, 76, 116, 134, 143, 148, 164, 214, 233, 239, 243f., 248, 257, 282, 287, 295, 300f., 313, 361, 440, 442
Tokyo 66, 453
Tomaschek, J. W. 62
Tomasini, Luigi 459, 537
Tomeoni, Irene 126n., 216f.
Tomich, Francesco 182f.
Tonkünstler Societät (Society of Musicians; Society of Musicians' Widows; Vienna) 209, 216, 225-8, 305, 456
Tookey, James (*pl. 10*)
Torezani, Signor 80
Torricella (music publisher) 229, 254
Toscanini, Arturo 501
Tost, Anna (*née* de Jerlischek) 141, 410
Tost, Jean 61
Tottenham Street Rooms (London) 41, 45
Tovey, Sir D. F. 411n., 422, 459n., 470, 518n., 533, 582
Tower of London 265
Townsend, Miss 412
Tozzi, Antonio 329
Traeg, Joseph (Giuseppe) 238, 480, 492, 570
Trauersdorf 614
Trautmannsdorf, Prince 215
Trevelyan, G. M. 50n.
Trento, Vittorio 254
Trier (Trèves) 261
Trieste 217
Trisobio, Signor (singer) 315
Troppau 64n.
True Briton 46, 311, 314
Tchaikovsky, P. I. 560
Turkey 184n.
Turkish music (instruments) 484, 492, 550, 559, 561f., 564, 600
Turin 167
Tuscany (Toscany) 56, 195; Grand Duke of 168, 195
Tusquin, see Depres, Josquin
Twining, Rev. Thomas 32, 49, 67, 74, 82
Twin Sicilies 196
Tyggeson, Tygge 323
Tyrol 211, 556
Tyson, Alan 119, 411n., 412n., 417n., 484

Uffizi Gallery (Florence) 133
Ugarte (Ugandi), Count 207
United States of America 92
Universal Edition (music publishers) 141n., 318n., 497n., 576
Unverricht, Hubert 27n., 46, 497n.
Upton 270

Valdesturla, Constanza 334
Valenciennes 222
Valko, A. 194n.
Vanhal (Vanhall; Wanhal; etc.), Johann Baptist 102, 191, 503, 506
Vauxhall 169, 172
Venice 56, 58, 142, 183, 199, 254, 298, 307, 330, 376f., 441, 503

Venier (music publisher) 229
Verdi, Giuseppe 126, 503
Verlag des Kunst- und Industrie-Comptoir, see Kunst-
und Industrie-Comptoir
Vermilly, M. (dancer) 69, 72
Verrio (Werrio), Antonio 262
Versailles, Château de 236; Petit Trianon 407
Vestris, Gaetano 39, 59, 69, 72, 79
Vestris, Madame (dancer) 52, 441
Vestris Senior (dancer) 79
Victor, M. (dancer) 39, 69, 72
Vienna (Vienne; Wien; Wienn) 22f., 27, 30f., 37n., 39,
41, 44, 46, 50f., 54-61, 63, 64n., 68, 72, 76, 80, 82f.,
85f., 88, 95, 97f., 102, 104-8, 112, 114, 116-8, 122-6,
129-31, 140f., 154, 156-9, 165, 169f., 179, 183, 189f.,
192-9, 202, 204-11, 215-26, 228-30, 237f., 242, 248n.,
254, 260, 266, 281, 285, 294, 303, 305, 309, 315, 317n.,
318, 320, 334, 355, 371-3, 375, 393-6, 413-7, 428, 434,
437-42, 452, 455-9, 479f., 483-7, 490ff., 502, 507, 512,
520, 526, 531, 534, 548f., 551-3, 557-60, 568, 586, 593,
611, 613; Stadtbibliothek 372, 457f.; see also Wiener
. . . etc.
Vienna, Congress of 126, 461, 508
Vienna Philharmonic Orchestra 55, 486, 498
Vienna State Opera Orchestra 500
Vieweg Verlag 407n.
Viganò, Josefa Medina 217, 221
Viganò, Salvatore 217
Vigée-Lebrun, Elisabeth (*pl. V*)
Viguerie (printer) 439, 452
Vincent, Mr (singer) 299
Vinci, Leonardo (composer) 33
Viotti, Giovan(ni) Battista (incl. unid. Concertos for v.
and orch.) 13, (49), 50, 67, 169, 189, 213f., 232-7,
241f., 245-7, 250-3, 255-7, 277, 280, 282f., 286f., 291,
294-6, 303-5, 307, 309f., 313, 459, 595, *pl. 23*
WORKS:
Concertante (2 v.; unid.) 295;
Concertos (v.): — in E (Giazotto 96) 234; — No. 22
in A minor (Giazotto 97) 234; — in G (Giazotto 98)
234;
Duetto concertante (2 v.; unid) 291
Virgil 241, 327
Vogel, Johann Christian 295f., 312; *Demophöon*
(Overture) 295f., 312
Volpini, Angelo (*pl. 12*)
Vormärz 560

Wadleigh, Richard 324, 326n.
Wagenseil, Georg Christoph 189, 503
Wagner, Richard (481), (545), (553); *Die Meistersinger*
(545); *Das Rheingold* 553; *Tristan* 481
Waldstein, Ferdinand Count von 192, 442
Waldstetten, Baron and Baroness von 207
Wales, Prince of (later George IV) 23, 41, 43f., 47, 59,
64, 72, 109f., 117-9, 132, 159, 175, 177, 215, 256, 270,
275, 282-5, 288, 299-301, 303, 314, 317, 318n., 371,
408, 455, 487f., *pls. 8, 9*
Wales, Princess of, see Caroline
Walker, J. C. 230n.
Wallerstein, Castle of 215, 507, 549
Walpole, Horace 47, 83
Walter (Walther), Anthon (piano maker) 413-5, 450
Walter, Bruno 498
Walter, Horst 414n., 415
waltz 208ff., 424, 485f., 514, 530, 543, 553, 556
Wangermann, Ernst 196n.
Wappenschmitt, Oscar 560n.
Warren, Joseph 371
Warwick, Earl of 46
Washington, George 92
Washington, D. C. 66, 254

Wasserkunstbastei (Vienna) 106, 194
Waterloo 215
Watson, Henry (Library, Manchester) 142
Watteau, Antoine 407, 529, 587
Waverley (Waverly) Abbey 269
Webbe (Webb), Samuel 90, 170, 244; Glee (unid.) 244
Webber, Mr 279
Weber, Carl Maria von 461, 613
Wegeler, F. G. 192n., 413n., 456
Weigl, Joseph, Jr 98, 230; *La principessa d'Amalfi* 230;
Venere e Adonis 98
Weigl, Joseph, Senior ('cellist) 230
Weimar 31, 70, 117, 124, 245
Weinmann, Alexander 372n., 394, 497n.
Weissenwolf, Countess 199
Weissenwolf, Countess Lolotte 215
Weissenwolf, Countesss Maria Anna 199n.
Weissenwolf, Freiin Maria Elisabeth 199n.
Weißgram, Ignaz 220
Welch, Master (singer) 299
Weltjee, Mr (of Carlton House) 284
Welsh, Jr (singer) 170
Wendling, J. B. 51n.
Wendschuh, Ludwig 320n., 354n.
Wenman, Viscount 29
Went, Johann (oboist and composer) 225; Terzetto (2
ob., cor angl.) 225
Wesley, Samuel 139
Wessely, Othmar 354n.
West, Benjamin 264
Westminster Abbey 27, 83f., 103, 167, 170, 183, 279
Westphal (music shop, Hamburg) 192, 228
Wetenhall, Edward 66f.
Whitbread, Samuel 371
White, Charles 320n.
Whitehall 215
Whiting, Mr 264
Whyte (Edinburgh publisher) 318n., 401f.
Widow's Concert, see Royal Society of Musicians
Wieland, Christoph Martin 216, 274
Wiener Schriftsteller- und Künstler-Lexikon 487n.
Wiener Theater Almanach 226ff.
Wienerwald (Vienna woods) 195
Wiener Zeitung 198, 206, 224, 237, 372, 393f., 410, 413,
455, 456-8, 480
Wiesbaden 231
Wight, Isle of 263f.
Wight, Rev. Osborne 279, 364
Williams, Mr (ticket-seller) 250
Willis' Room 255, 300
Wills, Mr 43
Wilmot, Sir Robert 260
Wilson, T. (publisher) 564
Winchester (Winschester) 264
Windsor 23, 51, 67, 110, 175, 270, 285, 310; *pl. 28*
Winston Salem (North Carolina) 184n.
Witt, Friedrich 507f.; Symphony in C ('Jena') 507f.
Wlach, Leopold 486
Woden, (Wotan) 56
Wolcot (Walcott), John 108, 136f., 402
Wolf, Sándor 488
Wolfe (composer) 104
World 162, 233, 235
Worms 195
Wranizky (Wranitzky; Wraniezky; etc.), Paul 27f., 224,
249f., 534; Quintet (2 v., 2 va., vc.; unid.) 249f.;
Symphonie caractéristique (Peace of Campo Formio)
224
Wrbna (Würben; Wurben), Countess 207, 224
Wrbna, Eugen Wenzel Joseph, Count 207
Wrbna, Joseph, Count 207
Wren, Sir Christopher 88, 262n.
Wulkaprodersdorf 614

Wurzbach, Constantin von 194n.
Würzburg 183

Yaniewicz (Janowich; Janiewez; Jarnovick; etc.), Felice
   131, 133f., 139, 148-50, 157, 160, 162, 183f., 253f.,
   283f., 288, 297f.; Concerto (v. and orch.; unid.) 298
York (Yorck) 143, 180
York, Frederick, Duke of 23, 44, 76, **109f.**, 118, 215,
   248, 283f., 303; *pl. 8.*
York, Duchess of, see Friederike Charlotte Ulricke
York House (London) 109, 283
Young, Arthur 31
Young, Mary, see Barthelemon, Mrs

Zagersdorf 614
Zeitung für die elegante Welt 151, 373
Zillingtal 614
Zimmermann, Anton 251; Sinfonia Echo (E flat) 251
Zingaralli, N. A. 241, 305, 310;
   Aria (soprano, cor angl.) 310;
   Aria (unid.) 241; Sestetto (unid.) 305
Zinzendorf, Karl, Count 13, 50n., 112, 124, 126n., 201,
   215-7, 221f., 230, 294, 438, 593n.
Zitterer, Johann 22n.
Zoncada, Mr (horn player) 249, 251, 253
Zürich 214n.
Zweig, Stefan 491

INDEX OF COMPOSITIONS BY HAYDN

(HOBOKEN REFERENCES IN PARENTHESIS)

Alessandro (pasticcio; XXXII:3) 28n.
Alfred (XXX:5) 331
Andante con variazioni (pf.; XVII:6) 231, 317f., 423, 437ff.
Arianna a Naxos, see under Cantatas
ARIAS FOR VOICE AND ORCHESTRA:
— for Davide, 'Cara, deh torna in pace' (lost) 68f., 75-7, 81, 316f., 370;
— for Miss Poole (lost) 146, 317, 318n., 370;
— di Lindora, 'Son pietosa' (XXXII:1; for pasticcio *La Circe*, 1789) 169;
— di Merlina, 'Il meglio mio carattere' (XXIVb:17; for Cimarosa's *L'impresario in angustie*, 1790) 221

CANONS:
— 'Kenne Gott' (XXVIIb:13) or 'Denke mein' 185, 318n., 360;
— The Ten Commandments (XXVIIa:1-10) 93, 178, 273, 317, 318n., 360;
— 'Thy voice, O Harmony' (XXVIIb:46) 94, 178, 273, 318n., 360;
— 'Turk was a faithful dog' (XXVIIb:45) 268, 360
CANTATAS:
Arianna a Naxos (XXVIb:2) 27f., 47, 61, 76, 85, 97, 146, 371; contemporary criticism 47;
— for the Duke of Bedford (lost) 371;
— 'Miseri noi' (XXIVa:7) 61, 141, 146, 194, 371f.,
— *Scena di Berenice* (XXIVa: 10) 28, 72, 307-9, 310, 312, 317, 318n., 334, 370-5, 431; contemporary criticism 308;
— 'Der Versöhnungstod' 480
CANZONETTAS:
English Canzonettas (XXVIa:25-30) 23, 169, 257f., 283-6, 318f., 318n., 369, 377-93, 403, 502; complete titles 258, 315; contemporary criticism 393;
— 'Mermaid's Song' (XXVIa:25) 258, 378, 403;
— 'Pastoral Song' (XXVIa:27) 258, 379;
— 'Recollection' ('The Season comes'; XXVIa:26) 169, 258, 378;
— 'She never told her love' (XXVIa:34) 386, 389, 393, 396f.;
— 'Transport of Pleasure' (later ' . . . of Content'; Hoboken *deest*) 285, 315, 391f.
CATCHES:
Italian Catch in seven parts (*Maccone*; lost) 72, 77, 79, 85, 316, 317n., 357, 361;
Twelve Sentimental Catches and Glees (Earl of Abingdon; pf. by Haydn; XXXIc:15) 272, 317, 318n., 361-4
'Clock' Symphony, see Symphonies: No. 101
Concertante, Op. 84 (I:105; 'Sinfonia Concertante'), for ob., bsn., v., vc. and orchestra 144f., 147, 160, 194, 238-60, 257, 316, 317n., 412, 491, 501, 510, 516, 531, 533, 536-41; contemporary criticism 145, 147, 240
CONCERTOS:
— 2 hns. and orch. (VIId:2) 169, 537;
— 2 lire and orch. (VIIh:3) 63, 454f., 550, 558, 562f.;

— pf. and orch. (XVIII:11; 'Op. 21'; 'Op. 37') 416, 433, 505;
— trpt. and orch. (VIIc:1) 169, 201, 537;
— v. and orch. (VIIa:3) 11; — (Hoboken *deest*) 169f.;
— v., cemb. and orch. (XVIII:6) 536;
— vc. and orch. (VIIb:1) 11; (VIIb:2) 537
Contredanze (IX:29) 483
Coro, 'Su cantiamo' (Hoboken *deest*) 356f.
Country Dances 316f., 318n., 483f.; *Princess of Wales' Favorite Dance* (Hoboken *deest*) 206
Creation, The, see under Oratorios

DEUTSCHE TÄNZE (German Dances):
— (IX:10) 485;
Redoutensaal Dances (IX:12) 205-8, 221, 224f., 317, 318n., 322, 484-7; (IX:13) 487;
Six Allemandes (IX:9) 485
Divertimento a nove (II:17) 539, 549
'Dr. Harington's Compliment' (voices and pf.; XXVIb:3) 267, 316, 318n., 396, 403f.
'Drum Roll' Symphony, see Symphonies: No. 103
DUETS, VOCAL:
'Guarda qui' (XXVa:1) 39;
'Saper vorrei' (XXVa:2) 39;
'Quel cor uman e tenero' (Hob. II, p. 225) 254, 306-9; contemporary criticism 308

Fantasia (pf.; XVII:4) 117f., 129f.
Flötenuhr (musical clock), pieces for 201f., 557, 564-6; — (XIX:16) 202; — (XIX:26) 557; — (XIX:29) 202; — (XIX:30) 202; — (XIX:32) 202

'God save the King' (Hoboken *deest*) 317, 318n., 361, (533)
'Gott erhalte' (XXVIa:43) 14
'Gypsy Rondo', see Trios: (b) pf., v., vc., No. 39

'Jacob's Dream' (v. sonata; lost) 310, 316, 318n., 452

LIEDER (see also Canzonettas; Songs):
XII Lieder (XXVIa:1-12) 377f.
'London' Symphonies, see Symphonies: Nos. 93-104
'London' Symphony, see Symphonies: No. 104
'London' Trios, see Trios: (a) 2 fl. and vc.

Maccone (for Gallini), see under Catches
Madrigal, 'The Storm' (XXIVa:18) 135-7, 147, 194, 216, 226, 228, 316, 317n., **354-6**, 369, 383, 412, 519; contemporary criticism 136f., 147, 158
MARCHES:
— *for the Captain of a ship* (= Prince of Wales?) 72f.;
— *for the Derbyshire Cavalry Regiment* (VIII:1 and 2) 260, 317, 318n., **488-90**;
— *for the Prince of Wales* (VIII:3) 157f., 317, 318n., 408, **487-9**;
— *for the Royal Society of Musicians* (VIII:3bis) 26, 157f., 317, 318n., **487-9**;

— arrangement for wind band of Symphony No. 100/II (Hoboken *deest*) 562f.;
— (VIII:7) 207, 487f.
MASSES (arranged in chronological order):
  Missa brevis alla cappella 'Rorate coeli desuper' (XXII:3) 11;
  Missa Sunt bona mixta malis (XXII:2) 430;
  Missa Cellensis in honorem B. V. M. (XXII:5) 11, 365, 422;
  Missa Cellensis ('Mariazellermessse'; XXII:8) 11;
  Missa Sancti Bernardi de Offida (XXII:10) 532;
  Missa in tempore belli (XXII:9) 198, 470, 509;
  Missa in angustiis ('Nelson Mass'; XXII:11) 198, 356, 381, 500, 502;
  Missa ('Theresienmesse'; XXII:12) 532;
  Missa ('Schöpfungsmesse'; XXII:13) 383, 532;
  Missa ('Harmoniemesse'; XXII:14) 358, 532
'Military' Symphony, see Symphonies: No. 100
MINUETS (in chronological order):
  'Seitenstetten' Minuets (IX:1) 456f.;
  — Redoutensaal (IX:11) 205-8, 221, 317, 318n., 322, **484-6**;
  Twenty-Four Minuets (IX:16) 207, 317, 318n., 486, **551f.**
'Miracle' Symphony, see Symphonies: No. 96

Notturni for the King of Naples 64f., 75, 79, 159, 161-4, 194, 284, 317, 318n., **453-5**;
  — (II:25) 453, 455; (II:26) 453; (II:27) 65, 159, **454**; (II:28) 65, 159, 454; (II:29) 453; (II:30) 453, 455; (II:31) 65, 453, 455; (II:32) 65, 159, 161, 164, 453f.

OPERAS (arranged in chronological order):
  Le pescatrici (1769; XXVIII:4) 576n.;
  L'infedeltà delusa (1773; XXVIII:5) 329, 330, 337, 351;
  Philemon und Baucis (1773; XXIXb:2) 11, 369;
  L'incontro improvviso (1775; XXVIII:6) 330, 551;
  Das abgebrannte Haus (*Die Feuersbrunst*) (1776?; XXIXb:A) 11, 351, 549;
  Il mondo della luna (1777; XXVIII:7) 199n.;
  La vera costanza (1778?; XXVIII:8) 100, 125f., 348;
  L'isola disabitata (1779; XXVIII:9) 373;
  La fedeltà premiata (1780; XXVIII:10) 11, 28n., 61, 69, 122, 196, 225, 238n., 311, 320n., 351, 411, 480, 526;
  — 'Ah, come il core' 61, 69, (73), 75f., (81), (91), 351;
  Orlando Paladino (*Ritter Roland*) (1782; XXVIII:11) 100, 122, 124, 197f., 254, 306-9, 320, 323, 332, 356; — Duet 'Quel tuo visetto' (later adapted to Da Ponte's words 'Quel cor umano e tenero') 254, 306-9, 332;
  Armida (1784; XXVIII:12) 348, 505;
  L'anima del filosofo (*Orfeo ed Euridice*) (1791; XXVIII:13) 30, 38f., 54, 59, 70-2, 81, (122), 146, 194, 199, 205, 301f., 311, 316, 317n., **323-54**, 356f., 370, 372, 381, 388, 412, 483, 491, 505;
  — Overture ('Overture to an English Opera'), see Overtures: Windsor Castle'
ORATORIOS:
  The Creation (*Die Schöpfung*; XXI:2) 22, 24, 46, 53, 68, 86, 174, 178, 197, 269, 288, 316, 320, 330, 354-6, 369, 390, 441, 471, 501-3, 509, 511, 523, 532, 582f., 595, 609, 618;
  Mare Clausum (XXIVa:9) **271**, 317, 318n., **356**, 357;
  Il ritorno di Tobia (XXI:1) 74n., 83, 225f., 354; — Aria and Chorus, 'Ah, gran Dio', and Chorus, 'Svanisce in un momento' 74n.;
  The Seasons (*Die Jahreszeiten*; XXI:3) 151, 197, 344, 356, 390f., 501f., 532, 609;
  The Seven Words (*Die sieben Worte*; XX:1 & 2) 67, 81f., 85f., 130, 161, 320, 356, 359;
  Stabat Mater (XX bis) 11, 58, 422
OVERTURES:
  — in D (Ia:7) 42;
  — 'Windsor Castle' (Ia:3) 299-302, 324, **483**

'Oxford' Symphony, see Symphonies: No. 92

'Pietà di me', see Terzetto
Psalms, English (XXIII, Nachtrag) 360

QUARTETS (string; arranged by traditional *opera*):
  — Op. 9 (III:19-24) 430, 479; — No. 4 (III:22) 430;
  — Op. 20 (III:31-36) 422, 479; — No. 3 (III:33) 422;
  — No. 5 (III:35) 337, 422;
  — Op. 33 (III:37-42) 446, 479; — No. 6 (III:42) 460;
  — Op. 50 (III:44-49) 479; — No. 1 (III:44) 200;
  — Op. 54/55 (III:57-62) 24n., 479;
  — Op. 64 (III:63-68) 48, 60f., 65f., 70, 73, 147, 421, 455, 458, 479; — No. 1 (III:65) 458; — No. 5 ('Lark'; III:63) 202;
  — Op. 71 and 74 (III:69-74) 25, 48, 188, 219, 230f., 233, 235f., 236n., 242, 244-6, 316, 317n., 322, 417, 421, 424, **455-82**, — Op. 71, No. 1 (III:69) 455, **460-5**;
  — Op. 71, No. 2 (III:70) 207, 455, 460f., **466-8**, 557;
  — Op. 71, No. 3 (III:71) 431, 433, 455, 459-61, **468-72**; Op. 74, No. 1 (III:72) 455, **460-79**, 548; — Op. 74, No. 2 (III:73) 455, 460, **478f.**; — Op. 74, No. 3 ('Rider'; III:74) 70, 455, 458-60, 472, **479-82**, 516;
  — Op. 76 (III:75-80) 73, 421f., 446, 460f., 470, 479, 506; — No. 1 (III:75) 460; — No. 6 (III:80) 470;
  — Op. 77 (III:81-82) 155, 215, 446, 460, 470, 557; — No. 1 (III:81) 557; — No. 2 (III:82) 470, 557, 582;
  — Op. 103 (III:83) 381, 383, 460, 470

'Rider' Quartet, see Quartets: Op. 74, No. 3

'Salomon' Symphonies, see Symphonies: Nos. 93-104
Scena di Berenice, see under Cantatas
Scherzandi (II:33-38) 184
SONATAS (pf.; arranged numerically):
  — No. 33 (XVI:20) 418, 422;
  — No. 57 (XVI:47) 450;
  — No. 58 (XVI:48) 448;
  — No. 59 (XVI:49) 140f., 417, 426, 450;
  — No. 60 (XVI:50) (276), 316, 317n., **439-48**;
  — No. 61 (XVI:51) (276), 316, 317n., 396, 410, 439f., 442, **448f.**; contemporary criticism 449;
  — No. 62 (XVI:52) 276, 316, 317n., 428, 439-43, 445f., **449-52**; contemporary criticism 452
SONGS (see also Canzonettas; Lieder):
  'Eine sehr gewöhnliche Geschichte' (XXVIa:4) 273;
  'Ich bin der Verliebteste' (= 'Transport of Pleasure', see Canzonettas) 284f., 391f.;
  Irish songs 401;
  'O tuneful voice' (XXVIa:42) 315, 318n., **396-400**; contemporary criticism 397;
  Scottish songs for Napier (XXXIa:1-100, 101-150) 128f., 316-8, 318n., 377, **400-3**;
  'The Spirit's Song' (XXVIa:41) 315, 318n., **394-6**, 397;
  'Trust not too much' (XXXIc:17) 316, **394**, 408, 483;
  Welsh songs 401
Stabat Mater, see under Oratorios
Storm, The, see Madrigal
'Surprise' Symphony, see Symphonies: No. 94
SYMPHONIES (arranged numerically; numbers identical with Hoboken, Vol. I):
  — No. 2 – 541;
  — No. 5 – 506;
  — Nos. 6-8 ('Le Matin', 'Le Midi', 'Le Soir') – 513;
  — No. 7 ('Le Midi') – 539;
  — No. 9 – 541;
  — No. 11 – 506;
  — No. 13 – 517;
  — No. 16 – 568;
  — No. 20 – 541;
  — No. 22 ('Philosopher') – 330, 359;